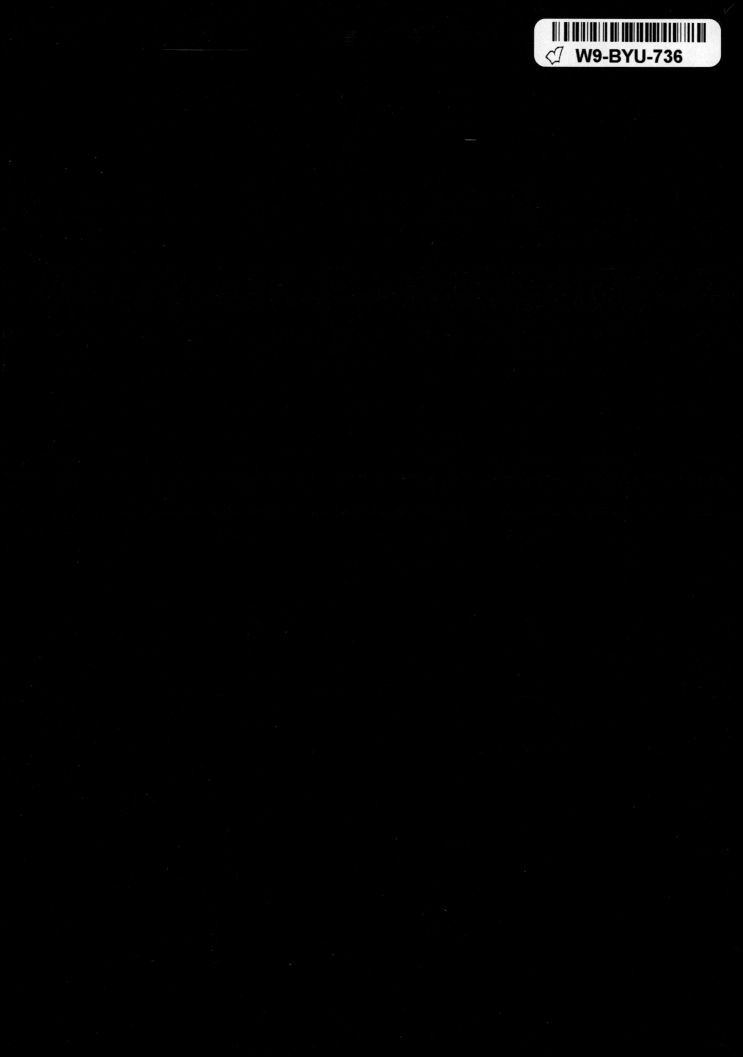

Encyclopedia of
Women *and*

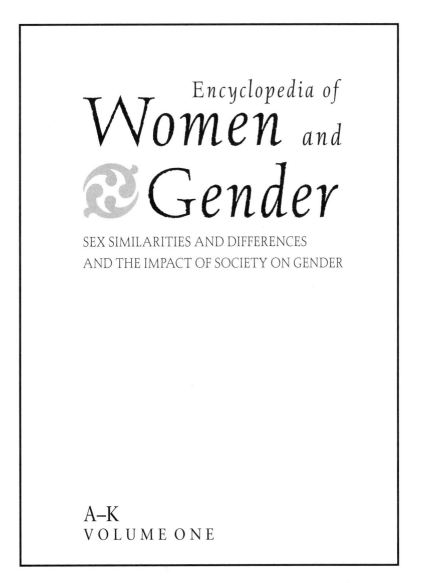

Gender

SEX SIMILARITIES AND DIFFERENCES
AND THE IMPACT OF SOCIETY ON GENDER

A–K
VOLUME ONE

Encyclopedia of
Women and
Gender

SEX SIMILARITIES AND DIFFERENCES
AND THE IMPACT OF SOCIETY ON GENDER

EDITOR-IN-CHIEF

Judith Worell

University of Kentucky, Lexington

A–K
VOLUME ONE

ACADEMIC PRESS
A Harcourt Science and Technology Company

San Diego   San Francisco   New York   Boston   London   Sydney   Tokyo

The sponsoring editor for this encyclopedia was Nikki Levy, the senior developmental editor was Barbara Makinster, and the production managers were Joanna Dinsmore and Molly Wofford. The cover was designed by Linda Shapiro. Composition was done by ATLIS Graphics & Design, Camp Hill, PA, and the encyclopedia was printed and bound by Edwards Brothers, Ann Arbor, MI.

This book is printed on acid-free paper. ∞

Academic Press
A Harcourt Science and Technology Company
525 B Street, Suite 1900, San Diego, California 92101-4495, USA
http://www.academicpress.com

Academic Press
Harcourt Place, 32 Jamestown Road, London NW1 7BY, UK
http://www.academicpress.com

Library of Congress Catalog Card Number:

International Standard Book Number: 0-12-227245-5 (Set)
International Standard Book Number: 0-12-227246-3 (Volume 1)
International Standard Book Number: 0-12-227247-1 (Volume 2)

PRINTED IN THE UNITED STATES OF AMERICA
01 02 03 04 05 06 EB 9 8 7 6 5 4 3 2 1

CONTENTS

F

G

H

I

CONTENTS OF VOLUME TWO

L

P

M

Contents ix

T

W

PREFACE

When I entered the field of psychology, theory and research related to women and gender were relatively invisible. The majority of research within the social sciences was based on the assumption that data obtained mainly from the lives and perspectives of men represented the totality of human experience. The rise of a revitalized women's movement provided the impetus for scholars and researchers to challenge the absence of knowledge about the lives of girls and women. In the ensuing years, a plethora of gender-related scholarship and research produced an abundant body of literature that changed the direction of the discipline. We began asking new questions, naming new problems, confronting the limitations of traditional research paradigms, and applying the fruits of our research to issues of human welfare, public policy, and social justice. The outcome of these efforts is a revised discipline that provides a rich source of theory and research on the psychology of women and gender.

Purpose and Scope

This encyclopedia provides comprehensive coverage of the many topics that encompass current research and scholarship on the psychology of women and gender. The content of these volumes is intended to be accessible to and informative for students and scholars from all academic disciplines, as well as interested readers in the public or corporate domains who wish to explore and expand their understanding of the factors that influence the diverse lives of women and men. Many articles will be particularly interesting and relevant to those in allied professions such as nursing, social work, medicine, and the law.

The authors include prominent and outstanding experts on gender, as well as some excellent emergent scholars. The articles cover a broad array of topics related to the psychology of gender, with additional contributions from allied social sciences including sociology, anthropology, and communications. In contrast to earlier considerations of gender as the study of sex differences, the authors of these articles present a wide range of perspectives on the multiple meanings of sex and gender. Many authors point out that differences among women and groups of women, for example, are greater than most differences that may be found between women and men. Thus, comparisons across the diversity of women is as important as those between the two sexes. Our main focus here is on understanding girls and women in the context of their lives and experiences. In particular, the importance of context is emphasized throughout, in recognition that all behavior is multidetermined and assumes meaning only if understood within particular cultures, situations, and historical time frames. Across the articles attention is given to multicultural issues of diversity in human experience, including those related to nationality, economics, sexuality, and racial/ethnic variables. Our overall goal is to explore through theory and research how social and cultural influences have structured and shaped the gender-related roles, behaviors, well-being, life events, and opportunities afforded to diverse groups of women and men.

Content

The articles in this volume are comprehensive and cover topics in depth rather than in condensed formats. Each article reviews a theme that is important to the psychology of gender in human experience and includes a glossary of relevant concepts and timely references that will be invaluable for further reading. Although the content is ordered alphabetically by title, we conceptualized and developed it more broadly according to significant topical areas. A sample of these topics is summarized below.

The basis of most psychological research rests on theoretical structures that provide a framework and assumptions about human nature and experience. Several articles discuss theories of gender development from the perspectives of evolutionary psychology, biology and genetics, social construction, psychoanalysis, social roles, social learning, gender schemas, the history of gender study, and the feminist movement. Next we considered that in examining theories and questions related to women and gender, researchers depend upon a variety of quantitative and qualitative methods. Standard empirical methods of research and analysis, as well as some newer approaches to understanding people's lives, are carefully explained and evaluated. Several articles examine the characteristics of feminist research and the implications of research on sex differences for our understandings of gender. Then, since gender development is multidetermined, we present reviews of major periods and issues in women's development, including cognitive development, gender acquisition and expression in childhood and adolescence, children's play patterns, marriage, motherhood, childcare options, divorce and child custody, mid-life, menopause, and aging.

Psychologists have traditionally been interested in personality; we review the research on gender-related personal characteristics such as social identity, self-esteem, empathy, emotional expressiveness, assertiveness, anger, humor, leadership, ethical/moral judgment, personal and social power, entitlement, and aggression. Health and mental health are important to the well-being of girls and women; we cover topics on life satisfaction, health care, stress and coping, trauma, depression, eating disorders, agoraphobia, anxiety, body image, attractiveness, safer sex behaviors, reproductive technologies, abortion, substance abuse, chronic illness, disability, psychiatric diagnosis, and recovered memories. Various approaches to psychotherapy and counseling are included to consider alternatives for women's healing and well-being. In all these articles, implications across cultures and social policy are integrated.

Moving to dyadic and community relationships, we explore research on friendship, love, intimacy, lesbian and heterosexual partnering, family, sexuality and sexual desire, and social support. Since most women are involved in heterosexual relationships at some time in their lives, we include an article on men and conceptions of masculinity. Societal or cultural contributions to gender development are reflected in articles on parenting in diverse cultures, academic and achievement options, educational settings, school climate, media influences, and participation in sports and athletics. Gender-related research on work and employment environments is covered in articles on affirmative action, mentoring, nontraditional careers, work–family balance, career achievement, women in the military, and employment-related sexual harassment.

The gender-related effects of biased experiences and minority status include articles on stereotyping, prejudice, androcentrism, test bias, self-fulfilling prophesies, ethnicity and sexual orientation, and poverty. A number of articles cover the critical research area of gender-related violence and implications for social policy. Violence in the lives of women is addressed in reviews of child physical and sexual abuse, emotional abuse, women-battering, rape, sexual misconduct with clients in therapy, hate crimes, prostitution and the sex industry, media violence, torture, and imprisonment. As an important factor in implementing social policy, we include an article on political behavior. We anticipate that the many exciting and interesting reviews in these volumes will stimulate readers to explore further in their own areas of interest.

Collaboration

An original and ambitious enterprise such as this could not have been accomplished without the collaboration of a distinguished, capable, and hard-working Executive Advisory Board. Together, we generated the topics to be covered and the names of article authors who could best contribute to the excellence of the reviews. I am grateful to these colleagues for their wisdom and perspective in selecting an outstanding group of eminent and accomplished authors. I appreciate their continuing interest and support in bringing these volumes to fruition. I am also grateful for and appreciative of the efforts of each of the superb article authors, who carved out time in their crowded schedules to help us complete this outstanding work.

Finally, I thank the staff at Academic Press for their sustained involvement and support. I thank Nikki Levy for her insight in initiating the development and production of these volumes and for her generosity in negotiating an acceptable range of ti-tles, and Barbara Makinster for her consummate patience and skills in arranging the mechanics of the production with both efficiency and grace. I am confident that these volumes will represent an outstanding and useful contribution to our understanding and appreciation of the lives of women and men in the context of the realities of contemporary society.

Judith Worell

ABOUT THE EDITOR-IN-CHIEF

JUDITH WORELL is professor emerita and past chair of the Department of Educational and Counseling Psychology at the University of Kentucky. She received her Ph.D. from the Ohio State University and is a licensed clinical psychologist. She has served as associate editor of the *Journal of Consulting and Clinical Psychology* and as editor of the *Psychology of Women Quarterly.* She served an eight-year term as member and chair of the Publications and Communications Board of the American Psychological Association and also has served on the editorial board of numerous psychology journals. She has over 100 publications and presentations, including eight books.

Dr. Worell has been highly active in both community and professional organizations on behalf of girls and women and was president of the Kentucky Psychological Association, the Southeastern Psychological Association, and the Society for the Psychology of Women, a division of the American Psychological Association. She has been named Outstanding Graduate Professor at the University of Kentucky, Lexington Woman of the Year, Distinguished Kentucky Psychologist, and Distinguished Leader for Women of the American Psychological Association. She was awarded a Presidential Citation from the American Psychological Association for her continuing work on the concerns of women, and an honorary doctorate of letters from Colby-Sawyer College. Dr. Worell's current research focuses on process and outcomes of feminist therapy with women and on a model of women's mental health that emphasizes women's empowerment and resilience.

ABOUT THE EXECUTIVE ADVISORY BOARD

JANET SHIBLEY HYDE is chair of the Department of Psychology and Helen Thompson Woolley Professor of Psychology and Women's Studies at the University of Wisconsin–Madison. She is the author of two undergraduate textbooks on the psychology of women and human sexuality. For more than a decade she has carried out a program of research using meta-analysis to synthesize the existing research on psychological gender differences. In addition, she is conducting a longitudinal study on maternity leave and how women balance work and family. She is a past president of the American Psychological Association Division 35, the Society for the Psychology of Women.

KEN POPE is in independent practice as a licensed psychologist. His practice, research, writings, and presentations specifically address the needs of people who have experienced political or governmental torture, contracted AIDS, endured racial, sexual, and other forms of discrimination or harassment, experienced physical or sexual assault, were exploited by therapists, or lacked access to traditional services. He has developed and implemented models for providing preventive, clinical, and other services in these areas. His publications include 10 books and over 100 articles and chapters in peer-reviewed scientific and professional journals and books. He is a charter fellow of the American Psychological Society (APS) and a fellow of the American Psychological Association (APA) Divisions 1, 2, 12, 29, 35, 41, 42, 44, and 51. He received the APA Division 12 Award for Distinguished Professional Contributions to Clinical Psychology, the APA Division 42 Presidential Citation "In Recognition of His Voluntary Contributions, His Generosity of Time, the Sharing of His Caring Spirit [and] His Personal Resources," and the APA Award for Distinguished Contributions to Public Service.

PAMELA TROTMAN REID is professor of psychology and education at the University of Michigan in Ann Arbor and a research scientist at the University's Institute for Research on Women and Gender. Dr. Reid earned her Ph.D. from the University of Pennsylvania and has been an educator for more than 30 years, holding faculty and administrative positions at several universities. Her research has focused on gender and ethnic issues, particularly on the intersections of gender and race as they impact African American women and children. Dr. Reid has published numerous journals articles and book chapters in this arena as well as on the socialization of girls and boys, issues of poverty, and prejudice. She is a fellow of the American Psychological Association and has been on the Board of Educational Affairs there as well as having been president of the Division of Psychology of Women. She has received a number of awards, including the Distinguished Leadership Award by the Committee on Women in Psychology and the Distinguished Publication Award from the Association of Women in Psychology. She has also been named one of 100 Distinguished Women in the Psychology of Women.

STEPHANIE RIGER is professor of psychology and gender and women's studies at the University of Illinois at Chicago. She received her doctorate from the University of Michigan and is the recipient of the American Psychological Association's Division 27 Award for Distinguished Contributions to Research and Theory and a two-time winner of the Association for Women in Psychology's Distinguished Publication Award. Dr. Riger is the author of numerous journal articles and books on gender psychology. Her current research focuses on the impact of welfare reform on intimate violence and the evaluation of domestic violence and sexual assault services.

JANIS SANCHEZ-HUCLES is a professor of psychology at Old Dominion University in Norfolk, Virginia, and a clinical psychologist in private practice in Virginia Beach, Virginia. She is also a faculty member of the Virginia Consortium in Clinical Psychology and a community faculty member of Eastern Virginia Medical School. Dr. Sanchez received her Ph.D. from the University of North Carolina–Chapel Hill, and she has been involved in developing and teaching courses titled The Psychology of Women, The Psychology of African Americans, and Diversity Issues in Psychodynamic Therapy. Her research has focused on clinical training, women and families of color, diversity, feminism, and issues pertaining to trauma and violence, and she is the author of numerous book chapters and journal articles and a book in this area. Dr. Sanchez is a fellow of the American Psychological Association (APA) and has served on a variety of APA committees, including an

APA Presidential Task Force on Violence and the Family, task forces on the restructuring of the council of representatives and on the integration of science and practice, the APA Council of Representatives, the Committee on Structure and Function of Council, the advisory board for the APA Science Directorate, the Board of Educational Affairs, and the Executive Board for Division 35, the Society for the Psychology of Women. She is also past chair of the APA's Committee on Urban Initiatives.

BRENDA TONER is currently head of the Women's Mental Health and Addiction Research Section at the Centre for Addiction Mental Health and professor and head of the Women's Mental Health Program, Department of Psychiatry, University of Toronto. Dr. Toner received her Ph.D. from the University of Toronto, followed by a postdoctoral fellowship in eating disorders. She has published and presented on a variety of health-related problems that are disproportionately diagnosed in women, including eating disorders, anxiety, depression, chronic pelvic pain, chronic fatigue, and irritable bowel syndrome. She is particularly interested in investigating factors in the lives of women that cut across diagnoses, including violence, body dissatisfaction, poverty, discrimination, gender role conflicts, and isolation. One of her major research interests is psychosocial assessment and treatment of functional gastrointestinal disorders.

CHERYL BROWN TRAVIS is a professor in the Department of Psychology at the University of Tennessee, specializing in gender-diversity issues and health psychology, with an emphasis on policy, planning, risk perception and communication, and decision making. She is a fellow of the American Psychological Association and a past president of the Society for the Psychology of Women. Publications by Dr. Travis include books on women's health as well as articles on medical decision making and physician practice patterns. Her professional activities have involved symposia on medical decision making and informed consent. She has participated in a briefing to members of Congress on women's health issues and has provided formal Senate testimony on authorization hearings for the Environmental Protection Agency, in which she advocated behavioral and psychological approaches to environmental health. She is currently an associate editor of *American Psychologist* and the founding editor of the *Psychology of Women* book series.

HOW TO USE THE ENCYCLOPEDIA

The *Encyclopedia of Women and Gender* is intended for use by students, research professionals, and practicing clinicians. Articles have been chosen to reflect major disciplines in women's studies and gender issues, common topics of research by professionals in this domain, and areas of public interest and concern. Each article serves as a comprehensive overview of a given area, providing both breadth of coverage for students and depth of coverage for research professionals. We have designed the encyclopedia with the following features for maximum accessibility for all readers.

Articles in the encyclopedia are arranged alphabetically by subject. Complete tables of contents appear in all volumes. The index is located in Volume 2. Because the reader's topic of interest may be listed under a broader article title, we encourage use of the Index for access to a subject area, rather than use of the Table of Contents alone. Because a topic of study is often applicable to more than one article, the Index provides a complete listing of where a subject is covered and in what context.

Each article contains an outline, a glossary, cross-references, and a suggested reading section. The outline allows a quick scan of the major areas discussed within each article. The glossary contains terms that may be unfamiliar to the reader, with each term de-fined *in the context of its use in that article.* Thus, a term may appear in the glossary for another article defined in a slightly different manner or with a subtle nuance specific to that article. For clarity, we have allowed these differences in definition to remain so that the terms are defined relative to the context of the particular article.

The articles have been cross-referenced to other related articles in the encyclopedia. Cross-references are found at the first or predominant mention of a subject area covered elsewhere in the encyclopedia. Cross-references will always appear at the end of a paragraph. Where multiple cross-references apply to a single paragraph, the cross-references are listed in alphabetical order. We encourage readers to use the cross-references to locate other encyclopedia articles that will provide more detailed information about a subject.

The suggested readings at the close of each article list recent secondary sources to aid the reader in locating more detailed or technical information. Review articles and research articles that are considered of primary importance to the understanding of a given subject area are also listed. This section is not intended to provide a full reference listing of all material covered in the context of a given article, but is provided as a guide to further reading.

Abortion and Its Health Effects

Henry P. David

Transnational Family Research Institute, Bethesda, Maryland

Ellie Lee

University of Southampton, United Kingdom

Glossary

Emergency contraception Method used to prevent pregnancy after unprotected intercourse. A woman has three options: (1) she can take what is equivalent to a double dose of certain combined oral contraceptives within 72 hours, repeated 12 hours later, (2) she can take pills composed of only progestrin with the same timing, or (3) she can ask her clinician to insert an IUD.

External cervical os A small round opening at the lower part of the cervix, which is also known as the neck of the womb or uterus.

Genital tract infection Caused by microorganisms in a woman's vagina or cervix. Following abortion, where tissue is inevitably bruised or damaged to some degree, infection can develop in the uterus and fallopian tubes. When severe, it can affect the peritoneum and ultimately the other pelvic organs. In some cases, infection can be severe, affecting a large number of organs in the pelvic region, and this condition is called pelvic inflammatory disease (PID).

Hemorrhage In all abortions, some bleeding occurs when the placental tissues separate from the uterine wall. Normally, between 50 and 200 ml of blood can be lost. However, in a small number of abortions (the proportion is greater where the abortion occurs at an advanced stage of pregnancy), a larger quantity of blood may be lost.

Induced abortion The deliberate ending of a pregnancy in such a way as to ensure that a live birth does not occur. Depending on global geographical location, 10 to 60% of pregnancies are terminated by abortion. Induced abortion is distinguishable from spontaneous abortion, also known as miscarriage, which occurs in between 10 and 15% of all pregnancies. There are two different types of induced abortion, surgical and medical (using pills), as discussed in the text.

Oral contraceptives Hormonal method of birth control, of which there are two types, the combined oral contraceptive pill and the progestin-only pill. The first type contains a combination of hormones and works principally by suppressing ovulation. The second contains only one hormone and suppresses ovulation in fewer than 50% of the women who take it, but it also works by causing changes in the cervical mucus, which make it difficult for the sperm to enter the womb, and by making the womb lining less receptive to the egg if it is fertilized. Both types of pill are considered to be medically safe.

Prophylactic antibiotics Antibiotics given as a preventative measure at the time of abortion to prevent genital tract infections.

Uterine perforation Piercing of the wall of the uterus, which may occur in a small number of cases when an abortion is performed by surgical means (for example, with a suction canula inserted via the cervix to reach the conceptus). The perforation may not cause significant problems and can heal. However, significant medical problems can result if the perforation is reentered with a medical instrument and if other organs are damaged as the instrument passes through the wall of the womb. Studies have shown that the risk of uterine perforation is far less when experienced clinicians perform the abortion. It is therefore preferable that abortion be carried out by specialized staff.

INDUCED ABORTION is as old as humanity and probably occurs in all cultures. Throughout recorded history, women have resorted to abortion to end unwanted pregnancies, regardless of religious, social, or legal sanction and often at considerable risk to personal health. Despite the growing awareness of population and environmental concerns, the right of women to make autonomous decisions, and international discussions of reproductive and sexual health and responsible parenthood, abortion has retained an aura of social ambivalence.

I. Introduction

More than 25 years after the Supreme Court's landmark *Roe v. Wade* decision, when the court ruled that the "right to privacy" was broad enough to encompass a woman's decision whether or not to terminate her pregnancy, polls suggest that although most North Americans believe that abortion should be legal on some grounds, there are nuanced views and discomfort about the circumstances and pregnancy stages under which it should be permitted. There is, however, substantial agreement that, regardless of personal opinions, the decision to end a pregnancy should be left to the woman and her physician.

Worldwide, the legal status of abortion ranges from complete prohibition for any reason to availability at the request of the pregnant woman. Despite the technological and social policy advances made since abortion was first legalized in Russia in 1920, it can still be said that no other elective procedure or public health issue evokes as much public debate, generates such emotional and moral controversy, or receives greater sustained attention from the media. The public debate is dominated by two opposing perspectives: (1) abortion as a woman's right and means for controlling her fertility and (2) abortion as a threat to morality and social cohesion. Abortion continues to be subject to conflicting ethical views, sensitive to varying interpretations, and divisive public policy concerns.

In the United States the abortion rate has declined from 24 per 1000 women aged 15 to 44 in 1985 to 20 per 1000 women of the same age in 1995. A continuing area of debate is how abortion may or may not impact a woman's subsequent physical health and psychological well-being. As will be further discussed, when performed by experienced practitioners, the health risks of abortion are very low and substantially less than the risk of dying as a result of pregnancy or childbirth. Mental health effects are less well defined or documented. There is no psychologically painless way of coping with an unwanted pregnancy. While an abortion may elicit feelings of regret, guilt, or loss, an alternative solution, such as a forced marriage, giving a baby up for adoption, or adding an unwanted child to an already strained partner relationship, is also likely to be accompanied by psychological problems for the woman, the child, and society.

This article begins by discussing the decision-making process in reproductive behavior and placing abortion in the broader context of factors that led to an unplanned pregnancy. The article then explores the question of why an unplanned pregnancy happens, assesses contraceptive method failures, summarizes women's reasons for ending a pregnancy, and discusses emergency contraception. The article also reviews research findings about the physical and mental health effects of abortion in early and late procedures. Primary focus is on studies in the United States with some consideration of findings in European countries. Allegations about a "postabortion syndrome" and factors likely to contribute to negative psychosocial outcomes are noted. The article also reviews barriers to abortion, the special needs of adolescents, and the acceptability of medical as compared to surgical abortion. This is followed by findings from the continuing study of the psychosocial development of 220 children, now adults, born between 1961 and 1963 in Prague, Czech Republic, to women twice denied abortion for the same pregnancy and pair-matched controls born to women who wished to conceive and did not request an abortion. The success of the public health program in the Netherlands in achieving the world's lowest abortion rate is described with an emphasis on lessons learned. Within this context it is important to remember that discussion of abortion, fertility regulation, and reproductive and sexual health are often influenced by ethical, political, and religious controversies that very likely color the vision of even the most objective social scientists and medical researchers.

II. *Reproductive Decision Making*

The physical expression of sexuality is universal. What differs is how cultures, religions, and societies construe and influence the setting in which heterosexual relations occur and in which pregnancy is encouraged or discouraged. In most developed countries, such as the United States, where early premarital sexual intercourse is widespread, childbearing before marriage is deemed undesirable for the young woman and for society. [*See* CROSS-CULTURAL SEXUAL PRACTICES.]

Throughout their fertile years, individuals are faced with many choice points and alternative courses of action, which are likely to determine the success of their efforts to control their fertility. The awareness of these choice points, the extent to which alternative courses of action are recognized, and the degree to which choices are based on realistic appraisals of benefits, costs, and consequences are the

cornerstones of rational reproductive behavior. Although most people acknowledge that both pregnancy and childbirth are life events that usually occur by choice, not chance, real-life experiences may be quite different.

Successful fertility regulation generally requires the coordination of three distinct human forces: (1) the desire to have sexual relations, (2) the wish to have or not to have a child, and (3) the will to practice consistent contraception. While these forces may be logically linked, they are not necessarily psychologically related. Nor are they always shared by the partners. Given the degree of vigilance involved, it is not surprising that unplanned pregnancy remains common. Although improvements have been made in the provision of health delivery systems, regular availability of contraceptives and method acceptability are elusive goals for some partners, at times confounded by contraceptive failures.

The decision to use or not to use a fertility-regulating method is often associated with the perceived risk of pregnancy, the openness of partner communications, the support of parents and peers, the community's attitude toward sexuality education, and the influence of specific guidance by health clinic staff. [*See* SEXUALITY EDUCATION.]

III. *Contraceptive Effectiveness and Practice*

Even in countries where contraceptives are freely available, unplanned pregnancy remains common. For example, Furedi reported in 1996 that almost a third of all births in Britain could be a result of accidental pregnancy. Added to pregnancies that end in abortion, this would indicate that perhaps as many as 50% of all conceptions are unplanned.

Contraceptive failure is an important issue raised by women in their explanations of why they find themselves with an unwanted pregnancy. A 1993 study of 769 women requesting abortion in the British National Health Service found that 68% of participants claimed to have conceived as a result of a contraceptive method failure.

All forms of contraception have a failure rate, often termed "method failure," which applies even when used according to manufacturer's instructions. According to Furedi, even with careful use, one couple per hundred will become pregnant when the pill is used, as will around two per hundred using the

IUD, diaphragm, or condoms. Perhaps more important is "user failure"—that is, when contraception is not used as instructed.

For female sterilization, injectable contraceptives or implants, and the IUD, failure rates are very low. With typical use, however, pregnancy rates for couples using the pill can be 3 in 100. For the diaphragm and condoms, as many as 15 couples in 100 will become pregnant; and with natural family planning, 20 in 100 couples will get pregnant.

As noted in a 1999 Alan Guttmacher Institute report, whether couples will be successful in preventing unplanned pregnancies is to a large extent determined by the effectiveness of their contraceptive practice. The chance of an unexpected pregnancy is almost nonexistent for couples who rely on sterilization and very low for users of an IUD, injectable, or implant. It is moderate for pill and condom users, and very high if couples depend on periodic abstinence, withdrawal, or spermicides.

The most obvious user failure is inconsistency of compliance with manufacturer's instructions. This is particularly true for oral contraceptives. A 1993 poll commissioned by the manufacturers of Norplant contraceptive implants found that 60% of 326 pill users had forgotten to take their pill at least once during the preceding 12 months, while a further 7% were unable to say with certainty that they had always remembered. Similar results have been obtained from other studies of pill users, including polls commissioned by manufacturers of oral contraceptives.

A 1995 study of pill compliance among women aged 16 to 30 from Denmark, France, Italy, Portugal, and the United Kingdom suggested that poor compliance was associated with a lack of established routine for pill taking, failure to read and understand written materials that came along with the contraceptives, and occurrence of side effects. Women who were inconsistent pill takers, frequently missing one or more pills per cycle, were almost three times as likely to experience an unintended pregnancy than women who took their pills consistently. Some of these issues could be resolvable through better education, information, and prescribing practice. Although suggestions for establishing pill-taking habits can reduce forgetfulness, it is unlikely that "perfect contraception" is achievable.

A second factor is users' knowledge and skill in contraceptive use. A 1994 study in the United States found that although 89% of a sample of more than 300 people attending a clinic said they were somewhat or very sure that they could put a condom on and take it off correctly, only 60% managed to demonstrate their perceived level of skill.

Even well-informed women may have problems with contraceptives that can usually be managed in a methodical and routine fashion away from the distractions of sexual excitement. For example, a woman may be aware that sickness and diarrhea may interrupt the action of oral contraception, but it might still be difficult for her to judge whether her own illness was severe enough to make a difference. She may know that some antibiotics can undermine her contraceptive's effectiveness, but not which ones. A woman may know that she needs to use spermicide with her diaphragm but be unsure how much.

Third, circumstances in which sexual intercourse occurs reflect that contraceptive use "in the real world" differs from "laboratory conditions." The possibility of sexual activity may be something that neither partner may wish to admit, especially if the relationship is in its early stages, or one or both partners feel uncomfortable about sex in general or their sexuality in particular. Even those who are comfortable with their sexuality, well informed about contraception, and able to communicate easily with their partner may fail to use contraception effectively. Sexual activity is not always prepared for and planned—nor do people always want it to be. A passionate, unpremeditated sexual relationship is something many hope to experience. However, passionless, fearful, intimate violence, including rape, battering, and childhood sexual abuse, is also linked with the risk of unintended and unwanted pregnancy, often requiring special counseling to cope with possible emotional trauma.

Finally, effective use of contraception requires exceptional motivation. Since the chance of pregnancy with a single act of intercourse at midcycle is less than 30%, more than 70% of women will "get away" with doing nothing. To expect consistent use of contraception in every act of intercourse during a woman's fertile life may be demanding more than most couples can deliver.

IV. *Reasons for Ending an Unplanned Pregnancy and Emergency Contraception*

Throughout the world, women give similar reasons for deciding to end an unplanned pregnancy. They include (1) being too young or too old to have or raise a child, (2) already having as many children as they want, (3) wishing to delay childbirth to a later time, (4) having problems with husband or partner, (5) not wanting to raise a child alone, (6) desiring to complete school or university training before having a child, (7) being infected with HIV/AIDS, (8) having been raped, (9) not wishing parents to know about pregnancy, and (10) being coerced by partner or parents.

Too few women are aware that emergency contraception (EC) can prevent pregnancy if taken within 72 hours after unprotected sexual intercourse. Too many women calling a national hot line listing EC health practitioners experience difficulty in obtaining and filling a prescription in a timely manner. Trussell found in a 2000 study that physicians do not routinely counsel women or prescribe EC pills in advance. Other studies have shown that women are much more likely to use EC when they need it if they already have it at home. Some practitioners decline to see women who are not established patients or are otherwise unavailable (as on weekends). Under some North American state laws, pharmacists can refuse to dispense EC pills if doing so would conflict with their moral or religious beliefs. In other states (e.g., Washington) pharmacists are allowed to dispense EC on request.

V. Risks to Physical Health

Much evidence attests to the low rate of risk to physical health associated with abortion. The risk of death is 0.6 deaths per 100,000 legal abortions in the United States. This is substantially less than the risk of dying as a result of pregnancy or childbirth (8.4 deaths per 100,000 live births).

In 2000, the British Royal College of Obstetricians and Gynaecologists (RCOG) published an evidence–based guideline, *The Care of Women Requesting Induced Abortion*. Based on systematic literature review and synthesis of the best available research results, the guideline advises that women considering abortion should be given certain information on the possible complications of abortion. For example, hemorrhage at the time of abortion is rare, occurring in around 1.5 of 1000 abortions overall. The rate is lower for early abortions (1.2/1000 at <13 weeks gestation and 8.5/1000 at >20 weeks). Uterine perforation at the time of surgical abortion is also rare. The incidence is about 1 to 4 per 1000 abortions. The rate of damage to the external cervical os at the time of surgical abortion is no greater than 1%. The rate for complications is lower when abortions are

performed early in pregnancy by experienced clinicians. Genital tract infection of varying degrees of severity, including pelvic inflammatory disease, occurs in up to 10% of cases. The risk is reduced when prophylactic antibiotics are given or when lower genital tract infection has been excluded by bacteriological screening.

For comparison, an American specialist in abortion services, Warren Hern, the author of the medical text *Abortion Practice*, has noted lower complication rates. In various published series, Hern reported a major complication rate (including hemorrhage requiring transfusion) of 0.2% (2 per 1000) in second-trimester abortion from 15 to 34 menstrual weeks. His 30,000 first-trimester patients have experienced a major complication rate of 0.01% with no uterine perforations. By contrast, patients carrying pregnancy to term in the United States routinely experience a caesarian rate of 25 to 30%, a major complication rate more than a hundred times greater than second or third trimester abortion and more than 2500 times greater than that experienced by first trimester abortion patients.

There has been some discussion in recent years that abortion leads to future infertility and breast cancer. Women's concern about these conditions may have been heightened by claims made mainly by abortion opponents that abortion leads to an increased risk of, or even causes, infertility and breast cancer.

The RCOG guideline states that women with previous induced abortion appear to be at an increased risk of infertility in countries where abortion is illegal, but not in those where abortion is legal. It notes that published studies strongly suggest that infertility is not a consequence of induced abortion where there are no medical complications. British gynecologist David Paintin has observed that in so far as abortion and reduction in fertility are linked, a proportion of the one or two per thousand women who have serious abortion complications are likely to experience reduced fertility or inability to conceive again because of these complications, but not where complications are absent.

The RCOG also reviewed available evidence about breast cancer for its guideline, and found that available evidence on an association between induced abortion and breast cancer is currently inconclusive. The RCOG noted however, that the validity of the evidence gathered from studies that compare incidence of breast cancer in women who have and who have not had an abortion may be questionable because of the reluctance of women studied to reveal whether they had an abortion. Studies based on national registers are less prone to inaccuracy because they do not rely on subject recall. Such studies have not shown any significant association between abortion and breast cancer. The guideline therefore states that when only those studies least susceptible to bias are included, the evidence suggests that induced abortion does not increase a woman's risk of breast cancer. [*See* HEALTH AND HEALTH CARE.]

VI. Risks to Mental Health

Of all the possible complications of abortion, psychological responses are the most difficult to assess and evaluate—far more so than mortality and morbidity statistics. Assuming that psychiatric or psychological morbidity is a real and measurable phenomenon, the explanation for the wide range of opinions expressed in the literature may well lie in the inadequacy of much of the published work. Included in the scientific deficiencies are (1) an overemphasis on clinical case histories that ignore the large majority of women who terminate unwanted pregnancies and never seek postoperative mental health consultation, (2) the absence of standardized followup procedures, (3) failure to reach consensus on diagnostic psychological criteria, or (4) disagreement on psychological variables related to the sociocultural context within which the abortion decision occurs.

There is a general tendency to treat women seeking abortion as a homogeneous group. Many reports do not consider age, marital status, parity, wantedness of pregnancy, gestational age, previous reproductive history, or sociocultural setting. These and other characteristics can have a substantial effect on a woman's motivation and may also influence the risk of psychological consequences. Results obtained in one sociocultural setting often are not applicable to others. In segments of society where abortion is socially and morally unacceptable, guilt will often be one of the commonly reported short-term effects, even in the absence of restrictive laws. In societies where abortion is legal and socially acceptable as a way to control fertility, psychological guilt reactions or shame are practically unknown.

A. POSTABORTION SYNDROME

Postabortion trauma was initially described by Rue in 1981 in United States Congressional Testimony as a variant of posttraumatic stress disorder. He as-

serted in 1995 that in 1987 the American Psychiatric Association had acknowledged in its newly revised manual of diagnostic criteria, the *Diagnostic and Statistical Manual of Mental Disorders III-R* (DSM-III-R) that abortion was a type of "psychosocial stressor." He claimed that psychological stressors were capable of causing posttraumatic-stress disorder and that postabortion syndrome (PAS) is a specific type of posttraumatic stress disorder. The only problem with Rue's assertion is that the American Psychiatric Association never published a statement suggesting that abortion is a psychosocial stressor. Neither the 1987 nor the 1994 revision nor the 2000 update of the *APA Diagnostic and Statistical Manual* (DSM III-R and IV) mention abortion in relation to posttraumatic stress disorder. Indeed, the only mention of abortion in DSM IV is spontaneous abortion.

As defined in DSM IV, posttraumatic stress disorder (PTSD) is a disabling condition "following exposure to an extreme traumatic stressor involving direct personal experience of an event that involves actual or threatened death or serious injury." Likely stressors cited by the DSM as examples of PTSD include military combat, violent personal assault, terrorist attack, and being held hostage. It is quite a stretch to claim abortion as a stressor likely to induce PTSD. Indeed, Rue concluded in a 1995 essay that "the American Psychiatric Association in no way supports the existence of, nor does it find any clinical evidence for the basis of the diagnosis of post-abortion syndrome." He then repeats his assertion that DSM-III-R lists abortion as a "psychosocial stressor," a claim for which there is no basis in fact.

One of the criteria for PTSD is experiencing "an event that is outside the range of usual human experience and that would be markedly distressing to almost anyone." Considering that more than 35 million women have experienced abortion in the United States since legalization of the procedure in January 1973, it can hardly be said that the abortion experience is outside the range of usual human experience. There has been no reported increase in public or private mental health services for women attributing their current psychological problems to abortion.

The rationale for PAS was developed in 1985 by Speckhard on the basis of 45 to 90 minute individual interviews with 30 women recruited for her doctoral dissertation in sociology at the University of Minnesota because these women deemed their abortion experience to have been "highly stressful." The time between the retrospective account and the most recent abortion varied from 1 to 25 years. Both legal and clandestine abortions were included. Moreover, 46% of the sample participants had second-trimester abortions, and 4% experienced third-trimester terminations, both known to be more psychologically stressful than first-trimester procedures. Whereas over 90% of all women having abortions in 1998 had them in the first trimester, only 50% of Speckhard's sample reported first-trimester abortions. More than 9 out of 10 (92%) of the women recalled feelings of anger, hostility, or rage toward individuals (including partner, medical professionals, and significant others) who were perceived as having been coercive in the abortion decision-making process. Moreover, 96% of the women "regarded abortion as the taking of a life or as murder," an observation very likely to heighten feelings of guilt and perceptions of stress. Speckhard later cautioned readers that "the generalizability of the results is severely limited by the size of the sample and the sampling methodology," adding that "the results presented do not necessarily apply to all women who have abortions, or even to that proportion of women who are highly stressed following abortion." [*See* DIAGNOSIS OF PSYCHOLOGICAL DISORDERS; POST-TRAUMATIC STRESS DISORDER.]

B. AMERICAN PSYCHOLOGICAL ASSOCIATION EXPERT PANEL

Recognizing the political, ethical, and moral issues intertwined with abortion and in response to questions raised in the United States Congress about the medical and mental health effects of abortion, the American Psychological Association (APA), in 1989, convened an expert panel to examine the psychological factors. The panel's mission was not to assess values but to review the best available evidence on psychological responses to abortion. It focused on studies with the most rigorous research designs, reporting findings on the psychological status of women who had legal abortions under nonrestrictive circumstances—that is, on request in the first trimester and not solely on grounds of physical or mental health.

Despite a wide variety of samples, methodologies, and differing times of assessment, the conclusions were consistent. The APA panel found that psychological distress is generally greatest *before* the abortion when the woman has to decide how to resolve an unwanted pregnancy. Responses after abortion reflect the range of psychological experience and the resources a woman has for coping with negative life events. While there may be temporary sensations of

regret, sadness, or guilt, the weight of the evidence indicates that legal abortion of an unwanted pregnancy in the first trimester does not pose a severe psychological hazard for the vast majority of women. Indeed, most women report experiencing a feeling of relief—of anxiety lifted.

In further examining the argument for the existence of PAS, the panel cited findings that patients averaged higher scores on the short form of the Beck Depression Inventory immediately after the abortion, and far lower scores three weeks later. None of the scores exceeded the threshold indicating depression. Women who blamed their pregnancy on their own character were significantly more depressed before the abortion, anticipated more negative consequences, and tended to have more severe negative moods immediately after abortion than women who were not self-blamers. Moreover, studies of other life stressors suggest that women who show no evidence of severe negative responses after a stressful life event are unlikely to subsequently develop significant psychological problems in conjunction with that event. Another empirical study found that women who had a strong, satisfying, and stable partner relationship and were capable of making independent decisions were less prone to early or late postabortion psychological difficulties.

In a longer-term study Russo and Zierk reported in 1992 that the well-being of 773 women, interviewed annually in a national sample of 5295 women, was unrelated to their abortion experience eight years earlier. The study considered many factors that can influence a woman's emotional well-being, including education, employment, income, the presence of a spouse, and the number of children. Higher self-esteem was associated with having a higher income, more years of education, and fewer children. Women who had experienced an abortion had a statistically significant higher global self-esteem rating than women who had never had an abortion. This difference was even greater when comparing aborting women with women delivering unwanted pregnancies (who had the lowest self-esteem). Women who had experienced repeat abortions did not differ in self-esteem from women who had never had an abortion. Women's level of self-esteem before having an abortion was the strongest predictor of their psychological well-being after an abortion. In all, the evidence confirmed earlier findings that factors other than the abortion experience itself determine postabortion emotional status. Some women continually reconstruct and reinterpret past events in the light of subsequent experience and can be pressured into feeling guilt and shame long afterward.

In light of the substantial amount of evidence against PAS, it is perhaps surprising that the claim for PAS retains any credibility. In part the continued debate about whether or not there is such a syndrome can be explained by the confusing degree of variation in the "symptoms" that are said to be associated with the putative condition. As already noted, Rue claimed that PAS is a form of PTSD. As such it would constitute a severe psychiatric disorder. If its occurrence could be measured on this basis, it would be found to be extremely rare if not nonexistent.

However, proponents of PAS tend to shift in their writings from a definition of the PAS "symptoms," where the proposed comparison with PTSD is made clear, to a much broader collection of "symptoms" that could perhaps more accurately be described as negative feelings. Rue has listed a wide range of feelings and forms of behavior that he argues might be evident in women who have had an abortion. These include feelings of helplessness, hopelessness, sadness, sorrow, lowered self-esteem, distrust, regret, relationship disruption, communication impairment or restriction, and self-condemnation.

Associating this broad range of symptoms with a diagnosis of PAS allows claimants to argue that large numbers of women may suffer from the syndrome. As the diagnostic criteria for PAS become broader, it is easier to claim that many women may suffer from the syndrome. A link between mild and severe psychological responses is generated: all become less serious versions of the same response. Feelings a woman might have after abortion, such as sadness or regret, are misinterpreted by Rue as a less serious version of a psychiatric disorder. If an accurate assessment of the psychological effects of abortion is to be made, an approach that combines psychiatric illness with negative feeling is unacceptable. As Stotland argued in a 1992 commentary in the *Journal of the American Medical Association*, a symptom or a feeling is not equivalent to a disease. Some women who undergo abortion experience feelings of sadness, regret, and loss, but this does not mean they are suffering from a disease.

In sum, for the vast majority of women, an abortion of an unwanted pregnancy will be followed by a mixture of emotions, with a predominance of positive feelings and relief. This holds immediately after abortion and for some time afterward. Little is known about long-term effects beyond 10 years.

However, the positive picture reported up to 8 years after abortion makes it unlikely that more negative responses will emerge later. Severe negative reactions are rare. The time of greatest stress is likely to be before the abortion decision is made. Evidence from the research literature suggests that, in the aggregate, legal abortion of an unwanted pregnancy in the first trimester does not pose a psychological hazard for most women. They tend to cope successfully and go on with their lives. As previously noted, there is no credible evidence for the existence of a postabortion syndrome.

C. EUROPEAN STUDIES

Denmark offers unique opportunities for research in reproductive health because it has a uniform national population registration system that provides access to national abortion, birth, and admission to psychiatric hospital registers. Linkage among these registers makes it possible to compare the risks of psychiatric hospital admission following abortion and childbirth. However, because there may be a bias against hospitalizing a new mother, particularly if she is nursing, the relative psychological risk of abortion compared with childbirth may be exaggerated by using hospital admission as an operational indicator of psychiatric illness.

Controlling for previous psychiatric history, first-time psychiatric hospital admissions were tracked three months postabortion and postpartum and for all other women under age 50 experiencing no fertility event and residing in Denmark. Data were obtained on 27,234 women terminating pregnancy, 71,378 women carrying to term, and the total population of 1,169,819 women who were 15 to 49 years old.

As reported by David in 1985, among women who were married or living in a stable partner relationship, the postpregnancy risk of admission to a psychiatric hospital was about the same for abortions or deliveries; approximately 1.3 per 1000 abortions and 1.2 per 1000 deliveries. While the difference between rates for abortions and deliveries was not statistically significant, the rate for the total population of women was considerably lower (0.7 per 1000). Among a smaller group of separated, divorced, or widowed women, those who had terminated pregnancies showed a substantially higher psychiatric admission rate (6.4 per 1000) than did separated, divorced, or widowed women carrying to term (1.7 per 1000). Women who are divorced, separated, or widowed may be relatively more likely to be terminating pregnancies that were originally intended, placing them at higher risk for negative postabortion psychological reactions. However, in the aggregate, there appeared to be little risk to psychological well-being after either abortion or delivery in Denmark.

In a longer term (up to 11 years) prospective cohort study of 13,261 women, organized jointly by the Royal Colleges of Obstetricians and Gynaecologists and of General Practitioners in the United Kingdom, there were four comparison groups: 6151 women who did not request abortion, 6410 who obtained an abortion, 379 whose request for abortion was denied, and 371 who requested an abortion and then changed their minds.

Among the study's key findings were that (1) there were no significant differences between women with equivalent past psychiatric histories and the comparison groups in overall rates of psychiatric illness; (2) women with a previous history of psychosis were more likely to experience a psychotic episode during the period of the study than those who had no such history and that termination of pregnancy did not appear to increase the risk; (3) women with a past history of nonpsychotic disorder or no history of psychiatric disorder who had a termination were significantly less likely to have a psychotic episode than those who did not request a termination; and (4) in women with no previous history of psychosis, the risk of psychosis after termination appeared to be lower than after childbirth.

It was noted that many women were lost to followup during the study and that at the end just 2122 (34.4%) of the termination group and 3000 (42.4%) of those who did not request a termination were still under observation but that comparisons between the groups were still valid.

D. FACTORS CONTRIBUTING TO NEGATIVE REACTIONS

Severe psychological reactions after abortion are infrequent. Psychoses are very uncommon, being reported in only 0.3 to 1.2 per 1000 legal abortions in women who had no known prior psychiatric history. Individual case studies and anecdotal reports of severe stress or psychopathology following abortion appear in the literature, but there is no clear evidence of causal linkage to abortion. While such responses can be emotionally overwhelming for the woman concerned and for her family, the number of such cases is very small and was characterized by former

U.S. Surgeon General C. Everett Koop in 1989 as "minuscule from a public health perspective."

In spite of the general conclusion that induced abortion for the majority of women is not a threat to their physical or mental well-being, research studies have identified certain women to be at some risk for negative psychological reactions and in potential need of special counseling and support. Included are women who (1) terminate a very much wanted pregnancy for medical reasons, (2) lack support from partners or parents for their decision, (3) were coerced into making a decision they subsequently regretted, (4) are conflicted about deeply held religious values, (5) are uncertain of their coping abilities beforehand, (6) blame themselves for the pregnancy, (7) delay into the second trimester, or (8) had a previous psychiatric episode. The identification of women at risk does not constitute a contraindication to abortion.

When a pregnancy is very much wanted, but abortion is indicated for medical reasons (either maternal or fetal), the woman (and often her partner) are likely to react with feelings of depression and guilt. However, in spite of the emotional trauma of the (usually second-trimester) experience, most couples have indicated that they would make the same decision again if faced with a defective fetus. Similarly, when delaying the abortion into the second trimester for reasons of ambivalence toward the pregnancy, the feeling of psychological loss may be more severe if the woman has noted fetal movements. Women identified in preabortion counseling as experiencing ambivalence should be given a chance to reconsider their decision.

E. REPEAT UNWANTED PREGNANCIES AND ABORTIONS

Reports of women having repeated unwanted pregnancies and abortions in the United States and Europe indicate that they did not use contraception because they did not expect to have sexual intercourse or that the side effects of contraceptives resulted in inconsistent or discontinued use. Some women are exceptionally fertile or "unlucky" in their contraceptive practice. The few studies in this area found that major life changes, depression, loneliness, and anger reduce contraceptive vigilance and expose women to greater risk of unwanted pregnancy. Psychological reactions to two or more abortions may range from none or mild feelings of regret or disappointment about the lack of contraceptive discipline to stronger feelings of guilt, anger, and sadness. These reactions are generally temporary and not significantly different from those experienced by women having a first procedure.

Repeat abortion appears to be more difficult for health practitioners. As Hern noted, they may feel frustrated by what is perceived to have been their failure to induce behavioral change in a patient after the first procedure. By inquiring how a patient decides to practice contraception, health professionals can help to raise consciousness and improve future vigilance.

VII. *Adolescents*

As noted by Adler and others, approximately 1 million adolescents become pregnant each year in the United States. Of these, about 20% experience a spontaneous abortion and about equal proportions of the rest end their pregnancies or carry to term. The vast majority of teenagers seeking abortion are unmarried and were ending first pregnancies. When asked the reason, over 75% respond that they are seeking an abortion because they do not believe they are sufficiently mature to raise a child.

A review by Adler and colleagues of research data in the American Psychological Association volume edited by Beckman and Harvey does not lend support to the view that adolescents are at substantial risk for adverse psychological health effects. The way an adolescent responds depends to a large degree on parental attitude and the approach of clinic staff. Consequences of abortion in early adolescence are probably less serious than the consequences of bearing and rearing a child. A 1989 Baltimore study followed 360 pregnant Black teenagers for two years. Those who obtained an abortion were better off economically, further advanced in their education, and showed a more favorable psychological profile over time than those who decided to carry to term. The weight of the evidence provides no compelling rationale for legislation restricting access to abortion for adolescents.

Another issue concerns the continuing debate over whether adolescents are competent to make autonomous decisions about having an abortion. Competence has been defined as the ability to (1) understand the information presented, (2) display reasoning in the decision-making process, (3) make a choice or decision, and (4) appreciate the consequences of the decision made. An informed choice requires (1) access to sufficient information, (2) understanding the information, (3) competence to evaluate potential consequences, (4) freedom to make a choice, and (5) ability to make and express the choice. With adults, the focus has been on providing information in a way that assures informed consent. With adolescents, the focus has been on competence to make an informed choice. Adler and colleagues cite study conclusions indicating that adolescents are often more capable of expressing preferences and participating in major life decisions than is generally recognized in medical settings or under the law.

Parental consent laws for abortion generally include a provision for judicial bypass, allowing a judge to provide permission in lieu of parental consent if there is a compelling reason why parents cannot be informed or asked to provide consent. Adolescents who do not consult at least one parent appear to have a good reason for wanting to avoid doing so as apparent in the finding that virtually all requests for judicial permission have been granted.

Most pregnant adolescents voluntarily consult with an adult and the majority involve their parents. Studies have found that the likelihood of parental consultation varies as a function of age: the younger the adolescent the more likely it is that she will involve her parents. Young women who chose not to tell their parents were more financially independent and more likely to live alone. Many of those who carried to term may have made an active decision to do so. For others, continuing an unwanted pregnancy may be a default choice, resulting from an inability or unwillingness to confront reality, lack of knowledge about alternatives, or both.

Many parents are too embarrassed to talk openly about sexuality and fertility regulation with their children. Too few schools are prepared to broaden their biology-oriented courses or to include practical information about contraception as part of life-skill classes. Policy makers tend to shy away from what they perceive to be politically sensitive topics, and governments are reluctant to initiate adolescent pregnancy prevention programs for fear of unfavorable public reaction. It is seldom acknowledged that unmarried teenagers will engage in sexual intercourse with or without contraceptive information and services. [*See* ADOLESCENT GENDER DEVELOPMENT.]

VIII. *Barriers to Abortion*

Experience in the United States and other countries has shown that legal authorization of elective abortion does not guarantee that abortion is equally available to every woman requesting termination of an unwanted pregnancy. Lack of clinical facilities or personnel, conservative medical attitudes, and restrictive regulations can effectively curtail access to abortion, especially for socioeconomically disadvantaged and young unmarried women. Nearly one-third of metropolitan U.S. areas lack any facility that offers abortion services. With the decline in the numbers of providers, especially in rural parts of the country, some women who want the procedure must now travel hundreds of miles. Additional impediments may involve difficulties in obtaining an appointment, gestation limits, harassment by antiabortion protestors, and increased costs imposed by the legal requirement of a 24-hour waiting periods in many states. The mergers of nonsectarian nonprofit health centers with Catholic Church–supported medical facilities has further reduced the availability of reproductive health services, including abortion and emergency contraception.

The legislative obstacles restricting access to abortion for adolescents increase the chances of delay into the second trimester when abortion carries increased risk of medical and psychological health effects. In sum, women's ability to obtain safe abortion services is affected not only by the laws on the books but also by how these laws are interpreted and by community and medical attitudes.

IX. Medical and Surgical Abortion

As of 2000, over 95% of abortions in the United States are performed using the vacuum aspiration method of surgical abortion. This method requires the insertion of a flexible plastic tube through the cervix into the uterus. The products of conception are then sucked out using an electric motor or manual pump. Although an extremely safe, efficient, and brief procedure, possible complications related to its surgical nature can occur, including infection and perforation of the uterine wall.

Medical abortion, another type of abortion, is induced by a drug or combination of drugs administered orally that cause the uterus to expel the conceptus. Developed in France, RU-486 was the first method of medical abortion to become available. It belongs to a class of synthetic agents known as antiprogestins that block the action of the natural hormone, progesterone, by binding with progesterone receptors in the lining of the uterus. This action re-

sults in a breakdown of the uterine lining, the occurrence of bleeding as in menstruation, and stimulation of uterine contractions. Called mifepristone in its generic form, it is safe and 92 to 95% effective with minimal serious side effects when used early in pregnancy (from the time a woman knows she is pregnant up to seven weeks after the beginning of her last menstrual period). The administration of mifepristone is followed 48 hours later by another pill, Misoprostol, a prostaglandin that enhances uterine contractions leading to faster expulsion of the conceptus, usually within four hours. Presently, medical abortion requires visits to the physician's office on three separate days over a two-week period, including a followup consultation to assure that the pregnancy has ended. Medical abortion is more time-consuming than the standard one-time appointment at a free-standing abortion clinic.

In acceptability studies in diverse countries reasons for choosing medical abortion consistently included anxiety about surgery and fear of general anesthesia, preference for the privacy and personal control attained by not having to go to an abortion-identified clinic, and a feeling that the procedure seemed less invasive, more "natural," and "like a premeditated miscarriage." Perceived disadvantages included the cost of time, inconvenience, greater cramping and bleeding, and a slightly higher failure rate. Most women who had experienced both a surgical and medical procedure preferred the latter. There were no differences in psychological effects. In trial centers in the United States, medical abortion was found to be just as safe, effective, and satisfactory in adolescents as in older women.

In France, RU-486 accounted for one-third of all abortions in 1998. Availability did not increase the total number of abortions. Rather, women sought to end unwanted pregnancies earlier. Now approved in 13 countries, Mifepristone was approved by the Food and Drug Administration (FDA) in the United States in September 2000 under the brand name Mifeprex. It is provided directly to physicians' offices or clinics and is not available through pharmacies. To prescribe Mifeprex, physicians must certify their ability to assess the duration of a pregnancy accurately, competence to diagnose an ectopic pregnancy (a pregnancy that develops abnormally outside the uterus, usually in the fallopian tube), and capability to provide or make an appropriate referral for a surgical backup in cases of incomplete abortion (presently about 5%) or to medical facilities in cases of prolonged or severe bleeding. Physicians must also follow certain guidelines for the use of Mifeprex, including counseling. It is anticipated that the availability of Mifeprex will result in earlier abortions obtained within a less contentious context without necessarily increasing the total number of abortions.

X. Abortion Denied

Reviews of studies of women who did not succeed in obtaining abortions for unwanted pregnancies in Sweden showed that a significant proportion of these women experienced adverse emotional reactions, less stability in their martial lives, poor interaction with their partners, less involvement in child rearing, and low work capacity.

Unique circumstances made it possible to organize, conduct, and continue for more than 30 years the study of 220 children born in 1961 through 1963 to Prague women whose request for termination of an unwanted pregnancy (UP) was twice denied (once on initial request and again on appeal) and 220 pair-matched controls born to women who accepted their pregnancy (AP) and did not request an abortion. The matching criteria included age and sex of the child, same school class, mother's age, number of children in the family, birth order, and socioeconomic status of the family as determined by its completeness and parental educational and economic levels.

The children were initially examined at age nine by a research team that did not then or later know which child belonged to which group. While differences between UP and AP children were not statistically significant, they were consistently in disfavor of the UP children. School, social, and family life were less satisfactory and less stable, especially for the "only" children (i.e., children who had no siblings).

In 1977, when the children were between 14 and 16 years of age, it was possible to locate 216 of the 220 UP children and 215 of the 220 AP children, achieving a 98% followup rate. Although intelligence test scores did not differentiate between UP and AP children, school performance continued to be poorer in the UP children. A significantly larger number of UP children did not continue their education to the secondary school level, but instead became apprentices or started jobs without prior vocational training. Many of the UP children described their mothers as inconsistent and variable in their emotional behavior toward them, whereas the fathers were often perceived to be "warmer" than the mothers. Analysis of the findings from the Czech Child-Marriage-Family Scale suggested that the emotional gap between UP boys and their mothers widened and deteriorated over time, whereas the relationship between the UP girls and their mothers remained about the same or improved.

A third followup wave was conducted in 1983–1984 when the study participants were young adults aged 21 to 23 years. Data were also obtained from child care councils and from drug, alcohol, and crime registers. The findings showed a significantly greater problem proneness among UP than AP study participants. Compared to to AP controls, the UP young adults reported significantly less job satisfaction, more conflict with coworkers and supervisors, fewer and less satisfying relations with friends, and more disappointments in love. Among the married young adults in both groups, the UP participants more often judged their marriages to be less happy and more often expressed the desire not to be married at all or not to be married to their present partner.

Another study was conducted in 1989 to assess partner choices among married UP and AP study participants. There were significantly more single and divorced women in the UP group than in the AP group. Significantly more UP than AP men had married, but there was no significant difference in their divorce rate. The partners of UP study participants were found markedly more often in the files of alcohol and drug treatment centers and on the crime register than the spouses of AP study participants. Compared to married AP women with children, married UP women with children more frequently reported that they were unprepared for their first pregnancy, felt "less happy" during pregnancy, and "felt like mothers" only after delivery (whereas many AP women experienced such a feeling in early pregnancy). For information on pregnancy, childbirth, and child care, UP women more often turned to the media and friends, whereas AP women turned more often to their mothers. UP women planned to stay at home with their child for a shorter period of time and returned to work earlier than AP women. The UP women also more frequently rated their marriages as "less happy" or "definitely unhappy."

A fourth followup was initiated in 1991 when the study group participants reached 30 years of age. It was possible to establish contacts with and obtain data from 84% of all original UP subjects and 88% of AP subjects (i.e., more than 90% of those still available for study). Except for the "only" children, differences between UP and AP participants had narrowed.

For the first time, the siblings of UP and AP participants were included. The objective was to distinguish which characteristics of the UP participants were shared by their siblings and which were specific to those born of unwanted pregnancies. Whereas the UP females were more frequently emotionally disturbed than their AP female controls, no such difference was noted between the female siblings of the UP and AP participants.

A fifth followup wave was conducted in 1997 when the participants and their siblings were around 35 years of age. It was possible to reinterview 75% of the original 440 participants plus 247 siblings. Initial findings reinforce the earlier observation of longer-term detrimental effects of unwantedness in early pregnancy on later psychosocial development. Differences in psychiatric morbidity are being explored.

XI. *Lessons from the Netherlands*

Among countries reporting reliable abortion statistics, the Netherlands has the lowest abortion rate. Similarly, Dutch teenagers have the lowest rate for pregnancies and abortions. By 1972 abortion was openly available on request, about a year before the U.S. Supreme Court Decision. Presently all costs are covered by national health insurance. Insofar as can be determined, there are no clandestine procedures and registration is believed to be complete.

As noted by David and Rademakers in 1996, there has been a considerable decrease in the number of births resulting from unplanned pregnancies in the Netherlands. During the late 1960s, 44.5% of first births were not planned. Twenty years later, unplanned births represented only 5.7% of all first births. The vast majority of Dutch pregnancies are wanted and unplanned pregnancy is rare. When an unplanned pregnancy does occur, the chances are that it will be terminated by abortion.

The birthrate of American teens has been consistently higher than that of adolescents in industrialized European nations. Studies have shown that American teens are not more sexually active than European adolescents but are less effective contraceptors. Compared to many American teens, Dutch teenagers have easier access to modern contraceptives and to emergency contraception.

A 1990 Youth and Sex Survey of Dutch adolescents found that 80% contracepted at sexual debut: 41% used condoms, 21% used the pill, 9% used both condom and pill (popularly known as Double

Dutch), 6% used withdrawal, 16% used nothing, and 6% did not respond to the question. A repeat survey in 1995 indicated that Dutch adolescents experienced sexual debut earlier (mean age 17.7 years), were more active sexually than five years before, and had more sexual partners. Contraceptive usage at sexual debut had further improved to 85%.

What is different in the Netherlands, compared to the United States, is a general attitude of openness and tolerance toward sexual activities. It evolved from 1965 to 1975, partially as a result of increasing recognition of the public health effects of unwanted pregnancies, especially among teens. At the same time, the influence of the Catholic church in daily life declined. Prevention of unwanted pregnancy was defined as a public duty, not just a personal concern. Modern contraceptives (pills and IUDs) were provided free of charge by the national health service. Efforts to impose a charge were so fiercely resisted that the government withdrew its proposals.

The lower abortion rate did not result from sexual abstinence, rejection of abortion as a means of resolving an unwanted pregnancy, widespread use of emergency contraception, or data manipulation. The explanation offered by Dutch researchers is that unplanned pregnancies are rare because most couples practice effective contraception. Abortion is deemed a last resort that should be prevented.

As the country transitioned from an agricultural to a modern industrial society, and with the evolution of mass media and more effective contraceptives, a broad consensus emerged regarding sexuality. It was considered a healthy and normal part of life, both for adults and adolescents. At the same time, everyone was cautioned to make their own decisions and take personal responsibility for their sexual behavior. The objective of sexuality education is to instill skills enhancing partner communication and negotiation about sexual relations. The Dutch are comfortable with the notion that adolescents are sexually active and should have ready access to contraception and open discussions.

Sexuality education begins at an early age, is non-judgmental and positive in tone, and is an ongoing lifelong process, involving a variety of approaches and media. Teenage periodicals and TV programs are explicit. The focus is on real problems and real feelings. For example, a prime-time TV program featuring a popular rock star regularly discusses topics ranging from sexual orientation and masturbation to oral sex. The approach to AIDS is similarly forthright. Instead of telling adolescents to say no to sexual activity, they are taught to practice safe sexual behavior, preferably by combining pregnancy and AIDS/STD prevention methods, such as the pill plus condom. Use of pill plus condom at sexual debut has increased from 9% in 1990 to 24% in 1995 and from 13% to 18% at most recent intercourse. Contraceptives are readily available and accessible to all, regardless of age. [*See* SAFER SEX BEHAVIORS.]

The Netherlands is a country where public policies about sexuality are congruent with private behavior. A gradual shift in public policies toward greater acceptance of private values and lifestyles was associated with a strong public emphasis on personal responsibility for reproductive behavior and parenthood. Meanwhile, in the United States, private sexual behavior has become far freer than publicly advocated sexual beliefs and fundamentalist religious views would suggest. It is quite likely that a more rational and less ambivalent public approach to sexuality would encourage more responsible reproductive behavior, thereby reducing unwanted pregnancies, the tendency to resort to abortion, and the dangers of AIDS. The Dutch experience is instructive.

XII. A *Final Note*

Even in countries where contraceptives are readily available, unplanned pregnancies remain common. There will always be a need for abortion. When performed by experienced practitioners in legal settings, risks to physical health are low and substantially less than dying from complications associated with pregnancy or childbirth. Psychological distress is generally greatest before the abortion when the woman has to decide how to resolve an unwanted pregnancy. Abortion is usually followed by a mixture of emotions with a predominance of positive feelings and relief. Severe negative reactions are rare. There is no credible evidence for a postabortion syndrome. In an enlightened community effective sexuality education, ready access to modern contraceptives, contraceptive vigilance, and the availability of emergency contraception constitute the public health approach to reproductive behavior, reducing unwanted pregnancies and reliance on abortion.

SUGGESTED READING

Adler, N. E., David, H. P., Major, B., Roth, S. H., Russo, N. F., and Wyatt, G. (1990). Psychological responses after abortion. *Science* **248**, 41–44.

Adler, N. E., David, H. P., Major, B., Roth, S. H., Russo, N. F., and Wyatt, G. (1992). Psychological factors in abortion: A review. *American Psychologist* **47**, 1194–1204.

Alan Guttmacher Institute (1999). *Sharing Responsibility: Women, Society, and Abortion Worldwide.* Alan Guttmacher Institute, New York.

Beckman, L. J., and Harvey, S. M. (1999). *The New Civil War: The Psychology, Culture, and Politics of Abortion.* American Psychological Association, Washington, DC.

David, H. P. (1985). Postabortion and postpartum psychiatric hospitalization. In *Abortion: Medical Progress and Social Implications.* (R. Porter and M. O'Connor, eds.), Ciba Symposium No. 45, pp. 150–161. Pitman, London.

David, H. P., and Rademakers, J. (1996). Lessons from the Dutch abortion experience. *Studies in Family Planning* **27**, 341–343.

Kubicka, L., Matejcek, Z., David, H. P., Dytrych, Z., Miller, W. B., and Roth, Z. Prague children from unwanted pregnancies revisited at age thirty. *Acta Psychiatrica Scandinavica* **91**, 361–369.

Rue, V. M. (1995). Post-abortion syndrome: A variant of post-traumatic stress disorder. In *Post-Abortion Syndrome: Its Wide Ramifications.* (P. Doherty, ed.), pp. 15–28. Four Courts Press, Dublin.

Russo, N. F., and Zierk, K. L. (1992). Abortion, childbearing, and women's well-being. *Professional Psychology; Research and Practice* **23**, 269–280.

Speckhard, A. C. (1987). *Psycho-Social Stress Following Abortion.* Sheed and Ward, Kansas City.

Academic Aspirations and Degree Attainment of Women

Helen S. Astin

Jennifer A. Lindholm

University of California, Los Angeles

Glossary

Contextual determinants Environmental factors, such as the sociohistorical times and available support systems, that influence an individual's sense of self-efficacy.

Normal schools Institutions established in the northeastern, eastern, and western regions of the United States in the late 19th century specifically for the purpose of training teachers. Most were closed or converted into colleges or universities during the rapid expansion of the state university system in the mid-20th century.

Self-efficacy The belief or conviction that one can successfully perform a given task or activity.

Structure of opportunity The combined effects of economic, social, and political forces on individuals' access within the educational system and workplace.

ACADEMIC ASPIRATIONS AND ACHIEVEMENT of women in the United States as well as some of the forces that have shaped their academic choices are examined in this article. We provide a brief overview of the sociohistorical forces that have influenced women's access to formal schooling within the United States, followed by national trends in women's postsecondary educational aspirations and degree attainment. We conclude with a brief overview of the social and legislative changes that have had an impact on the educational accomplishments of women and consider the potentially mediating role that personal characteristics play in affecting their educational choices.

I. Introduction

Within North American society, education has historically been viewed as a vehicle for occupational mobility and as a necessity for one's full participation in a democratic society. Far from this idealistic vision, however, is the reality of unequal opportunity and its resulting impact on the achievement of large segments of our society. The cumulative body of research on women's academic and career development reveals that although women in the United States have achieved relative parity of access to higher education, in the aggregate they have not fared as well as men. Moreover, while women's degree attainment at the associate, bachelor's, and master's degree levels now surpasses that of men, there is still considerable disparity within many fields in the percentages of women doctoral degree recipients. In the labor market, women also remain comparatively disadvantaged with respect to the economic returns on their educational investments.

In addressing the educational aspirations and attainment of women, it is important to consider the effects of personal and social forces that combine to shape individual perceptions of what is possible and what is acceptable. Taken together, these perceptions play a key role in influencing educational and occupational decisions.

II. Social Forces and Women's Educational Opportunities

Researchers in the fields of educational and vocational development have long recognized what Robert Lent, Steven Brown, and Gail Hackett referred to in their 1994 monograph on career and academic interest, choice, and performance as the "mutual interacting influences" between individuals and their environments. There are numerous theoretical perspectives on the specific nature of the relationship between personal and environmental factors and their resulting influence on educational and occupational choices. Common among them, however, is the important role that social forces, such as the structure of opportunity, play in affecting choice behavior. Also critical is the influence of personal characteristics, such as one's sense of self-efficacy, in shaping both academic and career development. As Lent and his colleagues indicated, "contextual determinants" help to explain the learning experiences that promote personal interests and choices. Thus, in examining changes over time in women's academic aspirations and attainment, it is essential to consider the social context for women's educational development over the past 200 years.

Today, it is taken for granted that, within North American society, both boys and girls have equal access to education. However, prior to the 19th century, formal schooling for women and girls of any age within the United States was nonexistent. In time, however, economic considerations facilitated girls' access to formal education. Thus, girls began to attend school in the early 1800s, most often early in the morning for abbreviated periods of instruction before the boys arrived, or during the summer when the boys were busy with farmwork.

When the first high school for girls opened in 1824, higher education was still viewed entirely outside the realm of possibilities for young women, both for practical and ideological reasons. Higher education was deemed unnecessary for women since its primary purpose was for professional training. Because the professions, including teaching, were exclusively men's occupations, there was no compelling reason to prepare women for advanced academic training. Beyond "practical" considerations, however, there were also a host of widely held social biases that thwarted women's educational opportunities. For example, as Mariam Chamberlain explained in her 1988 work on women's progress and prospects in academe, the prevailing mindset in the 18th, 19th, and even early 20th centuries was that intellectual activity was not only unfeminine but also potentially harmful to women's health and reproductive capacity. Compounding concerns for preserving women's health and femininity was a prevailing belief that women were less intelligent than men and thus incapable of succeeding in advanced courses of study. There was also concern that women's attendance would lower standards in coeducational institutions, as well as distract male students from their studies.

These social biases and the debates they fueled about the practicality of women having access to the same types of degree programs offered for men prevailed into the 1940s, despite the fact that faculty at Oberlin College one hundred years earlier had declared a commitment to include both sexes and all races in their educational programs. Oberlin first began admitting women students in 1837, providing them with equal access to the type of postsecondary curriculum available to men. Four years later, three women students graduated from Oberlin with degrees that were equivalent in rigor and scope to those earned by their male classmates.

With few exceptions, however, pre–Civil War higher education opportunities for women remained segregated. It was not until the Civil War and the years immediately following when declines in male enrollments and a subsequent need to maintain college operating costs lowered resistance to admitting women to traditionally male colleges. In the years following the Civil War, women also gained greater access to higher education because the rapid growth of the public school system resulted in an increased demand for teachers that could not be met exclusively by men. In addition, the Morrill Act of 1862, which paved the way for the establishment of state universities and land grant colleges, provided women with a new avenue of access to higher education. These new institutions were founded to provide students with both liberal and practical education. As such, they offered new fields of study within their curricula that were deemed "practical" for women, such as home economics. [SEE CAREER ACHIEVEMENT.]

III. *Women's Participation in Higher Education:* 1870–2000

By 1870, the first year that national college attendance records were kept, approximately 11,000 women were enrolled in U.S. postsecondary institutions, representing approximately 25% of the total number of students enrolled. However, because most women were attending non-degree-granting institutions, approximately only one in seven bachelor's degree recipients during this time were women. The overwhelming majority of women students in the late 1800s attended "normal" schools (approximately 5000) and private seminaries and academies (approximately 3000) that did not grant bachelor's degrees. In her 1959 historical review of women's participation in higher education, Mabel Newcomer estimates that of the entire population of women attending college in 1870, only about 3000 were attending degree-granting institutions. The vast majority of these (approximately 2200) were enrolled at women's colleges. Only about 600 women were enrolled in degree-granting programs at coeducational colleges. Another 200 attended the eight state universities admitting women at the time. However, these women were typically educated in what were referred to as exclusively "female departments" within the larger university. Within these environments, the curriculum was geared primarily toward developing women students' content knowledge and skills in areas such as home economics, with an ultimate goal of helping them to become better wives and mothers.

Besides the ever-increasing need for public school teachers, women's collegiate opportunities were aided by the growing participation of women in the workforce. The 1870 census, for example, lists at least one woman in every one of the 338 occupations in its classifications, including 525 female physicians and 5 female lawyers.

A. ENROLLMENTS

Despite these dismal early statistics, women's participation in higher education increased steadily during the latter part of the 19th century as more and more colleges and universities began admitting women. Whereas in 1870, roughly 30% of colleges and universities were coeducational, by 1900, 70% admitted both men and women, and by the turn of the century women comprised 36% of all students enrolled in higher education (Table I). While increasing numbers of women were participating in postsecondary education, it is also important to note that in 1900, the possibility of pursuing postsecondary education for both men and women was a reality for only a very small, and generally elite, segment of the

Table I
Enrollment in Institutions of Higher Education: 1870–1997[a]

Year	Total	Percentage of women
1870[b]	52,286	21.3
1880[b]	115,817	32.7
1980[b]	156,756	35.9
1900	237,592	35.9
1910[b]	355,213	39.6
1920	597,880	47.3
1930	1,100,737	43.7
1940	1,494,203	40.2
1950	2,659,021	30.3
1960	3,639,847	35.9
1970	8,004,660	40.7
1980	11,569,899	50.9
1990	13,538,560	54.3
1997	14,367,530	55.6

[a]Data for 1870 to 1950 are for resident degree-credit students who enrolled at any time during the academic year. The year 1997 includes degree-granting institutions.
[b]Estimated.
Source: U.S. Department of Education. National Center for Educational Statistics, 1999.

nation's citizens. Indeed, the entire college-going population in the United States at the beginning of the 20th century comprised less than 4% of the total population.

While women's enrollments, relative to those of men, continued to increase until 1920, a decline occurred during the 1930s, 1940s, and 1950s. Another shift occurred in 1960, leading to increases that continued through the late 1990s, when the majority of enrolled students were women. The declines during the 1930s, 1940s, and 1950s can be explained by the social and historical events that occurred during those decades: the Depression, World War II, and the postwar 1950s when colleges were populated by large numbers of veterans (most of whom were male) returning to, or entering, college on the GI Bill. For any veteran who wanted a college education, the GI Bill provided a means for subsidizing 100% of postsecondary education costs, including books and living expenses. Indeed, economic factors and the need to make space on college and university campuses for large numbers of veterans had a significant impact on women's participation in higher education during the mid-1900s.

B. DEGREE ATTAINMENT

With respect to degree attainment, the absolute numbers of both women and men completing undergraduate and graduate degrees increased dramatically during the Depression era, even though enrollments of women had begun to decline (Table II). In part, the observed increases in the absolute numbers of individuals earning degrees between 1920 and 1930 (bachelor's degree attainment nearly tripled during this decade, while master's and doctoral degree attainment more than tripled) can be explained by the tightening of the labor market due to the Depression. Lack of employment opportunities often results in students' remaining in school longer and, thus, completing their degrees. As indicated earlier, the declining enrollment of women relative to men that began in the 1930s continued into the 1950s, where we also see the most dramatic decline in women's degree attainment. In 1950, for example, 24% of those receiving bachelor's and first professional degrees were women compared to 41% only a decade earlier.

Historically, willingness to accommodate women within U.S. colleges and universities has been dependent primarily on ideological grounds (most notably whether educated women were "acceptable" to men).

Even once the concept of an "educated woman" became more acceptable within North American society, decisions to enroll women were commonly based on whether there was adequate space remaining after the population of men who wished to attend college had been accounted for. This bias helps to explain the dramatic drop in the proportion of women attaining degrees in the 1950s, when male enrollments rose dramatically following both World War II and the Korean War. The large influx of men onto increasingly crowded campuses, coupled with a trend toward earlier marriage and childbearing for women, resulted in a marked decline in women's participation in higher education. Women who wanted to further their education, particularly at the graduate level, had to be much better qualified academically and much less in need of financial aid than their male peers. Those who were married and raising children, but who also aspired to continue work on their degrees, were almost universally denied part-time enrollment. The decline in women's access to higher education during the 1950s is evident in degree attainment trends shown in Table II.

By 1960, the proportion of women earning bachelor's and first professional degrees rose to 35%, but ultimately, it was not until 1970 that women's overall degree attainment, relative to that of men, again returned to the prewar rates of the 1940s. Since the 1980s, women have earned a majority of the bachelor's and master's degrees awarded in the United States.

C. DEGREE ATTAINMENT BY FIELD OF STUDY

Beyond changes in women's enrollment and degree attainment during the 20th century, there have also been notable changes over time in the fields in which women have been most likely to earn undergraduate and graduate degrees. Since the 1970s, the diversity of the fields in which women earn degrees, particularly at the bachelor's and master's levels, has also increased (Tables III and IV). Not surprisingly, these signs of educational progress parallel progress in women's participation in the labor market. Over the past 30 years, women have made notable gains in embarking on professional careers once deemed "unacceptable" for their gender. In spite of these changes, women continue to lag behind, particularly in traditionally "male" fields. Moreover, despite their increasing proportions of undergraduate and graduate degree attainment, the vast majority of women continue to pursue careers in lower paying, less presti-

Table II
Women's Degree Attainment: 1870–2000

	Associate	Bachelor's	Master's	Doctorate	First Prof.
1870[a]					
Total	—	9,371	0	1	—
% Female	—	14.7	—	0	—
1900					
Total	—	27,410	1,015	149	—
% Female	—	19.1	19.1	1.3	—
1910					
Total	—	37,199	2,113	443	—
% Female	—	22.7	26.4	9.9	—
1920					
Total	—	48,622	4,279	615	—
% Female	—	34.2	30.2	15.1	—
1930					
Total	—	122,484	14,969	2,299	—
% Female	—	39.9	40.4	15.4	—
1940					
Total	—	186,500	26,731	3,290	—
% Female	—	41.3	38.2	13.0	—
1950					
Total	—	432,058	58,183	6,420	—
% Female	—	23.9	29.2	9.6	—
1960					
Total	—	392,440	74,435	9,829	—
% Female	—	35.3	31.6	10.5	—
1970					
Total	206,023	792,316	208,291	29,866	34,918
% Female	43.0	43.1	39.7	13.3	5.3
1980					
Total	400,910	929,417	298,081	32,615	70,121
% Female	54.2	49.0	49.4	29.7	24.8
1990					
Total	455,102	1,051,344	324,301	38,371	70,988
% Female	58.0	53.2	52.6	36.4	38.1
2000[b]					
Total	568,000	1,164,000	385,000	43,900	74,200
% Female	60.0	56.3	57.7	40.8	42.6

[a]Until 1970, numbers and percentages reflect bachelor's and first professional degree recipients combined.
[b]Projected.
Source: U.S. Department of Education. National Center for Educational Statistics, 1999.

gious, "female" occupations such as elementary and secondary school teaching, social work, and nursing.

Since 1970, we have also seen a dramatic increase in the proportions of women attaining doctoral and first professional degrees (e.g., law and medical degrees). In 1970, women received 13% of doctoral degrees. By 1990, they were 36% of all doctoral recipients, and by 2000, women are projected to earn 41% of doctoral degrees (Table II). The most dramatic increases in women's degree attainment at the doctoral level have occurred in traditionally "male" fields such as agriculture, business, engineering, and the physical sciences (Table V). Nevertheless, women's representation in these fields continues to remain relatively low. [See WOMEN IN NONTRADITIONAL WORK FIELDS.]

Besides changes in the fields of doctoral production, it should also be noted that there has been a shift in women's first professional degree attainment (Table II). In 1970, women were earning 5% of first

Table III

Bachelor's Degree Attainment by Field of Study

	1950		1960		1970[a]		1980		1990		1997	
	Total	Women (%)	Total	Women (%)	Total	Women (%)	Total	Women (%)	Total	Women (%)	Total	Women (%)
Agriculture	—	—	—	—	12,672	4.4	22,802	29.6	12,900	31.6	22,602	39.0
Architecture	2,563	4.8	1,801	3.2	5,570	11.9	9,132	27.8	9,364	39.1	7,944	35.9
Biological science	—	—	15,576	25.2	35,473	29.1	46,370	42.1	37,204	50.8	63,975	53.9
Business	—	—	51,076	7.5	114,729	9.1	184,867	33.7	248,698	46.8	226,633	48.6
Communications	—	—	—	—	10,802	35.3	28,616	52.3	51,308	60.1	47,768	58.8
Computer science	—	—	—	—	2,388	13.6	11,154	30.2	27,257	29.9	24,768	27.2
Education	61,472	48.9	89,002	71.3	176,307	74.5	118,038	73.8	105,112	78.1	105,223	75.0
Engineering	52,246	0.003	37,679	0.004	50,046	0.07	68,893	9.3	81,322	13.8	75,157	16.6
English	17,240	52.3	20,128	62.3	64,342	65.6	32,541	65.0	47,519	67.0	49,345	66.5
Foreign languages	4,477	61.0	4,527	65.8	19,055	75.2	10,816	76.1	11,092	73.8	12,261	71.0
Health professions	—	—	—	—	25,226	77.1	63,920	82.2	58,302	84.4	85,631	81.5
Math	6,382	22.6	11,399	27.2	24,937	37.9	11,872	41.5	15,176	45.7	12,820	46.1
Physical sciences	—	—	16,007	12.5	21,412	13.8	23,410	23.7	16,066	31.3	19,531	37.4
Psychology	9,569	36.7	8,061	40.8	38,187	44.4	42,093	63.3	53,952	71.6	74,191	73.9
Public administration	—	—	—	—	5,466	68.4	16,644	73.3	13,908	76.0	20,649	79.8
Social science/history	—	—	—	—	155,324	36.8	103,662	43.6	118,083	44.2	124,891	48.7
Visual/performing arts	—	—	—	—	30,394	59.7	40,892	63.2	39,934	62.0	50,083	58.6

[a]Data are from 1971.

Source: U.S. Department of Education. National Center for Educational Studies, 1999.

Table IV
Master's Degree Attainment by Field of Study

	1950		1960		1970[a]		1980		1990		1997	
	Total	Women (%)	Total	Women (%)	Total	Women (%)	Total	Women (%)	Total	Women (%)	Total	Women (%)
Agriculture	—	—	—	—	2,457	5.9	3,976	22.5	3,382	33.8	4,516	42.2
Architecture	166	4.2	319	4.4	1,705	13.8	3,139	28.5	3,499	36.3	4,034	42.1
Biological science	—	—	2,154	22.6	5,728	33.6	6,510	37.1	4,869	50.8	6,466	53.1
Business	—	—	4,643	3.6	25,977	3.9	54,484	22.4	76,676	34.0	97,619	38.9
Communications	—	—	—	—	1,856	34.6	3,082	50.5	4,362	61.0	5,601	64.2
Computer science	—	—	—	—	1,588	10.3	3,647	20.9	9,677	28.1	10,098	28.2
Education	20,069	40.1	33,433	46.0	87,666	56.2	101,819	70.2	84,881	75.9	110,087	77.0
Engineering	4,496	0.003	7,159	0.004	16,443	1.1	16,243	7.0	24,772	13.8	26,827	18.3
English	2,259	41.6	2,931	50.3	10,686	60.6	6,189	63.9	6,567	66.4	7,722	64.6
Foreign languages	919	50.4	832	52.9	4,407	66.1	2,152	70.8	1,931	69.8	2,244	70.7
Health professions	—	—	—	—	5,749	55.3	15,704	72.3	20,321	77.7	35,958	78.6
Math	974	19.5	1,757	19.1	5,695	27.1	3,382	33.1	4,146	38.1	3,783	40.8
Physical sciences	—	—	3,376	9.7	6,367	13.3	5,219	18.6	5,449	26.4	5,563	32.6
Psychology	1,316	28.0	1,406	30.2	5,717	40.6	9,938	58.8	10,730	68.5	14,353	73.2
Public administration	—	—	—	—	7,785	50.0	17,560	55.2	17,399	67.6	24,781	71.9
Social science/history	—	—	—	—	16,539	28.5	12,176	36.0	11,634	40.7	14,787	47.0
Visual/performing arts	—	—	—	—	6,675	47.4	8,708	53.3	8,481	56.3	10,627	57.9

[a]Data are from 1971.
Source: U.S. Department of Education. National Center for Educational Studies, 1999.

Table V
Doctoral Degree Attainment by Field of Study

	1950 Total	1950 Women (%)	1960 Total	1960 Women (%)	1970[a] Total	1970[a] Women (%)	1980 Total	1980 Women (%)	1990 Total	1990 Women (%)	1997 Total	1997 Women (%)
Agriculture	—	—	—	—	1,086	2.9	991	11.3	1,183	19.7	1,217	27.4
Architecture	1	0	17	0	36	8.3	79	16.5	103	29.1	135	31.1
Biological science	—	—	1,205	9.9	3,645	16.3	3,636	26.0	3,844	37.7	4,812	43.1
Business	—	—	135	1.5	757	2.8	753	14.7	1,093	25.2	1,336	29.1
Communications	—	—	—	—	145	13.1	193	37.3	273	46.9	300	48.3
Computer science	—	—	—	—	128	2.3	240	11.3	627	14.8	857	15.9
Education	953	16.4	1,591	19.6	6,041	21.0	7,314	43.9	6,502	57.3	6,751	62.8
Engineering	417	0.002	786	0.004	3,638	0.006	2,507	3.8	4,981	8.9	6,210	12.3
English	230	21.3	397	20.9	1,650	28.8	1,294	47.0	1,078	55.5	1,575	57.5
Foreign languages	168	19.6	150	33.3	703	39.5	522	58.4	475	61.5	622	60.3
Health professions	—	—	—	—	466	16.5	786	44.7	1,536	54.2	2,672	56.0
Math	160	5.6	303	5.9	1,249	7.6	763	13.6	966	17.8	1,174	24.1
Physical sciences	—	—	1,838	3.4	4,390	5.6	3,089	12.4	4,164	19.4	4,474	23.0
Psychology	283	14.8	641	15.1	2,144	24.0	3,395	43.4	3,811	58.9	4,053	66.7
Public administration	—	—	—	—	174	24.1	342	36.8	508	53.7	518	53.1
Social science/history	—	—	—	—	3,660	13.9	3,230	27.0	3,010	32.9	3,989	37.9
Visual/performing arts	—	—	—	—	621	22.2	655	36.9	849	44.4	1,060	50.1

[a]Data are from 1971.

Source: U.S. Department of Education. National Center for Educational Statistics, 1999.

professional degrees. By 1990, they earned 38% of all first professional degrees, and it is projected that in 2000 women will be 43% of first professional degree recipients. With respect to specific professions, in 1971, women earned 1% of degrees in dentistry, 9% in medicine, 7% in law, and 4% in business. By 1997, these percentages were 37, 41, 44, and 39 respectively (Table VI). Indeed, a dramatic change.

D. DEGREE ATTAINMENT AMONG WOMEN OF COLOR

Table VII shows trends since 1977 in degree completion rates for women of different races and ethnicities. With few exceptions, patterned growth in degree completion between 1977 and 1997 among women of color parallels that observed for White women: steady increases. In 1977, women earned nearly half of the associate, bachelor's, and master's degrees awarded in the United States. Among the larger population of women, African American women earned comparatively higher percentages of the associate (54%), bachelor's (57%), and master's (63%) degrees than did their male counterparts. Only among Asians did women earn notably lower percentages of master's degrees (39%) than men. Women's degree attainment relative to men was notably lower for doctoral degrees (24%) and first professional degrees (19%) in 1977. Compared with women of other racial and ethnic groups, African American women achieved the greatest parity with their male counterparts in doctoral (39%) and first professional (31%) degree attainment. Observed racial and ethnic differences in the comparative degree attainment rates of men and women are reflective of long-standing historical conditions and culture norms.

By 1997, women earned more than half of the associate, bachelor's, and master's degrees awarded in the United States. Compared to their male counterparts, African American women continued to fare the best in their proportionate degree attainment at the associate (66%), bachelor's (64%), and master's (69%) degree levels. While considerably better than in the 1970s, women's proportional degree attainment at the doctoral level still continued to lag behind that of men in 1997. White women continued to earn the overwhelming majority of doctoral degrees awarded to women and received nearly half (46%) of doctoral degrees awarded to Whites. Compared to their male counterparts, African American women continued to fare the best proportionately in terms of doctoral degree attainment, earning 57% of the degrees awarded within the population of African American doctoral recipients. Asian women continued to do the least well compared to their male counterparts, earning just 38% of the doctoral degrees awarded to Asians.

As indicated earlier, first professional degree attainments increased considerably between 1977 and 1997 for all women. Most notable, perhaps is that although the absolute number of White first professional degree recipients actually declined somewhat in 1997 (relative to 1987 figures), the percentage of degrees awarded to White women steadily increased (from 18 to 40%) between 1977 and 1997. Over the same time period, the absolute numbers of professional degrees awarded to people of color steadily increased, as did the relative proportion of women within each non-White racial or ethnic group who

Table VI
First Professional Degrees by Field

	1950		1960		1970[a]		1980		1990		1997	
	Total	Women (%)	Total	Women (%)	Total	Women (%)	Total	Women (%)	Total	Women (%)	Total	Women (%)
Dentistry	2,579	0.007	3,247	0.008	3,745	1.1	5,258	13.3	4,100	30.9	3,784	36.9
Medicine	5,612	10.4	7,032	5.5	8,919	9.1	14,902	23.4	15,075	34.2	15,571	41.4
Law	—	—	9,240	2.5	17,421	7.1	35,647	30.2	36,485	42.3	40,079	43.7
Business[b]	—	—	4,643	3.6	25,977	3.9	54.484	22.4	76,676	34.0	97,619	38.9

[a]Data are from 1971.

[b]Includes degrees in business management/administrative services, marketing operations/marketing and distribution, and consumer and personal services.

Source: U.S. Department of Education. National Center for Educational Studies, 1999.

Table VII

Degree Attainment by Ethnic/Racial Background[a]

	1997		1987		1997	
	N	Women (%)	N	Women (%)	N	Women (%)
Associate						
Total	404,956	48.2	436,304	56.3	563,620	60.8
White	342,290	47.9	361,861	56.3	424,364	60.7
Black	33,159	53.8	35,447	60.6	55,260	65.6
Hispanic	16,636	45.3	19,334	54.7	42,645	58.8
Asian	7,044	48.5	11,779	47.6	24,829	56.6
American Indian	2,498	51.3	3,195	60.5	5,927	65.6
Bachelor's						
Total	917,900	46.1	991,264	51.5	1,168,023	55.7
White	807,688	45.8	841,818	51.7	898,224	55.3
Black	58,636	57.1	56,560	60.2	94,053	64.4
Hispanic	18,743	44.9	26,988	52.3	61,941	58.0
Asian	13,793	44.6	32,624	47.1	67,969	52.8
American Indian	3,326	45.8	3,968	54.2	7,409	59.7
Master's						
Total	316,602	47.1	289,349	51.2	414,882	57.1
White	266,061	47.8	228,874	53.9	302,541	59.0
Black	21,037	63.0	13,873	62.9	28,224	68.5
Hispanic	6,071	46.2	7,044	52.7	15,187	59.7
Asian	5,122	39.0	8,559	38.8	18,477	51.9
American Indian	967	46.1	1,103	53.0	1,924	62.1
Doctoral						
Total	33,126	24.4	34,041	35.2	45,394	40.9
White	26,851	25.4	24,434	39.8	28,344	45.9
Black	1,253	38.9	1,057	54.1	1,847	57.4
Hispanic	522	26.6	751	41.3	1,098	47.9
Asian	658	17.9	1,098	27.7	2,607	38.4
American Indian	95	16.2	105	45.7	173	50.3
First porfessional						
Total	63,953	18.7	71,617	35.0	77,185	42.1
White	58,422	18.2	62,688	34.4	59,852	40.3
Black	2,537	30.6	3,420	46.3	5,251	58.5
Hispanic	1,076	17.0	2,051	36.5	3,553	45.1
Asian	1,021	24.0	2,270	37.4	7,037	46.0
American Indian	196	18.9	304	39.8	511	43.4

[a]Comparable data for degree attainment by race and ethnicity are not available for the earlier time periods covered in Table I though VI. Source: U.S. Department of Education. National Center for Educational Statistics, 1999.

earned professional degrees. Overall, however, the number of professional degree recipients among women of color remains substantially below that of White women, reflecting their representativeness in the overall population.

IV. Women's Degree Aspirations

Degree aspirations have been found to predict degree attainment. Trends in degree aspirations for men and women show that both sexes have increased their as-

pirations with respect to higher education attainment. In 1966, only 39% of first-year women college students (and 52% of their male counterparts) aspired to earn master's, doctoral, or first professional degrees. However, by 1999, the percentages of those aspiring to earn graduate degrees (combining the three degree levels) rose to 68% for women and 60% for men (Table VIII).

Degree aspirations among women of color tend, overall, to be higher than those of White women (Table IX). For example, in 1972, the first year for which data for racial categories by gender are avail-

Table VIII
Trends in Degree Aspircations of Entering College Students[a]

	1966		1972		1980		1990		1990	
	Men	Women	Men	Women	Men	Women	Men	Women	Men	Women
Associate	4.1	7.3	6.5	10.1	6.9	9.5	4.7	6.3	4.2	3.6
Bachelor's	32.5	46.1	33.9	41.3	37.2	38.1	30.7	27.6	29.0	24.8
Master's	31.2	32.3	26.0	28.9	29.3	30.1	36.1	38.1	38.6	41.3
Doctoral	13.7	5.2	10.6	6.8	8.5	7.3	12.3	12.5	13.8	14.6
M.D., D.D.S., D.V.M., D.O.	7.4	1.9	9.7	4.3	7.0	5.9	5.9	6.6	5.6	8.8
L.L.B. or J.D.	—	—	6.5	2.1	4.9	3.7	4.7	4.9	3.6	3.6

[a]All numbers are percentages.
Source: Cooperative Institutional Research Institute, UCLA Higher Education Research Institute.

able, 41% of White women aspired to earning an advanced degree (either master's, doctoral, or first professional). By comparison, 57% of African American women, 52% of Asian women, and 50% of American Indian women indicated similar aspirations for advanced degree attainment. Only Hispanic women reported lower advanced degree aspirations than White women (30%). By 1999, 66% of White women aspired to earn advanced degrees, compared with 76% of African American women, 82% of

Table IX
Trends in Women's Degree Aspriations by Race/Ethnicity[a]

	All	White	Black	Asian	American Indian	Hispanic
1972						
Associate	10.1	10.1	7.7	8.2	9.5	17.9
Bachelor's	41.3	43.2	28.0	31.6	33.6	35.3
Master's	28.9	28.7	35.6	31.8	26.0	21.7
Doctoral	6.8	5.9	12.9	10.2	12.6	3.9
First professional	6.4	5.9	8.8	9.8	10.2	3.9
1980						
Associate	9.5	10.2	3.8	6.3	10.0	15.8
Bachelor's	38.1	32.3	24.8	25.1	31.4	25.9
Master's	30.1	23.9	34.0	27.8	27.5	25.5
Doctoral	7.3	5.1	14.3	12.0	10.7	6.8
First professional	9.6	7.2	13.8	21.4	12.8	8.6
1990						
Associate	6.3	7.0	3.4	1.6	4.3	1.0
Bachelor's	27.6	29.2	21.3	15.7	25.6	24.9
Master's	38.1	38.4	37.0	36.0	26.1	39.6
Doctoral	12.5	11.4	17.3	21.2	20.1	17.0
First professional	11.5	10.4	15.9	22.1	17.9	11.4
1999						
Associate	3.6	4.1	2.7	0.6	3.3	0.7
Bachelor's	24.8	27.3	16.5	13.7	18.3	22.8
Master's	41.3	42.3	35.8	41.5	37.3	37.5
Doctoral	14.6	12.6	22.2	20.2	19.6	18.4
First professional	12.4	10.7	17.8	20.1	16.5	16.2

[a]All numbers are percentages.
Source: Cooperative Institutional Research Program, UCLA, Higher Education Research Institute.

Asian women, 74% of American Indian women, and 72% of Hispanic women. Although disparity in the percentage of White women (compared with women of color) who aspire to earn advanced degrees appears to have declined over the past 30 years, women of color remain comparatively more likely to aspire to earning doctoral or first professional degrees than do White women. These trends reflect the notion that education is a vehicle for upward mobility among members of racial and ethnic groups who have been traditionally marginalized in U.S. society.

V. Social and Legislative Changes as Forces in Women's Aspirations and Achievement

How can we explain the dramatic changes observed in the 1970s with respect to both degree aspirations and attainment? While women's proportional degree attainment rates in the 1960s continued to lag behind those of women in the 1940s, the late 1960s also brought dramatic change in women's expectations for equal opportunity in both academic and labor market domains. Changes in social attitudes brought about by both the civil rights movement and the women's movement, combined with a shift in the national economy (the 1970s were characterized by considerable inflation and a tightening job market), explain women's escalating degree aspirations and attainment. The structure of opportunity was, indeed, changing.

The revolutionary societal shift that began in the late 1960s and continued through the 1970s and beyond enabled women to make tremendous gains in achieving parity with men in postsecondary access and degree attainment. Increasingly, women began working outside the home, marrying later, and having fewer children. As societal awareness of damaging sex-role stereotypes increased nationwide, women's rights became a prominent political issue. For the first time in U.S. history, federal legislation was passed banning discrimination against women in educational institutions, as well as in the workforce.

Until 1968, when Executive Order 11246 was amended to include prohibition of discrimination based on sex by federal contractors, including higher education institutions, there were no legal remedies for sex discrimination in higher education. Since the passing of Title IX of the Educational Amendments Act of 1972, which prohibited sex discrimination in

any program within the educational system receiving federal financial assistance, two other key federal statutes have operated to help protect and promote women's rights in education.

The Women's Educational Equity Act (WEEA) was passed as part of the Special Projects Act of the Educational Amendments of 1974. This legislation was enacted to provide financial support to colleges and universities, state agencies, and other types of institutions for the purpose of creating educational environments that promoted gender equity through training programs for academic personnel, counseling and guidance activities, vocational education development, and the like. Two years later, the Vocational Education Amendments Act (VEA) of 1976, which required state educational agencies to be proactive in eliminating sex bias, stereotyping, and discrimination in vocational education at the secondary and postsecondary levels, was passed.

The effects of the women's movement and concomitant events of the 1970s redefined women's role in society. The effects are evident not only in the substantial increase in women's access to postsecondary education but also in women's changing aspirations and attainment at all degree levels. [*See* Affirmative Action; The Feminist Movement.]

VI. The Mediating Role of Personal Factors in Shaping Women's Academic Aspirations and Attainment

The sociohistorical context has played a central role in affecting women's opportunities for educational achievement in the United States. However, it is also essential to consider the influence of personal characteristics in shaping women's educational choice behavior. Why, for example, do some women challenge long-standing historical expectations and sociocultural norms regardless of environmentally based constraints while others do not?

Gender differences in educational and career outcomes have been well documented in the aspirations and achievement literature. However, as Lent, Hackett, and Brown noted in 1994, there remains much to learn about the "specific paths" through which sex and race or ethnicity affect these outcomes. There is also considerable debate surrounding the applicability of a single academic or career development model to the study of choice behavior for both sexes and all ethnic and racial groups. To understand why women and men generally remain concentrated in different educational degree programs and occupations, we must continue to explore the mediating role that personal forces play in determining how societal forces are perceived and internalized by women. Such exploration is also important for better understanding the differential effects of gender on the educational aspirations and attainment of people from different racial and ethnic backgrounds.

Girls' early relationships with parents, teachers, and other influential adults in the family and in the community provide the foundation from which educational aspirations and, eventually, achievement are built. The early messages they receive about what is possible and what is appropriate, and the emotional and instrumental support they receive in exploring a variety of options, play an intuitively central, but not yet completely understood, role in determining future achievement. Early learning experiences not only fuel girls' personal interests and motivation but also their self-efficacy expectations, defined in 1977 by Albert Bandura as the belief or conviction that one can successfully perform a given task or activity. These expectations, which are acquired through performance accomplishments, vicarious experiences, verbal persuasion, and emotional arousal, play an integral part in mediating the effects of the broader social context. The construct of self-efficacy also holds valuable potential for both research and programmatic efforts to further promote parity between women and men in educational and occupational decision making. It may also be a helpful construct in understanding the disparities across ethnic groups.

In 1994, Jacquelynne Eccles applied the model of achievement-related choices she developed with colleagues over the past 15 years to understanding women's educational and occupational choices. The model provides an integrated framework for considering the effects of (1) expectations for success and (2) individual value placed on various perceived options for educational, vocational, and other achievement-related choices. By relating achievement-related beliefs, outcomes, and goals to the impact of socializers, gender-role beliefs, self-perceptions, causal attributions and the like, Eccles and her colleagues provide a useful structure for further theoretical and empirical work geared toward developing a more complete understanding of women's educational aspirations and attainment. [*See* ACHIEVEMENT.]

VII. Conclusion

In examining trends in women's educational aspirations and degree attainment over the past 200 years in the United States, we find notable shifts both in the numbers of women enrolled in colleges and universities and in the numbers who are earning undergraduate, graduate, and first professional degrees. We also find significant changes over time in the fields women choose to pursue and in their degree aspirations. Overall, we attribute these changes to the combined effects of personal and sociohistorical forces. Both the real and perceived structures of opportunity play integral roles in shaping the achievement of all citizens. Through social change and legislative action, we have made significant progress over the past two centuries in opening access to postsecondary education to a broader segment of the population. However, as we embark on a new century, there remains much work to be done. We must establish new avenues for opportunity and create stronger support networks for segments of the population that have been historically underrepresented in various academic and vocational spheres and comparatively disadvantaged in pursuing their educational and career goals.

SUGGESTED READING

Bandura, A. (1977). Self-efficacy: Toward a unifying theory of behavioral change. *Psychological Review* 84, 191–215.

Bradley, K. (2000). The incorporation of women into higher education: Paradoxical outcomes? *Sociology of Education* 73(1), 1–18.

Chamberlain, M. K. (ed.) (1988). *Women in Academe: Progress and Prospects.* Russell Sage Foundation, New York.

Cohen, C. J. and Nee, C. E. (2000). Educational attainment and sex differentials in African American communities. *The American Behavioral Scientist* 43(7), 1159–1206.

Eccles, J. S. (1994). Understanding women's educational and occupational choices. *Psychology of Women Quarterly* 18, 585–609.

Gordon, L. D. (1990). *Gender and Higher Education in the Progressive Era.* Yale University, New Haven, CT.

Jacobs, J. A. (1996). Gender inequality and higher education. *Annual Review of Sociology* 22, 153–185.

Lent, R. W., Brown, S. D., and Hackett, G. (1994). Toward a unified social cognitive theory of career/academic interest, choice, and performance. *Journal of Vocational Behavior* 45, 79–122.

Newcomer, M. (1959). *A Century of Higher Education for American Women.* Harper Brothers, New York.

Pearson, C. S., Shavlik, D. L., and Touchton, J. G. (1989). *Educating the Majority: Women Challenge Tradition in Higher Education.* American Council on Education and Macmillan, New York.

Academic Environments
Gender and Ethnicity in U.S. Higher Education

Pamela Trotman Reid

University of Michigan

Sue Rosenberg Zalk

Graduate Center, City University of New York

Glossary

Affirmative action A policy or procedure intended to provide an advantage or an added opportunity for admissions or employment to a member of an underrepresented group, usually a woman or a person from an ethnic minority group.

Chilly climate An atmosphere or environment that is unwelcoming, unsupportive, and discouraging to students or employees.

Gender gap/ethnic gap The differences in achievement, attitude, or performance that are attributable to gender or ethnic group membership.

Glass ceiling A de facto barrier to advancement of women/ethnic group members, which can be felt, but not seen, since it is usually unwritten and unspoken.

Heterosexism The belief that heterosexuality is the only appropriate and acceptable lifestyle; the assumption or expectation that everyone will have a heterosexual lifestyle.

Imposter phenomenon The result of feelings of insecurity and low confidence that leads one to believe that success is undeserved and that others will uncover a reality that is negative and unflattering.

Stereotypic threat Feelings of stress and performance decrements resulting from an awareness that others believe negative stereotypes about one's group, even when the person affected does not believe the stereotypes.

Sexual discrimination Unfair or biased treatment based on gender or sex.

Sexual harassment Unwelcome sexual advances, requests for sexual favors, and other oral or written communications, as well as unwanted physical contact of a sexual nature.

ACADEMIC ENVIRONMENTS in this article refers to the contexts in which teaching, learning, and research occur at the post-secondary level (i.e., at colleges and universities). These contexts can be described in terms of the experiences that individuals have in academia. Such experiences may influence decisions, impact behavior, and color interpretations made by the people who serve in various roles. This article focuses on how these experiences are shaped by the way society has constructed gender.

I. *Academic Background, Mission, and Community Need*

From the most prestigious research universities to the humblest two-year colleges, features of the academic environment consistently reflect gender-typed beliefs, often creating a "gender gap" with respect to the distribution of power and prestige. Widely held beliefs about women and men in university settings appear to dictate policies and practices for all members of the academic community. They also set the standards of behavior by which students, faculty, and administrators are evaluated.

Gender interacts with a variety of environmental features in the academy, such as the following:

1. *Structure and organizational features* including institutional standing in the surrounding community, historic mission as public, private, or religious, relative status based on perceived quality, and administrative organization or leadership.
2. *Social roles, traditions, and practices* including formal and informal perspectives that are assigned, ascribed to, or adopted by individuals working within a particular postsecondary setting. Examples include the use of stereotypes and attitudes based on preconceived ideas.
3. *Interpersonal dynamics* including both positive interactions among members of the academic community, such as mentoring, and negative ones, such as harassment.

This article also examines how ethnic influences operate in higher education in the United States. There are differential expectations based on ethnicity and race in the U.S. academy. These expectations are also based on stereotypic beliefs resulting in an overrepresentation of White men and women in comparison to the general population and an underrepresentation of people of color. The relationship between representation and level of prestige or importance is remarkably linear, such that the more important or prestigious a position or institution is, the less represented are women and people of color. For this reason, the discussion will include concerns of power, status, choice, and interpersonal dynamics as they occur in academic settings.

An examination of academic environments begins with an understanding of the mission, community, and history of higher education in the United States. Using traditions set in England and other European countries, the colleges and universities that were first established in the U.S. limited their enrollment to men. These include schools such as Harvard University, Yale University, and the College of William and Mary (Yale and Harvard have been coeducational for fewer than 30 years). These privately funded institutions served an elite, powerful, and wealthy community of families. (William and Mary became a state-supported institution in 1906.) They were designed to prepare and train the leaders of government, industry, and society, who at the time were correctly assumed to be men.

The fact that men received the best education was consistent with a belief that White men were more deserving, more talented, and more suited to higher education. These notions fit easily with the early and pervasive beliefs of racial and social class superiority that persist to this day. Indeed, sexism and racism are compatible with the belief that White men are superior in intellectual abilities and better suited to lead any group from the most informal and unstructured to the most formal and structured. [*See* Gender Stereotypes.]

A. HIGHER EDUCATION FOR WOMEN

Women from the same elite families that sent their sons to the universities in the 1800s and early 1900s were often not considered capable of the intellectual rigors of higher education. There was also the question in some families about whether women were worthy of the investment of time and money that such privileged education required. Both the policy and the practice of female exclusion were the norm in higher education for almost two centuries. Indeed, it was not until generations after the earliest colleges in the United States were established in the 1700s that alternatives for women were considered. While a handful of determined women braved the all-male environment to attend college, these few were the rare exceptions. It was not until the late 1800s that several institutions were founded to provide higher levels of education for women. Among the first of their kind were Mount Holyoke College in Massachusetts (a prestigious private institution) and Hunter College in New York (a public college established to parallel the all-male City College of New York). Oberlin College in Ohio was the first to accept both men and women in 1833; Oberlin also accepted students without regard to race/ethnicity.

As the need for an educated populace increased and with the advent of public education for all children, additional colleges for women were established throughout the country. Many of these were founded as "normal schools" (i.e., schools for the training of teachers) or they were viewed as "finishing schools" (i.e., places for young women to learn enough about art and culture so that they might take their place in the social community). Thus, the curricular emphases were on the humanities, social sciences, and home economics. The education of women was to allow them to develop appropriate social skills for the intellectual life of their peers and to prepare them to be intelligent wives and mothers. The public colleges, more often than private ones, focused on educating women as teachers. The private colleges were most often affiliated with a religious denomination. In fact, two-thirds of women's colleges are still connected with a religious group (most are Catholic).

B. HIGHER EDUCATION FOR PEOPLE OF COLOR

As the expectations for women prescribed the curriculum for their colleges and limited their access, the educational opportunities for people of color were even more harshly restricted. Not only practice and tradition, but legal statutes as well, excluded particular ethnic groups (African Americans, Native Americans, and other people of color) from schools and colleges. Just as the colleges for women focused on assumed gender-appropriate areas of study, many of the institutions for ethnic minorities began with an emphasis on religion (to teach morality and prepare ministers), teacher education (to provide teachers for ethnic minority children), and vocational skills (to serve ethnic communities).

The effort to provide higher educational opportunities for African Americans was most extensive. Colleges designated for the recently freed men of African descent began after the Civil War (the late 1860s). These institutions paralleled White colleges with respect to the gender expectations (i.e., most were restricted to men at first and later provisions were made for women). Founded necessarily with the largess of White men and women, these institutions were controlled by White trustees and usually run by White administrators. Howard University (a historically Black university in Washington, D.C.), for example, did not appoint its first African American president, Dr. Mordacai Johnson, until 1926, almost 60 years after its founding.

Even today, many historically Black colleges and universities have substantial numbers of White trustees and faculty; at the same time they are subject to governance by White legislators and governors. They also remain, with few exceptions, dominated by men. Few of these institutions have ever had a woman serve as president, and fewer have had an African American woman serve in that capacity. Even the colleges whose mission it was to educate African American women rarely chose one to lead the institution. For example, Spelman College, a well-known liberal arts college for African American women, did not appoint its first African American female president until 1981 when Johnnetta Cole was named president.

With the bulk of Native Americans confined to reservations, few universities or colleges were provided for them. There was a notable exception, the Indian Charity School in New Hampshire, which enrolled young Native American men and women. Chartered in 1769 as Dartmouth College, it changed in 1770 to focus almost exclusively on male "English youths." There was attention to American Indian education initiated after the Civil War, but the efforts were intended to assimilate them into the American mainstream. Thus, Native American youth were enrolled (sometimes by force) in boarding schools where they spoke English only and studied a traditional curriculum. The current Tribal Colleges were established in recent decades and most are two-year institutions. Recent attention to higher education for other ethnic groups (e.g., Asian Americans, Mexican Americans) has been the result of the growing population needs and community demands.

C. RE-ENTRY WOMEN AND TWO-YEAR COLLEGES

Among the variety of educational institutions currently flourishing in the United States, two-year colleges have become an important source of educational and economic opportunity. Jean O'Barr, a women's studies scholar, noted that in addition to providing innovative vocational programs, two-year colleges have led the way in accepting re-entry women (i.e., women who enter college some years after graduating from high school). This group is one of the fastest growing segments of the college student body comprising adults who grew up without the opportunity, interest, or the resources to enter college in their youth and who enroll years after high school. Many of these students are women who married and became full-time wives and mothers rather than embarking on college or a career. For other re-entry students, earning an income was the priority after high school. However, the quickly changing marketplace and the burgeoning technological fields found them unprepared for the employment growth opportunities. The underprepared students are more often women than men.

The community or two-year colleges have also been found more accepting of ethnic minority students and older students, as well as those students from economically deprived and academically deficient backgrounds. They have also been most willing to accept and promote women and ethnic minority men in faculty and administrative ranks. Thus, according to data from the American Council on Education, two-year colleges have a greater proportion of female presidents and greater percentages of female faculty and ethnic minority and re-entry students. [*See* CLASSROOM AND SCHOOL CLIMATE.]

D. COED VERSUS SINGLE-SEX COLLEGES FOR WOMEN

Women as students in coeducational institutions must contend with male dominance in the classroom, in extracurricular leadership activities, and in the institution as a whole. They experience pressure for gender role conformity and challenges to their self-esteem and career ambitions. Women in women's colleges, in contrast, have less exposure to these undermining experiences and greater opportunity to take leadership positions and develop their potential in areas ranging from science to student government. Additionally, due to the proportionately higher number of women in top administrative and faculty positions, role models abound. The Women's College Coalition reports that Catholic women's colleges are particularly strong in offering innovative programs for women and for encouraging women's leadership potential.

Although it is difficult to know specifically which factors contribute to what outcomes (for example, there may be differences between women who choose coeducational as opposed to women's colleges), it is known that women in single-sex schools are more likely to pursue less traditional courses of study and career aspirations. In comparison to their peers in coeducational institutions, women in single-sex colleges are more likely to major in mathematics and the natural sciences. (Interestingly, men in single-sex institutions are more likely to major in the arts and humanities than are those in coeducational colleges.) Graduates from women's colleges are also more likely to pursue doctoral degrees and to achieve high levels of professional success. [*See* SEX SEGREGATION IN EDUCATION.]

II. *Status and Hierarchy in Academia*

Colleges and universities represent communities that include administrators, faculty, students, and staff. While traditions across institutions vary, in the main, they have had at their base patriarchal structures developed with the expectation of male dominance and male leadership. Even colleges established for women have, until recently, been directed in accord with gender stereotypes. Many have only accepted female leadership within the past few decades. For example, as of 2001, Hunter College, initially established for women, has had only four women presidents out of thirteen. Similarly, Vassar College (established for women in 1861) has had three women presidents out of nine; the first was in 1946. Even when women were named to head a college, many times they reported to higher male authorities, such as the case of Barnard College's dean and president who reports to the president of Columbia University.

A. FINANCIAL POWER AS STATUS

The denotation of prestige by financial status is one of the major indicators of social class differences existing in our society. At the university, even within departments and within faculty ranks, there are differences that are accounted for primarily by gender. The 1999 survey conducted by the American Association of University Professors found double-digit disparities between the salaries of male and female faculty members of equal rank. The most prestigious institutions (e.g., those granting doctoral degrees) had an average gap of 9.7%. It was also found that private institutions were likely to demonstrate disparities between average salaries of male and female faculty members that were greater than those of public institutions (12.1% compared with 11%).

Institutions may also be ranked by financial status that appears to match the status of their students. In other words, it appears that private institutions, historically male-only, are best endowed, most financially stable, and considered the most prestigious.

Women's colleges and historically Black institutions are typically among the lowest in financial standing and in prestige. Even among public institutions (where coeducation is required) within the same state, financial resources and status are paired such that the campuses serving minority and low-income populations appear to receive lower rates of funding than those serving middle-class White populations. This appears to be the case in Mississippi, Texas, and New York.

Financial success has also been strongly linked to professional areas or disciplines that are male-dominated, such as law, medicine, engineering, business administration, and the natural sciences (e.g., biology, chemistry, and physics). On the other hand, disciplines traditionally open to and dominated by women have lower access to funds from outside the institution. Thus, colleges of nursing, social work, and education are less likely to have major funding agencies or wealthy alumni to support their efforts. Not surprisingly, the academic disciplines with the most strongly rooted male hierarchies appear the most resistant to allowing access to women and low-status ethnic minorities.

B. ADMINISTRATIVE DIVISIONS AND STATUS

Administrative divisions within the college or university may also be used to indicate the distribution of power. For example, the academic affairs area traditionally holds the most prestige and is considered most central to institutional standing and mission. The vice president of academic affairs/chief academic officer is usually second to the president in authority. This vice president oversees the primary academic functions of the educational enterprise with supervisory responsibility for academic deans and faculty. Other vice presidents vary in power according to their centrality to the mission of the particular institution and their access to resources.

As we consider the administrative divisions across institutions, it can again be seen that gender and ethnic distributions in these offices tend to confirm and reify the expectation of male dominance in the academy. U.S. Department of Education data show that men predominate in all vice presidential offices and their proportions are greatest in the lines of greatest authority. Thus, there are more women and ethnic minorities who are vice presidents of student affairs than are vice presidents of academic affairs. Few women are selected to head areas such as vice president of research, finance, and administration, or institutional development. Although there are increas-ing numbers of women who do hold these posts, it is more likely that women have appointments at the associate and assistant level in these departments. Thus, the "glass ceiling" effect for women seems evident.

C. WOMEN FACULTY AND ADMINISTRATORS

When gender is considered, no matter what system of academic ranking is used, women are less likely to hold high-status positions. Additionally, demographic data indicate that the more prestigious the institution, the fewer women in administrative roles (e.g., vice presidents, deans, department chairs) and the fewer women in higher-level faculty ranks. (At most colleges and universities, faculty ranks range from low to high: instructor/lecturer, assistant professor, associate professor, or full professor, respectively). Data from the U.S. Department of Education for 1997 show that at two-year institutions women comprise 47% of those in full-time executive, managerial, and faculty positions, while at four-year institutions women comprise only 37% of those positions.

In part, the lower proportions of women and minorities in high-status positions results from the lack of professionals prepared to move into these positions. However, there is promise for the future. The survey of earned doctorates conducted by the National Opinion Research Center found that of doctorates awarded to U.S. citizens, women earned 41.8% of doctorates awarded in 1998 and ethnic minorities earned 14.7%, the highest percentages ever.

1. Gender Disparities

Administrative roles serve to establish the hierarchical system of leadership with male images of leadership relatively unchallenged. At the highest level, the presidency, women represented only 16% of all college and university presidents in 1995. While this is an increase from 1990 when women had only 12% of presidencies, as the American Council on Education's Office of Women in Higher Education analyses show, most women who are presidents head two-year colleges with fewer than 3000 students. Only 7% of institutions with more than 10,000 students are led by women. For example, of the prestigious Ivy League universities, the first woman president was appointed in 1998; she is Judith Rodin, president of the University of Pennsylvania.

Information from colleges and universities indicate that significant gender disparities also exist for other high administrative positions. A survey by the American Council of Education indicated that only 25%

of academic deans are women. Among these deans, women usually head schools of education or schools of social work more often than colleges of business or medicine. Fewer than 17% of the vice presidents of finance are women; among elite research universities, 18% of provosts or vice presidents of academic affairs are women. Among faculty, fewer than 19% of tenured full professors are women (the highest faculty level) and female professors are more often found in gender-stereotyped disciplines (e.g., nursing, education, social work) and least likely to be found in the sciences, engineering, or law.

Among students, women comprised more than 52% of college and university enrollees in 1999. The gender disparities favor women in schools of nursing and social work, as well as departments in the humanities and social sciences. Science departments and engineering still maintain overwhelmingly male majorities. Women are also more likely than men to be employed as part-time instructors and adjunct faculty, positions which hold neither stability, authority, or high salary.

2. Barriers for Female Administrators

The difficulty of reaching high-status administrative positions for women has often been attributed to their own shortcomings, such as their lack of experience or a relatively short tenure in the academy. The low numbers of women have also been blamed, in part, on stereotypic characteristics, such as the perception that women have problems handling power, lack ambition, and are not adequately prepared for the position. While these factors are not substantiated, it has been shown that the conflicting demands and expectations of family versus career goals have interfered with women's academic advancement.

Although the interference of family obligations may affect women more than men, Vivian Valian's review of research found that women often face a high level of resistance from peers and superiors. The reluctance of male leadership to change the status quo has been a major factor in women's slower career trajectories. There have also been harsher evaluations of women when advancement to leadership has been reached. Thus, women appear to receive more serious repercussions than their male peers do for similar mistakes.

Among the systemic barriers that exist for women in academia, until recently there were few female role models to emulate on the path to achievement.

Using male role models did not provide women with the strategies necessary to negotiate the balance apparently needed for women in male-dominated departments. Further, there is evidence that women are less likely than men to have mentors—that is, experienced professionals to assist, advise, and guide their careers. The lack of both role models and mentors seriously disadvantages women in career advancement. [*See* CAREER ACHIEVEMENT; MENTORING AND FEMINIST MENTORING.]

D. ETHNIC MINORITY FACULTY AND ADMINISTRATORS

An ethnic breakdown of data collected by the American Council on Education (ACE) in 1995 indicated that ethnic minorities are also less likely to be employed at the more prestigious research institutions, while greater numbers are found at less prestigious two-year and four-year institutions. Thus, despite the fact that the U.S. resident population in 1995 was only 73.6% White; executive, managerial staff, and faculty remain more than 85% White across all institutions according to 1997 Department of Education reports. While women and people of color remain least represented in doctoral and private institutions, the trend is in the positive direction so that the ACE 1999 report indicated that women now hold 19.3% and minorities 11.3% of the presidency positions.

Faculty members of color, like White women faculty, have higher representation in less prestigious colleges and universities. African Americans and Latinos, for example, represented only 4.9% of all full professors, 7% of associate professors, and 9% of assistant professors in 1998. This percentage has changed imperceptibly over the past 20 years, so at the current rate, parity with representation in the general population cannot be expected for many years. Interestingly, women of color do not even dominate those positions in academia that might be seen as their stereotypic domain. For example, fewer than 8% of collegiate women's basketball teams have an African American woman as the head coach, despite the large number of African American players; however, more than 35% of the women's teams are coached by White men!

Although almost half of all Black academics in the United States are found at the historically Black institutions, the Black colleges maintain highly integrated faculties. For example, at Xavier University, an historically Black institution in New Orleans, African Americans hold fewer than 35% of the faculty positions; at the historic Tuskegee University (founded by Booker T. Washington), African Americans hold slightly more than half of the faculty positions. Contrast this with the departments at predominantly White institutions; many have no faculty of color. It must be recognized that in part the scarcity of minority faculty reflects the low rates of participation and graduation through the pipeline; however, this does not explain the disproportionate representation across institutions.

On a positive note, comparisons of academic salaries of minority faculty and staff indicate that while the numbers employed increase slowly, salaries are reaching parity. Taken in context, however, this is not as impressive as it may first appear. Since most African American faculty teach at historically Black and state-funded schools, the salaries for all faculty and staff are skewed toward the low end. Even with recent improvements in pay levels, the U.S. Bureau of the Census indicates that the differences in earnings among all ethnic groups compare negatively to their White male counterparts.

It should be noted that when considering disparities across ethnic and gender group, an inclination of many researchers is to compare women of color with White women and men of color with White men. This type of comparison has been found to be misleading since the standard of comparison for all is actually White men. Thus, while it can be found that Asian American women and White women earn similar salaries when they have equivalent educational standing, all women and Asian American men earn significantly less than White men with the same academic standing. (Similarly, African American women and White women faculty members earn essentially the same lower salaries, but African American women earn almost $11,000 less than their White male peers according to the U.S. Equal Employment Opportunity Commission data.)

III. *Gender Roles and Stereotyped Practices*

In academic institutions, the formal titles that people hold (e.g., dean, professor, or student) indicate the roles they are expected to play. However, as Vivian Valian, a professor at the City of University of New York noted, gender also dictates certain expectations, thus, even for people with the same title, reactions to their roles may be different. Since society

often defines women as lacking in some basic competencies and as being deficient in the characteristics necessary for leadership, women in academia are often evaluated in stereotypic ways regardless of their actual status or their performance in the role. Women may be viewed as weak, indecisive, and easily influenced. Additionally, there may be an expectation that women will play the informally defined role of a nurturer, seductress, or subservient. Thus, gender expectations may interfere with the effectiveness with which women operate in leadership roles or positions of authority.

In assessing the effectiveness of women in academia, regardless of their roles, the impact of stereotyped expectations may be seen to influence not only others, but also the women themselves. Psychological research has demonstrated the deleterious effect of negative and biased attribution on self-esteem and self-respect. Women who are judged inferior by their supervisors, peers, or students may accept these judgments as reflections of their ability, whether accurate or not. Findings suggest that people in the context of negative evaluations and biased beliefs begin to perform less well even when they do not accept the assessments or believe the stereotypic assumptions. [*See* LEADERSHIP; SELF-ESTEEM.]

Claude Steele, a psychology professor at Stanford University, calls this negative reaction to others stereotyped beliefs "stereotypic threat." Steele's research has demonstrated that a number of subtle cues can trigger this reaction among African American students and women. For example, the awareness that a test will result in comparisons with White students, having a White instructor pass out tests, and simply knowing that Whites hold negative beliefs about Blacks are sufficient to induce a decline in African American students' academic performance. Similar responses have been demonstrated among women as well as White men when stereotyped beliefs are operative. While steps can be taken to reduce this reaction, they are often not, because the phenomenon itself is usually unrecognized. Instead, a "blame the victim" approach is the most frequent explanation. That is, poor performance is attributed solely to a deficit in the performer with little or no credence given to situational factors as contributing to performance difficulties. [*See* TEST BIAS.]

A. AUTHORITY FIGURES AND GENDER ROLES

The social expectations, which assign men to public duties and relegate women to private realms, remain difficult to shake. Indeed, stereotypes persist in defining men as excelling in intellectual areas, while ceding emotional and relational areas to women. The image of authority remains a father-like figure (i.e., nonfemale). Further, traditional social constructions of organizations insist on an apex with a single figure at the top. Even when the relatively infrequent opportunity arises for a woman to hold a position of authority, she may not be seen as the source of power. Female administrators in male-dominated institutions challenge both the system and the stereotype of power by their presence.

Women and people of color who find themselves in a role of authority or a position of privilege may sometimes question their own right and ability to maintain such status. This experience has been dubbed, the "imposter phenomenon" by Pauline Rose Clance, a Georgia State University professor of psychology. She and her colleagues found that women and others, unused to high-status positions, may feel insecure and undeserving leading them to worry that they have mistakenly been given the positions. Further, they may fear that their imagined inadequacies will be uncovered and they will be revealed as undeserving frauds.

In university settings it is not only the faculty who must overcome the expectation that men hold the authority role. Several studies of classroom performance indicate that students, too, appear to have an expectation that men are leaders and holders of knowledge. As Susan Basow's research demonstrates, gender is a factor in how students evaluate their instructors. For example, male students are more likely than female students to rate female instructors low on teaching performance. Students have also been found to give lower ratings to female faculty on knowledge and overall performance, and they expect women to be more nurturing and supportive. [*See* ANDROCENTRISM.]

Roles and expectations for students are also governed to a considerable extent by gender. Although there has been significant change in the past few decades, moving women from the minority to the majority group in most college and university student bodies, women remain significantly underrepresented in departments of physical science, computer science, and engineering. Indeed, the 1999 analysis of science departments at the Massachusetts Institute of Technology conducted by a committee of senior female scientists found that the pipeline of students into the advanced levels was particularly constrained by gender. The percentage of women faculty in the

School of Science had not increased for more than a decade. Further, their data found that an inverse relationship for percentages of women among science students and level of seniority; thus, undergraduate women were less likely than male students to gain acceptance to graduate programs, graduate women students less likely than males to have offers of postgraduate positions, and female faculty less likely to have key assignments.

IV. Curriculum Issues

Gender stereotypes in academic settings have also been found in the content of the curriculum. Since the content of academic courses is the purview of the faculty who teach them, it may be understood that the male-dominated faculty have set standards that supported their strengths and interests. Thus, women have often been excluded and ignored. In the humanities, the major thinkers and writers studied have been White and male; the scientists most exalted in both physical and social sciences also met these criteria. After considerable struggle among scholars, White women and people of color are now included among the major contributors in many of the academic disciplines presented in universities.

A. GENDER, DIVERSITY, AND MULTICULTURALISM IN THE CURRICULUM

In spite of the resistance to diversifying the curriculum, courses reflecting ethnic diversity, gender differences, and sexual orientation were introduced on most campuses throughout the United States. The Association of American Colleges and Universities report that 63% of all institutions now require some level of diversity education. Their survey also indicates that these changes are supported by a large majority of those polled. By seeking changes in course contents, there was an acknowledgement that diversity is necessary and important for today's graduates and it serves to strengthen our diverse communities.

Diversity in the curriculum has also been accompanied by changes in the student composition and changes in the faculty composition. The movement to transform curriculum from the exclusive European-male perspective began in the late 1960s with students of color in several universities in California demanding more faculty of color and the introduction of courses that better reflected their history and experiences. The impact of including female and ethnic minority scholars in the curriculum is significant in several ways. For example, female and minority scholars provide diverse perspectives that have broadened the field and introduced new questions. Recognizing the differences in expectations may change the interpretation of what people think and how they behave. It must be noted, however, that while women's studies departments, centers, and programs abound and ethnic studies has taken root on most campuses, these curricular offerings are still, to a some extent, regarded as marginal to the traditional academic agenda.

B. WOMEN'S STUDIES

The women's movement that emerged in the 1960s had a strong impact on college and university campuses. It fueled the growth of women's studies, which, in turn, contributed to the women's movement and to advancing the struggle for women's rights. Feminists on campus initially directed their attention to the unfair treatment of women faculty in such things as salaries and promotion. Attention was soon focused on the curriculum, a curriculum which ignored women's contributions to the knowledge base (for example, as authors and scientists) and which ignored women's experiences and perspectives in that knowledge base. [See FEMINIST MOVEMENT.]

By the late 1960s, academic departments throughout the United States were witnessing increasing numbers of courses specifically addressing such topics as women's health, women and politics, women's history, women's literature, the psychology of women, women and work, and the like. The number of courses continued to proliferate and, in the first half of the 1970s, a growing number of feminist scholars began to articulate Women's Studies as an integrated and distinctive field of knowledge. Journals such as *Sex Roles, SIGNS, Feminist Studies, Women's Studies Quarterly,* and *Psychology of Women's Quarterly* were founded to provide a forum for research and theory about women's lives, status, and experiences. The National Women's Studies Association was founded in 1977, thus providing a venue for networking and sharing of information among academicians and students interested in pursuing and teaching women's studies courses and related topics. By the early 1990s, there was some form of women's studies in the curriculum of more than 2000 accredited colleges and universities in the United States.

Simultaneous with the growth of women's studies, feminist scholars began to challenge the academic canon, that is, those courses set as required components of the curriculum. It was pointed out that these writings narrowly featured the works of Western, Caucasian men and assumed a heterosexual perspective. While recognizing the value of these works, they pointed out that there were also classic writings by women, ethnic minorities, and non-Western people that could be considered not only as a legitimate body of knowledge, but important for an educated populace. They argued that these diverse perspectives should be part of the canon and included in course requirements. The effectiveness of these arguments have varied considerably from campus to campus and over time, with some schools readily embracing such curriculum reform and others staunchly resisting. Curriculum changes also fluctuate within a particular college or university. They have been subject to local political moods and viewed as political statements as well as educational ones.

Coinciding with the growth of women's studies courses and efforts to expand the academic requirements are activities to incorporate knowledge by and about women into the traditional academic courses. Proponents for a diverse curriculum recommend that information including women, people of color, gay men, and lesbians not be treated solely as supplemental topics, but that they become an integral part of the total knowledge base. Efforts to incorporate this new literature were particularly visible in the late 1980s. Support for change was provided by philanthropic organizations, such as The Ford Foundation, which funded projects designed to assist faculty in incorporating knowledge about ethnically diverse women into their courses. Today, the integration of knowledge about women, ethnically diverse groups, gay men, and lesbians occurs in more and more courses, although certainly this broad view is still not representative of the majority of university courses.

V. Sex Discrimination in Academic Institutions

Notwithstanding the continued gender imbalance in faculty and administrative positions, sex discrimination is illegal in most employment settings, including educational institutions. In 1964, the U.S. Congress passed Title VII of the Civil Rights Act, which prohibits discrimination in employment on the basis of an individual's race, color, religion, sex, or national origin. Decisions about hiring, terminating employment, terms of compensation, and conditions of work based on sex were declared unlawful. The act also prohibits classifying job applicants or employees on the basis of sex. Academic institutions can be, and have been, held accountable for their employment practices that are not in compliance. For example, Vassar College, a prestigious private college, was censured when it was found that it had not tenured any married woman professor in the sciences for 30 years. While such actions were defended as the outcome of objective criteria, the court ruled that it was based on the belief that women with families cannot be productive and successful scientists. Women in a number of colleges and universities have sued and won compensation for discrimination in salary and tenure decisions.

When patterns of discrimination are blatant, pervasive, and affect a large class of individuals, such as women, they are easier to document and legal action is more likely. However, recent research by psychologists, such as Janet Swim, Monica Bernat, and John Dovidio, demonstrates that subtle patterns of discrimination are harder to prove. These would include individual instances of discrimination, inequity based on unarticulated stereotypes, and stereotypes that decision makers (e.g., promotion committees) may not even acknowledge or be cognizant they hold. The victim may not even be aware that the decision was based on gender since no two applicants will have the exact same background, experience, or education and there are so many factors that go into hiring and promotion decisions. Yet such discrimination does occur in academic settings. It may be represented by statements such as, "We would gladly hire a woman, we just cannot find anyone who is qualified," or in differential treatment of women and men during interviews, or by evaluations based on stereotypical assumptions.

A recent study by Rhea Steinpreis and colleagues found psychology faculty members more likely to judge a man as more qualified than a woman based solely on reading his or her academic credentials. This was true even when the applicants were represented by identical credentials—only the name was changed, one had a female name and the other a male name. In addition, considerable evidence suggests that research articles are judged differently when the reader thinks they were written by a woman as opposed to a man. A person's sexual orientation has also been a factor in sexual discrimination. For example, in one situation a college presidency of-

fered to a woman was rescinded after the board of trustees learned that she was a lesbian and that she planned to bring her female partner to live with her in the president's residence.

Clearly, the illegality of discrimination has not prevented it from impacting decisions based on race or ethnicity. The combined impact of ethnicity and gender has been shown in the scarcity of women of color in high academic rank. Sexual orientation may not be as obvious a marker and it has not been consistently counted, but it is also likely to combine with gender or race to the detriment of the faculty or administrator.

A. ANTIDISCRIMINATION LAW AND POLICY IN HIGHER EDUCATION

Academic institutions are not just enjoined to avoid discrimination in employment practices; it is unlawful to discriminate by gender in all aspects of the educational process. Title IX of the Educational Amendments of 1972 prohibits discrimination based on sex in all educational programs and activities if the institution receives any federal funds. This law applies to academic, educational, extracurricular, athletic, and other programs, whether they take place in the school or elsewhere. (Based on the criterion of federal funding, few colleges or universities in the United States are exempt from Title IX provisions.)

Title IX has had a far-reaching impact on funding practices in athletics, an area with significant rewards and recognition in many colleges and universities. It has served to raise the support for and awareness of women's sports, thereby enhancing the opportunities for women athletes. Title IX, however, is not limited to athletics; it also demands gender equity in admissions, financial aid, housing, access to classes, health services, student employment opportunities, and the like. The law does not, as some might suggest, require coed bathrooms or locker rooms or dormitories, but it does mean that such facilities need to be comparable for female and male students.

There are conditions under which simple equity (i.e., equal treatment) is not adequate for correcting the outcome of an historical legacy of gender and race/ethnic discrimination. Although the Civil Rights Act was enacted in 1964 to prohibit gender and racial discrimination, it was not until the 1970s that enforcement began. Affirmative action was initiated and it served as a policy and a guide, in both employment and educational settings. The intent was to provide some advantage for those groups who had been disadvantaged by law and by tradition. Through this policy, colleges and universities could provide financial incentives and support, as well as special educational programs, to encourage White women and people of color to pursue higher education. The policy enabled single sex schools wishing to become co-educational, or historically White schools seeking greater ethnic diversity, to take gender or race into consideration in students' admissions and financial aid decisions, and in faculty hiring. Affirmative action policies were also effective in bringing large numbers of White women into universities as students, faculty, and staff members.

Affirmative action practices have been successfully attacked in California, Florida, and Texas; other confrontations are currently being waged in the courts. The attacks have been aimed primarily at public institutions seeking to aid students of color, and the result has been to change policies and to close programs designed to foster ethnic minority students' education advancement. The long-term outcome of these efforts is yet to be determined, but the short-term impact has reduced ethnic minority enrollment. In the interim, however, many colleges and universities continue policies designed to correct for past sex discrimination and unequal treatment and opportunities for people of color. [See AFFIRMATIVE ACTION.]

B. SEXUAL HARASSMENT

Although litigation for sexual harassment claims began to appear in the courts during the 1970s, no official definition of sexual harassment existed until 1980 when the Equal Employment Opportunity Commission (EEOC) explicitly defined sexual harassment as a form of sex discrimination and, therefore, illegal in work settings. In 1984, the EEOC expanded the guidelines to include educational institutions. According to the EEOC, sexual harassment is defined as unwelcome sexual advances, requests for sexual favors, and other verbal or physical conduct of a sexual nature when (1) submission to such conduct is made either explicitly or implicitly a term or condition of an individual's employment or academic advancement, (2) submission to or rejection of such conduct by an individual is used as the basis for employment decisions or academic decisions affecting such individual, or (3) such conduct has the purpose or effect of unreasonably interfering with an individual's work or academic performance or creating an intimidating, hostile, or offensive

working or academic environment. The first two definitions of sexual harassment fall in the category of *quid pro quo* sexual harassment. The third definition is referred to as "hostile environment" sexual harassment.

1. *Quid Pro Quo* Sexual Harassment

Quid pro quo sexual harassment involves tangible benefits or losses. In other words, compliance with sexual requests, or tolerating sex-related behaviors, results in job enhancement or educational benefits, or the reverse (i.e., rejection of sexual requests or sex-related behaviors results in a demotion of some sort or academic penalties). Examples of *quid pro quo* sexual harassment experienced by a student might include promises of a higher grade for sexual favors (or being penalized for not complying). They could involve sexual bartering for good recommendations, scholarships, awards, or academic contacts. Indeed, any area in which an instructor, or anyone else in the school, has power over the student (e.g., residence hall director) can lead to this form of harassment. Interestingly, if the student complies with the sexual request and gets the promised award, or even if the student does not comply with the request and the threat (e.g., poor grade) is not carried out, it is still sexual harassment.

2. Hostile Environment Sexual Harassment

Hostile environment sexual harassment refers to unwanted and offensive sexual behavior not tied to conditions of employment or educational advancement. It is considered sexual harassment because it involves the use of sex-related behavior to create a hostile and intimidating work or educational environment—an environment that interferes with one's right and ability to work or study. It might include repeated requests for sexual intimacy or a social relationship, questions about sexuality or statements about one's own sex life, sexual jokes or teasing, comments about the person's body or derogatory comments about women. It may include sexual impositions, such as sexual or sexualized touching (e.g., pinching, rubbing, grabbing, unwanted kissing), cornering someone, and obscene gestures. It can also include pornographic materials or exposing someone to sexual objects.

Hostile environment sexual harassment is the most common form of sexual harassment. It is also more ambiguous and open to interpretation than is *quid pro quo* sexual harassment. Nonetheless, it is illegal and many plaintiffs (i.e., the individuals bringing a suit) have won cases against colleges and universities for being subject to hostile environment sexual harassment. Exactly how many students experience incidences of sexual harassment is not known. Dzeich and Weiner found that 20 to 30% of female students were subjected to sexual harassment. The numbers depend on how one defines sexual harassment.

3. Consequences of Sexual Harassment for Women

Psychologist Mary Koss reported that women who have been harassed suffer psychological, physical, and career-related consequences. They report symptoms of depression, anxiety, sleep disturbances, gastrointestinal disorders, headaches, self-doubt, low self-esteem, feelings of vulnerability, and helplessness. In her research in academic settings, Michele Paludi found that female students change majors and often, as a result, career directions in response to sexual harrassment. They avoid student activities, drop courses, and sometimes even drop out of school to avoid the harasser. Louise Fitzgerald found that male faculty members who engaged in sexual relationships with their students denied the power differential between them and students, as well as the psychological power they had over their students.

Little of the research on sexual harassment has considered the race or ethnicity of the students. Darlene DeFour, a professor at Hunter College, suggested that ethnic minority women students may be more vulnerable to sexual harassment than their White counterparts considering the negative stereotypes that many hold about them. It is also not known how many faculty members or employees in academic settings experience sexual harassment, but estimates are high assuming academic settings are similar to the federal workplace (and they may not be). A survey done by the U.S. Merit Systems Protection Board found that over 40% of the female employees in the federal workforce reported experiencing some form of sexual harassment during a two-year period.

Sexual harassment by a person with authority is an abuse of power. The act of sexually harassing someone is the assertion of power—the power to intimidate, humiliate, and create discomfort. Sexual harassment also suggests that the person's sexuality is primary, not her role as a worker, student, or colleague. It reduces the victim to a "sex object." Thus,

peers, or others, who have no objective power can also sexually harass. Academic institutions can be liable for incidents of sexual harassment, whether or not they were officially reported. Institutions are also liable if harassment was reported and no intervention was taken to stop it, if there is no well-publicized policy, and if a procedure for reporting occurrences of harassment is not in place.

It should be noted that laws prohibiting sexual harassment were instituted primarily to protect women workers and students from male supervisors, teachers, coworkers, and peers. Although women are many times more likely to be the victims of sexual harassment, men can also be victims of sexual harassment. This, too, is illegal. There may be, however, differences between women and men in their experience of sexual harassment. In her research on gender in the workplace, Barbara Gutek found that men are less likely than women to label sex-related behavior as harassment or to judge it offensive. They are also less likely to suffer negative job consequences, such as being transferred or traumatized as a result of such behavior. Sexual harassment can also occur between people of the same sex. [*See* SEXUAL HARASSMENT.]

C. CHILLY CLIMATE FOR WOMEN

While sexual harassment may vary from subtle to extreme illegal behavior, the academic environment also comprises other characteristics that may make the various constituents feel supported, comfortable and welcome—or not supported and unwelcome. For about two decades the Project on the Status and Education of Women of the Association of American Colleges and Universities has published reports on the status and experiences of girls and women in the classroom and on campuses. They have described conditions of unwelcoming, nonsupportive academic environments as the "chilly climate." In addition, they have chronicled the ways in which institutional settings discourage women from pursuing academic goals and how they encourage self-doubts.

Even when women and men take the same courses, the environment may be very different for them. In their classic 1982 report, Roberta Hall and Bernice Sandler suggested that teachers treat female students differently from male, that is, in ways that reflect gender stereotypes. Women students often reported feeling trivialized. A 1996 followup report on the "chilly classroom climate," conducted for the National Association for Women in Education, further discussed some of the classroom experiences that affect women negatively. The experiences included communication of lower expectations for women, differential treatment of women and men when their achievements are the same, exclusion of women from class participation, less attention and encouragement for women, and overt hostility toward women.

"Chilly climate" experiences can also result from the hostility and harassment of student peers. Gay men and lesbians similarly may experience a "chilly climate" in academe. Heterosexism, open hostility toward lesbians and gay men, and the assumption of heterosexuality reflected in the use of heterosexual examples, contribute to feelings of "invisibility," as well as to an unwelcoming and unsupportive educational experience.

While some researchers debate the idea that college teachers treat students differently according to their gender, there is general agreement that women and men experience the classroom differently. Women participate less in class than do men, who typically dominate classroom dynamics. There is also evidence that women and men respond differently to competition and cooperation. The research findings on learning styles, and attributions and expectations for success, are still conflicted, but it is clear that the academic experiences of women and men differ in these areas. For example, researchers suggest that the differential attitudes, expectations, and behaviors affect self-esteem and serve to disadvantage women.

Another area still underexplored is the experiences of women of color in the classroom. Gender stereotypes vary by race and ethnicity and the academic experiences of women of color may be, in part, an outcome of assumptions made about being a woman of a particular ethnic or racial group. In addition, as a result of the underrepresentation of women students and faculty of color, ethnic minority women students and faculty can feel alone and isolated, lacking a community that is familiar and comfortable. Similarly, in most institutions of higher education, there are few, if any, women role models for women of color, and there are few mentors of similar ethnic or racial backgrounds.

VI. *Summary*

Academic environments reflect societal attitudes and stereotypes about gender, ethnicity, and race. They frame the experiences of those studying and working in higher education settings. The first colleges and universities in the United States were intended to prepare White, middle-and upper-class men to lead government, industry, and society. It was not until the late 1800s that the first colleges were established to educate women. These early women's colleges primarily trained women as teachers or prepared them for their appropriate social standing. Higher-educational opportunities for people of color were also not available until after the Civil War. The institutions for newly freed Black men and women often focused on religious training and teacher preparation.

Today, women comprise more than half the number of students in colleges and universities. These women students, however, are concentrated in the humanities and social sciences and underrepresented in the physical sciences. In addition, men predominate in all the high-status and powerful administrative positions. For example, there are many fewer women college presidents or faculty of high rank. The numbers of people of color in high administrative or faculty positions remain disproportionately low.

Gender biases, stereotypes, and expectations contribute to this inequity between White men, women, and people of color. Such beliefs can negatively affect one's self-esteem and performance and undermine efforts to advance. They can also influence people's judgment about women's competencies in such things as student and peer evaluations of faculty.

Another arena in which gender and ethnic biases is evident is the curriculum. Historically, the curriculum has consisted of the works and achievements of White middle-class men. Women, men of color, gay men, and lesbians, among other groups, have been conspicuously absent from courses. In recent years, however, ethnic studies and women's studies faculty and students have actively promoted a more diverse and inclusive curriculum. Increasing numbers of colleges and universities are now offering a more multicultural curriculum, although the numbers of such offerings are still relatively few.

Although it is illegal to discriminate against women and people of color in academic institutions receiving federal funding (which is almost all higher-educational institutions in the United States), discrimination does occur. This can be seen in patterns of hiring and promotion. It is also evident in more subtle ways, such as treating women students' achievements differently than those of men, and it is often not recognized as discrimination either by the person demonstrating the behavior or the recipient of the behavior.

Sexual harassment, categorized as either *quid pro quo* or hostile environment sexual harassment, is also a form of discrimination. Not only does it relegate an individual's roles as student or worker secondary to her or his sexuality, but it can also have harmful physical, psychological, and career consequences to the victim. Sexual harassment, overt and subtle messages such as those that imply that women are not as competent as men or that they are not taken seriously, hostile comments about women, or lower expectations all contribute to a "chilly climate for women" in the academy.

SUGGESTED READING

American Psychological Association. (2000). *Women in Academe: Two Steps Forward, One Step Back: Report of the Task Force on Women in Academe.* American Psychological Association, Washington, DC.

Benjamin, L. (ed.) (1997). *Black Women in the Academy: Promises and Perils.* University of Florida Press, Gainesville, FL.

Chliwniak, L. (1997). *Higher Education Leadership: Analyzing the Gender Gap.* George Washington University, Washington, DC.

Collins, L. H., Chrisler, J. C., and Quina, K. (eds.) (1998). *Arming Athena: Career Strategies for Women in Academia.* Sage, Thousand Oaks, CA.

Mintz, B., and Rothblum, E. D. (1997). *Lesbians in Academia: Degrees of Freedom.* Routledge, New York.

Paludi, M. (1996). *Sexual Harassment on College Campuses: Abusing the Ivory Power.* State University of New York Press, Albany, NY.

Pearson, C. S., Shavlik, D. L., and Touchton, J. G. (1989). *Educating the Majority: Women Challenge Tradition in Higher Education.* American Council on Education, Macmillan, New York.

Sandler, B. R., Silverberg, L. A., and Hall, R. M. (1996). *The Chilly Climate: A Guide to Improve the Education of Women.* National Association for Women in Education, Washington, DC.

Solomon, B. (1985). *In the Company of Educated Women: A History of Women and Higher Education in America.* Yale University Press, New Haven, CT.

Valian, V. (1998). *Why So Slow? The Advancement of Women.* MIT Press, Cambridge, MA.

Achievement

Jacquelynne S. Eccles
University of Michigan

Glossary

Causal attributions Explanations people provide to themselves for their behavior, successes, and failures.

Expectancy How well a person expects to do on an upcoming task.

Gender The socially constructed characteristics of being male or female.

Gendered The extent to which a characteristic, outcome, occupational choice, or participation in various roles is more likely to be true of one gender or the other. For example, employment in information technology jobs is more common for males than for females.

Gender-role stereotyping The extent to which a role or activities is seen as more appropriate for one gender or the other.

Identity and identity formation Identity is the sense one has of who one is and what one should be doing with one's life. Identity formation is the process of deciding on, or committing oneself to, a specific identity.

Self-concept Beliefs about oneself and one's abilities and interests.

Self-perceptions Perceptions of oneself and one's successes and failures.

Stereotypes Generalized beliefs about particular groups of people such as males and females.

Task values The value one attaches to engaging (doing) particular tasks, activities, or roles.

ACHIEVEMENT is defined in *Webster's Collegiate Dictionary*, 10th ed., as "the act of achieving, a result gained by effort, and the quality and quantity of a students' work." Psychologists have typically used this term to refer to school grades, extent of education, level and type of occupation, and success in terms of income, status of job, awards, promotions, and so on. This article focuses on the ways in which gender (one's status as a female or male) is related to these various measures of achievement.

The relation of gender/sex to achievement is a massive and complex topic. Even defining what is included under the topic of achievement is complex. This article limits the discussion to school-related achievement during the childhood and adolescent years and educational and vocational achievement during the adult years, focusing on the gendered patterns associated with these objective indicators of achievement. But even within this limited scope, the relation of gender/sex to achievement is complicated. The patterns of sex differences are not consistent across ages and there is always greater variation within sex than across sex. To make sense of this heterogeneity, this article presents the findings in relation to the Eccles Expectancy-Value Model of Achievement-Related Choices with a specific focus on the ways in which gender as a social system influences individual's self-perceptions, values, and experiences.

This article focuses on studies of European Americans because they are the most studied population. Studies on gender differences in achievement in other populations are just becoming available, and even these focus on only a limited range of groups. In addition, none of the existing studies on other populations have the range of constructs presented in this entry, making comparisons of findings across groups impossible at this point in time. Consequently, rather than leaving the impression that the findings presented are universal, this article will be explicit about their limitations. More work is desperately needed to determine the generalizability of these patterns to other cultural and ethnic groups.

I. *Gender and Academic Achievement*

Over the past 10 years, there have been extensive discussions in both the media and more academic publication outlets regarding gender differences in achievement. Much of this discussion has focused on how girls are being "short changed" by the school systems. Most recently, the American Association of University Women (AAUW) published two reports on this topic in 1990 and 1993. This perspective on gender inequity in secondary schools has been quite consistent with larger concerns being raised about the negative impact of adolescence on young women's development. For example, in recent reports, the AAUW reported marked declines in girls' self-confidence during the early adolescent years. Similarly, Carol Gilligan has reported that girls lose confidence in their ability to express their needs and opinions as they move into the early adolescent years—she refers to this process as losing one's voice.

However, just 10 years earlier, in the 1960s, the big gender equity concern focused on how schools were "short changing" boys. Concerns were raised about how the "feminized culture" in most schools fits very poorly with the behavioral styles of boys, leading many boys to become alienated and then to underachieve. The contrast between these two pictures of gender inequities in school was recently highlighted by Sommers in her article in the May 2000 issue of the *Atlantic Monthly*.

So what is the truth? Like most such situations, the truth is complex. On the one hand, female and male youth (both children and adolescents), on average, fare differently in American public schools in terms of both the ways in which they are treated and their actual performance. On the other hand, it is not the case that one sex is consistently treated less equitably than the other: female and male youth appear to be differentiatly advantaged and disadvantaged on various indicators of treatment and performance. In terms of performance, girls and women earn better grades, as well as graduate from high school, attend and graduate from college, and earn master's degrees at higher rates than boys and men. In contrast, men and boys do slightly better than girls and women on standardized tests, particularly in math and science, and obtain more advanced degrees than women in many areas of study, particularly in math-related, computer-related, engineering, and physical science fields. Men are also more likely than women to obtain advanced graduate degrees in all fields except the social sciences. These patterns are most clear in European American samples. They are less extreme in other ethnic groups within the United States.

In terms of treatment, in most ethnic groups in the United States, male youth are more likely than female youth to be assigned to all types of special/remedial educations programs and to either be expelled from or forced to drop out of school before high school graduation. Low-achieving boys (in both White and Black samples) receive more negative disciplinary interactions from their teachers than any other group of students—disproportionately more than their "fair" share. In addition, in most studies of academic underachievers, male youth outnumber female youth 2 to 1. In contrast, high-achieving male youth (particularly White high-achieving male youth) receive more favorable interactions with their teachers than any other group of students and are more likely to be encouraged by their teachers to take difficult courses, to apply to top colleges, and to aspire to challenging careers.

More consistent sex differences emerge for college major and for enrollment in particular vocational educational programs. Here the story is one of gender-role stereotyping. Both White women and men are most likely to specialize or major in content areas that are consistent with their gender role—that is, in content areas that are most heavily populated by members of their own sex. This gendered pattern is especially marked in vocational education programs for non-college-bound youth; for physical science, engineering, and computer science majors; and for those seeking professional degrees in nursing, social welfare, and teaching.

II. *Gender/Sex and Adult Occupational Choice and Success*

Gendered patterns of achievement behaviors and choices among whites are still very clear in the arena of adult vocations. This is especially true in the blue- and pink-collar labor markets where technical and unionized skilled labor jobs are occupied primarily by men and pink-collar and other service-related skilled jobs are occupied primarily by women. In the white-collar and professional labor markets, men and women of all ethnic groups are much more evenly distributed across various job types. The entry of women into medicine, law, and business over the last 20 to 30 years has gone a long way toward equalizing the proportion of women and men in these fields. Although the proportion of jobs held by women (versus men) has increased some in the fields of chemistry, physics, engineering and computer science, women are still underrepresented in these fields, especially physics and engineering. Finally, the proportion of nurses, social workers, and teachers who are men has remained low.

These data suggest that, as was true for college majors, gender is still a major factor in the occupational choices of many men and women—with women of all ethnic groups seeking occupations requiring a college degree being most willing to cross gender-stereotyped barriers. Despite recent efforts to increase the participation of women in advanced educational training and high-status professional fields and in such male-dominated recreational activities as athletics, women and men of most ethnic groups studied in the United States are still concentrated in different educational programs, occupational fields, and recreational activities. Most important for this article, women (and people of color more generally) are still underrepresented in many high-status occupational fields—particularly those associated with physical science, engineering, and applied mathematics (the one exception being the high rates of participation of both Asian American men and women in the sciences and engineering). In addition, sex differences remain evident in such indicators of occupational success as salary, advancement up the status hierarchy, and awards for outstanding achievements in virtually all fields and for

most ethnic groups in the United States. Although the extent of the sex discrepancy on these indicators has declined to some extent over the past 30 years, men still fare better than woman on most of these dimensions of achievement.

Why? Many factors, ranging from outright discrimination to the processes associated with gender-role socialization, undoubtedly contribute to these gendered patterns of educational and occupational choices and of the level of occupational success. Discussing all possible mediating variables is beyond the scope of a single encyclopedia entry. Instead, this article focuses on a set of social and psychological factors related to the Eccles Expectancy-Value Model of Achievement-Related Choices and Performance (see Figure 1). [*See* Academic Aspirations and Degree Attainment of Women; Career Achievement.]

III. *Eccles' Expectancy-Value Model of Achievement*

Over the past 20 years, Eccles and her colleagues have studied the motivational and social factors influencing such achievement goals and behaviors as educational and career choices, recreational activity selection, persistence on difficult tasks, and the allocation of effort across various achievement-related activities. Given the striking sex differences in educational, vocational, and avocational choices, they have been particularly interested in the motivational factors underlying boys'/men's and girls'/women's achievement-related decisions. Drawing on the theoretical and empirical work associated with decision making, achievement theory, and attribution theory, they elaborated a comprehensive theoretical model of achievement-related choices that could be used to guide our subsequent research efforts. This model, depicted in Figure 1, links achievement-related choices directly to two sets of beliefs: the individual's expectations for success and the importance or value the individual attaches to the various options perceived by the individual as available. The model also specifies the relation of these beliefs to cultural norms, experiences, aptitudes, and to those personal beliefs and attitudes that are commonly assumed to be associated with achievement-related activities by researchers in this field. In particular, the model links achievement-related beliefs, outcomes, and goals to interpretive systems like causal attributions, to the input of socializers (primarily parents, teachers, and peers), to gender-role beliefs, to self-

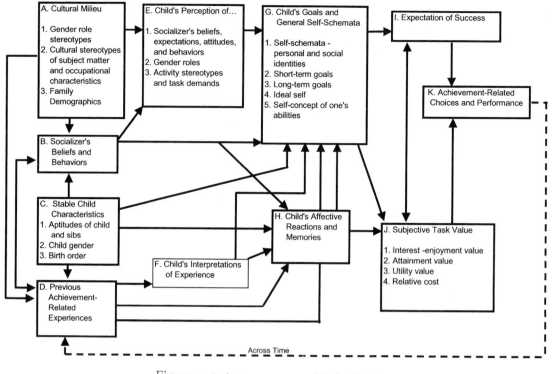

Figure 1   Eccles' expectancy model of task choice.

perceptions and self-concept, and to one's perceptions of the task itself.

For example, consider course enrollment decisions. The model predicts that people will be most likely to enroll in courses that they think they can master and that have high task value for them. Expectations for success (and a sense of domain-specific personal efficacy) depend on the confidence the individual has in his or her intellectual abilities and on the individual's estimations of the difficulty of the course. These beliefs have been shaped over time by the individual's experiences with the subject matter and by the individual's subjective interpretation of those experiences (e.g., does the person think that her or his successes are a consequence of high ability or lots of hard work?). Likewise, Eccles and colleagues assume that the value of a particular course to the individual is influenced by several factors. For example, does the person enjoy doing the subject material? Is the course required? Is the course seen as instrumental in meeting one of the individual's long- or short-range goals? Have the individual's parents or counselors insisted that the course be taken or, conversely, have other people tried to discourage the in-

dividual from taking the course? Is the person afraid of the material to be covered in the course? The fact that women and men may make different choices is likely to reflect sex differences in a wide range of predictors, mediated primarily by differences in self-perceptions, values, and goals rather than motivational strength or drive.

Eccles and her colleagues have spent the past 20 years testing the hypotheses implicit in this model on European American samples. They have just begun testing the hypotheses on African American samples. By and large these studies support most of the key components of this model for both populations. The next section reviews some of this support, focusing on the power of the two most proximal predictors of achievement-related choices—expectations for success and subjective task value. However, since the studies of African Americans is in the preliminary stage, the results reported focus on findings from the European American samples. Thus far, however, we have found no evidence that the model is any less appropriate for African Americans. The final section examines more specifically how gender roles relate to the model in Figure 1.

A. COMPETENCE AND EXPECTANCY-RELATED SELF-PERCEPTIONS

In the past 20 years, there has been considerable public attention focused on the issue of girls' declining confidence in their academic abilities. In addition, researchers and policy makers interested in young women's educational and occupational choices have stressed the potential role that such declining confidences might play in undermining young women's educational and vocational aspirations, particularly in the technical fields related to math and physical science. For example, these researchers suggest that young women may drop out of math and physical science because they lose confidence in their math abilities as they move into and through adolescence—resulting in women being less likely to pursue these types of careers than men. Similarly, these researchers suggest that sex differences in confidence in one's abilities in other areas underlie sex differences across the board in educational and occupational choices. Equally important, Eccles and her colleagues have suggested that the individual differences in women's educational and occupational choices are also related to variations among women in their confidence in their abilities in different domains.

But do girls/women and boys/men differ on measures commonly linked to expectations for success, particularly with regard to their academic subjects and various future occupations? Are girls/women more confident of their abilities in female gender-role stereotyped domains? In most studies, the answer is yes. For example, both Terman and Subotnik found that gifted White girls were more likely to underestimate their intellectual skills and their relative class standing than gifted White boys—who were more likely to overestimate theirs. Sex differences in the competence beliefs of more typical samples are also often reported, particularly in gender-role-stereotyped domains and on novel tasks. Often these differences favor boys and men. For example, in the studies of Eccles, Wigfield, and their colleagues (as well as in related work by John Nicholls and Virginia Crandall), high-achieving White female students were more likely than their White male peers to underestimate both their ability level and their class standing; in contrast, the White male students were more likely than their White female peers to overestimate their likely performance. When asked about specific domains, the sex differences depended on the gender-role stereotyping of the activity. For

example, in the work by Eccles and her colleagues, White boys and young men had higher competence beliefs than their female peers for math and sports, even after all relevant skill-level differences were controlled; in contrast, White girls had higher competence beliefs than White boys for reading, instrumental music, and social skills; and the magnitude of these differences increased following puberty. Furthermore, in these studies, the young women, on average, had greater confidence in their abilities in reading and social skills than in math, physical science, and athletics and, when averaged across math and English, the male students how lower confidence than their female peers in their academic abilities in general. By and large, these sex differences were also evident in the preliminary studies of African American students. This could be one explanation for the fact that the young men in these samples, as in the nation more generally, are more likely to drop out of high school than the young women.

Finally, the White female and male students in the Eccles and Wigfield studies rank-ordered these skill areas quite differently: the girls rated themselves as most competent in English and social activities and as least competent in sports; the boys rated themselves as most competent, by a substantial margin, in sports, followed by math, and then social activities; the boys rated themselves as least competent in English. Such within-sex, rank order comparisons are critically important for understanding differences in life choices. In the followup studies of these same youth, Jozefowicz, Barber, and Eccles were able to predict within-sex differences in the young women's and men's occupational goals with the pattern of their confidences across subject domains. The youth who wanted to go into occupations requiring a lot of writing, for example, had higher confidence in their artistic and writing abilities than in their math and science abilities. In contrast, the youth who wanted to go into science and advanced health field–related fields (e.g., becoming a physician) had higher confidence in their math and science abilities than in their artist and social abilities.

One of the most interesting findings from existing studies of academic self-confidence is that the sex differences in self-perceptions are usually much larger than one would expect given objective measures of actual performance and competence. First, consider mathematics; with the exception of performance on the most anxiety-provoking standardized test, girls do as well as boys on all measures of math competence throughout primary, secondary, and tertiary education. Furthermore, the few sex differences that do exist have been decreasing in magnitude over the past 20 years and do not appear with great regularity until late in the primary school years. Similarly, the sex difference in perceived sports competence is much larger (accounting for 9% of the variance in one of our studies) than the sex difference in our measures of actual sport-related skills (which accounted for between 1 and 3% of the variance on these indicators). [See SPORT AND ATHLETICS.]

So why do female students rate their math and sports competence so much lower than their male peers and so much lower than they rate their English ability and social skills? Some theorists have suggested that female and male students interpret variations in their performance in various academic subjects and leisure activities in a gender-role stereotyped manner. For example, girls and women might be more likely to attribute their math and sports successes to hard work and effort and their failures in these domains to lack of ability than do boys and men; in contrast boys and men might be more likely than girls and women to attribute their successes to natural talent. Similarly, girls and women might be more likely to attribute their English and social successes to natural ability. Such differences in causal attributions would lead to both the between- and within-gender differences in confidence levels reported earlier.

The evidence for these differences in causal attributions is mixed. Some researchers find that White girls and women are less likely than White boys and men to attribute success to ability and more likely to attribute failure to lack of ability. Others have found that this pattern depends on the kind of task used: occurring more with unfamiliar tasks or stereotypically masculine achievement task. The most consistent difference occurs for attributions of success to ability versus effort: White girls and women are less likely than White boys and men to stress the relevance of their own ability as a cause of their successes. Instead, White girls and women tend to rate effort and hard work as a more important determinant of their success than ability. Interestingly, so do their parents. There is nothing inherently wrong with attributing one's successes to hard work. In fact, Stevenson and his colleagues stress that this attributional pattern is a major advantage that Japanese students have over U.S. students. Nonetheless, it appears that within the context of the United States of America, this attributional pattern undermines girls'

and women's confidence in their ability to master increasingly more difficult material—perhaps leading young women to stop taking mathematics and physical science courses prematurely.

Gender-role stereotyping has also been suggested as a cause of the sex differences in academic self-concepts. The extent to which adolescents endorse the White American cultural stereotypes regarding which sex is likely to be most talented in each domain predicts the extent to which White girls/women and boys/men distort their ability self-concepts and expectations in the gender-stereotypic direction. Spencer and Steele suggested a related mechanism linking culturally based gendered stereotypes to competence: stereotype vulnerability. They hypothesized that members of social groups (like women) stereotyped as being less competent in a particular subject area (like math) will become anxious when asked to do difficult problems because they are afraid the stereotype may be true of them. This vulnerability is also likely to increase girls' and women's vulnerability to failure feedback on male-stereotyped tasks, leading them to lower their expectations and their confidence in their ability to succeed for these types of tasks. To test these hypotheses, Spencer and Steele gave college students a difficult math test under two conditions: after being told that men typically do better on this test or that men and women typically do about the same. The women scored lower than the men only in the first condition. Furthermore, the manipulation's effect was mediated by variations across condition in reported anxiety. Apparently, knowing that one is taking a test on which men typically do better than women increases young women's anxiety, which, in turn, undermines their performance. This study also suggests that changing this dynamic is relatively easy if one can change the women's perception of the sex-typing of the test.

In sum, when either sex differences or within-sex individual differences emerge on competence-related measures for academic subjects and other important skill areas, they are consistent with the gender-role stereotypes held by the group being studied (most often European Americans). These differences have also been found to be important mediators of both sex differences and within-sex individual differences in various types of achievement-related behaviors and choices. Such gendered patterns are theoretically important because they point to the power of gender-role socialization processes as key to understanding both girls' and boys' confidence in their various abilities. To the extent that gender-role socialization is key, it is important to study how and why young women differ in the extent to which they are either exposed to these socialization pressures or resist them when they are so exposed.

But even more important, all of the relevant studies have documented extensive variation within each sex. Both girls/women and boys/men vary a great deal among themselves in their intellectual confidence for various academic domains. They also vary considerably in their test anxiety, their attributional styles, and their locus of control. Such variations within each sex are a major set of predictors of variation among both young men and young women in their educational and occupational choices. White adolescent males and females who aspire to careers in math and science and who take advanced courses in math and physical science have greater confidence in their math and science abilities than those that do not. They also have just as much, if not more, confidence in their math and science abilities as in their English abilities.

B. OCCUPATIONAL ABILITY SELF-CONCEPTS

Eccles and her colleagues have extended the work on academic and athletic self-concepts by looking at White and Black adolescents' competence ratings for skills more directly linked to adult occupational choice. As their samples moved into and through high school, they asked the students a series of questions directly related to future job choices. First, they asked them to rate how good they were compared to other students at each of several job-related skills. Second, they asked the students to rate the probability that they would succeed at each of a series of standard careers. On the one hand, the results are quite gender-role stereotyped: the young women (both Black and White) were less confident of success than were their male peers in science-related professions and in male-typed skilled labor occupations. In contrast, the young men (both Black and White) were less confident of their success than were their female peers in health-related professions and female-typed skilled labor occupations. On the other hand, there were no sex differences in these seniors' ratings of either their confidence of success in business and law or their leadership, independence, intellectual, and computer skills. Furthermore, although the young men were more confident of success in physical science and engineering fields, the young women were more confident than their male peers of success in health-related fields that involve extensive scientific training.

The within-sex patterns were equally interesting. On the average these young women saw themselves as quite competent in traditionally female-typed jobs and skills related to human service, particularly in comparison to their confidence for science-related jobs and mechanical skills. Interestingly, these young women also saw themselves as quite competent in terms of their leadership and intellectual skills and their independence.

C. GENDER AND ACHIEVEMENT VALUES

Do women and men make gender-role stereotypic life choices because they have gender-role stereotypic values? In most studies, the answer is yes for the populations most studied (European Americans and African Americans). Gender-role stereotypic patterns in adolescents' valuing of sports, social activities, and English have emerged consistently. Interestingly, the gendered pattern associated with the value of math does not emerge until high school. Finally, the gendered pattern of valuing math, physics, and computer skills have emerged as the key predictors of both sex differences among White Americans and individual differences among White female students in adolescents' plans to enter math-related scientific and engineering fields.

It is important to note, however, that these gendered patterns have decreased over time for women of most ethnic groups in the United States. Young women today are more likely to aspire to the male-stereotyped fields of medicine, law, and business than their mothers and grandmothers. Although the numbers are not nearly as large, young women today are also much more likely to seek out occupations related to engineering and physical science. Finally, young women today are also much more involved in athletic activities than their mothers and grandmothers.

Because of their interest in understanding career choice, Eccles and her colleagues asked their Black and White senior high school participants to rate how important each of a series of job-related and life-related values and a series of job characteristics were to them. As was true for the job-related skills, they found evidence of both gender-role stereotypic differences and of gender-role transcendence. In keeping with traditional stereotypes, the young women more than their male peers, rated family and friends as important to them; the young women were also more likely than the male peers to want jobs that were people oriented. In contrast, but also consistent with traditional stereotypes, the young men placed a higher value on high-risk and competitive activities and wealth; they also were more interested in jobs that allowed for work with machinery, math, and computers. However, counter to traditional stereotypes, there were no sex differences in careerism (focus on career as a critical part of one's identity), and the women and men were equally likely to want jobs that allowed flexibility to meet family obligations, that entailed prestige and responsibility, and that provided opportunities for creative and intellectual work.

Evidence of both gender-role typing and gender-role transcendence was also evident in the within-sex patterns. Although these young women still, on the average, attached most importance to having a job with sufficient flexibility to meet family obligations and with the opportunity to help people, they also placed great importance on the role of their career for their personal identity (careerism) and on the importance of both prestige/responsibility and creativity as key components of their future occupations.

IV. *Predicting Occupational Choice*

Eccles and her colleagues next used the values and ability self-concepts to predict these young men's and women's occupational aspirations. As expected, ability self-concepts were key predictors of both between- and within-sex differences in career aspirations. Also as predicted by the Eccles Expectancy-Value Model of Achievement-Related Choices, the lifestyle and valued job characteristics were significant predictors of career aspirations. The within-sex analyses were especially interesting. Values did an excellent job of discriminating between these young women's occupational plans. Perhaps most interestingly, it was the value placed on helping other people that predicted which women aspired to advanced level health-related professions (e.g., a physician) and which women aspired to Ph.D.-level science careers. Both of these groups of women had done very well in their math and science courses and had very high confidence in their math and science abilities. In contrast, they differed dramatically in the value they placed on helping others: the women aspiring to the health-related fields placed more importance on this dimension than on any other value dimension. In contrast, the women aspiring to Ph.D.-level physical science and engineering careers placed less importance on this dimension than on any other dimension, particularly the value of being able to work with math and computers.

Evidence from other investigators also provides good support for a key role of perceived task value in achievement-related decisions. For example, Dunteman, Wisenbaker, and Taylor studied the link between personal values and selection of one's college major using a longitudinal, correlational design. In their 1978 report to the National Science Foundation, they identified two sets of values that both predicted students' subsequent choice of major and differentiated the sexes: the first set (labeled thing-orientation) reflected an interest in manipulating objects and understanding the physical world; the second set (labeled person-orientation) reflected an interest in understanding human social interaction and a concern with helping people. Students who scored high on thing-orientation and low on person-orientation were more likely than other students to select a math or physical science major. Not surprisingly, the women in their study were more likely than their male peers to be person oriented and to major in something other than math or physical science; in contrast, the men were more likely than their female peers to both be thing oriented and to major in math and physical science.

In summary, gendered patterns in the valuing of different academic subject areas and activities still exist. Although it is encouraging that girls value math during elementary school, the fact that young White women have less positive views of both their math ability and the value of math is problematic because these differences lead young White women to be less likely than young White men to take optional advanced-level math and physical science courses. It is likely that similar sex differences exist in other ethnic groups.

V. *Gender Roles and Gendered Occupational Choice*

This analysis has a number of important implications for understanding how gender leads to differences in educational and occupational achievement. Because socialization shapes individuals' self-perceptions, identity formation, goals, and values, men and women should acquire different self-concepts, different patterns of expectations for success across various activities, and different values and goals through the processes associated with gender-role socialization. Through the potential impact of the socialization practices linked to various gender roles on both expectations for success and subjective task value, these socialization experiences can affect educational and vocational choices in several ways.

First, because gender-role socialization-related experiences influence identity formation, such experiences could lead the two sexes to have different hierarchies of core personal values. Several studies have documented such differences for White populations. More work is needed to determine the generalizability of this pattern to other ethnic groups. What little evidence there is suggests that these differences are evident in most other groups.

Gender-role socialization could also lead the two sexes to place different values on various long-range goals and adult activities. The essence of gender roles is that they define what an individual should do with her or his life in order to be successful as a man or woman. If success in various gender-related roles is a central component of an individual's identity, then activities that fulfill these roles should have higher subjective task value than tasks linked to the opposite gender's stereotypic roles. Gender roles mandate different primary activities for women and men. Traditionally, in the gendered roles of wife and mother (within at least European American, Asian American, and Hispanic American cultures), women are supposed to support their husbands' careers and raise their children; men are supposed to compete successfully in the occupational world in order to confirm their worth as human beings and to support their families. To the extent that a woman has internalized this traditional definition of these female roles, she should rank-order the importance of the associated adult activities differently than her male peers. In particular, she should rate the parenting and the spouse-support roles as more important than a professional career role and she should be more likely than her male peers to resolve life's decisions in favor of these family roles. The men and women in the Eccles study described earlier did exactly this: the women indicated they would be more likely to make sacrifices in their professional life for the needs of their family than did the men. They were also more likely to mention both family and career concerns in qualitative descriptions of what they thought a day in their lives would be like when they were 25. Similar results were reported by Sears and Kerr in their studies of the career-related decisions of gifted women—many of whom ended up choosing to limit their career development after they had their families in order to fulfill their image of their role as wife and mother. Each of these studies, however, had primarily European American samples. Work is needed to see if these patterns are also evident in other ethnic groups.

Similarly, gender roles can influence the definition one has of successful performance of those activities considered to be central to one's identity. For example, women and men may differ in their understanding of the requirements for successful task participation and completion. If so, then men and women should approach and structure their task involvement differently even when they appear on the surface to be selecting a similar task. The parenting role provides an excellent example of this process. If men define success in the parenting role as an extension of their occupational and bread-winner roles, then they may respond to parenthood with increased commitment to their career goals and with emphasis on encouraging a competitive drive in their children. In contrast, if women define success in the parenting role as high levels of involvement in their children's lives, they may respond to parenthood with decreased commitment to their career goals. Furthermore, if staying home with her children and being psychologically available to them most of the time are central components of a woman's gender-role schema, then involvement in a demanding, high-level career should have reduced subjective value precisely because it conflicts with a more central component of her identity. Evidence from studies with White American samples confirms these predictions.

Women and men could also differ in the density of their goals and values. There is some evidence suggesting that White men, at least, are more likely than White women to exhibit a single-minded devotion to one particular goal, especially their occupational goal. In contrast, White women seem more likely than White men to be involved in, and to value, competence in several activities simultaneously. Becoming a leader in any field requires sustained and quite focused engagement with that field. Such intense engagement is easier if an individual is single-mindedly devoted to one goal.

One other pattern characterizes the responses of the White women and men in several studies: White men usually rate family and occupation as of equal importance while the White women rate family as more important than occupation. Several researchers have suggested that the perceived conflict of traditional female values and roles with the demands of male-typed achievement activities is very salient to women. How this conflict affects women's lives is a complex issue. Some studies emphasize its negative consequence. For example, recent interviews with the Terman women suggest they now have regrets about the sacrifices they made in their professional development for their family's needs. Similarly studies with predominantly White children and adolescents suggest that girls and young women feel caught between their need to be "nice" and their need to achieve.

Several investigators have pointed out that this conflict results, in part, from the fact that women have multiple roles and multiple goals. These multiple roles, however, provide richness to women's lives as well as stress. There is growing evidence (from studies of several different ethnic groups) that women with multiple roles are healthier both mentally and physically than women with few roles and than men in general.

Finally, as predicted in the model in Figure 1, gender roles could affect the subjective value of various educational and vocational options indirectly through their influence on the behaviors and attitudes of the people individuals are exposed to as they grow up. If, for example, parents, friends, teachers, or counselors provide boys and girls with different feedback on their performance in various school subjects, with different advice regarding the importance of various school subjects, with different information regarding the importance of preparing to support oneself and one's family, with different information regarding the occupational opportunities that the student should be considering, and with different opportunities to develop various skills, then it is likely that girls and boys will develop different self-perceptions, different patterns of expectations for success, and different estimates of the value of various educational and vocational options. Similarly, if the men and women around children engage in different educational and vocational activities, then girls and boys should develop different ideas regarding those activities for which they are best suited. Finally, if one's peers reinforce traditional gender-role behaviors and values, girls and boys will likely engage in different activities as they are growing up and thus are likely to acquire different competencies, different patterns of expectations or success, and different values and long-term goals.

In summary, it is likely that gender roles have their largest impact on life trajectories through their impact on both personal and social identities. As girls and boys grow up, some learn to value those aspects of life and personality that are consistent with their various gender-related roles. They learn to see themselves in terms of these gender roles. Such a socialization process affects their expectations and values, which, in turn, affect their life choices. Exactly why some women and men place great importance on such roles and others do not has been the subject of extensive theorizing and empirical work. Developmental psychologists link it to gendered socialization pressures from parents, peers, and the larger social context and to children's early need to form stable social categories and personal identities and then to become competent members of the groups they have identified with. To the extent that the child grows up in a gendered world with strong pressures toward conformity to that world, the child will come to attach great importance to behaving in accord with the norms of this gendered world. In contrast, to the extent that the child grows up in a world that both encourages and reinforces independence, flexibility, and individual choice and provides extensive models of gender-role transcendence, she or he is likely to place much less importance on conformity to gender-role stereotypic behavior norms. By and large research evidence supports these predictions for European American populations. More work is needed to determine the extent to which this is also true in other ethnic groups. What evidence there is suggests two conclusions: (1) the predicted relations are likely to be true in most ethnic groups, and (2) the exact extent and specific nature of both gender-role stereotyping and gender-role socialization will differ across ethnic groups—leading to ethnic group differences in the magnitude of sex differences on all of the constructs discussed in the article.

SUGGESTED READING

American Association of University Women. (1990). *Shortchanging Girls, Shortchanging America: Full Data Report.* American Association of University Women, Washington, D.C.

Baruch, G., Barnett, R., and Rivers, C. (1983). *Life Prints.* McGraw-Hill, New York.

Bell, L. A. (1989). Something's wrong here and it's not me: Challenging the dilemmas that block girls' success. *Journal for the Education of the Gifted* 12, 118–130.

Betz, N. E., and Fitzgerald, L. F. (1987). *The Career Psychology of Women.* Academic Press, Orlando, FL.

Crosby, F. J. (1991). *Juggling,* The Free Press, New York.

Eccles, J. S. (1994). Understanding women's educational and occupational choices: Applying the Eccles *et al.* model of achievement-related choices. *Psychology of Women Quarterly* 18, 585–609.

Eccles, J. S., Barber, B., and Jozekowicz, D. (1998). Linking gender to educational, occupational, and recreational choices: Applying the Eccles *et al.* model of achievement-related choices.

In *The Many Faces of Gender: The Multidimensional Model of Janet Taylor Spence.* (W. B. Swann, Jr., J. H. Langlois, and L. A. Gilbert, eds.) APA Press, Washington, D.C.

Eccles, J. S., and Harold, R. D. (1992). Gender differences in educational and occupational patterns among the gifted. In *Talent Development: Proceedings from the 1991 Henry B. and Jocelyn Wallace National Research Symposium on Talent Development.* N. Colangelo, S. G. Assouline, and D. L. Ambroson, eds.). Trillium Press, Unionville, NY.

Eccles, J. S., Jacobs, J., Harold, R., Yoon, K. S., Arbreton, A., and Freedman-Doan, C. (1993). Parents and gender role socialization. In *Claremont Symposium on Applied Social Psychology, 1992: Gender and Social Psychology.* (S. Oskamp and M. Costanzo, eds.), pp. 59–84. Sage, Thousand Oaks, CA.

Farmer, H. S. (1997). Women's motivation related to master, career salience, and career aspiration: A multivariate model focusing on the effects of sex role socialization. *Journal of Career Aspirations 5*, 355–381.

Gilligan, C., Lyons, N. P., and Tammer, T. J. (1990). *Making Connections: The Relational Worlds of Adolescent Girls at Emma Willard School.* Harvard University Press, Cambridge, MA.

Kerr, B. A. (1985). *Smart Girls, Gifted Women.* Ohio Psychology Publishing, Dayton, OH.

National Science Foundation. (1999). *Women, Minorities and Persons with Physical Disabilities in Science and Engineering.* National Science Foundation, Washington, D.C.

Ruble, D. N., and Martin, C. L. (1997). Gender development. In *Handbook of Child Psychology, Vol. 3, Social, Emotional, and Personality Development*, 5th ed. (W. Damon and N. Eisenberg, eds.). Wiley, New York.

Sommers, C. H. (2000, May) Girls rule! Mythmakers to the contrary, it's boys who are in deep trouble. *Atlantic Monthly,* 59–74.

Subotnik, R. F., and Arnold, K. D. (1991). *Remarkable Women: Perspectives on Female Talent Development.* Hampton Press, Cresskill, NJ.

Adolescent Gender Development

Lucia F. O'Sullivan

Julia A. Graber

Jeanne Brooks-Gunn

Columbia University

Glossary

Adolescence Period of development referring to the second decade of life.

Gender Societally defined concept of being male or female.

Gender identity Personal sense of self as female or male in terms of behaviors, attitudes, interests, and preferences.

Gender role A pattern or code of behaviors or attitudes considered appropriate for women and men as determined by changing sociocultural and historical forces.

ADOLESCENT GENDER DEVELOPMENT may be defined as the biological, psychological, and social processes contributing to attitudes, behaviors, and cognitions relevant to one's understanding of being a male or a female. Adolescence is a period of life representing what is commonly considered a transition from childhood to adulthood. Developmental experiences that characterize adolescence, such as the onset of puberty and the initiation of sexual and romantic behaviors, help to elaborate one's concept of gender identity and roles.

I. Introduction

Gender refers to societally defined concepts of being a female or a male. In Western cultures, gender is commonly treated as fixed binary code to which a person is assigned on the basis of biological characteristics and responds accordingly. However, one can experience considerable variation in one's gender roles, identity, and behavior across contexts and time. Gender should in fact be considered a dynamic process rather than a fixed construct. It is possible, for instance, to adopt more masculine standards of behavior in some situations than others or when interacting with particular groups of people. More important, it is clear that we are not appointed at birth to behave, think, feel, or develop according to a rigid binomial program representing female or male. Biological markers of gender, such as external genitalia or chromosomal patterns, may not match our self-identity as man or woman, boy or girl, and neither category may correspond to the gender roles we adopt.

However, the bias toward viewing gender as a fixed binary code and, in particular, speculation about gender differences amounts to what Carol Nagy Jacklin has referred to as a national preoccupation. Yet researchers typically uncover greater within-sex differences than between-sex differences as recognized, for instance, in relatively current reviews of the research summarizing male superior mathematical ability and female superior verbal ability. Eleanor Maccoby has argued, however, that there may be some universal themes that characterize gender differences between men and women across cultures, such as more aggressive physical activity found among males than females. These differences appear few in number, and the extent to which these differences are expressed is heavily influenced by the cultural context in which they are found. It is their universal nature that suggests that these gender differences correspond to differential roles of women and men in the process of reproduction because in these cases biology subverts culture. As such, understanding adolescence is critical to understanding the development of gender because key reproductive issues, such as the onset of puberty and the initiation of romantic and sexual relationships, are the hallmarks of this period of development.

Although researchers have addressed the wide range of biological, psychological, environmental, and social processes associated with gender development in both infants and children, there is almost no research at all concerning adolescents. For example, a search for articles focused on "adolescent gender development" published since 1967 produced almost no results. This research neglect is particularly interesting given that adolescence heralds considerable reorganization and adaptation vis-à-vis cultural roles and expectations for gender.

Our review of research relevant to adolescent gender development has focused instead on differential experiences for adolescent girls and boys that are related to gender phenomena or constructs, as well as the meaning, progression of events, and factors related to these experiences. Many of the developmental transitions adolescents experience may influence their understanding of gender. As the thought processes of adolescents become more abstract and self-reflective, adolescents also become better able to compare several complex mental constructs simultaneously and adopt the perspectives of others. According to Wyndol Furman and Valerie Simon, these cognitive changes prompt adolescents to elaborate

and integrate their views of their own roles and preferences to achieve some measure of personal identity. Moreover, these changes require integration of adolescents' views regarding men's and women's roles generally in romantic and sexual relationships. Cognitive developments occur in tandem with physiological changes associated with puberty and a number of significant contextual changes associated with this age group (e.g., transition to junior high school or middle school, ultimately influencing academic performance and career orientation).

Moreover, we have construed adolescent gender development as being steered in part by the biological factors on which the sexes differ, as well as the differences in socialization practices, influential models of learning, and meanings attributed to gender-related experiences. Research demonstrates increasing divergence between boys and girls in several important domains during adolescence, including self-esteem, behavior problems, academic achievement, and sex role attitudes which are likely to help further establish beliefs and expectations about experiences unique to girls and boys.

In the following sections, we review the available literature with an eye toward demonstrating the ways in which adolescents' developmental trajectories contribute to the formation of gender-related identities and roles. There are numerous experiences relatively unique to adolescence that help to establish one's concept of gender, the most significant of which may be puberty, initiation of dating and sexual relationships, altered relations with peers and parents, school transitions, marriage, child rearing, and work. Because gender should be understood within a particular historical and cultural context, we describe recent research conducted primarily in North America or Western cultures (more generally), as well as theories familiar to these cultures.

A. THEORIES RELATED TO ADOLESCENT GENDER DEVELOPMENT

The major theories addressing adolescent gender development in some form include (1) psychoanalytic, (2) social learning/scripting, (3) evolutionary, and (4) social constructionist theories. In brief, psychoanalytic theories contend that gender development in adolescence centers around the successful resolution of the oedipal complexes in youth, subsequent formation of sexual unions with the other sex, and reexamination of parental values and ideals. Social learning and scripting theories postulate that attitudes and behaviors become strongly associated with various societally condoned rewards and punishments during gender socialization. Gender roles result from the differential modeling and reinforcement of boys and girls for various behaviors considered "appropriate" for their sex. Society has expectations or scripts about how women and men or girls and boys should behave and actively shapes the adoption of different behaviors and attitudes during adolescence. Evolutionary theorists argue that evolution determines differential reproductive strategies for females and males via the processes of sexual selection. These strategies ultimately influence a wide variety of differential sexual attitudes and relationship orientations and behaviors for women and men. Finally, social constructionist theories focus on the influence of social and cultural forces on behaviors. Adolescent gender development is shaped by women's lesser value in society, weaker role in relationships with men, and higher likelihood of exploitation. [*See* GENDER DEVELOPMENT: EVOLUTIONARY PERSPECTIVES; GENDER DEVELOPMENT: GENDER SCHEMA THEORY; GENDER DEVELOPMENT: PSYCHOANALYTIC PERSPECTIVES; GENDER DEVELOPMENT: SOCIAL LEARNING.]

Our own focus on gender identity, gender roles, and gendered behavior during adolescence is somewhat eclectic. It embeds social learning/scripting and social constructionist approaches into the development context of adolescence, and an evolutionary perspective to understand what may be some fundamental differences between the sexes.

II. *Gender Identity*

Gender identity refers to a personal sense of self as a female or a male in terms of behaviors, attitudes, and preferences. The first step in developing gender identity is the task of labeling one's own gender. Kohlberg's work on the development of gender among children demonstrated that children are able to consistently label themselves and others as boys or girls at around two years of age. Between ages three and four, they learn that gender is a stable characteristic of a person across time, and by age five they also learn that gender is a stable trait across situations.

Research indicates that gender identity is fixed relatively early in a person's development. John Money and Anke Ehrhardt argued that there is a critical period for the development of gender identity. This window begins around 18 months of age and ends around four years. Once established, it is unlikely (although not impossible) to change even in face of

later biological developments at odds with one's gender identity. Those whose gender identity is incongruent with their external appearance typically seek medical treatment to alter their appearance to match their identity.

Some exceptions of gender reassignment do occur in adolescence. For example, J. Imperato-McGinley has conducted elaborate kindred studies of male pseudohermaphrodites with 5 alpha-reductase deficiency. These children are born with female-appearing external genitals (incomplete masculinized male genitalia). Many were raised by their families as girls, self-identified as girls, and adopted female gender role behaviors. At puberty, however, a male gender identity (and sometimes also male gender role behaviors) evolved for some of these individuals in conjunction with the masculinizing events of puberty. These cases are rare, as are the endocrine disorders that cause them. Although gender identity changes can occur beyond childhood, gender reassignment is extremely unlikely and becomes increasingly more difficult at later ages. These isolated cases do serve to illustrate, however, the plasticity of our gender-related concepts.

Janet Spence has argued that people vary in the extent to which they endorse attitudes, interests, and behaviors characteristic of females or males at any given time and across developmental periods. The fundamental sense of gender identity developed in childhood may be relatively stable for most people, but the actual content of this identity is variable across the life span. Recent research, such as the work of Cynthia Smith and her colleagues, supports the view of a more dynamic model of gender identity. How one defines what is appropriate for one's sex and the development of these changing definitions for identity are at the heart of the discussion of gender roles.

III. *Gender Roles*

Unlike gender identity, in most respects gender roles appear relatively malleable and able to incorporate ever-changing societally condoned notions of appropriate behavior for men and women. Traditional gender roles of masculinity have emphasized agency and instrumental behaviors and attributes, whereas traditional feminine roles have emphasized expressive and relational behaviors and attributes. Gender roles may correspond to a person's gender identity, but this is not always the case. Some girls with a female gender identity may adopt female gender role behaviors and attitudes, whereas others may adopt behaviors and attitudes typically associated with boys. Susan Golombok and Robyn Fivush have noted, as have others, that attributes associated with males tend to be more highly valued than those associated with females. For example, Western society values traits like independence and assertiveness but not weakness or gullibility. These researchers argue, however, that the labels used to describe female traits often carry negative connotations (e.g., "gullibility" rather than "trusting") and should be understood as reflecting most cultures' devaluation of the feminine in any form.

However, in many respects, only women and girls have significant flexibility in their adoption of gender roles because they are freer to adopt both feminine and masculine (the more valued) traits. Males report wanting to possess attributes considered stereotypically masculine, but not less desirable traits, which are those, considered stereotypically feminine. Indeed, Richard Eisler, Jay Skidmore, and Clay Ward found that men's identification with the masculine gender role contributed to elevated anger, stress, and health problems in situations requiring that they attempt to (even temporarily) adopt feminine behaviors. Connie O'Heron and Jacob Orlofsky maintain that men who fail to demonstrate these traditional male standards tend to report more anxiety and depression than do women who deviate from traditional female gender roles. Unfortunately, for girls, many traditional female characteristics are not psychologically healthy, such as passivity, dependence, and shyness. As such, adopting an extreme female gender role may be associated with negative consequences, including helplessness and depression. Conventional male characteristics, such as forcefulness and independence, are positively associated with self-esteem and confidence for both males and females.

Changes experienced in adolescence are largely defined by one's social context and an individual's interactions with roles and expectations for behavior based on identification or membership in social groups. Issues of group membership are particularly salient to adolescents as they struggle to attain membership in a new group, that is, adults. Within the broad group of adults are the subgroups with which adolescents also identify such as being a man, being a woman, being a member of a particular ethnic or racial group, and so on. Adolescents construct their roles via their perceptions of the norms and expectations for members of the group or groups with which they identify or want to belong.

Adolescence is also characterized by increasing dif-

ferentiation in gender roles between girls and boys through greater adherence to traditional gender role stereotypes. John Hill and Mary Lynch contend that early adolescents around puberty are overly concerned with the significance of gender to the point where they develop stereotyped, inflexible gender categories. Gender intensification helps adolescents clarify their understanding of gender during a period of uncertainty about their own changing bodies and social roles. Pressures to engage in gender-appropriate behaviors heighten during early adolescence, paralleling an increasing need to conform to these roles to ensure acceptance by peers. However, Hill and Lynch have suggested that as development during adolescence progresses, the pressure to conform to these roles attenuates. Specifically, they are able to form their own ideas of what it means to be female or male with less adherence to societally defined roles as they adapt to their adult-like bodies, form more stable identities, gain experience in romantic and sexual relationships, and develop the cognitive abilities to see multiple perspectives or options for roles. Although there is greater flexibility in gender roles in some respects for adolescents today, particularly for girls, Lynn Ponton has argued that the sharper distinctions in gender roles are still apparent for younger adolescents. [*See* GENDER STEREOTYPES.]

IV. Socializing Agents or Influences on Gender Roles in Adolescence

A range of socialization agents appears to influence adolescents' concepts of gender. These can include more proximate agents such as family, peers, friends, and teachers, as well as more distant agents, such as celebrities, the media, and so on. In addition, pubertal development influences gender concepts by ultimately producing an adult-like body that signals to others as well as to the adolescent that he or she is ready to assume the role of an adult.

A. CHANGES ASSOCIATED WITH PUBERTY

There is a range of physical, psychological, and social changes associated with puberty. Pubertal processes influence one's concept of gender like few other experiences of adolescence. The experience of puberty also varies significantly on the basis of gender. The onset of puberty among boys generally follows girls by approximately two years, although the reasons for this discrepancy are unclear. Puberty acts as a stimulus for further differentiating self from the other sex, and for developing interest in the other sex. It is also a period of marked social change in one's interactions with significant others.

Pubertal development involves numerous changes in nearly every system of the body with (1) changes in the central nervous in areas that serve as control centers for reproductive systems, (2) changes in the cardiovascular system with increases in endurance and strength, (3) growth in height and weight, and (4) development of secondary sexual characteristics. The initial hormonal-central nervous system paths that were established prenatally in girls and boys are dormant during much of childhood. In late childhood, this system is activated. It takes about four to five years for each adolescent to complete pubertal development from the time that the first external signs of puberty are apparent.

For girls, the first external signs of pubertal development are usually onset of breast development or appearance of pubic hair at nine to ten years of age. Recent studies have found that African American girls begin puberty about nine months earlier than their White age mates. Overall, most girls begin puberty sometime in late childhood. By their entry into middle or junior high school, most will have clearly visible signs of breast development and growth in height. Menarche occurs just after the peak of the growth spurt in height and during the growth spurt in weight. Menarche, the onset of menses, is one of the last events of puberty in girls, although menarche is often considered a key transition in the life course for most girls. It is an event frequently imbued with social and personal significance, and may signal the need for a realignment of a girl's self-definition with her altered status in society as a woman. The median age of menarche has been steadily declining over the last 150 years in all developed countries, although it may have plateaued at this point at 12.5 years. In the United States, African American girls have a slightly earlier rate of menarche (12.1 years) compared to White girls (12.9), which corresponds to their earlier onset of puberty. Researchers have not yet substantiated differences among other racial and ethnic groups. [See MENSTRUATION.]

For boys, pubertal development usually begins with initial growth of the testes occurring around 11 years of age, followed by growth of pubic hair. Acceleration in growth in height begins around 11.5 years of age and peaks around 14 years of age. The beginning of sperm production occurs early in puberty, but final adult levels are not reached until the late teens. First ejaculation usually occurs around 13.5 years of age. Notably, boys will likely experience pubertal changes that are only apparent to them and possibly their parents before having signs of puberty that are apparent to others in their social spheres. The more "private" experience of puberty is in contrast to girls' development in that breast growth is usually noticeable to others making pubertal development a more public event for girls. Thus, boys may have more time to adjust to puberty before having to deal with the reaction of others to their development. In addition, there are no truly comparable pubertal events for boys that have the same social and cultural significance as menarche in girls. It has been argued that a boy's first experiences of ejaculation may be analogous as a sign to the individual of reproductive maturity; however, menarche seems to be associated with more social rituals ranging from rites of passage ceremonies to a discussion with mom about "becoming a woman."

Jeanne Brooks-Gunn found that boys' experiences of pubertal development are generally positive. Girls, on the other hand, are more likely to report negative experiences of puberty, such as being teased about breast development or being shocked by their first period. In some sense, these patterns parallel the nature of gender roles in that becoming more like an adult female may entail taking on attributes that are deemed less desirable. By most accounts, girls also report more major life events and daily stressors (e.g., concerns about weight) than do boys during early adolescence, contributing in part to the higher incidence of depressive episodes and loss of esteem among girls. These reactions may be due to some extent with the timing of puberty, which coincides typically with the transition from protected elementary school social environments to junior high school—a stressful event for many adolescents.

B. THE INFLUENCE OF FAMILY AND PEERS

A hallmark of adolescence is the steady diminution of parental influence as socializing agents. Adolescence is characterized by increased conflict with parents reflecting adolescents' growing desire for autonomy and independence. Increased strain in relationships with parents occurs around the time of girls' menarche, and later in the pubertal process for boys. Jacquelynne Eccles has documented how parents play an important role in influencing their children to engage in gender role stereotyped behavior. Parents' stereotyped beliefs interact with the sex of their child to influence their views of their child's abilities. For instance, mothers with stereotyped views about math competency (i.e., boys are naturally more talented at math than are girls) tend to rate their sons' abilities as higher than their daughters' and encourage their daughters less than their sons to participate in math and science activities. Parents' perceptions of their child's abilities have a stronger influence on children's perceptions of their own abilities than do children's grades. Overall, research indicates that girls may be influenced more by parental evaluations than boys, often to their detriment. However, most parents and adolescents maintain warmth and closeness despite greater independence. Adolescents usually report an alignment with their parents' values and goals for achievement and careers, although peers may have a greater influence over decisions about social interactions.

Corresponding to the diminution of parental influence in some areas of adolescents' lives, both peers and older siblings gain ground during early adolescence as influential models of older, more gender-specific adult attitudes and activities. For example, research has shown that having a pregnant or parenting older sister in the home increases the likelihood that an adolescent girl will become an adolescent parent herself. Adolescents' perceptions of peers' sexual behavior corresponds in many respects to their own sexual behavior. The process of social comparison, which is key to peer influence, is actually reciprocal in nature—that is, adolescents express the desire to be similar to their friends, particularly in early adolescence, and adolescents become censured by peers for not adhering favorably to group norms, seeking those to whom their behaviors more closely match. The salience of peers ultimately diminishes in importance toward later adolescence favoring romantic partners.

C. DEPICTIONS OF GENDER ROLES IN THE MEDIA

Jane Brown found that adolescents spend an average of six hours each day with some form of media. Two-thirds of adolescents have a television in their bedroom and may have easy access to the Internet and computer games. Most forms of media incorporate heterosexual themes with stereotyped depictions of gender roles for women and men. Gay, lesbian, bisexual, and transgendered youth are rarely portrayed in the media. Attesting to the importance of this source of influence, the Kaiser Family Foundation indicated that adolescents typically report that the media was their primary source of information about sex and intimacy.

There is sparse research on the effects of sexual media content on adolescents' interpretation of media-depicted gender roles despite the media saturation adolescents currently experience and cultural interest in the phenomenon. In part, it is difficult for researchers to ascertain the nature of the effects media has on the development of gender roles and behavior because of the diverse range or sources of influence (television, movies, newspapers, magazines, books, videos, the Internet) and the presumed insidious nature of its influence.

Most media analyses in the social sciences focus on the impact of aggressive and sexual content, rather than the depiction of gender roles per se. Of course, depictions of aggression and sex fortify stereotypes of typical female and male behavior and attitudes in many ways. Male characters are more likely to conduct acts of violence, although victims are equally likely to be male or female. The sexuality of both girls and women is portrayed explicitly in most forms of media (typically through provocative dress), yet media directed at female consumers focuses on establishing and maintaining men's sexual and romantic interest and facilitating interpersonal interactions. Men are typically depicted as being strong, financial providers and taking the initiative in intimate relationships, whereas women are typically depicted as delicate, lacking humor, and responsible for the care of children and home. Thus, the information that is transmitted to adolescents about sex and intimacy via the media is also coupled with information on traditional roles in these relationships. [*See* MEDIA INFLUENCES; MEDIA STEREOTYPES.]

V. Enactment of Roles and Scripts in Dating Behavior and Sexuality

Adolescents gain greater exposure to romantic interactions during adolescence and advance their understanding of adult roles for men and women in these contexts. As a result of cognitive changes during this period, they are better able to conceptualize their future and consolidate ever more stable intimate relationships with the other sex.

There is relatively little research attention devoted to romantic relationships in adolescence. This is particularly significant when compared to the amount of attention devoted to adolescent sexual behavior, notably the reproduction-related behavior of mid- to late adolescent girls. Most studies of adolescent sexuality have disregarded romantic relationships altogether. Part of the reluctance of researchers to investigate these relationships may be attributed to the fact that these relationships are more transitory in nature, less intimate, and less likely to lead to marriage compared to adult relationships. Thus, they may be viewed as having less "substance." It is also the case that parents have historically held a vested interest in regulating or policing the sexual behavior of adolescents, arising from moral beliefs prohibiting premarital sexual activity and childbearing.

The importance of romantic relationships to adolescence, however, should not go unappreciated. Romance competes with adolescents' attention for school, career, family, and friends. These early relationships constitute an arena for unprecedented experiences of strong emotions such as love, anxiety, anger, jealously, despair, and elation. Marita McCabe has demonstrated that relationships and sexual experience are important contributors to adolescents' objective and subjective quality of life. In addition, adolescent romantic relationships provide a critical context for working through broader issues of identity, individuation, and other components of self-concept, including gender identity and gender roles. These relationships provide opportunities to enact relationship scripts and practice relationship behaviors, such as reciprocity and intimate self-disclosure. Although dating and sexual behaviors overlap for many adolescents, the nature of dating and sexual scripts will each be addressed in the following sections in order to describe the unique contributions of each to the development of gender. [*See* INTIMACY AND LOVE.]

A. ADOLESCENT DATING BEHAVIOR

It should be noted that the concept of dating is distinct from the broader concept of courtship, which refers more directly to committed relationships directed toward marriage. Compared to previous decades, current dating patterns in adolescence are less formal and incorporate less adherence to adult cultural scripts specifying progression of the relationship from first meeting to marriage. Adolescent relationships differ from adult relationships in that the goal of these relationships is not necessarily marriage or long-term commitment. The term "dating," though familiar in the research literature, is often not recognized by adolescents who prefer instead to describe their relationships in terms of hanging out or simply in terms of having a boyfriend or girlfriend. Furthermore, conventional concepts of dating activity involving circumscribed activities between unaccompanied couples no longer apply for most early to midadolescent relationships.

1. Development of Heterosexual Dating Scripts

Societal codes delineating masculinity and femininity play a critical key role in dating rituals. Eleanor Maccoby has argued that intimate relationships between boys and girls can develop only after an individual has overcome the gender segregation that characterizes most of childhood. This segregation leads to the formation of essentially different cultures for boys and girls and is largely accountable for many of the sex differences and associated tension between the sexes. Adolescents are required to learn how best to negotiate strategies of cooperation or to accommodate these differences in order to successfully establish intimate relationships with the other sex.

Adolescents are often able to describe in some detail the interpersonal scripts that characterize their dating experiences in early adolescence. Girls and boys typically report experiencing first romantic interest or "crushes" between the ages of 7 and 10 years. These crushes are typically directed toward unavailable targets (such as teachers and celebrities) at first, but soon are directed toward known others. Interestingly, hormonal changes associated with pubertal development occur around this same age range, although as yet, direct hormone links to these initial romantic feelings have not been made.

Around 10 to 12 years of age, girls begin to pay greater attention to clothing, makeup, and behaviors that emphasize their attractiveness, often to the consternation of their parents. Girls also initiate direct communication with boys that they find attractive, such as talking to boys on the telephone or hanging out with boys during breaks at school or in the evenings. Adolescents then begin to spend increased amounts of time in mixed-sex encounters around the ages of 10 to 14 years. Games with some sexual content (e.g., Spin the Bottle, Man Hunt, and Seven Minutes in Heaven) and usually kissing or touching of breasts and genitals over clothes, become more common among groups of both girls and boys. Sexual play of early adolescence is prescriptively heterosexual.

During mid-adolescence, groups of boys will mix with groups of girls with whom they are acquainted in some way (typically through school interactions). Mixed-sex groups are made up of some who become romantic couples and others who are just friends. Earliest romantic relationships frequently involve minimal interpersonal contact, with the couple spending little or no time together, but they are recognized among peers as "liking each other" or "going together." These relationships are often short in duration compared to relationships established later in adolescence. Most dating activity during this period occurs within group contexts, such as attending parties and movies or socializing after school in friends' homes without direct adult supervision. Couples are typically paired in these group encounters and are able to take time alone periodically from the group.

Wyndol Furman and Elizabeth Wehner have argued that peers are central to forming these early romantic attachments. Peers act both as a source of communicating expectations of societal norms about romantic involvement and a model of "gender-appropriate" dating scripts. They also frequently serve additional functions that include being a source of connections or contacts to romantic prospects and being "matchmaker" or facilitator of early romantic connections.

As adolescents get older, their romantic relationships are more likely to involve higher degrees of both romantic and sexual intimacy and are longer in duration compared to those formed in early adolescence. These relationships are also characterized by more solitary activities for the couple. Sexual intimacy commonly progresses with increasing romantic intimacy. Relationships in later adolescence involve shared activities and are less recreational compared to earlier relationships, and are more likely to focus on relationship development. Unlike earlier relationships where the motives for establishing relationships are often recreation or status related, both older male and female adolescents emphasize intimacy, companionship, and socialization.

2. Differential Experiences for Male and Female Adolescents in Dating Relationships

Thomas Wright has contended that women view love and sex as interrelated, whereas men have a tendency to differentiate sex and intimacy or love. Such findings fit with commonly held beliefs about which behaviors are appropriate for girls and boys, as well as girls' heightened focus on relationships. Although

data are lacking for younger adolescents, studies with older adolescents indicate that more men than women desire and experience sexual intercourse, and men desire higher levels of sexual intimacy than they actually experience in their relationships with women. This discrepancy between desired and experienced levels of sexual intimacy is less apparent among women, and the discrepancy between men and women is more apparent in couples subscribing to conventional gender roles. However, both male and female adolescents stress the importance of developing romantic intimacy prior to sexual involvement, even though this value is more strongly endorsed by female adolescents. Robin Simon and colleagues found that girls in grades six through eight endorse a norm that "one should always be in love," suggesting that cultural scripts prescribing girls' predominant interest in love and romance are alive and well.

Most research on intimate relationships support the contention that women and men approach relationships differently. Women express greater commitment to their relationships, greater expectations of monogamy, and less acceptance of sexual involvement outside of the primary relationship compared to men. David Buss and colleagues have demonstrated that women exhibit more distress to emotional infidelity of their dating or marital partner than do men, whereas men exhibit more distress to sexual infidelity than do women. Furthermore, Buss and his colleagues surveyed men and women across 37 cultures regarding partner selection criteria and found that women consistently valued earning potential in mates more than did men, whereas men consistently valued physical attractiveness more than did women.

However, with regard to personality characteristics, both men and women seek similar traits (such as sense of humor and kindness). They tend to select partners similar to themselves and who match their ideals. It is not clear, however, to what extent the mate selection findings with adults can be accurately applied to adolescents. Research with adolescents is lacking from the literature. Brett Laursen and Lauri Jensen-Campbell contend that cultural, peer, and familial messages emphasize the importance of status and physical appearance as "romantic resources" among young adolescents, paralleling the findings of the mate selection studies. Lucia O'Sullivan found that early adolescent girls placed higher value on boyfriends who were good looking, popular, or who provided gifts. It is likely that adolescents engage in greater exploration of different types of partners during their shorter-lived relationships and come to value more culturally prescribed notions of partners as the commitment levels and longer-term potentials of relationships advance.

American girls also place higher value on their own physical attractiveness and heterosexual attractiveness than boys do; as such, they experience greater dissatisfaction with their appearance. The higher incidence of eating disorders among girls is frequently attributed to the greater emphasis in girls' focus on meeting beauty ideals, particularly those related to maintaining a stereotyped lean body considered ideal for young women. Some have argued that boys' dissatisfaction with their bodies has been overlooked, and that many boys experience considerable dissatisfaction with regard to lack of physical strength, muscle size, and definition. Initially, it was suggested that this might be particularly true among homosexual boys where the emphasis on physical appearance is more notable than among heterosexual boys. More recently, it has been argued that heterosexual boys are also under increasing pressures about their appearance, especially to look muscled or "bulked up." Whereas the ideal figure for women as depicted in the media has been physically unattainable for most girls, ideal male figures are becoming increasing unattainable for most boys without the use of steroids or excessive exercise regimens. It seems that adolescents of both sexes perceive their own physical appearance as being of great importance in their success at forming romantic relationships, as well as defining their value as a potential dating partner. [*See* Beauty Politics and Patriarchy.]

3. POWER DIFFERENTIALS IN DATING RELATIONSHIPS

The existence or enactment of power differentials in dating relationships is another path through which adolescents test and construct their concepts of gender identity and "appropriate" gender roles. The power differentials between female and male adolescents and how these are enacted in relationships during this period are complex phenomena. Male and female adolescents approach their intimate relationships with peers differently. Unlike boys, girls will use physical gestures of intimacy among friends, comment on each other's physical appearance, and mutually self-disclose personal information. Girls focus on binding intimacy within their interpersonal relationships and establishing egalitarian connections.

Boys, on the other hand, tend to focus on establishing superior positioning within a social hierarchy of peers.

These differential approaches to peer relationships help us to understand how boys and girls express power and influence in romantic relationships. Adolescent girls tend to have less power in their heterosexual dating relationships compared to adolescent boys because girls are more invested, committed, and emotionally vulnerable in these relationships. Girls also desire greater intimacy in their relationships with boys than they report experiencing.

Historically, girls have been expected to defer to their male partners in their intimate relationships. Boys are more likely to be dominant in their relationships with girls with regard to decision making. In contrast, girls tend to control many sexual decisions (as will be discussed). However, many adolescents' perceptions of appropriate methods of resolving sexual tensions in relationships still conform to the view that the male's needs or desires are more powerful or important than the female's needs or desires. A substantial minority of both female and male high school students endorse the belief that it is appropriate to gain intercourse when the male "is so turned on he can't stop" or when "she gets him sexually excited," suggesting endorsement of traditional attitudes about power in intimate relationships. In contrast, adolescents report greater acceptance of girls' use of dating violence against boys than boys' use of dating violence against girls, in part because of perceptions that girls use violence in self-defense and are less likely to do physical harm to their partner. Indications that boys are more accepting of dating violence overall may be associated with their greater propensity to engage in it regardless of the belief that it is more acceptable for girls to engage in violence. In general, regardless of whether a conflict situation is sexual, girls are more likely than are boys to report actually experiencing verbal and physical coercion (including threats of physical force) from a dating partner. [*See* Power.]

B. DEVELOPMENT OF SEXUAL EXPERIENCE ACROSS ADOLESCENCE

Sexual experiences for female and male adolescents vary across a number of dimensions. Historically, boys date earlier than girls and engage in first intercourse at younger ages, although this gap has been narrowing in recent decades. Some researchers now report little or no differences in the proportions of male and female adolescents reporting various dating and sexual experiences. This convergence is generally attributable to greater change among female adolescents than among male adolescents.

What is clear from research on adolescents is that sexual activity has become an integral aspect to adolescent life with intercourse becoming a widely recognized milestone or transitional event into adulthood. Radical changes in patterns of marriage and sexuality over recent decades indicate that marriage is no longer the exclusive domain within which sexual activity occurs.

Early to mid-adolescents typically experiment with early sexual activities, such as kissing and breast fondling, and other activities short of sexual intercourse, within mixed-sex encounters previously described. Only recently have researchers addressed the types of "preintercourse" behaviors common among adolescents. Most boys and girls have considerable breadth of sexual experience prior to first intercourse.

Even though increasing sexual intimacy typically corresponds with both age and level of romantic intimacy or commitment within a relationship, there has been an increase in the number of adolescents having sex at ever-earlier ages in recent decades. The Alan Guttmacher Institute reported that approximately 9% of male adolescents and 1% of female adolescents nationwide had intercourse experience by age 13 compared to 80% of males and 76% of females by age 20. Researchers have identified a range of personal, demographic, and biological factors associated with the timing of first intercourse, including age, gender, race/ethnicity, socioeconomic status, and pubertal status. Girls and boys differ in the ages of their sexual intercourse partners with girls' partners being typically two or more years older.

Ethnic/racial differences in sexual activity are more apparent in early adolescence than mid- to late adolescence. African American male adolescents generally report higher rates of sexual behaviors (e.g., numbers of sexual partners) and earlier onset of intercourse activity than White and Hispanic male adolescents. Less discrepancy in sexual experiences across ethnicities/races is noted among female adolescents, although African American and Hispanic female adolescents are less likely to report using effective contraceptive methods consistently.

There is some controversy regarding conclusions drawn from these studies, however, as confounds between race/ethnicity and socioeconomic status are not consistently resolved. For example, prior studies have reported that White adolescents progress through a sequence of kissing and fondling, oral sex, then intercourse, whereas African American adolescents are less likely to engage in noncoital activities prior to intercourse. Shirley Feldman, Rebecca Turner, and Katy Araujo found that the sequence of behaviors was quite similar for African American, Asian, White, and Latino adolescents. Also, despite prior reports, first experience of oral sex typically occurred after intercourse. What seemed to differ by race/ethnicity, after controlling for sociodemographic factors, was the age of initiation of sexual behaviors and the length of time it took individuals to progress to intercourse. Specifically, Asian American adolescents initiated each sexual activity at an older age than their counterparts. African American adolescents also had the most rapid progression of sexual activities, initiating kissing a little before 14 years of age and intercourse by 15.5 years of age. In contrast, other youth took about 2 to 2.5 years for this progression. [*See* SEXUALITY AND SEXUAL DESIRE.]

1. Scripts Governing the Development of Sexual Behavior for Female and Male Adolescents

Socially learned sexual behaviors, experiences, and meanings are what John Gagnon and William Simon have referred to as sexual scripts. Sexual scripts are intricately related to society's views of gender. Bernie Zilbergeld and others have characterized the male sexual script as incorporating the following themes or characteristics: Men are the initiators and orchestrators of sex and are ready and interested in engaging in sexual intercourse without emotional involvement. They have considerable sexual appetites that may be uncontrollable, particularly when deprived of sexual access. The female sexual script, on the other hand, incorporates the following tenets: Women are reactive and passive in their sexual interactions with men, require seducing or coercing into sex, and are ultimately responsible for controlling the pace and content of sexual encounters with men even when faced with extreme physical force.

To a large extent, adolescents' sexual behaviors and feelings appear to conform to these rules for appropriate gender behavior. Male adolescents tend to report starting sexual and dating careers at younger ages than do female adolescents. They also report having more sexual partners, encounters, and sexual outlets generally, including masturbation. Male adolescents use sexually explicit words more frequently than do girls and report finding these words generally more arousing. They also tend to report finding sexually explicit visual stimuli as more arousing than do female adolescents. In support of these findings, James Geer and colleagues have documented gender differences in the organization of memory for sexual information. Specifically, women are faster and more accurate at remembering information that is romantic or affectionate in nature, whereas men are faster and more accurate at remembering information that is sexual in nature.

Female adolescents are more likely to report rejecting sexual advances from a partner than are male adolescents and controlling the pace of sexual intimacy early in the relationship. They also report assuming responsibility or being held responsible for avoiding pregnancy. Female adolescents also more often report that they have agreed to unwanted sexual activity either because they believed their refusals would be disregarded or overcome in some way, because they felt it was inappropriate to refuse, or because it would risk the stability of their relationship.

Anecdotal reports and a growing ethnographic literature indicate that the sexual double standard continues to be strongly endorsed indicating different standards apply for judging appropriate sexual behavior despite general convergence of girls' and boys' reported sexual experiences. Qualitative research by Lucia O'Sullivan indicates that girls experience considerable fear about being viewed as sexually permissive and experience significant condemnation from peers for engaging in permissive sexual behaviors, whereas boys experience enhanced social status from these activities. Interestingly, this "sexual double standard" has not been well substantiated in the experimental and survey research literature. Both male and female targets with histories of casual sexual partnerships (outside of committed relationships) tend to be evaluated as having more negative personality characteristics and are viewed as less desirable as friends or dating and marriage partners.

All in all, female and male adolescents approach sexual relations differently in many respects, although it would be a mistake to emphasize these differences in light of the many overlapping experiences they report. For example, even though boys may report initiating sexual encounters more often than girls, many female adolescents report initiating sex in their relationships and many male adolescents report refusing sexual advances from a female partner. The limited research on patterns of sexual activity indicates that both female and male adolescents may in fact engage in sexual intercourse relatively infre-

quently or inconsistently, particularly at younger ages. In addition, rates of sexual intercourse among adolescents appear to be decreasing nationwide in recent years, perhaps attributable in large part to public health efforts to reduce sexual risk behaviors. Mary Oliver and Janet Hyde published a much-cited meta-analysis of gender differences in sexual attitudes and behavior. Their analysis reviewed 177 sources reporting gender differences on 21 measures of sexual attitudes and behaviors. The largest consistent sex differences indicated that men report masturbating more frequently and have more permissive sexual attitudes compared to women (although women tend to have far more positive attitudes regarding homosexual interest and activity). Of particular importance, all other gender differences were small or moderate in size and have actually decreased in size between males and females over recent decades. [*See* SEX-RELATED DIFFERENCE RESEARCH: PERSONALITY.]

2. Foundations of Sexual Interest and Behavior

The literature on adolescent sexual behavior has grown out of the research addressing prevention of adolescent pregnancy. As such, much of the literature focuses on predicting intercourse without making connections to romantic relationships, preintercourse behaviors, or other normative adolescent experiences. Sexual interest or desire has long been thought to relate to hormone levels. In particular, testosterone has been linked to arousal and sexual interest in adult men and women. Thus, it would be expected that early adolescence would be a time of increasing sexual interest given the rise in hormones at this time.

However, actual engagement in sexual behaviors has social constraints along with a biological substrate, especially for adolescents. The patterns revealed from the adolescent literature indicate that variations in social context, peers, and family relationship affect emerging adolescent sexual behavior and relationships. Researchers find that initiation of sexual behavior among adolescents is closely related to perceptions of peer norms, although many studies of peer influences are plagued with methodological weaknesses. Usually peers' reported sexual behaviors correspond with one another within a group of peers. The direction of effects is unclear; that is, do adolescents choose friends with similar sexual interest and experience, or do peers influence adolescents' choices or decisions regarding sex? A recent study by Peter Bearman and Hannah Brueckner of peer influences using a large, multischool design found that a girl's initiation of intercourse was not associated with whether her best friend had had intercourse. Instead, girls were more likely to initiate intercourse over a one-year period if they were more popular (based on nominations from peers). The broader school context was also important for the initiation of intercourse in that girls were more likely to initiate intercourse if a higher number of other adolescents at their school had already had intercourse. Sara Kinsman, Daniel Romer, Frank Furstenberg, and Donald Schwarz have argued that sexual intercourse is not an unplanned or unexpected experience for many adolescents given the strong relationship between decisions to initiate sex and the normative behavior as defined by the social context of today's youth. At this level, social norms, beliefs, and values about sexual behavior are viewed as providing structure for behavioral decisions via the processes of socialization.

Studies of parental influence are fewer in number, but tend to indicate that more positive parent–adolescent relationships coupled with monitoring and rules result in later onset of intercourse. More specifically, supportive relationships with one's parents, open general communication (rather than communication about sex specifically), and close (not oppressive) supervision are related to delayed onset of sexual activity and higher rates of contraceptive use once sexual activity occurs.

3. Sexual Risk Behavior in Adolescence

Understanding how gender-based scripts for sexual behavior and relationships influence actual behaviors is important not only from the psychological perspective but also from a health perspective. Does adherence to traditional gender roles influence the engagement in risky sexual practices? Adolescents in the United States have high rates of adolescent pregnancy and are experiencing an epidemic of sexually transmitted diseases (STDs), including human immunodeficiency virus (HIV), gonorrhea, chlamydia, pelvic inflammatory disease, and human papillomavirus. Each year, approximately 1 million adolescent girls become pregnant and approximately 3 million cases of STDs are recorded. According to the Institute of Medicine, the rate of infection with STDs is higher among adolescents and young adults than among any older age group. In the United States, HIV has become the sixth leading cause of death among those aged 15 to 24 years. Those diagnosed with HIV in young adulthood were frequently unknowingly infected in adolescence. Poor prophylactic practices, multiple sexual partners, other STD histories, and use of alcohol and drugs during sexual encounters are factors that contribute to adolescents' heightened risk. Rates of contraceptive use in the United States are significantly lower than those of other Western nations, and their rates of adolescent pregnancies are significantly higher. This is true despite comparable ages of first intercourse for adolescence, reflecting important differences in the ways that adolescents are socialized and the quality of sex education available to them. [*See* AIDS/HIV.]

Female adolescents, particularly younger girls, are at greater risk of STD infection than male adolescents through heterosexual transmission because their genital structures are more susceptible to lacerations and abrasion permitting transmission of infection. Adoption of prophylactic and contraceptive measures has traditionally been a female concern and responsibility, requiring "gendered negotiation" of sexuality. Girls report higher contraceptive rates than do boys, although little comparative research is available. It is important to bear in mind that adolescent girls (and women) have had to rely on male partners to use male-controlled methods, most notably condoms. This reliance reinforces girls' dependence on boys to ensure their safety and results in a situation that requires cooperation and adequate communication within the couple. Adolescent girls are also more likely than their male counterparts to engage in independent health seeking behaviors and take greater responsibility for their health. When boys are targeted in intervention efforts, it is usually within the context of a relationship, led by the girls' interest in participation. [*See* Sexually Transmitted Infections and Their Consequences.]

VI. Conclusions

Youth in industrialized societies are granted a prolonged period of adolescence. The decreasing age of puberty and sexual maturation extends the boundaries of adolescence downward whereas heightened social emphasis on education attainment and career development also extends these boundaries upward in age. The transition into adolescence is not only typified by pubertal changes, but also by the initiation of new patterns of cognition, social cognition, family relationships, and peer relationships.

Despite the surprising dearth of research on adolescent gender development, current constructions that restrict gender development to early childhood years seem inadequate models for understanding the dynamics of the processes involved. Research has established that the key transitional events that move adolescents into adulthood help to refine individuals' understanding and expression of gender. Further, these events prompt the reinforcement by primary social influences of sociocultural standards for gendered behavior. As such, it is clear from the available literature that gender development continues at least into adolescence, and by all indicators, beyond into adulthood.

SUGGESTED READING

Golombok, S., and Fivush, R. (1994). *Gender Development.* Cambridge University Press, Cambridge, England.

Maccoby, E. E. (1998). *The Two Sexes: Growing Up Apart, Coming Together.* Harvard University Press, Cambridge, MA.

Rossi, A. (1994). *Sexuality across the Life Course.* Chicago University Press, Chicago.

Affirmative Action

Sirinda Sincharoen

Faye J. Crosby

University of California Santa Cruz

Glossary

Affirmative action Occurs whenever an organization goes out of its way to make sure that there is no discrimination against people of color, against White women, against people with disabilities, or against veterans.

Classical affirmative action The type of affirmative action established in 1965 whereby an organization monitors itself to make sure it employs and promotes talented women and talented people of color in proportion to their availability.

Equal opportunity employer An employer who refuses to discriminate.

Executive Order 11246 The mechanism by which President Johnson introduced widespread affirmative action into life in the United States.

Merit A positive quality, measured according to certain criteria in ways that may be explicit or implicit.

Preferential treatment Treatment that occurs when a person receives consideration by virtue of group membership.

Quotas A narrowly defined percentage of the whole that must be composed of people from a specific group. Quotas do not take into account the availability of people from the specified group. Quotas are forbidden by law and are not part of affirmative action.

AFFIRMATIVE ACTION is a topic that is often hotly debated. Yet when pressed, few people can provide an explicit definition. In principle, affirmative action involves taking positive action to increase the likelihood of creating or maintaining true equality for individuals of differing groups. How the principle of affirmative action is translated into practice has sometimes been a cause for concern as well as a cause for celebration. When affirmative action is misapplied, it can harm women; when it is properly applied, it has been proven to help women in terms of both employment and education. Recommendations for how to make affirmative work well are, therefore, included at the end of this article.

I. What Is Affirmative Action?

In general, affirmative action is a term used to indicate that organizations are taking positive steps toward providing equal opportunities for women and others from underrepresented groups. Strategies are needed in part to remove institutional barriers created by past discrimination and prejudice. One goal of affirmative action is to create access for women and minorities to fields in education and employment that were previously closed to them.

A. AFFIRMATIVE ACTION IN EMPLOYMENT

In 1965, President Lyndon Johnson signed Executive Order 11246 that included the term "affirmative action." EO 11246 required federal contractors (i.e., organizations that do business with the federal government) to take proactive steps to ensure that discriminatory practices were not being carried out in employment. Affirmative action was part of the civil rights movement and part of President Johnson's vision of a Great Society, in which individuals would have equal opportunities to reach the goals they wished to pursue and the disparities between rich and poor would be diminished. In recent years, scholars have labeled Johnson's affirmative action plans as "classical affirmative action" to distinguish them from unjustified preferential treatment.

Classical affirmative action plans consist of obligating organizations to keep conscientious employment records. First, a company conducts a utilization analysis of its particular job categories, ascertaining the number of women and minorities working in them. Then, using published data, the company calculates the number of qualified women and minorities that are theoretically employable for each job category. Whereas the former type of analysis determines utilization, the latter determines availability. Next utilization is matched against availability. If discrepancies exist, a corrective plan is devised. For example, if a company noticed a pattern of underrepresentation of women at a particular job title, the company would conduct an analysis to investigate if one of their practices was generating unintended discriminatory effects. The organization might also examine whether a certain type of subtle favoritism existed.

Some affirmative action strategies have veered away from the "classical" definitions. Such activities include instituting set-asides, in which organizations ensure allotted spaces for minority workers. Researchers Faye Crosby and Diana Cordova point out that some of these programs have been criticized for establishing "preferential treatment" for women and ethnic minorities. These means of achieving affirmative action goals tend to be fraught with controversy and are often the targets of strong criticism and bitter opposition. Thus, these types of affirmative action practices are not often employed and are not endorsed by federal government standards for implementing affirmative action plans.

It is also important to differentiate between affirmative action and equal opportunity programs. The difference between equal opportunity employers and those who institute affirmative action programs lies in how they approach the problems of discrimination. While equal opportunity employers hope to diminish discrimination against women and minorities within an organization, they may expend no energy toward the goal. Equal opportunity employers take action only if complaints of gender or race discrimination are presented by employees. Affirmative action employers, on the other hand, do not wait for complaints to arise. Instead, they have in place operating plans to monitor their own behavior. Unlike equal opportunity employers, affirmative action employers invest considerable effort and commitment in seeking out discrepancies between equality and opportunity within an organization. [See CAREER ACHIEVEMENT; WORKING ENVIRONMENTS.]

B. AFFIRMATIVE ACTION IN EDUCATION

In education, affirmative action strategies have been exercised in various ways. For instance, some universities reserve particular seats within an incoming class for women and other applicants from underrepresented groups. These applicants constitute a separate applicant pool and are evaluated for admission based on comparisons with one another, rather than against the larger pool of nonminority applicants. This affirmative action strategy has been controversial, however, and spurred the 1978 Supreme Court case of *Bakke* v. *University of California at Davis*. In the *Bakke* case, a White male student sued the university based on the premise that the medical school was utilizing discriminatory admissions standards in its creation of a separate pool for minority applicants. The majority opinion of the Supreme Court justices' ruling in the case indicated that this type of operationalization of affirmative action was unlawful and constituted a violation of the Equal Protection Clause of the Fourteenth Amendment.

An alternative form of affirmative action used by some universities is to allot so-called bonus points for minority applications. There are two rationales for bonus points: diversity and true merit. The diversity justification rests on the premise that a diverse campus enhances the education of all its students. Of course, campuses have the discretion to decide which attributes contribute to the desired diversity (participation in sports, work experience, geographic location of an applicant's residence, etc.) and thus deserve the allotted "bonus" points. Race or ethnicity can also be included as one of many preferred attributes.

The other rationale for bonus points concerns considerations of merit. According to this rationale, "standard" measures of merit may underestimate the potential of those from a nonstandard background and overestimate the potential of those from the mainstream. The Educational Testing Service (ETS) acknowledges, for example, that there is a difference between the scores of young men and young women on the math SAT in which calculators are allowed (Math IIC). ETS also acknowledges that the male scores are elevated compared to the female scores when one does a reverse "prediction" of high school SAT scores based on students' college grades, so that, for example, the typical female with a score of 600 on the Math SAT IIC earns better grades in college math classes than the typical male with the same score. When the entrance tests favor men, female applicants might receive bonus points to help rectify the imbalances. With bonus point programs, all applicants are evaluated in one applicant pool. In the *Bakke* case, the Supreme Court justices' majority opinion lauded this type of affirmative action practice as being exemplary for allowing colleges and universities to consider demographic characteristics in admissions in ways that are not discriminatory. [*See* TEST BIAS.]

Last, other universities implement affirmative action by utilizing outreach programs or in other ways that expend extra effort to attract and nurture minority applicants to apply to their university. Sometimes these outreach programs include special scholarship offers to minority applicants or White women. Outreach efforts also include having admissions personnel make special visits to high schools to recruit minority applicants.

In principle, affirmative action in employment or education is simple. In practice, its implementation is diverse. Some forms of affirmative action are more controversial than others; some involve taking more proactive measures than others; and some are more successful than others. When the practice of affirmative action is at odds with the principle, affirmative action becomes most vulnerable to criticism and attack.

II. Why Is Affirmative Action Needed?

Given that racial and gender discrimination have long been illegal in the United States, why is affirmative action still necessary? Some argue that in present-day North American society, we have achieved equal opportunity for members of all diverse groups. Others point out that discrimination continues to exist, and sometimes even the most well-intentioned individuals are often unable to detect the small everyday instances of discrimination that can add up to a large amount of problems. Affirmative action can serve as the external remedy that is needed to monitor for discrimination. It can ensure that people will be treated fairly, even in conditions where those who are disadvantaged do not recognize it themselves. The policy of affirmative action is the only legally mandated policy that prevents the buildup of inequities.

A. EVIDENCE OF CONTINUED EXISTENCE OF UNFAIRNESS

Categorical unfairness on the basis of gender has been well documented in contemporary North American society by researchers. As Faye Crosby and Diana Cordova reported, empirical studies of income, for example, show a disparity in the average earnings of men and women. Specifically, in 1997, employed women earned less money than comparably employed men, even after taking into account factors such as amount of education, tenure with current employer, union membership, and years in the paid labor market. In 1993, for example, White women in the paid labor force earned a little less than 69 cents to every dollar earned by White men, after adjusting for number of hours worked. Among African Americans and non-White Latino populations as well, women earned less money than their male counterparts.

B. FAILURE TO PERCEIVE UNFAIRNESS

The aforementioned statistics demonstrate that the objective status of women is lower than that of men. However, people's level of contentment with their circumstances is not simply a function of their objective position. Their subjective appraisal of their lives matters too; how they perceive their situation has an influence on whether they willingly accept their lot in life. Relative deprivation theory posits that people in disadvantaged groups (for example, women) become aware of their relative misfortune when they notice the discrepancy between their own circumstances and some reference standard, which usually includes comparison to others who are more privileged (such as men). The phenomenon of relative deprivation may be experienced at the individual level, the group level, or both. In other words, an individual may experience grievances on behalf of him or herself or on behalf of his or her membership in disadvantaged groups.

Under many conditions, there are discrepancies between feelings of personal deprivation and feelings of group deprivation. That is, people who belong to objectively disadvantaged groups tend to recognize the categorical unfairness facing group members in general, but are unwilling to accept that they may be personally disadvantaged because of their group membership. This phenomenon, commonly known as the denial of personal discrimination, was first documented in a 1978 study of working men and women in Newton, Massachusetts. There, Faye Crosby discovered that the employed women in her sample were more resentful about the situation of working women in general than were the working men, but that they were as satisfied with their own jobs as were the working men. In other words, the working women expressed no more dissatisfaction about their personal situations than did working men. The women did, however, recognize the disadvantages faced by working women in general. One explanation for these findings is that the women in the sample were in fact not objectively deprived. However, the women and men were similar with respect to various occupational characteristics, such as education, training, and status of occupation. Despite these similarities, the women earned significantly less money than did the men in the study. Yet the women in this sample all felt that they were the exception to the rule, as they felt that they themselves were not being personally discriminated against.

Further examination of denial of personal discrimination conducted by other researchers has revealed that the phenomenon is quite widespread. The tendency to report more discrimination at the group level than at the personal level has been documented in a number of different populations, including female undergraduate students in the United States and Canada, working women in the United States and Canada, gay men and lesbians in the United States, African American students in the United States, ethnic minority group members in the United States and Canada, and people with chronic psoriasis in Canada. The discrepancy between perceived discrimination at the group and personal levels seems to be the norm for members of most disadvantaged groups in the United States, Canada, and Europe.

What are the underlying mechanisms for the phenomenon? Donald Taylor, Karen Ruggiero, and Winnifred Louis have suggested that two different processes are at work: (1) the minimization of personal discrimination and (2) the augmentation of group-level discrimination. Broad social stereotypes about gender in society make it likely that people may exaggerate the level of group disadvantage when they think of women relative to men.

Why does minimization of personal discrimination occur? There are two classes of explanations: cognitive and motivational. The cognitive explanations focus on perceptions of patterns of discrimination and the type of information people use to make decisions about deservingness and discrimination. For instance, it is difficult to perceive discrimination when slightly ambiguous information is presented on a case-by-case basis rather than in aggregate form. Consider the situation of a working woman who knows that her salary is low but is unsure if the cause is discrimination. Such a woman may compare her outcomes to a male colleague. She may find it impossible to decide whether the salary differential is due to gender or to some other characteristic (such as seniority) in which she and the male colleague also differ. Unless the woman sees herself as a datum in a larger picture, she may not recognize the pattern of discrimination, as these statistics are not available to her in summary form.

Psychologist Brenda Major has argued that social comparison processes play an important role in the minimization of personal discrimination. People tend to compare themselves to similar others in order to determine whether their outcomes are fair. Members of disadvantaged groups thus are likely to focus on fellow group members when making these comparisons—they do not compare themselves to those who are better off (as they are dissimilar). For example, women compare themselves only to those in the same circumstances as themselves and thus do not become aware that they are relatively disadvantaged. They do not become aware of their relatively deprived state and do not realize that they may be the victims of discrimination. [*See* SOCIAL ROLE THEORY OF SEX DIFFERENCES AND SIMILARITIES.]

A second class of explanations for the minimization of personal discrimination invokes theories of motivation. Research has demonstrated that there are negative consequences to acknowledging that one is a victim of personal discrimination. People who recognize personal discrimination have been reported as experiencing decreased levels of personal control and personal self-esteem. [*See* SELF-ESTEEM.]

Recognition of personal discrimination is related to lower levels of well-being for several reasons. People experience distress when they consider the possibility that there are people in the world who do not wish them well. When they minimize discrimination, therefore, they avoid thinking about potential villains in the world who would do them harm. Another explanation is that people have a need to believe in a just world, where we are all treated fairly and get what we deserve: if we work hard, we should be rewarded. This type of world is predictable and stable, which gives people a sense of control over their outcomes. Finally, people tend to want to believe that they are special and thus somehow exempt from the harm done to others of their group. Minimization of personal discrimination is one way to maintain that belief.

Whereas people tend to minimize their experiences of personal discrimination for both motivational and cognitive reasons, they may exaggerate the level of group disadvantage. People may hold stereotypes that certain groups are mistreated. If ratings of group discrimination are derived in part from stereotypes, then there should be little variation between people in the "scores." Interestingly, some researchers have found less variability in group ratings of discrimination than in ratings of personal discrimination.

Everyday injustices against individual people often go unnoticed, even by the victims, and even when the victims know their group to be disadvantaged. These injustices—whether intended or not—build up until they become so dramatic and obvious that it would be impossible for disadvantaged group members to ignore them. When injustices become so dramatic, the response can be dramatic. Extreme reactions to injustice in either an employment or an educational setting tend to be costly both in human and financial terms.

In sum, it is clear that despite the increasing focus on promoting equality in our society today, unfairness continues to exist. People also have the tendency to minimize unfairness at the individual level, and this minimization has negative and costly consequences for society in terms of inaction and the buildup of explosive situations. Given the high stakes, we turn to affirmative action, which, as an external system, is needed in order to monitor society for injustices and compensate for people's difficulty in recognizing these injustices themselves. Affirmative action is needed both to ensure that all people are treated fairly and, in accomplishing this first goal, to prevent the buildup of unproductive and costly explosive situations in organizations and educational institutions.

III. *What Reactions Are Provoked by Affirmative Action?*

Affirmative action has attracted attention in diverse arenas. Journalists and other experts in the media have offered opinions, as have scholars. Much studied, too, are average Americans whom the pollsters often question about affirmative action. Examination of their answers allows for some tentative conclusions about the dynamics of people's reactions to affirmative action.

A. JOURNALISTS

It seems that journalists are not drawn to definitions, and that may be why so few broadcast the definition of affirmative action. Looking at the summer of 1995, just prior to a major policy statement on affirmative action by President Bill Clinton, Faye Crosby and Diana Cordova found that fewer than 6% of the newspaper and magazine articles included a definition of what was meant by affirmative action. This was so even though most of the 176 articles the researchers located came from the *New York Times* and the *Washington Post*. Some of the articles implied, mistakenly, that affirmative action was nothing more than unjustified preferential treatment.

Although many journalists have failed to educate the public about what affirmative action is or how it operates, newspapers and magazines have carried a number of very thought-provoking articles about issues related to affirmative action, and it is often these voices that shape the public's view about affirmative action. Heated discussions of individualism, identity, and community have arisen in the newspaper coverage of affirmative action. At one extreme, Ward Connerly, regent of the University of California, has argued against affirmative action in many editorial pieces, equating the policy with quotas. Connerly expressed concern that the existence of affirmative action promotes discrimination against students ineligible for affirmative action and discredits the admissions policies for the University of California campuses. He has gone as far as to say that "[affirmative action] is breeding hostility among the races." While most liberals would consider Connerly's views radically conservative, there are others who have expressed similar perspectives. In a *Los Angeles Times* editorial, Steven A. Holmes, frustrated by the vagueness that has plagued implementation of affirmative action, asks "At what point does 'socially disadvantaged' become defined so broadly that the only ones not included are Donald Trump and Bill Gates?" Other journalists have elaborated on the issues raised by Holmes and ask: When does a group cease to need or deserve affirmative action? How is one to decide, for example, if it is still necessary to take affirmative actions to promote fairness for Jews? For Asian Americans? For working women?

The news media have also presented numerous articles favoring affirmative action. A vocal supporter of affirmative action is former chancellor of the University of California, Berkeley, Chang-Lin Tien. In recounting his experiences with racial discrimination as an Asian American, he stated, "Like it or not, this history of racial division is linked with the debate over affirmative action. Although the U.S. has made great strides, race still divides our society. It is part of the debate over how we afford equal opportunities to everyone." Tien's implication that racial discrimination fuels opposition to affirmative action is a wake-up call for many who view America as the land of equal opportunity. The success of affirmative action programs is supported by findings reported by Ethan Bronner in 1997 in the *New York Times* that doctors who were admitted to medical school at the University of California, Davis, on the basis of affirmative action performed just as well as those who were admitted solely on academic merit. Success stories such as this are echoed across various populations. Perhaps one of the most poignant pleas for retaining affirmative action comes from former President of the United States, Gerald R. Ford. In an editorial for the *New York Times*, Ford wrote, "To eliminate a constitutional affirmative action would be to mock the inclusion vision Carl Sandburg had in mind when he wrote: 'The Republic is a dream. Nothing happens unless first a dream.' Lest we forget: America remains a nation with have-nots as well as haves. Its government is obligated to provide for hope no less than for the common defense."

The arguments presented are just a few examples of the types of debates that are carried out in the media about affirmative action. How affirmative action is portrayed and debated by the media has a strong impact on public views and opinions about affirmative action. Judging from the vastly differing viewpoints about affirmative action that are expressed by journalists, it is clear that feelings about affirmative action are as diverse as the groups of intended beneficiaries to which it is applicable. [*See* MEDIA INFLUENCES; MEDIA STEREOTYPES.]

B. SCHOLARS

Scholars are also active in the debate over affirmative action. Many scholars wholeheartedly support and promote the policy and practice. In her 1991 book, *The Alchemy of Race and Rights,* Patricia J. Williams described the trials and tribulations she faced as a Black woman working to earn her law degree. She states, "It is thus that affirmative action is an affirmation; the affirmative act of hiring—or hearing—blacks is a recognition of individuality that includes blacks as a social presence . . . [Affirmative action] is an act of verification and vision, an act of social as well as professional responsibility." Other scholars, such as Barbara Bergmann, have recognized that numerous alternatives to affirmative action exist, yet Bergmann found these "solutions" to racism and sexism to be inadequate. In her 1996 book, *In Defense of Affirmative Action,* her extensive list of affirmative action alternatives even includes a tongue-in-cheek recommendation of "just pray." But her tone becomes quite serious when she asserts, "Prayer has never taken us very far in solving this country's race an poverty problems. Only an activist policy—with affirmative action as a prime ingredient—will do that." Christopher Edley, Jr., an advisor to President Clinton on the issue of affirmative action, has also written about the importance of maintaining affirmative action in his book *Not All Black and White.* He confronted the issue of how to make the determination that affirmative action is no longer needed. He wrote:

When will affirmative action end in the United States? If we mean "end entirely and for all situations," the answer is simple: it should end when the justification for it no longer exists, when America has achieved racial justice in reality . . . President Clinton said it well: "Mend it, don't end it." Affirmative action will remain controversial, and we should expect it to, like any policy addressing an intractable and painful problem. The continuing controversy—whether flames or embers—is about values and vision. What does America want to see in the mirror? What kind of communities do we want for our children? What dreams will nourish the spirits of the least among us?

These views that have been expressed reflect the opinions of many scholars on the issue of affirmative action and the need to continue the policy.

As with any debate, the other side of the issue is just as passionately argued. Opponents of affirmative action warn of the negative consequences that can befall on "beneficiaries." In his book *Hunger of Memory*, Richard Rodriguez expressed his frustrations and guilt over wrongly being designated an affirmative action recipient. He asserted that

All Mexican-Americans certainly are not equally Mexican-American. The policy of affirmative action, however, was never able to distinguish someone like me (a graduate student of English, ambitious for a college teaching career) from a slightly educated Mexican-American who lived in a barrio and worked as a menial laborer, never expecting a future improved. Worse, affirmative action made me the beneficiary of his condition.

Shelby Steele, an African American professor, echoed Rodriguez's complaints. In his book *The Content of Our Character*, Steele warned of the ill consequences that can befall affirmative action recipients. He stated "under affirmative action the quality that earns us preferential treatment is an implied inferiority. However this inferiority is explained—and it is easily enough explained by the myriad deprivations that grew out of our oppression—it is still inferiority." Terry Eastland eloquently captured sentiments against affirmative action in his book *Ending Affirmative Action* by stating "We do not have to take the risk of affirmative action. And once free of it, those now eligible for it would be able to compete and achieve on the same terms as everyone else."

Do the views of journalists and scholars influence the public? It is hard to say. Certainly the complexities of debate as well as the level of engagement among scholars reflect the strength of feeling among the general public.

C. REACTIONS AMONG THE GENERAL PUBLIC

Affirmative action is a policy that ultimately must have public support in order to be successful. How is affirmative action perceived among the general public? A number of polls have tracked levels of support for or opposition to various types of affirmative action.

The clear message from the polls is that Americans dislike quotas or unjustified preferential treatment, but they like classical affirmative action programs. A 1995 Gallup poll found that fewer than one in eight respondents supported affirmative action programs that involved hiring quotas while 40 to 50% endorsed programs that were designed to give African Americans or women special treatment without using quotas. When affirmative action is described by

pollsters as not involving quotas or preferences, about 70% of Americans support affirmative action programs. National polls conducted in mid-1990s also show strong endorsement for affirmative action among the American public—70% of respondents reported strong support for affirmative action as it was currently practiced. This included a three out of four approval rate found by the 1995 Gallup poll for the use of outreach programs by employers to recruit qualified minorities and women. A 1991 Harris survey found that 75% of Whites and 85% of African Americans agree that employers should give special training and advice to women and minorities so they can perform better on the job. Similarly, in a 1996 study by Maura Belliveau, when affirmative action was framed as involving targeted recruitment, 71% of Whites and 87% of Blacks favored the procedure.

Psychologist Heather Golden and her colleagues were able to demonstrate that people's understandings of affirmative action vary along predictable grounds. Women, people of color, liberals, and Democrats (more than do men, White people, conservatives, and Republicans) think of affirmative action as a system by which organizations monitor utilization of available talent. Golden and associates also showed, through statistical analyses, that people's understanding of affirmative action influences their endorsement of the policy over and above the influence exerted by the demographic variables. Thus, for example, while women typically endorse affirmative action more than men do, within either sex endorsement is stronger among those who think of affirmative action as a monitoring system than among those who think of it as a quota system.

What accounts for differences in how ordinary people conceive of affirmative action and how much they endorse or oppose it? Several explanations have been proposed, each of which seems to have some merit. Factors that play a role in determining reactions to affirmative action include (1) prejudice, (2) self-esteem, (3) self-interest, (4) perceived scarcity of resources, and (5) perceptions of fairness.

1. Prejudice

Among privileged group members opposition to affirmative action has been linked to factors such as prejudice. Racism and sexism have been identified as two of the strongest predictors of opposition to affirmative action. For example, many Americans are more willing to support affirmative action for the elderly or handicapped than for Blacks. The case for racism accounting for opposition to affirmative action is further supported by the finding that Whites who have the most contact with Blacks show the most support for affirmative action. In addition, Whites generally are more supportive of affirmative action when it is presented in terms of gender than when it is presented in terms of race. Other studies have found that those who are racist or have strong belief in a "just world" (i.e., the belief that the world is fair and that individuals ultimately deserve or earn the fate that they receive) take issue with mild forms of affirmative action, and, generally, opposition to affirmative action increases as a function of racism and conservatism. Attitudes toward affirmative action are most positive among nonracist liberals who subscribe to egalitarian values. [*See* PREJUDICE.]

2. Self-Esteem

Another issue that may affect support for affirmative action is an individual's level of self-esteem. Research has found that those with lower self-esteem are more likely to think that affirmative action in the workplace impairs their future self-interest. Related to this is the notion of scapegoating, where individuals seek to blame others for their own disadvantaged situations. As Anthony Pratkanis and Marlene Turner have noted, when Whites feel relatively deprived, they may engage in an ego-defensive function such as scapegoating and blame the affirmative action recipient for their own shortcomings.

3. Self-Interest

One evident factor that determines support for affirmative action is self-interest. We are often the strongest supporters of policies, issues, laws, rules, rights, and so on that will benefit ourselves or our group. Research has found support for this assertion such that women and people of color favor affirmative action more than men and Whites, and respondents' attitudes are more positive when affirmative action is targeted toward their own group. Opposition to affirmative action is strongest among Whites when it is framed as discriminating against White people rather than as a policy designed to help Black people.

4. Perceived Scarcity of Resources

If some individuals perceive of affirmative action as unfair because they feel it deprives candidates of fair chance to compete, this opposition can be further fueled by existing economic factors such as perceived scarcity of resources. In some situations affirmative action may be seen as a redistribution of existing, limited resources. Recipients of affirmative action may be perceived as receiving charity rather than as contributing members who are deserving of the opportunity.

5. Perceptions of Fairness

Self-interest may provide one explanation for why beneficiaries of affirmative action and nonbeneficiaries differ in their support of the policy. However, it cannot explain why some intended beneficiaries oppose affirmative action. For example, why are some Blacks are so vehemently opposed to affirmative action? It would be naive to assume that endorsement or rejection of affirmative action can be accounted for solely by factors such as gender and ethnicity.

Opinions about affirmative action are also related to perceptions of fairness such that perceived fairness can be one of the most powerful predictors of attitudes. According to research on procedural justice, people will report unfairness if they perceive that the procedures leading to the outcome were unjust—separate from the actual outcomes received as a consequence of these procedures! The process of attaining diversity is a key determinant of whether unfairness will be perceived. A study conducted by David Kravitz and Judith Platania found that support for affirmative action increased when the hiring process involved recruitment of highly qualified applicants and special training programs. Decreased support occurred when attention was focused on ethnicity.

How affirmative action is framed or worded has a strong influence on resulting attitudes. Views of affirmative action are contingent on the understanding of what it entails. As the findings regarding public opinion about affirmative action indicate, generally everyone reacts more favorably to outreach and "soft" affirmative action programs and least favorably to programs that involve preferential treatment. When affirmative action is equated with preferential treatment, this is seen as a violation of the principles of procedural and distributive justice

Individual ideology also affects reactions toward affirmative action. From a cross-cultural perspective, support for affirmative action is stronger among collectively oriented cultures where the collective well-being of the group is the focus rather than individual well-being. On the other hand, North American cultural values are built on the meritocratic ideology that everyone has the opportunity to succeed economically. This ideology is based on the premise that success and failure are the products of individual characteristics such as hard work, capability, and perseverance rather than structural barriers. As a result, unequal outcomes are merely reflections of unequal contributions. Unfortunately, this strong subscription to merit can lead to perceptions of affirmative action policies as irrelevant or a form of reverse discrimination. Those who strongly subscribe to this ideology often oppose affirmative action, whereas those who are skeptical of this ideology or have little faith in the actual implementation of it see affirmative action as means to achieve fairness. The relationship between opposition to affirmative action and perceived unfairness of the policy is a strong one, and remains so even when it is measured independent of prejudice level. [*See* INDIVIDUALISM AND COLLECTIVISM.]

Related to ideology are perceptions of need and the types of attributions that are made for disadvantaged situations, and these factors play a role in influencing views of affirmative action. Positive attitudes toward affirmative action have been related to beliefs that the target group needs help and that affirmative action will not impair organizational performance. Important factors related to how the need is perceived include the magnitude of the need, perceptions of the target group's ability to fulfill the need in the absence of affirmative action, and the consequences of not making efforts to fulfill the need. Anthony Pratkanis and Marlene Turner reported that Whites who believe that the cause of poverty is due to inadequacy (i.e., lack of motivation or ability) often show less support for affirmative action than do individuals who believe that poverty stems from social factors (i.e., discrimination).

In sum, the average American values fairness. If she or he conceives of an affirmative action plan as enhancing fairness, she or he is likely to endorse the plan. Softer forms of affirmative action are seen by most Americans as better promoters of fairness than harder forms. Overall, women and people of color support affirmative action more than do men and White people.

IV. How Can We Make Affirmative Action Work Well?

One reason that affirmative action policies and programs have come under fire is because of the lack of uniformity in which they are operationalized and implemented. Among those who support affirmative action, a question of importance and uncertainty pertains to how to design the best affirmative action models. How can we make affirmative action work well?

Anthony Pratkanis and Marlene Turner have warned of two issues related to the implementation and practice of affirmative action that can result in negative consequences for beneficiaries and others; self-threatening affirmative action and implications of preferential treatment. Thus they use "the model of affirmative action as help" in guiding their recommendations for creating effective affirmative action programs. The model is based on the assumption that due to the prevalence of racial and gender stereotypes, affirmative action recipients are often viewed as needing "special" help. Ironically, some forms of help that affirmative action recipients receive can be self-threatening. There are three key conditions that can foster self-threatening affirmative action. Affirmative action can be perceived as self-threatening if the implementation strategy of the program conveys or implies negative messages to the recipient. For example, some affirmative actions may be structured so that they inadvertently imply that the recipient lacks basic qualifications required for the job, is inferior to other applicants and current employees, or could not have obtained the job without help. These implications create what is called an affirmative action stigma. Second, affirmative action can be self-threatening when it seems to conflict with societal values and norms. This can occur when information about qualifications for the position are not explicit and focused or are ambiguous. The resulting implications may convey that the recipient is dependent and lacks self-reliance. Finally, help from affirmative action can be self-threatening when it does not convey clear instrumental benefits. It is important for affirmative action programs to clearly confirm the possibility of the recipient's future success, ensure that the "help" does not imply a continuing dependence or need for future assistance, and work toward removing discriminatory barriers.

When affirmative action is perceived by intended beneficiaries as self-threatening, it can cause immediate negative self-perception of the recipient's ability, performance, and affect. This can produce self-doubt about task-related abilities. In addition, self-threatening affirmative action can result in negative evaluation of the selection procedure and provider. One response to self-threat among recipients may be to engage in defensive behaviors to protect the self. Thus beneficiaries may be undermined by this type of affirmative action.

In addition, Anthony Pratkanis and Marlene Turner have warned of creating a view of affirmative action as preferential treatment. The view of affirmative

Table I

Recommendations for Increasing the Effectiveness of Affirmative Action

Recommendation	Example
Focus helping effort away from the recipient and toward removing social barriers.	Direct help toward changing institutional norms that perpetuate prejudice and discrimination.
Establish unambiguous, explicit, focused qualifications criteria to use in the section process and promotion decisions.	Use concrete criteria that apply equally to all members of the organization.
Communicate clearly requisite criteria and procedures.	Make the hiring criteria and procedures open and public so that it increases the likelihood that the procedure is seen as fair. Reduce use of biasing decision factors such as stereotypes.
Make all efforts to ensure that the selection procedures are perceived as fair by relevant audiences.	Use the targeted attribute (i.e., sex or race) as one of many selection criteria (including competency and qualifications). Design a hiring procedure that is viewed as conforming to societal values.
Emphasize the recipient's contributions to organization and his or her specific competencies.	Promote the view of the recipient as a unique contributor to the organization. Emphasize the positive aspects of having diversity in skills and perspectives.
Develop socialization strategies that deter attributions fostering helplessness, such as behavior among beneficiaries.	Stop new members from making attributions that they are dependent on the organization for their jobs, status, and future advancement.
Reinforce that affirmative action is *not* preferential selection.	Emphasize that affirmative action is based on the proportion of qualified applicants. Describe the exact procedures and tactics used in hiring.
Establish equal status contact with superordinate goals.	Create conditions for positive intergroup relations that include equal status among group members, striving to achieve common goals, maintaining cooperative dependency among all group members, and positive support of authorities, laws, customs.
Implement affirmative action using the psychology of inevitability.	Have authorities create the perception that change is inevitable, and nothing can be done to prevent it. Authority support legitimizes the effort so that affirmative action is not seen as counter to societal norms. Focus on discriminatory barriers so that in-group members must change their attitudes to fit the new reality.
Be aware that affirmative action does not operate in isolation.	Frame affirmative action as part of a larger workplace context that affects the success of the program. Diffuse the program throughout the organization. Develop meaningful reward systems to reinforce the attainment of program goals. Allocate resources to monitor and maintain the program.
Recognize that affirmative action does not cure all problems.	Do not expect affirmative action to solve all the problems faced by the organization. Acknowledge that affirmative action needs to work in conjunction with other programs.
Monitor affirmative action programs.	Periodically assess and redesign policies and practices.

action as preferential treatment can be devastating to recipients and distasteful to observers. Preferential treatment causes recipients to become stigmatized as less qualified. In addition, outsiders view preferential treatment as unfair. Affirmative action is seen as more fair when the institution shows a history of discrimination. The problem is that the principle of affirmative action is often seen as fairer than the actual practice or implementation.

To counter conditions that lead to self-threatening behaviors, there are three conditions that foster self-

supportive affirmative action. First, the hiring process should carry positive, self-relevant messages highlighting the recipient's unique qualifications and ensuring that there are no implications that the person is inferior or in need of help. Second, the process should confirm societal norms and values of procedural fairness, independence, self-reliance, and merit. Ultimately, the process should make strides toward providing instrumental benefits such as the removal of discriminatory barriers.

Other recommendations such as those provided by

Weining Chang focus on strategies for easing the sense of unfairness that may be perceived about some affirmative action programs. These include the following:

1. *Have an open and merit-based selection process.* A selection process that is publicly observable and accessible and that includes salient features of objectivity and focus on filling positions with qualified members will be faced with less resistance and criticism.
2. *Ensure that there is equity in evaluation.* Hires under affirmative action should be given the same challenges and held to the same standards for evaluation as other employees.
3. *Promote functional integration.* It should be clearly demonstrated that affirmative action recipients do not receive or are denied special circumstances. They should be placed in positions where they work alongside others and suffer and enjoy the same fate as other employees.

Table I provides numerous recommendations on how to increase the effectiveness of affirmative action programs. These strategies are based on a synthesis of research by Anthony Pratkanis and Marlene Turner.

V. Conclusions

As a society, we value fairness. We want women and men to receive fair outcomes, determined by fair procedures. Ironically, it is partially our desire for fairness that impels many people to turn a blind eye to minor problems around them. Minor injustices accumulate. Because affirmative action, unlike any other American legal policy, is proactive, not reactive, it is uniquely well suited to interrupt the accretion of small injustices. By helping organizations preserve fairness, affirmative action can contribute to social stability. Misconceived or misapplied forms of affirmative action offend men and women in the United States, but properly conceived programs are at the heart of our democracy, assuring all people— no matter what their gender or ethnicity—the opportunities they deserve.

SUGGESTED READING

Bowen, W. G., and Bok, D. (1998) *The Shape of the River: Long Term Consequences of Considering Race in College and University Admissions.* Princeton University Press, Princeton, NJ.

Chavez, L. (1998). *The Color Bind: California's Battle to End Affirmative Action.* University of California Press, Berkeley, CA.

Clayton, S. D., and Crosby, F. J. (1992). *Justice, Gender, and Affirmative Action.* University of Michigan Press, Ann Arbor, MI.

Crosby, F. J., and VanDeVeer, C. (2000). *Sex, Race, and Merit: Debating Affirmative Action in Education and Employment.* University of Michigan Press, Ann Arbor, MI.

Heilman, M. E. (1996). Affirmative action's contradictory consequences. *Journal of Social Issues* **52**(4), 105–109.

Pratkanis, A. R., and Turner, M. E. (1996). The proactive removal of discriminatory barriers: Affirmative action as effective help. *Journal of Social Issues* **52**(4), 111–132.

Aggression and Gender

Jacquelyn W. White

University of North Carolina at Greensboro

Glossary

Aggression Any action directed toward another person with the intent to do harm.

Battered woman's syndrome A special case of post-traumatic stress disorder that explains how the psychological effects of battering create feelings of helplessness.

Externalizing disorders Symptoms that are directed toward others; includes conduct disorders and aggression.

Gender segregated play The separation of boys and girls into different play groups.

Gendered Affected by the sex of the person(s) involved.

Indirect aggression Harming others by use of indirect strategies, such as spreading rumors or instigating others to harm the target.

Internalizing disorders Symptoms that are directed inward; includes depression and anxiety.

Patriarchy A social system in which the father or other male is the chief authority.

Predatory aggression Use of force or strong-arm techniques to harm others.

Prosocial behavior Behaviors aimed at helping others or promoting positive social relationships.

Relational aggression Aggression in which the intent is to harm in some way the target's social goals or relationships.

THE ROOTS OF AGGRESSION AND VIOLENCE are gendered and can be found in the childhood experiences of girls and boys. Gendered in this context means that the who, how, and why of violence cannot be understood without considering the sex of the perpetrator, the victim, their relationship, and the context of the violence. Gender role expectations, socialization, and power inequalities are central to understanding aggression and violence in both women and men. A brief review of gendered aggression during childhood, adolescence, and adulthood, including the elder years, follows a discussion of the working definition of aggression used in this article. The article concludes with a presentation of an integrated developmental model of aggression and violence. It is beyond the scope of this article to review exhaustively all the gender-relevant research on aggression and violence. Therefore, each section is based on a representative sampling of studies, those dealing with violence in the public sphere, relying primarily on criminal justice statistics, and those dealing with violence in intimate relationships, relying on criminal justice statistics and empirical studies. Somewhat more attention is given to violence in intimate relationships because, unlike much of the literature on aggression and violence, it is a topic in which gender issues have been investigated extensively.

I. Overview

In looking at aggression and violence, this article discusses these experiences from a developmental perspective for three reasons. First, violence occurs across the life cycle. There are gendered patterns of aggression and violence in childhood play, forms of parental punishment, and child abuse. Gendered patterns of aggression continue into adolescence, adulthood, and the elder years. Second, childhood experiences with aggression and violence increase the risk of further victimization and perpetration during adolescence, and adolescent experiences increase the risk of further involvement with violence during adulthood. Third, there are serious long-term psychological and physical consequences of victimization at all ages. Thus, messages learned in, and the consequences of, early experiences are repeated and reinforced in adolescence and young adulthood.

Due to the notion that aggression is a predominantly male attribute, researchers have disproportionately used male as opposed to female participants in their research studies. From 1967 to 1974, only 8% of the studies conducted examined female aggression, whereas 54% focused exclusively on males. More recently, in a check on the number of citations on PsychInfo from 1984 to 2000, there were only 802 listings under sex differences and aggression, but 9872 under aggression; if the search were limited to entries under human aggression, there were 192, but only 11 dealt with sex differences.

Even when female aggression has been the research focus, the conceptualization and operationalization of aggression has stemmed from the "male" perspective on aggression. For example, much of the research on aggression has focused specifically on physical aggression. Typically, this work has involved the teacher–learner paradigm in which the participant, acting as teacher, punishes the learner with electric shocks for incorrect responses. Research has shown, however, that women perceive electric shock more negatively and a less effective deterrent than do men; thus, they are more reluctant than men to administer it. Research demonstrating gender differences in aggression might be reflecting gender differences in a willingness to behave physically aggressively rather than the potential for aggression.

A continued focus on types of aggression in which men consistently emerge as more aggressive than women fails to examine those situations in which women might aggress and the modes of aggression they might adopt. Cross-cultural analyses suggest that despite tremendous cross-cultural variation, men tend to be more physically aggressive but women may use more indirect aggression. Men are more likely to use aggression that produces pain or physical harm, whereas women are more likely to use aggression that produces psychological or social harm. Because the majority of researchers have been male, they may have chosen questions and contexts regarding aggression of greatest personal relevance. Cross-cultural research has identified an extraordinary range of harm-doing behaviors committed by women, including verbal, nonverbal, and physical aggression, passive-aggressive behaviors (i.e., nonperformance of duties), property damage, and locking someone out of the house. A search of the literature did not reveal any studies that examined a comparable range of behaviors in men. [*See* CROSS-CULTURAL GENDER ROLES.]

Thus, in reviewing the literature for this article, aggression was defined as any behavior directed toward another person or a person's property with the intent to do harm, even if the aggressor was unsuccessful. The behavior could be physical or verbal, active or passive, direct or indirect (i.e., aggressor may remain anonymous), and the consequence for the target could be physical or psychological. All forms of harm-doing behavior, including self-defense, were considered because in some cases, such as domestic violence, it is difficult to distinguish retaliative from self-defense motives. Also, aggression was broadly defined in order to examine more fully the broad range of harm-doing behaviors available to human beings.

II. Gendered Violence in Childhood

The gendered nature of violence is evident early in childhood and establishes a framework for patterns of adult behavior. From the beginning children learn, in peer interactions and in the family, the major lesson of patriarchy: the more powerful control the less powerful. Furthermore, they learn that power is gendered. They learn to associate men with power and dominance. [*See* POWER.]

A. CHILDREN'S PLAY EXPERIENCES AND AGGRESSION

Although young children below the age of 12 are unlikely to be involved in violent crimes as perpetrators, they do engage in aggressive behavior, usually directed toward peers and siblings, often in the context of play. Play is the "work" of children and the context within which they learn gender role expectations. Girls and boys learn very early that boys are supposed to be stronger than girls and that girls should follow boys. In particular, children receive very specific messages about aggression. Given that children often play in same-sex groups, it is not surprising that the forms of aggression expressed in these groups differ. For example, girls are more likely to use verbal persuasion, whereas boys are more likely than girls to establish dominance physically, for instance by shouldering. This leads boys to be the targets of physical aggression in play situations more often than girls.

School-age girls and boys show definite preferences for gender-segregated play. The pressure for children to differentiate themselves from other sex playmates is strong at this age. Although both boys and girls run from, chase, and tease each other, key differences in the play styles of girls and boys exist. Boys establish their identity as male by defining girls as different and inferior, scorn girl-type activities, and exclude girls from their play. In fact, boys' rougher play may be one reason for same-sex play groups. It is likely that girls learn to protect themselves from boys' displays of dominance by avoiding them. Girls develop a wariness of boys that they carry into adolescence. These patterns explain why girls and women may develop greater anxiety and feelings of guilt regarding aggressive behavior.

Gendered patterns of aggression show up not only in play, but in more serious ways. For most children the frequency of more serious aggressive behaviors, such as hitting, biting, and temper tantrums, declines from ages two to five for girls and boys. However, by the age of four gendered patterns in these more severe problem behaviors begin to emerge, with boys being 10 times more likely that girls to be diagnosed with externalizing (acting out) disorders. Social and developmental factors have been associated with this divergence between girls and boys. The suggestion is that gendered socialization (i.e., encouraging girls to play quietly, be fearful, be dependent), combined with faster maturation, leads girls to less externalizing and more internalizing behaviors (inward-directed, such as depression) over time. Boys are more likely than girls to show stability in aggressive behavior over time. Parents, teachers, and peers all contribute to the differential socialization of girls and boys, in part by being less tolerant of aggressive, acting-out behaviors in girls. Girls also receive more training in empathetic and prosocial behavior than boys. [*See* DEPRESSION; PLAY PATTERNS AND GENDER.]

B. MEDIA INFLUENCES

Children are exposed to sex-typed toys, cartoons, books, movies, and games from an early age. Many of these images not only send the message that boys and girls are different, but that violence is a factor in many social interactions. Children with very heavy diets of TV violence as youngsters are at much higher risk for involvement with the criminal justice system by the time they are 19 years old. In the United States it has been estimated that on average a six-year-old has watched 5,000 hours of television; by the age of 18 this number has increased to 19,000 hours. A *TV Guide* study found 1846 acts of violence in an 18-hour period on just 10 channels. It is not surprising that media exposure to violence tends to normalize violence for children. Furthermore, this violence is gendered. Typically the media messages suggest that boys and men are the aggressors and that girls and women are the victims. As we will see later, violence toward women is often sexualized. [*See* MEDIA INFLUENCES; MEDIA VIOLENCE.]

C. GENDER AND PARENTAL PUNISHMENT

In both normal and abusive homes, children receive gendered messages about aggression and violence via parents' discipline strategies and intervention in peer conflicts. Children, especially those from abusive homes, have many opportunities to learn that the more powerful person in a relationship can use aggression to successfully control the less powerful person. The majority of parents in American homes use verbal and physical aggression as disciplinary tactics. Over 90% of children are spanked sometime in their youth, with many parents reporting physical aggression against their children; this aggression includes pushing, shoving, and slapping. Fewer parents report using severe aggression, including hitting, kicking, beating, threatening, and using weapons against their children.

Punishment does not appear to be uniform, however; the sex of the child and parent affect the pattern and outcome. During early childhood, boys are at greater risk than girls for severe abusive punishment, whereas during preadolescence and adolescence girls' risk increases. This discrepancy is presumably because of boys' increased ability to inflict harm on others as they physically mature. Although parents do not differ in the frequency with which they spank girls and boys, mothers tend to spank more often than fathers and the effects of the spanking are different. Paternal spanking leads to reactive, angry aggression in both girls and boys, but only boys show unprovoked bullying aggression against others when spanked by their fathers. Fathers' spanking of boys may transmit a gender-stereotypic approach to interpersonal disagreements. Moreover, parents' reactions to their children's aggressive behavior differ. Although parents generally see aggression as an undesirable attribute for children, they view it as a tolerated *masculine* behavior. Furthermore, girls are more likely to be encouraged to yield to peers and to remain in control of their feelings and actions. Thus, as contradictory as it may seem, boys expect less parental disapproval than girls for aggression directed toward peers, although they are punished more harshly for aggression than are girls.

D. CHILDHOOD PHYSICAL AND SEXUAL ABUSE

According to the National Center on Child Abuse and Neglect, in 1996 52% of the victims of maltreatment were girls. However, female victims were three times more likely (16%) than boys (5%) to experience sexual abuse, but less likely to experience neglect (54%) than boys (62%), whose maltreatment was more likely to end in death (56% of fatalities were boys). The report also indicated that 80% of the perpetrators were parents, and most perpetrators were female, many single parents (54% female only; 24% male and female). However, whereas females were more likely to physically abuse younger children, men more often abused older children. The form of maltreatment most often committed by women was medical neglect (70%) followed by neglect (64%), then physical (41%) and psychological (37%) abuse. On the other hand, men were most likely to commit sexual abuse (62%) followed by physical (33%) and psychological (26%) abuse. [*See* CHILD ABUSE.]

E. GENDER DIFFERENCES IN THE SUBJECTIVE MEANING OF AGGRESSION

These various childhood experiences with aggression and violence help shape a person's understanding of appropriate norms. There is a rich developmental literature that shows gender-related patterns in both children's and adults' understanding and use of anger and various types of aggressive behavior. Girls are taught to be less direct in expressing aggression. Girls regard relational aggression more positively than boys who judge physical aggression more positively. Boys also expect more rewards and fewer punishments for behaving aggressively than girls. Self-presentational studies of aggression have found that women are more likely than men to make derogatory self-statements regarding their aggressive episodes to avoid incurring negative reactions from an audience. In adults, men see anger expression as a means of reasserting control over a situation, whereas women see anger expression as a loss of control. Apparently, women and men share the belief that his aggression is a means of control and hers is a signal of loss of control. Thus, women come to experience aggressive behavior as a loss of emotional control, whereas men find aggression rewarding and an effective way to control others.

F. SUMMARY

As studies of play patterns in girls and boys, media influences, parental punishment, and childhood physical and sexual abuse suggest, boys receive numerous messages that distance them from girls and condone their use of aggression to express interpersonal power and control. Girls, on the other hand, receive messages that encourage submission and discourage them from defending themselves physically against aggression. Additionally, some girls and boys learn that their bodies are not their own, and that caretakers may use them sexually. These experiences set the stage for patterns of behavior that emerge during adolescence in peer groups and in intimate, heterosexual interactions. Boys and girls learn, through observations in the home, from peer interactions, and from media depictions of male-female interactions, that boys are dominant and girls are submissive, that boys are agentic and girls are passive. During childhood, boys experience more physical aggression and girls experience more sexual aggression. Among adolescents, girls are at a greater risk than boys for both physical and sexual victimization. Girls who develop externalizing problems are more likely, relative to female peers, to show slower maturation and deficits in social, emotional, and communication skills.

III. Gendered Violence in Adolescence

Adolescence is a significant transition period for young people. During adolescence, young men and women experience extreme pressure to conform to traditional gender roles. Unfortunately, part of establishing a masculine identity for young men often involves distancing oneself socially and psychologically from anything feminine. Young men seek out companionship from other men and distance themselves from women except in social contexts involving "power-enhancing" or sexual opportunities. The result is manifested in both public (i.e., crime and juvenile delinquency) and private (i.e., intimate relationships) spheres.

A. JUVENILE DELIQUENCY

According to the 1999 report of U.S. Department of Justice on juvenile offenders and victims, during the 1990s males accounted for 84% of violent crimes (murder, nonnegligent manslaughter, forcible rape, robbery, and aggravated assault). Similarly, males accounted for approximately 71% of juvenile homicide victims. Juvenile victims over 12 years old were more likely to be male (81%) than female. Acquaintances were most likely to be the victim of a male juvenile homicide offender (54%), followed by strangers (37%), and family members (9%). Conversely, for female juvenile homicide offenders, victims were most likely to be family members (39%) and least likely to be strangers (15%). Gendered patterns were evident in the method of killing, with males (73%) more likely than females (41%) to use a firearm, whereas females were more likely than males to use a knife (32%) or other means (27%).

Typically, factors predictive of adolescent violence have included weak school and family bonds, other problem behaviors such as substance abuse, exposure to deviant social influences, low self-esteem, and rebelliousness, along with school and neighborhood characteristics. Different patterns of factors are predictive of adolescent violence in males and females. First, there is a lower frequency and range of violent acts for girls than for boys, and different factors predict relational and predatory violence for each. For girls, the strongest predictors of violence were low self-esteem and attending schools in low-income neighborhoods. For boys, on the other hand, exposure to drugs, early use of drugs, and perceived peer use of drugs were highly predictive, along with frequent school moves. Additionally, according to a recent report issued by the U.S. Department of Justice, physical, sexual, and emotional victimization has been identified as a unique pathway into the juvenile justice system for girls. [See ADOLESCENT GENDER DEVELOPMENT.]

B. DATING VIOLENCE: PHYSICAL AND SEXUAL

Studies indicate that dating violence during the teen years is pervasive, with as many as 35% of female and male students surveyed reporting at least one episode, with fewer experiencing recurring violence. A national survey of approximately 2600 college women and 2100 college men revealed that within the year prior to the survey 81% of the men and 88% of the women had engaged in some form of verbal aggression, either as perpetrator or victim. Approximately 37% of the men and 35% of the women inflicted some form of physical aggression and about 39% of the men and 32% of the women sustained some physical aggression. In this survey all types of heterosexual relationships were included from the most casual to the most serious, thus providing a comprehensive estimate of the scope of courtship violence. The measures of verbal aggression included arguing heatedly, yelling, sulking, and stomping. Physical aggression included throwing something at someone, pushing, grabbing, shoving, or hitting. The ubiquity of courtship violence among college students is apparent in that comparable rates of violence have been observed across gender, ethnic group, and type of institution of higher learning, such as private or public, religious or secular. All the evidence to date suggests that it would be unusual to find a high school or college student who had not been involved in some form of verbal aggression and a substantial number who have not been involved in physical aggression. Also it appears that the same people who report inflicting some form of violence are the same ones who report experiencing violence.

As men and women establish intimate relationships, dominance and violence also surface in the form of sexual aggression. A comprehensive survey asked more than 3000 college women from 32 institutions of higher education across the United States about sexual experiences since the age of 14. Of those surveyed, over half (53.7%) had experienced some form of sexual victimization; of these about half had experienced acts by a man that met the legal definition of rape or attempted rape; the remaining reported being verbally pressured into sexual intercourse or some other form of unwanted sexual contact, such as forced kissing or fondling with no attempted penetration. More recent studies confirm these high numbers among Canadians, as well as among a national sample of 8000 women in the United States.

Community-based surveys have found that 25% of African American women, 20% of White women, and 8% of Hispanic women reported at least one sexual assault experience in their lifetime. High school women also appear to be at greater risk for rape than previously thought. A recently concluded longitudinal study of college students provides data on the prevalence of sexual, psychological, and physical violence against women within a dating relationship during adolescence and while in college. Women reported high levels of victimization: 14% of the women reported being the target of unwanted sexual contact, 15% reported verbal coercion, and 20% reported rape or attempted rape. In this study, 10.8% of the men reported performing acts of unwanted contact as the most serious form of sexually aggressive behavior, while 5.9% admitted using verbally coercive tactics to obtain sexual intercourse, and 6.9% reported acts that met the legal definition of rape or attempted rape. [*See* RAPE.]

C. MEDIA INFLUENCES

Sexualized images of women's bodies are prevalent, not only in sexually explicit materials, but in general media images (e.g., advertising). Women become the objects of men's gaze and evaluation. Women learn that their bodies are evaluated by others. Our culture socializes girls to view themselves as objects for evaluation and approval by others. Moreover, girls themselves come to internalize an observer's perspective and may come to evaluate their self-worth based on the responses and evaluations of others. Many young women believe that being good looking, attracting men, and having dates and boyfriends are very important and that they will be judged more favorably if they have a relationship with an attractive man. Many young women also seem to believe that when a woman is more attractive than the man, he must treat her especially well as a means of equalizing power in the relationship; if the woman is less attractive than the man, he can treat her poorly to compensate for her unattractiveness. When mistreated, they blame themselves rather than the man for their victimization.

In the extreme, the sexual objectification of women, as depicted in pornography, may have an impact on both adolescent women and men. Many men report being exposed to pornography for the first time around the age of 12. Pornographic images are verbally or pictorially explicit representations of sexual behaviors that degrade and demean the role and status of women as mere sexual objects to be exploited and manipulated sexually. Although women are more negative toward pornography than are men, repeated exposure results in desensitization to the disturbing images and may make women more likely to fail to reject certain myths about rape. One study found the following exposure to R-rated films that portray coercive sex, women were more likely to endorse statements describing rape as a sexual act and male sexuality as uncontrollable.

The evidence of an impact of repeated exposure to pornography on young men is well documented. Exposure to pornography increases men's sexual callousness toward women, desensitizes men to violence against women, and increases men's acceptance of rape myths and willingness to engage in aggressive behavior toward women. Pornography consumption is an important risk factor for sexual aggression, in part by contributing to the social context in which men and women learn about gendered relationships. [*See* PROSTITUTION.]

D. SUMMARY

A host of factors predict adolescent violence, including engagement in early deviant behavior, weak school bonds, poor grades, and prodrug environments. However, girls and boys show differential patterns of risk factors. Furthermore, the various themes of "boy versus girl" that were learned in childhood are reinforced and played out with serious consequences for numerous young women and men during adolescence. Experiences with verbal, physical, and sexual aggression and violence are all too common. Young men continue to believe it is acceptable to dominate young women in ways that are not only harmful to their partner but that increase the risk of continuing these patterns of behaviors in young adulthood. Young women who are victimized during childhood and adolescence are at great risk for further victimization in young adulthood. Furthermore, young men who were victimized as children and were perpetrators of sexual and physical aggression during adolescence are at increased risk for further perpetration during early adulthood.

IV. *Gendered Violence in Adulthood*

The statistics on criminal behavior in adulthood parallel those of adolescence, not surprisingly since many adult offenders began offending as juveniles. As with adolescents, gender-related patterns of violence are apparent in the public as well as the private spheres. In the public sphere, such as businesses, parking lots, and open areas, men are most likely to be victimized by other men, frequently strangers (63%). The rate of homicide for men is 0.17 per 1000 persons age 12 or older (compared to 0.04 for women). Men have a substantially higher lifetime chance of going to prison (9%) than women (1.1%). Women constitute only 5% of all state prison inmates and 10% of local jail inmates. Women are more likely to be victimized in the private sphere, often in a private home (46%) or at school (13%), and by someone they know (62%). Strangers account for only 32% of reported rapes or sexual assaults. [*See* IMPRISONMENT.]

A. CHILD MALTREATMENT

As noted earlier, there are gendered patterns among adult perpetrators of child abuse. Most abused children are victimized by their parents, more often the mother in her role as primary caregiver. Furthermore, her abuse is most likely to take the form of neglect, with fathers more likely to commit physical or sexual abuse. Although it seems paradoxical that mothers would abuse their children, issues of power and mothering must be considered. Often women who sexually abuse their children are in situations of powerlessness and display serious psychological problems, including retardation and chemical dependency. It is not unusual to find that women are coabusers with men; 24% of all forms of maltreatment and 29% of sexual abuse cases had coabusers. Men who abuse their children, on the other hand, have been described as authoritarian, punitive, and threatening. The victims of incestuous abuse tend to feel overwhelmed by their fathers' authority and unable to resist. Perpetrators may convince their victims that others will be angry with them and will not believe them if they tell, or that the abuse is their fault. Incest is more common in families in which members are emotionally distant. Open displays of affection often are absent and the family system lacks intimacy and cohesion. There is little mutual affection displayed between family members. Incest is also more common in families with a rigid, traditional family structure. Fathers are the head of the household; women are viewed as subordinate to their husbands and children as subordinate to their parents. Obedience and control permeate all aspects of the parent–child relationship. Sexual child abuse is more common in families with a number of conflictual relationships between family members, particularly between parents.

B. VIOLENCE IN MARRIAGE AND OTHER COMMITTED RELATIONSHIPS

The patterns established in adolescent relationships may continue in adulthood. The greatest threat of violence to adult women is from their intimate partners; for men, the greatest threat is from other men. Women are more likely to be physically or sexually assaulted by an intimate partner than by a stranger. It is estimated that 2 to 3 million women are assaulted by male partners in the United States each year, and that at least half of these women are severely assaulted (i.e., punched, kicked, choked, beaten, threatened with a knife or gun, or have a knife or gun used on them). As many as 21 to 34% of women will be assaulted by an intimate partner during adulthood. Further, it is estimated that 33 to 50% of all battered wives are also the victim of partner rape. Studies have shown that 22 to 40% of the women who seek health care at clinics or emergency rooms were victims of battering.

Intimate violence may escalate, resulting in homicide. Approximately two-thirds of family violence deaths are women killed by their male partners; over one-half of all murders of women are committed by current or former partners. In contrast, only 6% of male murder victims are killed by wives or girlfriends. Murder-suicides are almost always cases where the man kills his partner or estranged partner and then kills himself. He also may kill his children or other family members before he kills himself. Although there are instances where a woman murders a partner who has been abusing her, this happens less frequently than men killing partners they have abused chronically.

When women kill their partners, they are often reacting to abuse rather than initiating it. A study of women who killed partners found several common factors. The women were in abusive relationships and the abuse was increasing in frequency and severity. The increased violence was associated with a rise in the number and seriousness of the women's injuries. It was common for these men to have raped their spouses, to have forced them into other sexual acts, and to have made threats against their lives. The men typically used excessive alcohol daily and used recreational drugs. The effects of this intense and repeated abuse has led attorneys to use "the bat-tered-woman syndrome" in court cases to describe the psychological state of battered women who kill.

Several studies report that more women than men report being aggressive in intimate relationships. National surveys of spousal abuse indicate that women are more likely than men to report physically aggressing against their spouses and report more acts of aggression, especially low-level, against their husbands than their husbands report against their wives. However, most research on female aggression in intimate relationships has been examined via self-reports of aggressive behavior in marital relationships. Although it is beyond the scope of this article to critique fully this literature, several cautions should be noted. Because most of the data are self-reports, it would be premature to accept these data as accurate reflections of the amount of aggression in intimate relationships. Women may be more willing to report negative behaviors than men; there may be gender-related differences in the salience of memories for certain verbal and physical behaviors; and the criteria that women and men use for labeling a certain action a "yell" or "slap" may be gender related. Despite the fact that women are as likely as men to report engaging in physical aggression against their spouse or dating partner, women are more likely to sustain serious injury than are men. The primary reason for women's visits to emergency rooms is injury due to battering by a male partner. Also, as noted earlier men are more likely to murder their partner than are women. In 1991, when some 4 million women were beaten and 1320 murdered in domestic attacks, 622 women killed their husbands or boyfriends.

Although women have been reported to initiate acts of violence against their spouses as frequently as men, the motives of women and men for aggression differ. In self-reports of reasons for spousal homicide, the most frequently cited reason among women is self-defense, whereas among men the most common justification is sexual jealousy or the wife threatening to terminate the relationship. Women who initiate acts of violence do so frequently in anticipation of an abusive attack from their partner. [*See* Battering in Adult Relationships.]

C. VIOLENCE IN SAME-SEX RELATIONSHIPS

Relationship abuse is not limited to heterosexual relationships. Although there have been no prevalence studies, research with convenience samples indicates that partner abuse is a significant problem for lesbian women and gay men. Gay male couples report slightly less sexual abuse than lesbian couples but more severe physical violence. Partner abuse has been associated with issues of power, control, and dependency in both lesbian and heterosexual couples. For lesbians and gay men, the internalization of societal homophobic attitudes may, in part, lead to aggression against partners and reduce reporting due to threats that their sexual orientation will be revealed ("outed") by their partner. For gay men, the fear of AIDS, the stress of having AIDS, or caring for a partner with AIDS may be associated with abuse. Fortunately, shelters and organizations are slowly beginning to assimilate information on the issue. For abused gay men there are still few resources available for support and assistance. [*See* Lesbians, Gay Men, and Bisexuals in Relationships.]

D. AGGRESSION AMONG OLDER ADULTS

Older adults are less inclined to use direct forms of aggression to deal with conflict, preferring more indirect forms. However, men still surpass women in rates of overall aggression. Aggressive older adults are more likely to endorse masculine values and have less well-connected social networks.

Power inequalities between women and men continue into the later years and result in the continued victimization of older women by men. Elder abuse is often spouse abuse that has continued for years. Although equal numbers of older women and men are victimized by spouses, women suffer more serious consequences. Although most data on elder abuse do not look specifically at spouse abuse or sexual assault, some patterns emerge from the available data. A survey of the over-65 population of Boston found that 2% were the victims of physical abuse; 58% were abused by a spouse and 24% by an adult child. Victimization by adult children reflects the change in relationship dynamics as parents age. Adult children often become caretakers of an elderly parent with chronic physical health, mental health, or cognitive problems. Adult children gain power and the aging lose power within a social context that values youth and devalues maturity. Submissiveness, self-blame, self-doubt, and lack of social support mediate the effects of older woman abuse.

Little is known about the sexual abuse of older women. This remains a taboo topic, although there is a growing recognition that the problem needs attention. Clinical evidence suggests that older women may be raped in their homes as well as in institutions, such as residential treatment facilities and nursing homes; elderly wowmen are also more likely to be more seriously injured than younger women during a sexual assault. However, there are many difficulties with verification because of dementia and other memory-related problems among this group. A study of elder sexual abuse in Great Britain found a ratio of 6:1, female to male victims, with perpetrators more likely to be sons than husbands. Additionally, one study suggests that men who sexually assault older women may suffer from more severe psychopathological processes and that their assaults are more brutal and motivated by anger and a need for power.

Gender-related patterns of death are also apparent in cases of assisted suicide and euthanasia. Two studies have documented a consistent pattern of women being the more likely target and men being the agent of death. It appears that gender-related attitudes toward suffering, being a burden on others, and caregiving, coupled with sexist attitudes toward older women, contribute to this pattern.

E. SUMMARY

Elder abuse occurs for many reasons, but consistent gender-related patterns are apparent. Often the violence that occurred in marriage and other committed relationships continues into the later years of life. Although it has been documented that violence and aggression decline with age, negative consequences of earlier patterns of interpersonal violence persist. Negative relationship outcomes persist. The long-term effects of childhood sexual abuse and domestic violence produce lasting symptoms that may include depression and revictimization. Unfortunately, the correct diagnosis of symptoms related to abuse in the elderly is complicated by their age and may result in misdiagnosis as dementia or mental illness. In 1992, the American Association of Retired Persons produced a report identifying similarities between elder abuse and other forms of violence. The report identified a variety of factors— power imbalances, secrecy and isolation, personal harm to victims, social expectations and sex roles, inadequate resources to protect victims, and the control perpetrators have—that contribute to elder abuse.

V. Consequences of Violence

The developmental pattern of continuing gendered violence is mirrored in the consequences for victims. Beginning in childhood, victimization experiences influence subsequent psychological, social, and emotional development. For example, sexually victimized girls suffer from several problems, including traumagenic sexualization, impaired self-esteem, feelings of

betrayal, and lack of trust. Young women who experience physical or sexual violence during adolescence are more likely to be injured and to feel surprised, scared, angry, and hurt by a partner's aggression than are men. Although men are two to four times more likely to use severe forms of violence, women are three to four times more likely to report injuries. An additional serious consequence of dating violence is an increased risk of marital violence either by the same or a different partner. There are many consequences of assault beyond the immediate physical trauma necessitating medical care. Abused women are at higher risk for a range of health problems that are not a direct consequence of physical blows to the body. These include clinical depression, post-traumatic-stress disorder, sexually transmitted infection, gastrointestional disorders, frequent urinary tract and vaginal infections, and decreased perceived health status. They also show a range of adverse behavioral outcomes such as suicide and substance use. There are also social and economic consequences. The abused woman's partner may limit access to household resources and control decision making, the quality of life for children in the home, and the woman's employment patterns. Domestic violence influences a woman's earnings and ability to remain in a job, reduces her educational attainment and income, and reduces her participation in public life, lessening her contribution to social and economic development. Violent partners also may prevent women from seeking immediate care even when it is needed. This is especially true among rural women where one of the common forms of domestic violence is denial of access to means of transportation and communication. Children witnessing abuse have many of the same problems as their abused mothers, including more emotional and behavioral problems and more physical health complaints. In many families where husbands abuse their wives, children are also abused. The children of abused women are more likely to be malnourished and more likely than other children to die before age five. Abused women are more likely to have an infant death or pregnancy loss from abortion, miscarriage, or stillbirth.

VI. An Integrated Contextual Developmental Model

The integrated contextual developmental model provides a metatheoretical framework within which to understand gendered violence across time and cultures. Derived from ecological models it describes five levels of interacting factors: sociocultural (including historical, cultural, and community traditions and values), social networks, dyadic, situational, and intrapersonal. The most distal influences are historical and sociocultural. These provide the backdrop for a number of interconnected relationships a person has or may have at different points across the lifespan. These include family, social, school, and work relationships. Also important is the relationship between two individuals, the potential perpetrator and potential victim. These two individuals have an interaction history that will influence their behaviors in any given situation; the situation provides the proximal cues for aggression and violence. All these factors coalesce to determine the particular behavioral manifestation of aggression (i.e., direct, indirect; verbal, physical, sexual). Certain situational factors will increase the likelihood of an aggressive encounter.

The model assumes that patriarchy operating at the historical/sociocultural level affects the power dynamics of all relationships. Shared patterns of ideas and beliefs passed down from generation to generation define one's social networks. Historical and sociocultural factors create an environment in which the growing child learns rules and expectations, first in the family network and later in peer, intimate, and work relationships. Early experiences define the context for later experiences. Embedded in these social networks are characteristics of the personal relationships in which individuals act violently. Power dynamics become enacted in social networks and result in the internalization of gendered values, expectations, and behaviors. Thus, cultural norms governing the use of aggression as a tool of the more powerful to subdue the weaker combine with gender inequalities to create a climate conducive to violence. Violence is inextricably bound to the social context of male domination and control. The patriarchal view of society gives men a higher value than women. In most cultures it is taken for granted that men should dominate in politics, economics, and the social world including family life and interpersonal relationships.

A. SOCIOCULTURAL LEVEL

The sociocultural level of analysis examines historical, cultural, social, institutional, and community influences on behavior. A great deal of macrolevel research, especially in the sociological tradition, has documented the role that sociocultural factors play in delinquency and crime in general. Other sociocultural factors implicated in violence include sexual inequalities, gender role prescriptions (including dating and sexual scripts), and cultural norms and myths about women, men, children, family, sex and violence, as well as scripts for enacting relationships. Expectations about the appropriate roles for men and women are communicated through various institutionalized practices of a society, including those of the legal system, organized religion, schools, media, politics, and the military. All set the stage for the evolution of cultural myths that perpetuate male violence against women and shape myths about female violence as well.

During adolescence, young men and women experience extreme pressure to conform to traditional gender role expectations. It appears that violence in adolescence is so prevalent, in part, because the overall structure and meaning of maleness, at least in North American culture, encourages boys to feel entitled to power at any cost. Scripts for being male or female are fairly well defined and have not changed much over several decades. A script is a set of rules to be followed. Dating and sexual scripts in particular afford men greater power relative to women. Women are assumed to be responsible for how "far things go," and if things "get out of hand," it is their fault. Men who endorse traditional scripts are more likely than men who do not to perceive force and coercion as acceptable means of obtaining desired outcomes regardless of the circumstances.

Cultures in which less traditional gender roles are prescribed and in which male dominance and female subordination are not encouraged show fewer instances of male violence against women, supporting the idea that sociocultural values contribute to violence. However, although all men within a given culture are typically exposed to similar sociocultural pressures to behave in accordance with their assigned gender roles, not all men are violent. One reason not all men are violent lies in the multiply determined nature of violence. Embedded within one's culture are situational, dyadic, and individual influences that may either increase the likelihood of violence or mitigate against it.

B. SOCIAL NETWORK LEVEL

The social network level of analysis focuses on one's history of personal experiences within various social institutions (family, peers, school, religion, and work settings). The gendered norms and expectations that contribute to violence are transmitted through these institutions. Witnessing and experiencing violence in the family of origin alters the likelihood of later involvement in violent episodes. Men who either witnessed or experienced violence as a child show a higher likelihood of delinquency, as well as being sexually or physically aggressive in dating situations. As with the family unit, other social networks may promote a system of values that reflect sociocultural understandings of gender inequality. Within these networks, the acceptance of interpersonal violence may be encouraged and rewarded. For example, exposure to delinquent peer groups, whether at school, work, or in the community at large, has been shown to be related to deliquency in general, as well as dating violence and sexual assault.

The gender-related patterns learned in childhood are played out in adolescent dating and committed relationships. Young people usually begin dating in high school, although children as young as kindergartners talk about having boyfriends and girlfriends. The idea of being paired with a member of the other sex is pervasive in our society. Traditionally, it has been assumed that children's "playing house" and later dating provide a context for socialization into later roles, including husband, wife, lover, and confidante. Dating also offers opportunities for companionship, status, sexual experimentation, and conflict resolution. However, courtship has different meanings for young women and men. Whereas for men courtship involves themes of "staying in control," for women themes involve "dependence on the relationship." Violence is one of the tactics used to gain control in a relationship.

C. DYADIC LEVEL

Whereas social networks focus attention on a perpetrator's and victim's history of interpersonal relationships, particularly within the family and peer groups, the dyadic level focuses on the nature of one specific relationship, the one between the perpetrator and victim. Crime statistics tell us that individuals are much more likely to victimized by someone they know than by a stranger; this is particularly true for women. Several researchers have found that violence is more likely to occur in serious than in casual relationships, suggesting that violence in more committed relationships may reflect the acceptance of violence as a legitimate mode of conflict resolution. On the other hand, violence in a developing rela-

tionship may be a way of testing the relative safety of making a greater commitment to the relationship. Forms of sexual and dating violence are more likely in relationships plagued by problems, including jealousy, fighting, interference from friends, lack of time together, breakdown of the relationship, and problems outside the relationship, as well as disagreements about drinking and sexual denial.

Nonverbal and verbal communication patterns between the members of the dyad may set the stage for violent interactions. More specifically, men and women do not always perceive behaviors in exactly the same way. Some men interpret a woman's behavior in a more sexualized way than it was intended, do not take her verbal protestations seriously, and perceive her rejection of sexual advances as a threat to their masculinity. Men who endorse adversarial sexual beliefs and interpersonal violence are more likely to misinterpret a woman's behavior as sexually connotative than men who do not hold such beliefs. Similarly, women may enter dating relationships with a cognitive set toward trust, companionship, and having a good time, and hence be less alert to the warning signs of assault.

D. SITUATIONAL LEVEL

This level of analysis focuses on situational variables that increase or decrease the likelihood of interpersonal violence. In order for violence to occur, the situation must be conducive to the violence. Features of the situation influence the likelihood that violence will occur by affecting the opportunity for the violent acts (i.e., times when privacy is available and detection minimal). The routine activities model of crime emphasizes the role of opportunity. Situations that include violent cues, such as the presence of guns, are likely to promote violence, especially for men. A number of situational variables, including time of day, location, and the presence of social inhibitors or disinhibitors, such as alcohol and drugs, are known to affect the likelihood of crime differentially for women and men. According to crime statistics, women are more likely to be the victim of crime during daylight hours than at dark, the more likely time for men. A private home, or a private vehicle if they are traveling, is the most likely site of victimization for women, whereas for men it is a public place and they are on foot. Not surprisingly then, courtship violence is most likely to occur in private settings and on weekends. Alcohol and drugs are also related to incidents of violence, including violence against women. Alcohol acts as a disinhibitor for the man, as an excuse for the violence after it has occurred, and as a means of reducing the victim's resistance. In cases of dating violence, alcohol use is common. In cases of acquaintance rape, alcohol may enhance ambiguity by increasing the likelihood that men may misinterpret a woman's friendly behaviors as sexual. Some men may interpret a woman's consumption of alcohol as an indication that she is "loose."

E. INDIVIDUAL LEVEL

The focus at the individual level is on attitudinal, motivational, and characterological features of a person. However, it is recognized that individual attributes typically emerge as the result of experiences in various social networks. Thus, there is a dynamic interplay between factors operating at these various levels. For example, the attitudinal underpinnings of violence—in particular, the endorsement of traditional sex-role stereotypes and cultural myths about violence—often stem from being reared in households where violence was considered normative.

Certain personality and behavioral variables have been identified in individuals with a history of violence. Many of these are factors identified in early childhood, such as hyperactivity, learning disabilities, conduct disorders, and rebelliousness. Other factors include antisocial tendencies, nonconformity, impulsivity, low socialization and responsibility, hypermasculinity, delinquent behavior, affective dysregulation, and self-centeredness coupled with insensitivity to others.

Violence in intimate relationships has been associated with the endorsement of traditional sex-role stereotypes and cultural myths about violence. Relative to nonsexually aggressive men, sexually aggressive men more strongly subscribe to traditional gender stereotypes. Similar findings have been obtained in studies examining the characteristics of men who abuse their dating partners or spouses. A history of promiscuous-impersonal sex, distrust of women, and gratification derived from dominating women represent factors associated with sexual violence toward a female partner, whereas relationship distress and verbal aggression are predictive of physical aggression.

Furthermore, a man's need for power, dominance, and control appears to play a role in violent behavior. A man who feels threatened by a loss of control, such as by being rejected, may attempt to regain that control by behaving aggressively. Violent acts perpetrated against women often include intimidation, co-ercion, and belittlement, suggesting the importance of power and dominance. Men who are quick to react to anger, believe that violence will aid in winning an argument, and have successfully used violence in the past are likely to do so again. Similarities between men who engage in courtship violence and wife-batterers have been found.

The extent to which these specific individual variables influence the incidence of violence depends on the degree to which cultural norms and the influence of social groups affect individual mental representations of the situation and the relationship with the victim. For example, although the legal definition of rape appears straightforward, the social meaning of the term "rape," the circumstances surrounding an act of forced sexual intercourse, and the likelihood of punishment make some reluctant to use the label. The term "rape" has been shown to have different meanings for women and men. College students in general, and sexually aggressive men in particular, believe that sexual precedence (i.e., a past history of sexual intercourse) reduces the legitimacy of sexual refusal. Moreover, some people are hesitant to label forced sex as rape if consent was not explicitly verbalized, even if threats, intimidation, or incapacitation are present. Although a woman may not realize that forced sexual intercourse by an acquaintance during a date is rape, this does not change the legal definition of the act as rape, nor does it reduce the culpability of the perpetrator. Furthermore, whether or not a sexual assault is labeled rape does not alter the consequences for the victim.

VII. Conclusion

The pattern of violence, where women are often the victims and men are the perpetrators, is not due to biological destiny. Women are not born victims and men are not biologically predetermined to be aggressors. Rather, stereotypes of how women and men are supposed to behave, experiences that reinforce stereotypical behaviors, and a social structure that supports power inequities between women and men all contribute to gendered patterns of violence across the life span.

To understand violence we must first recognize that culturally based socialization practices encourage men to be aggressors and women to be victims. In societies where there is no formal hierarchy that privileges one group over another and in which women and men exercise relatively equal power, general levels of aggression, and male violence against women are low. As this article has described, gendered violence is learned early in life and continues across the life span. Statistics allow us to examine larger social influences and overall patterns found in society. They reveal that women are the victims of intimate violence more often than men at every stage of development, with the exception of early childhood physical abuse.

Although women may be the perpetrators of aggression, this does not destroy the argument that intimate violence is related to gender and social roles. Patriarchy as a social system carries with it the message that the more powerful are entitled to dominate the less powerful. Aggression and violence are inherently gendered. Even when girls and women act aggressively, they are responding to and enacting male models of behavior and control, models Western culture has endorsed. Because men more often hold higher status positions than women, it follows that men will abuse more than women; and because adults are more powerful than children, children will be victimized more than adults; and because the young are more powerful than the elderly, the aged are at risk.

Inequality in relationships, coupled with cultural values that embrace domination of the weaker by the stronger, creates the potential for violence. The more powerful partner can control money, resources, activities, and decisions, and this is the case in lesbian, gay, and heterosexual couples. Both men and women learn that violence is a method people use to get their way. When individuals use violence and get their way, they are reinforced and thus more likely to use aggression in the future. However, men have historically received greater rewards for aggression and violence than have women. Women are as likely as men to aggress in situations that are congruent with their gender identities and where they hold relatively more power.

SUGGESTED READING

Bergen, R. K. (1998). *Issues in Intimate Violence*. Sage, Thousand Oaks, CA.

Koss, M., Goodman, L., Fitzgerald, L., Russo, N., Keita, G., and Browne, A. (1994). *No Safe Haven*. American Psychological Association, Washington, DC.

Meloy, J. R. (1998). *The Psychology of Stalking: Clinical and Forensic Perspectives*. Academic Press, San Diego.

Russell, D. E. H. (1993). *Making Violence Sexy: Feminist Views on Pornography*. Teachers College Press, New York.

Shrier, D. K. (1996). *Sexual Harassment in the Workplace: Psychiatric Issues*. American Psychiatric Press, New York.

Walker, A. (1982). *The Color Purple*. Washington Square Press, New York.

Warshaw, R. (1988). *I Never Called it Rape: The Ms. Report on Recognizing, Fighting, and Surviving Date and Acquaintance Rape*. Harper & Row, New York.

Aging

Janet Belsky
Middle Tennessee State University

Glossary

ADL limitations Impairments in the ability to perform daily life tasks produced by disease.

Alzheimer's disease Old age condition in which neural deterioration produces progressive and serious mental impairment.

Epidemiologic transition Early 20th-century shift in mortality from infectious to chronic diseases accompanied by a dramatic rise in average life expectancy in industrial countries.

Gender crossover Controversial theory in adult development that men and women become psychologically similar or adopt the traits of the other sex at the empty nest.

Instrumental help Concrete aid to an individual, typically a family member, in need.

Old-old Age group over age 80.

Osteoporosis Age-related skeletal disorder (most prevalent among European American and Asian American females) in which the gradual loss of density of the bones makes fractures likely.

Presbycusis Classic age-related hearing impairment most common in males caused by the selective atrophy of the hearing receptors that encode high-pitched tones.

Vascular dementia Old age condition in which small strokes produce progressive, serious mental impairment.

THE AGING PROCESS is universal. This article highlights the ways gender makes a difference in that path. In addition to focusing on differences, this article focuses on a certain point in history in a particular place. It describes aging in the United States and, to some extent, the developed world. This is why, before scanning the findings, Section I sets the stage. It outlines the demographic and research framework. It traces how we got to where we are today and explores issues relating to what we know. Section II turns to the data, exploring gender differences in physical and cognitive aging. Section III examines women, men, personality, and mental health. Section IV examines late life relationships and roles (and economic status) through a gender lens. The article concludes by spelling out some concerns specific to the baby boom men and women now moving into their older years.

I. The Demographic and Research Framework

A. A FAR LONGER LIFE AND A MORE FEMALE WORLD

When historians look back to the 20th century, they may list the life expectancy revolution as the main achievement of this miraculous human hundred years. Although its seeds were laid down in the Industrial Revolution, during the early decades of the

20th century an historic epidemiological transition took place. Due to medical and public health advances, infectious diseases no longer were the main cause of death. For the first time ever, people in industrialized countries routinely lived past youth to die from chronic diseases. During the second half of the century, life expectancy advances were slower and occurred at life's upper ends. In particular, the 1970s fitness movement, by pushing back the onset of heart disease, extended life expectancy and survival during the older years. During this brief century, U.S. life expectancy at birth shot up from age 46 to 77. Today, once reaching 65, the average American can expect to live to the mid-eighties, within striking distance of the estimated biological limit of human life (about age 100 to 105). In fact, as Japan, Australia, New Zealand, Canada and *every* Western European country outrank the United States in life expectancy, in this new millenium inching close to this ultimate marker is fast becoming routine—provided a person is fortunate to be born with advantages, and *she* happens not to be male.

With an average life expectancy at birth of almost 80 compared to 73, in 1999 U.S. women outlived men by about seven years. Although life expectancy has increased for everyone, notice from Table I that this wide gender gap in longevity has existed for the past half century. It exists throughout the developed world. In other words, once a country undergoes the epidemiological transition, women's small longevity edge becomes pronounced. With more people surviving to advanced old age, and fewer being born, we are undergoing a historic feminization of the world.

As we approach the midpoint of this century, this enduring shift in life expectancy will collide with a temporary childbearing trend to produce an unparalleled "older" and therefore more female world. During the 1970s, fertility plunged in industrial countries. Moreover, the baby boomers, the huge bulge in the population born between 1946 and 1961, are about to enter later life. To get a sense of how female the United States will be when the huge leading edge of this cohort moves into their 80s, the time of life called the old-old years, consider these statistics: in 2040 one in five Americans will be over 65. The fraction of the old-old will increase from its current 1% of the population to 5%. Today, in the age group over 85, there are approximately $2\frac{1}{2}$ women for every man.

The underlying framework for understanding gender and aging at this point in history centers on that

Table I
Life Expectancy at Birth for Selected Countries, 1900 to 1999 (in Years)

| Region/Country | Developed countries | | | | | |
| | Circa 1900 | | Circa 1950 | | 1999 | |
	Male	Female	Male	Female	Male	Female
Western Europe						
Austria	37.8	39.9	62.0	67.0	74.3	80.8
Belgium	45.4	48.9	62.1	67.4	74.3	80.9
Denmark	51.6	54.8	68.9	71.5	73.8	79.3
France	45.3	48.7	63.7	69.4	74.8	82.7
Germany	43.8	46.6	64.6	68.5	74.0	80.5
Norway	52.3	55.8	70.3	73.8	75.6	81.4
Sweden	52.8	55.3	69.9	72.6	76.6	82.1
United Kingdom	46.4	50.1	66.2	71.1	74.7	80.2
Southern and Eastern Europe						
Czech Republic	38.9	41.7	60.9	65.5	71.0	77.9
Greece	38.1	39.7	63.4	66.7	75.9	81.2
Hungary	36.6	38.2	59.3	63.4	66.9	75.7
Italy	42.9	43.2	63.7	67.2	75.4	81.8
Spain	33.9	35.7	59.8	64.3	74.0	81.7
Other						
Australia	53.2	56.8	66.7	71.8	77.0	82.9
Japan	42.8	44.3	59.6	63.1	77.0	83.4
United States	48.3	51.1	66.0	71.7	73.0	79.7

Source: Kinsella, K. (2000) Demographic dimensions of global aging. *Journal of Family Issues* **21**, 541–558.

simple fact. Although men do routinely live to later life, women inhabit the territory of advanced old age. A second theme running throughout our discussion relates to that other historic 20th-century change. This revolution revolves around gender too.

B. A DIFFERENT FAMILY AND A MORE VARIABLE, LESS GENDER-DEFINED ADULT LIFE

The life expectancy revolution took place more gradually, mainly during the first part of the 20th century. The sexual and women's movements quickly transformed society during the century's final decades. Suddenly, during the 1970s, workforce issues became women's issues and child care was expected to be a shared marital job. Divorce was transformed from atypical to predictable. Then, during the 1980s and 1990s, as nonmarital motherhood became far more common, the explosion of single-parent families catapulted hands-on grandmotherhood (always common in developing countries and earlier times) into a contemporary older female concern. [*See* DIVORCE; FAMILY ROLES AND PATTERNS, CONTEMPORARY TRENDS; MARRIAGE.]

Table II offers statistics that highlight this different gender balance of earlier adult life. As we enter the 21st century, the irony is that families are more matrifocal, or female centered, at the same time as other adult roles have become less rigidly gender defined. Women are just as well educated as men. They are much more similar in their occupational patterns, although not their income, to the opposite sex. With both men and women moving in and out of marriages and careers as they move through life, adult pathways are more variable and flexible than ever before. This unparalleled freedom to chart our own life path applies to choices made both in earlier and in later life. In fact, it is no accident that the struggle against sexism in the 1960s went hand in hand with a battle against ageism, or discrimination based on age. The leader of the Gray Panthers, the activist elderly rights group that fought against mandatory retirement and promoted our contemporary more age-irrelevant society, was a remarkable woman in her 60s named Maggie Kuhn.

C. RESEARCH TRENDS AND RESEARCH CAUTIONS

Because who we are as older adults is a function of our enduring life history, coming of age in this less predictable era will dramatically shape how men and women grapple with the predictable challenges of old age. Furthermore, while every cohort ages differently, at this moment, there are two *exceptionally* different cohorts in the aging phase of life. There is the very old group who spent much of their adulthood before the sexual and women's movements, and there are the post-liberation baby boomers about to enter their retirement years. Because our studies deal with the earlier, more traditional cohort, many

Table II
Two Examples of the Changing Gender Context of Earlier Adult Life

Educational and occupational trajectories are far less gender defined
Illustrative examples
Both women and men go on to higher education at equal rates. In 1998, roughly twice as many males over 65 were college graduates as females that age (20% compared to 11.2%). In contrast among the young adult population, women were as likely to graduate from college as men. In fact, partly because of the influx of adult returning students, not only do women outnumber men at U.S. universities today, but this gender gap is expected to widen over time.
After being married both men and women work outside the home: In 1960, fewer than one-third of married women were in the workforce compared to almost 90% of their male counterparts. By 1998, the sharp male/female differences in labor force participation at marriage no longer were apparent, with 61.9% of wives working compared to 77% of married men.
Families are far more matrifocal or female centered
Illustrative statistics
The two-parent family is being replaced by the single-mother family. In 1970, one in ten U.S. children were living in mother-headed families. By the early 1990s, the percentage had risen dramatically to almost one in four. During the 1980s there was a sharp rise in the fraction of single women giving birth. In that year, for instance, in the early 20s age group, 39.7 women per thousand single females gave birth. By the early 1990s, the comparable figure had risen to 68.5.

of the current facts about gender and late life may soon be obsolete. Our research has other limitations as well.

After gerontology became an established science at the end of the Second World War, gerontologists studied men. In fact, the pioneering American study of physical aging, the Baltimore Longitudinal Study, added women only in 1978. Since the 1980s, women have increasingly been a focus of behavioral science research in aging, particularly in the interpersonal and emotional realms. Our new challenge is to study the inner lives of *both* sexes and especially to chart the conditions under which women and men grow emotionally with age. Because the ways we decline are more obvious, of compelling social importance, and far easier to measure, research in gerontology has mainly centered on negatives, the losses and problems that occur. Despite a long research tradition probing adult personality, our understanding of physical and cognitive aging is still much more solid than our knowledge about age changes in the emotional side of life. While this article reports on tantalizing new research relating to gender and age-related emotional growth, be aware that these trends are tentative. They must be confirmed using longitudinal studies with multiple cohorts and representative samples of older women and men.

Finally, before exploring the research, another caution is required. The life expectancy gap between the most disadvantaged and the most affluent Americans exceeds the longevity difference between women and men. African American women are more likely to follow the male physical aging pathway. They are at much higher risk of developing diabetes and vascular illnesses and less prone to osteoporosis than their European American counterparts. Among this important segment of the aging population, the striking male/female disparity in late life economic status does not exist. In other words, within any single country, gender pathways tend to vary dramatically by ethnicity. Knowing someone's socioeconomic status may tell us more about that individual's aging path than knowing whether that person is female or male. Furthermore, as the world turns completely multicultural and earlier life less gender defined, making late life gender generalizations grows more hazardous. As we see now, gender is *one* influential marker that shapes the aging experience. However, to understand that experience in the flesh we need to adopt a contextual approach—looking at who we are as people, rather than at who we are as women and men. [*See* POVERTY AND WOMEN IN THE UNITED STATES.]

II. *Physical and Cognitive Aging*

A. LONGEVITY AND HEART DISEASE

Women's advantage in life expectancy has multiple causes. By almost every indicator, females are hardier. Their mortality rates at *every age* in the life span are lower, even in the face of many diseases. However, at the heart of why older women outlive men is one particular illness—heart disease. Cardiovascular illnesses, heart disease, and stroke cause about one of every two deaths in developed countries. Heart disease is the top cause of mortality for both females and males. However, because estrogen insulates women against the normal age-related buildup of atherosclerosis that causes the coronary arteries to become occluded or blocked, women almost never die from a heart attack before menopause. A few years after menopause, ovarian estrogen production shuts down; women lose this resilience and gradually become susceptible to heart disease and stroke. In fact, menopause is an overall female aging marker. It is implicated in a cascade of old age changes, from skin wrinkling to alteration in body fat distribution, skeletal disorders, and memory loss. But it is not until the 80s that the male/female ratio of deaths from heart disease floats down to 1:1. [*See* MENOPAUSE.]

Heart disease is a top ranking cause of disability. Impaired circulation due to the weakening heart muscle (congestive heart failure) and especially constricted coronary arteries (coronary artery disease) can seriously compromise cognition as well as limiting the ability to physically negotiate life. But, unlike cancer, when heart disease is fatal, especially before old age, it tends to kill abruptly. So even earlier in life, males tend to die more quickly than females without being disabled by disease. If we die at a relatively young age we are less likely to spend time incapacitated anyway because we often have only one disease. As Table III shows, as we progress through the older years the chance of developing a variety of chronic conditions accelerates. Most chronic illnesses are not fatal, but they do interfere with the ability to freely negotiate the world.

B. CHRONIC DISEASE AND DISABILITY

So simply by virtue of reaching advanced old age, women are more likely to develop *every* age-related disease. As these illnesses accumulate, women tend to have trouble handling daily life. The bottom line is that the female longevity advantage comes at a se-

Table III

Prevalence of Five Selected Chronic Conditions by Sex and Age in the United States, 1995[a]

	Male			Female		
	45–64	65–74	75+	45–64	65–74	75+
Arthritis	176.7	385.5	437.0	285.4	498.2	616.1
Hearing impairment	203.6	332.8	423.5	89.7	159.0	307.8
Heart disease	143	316.3	439.4	100	229.3	318
Cerebrovascular, disease	16.2	59.4	113.0	13.6	45.8	90.2
Cataracts	16.8	72.1	214.0	21.6	132.1	247.0

[a] Rates are per 1000 adults that age.

Source: National Center for Health Statistics, 2000; data based on the 1995 Health Interview Survey.

rious price. Women are at far higher risk of developing activities of daily living (ADL) impairments or to have difficulty coping with normal life tasks.

Although not everyone with an illness has limitations, ADL impairments rise in tandem with the age-related rise in disease. By their late 60s and early 70s, about one in four Americans reports some trouble in performing a strenuous activity such as gardening or housework. By the old-old years, these minor impairments are typical and can take a more devastating form. Over age 85, approximately one in five people living in the community suffers from a basic ADL limitation or elemental difficulty performing such tasks as eating, dressing, or getting out of bed. The risk of having these problems in advanced old age is actually higher, as it is these basic self-care difficulties that result in institutional care. In other words, there is something unique and qualitatively different about surviving to age 80 and beyond: *serious* physical losses become the norm.

Epidemiological surveys longitudinally tracing ADL impairments and comparing their rates over decades reveal other insights relevant to age and this distinctive female/male path. While disability pathways are variable, as we might expect, the likelihood of fully recovering once a person does develop an ADL problem is far less probable in advanced old age. Moreover, while in the 60s and 70s disability "episodes" tend to take place suddenly, due to a catastrophic event such as a heart attack or stroke, by the old-old years these limitations most often progress slowly as the person's chronic ailments accumulate. Finally, though the lifestyle revolution has increased active life expectancy, allowing us to live longer in health, it has left the rate of serious ADL impairments in our oldest years untouched. People

are *no more likely* to live healthily beyond the mid-80s today than they were a few decades ago—emphasizing, once again, that women's longevity is a double-edged sword. It is purchased at the price of higher morbidity, a more protracted, pronounced illness path.

This excess morbidity is not just due to living very long. By every index of illness, from number of doctors visits to days confined to bed, women "live sicker" than men throughout adult life. During the older years a primary reason for this inflated female morbidity is that musculoskeletal and vision disorders most often strike women at younger ages (see Table III). These are the types of chronic illnesses that directly lead to ADL problems, and when an older women is confined to bed by any disease, she is less likely to fully recover mobility, because the female body has comparatively less muscle mass to draw on in reserve. This lower female reserve explains why breaking a bone is especially dangerous for women, which brings us to two age-related chronic conditions well known for their gender path—osteoporosis and hearing loss. [*See* CHRONIC ILLNESS ADJUSTMENT; DISABILITIES AND WOMEN.]

C. SPECIFIC GENDER-LINKED DISEASES

The skeletal disorder osteoporosis, caused by the progressive loss of density of the bones, affects both women and men. However, because their bones are smaller to begin with and the estrogen depletion at menopause accelerates the erosion, women, in particular small-boned European American and Asian American women, are especially vulnerable to this disease. (Other risk factors for osteoporosis include genetics, poor diet, and living a sedentary life.)

Osteoporosis causes the old age spinal deformity called dowagers' hump, which interferes with mobility and compresses the internal organs. Most important, osteoporosis can cause permanent disability because the fragile bones break under little or no stress. Hip fractures in old age are especially dangerous. In about one-quarter of cases they result in admission to a nursing home. In fact, impairments in lower body functioning along with dementia are the main risk factors for institutional care. By their late 60s, about one in five U.S. women show hipbone erosion serious enough to qualify as osteoporosis. In advanced old age, half of all women show this type of change. This is why, although it is not immediately life threatening, osteoporosis is such a well-publicized public health concern.

The media is more quiet about late-life hearing loss. But the age-related hearing disorder called presbycusis may have more of an impact on later-life health than osteoporosis because, as Table III shows, it is extremely prevalent, has its onset at a comparatively young age, and can have devastating effects on life. Although presbycusis also leads to ADL problems, its main toll is social and interpersonal. Because it limits one's ability to engage in that fundamental human activity—a conversation—poor hearing can lead to depression, impaired cognition, and especially isolation in old age. Moreover, because presbycusis is caused by the selective atrophy of the hearing receptors responsible for encoding high-pitched tones, this classic old-age hearing problem cannot be completely compensated for by wearing a hearing aid. Notice from Table III that males, particularly White men, are far more likely than women to develop hearing impairments, especially at younger ages. Although their greater vulnerability to vascular problems (which impairs blood flow to the auditory system) plays a role, the main reason is environmental. Noise damages the hearing receptors. Males are much more likely to be subjected to intense levels of occupational noise. People in those traditionally male industries, such as factory and construction jobs, often suffer from hearing difficulties even in midlife.

Government noise abatement regulations were passed in the 1980s to limit the amount of occupational noise. We might have expected these primary prevention measures and, more important, the dramatically declining fraction of American workers with factory jobs to reduce the prevalence of this disease. But for some reason (noise in the overall environment, perhaps) the rate of age-related hearing problems *rose* over 100% during the past two

decades in the United States. Medications and estrogen replacement therapy show promise of slowing the high rates of bone erosion that occur during the early post-menopausal years. But so far, other than prevention, there is little that can be done to stem the strangely silent epidemic of hearing loss among middle-aged and older men.

D. COGNITION

As we just saw, gender is a salient marker in discussing physical aging. Distinct male/female age patterns in cognitive pathways are not as clear-cut. However, by combining the findings of two landmark studies in cognitive aging, we can get tentative insights into the different intellectual pathways men and women follow as they travel through their older years. In K. Warner Schaie's pioneering Seattle Longitudinal Studies, begun in the early 1960s, in which adults were tested every seven years using Thurstone's test of primary mental abilities, heart disease was the main risk factor linked to excessive losses on every facet of intelligence in late middle age and early late life. In the more recent 1990s Berlin Aging Study, which comprehensively explored a wide array of abilities in people mainly over age 80, Paul Baltes' research team found a close link between sensory-motor capacities and intellectual performance. In particular, scores on tests of gait/balance, or lower body functioning, and vision are a remarkably good barometer of the quality of our thinking during the old-old years.

So, if we can generalize, their lower susceptibility to vascular disease gives women a cognitive edge earlier in life. In their 50s, 60s, and early 70s, females seem more resilient intellectually than males. In previous cohorts, this biological advantage was probably obscured by the gender differences in college attendance and occupational histories. Education correlates with late life cognitive resilience, as does working during ones younger years at a complex, intellectually demanding job. However, their vulnerability to visual and musculoskeletal problems puts women at special risk as they travel further up the age rungs. Interestingly, underlining the principle that females survive sicker, among the Berlin elderly, the women were $2\frac{1}{2}$ times more likely than the men to be classified in the "most dysfunctional" category, the group showing serious cognitive impairments as well as widespread deficits in every area of life.

In the same way as with physical ADL limitations, the risk of serious cognitive deficits accelerates in advanced old age. While during the 60s and early 70s a tiny percentage of people suffer from symptoms of dementia, over age 80 the fraction jumps. More than one in three Americans living outside of institutions has memory problems serious enough to qualify as a dementing disease. Although not everyone who lives to the century mark is destined to develop dementia, because it is the end point of normal brain aging, as people inch close to this ultimate human limit, their odds of developing this condition are very high. For instance, by their 90s, 60% of the Berlin elderly had clear-cut psychiatric diagnoses of this disease. Their greater vulnerability to artery problems puts men at higher risk of developing Vascular dementia, the more stepwise type of dementia caused by small strokes. Women are more likely to suffer from Alzheimer's disease, the illness caused by the deterioration of the neurons themselves. Postmenopausal estrogen loss may be partly responsible for the fact that females face roughly twice the risk of developing Alzheimer's as males. However, the main reason, once again, is that women survive longer and thus are more physically impaired for a longer time. In fact, as Table III shows, by their old-old years, women also often have vascular problems. When the actual symptoms of dementia erupt, both vascular and neural deterioration is often involved.

A final note: despite its other benefits, as of this writing, there is *no clear evidence,* at least in humans, that estrogen replacement can postpone postmenopausal age declines in memory and reasoning, prevent the onset of Alzheimer's disease, or affect the course of that illness once a woman is diagnosed with this disease.

E. LIFE STYLE CONSEQUENCES

Table IV spells out the life consequences of surviving longer while more frail. Women are more likely to spend time living alone in the community and coping with ADL problems. On average they live for about a decade as widows; they have a far higher risk of entering nursing homes. Females make up the overwhelming majority of the residents in long-term care. On the other hand, women have advantages when confronting these hardships that their survivorship confers. Although, as we will see, both sexes tend to become depressed when they develop these impairments, the physical reversals of old age seem more difficult emotionally for men. Men have less practice with being dependent and out of control, so they lack the coping skills that females' help seeking and caregiving practices provide. The fact that women are more embedded in relationships also serves as an emotional cushion in confronting the dependencies of old age. Interestingly, this female interpersonal superiority in the face of greater physical decline is accentuated by the actual gender pattern of age-related chronic diseases. Notice that the male old age problem, hearing loss, takes its toll mainly

Table IV

Three Important Life Consequences for Women of Surviving Longer While More Frail

---

Living alone and having trouble coping is a more probable path

In 1997 in the 75–84 age group, almost half of all U.S. community-dwelling women lived alone. By age 85+, the figure was more than 60%. Moreover, beyond this age, about half of this female noninstitutional population report at least one life activity, such as housework, as being "difficult."

Being widowed is a genuine life-state

In 1997, about one in four U.S. women aged 75–84 in the community was still living with her spouse. By 85+ the figure dipped to less than 10% (compared to more than half of all men in this same age). The tendency to marry men a few years older plus their longevity advantage suggests that the typical woman can expect to outlive her husband by about a decade.

Living in a nursing home is a more likely event

In 1985, 4.6% of the U.S. population over 65 lived in nursing homes. Women comprised about three-fourths of this group. Among the age group over 85, the fraction jumps to 22% and women make up more than 80% of the residents in long-term care. Moreover, researchers estimate that once she has reached age 65, a U.S. woman's odds of entering long-term care at least *at some point* before she dies are higher than 50/50.

Sources: The concrete statistics in this list were derived from data compiled by the U.S. Bureau of the Census (1997 population reports) and the National Aging Information Center of the Administration on Aging (1997).

on relationships, while female chronic illnesses require reaching out to others for help in handling life!

III. *Personality and Mental Health*

The previous discussion suggests that men and women adjust differently to the aging process. Is there a gender difference in personality and mental health in the second half of adult life? Answers come from exploring two lines of research: studies probing age changes in personality and epidemiological investigations exploring the prevalence of mental disorders at different times of life.

A. MIDLIFE PERSONALITY DEVELOPMENT

In the pioneering 1950s Kansas City studies that launched the study of adult personality development, the central finding related to gender and midlife change was that men and women become more androgynous, or "cross over" to adopt the traits of the opposite sex at the empty nest. According to psychologist David Gutmann, traditional gender roles are important in the first half of adulthood because of what he calls the parental imperative. Optimal child rearing requires a division of labor in which one partner assertively provides for the family and the other performs the nurturing role. Once children have left the nest, women "reclaim" the masculine qualities they had dampened down to ensure their children's development. Men relax, giving play to their softer, more "female" side.

Gutmann's influential theory about gender and aging makes intuitive sense. It dovetails with phenomena from the male age-related declines in testosterone and sexual potency, to the female midlife marker called menopause, to the unflattering image of the old woman as harpy or witch that, as Gutmann's cross-cultural surveys reveal, has been a staple myth in cultures around the world. However, after decades of research, the data supporting a gender crossover is flimsy. For one thing, women's caregiver orientation does not evaporate at the onset of the empty nest. It is resilient and lifelong, extending into the postmenopausal years. Studies supporting the shift to androgyny were carried out in a more traditional era with middle-class European American women and men. Distinct personality differences between the sexes are hard to pinpoint at any time of life in our current multicultural, less gender-defined age. Moreover, there is no consensus on what qualities being androgynous actually entail. Finally, notice that Guttmann's parental imperative conjures up images of the breadwinner father and homemaker mother, a vanishing family form.

Actually, the evidence that personality remains stable as we travel though life is more compelling than the data showing that men and women change in *any* specific way with age. In landmark 1980s studies using a five-factor model of personality, Paul Costa conclusively showed that basic personality traits such as extroversion, openness to experience, and neuroticism stay fairly stable from youth to old age. However, given that "who we are as people" endures, growth and development over time is a heartening minor chord. For instance, in a 1990s study exploring dimensions of well-being such as feelings of competence, autonomy, and control among adults of different ages, Carol Ryff found that the middle years rank as a high point in life. Moreover, the women's movement has been beneficial for midlife female mental health. In following graduates of an elite college for women (Mills College), researchers found increases in competence and well-being from their 20s through their 50s. This led the authors of this study to label the empty nest as women's "prime of life." But, the message of this study and others is that for women the historical context is critically important in promoting this age-related growth. The Mills parent generation who reached their 50s before the women's movement reported lower feelings of confidence and decreased well-being at the same point in life. [*See* MIDLIFE TRANSITIONS.]

B. LATER-LIFE MENTAL HEALTH

Many of the best designed longitudinal studies tracing personality over decades end at the 50s. It is also important to emphasize that the message of midlife as "life's prime" applies to *advantaged women* because in recent decades there has been a feminine tilt to studies exploring adult personality change. However, researchers are now supplementing information derived from following women attending elite colleges such as Mills and so extending the growth and development theme to both sexes and older ages. Cross-national surveys show that, despite being disadvantaged along dimensions ranging from wealth to health, people over age 65 in virtually every country report just as high life satisfaction as younger adults. Recent (albeit cross-sectional) studies in the United States go one step further. They suggest that, because over the years we learn to manage our emotions better, well-being is at its peak in late life. The encouraging message that age brings better mental health gains real weight when we consider data on psychiatric disorder rates. The National Comorbidity Study (NCS) and the Epidemiological Catchment Area Study (ECA), the two major late 20th-century U.S. surveys of these problems, both pinpointed the early 20s as the time of life when mental disorders are at their height. The fall off in prevalence is especially steep for substance abuse. But the finding of lower illness rates, especially after mid-life, extends to *every* psychiatric disorder (with the exception of dementia). It even is apparent for depression, that classic problem people traditionally have linked with being old. In the ECA study, the well-known pattern showing that women face more than twice the risk of developing this disorder remained. However, rates of major depression were substantially lower among both women and men over age 65.

There are qualifications. These surveys used the stringent DSM (diagnostic manual) definition of this psychiatric disorder. Dysphoria or subclinical depressive symptoms are very common in later life. Most important, the ECA study lumped together all people over 65. As we saw in our earlier discussion, the old-old are a qualitatively different group. In fact, over age 80, rates of depression do accelerate and gender differences may blur. Both men and women are at high risk for developing this disorder, particularly when they experience the kinds of ADL problems that warrant nursing home care.

Finally, there is one disturbing epidemiological gender finding that paints a much less rosy portrait of late life mental health. Elderly males commit suicide at almost twice the rate of every other U.S. group. The prevalence of suicide over age 85 among European American males is genuinely alarming. One likely reason is that, as was suggested earlier, for men, particularly those accustomed to being at the top of the social hierarchy, old age dependencies are a devastating emotional blow. But an equally likely cause has to do with relationships. By this time in life many men are widowed. It is emotionally and socially harder for men in advanced old age to find a new mate. This brings us to that final area where our gender shapes our aging path—in our relationships and roles. [*See* DEPRESSION; DIAGNOSIS OF PSYCHOLOGICAL DISORDERS.]

IV. Relationships and Roles

A. MARRIAGE, WIDOWHOOD, AND FRIENDSHIPS

Although the specific health advantages of marriage may have declined in recent decades now that such a high fraction of people are living outside of that state, the gender pattern endures: being married or having a partner is especially beneficial for men. This seems especially true in later life. Although the ranks of divorced older people are rapidly increasing, widowhood is still the number one cause of relationship loss in later life. So to make this case, we turn mainly to research on the death of a spouse.

In predicting how people adjust to being widowed, it is critical to adopt a contextual approach. Economic status, life options, being an immigrant, ethnicity, previous experience with living alone (i.e., through divorce), the quality of one's marriage, age, and especially ones enduring personality are just a few of the complex forces that shape how a particular woman or man reacts to this life stress. Many longitudinal studies show no gender differences in spousal bereavement at all. However, in addition to the alarming suicide rates in advanced old age, there are clear signs that, unless they remarry or find a new partner, men suffer more severe problems after their spouse dies. Although its prevalence normally declines steeply after youth, alcoholism rates among elderly widowers are unusually high. In fact, among widows and widowers, the gender imbalance in depression is reversed. Older widowers have higher rates of depression than older widows do.

The most tantalizing research shedding light on the emotional importance of being married for aging men comes from studies of emotion regulation touched on in the previous section. In a 1998 investigation probing these emotions at different times of adult life among several thousand U.S. adults, the researchers found, consonant with the growth and development theme, that negative affect steadily declined for males and positive affect rose from youth to the early 70s for both sexes. But the age decline in unpleasant emotions *only* occurred among married men, not those without a spouse. In other words, marriage may be an important life context shaping age-related emotional growth, but only for males.

Another line of evidence suggesting men need marriage more than women as they age involves that well-known gender difference in the ability to form connections with friends. Friendships are highly associated with late life mental health. In fact, close friends, more than family ties, predict well-being in old age; the truism that women have closer friendships seems even truer in old age. In one comparative study, the researchers found that while males withdrew from friends as they traveled into their old-old years, female friendships endured. Not only do women preserve their very closest friends as they age and develop disabilities, but they also draw on these widowed friends for instrumental (concrete) help after their spouse dies. This widow-to-widow caregiving has limits. It is *family members* who are the lifeline when older people require ongoing ADL help. However, the fact that the male/female "friend chasm" may widen in old age spells special vulnerability for elderly men. [*See* FRIENDSHIP STYLES.]

Once again there are cautions. These studies were conducted with the older traditional cohort. The late-life male bonding experience may be different among the new "sensitive" baby boom men. Moving in and out of marriage may make this new cohort of males more resilient emotionally to losing a spouse in their older years. Women who are unusually dependent on their husbands for instrumental help have a great deal of difficulty coping with widowhood. And, men do have two clear advantages in confronting this central life loss. They do not suffer the economic reversals of widows, and, of course, they are far more likely to find a new partner after their wife dies. This brings up another topic relating to relationships with a distinctive gender path—sex.

B. SEXUALITY

Sexuality is the area of life where the principle of female social superiority amidst greater physical decline is reversed. As Table V shows, males decline more than females in their physiological sexual capacities with age. However, women are more socially isolated sexually during their aging years. The gender gap in sexual interest and activity that begins at puberty widens after midlife. Women report less sexual interest and lower rates of intercourse than men do at each comparable older age. For instance, in the

only epidemiological study of U.S. adult sexuality, the 1990s National Opinion Research Center (NORC) poll, among the age group in their 50s, two in three men reported regularly having intercourse several times a month in the previous year or several times a week. More than half of the women the same age reported having heterosexual intercourse only a few times that year or less often. In fact, in the 50s the largest fraction of the female sample—30% of respondents—reported not having had any sex at all.

Being rendered partnerless by widowhood, divorce, or having an ill spouse is the event that is likely to spell the end of a woman's sexual life. Physical problems, especially vascular disease, diabetes, prostate conditions, and the sexual side effects of medications, are the main barriers to sexuality for older men. Some women do continue to enjoy regular heterosexual sexual relations well into old age. An unknown (probably miniscule) percentage of contemporary older women may either remain in enduring sexually active lesbian relationships or turn to a female partner in later life for their sexual needs. However, the male preference for younger mates, women's greater numbers, their tendency to marry older men, and, most important, society's *continuing* messages that they are no longer physically appealing almost certainly doom many females to spend a significant portion of their adult lives without having any sex.

C. FAMILY CAREGIVING

The life expectancy revolution plus the explosion of female headed families has embedded aging women more deeply into that other gender-linked job—care-

Table V

Physiological Sexual Changes with Age

Midlife changes in the male sexual system	Midlife changes in the female sexual system
1. Erections take longer to develop, and once achieved are more apt to be lost.	In response to the loss of estrogen, after menopause the vagina shortens, the vaginal walls become more fragile, and lubrication becomes less copious. The main impact of these changes is to make intercourse more painful, not reduce a woman's capacity to become aroused or achieve orgasm.
2. Orgasms are less explosive. Older men experience a seepage of fluid during ejaculation.	
3. Penile deflation after orgasm is more rapid.	
4. The refractory period, or interval required for sexual activity, lengthens. By the 50s, after ejaculation, men typically cannot achieve another erection and reach orgasm for 12 to 24 hours.	
5. Manual stimulation is more likely to be required to achieve an erection and orgasm.	

giving. Women are likely to care for their spouse because he typically precedes them in illness and death. The late 20th-century declines in heart disease mortality in particular translate into more men living to ages where they encounter the kinds of ADL difficulties that require extended care. Married couples, *both men and women,* are apt to shoulder this caregiving job alone. They tend not to rely on their children or formal sources of help. For emotional and financial reasons (the assets of *both* partners are quickly depleted), even when a spouse needs this intervention, husbands and wives are often reluctant to contemplate nursing home care.

While the gender tilt to spousal caregiving lies mainly in the fact that women outlive men, this is not the case with parent care. Although sons do take on this responsibility if there are no other siblings, they are the only child who lives close by, and the care recipient is male, it is daughters or other female relatives who typically provide ongoing help when the older generation needs daily ADL care.

How common and how burdensome is this typically female role? Although parent care is far from universal, it is a more normative contemporary experience for older women today. In one 1990s New York State poll, by their later 50s to early 60s two-thirds of the women reported having provided some parent care. In another genuinely representative survey (The 1987 National Survey of Families and Households), one in five women aged 35 to 65 reported *currently* providing some form of regular care to a family member, most often a parent, who was chronically ill. Unfortunately, studies consistently show that women experience more psychiatric symptoms when thrust into this care-provider role. One reason for this gender split may lie in the enduring female propensity to experience negative affect. Women *in general* report higher levels of daily distress and are much more susceptible to depression than men. However, some of the excess morbidity is specific to the care-providing experience itself. Women take on heavier daily caregiving responsibilities. They are less comfortable about utilizing formal help. They get less interpersonal support than men when providing parent care because they are performing an expected "female job." Being more reactive to relationship issues, they may feel more overwhelmed by the distressing interactions that adult-to-adult family care provokes. However, emerging research suggests that a major problem is role overload. If women do not feel pressed in two many different directions when providing care, the experience is more apt to be a positive one.

In recent years there has been considerable publicity about "women in the middle," empty nest women providing care to the family's older and younger rungs. The true prevalence of women in this situation is small. A more typical reason for the feelings of overload may lie in being pulled between the demands of a career and often needing to give up working, or, in her 60s and 70s, when a woman feels pressed between her marital responsibilities and the need to provide parent care. However, while the frazzled image of women juggling the demands of older and younger generations does not often fit reality, hands-on grandparenthood has become a more common role.

Once again, it is hard to generalize about grandparents. The diverse contemporary family, the less gendered nature of society, plus that fact that women and men now enter this "older" role for half of adult life, has produced a dazzling array of grandparent styles. However, gender is one salient dimension that shapes the experience of grandparenthood. Women are typically more physically and emotionally involved with their grandchildren than men. Due to the matrifocal tilt of the family (and because they tend to be the youngest in the grandparent set), maternal grandmothers are especially intensely involved. This is particularly true if a woman lives near her daughter and—very important—has a close relationship with that female child. The fraction of grandparents providing daily care to grandchildren has also escalated as a function of the legions of women with young children who work outside the home. When there is an intact two-parent family, this ongoing care usually involves regular baby sitting and some financial help. However, grandparents, particularly grandmothers, take on heavier instrumental responsibilities when a daughter is a single parent or during times of crisis such as a child's divorce.

Although once again its prevalence has been exaggerated, more grandparents are now taking *primary* responsibility for a grandchild's care. From 1970 to 1997, the fraction of grandparent-headed households rose over 76% in the United States. In that year, 6.7% of U.S. children were living in this family form. Grandparent-headed households are most prevalent among African Americans. Usually at least one parent in these families, typically the mother, is living in the house. But in more than a third of these cases, the parents are absent and the older generation has sole custody of the child. Grandmothers in this situation (in 1997 about 14% of this total U.S. group) are in the worst straits. The tiny fraction of solo grandfather families did rise during the 1990s. However, the unfortunate fact is that the most at-risk people—very poor women in the poorest health—are the still the group most likely to be taking on this most demanding family job. [See WORK–FAMILY BALANCE.]

D. RETIREMENT

The increasing diversity of work pathways among both sexes also translates into more trouble making retirement generalizations about women and men. Everyone—both male and female—tends to adjust well to this life transition. Although retiring well before age 65 is the norm, blurred workforce transitions in which people leave the labor force gradually or return to work after retiring are becoming more common among both females and males.

However, fascinating married couple retirement comparisons highlight the enduring gender dimension of late 20th century older family roles. Data from the National Survey of Families and Households shows that if a husband is retired and his wife still works full time, the man steps in to do more than half of the housework. But once both spouses retire, the standard gender pattern reasserts itself. Even though *neither partner* is working, the woman assumes the traditional household chores. Moreover, married women often time their retirement decisions to fit their spouse's retirement timetable. Because the man's assets tend to be higher, it is her husband's pension and benefits that are apt to influence when a married woman retires.

Actually, because of their more tenuous workforce status, the U.S. female retirement experience tends to mirror that of other disadvantaged minority groups. As is true for Hispanic and African American males, involuntary retirement due to joblessness is more common among late middle-aged women. Moving in and out of the labor force, plus being in lower-paying jobs, means women are far less likely to retire with pensions. They have comparatively lower Social Security benefits when they leave a job.

There are some caveats. Women with comparable work histories do retire with the same assets as men. As is true for males, females who are highly work oriented and more in need of money try to work longer into old age. Moreover, these male/female differences in retirement pathways apply *only* to European American adults. African American labor force

patterns do not differ much by gender. Both men and women in this ethnic group are equally disadvantaged with regard to pensions and other income sources when they retire.

E. ECONOMIC STATUS

In fact, just as clear-cut ethnic differences in economic status persist into the retirement years, the feminization of poverty applies at every age. However, it has its most dramatic consequences at the end of life. Old-old women are more likely to be living in poverty than *any* other group, including single mothers. Why is falling into poverty such a likely pathway for women when they live to advanced old age?

One reason is that, just as with divorce, after being widowed women suffer a loss in income because, although they still get their husband's social security, other spousal money can dry up. Interestingly, however, researchers trace the onset of this economic loss to the months before actually being widowed, as the soon-to-be single person's assets are eaten up by the health care costs incurred by having a seriously ill spouse. When we add this earlier late life blow to extended years of postretirement living and her own even more serious subsequent old-age health care bills, it is no wonder that even if a woman enters her 60s upper-middle class and married, she is likely to end her older years poor. And, because of their different work histories, single women begin their retirement years already at an economic disadvantage compared to men!

V. Final Thoughts

Baby boom women and men are approaching late life with unparalleled resources. Their midlife pathways seem so positive. All signs point to the fact that this will be the first cohort in history where the phrase "golden years" really rings true. Population aging has already dramatically altered our cultural priorities. From the intense attention to modifying so-called inevitable old-age handicaps such as osteoporosis and erectile problems, to creative alternatives to institutionalization, to new apartment-like nursing homes, the postindustrialized world is finally squarely confronting—and dealing constructively with—the realities of *being* old. Breathtaking advances in the genetics of aging may soon make even these interventions obsolete. At some point in this century, we will almost certainly have the tools to lengthen the human life span and permit people to live to advanced old age relatively disability-free. However, keeping this positive underpinning in mind, we conclude by highlighting the main problems facing each sex as this huge new cohort travels into old age.

A. FOR BABY BOOM WOMEN

Sexuality (and finding an intimate partner), economic problems, and dealing with old-age disabilities are enduring concerns. Despite giving lip service to the idea that elderly women are sexual, there are no signs that the cultural zeitgeist has shifted from prizing looks and female youth. Cross-national surveys consistently show physical appearance is by far the main correlate of human self-esteem. Comparative cross-cohort U.S. data suggest that among contemporary young adults "looks" looms larger than ever in importance in selecting a mate. These findings do not bode well for baby boom females' chances of finding a sexual partner in later life. Another ominous earlier adult sign for this group lies in the gender income gap due to single parenthood. Old age poverty will be even more likely among baby boom women because a higher fraction of this cohort are entering late life divorced. Finally, there is the fact that elderly females both live poorer and more physically impaired. Formal caregiving services for older people with disabilities are paid for out-of-pocket. Alternatives to nursing homes are often only available to U.S. elderly with considerable means. Now couple this societal reality with the declining pool of family caregivers produced by the drop in late 20th century fertility plus a higher fraction of single parent daughters who *must* work full-time. What will happen to the millions of baby boom women (and men) who will need ongoing help coping with ADL problems in advanced old age?

B. FOR BABY BOOM MEN

Isolation from family relationships and family caregiving help are emerging concerns. While their experience with divorce *may* provide resilience to being widowed, this event also presents hazards to baby boom men. It weakens what gerontologists call the filial imperative, the moral duty to provide for one's parents in old age. As should come as no surprise, researchers find that children are not as willing to provide parent care to a father who has not been present during their childhood to care for them. So the smaller cushion of child caregivers may have its most ominous consequences for the large cohort of divorced baby boom men entering old age. Moreover, since having a partner may be a special life context fostering age-related growth for males, living partnerless even periodically might produce poorer late-life mental and physical health. It may accentuate the male risk of isolation in old age. In other words, for both sexes the impact of the divorce and single parent revolution does not end earlier in life—it will continue to reverberate well into the older years.

SUGGESTED READING

BOOKS

Masoro, E., and Austad, S. (2001). *Handbook of the Biology of Aging,* Fifth edition. Academic Press, San Diego.

Birren, J., and Schaie, K. W. (2001). *Handbook of the Psychology of Aging,* Fifth edition. Academic Press, San Diego.

Binstock, R., and George, L. (2001). *Handbook of Aging and the Social Sciences,* Fifth edition. Academic Press, San Diego.

These three edited reference works in gerontology, published every six years or so, offer authoritative overview chapters of the latest research in these domains.

Lachman, M., and James, J. P. (eds). (1997). *Multiple Paths of Mid-life Development.* University of Chicago Press, Chicago.

This edited book showcasing 1990s studies probing personality change during midlife, illustrates the creative ways used to probe midlife personality development (mainly in women).

Willis, S., and Reid J. D. (eds). (1999). *Life in the Middle: Psychological and Social Development in Middle Age.* Academic Press, San Diego.

This edited book offers an authoritative review of research on all aspects of midlife.

JOURNALS

Journals of Gerontology, A and B, and *The Gerontologist*

These journals, published by The Gerontological Society of America, are the leading outlets for research in the field. *Journal of Gerontology A* covers biomedical research; *Journal of Gerontology B* covers research in the social sciences. *The Gerontologist* covers more applied practice-oriented aging research.

Generations

Each issue of this provocative, policy-oriented journal published by The American Society on Aging covers a timely gerontological topic in depth. Recent late 1990s gender-relevant topics include the financial aspects of aging, grandparenthood, and baby boomer aging.

Psychology and Aging

This is the premier journal covering basic research in the psychology of adult development and aging, published by the American Psychological Association.

Women and Aging

This publication by Haworth Press is the only journal specifically devoted to research on women and aging.

Agoraphobia, Panic Disorder, and Gender

Iris Fodor

Jamie Epstein

New York University

Glossary

Agoraphobia "Anxiety about, or avoidance of, places or situations from which escape might be difficult (or embarrassing) or in which help may not be available in the event of having an unexpected or situationally predisposed panic attack or panic-like symptoms. Agoraphobic fears typically involve characteristic clusters of situations that include being outside the home alone; being in a crowd or standing in a line; being on a bridge; and traveling in a bus, train, or automobile" (*DSM-IV*, American Psychiatric Association, 1994. p. 396). Situations eliciting distress are to be avoided given the anxiety about panic attacks and often a companion's presence is required.

Panic Panic disorder represents "recurrent unexpected (out of the blue) panic attacks with no situational trigger. . . . There are persistent concerns about having additional attacks and a change in behavior related to the attacks." Panic attacks feature "a discrete period of intense fear or discomfort, on which four (or more) of the following symptoms develop abruptly and reached a peak with 10 minutes" (p. 395, *DSM-IV*, American Psychiatric Association, 1994).

Bodily and psychological symptoms of panic include the experiences of pounding heart, sweating, trembling or shaking, shortness of breath, smothering, choking, chest pain, nausea, dizziness, unsteadiness and lightheadedness. In addition there may be feelings of depersonalization, fear of losing control or going insane, fear of dying, tingling, hot flashes, or chills.

AGORAPHOBIA—the fear of being out in the world—has become the most common and debilitating phobic disorder since it was first documented by Westphal in 1871. In fact, agoraphobic individuals represent half of the phobic population, with recent surveys suggesting that agoraphobia may affect many more individuals than are currently identified, crossing all classes and ethnic groups. Until recently, however, clinicians and researchers alike have not focused on gender issues. Regardless of whether clinical or community samples are considered, the chance of an agoraphobia diagnosis is about four times higher for women than for men. This article focuses on agoraphobia, as well as its latest variant panic disorder. Agoraphobia is a representative anxiety disorder that has high prevalence among women and has been the locus of a biological versus psychological etiology debate among contemporary researchers and clinicians. We will survey the clinical, research, and theoretical literature on the relationship between agoraphobia, panic, and gender highlighting the agoraphobic syndrome, its relation to panic disorder, and common characteristics, triggers, and onset. Given that agoraphobia is considered a "women's syndrome," we will utilize a feminist framework, highlighting sex-role socialization variables and social learning theory in an attempt to understand the gender disparity, as well appraise current research on the most effective treatment.

I. *Agoraphobia: An Overview*

In 1949, William Terhune described an agoraphobic woman who was chronically anxious and feared death or sudden illness if she went out in the street, on trains, in cars, or to the theater or church. She had reached the point at which she could not perform any of her duties and was helpless. Her husband had to remain home with her, and even then she continued to be frightened. His description a half century ago is still typical for today's agoraphobic individuals. Most agoraphobic people are women (75%): the problem begins when they are in their 20s, and their symptoms may immobilize them, keeping them dependent and confined to the home throughout their life.

During the past 25 years there has been a rapid increase in the research, theoretical and clinical literature on anxiety disorders, agoraphobia, and panic disorders. Generally, there has been a shift from viewing agoraphobia as a variant of anxiety neurosis to a more behaviorally based anxiety avoidant disorder and even more recently to a view of agoraphobia as linked to panic disorder.

Psychoanalysts from Freud on viewed agoraphobia as representing an anxiety neurosis with neurotic conflicts. In the 1960 through the 1980s, the major writers and researchers following Joseph Wolpe's pioneering work in behavior therapy viewed agoraphobic symptoms as variants of learned avoidance behaviors. They made major contributions to the clinical and research understanding and treatment of agoraphobia. With the advent of cognitive behavior therapy, developed by Albert Ellis and Aaron Beck, the cognitive aspects of agoraphobia were highlighted. In particular, catastrophic thinking and the "fear of fear" were featured as eliciting panic and driving the avoidance behaviors by such authors as Dianne Chambless, Alan Goldstein, and David Clark. At the same time, another shift occurred: biologically oriented psychiatrists, Donald Klein among others, presented strong evidence for a biological basis for agoraphobia emphasizing the sudden panic component of the disorder, which support pharmacological treatments.

II. *Agoraphobia and Panic Disorder: DSM-IV*

The debate over the etiology of agoraphobia can best be seen in the shifts in the American Psychiatric Associations (APA) diagnostic descriptions over the past three decades. The changing diagnostic framework reflected the shift in membership on the panels from a more psychoanalytic perspective in the 1960s to increased representation of the behavior, cognitive, and biological points of view.

The American Psychiatric Association in 1968 placed phobias in the category of anxiety neuroses and proposed a psychodynamic etiology. In the 1970s and 1980s, with attention to agoraphobia by behavioral and cognitive behavioral researchers, a more cognitive behavioral diagnosis of agoraphobia was featured stressing the learned avoidance characteristics of agoraphobia. However, as the biological perspective gained prominence, a debate over psychological versus biological triggers resulted in two categories for what had been viewed as one disorder. By 1994, the American Psychiatric Association's diagnostic manual no longer featured a single diagnosis of agoraphobia, but two variants, one with and one without accompanying panic disorder, as well a separate diagnostic category for panic disorder. This distinction between agoraphobia with or without accompanying panic disorder has influenced the research and writing on agoraphobia since that time, with most of the numerous books and articles featuring panic in the title.

Panic disorder is described in the *DSM-IV* as representing "recurrent unexpected (out of the blue) panic attacks with no situational trigger with persistent concerns about having additional attacks and a change in behavior related to the attacks." Panic attacks feature "a discrete period of intense fear or discomfort, on which four (or more) of the following symptoms develop abruptly and reached a peak with 10 minutes" (p. 395). These bodily and psychological symptoms include the experiences of pounding heart, sweating, trembling or shaking, shortness of breath, smothering, choking, chest pain, nausea, dizziness, unsteadiness, and lightheadedness. In addition there may be feelings of depersonalization, fear of losing control, or going insane, fear of dying, tingling, hot flashes, or chills. [*See* ANXIETY; DIAGNOSIS OF PSYCHOLOGICAL DISORDERS.]

Most of the clinical and research reports on agoraphobia prior to 1994 emphasized the avoidance features, while after that time the writers tended to feature panic and either compare and contrast or combine the two disorders in their clinical writing and research. For the most part, cognitive behavioral writers and researchers, who are mainly psychologists, have tended to view these two disorders as integrated, while the more biologically oriented psychiatrists have focused on panic and the bodily based symptoms as central.

III. Clinical Characteristics of the Agoraphobic Syndrome

An adaptation and expansion of the framework provided by Alan Goldstein and Dianne Chambless in 1982 gave an extensive description of the core clinical features of the agoraphobic syndrome, which have informed most cognitive treatment programs and provides a framework for discussing gender issues.

This framework features "fear of fear" as a central premise. Agoraphobic individuals are afraid of becoming anxious or panicking. They are fearful that when they are anxious, physical symptoms will emerge in a manner that is out of control. To ward off the fear, they engage in avoidance behaviors. What they fear most are not the feared objects themselves (closed spaces, etc.), but they fear the feelings

that might emerge from being trapped in these situations. They fear most becoming hysterical (out of control) and manifesting the physical symptoms (dizziness, hyperventilation, and nausea) with no help or escape available. Avoidance helps them maintain control.

Additionally, agoraphobic individuals also suffer a lack in the development of self-sufficiency. They usually rely on a significant other to be with them most of the time. They exhibit "anxious attachment, " or anxiety about not being adequately taken care of. Another aspect of the lack of self-sufficiency is the lack of skills to control themselves when they panic or try to negotiate the world as adults. They also demonstrate an inability to solve problems when stressed. They often exhibit a mislabeling of emotions. They fear arousal and show a tendency to overgeneralize and to label most arousal as anxiety or panic. Furthermore, persons with agoraphobic symptoms show poor discrimination of others' feelings (particularly anger). They are also reported to have widespread lack of assertiveness. They cannot express angry feelings or take risks in interpersonal confrontation, since there is likelihood that such expression elicits anxiety, and anxiety must be avoided at all costs. Control is a central issue for persons with agoraphobia. They fear loss of control during anxiety attacks and try to maintain control over themselves by controlling their significant other to be with them. Self-esteem is linked to control. It is high when they feel in control and low when they feel out of control. [*See* SELF-ESTEEM.]

IV. Agoraphobia and Panic Disorder: Gender Questions

After the *DSM-IV* was published in 1994, most of the research and clinical studies did not differentiate between agoraphobia with and without panic disorder, since panic attacks were a prominent feature of the disorder. While women were always reported to be in the majority in reported case studies in the literature, and a small number of feminist writers espoused a feminist approach to agoraphobia, until recently there has not been much interest in gender differences. What is surprising, given the thousands of articles and dozen of books published on agoraphobia and panic disorder in the past 20 years, is how little attention has been paid to gender as a feature of the syndrome. Most of the books, except for mentioning the high prevalence rates for women, ignore the topic, and almost none of the research attends to gender differences. Additionally, with a few exceptions, almost no attention has been paid to cultural variations or ethnic and racial differences. Agoraphobia and panic disorder are mainly described in Western cultures. Richard McNally, who reviews cross culture issues for panic disorders, cites a paucity of research on this syndrome in Asian or African cultures.

In the past decade, there have been a few large clinical research studies conducted mainly in the United States and England that have specially addressed gender issues in agoraphobia and panic disorder. While the handful of feminist writers who address clinical issues from a gender perspective are psychologists surveying the psychological literature and using case illustrations, these large research studies were mainly conducted by teams of psychiatrists using symptom check lists on surveys of hospital patient populations.

Given that women are overrepresented in clinic and community populations reporting agoraphobia and panic attacks, to further understand gender issues relevant to the agoraphobic syndrome, we need to ask the following questions. Why does agoraphobia develop (etiology)? Are the roots familial, cultural, or biological? Why are females more prone to agoraphobic symptoms? Where are the men? Are specific features of the disorder more prominent in women than men or visa versa? What are the risk factors associated with the development of agoraphobia and the gender ratio? What are the immediate triggers, the stressors that elicit the symptoms? What are the various theoretical approaches to understanding agoraphobia and gender variables? Given all of these considerations, what is the most effective treatment?

A. PREVALENCE RATES AND GENDER DIFFERENCES

Epidemiological studies have been mainly conducted on Western populations. These studies report that agoraphobia without a history of panic occurs in 5% of the population in the United States. Women are three times more likely than men to have agoraphobic symptoms and are twice as likely to have panic attacks with or without agoraphobia. However, the ratio may differ in other cultures. For example, Richard McNally (1994) in his survey of cultural factors in panic disorders reported on a study in India that suggested that 85% of agoraphobic

patients in that culture are men. Because women do not leave home alone in India and in other eastern and Middle East cultures, panic and agoraphobic symptoms may appear only for men.

From clinical studies of male and female agoraphobics in Western cultures, men and women report a similar pattern of panic attacks, while women reported more agoraphobic avoidance symptoms. One big difference, however, is that men with panic disorder report a high rate of alcoholism. Also, the more the men used alcohol, the lower the rate of agoraphobic avoidance symptoms. For men, alcohol appears to be a strategy to combat anxiety and panic.

Panic disorder with agoraphobia appears to be a more severe disorder in women than men. Women report more severe agoraphobic avoidance when facing situations or places, are more afraid of leaving home alone or staying home alone, and report more bodily sensations than men. In addition, compared to men, they report more catastrophic thoughts and higher scores on fear surveys. Women are also less likely to be employed full time than men.

Many more women than men are diagnosed with other anxiety disorders and symptoms of depression. Many agoraphobic women are also found to have post-traumatic stress disorder (as high as 23% in one study).

B. MALE UNDERREPRESENTATION IN RESEARCH POPULATIONS OF AGORAPHOBIC PERSONS

Are men underrepresented in samples of agoraphobic persons? In general, gender differences with respect to the incidence of agoraphobia have been derived from men and women in studies of help-seeking behavior or from reports in research based on community samples in Western cultures. Since both sources of information rely on self-report measures, they may be considered subjective and may not accurately represent the true agoraphobic population. It has been argued that traditional masculine sex-role stereotypes make it more difficult for men to openly admit their feelings of agoraphobic anxiety, since compared to women, men are expected to be stronger and braver. Alan Goldstein in 1987, the director of Temple University's Agoraphobia and Anxiety Program, has proposed that male agoraphobics may find it difficult to seek out help because most Western cultures "teach men to be self-sufficient and not admit to having fears." He reported that "many men will only come for treatment when their lives are seriously disrupted by panic attacks, often to the point where they are threatened by the loss of their family or employment" (p. 145). Hence, it is not known how many more men than women fail to be diagnosed as agoraphobics because of a masculine reluctance to admit anxiety.

C. MEN AND ALCOHOL

A second source of potential sex-ratio bias involves the relationship between sex-role stereotypes and the use of alcohol as a coping mechanism for anxiety symptoms. Excessive use of alcohol may distract diagnosticians, and patients themselves, from the seriousness of the agoraphobic syndromes. Matt Kushner, Kenneth Abrams, and Carrie Borchardt in 2001 compiled a review of the relationship between anxiety disorders and alcohol use. In one research study, many of the male patients who were treated for alcoholism had severe, disabling agoraphobia, anxiety, and other social phobias. In another, there were research reports that found that 21% of outpatient agoraphobics were alcoholic (18% of the women and 36% of the men).

In a study that explored alcohol use in agoraphobic patients, the males were found to report more alcohol use and to view alcohol as an effective strategy for coping with anxiety problems compared to females. Some researchers suggest that alcohol has the potential to interact with clinical anxiety in a circular fashion, resulting in an upward spiral of both anxiety and problem drinking. [*See* SUBSTANCE ABUSE.]

D. EMPLOYMENT

Another variable relevant to the sex ratio of disclosed agoraphobics is employment. Cultural expectations may put added pressure on men to go outside the home and keep a job. It may be easier for women homemakers than for employed men to avoid being out in public. One may ask if unemployment is a risk factor for becoming agoraphobic, rather than a consequence of the disorder? There is some evidence to suggest that the onset of agoraphobia often precedes unemployment. In one study, researchers found that prior to the onset of agoraphobia, the employment rate for a sample of agoraphobics did not differ from those in the general population. However, the employment rate in men fell from 81% of the sample before the onset of agoraphobia to 49% after an agoraphobic period of five years. For agoraphobic women, the employment rate fell from 46%

of the sample to 18% during a five-year period. Dianne Chambless suggested that having a job outside the home is a protecting factor for agoraphobiacs. Julian Hafner and Priscella Minge, in their 1989 study of agoraphobic married women, reported further that a majority of the wives in their study viewed agoraphobia as a barrier to being more independent and returning to paid employment.

V. *Onset and Life Course*

Agoraphobia usually starts in early adult life, with two probable peaks of onset at about 20 and 30 years of age. The onset may include a panic attack, which is followed within hours by incapacitating anxiety and avoidance behavior. This may lead to a whole range of life restrictions, which affect both the agoraphobic and their family. Researchers report that women and men suffering from agoraphobia demonstrated a wide range of problems, which appear to be a direct consequence of the condition. These include an inability to work, lack of social contacts, poor self-esteem, marital disharmony, and depression. Since most research has not focused specifically on gender differences and potential risk factors for developing agoraphobia, in this article we will review the risk factors and try to highlight relevant gender variables.

VI. *Childhood Antecedents*

A. ANXIETY SENSITIVITY/TEMPERAMENT

Recently there has been interest in studying childhood anxiety sensitivity and temperament and its relationship to vulnerability for the development of anxiety disorders. Longitudinal studies of infants and children addressing temperament serve as a foundation for this research. In addition, there have been retrospective studies that have studied children of phobic patients, as well as retrospective interview studies with agoraphobics and panic disordered patients, asking them about their childhood anxieties and fears. This research has not focused on gender differences. To date, this line of research suggests that as children agoraphobic individuals may have exhibited anxiety sensitivity; behavioral inhibition in the preschool years; avoidant, phobic, or anxious behavior in childhood; and separation anxiety in adolescence. A similar pattern of anxiety sensitivity and anxious phobic behavior was also found in the children of agoraphobics. School refusal behavior could be considered a childhood version of agoraphobia. Generally, researchers report high incidences of school refusal behavior and/or fear of going to school in clinical studies of persons with agoraphobia. Over 30% of adults with agoraphobic symptoms report childhood school refusal behavior. In summary, parental protectiveness, school refusal behavior, and family history of phobias appear to be risk factors related to the development of agoraphobia.

B. PARENTAL PROTECTIVENESS

Most clinical writers reviewing histories of agoraphobics neglect to mention parental overprotectiveness, but stress maternal overprotectiveness as a factor in promoting dependency and phobias in both females and males. In extensive reviews of the literature that focuses on phobic and adult agoraphobic case descriptions from the psychoanalytic and behavioral literature, strong evidence is presented for phobic symptoms as coexisting with personality patterns of dependency and avoidance. In childhood cases, when parent's behavior could be observed, parental overprotection was the rule. The writers suggested that phobics may experience early interpersonal familial learning situations in which the avoidant-dependent pattern is an adaptive role for the child. The fathers' role, in this literature, has generally been ignored.

For the most part, there are few differences reported in the clinical literature pattern of maternal overprotectiveness for male and females suffering from agoraphobia. In several clinical case studies of male agoraphobics, there are reports of their being overprotected and of being considered their mother's pet.

Contrary to the clinical reports, in recent research studies, there are inconclusive findings on scales to measure overprotectiveness in the mothers of agoraphobics. However, high fear or agoraphobic scores were correlated with the agoraphobics' ambivalence toward mothers. There are also reports of trauma in childhood, experiences of parental illness, conflict in the family, violence, separation, and sexual abuse. Agoraphobics report more emotional problems, more parental separations, alcohol problems, verbal aggression, and violence to solve conflict in their childhood families compared to other clinical populations.

D. PHOBIC DISORDERS IN OTHER FAMILY MEMBERS

There are reports in the clinical literature of a high rate of phobic disorders for female relatives of agoraphobic individuals. In one research study, 34% had phobic mothers, whereas only 6% had phobic fathers. There are also case reports of multigenerational agoraphobia in mothers, daughters, and even grandmothers. In a controlled study of first-degree relatives of patients matched with controls, the rate of panic disorder was 17%. These findings appears consistent across studies. In general, more females than males are likely to have relatives with these disorders.

Twin studies report a concordance rate in monozygotic (identical) twins of 31%, with none for dizygotic (fraternal) twins. Others have estimated the heritability factor for panic disorder at 35 to 40%, and rates of agoraphobia found in near relatives was also high. Researchers also point to a familial relationship between agoraphobia, panic disorder, and depression.

VII. *Triggers/Stressors*

A. INTERPERSONAL STRESS/TRAUMA

There is considerable agreement among the psychoanalytic, cognitive/ behavioral, and biological communities for viewing stress, particularly interpersonal stress, as a trigger for emergent agoraphobic symptomology. From the earliest case reports, psychoanalysts described the stress of interpersonal "trappedness" as a factor in the development of agoraphobic symptoms. Thus, psychoanalysts view the agoraphobic as remaining the mother's child with conflict in the separation individuation process and clinging to passive dependent behaviors.

Cognitive /behavioral theorists posit a similar interpersonal trigger. Many claim that phobic symptoms are the result of psychological avoidance behavior in conflict situations with a dominating parent or spouse with a lack of development of assertive behavior. Researchers, in comparing the childhoods of agoraphobics women to clinical controls, reported significantly more emotional problems and more conflicts with parents.

Most writers additionally pointed to stress in the marital or couple relationship as a prime trigger. Reports from clinical studies suggest that the majority of agoraphobic individuals in treatment report marital difficulties, although these findings are not clear-cut in research studies and will be addressed later. Clinicians have suggested that the conflict centers on unhappiness with their marriage and resentment of the spouse's domination. Given their dependency, agoraphobics may reasonably seek out dominating partners, whom they grow to resent.

While the previously mentioned stressors are most frequently noted in the agoraphobia literature, more recent work has suggested other triggers. The development of panic symptoms is also a feature of posttraumatic stress disorder. Panic disorder and an increase in anxiety and fearfulness has been reported in women following rape. There are recent reports of childhood sexual abuse and other family trauma in persons with agoraphobic symptoms. What *is* clear is that stress plays a major role in creating a climate that triggers anxiety and panic attacks, and real-life experiences of trauma may contribute to the development of agoraphobia and panic. However, most agoraphobic individuals do not have a history of trauma; rather, the major stressor often lies in the dynamics of their current relationships.

B. THE MARITAL RELATIONSHIP

Many writers have argued that the marital relationship, particularly the feeling of being trapped in the marriage, assertiveness issues, and reinforcement of the phobia by the spouse are factors in the etiology and maintenance of agoraphobia. A review of the literature on marital factors for women shows that the findings are not clear-cut. Many studies divide female agoraphobic women into groups with functional and dysfunctional marriages and do indeed find a group of dysfunctional relationships and "neurotic" spouses that appear to contribute to the maintenance of the phobia. However, there are also many reports of functional, nondistressed marriages and nondistressed, non-neurotic spouses among the population of married agoraphobic women. (Sexual functioning within the marriage, while problematic for some agoraphobic women, seems to show a similar pattern to that reported for females with other neurotic disorders.)

Julian Hafner has been among the most active investigators of the role of marital relationship issues in the development of agoraphobic symptoms. In 1989, Julian Hafner and Priscella Minge studied sex-role stereotypes, personality, and marital adjustment of a population of diagnosed agoraphobic women and their husbands with matched controls. Agoraphobic women scored significantly lower than the controls on the sex-role measure of autonomy and higher on the trait of intropunitiveness (self-critical). The husbands' ratings of marital satisfaction correlated strongly with their wives' self-ratings of femininity among the agoraphobic group. The authors concluded that sex-role stereotyping plays an important role in the development of agoraphobia, especially in cases where the symptoms coexist with high marital dissatisfaction.

Several extensive literature reviews and research studies have been conducted in an effort to study unhappy marital relationships among agoraphobic spouses. Most of the sample participants have been married women and their husbands, and the evidence suggests that unhappy marriages are not common in this population. However, one recent study compared the gender-role constructs, interpersonal behaviors, and marital relationships of agoraphobic persons with controls. The agoraphobic respondents scored significantly higher on measures of marital conflict and interpersonal dependency and lower in self-confidence and self-agency than controls. This sample of persons with agoraphobia also viewed their marital relationships as significantly less satisfactory than controls, in terms of level of support, depth of relationship, and characteristic level of conflict. Little research has been done on agoraphobic husbands, and to our knowledge there has not been research on agoraphobia among gay and lesbian couples.

In summary, support for the importance of the role of marital relationship problems in the development and maintenance of agoraphobic symptoms has been mixed. A few studies, however, have reported marital difficulties arising after successful treatment. These findings may indicate that a more accurate rating of marriage satisfaction is likely to be given after the patient has come to trust the therapist, or the findings may indicate that treatment alters sex-role expectations, or that the new freedom to be away from the home was threatening to the partner who was the "caretaker."

VIII. *Theoretical and Treatment Perspectives for Agoraphobia*

The large body of clinical writings about research and treatment of agoraphobia over the past century have been a testing ground for all the controversies among mental health professionals. In spite of the volume of work, few of the major theorists writings about agoraphobia directly address the question as to why women are more prone than men to develop this disorder, nor discuss treatment planning with gender issues in mind. An overview of the major theoretical perspectives and treatments for agoraphobia and panic will follow. We conclude with an integrative feminist cognitive perspective on agoraphobia, gender, and treatment.

A. BIOLOGICAL EXPLANATIONS OF AGORAPHOBIA AND PHARMACOLOGICAL TREATMENTS

Recent research on the brain suggests that the locus ceruleus may be the center for the physiological, emotional, and behavioral origin of fear and anxiety. The biological focus posits that patients with agoraphobia and panic disorders have an inherited genetic vulnerability or constitution predisposition (i.e., anxiety sensitivity) that sets off the nonadrenergic bodies of the locus ceruleus.

To bolster their belief in constitutional vulnerability, genetically based theorists stress that anxiety disorders tend to run in families. (See the previous section on family variables.) Generally, researchers estimate the heritability factor for panic disorder at 35 to 40%, and rates of agoraphobia found in near relatives was also high.

Other biological studies have used sodium lactate as a research tool to set off panic attacks in panic disordered patients. Agoraphobics and panic disorder patients respond differently to sodium lactate, eliciting neuroendrocrin changes compared to normal controls. Other biological markers studied have included serotonin, which points to neurotransmitter system irregularities in patients with panic disorder. This line of research suggests that increased activity or reactivity of the noradrenergic neurotrsansmitter systems is associated with panic anxiety.

Given the growing interest in biological factors, genetic, and constitutional determinants, it is suprising how little of this work addresses gender issues. The one exception is that the higher incidence of agoraphobia in women has been attributed to hormonal influences on the acquisition of anxiety responses. Donald Klein, among others, has suggested that estrogen fluctuation may be partly responsible for the acquisition of phobic avoidance. Other researchers have suggested that that because testosterone is linked to dominance behavior, men will

more likely face situations rather than avoid them. This research is ongoing and complex and most writers tend to disconfirm any simple relationship between hormonal factors and the development of agoraphobia and panic disorder.

Given the biological focus of research, pharmacological treatments have been developed. Donald Klein was one of the pioneers in demonstrating that the symptoms of panic were relieved by tricyclic antidepressant medication. Additionally, he was also able to demonstrate a differential responsiveness to drug therapy for panic attacks from other anxiety disorders. Now there is impressive evidence that tricylic antidepressants work effectively to reduce panic attacks and are moderately effective in reducing phobic avoidance. Other medications, such as alprazolam and serotonin inhibitors (clolpramine), are also widely used and reported to be effective. However, relapse rates are high when medication is discontinued. Many treatment programs combine pharmacological with psychological treatment, primarily cognitive behavior therapy. However, gender effects in responsiveness to pharmacological treatment have not been fully studied.

B. PSYCHOANALYTIC VIEWS OF AGORAPHOBIA

Psychoanalysts were the first to describe and treat agoraphobia. Psychoanalysts view phobias as a symptom neurosis characterized by a pathological fear of a particular object or situation and the consequent attempts to avoid them. This definition derives from Freud's 1909 psychoanalytic approach to phobias emerging from his case of five-year-old Little Hans's phobia of horses. Central to the classical psychoanalytic approach is the view elaborated by Otto Fenichel in 1945. What a person fears, she or he unconsciously wishes, so there is an attempt to escape from an internal dangerous impulse by avoiding a specific external condition that represents the impulse.

Other early psychoanalytic theorists highlight interpersonal conflict as primary for the translation of anxiety into concrete symbolic symptoms. This view was presented in 1929 by Helene Deutch, who provided the first analytic agoraphobic case description. The woman that Deutch described had demonstrated an ambivalent and conflict-ridden identification with her mother. She reported that the agoraphobic woman harbored unconscious death wishes against her mother, so she needed to keep her close by. Edoardo Weiss, who wrote a psychoanalytic book on agoraphobia in 1958, saw as central to agoraphobics "a conflict between symbiotic union with the mother and the need for separation from her in order to establish one's own autonomous ego" Weiss (1966), p. 386. Melitta Sperling described the transfer of mother–daughter conflicts to the marital relationship in her analysis of an agoraphobic woman. She reported that the patient expressed feeling trapped in her marriage, as she had felt trapped with her mother.

Alexandria Symonds, in 1971 broadened this viewpoint by adding a feminist perspective. In a paper titled "Phobias after Marriage: Woman's Declaration of Dependence," she described a young woman who was apparently independent, self-sufficient, and capable, but who had changed after marriage and developed phobias and other signs of constriction of self. She reported that the phobic women she saw clung to their husbands for constant support, apparently changing from a capable person into the classically helpless female (p. 144).

While there is not a psychoanalytic literature focused on agoraphobia, the views of Nancy Chodorow seem relevant for understanding the psychodynamics of agoraphobia, as well gender issues in self-development. In 1978 Chodorow wrote *The Reproduction of Mothering* in which she proposed the view that the growth of the self and the lessening of dependency occurs by progressive differentiations from the mother for both girls and boys. She went on to suggest that such separation is particularly difficult for daughters and mothers, because mothers of daughters tend not to experience these daughters as separate from themselves. Following this line of thinking, we can theorize that agoraphobic persons, who are primarily female, may be suffering from an exaggerated case of the prototypical female separation experience. Furthermore, since some of the mothers of agoraphobic individuals may themselves be agoraphobic, daughters of such women may have even more difficulty separating in that they identify with their mothers and therefore model agoraphobic behavior patterns.

Luise Eichenbaum and Susie Orbach, in a feminist psychoanalytic book in 1982, devoted several pages to discussing agoraphobia. They followed this line of thinking and espoused the view that the boundaries of home are substitutes for psychological boundaries because the agoraphobic person has difficulty being separate.

While psychoanalysts do treat agoraphobic patients, with the exception of the previous authors they have not written much about the specifics of their treatments or provided rich case histories. Very little research has been conducted on the psychodynamic treatment in general and for agoraphobics in particular. Weiss reported in 1958 that agoraphobic patients were long-term treatment cases, difficult to treat, and often had unsuccessful outcomes. A handful of recent clinical studies report positive outcome, provide little detail on the specifics of treatment, and do not address gender issues. [*See* GENDER DEVELOPMENT: PSYCHOANALYTIC PERSPECTIVES.]

C. BEHAVIORAL APPROACHES TO UNDERSTANDING AND TREATING AGORAPHOBIA

In the 1960s and 1970s, agoraphobia and anxiety disorders became a prime focus of the newly emerging field of behavior therapy. Behavior therapy theory developed from the pioneering work of Joseph Wolpe in 1958, who suggested that phobias arose from classically conditioned autonomic disturbances that are reinforced by developing avoidance behaviors. Wolpe viewed phobias as developing by autonomic conditioning from "situations which evoke high intensities of anxiety." In describing his therapy, he described the case of an unhappy married woman, resentful of her children, family responsibilities, and exhausted, who one day went food shopping. She felt she wanted to erupt, to scream, but she did not. A few days later, when out in the city, all of a sudden she began to feel very strange. That was the day she tried to walk home from the bus and could not walk. She developed a phobia, which Wolpe presumed constituted the avoidance behavior. The woman feared leaving the house, and Wolpe suggested that "the prospect of taking the action that would lead out of the situation simply adds new anxiety to that which already exists and this is what inhibits action" Wolpe (1970), p. 302. The avoidance alleviates the anxiety, but what maintains the avoidance behaviors is usually some form of social reinforcement. The behaviorists believe that the avoidance behavior is often reinforced by the family.

The advent of behavioral therapy for agoraphobia in 1958 reversed a long-standing clinical pessimism about successfully treating agoraphobia by psychodynamic therapists. Over the course of the past 40 years, literally hundreds of studies have been conducted to examine and compare various behavioral treatment methods. The results of this research have demonstrated that prolonged exposure (confronting the situation in real life) along with learning relax-ation techniques is the treatment of choice. Sixty to seventy-five percent of agoraphobic patients showed substantial improvement with prolonged exposure on measures of phobic severity. Previous recovery rates with traditional psychoanalytic or supportive therapy were reported to be about 24%.

Behavioral researchers also recommended treat-ment techniques that facilitated home-based practice (homework) between exposure sessions as the effec-tive ingredient in overcoming agoraphobia. The best results were produced when exposure was conducted in socially cohesive groups of patients.

Nonetheless, other researchers such as Paul Em-melkamp have claimed that behavioral treatment has definite limitations and its share of failures. He re-ported that many agoraphobic patients drop out of treatment or fail to improve, while other agoapho-bic patients develop new symptoms or retain signif-icant residual problems following behavioral treat-ment. In general, although behavioral treatment does lead to considerable improvement, relatively few pa-tients were entirely free of agoraphobic symptoms. What is also suprising, given all the research, most of which was conducted with women, is how little gender differences or women's issues were consid-ered in the study of responsiveness to treatment.

D. COGNITIVE BEHAVIORAL PERSPECTIVES AND THERAPY

Spawned by the cognitive revolution in psychology, behavior therapy became more cognitive in the 1970s and 1980s, which in turn affected theorizing about agoraphobia. Most influential were the ideas of Aaron Beck and Albert Ellis. They both presented somewhat overlapping theories. In 1985, Beck pre-sented his fully developed cognitive approach to un-derstand anxiety disorders. In particular, he empha-sized the importance of two types of cognitions central to agoraphobia and panic: attribution of causality and cognitive set. In panic attacks, there is a misattribution of causality. That is, the person makes an interpretation of symptoms as a threat to life or ability to function (i.e., "I am going crazy"), which in turn leads to their intensification. Ellis la-beled this misattribution "catastrophic thinking." Furthermore, as agoraphobic persons approach their phobic situation, their cognitive set leads to an an-ticipation that something terrible is about to happen to them. Central for both Ellis and Beck is the idea that anxiety-evoking cognitions by themselves simul-

taneously elicit anxiety, serve to justify the fear and maintain and drive the avoidance behaviors.

In 1993, Vittoria Guidano and Gianni Liotti high-lighted patterns of interactions characteristic of ago-raphobic parent–child interactions from an Italian clinical sample. They emphasized that such parents set up "agoraphobic belief systems" (an agoraphobic cognitive organization) that places limits on the child's personal freedom to explore the world and encourage the child to view the world as a danger-ous place (home as safe, and the child as weak). Family patterns for these children include being dis-couraged by their parents (usually their mother) from leaving home alone even for a short outing, being kept at home for longer periods of convalescence than necessary after minor illnesses, and not being allowed to go out and play with friends.

David Clark, a major cognitive behavioral re-searcher on panic disorder, reported that when ago-raphobic individuals experience conflict, they are un-able to connect the high level of anxiety to their distress. In particular, they do not know how to han-dle their symptoms. According to the cognitive model, an agoraphobic person perceives the world through a fear schema—an integrated cognitive, emo-tional, and behavioral lens that is particularly sensi-tive to particular environmental cues, bodily based symptoms, or fear-driven thoughts. For example, panic attacks can occur when individuals, upon en-countering a feared stimulus, perceive anxiety-based somatic symptoms as more dangerous than they are. They misinterpret heart palpitations as signaling an impending heart attack or the shaking, jittery feeling as indicating loss control or going crazy. As these so-matic sensations are experienced, the individual be-comes increasingly apprehensive until full-blown panic occurs. Once the anxiety schematic process be-gins, the whole pattern plays out and the individual is unable to stop it.

Researchers on cognitive variables linked to ago-raphobic behaviors have emphasized the following. Individuals with panic disorder plus agoraphobia score higher on measures of anxiety sensitivity. The greater the anxiety sensitivity, the greater the avoid-ance. Women in these studies exhibit greater anxiety sensitivity and expect that panic is more likely to oc-cur more than men do. Women too often believe that their catastrophic thoughts are true and that the con-sequences they anticipate, such as suffocating or be-coming crazy, might happen. They also exhibit stronger beliefs about the physical symptoms, heart attack, and loss of control compared to men. In general, they show more thinking errors, and they catastrophize and overestimate the threat more than do males with similar symptoms. In addition, women demonstrate a higher phobic avoidance and more fear of being alone than men.

Cognitive behavior therapy is generally considered the treatment of choice for agoraphobia and panic disorder. In 2000, William Sanderson and Simon Rego compiled an excellent descriptive review of empirical studies that support the claims of the effectiveness of cognitive behavior therapy for agoraphobia and panic disorder. In spite of some criticisms, discussed earlier by Emmelkamp, there is no question that cognitive behavior therapy provides a psychoeducational treatment package that addresses the main clinical problems of agoraphobic patients.

The cognitive behavioral treatment package features the learning of coping skills to master anxiety and encourages real-life practice in learning new behaviors. Central to the program, whatever techniques are used, is the focus on schematic patterning, particularly cognitive therapy for catastrophic thinking, as well as the teaching about the mind-body link. However, researchers stress that improvement is most dependent on the cognitive changes and the willingness to expose oneself to the feared stimuli during the course of treatment.

1. The Cognitive Behavioral Treatment Package

Most programs feature the following, alone or in combination.

- *Psycho-education/teaching about anxiety, panic, and bodily based symptoms.* Clients are given self-help books that teach anxiety mastery.
- *Cognitive restructuring.* Clients learn to think differently about anxiety and catastrophic thinking. This typically involves challenging the dysfunctional beliefs and helping the client substitute adaptive or coping self-statements for maladaptive or noncoping self-statements. For example, an agoraphobic could substitute the coping statement "I can learn to control my anxiety" to counter the belief that "I am helpless and cannot control my anxiety."
- *Relaxation training.* Clients learn techniques for relaxation.
- *Respiratory control.* Clients learn about breathing to increase relaxation and prevent hyperventilation

- *Visualization.* Clients learn how to construct imaginal calming scenes as an aid in relaxation and mastery.
- *Exposure.* Clients build a fear hierarchy by setting up a real-life program to confront anxiety-provoking stimuli.
- *Coping skills training.* Clients learn self-sufficiency and are shown how to handle oneself when panic symptoms emerge (anxiety management).
- *Work with families and significant others.*
- *Combined pharmacological treatment.* Often medication is used as a treatment aid.

While gender has not been specifically addressed in the cognitive behavior therapy literature, a handful of cognitive behavior therapists have featured a feminist framework for understanding and treating women. This approach has been at the cutting edge for the understanding of gender issues relevant to the disorder. We believe that feminist approaches provide an integrative framework for understanding and treating agoraphobia and addressing gender issue.

2. Social Learning Theory and Sex Role Expectations

Social learning theory, which stresses social factors in the development, reinforcement, and maintenance of behaviors, seems to provide the most straightforward and coherent response to understanding the sex differences and clinical features of agoraphobia. While Western culture is changing, for the most part there are still differential sex-role expectations for females and males. Traditionally, males are expected to exhibit traits of aggressiveness, independence, coolness, objectivity, adventurousness, and ambition, whereas females are socialized to exhibit their opposite—passivity, emotionality, subjectivity, submissiveness, excitability, dependency, lack of adventurousness, and so on.

In the clinical literature, persons with agoraphobia are described as having the personality traits of passivity, dependency, avoidance, and nonassertiveness more often than other neurotics, and these traits are descriptive of women and men. On self-report questionnaires, agoraphobic women achieve more stereotypically feminine scores than do normals and anxiety neurotics. In addition, Kathleen Brehoney reported that women who are high scorers for agoraphobic traits are also reported to be high scorers for stereotypic feminine traits.

Social learning theorists have suggested that parental and societal reinforcement as well as modeling are important influences in the socialization of children. Researchers on socialization suggest that autonomy is often not reinforced in girls. Girls are reported to have less encouragement for independence, more parental protectiveness, less cognitive and social pressure for establishing an identity separate from the mother, and more dependent on adults for solving their problems. The first author, from reviewing the socialization theory and agoraphobic clinical characteristics in previous writings, has proposed that children who later become agoraphobic are socialized more like stereotypical females in U.S. culture. That is, they are allowed to retain childhood fears, are reinforced for dependency (overprotected), and, following modeling theory, may have been subjected to less effective, even phobic, parental models. According to this theory, female and male agoraphobics seem to have similar characteristics, but different socially accepted responses to fear and anxiety. [*See* GENDER DEVELOPMENT: SOCIAL LEARNING.]

3. Agoraphobic Women

For most of history, women were rewarded for their stereotypic feminine behavior, but today we are confronted with a complex and often contradictory situation for women. In this new century, women are still socialized to some extent into a role that puts family first; yet they are expected to participate more fully in the world. Today we are still seeing agoraphobia in young women who display many stereotypical sex-role behaviors and have conflicts over sex-role expectations. Now, however, such stereotypic feminine behavior is considered somewhat dysfunctional, and even marriage is no longer considered an easy escape route from being out in the world. Today's women are expected to function more autonomously, by society and often by their mates and significant others. We are also seeing more single women with agoraphobic symptoms.

Given contemporary expectations for women, today's agoraphobics may be under even more stress, have lower self-esteem, and feel even more hopeless than before. Perhaps they may be going on strike against the contradictory messages they are getting to be feminine and to put family first but also to go out in the world and achieve mastery. However, it is clear that stereotypic patterns are still present in many women today.

In 1974, Iris Fodor argued that agoraphobia may reflect overtraining in stereotypic aspects of the female role. In this early discussion of agoraphobia, texts from the media, children's readers, and research on the differential socialization of males and females with respect to fears and mastery were presented. It was argued that agoraphobic women were overly socialized into the female role, and their helplessness, dependency, emotionality, excitability, and giving up under too much stress were part of their "feminization training," which was the stereotypic way women at that time were socialized. Furthermore, such feminine items on the sex-role stereotyping, scales such as emotionality, submissiveness, excitability, passive, house oriented, not at all adventurous and showing a strong need for security and dependency, could just as well have described agoraphobic behavior.

A similar position was proposed by Alexandria Symonds, a psychoanalyst, drawing on her clinical work with agoraphobics. She proposed that many women, and men too, equate morbid dependency and helplessness with femininity. She reported on patients who had some confusion and uncertainty about their femininity and who feared the ordinary aggression and assertiveness, which accompanies growth and involvement. She said these patients worried that their growth would hurt others.

Later, several cognitive/behavioral writers, such as Barry Wolfe and Kathleen Brehoney, among others, adapted the same basic arguments. Essentially they argued that the sex-role training of women as helpless and dependent leads to their socialization into a prescribed role that promotes fearfulness and nondevelopment of mastery skills and leads them to be more vulnerable to phobic conditions.

Furthermore, many agoraphobic women come from families where the mother is also phobic and therefore they have female familial role models that present fearful, avoidant behavior. Many of the familial childhood patterns are still present in the agoraphobics' ongoing family life. Parents, particularly mothers, who are also agoraphobic may be continuing to support the avoidance behaviors. Alan Goldstein reported on a number of adult agoraphobic cases in which the daughter, who is still living with the mother, is the identified client. He reported seeing the mother, who is usually also agoraphobic, deteriorate as the daughter improves. The daughter, being overwhelmed with guilt, relapses, and then the mother improves. Furthermore, spouses often became additionally involved in keeping the agoraphobic at home. Julian Hafner talked about jealous husbands who become symptomatic themselves as their spouses phobias improve and who may not support more independent behavior.

Researchers have also studied stereotyping and cultural expectations in agoraphobics. Dianne Chambless in reviewing studies of fearfulness reported that when "men report being highly fearful, they are more likely to approach a feared object, than women who describe themselves as equally fearful, presumably due to the incongruence of fearful behavior with the male sex-role stereotype." They suggested that passively avoiding, rather than conquering, a feared situation may be more typical of women than men (pp. 3–4). Dianne Chambless, in another study of gender-role stereotypes in agoraphobics, found that agoraphobic women and anxiety neurotics were no more stereotypically feminine than normals, but they had lower masculinity scores (less instrumental, active, and assertive). Other researchers have also found that women agoraphobics score low on the masculine scales.

Recent research and clinical writing about female agoraphobia has stressed the role of trauma, rape, and possibly child sexual abuse, as well as violence and family emotional problems in the backgrounds of some women who develop agoraphobia. Given that stress, particularly interpersonal stress, is considered a trigger for the development of agoraphobic and panic disorder, and given that women are more subject to rape and other sexual abuse and are vulnerable to family conflict, it is not suprising to see this co-occurrence. However, given the socialization pattern described earlier, one could expect that many women are not well enough trained to master anxiety and cope with stress, so given the trauma and sexual abuse as an added stressor, they may develop phobic symptomology.

4. Outcome of Treatment

Given that effective treatment programs are available, it is somewhat disheartening to see that in comparative studies, women do not do as well as men in the maintenance of treatment success. Seventy-five percent of the participants in treatment studies are women. In four-year followups tracking both psychosocial and pharmacological treatment, researchers have reported that women exhibited double the rate of symptoms compared to men, regardless of whether they had panic disorder or agoraphobia. In addition, women scored higher on fear measures and had higher medical care usage.

Since gender is not considered in the treatment design—and given the lower success rate of women in treatment and the reluctance to acknowledge anxiety and use of alcohol for anxiety management among men—we would like to propose an integrated, cognitive, behavioral, feminist treatment approach for working with agoraphobic women and men. Such an approach would take into consideration the familial, societal, and cultural sex-role learning specific to each gender, as well as the particular gender-related features of the disorder.

5. An Integrated Feminist Approach for Working with Agoraphobic Women

Feminist psychotherapy involves the consideration of cultural stereotypes and gender barriers in understanding the agoraphobic syndrome. The personal is the political. The way the agoraphobic woman constructs her experience has been shaped and rewarded by society. While the model presented is written for women, given the similar profiles of male and female agoraphobics, it can also be adapted for men. Before this era, most White European American women were not expected to be in the workplace and they had a high incidence of agoraphobia. Now, when most women do work, the prevalence rate is the same, but it is now considered even more unacceptable for women to be anxious and afraid to go out into the world. Thus, modern women feel even worse about their anxiety and panic. It may be that women, if the biologically focused theorists are right, may be more prone to anxiety sensitivity and emotional vulnerability. However, in working with agoraphobics therapeutically, feminist therapists need to take into account the stressors in a modern woman's life that make her at risk for the development of agoraphobia. Most modern women are not taught how to manage emotions or anxiety, or how to juggle work, family, and personal time. Married women have often been encouraged by their husbands for staying at home and not pushing themselves to handle the multiple stresses on a woman's life. The ultimate goal of feminist therapy is to foster coping skills, as well as cognitions that counter feelings of helplessness, dependency, and being out of control of one's life. Feminist therapists can model different attitudes toward arousal and anxiety. Women need to be taught that everyone gets anxious, and that it is not so unusual to feel anxiety when trying new things. The therapists can model their own successful and unsuccessful attempts at coping with anxiety. Often the agoraphobic woman has only had family members who believe anxiety is dangerous and avoidance is the only way to cope.

The therapists own attitude toward women's roles is a factor in the treatment. Research has shown that therapists who do not espouse traditional gender roles for women are better able to foster positive changes with more satisfaction reported by their female clients.

While cognitive behavior therapists have integrated a feminist approach in working with other women's disorders (trauma, eating disorder, sexual abuse), there have been very few papers presenting an integrated feminist cognitive behavioral model for agoraphobia. Cognitive behavior therapy (CBT) provides an ideal integration with feminist therapy.

CBT is based on social learning theory. Problematic behavior is viewed as learned and shaped by the environment. The therapist is seen as a consultant/ teacher. By focusing on cognition's, the client can see the way she has constructed her worldview and its consequences. She can recognize that there are other ways to interpret her experiences. CBT puts the client in charge. The emphasis is on using therapy as a tool for teaching the client about herself, setting her own goals, and learning techniques for change.

CBT is optimistic about change. Any motivated person with enough support can learn to assess and combat catastrophic thinking, learn new coping strategies, and so on. Moving beyond a focus on anxiety management and working on catastrophic cognitions, the feminist therapists might assist their agoraphobic clients through assertiveness training and role play while helping them learn independence and autonomy. [*See* FEMINIST APPROACHES TO PSYCHOTHERAPY.]

6. An Integrated Feminist Approach for Working with Agoraphobic Men

Agoraphobic men, like their female counterparts, are reported in the clinical literature to be dependent and to come from families with maternal overprotectiveness or other family conflict, violence, or emotional problems. They appear to lack many of the same personal and social competencies as female agoraphobics. They are also more likely to suffer from physical illness prior to the first agoraphobic episode and are reported to be hypochondriacal. Often they come for help when they are more severely impaired by the panic attacks and agoraphobia or are afraid of dying of a heart attack.

There is a consistency among the researchers that males with panic disorder are less likely to admit to fears on self-report scales or engage in avoidant behavior when anxious. The dependent personality style and staying at home are in direct variance with prescribed sex-role behavior for a male. Thus, male agoraphobics are more likely to be employed. Also, while males are less avoidant, researchers suggest that males are more likely to use alcohol for managing anxiety.

First of all, boys and men need to be educated about anxiety early on. While boys and girls report anxiety and fears as children, men are less likely to continue to report fears and anxiety later in life. They come for help only when their agoraphobia is severe and they are terrified they are having a heart attack. Hence, psychoeducational programming, from childhood on, is essential for males as well as females. Boys have to be taught that anxiety is a normal feature of life; some clinicians, for example, Gestalt therapists even consider anxiety suppressed excitement, an arousal associated with challenge. However, given boys' socialization to be brave and to master fears, this anxiety is considered unacceptable for boys. They either will not admit it or engage in activities to prove to themselves and the world that they are not anxious. (We see a lot of high-risk, athletic activities and often-dangerous behavior in males from adolescents on.) While the biologically oriented might say that tetestrone is a factor in taking action, this denial of anxiety can often be dangerous. Most important, given that many researchers now point to alcohol as an anxiety management technique, and considering the high rate of alcohol use among men with agoraphobia and panic disorder, teaching anxiety management to boys and men becomes even more urgent.

Another aspect of a feminist approach to treatment would be to look at how men who may need to appear brave and strong may foster the dependency, helpless, and staying-at-home behavior in their mates.

IX. Conclusions

The goal of this article was to highlight the central features of the agoraphobic syndrome, to address gender issues, and to explore potential explanations for the disproportionate number of women who suffer from this disorder as compared to men. Several potential biases were addressed, such as alcohol abuse, gender-role expectations, and employment to help explain this gender difference. Social expectations and gender roles seem to contribute to the higher incidence of female agoraphobics. Contemporary social expectations *are* evolving, but it is still more likely that men will feel that they are required to work, no matter how stressed they are, while it is more acceptable for women to choose to stay at home. These gender roles afford the female agoraphobic greater opportunity to reinforce her phobic avoidance, while exposure to new and fearful situations may force the male agoraphobic to mask his phobic tendencies. Further exploration and research studies will provide clinicians with a better understanding of the variables associated with the development and maintenance of agoraphobia, as well as the role played by the larger culture in maintaining this gender difference.

Along with other feminist authors, Dianne Chambless, Barry Wolfe, and Jan Mohlman, among others, we believe that cognitive behavior therapy is an ideal feminist therapy to promote self-sufficiency and mastery and to help agoraphobics face fears and manage anxiety. In many ways, the treatment provides a structure that will allow agoraphobics to learn as adults what they did not learn as children. The research suggests that agoraphobics need help in mastering out-of-control feelings, thereby allowing them to be active and assertive in the world. Men as well as women need this approach.

Also, given the research on biological and constitutional factors, particularly anxiety sensitivity, and lifelong issues with anxiety, children who are anxious need to learn about anxiety, how it is to be managed, and how to develop self-confidence in handling themselves in a variety of situations. Given the association of alcohol as an anxiety-management technique, it may be that cognitive behavior therapy (particularly anxiety-management techniques and active coping skills training) need to be instituted earlier in schools, as part of a general emotional education program. For girls, there is a need to learn to transcend the limitations of the traditional stereotypic female role that promotes dependency, helplessness, and avoidance. For boys, there is a need to learn to admit and face up to fears, as well as learning techniques for managing anxiety.

SUGGESTED READING

American Psychiatric Association. (1994). *Diagnostic and Statistic Manual of Mental Disorders: DSM-IV*, 4th ed. Author, Washington, DC.

Barlow, D.H. (1988). *Anxiety and Its Disorders*. Guilford, New York.

Chambless, D. I., and Goldstein, A. J. (1982). *Agoraphobia: Multiple Perspectives on Theory and Treatment*. Wiley, New York.

Fodor, I. G. (1992). The agoraphobic syndrome: From anxiety neurosis to panic disorders. In *Personality and Psychopathology: Feminist Reappraisals* (L. S. Brown and M. Ballou, eds.), pp. 177–205. Guilford Press, New York.

Goldstein, A. (1987). *Overcoming Agoraphobia: Conquering Fear of the Outside World*. Viking Press, New York.

Hafner, R. J., and Minge, P. J. (1989). Sex role stereotyping in women with agoraphobia and their husbands. *Sex Roles* 20, 11–12.

McNally, R. (1994). *Panic Disorder: A Critical Analysis*. Guilford Press, New York.

Rachman, S., and Maser, J. D. (1988). *Panic: Psychological Perspectives*. Erlbaum, Hillsdale, NJ.

Sanderson, W., and Rego, S. (2000). Empirically supported treatment for panic disorder. *Journal of Cognitive Psychotherapy* 14, 3, 219–244.

Turgeon, L., Marchand, A., and Dupuis, G. (1998). Clinical features in panic disorder with agoraphobia: A comparison of men and women. *Journal of Anxiety Disorders* 12(6), 539–553.

Weiss, E. (1966). Psychodynamic formulation of agoraphobia. *The Psychoanalytic Forum* 14, 378–386.

Wolfe, B. E. (1984). Gender ideology and phobias in women. In *Sex Roles and Psychopathology* (C. S. Wisdom, ed.). Plenum, New York.

Wolfe, B., and Maser, J. (1994). *Treatment of Panic Disorder: A Consensus Development Conference*. American Psychiatric Press, Washington, DC.

Wolpe, J. (1970). Identifying the antecedents of an agoraphobic reaction: A transcript. *Journal of Behavior Therapy and Experimental Psychiatry* 1, 299–304.

Yonkers, K., Zlotnick, G., Allsworth, J., Warshaw, M., Shea, T., and Keller, M. (1998). Is the course of panic disorder the same in women and men? *American Journal of Psychiatry* 155, 5.

Androcentrism

Susan A. Basow

Lafayette College

Glossary

Gender polarization Seeing males and females as opposites; imposing that polarity on everything from feelings (male feelings and female feelings) to jobs (male jobs and female jobs).

Glass ceiling The invisible yet persistent attitudinal and structural barriers that limit women's advancement in an organization.

Patriarchy Rule of the fathers. A sociopolitical system in which men and their experience have power over women and their experience.

Positivist The belief that there is an objective truth, which scientists can discover.

Sexism The systematic privileging of one gender over the other. More than personal bias, sexism is institutionally supported and involves both prejudicial attitudes and discriminatory behaviors.

Social construction The way society shapes our views and even the phenomenon in question. Gender is socially constructed since what is feminine and what is masculine is determined and shaped by culture.

ANDROCENTRISM literally means male-centeredness. It is the habit of viewing males and male experience as the norm for human behavior. Females and female experience, when considered at all, are viewed as deviations or exceptions from the norm. This article examines how androcentrism functions in theories, language, research, the workplace, and the family, using research primarily focused on the United States.

I. Theories

Until the 1970s, virtually all theories were un-self-consciously based on male lives and experiences, which were assumed to be the universal human experience. Males are the norm; females are the "other." Thus theories of human behavior were constructed based on male behavior, with females viewed (if they were viewed at all) as exotic or annoying exceptions. As early as 1911, Charlotte Perkins Gilman noted that our culture is androcentric and what has been called "human nature ... was in great part only male nature."

Several examples illustrate how androcentrism operates as a core assumption of our thinking. Indeed, Sandra Bem in 1993 referred to androcentrism as one of three "lenses" of gender through which we perceive the world. (The other two lenses are gender polarization, seeing males and females as opposites, and biological essentialism, seeing gender differences as innate.) Androcentrism fits in with a patriarchal power structure, one in which males and their experience are privileged. Whereas patriarchy reveals *who* has the power, androcentrism reveals *how* that power is perpetuated psychologically and culturally. [*See* DEVELOPMENT OF SEX AND GENDER.]

Psychological theories are meant to explain human behavior. But in a world where males are privileged over females and where males are constructing the theories that both rationalize and create the cultural ideology, it is perhaps not surprising that such grand theories, in fact, have been partial ones. Beginning with Adam and Eve, the story of human behavior has focused on men at the center, created first and in God's image, with women as marginal and subordinate to men. Ancient Greek philosophers also viewed women as subordinate and inferior to men. For example, Aristotle viewed females as "mutilated" males, characterized by a lack of qualities (such as reason), which men, by nature, have.

Psychological theorists followed this androcentric tradition. Three examples are Sigmund Freud's psychoanalytic theory of personality, David McClelland's theory of achievement behavior, and Lawrence Kohlberg's theory of moral behavior. Perhaps the most influential was Sigmund Freud, whose psychoanalytic theory of human behavior was created in the early 1900s. Although many of his patients were women, his theory of human behavior assumed the male as norm. For example, one of the most critical stages of personality development was termed the "phallic stage." Freud claimed that between ages three to five, both boys and girls become aware that boys have a penis and that girls do not. Further, claimed Freud, both boys and girls recognize that the penis is the "superior organ." This "recognition" makes boys anxious about losing their penis ("castration anxiety"), and girls jealous of what boys have ("penis envy"). These developments supposedly have far-reaching effects on a child's personality: boys subsequently develop an active dominant personality with a strong conscience, while girls subsequently develop a sense of inferiority and passivity, along with a desire for a (male) child. Thus, in Freud's androcentric theory, the possession or lack of a penis is pivotal in a child's psychological development.

Later theorists challenged this and many other aspects of Freud's theory. Although having a penis (or not) certainly might affect certain aspects of one's life (one's future reproductive role, for example), it is not intuitively obvious that a penis is "superior" to a clitoris, nor that its possession (or lack) automatically leads to personality differences. For example, Karen Horney, a contemporary and student of Freud's, thought it was equally plausible for males to develop "womb envy" based on women's central role in the reproduction of life. Kate Millet and other feminist critics of the 1960s and 1970s pointed to Freud's mistake of confusing societal privileging of males with biological privileging of the penis. Thus, some girls may indeed envy boys, but they are more likely to envy the power and privileges that boys have in a patriarchal culture rather than the anatomical penis.

Another example of androcentrism in psychological theories is David McClelland's 1953 theory of achievement motivation. Although he studied only males, McClelland created a theory that was meant to explain human variations in achievement behavior. He posited that an individual's level of achievement varied with that person's motivation to achieve (how important achievement was to the individual), the individual's expectations of the likelihood of success, and the value attached to success. His model worked very well to predict the achievement behaviors of males. However, it did not work well to predict the achievement behavior of females. Rather than modifying the theory so that it could encompass the behavior of females as well as males, McClelland and others simply stopped studying females and continued to promote a model of *human* achievement behavior based on *male* behavior.

As later theorists, beginning with Matina Horner in the late 1960s, have discovered, the original achievement model suffered from androcentrism. It failed to consider the consequences of success for women. Although success for males may be associated with a variety of unambivalently positive consequences, such as social esteem and financial reward, success for females may be perceived ambivalently. Successful women may be viewed as socially unattractive and reacted to quite negatively, especially by males. We now know that both men and women will avoid success if they expect negative consequences to follow. Thus, using males as the norm obscured an important aspect of human behavior.

Another androcentric aspect of the original achievement theory was the definition of achievement used. Achievement was defined primarily in ways applicable to men's lives and emphasized mastery and competitiveness, especially in such areas as sports, school, and occupations. Yet achievement can occur in other domains as well, such as in personal or interpersonal arenas. Achievement also can take forms other than mastery and competitiveness, such as working hard. When all these neglected aspects of achievement are considered, we have a more complex but more accurate understanding of human behavior. [*See* ACHIEVEMENT.]

Kohlberg's 1969 theory of moral development provides another example of androcentrism. Kohlberg created his theory by studying males of varying ages thinking out loud about several moral dilemmas, such as whether to steal a drug if the life of one's wife depended on it. He concluded that children passed through a series of six invariant stages in terms of their moral reasoning, from a concern with obedience and punishment to a concern with individual principles. The average male tended to function at stage 4, a concern with authority. When females were studied, they were found to function more at stage 3, a concern with feelings and social opinions. The conclusion was drawn that females were less morally developed than males, a position already theorized by Freud and attributed to the phallic stage.

The androcentrism in Kohlberg's theory is obvious from the fact that a theory based on male reasoning using dilemmas involving only male protagonists was promoted as a theory of *human* behavior. Studying female moral reasoning directly, as Carol Gilligan and others have done during the past 20 years, reveals a more complex picture. There are at least two different types of moral reasoning, one concerned with rights and the other concerned with care. Males and females use both, although females may be more likely to use the care orientation than are males under some circumstances. More important, as a society we need both orientations—justice and care—to deal with moral issues. It is androcentric to value individual rights over interpersonal concern and to state that one is superior to the other. [*See* FEMINIST ETHICS AND MORAL PSYCHOLOGY.]

II. *Language*

Language conveys messages beyond the meaning of words. A prime message in the English language is that males are the norm and females are exceptions. Androcentrism in language can be recognized easily in several linguistic patterns: ignoring females, stereotyping females, and deprecating females.

The most obvious way that language marginalizes females is by ignoring them. Male nouns and pronouns are supposed to represent humans in general; female nouns and pronouns represent only particular female individuals. Thus, words and expressions like "chair*man*," "*man*kind," and "everyone should do *his* best" are supposed to refer to males and females alike. However, researchers like Nancy Henley have demonstrated that people read such words and think primarily of males, not males and females equally. For example, androcentric language affects people's perceptions of what jobs are appropriate for whom (fewer people see women as suitable for a job as a "mail*man*" than for a job as a "mail *carrier*"). In fact, even seemingly neutral nouns like "person" and pronouns like "they" appear to connote primarily males due to androcentrism in the culture at large. Only a concerted effort to include females in examples and illustrations, as well as in nouns and pronouns (*"he and she," "hers and his"*) appears likely to bring females into the center of our consciousness.

Another aspect of androcentrism in language relates to stereotyping and marking. Since males are the norm, their gender goes unmarked. Since females are "other," their gender gets marked. For example, there are doctors and then there are *women* doctors; there are lawyers and there are *female* lawyers. Marking occurs for other nonnormative groups as well, as in *the African American doctor, the Jewish doctor,* or *the gay doctor.* Thus, the norm not only is male, but it is White, Protestant, and heterosexual as well. Such characteristics are implied in the unmarked noun "doctor." We become aware of the norm only when trying to describe those who don't fit it.

The convention of putting male terms first when linking male and female terms, as in "husband and *wife*," "his and *hers*," "he and *she*," also signals that men are primary and women secondary and subordinate. We need to take care to alternate whom we note first, or even put women first more often in order to counter the broader cultural pattern. A similar message is conveyed when women are referred to as possessions, as in "the pioneers moved West, taking their wives and children with them." This linguistic construction also erases the fact that women were pioneers too. It would be preferable to say "pioneer families moved West," or "female and male pioneers moved West, along with their children."

Linguistic stereotyping also focuses on males as the norm by emphasizing different qualities when females are described. Women are stereotyped both as sexual objects and as homemakers. As sexual objects, their appearance is commented upon in all arenas. For example, descriptions of male political candidates typically focus on the content of their speeches or positions whereas descriptions of female candidates more often include comment on their appearance and family roles. Thus, Hillary Clinton probably had more written about her hairstyles and her marital role than her policies. Newspaper reports are more likely to note that someone is "grandmother of five" rather than "grandfather of five." Or that the victim of a crime is a "blonde," which almost always means a woman, since men are virtually never referred to by their hair color alone.

Not only are men rarely referred to by their hair color, they also are rarely referred to as perpetrators of sexual assaults and battering. Instead, women continue to be linked with sex and with being victims by language describing how many women "get raped" or "battered." Such passive sentence construction makes it appear that rape and battering just happen to women, rather than conveying the actual reality of men as the typical perpetrators of such crimes.

Perhaps most obviously, women are linguistically stereotyped by being traditionally referred to by their husband's name—*Mrs. John Doe,* rather than *Ms. Mary Doe.* Even the convention of marking a woman's marital status (through the titles *Miss* or *Mrs.*) and not men's (both married and single men are *Mr.*) conveys a message about women's "proper" roles.

Another way androcentrism operates in our language is by deprecating or trivializing females, subtly or not so subtly making them subordinate. For example, adult males typically are referred to as *men* while adult females often are referred to as *girls.* Calling an adult male a *boy* is generally considered to be insulting, yet it is acceptable to juvenalize adult females. Women do this as well as men, about themselves and others, suggesting the power of cultural androcentrism.

Trivialization also occurs when women typically are referred to by their first names alone, when similarly situated men are referred to by their first and last names or last names alone. Thus, a female employee may be referred to as "Kathy" while a male in the same position might be referred to as "Mr. Jones" or just "Jones." This is another way to convey the subordinate status of women since we typically refer to children by their first names. Although this pattern may appear to convey friendliness, its privileging of males may become more evident when salary and promotion decisions are being made.

Other forms of deprecation can be seen in the tradition of attaching "feminine" endings to generically male terms, such as "sculpt*ress*" and "major*ette.*" Such constructions emphasize the male norm. Fortunately, there has been some change in this area. For example, it is becoming more acceptable to refer to both male and female movie and stage performers as "actors," rather than "actors and actresses." The term *actor* carries more weight, again illustrating the inequality between two supposedly parallel terms.

Another form of deprecation can be seen in the fact that there are many more sexual and sexualizing terms relating to women than there are to men. For example, terms such as *madam* and *dame* have a double meaning, unlike their male counterparts *sir* and *duke.*

Because sexism and androcentrism are so endemic to our language, a concerted effort needs to be made to avoid replicating them. Fortunately, beginning in the 1980s, virtually all publishers, including the American Psychological Association and such newspapers as the *New York Times* have issued strict guidelines mandating nonsexist language usage. Even the 1982 edition of *Roget's Thesaurus,* a book of synonyms and antonyms first published in the 1850s, started eliminating sexist words. For example, it changed *mankind* to *humankind.* The fact that androcentric language still is with us, however, suggests that this will be a difficult area to change unless the rest of the culture changes as well.

III. Research

As was noted in the discussion of McClelland's theory of achievement behavior and Kohlberg's theory of moral development, research itself frequently suffers from androcentrism by focusing on males as representing all humans. For example, until the 1980s, males were twice as likely as females to be participants in psychological research. Yet results from studies conducted with just males typically were generalized to all humans, often leading to incorrect theories and practices.

Sometimes this type of androcentrism is downright dangerous. Medical research traditionally has used only White male participants, such as the important research on the effectiveness of aspirin in preventing heart attacks. Although results were generalized to all people, it actually was unknown how aspirin affected women or minority men. Since women typically differ from men in body size and hormonal fluctuations, as well as presenting different heart attack symptoms, it is critical for research to include women. In fact, the very reasons women typically are excluded from medical research—the variability of the menstrual cycle and the possibility of pregnancy—are reasons why results based only on males may not generalize to females. Recognizing this fact, the National Institutes of Health in 1990 issued stringent guidelines for research funding to ensure that women and minorities are adequately represented in all future federally funded research.

Another example of androcentrism in research relates to defining problems or illnesses. In an androcentric society, men typically are in the position to define the nature of "reality" and the nature of women. Traditionally they have defined women's "nature" in terms of their own interests. For example, it benefits men to view women as "naturally" nurturant and noncompetitive since such a construction encourages women to take care of children and avoid competing with men in the work world. If a woman enjoys competition, or dislikes caring for children, she is seen as abnormal, a problem to be explained. Between the 1850s and 1950s, many such women were sent to sanitariums for a "cure," such as Charlotte Perkins Gilman, author of *The Yellow Wallpaper* and other books. With the advent of tranquilizers in the 1950s, many women who didn't "fit" their roles were given these prescription drugs, often known as "mother's little helpers." Betty Friedan wrote about this way of pathologizing women who weren't happy with the confining domestic role prescribed for them in her 1963 classic, *The Feminine Mystique*.

In addition, with males used as the "standard" human, research has tended to consider things that happen primarily to women as abnormal. A prime example relates to hormonal fluctuations. Women's menstrual cycles are overt evidence that their hormones fluctuate in regular cycles. Emotional changes that precede menstruation, if perceived as "too strong," may be considered a form of mental illness. Because men set the norms and they do not appear to cycle, women are viewed as more emotionally labile than are men. A great deal of research has focused on women's emotional changes as a function of menstruation, pregnancy, and menopause. Most of this research views these changes as a form of pathology to be treated by drugs of some type. It is only recently, as more women establish careers as researchers, that it has been recognized that men, too, have hormonal fluctuations as well as mood fluctua-

tions. Such fluctuations appear to be human, a fact obscured when a man's apparent functioning is considered normative.

Men, especially White men, and their behavior often serve as the standard against which all others are judged. We've already noted that the medical norm is "male." In fact, male figures and overlays typically are used in medical textbooks as representing the "generic" human; figures of females typically are presented only when discussing problems affecting women (for example, ovarian cysts). But using White male behavior as the norm occurs in all fields, including psychology. For example, if we consider White male's typical level of emotional expressiveness (low) as the norm, then other groups appear more emotional. Indeed, even the definition of emotional expressiveness is androcentric, since it typically excludes anger as an emotion, one more frequently expressed by men. Because observer ratings do not always have some identified standard against which behavior is judged, it's not always clear what a rating means. When rating a female's emotional expressiveness on a 7-point scale, from low to high, does a high number assigned to a female indicate that she is highly emotional compared to a standard male, or highly emotional compared to other females?

Research on gender typically suffers from one of two possible biases. One bias is to focus on and consequently exaggerate gender differences, such as viewing men as active and women as passive. A second bias is to minimize differences between men and women, often obliterating important aspects of women's lives; for example, ignoring women's greater child care responsibilities in research on workplace productivity. Both biases support the existing gender hierarchy by not challenging "male as norm" and by focusing on individuals rather than on the power differential embedded within the organization of society. Research suggests that women and men are both similar and different, depending on what aspect of functioning is being considered by whom in what social context at what point in time. The context is critical since gender is so much a construction of culture—that is, what we think of (and perceive) as masculine and feminine is a social construction, not a biological given. [*See* SOCIAL CONSTRUCTIONIST THEORY.]

The whole empirical research enterprise so characteristic of science has been criticized as using male standards and criteria as the ideal. The emphasis on objectivity, replicability, and isolation of variables that characterize the positivist empiricist model of research in psychology and other natural sciences can be viewed as a model based on male values. Rhoda Unger, Mary Gergen, and others have criticized such a model as androcentric and as leading to only a partial understanding of our world since only some topics lend themselves to such methods. We also need qualitative research that allows for in-depth understanding of complex phenomena, research that considers contextual variables such as status and power, and research that recognizes that the experimenter is a person in a reciprocal relationship with the "object" of study. For example, Barbara McClintock won a Nobel Prize in biology for her research on genetic variations in corn based on, in her words, "a feeling for the organism."

Indeed, our entire discussion of androcentrism reveals the fallacy of scientific "objectivity." For centuries, scientists have insisted they were objective; yet they were so imbued with the biases and values of their culture that they literally could not see them. As feminist critics of science, such as Evelyn Fox Keller, have pointed out repeatedly, there is no such thing as "pure objectivity." Science is performed by people, and people are affected by their culture. What is critical is for scientists, and all of us, to become aware of our values and biases, including the role they play in shaping what we do and how we do it. We may not be able to be "free" of our values, but we can become more sensitive to them and their effects.

IV. Workplace

Androcentrism in the workplace can be seen in several ways. Men's lives and interests define what we think of as work, and women's work is undervalued and underpaid. Androcentrism is so strong in the workplace that women and men typically do not even hold the same jobs, with the jobs available to women being based primarily on men's views of women's "nature." Because women in an androcentric society are defined primarily in terms of their reproductive and domestic roles as well as their subordinate status, most of the jobs that have traditionally been available to, and considered suitable for, women have followed suit. Thus, typical jobs for women involve serving and taking care of others, whether children (such as child care work and teaching), the ill (such as nursing and health aide), bosses (such as secretarial work), or the general public (such as waitressing). Three out of four female employees work in just one of three job categories—clerical/administrative support, managerial/professional (mostly as teachers and administrators), and service—while male employees are spread across a wider variety of job categories. Furthermore, most men and women work predominantly with members of their own sex.

Women also are typically defined in terms of their sexual attractiveness to men. This quality also affects their workforce opportunities. Many jobs informally "require" female attractiveness, such as receptionist and flight attendant, and most "sex workers"—prostitutes, strippers, and so on—are women.

What all these jobs have in common, besides their link to female stereotypes, is their low status and low pay. On average, women employed full time earn less than three-quarters of the salary earned by men employed full time. This does not mean that women and men doing the same job for the same company receive different wages, although this does happen. The main reason for the salary differential is the gender segregation of the labor force. Men and women typically work in different occupations and the ones where women work pay the most poorly.

Why are the jobs in which women work so low paying? Because of androcentrism as well as patriarchy, whatever men do is seen as having more value than whatever women do. Thus child care jobs, done primarily by women, are lower paying than animal care jobs, done primarily by men. Furthermore, men expect to earn more and have higher status in their jobs than do women. Consequently, when salaries in a field start increasing (because of labor shortages), more men enter the field. Such is happening with the profession of nursing. However, as Barbara Reskin and Patricia Roos discovered in 1990, when salaries and status in a field start decreasing, the opposite occurs: men are less likely to enter the field, leaving more openings for women. Such is happening today with health care professions like psychology and medicine.

Because men historically were viewed as the breadwinners of families, their salaries were viewed as the family wage. Women, at least White middle-class women, were expected to be homemakers. When they did enter the labor force, they typically were viewed as working only for supplementary income (supplementing that of their fathers or husbands). Furthermore, they were viewed as incidental workers, likely to leave the labor force for marriage and children. Indeed, many women did move in and out of the labor force and most were geographically restricted by family responsibilities in their search for employment. Therefore, "women's wages" were set low initially and stayed that way until challenged by the second wave of the women's movement in the 1960s and 1970s.

In reality, women, especially African American and working-class women, have always been an important component of the labor force in the United States. U.S. women hold 46% of all full-time jobs today and the majority of women are employed, even the majority of mothers with young children. Many employed women are single or single parents and their income is critical for their own and their family's survival. Many more are married, yet their income too is important to the welfare of their families. Few families in the United States today can afford to live on just one salary.

Yet the normative worker is still viewed as male. The very definition of work as consisting of continuous full-time employment is based on men's work lives. The work women do in the home or for their families is not even defined as "work" and is not considered in the country's gross national product. This view reinforces the cultural value attached to men and men's lives. "They" are important for the nation's economy; women are economically "dependent." Yet it is often the unpaid work that women do at home that allows a man to pursue a career and succeed at it. In fact, many professional careers (such as CEOs or presidents of a college or a country) are really two-person careers. If his wife didn't see to the shopping, cleaning, child care, and entertaining that frees a husband to concentrate on his work and his professional networks, many a man's career would founder. Married women may have a difficult time holding such positions since they don't have "a wife" to do all the necessary behind-the-scenes work. It is no wonder that most women CEOs are unmarried or without children.

As suggested by this example, employer expectations of their employees often use men as the norm. Since men both stereotypically and historically have not been primarily responsible for children, they generally have been "free" to engage in overtime work, travel assignments, and networking opportunities, such as golf games and professional conferences. When such behavior is viewed as normative, women often have to try twice as hard to "prove" they can perform as well as men. Although it has been illegal in the United States to discriminate directly against women in employment since the 1970s, many em-

ployers still view men as more suitable for certain, especially high-paying, jobs. Women who have domestic responsibilities often are considered suspect workers who are not really committed to their profession, and those without such responsibilities may be suspect as women!

Men as the norm can be seen in other employment decisions. Historically, men have been viewed as "natural leaders," more suitable than women for supervisor, management, and other leadership positions. For example, although most elementary and secondary schoolteachers are women, most principals and school superintendents have been men. Since the 1980s, however, research has indicated that although some women may have a different leadership style than men, one emphasizing cooperation and democratic decision making, that style is equally if not more effective than the more authoritarian and competitive style traditionally associated with men.

So ingrained is the perception of the male as the normative leader that even in situations where a woman is clearly in charge, others may not perceive her that way. For example, research has shown that the person who sits at the head of a table is typically perceived as the leader. This is true for men, but not for women. Thus women are at a marked disadvantage when trying to gain and advance in leadership jobs. The male norm is so strong that during the 1970s and 1980s, women who aimed for success in the business world were encouraged to adopt the male professional uniform (a suit and "feminine" version of a tie), as well as male behaviors (strong handshake, direct eye contact, lower voice register). Yet there was the danger of going too far in the "masculine" direction and thereby being seen as unfeminine, also undesirable.

Having a mentor is very helpful in professional careers, but obtaining a mentor is not easy for "nontraditional" workers. Those in leadership positions often look to younger versions of themselves when looking for someone to groom for advancement. Because White men dominate the higher levels of management, younger White men have an advantage over women in gaining a mentor. This is true with respect to minority men as well.

The 1990s brought some welcome progress, with the range of acceptable dress and behavior for women expanding. Women's managerial style also received many positive comments, as evidenced by books with such titles as "The Female Advantage: Women's Ways of Leadership." Also, the percentage of women in managerial positions has increased to 45%. Yet androcentrism in the workplace still is alive and well. For example, most of these women are in the lower levels of the management hierarchy. The subjective nature of promotion decisions at the highest levels, often based on such subjective qualities as the ability to "fit in" and be perceived as a leader, are likely to keep women hitting their heads against "the glass ceiling" for a long time yet.

Women are disadvantaged in blue-collar work environments, as well. Men have dominated these jobs, such as construction and the trades, and the pay is considerably higher than that in traditionally female pink-collar jobs, such as manicurist. Many male blue-collar workers feel threatened by women's encroachment on "their" territory, and they try to keep women out by both direct and subtle means. For example, they may be overtly hostile and threatening, or they may make sexual innuendoes, tell sexist jokes, or decorate the workplace with sexist pictures. Three out of four women in traditionally male jobs report experiencing some form of sexual harassment. Unfortunately, such harassment seems to work since many women who enter these fields wind up leaving because they do not feel comfortable.

The workplace itself is based on men's lives. There are few accommodations to the fact that many employees, men and women, have children, and only women give birth. Although the number is increasing, most employers do not provide on-site child care, paid pregnancy, or child care leave. The United States stands alone among advanced industrialized countries in having no statutory provisions to guarantee paid infant care leave. Although workers covered by disability insurance might get paid for pregnancy-related "disability" (another example of the androcentric bias of pathologizing what is normal for women), such leave is short, usually six weeks, and many female employees (about one-third) are not even covered by such insurance. The Family and Medical Leave Act (1993) provides for 12 weeks of leave, but this leave is unpaid and most workers cannot afford to take it. Furthermore, most women work in jobs with fewer than 50 employees, so even that meager leave is unavailable to them. The result is that most new mothers take minimal time off and many feel the strain of juggling job and domestic responsibilities. They often accommodate by taking less demanding or part-time jobs, which further adds to the salary differential and the perception that women are not "real workers."

Every aspect of the workplace is permeated by androcentrism. Although the salary differential has been decreasing over the past 50 years, especially in the past 20 years, it still exists. Women employed full time earn approximately three-fourths of what men earn. Although this is an improvement over previous years, the narrowing of the wage gap is due mainly to a decline in men's wages rather than an increase in women's wages. For all the press about the influx of women into such high-status fields as law and medicine, the reality is that most women are employed in low-paying, low-status jobs. The changes that have occurred in terms of job segregation have been due to women entering traditional male fields rather than men entering traditional female fields. Thus the status of the latter (such as teaching and child care) remains low, and the workplace still is an unfriendly one for those with family responsibilities, mainly women. Until the workplace becomes more accommodating to families, women will continue to be disadvantaged there. [See CAREER ACHIEVEMENT; CHILD CARE; LEADERSHIP; POWER; WORK–FAMILY BALANCE; WORKING ENVIRONMENTS.]

V. Family

"Father knows best," the name of a popular TV show in the 1950s, could also be the motto summarizing idealized family life in Western cultures. This ideal is both patriarchal and androcentric. The father/husband is considered the traditional head of the household, with the wife and children subordinate to him. His home is "his castle," and the rest of the family is supposed to respect and cater to him. Everything is done to support his well-being and to facilitate his activities. He is not expected to engage in any of the routine domestic responsibilities, such as housecleaning or food preparation, although he might do the more occasional home repair or outdoor maintenance. Nor does his role as father involve much daily contact with his children, although he may occasionally "baby-sit." In this mythic picture, breakfast is prepared for him to eat before work, sometimes lunchboxes as well, and dinner is served when he comes home. Social activities may revolve around his social or professional networks, and he may need "a night out with the boys." Whatever he needs, he should have, for he is "lord and master" of the house.

In this idealized family, the wife's main role is to support her husband. As we have seen, women have traditionally been defined by their domestic and reproductive roles. This view of women and men as functioning in "separate spheres" was embedded in legal history in the 1873 case of *Bradwell* v. *Illinois*. In that case Myra Bradwell was denied permission to practice law in the state of Illinois because the Supreme Court viewed that it was woman's "mission . . . to fulfill the noble and benign offices of wife and mother." Thus, women are presumed to be best suited not only to bearing children, a biological reality, but to raising them as well. Somehow female reproduction also has become associated with other domestic duties, such as cleaning house and clothes, preparing and serving food, providing an aesthetically pleasing and restful atmosphere for the primary breadwinner/husband, and so on.

Marriage, for women, has historically meant a loss of individual identity. Under the doctrine of coverture in English common law, upon which U.S. laws were based, marriage meant that "two become one" and that one is the husband. A woman assumed her husband's identity (she stops being *Mary Doe* and becomes *Mrs. John Smith*). Until the 20th century, married women were unable to sign contracts or hold property in their own names. It wasn't until 1975 that married women were entitled to credit in their own name. In a few remaining states, it still is legal for a husband to rape his wife since husbands were presumed entitled to their wife's "sexual services." Wife beating, too, traditionally has been viewed as a husband's prerogative and in many communities it still is difficult to get police or the courts to take such assaults seriously.

The reality of family life at the turn of the 21st century is very different from the idealized 1950s version. The traditional family, with father as breadwinner and mother as full-time homemaker and child caretaker, represents less than 10% of all families today. Indeed, as Stephanie Coontz noted in her 1992 book, *The Way We Never Were,* the reality of the 1950s didn't match the idealized version either. Working-class women have always been in the labor force. Today, the mythic 1950s family is even more unreal. As we have seen, most mothers are in the labor force, even those with preschool children. At least half of all children spend part of their childhood living with only one parent, most often the mother. And more and more gay and lesbian couples are raising children.

Families without a father as head have typically been devalued (as in "broken" families or "illegitimate" children) or not considered families at all (such as lesbian and gay families). In a controversial article in *The American Psychologist* in 1999, Louise

Silverstein and Carl Auerbach challenged the androcentrism of defining families only in terms of "the essential father." Although fathers are indeed important in the lives of their children (and children important to fathers), children can grow into mature healthy individuals in a variety of families, including lesbian and single-mother families. Children need love and guidance and attention, but these qualities are not necessarily best or only provided by two biological married parents.

The androcentrism involved in idealized patriarchal family life is readily apparent when the reality of women's lives is examined. Most married women and most mothers must juggle domestic and work-related responsibilities on a constant basis. We already have seen how the workplace functions androcentrically. Little accommodation is made in the United States for employees who also are responsible for children and domestic chores, as most mothers are. Women who give birth often are allowed only minimal paid leave, covered under disability insurance only for those entitled to it. Therefore, most new mothers take only minimal time off since few can afford to take unpaid leave. Adoptive parents and men don't even get disability coverage and very few work in situations that allow paid parental leave. Time off when a child is ill or for school functions is rare in the workplace.

The burden of combining work and family life falls unevenly on women's shoulders due to the androcentric view of the family as women's responsibilities. Men have traditionally combined work and family life by having the wife be in charge of the latter. Women rarely have that option, although there are increasing numbers of men who wish to be more involved than their fathers were in child care. Many are willing to sacrifice career advancement for more time at home. Still, new mothers typically find themselves more involved in child care activities than they had expected. They also find themselves doing more of the housework, regardless of the previous division of labor between couples and regardless of their employment status. In fact, women with children generally work a double shift—35 hours per week in paid employment and about the same amount in home and child care activities. In contrast, fathers spend less than 8 hours a week in childcare or domestic activities, even if their wife is employed.

Contrary to androcentric myths, women do not necessarily feel happiest and most fulfilled when they have a child and concentrate on domestic activities. Marital satisfaction tends to be lowest, especially for the wife, when a young child is present in the home. Dual roles appear to be important to women's mental health, even though they are challenging. It is women who feel trapped in the home—because they cannot afford to pay for child care in order to gain paid employment or because their partner doesn't want them to work—who are the most unhappy and stressed. The critical issue is choice. Mothers who are forced to stay home as well as those forced to join the labor force tend to be more conflicted and troubled than mothers who choose either option.

Unfortunately, androcentrism in the family and in the workplace may make mothers feel guilty for choosing employment. Research repeatedly shows, however, that such mothers typically are happier and less anxious and depressed than stay-at-home mothers, at least when they have social support and positive employment attitudes. Furthermore, their children appear unharmed by nonmaternal care, whether that care occurs in family day care situations or child care centers. Certainly some caregivers are better than others, but that is true of biological mothers as well as employed professionals.

Even egalitarian couples experience the pressure of androcentrism once a child is born. If the decision of who will stay home with the baby is based on economic grounds, then it more often makes sense for the father to keep his job than the mother, since he probably earns more than she does. Moreover, because it is more typical for the mother to take time off to care for a baby, a father who does so may lack social as well as professional support. Indeed, his coworkers and others might question his masculinity as well as his career commitment.

Thus, society at large supports androcentrism in the family. Even in the current situation of most mothers working outside the home, service calls (for appliance repairs and so on) still are scheduled during the workday, since it is assumed "someone" (read, "the wife") will be home. Children are sent home from school early on snow days without warning because it is assumed "someone" (read, "the mother") will be home. There are endless examples of societal assumptions that mothers belong at home, starting with the lack of sufficient quality affordable child care and after-school care in the United States. Rather than helping to ensure the availability of such care, society tends to reinforce the view that children are best cared for by full-time, stay-at-home mothers. That is, unless the mother is on welfare. Then she should be in the labor force. Implicit in this hypocritical view is the androcentric assumption that the only proper family is one with a breadwinning father at the head.

Women who do conform to the traditional role assigned to them often find themselves in difficult straits later in their lives if they become divorced or widowed. Without labor force resources of their own, displaced homemakers suffer financially. Upon divorce, the standard of living of the custodial mother generally decreases dramatically while the standard of living of the typical noncustodial father increases. Less than one out of four single mothers receives regular and full child support. Elderly women who spent most of their lives as homemakers or in low-paying jobs with few benefits rarely have pensions of their own and only 10% receive pension benefits from their husband's plan if they outlive him. The result is that 40% of all women over 60 years of age have incomes below or only slightly above poverty level.

Although we give great lip service as a culture to families and family values, what is being supported is a narrow androcentric definition of families, one that benefits men much more than women. If we are truly concerned with raising the next generation of children well, we need to have many more social and structural supports available to the wide array of family types that exist. [See DIVORCE AND CHILD CUSTODY; FAMILY ROLES AND PATTERNS, CONTEMPORARY TRENDS; MARRIAGE; MOTHERHOOD; PARENTING.]

VI. Conclusions

Men and their experiences are considered the norm in the United States as well as in most other countries. Theories are based on men as the quintessential human, as is language. Women's lives and experiences are typically invisible, marginalized, or devalued. This is seen in research as well, from the problems studied, to the populations used, to the conclusions drawn. When we look at the workplace and the family, we see clearly how these institutions are shaped to fit men's lives. Workers are expected to work continuously, without any disruption for childbirth and child care. That is, the workplace is based on a man as the typical worker. In families, men are the breadwinners and heads of households. A woman's main role is to provide reproductive and domestic services, so that the husband can focus on his work role.

One main result of androcentrism is male advantage and female disadvantage, especially economically and politically. Until we eradicate androcentrism, we will be unable to create a society in which all individuals have equal opportunity to actualize their potentials. Change has begun, but it will take a concerted commitment on many levels for much progress to occur.

SUGGESTED READING

Basow, S. A. (1992). *Gender: Stereotypes and Roles,* 3rd ed. Wadsworth, Belmont, CA.

Bem, S. L. (1993). *The Lenses of Gender.* Yale University Press, New Haven, CT.

Hochschild, A. (1989). *The Second Shift: Working Parents and the Revolution at Home.* Viking, New York.

Jamieson, K. H. (1995). *Beyond the Double Bind: Women and Leadership.* Oxford University Press, New York.

Keller, E. F. (1985). *Reflections on Gender and Science.* Yale University Press, New Haven, CT.

Lakoff, R. T. (1990). *Talking Power: The Politics of Language in Our Lives.* Basic Books, New York.

Reskin, B. F., and Padavic, I. (1994). *Women and Men at Work.* Pine Forge Press, Thousand Oaks, CA.

Silverstein, L. B., and Auerbach, C. F. (1999). Deconstructing the essential father. *American Psychologist* **54**, 397–407.

Anger

Dana Crowley Jack

Fairhaven College/Western Washington University

Glossary

Cognitive schemas Verbal or pictorial images in the stream of consciousness organized by attitudes and assumptions developed from previous experiences.

Evolutionary psychology A field of psychology using current understandings of evolutionary mechanisms to help explain human commonalities in human social psychology and behavior, including emotions.

Display rules The social and cultural rules that dictate when, where, and how a person may express an emotion.

Social norms Social conventions that regulate human life, including implicit cultural standards and explicit laws.

Type A personality A particular configuration of behaviors and traits, particularly a sense of urgency, competitiveness, goal-directedness, hostility, and anger found to be associated with heart disease, particularly in men.

ANGER is an adaptive emotion that arouses a person physically and mentally to take action in response to perceived social threats, violations, or frus-trations. As an activator, anger itself is neutral; the behaviors it leads to can be constructive or destructive. Cultural rules dictate when and how to express anger and who has the prerogative for its obvious display. The social stereotypes of women's anger as "unnatural" or as aggressive and linked to negative outcomes often cause difficulties for women's positive use of this strong emotion, especially among White middle-class women. This article presents an overview of physiological, social, and cognitive aspects of women's anger and discusses therapeutic interventions for women's anger-related difficulties.

I. The Emotion of Anger

Anger is an emotion, accompanied by physiological changes that prepare persons to take action. Anger is manifested in the body through such changes as an accelerated heart rate, elevated blood pressure, adrenaline, and noradrenaline, as well as peripheral vaso-constriction. Anger also has cognitive components, which include the perception of feeling angry and at-tributions about what caused the anger. Though theorists disagree about precisely how emotions func-tion, the most widely accepted view is that emotions occur as complex interactions of physiology, cognitions, and social appraisals.

From the perspective of evolutionary psychology, emotions evolved to serve biologically adaptive functions necessary for survival. Anger, for example, can trigger aggressive feelings and behaviors for self-defense when a person is attacked. Robert W. Levenson describes specific autonomic nervous system patterns, found in western and nonwestern cultures, in individuals of all ages, that characterize anger and distinguish it from fear. He cites numerous studies that link fear to lower diastolic blood pressure and with cooler surface temperatures, greater vasoconstriction, and lesser blood flow in the periphery. Facial blushing accompanies anger-like states in daily life, and facial pallor occurs in fearlike states. Such autonomic patterns have provided a basis for arguing that fear is associated with a "flight" response, while anger activates a tendency for a "fight" response. [See GENDER DEVELOPMENT: EVOLUTIONARY PERSPECTIVES.]

Though on a biological level, anger may be linked with an action tendency to aggression, at other levels such as the interpersonal and sociocultural, anger serves to *communicate*. Paul Ekman, following Darwin's ideas, found that people across literate and nonliterate cultures agreed in how they labeled photographs of the following facial expressions: enjoyment, anger, fear, sadness, disgust, and surprise. One explanation for the universal ability to identify anger across cultures posits a central, hard-wired connection between the motor cortex and other areas of the brain involved in directing the physiological changes that occur during anger. A second group of explanations proposes that such a connection is learned, not hard-wired. Such learning could be common to all members of our species, or culture specific. Regardless, the powerful communicative aspects of anger suggest that it is a highly interpersonal emotion that informs others about feelings and intentions. From this perspective, anger's function is social as well as biological; it results from biology interacting with culture, mind interacting with body.

James Averill's model of emotion presents five, interrelated levels of organization and graphically portrays the interrelatedness of social, biological, and individual aspects that come into play when a person gets angry (see Figure 1). As indicated by the arrows on the figure, the levels and components are reflexive and interactive. At level 1 are the biological and social potentials, including our genetic endowment and social patterns of response that help

ensure the survival of a society. Biological and social potentials interact within individual experiences and endowments to form a person's emotional traits (level II), commonly called one's temperament, which includes idiosyncratic aspects like being quick to anger. Emotional traits also include emotional intelligence and emotional creativity, defined as the capacity to originate novel yet effective emotional responses. At level III, specific abilities, social rules and roles define when one is able to engage in an emotional behavior. Social rules for emotions dictate when and how a particular emotion can be expressed, while social roles confer privileges, restrictions, and obligations regarding emotional expression, such as when and at whom one is allowed to overtly express anger. Level IV, episodic dispositions, represents the activation of an emotional state, which is a relatively short-term predisposition to respond in one of a variety of ways consistent with the rules and expectations that govern emotions. Level V, component responses, includes six categories through which emotions take form and are expressed: cognitive appraisals, physiological change, expressive reactions, instrumental acts, verbal behavior, and feelings.

In everyday life, people are not consciously aware of aspects that organize their experience of anger, such as their biological potentials or even social rules. Numerous theorists make the point that the cognitive appraisals of situations, the interpretations we make of our bodily states, and the actions we take in response to them most strongly determine our subjective experience of anger. People are most consciously aware of their anger when they are expressing it (level 5). Gender differences in anger formation and expression are affected at every level of organization in this model, but most particularly in levels 3, 4, and 5.

II. The Relationship of Anger to Aggression

Because anger is an emotion that physiologically arouses an individual, many theorists consider anger as the mediator between provocation and aggression. That is, they regard anger as creating a readiness for instrumental acts of aggression. However, not all anger leads to aggression. Anger can lead to varied outcomes, including constructive actions that foster self-definition and social change, or destruc-

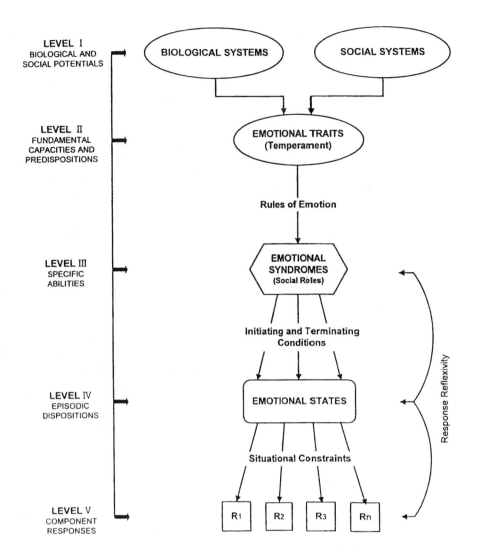

Figure 1 A framework for the analysis of emotional behavior. From Averill, J. R. (1997). The emotions: An integrative approach. In *Handbook of Personality Psychology* (R. Hogan, J. Johnson, and S. Briggs, eds.). Academic Press, San Diego, CA.

tive behaviors that hurt others, or to physical illness resulting from habitual anger suppression. Conversely, acts of harmful aggression are often caused by factors other than anger, such as shame, fear, self-defense, and dominance.

Most investigations of anger's relation to aggression have occurred in settings involving strangers, where relationships are transitory and stripped of their social context. Such studies often label the verbal, outward expression of anger as "aggression," to distinguish it from anger that is suppressed or not communicated. When these studies find that provocation leads to "aggression," their findings add to the common belief that anger is a destructive emotion, even though the distinction between assertive self-expression and aggression may not have been drawn. As well, in most experimental studies, gender is considered to be an aspect of the individual; the larger social characteristics of gender, such as power and status, remain invisible and uninvestigated. Thus the social aspects of gender often go unanalyzed in experimental research on the relation of anger to aggression.

Studies of anger in daily life find that when recognized and acknowledged by others as appropriate, anger is not problematic to an individual and more often leads to positive rather than destructive interpersonal outcomes. In a now classic study, James Averill found that a majority of 523 respondents from a community sample and from university samples (whose ethnicity was unidentified) believed their anger was more beneficial than harmful, by a ratio of 2.5:1. Seventy percent indicated that expressing anger helped improve the relational situation. Not surprisingly, the most commonly reported target of anger was a friend, acquaintance, or loved one. Further, 62% of the women said that they "somewhat" or "very much" felt a desire to talk the incident over with the person who instigated the anger; 40% of the men said the same thing. If the direct, positive expression of anger successfully "clears the air" in a relationship, each of the parties feels better. Among his respondents, anger was most often constructively motivated: the primary objective was not to harm or inflict pain on the target, but rather to change the situation that created the anger.

People attribute their anger, most often, to a perceived wrong. This might be an action on the part of another that is potentially hurtful (and that is regarded as unjustified by the angry person) or an act that, while not intentional, could have been avoided. Commonly reported causes of anger, in both women and men, are a loss of personal pride, self-esteem, or sense of personal worth that follows the distressing actions of another person. Anger is a very common emotion, occurring among 85% of the participants in Averill's naturalistic study at least once during the prior week. The findings that anger is typically initiated by a perceived wrong, is directed toward a friend or loved one, and is constructively motivated are consistent with the notion that anger serves a positive social function by helping to regulate interpersonal relations. [See AGGRESSION AND GENDER.]

III. *The Social-Relational Perspective on Anger*

Research on anger is increasingly focusing on the social contexts in which emotions arise and the interpersonal purposes they serve. A number of researchers find that people most often become angry in interpersonal situations and stress that anger cannot be fully understood apart from the social context in which it occurs—most often in close relationships. Theorist John Bowlby, who investigated attachment behaviors in humans and other animals, described anger as a response to disconnection or obstacles in relationship. Anger's functions are to restore rela-

tionship and discourage the loved person from going away. Positive anger expression, an "anger of hope," as Bowlby called it, requires a belief that one can communicate and be heard and that anger and conflict can have positive benefits to relationships. In contrast, the "anger of despair" often arises from a feeling of being powerless to restore the relationship or when hostility over separation has replaced the bonds of attachment. Dana Crowley Jack's investigation of anger and aggression in 60 women found that their anger of despair most often finds expression through hostile aggression toward others or toward the self.

Women are more interpersonally focused than are men, and researchers find that women's anger is more likely to result from another's actions within a close relationship, whereas men are more likely to be angered by the actions of strangers. Sandra Thomas reports that women describe their anger primarily in relational terms, placing their anger squarely in stories about relationships and focusing on the interpersonal effects of their anger, while men's stories are more impersonal and self-focused.

People develop working models, or cognitive schemas of their relationships, that directly reflect their interpersonal experiences and that guide their behaviors in relationships. These relational schemas include self, other, and expected interactions that have come from past regularities in interactions, especially around heightened emotions such as anger, fear, and sexual desire. Beverly Fehr and colleagues, in a study of university undergraduates exploring interpersonal scripts for anger in close relationships, found that women reacted to interpersonal events with more anger than did men. They surmise that women's greater tendency to be angered in these contexts may reflect their greater sensitivity to the quality of their close relationships and their higher motivation to achieve intimacy in these relationships as well as, perhaps, their reported tendency to derive self-esteem from close relationships. Mario Mikulincer found that people who are securely attached (in terms of general attachment theory) to a loved one are able to see their anger as functional to remove barriers to relationship. When angered, they are able to bring anger into dialogue with a target person positively. However, the ability to express anger positively relates not only to feeling securely attached, but also to a relative equality in social hierarchy with the person with whom one is angry.

IV. Women's Anger in Social Context

A. SOCIAL RULES GOVERNING ANGER EXPRESSION

Within cultures, social rules dictate who gets to be overtly angry, in what situations, and at whom. These rules allow those with more social power and dominance to more openly display their anger than those who are less powerful. Following the hierarchy of gender in our society, men have much more permission than women to show anger, both publicly and privately; women have less freedom to overtly express anger, and more often fear reprisal after showing their anger than do men. As Carol Tavris observed, many negative stereotypes surround angry women and differentiate between the value of women's and men's anger: an angry man is considered assertive and strong; an angry woman is considered "bitchy" and overbearing. Women get much more sympathy and support when they define their problems in medical or personal terms, such as "I am sick" or "It's my problem that I get angry," than if they confront with anger the situations that distress them. Further, White middle-class women are usually socialized into indirect patterns of anger expression. Jerry Deffenbacher found that women are more likely than men to raise their eyebrows, sigh pointedly, or shake their heads when angry. A number of additional studies reveal the classic "silent treatment" and various passive-aggressive modes of anger expression such as engaging in destructive gossip. Dana Crowley Jack found that women most often resort to indirect anger expression because of unequal power, socialization, and cultural expectations, and that respondents in her study easily describe the forms of indirect anger they use, and for what reasons and purposes. [See GENDER DEVELOPMENT: SOCIAL LEARNING; GENDER STEREOTYPES.]

Much of the research on women's anger has used White middle-class respondents; we know much less about anger in women of color, women in poverty, and women who live with disability. Yet, clearly, different social contexts carry different expectations about women's display of anger. In subcultures that equate femininity with suppression of anger, women learn to present less direct anger display and more controlled manipulation of situations, while in subcultures that encourage more open forms of speech, including anger and opposition, women use a wider, more visible range of angry behaviors. Lyn Brown has found that poor and working-class White girls appear more willing to engage in open conflict and to exhibit angry, aggressive behavior than many White, middle-class girls who are socialized to suppress their anger and rely on indirect expression. Dana Crowley Jack's study of anger and aggression in 60 women of different ethnicities reveals that in contexts where their survival is at stake, women often develop an attitude of aggressive anger as a strategy of self-protection. In contexts that stress an absence of anger as "feminine," she found that women perceive any outward manifestation of their anger as aggressive, including as innocuous an act as opposing someone by simply stating a differing opinion. Anger and its expression never exist in a social vacuum; culture and class affect who keeps quiet about their anger, who releases it indirectly, who feels their anger is righteous and should be expressed, and who uses anger for self-protection. [See CROSS-CULTURAL GENDER ROLES.]

B. INEQUALITY AND WOMEN'S ANGER

The complexities of women's anger can only be understood within social, historical context. Within male-dominated cultures, women historically have been denied the direct expression of their anger. A number of theorists have described women's conflicts about anger that result from living in conditions of subordination. Jean Baker Miller observed that women's problems with anger arise from "a situation of subordination that continually produces anger, along with the culture's intolerance of women's direct expression of anger in any form." In her view, this double bind creates indirection and confusion among women regarding their anger.

In a national probability sample of 2031 adults, Catherine Ross and Marieke Van Willigen found that women had higher levels of anger than men did. Economic hardship and inequitable distribution of parental responsibilities were found to explain this difference, which supports a hypothesis that women's anger results from experiencing their social inequality, both within the family and in the wider society. In general, clinical studies support the assertion that women perceive less freedom for the direct expression of anger than men do. Patricia Droppleman, Sandra Thomas, and Dorothy Wilt found that women internalize or suppress their anger at higher rates than men, which carries a variety of somatic and psychological consequences. In the workplace, women perceive that angry displays directed at coworkers have greater relationship cost and personal cost for themselves than for men.

Additional studies affirm that women's anger is affected by a context of social inequality relative to men. Catherine Lutz has argued that there is no avenue for a woman's expression of anger that will not be considered irrational by the culture. In analyzing men's and women's narratives, she found that women talk about the control of emotions, such as anger or hate, more than twice as often as men do as a proportion of the total speech each produced in interviews. Women's discourses of emotional control offer evidence of a widely shared cultural view of the danger of both women and their emotionality. Lutz has argued that when women speak of self-control, they are engaging in a process by which they obviate the necessity for more coercive outside control from others.

Anne Campbell found that women and men have different social representations of anger and aggression based on their different relationships to power and socialization. Arguing that the actual experience of anger depends on the social representation of the meaning and management of that emotion, Campbell's research details how women envision that their anger and aggression result from a breakdown of their own internal control leading, in turn, to a breakdown of normal social interaction. Campbell found that anger feels good to most men because it confers the reward of dominance and control over others, whereas most women view an angry outburst as a failure of control, and they feel guilty about it rather than good. Dana Crowley Jack also found that women's schemas of angry, aggressive interactions include a fear of unpredictable negative consequences (chaos), which may arise from awareness that a woman's anger or aggression interrupts dominant social expectations and opens the door to retaliation. In agreement with Lutz, both Campbell and Jack found that after displays of anger and aggression, women engage in "preemptive self-condemnation." They place themselves in the role of an observer and offer the kind of condemnation that would be expected from an unsympathetic onlooker. A woman often employs preemptive self-strikes, such as criticizing herself publicly for any anger display, to convey to others that she is fully aware of the negative connotations that could be placed on the behavior and that she has already condemned herself for the behavior, thus rendering further social punishment unnecessary.

C. WOMEN'S ANGER IN INTIMATE RELATIONSHIPS

Neil Jacobson, John Gottman, and colleagues found that when heterosexual couples engage in violent, physical arguments, women fear men's anger and aggression; men do not fear women's. When Jacobson and Gottman studied such couples with a male batterer, they found that fear is the major gender difference between male and female violence. The women consistently manifested fear in the laboratory during arguments, whereas the men did not. The women consistently reported fear when describing arguments at home, whereas the men did not. Women fear that behind men's anger lies the threat of physical violence, and that their anger expression will create anger in their partners. In spite of their fear, some of the women with male batterers continued to stand up for themselves and to express anger. [See BATTERING IN ADULT RELATIONSHIPS.]

Further, a study examining the display of emotion in 30 heterosexual couples found strong differences in the ways women and men communicate negative feelings. John Gottman and Robert Levenson used measures of physiological responses, self-report, and video data to look at interaction in unhappy couples. At first glance, it appears as if each partner receives and gives back negative feelings to the other. Yet the wife and the husband are communicating different negative emotions: 78% of the husband's negative affect is anger and contempt, while 93% of the wife's negative feelings are expressed as "whining [sic], sadness, and fear." The data reveal "a clear dominance structure. . . . He reciprocates her anger, but she does not reciprocate his; instead she responds to his anger with fear, which leads back to his anger." In situations causing anger in couples, women's responses may initially reciprocate their partner's anger, but women's anger is quickly replaced with fear. As well, a common pattern is for women's anger expression to be met with emotional withdrawal by her male partner, thus increasing her anger over his refusal to address issues that arouse her anger, and thus continuing his emotional control.

In lesbian couples engaging in battering (which occurs at a rate similar to that of heterosexual couples), fear of the partner's anger is also associated with fear of the partner's physical attack. However, in her nationwide study of lesbian couples, Claire Renzetti found that jealousy and power imbalances, including economic inequality, predicted abuse more than did anger. [*See* LESBIANS, GAY MEN, AND BISEXUALS IN RELATIONSHIPS.]

D. ANGER AS A POLITICAL EMOTION

Elizabeth Spelman described a "politics of emotion": the systematic denial of anger can be seen as a mechanism of subordination and the existence and expression of anger as an act of insubordination. Anger may be the "essential political emotion" because it recognizes a violation and motivates a person to make personal and political change. When used politically, anger expression does not follow rules of status and hierarchy.

Social inequalities that instigate anger on a daily basis attach to race and class as well as to gender, to sexual preference, and to disabilities. Anger can become a powerful fuel to create political and personal change. Aida Hurtado and bell hooks describe using anger explicitly for political purposes. Hurtado recounts employing her anger to challenge the devaluing discrimination she faced growing up Latina in South Texas; hooks describes the importance of using anger creatively to oppose racism and insidious acts of discrimination.

Social rules not only affect women's anger display, social realities affect what choices women actually have for resolving discord and directly expressing their anger. Many women are convinced that voicing opposition or anger will be met with some type of negative consequence. Behind this fear, which often feels "inner" or uniquely personal, lie specific conditions that influence fear, such as violence, sexual and racial discrimination, and poverty. Women do face higher risks of negative economic, physical, or interpersonal consequences for voicing their anger, opposition, or demands than men do. It is difficult to separate the effects of gender socialization from the effects of status in women's likelihood of expressing their anger. Women more often occupy the lower rungs of economic and social hierarchies than men do. Even though many women have been socialized to suppress anger rather than express it directly and have learned to question themselves rather than the conditions that create anger, their social status also powerfully affects their anger expression. [*See* POLITICAL BEHAVIOR.]

E. SUMMARY OF THEMES REGARDING WOMEN'S ANGER

Summarizing research on women's anger and themes from their focus group interviews with selected girls and women, Deborah Cox, Sally Stabb, and Karen Bruckner have listed the following feminist issues:

1. *Fundamental tension between adaptive function and societal inhibition.* Women describe the tension of feeling their anger while experiencing societal messages not to feel, to control, to suppress, or to redirect their anger away from its instigators and into a "safe" direction.

2. *Exquisite sensitivity to power differences and degrees of affiliation/relational context.* Anger expression most often follows hierarchical lines, with the safest targets being close friends. Decreased affiliation and increased social power of the target results in decreased safety for anger expression. Some women express indifference to the status or affiliation of their anger's target.

3. *The implied fear of anger leading to aggression in both self and others.* Women often associate anger with abuses of power and destructive aggression, both in others and in themselves.

4. *Men's withdrawal from girls' and women's anger.* Women are further angered by men's refusal to engage with the causes of their anger.

5. *Sexual harassment as a source of anger.* A woman's social context and support influence the way she channels anger resulting from harassment into positive action or diverts it.

6. *Anger specific to prejudice identified by all minority groups.* Discrimination arouses anger; chronic, unexpressed anger can carry negative health effects.

7. *Recognition of individual differences in personality and dysfunction in both women and men.* Women recognize that anger can attain dysfunctional levels in both its expressed and suppressed forms.

V. Anger and Physical Illness

Anger has been linked to many adverse psychological and physical consequences, including depression, eating disorders, irritable bowel syndrome, hypertension and cardiovascular disease, and suicide. A number of researchers have hypothesized that the manner in which people express or control their anger is a critical variable relating to health consequences, yet findings regarding how styles of anger expression associate with specific negative health outcomes are complex and contradictory. For example, some studies suggest that the outward expression of anger, reflected in the Type A personality and other hostile behaviors, is associated with the development of coronary heart disease. Other studies conclude that the suppression of anger increases the risk of hypertension and coronary heart disease and is associated with higher rates of suicide.

One difficulty in determining how style of anger expression relates to physical and mental ill health may derive from the inadequacy of instruments used to measure anger expression. Numerous reviewers have commented on the problems with existing anger assessment instruments, including false dichotomies between suppression and expression of anger, artificial quantification of anger severity, inadequate distinction between explosive, aggressive displays and more constructive outward forms of expression, anger vignettes that are relevant only to specific populations, and conflation of categories such as shame, hostility, and guilt with anger.

Anger measures are rarely sensitive to gender-related ways of expressing emotion. Sandra Thomas, in her study of 535 women, used a wide range of somatic, cognitive and anger proneness anger measures in the first phase of her research. Concerned that women may have other ways of expressing their anger that are not measured by existing tests, Thomas asked recipients for written descriptions of "anything else that you do when angry that has not been mentioned on our questionnaires." She found specific strategies and behaviors that are not assessed by current measures, such as crying, physical activity, reflection, prayer, writing, and planning for a problem-solving discussion with the offender. Reflection, for example, includes the ability to look at the situation from the other person's perspective and offers a valuable behavior for increasing effective conflict. Thus, instruments widely used to assess anger expression may be insensitive to gender-related styles and may be omitting behaviors that determine whether anger expression is beneficial or harmful.

For example, though studies find that women are four times more likely than men to cry when angry, many anger measures do not include crying as a form of anger expression. Women's tears are a socialized, behavioral display of women's anger. They offer solution to the puzzle of how to express anger in ways that do not threaten the other person and provide a safe means to express anger without being aggressive to another or without violating social norms regarding how women "should" behave interpersonally in a nondominant manner. Onlookers often misconstrue women's crying as weakness and often trivialize and pathologize tears or label them as manipula-

tive. In experimental studies, women have been found to be less reluctant than men to express powerless emotions, such as sadness and fear, whereas men are more motivated to stay in control and tend to express emotions, such as anger, that reflect their power. [*See* EMPATHY AND EMOTIONAL EXPRESSIVITY.]

Despite problems in measurement that may not reflect women's experience, research suggests a relationship between racial discrimination and higher blood pressure in African American women due to anger's arousal and its suppression. For example, Nancy Krieger conducted a study with 51 African American women and 50 White women, ages 20 to 80 years, who described how they dealt with unfair treatment from others. Among Black women, those who stated they usually accepted and kept quiet about unfair treatment were 4.4 times more likely to report hypertension than those who said they took action and talked to others. No clear association between anger expression and hypertension was found among White respondents. Additionally, in a study of 1323 African Americans examining the prevalence of hypertension and the frequency that anger is expressed outwardly toward people and objects in the environment, Ernest Johnson and Larry Gant found that a significantly greater number of women with high blood pressure scored low on anger expression, while there was no significant difference between anger expression styles and hypertension for Black men. Clearly, racial and gender contexts affect whether or not people choose to reveal their anger. Suppressed anger can affect health when the stressful situation continues; expressed anger can affect health when it results in even worse interpersonal consequences.

Further, studies have linked the construct of self-silencing (what is often called anger suppression) to a number of specific illnesses in women, such as irritable bowel syndrome, eating disorders, and depression. Dana Crowley Jack defined "silencing the self" as keeping vital aspects of self (thoughts, feelings, goals) hidden out of fear that exhibiting them would threaten one's relationships or one's safety. Self-silencing is a cognitive activity in which a person monitors the self, tries to eliminate thoughts and feelings perceived as dangerous to relationships, and attempts to bring feelings into line with perceived notions of how one "ought" to feel and behave. Self-silencing includes suppressing one's anger, that is, not expressing anger directly but keeping it out of relationships; doing so means that the situation that causes the anger remains unaddressed. Comparing women who had irritable bowel syndrome (IBS) with those who had inflammatory bowel disease (IBD), Alisha Ali and colleagues found that women with IBS scored higher on self-silencing (as measured by Jack's Silencing the Self Scale), self-blame, and emotional abuse from others. [*See* HEALTH AND HEALTH CARE.]

The emotion of anger has been linked to women's eating disorders in numerous ways. Most basically, food is used to alter moods; eating (overeating, not eating, or bingeing and purging) to alter moods may become an addictive behavior. Estimates are that 30 to 85% of women who are bulimic have been physically or sexually abused and experience problems with depression, anxiety, interpersonal relationships, and anger. Numerous studies report that overweight women use food to deal with depressed, anxious, or angry feelings. As well, the bingeing and purging of bulimia often relate to crises and upsets involving anger. Suppressing anger is also tied to eating disorders. Among such studies, Romy Cawood found that self-silencing predicted level of eating disorders in a sample of college women as measured by the Eating Disorders Inventory and the Questionnaire for Eating Disorders Diagnosis. [*See* EATING DISORDERS AND DISORDERED EATING.]

VI. Women's Anger in Relation to Their Depression

The popular belief is that anger turned inward can lead to depression. Yet, interestingly, depressed people are often outwardly angry. In fact, increased irritability is one of the symptoms of depression. Also, depression may result from the ineffective use of anger, as when anger does not accomplish its intent of changing an ongoing situation that causes anger or fails to remove obstacles to relationship or impediments to achieving one's goals. After anger has been ineffective, it is easy to feel more hopeless about having any control over one's life.

The relationship of women's anger to their depression is complex. Similar social realities affect both women's anger expression and women's vulnerability to depression. These social realities include poverty, violence against women, and women's general social inequality, as well as their inequality in intimate relationships with men. Women's fears about the negative consequences of overt anger expression, which many equate with aggression, appear to be re-

lated to the inhibited behaviors and cognitive styles researchers find associated with female depression. Cognitive-behavioral studies have revealed that directing angry hostility inward creates depressed feeling; when anger cannot be expressed, it often finds an outlet in negative self-talk and self-deprecation. Whether a woman's anger is related to her depression in any given instance depends on a number of factors: the social situation that precipitated her anger and depression, the woman's interpretation (or cognitive appraisal) of the situation, the social supports she has available, and on her perception of the choices she has in response to the situation.

Studies find that the construct of self-silencing, measured by Jack's Silencing the Self Scale, reliably predicts depression across a number of populations. Suppressing anger, or keeping it out of relationship, appears particularly linked to depression because anger demands positive, interpersonal expression; its function is to regulate relationships, to restore connection, to have an interpersonal effect. Suppression of anger eliminates the possibility that ongoing conditions affecting the anger, including misattributions as well as inequities, will change. Self-silencing can lead a woman to feel separated from others and from herself, and to the experience of presenting a "false self" to others. Her anger over disconnection can contribute to depression, as can hopelessness about changing the conditions that instigate anger. Currently, the physiological relationship of chronic anger arousal and suppression to the biochemistry of depression is not well known.

Uncontrolled, explosive anger expression does not protect women against depression. The critical issue regarding anger appears to be how a person brings it into relationship, whether doing so facilitates dialogue and connection, and whether the situation that relates to the anger is open to influence and change.

As well as suppressing anger, women often turn their anger against themselves. If a woman perceives some aspect of her *self* as the barrier to what she desires—positive relationships, inclusion, success—then she may direct her hostile anger against herself for not being "pretty" enough, smart enough, or lovable enough. Culture plays a vital role in women's tendency to self-blame and self-attack, providing images of how they "should" be and look, and holding them responsible when relationships fail. In self-attacks, social factors contributing to women's feelings of powerlessness become converted into hated personal deficits as a woman perceives herself as creating the problem. As cognitive-behavioral studies have revealed, directing angry hostility inward creates depressed feeling. [See DEPRESSION.]

VII. Therapeutic Interventions for Women's Anger-Related Conflicts

Therapists working with women's anger in therapy use a number of approaches. Feminist therapy, as defined by Judith Worell, Pam Remer, and others writing from a feminist perspective, works toward facilitating a woman's empowerment, both at the personal and at the social level. Empowerment means validating women's experiences, fostering awareness of power imbalances within clients' relationships that reflect the wider society (including the power imbalances inherent in the therapist-client relationship), and facilitating the client's ability to control her own life, define her own goals, and make the changes that she desires for her own well-being and circumstances. Women who have been victims of others' destructive anger and aggression can fear the consequences of anger expression, which can create a prohibition against exploring their own anger. As well, it is useful to explore relational binds that have made a woman angry, such as suppressing anger in discriminatory situations or feeling a forced choice between self-definition (anger expression) and anger suppression.

Women rarely name their anger as the problem for which they are seeking therapy. More often, anger comes to attention as it relates to the issue for which a woman seeks help, such as depression, eating disorders, anxiety, or physical illness. When anger is the presenting problem, clients often seek anger-control strategies or have been ordered to therapy for help with anger management. Representative feminist approaches to working with women's anger-related conflicts in therapy are summarized next. [See COUNSELING AND PSYCHOTHERAPY; FEMINIST APPROACHES TO PSYCHOTHERAPY.]

1. Jean Baker Miller and colleagues at the Stone Center have taken a relational and psychodynamic approach to women's anger. Not only does anger remind a woman of her separateness, it brings to the fore a seemingly irresolvable conflict between autonomy and intimacy, which needs to be addressed in therapy. Miller and Janet Surrey have suggested helping women rethink the common assumption that anger is a destructive and negative emotion. Those in power have an investment in women's perception of their anger as something negative to be feared; such a belief can be used to maintain positions of power and subordination. Within relationships, the signal of anger may serve a communicative function and be a necessary part of dynamic, changing relationships. Therapy can be aimed at deconstructing a woman's fear that expressing anger will cause conflict, which may threaten her connections. It can also focus on helping a woman find positive, direct ways to communicate her anger.

Miller has suggested reframing anger as a signal, an emotional response to having been wronged, and as a powerful motivation to bring about change. If, for example, anger is tied to trauma, such as rape or battering, the client can not only work through the trauma, but connect her anger with groups working to create social change.

2. Cognitive-behavioral approaches to anger management consider that anger is triggered by irrational thoughts in response to situations, especially thoughts related to unconscious demands and expectations. People are able to control and change their thoughts, which allows greater freedom of response to anger-provoking situations. Cognitive-behavioral techniques can be used to help women with a range of difficulties, from uncontrolled, destructive anger to habitual suppression of anger. Goals are set by the client and revolve around identifying sources of anger (both external situations and irrational thoughts) and developing cognitive-behavioral coping techniques to deal with anger. Commonly used techniques include thought-stopping, self-talk to prevent the escalation or suppression of anger, timeouts or other self-calming techniques, changing negative self-talk to positive self-talk, and disputing irrational beliefs about anger expression. Since physiological arousal is part of anger (both suppressed and expressed anger), techniques may also include relaxation methods such as muscle tensing and relaxing, deep breathing, and self-guided imagery. One common type of self-guided imagery consists of imagining a relaxing place, such as a beach, and conjuring the recollections of sun, the sound of surf, the sensations of warm sand, and so on in order to relax. Many cognitive-behavioral therapies also focus on values clarification, in which the client identifies the source of her anger and assesses what actions she can take to resolve the situation, including addressing or leaving it. Role-playing scenarios can be used to practice assertive, constructive

expressions of anger rather than aggressive or passive responses. In situations where expressing anger will make the problem worse, such as in certain work situations, the client can actively choose alternative outlets for anger's energy, such as exercise, creative pursuits, or joining groups working for social change on the issue that is causing the anger.

3. Rather than "anger management," Deborah Cox, Sally Stabb, and Karin Bruckner advocate a method of therapy that involves two dimensions. First, the revelation of anger to self—the release of anger in a safe and empowering manner so that anger becomes a less threatening emotion. Second, the revelation to others—the appropriate and respectful expression, or clarification, of anger to others. These revelations of anger require safety from a risk of loss of control or shaming by others. Becoming acquainted with one's anger in these ways allows for its integration and for its creative, positive expression.

4. Anger awareness can be linked to body awareness, and women can learn to reintegrate feelings of anger with positive instrumental actions, including carrying out their own will. Possible avenues include martial arts and self-defense training, as well as practices that teach one to recognize bodily sensations and physicality, such as yoga and tai chi. The body gives signals about health, safety, and emotions as well as being a source of force; many women have become so split from their bodies and emotions that they do not recognize their anger. Moreover, knowledge of one's power includes knowledge of one's potential for both creativity and destruction.

In summary, women face many obstacles to using their anger in positive ways, yet positive anger expression is necessary to define one's self and goals and to oppose conditions that are oppressive. The changing norms of today's society regarding women's behavior allow more freedom for women to utilize this powerful emotion in positive ways for personal and societal change.

SUGGESTED READING

Cox, D. L., Stabb, S. D., and Bruckner, K. H. (1999). *Women's Anger: Clinical and Developmental Perspectives.* Brunner/Mazel, Philadelphia.

hooks, b. (1996). *Killing Rage: Ending Racism.* Henry Holt, New York.

Jack, D. (1999). *Behind the Mask: Destruction and Creativity in Women's Aggression.* Harvard University Press, Cambridge, MA.

Lerner, H. (1997). *The Dance of Anger: A Woman's Guide to Changing the Patterns of Intimate Relationships.* HarperCollins, New York.

Miller, J. B. (1991). The construction of anger in women and men. In *Women's Growth in Connection: Writings from the Stone Center* (J. V. Jordan, A. G. Kaplan, J. B. Miller, I. P. Stiver, and J. L. Surrey, eds.). New York: Guilford Press.

Stearns, C. Z., and Stearns, P. N. (1986). *Anger: The Struggle for Emotional Control in America's History.* The University of Chicago Press, Chicago.

Tavris, C. (1989). *Anger: The Misunderstood Emotion,* rev. ed. Simon & Schuster, New York.

Thomas, S. P. (1993). *Women and Anger.* Springer, New York.

Valentis, M., and Devane, A. (1994). *Female Rage: Unlocking Its Secrets, Claiming Its Power.* Carol Southern Books, New York.

Anxiety

Shawn P. Cahill

Edna B. Foa

University of Pennsylvania

I. Anxiety as a Construct and the Measurement of Anxiety
II. Anxiety as a Normal Emotion
III. Anxiety as a Symptom
IV. The Anxiety Disorders
V. Conclusions

Glossary

Anxiety disorders A group of psychiatric disorders in which the central feature is excessive, unrealistic, and persistent anxiety that is associated with extreme distress or impairment.

Anxiety sensitivity A stable tendency to fear anxiety symptoms because they are believed to cause harm such as heart attack.

Comorbidity The co-occurrence of two or more psychiatric disorders in the same person.

Epidemiology The study of the incidence and distribution of psychiatric disorders in the population.

Heritability Estimates of the degree to which variation in some physical or psychological characteristic within a given population is genetically determined.

State anxiety An emotional reaction in response to threat, characterized by subjective distress and physiological arousal.

Trait anxiety A stable tendency to experience state anxiety across a variety of situations.

ANXIETY can be viewed from several perspectives. One perspective views anxiety as a normal emotional experience characterized by a subjective feeling of fear or apprehension in response to perceived threat or danger, accompanied by physiological arousal and activation of fight or flight behavior. Another perspective views anxiety as a sign, symptom, indicator, or consequence of some underlying psychological or biological condition. Finally, from the psychiatric perspective, anxiety is a pathological condition and several specific disorders have been identified in which anxiety is the main feature. By definition, anxiety disorders are characterized not only by symptoms of severe anxiety, but also by distress and functional impairment associated with the symptoms. Regardless of the perspective, anxiety has commonly been conceptualized as a multifaceted construct that may be measured via three partially independent systems: (1) the subjective system, involving self-reports of feelings and cognitions; (2) the motoric behavior system, involving emotionally expressive behavior (e.g., facial reactions) and avoidance behavior; and (3) physiological arousal (e.g., increased heart rate, perspiration). Anxiety has sometimes been distinguished from fear, where fear reactions are triggered by the presence of actual threat, and anxiety involves the anticipation of threat. This article first describes several important issues related to the definition and measurement of anxiety and then discusses anxiety from each of the three perspectives outlined earlier.

I. Anxiety as a Construct and the Measurement of Anxiety

What is anxiety? How is anxiety measured? No single answer exists to either of these questions and, in fact, how one answers either of these questions influences the answer to the other. For example, if anxiety is viewed as a subjective emotional state, then by definition it can only be observed by the person experiencing it. In this case, the measurement of anxiety would have to rely exclusively on the person's self-report of the emotional experience. If the emphasis is on the motoric system, the measurement will focus on overt behaviors such as facial expressions, escape, and avoidance. Finally, if anxiety is viewed in terms of physiological arousal, then measurement will focus on indicators such as heart rate and respiration. While each of these three measurement approaches has helped to advance our knowledge about anxiety, no single approach by itself provides a complete picture. Thus, anxiety is best viewed as a multifaceted construct that calls for measurement in several response systems (subjective, behavioral, and physiological), none of which uniquely defines anxiety.

II. Anxiety as a Normal Emotion

Anxiety is a normal emotional reaction that is experienced sometimes by everyone. Subjectively, it is experienced as a negative affective state most often accompanied by physiological arousal, which occurs in response to perceptions of threat or anticipation of harm. As a normal emotional reaction, anxiety fluctuates according to the situation, increasing when threat is perceived and decreasing when the threat disappears. The primary function of anxiety reactions is to prepare the person to respond adaptively to the threat. Thus, the cognitions and subjective anxiety help the person appraise the degree of danger, and the physiological arousal (increased heart rate, increased respiration) helps support adaptive responding to a threatening situation (e.g., running away from an attacking dog).

Although anxiety is a common emotional state experienced by most, individuals differ considerably in their proneness to experience anxiety: while some people seldom feel anxious, even in the face of danger, others feel anxious in a wide range of daily situations. Further, the tendency to be calm or anxious appears to be stable over time. Thus, a useful distinction may be made between state anxiety, referring to an acute emotional reaction to threat, and trait anxiety, referring to stable tendency to view the world as a dangerous or safe place. As such, trait anxiety reflects the frequency of experiencing state anxiety over extended periods of time.

Another important individual difference relates to anxiety sensitivity, that is, the degree to which anxiety is itself distressing. While most people regard anxiety as being unpleasant, some individuals experience anxiety reaction as most upsetting. Indeed, the history of the anxiety sensitivity concept lays in the earlier "fear of fear" concept, wherein people respond with fear to normal bodily reactions to threat. Conceptually, state anxiety, trait anxiety, and anxiety sensitivity are orthogonal to one another, such that levels can independently vary on each factor. In reality, however, measures of all three factors are often intercorrelated with one another. The research evidence on the relationship between trait anxiety and anxiety sensitivity is mixed. On the one hand, studies have found substantial correlations between measures of state anxiety and anxiety sensitivity, suggesting considerable overlap between the two constructs. On the other hand, several findings suggest that the two constructs tap different phenomena. These include the following: (1) anxiety sensitivity predicts fearfulness even when the overlap with trait anxiety is statistically controlled, (2) factor analytic studies yield separate factors that correspond with the items on the two different measures, and (3) trait anxiety is generally elevated among individuals with any of the anxiety disorders, whereas anxiety sensitivity appears to be uniquely associated with panic disorder. This latter finding is particularly important because it supports current conceptualizations of panic disorder as involving fear of the bodily sensations associated with panic. Furthermore, longitudinal studies have demonstrated that elevated anxiety sensitivity predicted the development of panic attacks among individuals with no prior history of having them.

To reconcile the inconsistent findings about the relationship between trait anxiety and anxiety sensitivity, some experts have proposed a hierarchical model in which anxiety sensitivity, along with fear-of-injury sensitivity and for fear-of-social-evaluation sensitivity, are lower-order traits nested within the higher-order trait anxiety dimension. This model accounts for the overlap between trait anxiety and anxiety sensitivity, as well as the specific relationship between anxiety sensitivity and panic.

III. Anxiety as a Symptom

As noted earlier, normal anxiety is viewed as the activation of adaptive reactions to potential or actual threat. However, the various systems of anxiety can be activated by events other than realistic threat, in which case the experience of anxiety may reflect the activation of some other underlying psychological or biological process. In other words, anxiety may be viewed as a symptom of some other condition. For example, people may experience subjective anxiety and physiological arousal in response to a variety of substances such as caffeine, and anxiety can be a side effect of different medications. Anxiety may also be the result of an abnormal medical condition, such as hyperthyroidism. In each of the preceding examples, anxiety is not seen as the focus of the condition itself and is expected to be alleviated when the underlying condition is removed (e.g., discontinuation of the anxiety-producing substance or medication, treatment for the medical condition). In contrast to anxiety as a symptom, the anxiety disorders constitute a class of psychiatric conditions in which anxiety is a defining feature of the syndrome and the goal of treatment is the alleviation of the anxiety itself, rather than correcting some other (nonanxiety) underlying problem.

IV. The Anxiety Disorders

The *Diagnostic and Statistical Manual of Mental Disorders* (DSM) defines the term "mental disorder" and specifies the criterion for all mental disorders that are officially recognized by the American Psychiatric Association. According to the current edition of the manual, *DSM-IV,* a mental disorder is a clinically significant behavioral or psychological syndrome or pattern that is associated with significant distress or disability. *DSM-IV* recognizes nine specific primary anxiety disorders, all of which involve anxiety that is excessive, unrealistic, and persistent. The various anxiety disorders differ from one another with regard to the circumstances that activate the anxiety and how the anxiety is expressed. A defining criterion common to all of the anxiety disorders is that the avoidance or emotional distress associated with the anxiety must be significant enough to interfere with the person's social and occupational functioning. [*See* DIAGNOSIS OF PSYCHOLOGICAL DISORDERS.]

A. PANIC DISORDER AND AGORAPHOBIA

The *DSM-IV* specifies three disorders associated with the phenomenon of panic attacks or a pattern of extreme behavioral avoidance called agoraphobia. These are panic disorder without agoraphobia, panic disorder with agoraphobia, and agoraphobia without a history of panic disorder.

Central to the diagnosis of panic disorder (PD), with or without agoraphobia, is panic. A *panic attack* is a sudden, intense rush of fear, anxiety, or impending doom that reaches a peak very quickly and is associated with at least 4 of 13 physical and cognitive symptoms (e.g., shortness of breath, dizziness, heart palpitations, fear of dying, fear of going crazy or losing control). Panic attacks may be cued by a specific situation, as when someone who is afraid of snakes encounters one, or they may be unexpected and perceived by the individual as coming out of the blue.

Although the experience of one or more unexpected panic attacks is necessary for the diagnosis of panic disorder, it is not by itself sufficient. Rather, the diagnosis of panic disorder requires a minimum period of one month during which time the individual must have recurrent unexpected panic attacks, at least one of which is followed by persisting concerns about having additional attacks or persistent worries about the physical or psychological consequences of the attack (e.g., having a heart attack, going crazy).

Panic disorder may or may not be accompanied by a pervasive pattern of avoiding situations in which help may not be available in the event of a panic attack. This avoidance pattern is known as agoraphobia. Typical agoraphobic situations include a variety of crowded public places (e.g., malls, restaurants, theaters), wide open spaces, and enclosed spaces (e.g., closets, elevators, cars). In addition, those with panic disorder (with or without agoraphobia) may avoid things that produce physical sensations similar to their panic attacks, such as strenuous exercise (heart palpitations, difficulty breathing, hyperventilation), amusement park rides (dizziness, nausea), or even foods and beverages that contain caffeine.

Epidemiological studies indicate that panic attacks are relatively common in the general population. As many as 30% of the population will have experienced some kind of panic attack (cued or uncued) in the past year, and between 9 and 14% will have experienced an entirely unexpected panic attack of the sort required for the diagnosis of panic disorder. Yet only 2 to 6% of the population will develop the full PD syndrome (with or without agoraphobia). Although most experts believe that agoraphobia is a consequence of experiencing unexpected panic attacks, *DSM-IV* does permit the diagnosis of agoraphobia without a history of panic disorder. Clinically, this condition is rare and most often presents with a history of anxiety attacks that, although not meeting the full criteria for a panic attack, appear to instigate the agoraphobic avoidance. [*See* AGORAPHOBIA, PANIC DISORDER, AND GENDER.]

B. SPECIFIC PHOBIAS

The key feature of specific phobias is the presence of a persistent and intense fear or avoidance of specific objects or situations that the individual recognizes as being excessive or unreasonable. In addition, fear and avoidance must significantly interfere with the person's social and occupational functioning or the person experiences marked distress about having the phobia. In children, the fears must persist at least six months in order to distinguish them from normal transient childhood fears. Further, insight into the excessive or unreasonable quality of the fears may be absent in children. Although the full range of phobic situations is quite broad, the most common are animal phobias (e.g., dogs, insects), natural environment phobias (e.g., heights, storms, water), blood-injury phobias (including receiving or viewing injections), and situational phobias (e.g., bridges, flying, enclosed spaces). Epidemiological studies indicate that between 5 and 10% of population experience the combination of intense fear, avoidance, and impairment that meet criteria for specific phobia.

C. SOCIAL PHOBIA

Human beings are highly social animals who most frequently live, work, and recreate within groups. Despite this, shyness is very common. For example, in one large survey of college students, 80% of participants indicated they had been shy at one point in their life, and 40% identified themselves as being currently shy.

Social phobia, however, is more than just shyness. Rather, socially phobic individuals experience marked and persistent fear or avoidance of one or more social or performance situations. In such situations, the person may fear doing or saying something embarrassing or fear manifesting the signs of anxiety (e.g., blushing, sweating, trembling). Most individuals with social phobia fear and avoid multiple situations, falling within the generalized subtype of social phobia. Generalized social phobia is a debilitating disorder that often severely disrupts social and occupational functioning. It is associated with extreme distress, failure to establish and maintain both casual and intimate relationships, and underemployment.

Prevalence estimates of social phobia vary significantly across different studies, ranging from a little more than 1% of the general population to as high as 13%. Although the reasons for the disparity among different studies are unknown, one factor appears to be the differing criteria across successive editions of the *DSM*, with the most recent editions being less restrictive than were earlier editions.

D. OBSESSIVE-COMPULSIVE DISORDER (OCD)

As the name implies, the person afflicted with obsessive-compulsive disorder (OCD) suffers from one or more obsession or compulsions. Obsessions are recurrent thoughts, images, or impulses that are experienced as intrusive and unwanted and cause extreme distress. Compulsions are defined as thoughts or behaviors that are usually carried out in response to an obsession or according to rigid rules with the goal of reducing distress associated with an obsession or to prevent some feared consequence.

One common obsession involves concern with being contaminated by germs or dirt. Individuals with such obsessions are driven to wash their hands and shower excessively or to go to great lengths to avoid situations in which they may come into contact with feared contaminants. Another common obsession involves a person doubting her or his performance of such routine activities as locking a door or turning off an iron, stove, or other appliance. These fears often lead to excessive checking and repeating these activities in order to prevent catastrophic accidents. In severe cases, the obsessions and compulsions occupy several hours of the afflicted person's day and secondary complications may develop as a consequence of the compulsions, such as severe skin problems produced by repeated washing with harsh cleansers in the effort to decontaminate. OCD used to be thought of as a relatively rare condition with a prevalence rate of 0.5%, and that it was especially resistant to psychological or pharmacological treatment. Current research indicates it is neither rare, with an actual prevalence rate of approximately 2.5%, nor is it impervious to treatment. Indeed, both psychological and pharmacological treatments have been shown to be helpful in ameliorating the symptoms of this disorder.

E. POSTTRAUMATIC STRESS DISORDER AND ACUTE STRESS DISORDER

While a stressful life event may precipitate the onset of any anxiety disorder, posttraumatic stress disorder (PTSD) and acute stress disorder are unique in that their diagnostic criteria require that the symptoms develop subsequent to a traumatic event. For a stressful experience to be classified as a traumatic event, it must first involve actual or threatened death, serious harm, or other threat to the physical integrity of the self or others, and second, the person must experience the event with intense feelings of fear, helplessness, or horror. Despite this strict definition, the prevalence of traumatic events is extremely high, with 50 to 70% of the United States population reporting exposure to one or more such events. Examples of common traumatic events are physical or sexual assault, combat, life threatening-accidents or illnesses, and natural or human-caused disasters.

Following exposure to a traumatic event, people are frequently bothered by persistent symptoms that form three clusters: (1) reexperiencing the traumatic event through distressing memories, nightmares, or flashbacks, and the intense fear of trauma reminders; (2) avoidance of trauma reminders, social withdrawal, and numbing of emotional responsiveness; and (3) hyperarousal, including sleep difficulties, irritability, and exaggerated startle response. For most people, these symptoms substantially decline in the course of the following one to three months. Those who continue to experience severe symptoms three months after the trauma are not likely to recover. Because most people recover during the first month post-trauma, *DSM* requires the symptoms to be present for at least one month before a diagnosis of PTSD can be made, and if the symptoms persist three months or longer, it is classified as chronic PTSD.

Acute stress disorder is a recent addition to the *DSM* classification system. The diagnostic criteria specify that the person must experience a traumatic event and develop PTSD-like symptoms within four weeks of the traumatic event for at least two days but do not last for more than four weeks. Beyond these temporal differences, what distinguishes acute stress disorder from PTSD is that diagnosis of the former also requires the presence of several dissociative symptoms, such as feelings of derealization and depersonalization. [*See* POSTTRAUMATIC STRESS DISORDER; TRAUMA ACROSS DIVERSE SETTINGS.]

F. GENERALIZED ANXIETY DISORDER

The key feature of generalized anxiety disorder is the presence of excessive worry and anxiety. The content of the worry encompasses a range of domains (e.g., school or work performance, personal finances) and cannot be limited to features of another specific disorder, such as worrying about having a panic attack (as in panic disorder). The anxiety and worry are associated with several symptoms of arousal or distress, at least some of which are present more days than not for a period of six months or longer. Further distinguishing pathological worry, as it appears in generalized anxiety disorder, from normal worry is that the frequency, intensity, duration of the worry and associated anxiety are far in excess to the actual probability or impact of the feared event and that the worry is experienced as difficult to control. The lifetime prevalence rate for generalized anxiety disorder is approximately 5%.

Recent theories of generalized anxiety disorder have attempted to provide functional accounts for the presence of the excessive worry. For example, active worrying has been found to decrease spontaneous aversive emotional imagery and is associated with a dampening of physiological arousal. Accordingly, it has been suggested that some individuals may adopt worry as a strategy to regulate their anxiety.

G. EPIDEMIOLOGY AND ETIOLOGY OF ANXIETY DISORDERS

Anxiety, as manifested in the various anxiety disorders, is the most prevalent form of psychiatric problem. The National Comorbidity Survey (NCS), an epidemiological study of a nationally representative sample of more than 8000 people in the United States, found that 17.2% of the sample met diagnostic criteria for at least one anxiety disorder during the preceding year. This compares with 11.3% for one of the affective disorders (e.g., depression, bipolar disorder) and 11.3% for a substance abuse disorder, the two next most common psychiatric conditions.

Two other important facts about psychiatric disorders in general, and about anxiety disorders in particular, emerge from epidemiological studies. First, there is substantial comorbidity among psychiatric disorders. Indeed, among individuals in the NCS who met criteria for at least one psychiatric disorder in the past year, nearly 60% also had three or more psychiatric disorders over the course of the individual's life. Anxiety disorders are frequently comorbid with one another, so that it is common for an individual to meet criteria for two or more anxiety disorders (e.g., panic disorder and generalized anxiety disorder). Also, individuals with anxiety disorders frequently meet diagnostic criteria for major depression and substance abuse disorders.

Second, psychiatric disorders are not evenly distributed between men and women. Rather, anxiety and most affective disorders are more prevalent among women than among men, whereas the reverse is true for substance abuse and antisocial behavior. Women are 2 to 2.5 times more likely than men to have panic disorder, agoraphobia without panic disorder, simple phobia, generalized anxiety disorder, and PTSD. Gender differences, although less pronounced, also exist for obsessive compulsive disorder and social phobia.

What are the causes of anxiety disorders and why are some people, particularly women, at greater risk than others to suffer from them? Research suggests that these disorders are caused by a combination of genetically determined biological vulnerabilities and by psychological vulnerabilities acquired through experience. Family studies have shown that anxiety disorders run in families, so that individuals with an anxiety disorder are more likely to have first-degree relatives who are similarly afflicted than individuals who do not have an anxiety disorder. Twin studies have further demonstrated that identical twins are more likely to be concordant for the presence or absence of an anxiety disorder (e.g., both twins have an anxiety disorder) than are fraternal twins. However, studies also suggest that the inherited vulnerability is for a general tendency to strongly respond to stressful experiences with anxiety or depression, rather than for a tendency to acquire a specific disorder. Moreover, heritability estimates suggest that genetics account for 30 to 50% of the variance in anxiety disorders with the remaining 50 to 70% of the variance being accounted for by a number of experiential (environmental) factors.

Two experiential factors that feature prominently in a number of psychological theories of anxiety and depression are (1) a psychological vulnerability factor of a diminished sense of control acquired through prior repeated experiences with uncontrollable aversive events and (2) current stressful life events. Specifically, as discussed earlier, stressful life events activate unpleasant emotional states in most individuals, which mobilize adaptive behaviors and subside when the stressful event has passed. Among vulnerable individuals, however, stressful life events can result in the kind of severe emotional distress and functional impairment that are characteristic of the anxiety and affective disorders. [See STRESS AND COPING.]

As with the biological vulnerability for experiencing strong negative emotional states, a diminished sense of control and the experience of stressful life events are general factors associated with the etiology and onset of a range of psychiatric disorders and are not specific to any particular disorder or class of disorders. In other words, these general factors help to identify which individuals are more likely to develop a psychiatric disorder than others and when a psychiatric disorder is likely to be expressed. However, these general factors cannot predict which of several possible disorders will be expressed.

Psychological theories have proposed two additional factors that influence how an emotional disorder will be expressed in different individuals. First, gender roles may explain some of the gender differences in the distribution of the various psychiatric disorders. For example, anxiety and depression are more consistent with female gender roles, while substance abuse and antisocial behavior are more consistent with male gender roles. Second, the individual's unique history with stressful events helps determine the specific way in which a psychiatric disorder will be expressed. In the case of anxiety disorders, different experiences will determine the situations that elicit anxiety. For example, a person who had experienced a spontaneous (i.e., unexpected) panic attack in the presence of an unfriendly dog is likely to develop a dog phobia, whereas the individual who had experienced a spontaneous panic attack during a public speaking engagement would be more likely to develop social phobia.

H. TREATMENT OF ANXIETY DISORDERS

1. Psychological Treatments

Effective cognitive-behavioral treatments have been developed for all anxiety disorders. These treatments consist of one or more of the following components: systematic exposure to feared but safe stimuli, cognitive restructuring of unrealistic fear-related thoughts, and training in specific anxiety management (e.g., relaxation) and other relevant skills (e.g., social skills training in the treatment of social anxiety).

a. Exposure Therapy. A large body of research demonstrates that exposure therapy, in which individuals repeatedly confront fear-provoking situations, objects, or memories, results in gradual reduction (habituation) of the fear reaction. Exposure therapy utilizes three modalities. In imaginal exposure, the person undergoing treatment is instructed to create mental images of the feared situations (e.g., imagining using a "contaminated" public telephone) or the feared consequences of confronting the feared situation (e.g., contracting a terrible disease). *In vivo* exposure involves direct contact with the actual feared situation, such as helping someone who is afraid of dogs to approach, pet, and play with a friendly dog. Interoceptive exposure involves intentionally arousing feared bodily sensations and is primarily used to help people overcome fears of sensations related to anxiety and panic, such as rapid and heavy breathing accompanied by dizziness, hyperventilation, and chest pains. Individuals with panic disorder frequently interpret these sensations as indicating they are having a heart attack or are going crazy and therefore, avoid activities that elicit these sensations. Common interoceptive exposure exercises to target this "fear of fear" include overbreathing to induce hyperventilation, spinning in a chair, breathing through a small straw, and bursts of intense physical activity (e.g., stair stepping). The key feature for selecting among the different modalities in treating a particular individual is that the stimulus content for the exposure exercise must match the stimulus content of the person's fear-related perceptions.

Individuals with anxiety disorders frequently have unrealistic, catastrophic thoughts related to their feared stimuli. For example, individuals with panic disorder may interpret their panic attacks as evidence of a serious medical problem; those with contamination obsessions may fear contracting venereal disease from using a public toilet; and those with a dog phobia may expect all dogs to viciously attack. Exposure therapy helps to modify the unrealistic evaluations associated with the unrealistic fear by demonstrating that the anticipated aversive consequences do not actually occur.

b. Cognitive Therapy. Another method for changing unrealistic evaluations is cognitive therapy (cognitive restructuring), in which individuals are taught how to evaluate the evidence for and against their beliefs, challenge the negative evaluations, and replace them with more realistic ones. For example, trauma survivors often develop exaggerated beliefs that the world is utterly dangerous and thus overestimate the likelihood of their being traumatized again. Cognitive therapy helps them to reevaluate their estimations of retraumatization by considering objective information.

c. Anxiety Management and Social Skills Training. Anxiety management training is often used as one component of treatment programs for anxiety disorders. This involves teaching people skills to manage the physiological arousal associated with anxiety, such as breathing retraining and progressive muscle relaxation. Other techniques, such as role playing, are employed in order to help individuals develop skills that they failed to acquire because of high levels of anxiety. Social skills training is particularly relevant in the treatment of social anxiety, where the socially anxious individual often acts in ways that fail to elicit positive responses or even trigger negative reactions from others, thereby reinforcing fear and avoidance of social situations.

2. Pharmacological Treatments

Several classes of medications have also been found to be helpful in the treatment of anxiety disorders. Two early classes of antidepressant medications, the tricyclics (e.g., imipramine) and monoamine oxidase inhibitors (e.g., phenelzine), have demonstrated efficacy in the treatment of several anxiety disorders, notably panic disorder and social phobia, respectively. Recently, they have been replaced as "front line" medications by selective serotonin reuptake inhibitors (SSRIs; e.g., fluoxetine, paroxetine, sertraline), another class of antidepressant medications that have also proven to be effective and have more favorable side effect profiles. Indeed, one or more of the SSRIs have received approval from the Food and Drug Administration (FDA) in the treatment of panic disorder, social phobia, posttraumatic stress disorder, and obsessive compulsive disorder. A disadvantage of all antidepressant medication is that they require several weeks of administration before anxiety is substantially reduced.

Another class of medications frequently used in

the treatment of anxiety is the high-potency benzo-diazepines (e.g., alprazolam, clonazepam). Compared to other medications used for anxiety, benzodiazepines have the advantage of being fast acting, usually reaching their peak blood level within 90 minutes of taking the medication. Thus, when encounters with feared situations can be accurately anticipated and planned for, such as an airplane flight or a trip to the dentist, these medications can be very helpful. In chronic anxiety conditions (e.g., generalized anxiety, panic attacks), a benzodiazepine may need to be taken regularly for longer periods of time under the supervision of a health care provider. However, the chronic use of benzodiazepines have several disadvantages, the most important ones being cognitive impairment due to the medication's sedating effect, the development of tolerance to the antianxiety effect of the medication, the potential for physical dependence, and aversive withdrawal symptoms upon discontinuation.

Two other medications that have received Food and Drug Administration approval for use with generalized anxiety disorder are briefly mentioned. Venlafaxine is an antidepressant medication that inhibits not only serotonin reuptake, like the SSRIs, but also the reuptake of norepinephrine. Buspirone is a non-benzodiazepine anxiolytic whose mechanism of action is not yet known.

One disadvantage associated with all medications used for the treatment of anxiety disorders is the high relapse rate when the medications are withdrawn. A strategy that has shown great promise is the addition of cognitive-behavior therapy for individuals who already are on medication and wish to discontinue their use.

V. Conclusions

This article examined anxiety from three perspectives: anxiety as a normal emotion, anxiety as a sign or symptom of a psychological or biological condition, and anxiety as a psychiatric condition. Regardless of the perspective taken, anxiety is best conceptualized as a multifaceted construct that calls for measurement in several response systems (e.g., subjective, behavioral, and physiological), none of which

uniquely defines anxiety. Normal anxiety is evoked when the individual perceives realistic threat and diminishes when the threat is terminated. In contrast, pathological anxiety, as manifested in the various anxiety disorders, is excessive, unrealistic, and persistent. Epidemiological studies indicate that pathological anxiety is the most prevalent psychiatric problem, occurring about twice as frequently in women than in men. Etiological theories of anxiety postulate both biological and psychological vulnerabilities. Both psychological and pharmacological treatments are effective in ameliorating symptoms of anxiety disorders. Cognitive behavioral interventions, including exposure therapy, cognitive therapy, and anxiety management training, have proven quite helpful. The most commonly used medications are the SSRIs. While cognitive behavior therapy produces significant, lasting improvements, it requires expertise and therefore is not always readily available. Medication treatment is widely available, but side effects and relapse upon discontinuation provide a considerable disadvantage.

SUGGESTED READING

Borkovec, T. D., and Lyonfields, J. D. (1993). Worry: Thought suppression of emotional processing. In *Attention and Avoidance* (H. W. Krohne, ed.), 101–118. Hogrefe & Huber, Seattle, WA.

Clark, D. M. (1986). A cognitive approach to panic disorder. *Behaviour Research and Therapy* **24**, 461–470.

Craske, M. G. (1999). *Anxiety Disorders: Psychological Approaches to Theory and Treatment.* Westview, Boulder, CO.

Foa, E. B., and Kozak, M. J. (1986). Emotional processing of fear: Exposure to corrective information. *Psychological Bulletin* **99**, 20–35.

Foa, E. B., and Rothbaum, B. O. (1998). *Treating the trauma of rape: Cognitive-behavioral therapy for PTSD.* Guilford, New York.

Gabbard, G. O. (ed.) (1998). *Treatments of psychiatric disorders,* 2nd ed., Vol. 2. American Psychiatric Press, Washington, DC.

Heimberg, R. G., Liebowitz, M. R., Hope, D. A., and Schneier, F. R. (eds.) (1995). *Social Phobia: Diagnosis, Assessment, and Treatment.* Guilford, New York.

McNally, R. J. (1994). *Panic Disorder: A Critical Analysis.* Guilford, New York.

Nathan, P. E., and Gorman, J. M. (eds.) (1998). *A Guide to Treatments That Work.* Oxford Press, New York.

Swinson, R. P., Antony, M. M., Rachman, S., and Richter, M. A. (eds.) (1998). *Obsessive-Compulsive Disorder: Theory, Research, and Treatment.* Guilford, New York.

Assertiveness

Linda L. Carli

Wellesley College

Glossary

Assertiveness Self-expression; also directness or defense of one's rights.

Descriptive stereotype A generalized belief that all members of a group of people share particular traits and behaviors.

Effect size A statistic that measures the size of the effect of an independent variable.

Exert power The capacity to influence others as a function of one's presumed knowledge or expertise.

Legitimate power The capacity to influence others as a function of one's right or authority to do so.

Meta-analysis A statistical technique that combines the results of two or more studies to assess the size and variability of an independent variable.

Negative assertion A forceful, controlling, or aggressive form of self-expression.

Prescriptive stereotype A generalized belief that requires members of a group of people to exhibit particular traits or behaviors.

Positive assertion Self-expression that acknowledges and supports the rights of others.

Referent power The capacity to influence others as a function of one's likableness or social attractiveness to others.

ASSERT, according to *Webster's Collegiate Dictionary,* 10th ed., is defined as "to state or declare positively and often forcefully or aggressively." In psychology, assertive behavior has been defined in a variety of ways, including directly and honestly communicating one's views; speaking up for oneself or defending one's rights; using competent forms of communication, such as rapid and fluent speech and a direct gaze; making strong statements, and openly expressing a contradictory point of view. In their 1993 book, *Assertion and Its Social Context,* Keithia Wilson and Cynthia Gallois compiled definitions of assertiveness from popular and scholarly sources, as well as a sample of adult laypersons. Wilson and Gallois were looking for common themes in the many ways in which assertiveness has been defined. They found that for all sources, assertiveness was most often defined as involving self-expression. Other common themes included directness, defending one's rights, respecting the rights of others, and behaving in a socially appropriate manner.

I. Introduction

Although the research of Wilson and Gallois revealed considerable agreement in the definitions of assertiveness, it also revealed that laymen were unique in their views. Unlike laywomen and popular and scholarly writers, laymen did not mention the rights of others in their definitions, but emphasized power, control of others, and getting one's way. Additional evidence that males may view assertiveness differently than females has been reported in research on children. For example, researchers Jane Connor, Lisa Serbin, and Regina Ender asked elementary school children how children should assert themselves with adults and peers. Results revealed that boys endorsed aggressive behavior as a means of self-assertion more than girls did. In contrast, in the professional literature, writers, such as Robert Alberti and Michael Emmons in their book *Your Perfect Right,* have often explicitly distinguished assertiveness from aggressiveness by noting that, unlike aggression, assertion involves socially appropriate behavior that does not violate the rights of others and does not involve rejection, punishment, threat, or negative evaluation of others. Nevertheless, because even in the professional literature assertiveness has sometimes been equated with aggressiveness or forcefulness, Wilson and Gallois distinguished the two styles of assertive self-expression by labeling the aggressive approach as *negative assertion* and the more socially appropriate approach as *positive assertion.* Generally, research indicates that positive assertion is a more effective strategy for interacting with others and achieving one's goals because it evokes more favorable reactions from others than does negative assertion. For example, Jeffrey Kern asked undergraduates to evaluate assertion that was either warm and emphatic or more affectively neutral; results revealed that the speakers using the more positive style of assertion received more favorable evaluations and, in particular, were liked more than those using the less positive style. Clearly, use of positive assertion is not only endorsed more strongly by experts and scholars than is negative assertion, but positive assertion evokes more favorable reactions from others.

The gender difference in defining assertiveness, with men and boys endorsing negative assertion more than women and girls, suggests that men and women may differ in their assertive behavior. Clearly, negative assertion is more congruent with the traditional male than the traditional female gender role. Research on gender role stereotyping reported by John Williams and Deborah Best in their book, *Measuring Sex Stereotypes: A Multination Study,* reveals that men are considered to be more direct, controlling, and aggressive, whereas women are considered to be more concerned with the needs of others. More specifically, Elizabeth Hess and her colleagues found evidence that both women and men consider positive assertion to be more stereotypically feminine than negative assertion. In addition, researchers Bruce Sterling and John Owen reported evidence that negative assertion conflicts with the traditional female role; they found that people consider the use of negative assertion to be unfeminine. These descriptive stereotypes, which are generalized beliefs about the traits or behaviors of a particular group of people, parallel the gender differences in definitions of assertiveness. Based on gender stereotypes, therefore, people would certainly expect women to use more positive forms of assertion than men and men to use more negative forms of assertion than women.

Although gender stereotypes are often thought of as descriptive generalizations about how women and men typically behave, stereotypes do not merely describe beliefs about gender differences in behavior, but are also highly prescriptive. Prescriptive stereotypes are generalized beliefs that members of a group of people should exhibit particular traits or behaviors and should be penalized when they do not. Indeed, there is ample evidence that people consider certain components of gender stereotypes to be desirable and necessary. In particular, people demand greater warmth and other-directedness from women. Furthermore, as noted in Carli (1999), men possess greater social power than women possess, with men more often attaining higher leadership positions, exerting greater influence over others, and having more control over resources than women do. Men, therefore, are perceived as having more legitimacy as leaders and are given greater latitude to behave in an aggressive, direct, and self-enhancing manner than women are. Consequently, people penalize women for behavior that appears direct or aggressive more than they penalize men. As a result, even though negative assertion is more likely to evoke negative reactions from others than is positive assertion, women who exhibit negative assertion or directness risk greater penalties than men for doing so. Therefore, compared with men, women's greater endorsement and use of positive assertion and avoidance of negative assertion and directness can be viewed as pragmatic. For women, positive assertion is much more likely to be effective than negative assertion; for men, the advantage of using positive assertion is less clear. This analysis leads to two hypotheses regarding gender and assertiveness: first, that females and males differ in the way they assert themselves, with females showing more positive assertion than males and males more negative assertion and directness than females, and second, that people react less favorably to female than male assertiveness, especially negative and direct forms of assertiveness. [*See* GENDER STEREOTYPES.]

II. Previous Reviews

Several reviews have been conducted of the literature on gender differences in assertiveness. These reviews have relied primarily on studies using personality scales and questionnaire measures of assertiveness rather than behavioral measures. None of the previous reviews have included separate analyses of positive and negative assertion, but instead tested for gender differences in general assertiveness, combining measures of positive and negative assertion.

A. EARLY REVIEWS

The first review, conducted by James Hollandsworth and Kathleen Wall, identified seven studies that examined gender and assertiveness. These seven studies contained 14 separate tests of gender differences, all of which used questionnaire measures of assertiveness. The means of all 14 tests were in the direction of greater male assertiveness, but only 4 of them revealed significant effects. The results of this review indicated that men report being more assertive than women. In order to examine the gender effect further, I computed the effect size associated with the gender difference. Effect size is a statistical measure that reveals how big a difference is rather than simply whether a difference exists. Based on my computation, the average effect size for the studies in the Hollandsworth and Wall review was small.

Judith Hall conducted a second review of gender differences in assertiveness and published the results in her 1984 book, *Nonverbal Sex Differences*. Hall performed a meta-analysis of studies published between 1975 and 1983 in four journals: *Journal of Personality and Social Psychology, Journal of Personality, Journal of Personality Assessment,* and *Sex*

Roles. Meta-analysis is a statistical procedure that combines the results of two or more studies to assess the size and variability of an independent variable, in this case the gender difference in assertiveness. Hall's purpose was to compare the effect size of the gender differences in nonverbal behavior, her primary interest, with the effect size of gender differences in other variables, including assertiveness. She did not intend to conduct a comprehensive review of gender differences in assertiveness, and, in fact, included just seven studies, most of which employed self-report personality measures. Hall reported a very weak correlation between gender and assertiveness, indicating a very small gender difference, with men reporting or displaying slightly more assertiveness than women did.

B. MORE RECENT REVIEWS

A meta-analysis by Alan Feingold included four samples of studies: those previously examined in a qualitative review by Maccoby and Jacklin, those published between 1984 and 1992 in the same journals used by Hall, those used to establish norms for personality scales in the United States, and those used to establish norms for personality scales for non-U.S. samples. Most of the 22 studies obtained from the earlier Maccoby and Jacklin review included children as participants and 17 of these studies relied on behavioral measures of assertiveness. For this sample, Feingold reported a small to medium mean gender difference showing greater assertiveness among males. However, when he repeated the analysis excluding two studies with extreme results, the gender difference was reduced dramatically, yielding a trivial and essentially meaningless effect. Feingold's second sample, which replicated and extended Hall's review, contained 15 studies, all employing self-report or personality measures of assertiveness with participants of high school age or above. This sample revealed a very small gender effect, with more self-reported assertiveness among male than female participants. The third sample consisted of 25 studies conducted to assess the norms for eight different self-report personality measures of assertiveness. Most of these studies used samples of high school or college students; a few used a nonstudent adult sample. Overall, the meta-analysis revealed greater self-reported assertiveness among men than among women. However, although the overall effect size was moderate, the size of the gender difference depended on the particular scale being assessed; some scales revealed no gender differences, some revealed small ones, some revealed medium ones, and some revealed large ones. Finally, the fourth sample consisted of 11 studies assessing the assertiveness norms for the Personality Research Form using samples outside the United States. Results revealed a small gender difference, with men reporting greater assertiveness than women. [*See* SEX-RELATED DIFFERENCE RESEARCH: PERSONALITY.]

III. *Limitations of Past Research*

Overall, the reviews show a small gender difference in assertiveness. Although this suggests that any actual gender effect is trivial and probably of little theoretical interest, there are limitations of the reviews that make it difficult to form clear conclusions about gender differences in assertiveness. First, because the reviews did not include separate measures of positive and negative assertion, they do not provide any evidence about whether females and males assert themselves in different ways or whether assertive behaviors reflect pressures to conform to traditional gender stereotypes.

Second, even if the previous reviews had distinguished positive and negative assertion, they would still be somewhat limited because of their reliance on self-report measures of assertiveness rather than behavioral measures. Respondents' self-reports may not be accurate. To conform to gender role norms, men may exaggerate their assertiveness and woman may underestimate theirs. Moreover, individuals may not be aware of how they actually behave and may resort to guessing how they think they might behave. In fact, the only sample that was based primarily on behavioral rather than self-report measures—Feingold's meta-analysis of Maccoby and Jacklin's qualitative review—showed no meaningful evidence of a gender difference, except in two studies with extreme and atypical results.

In addition to the problems associated with self-report data, research on gender may sometimes be subject to reporting biases. Reporting biases are probably more common when gender effects are nonsignificant and authors have the option to report the effects or not. Under such conditions, authors may be more inclined to report a result when it is consistent with their hypotheses or theoretical perspective. Feingold noted that researchers might also choose not to report gender effects that are politi-

cally incorrect. He argued that because reporting biases should not be present in studies designed to assess norms for personality scales, gender differences found in these samples should be more accurate than in other types of studies. Indeed, Feingold did find somewhat larger, although still small, gender differences in assertiveness in the studies assessing personality scales than in the other studies. However, the size of the sex difference varied widely across the various personality scales, some of which showed no evidence of a difference. This suggests that the personality scales are measuring assertiveness somewhat differently, capturing different dimensions of the construct. Given the diversity of definitions of assertiveness, this is hardly surprising. However, the implications for understanding the gender effect are unclear. Perhaps the scales that reveal gender effects obtained those differences primarily for items reflecting negative assertion or directness and not those reflecting positive assertion. Unfortunately, there is no way to determine whether this was the case in most personality scales measuring assertiveness.

IV. *Behavioral Studies of Gender and Assertiveness*

Although past reviews of gender and assertiveness have generally focused on self-report measures, many additional studies have examined gender differences in specific behaviors that reflect assertiveness. Such behaviors include self-expression, defending one's rights when someone violates them, and using direct forms of communication. Moreover, behavioral studies of assertiveness typically allow separate examination of positive and negative assertion. Behaviors reflecting positive assertion include self-disclosure and expressing positive feelings and social support of others, whereas behaviors reflecting negative assertion include disagreeing, attempts to control others, and expressing negative emotions.

As noted earlier, self-expression through positive assertion is congruent with the traditional female gender role and should therefore be more common among women. Directness and self-expression through negative assertion are congruent with the traditional male gender role and in conflict with the traditional female role; consequently, they should be more common among men than women. Do females show higher levels of positive assertion than males, and do males show higher levels of negative assertion and directness than females?

A. POSITIVE ASSERTION

Research does reveal that women show higher levels of positive assertion in their emotional expressiveness. Women express more positive emotion than men, both verbally and nonverbally. For example, Jack Balswick, in his book *The Inexpressive Male*, reported that women verbalize positive emotions more than men do. Similarly, Judith Hall reported evidence that women smile more, laugh more, and show more head and body movement than men do. Hall's meta-analytic review of these gender differences indicates that the gender differences in nonverbal expressiveness is moderate to large in size. Kathryn Dindia and Mike Allen conducted a meta-analytic review of gender differences in self-disclosure and found a small to moderate gender difference, with women expressing their feelings through self-disclosure more than men do. Overall, the evidence clearly demonstrates that women show higher levels of positive assertion through expressing positive emotions than do men.

Women also express more support of others than men do. For example, Sherry Pitcher and Stewart Meikle found that in role-play exercises women express more appreciation of others than men do. Victoria DeFrancisco's research on marital conversations and Linda Carli's research on conversations between strangers both revealed that, compared with men, women maintain conversations by verbally and nonverbally reinforcing and encouraging others' speech. For example, when others are speaking, women make more appreciative comments, express more agreement, communicate interest in what others say, and nod their heads more often than men do. Carli has found additional evidence of women's greater support of others in a review of studies examining verbal interactions in small task-oriented groups or dyads. In these studies, men express a higher proportion of opinions or ideas than women do, but women express a higher proportion of socially supportive behaviors toward others, such as agreeing and complimenting, than men do. Analyses of these differences indicate that they are moderate in size. However, because the analysis of group interaction is based on percentages of each behavior to control for overall talkativeness, these results should not be interpreted as revealing gender differences in

the overall amount that participants assert themselves generally, but only that compared with the other gender a smaller proportion of men's talk involves expressing positive emotion or support of others and a smaller proportion of women's talk involves expressing opinions. Finally, in a comprehensive meta-analysis of gender differences in leadership style across a wide variety of settings, Alice Eagly and Blair Johnson found that women leaders lead in a more democratic manner than men, involving subordinates in decision making more than men do. The overall conclusion, then, is that women's assertions are more socially supportive than men's. [See LEADERSHIP.]

Similar findings have been reported in research on children. Studies by Marjorie Goodwin, Lynne Zarbatany, and other researchers have revealed that girls express more positive emotion and social support of others than do boys. Even when girls disagree or refuse requests, they tend to temper their assertions and to mitigate conflict with explanations, compromise, or other socially supportive behaviors more than boys do. Girls also show greater positive assertion by more often inviting others to join in games and encouraging others to speak than boys do.

In general then, women and girls employ more positive assertion than do men and boys. Across a variety of settings, both verbally and nonverbally, females show more self-expression in ways that respect the rights of others than males do. Research on positive assertion indicates that the style of assertiveness used by women and girls corresponds quite closely with the demands of the female gender role and with prescriptive stereotypes about appropriate behavior for women and girls and with gender difference in power.

B. NEGATIVE ASSERTION

Research for the most part confirms that males show higher amounts of negative assertion through more frequent attempts to direct and control others than females show. For example, a study by D. S. Moskowitz indicated that men issue more directives and commands than women do. Similarly, Pitcher and Meikle's role-play study revealed that men express more aggression toward others than do women. In a review of studies of small group interactions, Carli found that men express greater disagreement and negative emotions toward others than women do. Likewise, Alice Eagly and Blair Johnson found evidence that across a wide variety of settings male leaders lead in a more autocratic manner than women leaders, exhibiting more directiveness of subordinates and discouraging them from participating in decisions.

Negative assertion is also more common among boys than girls. L. Lowenstein found that boys bully others more than girls do. Research on gender differences in communication by Marjorie Goodwin and many others has shown that compared with girls, boys disagree and argue more, issue more directives, express more negative emotions and threats toward others, and more often attempt to exert control over others. In general, boys, like men, show higher levels of negative assertion in a wide variety of common interactions with peers. Research on young children indicates that these differences begin to emerge in preschool and continue throughout childhood and adulthood.

Although males generally show more negative assertion than females, there is one exception to this finding. Women and girls do not show less negative assertion than men and boys do when someone else violates their rights. For example, Mary Harris reported that both men and women are equally likely to verbally protest when someone cuts in front of them in line and, in fact, women showed higher levels of nonverbal dissatisfaction than men did in her research. Likewise, Robert Deluty and other researchers have reported that both girls and boys are equally likely to stand up for their rights to resist unfair treatment by others and to use the same amount of negative communication in self-defense.

Clearly, research on negative assertion indicates that males generally employ more negative assertion than females, except when their rights are violated. Under these conditions, women and girls match or exceed males in their use of negative forms of assertion. These findings suggest that, unlike males, females do not typically use negative assertion to control others but rather to ensure that their own rights, as well as the rights of others, are respected. Again, the results of research on negative assertion reveal that females' use of negative assertion is more socially appropriate than males'. The gender differences in negative assertion reflect gender differences in power; males' power advantage gives them greater latitude to use negative assertion, whereas females use negative assertion primarily as a form of self-defense.

C. DIRECTNESS

Research on gender differences in directness has yielded mixed findings. Studies involving role-playing have revealed no gender differences in directness. For example, Cynthia Smith reported that women and men claim that they would be equally direct in a conflict with a boss. Michael Papa and Elizabeth Natalle likewise reported no gender differences in directness when respondents role-played a conflict with a coworker. Studies that involve observation of actual behavior have revealed mixed results. Among adults, research by Carli and others has revealed that women speak in a more mitigated or indirect style than men do. Examples of speech forms that are mitigated or indirect include the use of polite expressions; hedges, which are adverbs or adverb phrases, such as *sort of, kind of,* and *maybe,* that temper the strength of an argument; and tag questions, which are questions added to the end of declarative statements, such as "spring comes after winter, *doesn't it*?" Although not all studies examining gender differences in indirect or mitigated speech have revealed greater mitigation by women, when gender differences occur they usually are in this direction.

Research on children's use of direct or indirect assertion has revealed similar mixed findings. For example, Jacqueline Martin observed interactions among siblings and found that boys and girls were equally direct. However, Marjorie Goodwin and others have found that in interactions with peers, girls use more mitigating language, by hedging and using tag questions, and make suggestions or requests more politely than boys. Boys, on the other hand, issue more direct demands than girls.

Finally, research on nonverbal behavior also reveals greater directness among males than females. Steve Ellyson and John Dovidio and their colleagues have reported studies revealing that men show higher levels of visual dominance than women. Visual dominance involves maintaining relatively more direct eye contact with others while speaking and less while listening to others. It is associated with power and status and is an index of perceived expertise or authority.

Overall, the results of research examining gender effects on directness are quite mixed. Still, given the preponderance of the findings showing more male than female directness, it appears that males are somewhat more direct in their self-assertions than are females, a gender difference that corresponds to gender differences in power, as predicted. However, based on the variability in the findings, it is likely that gender differences here are small and dependent on the situation.

V. *Effect of Others' Gender on Assertiveness*

Most studies examining gender and assertiveness have ignored contextual or situational variables that might moderate gender differences in assertive behavior. Nevertheless, research does reveal that the gender effects in assertiveness do depend not only on the gender of the participant but also on the gender of the person with whom the participant is interacting.

Research on both adults and children has revealed that positive assertion is more often used in interactions with females than with males and that negative assertion is used more often with males than with females. Considerable research, including work by Elizabeth Aries, Cathryn Johnson, and others, has demonstrated that both women and men verbally express more positive emotion and social support when communicating with women than with men and more negative emotion and disagreement when communicating with men than with women. People smile more, have more warmth in their voices, disclose more personal information, and are more likely to nod their heads and use expressions that encourage others to speak when speaking to a woman. Recent research by Cynthia Smith examined how people assert themselves when refusing the requests of others. Smith found that both men and women are more likely to justify and explain their refusal with a woman. The same pattern of findings has been reported in research on children. Studies by Campbell Leaper and by Melanie Killen and Letitia Naigles revealed that boys speak in a more supportive manner when speaking to girls than they do with boys.

What explanation is there for these findings? Although gender differences in assertiveness reflect gender differences in power, this explanation cannot account for the greater use of positive assertion with women and negative assertion with men. Positive assertion is generally more pleasing, less controlling, and less likely to evoke resistance from others than negative assertion is. Consequently, positive assertion might logically seem to be the preferred method to use when interacting with relatively powerful individuals, such as men. Instead, the greater use of positive assertion with women appears to correspond with other research revealing a tendency for people to be generally warmer and more pleasant toward females than males. There are two possible explanations for this. First, as Alice Eagly and her colleagues have demonstrated, people generally have more favorable attitudes toward women than men and expect women to be nicer to others than men are. Perhaps the belief that women are nicer leads people to expect interactions with females to be more pleasant and warm, which in turn leads them to show greater warmth toward women than men. Second, people may believe that women are more amenable and receptive to warm behaviors than men are, and therefore may employ such behaviors in order to be influential or effective with women. Likewise, people may use more negative assertion with men because they view interactions with men to involve more conflict, competition, and negative assertion than interactions with women, or people may expect men to be more accepting and tolerant of negative assertion than women are. This analysis suggests that others may see men as enjoying negative conflict and responding more favorably to it than women do, an effect that would work in opposition to the demand that people defer to men more than to women.

Both men and women use more positive assertion with women and negative assertion with men, which might suggest that both genders use more masculine forms of assertion when interacting with men. However, this is not the case; people are not more direct with men than women. On the contrary, a number of researchers, including most recently Patricia Bresky, have found evidence that people assert themselves in a more mitigated and less direct manner while interacting with men than with women, as would be expected given the greater power of men compared with women. Likewise, Ellyson and Dovidio's work reveals that both women and men show less visual dominance with men, spending relatively more time looking while listening when speaking to men than to women.

Use of indirect speech can involve other people in a conversation or reduce their resistance to influence, a particular concern when the others are relatively high in power. In effect, indirect speech can facilitate interactions with others. Because men are more likely than women to ignore the direct communications of other people or to resist their influence, speaking indirectly to men may be particularly functional, especially when trying to assert one's opinion or point of view. Men may be concerned that direct communications are overt attempts to control, manipulate, and influence them, and thereby undermine their power advantage. Consequently, sprinkling one's speech with indirect forms of communication when speaking to men may help to reduce these concerns. Indirectness may simply be perceived as superfluous in interactions with women, who are generally considered to be more responsive to the contributions of others.

VI. Gender Differences in Power

Clearly, gender composition affects assertiveness behaviors. People behave differently toward men than toward women. Similarly, people behave differently depending on their relative power in interactions with others. Carli found considerable evidence that women and men differ in power. In general, compared with women, men possess greater expert power, which is based on the common stereotype that men are more competent and expert than women, and more legitimate power, which is based on the prescriptive stereotype that men's higher status gives them the right to exert influence and have authority over others. Because of their greater expert power, in the absence of evidence to the contrary or a situation that stereotypically favors female expertise, men are expected to be more knowledgeable, competent, and expert than women are. Moreover, because of the greater legitimate power of men, people are more likely to defer to a man, give him opportunities to speak, and assign him to a leadership role than they are to a woman, even when the woman is just as competent as the man. On the other hand, research indicates that women have greater referent power, which is based on how likable a person is, because people generally have more positive feelings about women and like them more than they do men. Nevertheless, this does not preclude men from using referent power. Being likable and having good relationships with others is an appropriate source of power for men and other high-status individuals, even if they may not always take advantage of this source of power. There is no prescriptive stereotype requiring men to avoid being warm and likable. But because women in many situations may lack expert or legitimate power, but still have access to referent power, women probably rely on referent power more than men do.

In fact, gender differences in power parallel those in assertiveness. Of course, depending on their occu-

pational roles, income, and other factors, men do vary in power, as do women, and there is evidence that these variations in power affect assertiveness. For example, Judith Howard, Philip Blumstein, and Pepper Schwartz found some self-report evidence that in heterosexual and homosexual couples, the less powerful member of the couple is more indirect than his or her partner. Nevertheless, on average, men possess greater expert and legitimate power than women. Consequently, men are freer to use negative assertion more than women because women who are presumed to lack expertise and formal authority would be penalized for using such aggressive means of self-expression. However, women would still be able to employ positive assertion, which is congruent with females' greater referent power. Hence the typical gender differences in assertiveness appear to derive from gender differences in power. This suggests that people would be expected to penalize women more than men for being too direct or for exhibiting negative self-assertion. Moreover, when the balance of power shifts from one gender to the other, the typical gender differences in assertiveness should be eliminated or reversed. For example, in situations that involve stereotypically feminine domains, such as domestic settings or contexts involving women's health issues, females would have greater expertise and legitimacy than males. Consequently, in such situations, females would be expected to employ more negative or direct assertiveness as much as or more than males and males would be expected to increase their use of positive assertion.

What is the effect on directness and negative and positive assertion when women possess more exert and legitimate power? As would be predicted if gender differences in assertion were based on gender differences in power, research by Wendy Wood and Stephen Karten, among others, indicates that when participants interact in a domain in which women are more expert and authoritative, women express more direct opinions, express fewer positive emotions, and show less social support of others than when interacting in a domain favoring men. Men, under these circumstances, express fewer direct opinions, express more positive emotions, and show more social support of others. Both men and women use more mitigated speech when they have less education than when they have higher levels of education. John Dovidio and his colleagues have likewise found that women's visual dominance increases when they are working on a task that favors female expertise and that gender differences in visual dominance can be eliminated by increasing female expertise at a task. Therefore, gender differences in expert power affect gender differences in the use of positive and negative assertion.

Studies by Cathryn Johnson, as well as others, have revealed that the gender difference in legitimate power also affects gender differences in assertiveness. When assigned to the same formal leadership role, and therefore possessing equal legitimate power, adults display no gender differences in the extent to which they command or direct others or the extent to which they show positive assertion, such as expressing positive emotions or showing social support. Moreover, both women and men use less mitigated speech when they possess relatively high status compared with their lower status peers. Both genders also issue more direct than indirect requests to their subordinates when possessing more authority than when possessing less authority, although even under these conditions women are more indirect than men.

Research on girls and boys reveals the same pattern of results. For example, Amy Kyratzis and Jiansheng Guo examined gender effects on assertiveness in a sample of Chinese boys and girls and found that although girls generally use less negative assertion than boys do, in stereotypically feminine domains, where girls have more expert and legitimate power, girls express more negative emotion and issue more commands than boys do, whereas boys are more deferent and agreeable toward girls. McCloskey reported that girls assigned the leadership role of tutor, which increases their legitimate power, express more direct opinions and give more directions than boys in the same role. These results show that among adults and children, the typical gender differences in positive and negative assertion and directness are reduced or eliminated when gender differences in power are equalized and reversed when females possess more expert and legitimate power than males.

Finally, additional support for the notion that gender differences in assertiveness depend on gender differences in power comes from research on African American participants. Marjorie Goodwin's research on children has revealed that when gender differences are found among African Americans, they are similar to those found among Whites. Nevertheless, gender differences in status are smaller among African Americans than Whites because, compared with Whites, African American women have had higher rates of workforce participation, African American males have relatively lower status, and

African Americans are more inclined to endorse gender egalitarian beliefs. This suggests that gender differences in assertiveness should be smaller among African Americans than among Whites. Indeed, Mitchel Haralson, Jr., recently surveyed African Americans and found no gender differences in self-reported assertiveness among them. More important, Emily Filardo specifically compared gender differences in assertiveness in White and African American adolescent samples and revealed some evidence that gender differences in assertiveness are less pronounced among African Americans than Whites. In this study, gender did not interact with race for use of mitigated speech or expressions of negative emotions; however, interactions were found for the total contribution of ideas to the interaction and for expressions of positive emotions. Among Whites, girls contributed fewer ideas and expressed more positive emotions toward others than did boys, whereas no gender differences were found for the African American participants.

Gender differences in assertiveness do appear to depend on the lower expert and legitimate power of females compared with males. Clearly, women and girls can express themselves directly and through negative assertion, but may choose not to unless they find themselves in situations that favor their expertise or authority. Men and boys likewise avoid directness and negative assertion in situations where females possess higher levels of expert or legitimate power, but instead rely more on positive assertion in such situations. These results indicate that, although somewhat moderated by the race of the interactants, under most conditions use of negative assertion and direct self-expression are less acceptable in females than males, and as a result people denigrate and resist females who employ such forms of assertiveness or resist and ignore their ideas. [*See* POWER: PERSONAL AND SOCIAL DIMENSIONS.]

VII. Resistance to Assertiveness in Women and Girls

If gender differences in power affect gender differences in assertiveness and if prescriptive stereotypes preclude women and girls from using direct and negative forms of assertiveness, then there should be evidence of resistance to women and girls who violate these prescriptions. Not all studies have found resistance to female assertiveness, however. This has generally been the case because the studies examining reactions to assertive individuals have not clearly distinguished positive and negative assertion, but have instead depicted those individuals showing behavior that is a combination of positive and negative assertion.

More often, research has revealed that women receive less favorable evaluations for displaying direct or negative assertion than men do, or than women do for displaying positive assertion. Numerous studies, including studies by Jeffrey Kern and Jeffrey Kelly, have revealed that women are rated as less likable or popular than men are for disagreeing with the participants of the study, for directly refusing requests, or for exhibiting other forms of negative assertion. In studies by Linda Pendleton and others that examined participants' reactions to females only, participants reported more positive feeling toward females who exhibit positive than negative assertion. Moreover, even women leaders, who have relatively high legitimacy and expertise, are still evaluated differently than male leaders for use of direct or negative assertion. For example, Dore Butler and Florence Geis found that people express more negative emotion when a woman attempts to lead or direct them than when a man does. Alice Eagly, Mona Makhijani, and Bruce Klonsky conducted a meta-analytic review of studies examining the evaluation of female and male leaders. Their results likewise revealed that female leaders are evaluated more negatively for displaying autocratic than democratic behaviors, whereas male leaders are not. Finally, Jane Connor and her colleagues found children also approve less of females who display direct self-assertion than those who are more indirect, whereas they approve equally of males who are direct and those who are indirect.

It appears then that people prefer women who avoid direct and negative assertion and rely instead on positive assertion. This bias in reacting to female assertiveness is also reflected in the tendency of people to resist the influence of women or girls who are direct or negatively assertive and to be more open to their influence when they use positive assertion. For example, research by Beverly Fagot and her colleagues showed that preschool teachers ignore the negative assertions of toddler girls more than the negative assertions of toddler boys. In research by Carli and research by Michael Burgoon and his colleagues, women who showed negative assertion exerted less influence over others than did men showing negative assertion. Holly Buttner and Martha McEnally reported that managers are less likely to hire female job applicants who communicate directly than they are to hire direct male or indirect female applicants. Similarly, research by Steve Ellyson and John Dovidio demonstrated that women who display nonverbal directness through visual dominance are less influential than women who are less direct whereas men's use of visual dominance actually increases their influence. On the other hand, Cecilia Ridgeway, among others, reported that women who display positive assertion exert greater influence than women who do not, but the display of positive assertion does not increase men's influence.

Although not all studies have revealed gender differences in reactions to assertiveness, when such differences are found they typically show that men are more critical of female assertiveness than are women. Krystyna Rojahn and Tineke Willemsen found that men evaluated directive female leaders are negatively than directive male leaders and female leaders showing positive assertion more favorably than male leaders showing positive assertion. They found that women, in contrast, rated a male or female leader equally favorably, regardless of his or her assertive behavior. Pamela Geller and Stevan Hobfoll reported that although male and female participants gave equally favorable ratings to men who expressed disagreement, men gave less favorable evaluations than women did to a woman who disagreed. Other research reveals that whereas both men and women like men equally well whether they communicate directly or indirectly, men prefer women who communicate indirectly to those who communicate directly. Similarly, both men and women like men equally well when they display directness or positive assertion, but men prefer women who use positive assertion to women who are direct. Finally, Mary Crawford reported that male participants disliked female direct assertion more than their female counterparts, but this result was found only for older and not for college-age participants.

In addition to research showing that males dislike direct or negatively assertive females more than females do, research reveals that males are more resistant to the influence of direct or negative female assertions than females are. Several studies by Carli on adults have demonstrated that a man exerts equal influence over both women and men whether he expresses himself directly or indirectly or whether he uses positive assertion or not. A woman, on the other hand, exerts greater influence with men by expressing herself indirectly or by using positive assertion and exerts greater influence with women by speaking directly. In their meta-analytic review of studies examining the evaluation of male and female leaders, Eagly Makhijani and Klonsky found that, across a variety of leadership settings, men resist female leadership more than women do.

Research by Lisa Serbin and her colleagues has revealed the same effects among children. Boys' direct requests are equally influential with male and female peers, but girls' direct requests are influential with female but not with male peers. Moreover, male resistance to female influence begins very early, as Eleanor Maccoby and Carol Jacklin have shown. Male toddlers ignore the directives and prohibitions of female toddlers but are influenced by other male toddlers whereas female toddlers are equally responsive to their male and female peers. Amy Kyratzis and Jiansheng Guo likewise found that in their U.S. sample, boys resisted the direct assertions of girls more than girls resisted the direct assertions of boys.

Clearly, women and girls do receive more severe penalties than men and boys for displaying direct or negative assertions; people like females less and are less influenced by them for such displays. Although use of negative assertion is risky for everyone, in that it evokes more negative reactions from others than does positive assertion, males experience less of this risk than females do. Moreover, males, more than females, penalize women and girls for showing negative or direct assertion. The stronger reaction of males to female gender role violations provides further evidence that gender differences in power—and greater male expert and legitimate power, in particular—mediate gender differences in assertiveness.

VII. Conclusion

Overall, research reveals that both males and females are assertive, but they assert themselves differently. Women report being more concerned with balancing their needs with the needs of others, females show greater mutuality in their assertions than males do, and women and girls generally use positive assertion more than boys and men do. Men perceive assertiveness to be a means of expressing one's power over others and exerting influence, and males' behaviors reflect this perception. Men and boys display negative assertion, and, to some extent, direct assertion more than females do. However, women and girls can be very direct and negative, and they are when defending their rights. When others treat them

inappropriately, females match or exceed males in their use of negative and direct assertion, which provides further evidence that females are more concerned with a balance of needs and rights, including their own, whereas males are more concerned with asserting influence over others.

The pattern of gender differences in assertiveness reveals a greater mutuality and social appropriateness in the behaviors of females than males, a mutuality that corresponds to the standard of assertiveness set by experts in the field. Women and girls exhibit assertiveness in the very ways that are endorsed by assertiveness trainers and scholars. Curiously, in spite of this, there have been many popular assertiveness training guides specifically directed at women. A casual search of this literature uncovered more than 20 such guides in public libraries in eastern Massachusetts, but none specifically directed at men. Why this emphasis on assertiveness training for women when they seem to have little need for it?

According to Mary Crawford, one explanation is that professionals have considered women to have passive personalities and have blamed gender inequality on female passivity. Therefore, the past focus on women may reflect an implicit tendency to blame women, and their unassertive personalities, for gender discrimination against women. Wilson and Gallois have posited another explanation: that trainers may have had less luck attracting men to assertiveness training. They suggest that this may have occurred because men are less likely to accept training that requires balancing one's needs with the needs of others. However, there is no evidence that men have been aware that professionals explicitly endorse positive over negative assertion. Instead, men equate assertive behavior with negative and direct assertion and may not feel deficient or in need of training in these areas. A final explanation is that, in spite of their rhetoric endorsing socially supportive forms of self-assertion, experts in the field may tend to emphasize negative forms of assertion and the need for individuals to protect their rights, an emphasis that reflects a bias in favor of traditional masculinity and creates the misguided impression that women need assertiveness training more than men. Unfortunately, training women to display more negative and direct assertion would not have the desired effect of increasing female influence. Moreover, such training ignores the power differential between men and women.

In truth, gender differences in assertiveness depend to a large extent on the relative power of males and females and vary in accordance with shifts in power.

This accounts for the less pronounced gender differences in assertiveness among African Americans, where there is greater gender equality in power. Participants, male or female, who possess relatively greater expert or legitimate power are freer to express their self-assertions in less socially acceptable ways, through negative assertion and being direct. Those who lack these forms of power rely more on positive assertion. Because of traditional gender role stereotypes, the presumption of greater male expertise, and the prescriptions against female displays of authority, women and girls are generally the ones who are more constrained in their assertive behaviors and therefore rely predominantly on positive assertion. The relation of power to assertiveness is further underscored by negative reactions to women and girls who use negative and direct assertion. Females who assert themselves in a negative or direct manner are more likely than males to be disliked and are less likely to exert influence than males are. Men and boys, who possess greater expert and legitimate power, are particularly indifferent to direct assertions by women and girls. This undoubtedly accounts for the finding that female self-assertions are less direct with males than with females, because indirectness reduces male resistance to female assertion. In fact, both genders modify their assertive behavior to reflect their relative power in an interaction, and to reflect, as well, the gender of the person with whom they are interacting. In conclusion, both males and females are pragmatic and assert themselves in ways that are likely to be acknowledged and effective. Gender differences in self-assertion, therefore, do not reflect inherent differences between males and females in their ability to use direct, negative, or positive assertion, but instead reflect the continued potency of traditional gender stereotypes.

SUGGESTED READING

Alberti, R. E., and Emmons, M. L. (1990). *Your Perfect Right: A Guide to Assertive Living.* Impact, San Louis Obispo, CA.

Carli, L. L. (1999). Gender, interpersonal power, and social influence. *Journal of Social Issues* **55**, 81–99.

Feingold, A. (1994). Gender differences in personality: A meta-analysis. *Psychological Bulletin* **116**, 429–456.

Hall, J. A. (1984). *Nonverbal Sex Differences: Communication Accuracy and Expressive Style.* Johns Hopkins University, Baltimore.

Hollandsworth, J. G., Jr., and Wall, K. E. (1977). Sex differences in assertive behavior: An empirical investigation. *Journal of Counseling Psychology* **24**, 217–222.

Wilson, L. K., and Gallois, C. (1993). *Assertion and Its Social Context.* Pergamon, Tarrytown, NY.

Battering in Adult Relations

Lenore E. A. Walker

Nova Southeastern University

Glossary

Battered woman syndrome The collection of psychological symptoms that are often seen after a woman has been abused by her partner. It is considered similar to the symptoms seen by many psychologists in a posttraumatic stress disorder. Legal decisions have broadened the psychological definition by adding the dynamics of a battering relationship in the description contained in their opinions.

Battered woman A woman who has been physically, sexually, or seriously psychologically abused by her partner.

Abuse A term that is often used interchangeably with violence and battering behavior when describing partner abuse, child abuse, domestic or family violence.

Ex-parte orders An order in which only one party is heard before the judge. These were granted to battered women because of the danger testifying might place them in when asking a judge to issue an order of protection to keep the batterer from further harming them.

Order of protection A civil order that is issued to stop the batterer from continuing to harm the woman. While no longer the empty pieces of paper they once were thought to be, it is still difficult to get the courts to enforce a batterer's violation of this order. They are also called "restraining orders" in some places as the order demands that the batterer restrain himself from a variety of actions including contacting and threatening the victim.

Victim A term, often considered not politically correct by feminist advocates, to describe women who are attempting to keep themselves and their children as safe as possible from further abuse. However, it is a term used by agencies and others to denote that it is not the woman's responsibility to stop the violence—only the batterer can do so. Although the term remains controversial, it is used throughout this chapter as a clear way to denote who is responsible for the violence.

BATTERING IN ADULT RELATIONSHIPS is known to have occurred since we have records, although beginning in the early 1970s a new interest in protecting women and stopping male violence against them grew out of the new women's movement. As women came together to both end violence and create a new social order where women and men were equal in all relationships, psychology began to study the domestic violence relationship and its psychological impact on women. These data began to influence many of our societal institutional policies as barriers to prevention and intervention were explored. This included politics, health care, social services, criminal and civil justice, family law, and religion. It soon became clear that some of our most cherished beliefs were maintaining if not actually facilitating men's use of violence against women. Violence is learned behavior, and children who are exposed to violence in their homes are far more likely to grow up and use violence in their own lives. Violence and sexism are linked together, and both social role expectations and attitudes toward violence must be changed in order to stop battering in adult relationships.

I. History

Women have been battered by men as far back in history as we have records with attempts to deal with this important social problem. It was not until the mid-1970s when the new wave of the women's movement began to publicize the prevalence and negative effects of violence on women's search for equality that the right of a husband to punish his wife was seriously challenged and declared a violation of human rights. Many believe that the success of this new effort to stop men's abuse of women was due to the creation of a new social agency, the battered woman's shelter, that was both to transform the social order between men and women to one of equality and to protect battered women and their children. Erin Pizzey, a social reformer in England, opened the first known battered woman's shelter in 1971 in Chiswick, a suburb of London. Her goal was to give any woman who needed it a place to come with her children, but the small house soon filled with battered women who were seeking refuge from abusive men. Pizzey began a campaign of social reformation in England, enlisting the support of the Church and Parliament to study the problem and provide shelter for "battered moms" and their children. She quickly ran into difficulty with those who called her a "home-wrecker" and those who wanted to use the battered woman's movement to campaign for a more egalitarian society.

Pizzey was not considered a feminist in that she viewed the problem as one in which women contributed to their abuse through an inability to stand up for their rights and to sometimes use violence themselves toward their husbands. She intentionally designed the intervention model she used at Chiswick Women's Aid, which was similar to the then popular therapeutic community developed by Maxwell Jones and the Tavistock School in London. Despite the controversies she stirred up, some of which still exist today, she was known for her ability to work with some of the most violent and distressed battered women who were sent to her refuge from all over the British Isles. Pizzey held herself out to be the leader upon whom the rest of the women could model their own behavior change.

An immediate protest to Pizzey's model was raised by a more politically leftist and feminist group, the National Federation of Aid to Battered Women, who perceived the battering as solely the responsibility of the usually male batterer. The group felt it was only necessary to provide the battered woman with shelter and intervention for daily living needs, along with public education, to overturn the patriarchal institutions. Led by sociologists, Rebecca and Russell Dobash, the group quickly labeled the type of therapeutic community set up by Pizzey as a way to continue to blame the victim by inferring that the abuse was this imperfect woman's fault. Instead, the group advocated for a more feminist grassroots model without any type of intervention and the development of shelters, or refuges as they were called back then, quickly spread to other cities in the British Isles. In some ways, the battle for control by both groups called even more attention to the problem of woman abuse than might have happened otherwise. This attention to woman abuse quickly spread to other European countries and the United States where different models developed even though each continued the development of shelter as the cornerstone while modifying what other services were available. The battered woman shelter, then, became the symbol upon which was based the message to abusive men in the community—beat your partner and we will protect her! Table I outlines some of the important historical events in the development of protection for adults in battering relationships.

A. SOCIO-POLITICAL VERSUS HUMAN SERVICES MODELS

In Europe the shelter models continued to follow a sociopolitical approach that emphasized giving power back to the woman without any intervening

Table I
Important Historical Events

1970s	First battered woman shelter opened in England. Some controversy about who opened first battered woman shelter in the United States with the major contenders being Save Our Sisters in Hackensack, New Jersey, Women's Advocates in St. Paul, Minnesota, Haven House in the Los Angeles area, Bradley Angle House in Portland, Oregon, Women's Survival Space in Brooklyn, New York, Safe House in Denver, Colorado, and Casa de las Madres in San Francisco, California. Others claim earlier shelters but they were not part of the feminist movement towards a new egalitarian world order.
1973	Sociologist Richard Gelles examined police records and found large numbers of battered women who were unprotected even though their abuse was documented in the records. He joined with Murray Straus and Susan Steinmetz to conduct a national survey and found that over 28% of women stated they had been battered during that year. Later they founded the Family Violence Research Center at the University of New Hampshire, site of several conferences bringing together researchers, clinicians and advocates in the field. They also trained many of the later researchers and continue to update their national surveys.
1974	Marjorie Fields, then director of Legal Aid Services in Brooklyn, New York studied 500 divorce cases and found that over one-half of the female litigants had been physically assaulted by their husbands prior to the divorce. Later she led the successful lawsuit against New York City police and courts for failure to protect battered women, winning them new procedures.
1976	First book was published on the subject of battered women. Written by active lesbian and NOW member Del Martin, *Battered Wives* described what later became known as the "Battered Woman's Movement."
1977	The National Coalition against Domestic Violence is founded organizing approximately 250 battered women shelters and groups in the United States. Erin Pizzey came to Denver, Colorado, to describe the British experience sponsored by the Law Enforcement Assistance Agency (LEAA) grants and the National Institute of Mental Health.
1977	Frances Hughes, a battered woman with four children who had endured 12 years of abuse against herself and her children, burned the home where her husband slept after beating and raping her. She was later found "not guilty by reason of insanity" rather than the so-called battered women self-defense.
1977	The National Conference on Women held in Houston, Texas, ranked domestic violence as one of the issues to receive highest priority.
1978	National conference held in Denver, Colorado, by the Colorado Coalition against Domestic Violence brought together 10 models, representing different types of shelters, under a federal grant by Health and Human Services.
1978	First large-scale research study about the psychological effects of battering on women began in Denver, Colorado.
1978	The *Oregon* v. *Rideout* decision, which found that Greta Rideout was raped by her estranged husband, led more states to take seriously marital rape. The protest was led by Laura X from Berkeley, California.
1979	The Belmont Conference was held in Maryland with 30 leaders in the field coming together to brainstorm various intervention programs for batterers.
1979	U.S. Congressional Committee on Science and Technology took testimony about the problem of domestic violence. More than 1000 groups providing services to battered women were located in the United States.
1979	National Council on Christians and Jews organized a conference at the California Polytechnical Institute in the Los Angeles, California, area where prosecutors and advocates met to brainstorm changing prosecution of batterers.
1979	The Domestic Abuse Project (DAP) is founded in Minneapolis, Minnesota, to provide a new community treatment model for working with domestic violence.
1979	The U.S. Commission on Civil Rights took testimony in Washington, D.C., about domestic violence.
1980	First Office on Women was founded within the Health and Human Services Department but was closed prior to the inauguration of President Reagan.
1980	The Domestic Violence Intervention Project was created in Duluth, Minnesota, organizing police, prosecutors, judges, shelters, legal advocates, probation officers, and mental health professionals in an effort to stop domestic violence.
1980	Funding from federal groups such as VISTA to the Colorado Coalition Against Domestic Violence created a structure for grassroots organizing of state domestic violence coalitions.
1982	Lois Herrington, appointed by President Reagan to chair the Presidential Commission on Violence and Victims, agreed to take testimony from domestic violence victims after protests in Boston and San Francisco. The next year, she was appointed to chair the Attorney General's Task Force on Violence and Victims, resulting in the formal recommendation to criminalize all forms of violence in the family and the first Office on Victim Rights in the U.S. Department of Justice.
1984	The U.S. Congress passed the Family Violence Prevention and Services Act and the Victims of Crime Act, which not only recognized the serious problem of domestic violence but also provided the first federal government funding for battered

continues

women shelters and statewide advocacy organizations. Controversy with the feminist advocates over the language about lesbian victims of violence on the first brochure to be printed by Herrington's office led to her dismissal and the first of many clashes between the advocates and professionals about how the money was to be spent.

1984   Richard Berk and Larry Sherman's study in Minneapolis, Minnesota, found that arresting the batterer and holding him overnight in jail was the most effective intervention in stopping repeat violence. The National Organization of Police Chiefs encouraged the discontinuation of mediation as an intervention.

1984   Tracey Thurman won a $2 million dollar verdict against the police department in Torrington, Connecticut, for failing to protect her while they watched her husband beat and stabbed her, eventually breaking her neck.

1984   The coalition for Justice for Abused Women (JAWS) was founded in Denver, Colorado. It successfully brought forth new procedures from the criminal justice system including a proarrest policy and established the first domestic violence court in the country. Other counties in Colorado, including Durango where advocates had filed a lawsuit against the police department, followed suit. Shortly after, a similar court was founded in Quincy, Massachusetts, which was later followed by one in Miami, Florida, and others.

1985   The U.S. Surgeon General convened a conference between researchers, practitioners, and advocates in Virginia and declared that domestic violence was a public health menace. Some statistics published in the book resulting from that meeting held at the technologically sophisticated Xerox center indicated that as many as 50% of all women admitted to emergency departments in hospitals were injured by a male partner. Although a campaign to stop domestic violence was begun by Dr. C. Everett Coop, the U.S. Surgeon General at that time, the public health service was politically weakened by Congress who were dominated by those angered by its stand favoring gun control as one way to reduce violent deaths. Later, the U.S. Surgeon General reported that partner abuse against women was the number 1 cause of injury to American women between the ages of 15 and 44.

1985   The United Nations (UN) Third Conference on Women in Nairobi, Kenya, gave stopping violence against women one of the highest priorities and required member nations to develop strategies and prepare reports on their efforts for the next decade.

1986   Attorney Jeanne Elliott was shot and paralyzed by a police officer in the courtroom while legally representing his ex-wife in a domestic dispute over failure to pay court-ordered maintenance and child support. Later, the wife denied being a battered woman and the police officer was found guilty of attempted murder and sentenced to 16 years in prison. He has since been released; she, however, is still in a wheelchair.

1987   Missouri, one of the states that did not permit expert witness testimony in trials of battered women who killed abusive partners in what they claimed was self-defense, passed legislation permitting testimony on battered woman syndrome. Other states followed and today such testimony is permitted in all states.

1990   Ohio Governor Celeste was the first to commute the sentences of several battered women who were convicted of first-degree murder after killing their abusive partners. One year later, Governor William Schaefer of Maryland commuted the sentences of 12 women, and governors of other states shortly followed (including Governor Lawton Chiles of Florida, who set up what is considered the most comprehensive evaluation procedure). Despite the efforts of some advocate groups, other governors, such as the governor of California, denied all clemency efforts. Prisons around the world are filled with women serving long sentences for murder who might not have been convicted had testimony about the abuse they experienced been offered in their cases.

1990   Congress passed a resolution that no state should allow batterers to get custody of their children without demonstrating their ability to properly parent them. Supervised visitation was recommended until batterers completed an offender-specific treatment program and could prove their fitness to parent. Nationwide, it was found that more than 50% of all child abductions were the result of domestic violence.

1993   Congress passed the Violence Against Women Act modeled after the Civil Rights Act of 1964 declaring domestic violence to be a human rights violation and specifying federal civil and criminal penalties for violators.

1993   Both Lorena Bobbitt and her husband, John Wayne Bobbitt, each went on trial in Manassas, Virginia, after she cut off his penis following the last of many sexual batteries he had committed on her without consequences. Both were found not guilty and the issue of marital rape in domestic violence cases achieved greater national attention. He later was convicted of domestic violence against at least one other woman after his penis was resutured.

1994   The American Medical Association (AMA) announced a campaign to help stop violence in the family. The American Psychological Association (APA) formed its Presidential Task Force on Violence and the Family following successful initiatives to apply research and clinical efforts by psychologists in youth violence and violence against women. The American Bar Association (ABA) and several judges associations also formed campaigns to better educate their members and the community about the dangers of unchecked family violence.

1994   Nicole Brown was found brutally murdered in Los Angeles with a friend, Ron Goldman. Her former husband, O. J. Simpson, was charged with the murder and prosecuted for the crime in 1995. The prosecutors attempted to introduce evidence of his battering behavior as motivation for the murder. He was found not guilty by a criminal jury and the following year was found guilty in a civil court of placing her in danger of being killed, an artifact of California civil statutes. The extensive media coverage of the trial placed domestic violence and its terrible consequences in the public eye for months.

1995   The U.N. Conference on Women in Beijing, China, collected statistical data and a description of efforts to end violence against women from member nations.

1995   President Clinton established the first Violence Against Women Office in Justice Department to coordinate efforts to enforce the Domestic Violence Act.

1996   U.S. Congress passed a weapons specification law stating that anyone convicted of domestic violence (felony or misdemeanor) is prohibited from owning, carrying, or transporting a gun. This law is modeled after the section in the Violence Against Women Act that prohibits any police officer convicted of domestic violence from carrying a gun.

1996   Thirteen states passed legislation to prohibit insurance companies from denying benefits to victims of domestic violence or increasing premiums due to ongoing abuse.

1990s   Welfare reform laws were passed nationwide that imposed limitations on Aid for Dependent Children and general welfare benefits, impacting many poor battered women's abilities to leave their abusive partners.

2000   There are still less fewer 2000 battered women shelters in the United States and statistics indicate that for every two women accepted into shelter, five are turned away. For every two children sheltered, eight are refused. Despite continued efforts to obtain reliable and valid data on the numbers of battered women and children around the world, the actual count remains illusive due to the continued need to keep the violence as a private matter and inability to complete interviews without compromising the woman's safety.

psychological services. This model is defended by the attempt to demonstrate that it is the patriarchy resulting from sexism in the culture that perpetuates all forms of woman abuse. Violence against women is seen as a violation of human rights. While certainly true, the "cure" for those women who have been negatively affected by the abuse cannot simply be the demise of patriarchy and restoration of equality, as the past 30 years have shown. In the United States and Canada, the shelter model added psychotherapeutic and case-management types of interventions for both the batterer and the battered woman since it was felt that violence often creates psychological damage to both parties and their children. It was believed that without such intervention, it would be difficult for women to better protect themselves and for men to stop their violent behavior. Without the self-esteem and belief in themselves, it is difficult for women to band together and organize against the tyranny that oppression brings. Susan Schechter and Lenore Walker have documented the development of the politics that has accompanied the attention to the problem and describe services that battered women have received over the past 30 years. While only a small number of battered women will ever need to use a battered woman's shelter, its presence in a community provided the visibility needed to mobilize the more traditional institutions and agencies to become more supportive of protecting women and children from further abuse.

The feminist, sociopolitical ideological fear was that professionals would continue to blame the victim, treat the woman as if it were her problem, let the man get away without taking responsibility for his behavior, and continue the patriarchal attitudes and abusive behavior toward women. While the feminist sociopolitical model does not per se reject services for the battered woman, it does not encourage a clinical therapeutic ideology. Barbara Hart, a Pennsylvania attorney who helped start state and national battered woman's coalitions and wrote most of the model legislation for civil protection statutes, has argued that safety must be the first concern when working with abused women. She cautions therapists that they must give a great deal of thought to whether their techniques will place the woman in more danger. Evan Stark and Anne Flitcraft reviewed charts of women who came for medical treatment at the emergency departments in Yale University's hospitals and found that doctors rarely asked if obvious injuries were caused by domestic violence and even if they obtained the information, they rarely noted it on the patient's chart or made appropriate referrals. Karil Klingbeil at Harborview Hospital in Seattle and Carole Warsaw at Cook County Hospital in Chicago began a training program for physicians to assist them in identifying and assisting battered women when they presented for medical services. Jacqueline Campbell did the same within the nursing profession.

Walker's work on theories that attempted to explain the psychological damage from violence on women was often met with skepticism and denouncement by those who viewed the entire field of psychology as antifeminist. Sociologist Kirsti Yllo and her coauthor, psychologist Barbara Bograd, attempted to bridge the gap and document a feminist perspective on interventions with battered women. The human service model insisted that there must be planned steps to assist victims to heal and prevent further victimization along with social change, which is typically longer term. In fact, the Freudian-based psychodynamic therapy orientation that had typically been used to keep women oppressed, so clearly described by feminist psychologist Phyllis Chesler in her book *Women and Madness,* was replaced in the 1980s by the addition of feminist theory and techniques into most of the common therapy models, such as those focusing on object-relations, cognitive-behavioral areas, and existential theories. In addition, a group of feminist psychologists, who eventually formed the Feminist Therapy Institute, were at work developing a new therapy model based on feminism and a trauma-oriented model that better explained the psychological damage from the victim-survivor's perspective. They included names like Laura Brown, Mary Ann Dutton, Hannah Lerman, Natalie Porter, Elizabeth Rave, Lynne Bravo Rosewater, Adrienne Smith, Lenore Walker, Rachel Siegel, Paula Caplan, Ellyn Kashak, Jeanne Adleman, Sara Sharatt, and Jan Faulkner.

These tensions have never been totally resolved to either group's satisfaction even though there is much overlap between the two seemingly polarized ideologies. Those following a more sociopolitical model have found that the complexities in the individuals who come to shelter or present for different types of intervention, including legal services, are sometimes beyond their capabilities. At the same time, those following a more human services–oriented model find the pull toward pathologizing the victims and perpetrators still remains very seductive despite professional guidelines that admonish against it. Nonetheless, there are a number of items of agreement, such as the demographics and dynamics of adult battering relationships, that are incorporated within the different ideologies.

B. JUDICIAL VERSUS PUBLIC HEALTH SYSTEM MODELS

During the 1980s, another interesting turn occurred when the United States became more focused on using the judiciary as the gateway to other services for the victim and the perpetrator rather than the public health system as is used in other countries, as noted by Laurie Heise in a 1992 report commissioned by the World Bank. The focus on the judiciary probably was more politically driven than ideologically because in the early 1980s the United States government was under the control of the conservatives who promised a greater focus on "law and order" than on mental health or rehabilitation. The extensive community mental health system that had a strong public health focus was also dismantled during this period. Ironically, today the criminal justice system in the United States has become more like the old mental hospitals dismantled in the 1960s under the advent of the community mental health system. These hospitals were considered to be warehouses for the seriously mentally ill who received little if no treatment. Upward of 25% of the inmates in the U.S. prisons and 50% of those held in custody in the local jails are estimated to have some form of mental illness with most being warehoused with little or no treatment. Sadly, most of the women and many of the men who are incarcerated have long histories of being abuse victims both as children and as adults. The research on family violence indicates that early intervention with these victims may well reduce the number of violent crimes dramatically, but such prevention efforts are rarely funded or undertaken by communities.

Focusing on the judiciary was positive in bringing about both the change of laws and their enforcement to make it possible for poor as well as financially stable battered women to gain access to the courts, including the ability to file for court orders of protection. Women first are helped to find protection and safety and then given referrals to community shelters and other services at the time the police intervene or an arrest is made. Police were trained in making arrests upon probable cause, domestic violence was taken off the bonding schedule so the man would be held in jail until the next regularly scheduled court appearance, and special domestic violence courts sprang up around North America. Battered women were permitted to seek a greater distribution of the marital assets as a result of the man's violent behavior in either divorce or personal injury tort cases. These changes are more clearly explained in a separate section later.

As is necessary in a judicial system based on British Common Law, the focus is on the behavior of the accused, which means that the alleged perpetrator must be considered innocent until proven guilty. The abuse is seen through the perpetrator's intentions, not just the impact it has on the victim. This is not true in the inquisitor legal models such as those based on Roman law or the Napoleonic code where the accused must prove his or her innocence. When the public health model is the perspective to organize the intervention and treatment of the battered woman, it is more difficult to hold the batterer accountable for his actions. Psychological abuse, which is often the most damaging to the victim, is not given much importance in the judicial system where observable violent behavior gets more serious penalties. On the other hand, the emphasis on criminal responsibility for the perpetrator in the criminal justice model does help stop recidivism especially with those who have participated in the offender-specific treatment programs. Psychological abuse is given a great deal of attention in the stress-based model often used in public health systems, particularly those that have been recently developed in Latin America and some European countries. However, public health interventions are often more environmentally based and psychotherapy is not emphasized.

II. Dynamics of Domestic Violence

The research on the dynamics of domestic violence has debunked a number of myths that were commonly misunderstood about the behavior of batterers and battered women. They include the following:

Myth: Batterers are just being men and they can't control their use of violence, which is biologically caused.

Research: Battering behavior is learned behavior that can be unlearned and controlled by men or women.

Myth: Battering behavior is a man's response to provocation by the woman.

Research: Battering behavior is used by the man to intentionally demonstrate his power and control the woman.

Myth: The man only uses violence because he is drunk or high on drugs.

Research: Although there is an association between increased levels of violence with alcohol and other drugs, there are no data to suggest that alcohol causes the battering behavior.

Myth: Battered women stay in battering relationships, so therefore they must be masochistic or like being beaten up.

Research: Battered women stay in battering relationships because of many complex reasons including being terrified that they will get hurt worse or killed if they try to leave. In fact, terminating a battering relationship is the most dangerous time for the woman. There are no empirical data to demonstrate that masochism or the belief that one somehow deserves being hurt because of bad thoughts or deeds actually exists or that it influences why women remain in battering relationships.

Myth: Battered women are poor, uneducated women who have no resources.

Research: Domestic violence cuts across every demographic group including age, race, culture, socioeconomic level, education, and religion.

Perhaps the most often asked question about battering relationships is, "Why doesn't the battered woman leave the batterer?" The dynamics of battering relationships demonstrate that this is really the wrong question to ask, as there are psychological effects of the abuse in addition to the fear and terror of escalating danger that can explain the woman's behavior. The better question to ask is, "Why doesn't the batterer let the woman go?"

A. FEMINIST ANALYSIS OF THE BATTERER'S BEHAVIOR

The analysis of the batterer's behavior begins with the feminist analysis that violence against women is an abuse of power and control that requires intervention and consequences to stop it. Batterers are seen as having control over whether or not they use violence and therefore, if the consequences were made high enough, then they would stop it. This analysis looks at batterers' nonviolent behavior toward their employers, people on the street, or others in the community who get them angry as proof of the position. However, the recent observations of the spread of violence from the home into the workplace, schools, and other places in the community suggest a more complex analysis may be needed.

Early research by sociologists Richard Berk and Larry Sherman into effective interventions at stopping domestic violence demonstrated the effectiveness of arrest and post-adjudication offender-specific treatment programs rather than the "take-a-walk-around-the-block-and-cool-down" mediation policies previously subscribed to by law enforcement. Dissatisfaction with the typical psychological treatment programs that excused the batterer's behavior in favor of long-term analysis of his personality caused the battered woman advocate community to call for offender-specific treatment programs that were approved by or somehow attached to the court.

Programs, often modeled after the program begun in Duluth, Minnesota, by advocate Ellen Pence and psychologist Jeffrey Edelson, quickly sprang up around the country. They were usually six to twelve-weeks long, were psychoeducational in nature, and focused on dealing with anger management using a strong behavioral psychology ideology. Other, more comprehensive treatment programs were developed by Michael Lindsay and his colleagues at AMEND program in Denver, Daniel Sonkin in San Francisco, Alyce LaViolette in Long Beach, California, and RAVEN in St. Louis, which recommended longer attendance and added more psychological treatment. Court-ordered batterers were required to attend these groups, usually once a week, and if they did not appear, then this was reported to the court. Confidentiality, a cornerstone of psychotherapy, was not granted and the batterer was required to sign a waiver so that the therapist could discuss his progress, or lack of progress, with both the court and his partner.

Although these offender-specific intervention programs did not deal effectively with all batterers, and few men who were referred actually completed the program and stopped all of their abusive behavior, a sufficient number of those who attended did change (25 to 60%), suggesting that it is a worthwhile strategy to try. Besides, when treatment rather than prison was the sanction for battering, most battered women were more cooperative with the legal system and testified to the abuse. Most of the short-term, offender-specific, court-ordered treatment programs have been found to be too superficial to deal with the complexities presented by many batterers, and to date there are very few complete therapy programs that take into account the safety of the victim, the mental status of the offender, and the social conditions that tolerate if not facilitate the violence against women.

Research has now identified different types of batterers suggesting the need for different types of intervention programs rather than just one that fits all offenders. For example, University of Washington psychologists Neil Jacobson and John Gottman used physiological measures and found two groups of batterers, who they labeled "cobras" and "pit bulls." The pit bulls had the type of physiological reaction expected when angered: their hearts beat faster, their blood vessels dilated, and they continued to escalate their abuse. In contrast, the cobras were less reactive to stimuli, their heart rate slowed down, and they became more deliberate in their threats, sometimes patiently waiting to stun their prey. Although both were dangerous, the cobras who often used less overt physical abuse were more deadly. Obviously they were not responsive to the same treatment as the pit bulls. This is further described in a separate section later.

Traditionally trained psychotherapists were dismayed that the courts, in referring batterers for required treatment, did not always refer to them and utilize their treatment skills. Many did not have the requisite training in either gender or trauma issues and did not have the knowledge base for conducting offender-specific treatment from a cognitive behavioral perspective. In one research study, psychologists Michele Harway and Marsali Hansen found that fewer than one-third of surveyed mental health professionals were able to correctly identify or take seriously reports of domestic violence in a case study where, unbeknownst to the participants, the man later killed the woman. As more batterers became identified by the legal system, psychologists such as Donald Dutton in Vancouver, Canada, were able to conduct research to better understand batterers' personalities and behavior. Not surprisingly, it was found that batterers, like the women they abuse, are a varied group with mental illnesses, neuropsychological deficits, substance abuse problems in addition to their learned abuse of power and control. It is the interaction of these factors that results in domestic violence.

B. PSYCHONEUROIMMUNOLOGY

Interesting new research on psychoneuroimmunological changes from trauma that take place in the midbrain have added fascinating new data to what we already know about batterers and battered women. The biochemical changes that occur in the hypothalamus and other midbrain areas from the autonomic nervous system response to danger have been documented in those who have been exposed to family abuse. These changes may impact on the developing brain structures in children exposed to or experiencing violence in their homes as well as the functioning of the areas of the brain, particularly in those areas that control emotions as psychologist Daniel Goleman described in his book *Emotional Intelligence*. Physiological research has suggested that memory for trauma may reside in areas other than the cognitive areas of the brain cortex. Goleman reviewed data to suggest that the midbrain may have storage areas for nonverbal and unprocessed memory of trauma. Others, such as psychiatrist Bessel Van der Kolk, suggest that cells have memory for trauma. The recent controversy about the variable memories of women who claim to have been sexually abused as children may be because trauma memories are not cognitively processed by the brain in the same way that nontrauma memories are processed, causing the periods of forgetting and remembering that may be uncovered in feminist psychotherapy.

C. CYCLE THEORY OF VIOLENCE

Early stories of battered women that were systematically collected and analyzed found that battering relationships had periods of loving behavior in addition to the violence. Walker's *The Battered Woman,* published in 1979, updated the research in *The Battered Woman Syndrome,* which was first published in 1984 and compared those findings with newer research in the second edition published in 2000. Although most battered women were unaware of any pattern to the violence, this research uncovered a three-phase cycle of the violence that has been helpful in understanding the dynamics of domestic violence. The first phase was labeled, the "tension-building" period because the woman described the escalation of small events that led up to the second phase or the "acute battering incident." The women described their behavior during the first phase as causing the batterer to either calm down or speed up his abusive behavior.

Survivor therapy strategies incorporate this knowledge into treatment so the woman becomes consciously aware of how she can better protect herself from the acute battering incident where most of the physical injuries occur. After the second phase is over, which is usually the shortest period of the three phases, the batterer ceases his violent behavior and sometimes behaves in a loving and contrite manner. This third phase was named "loving-contrition" to reflect his nonviolent and non-tension-producing behavior at this time, even though he may not directly apologize or acknowledge his responsibility for the abuse. This third phase is the reinforcement for the woman staying in the relationship. She is reminded again of the "man she fell in love with" and believes if only the first two phases drop out, she will have the loving relationship she wanted during their courtship period.

In most battering relationships the abuse escalates while the loving behavior decreases. Even in those relationships where the batterer is truly sorry for what he has caused, the loving behavior can be excessive and become burdensome. In one case the batterer bought the woman a new car on credit, but she was then required to make the new financial payments. As the relationship progresses, the third phase of loving-contrition may change and an absence of tension and abuse may be the reinforcer for staying in the relationship. Many of these women are too frightened to leave the relationship or they have become so depressed that they do not have the energy to do so. Over time many of the social institutions that provide assistance have relaxed the barriers that once stopped women from seeking help. Even so, it is still embarrassing and in some communities stigmatizing to disclose the abuse, especially if there has been an outward appearance of being a successful, happy, and functional family.

D. LEARNED HELPLESSNESS

The social psychology construct of learned helplessness can give some direction to understanding how battered women learn to cope with the abuse rather than believe that they can ever totally escape from it. Martin Seligman first described the effects of aversive stimulation with intermittent reinforcement on a person's belief that he or she could have control over the environment so that the person would know whether or not his or her actions would keep him or her protected and safe. Although Seligman named his theory around the helplessness he observed in his animals, his work with people led to a reformulation of the theory demonstrating the coping strategies used when people (or animals) give up the belief in their ability to escape from the aversive stimuli. In his work with dogs, for example, Seligman found that they sat in a corner of the cage on top of their own excrement. While that might appear as if the animals had given up, in fact, fecal matter is a good insulator from electrical shock, so the animals apparently had found the least painful position in which they remained.

So too for battered women. They often try numerous coping strategies and favor the least painful ones, understanding that escape may be impossible or at the very least it might place them and their children at high risk for further harm from batterers who continue to stalk and abuse them. Leaving a battering relationship does not necessarily stop the abuse; rather, the batterer may escalate his violent behavior to the point of killing the woman, the children, and himself.

Applications of the theory of learned helplessness have been controversial in the field of domestic violence. The social-learning theory is interpreted by its name and used as if the woman is considered helpless rather than understanding its psychological process. Some have misinterpreted learned helplessness as a statement against the battered woman's incredible resiliency. Others, such as Ola Barnett and Alyce LaViolette, have applied the theory to develop effective intervention programs where the contingency between response and outcome is relearned. Seligman has developed a theory of optimism and positive psychology that he suggests will provide resiliency against developing learned helplessness even when exposed to the conditions of random and variable aversive behavior such as domestic violence.

III. Demographic Data

In 1994, the American Psychological Association (APA) president Ronald Fox appointed Lenore Walker to chair his Presidential Task Force on Violence and the Family to study the problem from a psychological perspective. A report was presented to the APA in 1996 detailing the findings of the committee, and suggestions for the practitioner facing a number of dilemmas when working in this area were also published. Although statistics are difficult to verify, since many women who are battered in adult relationships do not report their abuse, there are certain findings that are reliable and valid as they appear consistent in multiple data sources. Epidemiological studies together with clinical data demonstrate that domestic violence cuts across every demographic group including the rich and the poor, the educated and the uneducated, the young and the old, and people from every racial, ethnic, and cultural group. Although some studies have found that violence in the home is more prevalent in poor families, in fact, the data demonstrate that it is common for professional women to be battered and professional men are known batterers.

The greatest risk for becoming battered in an adult relationship in your own home is to be female. Although male children are abused more frequently than adult males, females are more likely to be physically and sexually abused by males in their household. Even the child abuse statistics demonstrate that

when child maltreatment through neglect is removed, more men abuse children and they abuse more seriously than do women. Male children exposed to these men are more likely to use violence in their own adult relationships. Interestingly, although the prevailing opinion is that caretakers and adult children are more likely to abuse the elderly, if the numbers of known older battered women are included in these data, again, it is more likely for an elderly woman to be abused by her male partner than by anyone else.

In domestic violence, 95% of the cases we know about are women who are battered by current and former male partners. Although stable over many years, these numbers have always been challenged as an underestimate of the numbers of men who are abused by women. It is suggested that more men are battered by women than report it because shame prevents them from disclosure. However, men have been able to report mutual violence and sexual abuse as a child without letting shame stop their disclosure. Battered women and batterers come from every social, economic, racial, ethnic, and educational class. Although finding resources may be more difficult for poor women, even those women with their own careers or sources of money are often unable to find help to protect themselves and their children. In the United States it is estimated that at least 2½ million women are battered every year using the sampling studies of sociologists Murray Straus and Richard Gelles.

In other countries the estimates are similar although there appears to be a higher rate of domestic violence in countries where wars and other state-sponsored violence is also occurring. In preparation for the United Nations (UN) Fourth Conference on Women held in Beijing in 1995, member countries were asked to provide estimates of the rates of violence against women in their country. These data are available in various reports put out by the UN. The World Health Organization (WHO) has a Web site that provides other demographic data it has collected. Data from a recent study conducted by the U.S. Centers for Disease Control (CDC) and the National Institute of Justice (NIJ) are also available on their Web sites.

Women don't leave battering relationships for complex reasons that include fear of further harm, no place to go or no money on which to survive, low self-esteem and self-blame, desire to keep the marriage together for the children's sake, and dependency needs. However, the major reason why women don't leave is that *leaving doesn't stop the violence.* In fact, women are more likely to be seriously injured or killed when they leave the battering relationship. In the United States it is estimated that one-half of the 2000 women who are killed each year are murdered by their current or former partners, often around the time of separation. Thus, to protect the woman and child, it is imperative to stop the batterer's abusive behavior, which can only be done with the total cooperation of the legal profession. A small number of women who are desperate may kill their batterers in self-defense. Their legal right to introduce details of the abuse into their legal defense, including the right to expert witness testimony, has been affirmed both by case and legislative law in most states and many other countries. This testimony has typically been provided by psychologists who usually describe the dynamics of domestic violence and its psychological effects including battered woman syndrome and learned helplessness to explain the woman's state of mind and to justify her use of deadly force when the batterer's danger to her might not appear that way to others. This is particularly important when the man appears to be sleeping or has stopped his violence for the moment. Testimony about what triggers the battered woman's continuous fear response as different from someone who has not previously experienced the danger of repeated violence is important to meet the legal standards regarding a "reasonable perception of imminent danger" needed to make a self-defense showing.

So far, the most effective way to stop battering behavior is to arrest and detain the batterer. Typical community responses include a proarrest policy so that a batterer can be arrested upon probable cause based on the affidavit of the arresting law enforcement officer who may not have witnessed the actual violence but has witnessed the aftermath of a crime scene. The man is taken to jail and held until the next regularly scheduled court appearance, usually overnight. No bond is permitted without sanction of the judge. In some communities, however, research has demonstrated that arrest and detention is not sufficient to stop the abuse. If the batterer is a marginalized member of the community then this arrest policy may even make him angrier and more dangerous. A system of domestic violence courts, with easier access to restraining orders for battered women described later, has created more safety for women; still, if the batterer decides he will harm or kill the woman, the community cannot always protect her.

IV. Theoretical Models

A. FEMINIST

The feminist model that is the prevailing viewpoint about domestic violence around the world is that battering behavior is an abuse of power and control by a man toward a woman. The man is seen as having special privilege by being male and he abuses that privilege for his own satisfaction, without regard for the woman's needs or rights. Although men can also be battered by women, its occurrence is rare and often in conjunction with what has been termed "mutual violence," which usually starts out as self-defense. Battering behavior is used by the ruling majority to enforce compliance of the minority members when they do not do what the oppressors require. Although members of the oppressed class may also use abuse against someone viewed as more oppressed than they are, it is not seen as normative as when it is used by the oppressors. The oppression of women from all forms of discrimination adds to the negative psychological impact from violence. Thus, racism, poverty, disability, membership in a minority class, sexual orientation, and other forms of diminished social power all multiply the effects of domestic violence.

Treatment of those who have been beaten into submission must include the reempowerment of the woman by using a positive approach that emphasizes her strengths, assists in her becoming more safe, validates her experiences, and helps her heal. Therapists must pay close attention to the potential to misuse their own power in the therapeutic relationship and at the same time, protect themselves from developing their own vicarious trauma reactions from exposure to their client's traumatic experiences. Even when the battered woman has numerous other problems, such as substance abuse, concomitant serious mental illness, and neuropsychological deficits, a nonpathologizing, nonauthoritarian relationship that respects each person's need for her own power is recommended in this model. Other forms of oppression are also considered during this type of intervention. New training models in feminist therapy and cultural diversity are being introduced so that clinicians will have these skills.

B. TRAUMA

Repeated exposure to trauma can cause physical as well as psychological problems, even in those who were mentally healthy prior to the occurrence of the event(s). Repeated violence, especially in the relationship that includes both loving and abusive behavior, is trauma that causes the same types of psychological injuries as does exposure to a plane crash, an earthquake, a war-related scene, or seeing someone killed. It is the fear of further harm or death that makes domestic violence such a severe trauma. Physiological psychology has provided a model for understanding extreme stress from trauma. Early in psychology it was discovered that people had a natural response to danger, which was labeled the "fight and flight" response. In the classic analogy, a person sees a bear, becomes afraid, has the normal psychophysiological reaction moderated by the autonomic nervous system, becomes stronger, more anxious, more focused on the danger, and then begins to run away from the bear toward safety. In the typical response to trauma and stress, the person who faces danger has the expected psychophysiological reaction that is moderated by the biochemicals released by the autonomic nervous system. He or she becomes more anxious, may focus on the danger repeatedly whether or not it is still present, and avoids people, places, and things that might remind the person of the trauma while possibly distorting emotional reactions. Memory for details of the trauma changes, with the person sometimes becoming almost obsessively concerned about details and reenactments of the incident and sometimes appearing to forget what happened for different periods of time. When the trauma response lasts longer than expected (usually that means more than one month after the incident), then it may be diagnosed as a posttraumatic stress disorder (PTSD) and treated with special methods. When it is a woman who has a PTSD reaction, a combination of feminist and trauma therapy, such as Walker developed in *Survivor Therapy*, is recommended.

C. RISK AND RESILIENCY

The community mental health model from the 1960s that has been integrated into the public health model currently in use suggests that the impact from any type of trauma, including domestic violence, is a result of the combination of the strength or resiliency of the woman prior to the victimization and the risk factors to which she has previously been exposed. Social policy that follows from this model suggests that prevention of serious psychological impact from domestic violence can be obtained through strengthen-

ing all women who are potential victims. This includes "normalizing" the experiences of violence so that the woman does not perceive herself as the only person who has been traumatized, does not blame herself, and does not succumb to the depression and isolation that can be a serious effect. Some of the woman's other coping strategies are understood in part as a way to mitigate the impact from the abuse rather than described as something wrong with the woman. For example, it is not paranoid to feel that someone is out to get you or to feel betrayed by someone who loves you, when in fact that is a common experience of a battered woman. Nor is the love and anger felt by the battered woman seen as unusual given the dynamics of the domestic violence situation. Once the cycle theory of violence is understood, the fact that both loving and violent behavior occurs in a battering relationship can be better understood and the reinforcing nature of the loving-contrition phase of the cycle can explain how the woman can feel both love and anger simultaneously.

1. Public Health Model

A public health model that builds in resiliency to better protect victims usually has three major areas for intervention: primary prevention, secondary intervention, and tertiary level care. The hospital, which is often seen as a tertiary-level care institution, is actually the battered woman shelter in the domestic violence analogy. A battered woman can go here for a short time in order to get strong enough to deal with the situation in her own way. The safety provided by the battered woman shelter is an important factor in many women's healing process. Some women need the security of the battered woman shelter or day-treatment type of programs in order to begin their healing. Others might need a short stay in a hospital, especially if they are so suicidal that they cannot be contained in the community at that time. These are all tertiary-level care components for victims.

While it would be nice to think that perpetrators would get tertiary-level support to stop their violence while detailed in jail, in fact this is rarely the case. They may learn to become even more violent when exposed to the different types of abuse that can occur among inmates. Some communities in the United States have programs for batterers that they can attend while incarcerated. However, there are too few of these programs to determine if they are helpful or not. Substance abuse treatment centers rarely deal with the abusive behavior using the newer offender-specific methodology reported earlier. Neither do mental hospital treatment programs.

Secondary intervention is needed when the woman has already been abused but the impact is not yet so severe that she cannot use community-based agencies to provide her with assistance. Out-patient programs offered by the courts and in the psychology community are the typical secondary intervention programs. They are designed to stop the offender behavior and help the victim to recover. The programs vary widely; some are excellent and others completely miss the point. It is important to note, however, that these intervention programs are available and some do work to help stop violence and better protect women, children, and men.

Prevention programs are the most important part of a public health approach as they teach people to recognize the possibility of abuse and the dangers it poses to the health and mental health of not only women and children but also the perpetrator himself. In primary prevention programs, everyone gets the same message—an educational campaign that battering behavior is wrong and against the law is one such type of program. High-risk groups can be targeted for special prevention programs, such as children who have been exposed to domestic violence in their homes. Boys, for example, are thought to face 1000 times the risk of becoming batterers if they have been abused and were exposed to their fathers battering their mothers. Pregnant teens are at higher risk to become physically and sexually abused, as are their babies. So are women who have recently become immigrants after being forced to flee their own countries. Many young girls who are abused by their boyfriends have been exposed to domestic violence in their own homes.

V. Interventions

Numerous interventions have been used in what has become known as the battered woman's movement. These include the social changes to overthrow the patriarchal order of society and bring about equality for women and men that have been described earlier, institutional reforms such as those necessary within the health, mental health, legal, and social services systems set up by government, prevention services, and immediate crisis intervention centers that protect an individual victim and her children. Described next are only a few of the interventions that are taking place all over the world today.

A. SHELTER

The most important intervention in the campaign to stop men's abuse of women has been the shelter movement described in the history section of this article. It can be thought of as the hub of the wheel from where all other services must be viewed. Interventions that do not take into account every battered woman's safety needs, which is the symbol that the shelter stands for, rarely will be effective in protecting and stopping the violence against women. In the United States there are more than 2000 battered women shelters that receive government funding and countless task forces that receive private funding to assist battered women and children. Although feminist philosophy to change the social order to one of equality between men and women is not included in the operation of all of these shelters, they are saving women's and children's lives.

B. FEMINIST THERAPY

In the 1970s, paralleling the feminist movement in the United States and other countries, a psychotherapy approach called "feminist therapy" was developed by a number of feminist leaders in the mental health field to attempt to overcome the psychological effects of oppression and discrimination against women, as well as to help alleviate other types of emotional distress in women and girls. The Feminist Therapy Institute, which was begun in 1981, has held meetings each year bringing together hundreds of feminist therapy leaders. Several books have been published including a series of feminist ethics that guides the feminist practice of psychology. This has been especially helpful for those working with battered women, as violence against women has been a major area of concern. In the mid 1990s a major conference bringing together the major leaders within organized psychology in the United States was held in Boston. Although there was doubt that the feminist therapy approach would survive—many leaders of earlier psychotherapy theories found it to be seriously flawed in its understanding of women—it is now integrated into the various therapy systems as is described by Mary Ann Dutton and Lenore Walker in *Feminist Psychotherapies: An Integration of Feminist and Psychotherapeutic Systems* and Laura Brown in *Personality and Psychopathology: Feminist Reappraisals* and stands as its own treatment system. The feminist therapy approach has been incorporated by Ola Barnett and Alyce LaViolette, *It*

Could Happen to Anyone, Why Battered Women Stay; Laura Brown, *Subversive Dialogues: Feminist Therapy Theories,* Marsali Hansen and Michele Harway, *Feminist Family Therapy;* Lenore Walker, *Abused Women and Survivor Therapy: A Practical Guide for the Psychotherapist;* and Lynne Rosewater and Lenore Walker, *Handbook of Feminist Therapy: Psychotherapy with Women.* It can be applied in individual therapy as well as in groups or family treatment. Videos are available to demonstrate the treatment (see Lenore Walker in *Survivor Therapy and Abused Women,* available from Walker, and *Feminist Therapy,* available from Allyn & Bacon). In the 1990s, this gender-specific approach to the treatment of mental illness was applied to men and boys by Gary Brooks in *A New Psychotherapy for Traditional Men* and Ronald Levant and William Pollack in *A New Psychology of Men.* Perhaps one of the most important additions to the treatment modality is the inclusion of an analysis of the context in which any events occur. Feminist therapy also pays attention to the power differential between client and therapist, which makes it the ideal modality to develop and reempower the battered woman whose power has been taken away by the controlling batterer. Assessing for and emphasizing the development of positive coping strategies rather than focusing on the things the woman does not do well helps to avoid the tendency to overpathologize behavior that feminists have stressed. [*See* FEMINIST APPROACHES TO PSYCHOTHERAPY; FEMINIST FAMILY THERAPY.]

C. PTSD DIAGNOSIS

At the same time, another treatment approach that dealt directly with victims of trauma also was developing, especially in the United States where large numbers of war veterans returning from Vietnam were requiring treatment for stress-based disorders. Although many of the symptoms were similar in anxiety and avoidance disorders such as depression and dissociation, the pattern in which they occur along with the intrusive memories and flashbacks to the trauma differentiate the posttraumatic stress disorder (PTSD) from other mental disorders. In fact, the PTSD is the only category in the Diagnostic and Statistical Manual of Mental Disorders (DSM-IV) that does not have a predisposition or pre-existing condition that contributes to its severity. Rather, the type of trauma, history of prior traumatic experiences, the risk factor exposure, and the resiliency of

the individual all contribute to the impact from the current trauma. As was mentioned earlier, PTSD is considered a normal reaction to abnormal situations even though the symptoms may become maladaptive. The perception of reexperiencing the trauma even after the abuse stops continues the impact of the trauma as if it were still occurring. The trauma that causes a PTSD can be a natural disaster or a "man-made" trauma such as battered woman syndrome, rape trauma syndrome, and battered child syndrome.

Victimization can also produce psychological effects that are diagnosed under different mental health categories. Since domestic violence occurs across all demographic groups, some women who have been battered also had a diagnosable mental illness prior to the abuse. Thus, it is important for a psychologist to check for other mental health issues that may call for different or additional treatment and intervention strategies. For example, new treatment programs for the chronic and seriously mentally ill combine various psychotropic medications together with environmental community-based interventions along with various forms of psychotherapy such as day treatment centers, groups, family therapy, and individual therapy. Using a trauma-based approach that focuses on the positive coping strategies of the individual may help victims overcome serious illnesses such as schizophrenia and bipolar disorders that once were not thought to be amenable to treatment. This is also true for many who have been previously diagnosed as having a personality disorder, either mistakenly or without considering other diagnoses such as PTSD that are more amenable to treatment. [*See* POSTTRAUMATIC STRESS DISORDER.]

D. THERAPISTS' ATTITUDES

Therapists and others in the social service institutions at first were unable to meet the battered woman's needs because of a basic lack of understanding about domestic violence as well as acting out the long-ingrained socialization patterns between men and women that do not promote equality. Most therapists, male or female, who have not been trained in the feminist gender perspective still do not find women's reports credible. If they do believe that the abuse really did occur, they are critical of the woman's behavior and are more likely to blame the victim and hold her responsible for her own victimization. Traditional psychological theories that were psychoanalytically based and focused on the victim's internal personality or even the more modern family systems theories that looked at the environment without a power analysis have been unable to provide a framework or lens through which the women's perspective was clearly viewed. It took the development of a trauma-based model together with the feminist-based theoretical model, described further later, to account for all the dynamics found in domestic violence and its impact on the victim.

Today, it is more likely that the feminist perspective on domestic violence is integrated in a psychological model that also looks at the mental health and neuropsychological integrity of both the victim and perpetrator. Subtle deficits in the coordination of all parts of the brain from frontal lobe dysfunction, damage from minimal brain trauma incidents from being violently shaken, and changes in brain chemistry from anoxia resulting when choked are seen in neuropsychological evaluations of seriously battered women. Damage from direct trauma to the brain from deliberate or accidental blows on the head can also be measured. A lifetime of serious mental illness in women is also accompanied by histories of battering in their adult relationships. While some battered women can heal on their own with family and community support, others need professional psychological treatment in order to survive and move on with their lives.

E. BATTERER'S "OFFENDER-SPECIFIC" TREATMENT

As described earlier, the most common type of treatment programs for batterers are 6- to 12-week psychoeducational programs that deal directly with the offender's attitudes toward women, toward violence against women, and anger management. Some of these programs assist the batterer in separating from his partner in a nonviolent way. A model called the Duluth Program is often used to design these programs. Relatively inexpensive to operate with a high initial success rate of stopping physical violence, these programs are popular in countries all over the world. Rarely does a batterer's treatment group specifically deal with multiple diagnosis of clients, such as those who may have major mental illnesses such as bipolar disorder, paranoid schizophrenia, and personality disorders, although sometimes batterers' can be court-ordered into multiple forms of treatment. It is estimated that at least one-third of all abusers have a mental illness diagnosis, but it is rare that they get appropriate treatment for their disor-

der. Sometimes the mental illness interacts with their violent behavior and neither can be properly treated without the other. In cases where batterers are also abusing substances, it is important to treat each problem separately without expecting the violence to stop with just substance abuse treatment.

A leading researcher into understanding the batterer, social psychologist Don Dutton has evaluated those who have completed treatment in Vancouver, Canada, and found another commonly seen type who he labels as having "borderline personality organization." Although this diagnosis is not an official one, its symptoms are close to the more popular borderline personality disorder that is also listed in the DSM-IV. It may be important to manage those batterers who have delusions with appropriate medication. As many as 60% of all battering incidents may also be associated with alcohol and other drug abuse, but rarely do the substances cause the violent behavior. Rather, alcohol and some other drugs do heighten the risk for more serious injuries. Although it appears that battering behavior often escalates, psychologist K. Daniel O'Leary and his colleagues at State University of New York at Stoney Brook have found that some batterers remain psychologically and verbally aggressive without crossing the line to using physical abuse, others become physically abusive early in the relationship and then continue maintaining power and control over the woman by intimidation and bullying techniques that threaten more violence, and still others remain at a fairly constant level of violence over a long period of time.

Approximately 20% of batterers also commit other criminal acts and meet the definitions for the new research on psychopathy and the antisocial personality disorder diagnosis. Described earlier, Jacobson and Gottman's "cobras" and some of the "pitbulls" may fit into this category. The pitbull is identified by his escalating angry behavior, including heightened psychophysiological measures such as a more rapid heartbeat, sweating, and other autonomic nervous system responses typical of rage responses. He is the dependent batterer who may choose his partner by trial and error but fears abandonment once he has made his choice. The cobra, on the other hand, is identified by his decreasing heartbeat, cool and calm exterior, and more deliberate actions. He is more independent and chooses his partner after careful planning. He does not let the woman go and is more likely to keep his threat to kill her in retaliation if she does not do as he demands.

Others have suggested different classifications including a tripartite division with power and control batterers making up one group, mentally ill and substance abusing batterers who also may have control problems making up the second group, and the psychopaths making up the smaller third group. Given these different classifications of batterers, it is apparent that the single intervention approach to offender-specific treatment is simplistic and not effective enough to help stop violence in adult relationships.

F. SOCIAL SERVICES AND CHILD PROTECTION

Many children today live in homes where their fathers are battering their mothers even if they are not beaten themselves. The harm done to children who are exposed to domestic violence has now been documented and found to negatively affect the child's emotional, intellectual, and social development by researchers such as Robert Geffner, Leslie Drozd, Geraldine Stahly, Honore Hughes, Peter Jaffe, Mindy Rosenberg, Robbie Rossman, and David Wolf. The social services system in the United States, which is one of the more widely developed protection systems around the world that tries to protect children from all forms of abuse, has not been able to provide nonpunitive services to these children or their families, without regard for economic, cultural, or educational status. Child Protective Services in the United States has helped to identify children who are in danger of serious physical harm from the same adults who are harming adult women, but has not been able to provide adequate services for these children and their families. Fear of having their children taken away from them by the state makes a large segment of the population afraid to ask for assistance, especially undocumented immigrants to a country. It is far better to add a helper or advocate to the family whose close access to all members make him or her acceptable. Newly educated caseworkers quickly become overburdened with a large caseload, resulting in a high turnover rate in the job.

The needs of the child, mother, and father are so different that it makes for numerous conflicts in the treatment approach. Children need to be protected from high-conflict stress situations, mothers need to be reempowered, and fathers need to have a nonviolent, loving, and noncontrolling relationship with their children. For the most part, social service caseworkers cannot provide all these services given the structure of the social services system, which is a

branch of state government. They must answer to the legal system, which demands that the parents conform to a rehabilitative treatment plan or parental rights can be terminated. Even if the caseworkers have a feminist perspective, the child protective system itself does not permit them the time to be particularly effective in dealing with everyone's individual needs in domestic violence situations.

Child custody disputes between mothers and fathers are common today in the United States where the legal standard of "best interests of the child" has changed from the child being raised by the mother to joint custody or parental responsibility. Obviously, it is not possible for most battered women to share parental responsibility with a man who has beaten and abused them. The impact on the child from remaining in the middle of high-conflict and abusive homes has not been considered by the courts and custody evaluators as will be detailed later. In other countries where children are still considered property of the father, battered women often remain in abusive homes in order to keep control of raising their children. This also occurs in the United States, although it is not as obvious.

G. MEDICAL INTERVENTION

Early data suggested that battered women did not tell their physicians about the violence that they were experiencing, even when the doctors inquired about suspicious injuries. The women told of being fearful of the punitive approach taken by social services and the lack of knowledge and skill on the part of the medical personnel who they saw. Feminists doctors such as Carole Warsaw from Cook County Hospital in Chicago and nurses such as Jacqueline Campbell at Johns Hopkins School of Nursing in Baltimore have been training the medical professionals to recognize the high rate of injuries from domestic violence in the emergency rooms, obstetricians' offices, and other doctor's offices. The failure of emergency room doctors to properly question women who came in when they needed stitches or broken bones set caused the medical profession to develop protocols that could be followed by any doctor in any type of institution. Battered women who are exposed to HIV infections and other sexually transmitted diseases need specialized treatment from both medical and mental health providers. M. Ross Seligson and Rebecca Bernas have attempted to train those in hospital centers dealing with AIDS to better understand battered women as well as shelter workers to better understand battered women with HIV infections. It is a difficult task due to the misinformation and myths held by professionals and clients alike about both issues.

At first it was the nurses rather than the doctors who were most willing to be trained, so protocols were developed that helped provide better procedures to facilitate disclosure and access to community resources from physician's offices. Sometimes all it took was a simple change, like interviewing the woman separately from her husband. Other times it took a change in the medical treatment protocol such as no longer prescribing tranquilizers for anxiety without first checking to see that if the anxiety was part of a trauma reaction from the abuse. Proper documentation in the patient's chart is also important especially since most abusers and abused women end up in one court or another. Psychologists have worked together with physicians to provide proper intervention on a case-by-case basis and the American Medical Association's campaign, which was begun in the early 1990s to educate doctors about domestic violence, has been important in helping to make doctors better assist battered women and their partners.

VI. Legal Profession

It is rare that a battered woman does not have some interaction with a part of the legal system, even if it is brief and anonymous. As was described earlier, the entire system needed to make accommodations for better serving women once it was determined that the legal system would be the gateway to further services. The gender bias task forces that were formed in most states in the United States during the 1980s and some other countries helped judges and others in the legal system make necessary changes to treat women professionals and litigants more equitably. Even though the legal systems vary in different countries, encouraged by the United Nations' initiatives on equality for women during the past 20 years, changes in laws were adapted to better protect women and children and hold batterers accountable for their unacceptable violent behavior. It has been difficult to get the legal system in the United States to accept that battering is a violation of human rights' doctrines, as this would place the violation into federal rather than state court where criminal and civil injuries from assaults are usually heard. The new federal laws on violence against women may remedy

this difficulty although they are meeting serious challenges in the appellate courts at this time.

A. CIVIL LAW

Victims of abuse are more likely to be awarded some financial compensation if they can prove that their injuries result from the abuse. In the civil codes in both the United States and Canada, there has been a removal of the interspousal tort immunity, allowing wives to testify against husbands that have injured them. Awards that have gone as high as $1 million in punitive damages, designed to punish the batterer, have encouraged attorneys to take these cases on a contingency basis often permitting battered women with limited financial resources to obtain needed resources from an otherwise recalcitrant batterer. In European and other countries where criminal cases have provisions for restitution, it is becoming more likely that batterers are required to contribute money directly to pay for the victim's expenses. In the United States some judges assess large monetary fines against corporations found guilty in unrelated charges and donate those assets to battered women services as a social policy.

B. CRIMINAL JUSTICE SYSTEM

The criminal justice system—which includes law enforcement, prosecutors and defense lawyers, judges and their support staff—has changed the way it deals with battered women in the past 20 years. The first change that occurred was the clarification of the assault laws to criminalize domestic violence. In 1983, the President's Commission on Violence and Victims and, in 1984, the U.S. Attorney General Task Force on Family Violence put in motion the criminalization of violence in the family and against women. No longer could men claim that they were immune from criminal prosecution because of a marital exclusion. Domestic violence was defined as an assault, stalking and surveillance were defined as harassment, and penalties were issued and enforced. By 1996 most states had added both misdemeanor and felony stalking laws to help prosecute batterers who would not let the woman leave. The protocol was for law enforcement to make an arrest upon probable cause, the prosecutors were not permitted to drop charges even if the victim requested it, and judges were trained to listen to and find women's reports of abuse credible with a variety of evidence including pictures taken by law enforcement at the scene. Psychologists began to provide expert witness testimony in the court as a way to bolster the victims' credibility and give voice to their stories. It was seen as unreasonable to expect the victim to testify against her partner, especially if she knew she would have to go home with him after the court proceedings were done. This area of the law has met with success in getting these changes adopted.

1. Orders of Protection

New laws were passed that permitted women to obtain orders of protection restraining or keeping abusers from hurting them and giving them the right to live in their homes and use their jointly owned possessions. Temporary child support and maintenance also could be ordered ex-parte (without the batterer present when the judge made the order), with the batterer being given the right to a hearing after a specified time period. Notices could be published when the batterer could not be found and personally served with a summons to come to court. These changes permitted the family to function with a lower risk of the abuser harming them whether or not he agreed. But, perhaps even more important, it sent a message to the batterer that he was no longer allowed to beat his wife without consequences. Unfortunately, far too many restraining orders are not enforced, sometimes making a mockery of the system.

2. Domestic Violence Courts

As was described earlier, batterers were frequently adjudicated and sentenced to treatment program(s) based on expediency—either what was available or what they or their attorneys wanted them to do. Sometimes, the batterer began to attend a program before the case was adjudicated, often to win more favorable treatment before the court, which could make it more difficult to later prosecute if the man did not follow through on his agreement. However, the incentive to erase the record did have a positive effect on subsequent arrestees. In some places in the United States, the domestic violence court, which is a new kind of treatment court that is based on a combination of feminist and mental health jurisprudence, was developed, giving battered women greater access to legal redress and batterers better access to court-ordered treatment. Experimental programs in places such as Quincy, Massachusetts, Denver, Colorado, and Miami, Florida, demonstrated that do-

mestic violence could be reduced in the community with sensitive interventions designed specifically for battered women and batterers. It is common to have the "dual-diagnosed" batterer placed in a substance abuse treatment program in addition to a batterer's treatment program. Parallel programs for women abusers are also available in selective areas. However, it is important to note that women abusers are most likely to use violence in self-defense rather than be the ones who start the fight.

3. Battered Women and the Justice System

Some battered women have multiple problems that bring them to the attention of the criminal courts. A new type of jurisprudence that takes into account both abuse issues as well as other mental health diagnosis and sometimes substance abuse began in 1997 in Broward County, Florida. Called the mental health court it is a voluntary diversion court for those who are arrested for nonviolent misdemeanor acts and have previously been treated for a mental illness. Many have had substance abuse problems. Some also have neuropsychological problems. Almost all have been abused as children and or adults. The U.S. Congress has authorized the establishment of 100 more of these mental health courts around the country using the Ft. Lauderdale court as a model.

Doctoral-level psychology students from Nova Southeastern University screen the 10 to 20 women who are arrested daily and make recommendations to the judge. Nova Southeastern University also designed and developed an out-client treatment program for these women called the OPTIONS program. Modeled after the positive feminist trauma approach together with the newer integrated treatment for seriously mentally ill, this program appears to be more successful than previous efforts to engage these women and their families in treatment. This calls for a comprehensive psychological, neuropsychological, and neurological evaluation, a review of all prior medical and psychological treatment charts, an evaluation of proper psychopharmacological intervention that may stop the PTSD symptomology, and, finally, a treatment plan that also deals with daily living needs.

4. Battered Women Who Kill

In the late 1970s, at a speech at the University of Washington in Seattle, together with a group of other feminists, Walker urged women that battered women should kill the abuser rather than die themselves. Susan Brownmiller, a feminist historian and author of *Against Our Will: Women, Men and Rape,* has documented this meeting in her book *In Our Time: Memoir of a Revolution,* and describes the zeitgeist of that meeting when reporters in the audience made headlines of Walker's promise to provide expert witness testimony to describe the psychological processes by which a battered woman reasonably can believe that she is in imminent danger of being killed, even if the crime scene itself does not yield up such clues.

Since then Walker has testified in more than 400 cases of battered women who have killed in what they believed was self-defense using psychological theories to explain what must have been the cognitive processes and terrorizing emotions when a battered woman kills her abusive partner. These theories have now been accepted in cases where battered women fail to protect their children from being harmed or killed by the abusive partner and to explain how battered women can be coerced into doing some other criminal act by an abuser, even if she would not ever do such an act by herself. This is particularly important in cases where women carry drugs into the United States and are prosecuted under federal guidelines that often require a judge to sentence them to more prison time than the actual drug dealer. Some of the early cases are reported in the book *Terrifying Love: Why Battered Women Kill and How Society Responds.* Angela Browne also documents the issues around battered women who kill in self-defense in *Battered Women Who Kill.* Although there has been controversy about the use of testimony about the effects of battered woman syndrome and PTSD in these criminal cases, primarily because the same testimony has been used to prove battered women's unfitness to parent their children during divorce cases, in fact, many women are alive, safe, raising their children, and not in prison because of the acceptance of such testimony in courts.

C. FAMILY LAW

The one most often mentioned reason for battered women to return to their abuser is their fear that neither they nor their children will be protected from the increasing danger from the batterer. Divorce reform that took place in the 1960s and 1970s in the United States providing for no-fault divorces and joint custody of children actually has left more women destitute and unable to support themselves and their children adequately. The new "back to work" laws that attempted to push people off welfare in most states during the late 1990s discovered that many women receiving benefits who could not hold a job and support themselves were untreated battered women.

Unfortunately, the social zeitgeist to give joint parental responsibility to mothers and fathers came about simultaneous to when battered women were fighting for the power to better protect their children from abusive partners, causing a clash in the legal system between protective mother's, children's, and father's rights. Despite the fact that mothers are more often custodial parents of children in divorces, contested custody battles are more often from homes where domestic violence has occurred and fathers are awarded sole custody in over 70% of these cases, according to recent statistics. Psychologists Phyllis Chesler, Martha Deed, Leslie Drozd, Robert Geffner, and Geraldine Stahly have been providing training workshops and materials to assist attorneys and mothers in avoiding the misattributions of being an alienating parent or having some kind of mental problems when all they are doing is trying to protect their children from further exposure to abuse and violence.

Psychologists who perform custody evaluations are often untrained in identification and assessment of danger from domestic violence and the belief that the child has not been harmed if the physical abuse only occurred to the woman and not the child prevails despite empirical data of psychological harm when exposed to a home where battering has occurred. This appears to be changing with California leading the way by requiring courses in domestic violence before a custody evaluator may be appointed by the court. This is of critical importance as evaluators must be able to assess the credibility of abuse allegations using the data on psychological impact from trauma for both the woman and the children. Allegations of "parental alienation syndrome," "psychological Munchausen by proxy," and other nonexistent syndromes that are attributed to mothers are often used as counterattacks to legitimate claims of battering. While mothers as well as fathers are capable of behavior that tries to alienate the other parent from the child, in fact, that is not a syndrome and should not be used in that way.

Munchausen disorder is a rare disorder whereby someone hurts themselves physically as an unconscious attention-seeking behavior. When it occurs "by proxy," usually when one parent harms a child and then lovingly care for the child in order to get the attention and approval from medical personnel, the harm is physical, such as injecting the child with harmful materials. Psychological Munchausen by proxy has been suggested as a counter to a mother's charges of sexual abuse to her child, but there are no data to differentiate the symptoms from the impact that would occur if the child really was being sexually abused or if the mother really was being battered herself. Therefore, it is inappropriate to use a nonexistent diagnosis that cannot be empirically or clinically proven.

VII. *Changing Public Policy and Norms*

One of the most important issues for those who work with abused women is to change the public policy and norms of the community so that the social conditions that facilitate violence against women are eradicated. When women are empowered and have easy access to community resources, they are less likely to remain in domestic violence situations. They are also less likely to experience the impact from domestic violence in a severe way, especially if they are taught to recognize the early warning signs. Legislators who set public policy need to be aware of the types of changes needed in the laws to better protect women and children from abuse. In the early 1980s, the U.S. Department of Justice formally criminalized violence in the family giving the police and the courts additional ways to stop perpetrators. It remains to be seen how effective this policy has been in protecting battered women and children and what its costs have been both in dollars and families.

Feminist psychologists have provided testimony to the U.S. Congress and Canadian government and have developed materials to assist others in testifying before local legislative bodies. The APA Task Force on Violence against Women has reviewed research and summarized it in a book, *No Safe Haven*. Those who set policies in various institutions and government agencies around the world need the data that feminist psychology can provide to make access easier for women and children (and some men) who have been battered. Delaware Senator Joseph Biden

in 1993 introduced feminist psychological analysis prepared by the APA Task Force on Violence against Women during the U.S. Congressional legislation on the Violence Against Women Act, with favorable results. The United Nations conferences on women during the past 20 years have collected data on violence against women from member nations and disseminated the statistics together with psychological data. There has been encouragement for countries around the world to take steps to deal with the serious impact domestic violence has on women's health and mental health. Most important, the social norms have dramatically shifted during the past 30 years—no longer is there social approval to "beat your wife with a stick no wider than your thumb," an admonition that was actually in legal citations up until recently. The psychological impact from partner abuse has been empirically and clinically documented, and society appears no longer willing to pay the high costs for it to continue.

SUGGESTED READING

Barnett, O. W., and LaViolette, A. (1993). *It Could Happen to Anyone: Why Do Battered Women Stay?* Sage, Newbury Park, CA.
Hansen, M., and Harway, M. (eds.) (1993). *Battering and Family Therapy: A Feminist Perspective*. Sage, Newbury Park, CA.
Holden, G. W., Geffner, R., and Jouriles, E. N. (eds.). (1998). *Children Exposed to Marital Violence: Theory, Research, and Applied Issues*. American Psychological Association, Washington, DC.
Jacobson, N. S., and Gottman, J. M. (1998). *When Men Batter Women: New Insights into Ending Abusive Relationships*. Simon & Schuster, New York.
Koss, M. P., Goodman, L. A., Browne, A., Fitzgerald, L. F., Keita, G. P., and Russo, N. F. (1994). *No Safe Haven: Male Violence against Women at Home, at Work, and in the Community*. American Psychological Association, Washington, DC.
Martin, D. (1976). *Battered Wives*. Glide Publications, San Francisco.
Schechter, S. (1982). *Women and Male Violence: The Visions and Struggles of the Battered Women's Movement*. South End Press, Boston.
Walker, L. E. A. (1979). *The Battered Woman*. Harper & Row: New York.
Walker, L. E. A. (1994). *Abused Women and Survivor Therapy: A Practical Guide for the Psychotherapist*. American Psychological Association: Washington, DC.
Walker, L. E. A. (1999). Domestic violence around the world. *American Psychologist* 54, 21–29.
Walker, L. E. A. (2000). *The Battered Woman Syndrome*, 2nd ed. Springer, New York.

Beauty Politics and Patriarchy
The Impact on Women's Lives

Cheryl Brown Travis
University of Tennessee

Kayce L. Meginnis-Payne
Peace College

Glossary

Beauty culture Context of behaviors and beliefs that supports the pursuit of beauty among girls and women and is used as a mechanism for socializing them into the feminine role.

De-selfing Process by which the preferences and needs of others become defining features of the self. Usually occurs when people attempt to gain approval, acceptance, and recognition from those who have more power, influence, and status.

Evolutionary perspective Assumes a genetic basis for human behavior by focusing on the primacy of biological influences, heterosexual mate selection, and the natural selection of adaptive characteristics.

Familiarity effect Tendency of people to endorse and seek out that which is familiar.

Halo effect The phenomenon in which positive evaluations in one area are indiscriminately generalized to a wide range of other judgments.

Matching hypothesis Suggests that people develop relationships with those of similar levels of attractiveness.

Neoteny Physical characteristics of infants and young children that include a proportionally larger head, round face, large eyes, and a short nose and chin.

Objectification theory Proposes that when girls and women internalize an observer's perspective of their physical appearance, they relate to themselves as "objects" in need of habitual self-monitoring and manipulation.

Patriarchy A sociopolitical system characterized by male privilege and power.

Symmetry effect The tendency to prefer faces with a high degree of symmetry between the right and left sides.

Social construction A philosophy of knowledge that suggests meaning varies over time and is shaped by social, economic, and political factors.

ATTRACTIVENESS is traditionally defined as "having the power to attract" or "arousing interest and pleasure." Inherent in this concept is the notion of relationship: in order to be considered attractive, one must have the ability to ignite a positive reaction *in another*. In North American culture, attractiveness is considered an essential quality for women. Indeed, the very notion of femininity is to be pleasing and aesthetically appealing to others. Thus, the interactive nature of attractiveness that determines how one is perceived, evaluated, and treated is especially pertinent to women. A number of cultural beauty myths help to secure the primacy of beauty and attractiveness in women's lives. However, beauty is not simply an "individual" quality. Standards of attractiveness vary not only by gender, but also by social, economic, and political trends of a given period. Despite its malleable nature, messages about beauty are ubiquitous. It is literally impossible to escape culture messages that reinforce the idea that beauty is a central feature of women's identity and worth. In addition, attractiveness seems to influence a wide range of evaluative judgments, including, for instance, applications of law and justice where jury decisions may be influenced by the attractiveness of plaintiffs and defendants. Ultimately, the consequences of this preoccupation with appearance establish a psychological oppression of women that is played out in intimate relationships, self-identity, and objectification.

I. *Theory and Myth*

A. BEAUTY MYTHS

Beauty myths give meaning to women's beauty as they serve to uphold the importance of attractiveness in women's lives. These myths reveal the complexity of messages, many of which are contradictory, that women receive about beauty. One such myth is that beauty is an inherited aspect of one's biology and, therefore, certain women "inherently" occupy a privileged position from which others are excluded. In accord with this myth, it is imperative that the various forms of illusion and artifice surrounding beauty be undetectable and appear completely "natural." A contradictory myth is that one must continuously strive and labor to be beautiful. This countermyth is captured in the workout exhortation that "beauty knows no pain."

Another myth is that beauty is something that "comes from within," namely that beauty is an indication of goodness and virtue. A contradictory myth is that beauty is a powerful and destructive evil force that lures men to their doom. The most com-

mon myth about beauty is that there can be only a single most perfect, most beautiful woman—"the fairest of the fair." Implicit in this myth is that each woman should strive to become the chosen one; and if she does not achieve this, she is considered in some way inherently deficient.

In addition to promoting mixed messages about the role of beauty in women's lives, beauty myths foster competition, divisiveness, and distrust among women. These myths undermine the collaborative, supportive relationships women create with one another. All beauty myths promote the idea that beauty is the most vital aspect of a woman's being. Ultimately, this conflation of beauty and being fosters the social control of women.

B. FEMINIST PERSPECTIVES

Feminist perspectives of beauty not only evaluate the impact of beauty myths, but also focus on the social and political influences on the expectations of physical attractiveness for women. Feminist perspectives contend that beauty is rarely a benign expression of individual aesthetic preference, but is integrated within a larger system of meaning. These systems reflect societal values, beliefs about gender roles, and, most important, power (i.e., who has it, how it operates, and how to get it). Standards of beauty are *socially constructed*; they evolve and change over time in response to social, economic, and political factors. One example of the social construction of beauty comes from anthropological and sociological research that suggests that the preference for a certain kind of body shape for women is not random, but is linked to economic factors. When women have access to economic independence, a thin standard is preferred. When women are denied access to economic power, marriage is favored and the standard becomes more curvaceous. Thus, it appears that when women are less likely to be controlled by traditional institutions such as marriage, another form of social control is introduced, in this case the expectation of extreme thinness. [*See* SOCIAL CONSTRUCTIONIST THEORY.]

According to this framework, Euro-American standards of attractiveness reflect aspects of the larger culture. One such aspect is *patriarchy,* the sociopolitical system characterized by systemic male privilege and power. Patriarchal societies expect women to achieve a certain standard of aesthetics even when it becomes physically, emotionally, and financially costly.

A patriarchal emphasis on beauty exerts control of women on a number of levels. To the extent that women see attractiveness as a normal and desirable means to identity and happiness, they are less likely to pursue more authentic routes to empowerment, such as education, advancement in employment, and financial independence. Additionally, to the extent that women's value is linked to observable markers and signs that are readily available for public monitoring, comment, and sanction, they can be more easily controlled. For example, when women are criticized for "not taking care of themselves" or when they are condemned for failing to participate in common beauty rituals, they are, on some level, being punished for failing to assume a submissive stance in relation to men and the patriarchal culture at large.

C. EVOLUTIONARY PERSPECTIVES

In contrast to feminist perspectives that emphasize the role of social and political influences, evolutionary perspectives suggest that attractiveness standards for women are based primarily on biological factors related to heterosexual mate selection and reproductive fitness. According to these perspectives, males are genetically inclined to mate with a variety of females and use females' physical attractiveness to judge their health and fertility. Although females are also thought to evaluate men by their appearance, this evolutionary model suggests that females are motivated to mate with a single male partner in hopes that he will commit himself to supporting her offspring. As a consequence, females are thought to use cues other than attractiveness to assess males' desirability.

Some researchers have attempted to establish an evolutionary basis for a specific beauty ideal. Studies based on this idea have attempted to document a universal preference for a particular female body shape characterized by slender, relatively narrow hips and normal body weight (i.e., what we might call a mesomorphic, athletic shape). This preferred body shape is characterized by a waist-to-hip ratio of approximately 0.7 to 0.8. (For women with a hip measurement of 36, the supposedly most preferred waist measurement would be 25 to 29 inches.) In these studies, silhouettes of female figures with a waist-to-hip ratio of 0.8 have been judged to be more attractive and more desirable for long-term relationships than silhouettes with other body shapes. The hypothesized evolutionary link proposes that women with the preferred body shape are more healthy and also more fertile than women of other body shapes and that natural selection has favored men who hold such a preference.

D. DECONSTRUCTING EVOLUTIONARY PERSPECTIVES

Evolutionary perspectives sound pretty scientific and precise. With the use of quantitative analysis and numeric measurements, the idea that women's beauty is part of a genetic predisposition for advancement of the species may seem compelling. However, the proponents of this theory have never been able to provide the biological evidence to substantiate an evolutionary basis for the preferred shape. Although it is true that emaciated women with low body fat will probably not ovulate and that very obese women often have trouble conceiving, the vast majority of women fall in a variable midrange of sizes and shapes that do not seriously impair or enhance their fertility. Despite the conclusions presented by evolutionary perspectives, there is little evidence to suggest that individuals with a waist-to-hip ratio of 0.8 are significantly more fertile than individuals with smaller or larger ratios. Research participants who are asked to judge the attractiveness of certain silhouettes are then also asked to "judge" or "evaluate" or "estimate" what they "think" might be the more healthy body shape. No actual biological reproductive data have ever been supplied in any of the studies. Thus, the supposed biological basis for the male preference, namely increased fertility among the slender-hipped "normal weight" female with a waist-to-hip ratio of 0.7 to 0.8, has not been documented.

With few exceptions, virtually all the research on this idea of an evolutionary basis for a preferred waist-to-hip ratio (WHR) has been conducted on samples of North American college students. What these studies demonstrate is that young college students of the 1990s report liking the body shape that is currently idealized in Western culture. They additionally give favorable evaluations on a number of other dimensions in accord with this beauty bias. Few cross-cultural studies of this preference for a specific WHR can be found, but in any case the methodology as well as the biological basis for this proposition contain fundamental flaws.

Waist-to-hip ratio was first used in medical research, usually on men, to indirectly infer percentage and distribution of body fat. This offered a relatively simple operation in the data-collection phase of medical studies because it was easier to take waist and hip measurements than to make direct measures of body fat (e.g., caliper measurements of skinfold or submersion in water).

Medical research on men, and later on women as well, found that individuals with a high percentage of body fat (reflected in a high waist-to-hip ratio) were more likely to have high levels of low-density cholesterol associated with heart disease. A high percentage of body fat (reflected in a high waist-to-hip ratio) was also associated with adult-onset diabetes. This body shape and these health outcomes also correlate with older age, lower education, and lower social class. Thus, the waist-to-hip ratio has been a shorthand marker for body fat and the chronic diseases associated with a high percentage of body fat. Popular accounts of this medical research discuss the cardiovascular risks associated with body shapes similar to an apple (a shape common for overweight men that is less politely described as a "beer belly").

There are some additional problems with the supposed evolutionary basis for a preferred female body shape. Diseases such as heart disease that are supposedly associated with the apple shape of high body fat would usually have reached clinical significance only *after* an individual had reproduced. Among populations of early humans and the time period during which such body shape preferences ostensibly would have evolved, most individuals would have been dead before these diseases could have been manifested. Furthermore, an ability to store fat during these early times could well have been a positive marker for health, due to probable periods of scarcity and famine. In the evolutionary time period when a preference for body type is presumed to have emerged, substantial body fat would likely have made a positive difference in survival. Additionally, the evolution of a relatively larger brain in human infants required a *wider* pelvic structure, not a more narrow one.

If there were an evolved genetic basis for such a preference one would expect the preference to be consistent over time. However, we know that the idealized body shape of women has varied dramatically in other eras and cultures. This knowledge leads one to conclude that context has a greater impact on preferences than does biology. For example, in the mid-1800s a handspan waist was idealized as tiny enough for a man's hand to span. This image was captured in the corseting scene of Scarlet O'Hara in the movie *Gone with the Wind*. In addition to corsets, during the late 1800s and early 1900s women wore bustles to present even greater contrast between waist and hips. The popular Barbie doll actually has a waist-to-hip ratio of 0.6 and thus represents a figure that is somewhat more curvaceous than that preferred in these opinion studies. A retrospective look at changing ideals in body size and shape for American women alone can identify a number of Hollywood bombshells that would be considered plump by today's standards (e.g. Marilyn Monroe, Kim Novak, Jane Russell, and Mae West). Further, these women represent an idealized hourglass figure and not the slender, narrow-hipped athletic idea of the 1990s. The ideal shape has been different in other time periods as well. Renaissance ideals of a preferred female shape and size were quite different from those of college students in the 1990s. Major artists of the period, such as Ruben and Michelangelo, depicted women that would be judged stout by today's standards. Anthropological artifacts from still other time periods for societies in precolonized Hawaii, Africa, and South America suggest that heavy female figures may well have been revered as tokens of fertility. [*See* GENDER DEVELOPMENT: EVOLUTIONARY PERSPECTIVES.]

II. Media Blitz

One might dismiss the hubbub about beauty as a minor and trivial phenomenon, of concern only to self-absorbed and narcissistic women. However, appearance and display have become major considerations in North American culture. It is impossible to escape or remain aloof, and everyone is affected in some manner. Messages about the relevance and importance of being attractive (rather than earnest) abound.

Each year, for instance, *People* magazine compiles a list of the 50 most beautiful people in the world. The celebrities making the list are exemplars of current trends in attractiveness. The beauties of 2000 included men such as Ben Affleck, George Clooney, Tom Cruise, Ricky Martin, and Denzel Washington, and women such as Neve Campbell, Heather Graham, Faith Hill, Julia Roberts, Brooke Shields, and Tina Turner. With few exceptions, these celebrities are Euro-American, and although the list has become more diverse over time, most of them are young, Caucasian, and extremely thin. Although each of these superstars has the financial resources to employ personal trainers, hair stylists, makeup artists, and chefs, the average reader makes the inevitable comparison, thinking, "Why don't I look like that?"

Consequences of the sexist media blitz on women are well established and disconcerting. Experimental studies have shown that exposure to unrealistic images through the media often results in increased weight concern among women. Additionally, advertising that portrays women with "ideal" and unrealistic body shapes has been shown to negatively affect women's perceptions of their own physical attractiveness and self-esteem. Both of these findings are even more troublesome in light of the fact that the "ideal" beauties seen within the media are becoming thinner and thinner. Thus, more and more women are finding themselves outside the bounds of what is portrayed as attractive. [*See* BODY IMAGE CONCERNS; MEDIA INFLUENCES; MEDIA STEREOTYPES; SELF-ESTEEM.]

A. COMMON MESSAGES AND DOUBLE STANDARDS

Cultural ideals, values, norms, and expectations about physical attractiveness are ubiquitous; these messages occur in magazines, television commercials, and music videos, and are even covered as noteworthy items in the news. Media images not only make current standards of attractiveness salient, but they also give meaning to physical appearance by associating it with well-being, happiness, and success. This association is especially strong for women.

In fact, it is virtually impossible for women to escape the media's reminders of just how important it is for them to be attractive. These reminders promise rewards, but also forecast social and psychological penalties for women who fail to meet minimum standards. These reminders may be explicit, by instructing and advising women on attractiveness-related issues, or they may be implicit, by conveying messages that "beautiful" people are sophisticated, successful, popular, and happy. Even in televised sitcoms, female characters who are below average in weight, and who thus more closely represent the "ideal," receive more positive comments from male characters than do heavier female characters.

Furthermore, there is a clear double standard with regard to the relevance and significance of beauty. Although mass media messages convey stereotyped role images and idealized physical attractiveness for men, men typically do not face the same degree of comment, observation, or censure if they vary from these ideals. Additionally, men are less likely to feel guilty about not meeting such standards. While attractiveness standards are made salient for men by the media, other qualities and characteristics are judged to be of equal or greater importance, such as occupational success, social eminence, or athletic competence.

The double standards portrayed in the media may both result from and contribute to double standards that exist in real life. Experimental research concludes, for instance, that people tend to rate older women as less attractive, and thus less desirable, than older men. Additionally, men consider youth to be *essential* for women's attractiveness, even when the men themselves are not young. A similar finding does not exist regarding women's evaluation of men's attractiveness; women consider men of all ages potentially attractive.

Multiple types of media promote double standards of attractiveness for men and women. Within film and television, for instance, younger actors typically play female objects of desire, whereas male objects of desire are played by actors of all ages. Males are thus given a far greater age range within which to be attractive, sensual, and sexually appealing. For women to be perceived as similarly sexy, they must meet much more narrow and limited expectations.

These messages to women are no more neatly summarized then in a cover story of *People* magazine (2000): "Staying sexy: Trade secrets for looking great and taking charge from some of Hollywood's leading ladies." The article conveys how surprising, unique, and rare it is for "older" women to be perceived as attractive and to be able to elicit sexual attention and approval from the culture at large. The article reviewed how Sarah Jessica Parker, 35, Michelle Pfeiffer, 42, Madonna, 41, Shakira Caine, 53, Jane Fonda, 62, Goldie Hawn, 54, Vanessa Williams, 37, Rene Russo, 45, and Angela Bassett, 41, are able to maintain their appeal through daily workouts, diets, and cosmetic surgery. It is notable that two of these women are still in their 30s. How young must women be to begin preparing to face the consequences of aging? The article was written solely about women, sending the message that it is women, not men, who must "work" to stay attractive and sexy.

B. ADVERTISING

Advertising is one of the most powerful forms of media that influences conceptualizations of attractiveness. Images of the "ideal beauty" are routinely paired with products designed to take advantage of the fact that most women do not meet current beauty standards. "Successful" advertising typically exhorts women to worry about their appearance and to feel anxious about their failures to emulate ideal standards. Advertising suggests that women should be purposeful in their pursuit of attractiveness. The message is that beauty is something that takes time, money, effort, and vigilance.

In addition to promoting the ideal, much of advertising conveys the need for women to camouflage unacceptable physical features. Women are told to suppress underarm odor, to rely on "intimate cleansers" to purify their genitals, and to eliminate "unsightly" body and facial hair. Despite the fact that human bodies are designed to store excess fat, advertising urges women to work to improve their appearance with the use of anticellulite creams and lotions (which, incidentally, do nothing to reduce cellulite and are quite expensive). In general, advertising tells women that signs of aging are unacceptable, asking, "Is your skin aging faster than you are?" New products are constantly created to perpetuate this message. For instance, antiwrinkle creams that once were the standard have now been supplemented by products to handle "embarrassing" age spots, which remove upper layers of the skin by using chemicals or abrasives.

In addition to admonitions about what must be disguised or hidden, there are a plethora of advertisements that promise magical ways to sculpt the body size and shape. An advertisement for breast enhancement states, "Put an end to your loneliness and become the woman with the full breasts. You can feel great and get the attention you deserve!" Despite class action lawsuits involving breast implants, the McGhan medical group (an INAMED company) regularly advertises their anatomical breast implants designed to better emulate a "natural" breast shape and even offers women a $50 gift certificate toward the procedure.

Advertising often presents unattainable images of physical attractiveness as normative. These images are crafted not only by using supermodels of uncommon proportions to represent "normal women," but also by using computer-enhancement techniques to "perfect" the images. Supermodel and spokesperson Tyra Banks once commented on her *Sports Illustrated* swimsuit cover that even *she* wished she looked as good as she did in the photograph.

Messages about the importance of beauty become even more powerful when paired with generally sexist messages that make alternative pathways for happiness and self-actualization seem improbable or less than satisfying. The subjective value of pursuing beauty is balanced against the probability of achieving equivalent happiness through other means. Thus, to understand the power of beauty messages in advertising it is important also to understand the general context of other messages given to women about who they are and about alternatives they might find rewarding.

Advertising does more than promote happiness associated with having the right appearance. Alternative pursuits and identities are presented as more problematic, less satisfying, and in any case as having a lower likelihood of being accomplished. The power of this message is conveyed in part by a constellation of messages that demean and diminish women in general. One result of such demeaning and devaluing is that girls and women come to have lower expectations about the likelihood and the value of success in endeavors outside that of having a pleasing appearance. These messages make personal appearance all the more significant, because it is the one area where women are depicted as capable of achieving marvelous results that will consistently bring happiness and pleasure. How does this happen?

The relative devaluing and limiting of alternative visions of women occurs in a number of subtle ways. Women tend to be depicted in highly stereotypical ways that restrict alternative views. For instance, women are often shown as being small in size relative to men, as having subordinate occupational roles, as assuming subordinate postures or positions relative to men, and as being excluded from the main action. In general, these messages convey the idea that women seldom venture outside the home, hence their place is in the home. When women do appear in advertisements outside the home they typically are portrayed in relatively low-status positions, hence the message is that women do unimportant things. All of these messages sustain an emphasis on traditional roles for women and on the importance of presenting oneself as pleasing and attractive to men. Research suggests that in the 1990s, sexism in magazine advertisements has persisted and, in some respects, increased.

Who benefits from such arrangements? Surely not the general populations of girls and women who come to feel insecure and inadequate. The cosmetic industry has a clear vested interest. Cosmetic sales fall into the tens of millions of dollars annually. These sales figures and profit margins also affect stock value as these corporations are traded on the stock exchange.

III. *Principles of Attractiveness*

A. GENERAL AESTHETICS

Despite the fact that attractiveness standards vary across time and culture and emerge from social and political factors, some general patterns of attractiveness are commonly observed. One of the most consistent patterns is a preference for people with smooth, unblemished skin. This preference applies to both adults and children, and to men as well as women. Other general principles of aesthetics have also been established.

1. Familiarity

Research shows that women and men tend to prefer appearances that are "average" or typical. Familiarity often leads to approval, even when the familiarity is due solely to mere frequency of exposure, a principle long exploited in advertising and political campaigning. The *familiarity effect* is seen when two photographs of the same person are presented for evaluation: an original photograph and a photograph that is reformatted by computers so that the features are actually a composite average of many people. In controlled studies, people consistently rate the reformatted photographs as more attractive than the original photographs. Interestingly, the greater the number of photos used to form the computerized composite average, the more the reformatted photographs are liked. In this case, being "average" results in greater approval, probably because it is more familiar.

2. Symmetry

People tend to prefer faces that have a high degree of symmetry between the right and left sides. Evidence of this *symmetry effect* is seen in studies where computer-manipulated photographs composed of the same side of the face (i.e., the right side and the right side) are ranked as more attractive than the original photographs that show the left and right sides as they occur naturally. Not surprisingly, the faces of some of the most successful super models and actresses reveal a high degree of symmetry.

3. Neotony

Infants and young children are widely considered to have endearing features. Features of infancy and youth that are typical of neoteny include a large head-size to body-size ratio, a rounded face, plump cheeks, large eyes, pug nose, and short chin. Collectively these characteristics are termed neoteny and are thought to account for the inherent appeal of infants. Preferences for neoteny can be seen across species; for example, puppies, kittens, and most young animals are considered cuter than their adult counterparts. Researchers believe that neoteny reduces the likelihood of aggression, particularly aggression of adults against helpless young. Neoteny is also thought to elicit caretaking and nurturing behaviors.

Interestingly, adults who embody characteristics of neoteny are often considered more attractive than adults who do not embody such characteristics. Further, it has been hypothesized that women use certain makeup techniques in order to simulate neoteny, such as using mascara to create the appearance of large, wide-spaced eyes, and that this effect is designed to elicit the protective response often associated with such appearances.

B. DIVERSITY IN BEAUTY IDEALS

In the many Westernized countries, standards of attractiveness have become increasingly stringent, especially for women. Light hair, tanned skin, taut cheekbones, and thin but full lips are just some of the many characteristics that are expected if one is to be considered attractive.

There is a lot of pressure to pursue these beauty ideals because real consequences (benefits and costs) may accrue to women on the basis of how well they adhere to these arbitrary and singularly narrow demands. Some characteristics, such as youth and a classic body shape, are vital to positive evaluations of beauty for women. For instance, there has been an increased desire for, and valuing of, exceptionally thin women. Research reveals that women larger than the ideal are consistently rated lower on attractiveness, intelligence, job success, relationship success, happiness, and popularity than average-sized or thin women.

Youth is also revered in Western culture. Research demonstrates that as the age of the face increases, perceived attractiveness declines. People who are considered most attractive are those who are young, or those who have been able to maintain the *appearance* of youth. Such an appearance is rarely achieved without the assistance of hair dyes, tanning lotions, teeth whiteners, hair growth creams, and cosmetic surgery. These "youth elixirs," often targeted toward aging "baby boomers," are increasingly marketed toward baby boomers' children. Advertising suggests that it is never too early to start worrying about aging. In fact, some advertisements suggest that 25 is the age at which women need to begin worrying about and concealing the signs of aging.

Most of these attractiveness standards are based on Euro-American norms. Such narrowly defined notions of attractiveness often exclude people of color, especially women of color, from being perceived as attractive. As a result, women of color are not typically afforded the benefits that "attractiveness" may provide. Additionally there are a plethora of products (e.g., to lighten skin and straighten hair) marketed to make the features of women of color conform to Western standards.

Some research has found distinct differences in attractiveness preferences among various ethnic groups. For example, several studies found that African American men tend to prefer larger body types for African American women than Caucasian men prefer for Caucasian women. Additionally, African American women are less likely to pathologize large African American women than Caucasian women are to pathologize large Caucasian women. It has been speculated that African American women have purposely turned away from mainstream ideals about body size as a means of resistance to racial oppression.

It is important to note that the research methodology used to assess the supposed flexibility afforded to African American women is questionable on philosophic grounds. As with much of the research on attractiveness, it is often *men* who are asked about their preferences, not the women. Thus, although the preferred shapes may vary slightly across groups, the research emphasis, regardless of race and ethnicity, remains on how pleasing or acceptable women are to men.

Although the standards of thinness and youth may seem generic and universal, they, like all beauty standards, are shaped by culture. Some non-Western cultures, for instance, value prominent buttocks, elongated necks, lips that are extended with plates, stretched earlobes, and comprehensive body tattoos. Features that are minimized or strenuously disguised in one culture may be a source of erotic appeal in others. For example, among the Efe peoples of West Africa, women are considered sexy if they have hair on their chests.

C. BEAUTY BIAS: WHAT'S BEAUTIFUL IS GOOD

There is a strong *halo effect* for physical attractiveness such that high ratings in physical attractiveness are generalized to a wide range of other judgments and evaluations. Compared to ordinary people, "beautiful people" are perceived as having more desirable qualities. Attractive people are generally viewed as more interesting, sociable, sexual, competent, successful, intelligent, and well adjusted than unattractive people. Compared to less attractive people, attractive people are not only perceived more positively, they also tend to be treated more positively by others. People are more likely to engage with and cooperate with others they perceive as attractive.

One explanation for these findings may be that attractive people develop better social skills and have a more positive demeanor in encounters with others precisely because of the favorable treatment they have received in the past. Their social skills and positive demeanor may then help to reinforce continued positive regard from others. Indeed, research has shown that attractive children and adults actually exhibit more positive behaviors and traits than unattractive children and adults. Thus, attractiveness may be a critical element in shaping expectations and experiences, and ultimately, the quality of relationships.

1. Hiring Practices and Employment

Attractiveness is often seen as an asset in hiring practices and employment evaluations. Studies involving a range of occupational groups have found that, compared to less attractive people, attractive people tend to rise more easily to the top and are at the higher end of the pay scale. A number of studies have found small associations between attractiveness and later occupational success. [See WORKING ENVIRONMENTS.]

2. Persuasion and Marketing

Within marketing and advertising, physically attractive people are typically seen as more credible and trustworthy and are assumed to have more expertise than unattractive people. In general, audiences find attractive communicators more likeable than unattractive communicators. In person-to-person encounters, attractive individuals are often more persuasive than unattractive people. For instance, attractive people are more successful in getting people to sign petitions than are ordinary-looking people.

3. Jurisprudence

Even within contexts that are designed to be objective, attractiveness appears to be influential. In trial situations, attractive defendants are less likely to be judged guilty of a crime than are unattractive defendants. Additionally, when attractive defendants are convicted, they are likely to receive lighter sentences or penalties than less attractive defendants. Judges tend to set lower bail and lower fines for attractive defendants. Even when their actions are in direct violation of norms or laws, attractive people are typically perceived as less offensive than is the case of ordinary looking people. These patterns seem to be true for both criminal and civil proceedings. For example, sexual harassment is likely to be seen as less flagrant when perpetrators are themselves relatively attractive.

4. The Lives of Children

The halo effect favoring attractive people is also seen among children. For instance, teachers who receive identical academic information about a child, but with photos depicting children or greater or lesser attractiveness, assume that the attractive children will do better academically. Additionally, compared to other mothers, mothers of especially attractive infants have been found to be more attentive, affectionate, playful, and responsive.

IV. Patriarchal Connections

Feminist principles suggest that issues of beauty and attractiveness be considered in terms of the extent to which the equality of women and men is advanced or impeded. Feminists also attend to the costs imposed on the lived experience of women and the ways in which individual experience and identity may be authenticated or silenced. When considering these issues, systems and traditions that seem benignly impersonal can be recognized as limiting and costly for both women and men and as especially dangerous for women.

A. ROMANTIC RELATIONSHIPS

Feminists point out that patriarchy influences not only employment and wage discrimination, but ad-

ditionally shapes close personal relationships. The fact that women have limited alternatives and fewer resources with which to pursue them makes the socially prescribed roles of wife and mother relatively more appealing and emotionally and psychologically important. Research has indicated that much of the interpersonal "intuition" and "sensitivity" of women can be explained by their generally lower status and limited alternatives. Additionally, women receive approval for and encouragement in these traditional roles. They come to expect that the most significant aspects of their identities will be realized in close romantic relationships. Indeed the monitoring and management of close personal relationships are deemed by many women to be important forms of achievement and skill.

The *matching hypothesis* suggests that people develop relationships, romantic and otherwise, with people of similar levels of attractiveness. People not only prefer associating with those considered attractive, but they actually base many relationship decisions on physical attractiveness. For instance, after blind dates, whether or not a second date is sought seems to depend on how physically attractive each person finds the other.

While social conventions require that men at least appear to take the first step in initiating these relationships, establishing a permanent romantic relationship is of singular importance for a majority of women. Patriarchal guidelines impose a handicap that they initially must appear to assume a passive stance in these matters. Drawing attention by presenting and packaging the self is one of the avenues allowed women in their pursuit of fulfillment through relationship with a man. It is in this patriarchal context that beauty and beauty myths become even more significant in women's lives.

Unfortunately, being considered unattractive appears to impact women more than men. If women are not perceived as attractive, their pool of available partners is significantly smaller than the pool for women who are perceived as attractive. Men, on the other hand, regardless of their physical attractiveness, are more able to generate a positive sense of self through a variety of avenues and have available to them a larger pool of potential partners.

Studies of campus dating situations generally find that men rate attractiveness as more important than do women. When asked to indicate the most desirable feature of a potential dating partner, college-aged males place highest significance on appearance. Personal advertisements ("Personals") in newspapers also reveal this effect in that ads from men are more likely than the ads from women to specify a certain kind of appearance that is desired. Women are apparently aware of these contingencies and are more likely to provide information about their appearance in their ads for men to evaluate.

When men do provide information on their own appearance in personal ads, it is most likely to involve their height. Studies show that men assume women are especially attentive to height. Content analyses of personal ads indicate that in general women want a male partner to be about four inches taller than themselves, while most men want a female who is of small or medium stature. There is some basis for men's assumption that their height is especially relevant to women, because men who describe themselves as tall in their advertisements receive more responses than other men receive.

One reason men seem to place more emphasis on women's attractiveness is that, compared to women, men are more likely to be evaluated on the basis of their association with an attractive partner. Unattractive men with attractive women partners are more likely to be admired by other men and to be rated positively on dimensions such as character, likability, income, occupational status, and success. Thus, female beauty may be an asset, not only of personal significance for individual women, but it also may be of additional social significance for men. Association with an attractive partner often confers higher status on her male partner. Therefore men's desire for attractive female partners may be based on the fact that it is a way to enhance their own status and prestige among other men. Such vested interests for men belie the air of superiority with which some men belittle women's efforts to be attractive, whereas men support the system by encouraging, paying special attention, commenting, and giving approval to women who appear to meet idealized standards.

Although there is evidence across cultures that compared to women, men have a stronger preference for attractive partners, this finding may be more prevalent in cultures where wives are seen as "belonging" to their husbands. Indeed, the emphasis on female beauty is strongest in societies where women have lower status and less economic autonomy. Research has shown that women perceived to be physically attractive are more likely to marry and to marry socially upward. These marriages are nevertheless understood to lack emotional connection and to be relatively superficial. In fact in this culture, the arrangement is deemed somewhat laughable and jokes are regularly made about "trophy wives."

B. INTERNALIZATION, SEXUALITY, AND IDENTITY

Women's bodies have become an arena where cultural meanings and values are projected and played out. In many cases, these cultural frameworks are ultimately internalized by women themselves. This phenomenon enables the culture to regulate and control individual women and women as a group. A critical feature of this internalization process is that it is often unconscious and therefore escapes reflection, analysis, and choice. Unlike other forms of oppression that require external policing, attractiveness standards impose control with more subtlety. Internalization of social messages leads girls and women to accept all manner of self-manipulations as normal, appropriate, and even desirable. There is an expectation that adherence to these arrangements leads not only to practical benefits but also to inner peace and a sense of satisfaction and completeness. This sort of internalization is an effective form of control and is an integral aspect of modern patriarchy.

For women, physical attractiveness is connected to the most profound aspects of self-identity. For instance, women's attractiveness is strongly related to their overall feelings of self-esteem. With regard to males, although adolescent boys may be distressed by the slow development of masculinity or may worry about their general grooming and appearance, the preoccupation is typically limited to adolescence. Adult men are much less likely than adult women to be tormented by imperfections in their body shape or size. Women do not come to this understanding alone. Attaining standards of beauty is considered by society in general to be a pivotal feature of "being feminine." In fact, research documents a correlation between judgments of women's attractiveness and their femininity.

Emulating cultural standards of beauty is often a way for women to display gender and establish a sense of identity and self. This display often requires an ongoing participation in the beauty culture where clothes shopping, experimenting with cosmetics, tanning, sharing diet tips, and participating in exercise focused on weight-loss are considered "recreational activities."

Women who fail or refuse to participate in these beauty rituals are often perceived by others as mannish, sexually neutered, or lesbian. Indeed, cultural views on attractiveness link beauty with sexuality and sexual identity. Since women are members of their own culture, it is understandable that many women have come to believe in the beauty-sexuality connection for themselves. Research shows, for instance, that women's sense of their own attractiveness is related to their perceptions of being sexual. The more a woman views herself as attractive, the greater her sexual self-esteem. Thus, external presentation, appearance, and evaluation by others are shaping an aspect of identity that ideally emanates from a private, interpersonal, and sensual realm.

When standards of beauty are internalized as aspects of identity, a number of psychological consequences are likely to follow. By emulating beauty ideals, girls and women often hope to win the approval and acceptance of others. As a result, opinion and social judgment become a major basis for defining women's sense of identity and worth. There is an increased internal motivation to attract the attention and affirmation of others and the preferences and needs of others become defining features of the self. With de-selfing, the "true" self becomes less worthy and more silent in deference to the needs and intimations of others. [*See* SEXUALITY AND SEXUAL DESIRE; SOCIAL IDENTITY.]

C. CONSEQUENCES OF OBJECTIFICATION

Objectification theory proposes that when girls and women internalize an observer's perspective of their physical appearance, they relate to themselves as "objects" in need of habitual self-monitoring and manipulation. Relating to oneself in this way not only increases anxiety and shame, but also increases the likelihood of eating disorders, sexual dysfunction, and depression.

A simplistic solution is to follow a regimen that produces the "right" body size and shape. However, striving for perfection is likely to produce feelings of failure and inadequacy, rather than a sense of satisfaction or self-acceptance. Meeting standards of attractiveness can produce other negative effects as well. It may actually lower self-esteem and self-assurance. For example, attractive women may attribute their academic success or positive evaluations at work to their appearance, discounting the merits of their actual achievements. Attractive girls and women may doubt the objective, merit basis for positive evaluations of their achievements and assume instead that ratings are actually based on their appearance. Although culture to some extent rewards the traditional pursuit of beauty, the emotional and physical risks to the women's sense of self are clear.

For women especially, there are a variety of negative associations to being "too attractive." For instance, women who are viewed as physically attractive are actually considered less likely to possess achievement-related traits than are physically attractive men. Additionally, women with curvaceous figures, as compared to underweight, normal, and overweight women, are more likely to be judged as incompetent. Women's attractiveness is also associated with weight preoccupation, regardless of their actual body size and general level of perfectionism. Thus, for women, being physically attractive may be a risk factor for disordered eating. Indeed, studies have revealed a general increase over the past 50 years in the numbers of women who have poor body image and who suffer from eating disorders. In addition, cosmetic surgery is increasingly performed on adolescents and patients under 50. [*See* EATING DISORDERS AND DISORDERED EATING.]

V. Conclusions

Fairy tales regularly link female beauty to romance, marriage, and happiness. In fairy tails, where there is often little social or economic alternative to marriage, beauty might be understood as a tool for women's self-advancement. One would expect, however, that in the real world an emphasis on beauty would be minimized as gender roles have become more flexible over time and as women have acquired more economic opportunity and power. Unfortunately, women continue to be evaluated by unrealistic and arbitrary standards of beauty that are emotionally, physically, and financially costly.

Thus, "makeovers" have much less to do with changing one's hair color or learning a new technique to apply lipstick, and have more to do with an attempt to allay anxiety by obtaining approval from others. However, the privileges and power to influence others that come from meeting beauty standards are limited, and only compensate in part for the social status and opportunities that otherwise are denied to women in patriarchal societies.

Feminist perspectives on attractiveness standards and stereotypes contend that beauty is not an independent, external, and objective quality, but is entangled with power, gender, and sexuality. Because the self resides in the body, feminist efforts to change women's roles in society and to transform gender stereotypes must address the degree to which beauty-related oppressions limit and control women. The gains to be had from challenging these oppressions include the possibility of greater freedom from the tyranny of beauty myths and patriarchy itself. There is additionally the possibility of greater authenticity and the confidence for women to become intentional agents in other realms of life as well. Benefits might include increasing equality between women and men, greater tolerance, more personal resilience, and a greater energy to challenge oppression and to pursue social change.

SUGGESTED READING

Callaghan, K. A. (ed.) (1994). *Ideals of Feminine Beauty*. Greenwood Press, Westport, CT.

Chaps, W. (1986). *Beauty Secrets*. South End Press, Boston.

Freedman, R. (1986). *Beauty Bound*. Lexington Books of D.C. Heath, Lexington, MA.

Jaggar, A. M., and Bordo, S. R. (eds.) (1992). *Gender, Body, Knowledge: Feminist Reconstructions of Being and Knowing*. Rutgers University Press, New Brunswick, NJ.

Lakoff, R. T., and Scherr, R. L. (1984). *Face Value: The Politics of Beauty*. Routledge and Kegan Paul, Boston.

Orbach, S. (1987). *Fat is a Feminist Issue*. Berkley Publishing Group, New York.

Travis, C. B., Meginnis-Payne, K. L., and Bardari, K. (2000). Beauty, sexuality, and identity: The social control of women. In *Sexuality, Society, and Feminism* (C. B. Travis and J. W. White, eds.), pp. 237–272. American Psychological Association, Washington, DC.

Wolf, N. (1992). *The Beauty Myth: How Images of Beauty Are Used against Women*. Doubleday, New York.

Body Image Concerns

Linda Smolak

Kenyon College

Ruth H. Striegel-Moore

Wesleyan University

Glossary

Body image Feelings and beliefs about, perceptions of, and attitudes toward the attractiveness of one's body.

BMI A ratio of body weight to height that is a commonly used indicator of fatness. It is typically calculated as weight (in kilograms) divided by height (in meters) squared.

Eating disorders The full clinical syndromes of anorexia nervosa (AN), bulimia nervosa (BN), and binge eating disorder (BED) as defined in the Diagnostic and Statistical Manual, Fourth Edition (*DSM-IV*; American Psychiatric Association, 1994).

Eating problems Individual symptoms of disordered eating attitudes and behaviors including calorie restrictive dieting, body dissatisfaction, binge eating, and use of severe weight loss techniques.

THE TERM "BODY IMAGE" is bandied around in the popular press, on talk shows, and over lunchroom tables. These discussions are often predicated on the assumption that body image is more problematic among girls and women than among boys and men. They are further marked by the belief that these body image problems are correlated with, and are perhaps casually related to, the eating disorders that people frequently think are epidemic among adolescents girls: anorexia nervosa and bulimia nervosa. Finally, it seems common to argue that these body image problems are attributable to sociocultural factors, particularly media portrayals of ultrathin women. This article examines these widely held assumptions. In particular, we aim to examine the gendered nature of body image concerns in terms of prevalence and causation. The basis for this review is mainly studies done in the United States, often with predominantly White participants. However, studies from Great Britain, Canada, and Australia were also considered when possible. Whenever the evidence provided the opportunity to do so, we tried to highlight similarities and differences among the different ethnic groups in the United States.

I. Defining Body Image

There is little doubt that body image is a complex concept that can be described as having several different dimensions: perceptual, cognitive, affective, and attitudinal. The concept of body image concern encompasses disturbances in these perceptual, cognitive, affective, and attitudinal dimensions of body image. The perceptual component refers to accuracy in appraising the actual size and shape of one's body or body parts. So, for example, several measures use adjustable light beams or calipers to assess individuals' perceptions of the width of their bodies or body parts. This perceptual component, specifically perceptual distortion, is central to the definition of Body Dysmorphic Disorder (BDD). People suffering from BDD perceive a particular body part as being abnormal or deformed. This represents an exaggerated or imaginary defect.

Most studies of "body image," however, do not focus on this perceptual component. Rather, the emphasis tends to be on the cognitive, affective, or attitudinal components. Body image concerns related to these components include overvaluation of physical appearance and body image dissatisfaction. These components can be distinguished in theory; in reality, however, they are strongly interrelated. Indeed, many measures combine questions asking about beliefs ("I think . . .") and affect ("I like . . ."). Body image measures tapping these subjective components often assess body dissatisfaction (i.e., beliefs and feelings about one's own body relative to a personally held ideal or preferred body). By far the most commonly studied aspect of body image concern is dissatisfaction with body weight or shape. Most measures used to study weight and shape dissatisfaction emphasize concerns about being or becoming *overweight*. It is in these measures of weight and shape concerns where the largest and most consistent gender differences emerge.

II. *The Gendered Nature of Body Image*

A. WEIGHT CONCERNS

The more clearly a researcher focuses on weight and shape concerns, the more likely she or he will find significant gender differences. Beginning in elementary school, girls are more dissatisfied with their weight and shape than boys are. Body dissatisfaction increases among girls as they move into adolescence and early adulthood. The gender difference continues into adulthood. Thus, at virtually all ages, girls and women are more dissatisfied with their weight and shape than are boys and men. Furthermore, the

size of the gender difference has apparently increased during the past 30 years.

It is important to keep this caveat in mind: some of the gender differences in body dissatisfaction may be a methodological artifact. Specifically, many of the measures of body dissatisfaction that focus on weight and shape ask about concerns about being overweight but not about being underweight. The widely used Body Dissatisfaction subscale of the Eating Disorders Inventory (EDI) is an example of such a scale. At least among prepubertal boys, concerns about being too small may be as common as worries about weighing too much. Girls are more likely to choose the thinnest available option in an array of body shapes as their ideal, while boys are more likely to choose the heavier shapes. Note that boys are not generally interested in being fatter; rather they want to be more muscular and generally "bigger." These differences are consistent with the differences in the female (thin) and male (lean and muscular) beauty ideal. A few recent studies indicate that among adolescents, boys were more likely than girls to want to be more muscular. An interest in being more muscular appears to be associated with poor self-esteem and elevated levels of depression among boys but not girls. Note, however, that in this research the term "muscular" refers to larger, more prominent muscles. When the focus is on "muscle tone," a term often associated with a more slender look, women report greater dissatisfaction than do men.

B. BODY MASS INDEX (BMI)

At least two variables seem as if they might potentially mediate the gender difference in weight and shape concerns: body mass index (BMI) and ethnicity. At all BMI levels, girls and women routinely are more concerned about being too heavy, compared to boys or men. Studies further show that at higher weights, body dissatisfaction rises in males and females, yet the threshold for males to experience body dissatisfaction is at a relatively greater degree of overweight than is the case for females. Indeed, even a minority of adolescent girls who are clearly underweight want to lose weight. Among average or normal-weight girls, a majority would like to be thinner. On the other hand, boys who want to lose weight are usually actually overweight, at least compared to national norms. Hence, body weight is associated significantly with body dissatisfaction in males and females, but compared to girls or women, it takes a relatively greater degree of overweight for boys or men to be weight dissatisfied.

C. ETHNICITY

Reviewers have commonly noted that African American women appear to have higher levels of body satisfaction than do White women. Nevertheless, beginning in elementary schools, African American girls and women show more body dissatisfaction than do African American boys and men. This gender difference is also evident in adults. Studies routinely find differences *between* ethnic groups in terms of body dissatisfaction, with African Americans scoring higher on appearance evaluation and lower on weight preoccupation than either European Americans or Latina Americans. But there are typically no significant gender by ethnicity interactions, suggesting that the gender difference is comparable *within* each ethnic group. [*See* ADOLESCENT GENDER DEVELOPMENT; CROSS-CULTURAL GENDER ROLES.]

D. SUMMARY

A quick perusal of studies in which body image serves as an independent or dependent variable indicates how widely researchers hold the opinion that body dissatisfaction and weight concerns are a women's issue. Indeed, body dissatisfaction is associated so strongly with being female that many studies explicitly exclude male participants because such concerns are seen as a women's issue. A brief review demonstrates that there is a gender difference in weight concerns. This difference is evident in two ways. First, beginning in elementary school, girls are more worried about being or becoming too fat and are more dissatisfied with their weight and shape than boys are. This difference may actually increase with development, particularly, perhaps, as girls gain body fat at puberty. Furthermore, although the data are limited, this difference does not appear to be attributable to greater incidences of overweight status among girls. Nor does the gender difference seem to be the province of one ethnic group although, again, the data are limited.

Second, the data suggest that the direction or nature of dissatisfaction with weight and shape of boys and girls may differ. Boys (and men) may be more concerned about being too small than are girls and women. Methodological limitations have not permitted a full examination of this contention. However, the data do not seem to suggest that considering this concern will eliminate the gender gap in overall body dissatisfaction.

This gender gap is of great interest because research clearly indicates that body dissatisfaction, particularly in relation to weight and shape, is not a trivial characteristic. Indeed, research indicates that it is not only related to eating disorders but also to depression.

III. *Body Image Concerns and Problem Behavior*

Why are we so concerned about negative body image, particularly weight concerns? Might not body dissatisfaction serve as a motivator for weight loss? Given that obesity is widely considered to be a major public health problem in the United States, wouldn't weight dissatisfaction, at least among those who are overweight, be desirable? Research on this question is limited and ambiguous. Body dissatisfaction does seem to help some people, perhaps especially men, in their efforts to lose weight. But in other cases, body dissatisfaction alone will not lead people to lose weight or even fail to gain weight. What is more clear is that negative body image is related to potentially health endangering behaviors including calorie-restrictive dieting and other weight-loss behaviors (e.g., purging, smoking, or illegal drug use to control weight) and to various forms of psychopathology, most notably anorexia nervosa, bulimia nervosa, and depression.

A. DIETING

Body dissatisfaction is more likely to translate into dieting or other weight-control practices among girls and women than among boys and men. As early as elementary school, girls are more likely than boys to try to lose weight even when there are no gender differences in overall body esteem. Throughout adolescence and adulthood, the data indicate that women routinely try to lose weight much more frequently than men do. Some studies suggest that high school girls are two to three times more likely than boys to be engaging in weight loss attempts. Among adults, the differences may not be as pronounced, but women are still more likely than men to try to lose weight.

It is noteworthy that these weight loss attempts may be health endangering. In the short run, people who are dieting are irritable, have difficulty concentrating, are fatigued, and may suffer from headaches or stomachaches. Clearly, these symptoms have the potential to interfere with school performance among children and adolescents. There is also potential for long-term problems, including decreased bone density and growth stunting. Dieting may create special risks for some people, including adolescent girls who have diabetes and who stop taking insulin in order to lose weight. The continued use of cigarettes by middle-class White girls has also been linked to their desire to lose, or at least not gain, weight. Some adolescents report the use of more extreme weight control measures such as purging or using drugs to control appetite or induce weight loss. Although the percentage of girls purging or using diuretics may be small, the health consequences of such extreme weight loss means are potentially quite serious and may even be fatal.

The significant association between weight dissatisfaction and dieting, established in most studies based on concurrent, correlational data, commonly has been interpreted as follows. Being overweight or the fear of becoming overweight creates weight dissatisfaction which, in turn, then prompts dieting and other weight loss behaviors. Recent prospective studies have added provocative findings to this hypothesized temporal sequence. Prospective research findings are particularly important because they can clearly indicate the temporal precedence of one behavior relative to another and thus elucidate causal relationships. Prospective longitudinal data indicate that dieting is related to weight gain and obesity, at least among adolescent girls. The reason for this link is not clear although it is possibly related to weight cycling. Dieting may lower basal metabolism so that when normal (or at least higher-calorie) eating is resumed at the end of a diet, weight gain is facilitated. Some people have also argued that dieting is linked to binge eating which, in turn, may contribute to obesity in some people. Additional research is needed to provide more information about the link between dieting and obesity.

Prospective longitudinal data also indicate that dieting is related to the onset of bulimic symptoms. There are several potential explanations for this link. One possibility is that dieting may be associated with restrained eating, which, when violated, may result in binge eating. In other words, when eating is severely restrained, the mind and body eventually rebel, requiring the intake of large amounts of food. Such behavior has been observed in calorie-starved men as well as in eating-disordered women. It is also possible that even moderate calorie restrictive dieting reduces levels of 5-HT (serotonin) in women's brains, though not, apparently, in men's. Reduced serotonin levels seem to be associated with carbohydrate crav-

ing and overeating, perhaps even binge eating. Interestingly, low serotonin levels are also evident in depressed mood and in clinical depression. Depression is also marked by a substantial gender difference and is frequently comorbid with eating disorders.

Thus, body dissatisfaction may lead to dieting. Dieting, in turn, may be related to obesity, eating disorders, and perhaps even depression. In addition to these indirect links, there is also evidence suggesting that body dissatisfaction is directly related to depression and eating disorders.

B. DEPRESSION

Numerous studies have established significant correlations between body dissatisfaction and depression among adolescent girls. Thus, girls who are depressed tend to have higher body dissatisfaction. More recently, investigators have begun to examine the relationship between body dissatisfaction and depression in prospective studies and results suggest that body dissatisfaction is a significant risk factor for adolescent depression. For example, in a longitudinal study by Eric Stice and his colleagues, girls ages 13 to 16 with higher body dissatisfaction scores in the first year of the study were 31% more likely to develop major depression four years later. The adverse effects of body dissatisfaction in terms of risk for depression do not appear to be limited to White girls.

Body dissatisfaction has also been found to mediate the relationship between gender and depression. There are no gender differences in depression in childhood. The gender difference emerges in adolescence, probably around age 15. Longitudinal research suggests that body dissatisfaction may be the single largest contributor to the development of the gender difference. Body dissatisfaction has been shown to be more influential than pubertal development or gender-role orientation in contributing to the onset of the gender difference in depression during adolescence. [*See* Depression.]

C. EATING DISORDERS

Many studies indicate that body dissatisfaction, particularly in the form of concern about weight gain, is prospectively related to the development of eating disorders. Middle-school girls with high body dissatisfaction or high concerns about weight and shape are more likely to develop problematic eating attitudes and behaviors later in adolescence. Symptoms of bulimia nervosa are among the problem behaviors predicted by earlier weight concerns. Arguably, body dissatisfaction is the most consistently documented precursor to anorexia nervosa and bulimia nervosa.

Internalization of the culturally proscribed thin ideal would seem to be a prerequisite for body dissatisfaction. This means that one's personal values include the culturally defined ideal (i.e., that a person agrees that the unreasonably thin body is attractive and attainable). More dangerously, a girl may adopt the thin ideal and integrate it into her self-definition, convincing herself that being thin is an important part of who she is. Internalization of the culturally defined ideal appears to be more of a problem for girls than for boys. This is true even when boys are asked about muscularity while girls are questioned about thinness. Thin-ideal internalization has been strongly linked to eating problems, both in prospective studies and in experimental designs. This combination of prospective and experimental data helps build a particularly strong case for a possible causal link between thin-ideal internalization and eating problems. More research is needed to confirm and explain this link.

It is possible that body dissatisfaction represents the earliest phases of an eating disorder. There is substantial reason to believe that there is at least a partial continuum of eating disorders. There are quantitative increases, but no evidence for a qualitative shift, in body dissatisfaction as one compares restrained eaters to subclinical eating disorders clients to women with eating disorders. Thus, at least in some cases, body and weight dissatisfaction may be signs that the person is on the road to developing an eating disorder.

Thus far we have focused on behavioral problems that might be associated with body dissatisfaction. It is also possible that body dissatisfaction might be addressed in ways that the culture does not deem as problematic. Some people think that dieting is such a coping mechanism in that dieting for weight loss might lead to a healthy change in weight. As has already been discussed, this is not as much of a straightforward relationship as some may think. There are real dangers associated with calorie restrictive dieting and it is often not a particularly effective means of losing weight. Indeed, dieting, at least among adolescent girls, may actually lead to obesity. [*See* EATING DISORDERS AND DISORDERED EATING.]

C. SURGICAL APPEARANCE ALTERING

Cosmetic surgery is another culturally sanctioned means of coping with body dissatisfaction. Increasingly, people turn to cosmetic surgery to feel better about their bodies. According to the American Society of Plastic Surgeons, the number of cosmetic surgeries doubled from 1997 to 1999, and liposuction and breast augmentation were the most commonly performed procedures. For example, more than 230,000 people underwent liposuction in 1999 and most of these patients (87%) were female. More than 1600 of these liposuction clients were under age 18. Scientific studies are needed to determine the medical safety and psychological impact of cosmetic surgery. Research to date is limited by the reliance on survey studies of samples of convenience, low participation rates, and grouping together different surgery procedures (e.g., face lifts, liposuction, breast augmentation).

Serious concerns have been raised about the medical safety of liposuction; indeed, there have been some deaths associated with the procedure. Current data may underestimate the medical risks because they are based on voluntary reporting by plastic surgeons. Both the voluntary nature of the reporting and the fact that not all cosmetic surgeries are performed by board-certified plastic surgeons may contribute to the underestimation.

Psychological studies of cosmetic surgery have focused on the question of whether there are certain patients for whom cosmetic surgery is counterindicated and on the question of whether cosmetic surgery results in lasting improvement in psychological well-being. There are several challenges involved in doing this research. What constitutes "lasting" improvement? Who will evaluate the potential patient, a plastic surgeon or a psychologist? What constitutes problematic body image concerns? Given the methodological problems it is not surprising that the evidence regarding the psychological benefits or risks associated with cosmetic surgery is mixed.

Women seeking cosmetic surgery do report dissatisfaction at least with the feature being altered and perhaps with their body overall. Research evaluating prospective cosmetic surgery clients does not indicate serious psychopathology in most of them. However, recent research suggests that 7% of women presenting for cosmetic surgery may suffer from Body Dysmorphic Disorder (BDD), a rate three to four times that observed in the general population. BDD is marked by exaggerated, unrealistic concern about a particular physical feature. Cosmetic surgery is not likely to alleviate BDD, given that, by definition, the individual's concerns are not justified. Indeed, individuals suffering from BDD may seek repeated surgeries to try to achieve their ideal. Outcome of cosmetic surgery among individuals with BDD is unknown; evidence to date is based on small case series and unrepresentative samples. On the basis of this preliminary evidence, experts suggest that surgery does not substantially improve BDD and may, in some cases, exacerbate symptoms. Similarly, if someone is suffering from anorexia nervosa (AN) or bulimia nervosa (BN), cosmetic surgery is not likely to provide long-term relief from body image concerns. Given the physical effects of BN and AN on the immune, cardiovascular, and gastrointestinal systems, surgery of any sort may be unusually dangerous for people suffering from these disorders.

Cosmetic surgery, like any surgery, carries with it risks of anesthesia errors, infection, and hemorrhaging. When surgery is being performed to correct a serious medical problem, the potential benefits typically outweigh the risks. This is not so clearly true of cosmetic surgery. When the surgery is motivated by BDD, AN, or BN, the risks may be particularly high. [*See* HEALTH AND HEALTH CARE.]

D. SUMMARY

Body image concerns are clearly more than a nuisance. They do not simply reflect vanity or narcissism. Nor are their long-term effects harmless. Body image concerns may lead to depression and eating disorders. Body dissatisfaction may also lead to dieting, which in turn may lead to obesity and eating disorders. These are not negligible problems.

Treatment and prevention programs may aim to reduce body dissatisfaction, particularly in terms of weight and shape concerns. Preventing body dissatisfaction in girls may decrease the incidence of obesity, depression, and eating disorders. Successfully designing such prevention programs, as well as treatment programs, requires some understanding of what causes body dissatisfaction.

IV. *Influences on Body Image*

Body image disturbances, or at least their body dissatisfaction components, are substantially learned. Certainly biological factors such as BMI and temperamental predispositions such as negative affect may contribute to the likelihood that such attitudes and belief systems are acquired. But body dissatisfaction is substantially environmentally induced. Three widely supported findings indicate that many women have adopted a cultural norm for an unattainable body type. These findings are (1) body dis-

satisfaction is a gendered phenomenon in terms of both the nature and the severity of the disturbance; (2) body dissatisfaction is so widespread that, at least among White women, it is considered normative; (3) as would be expected with a culturally proscribed attitude, there are ethnic group differences in the nature and severity of body dissatisfaction. These phenomena raise several important questions. First, what is the cultural message concerning women's bodies? Second, how is this message conveyed? Third, what are the effects of this message on women's attitudes and behaviors?

A. THE MESSAGE

Simply stated, women's bodies are treated as objects. Women are supposed to be beautiful rather than active or decisive. Furthermore, they are supposed to be available (though not promiscuously so) for men to enjoy. Women are supposed to be desirable. This cultural mandate takes many forms. For example, women are often posed in advertisements so as to take a subordinate role to men. Only certain types of women are routinely seen on television, and they are young and unrealistically thin. The common occurrence of sexual harassment, even among school-aged children, underscores the freedom with which boys and men comment on and touch girls' and women's bodies. That boys seem unaware that their teasing is upsetting to girls may be interpreted as further evidence of the "naturalness" of this behavior. Furthermore, non-appearance-related opportunities for success, though increasing, continue to be more limited for women than for men. Women continue to make less money than men in most occupations and are particularly underrepresented at the highest levels of government and business. In addition, women who are thin are more likely to get dates, be admitted to college, and be hired for and promoted at work. For example, there is a significant relationship between the degree to which a girl is overweight and dating for both Black and White adolescent girls: the heavier the girl, the less likely she is to be dating. For Black girls, this relationship may be apparent only among girls from higher socioeconomic backgrounds. [*See* BEAUTY POLITICS AND PATRIARCHY; WORKING ENVIRONMENTS.]

This message is an integral part of objectification theory. The core premise of this theory is that the dominant White male culture in the United States endorses very different conceptualizations of men's and women's bodies. Women's bodies are much more likely than men's to be looked at in a way that is evaluative and hence may, at any time, be objectifying. Women's bodies, then, are treated like objects to be rated and commented on, in much the same way one might evaluate a painting one is thinking of purchasing. The objectification of women's bodies includes a sexual aspect so that not only are women treated as objects to be looked at but also as objects that can be possessed by men. On the other hand, men are seen as active agents whose bodies are functional more than they are decorative.

Girls learn early on that boys (and men) look at them in this sexualizing, objectifying manner and are made uncomfortable by it. Nonetheless, with the experience of being rewarded or seeing others rewarded for meeting the societal expectations for attractiveness, girls gradually internalize this objectifying gaze. They know that others are watching and evaluating them, so they watch themselves so as not to fail in the eyes of others. They learn to monitor themselves and each other to ensure that societal standards are being met. Thus, girls may actively enforce the objectifying standards. Furthermore, the self-monitoring means that girls and women are likely to be anxious in situations where they are worried about failing to meet the standards. Thus, in an ingenious experiment, Barbara Fredrickson and her colleagues demonstrated that compared to men and to women wearing sweaters, women in bathing suits show decreased body esteem and even perform more poorly on math problems.

What exactly are these standards? First and foremost, they involve unrealistic standards for thinness. For example, the "supermodels" who sell clothes, makeup, and the general image of what is beautiful fall into the thinnest 10% of the female population. Camera angles, computer enhancement, and high-heeled shoes are used to make them look taller, leggier, and thinner than they already area. Despite being extremely thin, many of these women have relatively large breasts. Breasts are composed mainly of fatty tissue and so it is unlikely that most women can be very thin and have large breasts. This image probably contributes to the growing use of liposuction and breast augmentation surgery even among adolescent girls.

But the clearest component of the image is indeed the glorification of thinness and the vilification of fat. Both awareness and internalization of this message are related to body dissatisfaction, weight concerns, and the use of weight loss techniques in female children, adolescents, and adults. Thin-ideal inter-

nalization appears to be a causal risk factor for the development of bulimic symptoms, though more research is needed.

Recently, there has been some argument that an unrealistically muscular body is an analogous message for boys and that this message might be associated with BDD (especially a form known as muscle dysmorphic disorder) and steroid abuse. These links have not yet been empirically demonstrated. However, research does indicate that middle-school boys are aware of and may even internalize this muscular ideal. This awareness and internalization is, in turn, associated with concerns about being muscular, the use of muscle building techniques, and the use of weight loss techniques. Internalization, but not awareness, is also related to body esteem. These relationships are not as strong for boys as are the comparable ones for girls suggesting that the messages are not as powerful for boys. Nonetheless, the possibility that such messages may lead to body dissatisfaction deserves further attention because that body dissatisfaction may in turn be linked to dangerous muscle building techniques including excessive weight lifting and the use of food supplements or steroids.

B. THE MEDIUM

So how is the message concerning the importance of thinness for girls conveyed? This is fundamentally a social learning process, involving both modeling and direct reinforcement by a variety of socialization agents. More specifically, parents, peers, and media are all instrumental in conveying this message.

1. Parents

Parents are generally satisfied with their children's appearance, though parental satisfaction declines as their children get older. Yet many parents do comment on their children's weight and shape. There is now considerable research indicating that parental comments and teasing directed at a child influence that child's body image. Research examining concurrent relationships between parental comments and child body image has documented such relationships in elementary school children as well as in adolescents.

Studies examining the effects of parental modeling are more equivocal. Several studies have not found relationships between parental dieting or attitudes about their own bodies and children's eating attitudes and behavior, including body image. However, some researchers have found significant correlations. In studies looking at both direct parental comments to the child and parental modeling of undesirable eating attitudes and behaviors, parental comments seem to be more strongly related to child body esteem and use of weight loss techniques. In the long run, though, it would be surprising if parental modeling was completely unrelated to children's body image. It may be that the relationship only exists under certain circumstances or for certain components of body image. This is a question for future research.

The few longitudinal studies that have considered parental transmission of the cultural messages about body shape have also documented significant relationships. For example, girls and boys whose fathers comment on the children's weight are more likely to become constant dieters.

It is noteworthy that researchers often find that boys' parents make comments about their weight. In fact, parents seem to make weight-related comments to their sons and daughters about equally, though it is possible that mothers are marginally more likely to comment on daughters' weight. There is some debate concerning the impact of these comments. Some research finds that parental influence is roughly equal for boys and girls, while others report that girls are more affected by parental comments. Again, there are probably factors that mediate the effects of parental comments on children's body satisfaction. These mediators might include, for example, the children's age and the number of weight-related comments they also hear from peers, coaches, or teachers. More research is needed to elucidate such relationships.

The evidence is clear that many parents are conveying a cultural message about the importance of body shape to their children. Research also demonstrates that these messages are taken to heart by both boys and girls. Girls may be more affected, despite the fact that parents do not apparently make more comments to their daughters than their sons. The greater effect on girls may be attributable to the consistency, across socialization agents, of the message that girls receive.

2. Peers

As is true of parents, peers may either model body dissatisfaction or make comments directly to a child about weight and shape. Many of these comments will take the form of weight- and shape-related teasing, given that appearance-related teasing is more common than any other form of teasing. In addition, peer relationships, unlike parent–child relationships, involved *earned* status. Thus, children and adolescents will be motivated to do things, including achieve a particular look, in order to become more popular. Research suggests that peers do indeed influence children's body esteem and level of weight concerns in all of these ways.

When girls think they will be better liked if they are thinner, they have higher weight concerns. Girls who are teased, particularly those who take the teasing seriously, have higher body dissatisfaction. Peer modeling and teasing may be more strongly related to young girls' body dissatisfaction than are parental factors. Peer modeling of body dissatisfaction may actually be institutionalized in "fat talk," a phenomenon in which adolescent girls disparage their weight and shape despite being relatively satisfied with their average (or thinner) bodies.

Teasing may interface with the cultural objectification of the female body in the form of sexual harassment. Research with elementary school children suggests that sexual harassment, and girls' reaction to it, is related to body esteem. This is not true for boys, although they, too, report harassment. Studies with adult women suggest that sexual harassment may be a risk factor that is specific to body image and eating disturbances.

Few studies have examined peer comments about weight and shape among boys. Limited research suggests that compared to girls, elementary school boys report fewer peer interactions concerning weight and shape. Perhaps as an outcome of this, boys who think that peers will like them better if they lose weight do *not* demonstrate higher levels of weight concerns. Peer groups' norms about weight and dieting are correlated significantly with girls' dieting behaviors, however. It will be interesting to see whether future research uncovers comparable relationships between pressure from boys' teammates and coaches to increase muscularity and the boys' weight lifting and steroid use.

Thus, peers do appear to influence children's and adolescents' body esteem and weight concerns. Both the extent and the effect of these peer influences appear to be greater for girls.

3. Mass Media

Media, of course, can only model behavior. The modeling, in this case, includes both presenting the ideal image and demonstrating that failure to achieve that appearance will be punished. Mass media also send the message that the ideal body is attainable by everyone with a little effort and the right products. There can be little doubt that the image of women presented in magazines and on television is extraordinarily thin. It is unusual to see an average weight, much less an overweight woman, in a dramatic or romantic role. Furthermore, an analysis of situation comedies indicates that overweight female characters receive fewer positive comments than do the thinner characters. This message is not lost on children; boys who watch more television are more likely to negatively stereotype a fat female target.

Correlational data indicate that messages in the media about a thin body ideal indeed influence body esteem. Both print media, mainly in the form of teen or fashion magazines, and television effects have been documented. The cognitive element of this effect, which was implied in the peer comments–body image relationship, is particularly evident. The effects of the media are not primarily attributable to simple exposure (though such effects are sometimes reported). Rather, it is belief in these messages (i.e., internalization of the thin ideal as conveyed by the media) that appears to create the effect.

It is clear that exposure to these messages is widespread. As many as 25% of elementary school girls read teen magazines twice weekly, while almost double that read them at least occasionally. By early adolescence, upwards to 90% of girls see the magazines at least occasionally. The use of such magazines to obtain information about body shape and its attainment has been related to body dissatisfaction and weight concerns in children and adolescents. Beginning in late elementary school (and perhaps earlier) and continuing into adulthood, girls and women compare themselves to media images, including fashion models, and feel bad about it. As an interesting counterpoint to these findings, young girls whose favorite female television characters are closer to average weight seem less likely to internalize the thin ideal.

Boys, too, may be affected by exposure to male images, at least on television. Research concerning boys is so limited, however, that it is difficult to ascertain how strong these effects are and how they compare to the effects on girls. It is clear that the message concerning an ideal body is less consistently delivered to boys than to girls. Magazines aimed at men and boys carry fewer articles and advertisements about body shape and weight, for example.

Indeed, it is difficult to think of a male equivalent of *17* or *YM* or *Teen*. [*See* MEDIA INFLUENCES; MEDIA STEREOTYPES.]

4. Message Consistency

It seems possible that girls receive a more consistent message about how their bodies should look than do boys. This consistency is true both in terms of the strength and frequency of the message, especially in the media, and the number of sources conveying the message. This may be instrumental in creating the greater levels of dissatisfaction with weight and shape seen among girls of all ethnic groups (relative to boys) beginning by late elementary school. This argument is strengthened by data suggesting that middle-school girls living in a "subculture of dieting," who frequently use magazines as a source of body information and who also have parents and peers who are invested in dieting, have high levels of body dissatisfaction.

C. THE EFFECTS

Girls and women have higher levels of body shape dissatisfaction, weight concerns, and use of weight loss techniques than do boys and men. These differences emerge in elementary school and are true for all ethnic groups in the United States that have been studied. Sociocultural influences clearly affect girls' body image as outlined here. Boys, too, are affected by sociocultural factors. However, several of these factors seem greater for girls. Most notably, the media messages are more consistent in defining an ideal body for girls. Peer influences, including sexual harassment, also seem to be greater for girls.

All of this may create more internalization of a single, culturally defined ideal by girls. This ideal, in turn, when compared to one's own body, may create body dissatisfaction. Body dissatisfaction indices, including thin-ideal internalization, have been related to the use of weight loss techniques as well as the onset of bulimic symptoms. Indeed, since both prospective and experimental data supporting such relationships are available, it appears that body image problems may be a causal risk factor for the development of eating problems. Body dissatisfaction is also certainly related to the increasing use of cosmetic surgery by teenaged girls and women.

Evidence accumulating over the past three decades has indicated that there is a message strongly endorsing a "thin ideal" for U.S. women. While this message is most evident for White women, it also exists for women of color. This thin ideal is part of the process of objectifying women's bodies, treating them as ornaments to be used for the sexual pleasure of men. Because the thin ideal is rewarded socially and economically, women come to internalize the objectification through a combination of social learning and cognitive processes. The internalization of the thin ideal from cultural messages is then associated with, and possibly a causal factor in the development of, body dissatisfaction, the use of weight loss techniques to control an already normal body shape, and bulimia nervosa.

V. Conclusions

Both women and men exhibit body dissatisfaction. However, it is clear that there are important and substantial gender differences in this phenomenon. First, beginning early in childhood, girls show more body dissatisfaction than boys do. This is true in all U.S. ethnic groups that have been studied. Furthermore, it appears that body dissatisfaction, especially when focused on weight and shape, is both stronger and more common among girls and women. Body dissatisfaction seems to increase among girls as they move from childhood into adolescence.

Second, body dissatisfaction appears to be related to a wide range of eating, behavioral, and even physical problems, particularly among girls and women. Girls and women who are body dissatisfied are more likely to engage in potentially dangerous weight control techniques, including dieting. They are also more likely to develop depression, eating disorders, and, ironically, obesity. These relationships appear to be stronger for women than for men.

Finally, messages concerning ideal body type and the importance of attaining that ideal differ by gender.

Women are supposed to be thin, an ideal that is enforced by family, peers, and the media. This message is clearer, perhaps, for White, Hispanic, and Asian women than for Black women. However, it is clear enough for Black women that they are more body dissatisfied than Black men are. Research further suggests that this may be true in a variety of Western and Asian countries, though it would be premature to conclude that it is a universally held standard.

The cultural message impacts thin-ideal internalization and hence body dissatisfaction. There are still empirical questions to be addressed concerning this message and its effects. Nonetheless, there is sufficient evidence documenting the relationship that we can suggest that attempts to change the message should change the levels of body dissatisfaction among girls and women. This, in turn, should change the levels of at least eating problems and possibly eating disorders, depression, and obesity. In a similar vein, ensuring that the cultural messages concerning boys' bodies do not become as strong and pervasive as those concerning girls' bodies should be viewed as a preemptive strike against the future development of body dissatisfaction among boys.

SUGGESTED READING

Bordo, S. (1993). *Unbearable Weight: Feminism, Western Culture, and the Body.* University of California Press, Berkeley.

Brumberg, J. J. (1997). *The Body Project: An Intimate History of American Girls.* Random House, New York.

Striegel-Moore, R. H., and Smolak, L. (2001). *Eating Disorders: Innovative Directions in Research and Practice.* American Psychological Association, Washington, DC.

Thompson, J. K., Heinberg, L., Altabe, M., and Tantleff-Dunn, S. (1999). *Exacting Beauty: Theory, Assessment, and Treatment of Body Image Disturbance.* American Psychological Association, Washington, DC.

Thompson, J. K., and Smolak, L. (2001). *Body Image, Eating Disorders, and Obesity among Youth.* American Psychological Association, Washington, DC.

Career Achievement
Opportunities and Barriers

Audrey J. Murrell

University of Pittsburgh

Glossary

Affirmative action A variety of policies, programs, and procedures put in place to monitor and correct discrimination based on dimensions such as race, sex, and age.

Careerism The propensity to pursue career advancement through non-performance-based means.

Contingent work Any job in which an individual does not have an explicit or implicit contract for long-term employment.

Glass ceiling The concept of an invisible barrier that prevents women and minorities from advancing into top positions within organizations.

Mentoring Relationships at work that involve activities such as sponsorship, coaching, counseling, and role modeling.

Sex-role spillover When gender roles within society spill over into the workplace and compete with or replace work-related roles and expectations.

Sexual harassment Behaviors such as sexual remarks, sexual coercion, and intimidation that create a hostile work environment.

THE ISSUE OF WOMEN AND CAREER ADVANCEMENT has received considerable attention, especially over the past few decades. A variety of factors have been shown to influence women's advancement, including overall corporate climate, gender discrimination, sexual harassment, occupational segregation, and exclusion from mentoring opportunities. While issues facing women are careers are complex enough to fill several volumes, this article reviews some of the recent trends in changes within the workplace that create both opportunities and barriers to the advancement of women. The goal of this discussion is to highlight some of the ways in which the nature of careers have changed over the past decade and to review the unique implications of these changes for women. In addition, some of the key strategies for enhancing career opportunities for women are part of this discussion.

I. Overview

One of the featured stories in *Fortune* magazine in 1992, titled "When Will Women Get to the Top?"

examined changes in women's career advancement in organizations since the women's movement. While opportunities for women and careers outside of the home have clearly increased over the past several decades, the article suggested that the top levels of corporate America are still dominated by men. The question posed in this story was simply put: "Will we have women as CEOs within the next decade?" Almost a decade later, a study by Catalyst examined women in corporate leadership. The research found that just under 11.2% of corporate officers were women, and among the 40 corporate officers who held senior titles in research, only 2 were women. To date, within *Fortune* 500 corporations, only two are headed by women.

II. *The Glass Ceiling*

One of the most widely studied areas that examines the barriers to women's career advancement is the consequences of discrimination in the workplace. The most well-known illustration of discrimination in the workplace is the concept of the "glass ceiling," which defines the invisible barrier that prevents many women and minorities from advancing into senior and executive management positions within organizations. A number of studies have explored discrimination at work across factors such as job type, organization size and composition, industry, and target group involved. A study by the Federal Glass Ceiling Commission reported lower representation of women and minorities in occupations with high status, executive-level positions, and boards of directors. In addition, studies show that women experience barriers at all levels, not only at the top, and these barriers significantly retard a woman's career advances and detract from her performance in the profession. Work by a nonprofit organization known as Catalyst, Inc., has devoted substantial attention to the issue of women's advancement in organizations. Examples of differential treatment within organizations is one of the most widely cited reasons why women fail to advance to levels of authority and visibility within organizations.

Misconceptions and negative attitudes that have been shown to derail the careers and success of women in the workplace also have a clear and negative impact on members of other racial and ethnic groups. Research shows that women are often segregated in organizations by specialty, based on prevailing stereotypes. For example, previous work by Dobbins, Cardy, and Truxillo identified discrimina-

tion in job assignments that lead to future promotions as the number one barrier for women, particularly African American women in management jobs. The concept of occupational gender segregation describes the disproportionate overrepresentation of women and minorities in low-paying, low-status occupations compared to men and nonminorities. Clearly these differences decrease the earnings potential of women and minorities, as well as their career mobility and access to leadership and decision-making positions within organizations. In addition, discrimination by occupational type is more likely to exclude women and minorities from access to informal networks of information and support that can help in career advancement. Last, the disproportionate representation of women and minorities in low-status jobs puts them at greater risk of workplace discrimination, including sexual (and racial) harassment. [*See* SEXUAL HARASSMENT.]

Another area that has received a great deal of attention in research on the glass ceiling focuses on earnings disparities between men and women. Legislation of the 1960s drew considerable attention to discrimination at work as manifested in wage gaps and inequities in incentives and benefits. The notion of comparable worth and pay equity has received a great deal of attention during the past two decades. Efforts such as "equal pay for equal work" and affirmative action helped reduce some of this well-documented wage gap based on gender, but the pay for women of color continues to lag behind their White counterparts. Recent attention has focused on why sex discrimination in wages in some occupations and industries continues, particularly regarding the issue of wage differences for women in top positions within organizations.

One explanation for the persistence of earnings discrimination that is frequently cited is the existence of what has been labeled as "dual labor markets." A greater number of men are employed in the "primary labor market" compared to women. This primary market offers better jobs with higher pay rates. The "secondary labor market" is dominated by women and minorities and contains low-paying and low-status jobs. The notion of different labor markets based on demographic factors such as sex and race is quite consistent with the notion of occupational segregation based on sex and race previously discussed. What is key to the notion of the dual labor market is that it represents a structural barrier to women's career advancement that explains why there is relatively little movement between the two markets, especially for women and minorities. This dual labor market for women provides an impermeable barrier for career advancement and is of critical importance in explaining the gender gap in earnings.

A significantly underresearched area within the literature on the glass ceiling is the intersection of race and gender on career outcomes and advancement. Some writing in this area focuses on the double disadvantage experiences by minority women in professional settings. Ella Bell argued that for women of color, a "push and pull" exists between issues of race, ethnicity, and gender that uniquely affects career outcomes. This dual pressure puts this group in the unique position of being both visible and isolated within a traditional male (and White) work environment. In addition, these women are likely to experience job stress, dissatisfaction, and interpersonal conflict that results from high visibility, performance pressure, and isolation.

In her classic work on the effect of token or solo status and gender, Rusabeth Moss Kanter argued that proportional representation affects the dynamics of social interactions at work. A workplace that is homogenous in terms of master statuses such as sex or race will differ qualitatively from environments that are "skewed" (those with a 15% or less minority population) or "balanced" (those with a 40 to 50% minority population). Specifically, she contended that in skewed work environments, token or solo status results in stereotypical assumptions about what those characteristics mean that disadvantage women and minorities in organizations. Kanter argued that women who enter male-dominated organizations are more visible to others due to their uniqueness, more likely to be viewed as different from the dominant gender group, and more likely to be stereotyped within the workplace. [See WOMEN IN NONTRADITIONAL WORK FIELDS.]

As women are underrepresented in positions of power, barriers to advancement for women may persist. Robin Ely examined women in law firms with either few women in senior positions ("male-dominated" firms) or a significant number of women in senior positions ("sex-integrated" firms). She found that the proportion of women in senior positions shaped both the peer and supervisory relationships women had in the firms. More specifically, she found that early-career-stage women in male-dominated firms were less likely than those in sex-integrated firms to view senior women as good role models. Ely explained this finding by arguing that in male-dominated firms, junior women perceived that being female was incompatible with power and status within the organization. Junior women in her study would either see senior women as lacking in power and therefore not "legitimately senior," or they would view them as having obtained their positions by acting like men rather than women.

Clearly, career strategies have changed substantially for women in organizations since the early studies on the glass ceiling. While organizations attempt to restructure career patterns of their employees, there has also been a corresponding change in individual career attitudes. *Fortune* magazine described college graduates of 1989 as having their eyes on "new realities" in reference to career mobility. Daniel Feldman has described the changing career values and goals as "the propensity to pursue career advancement through non-performance-based means." These non-performance-based means include career mobility tactics (e.g., lateral transfers, downward movements, changing companies) and the instrumental use of social relationships with coworkers, supervisors or other organizational mentors. Ironically, the careerist attitude is seen as a double-edged sword. When individuals place a great deal of weight on career advancement, the desire for success is often at the expense of both relationships within organizations and coworkers who resent the instrumental and deceptive relationships maintained by careerists. The fact that career paths increasingly extend beyond organizational boundaries and span different organizations calls for a special consideration of the impact of these "boundaryless careers" and key outcomes and obstacles.

This "new career" reality has unique consequences for the experience of women compared to men in organizations. Research by Audrey Murrell and her colleagues showed that gender has an important effect on whether career mobility has positive versus negative outcomes on earnings, satisfaction, and breaking through the glass ceiling. Thus, while career mobility factors may enhance flexibility for males, they often involve mobility strategies (interruptions, job changes, part-time work) that may have a negative effect on career outcomes, particularly for women.

III. *Career Mobility versus Job Interruptions*

While there has been little theory developed to explain the impact of career mobility strategies on income, previous research together with public attention to the changing nature of careers support the importance of this area of study. Classical career theory assumes a linear progression that involves upward, uninterrupted movement across both explicit and embedded career ladders within organizations. Some have argued further that job changes and interruptions produce an especially strong negative effect on earnings for women in managerial and professional occupations.

Other studies that focus specifically on interrupted careers examine the impact of leaves of absence defined almost exclusively as maternity or parental leaves. This research finds that while leaves of absence negatively impact earnings, women often experience more negative effects because they are more likely to take this type of leave than men. Recent studies examine leaves of absence in the wake of the Family and Medical Leave Act. These researchers found that regardless of the reason for the leaves, this type of interruption had only a small negative impact on earnings for both male and female managers. However, women received a more negative performance review relative to men for taking time off from work. Periods of nonemployment often include both voluntary and involuntary exclusions from the workforce and are particularly detrimental to earnings when they are involuntary in nature (layoffs, downsizing, etc.). While some research finds gender differences in coping with nonemployment, there is little research on how displacement and interruptions produce long-term effects for men compared to women in overall earnings.

Recent research by Joy Schneer and Freida Reitman examined the consequences of career choice and outcomes for females compared to males in managerial careers. They found that the impact of gender differences on the overall work environment for female compared to male MBAs was greater in later compared to earlier career stages. Many have argued that organizations are "gendered," and thus judgments of career strategies, regardless of type or reason, are likely to have more negative consequences for women compared to men. While flexibility is important for new career entrants, what matters most is perhaps not the quantity of work but the type and quality of that work, especially for women in organizations.

Another key area that has received attention in the past decade is the debate over whether part-time work represents positive flexible work arrangements or detrimental reduced work (and earnings) for employees, especially women. Some research indicates that women are more satisfied with part-time work than men, because such absences from or interruptions in full-time work provide flexibility. In addition, periods of movement outside of the work environment may permit opportunities for individuals to seek additional education and training that will be beneficial once these individuals return to the work environment. However, periods of voluntary part-time work in midcareer also have negative impacts on salary, and women are more likely than men to work part time. This suggests that previous notions that professional women with children can benefit from reduced work without significant costs to current and future career outcomes (specifically earnings) may be unreliable, particularly in early career stages. Perhaps these types of interruptions not only are reductions for time worked (from full time to part time), but also represent a reduction in status that is detrimental for the future careers of women. Some argue that the greater likelihood of a woman working part time compared to a man working part time represents the potential for perpetuating women's subordinate status and position within society.

Recently, we have witnessed an increase in the number of employees who work part time or who are part of what has been called the "contingent workforce." The contingent workforce includes employment categories such as part-time, seasonal, temporary, and self-employed workers, as well as multiple job holders. Contingent work is defined as "any job in which an individual does not have an explicit or implicit contract for long-term employment, and one in which the minimum hours worked can vary in a nonsystematic manner." The Bureau of Labor Statistics (BLS) has noted a substantial rise in the number of employees that can be classified as "contingent workers" over the past decade. For example, BLS estimates that 1.4 million workers constituted the temporary help industry in 1992.

A number of authors have likened the rise in contingent work as indicative of an increasing dichotomy between well-paying, stable, and permanent or "core" jobs and poorly paying, unstable, or "peripheral" jobs. Some have argued that recent trends toward greater flexibility in work arrangements, while having some benefits to organizations, are harmful to employees, especially women. Contingent workers are paid less, have fewer fringe benefits, have little or no long-term security, are unlikely to be part of the union, and often are not protected by labor legislation. In addition, women and minorities tend to be overrepresented in careers in which the use of contingent forms of work has risen substantially over the past decade. Similar to the case with other types of "interruptions" from full-time work (e.g., leave of absence), the impact of part-time work on the career advancement of women is a complex picture that requires substantially more research.

IV. Sexual Harassment

Another key barrier for women's careers that has received considerable attention is sexual harassment as a form of gender discrimination. Behaviors such as sexual remarks, sexual coercion, and intimidation are examples of discriminatory acts that fall under the legal definition of harassment. In addition, aspects of the environment that are seen as hostile constitute harassment. While sexual harassment in the workplace is not a new issue, the attention focused on defining, prosecuting, and preventing harassment has increased substantially over the past decade. Still, a vast number of incidents of gender-based harassment go unreported because victims fear retribution by the perpetrator and by the organization.

Attention to the issue of harassment has increased substantially over the past two decades. By 1980, only 15% of workers had not heard of the term "sexual harassment." There is some evidence to support the speculation that marginality, or low-status characteristics, increase an individual's vulnerability to harassment. Younger women are more often the targets of harassment, and unmarried women are also reported as somewhat more likely than married women to be victims of harassment.

In addition, women who represent a minority within the organization such as those in nontraditional occupations face an increased risk of being harassed. Black women auto workers not only receive more harassment than Whites, but these women are also harassed more severely than their White counterparts. These incidents ranged from what these researchers labeled "moderate" harassment (sexual propositions, sexual innuendos) to "severe" harassment (demands for sexual activity, physical assault). A study examining Chicanos in white-collar jobs found evidence for incidents of both sexual harassment and race discrimination. Research that disentangles issues such as gender, race, and class, or race and status within the workplace (e.g., low-level workers, contingent workers), is clearly needed. In addition, comparing the frequency of sexual harassment for women of color across different occupational levels is necessary in order to confirm that these women, regardless of power or status within the workplace, are more prone to harassment.

While limited evidence examines the frequency and severity of harassment among women of color, there has been some research investigating the factors that predict whether women will report incidents of sexual harassment and the impact of sexual harassment on work outcomes for these women. For example, Barbara Gutek found that women who experience sexual harassment experience isolation and lack of access to mentoring and informal networks. Some suggest that these women may limit the nature of their interpersonal contacts at work, in part because of fear over exposure to harassment. Women may also be likely to quit their jobs because of harassment; harassment can thus derail their career advancement.

Previous scholars have suggested that sex-role spillover occurs when gender roles spill over into the workplace and either replace or compete with work-related roles and expectations. As a consequence of this spillover, experiences with sexual harassment are more likely to occur within environments that are highly sexualized, or when gender roles are highly salient. According to this argument, women in nontraditional, male-dominated occupations and men in nontraditional, female-dominated occupations are more likely to experience sexual harassment experiences at work compared to women and men working in traditional jobs. Gutek and her colleague argued that often "male sexuality becomes incorporated into male-dominated work environments." Such an orientation tends to cause people to respond in stereotypic ways. Young, attractive women may be seen as "sex objects" by their male coworkers rather than as employees, resulting in higher levels of sexual harassment. Within this type of stereotypic thinking, once a woman is labeled as "sexual" within a work environment, most of her behavior is perceived within this framework. Thus, it appears that individuals in male-dominated or highly sexualized workplaces are more likely to have highly stereotyped beliefs about the more general roles of women and men. Thus, stereotyped views of males and females, often pervasive in work environments that have a skewed gender ratio (e.g., are male-dominated), serve as a key barrier for women's career outcomes and well-being at work. [See WORKING ENVIRONMENTS.]

V. Affirmative Action

The variety of barriers that can derail women's advancement in organizations, coupled with recent attacks on antidiscrimination policies and programs, raise several questions about our ability to monitor the progress of women and minorities as well as correct incidents of discrimination and bias when they occur. Methods for measuring the negative or adverse impact of a variety of different employment practices on employees are a key feature of antidiscrimination policies and programs such as affirmative action. These monitoring systems are usually put in place either to assess progress of some existing antidiscrimination effort or to determine the need for future intervention. Recently, there has been a substantial amount of debate over the need for antidiscrimination programs such as affirmative action. Work by Faye Crosby and her colleagues suggested that macrolevel initiatives that monitor the progress of women and minorities in organizations are essential for the accurate detection of discrimination in the workplace. However, some critics of antidiscrimination policies such as affirmative action argue that these measures are no longer needed given the gains of women and coupled with claims of "reverse discrimination." Unfortunately, critics of antidiscrimination policies such as affirmative action often base these criticisms on employment practices and policies of the past. It may be the case that while affirmative action and similar policies and programs generate some resistance, changes in the nature of the employment relationship and the reduction of stable or full-time work may increase their importance and necessity in the future. [*See* AFFIRMATIVE ACTION.]

VI. Mentoring

One area that shows a great deal of promise for advancing the careers of women in various organizations is the impact of mentoring. Kathy Kram's influential work distinguished between the classic mentor relationship and "other less involving, exclusive, and intricate forms like the sponsor relationship" and peer support. Kram argued that there are two basic types of "mentoring functions." The first type, "career functions," involves sponsorship, exposure and visibility, coaching, protection, and challenging assignments. The second type of function, called "psychosocial," includes role modeling,

acceptance and confirmation, counseling, and friendship. While career functions are closely related to individuals' advancement in an organization, psychosocial functions focus on the enhancement of competence, identity, and personal effectiveness.

Kram proposed that developmental relationships can serve different functions at different stages in the life of a person's career. Belle Ragins also noted that under some conditions career advantages for a protégé are achieved because a more senior person undertakes key mentoring functions. Recent evidence provides support for the positive impact of these developmental relationships. A recent study showed that women and minority MBAs who had a mentor earned significantly more money than those who had not had a mentor. Protégés of White male mentors earned $22,454 more than those without formal mentors.

Recent work focuses on the developmental and relationship aspects of mentoring, particularly as it is related to the protégé's development of status and power within organizations. Research indicates that individuals who receive mentoring report more positional power and receive more promotions and compensation than individuals without either formal or informal mentoring relationships. Protégé's affect a mentor's status and credibility in the organization and can provide a loyal base of future support and expertise. In addition, an individual's experience as a protégé has been found to be a significant predictor in the decision to become a mentor. Clearly, when individuals see the value in these types of developmental relationships, they are likely to enter the relationship again as a mentor.

Mentoring relationships may take a variety of forms. Key dimensions that have been the focus of previous research include the specific position of the mentor and status within the organization. Previous work in this area shows that mentors who are at higher ranks than protégés differ from mentors who hold lateral or peer positions within the organization. These issues are particularly relevant with respect to gender and race and career outcomes. Because women face greater barriers to mentoring relationships, they may be more likely to develop relationships with their immediate supervisor and senior peers. Work by David Thomas showed that minority employees often go outside their department and their organization to find mentoring. These types of "external mentors" are an increasing trend in developmental relationships, particularly as organizations and careers become more "boundaryless."

Clearly, these various types of mentoring relationships have implications for women and other minorities in organizations who are faced with the glass ceiling and barriers to advancement. Women and minorities in organizations face somewhat of a paradox; they may have a special need for mentoring relationships but are unlikely to have limited access to both external and internal mentors.

Recently, Ragins proposed the diversified mentoring construct to capture the challenges and advantages of same-sex and cross-sex relationships within organizations. Gender, race, age, career stage, organizational tenure, socioeconomic class, and education may influence mentor functions and protégé outcomes, and they may also vary by the culture and composition of the workplace. Previous research found that gender differences in career stages affect the mentoring relationship. Because of interrupted careers, female protégés are frequently older than their male counterparts; this may impact the ability of the mentor to serve as a role model. Clearly, the gender composition of the mentoring relationship affects not only mentoring functions but also career outcomes that have both promise and many challenges. [*See* MENTORING AND FEMINIST MENTORING.]

VII. Summary

This article reviews some of the opportunities and barriers facing women's careers in the new U.S. economy. Issues such as the "glass ceiling" as barriers to career advancement are complicated by new career strategies and demands such as job interruptions, career mobility, part-time work, and leaves of absence. Whereas many of these strategies help to enhance the flexibility of work, they also pose some concerns for women's advancement and earnings. A variety of research also found that women and minorities often receive fewer promotions than their White male counterparts. These differences are further exacerbated by necessary interruptions from full-time work that negatively impact women more than men.

While numerous barriers still exist for women's career advancement, recent advances because of antidiscriminatory policies such as affirmative action have had an important impact. In addition, the positive benefits of mentoring for women and minorities are receiving a great deal of attention by current scholars. The combination of social policy (affirmative action) and organization policy (mentoring) appears to provide a critical alliance of forces that help

to remove historical barriers for women and minorities in organizations.

The focus of future research and managerial efforts should be toward designing effective systems to monitor the progress of women and minorities within organizations. These systems must be sensitive to emerging patterns of work, such as contingent employment across its various forms. In addition, legislative efforts should focus on more inclusive protection for contingent and other externalized employees. Finally, previous antidiscrimination policies and programs such as affirmative action may serve as useful models for the design of effective monitoring and intervention systems. Innovative efforts also may be needed to enhance diversity not only in terms of gender (and racial) group representation within organizations, but also in terms of the long-term career and professional success of women and minorities within these institutions.

SUGGESTED READING

Crosby, F. (1982). *Relative Deprivation and Working Women*. Oxford University Press, New York.

Crosby, F. (1984). The denial of personal discrimination. *American Behavioral Scientist* **27**, 371–386.

Dreher, G. F., and Cox, T. H., Jr. (1996). Race, gender, and opportunity: A study of compensation attainment and the establishment of mentoring relationships. *Journal of Applied Psychology* **81**, 297–308.

Federal Glass Ceiling Commission. (1995). *Good for Business: Making Full Use of the Nation's Human Capital*. U.S. Government Printing Office, Washington, DC.

Feldman, D. C. (1985). The new careerism: Origins, tenants, and consequences. *The Industrial Psychologist* **22**, 39–44.

Feldman, D. C., and Weitz, B. A. (1991). From the invisible hand to the gladhand. *Human Resource Management* **30**(2), 237–257.

Ibarra, H. (1995). Personal networks of women and minorities in management: A conceptual framework. *Academy of Management Review* **76**, 79–85.

Kanter, R. M. (1977). Some effects of proportions on group life: Skewed sex ratios and reponses to token women. *American Journal of Sociology* **82**, 965–990.

Kram, K. E. (1983). Phases of a mentor relationship. *Academy of Management Journal* **26**, 608–625.

Morrison, A., White, R., and Van Velson, E. (1987). *Breaking the Glass Ceiling*. Addison-Wesley, Reading, MA.

Murrell, A. J. (1999). African American women, careers and family. In *African American Women: An Ecological Perspective* (N. J. Burgess, E. Brown, and S. Turner, eds.). Garland, Ann Arbor, MI.

Murrell, A. J., Frieze, I. H., and Olson, J. E. (1996). Mobility strategies and career outcomes: A longitudinal study of MBA. *Journal of Vocational Behavior* **49**, 324–335.

Olson, J. E., and Frieze, I. H. (1989). Job interruptions and part-time work: Their effect on MBAs income. *Industrial Relations* **28**, 373–386.

Ragins, B. R. (1989). Barriers to mentoring: The female manager's dilemma. *Human Relations* **42**, 1–22.

Ragins, B. R. (1995). Diversity, power, and mentorship in organizations: A cultural, structural and behavioral perspective. In *Diversity in Organizations* (M. Chemers, M. Costanzo, and S. Oskamp, eds.). Sage, Newbury Park.

Ragins, B. R. (1997). Diversified mentoring relationships in organizations: A power perspective. *Academy of Management Review* **22**, 482–521.

Schneer, J. A., and Reitman, F. (1990). Effects of employment gaps on the careers of MBAs: More damaging for men than for women? *Academy of Management Journal* **33**, 391–406.

Thomas, D. A. (1990). The impact of race on managers' experiences of developmental relationships (mentoring and sponsorship): An intra-organizational study. *Journal of Organizational Behavior* **11**, 479–491.

Thomas, D. A. (1993). Racial dynamics in cross-race developmental relationships. *Administrative Science Quarterly* **38**, 169–194.

Child Abuse
Physical and Sexual

Angela Bissada
Childrens Hospital Los Angeles and University of Southern California/University Affiliated Program

John Briere
Keck School of Medicine, University of Southern California

Glossary

Abuse specific therapy A therapeutic approach that addresses the specific effects of child abuse. Such therapy may incorporate theory and interventions from behavioral, cognitive, systemic, and psychodynamic therapies.

Cognitive distortions Negative thoughts and beliefs about self and others. They may be formed in response to abusive events and may represent the victim's subsequent efforts to make sense of the abuse.

Corporal punishment A discipline method used by an adult that involves physical blows (e.g., spanking) as a method of punishing a child.

Dissociation A defensive alteration in the normally integrated functions of consciousness, memory, identity, or perception of the environment.

Grooming process A series of progressive behaviors engaged in by a sex offender in order to establish a relationship with the child that will eventually allow the offender to abuse him or her.

Insecure attachment The result of negative alterations in the normal parent–child bond, leading to a child's anxious, avoidant, or especially dependent responses toward his or her caregiver(s).

Posttraumatic stress disorder (PTSD) A psychological disorder that sometimes follows a traumatic event, including child abuse. PTSD symptoms include episodes of reliving the trauma, attempts to avoid being reminded of (or thinking about) the trauma, and signs of autonomic nervous system arousal, such as jumpiness, tension, or hyperactivity.

Psychological abuse Nonphysical forms of child abuse, wherein the child is repetitively made to feel criticized, humiliated, rejected, degraded, or otherwise devalued.

Somatization Bodily symptoms (e.g., stomach problems, headaches, pain) that are at least partially due to psychological factors and that occur on a regular basis.

CHILD ABUSE is said to have occurred when an adult or someone substantially older than a child intentionally injures, exploits, or significantly maltreats that child. Childhood physical abuse refers to any such acts committed by a parent or caretaker that results in tissue damage (e.g., bruises) or injury (e.g., broken bones). Child sexual abuse is defined as either (1) sexual exploitation of a child, (e.g., in pornography) or (2) any sexual contact with a child by a substantially older person for the purposes of sexual arousal or gratification. This article reviews the prevalence, causes, effects, legal ramifications, and treatment of physical and sexual child abuse.

I. *Incidence and Prevalence*

Child abuse is an unfortunately common event in North American society. The federal government reports, for example, that nearly 3 million allegations of child abuse were made to child protective service agencies in the United States in 1998. However, even these numbers are likely to be an underestimate. The maltreated child may not disclose abuse to authorities or to a responsible adult, often because of fear of the perpetrator, concerns about breaking up the family (in cases of parental abuse), or because the child is discouraged or prevented from doing so by others. Apropos of this, a study by Diana Russell found that over 95% of 647 women who had been sexually abused as children indicated that the crime had not been reported to the police.

Once reported, child abuse cases are usually investigated and determined to be *substantiated, unsubstantiated,* or *unfounded.* Substantiated means that sufficient evidence was uncovered to warrant a determination that abuse did, in fact, occur. Unsubstantiated, on the other hand, means that insufficient evidence was found to support a decision, one way or the other. Unfounded means that the evidence suggests that no abuse actually occurred. According to the United States Department of Health and Human Services (HHS), of reported child abuse cases in

1998, 66% were investigated and 903,000 were substantiated. Of these substantiated reports, 54% involved neglect, 23% were of physical abuse, 12% were of sexual abuse, and the remaining 11% consisted of psychological abuse, medical neglect, or "other" forms of abuse. It should be noted, however, that an unknown proportion of unsubstantiated abuse allegations represent true cases, despite insufficient evidence for a determination. As a result, data on substantiated cases tell only part of the story.

The prevalence of child abuse varies, to some extent, according to sex. According to a 1997 report released by the HHS, all forms of abuse combined are slightly more common in girls than boys (52 versus 47%, respectively). Of the various types of child abuse, the largest sex difference is for sexual abuse, wherein, according to the HHS, 77% of the victims are girls and 23% are boys. The likelihood that a child will be abused also varies as a function of his or her age, with younger children being more at risk. Among all children reported to be victims of abuse, 25% are between the ages of 12 and 18, 22% between 8 and 11, and 50% are age 7 or younger. Within the latter 50%, 25% are younger than 4 years of age. Type of abuse also varies according to the child's age: a greater proportion of neglect and medical neglect cases occur in those under 8 years, whereas children age 8 and older are more commonly victims of physical, sexual, and emotional abuse.

Offenders of abuse are often well known by their victims. HHS reports that approximately 80% of all child abuse victims in 1998 were victimized by one or both parents. Parental abuse is more common, however, for physical abuse and neglect than for sexual abuse. Although up to 21% of girls in the general population will experience sexual abuse by a nuclear family or extended family member by the age of 18, boys are considerably more likely to be sexually abused by nonfamily members, typically individuals who have abused other children and who are in their mid-20s or older.

Because a significant proportion of child abuse victims do not disclose their abuse at the time it occurred, and are not recognized as such by authorities, many researchers turn to retrospective surveys of adults to determine child abuse rates. In these studies, adults are asked specific questions about their childhood experiences, and their answers are categorized according to whether they satisfy current definitions of the various types of child abuse. Such retrospective reporting is thought by many scientists to be more accurate than governmental reports of substantiated abuse cases. However, the retrospective reports of adults also may be somewhat problematic, since the adult's recall of childhood events may be subject to distortion or forgetfulness.

In one of the most cited retrospective studies, David Finkelhor and his colleagues conducted a national telephone survey of adults in which 27% of women and 16% of men reported sexual abuse by the age of 18. A similar mail-out survey, distributed nationwide by Diana Elliott and John Briere, yielded similar findings: 32% of females and 13% of males reported a history of sexual abuse.

Unfortunately, child maltreatment results in death in some cases. The federal government reports that more than a thousand children are killed each year as a result of extreme child maltreatment. This number is likely to be an underestimate, since many municipalities and counties do not have specialized death review teams, and the determination of a child's cause of death may be made by those less trained in the signs of fatal child abuse. Approximately 40% of identified abuse-related deaths appear to involve children who had current or prior contact with local child protective service agencies. In other words, allegations had been brought to the attention of protective agencies but, for whatever reason, the death was not prevented. The U.S. Department of Health and Human Services reported that, in 1996, children under the age of four accounted for 76% of all abuse-related fatalities.

II. *Reporting Laws*

There are potentially two types of reporters of child abuse, mandated and nonmandated, the specific definitions of which vary from state to state. Mandated reporters are individuals who, in the course of their work, are exposed to children and are uniquely qualified and required by law to report suspected child abuse. Nearly 40 different professions are named as mandated reporters in one state or another. In many states, these include medical and mental health professionals, school and child care personnel, law enforcement and prosecution personnel, other government personnel (firefighters, licensing evaluators, community service and public assistance personnel), clergy, animal control officers, humane society officers and photographic film processors. In addition,

there are a few states in which every person, whether professional or layperson, is mandated to report child abuse.

Mandated reporters have a legal obligation to report any reasonable suspicion of child abuse. In California, "reasonable suspicion" is a case in which: "it is objectively reasonable for a person to entertain a suspicion, based upon facts that could cause a reasonable person in a like position, drawing, when appropriate, on his or her training and experience, to suspect child abuse," as cited in California Penal Code Section 11166(a), Most states require that a report be made to local law enforcement or the local child protection agency as soon as practically possible. Law enforcement and child protection agencies may be obligated to cross-report to each other and to the local district attorney.

In most states, a nonmandated reporter is anyone else who suspects abuse and chooses to make a report. These individuals are not required by law to do so and will not be penalized for deciding not to report. If a nonmandated report is made, most states allow this to be done anonymously.

III. *Physical Abuse*

A. DEFINITIONS

Varying cultures hold different perspectives as to what constitutes child abuse and what constitutes appropriate disciplinary practice. Physical abuse is defined by California law as an act against a child that results in a nonaccidential physical injury. Federal guidelines, such as the Family Court Act of 1976, define physical abuse further as the act of a parent or a person legally responsible for a child less than age 18 who inflicts or allows inflicton of physical injury upon the child by other than accidental means. Physically abusive acts can include punching, beating, kicking, biting, burning, shaking, or otherwise harming a child. The offender's intention may not have been to hurt the child but due to excessive discipline or physical forms of punishment, injury resulted. Corporal punishment, as defined by the American Academy of Child and Adolescent Psychiatry in 1988, is a discipline method used by a supervising adult that inflicts pain on a child. Various cultures (including some within the United States) view corporal punishment as acceptable or unacceptable and may or may not consider such physical discipline abusive.

B. CAUSES OF PHYSICAL ABUSE

A number of explanations have been offered for why physical abuse occurs. Although traditional models stress the role of parental psychopathology in physical abuse, more recent approaches attempt to determine the actual underlying mechanisms that allow or support physical abuse of children. Cognitive-behavioral models, for example focus on parents' ways of thinking about themselves and others that affect the level of their parenting skills and their responses to children in their care. Social learning models, on the other hand, emphasize the role of abusive parents' own maltreatment experiences as children. From this perspective, abused children learn maladaptive disciplinary practices through their own experience of abuse and later, as adults, repeat this behavior with their own children.

A broader approach to understanding abusive behavior is often referred to as the ecological or interactional model. This perspective incorporates the models just described, as well as emphasizing the role of parental stressors, characteristics of the child, the parent–child interactional style, and the role of society. Because the ecological approach is the most comprehensive, its various elements are considered individually next.

1. Parental Factors

A number of parental factors are associated with higher risk or potential to abuse children. Parents who abuse their children often have their own history of abuse and may believe that physical methods of discipline are the most effective. Perhaps as a result, studies suggest that as many as one-third of all individuals who were abused or neglected in childhood will abuse their own children in some manner.

Parents who are under increased amounts of stress are, overall, at greater risk for physically abusing their children. Yet not all parents who are exposed to stressors abuse their children. Those parents who have a history of poor coping, inadequate problem-solving skills, and innappropriate models of disciplining practices may be more likely to revert to abusive practices when parenting children amidst a stressful lifestyle.

Psychological factors can increase the risk of physical abuse. However, there do not appear to be any particular psychological characteristics that conform to a specific profile for physically abusive parents. Instead, a variety of psychological symptoms experienced by parents can impair their functioning and parenting abilities. Maternal depression and poor physical health appear to contribute to distant, irritable, and punitive interactions with children, and use of alcohol and drugs may foster neglect and reduce a parent's impulse control. Regarding the latter, at least one study suggests that 40% of adults reporting abusive behaviors will meet criteria for substance abuse disorders at some time in their lives. In addition, a number of studies demonstrate a long-standing history of poor self-esteem in physically abusive parents. [See SUBSTANCE ABUSE.]

Neuropsychological factors have also been implicated in physical abuse. Minimal brain dysfunction may lead to poor stress management and increased risk for abuse. In addition, cognitive deficits, including verbal processing problems and the inability to read interpersonal cues, also can increase a parent's likelihood of abuse. In 1995, Madhabika Nayak and Joel Milner compared high-risk to low-risk mothers and found that high-risk mothers demonstrated significantly inferior performances on neuropsychological measures that tapped conceptual ability, cognitive flexibility, and problem solving. Abusive parents also have been found to be hyperreactive to stress in general. Some physically abusive parents show autonomic nervous system hyperarousal, as assessed through measures of skin conductance, in response to stressful child-related stimuli.

As compared to their nonabusive peers, parents prone to physically abusive behavior tend to experience difficulty in the interpersonal realm. Their relationships with family as well as nonfamily members are often negative and nonsupportive. As a result, such parents may falsely perceive that support is not available from others and respond by isolating themselves further, which in turn increases the risk of abuse. [See SOCIAL SUPPORT.]

Physically abusive parents often possess a poor understanding of basic child development. They may expect their children to function at a much higher cognitive and emotional level than is appropriate for a child their age. When the child engages in age-appropriate or minimally problematic behavior, the abusive parent often views the child's actions in an especially negative light. In addition to unrealistic expectations, abusive parents often possess negative cognitive attributional styles. These may include a distorted sense of what is and what is not the child's responsibility. In one study, for example, abusive mothers attributed a child's negative behaviors to internal and stable characteristics while also attributing the child's positive behaviors to external and unstable characteristics. In other words, these mothers believed that the children's negative behaviors were the children's fault and choice but viewed their children's positive behaviors as due to external factors that had nothing to do with the children's efforts or inherent positive characteristics. In addition, even when offered information that accurately challenges these false perceptions of responsibility, abusive parents tend to continue to hold to their misperceptions. In combination, these cognitive distortions may lead to parents' overall negative perceptions of their children. Such children are rarely able to live up to parental expectations, are blamed for negative behaviors, and are not given credit for positive behaviors—all of which may serve to justify abusive behavior in the eyes of their parents.

2. Child Factors

It should be noted at the outset of this section that children should not be held responsible for their own abuse. Physical abuse, by definition, involves inappropriate and deleterious actions against a child, and thus can be never deserved—regardless of the unacceptability of the child's behavior. However, there are certain factors or characteristics in children that may lead to increased stress for the parent and, as a result, increase the risk of abuse. Infants who are born prematurely or come into the world with medical challenges present a unique set of stressors for parents, and their difficulties may discourage optimal parent–child attachment. When an infant has a prolonged hospital stay following birth, the parent may not have the opportunity for immediate bonding—a problem that may decrease parental emotional connection to the infant and contribute to the infant's insecure attachment to the parent. Further, chronic health problems may lead to increased parental concerns, feelings of responsibility, disruptions in family routine, and an inability for the caretaking parent to work outside of the home, leading to financial difficulties. Children also are born with different temperaments. A child with a relatively calm temperament may allow for an easier bonding experience than, for example, a child who cries often, has feeding difficulties, is hypersensitive, and has emotion regulation problems. The latter child, by virtue of not activating as much (protective) parent–child attachment as the former is at greater risk for being physically abused.

3. Parent–Child Interactions

A number of factors can contribute to a poor attachment, bond, or fit between the parent and child, which in turn increases the risk for abuse. As stated previously, early separations during the postpartum period can contribute to a poor attachment between infant and parent. John Bowlby described two general types of attachment styles displayed by infants. The first type, a secure attachment, results from a nurturing, supportive, stable, and consistent response by the primary caregiver. An insecure attachment, on the other hand, results from early neglect, inconsistency, lack of affection or nurturance, and general maltreatment. Not surprisingly, abusive mothers have infants with insecure attachments far more often than do nonabusive mothers.

In addition to strained attachment, parent and child may also exhibit dysfunctional communication styles. On the whole, abusive parents have fewer interactions and communicate less with their children as compared to nonabusive parents. Abusive parents tend to have increased difficulty assessing their child's emotional state correctly. When they do interact with their children, these interactions tend to be negative. Their overall interactional and disciplinary style may be critical, hostile, and aggressive.

Due to the negative interactions of the parent toward the child, the child may learn that the only way to receive attention from the parent is to act in a coercive and negative manner. Since the parent is unable to acknowledge the child's positive behaviors or attributes them to outside factors, the child may use noncompliant and aggressive behaviors to engage with her or his parent. The dyad seems to interact in negative, provocative ways, which can then place the child at risk for physical abuse.

4. Societal Factors

Several societal or contextual factors may increase the likelihood of physical abuse. Poverty and its resultant effects on the family are significant risk factors for abuse. For example, economic strain, lack of transportation, inadequate housing, and unemployment can lead to increased parental stress, which can place a child at risk. In addition, as noted previously, abusive parents tend to be isolated from the larger community and the societal supports it can afford. Abusive parents may perceive their environment as hostile and unwelcoming, which leads to a general lack of effort in initiating and maintaining community support networks. This lack of social interface may not only further stress vulnerable parents, but can reduce the likelihood that abusive parenting practices will be witnessed by others and discouraged. [*See* POVERTY AND WOMEN IN THE UNITED STATES.]

Beyond the relative availability of social supports, society may influence the prevalence of physical abuse through culturally transmitted attitudes and beliefs. Notions such as "spare the rod and spoil the child" still pervade many sectors of North American society, suggesting that corporal punishment is a necessary aspect of child rearing. Several studies suggest, in fact, that adults who were physically disciplined, if not abused, in childhood tend to hold beliefs that the same sort of treatment should be imposed on their own children for "bad" behavior. Although this belief system does not directly support the notion of physical child abuse per se, authoritarian models of discipline are likely to translate into more abusive actions for at least some vulnerable parents.

C. SYMPTOMS ASSOCIATED WITH PHYSICAL ABUSE

The effects of physical abuse on children are thought to begin very early in the child's life. Various writers suggest that the infant who has been abused experiences a disruption and distortion in the developmental tasks of social relations, self-identity, and the establishment of a secure, stable, and trusting relationship with the primary caregiver. As a result, the infant may show elevated levels of anxiety and distress and may exhibit disruptions in his or her normal attachment style or pattern with caretakers and other adults.

During middle and late childhood, there are often gender differences in symptom expression. Overall, boys tend to act out their distress through outward expressions of anger, aggression, and general noncompliance. Girls on the other hand, tend to experience their distress more internally, through depressive or anxious symptomatology. In general, the children in this age group may experience repeated, intrusive memories of abusive episodes. They may engage in aggressive play or behaviors that reenact the abusive experience. It appears that children who have been physically abused, as compared to their nonabused peers, tend to interpret the social cues around them as indicative of danger. They may begin to view the world as a hostile place and may come to assume that they are doomed to be exploited and harmed by others. These perceptions can develop into more chronic feelings of helplessness,

hopelessness, and a preoccupation with the possibility of danger in the interpersonal environment.

During adolescence, males and females may express somewhat different sets of symptoms. Boys often display academic and disciplinary problems, early school dropout rates, substance abuse, and general externalizing or acting out behaviors. Girls may also experience these problems, but usually to a lesser extent. Instead, they may be more likely to express distress through running away, experience "internalized" symptoms such as depression, and, in some cases, engage in sexual behavior. With regard to the latter, the physically abused adolescent female may yearn for love and affection and seek gratification of these needs through premature sexual relationships.

Arthur Green described a cluster of symptoms that is found among physicallly abused children. Within this framework, children who are exposed to chronic physical and psychological assault may employ a number of defensive strategies. For example, abuse victims may attempt to avoid future abusive attacks by becoming hypervigilant within their environments. These children may display a frozen watchfulness in which they sit passively yet in a constant state of alertness so as to detect cues of danger. When children engage in constant hypervigilant activities, the opportunity for exposure to, or focus on, other more age appropriate interests is significantly decreased. This lack of opportunity can result in compromised learning. In this regard, a number of studies report a decrease in intellectual, language, and perceptual motor skills among child physical abuse victims.

Child victims also may deny that their parents are at fault and instead may displace responsibility onto others or onto themselves. This allows victimized children to maintain the belief that their parents are good, but also reinforces that the children are bad and deserving of the abuse. This belief system places the children in negative positions. If the children are to blame for the abuse, then it follows that if they were to improve in some way, the abuse would stop. Faced with the reality that abuse usually continues despite the children's efforts at compliance, the children often develop feelings of helplessness and despair.

Abused children may express the anger and rage associated with the experience of abuse through aggressive acts toward others. A number of studies report that aggression is particularly common among physically abused children. Such aggression may represent social learning, whereby children learn during the process of abuse that the appropriate resolution of angry feelings is to hurt others. In addition, some authorities believe that aggressive behavior in such contexts represents the child's efforts to recreate, master, and control the painful emotions that surface during abusive episodes. Unfortunately, whether by virtue of social learning or the desire to gain control, such violent behavior often leads to compromised relationships with other children and adults. In this regard, physically abused children are less likely to initiate peer interactions and are less well liked by their peers. This lack of meaningful interpersonal relationships can lead to alienation and isolation. These consequences further reinforce negative self-attributions and a sense of inherent badness and may motivate further aggression. [*See* AGGRESSION AND GENDER; ANGER.]

Other common symptoms also have been reported among child victims of physical abuse. For example, Richard Famularo and colleagues have found an increaced incidence of attention-deficit/hyperactivity disorder, oppositional defiant disorder, and posttraumatic stress disorder among child victims of physical abuse. Although posttramatic stress disorder will be presented in more detail later in this article, when sexual abuse symptoms are described, posttraumatic stress is also reported among children who have been physically abused. For example, children may experience intrusive thoughts or memories of the abusive episodes, demonstrate repetitive play that reflects abusive themes, display hypervigilance, become easily startled, experience difficulty concentrating, and display angry or aggressive behaviors.

There is surprisingly little information on the long-term effects of physical abuse, as opposed to the considerable amount written about children. In general, however, the adult impact literature parallels the child literature, especially stressing the potential for physical abuse to be associated with an increased likelihood of anxiety, depression, low self-esteem, posttraumatic stress, and aggression toward others. None of these effects necessarily occur in any given adult abused as a child, given the wide number of variables that can intervene between abuse as a child and the symptoms as an adult.

IV. *Sexual Abuse*

A. DEFINITIONS

Sexual abuse can be divided into two categories. The first category, sexual assault, includes acts imposed on a child by an adult or significantly older child, which may include fondling, masturbation in a child's presence, oral copulation, incest, rape, sodomy, or penetration of a genital or anal opening with a foreign object or a penis. The second category, sexual exploitation, includes conduct or activities related to pornography depicting children, promoting prostitution of children, or exposing a child to sexual acts or sexual material.

Legally, at least in North America, any sexual activity with a child by an adult is considered sexual abuse. This is because children are immature cognitively and are dependent on adults, and thus are deemed incapable of rendering true consent. Although some such acts occur through force or the threat of force, physical coercion is not required in legal or most research definitions. This issue becomes more complex in instances where the initiator of the sexual acts is also a child or adolescent. Such acts may or may not be abusive depending on a number of factors including differences between the two children in age, status, and size, as well as whether coercion or force was used, the developmental inappropriateness of the sexual behavior, and whether the child perceived the contact as wanted or unwanted.

Current studies suggest that sexual offending begins early (often in adolescence) and is far more prevalent among males than females. Contrary to popular belief, many offenders do not limit their victims to one "type" (e.g., according to sex, age, or relation to the offender). For example, research conducted by Gene Abel, Judith Becker, and colleagues indicates that incest offenders often have offended against children outside of their families as well as within, and have also, in 6 to 20% of cases, engaged in rape of an adult woman, exhibitionism, voyeurism, frottage, or sexual sadism.

B. CAUSES OF SEXUAL ABUSE

A number of researchers have examined why some adults sexually abuse children. Studies repeatedly indicate gender differences among offenders of sexual abuse. In general, women are much less likely than men to report sexual feelings toward children or to commit any type of sexual offense against them. David Finkelhor attributes this difference to ways in which males and females are socialized in North American culture. Men are socialized to be less able to distinguish between sexual and nonsexual forms of affection and to be attracted to partners who are smaller, younger, and less powerful than themselves.

Accordingly, Kathy Smiljanich and John Briere surveyed 180 male and 99 female university students regarding their sexual interest in children. Their results demonstrated a much higher level of sexual response to children among males than among females (22.2 versus 2.8%, respectively). This increased sexual interest and other differences between male and female socialization (e.g., training of males to seek dominance), in turn, is likely to contribute to the significantly greater amount of sexual abuse perpetrated by males as opposed to females.

In general, most studies identify significant sexual maladjustment and psychological dysfunction among incarcerated sex offenders. However, it is not always clear whether research on convicted sexual abusers generalizes well to those who have not been apprehended but, nevertheless, commit sexual offenses against children. It may be, for example, that those sexual abusers with greater psychopathology generally are less successful in their commission of crimes and thus are more likely to be caught and incarcerated. At minimum, current research suggests that there is no specific pattern of psychological symptoms or disorder that discriminates sexual abusers from other people.

Of the various theories for why some individuals sexually abuse children whereas others do not, David Finkelhor's Four-Factor model is perhaps best known. His first factor, *emotional congruence,* suggests that sexual abusers often have unmet emotional needs that are met through sexual interactions with children. In such cases, the abuser may be seeking a nonsexual, as well as sexual, relationship with the child. The second factor, *sexual arousal,* involves the degree of sexual attraction the offender has toward children. The third factor, *blockage,* includes phenomena that have interfered with the development of appropriate adult relationships by the offender. The fourth and final factor, *disinhibitions,* includes all phenomena that allow the offender to overcome social and internal inhibitions against child molestation. Each of the four factors has two levels, individual and sociocultural, that interact between characteristics of the offender and environmental influences, including the media and the general socialization practices highlighted earlier in this section.

Finkelhor's sexual arousal factor has been linked in some theories to the sexual abuse experiences found in the life histories of some child molesters. Overall, it appears that approximately 30% of (primarily male) child sexual abusers report having been sexually abused themselves as children, although some studies report significantly higher or lower rates. Because this percentage is at least twice the sexual abuse rate for males in the general population, a history of sexual abuse appears to be a risk factor for later sexually abusive behavior.[1] Such abuse may classically condition sexual feelings to the various stimuli asssociated with sexual abuse, leading to deviant sexual arousal to children once the victim matures to adulthood.

Finkelhor's disinhibition factor includes attitudes or beliefs offenders may have that allow them to engage in sexual acts against children without overwhelming guilt or other internal inhibitions. Several studies suggest that, like rapists of adult women, sexual child abusers often may engage in thought patterns that normalize sex with children as acceptable under certain circumstances, justify it in terms of children's supposed desires for sex and their supposed seductive or "provocative" behavior, and may deny or minimize the negative effects on children of sexual victimization. Such attitudes sometimes occur in the context of adult–child sexual fantasies and may involve the use of pornography, child-specific or otherwise. It is unlikely, however, that holding attitudes or beliefs about the acceptability of sex with children is sufficient to produce sexually abusive behaviors in most people. Instead, it is likely that abuse-supportive attitudes interact with other psychological, social, historical, and perhaps, in some cases, even neurobiological variables to produce actual sexual acts against children.

C. THE GROOMING PROCESS

Unlike physical abusers, many sexual abuse perpetrators engage in behaviors to entice children into intimate contact with them, and may utilize various techniques to accommodate their victims to the idea of being sexually used. In some cases, this process may result in prematurely sexualized children who appear to voluntarily accept sexual contact from adults.

In this regard, Jon Conte and his colleagues interviewed 20 adult sexual offenders (gender unspecified) who were making successful progress in treatment. The interview focused on how the offenders selected, recruited, and maintained children in sexually abusive situations. The offenders were found to fre-

---

[1]It should be emphasized, however, that most sexually abused children do not go on to molest as adults, and many sexually abusive adults do not appear to have been sexually abused as children.

quently engage in a "grooming" process wherein they establish relationships with children and set them up for victimization. This process usually begins with a period of engaging children in pleasant, need-satisfying relationships. The offenders often choose children who they perceive as emotionally needy, who have poor histories of attachment, poor relationships with peers, and live in abusive home environments. These childen typically are vulnerable to persuasion through attention, gifts, and compliments offered by an adult who seems truly concerned and trustworthy. The offender then engages in nonsexual types of touching which the children may find pleasurable or nurturing. Eventually, within this seemingly positive and supportive relationship, the offenders begin to engage in sexual touching.

As described by Conte and his colleagues, when children seem interested in an interaction with the offenders, the offenders will often touch children on the arms, legs, or offer a hug. As time progresses, offenders begin to engage in progressively more extreme and direct sexual touching and devote considerable time and attention to convincing the children that any positive sexual or emotional feelings they might have are evidence of the validity of the relationship. Over time, the children may begin to believe that they are actively choosing the interaction and, as a result, may hesitate to disclose the abuse. As will be described in subsequent sections, child abuse victims often develop cognitive distortions in regards to blame and responsibility for the abuse. Such self-blame and guilt may be especially prevalent in instances where grooming has occurred.

It should be noted that grooming is usually used by offenders in cases where they desire ongoing sexual access to children and where they wish to see the abuse as a voluntary, even romantic act. Other sexual offenders may use little or no grooming, either when the abuse involves a single episode or when the child's pseudo-participation is not important to the offender. These individuals may use force, aggression, and threats to frighten and overwhelm the child.

D. EFFECTS OF SEXUAL ABUSE

Contrary to earlier thinking in the field, one characteristic symptom or syndrome does not exist for sexual abuse victims. Instead, some children may appear asymptomatic while others may be quite distressed and exhibit significant symptomatology. Recent studies suggest that approximately 10 to 28% of child victims show no observable symptoms following sexual abuse. Similarly, although many adults who were abused as children present with significant symptomatology, others seem to be far less affected. As described later in this article, this apparent lack of symptomatology is probably due to a variety of factors, including the child's psychological and temperamental resiliency, level of family support, and the severity of the abuse experience. In addition, some children may not experience significant symptoms immediately following sexual abuse, but may develop significant problems later on in childhood. Beverly Gomes-Schwartz and her colleagues, for example, found that children who appeared to be asymptomatic soon after the abuse were most likely to worsen by the time of an 18-month followup; in fact, 30% of these formerly asymptomatic children developed significant symptoms when reevaluated. Finally, it is likely that some sexual abuse effects or symptoms are missed or misdiagnosed by clinicians and that the psychological tests used to detect abuse-related symptoms in some studies are not sufficiently sensitive to uncover all significant abuse effects.

Beyond those for whom no obvious effects of sexual victimization are apparent, a number of studies demonstrate that, on average, childhood sexual abuse is associated with a wide variety of psychological symptoms and disorders, both initiallly and later in life. The most important of these will be described briefly here in the context of six categories: negative mood, cognitive distortions, post-traumatic symptomatology, sexual disturbance, relationship disturbance, dissociation, and somatization. It is important to note, however, that each of these symptoms and disorders also can arise from other forms of child maltreatment and from other, non-abuse-related, factors. This, in no instance should the presence of a specific symptom or diagnosis be considered to be proof of sexual abuse per se.

Negative mood states, specifically depression, anxiety, and anger, are among the most common phenomena associated with childhood sexual abuse experiences. Such emotional distress may present as a symptom or as a full-blown psychiatric disorder. Cheryl Lanktree and her colleagues, for example, found that sexually abused children in an outpatient psychiatry clinic were more than four times as likely to have received a diagnosis of major depression than similar clinic patients who did not have a sexual abuse history. Depressed children or adults, in turn, may be at risk for suicide or other self-destructive behavior. In a similar vein, studies suggest that, as compared to their nonabused counterparts, sexually abused children may have as much as five times the likelihood of being diagnosed with at least one anxiety disorder. Some sexual abuse victims may also complain of chronic feelings of anger and irritability, in some cases resulting in problematic behavior such as bullying, fighting, or attacking other children.

Cognitive distortions, involving low self-esteem, self-blame, guilt, shame, and distrust of others, are commonly documented among abused children and adults with child abuse histories, including those who have undergone sexual abuse in particular. Child victims of sexual abuse often experience what Finkelhor and his colleague Angela Browne refer to as *stigmatization,* which can lead to children having negative thoughts about their value and entitlements. For example, blaming or degrading comments made by offenders during or after abuse may lead children to feel that they are deserving of what has happened to them. In addition, other individuals in the immediate and larger community may communicate blame by asking questions regarding why a child did not protest or why she or he did not disclose the abuse sooner, for example.

Posttraumatic stress disorder (PTSD) has been associated with childhood sexual abuse in a number of studies. The primary symptoms of abuse-related PTSD in children include nightmares; sudden intrusive sensory memories of the abuse; emotional distress upon being reminded of the abuse; repetitive play that involves themes or memories of the abuse; avoidance of thoughts, feelings, and activities that otherwise might remind the child of his or her victimization; sleep disturbance; irritable mood; attention and concentration problems; and hypervigilance to the possibility of being abused again. Some studies suggest that up to 80% of sexually abused children in clinical samples have at least some PTSD symptoms, although the majority typically do not meet full criteria for the disorder. Similar findings have been described for adult survivors of childhood sexual abuse. [*See* Posttraumatic Stress Disorder.]

One of the most common symptoms reported in studies of sexually abused children is the presence of sexual behavior problems, including sexual preoccupation, excessive or developmentally premature sexual behavior, the intrusion of sexual themes and behaviors during play, and sexual fears and phobias. William Fredrich and others, for example, have shown that, as compared to non-sexually-abused children, children who have been sexually abused tend to display more sexual behavior and engage in behaviors that imitate adult sexual acts. Such activities may reflect the premature sexualization of abused children, such that they become prematurely aware of (and responsive to) sexual thoughts and feelings, as well as the results of modeling of sexual behavior engaged in by sexual abusers. In addition, sexually abused children may come to assume that their sexuality is the most interesting or attractive thing about them, and thus may engage in sexual behaviors as ways to receive attention, acceptance, or affection. In a minority of cases, sexually abused children may initiate sexual acts against other children. The sexual problems of sexually abused children may continue to develop into adulthood, leading to excessive or indiscriminate sexual behavior, increased vulnerability to further sexual victimization, and, in some cases, an increased likelihood of sexual aggression against others.

Sexual abuse victims, like victims of other types of child abuse, have been shown to exhibit more problems in interpersonal relationships. Sexually abused children tend to be less socially competent as compared to their nonabused peers and to be ambivalent or avoidant in interpersonal contexts. Child victims tend to perceive themselves as different from others and as in some way damaged, leading to withdrawal from the social milieu. Once children disclose abuse to other children, their peers may react in confused or rejecting ways, which can further reinforce a poor sense of self and withdrawal from social situations. As the children develop into adolescence and adulthood, there may be continuing difficulties with intimacy, trust, and the ability to maintain ongoing romantic or friendship relationships. [*See* Self-Esteem.]

Dissociation is another relatively common symptom among sexually abused children. This symptom pattern may be evidenced by incomplete memory for an abusive episode, a tendency to seem "in a fog" or to be "walking around in a dream world," problems with attention due to daydreaming or reduced responsiveness to the social environment, and a generalized numbing of feelings associated with both negative and positive events. Children may also report the experience of having floated above their body, thereby watching the abusive episode from another perspective (depersonalization), or feeling as though they, people around them, or the environment does not seem real (derealization). Adults with histories of childhood sexual abuse are similarly prone to dissociative symptoms, as well as more complex dissociative disorders.

Finally, children may express somatic or physical symptoms following sexual abuse that are based in psychological reactions to the abuse. These symptoms can include headaches, stomachaches, nausea, shortness of breath, chronic muscle tension, and elevated blood pressure, as well as (especially later in life) diffuse complaints of bodily dysfunction without obvious physical or medical bases.

V. Variables That Affect the Injuriousness of Child Abuse

A number of variables appear to affect the extent to which abuse results in negative psychological effects. These include age at the time of the abuse, history of a good attachment with caregivers, level of psychological functioning prior to the abuse, a history of previous trauma or abuse experiences, whether the abuse took place within the family (i.e., was perpetrated by a family member) or outside of it, and the general level of family functioning prior to and after the abuse, including how supportive any nonoffending caregivers were of the victim in general and after any abuse disclosure in specific.

The issue of parent–child attachment before and after abuse is considered of great importance in determiniing whether children will emerge from the experiences with greater or lesser psychological injury. In the optimal situation, well-loved children develop strong positive attachments to their caregivers in the first several years of life, during which time they internalize positive perceptions and expectations of self and others and begin to form an identity as separate from others. Such a positive, secure attachment may be a significant protective factor: children with strong, consistent, and secure attachments to their primary caregivers typically will fare better after child abuse than will children with histories of insecure attachment.

Attachment issues may also arise *from* abuse, in addition to moderating its effects. Children abused early in life by caregivers often form poor, inconsistent, and insecure attachments to said caregivers by virtue of the neglect, rejection, and sometimes aggression they experience in abusive contexts. As a result, abuse effects may be magnified by a concomitant insecure attachment and associated psychological disturbance.

The general level of positive family functioning and supportiveness after children disclose abuse has also been found to affect adjustment. Positive parental response to disclosure and continued emotional support is associated with fewer psychological symptoms as compared to a parental response characterized by disbelief or punitive action.

Other mediating factors of abuse effects include specific aspects of the abuse episode itself, especially in the case of sexual abuse. For instance, sexual abuse may have more negative effects if the perpetrator was a trusted adult (especially a parent), if there were a number of sexual acts that occurred over an extended period of time, if force or violence was present, if there were multiple perpetrators, and if the sexual abuse included oral, anal, or vaginal penetration.

Children's sense of personal responsibility for the abuse and how they interpret the abuse experiences themselves have been cited as significant mediators of abuse effects. For example, if children experience significant feelings of self-blame, powerlessness, betrayal, or stigma during or following abusive episodes, they may be at higher risk of developing symptomatology.

Finally, it is likely that genetic and biological variables have an impact on the outcomes associated with child abuse, such as children's overall temperament and resilience in the face of stress. In this regard, some children may be less vulnerable to child abuse effects than others because their nervous systems respond less powerfully to abuse experiences than do other children.

VI. Treatment of Child Abuse

Given the wide variety of symptoms seen in some victims of child abuse, there is generally no single treatment strategy or program that is effective for all. Instead, certain symptoms (e.g., of PTSD) may respond well to cognitive-behavioral therapy, whereas others (e.g., relationship problems) may be best treated from a more psychodynamic or interpersonal therapy perspective. Some writers suggest that the quality of the relationship between the child and his or her therapist may be as important as the specific techniques or approaches employed.

Abuse-specific therapy often includes cognitive-behavioral techniques for symptoms of posttraumatic stress, but also may utilize a variety of other interventions such as psychodynamic therapy, play therapy, family therapy, and group therapy. Psychiatric medication is occasionally used if depression or posttraumatic symptoms are especially severe, or to treat copresent conditions such as attention deficit disorder.

Typically, treatment of children who have symptoms associated with child abuse involves several components. Most importantly, the therapist must establish trust and rapport with the child, and provide a safe environment in which treatment can occur. The child is usually asked to recall and talk (or engage in directed play) about the abuse, as well as express feelings associated with it. This emotional processing of the trauma typically continues until recollections of the abuse no longer produce significant distress. The therapist also works to clarify erroneous beliefs the child may have about herself or himself or about the abuse. This component especially focuses on children's feelings of having caused or deserved abuse, as well as their general sense of self as bad or unworthy and the environment as intrinsically dangerous. Finally, most abuse-specific treatment approaches teach safety skills regarding future abuse. Children are not expected to control the initiation of abuse or to fight off an offender, however, they are usually taught strategies that reduce risk, call for help, and encourage speedy disclosure.

Parent interventions also are an important part of the child's treatment. In the case of physical abuse, the focus is often on teaching parents positive, nonviolent disciplinary techniques. As noted earlier, physically abusive parents often hold unrealistic expectation of their children and blame negative behaviors on the child's internal character, leading to "punishment" (physical abuse) for these assumed failings. Typically, therapy aids parents in forming age-appropriate expectations of their children and in making correct attributions for their behavior. In addition, primary caregivers may receive collateral, individual, or group therapy to address issues as disparate as anger management, substance abuse, depression, and the development of an appropriate support network.

Interventions also are frequently provided to the nonoffending caregiver of sexually abused children and adolescents. The goal of caregiver treatment include an improvement in overall parenting skills, greater danger awareness and risk assessment skills vis-à-vis potential spouses or partners, education regarding sexual abuse and its efffects, and generally implementing positive change (e.g., role clarification) within the family system. As well, some parents may need assistance in overcoming any abuse-related difficulties that may otherwise interfere in their parenting.

Treating sex offenders is usually seen as a separate issue from treating children, in relative contradistinction to physical abuse. This is because the extremity and social unacceptability of the act, legal penalties, and the significant likelihood of additional, new offenses typically preclude the sexual abusers from having much further contact with their victims. A variety of treatment approaches have been developed for adults who sexually abuse children. These include biological treatment (i.e., reducing sex hormone levels or treating psychological disorders, usually via medication), group therapy, family therapy, individual psychodynamic therapy, cognitive-behavioral therapy (CBT), and relapse prevention. Outcome studies generally suggest that CBT and relapse prevention approaches are most helpful, although the majority of successful treatment programs use a variety of different therapeutic techniques. However, even the most successful of programs rarely, if ever, prevent reoffending for all of those they treat. [*See* COUNSELING AND PSYCHOTHERAPY; FEMINIST FAMILY THERAPY.]

VII. Child Abuse Prevention

Treatment of child abuse victims, although of extreme importance, occurs after the fact. By the time abused children have seen a clinician, they have already undergone frightening and often painful traumatic experiences and have suffered whatever negative effects ensued for some period of time. The most efficient and humanitarian approach to child abuse, therefore, is to prevent its occurrence in the first place. For this reason, child abuse prevention programs can be found in many school systems and governmental institutions, and abuse prevention messages are often presented in radio, television, and billboard media. At the same time, however, such programs have yet to be implemented at the level required to substantially reduce child maltreatment in North American society. This is unfortunate, because it is prevention, not treatment alone, that offers the most hope for ending the widespread victimization of children.

VIII. Conclusions

Although childhood physical and sexual abuse is relatively common in North American society and can be associated with short- and long-term psychological effects, modern treatment approaches often are very helpful in resolving abuse-related distress and disorders. The scope and impacts of child maltreatment in North American culture strongly supports the need to intervene in this serious social problem, both in terms of identifying and treating abused children and, even more important, in the development of effective child abuse education and prevention programs.

SUGGESTED READING

Abel, G., Becker, J., Cunningham-Rathner, J., Mittleman, M., and Rouleau, J. L. (1988). Multiple paraphiliac diagnoses among sex offenders. *Bulletin of the American Academy of Psychiatry and the Law* **16**, 153–168.

Briere, J., Berliner, L., Bulkley, J. A., Jenny, C., and Reid, T. (eds.) (1996). *The APSAC Handbook on Child Maltreatment.* Sage, Thousand Oaks, CA.

Briere, J., and Elliott, D. M. (1994). Immediate and long-term impacts of child sexual abuse. *The Future of Children: Sexual Abuse of Children* **4**(2), 54–69.

Finkelhor, D. (1994). Current information on the scope and nature of child sexual abuse. *The Future of Children: Sexual Abuse of Children 4(2), 31–53.*

Friedrich, W. N. (1990). *Psychotherapy of Sexually Abused Children and Their Families.* Norton, New York.

Kolko, D. J. (1992). Characteristics of child victims of physical violence: Research findings and clinical implications. *Journal of Interpersonal Violence* **7**(2), 244–276.

McLeer, S. V., Deblinger. E. B., Henry, D., and Orvaschel, H. (1992). Sexually abused children at high risk for post-traumatic stress disorder. *Journal of the American Academy of Child and Adolescent Psychiatry* **31**, 875–879.

Child Care
Options and Outcomes

Marsha Weinraub

Candace Hill

Kathy Hirsh-Pasek

Temple University

Glossary

Day care Care for infants and children provided on a regular basis by someone other than the child's mother, father, or siblings.

Family day care Care provided by an unrelated adult in the provider's home.

In-home care Care provided by non-relatives in the child's home, e.g. a nanny.

Organized facility care Care provided by nursery schools, day care centers and programs such as Head Start.

Relative care Care provided by someone related to the child in or out of the child's home.

THE CHANGING FACE OF CHILD CARE in the United States today is examined in this article. We review what is known about the effects of child care on children's development. We describe some of the significant changes in maternal employment that have occurred over the past 25 years that have changed the face of child care in the United States, and we examine why child care is often perceived as a women's issue. Next, we briefly review the history of child care, offering a historical perspective on today's child care concerns. Then, we specifically address three questions. First, what are the current patterns of child care use in the United States? Specifically, what types of child care do American families rely on, what does each type of child care cost, and are there individual differences in the families that use each type of care? Second, what is "quality" child care, and is quality child care equally distributed across U.S. families? Third, what do we know about the effects of child care usage on three particular child developmental outcomes: the child's attachment to parents, the child's ability to get along with others, and the child's cognitive and language development? The discussion in this article is limited to child care in the United States and relies heavily on reviews of child care by Michael Lamb in 1998 and the report by the National Research Council and Institute of Medicine in 2000.

I. Recent Changes in Maternal Employment That Have Affected Child Care Today

Over the past 25 years, dramatic changes have taken place in women's employment in the United States. In 1975, 39% of mothers with children under six years of age were in the labor force. By 1999, that percentage had increased to 61%. The percentage of mothers working full-time and year round nearly tripled from 11 to 30%. More significant have been the changes with regard to mothers of infants. In 1977, 24% of mothers with children under one year of age were active in the labor force. By 1999, this percentage had doubled, with 54% of mothers in the labor force.

These numbers tell the story of what has become one of the most important issues facing families today. Enormous shifts in women's employment go hand in hand with a growing need for adequate child care. For the first time in the U.S. history, more than half of all children under the age of six regularly spend some time each week in some form of formal, nonmaternal care.

II. Child Care as a Women's Issue

The link between increased maternal employment and changing patterns of child care is largely responsible for the perception of child care as a women's issue. These changes in maternal employment have resulted from at least four different, but related, factors. First, the feminist movement of the 1960s and 1970s reflected the growing expectation that women can and should work for pay outside the home, and changes in the workplace have made it easier for women to obtain and keep satisfying jobs. Second, there are more single women who are heads of households than ever before, and their families depend on their earnings. Third, changing economic conditions have led families to feel that two incomes are necessary to support a family in today's world.

Fourth and finally, recent changes in federal welfare legislation have required mothers of very young children who receive public assistance to enter the labor force in record numbers. These changes in maternal employment have necessitated dramatic developments in child care.

Although fathers are more involved in day-to-day care now than they were in past generations, their increased participation does not compensate for the decrease in care provided by employed mothers. Even with continued assistance from older children, other relatives, and neighbors, families are forced to increasingly rely on paid care by nonrelatives. This care comes in many forms, from care in neighbors' homes to care in day care centers. The number of children requiring long hours of nonmaternal care has risen along with the increases in maternal employment. A growing reliance on nonmaternal care focuses new attention on child care in the United States, both in terms of the options available to families and in terms of the effects that this care will have on the nation's children.

While child care is a family issue, one that has implications for the roles of men and women equally, traditionally child care has been viewed as a women's issue. Child care is considered a women's issue because of the female's link to the child through conception and gestation, birth, and breast-feeding. Biological links forge cultural associations. In societies across the world, child care is viewed as a critical component of the feminine role. Cross-culturally, physical care of the young child is viewed as a women's role, whereas the provision of food for the family is seen as a male role. In her 1949 book, *Male and Female: A Study of the Sexes in a Changing World*, Margaret Mead noted that this gender role distinction is so deeply rooted "that only fairly complicated social arrangements can break it down entirely" (p. 197).

Because of this close mother–child biological relationship, societies are very hesitant to interrupt the mother's intimate relationship to the child in the first years of life. Indeed, within the United States, the closeness between mother and child was considered legally sacrosanct in the twentieth century until federal legislation (the Personal Responsibility and Work Opportunity Reconciliation Act [PRWORA]) was enacted in 1996. This legislation overturned 60 years of welfare legislation in the United States that prohibited states from requiring single parents caring for infants to engage in work-related activities. Today, 14 states require that parents return to the workplace when their welfare time limits have expired, even if their youngest child is less than one year old. This legislation, and the growing awareness that extensive child care initiated early in children's lives may have lasting effects on children and families, may be helping to move child care from a "women's issue" to a national issue, with implications for men as well as women.

III. *Child Care in the United States: A Historical Perspective*

In a variety of countries, particularly those with socialist governments in power, child care is assumed to be the responsibility of everyone, and child care programs have been organized by the community or the government. However, in the United States, child care has historically been considered the responsibility of the individual or the individual family unit. In her 1989 book, *Past Caring*, Emily Cahan chronicled child care in the United States, tracing the evolution of a *two-tiered system* that has developed uniquely in the United States. One tier of child care was a custodial system designed to provide care for lower-class children. The sole purpose of this type of care was to provide a safe and clean place to care for children during the days, or *day care*, while their parents, mothers in particular, worked outside the home. The second tier of child care in the United States catered to the interests of middle- and higher-class families and included child care in the form of nursery schools and kindergartens. Unlike the day nurseries that evolved in the first tier, the second tier of child care was created to provide additional education and socialization to children of more affluent families. Eager to benefit from new ideas about pedagogy and educational theory, families hoped that the educational and socialization activities available to children in nurseries and kindergartens would enrich their children's growth and help them become better prepared for entry to formal education.

The first tier of child care, the tier designed to provide custodial care for immigrants and lower-class families, had a cyclical history in the United States. Day care expanded to meet national crises of employment and wartime and receded at other times. When the urbanization and the Industrial Revolution of the 19th century required an expanding labor force, impoverished and immigrant mothers were exempted from the traditional requirements that

mothers raise their own children in their own homes. Day nurseries arose to meet the custodial care needs of poor and working-class families. Given the social climate, day nurseries were not publicly supported, and they fell under the responsibility of the charitable welfare system, with occasional support from social reformers eager to help disadvantaged children. The lack of funding for a centralized system resulted in poor quality child care, and this poor quality care continues to the present.

According to the 1993 book *Daycare*, by Alison Clarke-Stewart, the first U.S. day nursery was founded by Mrs. Joseph Hale and opened in Boston in 1838 to serve the needs of widows and seamen's working wives. These women, functioning as single parents, were required to work to support their families, and thus, the demand for child care emerged. In the decades to come, several more day nurseries were established for similar reasons in other cities such as New York and Philadelphia. Eventually in 1898, the National Federation of Day Nurseries was founded in response to the 175 nurseries operating in many different areas of the country. However, in the decades to follow, child care lost popular support and the number of day nurseries declined, leaving the struggle for child care once again a problem for individual families. This was the first of many recurring cycles to come for day care in the 20th century.

The national labor crises stimulated interest in day care, and public funding was provided to set up day nurseries. To counteract the effects of the Great Depression, for example, President Roosevelt initiated the Federal Recovery Act and the Works Project Administration (WPA) in 1933. Funding was given to day nurseries to supply jobs for out-of-work nurses and teachers. Emphasis was placed on programs for preschool-aged children, and nurseries were typically set up in conjunction with already established schools. By 1937, 1900 day nurseries serving more than 40,000 children were in existence. However, when the WPA was dismantled in 1939, the number of day nurseries once again decreased dramatically.

When women were needed for the war effort, child care was again on the upswing. During World War II, societal prejudice against working mothers was replaced with nationalism. *Rosie the Riveter* was needed in the factories, and women all over the United States were needed to staff hospitals, retail stores, and offices while men were away at war. To enable women and mothers to work, more day nurseries were required. In 1942, the federal government provided funding through the Lanham Act, and by 1945, 1½ million children were enrolled in day care. But once again, day care history repeated itself. As the war effort receded and the Lanham Act ended in 1946, national support for child care also receded. By 1950, day nurseries served only 18,000 children.

In contrast to the intermittent support that the first tier of the day care system experienced, support for the second tier of the day care system grew slowly but steadily. Because of the reliance on private funding, growth in the second tier was smaller and more gradual. In 1915, at the University of Chicago, wives of some of the male faculty members organized the country's first nursery schoool. For this school, and others like it to come, the goal was to provide an enrichment program for children before they entered formal schooling. Children entering these programs were generally between four and five years old, safely beyond what was considered the tender ages of childhood. These nursery schools became more and more popular as a supplement to the home educational experiences enjoyed by middle- and upper-class children.

Eventually, these two tiers of child care were united, at least philosophically. Support for lower-class, working mothers and educational enrichment for children in middle- and upper-class families offered two seperate goals that eventually converged in President Lyndon Johnson's War on Poverty. In the 1960's, educators began to view child care as an exciting way to enrich the lives of impoverished children—as a way to provide poor children with an intellectual "head start." Project Head Start, directed by Yale University psychologist Edward Zigler, was a massive investment of federal dollars and energies designed to improve the intellectual abilities of "disadvantaged" children.

While Head Start was a monumental, large-scale commitment to early education for disadvantaged children in the United States, it would take years for child care to surface as a major issue in national politics. Children of working-class parents were not considered at risk intellectually, and so they were not qualified for the model educational programs that characterized Head Start. Head Start was not designed to support the needs of working parents, if only because the hours of operation made it impossible for mothers to hold down full-time jobs.

Demands for child care did not enter the national dialogue until middle-class women entered the workplace in large numbers demanding full-time, high-quality care. These demands were further augmented in 1996 when new federal legislation required poor mothers to be employed, because they too needed full-time care for their children. Today, at the beginning of the 21st century, more than half of women with young children are in the workforce, and their children require nonmaternal child care on a regular basis. Increasingly, day care for mothers employed outside the home is incorporating many of the early educational goals previously reserved for supplemental nursery schools. How do families use child care, what options do families have, and what are the factors that affect the choices parents make for their children? [*See* FAMILY ROLES AND PATTERNS, CONTEMPORARY TRENDS; PARENTING; WORK–FAMILY BALANCE.]

IV. *Current Patterns of Child Care Use in the United States*

According to the U.S. Census Report of October 2000, most U.S. families are not deciding whether or not to use nonmaternal care. Rather, they are deciding what type(s) of care to use and at what age to enroll their child in care. In making these decisions, families have several options from which to choose. These options can be categorized as *relative care, in-home care, family day care,* and care by an *organized facility.* In 1995, about half of all children under the age of five were in relative care, with the majority in the care of their grandparents (30%). Approximately 49% of children were cared for by nonrelated adults, 30% of whom were enrolled in some kind of an organized facility. Many children were enrolled in multiple types of care for different times of the week.

Given the large number of options, how do parents decide which type of care to choose for their children? Several factors play a role in this decision-making process, including the demographic characteristics of the family, geographic location and access to child care, and the families' views of what is appropriate for their children. Table I shows the percentage of children in each type of care based on the family's marital status, race and ethnicity, educational level of the parents, and family income, using data the U.S. Census Bureau collected in 1995 and made available in the year 2000. This table shows that, not surprisingly, children living in two-parent

Table I

Children under Five Years Receiving Care by Selected Arrangements and Family Characteristics, Fall 1995 (number in thousands)

Characteristics of parent/family	Number of children	Percent in selected arrangement							Percent in multiple care
		Relative care				Nonrelative care			
		Total[a]	Designated parent	Other parent	Grandparent	Total	Organized facility	Other non-relative	
Children under 5 years	19,281	50.1	4.9	18.2	30.0	48.5	29.9	28.8	44.0
Marital status									
Married	13,722	48.7	5.3	20.7	27.6	49.1	29.3	29.9	42.4
Separated, divorced, widowed	1,956	50.7	3.5	11.2	29.3	58.7	39.1	34.0	54.9
Never married	3,554	54.9	4.0	12.6	39.5	40.4	26.9	21.7	44.1
Race and Hispanic origin									
Non-Hispanic White	12,998	51.9	5.6	20.7	32.2	51.5	30.2	32.1	46.1
Non-Hispanic Black	2,632	47.9	3.0	11.5	27.9	49.9	34.9	27.6	49.2
Non-Hispanic other races	835	52.9	8.1	19.6	31.8	45.6	30.8	25.6	48.0
Hispanic (of any race)	2,816	43.0	2.6	12.7	21.1	33.9	23.3	15.7	28.4
Educational level									
High school or less	9,752	48.0	4.0	13.3	30.0	37.9	25.2	20.9	36.3
College, 1 or more years	9,529	52.3	5.8	23.3	30.0	59.3	34.6	37.0	51.9
Poverty status[b]									
In poverty	4,332	40.8	2.8	9.4	25.0	32.4	23.4	15.2	31.2
Not in poverty	14,748	52.9	5.5	21.0	31.3	53.5	32.1	32.9	48.0

[a]Total includes care by siblings and other relatives not shown separately in this table.

[b]Excludes those with missing income data.

Note: Because of multiple arrangements, the total numbers and percentages may exceed the total number of children.

Source: U.S. Census Bureau, 2000.

households are more likely to be cared for by a parent than children living with a single parent (21% versus 12%). Hispanic parents are more likely to put their children in the care of relatives than nonrelatives (43% versus 34%). The educational level of parents also affects the choice of care. Parents with at least some college are more likely to entrust their children to unrelated caregivers than parents holding a high school diploma. Perhaps this is because parents with a higher education value the fact that caregivers in center care arrangements often have more formal education and more experience; perhaps this also reflects the greater ability of more educated parents to afford this kind of more expensive care.

Finally, families living in poverty use relative care more extensively than they use care by nonrelatives (41% versus 32%). In contrast, families living above the poverty level are more evenly distributed in their use of relative and nonrelative care. This may be due to the high cost of child care in general and of center care in particular, and poor families simply may not be able to afford care provided by nonrelatives as often as other families. The percentage of family income spent on child care by poor families (35%) is five times more than the percentage of income spent by nonpoor families. In 1997, the researchers on the National Institute of Child Health and Human Development (NICHD) Study of Early Child Care found that income and quality child care have a curvilinear relationship to one another. Of those families using child care centers, those slightly above the poverty line receive poorer quality care than those who live in poverty or those who are in the middle- to upper-income ranges. Government subsidies may play a large role in elevating the quality of care provided for the poorest families. [*See* POVERTY.]

Beyond the more standard social addresses of race, ethnicity, and family income, the child's age also plays a large factor in determining what kind of care parents will select. Fifty percent of children three and four years old are cared for in an organized facility while their parents are working or in school, while only 19% of children less than one year old are similarly enrolled in an organized facility. Because the overwhelming majority of mothers who are employed during their infant's first year return to work and place their child in some kind of routine nonmaternal care arrangement before the child is six months of age, most infants are cared for by relatives, by nonrelatives in their own homes, or by nonrelated caregivers in their own homes. Whether this pattern reflects parental preferences for homelike care for infants, the high costs of formal infant care, or the limited availability of organized, formal care for infants is not fully understood. Possibly, parental decisions regarding early infant care may also be affected by factors such as access to parental leave, the ability to take a loss of income for a period of time, new work requirements for welfare recipients, availability of subsidies, the availability of particular kinds of child care arrangements, and parents' beliefs concerning the costs and benefits of nonmaternal care.

What becomes clear from examination of the usage patterns in the United States is that public policy regarding child care must be sensitive to the heterogeneity of the population. There are no single or easy solutions to problems relating to increased needs for child care. This point is highlighted by the fact that 44% of children under the age of 5 and 75% of children between the ages of 5 and 14 were in two or more different child care arrangements during a typical week in 1995. Twenty-eight percent of families combine organized facility care and other nonrelative care during the parents' work or school hours. Families juggle multiple arrangements to compensate for the limited child care available for infants and toddlers, for mildly sick children, for children whose parents work nonstandard hours, and for disabled children. The publicly available, formally organized child care that does exist is geared primarily to normal children aged three years and older, with many programs for preschool and after-school care often organized in public schools. Surveys of parents often reveal that parents want their children to be in a safe, homelike setting where their children get caring, one-on-one attention, and they fear that center care cannot deliver the quality of care that they desire for their children.

Thus, it is important to examine the quality of the care that is available. What is quality care? How is quality measured in child care? How much quality care is available today to U.S. families? Is this quality child care equally distributed across U.S. families?

V. Quality of Child Care in the United States

Parents making decisions about care arrangements, researchers measuring child outcomes, and policy makers implementing child care policy all want to understand the effects of quality child care. Before that can be assessed, however, one must define quality care or at least find some way to know quality when it is seen. On the surface, there is widespread agreement on the definition of quality care. In her 1998 article in *American Psychologist,* Sandra Scarr defines high quality care as "warm, supportive interactions with adults in a safe, healthy and stimulating environment where early education and trusting relationships combine to support individual children's physical, emotional, social, and intellectual development" (p. 102).

To assess these characteristics of care, however, researchers had to find some quantifiable measure of care, and this has been a most thorny issue within the field of child development and early education. Generally, the quality of care is measured along two dimensions, structural and procedural.

A. STRUCTURAL MEASURES OF QUALITY CARE

Structural parameters of care are thought to mediate quality by ensuring adequate staff-to-child ratios, group sizes that are developmentally appropriate, and appropriate levels of care provider training and experience. Staff stability and the turnover rate and the adequacy of the physical facilities in relation to the group size are also sometimes included as structural properties of care. It is widely assumed that these more easily observable characteristics of care are important in ensuring that children have appropriate supervision, stimulation, and responsiveness by those entrusted with their well-being. For these reasons, and because the structural parameters of care are easily measured, these structural characteristics are often regulated by the government for both organized center care facilities and for larger family day care operations. Most studies of child care have used structural parameters as a metric for the quality of care. High-quality care, then, would be defined as that found in environments with high staff-to-child ratios, low group sizes, and teachers with a high degree of formal training and education. Thus, quality can be monitored on structural dimensions of care, such as staff–child ratios, group size, and caregiver education through governmental policy and state regulations. State guidelines vary considerably, and this can have great impact on the quality of care families will have access to in their area and the costs that will be associated with this care.

Structural measures of quality care are clearly correlated with optimal developmental outcomes for children. A recent paper published in 1999 by the NICHD Study of Early Child Care underscores this position. The NICHD researchers focused on the regulable features of quality care—the structural indicators—and asked whether developmental outcomes varied as a consequence of whether centers met or did not meet suggested guidelines. The number of standards met did not seem to make a large difference for two year olds, but it did for three year olds. In the latter, the higher the number of standards met, the better the children scored on measures of school readiness, language comprehension, and behavior problems in classes that met the standards for caregiver training and higher education. Developmental outcomes at 36 months of age also reflected fewer behavior problems and more positive social behaviors for children when their classes met the guidelines for child–staff ratio.

In evaluating care settings for infants, NICHD researchers report that home-like settings often do offer better quality care. Five hundred and seventy-six infants were observed at 6 months of age in five types of child care. These settings included care provided by fathers, grandparents, in-home sitters, child care homes, and centers. Structural characteristics, such as group size, child–adult ratio, and physical environment and caregivers' characteristics (formal education, specialized training, child care experience, and beliefs about child rearing) were used to assess each setting. In all types of care, positive caregiving, measured in terms of frequency counts and qualitative ratings, was higher when group sizes and child–adult ratios were smaller, when caregivers had nonauthoritarian beliefs about child rearing, and when the physical environments appeared safe, clean, and stimulating. Overall, sensitive, positive, and involved care was most likely in in-home arrangements, such as in father, grandparent, and sitter care, where group sizes and child–adult ratios were significantly smaller than in child care homes and centers. As caregivers in child care homes and centers were found to have more formal education and specialized training than caregivers in in-home arrangements, the findings suggest that caregiver experience plays less of a role with positive caregiving for infants than it does, as indicated above, for older children.

Unfortunately, care that meets guidelines for structural features of quality care can be expensive. In 1995, the Cost, Quality, and Child Outcomes researchers reported that a 25% increase in quality, from mediocre quality care to good quality care, is associated with a 10% rise in cost. Some observers have argued that too much emphasis on quality will increase costs to the point where families will no longer be able to afford childcare. Thus, there may be a trade-off between high quality care and affordable care. The challenge is to make high quality care affordable and availiable to families of varying income levels.

B. PROCEDURAL MEASURES OF QUALITY CARE

Whereas structural features of care are distal in nature, affecting children at a distance through other factors, procedural measures of care are more proximal in nature. In procedural measures of the care environment, the types of interactions caregivers have with the children and the children's interactions with peers and caregivers are examined. Procedure measures may also take into account the curriculum followed by careproviders, the games that children and caregivers play together, and the health and safety practices generally practiced in the child care setting.

Several operational measures have been developed to look at hands-on interactions and practices within a particular child care arrangement. The Early Care Environment Rating Scale (ECERS), published in 1980 by Thelma Harms and Richard M. Clifford, was developed for children two-and-a-half to five years of age to evaluate personal care routines, furnishings, language reasoning experiences, motor activities, creative activities, social development, and staff needs. Each of the 37 items on the scale is rated from 1 to 7, with a higher score indicating a better rating. The Family Day Care Rating Scale, also developed by Harms and Clifford and published in

1989, is a measure similar to the ECERS that was modified to include items applicable to child care in a home setting. The Infant/Toddler Environment Rating Scale (ITERS), developed by Harms, Debby Cryer, and Clifford and published in 1990, offers an alternative to the ECERS for children age two and younger who are placed in center-based care.

Finally, the most extensive procedural measure available is the Observational Record of the Caregiving Environment (ORCE) introduced by the NICHD Study of Early Child Care in a 1996 publication. With this measure, children are observed for two 44-minute cycles in their care arrangements on two different days about a week apart. Observers record and rate the incidence and quality of the responsiveness, stimulation, and sensitivity care providers direct toward the child across a variety of situations in the caregiving environment. Correlations between scores on the ORCE, measures of structural characteristics of care, and measures of child outcome have lent construct validity to this measurement.

Numerous studies have applied structural and procedural measures and even combinations of the two to derive some metric for the study of child care quality and its effects on children. Though the field of child care is riddled with conflicts over whether high-quality care is necessary or sufficient to guarantee optimal child outcomes, there is no disagreement about the ingredients that make up high-quality care. Regardless of the child's age or the type of care arrangement, in 1998 and in 2000, NICHD researchers found that sensitive and responsive caregivers who supply appropriate verbal and cognitive stimulation serve as important indicators of high-quality care. Likewise, in 2000, the National Research Council and Institute of Medicine concluded that quality of child care is highly contingent on the quality and preparedness of the care provider.

Good caregivers are generally those who have more formal education and better training in how to work with children. Thus, it should come as no surprise that centers with more experienced and higher trained staff also boast higher wages for their personnel. In fact, an extensive body of research, including findings by Deborah Phillips and her colleagues in 1995 and Sandra Scarr and her coauthors in 1994, confirms that teachers' wages are more closely related to quality of care than are other structural center care variables. Teachers' wages correlate not only with training but also with structural and procedural indices that are linked to better outcomes

for children. The U.S. military provides a successful story in how to increase care quality through focusing on improving the conditions for child care workers. As reported by the National Research Council and Institute of Medicine in 2000, the U.S. armed services was able to decrease the annual staff turnover rate by improving the workers' compensation and training. These improvements began in 1989; today, the U.S. military provides the country with a model child care system.

While the U.S. military provides a vision of how higher quality child care environments can be created, surveys of child care quality around the country present an abysmal picture of the quality of care made available to most children in the United States. The Cost, Quality, and Child Outcomes Study as reported in 1995, the Child Care Staffing Study as reported in 1990, and the Study of Children in Family Child Care and Relative Care as reported in 1994 have all investigated the quality of nonmaternal child care in various regions of the country and have found high proportions (25 to 40%) of inadequate care and low proportions (8 to 12%) of "good" care. Because many large-scale child care studies such as those listed above have refusal rates of about 45%, these figures may be overly optimistic, as it is likely that child care facilities not willing to participate in these studies may also provide lower-quality care.

In another examination of the characteristics and quality of child care, the NICHD Study of Early Child Care conducted 600 observations of nonmaternal child care settings in nine states. These NICHD researchers showed that most often, child care used by families for children from six months to three years is rated only "fair" in quality. Only 11% of the settings were considerered excellent. Their findings were extrapolated to the distribution of U.S. families in the national household education survey of 1995. Estimates were that 8% of care settings for children under three are likely to be rated "poor," 53% "fair," and 30% "good"; only nine percent are rated "excellent" in measures of procedural quality.

Similar results were reported by the NICHD researchers in the *American Journal of Public Health* using structural measures of quality of care. According to this report, most child care centers are not meeting recommended standards for the structural characteristics of care. The researchers imputed figures to project the percentage of care facilities that met guidelines for child-to-staff ratios, group size, formal training, and education of caregivers across nine states in the nation. The conclusion is clear.

Most child care centers, at least those responsible for infant care, are falling short of providing "good" quality environments for the children they serve. Studies also show that lower-income working-class families are less likely to get the quality of care that middle- and upper-income families obtain.

Is this lack of quality harming the nation's children? How does the use of child care relate to child outcome, and does the use of quality care enhance the changes of optimal child outcome?

VI. *Outcomes of Child Care*

Questions dealing with the relationship between child care and child outcomes are not straightforward. Indeed, just as there have been major fluctuations in the use of child care and the political attitudes toward child care, so too have there been fluctuations in our interpretation of whether child care is good or bad for children. Early reviews of the effects of early child care on infants and preschoolers to determine whether early child care posed risks to children's early development suggested that child care was not necessarily harmful to infants and young children. However, this early research was based on children in university-based child care centers of high quality using limited psychological measurement techniques. When Jay Belsky reviewed the growing literature in the 1980's, he came to a very different conclusion from the one he had reached just a few years earlier. In 1986, 1988, and again in 1990, Belsky argued that child care might well be a "cause of concern." Other researchers, including Alison Clarke-Stewart, Deborah Phillips, Kathleen McCartney and Sandra Scarr disagreed with Belsky's reading of the literature. These papers, along with those by other researchers, fueled a growing national debate about whether child care posed risks or benefits to young children and their families.

In the 1980's, women were entering the workforce in unparalleled numbers, and there was no guarantee that their children in nonmaternal care were safe from harm. What was needed was a comprehensive study of children in varying types of care that would assess the effects of varying types of quality, quantity, and stability. Only then could there be empirical data that spoke to the debate. Two studies were initiated to meet this challenge. Launched in 1990, the NICHD Study of Early Child Care followed 1300 children prospectively at 10 sites across the nation into their homes and into their child care settings.

Though not nationally representative, the study offered a glimpse at varying samples across varied settings and the outcomes that emerged. A second comprehensive investigation of child care centers, the Cost Quality and Outcomes (CQO) Study, examined children's development from preschool through second grade. An initial sample of 401 child care centers was recruited from four states, California, Connecticut, Colorado, and North Carolina. Nonprofit and for profit centers included 509 preschool classrooms and 224 infant/toddler classrooms. These studies have contributed a great deal to our understanding of the developmental trajectories of children from different backgrounds and the effects of different types of environmental contexts on children's development. Already, they have offered some important answers to the question of how early child care experiences affect the children's outcomes in several areas: children's attachment to parents, children's ability to get along with others, and children's cognitive and language development.

A. ATTACHMENT AND THE MOTHER–CHILD RELATIONSHIP

Child care researchers have long debated the effects of nonmaternal care on infants' attachment to their mothers. Since Jay Belsky issued his first 1986 warning, he has consistently argued that extensive nonmaternal care of children at an early age could increase the risk of insecure infant–mother attachments.

Most of the studies that Belsky reviewed, as well as the many others reviewed by Michael Lamb in his 1998 chapter published in the *Handbook of Child Psychology*, assessed infant–adult attachment using the standard procedure developed by Mary Ainsworth and her colleagues know as the "strange situation." Using the strange situation, the infant's behaviors toward the mother and a stranger in a series of separations and reunions are observed in an unfamilar laboratory environment. Based on the observations of the child's behavior, children can be categorized as either "securely" or "insecurely" attached to their mothers. Infants who show evidence of using the mother as a secure base from which to explore the strange environment, who greet the mother positively and seek proximity with her on reunion, and who can calm quickly and return to play are considered "securely attached."

In the early research looking at the effects of early child care, researchers were not able to tease apart differences in pre-existing characteristics of families who chose early child care—what are known as "selection factors"—on children's attachment to their mothers. Nor were they able to assess or control for the effects of the quality of the substitute care families used when they chose nonmaternal care. However, because they had a large sample of families using a wide variety of child care settings, researchers from the NICHD Study of Early Child Care were able to evaluate the effects of amount, quality, and stability of early nonmaternal care on children's attachment to their mothers while controlling for the effects of a number of different selection factors. In 1998, the NICHD researchers reported that the strongest factor predicting children's attachment to their mothers was the mother's sensitivity to their children. Whether the child was in long hours of care, poor quality care, or unstable care did not, in and of themselves, predict children's attachment security to their mothers. Also unimportant in predicting the child's attachment to the mother was the type of care the child was in, whether it was in-home care by a relative or nonrelative, family day care, or center care. Only when mothers scored very low in their sensitivity toward their children did being in longer hours of care, lower quality of care, or more than one child care setting predict insecure attachment. Thus, early child care was observed to affect child attachment only when the mother was already insensitive to the child.

Maternal sensitivity is generally measured by the supportive presence, positive regard, and lack of intrusiveness and hostility of the mother toward the child. Researchers with the NICHD Study of Early Child Care found that children under the age of two had a greater chance of experiencing insensitive mothering when they were exposed to risk factors at home and extensive or poor-quality early child care. The relationship between extensive and poor quality child care in the first two years of life raises some important questions. Does the use of child care at an early age diminish the monther's ability to respond sensitively to her child? These mothers may know less about how to respond to their children because they see them less and are with them for fewer hours each day. Or is it that more insensitive mothers, or mothers likely to be more insensitive, enroll their infants in more hours of child care at an early age? That is, are mothers who are less responsive to children those who choose to put children into early and extensive care? Though family characteristics play the most significant role in the child's development, it is often difficult to completely control for family influences when studying the effects of child care.

Does the quality of care affect maternal sensitivity and hence later attachment? There is some evidence that it does, but only for high-risk children. High-risk children, including those raised in poverty or with depressed mothers, seem to be more likely to reap the benefits of high-quality care. In a 1997 report from the NICHD researchers, mothers living in or near poverty with infants placed in full-time, high-quality child care showed more positive involvement with their six-month-old children than other poor moms raising their children alone or placing their children in low-quality care. Perhaps in these cases, then, high-quality care arrangements serve to buffer the child from the effects that result in insecure attachments. As further studies of the continuing effects of early child care become available, researchers will want to evaluate how the amount of care, the type of care, and the quality of care affect mothers' interaction with their children and their children's resulting attachment and relationship to their parents.

The literature to date in mother–child relationships, therefore, suggests that placing children in care environments does not, in and of itself, create a risk factor for children. Rather, family characteristics, particularly sensitive and responsive parenting, appear to be the greatest contributor to the parent–child attachment relationship. High-quality care for those children from environments that do not provide sensitive parenting may actually buffer the child from ill effects, while low-quality environments for these children may place them at increased risk. The resulting mother–child relationship prepares the child for subsequent interactions with others. With this early relationship, the child may begin building a personal narrative that influences the child's experiences in each of the subsequent periods of life.

B. SOCIAL-EMOTIONAL FUNCTIONING

In many ways, the child's socio-emotional functioning can be seen as an offshoot of the attachment relationship. The child's socio-emotional functioning is measured by the quality of the child's relationships not just with parents, but also with friends, caregivers, and teachers, and by the child's personal and interpersonal adjustment. Measures of young children's socio-emotional functioning generally include measures of emotional adjustment, social competence, behavior problems, and self-regulaton. These measures have also been considered as important child outcomes in the child care quality debate. Do children in child care have fewer friends? Are children that spend more time in child care more likely to be antisocial, more disruptive, and aggressive? Does the quality of that care affect child outcome?

Conflicting answers have been found so far with respect to the question of the role of child care experiences on children's social competence and adjustment. Some researchers have reported negative peer behavior as a function of early child care experiences, but some researchers have also suggessted that these negative associations could be due to poor quality child care. When enrolled in high-quality care, early entry into care and more time spent in care foster greater social competence over time and even into the child's school years. In 1999, the CQO study found that children's relationships with their caregivers were important variables that predicted social outcome. Children with closer relationships with their caregivers in child care centers rated higher on sociability and lower in problem behaviors than children with less close relationships with their caregivers. These findings were reported for children from the preschool years into elementary school. This effect was even greater for children with less-educated mothers with whom closer child–caregiver relationships were more strongly associated with fewer problem behaviors through second grade.

In the preschool years, research has also suggested that early and extensive care often predicts more aggression, noncompliance, and behavior. In evaluating more than 1000 children, NICHD researchers found that mothers reported less social competence and caregivers reported more behavior problems in two-year-old children when there were longer hours of nonmaternal care in the first two years of life. However, these findings did not hold true at 36 months. In addition, at 24 months, children in higher quality care were reported to have fewer behavior problems by both their mothers and their caregivers and were rated higher on social competence by their mothers. At 36 months, higher quality care was associated with greater compliance and less negative behavior during mother–child interactions and also fewer caregiver-reported behavior problems.

Further research is necessary to establish a solid relationship between the quantity of child care, the age of onset of the care, and the child's subsequent social competence and adjustment. Developmental transitions in addition to family factors and the quality of the child's care experiences may influence childen's socio-emotional development. Thus, quality of care seems to be relative to social outcomes

in terms of peer relations and problem behavior. That relation, however, may be neither simple nor direct.

C. COGNITIVE DEVELOPMENT

Finally, areas of great concern in the child care quality debate center on child cognitive and achievement outcomes. Does time away from the mother in nonmaternal care result in elevated or lower language, cognitive, and achievement outcomes? Cognitive development in children is measured by assessing the child's global intellectual functioning, knowledge and achievement (school readiness and literacy), cognitive processes (attention, problem solving, memory), and language development. Here the results are quite consistent across a number of studies. Quality of nonmaternal care emerges from a number of studies as a reliable and positive predictor of language, cognition, and achievement during the first three years of life.

Perhaps most exciting is that research has now gone beyond looking merely at structural indicators of quality to look at process indicators. In both a followup study, conducted by D. S. Chin-Quee and Scarr in 1994 to the Bermuda project originally conducted by Kathleen McCartney and her colleagues in the 1980's, and the NICHD Study of Early Child Care as reported in 2000, the amount of observed language stimulation positively relates to children's performance on measures of cognitive and linguistic abilities at ages 15, 24, and 36 months.

Intervention studies also support favorable cognitive and language developmental outcomes when children are placed in high-quality care during infancy. A Head Start summary report in January 2001 concluded that children enrolled in an Early Head Start program scored higher on a standardized assessment of infant cognitive development than the control children and were reported by their parents to have larger vocabularies and to use more grammatically complex sentences at the age of two. The Abecedarian and CARE early intervention projects found that preschoolers experiencing high-quality child care show better progress on tests of language and cognitive functioning than preschoolers who were not placed in similar child care situations. It seems that child care quality is most strongly related to optimal developmental outcomes for disadvantaged children.

Although the findings are consistent, more research is needed to determine practical significance of the effects of quality on child outcomes. Although the effects of quality have been demonstrated to be statistically significant, often the amount of variance that quality of care accounts for is a relatively small percentage of the total amount of variance in child outcomes. Thus, small variations in the quality of care may or may not have important practical meaning. Sandra Scarr pointed out that enhanced child care quality may not have long-term effects, and the effects that increased child care quality do have may not be large enough to justify the costs of that increased quality. For example, in the Bermuda study described earlier, the relation of quality care to cognitive competence diminished by the time the children were five to eight years old. Other researchers, though, have found more enduring effects. In particular, a 2001 report by the Cost, Quality, and Outcomes Study tracked the longitudinal effects of early child care experiences following school entry. The researchers documented that higher quality care was associated with better cognitive outcomes for children of different gender and ethnic backgrounds and with mothers of varying levels of education. However, while enduring, the researchers noted that these effects of quality were relatively modest ones.

VII. Conclusion

The article only scratches the surface of what developmental psychologists know about early child care and its effect on families and children. In many ways, the history of child care in the United States places child care squarely within the women's domain. Child care grew in response to women's entrance into the labor force. As U.S. women became more invested in job opportunities, national concern over their children became a more pressing issue. Indeed, all or most of the research on the subject of child care studies mothers as the primary caretakers. All of this debate has played out in a sociopolitical climate in which women are forced to question whether their role is best spent in the workplace or in the home.

Amazingly, many in the United States still hold on to the image that the real American family is like Ozzie and Harriet's, a model of two parents and two children. Demographic patterns show quite clearly that the structure of families has changed. Similarly, the role of women is changing. No longer is the American woman a single caricature of "Harriet" who is home with the children. Women are now found in numerous roles from CEO to industrial de-

signer to homemaker, and most women are employed for at least some part of their week.

These changes force researchers and policy makers to reevaluate the options available to families and the effects of child care on children. They also call for a shift in the way we think about the child care "problem." Because children may be affected by child care in significant and enduring ways, because both men and women are parents, and because children are the United States' most valuable economic and social resource, child care needs to be viewed not as a women's issue, but as a national issue. The challenge facing our nation is to establish family policies that enable parents to care for their young children while providing for their families, and to seek creative ideas to fund child care so that children from all segments of American society can have access to high quality care.

ACKNOWLEDGMENTS

This article was prepared with support from grant #U10 HD 25455-11 from the National Institute of Child Health and Human Development to Temple University.

SUGGESTED READING

Cahan, E. D. (1989). *Past Caring: A History of U.S. Preschool Care And Education For The Poor, 1820–1965*. National Center for Children in Poverty, New York.

Clarke-Stewart, K. A. (1993). *Daycare: Revised Edition*. Harvard University Press, Cambridge, MA.

Lamb, M. E. (1998). "Nonparental child care: Context, quality, correlates, and consequences." In *Handbook of Child Psychology, Vol. 4: Child Psychology in Practice*, (W. Damon, I. E. Sigel, and K. A. Renninger, eds.). New York, John Wiley.

National Research Council and Institute of Medicine. (2000). *From Neurons to Neighborhoods: The Science of Early Child Development*. Committee on Integrating the Science of Early Childhood Development (J. P. Shonkoff and D. A. Phillips, eds.). Board on Children, Youth, and Families, Commission on Behavioral and Social Sciences and Education. National Academy Press, Washington DC.

NICHD Early Child Care Research Network. (1999). Contexts of development and developmental outcomes over the first seven years of life. In *Young Children's Education, Health, and Development: Profile and Synthesis Project Report* (J. Brooks-Gunn and L. J. Berlin, eds.). Department of Education, Washington, DC.

Scarr, S. (1998). American child care today. *American Psychologist* 53, 95–108.

U.S. Census Bureau and Smith, K. (2000). *Who's Minding the Kids? Child Care Arrangements: Fall 1995*. Current Population Reports, P70-70. U.S. Census Bureau, Washington DC.

Zigler, E. F., and Finn-Stevenson, M. (1996) The child care crisis: Implications for the growth and development of the nation's children. *Journal of Social Issues*, 51, 215–231.

Chronic Illness Adjustment

Tracey A. Revenson

The Graduate Center of the City University of New York

Glossary

Adaptive task A specific stressor or challenge posed by living with a chronic illness (e.g., treatment demands, maintaining interpersonal relationships).

Autoimmune disorders The failure of the immune system to distinguish between the body (self) and foreign antigens (nonself), attacking the body's own cells.

Coping A psychological mechanism for managing stress, involving thoughts, feelings, or behaviors.

Downward social comparison A cognitive coping strategy in which people enhance their self-esteem by comparing themselves to someone worse off.

Resilience The personality attribute or coping process by which individuals are able to maintain strength and experience personal growth in the face of severe or prolonged adversity.

ADAPTATION TO CHRONIC ILLNESS is a broad topic that encompasses (1) the short- and long-term stresses and strains presented by living with a chronic condition; (2) the cognitive, behavioral, and emotional responses to these stresses and strains; and (3) the psychosocial outcomes that occur as a result of this coping process. This entry weaves together three basic themes. First, adaptation to illness cannot be defined or measured without asking the questions, "Adaptive in what ways? Adaptive at what point in the illness? Adaptive relative to what other possible outcomes?" Second, adaptation is inherently gendered—that is, one cannot answer these questions without taking gender into context. This goes beyond determining sex differences in health and illness phenomena, and assuming that the experience of chronic illness is qualitatively different for men and women. Finally, it is critical to look at both positive and negative aspects of the adaptation process. Resilience is offered as a component of positive adaptation that may be especially relevant for women.

I. Introduction

The onset, treatment, and progression of physical illness are well-recognized stressors for women and their families. Virtually every woman can expect to experience at least one chronic illness or disorder in her lifetime, and the incidence of chronic health problems increases with age. By age 55 over 80% of women experience at least one chronic health problem. Although mortality rates are higher for men, morbidity rates are higher for women, even when taking reproductive health and age into account.

Many illnesses are linked to gender, either by genetics, physiology, or lifestyle factors. For example, many autoimmune disorders (such as rheumatoid arthritis and systemic lupus erythematosus), some gastrointestinal disorders (irritable bowel syndrome), some forms of cancer (e.g., breast cancer), and osteoporosis are more prevalent among women. Recent studies show that lifestyle factors such as stress and smoking not only differ in their prevalence between women and men, but may be articulated physiologically in different ways (i.e., have different effects on the endocrine system).

There have been hundreds of studies of adjustment to chronic illness. Most are self-report or interview studies and use some measure of psychological distress, symptoms of depression, or quality of life as the indicator of adjustment. Some studies focus on a single disease, whereas others compare diseases. From these studies we can conclude that most adults adjust well to chronic illness: their scores on measures of depression or psychological distress are only slightly higher than the scores of people without a chronic illness. Moreover, those people who are more depressed tend to be in greater pain, experience greater physical limitations, and have more life-threatening conditions. People with chronic illness draw on a large reservoir of coping resources to help them adjust to illness, including personality characteristics such as optimism and social resources such as help from friends and family. However, most research on adaptation to chronic illness among women has ignored sexual orientation or race/ethnicity as factors affecting adaptation, so most of our knowledge at this time is based on studies of White, middle-class, heterosexual women.

It is impossible to review all studies of sex differences in illness and examine the roles that gender plays in adaptational processes within the page limits of this entry. Thus, two choices have been made. First, this article will use a broad rubric of "chronic illness," as many chronic conditions share common stressors or adaptive tasks. Emphasis will be placed on illnesses that are more prevalent among women or some subgroups of women. Second, the article will focus more on gender roles as they impact adaptational outcomes than on describing gender differences in chronic illness per se, as many sex differences in health outcomes are explained, at least in part, by cultural norms about gender roles.

II. The Stresses of Chronic Illness

By using a broad rubric of "chronic illness," some stressors posed by particular illnesses may be overlooked or minimized. However, most chronic illnesses produce common transient stresses and enduring life strains that require psychological adaptation. These include severe, intermittent, or unpredictable pain; physical changes in one's body and appearance; physical disability; uncertainty about disease progression; regular contact with health providers; treatment regimens that may be ineffective or uncomfortable; required changes in work or leisure habits; and emotional, social, marital, and sexual difficulties. Having a chronic illness may create or inflame existing financial strains or marital problems, as well as force unwanted changes in living arrangements, family routines, or work roles.

Chronic illness does not always forecast a shortened life span, but it does imply a long-term—sometimes, lifetime—process of coping with the stressors and challenges posed by the illness. However, a key point to remember is that there is great variation in the ways that women (and men) are affected by chronic illness. For some people, chronic illness impacts quality of life and daily functioning in major ways, while for others its impact is minimal or intermittent. Adjustment depends on the confluence of many intrapersonal, interpersonal, and environmental factors.

III. The Process of Adjustment/Adaptation

How does one define *adjustment?* It is useful to view psychosocial adjustment as an umbrella term that encompasses many dimensions and constructs. The words *adjustment* and adaptation often are used interchangeably, and will be here. Many therapists and researchers have advanced definitions of adjustment that emphasize the absence of psychological disorder: people with chronic illness are considered to be well adjusted when they do not evidence symptoms of depression; are able to maintain a balance of positive and negative emotions; are able to function in their usual family, work, and social roles; and are generally satisfied with their life. Sometimes psychologists use the terms well-being, mental health, or quality of life when assessing adjustment to illness. More recently, attention has been turned toward positive outcomes such as *stress-related growth* or *resilience*. No matter which definition is adopted, adaptation involves a number of fundamental themes.

A. COPING CONTRIBUTES TO ADJUSTMENT

It is difficult to write about adjustment without bringing in the concept of coping. Coping has been conceptualized variously as "adaptation under relatively difficult conditions," "any response to external life strains that serves to prevent, avoid, or control emotional distress," and "constantly changing cognitive and behavioral efforts to manage . . . environmental and internal demands . . . that are appraised as taxing or exceeding a person's resources." In all these conceptualizations, coping is defined as responsive to (perceived) psychological stress, can be cognitive, behavioral, or emotional, and is goal-directed toward adjustment.

Coping serves as an intervening process, between cognitive appraisal of a situation as stressful and psychological adjustment outcomes. That is, psychological appraisal of a stressor influences coping efforts, which subsequently impact psychological adjustment. An early paper in the field of coping, based on case studies of polio patients, laid out five criteria—essentially modes of coping—for successful adaptation: solving or eliminating the stressor, acquiring information, keeping emotional distress within manageable limits, maintaining a sense of personal worth, and moving toward greater autonomy, mastery, and growth. These themes remain the core of current theories of coping and adaptation.

If one adopts a process perspective (discussed later) then it is clear that coping and adaptation are two different concepts. Coping involves efforts to manage the stressful demands of illness *regardless of outcome*. This means that no one strategy is considered inherently better than any other is. A coping strategy that is adaptive at one time may be maladaptive at other times or with stressors other than illness. For example, denial of symptoms has been shown to be maladaptive upon discovery of a breast lump, as it leads to delays in seeking treatment, but denial may be adaptive at later stages of illness if it allows women to maintain a positive self-image. Thus, we cannot categorize coping strategies as unilaterally adaptive or maladaptive.

Recently there has been a focus on *cognitive* modes of coping. Based on her research with breast cancer patients, Shelley E. Taylor has suggested three cognitive mechanisms that lead to positive adaptation: (1) the search for meaning in the illness experience, (2) attempts to regain mastery over the illness and over one's life, and (3) the use of self-enhancement strategies to maintain one's self-esteem. The search for meaning often takes the form of the question "Why me?" (or as some breast cancer survivors have been asking, "Why *not* me?"). Taylor found that over 90% of the women with breast cancer whom she interviewed made some causal attribution for their cancer. This answer can take many forms—it may be spiritual ("Because God thought I could handle this"), biologically based ("Breast cancer runs in my family"), or logical ("At some point in your life you or someone in your family is going to become ill"). Taylor found that the answer itself doesn't affect adjustment, but that it is important to have some answer to that question, in order to place the illness in the context of one's life and to find some positive meaning in the experience.

Taylor found that the primary psychological mechanism for boosting self-esteem was the cognitive process of downward social comparisons—that is, women found someone worse off to compare themselves to, and in doing so, felt better about themselves. All the women in Taylor's study were able to make some type of downward social comparison by finding an appropriate target. For example, the older women stated that it would have been worse if they had been younger: "The people I really feel sorry for are these young gals. To lose a breast when you're so young must be awful. I'm 73; what do I need a breast for?" In contrast, the younger women in Taylor's study often would compare themselves with women of the same age with more advanced cancers or more debilitating treatments. All women were able to pinpoint some person for comparison who would make them feel better.

B. ADAPTATION IS MULTIFACETED

There are many domains in which to measure adjustment, including emotional adjustment, social adjustment, global adjustment to the illness, and adherence to prescribed treatment. Thus, it is not particularly useful to classify someone as being "well adjusted" or not, without specifying which domains of adjustment are being considered. Let us consider three women with very advanced rheumatoid arthritis (RA), an immunological joint disease that often involves severe pain and severe limitations in physical functioning. One of these women, an author, might be confined to her apartment because of lower-extremity limitations, but may still be able to write on her computer and to maintain professional and social relationships by telephone and visitors. Another woman, for whom RA has affected only the joints in her hands and wrists, may have given up her job on the factory line, but can fulfill her mothering role quite well. Yet another woman, in constant pain and with little ability to perform even the basic tasks of daily living, may retire and move in with a daughter. Who is better adjusted? One cannot define, measure, or study adaptation without asking the questions "Adaptive in what ways? Adaptive at what point in the illness? Adaptive relative to what other possible outcomes?"

C. ADAPTATION IS A PROCESS

Adaptation is not a static end point, but a dynamic process. The same can be said for chronic illness and the coping demands posed over the course of the illness. As a result, the person's life context and interpersonal relationships also change. Some theories have described stages of adaptation to illness as similar to the stages of dying outlined by Kubler-Ross (e.g., denial or minimization, followed by anger and emotional release, and then acceptance), but little research supports these stage theories. Instead, one's adaptation level may change frequently.

One set of factors that shape adaptation involves the nature of the illness. Disease stage, severity, rate of disease progression, and the extent to which the disease affects multiple body systems influence treatment demands and adaptive tasks. For example, a slower disease process probably allows a gradual and smoother adaptation, as people cope with their illness in smaller bites and as anticipatory coping efforts are made for future problems. A disease course marked with frequent transitions from health to illness—sometimes without warning—may prove a harder road to follow. For example, the nature of rheumatoid arthritis involves a long time horizon with periods of relative severity of joint pain, swelling, and stiffness, alternating with periods of relative comfort. This suggests that individual coping efforts must accommodate to rapidly changing illness demands.

As illness progresses, interpersonal relationships also change. Friends and family support must learn when to give and when to withhold help, as providing too much support or providing it at the wrong time may have negative consequences for adjustment. Interactions with health care providers also change, as patients move from crisis phases to more stable, long-term phases of medical care. [*See* SOCIAL SUPPORT SYSTEMS.]

The initial diagnosis of breast cancer provides a vivid illustration of how adaptation must be seen as a dynamic process. Upon being informed that a breast lump is malignant, women are faced with the immediate coping tasks of making medical decisions (type and timing of surgery, choice of surgeon), informing one's family, setting aside, at least temporarily, all other demands in one's life (e.g., work), and acknowledging the threat that the diagnosis places on survival. During the post-operative phase, patients are faced with new treatment decisions (e.g., chemotherapy, radiation, hormones, or some combination of these) and then must endure the noxious physical side effects of that treatment. At the same time, patients are working to maintain social relationships, resume or reconfigure work and family roles, and grapple with the long-term meaning of the illness. Later in the illness, women may be faced with a changed self-concept, a changed physical self, repeated or novel treatments, fears of disease recurrence, and in some cases, actual disease recurrence.

D. ADAPTATION ONLY CAN BE UNDERSTOOD IN CONJUNCTION WITH THE LIFE CONTEXT IN WHICH ILLNESS OCCURS

It is useful to consider four contexts: the sociocultural context, the situational context, the interpersonal context, and the temporal context. The sociocultural context involves ascribed or achieved characteristics, such as age, gender, social class, and economic status, that serve as proxy variables for health-promoting or health-damaging processes. The situational context involves the nature of the illness and medical treatment. The interpersonal context spans relationships with family, friends, work colleagues, and medical professionals. The temporal context refers to the patient's age/life stage and the timing of the illness within the individual's life. This contextual approach recognizes the interdependence of individual's behavior and their life situations, as well as the complex associations among contexts.

Some contextual factors are more strongly linked to gender than are others. Age is one such factor. Chronic illnesses and disability are more prevalent in old age, and women live longer than men; therefore women are likely to be living with at least one chronic condition for some part of their life. In assessing adjustment, it is important to consider whether the illness is occurring "on" or "off-time" in the normative life cycle. Chronic illnesses that are "off-time," for example, being diagnosed with Parkinson's disease in your 30s, are likely to be more stressful than when the illness occurs on-time. Why? First, the individual is not prepared for the changes that illness brings—there is no period of "anticipatory coping." Second, with off-time events, relatively few age peers are simultaneously experiencing the same life situation, so there are fewer individuals with whom to share concerns.

E. ADAPTATION IS RELATIVE

Stated more simply, the ease with which one adjusts to living with a chronic illness depends not only on immediate concerns, but also on long-term goals. The relative value of different outcomes may differ across individuals, across illnesses, or even *within* individuals over time. One woman may choose a particular treatment to maximize survival time but may sustain a great deal of pain and disability, while another woman might choose the risk of a foreshortened life in order to maintain a certain quality of life. It is also important to consider prior mental health in assessing adjustment. For example, a person who has survived a heart attack may be depressed, but perhaps this person was depressed before the attack.

F. ADAPTATION IS GENDERED

It is difficult to understand adaptation without considering how gender influences the entire adaptational process. Gender becomes a verb instead of a noun (you have a gender) or adjective (as in gender differences). Already, by discussing adaptation within life contexts, this article has taken a gendered perspective.

Most psychological theories of "healthy adjustment" are silently dominated by beliefs about gender roles. For example, dominant assumptions of mental health are that one should fight an illness, use active, instrumental, problem-solving efforts, and be self-reliant, drawing on one's inner resources. These ways of coping are not only correlated with better adjustment; in many studies, they also constitute the definition of better adjustment.

For example, many studies of coping conclude that men use more instrumental or problem-focused strategies, whereas women use strategies that focus on emotional regulation and seek emotional support to a greater extent than men do. Moreover, emotion-focused strategies are correlated with poorer mental health outcomes (e.g., fewer symptoms of depression). Putting these two findings together, the implication is that the strategies that women use are less effective.

However, recent studies suggest that the processing and expression of emotions may be adaptive, particularly for women. Thus, what constitutes effective coping may be different between men and women not only in *quantity* (e.g., men do more active coping) but also in *quality*. A number of researchers, coming from different theoretical perspectives, have concluded that interpersonal relationships are essential components of women's coping with major stressors such as illness. Women draw on their support networks more often; these interpersonal contacts serve as a place to express negative emotions, acquire feedback on coping choices, and obtain assistance with life tasks such as child care. Women are more likely to ask for support, use support, and not feel demeaned by it. (At the same time, women's focus on interpersonal relationships may create additional stresses, as women are often taking care of others while they themselves are coping with a chronic condition.)

The next two sections illustrate the six themes just described by exploring adaptation to two very difference chronic conditions that are prevalent among women: *musculoskeletal* and *rheumatic disorders* and breast cancer.

IV. Adaptation to Chronic Physically Disabling Illness

The rheumatic diseases, arthritis, and musculoskeletal conditions constitute more than 100 different illnesses and conditions, affecting nearly 40 million people in the United States. Arthritis and musculoskeletal disorders are the most common self-reported chronic conditions affecting women and, in national health surveys, arthritis is the most frequently cited reason for activity limitations. Rheumatoid arthritis (RA) is a chronic, systemic disease thought to be an autoimmune disorder. Its cardinal manifestations of joint inflammation, swelling, and stiffness result in severe pain, joint destruction, fatigue, and physical disability. For most patients, there is a steady progression toward increasing disability over the life span, although the course of RA is unpredictable and highly variable, with symptoms that flare and remit. The average age of onset of RA is between 25 and 50, although the incidence and prevalence of the disease increase with age, and at different points in the life span two to six times as many women as men have it. Systemic lupus erythematosus (SLE) is also an autoimmune disease that involves multiple systems of the body. Symptoms may include malaise, fever, weight loss, joint pain, renal, cardiac, neurological, and liver problems, and skin and mucous membrane problems. Almost 90% of patients with SLE are female, and it occurs more often among African American women. Osteoarthritis (OA) is the most common form of arthritis. It is most prevalent among older people and is marked by pain in an involved joint (or joints) that worsens with activity, joint stiffness and enlargement, and functional impairment. Women are twice as likely as men to have OA of the knee; similarly, African American women are twice as likely as White women. OA of the knee is more likely to result in disability more than OA in any other joint.

Most forms of arthritis pose a set of common stressors, including recurrent and severe joint pain, potential disability and loss of role functioning, increased risk for developing depression, and frequent medical care. The treatment regimens, especially for RA and SLE, can involve medications with unpleasant side effects. Except for SLE, most forms of arthritis pose no immediate life threat, but the experience of symptoms and the course of the disease are unpredictable. Therefore successful adaptation requires that one cope with uncertainty as well as with concrete illness symptoms.

Women with RA report more symptoms than men do, but when disease severity is taken into account, women actually have *fewer* symptoms than men do. This finding suggests that women do not overreport symptoms but rather have more severe disease and may, in fact, be less likely to complain about symptoms than men are.

The symptoms associated with arthritis often lead to functional limitations. As a result, women with arthritis have lower participation in the labor force, and it is generally reported that the economic impact of arthritis is much more severe for men than for women. The economic impact of women's work disability due to arthritis is underestimated, however,

because arthritis and its disability significantly affect women's "home" work (nurturing, raising families, housework), which is economically undervalued for ill and nonill women alike. Limitations impact quality of life in other ways as well. In one study of women with rheumatoid arthritis, approximately 40% of the women studied reported limitations in important role activities such as making arrangements for others and taking them places, maintaining social ties by writing or calling, and visiting or taking care of sick people. In addition, women who experienced these types of limitations were less satisfied with their ability to provide support to family and friends compared to unimpaired women. The nurturing role—a very important role for women—has been neglected in most past research on adaptation to illness. The presence of chronic disease is a risk factor for depression when it involves the loss of the ability to perform valued social roles. Again, this suggests that to understand the impact of chronic disabling illness, we must examine not only physical limitations but also women's psychological interpretations of the meaning of those limitations.

The most frequently studied effect of arthritis on psychological functioning is its impact on depression. Depressive disorders and depressive symptoms are more prevalent in people with rheumatic diseases compared to people without any serious, chronic illness. Women not only are at greater risk than men for some of the more common and serious rheumatic diseases, but they are also at greater risk for depression. If depression in women with rheumatic diseases is overlooked, then declines in functioning caused by depression could be mistakenly attributed to the rheumatic disease and result in overtreatment. Alternatively, if symptoms of depression are mistakenly assumed to be a natural part of the disease process that does not warrant treatment, women may suffer unnecessarily. [See DEPRESSION.]

Wishful thinking, self-blame, and other avoidant coping strategies have been associated with poorer psychological functioning for both women and men with rheumatic disease. Active coping strategies, and strategies such as information seeking and cognitive restructuring, have been associated with better psychological functioning. However, in a study of daily coping processes in which RA patients were studied over 75 consecutive days, women and men differed in the use of only one of seven coping strategies. (Women tended to seek social support to a greater degree.) Women made a greater number of coping efforts overall and used a greater diversity of coping strategies than men. These findings suggest that women may be more flexible in their coping efforts.

V. Adaptation among Women with Breast Cancer

The incidence of breast cancer in North American women has increased steadily over the past 50 years, culminating in the present 1 in 8 lifetime risk for developing the disease. As scientists improve methods of prevention, early detection, and treatment, growing numbers of women are living with breast cancer for longer periods of time. In response to this trend, clinical researchers have increasingly focused on quality of life issues and psychosocial adjustment to the disease. Although 20 to 30% of women with breast cancer experience significant psychological distress, this distress is substantially reduced in the year following diagnosis, and the majority of women with breast cancer are well adjusted. One to two years after treatment, women with breast cancer do not differ in from healthy women in psychological status.

Research has documented numerous psychosocial and physical effects of breast cancer, including emotional difficulties, problems associated with sexuality, negative changes in body image, challenges to one's sense of femininity, insurance and financial difficulties, pain and suffering, threats to one's self-esteem or self-concept, disruptions in daily activities, barriers to carrying out responsibilities, fulfilling important roles, setting or reaching goals, challenges to one's beliefs about the world, and problems with interpersonal relationships.

One difficulty that appears to be shared by many women with the disease is the fear of recurrence. Across studies, 60 to 99% of women voice this fear. Moreover, fears about breast cancer recurrence, unlike overall psychological distress, do not necessarily dissipate over time. Although 57% of women survive to 15 years after diagnosis, approximately 70% of breast cancer survivors still fear the possibility of recurrence 5 years after diagnosis. These fears have been associated with psychological distress among both current cancer patients and cancer survivors. Younger women have stronger fears, a finding that may be due to the generally more aggressive nature of breast cancer among younger women or a sense that a cancer diagnosis early in the life cycle is particularly unexpected or "off schedule."

A number of medical characteristics influence psychosocial adjustment to the initial breast cancer diagnosis. Treatment decision making (e.g., choosing mastectomy as opposed to breast-conserving surgery), undergoing treatment (e.g., chemotherapy, radiation, hormone therapy), and time since diagnosis have been associated with adjustment. Chemotherapy has been associated with decreased adjustment, varying with its toxicity and assaults on the body (nausea and vomiting, hair loss, weight gain, fatigue). In some studies, however, psychological distress increases again after the termination of treatment because women no longer feel they are actively fighting the disease and have no concrete evidence of disease processes (e.g., a shrinking tumor).

Results regarding the type of surgery have been equivocal. A recent meta-analysis (a statistical technique for combining the results of many studies) suggests that there may be modest benefits to having breast-conserving surgery (BCS), in terms of psychological, marital-sexual, and social adjustment, body/self-image, and cancer-related fears. In contrast, a longitudinal study showed that women who had BCS were more distressed and perceived less social support than women who had mastectomies. In another study, women who had chosen BCS rated their physicians' support of their choice as more important than did women who chose mastectomy, perhaps because they needed reassurance that BCS was as likely to have a positive medical outcome.

To understand adaptation to breast cancer, we must acknowledge the multifaceted nature of cancer. Not only are women coping with the various medical stressors described here, but these stressors may be symbolic of the controllability, predictability, intrusiveness, and degree of life threat of their disease. It is likely that individuals may use many different strategies to cope with different aspects of a multifaceted stressor such as breast cancer.

Most studies of coping and adjustment to breast cancer are framed within a stress, appraisal, and coping paradigm that has come to be recognized as the gold standard in the field. When faced with a stressful event, individuals make primary appraisals of the degree to which the event poses harm or loss, future threat, or challenge, and secondary appraisals of whether they are able to cope with the event. These appraisals both affect one's emotional response (distress) and behavioral response (coping efforts). Coping, in turn, affects adjustment, and the cycle begins anew. The importance of appraisal as a predictor of coping and adjustment has been highlighted in past research on women with breast cancer (as well as research with other illnesses); appraisals of threat, in particular, are associated with increased psychological distress.

Several studies have provided descriptive information on how women cope with a cancer diagnosis and initial treatment. Coping with breast cancer, or any cancer, means different things for different people at different points in the illness, in part because it occurs in the context of other life occurrences. Instead of producing global distress, cancer often produces what psychosocial cancer researcher Barbara Andersen has termed "islands" of psychosocial disruption that vary across the course of the illness. That is, not only are there many different aspects or adaptive tasks of breast cancer to cope with, but the "islands" rise above the water at different times. Thus, when women are asked to report how they cope with their breast cancer, it is impossible to know which aspects of breast cancer they are thinking about. Which aspects of having cancer are most salient for that woman *at that time?* For example, studies of women undergoing chemotherapy or taking Tamoxifen suggest that adjustment may be disrupted with new treatments or even in the absence of treatment, which gives no cues of remission or recurrence. Even asking women how they cope with a more focused aspect of their cancer, such as chemotherapy or cancer-related pain, has limitations. A woman undergoing chemotherapy may have to deal with excessive fatigue, fears about the long-term physical effects of this treatment, or sexual difficulties resulting from induced menopause. Likewise, the pain caused by a woman's cancer may prevent her from completing daily activities or may heighten fears about the progression of her illness.

As with other stressors, women with breast cancer use a wide range of coping techniques: cognitive, behavioral, problem-focused, and emotion-focused strategies, involving approach and avoidance of the stressor. The coping strategies of cognitive reappraisal, seeking social support, and avoidance have consistently been identified as among the most common strategies for coping with breast cancer. But which strategies lead to better adjustment?

Overall, the strategies of acceptance, positive reframing, and seeking and using social support have proved to be beneficial for women with breast cancer. Accepting the illness, or "learning to live with it" (as opposed to accepting responsibility for the illness), is conceptualized as a functional or beneficial coping response, and research with breast cancer patients has found it to be related to improved adjustment. Similarly, positive reframing involves a cognitive attempt to reappraise the stressor of illness, to change its meaning, in order to view it in a more positive light. For example, a woman undergoing chemotherapy may think of the accompanying nausea as evidence that the treatment is working, rather than evidence that the drugs are harming her body. Positive reframing has been identified as one of the most common strategies for coping with breast cancer and has been related to greater psychological adjustment.

Avoidant coping, including denial, behavioral or cognitive disengagement, and some tension-reduction strategies, such as using drugs or drinking, are consistently related to increased distress. Denial is the refusal or inability to acknowledge facts about the breast cancer. There is some controversy over whether denial is a beneficial coping strategy for women with breast cancer. Evidence suggests that it may be helpful at the time of diagnosis, when the woman is flooded with emotional reactions, but detrimental if it delays treatment decisions or is used continually or as a primary coping strategy. Avoidant coping has predicted greater distress after cancer diagnosis and after surgery, and in one study avoidant coping predicted cancer progression one year later.

VI. Marriage and Adaptation to Illness

Of all family members, spouses bear the lion's share of the stresses and burdens of chronic illness. There are also societal expectations that the healthy spouse care for her or his ill partner. Thus, spouses occupy a dual and sometimes conflicting role: they serve as the primary support provider to their partner, but at the same time, they need support for the illness-related stresses they experience.

The research literature on this topic suggests that wives face a greater burden than men, as patients or as spouse-caregivers. Two studies have compared couples in which the husband or wife had a chronic condition to couples in which neither spouse was ill. Compared to their counterparts in nonill families, wives who were chronically ill did more housework (an average of seven hours more a week in one study!) although they spent six hours less in the labor force. There were no differences between the groups in global marital satisfaction, although women with chronic illness were less satisfied with their role performance as wives and mothers. In contrast, wives whose husbands had a chronic illness were less satisfied with their marriages and with the social support they received from their partners than wives in nonill families. Compared to healthy families, wives in marriages in which the husband was ill were significantly less satisfied in many areas—with their husband's understanding of their feelings, the amount of attention received from their husbands, with their husband's help around the house and his role performance as a husband and father, and with the amount of time the couple spent together and the way they spent it. They were also less satisfied with their role performance as a mother but, surprisingly, *not* with their performance as a wife. Thus, a husband's illness appears to have a greater impact on women than their own illness. Clearly the women with ill husbands felt a responsibility to keep the family and home intact, but at great personal cost.

Studies of couples' coping with a myocardial infarction (MI, heart attack) present a similar picture. Men tend to reduce their work activities and responsibilities and are nurtured by their wives; in contrast, after hospitalization, women resume household responsibilities more quickly, including nurturing other family members, and tend to receive more help from adult daughters and neighbors than from their husbands. As John Michela wrote about a study of 40 couples he had conducted, in which the husband had suffered a first heart attack during the previous year: "*His* experience is filtered through concerns about surviving and recovering from the MI with a minimum of danger or discomfort, while *her* experience is filtered through the meaning of the marital relationship to her—what the marriage has provided and, hence, what is threatened by the husband's potential death or what is lost by his disability."

James Coyne has proposed that in order to understand adaptation to chronic illness, one must look at the interpersonal context of coping, or what he calls "relationship-focused coping." Within this approach, couples' coping might be envisioned as a tradeoff between protecting one's own health and well-being and attending to the other partner's. His study of men who had had an uncomplicated heart attack within the past six months and their wives unveils some of the hidden differences in women and men's coping styles and their outcomes on the individual and the marriage. Two relationship-focused coping strategies were examined: *active engagement* (which involved coping efforts such as problem solving with the spouse and discussing the partner's reaction to the illness) and *protective buffering* (hiding concerns, denying worries, and yielding to the partner to avoid disagreements). The study found that each partner's coping behavior affected how the other person coped with the illness, with some surprising gender effects. When wives used protective buffering their own distress increased; when husbands used protective buffering their *wives'* distress also increased. Thus, wives' efforts to shield their husbands from stress may increase their own psychological distress, as may husbands' efforts to protect their wives. The relationship-focused coping approach holds much promise for understanding gender differences in adjustment.

Couples' experience of coping with illness cannot be extricated from gender. Whether they are patients or caregivers, women assume a disproportionate share of the responsibilities for maintaining the family's organization and providing nurturance to family members. Carol Gilligan, among others, has noted that women tend to be socialized into caretaking roles in close relationships and are more responsive to the well-being of others. One national survey found that women were 10 to 40% more likely to support a loved one during a crisis, depending on the nature of the problem. In fact, when asked about stressful events that have happened to them in the past year, women are more likely to report not only their own life events, but also life events related to loved ones, than are men. This may account, in part, for gender differences in psychological distress when living with a chronic condition.

Although gender roles have changed in a major way over the past quarter century, chronic illness may constitute such a severe stressor that families revert to more traditional gender roles. This is an important area for future research.

VII. *Adaptation as Growth and Resilience*

As we have discussed throughout this article, psychological adjustment is a broad term that often includes both distress (e.g., depression and anxiety) and well-being (e.g., positive affect). In most studies, however, only distress is examined. Recent trends in psychology have highlighted the importance of positive psychology, and accounting for both aspects of psychological adjustment. Virginia O'Leary and Jeannette Ickovics have suggested that it is critical to acknowledge women's strengths in the face of adversity rather than focusing solely on their weaknesses.

From a clinical vantage point, one might expect that the primary and most direct outcome of living with chronic illness would be feelings of anxiety, depression, and hopelessness. Indeed, many research studies have demonstrated this. However, recognizing women's strengths means focusing on positive aspects of well-being, such as personal growth or strengthened social ties, as well as on distress. In qualitative studies of women with breast cancer, women spontaneously describe positive outcomes of their experience.

The concepts of resilience and thriving have been suggested as new ways to look at health outcomes in response to major stressors. Resilience refers to how some individuals are able to maintain strength and experience personal growth in the face of severe or prolonged adversity. Sometimes resilience is described as a personality attribute, other times as a coping process, and other times as the outcome of successful coping with adversity, making it a difficult construct to study. Some researchers propose that there are resilient individuals who have a definable set of characteristics that enable them to adapt successfully to stressful circumstances. Others suggest that resilience may be the coping process of fending off maladaptive responses to stress, thus leading to better mental health. Resilience can also be thought of as the long-term end product of adaptation to a severe stressor or challenge, such as chronic illness. Whichever approach is used, the focus of a resilience perspective is one of positive adaptation, not simply the absence of pathology.

Most theories of adaptation have defined successful adaptation as the individual's return to a baseline level of functioning after experiencing a major stressor. That is, if an individual faced with a serious chronic illness can return to her pre-illness level of psychological functioning and stave off long-term depression, she has adapted successfully to her illness. In contrast, the psychological construct of thriving calls for personal growth as a result of having "come through the storm": an individual goes beyond survival and recovery to thrive. As a result, thriving does not depend solely on physical health outcomes, but includes psychological, social, and spiritual growth. More to the point, thriving may be possible in the absence of physical recovery from disease, as in the case of an individual fighting an illness such as ovarian cancer or HIV/AIDS.

Resilience and thriving offer a new way to "include" gender in our definitions of adaptation, because it moves beyond viewing health issues solely in terms of vulnerability, deficits, or risk factors and refocuses on strengths and capabilities. Although women experience greater degrees and different types of stress than men, they also have a broader fund of stress-resistance resources. On the biological level, hormones provide a protective health advantage to women, at least until menopause, reducing risk of cardiovascular disease and osteoporosis. On the psychosocial level, social relationships may be a key to women's resilience. Research has found that women have stronger support networks and are able to mobilize help in a crisis more easily than men, both of which have been linked to better adaptation. Moreover, there is recent evidence that the expression of emotions, long considered a coping strategy that is linked to depression, may be an adaptive strategy for women and not for men. Clearly, in future research on adaptation to illness, we need gendered approaches, not simply defining phenomena relative to a male norm, but as they vary within a heterogeneous population of women.

SUGGESTED READING

Baum, A., Revenson, T. A., and Singer, J. E. (eds). (2001). *Handbook of Health Psychology*. Erlbaum, Mahwah, NJ.

Blechman, E. A., and Brownell, K. D. (1998). *Behavioral Medicine and Women: A Comprehensive Handbook*. Guilford Press, New York.

DeVellis, B. M., Revenson, T. A., and Blalock, S. J. (1997). Rheumatic disease and women's health. In *Health Care For Women: Psychological, Social, and Behavioral Influences* (S. J. Gallant, G. P. Keita, and R. Royak-Schaler, eds.), pp. 333–348. American Psychological Association, Washington, DC.

Gallant, S. J., Keita, G. P., and Royak-Schaler, R. (1997). *Health Care for Women: Psychological, Social, and Behavioral Influences*. American Psychological Association, Washington, DC.

Moyer, A. (1997). Psychosocial outcomes of breast-conserving surgery versus mastectomy: A meta-analytic review. *Health Psychology* 16(3), 284–298.

O'Leary, V. E., and Ickovics, J. R. (1995). Resilience and thriving in response to challenge: An opportunity for a paradigm shift in women's health. *Women's Health: Research on Gender, Behavior, and Policy* 1, 121–142.

Royak-Schaler, R., Stanton, A. L., and Danoff-Burg, S. (1997). Breast cancer: Psychosocial factors influencing risk perception, screening, diagnosis, and treatment. In *Health Care For*

Women: Psychological, Social, and Behavioral Influences (S. J. Gallant, G. P. Keita, and R. Royak-Schaler, eds.), pp. 295–314. American Psychological Association, Washington, DC.

Stanton, A. L., Collins, C. A., & Sworowski, L. A. (2001). Adjustment to chronic illness: Theory and research. In *Handbook of Health Psychology* (A. S. Baum, T. A. Revenson, and J. E. Singer, eds.), pp. 387–403. Erlbaum, Mahwah, NJ.

Stanton, A. L., and Gallant, S. J. (1995). *The Psychology of Women's Health: Progress and Challenges in Research and Application*. American Psychological Association, Washington, DC.

Taylor, S. E. (1983). Adjustment to threatening events: A theory of cognitive adaptation. *American Psychologist* 38(11), 1161–1173.

Classroom and School Climate

Denise M. DeZolt
Stephen H. Hull
University at Albany, State University of New York

Glossary

Bullying Behaviors such as hitting, kicking, picking on someone, intimidation, ignoring, repeated hostile teasing directed toward a person by an individual or group of people.

Gender equity Freedom from bias or favoritism of one gender group over another. An environment in which fair and equitable opportunities, access, benefits, and resources are available to both sexes.

Sexual harassment A range of unwanted and unwelcomed sexual behaviors such as sexual looks and comments, inappropriate touching or brushing against a person, and derogatory comments and slurs.

Special education A range of services provided to students identified as having special learning needs according to criteria established by federal legislation.

Title IX Civil rights law that prohibits sex discrimination in federally funded educational activities and programs.

Violence Physical or verbal assault, harm, or threats of harm against persons; may also involve the use of weapons or incendiary devices.

SCHOOL AND CLASSROOM CLIMATE includes the safety, relational, social-emotional, and environmental factors that influence the quality of learning experiences, academic achievement, and the psychological well-being of learners.

I. Introduction

Ms. Lamont teaches fourth grade, and she is as much mother as mentor and teacher to her students. When she reads during story time the boys and girls hold their breaths and their muscles are frozen in time. Her classroom is a warm and safe place to be, and her students want to come to school to be with Ms. Lamont. They feel understood, challenged, and respected. They know the boundaries in the classroom and follow the school authority structure.

What is the experience of a fourth grader in a classroom on any given day in a school in the United

States? How is it similar to the experiences of a tenth grader? In many instances, the answers to these questions depend on if you are a girl or a boy. Yet each hopes to experience a sense of community and connection, to be respected and understood, to feel safe, to be intellectually challenged, to find learning related to their real world, to have their learning needs addressed in the instructional strategies used by their teachers, and to find themselves reflected in their textbooks and other instructional materials. Although there are differences along gender lines, these factors comprise key elements of school and classroom climate. How the climate of the school and the classroom *feels* and *is perceived* by all students is a large factor in the successful academic and social development of all students.

Schools are places where children and youth need to learn not only academics, but also how to problem solve, get along with others, respect authority, and celebrate diversity and commonality. The climate of the school environment affects their ability to succeed in each of these areas.

II. Gender Issues in U.S. Elementary Schools

In U.S. elementary schools, girls may perceive the climate of the school or the classroom in ways that differ significantly from their same-age male peers. This section examines research findings that are relatively consistent across race and ethnicity. For example, compliance, following rules, and being neat and orderly (behaviors typically associated with girls) are valued and reinforced in elementary classroom settings. Thus girls are likely to receive praise, to feel accepted, and to be validated based on their behavior. Across all elementary grades, girls tend to be more engaged with academic material. That is, they are more likely to put forth effort in class, pay attention, and participate in class. In addition, they appear to have greater concern for their academic performance. In contrast, many boys in all grades, particularly in kindergarten through grade 6, appear to perceive the school and classroom climate to be less than hospitable, more feminine (more female teachers, stereotypically feminine norms), and at times unresponsive to their needs. This is particularly salient for boys of color whose school experience is more negative than their Caucasian male peers and than girls regardless of race or ethnicity.

During the elementary school years students are developing their feelings and beliefs about school in general and their school in particular. It is a time when they decide if school is a friendly place where they feel safe, understood, and encouraged, and where they are presented with a curriculum that interests them. Or they may decide it is an indifferent and unfriendly place where they feel misunderstood, are not encouraged to learn, and the curriculum is uninteresting. For many girls and boys, school is often viewed as just such an unfriendly place in which they do not feel safe emotionally and where they are forced to interact with a curriculum that, for them, is boring. In addition, the preponderance of attention boys receive is related to their difficulty remaining seated, following the rules, engaging with the material, and respecting others' personal space.

Academic and social success in the early school years are critical factors in future academic, social, and career success for all students. In general, a growing body of research on school and classroom climate indicates that elementary school climates often favor girls with regard to several factors and handicap boys on others. Compared to girls, boys read fewer books and get poorer grades in all subjects in all grades with the exception of some math and science courses. Girls are more likely to do their homework than their male counterparts. Girls, therefore, are reinforced for their gender-stereotypic behavior, whereas boys are punished for theirs. This places boys at greater risk for being suspended from school, getting into more fights, dropping out of school early, being placed in special education programs, becoming involved with the law or crime, using alcohol or other drugs, and committing suicide. Although it may appear that girls are at an advantage due to their behavioral status, those same gendered characteristics that are reinforced in elementary school may put them at risk in secondary school, where the demands for more teacher attention and support in content areas are related to academic success.

The quality of learning that occurs in the elementary grades is highly correlated with the level of academic success achieved later in school for both sexes. Girls' achievement in math and science approximates that of their same-grade male counterparts. Mastery of fundamental reading and writing skills is deemed by most educators to be a primary requirement for academic success in secondary school and college. In the elementary grades, boys experience reading success later than girls. Additionally, the gap between their skill levels and the comparative reading skill levels of girls increases as they progress through middle and high school. One U.S. national reading test found that the average 11th grade boy reads at the same level as the average 8th grade girl. More boys than girls are diagnosed with reading problems. Not only are boys more challenged in reading, but there is also evidence that boys struggle to achieve grade-level writing skills. Because reading and writing are necessary for nearly all subjects in school, a lack of these essential language arts skills has the natural effect of lowering achievement across all subject areas. Thus in the elementary years, boys tend to be punished by their teachers more than girls, to fall behind their female peers in reading and writing skills, and to be identified as students with learning problems. Across handicapping conditions and special needs, boys are overrepresented in the population who are classified and receiving services.

A. GENDER AND SPECIAL EDUCATION IN ELEMENTARY SCHOOL

The elementary school years are the time when many students are classified as having special needs deserving of special education services. There are two to three boys for every girl who receive special education services in the elementary grades. One of the most common classifications is attention deficit disorder or attention deficit hyperactivity disorder (ADD/ADHD). The large majority (estimates as high as 90%) of those diagnosed with ADD/ADHD are boys. The disorder is diagnosed in approximately 3 to 5% of school-age children and is 4 to 9 times more frequent in boys than in girls. It has been suggested that both underidentification in girls and overidentification in boys may account for the higher incidence reported for boys. Children who exhibit attentional and behavioral problems that are developmentally inappropriate relative to their age, typically boys rather than girls, are often referred to psychologists or physicians for assessment for ADD/ADHD. One possible reason why boys are overidentified for ADD/ADHD is that the climate in the school or classroom does not accommodate their learning styles and physical needs. They are expected to conform to behavioral rules that may favor the style of girls, and which are, for the most part, designed and reinforced by female teachers. Conforming to acceptable behavioral standards in the classroom tends to be easier for girls than for boys and may account for the higher percentage of boys that are referred for behavioral problems, disruptive behavior, or special education

assessment. [*See* Diagnosis of Psychological Disorders.]

III. *Gender Issues in Middle and High Schools*

As youth enter middle and high school, academic and social-emotional differences by gender persist, though the nature and direction may change. These differences continue to have implications for the classroom climate. The preponderance of research about gender issues at these levels has been rooted in a desire to enhance our understanding of the strengths and needs of girls. In middle and high school, girls seem to benefit from a learning environment that capitalizes on their academic competence through use of both cooperative and competitive learning strategies. In addition, they need leadership opportunities as well as female leaders to serve as role models.

Although much work has been done to document how girls' academic and social-emotional needs are or are not being met in schools, recent research indicates that boys' needs are also going unmet in key areas. According to William Pollack in 1998, school personnel tend to ignore the fact that many boys are clearly having academic problems, particularly in the language arts. In addition, school personnel typically are unaware of and ill equipped to adequately address the unique social and emotional needs of boys. Thus Pollack recommends that school professionals suspend their tendency to characterize boys' behavior as problematic. He further suggests that rather than allow a climate that is antagonistic toward boys, they attempt to create a school environment that is more appropriately responsive to boys' educational and social emotional needs. These findings are consistent with those from more qualitative studies of boys' school experiences. For example, boys' narratives about their lives in school reveal that many feel singled out by teachers and feel at a disadvantage academically. Still others feel like they are unfairly disciplined in schools and tell stories about their frustration when their attempts to have their voices heard and needs known consistently go unnoticed. Many boys feel disenfranchised in their schools and respond by disengaging from academics, while often simultaneously engaging in disruptive activities such as bullying, noncompliance, fighting, or resisting authority. These behaviors are likely to have a powerful and negative influence on the climate of the school and classroom for both girls and boys.

What happens to the differences between girls and boys in language arts and math and science in middle and high school? The lag in reading and writing skills that many boys experience in the elementary years tends to gets worse in middle and high school. At this time, even the slight advantage that some boys may have had over some girls in achievement in math and science is dwindling. That is, the gap between boys' and girls' achievement in math and science scores in high school is narrowing, with the girls gaining ground and nearly overtaking the boys. Despite the fact that boys more so than girls tend to choose less demanding courses in general, boys are more likely to take advanced courses in math, science, and technology. In the information technology arena, rather than enroll in the more challenging advanced courses, girls often select more basic (e.g., clerical and data entry) courses. Thus, girls seldom place in the top 5% in advanced math and science classes or in advanced technology classes. A close examination of girls' attitudes and behaviors related to information technology reveals that girls are less likely than boys to consider it as a possible career, in part due to their misperception that it is an isolated and solitary profession. In addition, software programs in general, and for schools in particular, tend to promote gender-based stereotypes and biases, further contributing to the gender differences in information technology.

Recent evidence suggests that the bottom half (academically) of regular education high school classes are *predominantly* made up of boys. That is, although many boys perform at an average level and a few may be gifted students, the bottom 50% of classroom performers in many high schools is made up mostly of boys. For many of these boys, and for girls who have not met with academic success, school holds little hope and they choose to drop out. Still others remain in school for social rather than academic reasons. They may become disruptive to the educational process in the classroom, thus interfering with the learning of their peers.

A. EXTRACURRICULAR PARTICIPATION

High school students enhance their social, physical, and emotional development through participation in school-related, nonacademic activities. The climate of the extracurricular arena seems to foster greater involvement of girls in student government, school

newspapers, and honor societies. In contrast, boys still dominate in sports. In the nearly 30 years since the passage in 1972 of Title IX of the Elementary and Secondary Education Act, there has been a dramatic increase in girls' access to and participation in high school and collegiate athletics, and in some sports that both sexes participate in, such as soccer and basketball, girls are represented in equal numbers. In general, however, more funding overall is allocated for boys sporting activities (especially football) than for girls sporting activities. [See SPORT AND ATHLETICS.]

B. GENDER AND SPECIAL EDUCATION IN MIDDLE AND HIGH SCHOOL

When youth with special needs enter middle and high school, their special education classifications typically follow. In fact, very few of the girls or boys who are identified as special needs students in elementary grades are declassified in the middle or high school levels. Thus, once classified, students tend to stay classified until they either drop out of school or graduate. There is growing evidence, however, that boys in particular may be overrepresented in special education, partly because they are identified in the elementary years as having learning and behavioral problems due to poor skills in reading and writing. This places them at a disadvantage because very few boys or girls are ever declassified. For these students, the stigma associated with their special needs status is further complicated by their developmental press for peer acceptance and belonging. Students with special needs in middle and high school are more likely to be successful in school settings in which the climate is one of acceptance of a broad array of diversity and where all members of the school community experience a sense of belonging.

C. TRANSITION TO COLLEGE

Since the passage of Title IX, the percentage of girls attending college and universities and obtaining professional degrees has increased dramatically. In contrast, according to the National Center for Education Statistics, recent trends in college enrollment show a gradual decline in the enrollment of boys as a percentage of all students. The percentage of boys among all college students in the 1950s was near 60%. Now the percentage of boys enrolled in classes in four-year colleges is nearing 45%, and declining each year.

Individual girls or boys in any given school may experience greater or lesser risk for success and failure than the group norm. Individual boys or girls may place at the top of their class in every subject and be accepted at the best colleges and universities. Individual girls or boys may excel in the extracurricular activities in school and develop healthy social and interpersonal skills. Yet for many, the experience of school is a very painful one indeed and an experience that is shaped in some ways by the climate of the school and the classroom.

Both girls and boys in middle and high school are likely to be academically successful when they are held to high academic expectations and a demanding curriculum. To facilitate both their academic and social-emotional development, learners at these levels also benefit from an environment in which they are academically engaged, experience positive teacher–student relationships, and navigate their daily lives in school with shared prosocial norms.

IV. Single-Sex Schooling

Single-sex classrooms and schools have been suggested as a partial solution to gender biases in education. Proponents of single-sex schools and classrooms contend that such settings provide an environment that is more conducive to academic achievement, especially for girls. For example, they hypothesize that for girls, the decreased competition with male counterparts corresponds with increased achievement in math and science.

In general, research about single-sex schools and classrooms presents mixed findings with regard to better academic achievement, more gender-appropriate instructional methods and materials, and a more gender-equitable overall climate for girls and boys. In fact, there is little support overall that single-sex schooling is free from sexism in terms of curricula or behavioral norms than coeducational schooling. Yet the most consistent findings indicate that the factors such as small class size, high academic standards, demanding curriculum, and gender-equitable classroom environments and teaching strategies are essential for the academic success of all students regardless of gender or type of setting. [*See* SEX SEGREGATION IN EDUCATION.]

V. Teacher–Student Interactions

Perhaps the most commonly shared event in schools is students' interactions with their teachers. Students and teachers relate on a daily basis about such issues as academic content, praise, feedback, discipline, and classroom behaviors and norms. An examination of teacher–student interactions reveals that absent any gender-equity training, teachers tend to exhibit a pattern of gender bias in their interactions with students.

A consistent body of evidence reveals that teachers give more attention of all kinds to boys in the classroom. This includes attention for instructional purposes, misbehavior, and simple communication in general. Girls are less likely than boys to be the recipients of critical attention from teachers and have more days when their interactions with teachers are minimal. Girls are more likely than boys to be reprimanded for calling out an answer without raising their hands. Thus, boys are more audible in the classroom and are given more communicative leeway. Teachers tend to interact more with high-achieving boys than with high-achieving girls. In addition, they are likely to give girls the answer when they ask for help, but tend to help the boys to employ strategies to ascertain the answer themselves. To ameliorate the effects of gender bias in teacher–student interactions, gender-equity training programs have been developed and implemented. Teachers who receive gender-equity training are more sensitive to issues of gender bias. They are also more likely to exhibit gender-equitable interaction patterns with their students.

VI. Gender in Reading Materials

What learners read informs who they are, how they fit in their worlds, and how others view them. When learners' experiences are ignored or omitted, marginalized or trivialized, rendered invisible, presented in fragmented ways as add-ons to the curriculum or stereotyped in texts, so too are they. When they read depictions of themselves as competent people who have voices that are heard and experiences that are honored, they are likewise honored and see themselves as competent. Despite efforts to be more inclusive of and sensitive to matters of gender, race, class, and ethnicity, textbooks typically used in schools continue to perpetuate gender-based and heterosexist paradigms. In fact, even within these efforts there is a tendency to oversimplify the unique and combined contributions of gender, class, ethnicity, and race. In addition, although the number of female authors and authors of color is increasing, most textbooks are still written by White male authors whose experiences typically do not reflect those of the female and minority students that comprise the vast majority of learners in many classrooms across the country. Authors of recent editions of commonly used school texts have attempted to be more attentive to gender, class, race, and ethnic stereotyping in the language, examples, and illustrations they use.

Concerns about gender inclusivity and appropriate representation extend to children's literature, especially given its high level of use in elementary classrooms. An analysis of children's literature reveals that boys' names are more often represented in titles of children's books than are girls' names. It is also quite common to find that even when the protagonist is a girl, or if a girl's name is in the title, the story has a boy as a central figure. To the further detriment of readers, both boys and girls are often portrayed as engaging in gender stereotypic behaviors. For example, girls are typically portrayed as kind, nice, passive, and dependent, whereas boys are typically resourceful, active, and independent. As problem solvers, boys are usually portrayed as clever, ingenious, and capable of resolving their own difficulties. In contrast, girls are likely to be depicted as able to resolve their difficulties only through the assistance of others. Children's literature that portrays both boys and girls across race and ethnicity in nonstereotypic and stereotypic behaviors allows readers to expand their points of view and depictions of the self. [*See* GENDER STEREOTYPES.]

In a gender-sensitive classroom climate, all learners are able to explore their constructions of gender in the texts that they read and in the stories they share in an atmosphere of acceptance and freedom to explore all aspects of gender without sanction. They have the opportunity to engage with texts that represent both boys and girls as mutually able to be caring, sensitive, able to offer and receive assistance, competent, capable, and intelligent across a variety of situations. To this end, reading materials in the classroom environment must be examined with regard to the diversity of gender experiences represented and to be supplemented to ensure a broad representation. School personnel need to remain aware of the potentially powerful overt and covert messages about gender in reading materials for situating boys' and girls' understanding of themselves in their worlds.

VII. Violence, Bullying, and Sexual Harassment

Although violence, bullying, and sexual harassment are typically discussed as separate issues, there is overlap in their definitions and descriptive criteria. Therefore, they are presented here as a cluster of negative behaviors that adversely affect school climate; have negative effects ranging from mild to severe on students' physical, academic, personal, and interpersonal lives; and have implications for gender concerns in school settings.

In general, boys are responsible for the preponderance of violence, bullying, and sexual harassment that take place in the schools. Girls are more generally the victims of these negative behaviors, although more recently there is concern about a rise in the incidence of violence among girls. [*See* AGGRESSION AND GENDER.]

A. VIOLENCE

Despite the introduction of dress codes, metal detectors, security personnel, and zero-tolerance policies, violence in the schools continues to be a major concern for school personnel, students, parents, communities, and law enforcement officers. A variety of attitudinal, experiential, and normative factors contribute to our understanding of violence in schools as well as to related gender differences. For example, boys report more favorable attitudes toward guns and violence than girls. Yet for both girls and boys exposure to school violence is a predictor of aggression. Boys who place a priority on academics are less likely to engage in violence than their nonacademically oriented same-sex counterparts. When there are personal and group norms that discourage violence, both sexes are less likely to engage in violent behavior. School climate has been found to be a factor in the incidence of school violence. Specifically a school climate that allows and tolerates minor expressions of aggression tends to promote school violence. Similarly, whereas a militaristic approach to school violence may have as its intended effect lowering the incidence of school violence, it often results in increased incidence of violence. In contrast, school norms that promote a strong sense of community, caring, inclusion, and connection, and where all students feel known and understood by at least one adult, create a climate where violence and aggression are less likely to occur. In addition, realistic and enforceable discipline policies that are consistently employed contribute to a more equitable and just climate. School personnel who are concerned about reducing violence often struggle with their own feelings of inadequacy to deal with the perceived magnitude of the problem, how best to intervene, and how to deal with the immediate crisis management of a violent situation. Thus they would benefit from preservice and in-service training, ongoing professional development, and supervised practice related to addressing the precursors and sequela (including posttraumatic stress) of violence. Further professional development in the areas of risk reduction, enhancing coping and resilience, and negotiating the community support systems also contribute to the creation of a climate that reduces the risk of violence. Finally, school personnel need to examine the emergent research on the efficacy of nonviolence and prosocial normative curricula to ascertain the components that are most successful in violence reduction.

B. BULLYING IN SCHOOLS

Bullying occurs when a student intentionally or repeatedly harms another student, either psychologically or physically. Boys and girls alike are victims and perpetrators of bullying in school environments. Both are likely to bully others of both sexes, but boys are more likely to bully girls than to bully other boys. According to self-reports of bullying, up to 70% of students experience bullying at some time in their school career, and 14% of students indicate that bullying has a significant negative impact on their lives. Although social and verbal bullying are experienced more by girls, threats and violent forms of physical bullying are experienced more by boys. Social bullying for girls may take the form of the "silent treatment" or by having rumors spread about them. In addition, girls more commonly use teasing and ridicule when bullying than do boys.

The attitudes and actions of teachers and school staff help create a climate that encourages or discourages bullying in the schools. There is significant evidence that teachers and school staff may tend to ignore bullying in the school. For example, less than one-third of teachers reported becoming involved in incidences of bullying. Support for the notion that students should not "tattle" on their peers perpetuates a school climate that tolerates bullying. School personnel who choose to recognize bullying, and who provide a supportive and protective environment for students who are bullied, create a school climate wherein bullying is reported and is likely to decrease.

Particularly for boys, gender socialization and social norms tend to support the beliefs that the tough survive and that pretending that you are unhurt physically or emotionally is a sign of strength and manhood. Interventions such as systemwide discipline policies, curricula that include components designed to educate students about the nature and extent of bullying, in-service training for teachers and staff, and a proactive home-school connection have been found to be effective in decreasing bullying in the schools. In addition, programs such as peer-mediation training and empathy building have been found to decrease the likelihood of bullying in the schools or provide for a more suitable method of identifying bullying and providing therapeutic services to both bully and victim.

C. SEXUAL HARASSMENT

In high schools across the country the majority of girls and boys are likely to report some form of sexual harassment by peers and school personnel. Although both adolescent boys and girls report incidences of sexual harassment, girls appear somewhat more likely to experience sexual harassment and to view it as problematic. When girls are sexually harassed, they are likely to experience concomitant effects such as academic difficulties, physical symptoms (e.g., headache, gastrointestinal problems), interpersonal relationship and sexual difficulties, and changes in behavioral and recreational activities. For these young women, the quality of their educational experience is negatively affected by sexual harassment. Boys who experience sexual harassment tend to report similar patterns of negative effects.

In a classroom of 30 students, 1 to 3 of them may be gay, lesbian, bisexual, or transgendered youth who are likely to encounter further alienation related to sexual harassment in school settings. Sexual minority youth, many of whom are struggling with sexual identity concerns, the coming out process, and antigay violence, are typical victims of harassment including name calling, slurs, gay bashing, and physical assault. It is not uncommon for them to hear routinely in elementary and secondary school hallways such comments as "You fag" and "It's so gay," and to know that this name calling is only the beginning of a broader range of harassing and damaging behaviors. Again, although both girls and boys report being harassed on the basis of sexual orientation, this issue is more prevalent and more stigmatizing for boys. Furthermore, boys of color who are harassed in relation to sexual orientation face the combined negative effects of their dual minority status—race and sexual orientation. Sexual minority youth report high levels of physical violence, verbal abuse, and harassment in schools, and a quarter attribute their dropping out of school to such negative treatment. In addition, sexual minority youth are likely to experience isolation, stigmatization, internalized homophobia, and high absenteeism. Also, a significant number of sexual minority youth who attempt or succeed at suicide may do so because of anxiety, fear, or depression surrounding sexual identity issues. Despite this bleak picture, for those sexual minority youth who are strong academic achievers the school setting may be viewed as a potential source of support.

Both the National Association of School Psychologists and the American Psychological Association have enacted policies related to the equitable and safe support of gay, lesbian, and bisexual youth and have worked to address the needs of these youth in school settings. Their efforts are directed at enhancing school climate factors that confront sexual harassment at multiple levels.

A school climate that supports and understands the importance of confidentiality when reporting incidences of sexual harassment increases the likelihood that incidences will be reported and handled appropriately. A supportive school climate includes availability of information regarding the nature of sexual harassment, the formation of a crisis team or intervention team designated to handle sexual harassment complaints, and a safety and security plan for harassed students. A school climate that ignores reported sexual harassment or dismisses perpetrators without consequence decreases the likelihood that incidences will be reported and increases the likelihood that future incidences will occur. Teacher and staff attitudes toward the significance of sexual harassment also affect the school climate. Those who consider it a significant issue tend to become more versed in effective strategies for identifying sexual harassment and for creating a school climate that fosters an ethos of safety and respect. Students of both sexes need to feel that school is a place where they are safe from sexual harassment, and that if it does occur, there will be adults in the school who will support and protect them and to follow the appropriate ethical and legal guidelines. [See SEXUAL HARASSMENT.]

VIII. Conclusions

School and classroom climate is related to students' academic, social-emotional, and developmental maturity in gender-biased ways. School climate is a powerful tool in helping to create schools with little gender bias. Although school climate is a construct with many components, it is a necessary part of any systemwide change that attempts to address issues of gender bias in the schools. Many of the gender-biased attitudes in schools are below the level of awareness and are deeply entrenched in and supported by the general culture. Increasing the awareness of gender bias in the schools is therefore a necessary step toward reducing and ultimately eliminating it in our schools. Creating a climate in the schools that encourages open and honest communication between and among school personnel and students will go far in beginning to raise the level of awareness of gender bias in the schools.

What, then, are characteristics of school and classroom climates that promote the academic achievement and social well-being of all girls and boys? To begin, it appears that teachers who receive gender-equity training are more likely to be responsive to equity concerns in their classrooms. In general, a supportive classroom climate includes an atmosphere where learners' voices are heard; where the classroom operates as a community of learners; where a sense of caring, belonging, and acceptance is perceived and practiced; where normative and clear limits and expectations for classroom behavior are clearly expressed; where freedom to take risks is celebrated; and where learners take responsibility for their learning and for setting realistic goals for themselves. Learners across all grades need to see positive male and female role models in teaching and leadership positions. A positive school climate that places a high priority on the respect and celebration of gender diversity issues will greatly contribute to the reduction of gender bias in our schools.

SUGGESTED READING

American Association of University Women at http://www.aauw.org

Duncan, N. (1999). *Sexual Bullying: Gender Conflict and Pupil Culture in Secondary Schools.* Routledge, New York.

Johnson, N. G., Roberts, M. C., and Worell, J. (1999). *Beyond Appearance: A New Look at Adolescent Girls.* American Psychological Association, Washington, DC.

Katz, M., Noddings, N., and Strike, K. (eds.) (1999). *Justice and Caring: The search for Common Ground in Education.* Teachers College, New York.

National Center for Education Statistics at http://www.nces.ed.gov

Pollack, W. (1998). *Real Boys: Rescuing Our Boys from the Myths of Boyhood.* Henry Holt, New York.

Counseling and Psychotherapy
Gender, Race/Ethnicity, and Sexuality

Lucia Albino Gilbert

Jill Rader

The University of Texas at Austin

I. Counseling and Psychotherapy: Historical Roots and Definition
II. Traditional Considerations of Gender, Ethnicity, and Sexuality in Counseling and Psychotherapy
III. Evolving Conceptualizations of Gender, Ethnicity, and Sexuality
IV. Practice Issues with Regard to Gender, Ethnicity, and Sexuality
V. Contemporary Concerns for Clients
VI. Conclusions

Glossary

Counseling and psychotherapy A complicated process that occurs between a client and a trained psychologist that is focused on assisting the client.

Culture Broadly, the pattern of arrangements, material or behavioral, characterizing a particular society. It includes social institutions and knowledge, belief systems, morals, and customs.

Dominant discourses The mechanisms through which traditional views of various groups, and members of groups, are presented and preserved in the majority culture. Dominant discourses are linguistic (including verbal and nonverbal communication) and nonlinguistic (including everyday practices and institutional structures) and typically preserve the "status quo" by perpetuating the values of the most powerful group(s) in society.

Ethnicity A complex multidimensional construct that refers to culture, ethnic identity, and minority status often used in describing ethnic groups of color in the United States.

Gender The psychological, social, and cultural features and characteristics that have become strongly associated with the biological categories of female and male. Gender can become manifest in a culture as essential sex differences, as ways to organize women and men via laws and implicit policies, as the language and discourse to describe what is normative for women and men, and as interpersonal processes reproducing that society's meaning of what it means to be a woman or a man.

Sex Refers to whether one is born biologically female or male.

Sexual orientation Defined by the sex of the person with whom one forms an emotional and sexual bond. Behavior is not necessarily reflective of one's sexual orientation.

Sexuality One's biological and psychological capacity to engage in sexual feelings, activity, or intercourse. For heterosexual couples, sexuality may include the capacity to reproduce.

GENDER, ETHNICITY, SEXUALITY, AND CULTURAL ISSUES must be considered in the theoretical approaches and practice of counseling and psychotherapy. This article first describes the powerful critiques of the patriarchal nature of psychological theories and psychotherapeutic practice and then describes current and emerging theories and practice that bring an explicit discussion of gender, race, and sexual orientation into the therapy room. Particularly crucial to current theories is understanding that ethnicity, gender, and sexuality are contextual and socially constructed.

I. *Counseling and Psychotherapy: Historical Roots and Definition*

Sage counselors have always existed. Psychologists professionally trained to engage in counseling and psychotherapy, however, represent a relatively recent phenomenon. Counseling has its early roots in vocational guidance and normal human growth and development. Psychotherapy, in contrast, has its early roots in mental health, intrapsychic conflicts that interfere with normal development, and abnormal personality development.

The confluence of the vocational guidance and mental health movements occurred in the years following the outbreak of the Second World War. In 1944, the Veteran's Administration (VA) established counseling centers within their hospitals and used the term "counseling psychologist" for individuals trained to work with the psychological problems of "normal people." Attention was focused on the psychology of human differences, especially the study of individual differences in intelligence, aptitudes, interests, and personality, which were viewed as important for effective assignments during the war and for postwar job placement. At about this same time, the VA initiated large-scale training programs to meet the heavy demands for mental health services occasioned by the war and the more severe mental problems experienced by veterans. Clinical psychology as we know it today also largely evolved from these VA initiatives. Clinical psychologists were called upon to do "mental testing" and to provide interpretations of their findings using perspectives of mental health closely tied to medical models and psychoanalytical theories of human behavior.

The development of counseling and psychotherapy separate from medical and psychoanalytical perspectives is largely attributed to the work of Carl Rogers and the publication of his first book, *Counseling and Psychotherapy*, in 1942. In marked contrast to the psychoanalytical theories heavily influencing U.S. psychology, which emphasized psychotherapy as a medical therapy performed by medically trained psychiatrists, Rogers' book espoused a counseling relationship whose characteristics were warmth and responsiveness of the therapist and a permissive climate in which the feelings of the client could be freely expressed. According to Rogers, a client in such a relationship would gain self-understanding and would be empowered to make decisions without an authoritarian therapist. Rogers' theory emphasized trust in the client and the importance of the relationship between the therapist and the client.

Originally Rogers chose the term "counseling" to describe his theoretical approach because it was less controversial than using the term "psychotherapy." Psychiatry had long considered psychotherapy as its field. Rogers' theory proved to be highly influential and popular among U.S. psychologists, however. Its explicit assumption that one could perform psychotherapy without a medical degree became an important factor in expanding counseling psychology and clinical psychology to include not only personal counseling and vocational and mental assessment, but also psychotherapeutic interventions. Another important factor facilitating psychologists' role in providing psychotherapy was the report of the Joint Commission on Mental Illness and Health in 1961. This report authorized increased government funding for mental health services and training and emphasized psychotherapy as a basic service to be provided by psychologists in outpatient mental health clinics. This focus on psychotherapy was accompanied by an increased acceptance of psychotherapy as an intervention for psychological problems and disorders, particularly among the middle and upper classes of our society.

The field of counseling and psychotherapy is characterized by a variety of schools and theoretical viewpoints: feminist, humanist, cognitive, person-centered, behavioral, psychodynamic, and psychoanalytic, among others. Many practicing psychologists, however, identify themselves as eclectic or integrative in that they do not limit themselves to the procedures of any one theoretical orientation but rather combine aspects of various approaches in their therapeutic work with clients. Feminist therapy, for example, takes a number of forms and can be incorporated in a variety of theoretical approaches to counseling and psychotherapy, including the cognitive-behavioral and person centered. Moreover, despite the diversity of theoretical approaches, a large body of research shows that the psychotherapeutic relationship is central to effective therapeutic change and that the burden of work for therapeutic change is on the client. The highly confidential nature of the relationship, the role of the therapist as an interested and understanding expert, the motivation of the client for making possible changes, and the working alliance that develops between the client and therapist are all aspects of the psychotherapy that contribute to making the ongoing interactions useful for the client.

II. Traditional Considerations of Gender, Ethnicity, and Sexuality in Counseling and Psychotherapy

Historically, the field of counseling and psychotherapy largely ignored people of color and issues of cultural background. Gender, when considered, focused on how women differed from, and were lesser than, men. Only one sexual orientation, heterosexuality, was considered normal.

A. INVISIBILITY

Despite the significant role that women have played in U.S. society and despite the cultural diversity that has typified this country since its origins, the functioning and needs of women; gay, lesbian, and bisexual (GLB) people; and people of color has remained unexplored until fairly recently. In the 1968 classic paper, "Psychology Constructs the Female," Naomi Weisstein described how psychology as a field could say nothing about women because women had not been studied.

The invisibility of women, GLB people, and racial minorities has manifested itself in several ways. First, because oppressed groups have held an unequal political and economic status in society, they have not been visible leaders in our communities. Those who assume leadership positions in government, educational institutions, and the workplace, as well as in the family unit, have therefore had the power to set the agendas. The policies and laws in our country reflect the majority-culture bias and the lack of representation of women, people of color, and GLB people. Therefore, the invisibility of oppressed groups extends beyond the lack of role models. Invisibility also occurs with regard to whose rights are pro-

tected, whose needs are met, and whose psychological functioning is studied. For example, until the 1970s, the vast majority of psychological studies have relied on data collected from male, Caucasian, middle-class college students. Thus, most of our theories of human behavior have been based on data that have not been reflective of the population as a whole with regard to sex, race, and socioeconomic status.

B. BETWEEN-GROUPS DIFFERENCE

Traditional views of gender, race, and sexual orientation have also focused on differences between the groups, using the White heterosexual male as the site of comparison. With regard to sex and gender, psychology has historically followed a gender-as-difference model that emphasizes "essential" differences between women and men and ignores the great degree of overlap in the cognitive abilities and personality characteristics between the two sexes. Theories relied entirely on the unquestioned cultural assumption that women and men are "opposite" in their abilities, life roles, and choice of sexual partners and that their "opposite sex" nature was biologically determined. [See GENDER DIFFERENCE RESEARCH: ISSUES AND CRITIQUE.]

Similarly, a between-groups difference has been overstated in social science research with regard to people of different races and sexual orientations. Again, the emphasis has been how such groups deviate from the norm rather than on the considerable overlap between majority and minority culture people, or on the considerable within-groups variability found among gay and lesbian people, people of the same race, and so on. This research on difference is not always conducted with the intent to present diverse groups in an unfavorable light. For example, the presumed high academic achievement of Asian Americans and the presumed equity of lesbian and gay partnerships have become social stereotypes and the focus of research activity. Nonetheless, the emphasis on between-groups difference, whether that difference favors the majority or minority culture, overestimates the dissimilarities between cultural groups and may foster an "us/them" mentality.

C. PATHOLOGY

Though, as mentioned earlier, comparisons can be advantageous for a minority group, the differences between the White heterosexual male norm and "other" are often pathologized at the expense of nonmajority groups. For example, it was not until the mid-1970s that homosexuality was removed as a disorder from the *Diagnostic and Statistical Manual of Mental Disorders (DSM)*.

The tendency of the majority culture to pathologize women has been well documented. As far back as the 19th century, early feminist critics called into question practices that unfairly labeled women as sick, psychologically inferior or deviant. For example, Charlotte Perkins Gilman, in *The Yellow Wallpaper*, presented a chilling account of how one male doctor's "resting cure" for women drove a once prolific writer to madness. Phyllis Chesler's groundbreaking work, *Women and Madness*, published in 1972, documented how standards and practices of mental health pathologized women for the stresses and discrimination they endured and for asserting themselves as human beings who deserved respect. Consistent with the psychodynamic theories of the time, the female role was itself viewed as a model for pathology, a situation that placed women in a double bind. On the one hand, women were viewed as disturbed because they engaged in behaviors consistent with the traditional female role, such as acting passive and submissive, or living their lives through others. However, they were also viewed as disturbed if they engaged in behaviors outside of the female traditional role, such as promoting their own interests and abilities and not centering their lives around men's wishes and desires.

Ethnic group differences have also been pathologized. Multicultural researchers have explored how explanations of the psychological functioning of minority people have historically adhered to either a genetic-deficient model or a cultural-deficit model. According to the genetic-deficient model, racial minorities were believed to be intellectually inferior to Whites. The majority culture traditionally considered people of color to be uneducatable and, therefore, undeserving of equal academic, social, and occupational opportunities. The cultural-deficient model was more compassionate but had serious flaws. The cultural-deficient model considered minority people to be disadvantaged due to their nonadherence to White, middle-class attitudes, behaviors, and language. Both the genetic-deficient and cultural-deficient models have since fallen into disrepute in the psychological literature due to their cultural biases, gross inaccuracies, and social ramifications (e.g., discrimination).

Sexual orientation is one of the last remaining battlefields with regard to ending the pathologization of difference. Virginia Woolf used the phrase "other sexes" to point out the need to expand our way of thinking about sexual difference. We live increasingly in a world where genders, sexes, and sexualities are more fluid, and where individuals do not view sexual expression as defining their biological sex or their socially constructed gender. Yet heterosexuality remains the norm, which is reflected in the relative lack of attention to GLB clients in the psychological literature and in graduate psychology program curricula. Furthermore, much of the existing research on the psychological functioning of GLB people continues to fall prey to damaging and pathologizing stereotypes. For example, with regard to lesbian relationships, much has been written on the tendency for lesbian couples to "merge" or to lose their autonomy. Lesbian "bed death" (cessation of sexual activity) has been another area of research that has received undue attention in social science research and which has not been empirically validated. With regard to diagnosis, "Gender Identity Disorder," a diagnostic category that pathologizes a preference for transgender behaviors, remains in the *DSM-IV*. [*See* LESBIANS, GAY MEN, AND BISEXUALS IN RELATIONSHIPS.]

III. Evolving Conceptualizations of Gender, Ethnicity, and Sexuality

Carolyn Sherif was among the first prominent psychologists to question the validity of a psychological science that seeks to develop general laws by erasing the fact that individuals develop in a social and cultural context. This science has stripped the individuals of their cultural background, personal history, and gender, factors that have a profound impact on how they develop, how they are viewed and treated by others, and how they respond to particular situations. Other writers have provided powerful critiques of the patriarchal nature of psychological theories and psychotherapeutic practice, of White middle-class bias in the study of gender and sexuality, and of the White male bias in racial ethnic studies and studies of homosexuality.

These criticisms have led to significant theoretical advances and to major reconsiderations of gender, ethnicity and sexual orientation in counseling and psychotherapy. Most wide-reaching and compelling are those theories that shift the notions of gender, race, ethnicity, and sexuality from static, biologically located and determined concepts to gender, race, ethnicity, and sexuality as fluid and socially located and constructed concepts. Women and men are not born with gender; they become women and men within the context of their culture. Similarly race and ethnicity are dimensions, not categories, of human experience, and their psychological meaning comes from an individual's social and cultural locations.

A. GENDER AND BIOLOGICAL SEX: TRANSCENDING ESSENTIALISM AND SEXISM

The current definition of gender reflects a more sophisticated awareness of the roles of social forces and power structures in creating and influencing human behavior and signals a rejection of essentialist explanations of sex differences. Researchers in the field hypothesized that behaviors and attitudes previously believed to be determined by sex (female or male) were societal and situationally created rather than intrinsic to the individual. Research emerged to counter prevailing beliefs about sex differences and to provide evidence that differences in power status might better explain sex-related behaviors. With a greater understanding of gender came a better understanding of the power inequities in society—and in the therapy room. Feminist therapy, for example, now positions gender as a locus for understanding oppression and power imbalance. [*See* FEMINIST APPROACHES TO PSYCHOTHERAPY; FEMINIST FAMILY THERAPY.]

In her book with Murray Scher, *Sex and Gender in Counseling and Psychotherapy*, and in other writings, Lucia Albino Gilbert highlighted the ongoing difficulty that many psychotherapists have in differentiating between the constructs of gender and sex. This difficulty may arise from the fact that, although gendered behavior is socially determined, gender as a definition is inextricably bound to biological sex as a point of comparison or reference. Moreover, many practicing therapists remain uninformed about current theories of sex and gender. The view that sex is a construct separate from gender, and that sex is restricted to a biological label, or whether one is born female or male, is often not understood. As a consequence, many therapists are unwittingly replacing the old term "sex" with the new term "gender" and perpetuating stereotypic views in their work with clients.

In their book, Gilbert and Scher identified several "faces of gender" that are particularly salient in the therapy room. These include "gender as difference," "gender as structure," "gender as language and discourse," and "gender as interactive process." Such conceptualizations illuminate how gender processes impact all levels of women's and men's lives, including their work with therapists.

Gender as difference enters the therapy room if therapists advocate roles that are stereotypically male or female, even if challenging such roles might be in the client's best interest. For example, a therapist uninformed of current thinking about gender and sex may fail to challenge a female client's subordination of her own needs and self-definition in relation to those of her husband or family, particularly if she or he assumes that this client is assuming her "natural" biological role and acting out of "essential" female characteristics of caring and nurturance of others.

Gender as structure is evident at the organizational level, including with regard to how therapy services are delivered. Gendered beliefs profoundly influence our social, political, and religious institutions and organizations. In addition, one need only look at the representation by sex in our government, in our churches, synagogues, and temples, and in our *Fortune* 500 companies—which are overwhelmingly male. Therapy and counseling settings may intentionally or nonintentionally perpetuate these institutional inequities. For example, directors of community clinics, hospitals, and counseling centers are more often male than female. In addition, policies at some therapy settings may not be "gender-fair." For example, it is not unusual for settings to use the *DSM-IV* in a way that is pathologizing toward women clients. Another factor to consider is that female clients—who, on average, earn less than male clients—may not have the same access to mental health care providers.

Another important face of gender in counseling and psychotherapy is gender as language and discourse. The role of dominant discourse in shaping what it means to be female versus male, White versus non-White, and heterosexual versus lesbian, gay, or bisexual is discussed in a later section. Therapists who lack an awareness of gender, specifically, may perpetuate damaging and limiting beliefs about women in counseling. Language is profoundly powerful. It shapes our conceptualizations of who we are, and it names what ails us. Feminist critics have argued that some *DSM-IV* diagnoses, for example, are based on gender stereotypes or are disproportionately assigned to either women or men (e.g., the labels of dependent personality disorder, histrionic personality disorder, and borderline personality disorder are almost always given to women). Thus, the *DSM-IV* may overpathologize women or pathologize traits that are fostered in girls and women in this society. [*See* DIAGNOSIS OF PSYCHOLOGICAL DISORDERS: DSM AND GENDER.]

Gender as an interactive process refers to gender's active, alive quality. This active quality or process engaged in by women and men is referred to as the *doing or reproducing of gender*. The doing of gender refers to the process in which one not only internalizes societal constructions of women and men, but also is reinforced for playing them out in her or his interpersonal interactions, particularly in interactions where gender is salient.

A common example of the doing of gender concerns physical height. Many women are taller than, or as tall as, many men. Yet if we conducted a study of the heights of women and men in heterosexual couples, we would conclude that male partners are almost always taller than female partners. It is important in the culture to project an image that the man is taller than the woman; both women and men engage in interpersonal behaviors to preserve this view, either by whom they select as partners or the size heel they wear when they are with their partners. The motivations for doing this are likely tied to views held by both women and men, that men should be bigger and stronger than women. The doing of gender in psychotherapy is further considered in a later section.

B. ETHNICITY AND CULTURAL ISSUES: TRANSCENDING RACISM AND HETEROSEXISM

Ethnicity is becoming an increasing important topic in psychology, particularly the study and considerations of ethnic groups of color in the United States—that is, groups of non-European origin, primarily African Americans, Asian and Pacific Islander Americans, Latinos, and Native Americans. The work of Jean S. Phinney described aspects of ethnicity important for psychological theory and practice. These include the cultural values, attitudes, and behaviors that may distinguish ethnic groups, the subjective sense of ethnic identity that may be held by ethnic group members, and the experiences associated with minority status, including powerlessness, discrimination, and prejudice.

The current definition of multicultural counseling reflects this complex view of ethnic identity. It has also broadened its scope to be more inclusive of other potential identities, such as sexual orientation, socioeconomic class, age, and so on. The rationale is that each of these group memberships involves unique experiences and viewpoints that typify cultural experience. In addition, multicultural counseling acknowledges the multifaceted nature of identity while building on the strengths of existing therapy modalities. The culturally competent therapist blends culturally specific knowledge about a client with effective therapeutic skills within the particular theoretical approaches to counseling and psychotherapy adhered to by therapists. Effective therapeutic or "universal" healing skills are those common factors across the different therapy approaches that promote client growth and improvement, such as a strong therapeutic alliance, empathy, and a shared worldview.

The tension between the specific and the universal aspects of human experience has been defined in the multicultural literature as the balance between "etic" and "emic" approaches to counseling and psychotherapy. Etic approaches are those universal, culturally generalizable modes of relating one finds across all successful therapeutic relationships. Emic approaches are counseling strategies that specifically target a client's unique culture. For example, a therapist might employ a systems approach when dealing with a Latina client who places a strong value on group decision making among her family members (emic approach), while engaging in the empathic, affirming dialogue that promotes rapport (etic approach).

The effects of oppression may affect decisions to seeking counseling or willingness to trust a therapist. In addition, clients who are members of several oppressed groups—minority lesbian, gay and bisexual clients, for example—present added challenges and strengths in a therapy situation. For instance, an African American lesbian brings to the therapy room four social reference groups—the majority culture, her minority culture, and her lesbian and gay culture, as well as the cultural meanings attached to her sex and gender. Each culture presents unique resources and difficulties, and some cultures may be in conflict with other cultures. For members of groups of color, the significance of their group membership may lie in part in the struggle to gain equality, recognition, and acceptance within a predominately White society.

Culturally aware counselors acknowledge these many layers of identity, and address the differences, as well as the overlap, between these multiple cultures. Besides highlighting differences between group identities, the counselor recognizes within-group variability and the uniqueness of each client's multifaceted identity. This recognition is critical, because multicultural counseling research consistently demonstrates that minority-culture clients are far more likely to terminate prematurely than majority-culture clients. These terminations have been attributed to a lack of cultural knowledge on either side of the therapeutic equation—cultural mistrust on the part of the client or therapist insensitivity to the client's cultural issues.

IV. Practice Issues with Regard to Gender, Ethnicity, and Sexuality

Understanding issues with regard to gender, race, and sexuality are central to all theoretical approaches to counseling. Counselors and therapists not only need to understand how each of these issues affects individuals in their day-to-day living, but also how these issues are perpetuated by cultural discourses and by dynamics played out in the therapeutic setting. Particularly crucial is understanding that ethnicity, gender, and sexuality are contextual and socially constructed. Their meanings vary not only across historical time periods but also across nations and regions during the same time period.

A. DOMINANT DISCOURSE AND THE PERPETUATION OF DISCRIMINATION

Dominant discourses are the mechanisms through which traditional views of the various members and groups within a culture are presented and preserved. Rachel Hare-Mustin has defined discourse as a system of statements, practices, and institutional structures that share common values.

Dominant discourses are pervasive and can assume many forms of expression, particularly in our mass media-driven culture. They reflect and perpetuate the values of society, and those values oftentimes support the status quo. For example, "Women are more nurturing than men" is a dominant discourse that may shape how a therapist conceptualizes treatment for both female and male clients. Dominant discourses limit our conceptualizations of other, less-powerful groups of people, as well. For example, popular misconceptions such as "Gay men are nonmonogamous," "Native Americans are alco-

holics" or "African American men commit more crimes than White men" are damaging not just on a societal level but on a therapeutic level as well.

Without an awareness of dominant discourse, the therapeutic relationship can mimic the patriarchal, White, heterosexist interactions encountered in the client's external world. A therapist who has not dealt with his or her own inner attitudes surrounding gender, race, and sexual orientation will inevitably be less effective in helping clients to deal with discrimination and with their own internalized sexism, racism, and homophobia.

Discrimination on the basis of sex and race continues as a problem in our culture, although its manifestation may be more subtle today than in past times. For example, despite the existence of federal laws that prohibit sexual discrimination, women today are paid approximately 70% of what men in comparable positions are paid. Discrimination is also seen in higher education and the workplace in terms of differential evaluations and rewards based on gender and ethnicity.

The management of racism and sexism is among the many issues whose importance will vary from client to client and which will be a function of the multiple factors that help shape a client's psyche. Because of the ongoing and unpredictable nature of racist and sexist comments, reactions, and behaviors in one's daily life, dealing with racism can be a major source of stress that needs constant managing. In the essay "Sexism: An American Disease in Blackface," Audre Lorde described the double effect of racism and sexism: "As Black women and men, we cannot hope to begin dialogue by denying the oppressive nature of male privilege." Similar to partners in heterosexual European American families, African American partners also struggle with women's and men's views of gender roles and male power, privilege, and superiority vis-à-vis women.

Sexual harassment also remains a common experience for all women. Most broadly defined, sexual harassment refers to the unwanted imposition of sexual requirements in the context of unequal power. Sexual harassment is about power and the need to dominate, not physical attraction. It occurs in many forms—innuendo, "friendly harassment," overt sexual comments, unwanted touching, or even sexual coercion. Sexual harassment also includes subtle forms of intimidation—lingering, sexually suggestive remarks, and behaviors and attitudes that demean or exclude women—that create a "hostile environment" and unreasonably interfere with an individual's performance. As one client noted, "It's the daily little insults that wear you down. We are expected to go along with jokes about women's sexuality or stupidity, pinups in the office, demeaning attitudes, lewd remarks, and 'joking' requests for sexual intimacy." [*See* SEXUAL HARASSMENT.]

The final kind of discrimination to be considered is one less talked about: homophobia and heterosexism. Homophobia is the irrational fear, intolerance, and, in its most severe form, hatred of people who are gay or lesbian. This type of prejudice leads to persistent beliefs in negative stereotypes toward gays and lesbians and supports discriminating actions against these groups in areas such as jobs, housing, and child custody. Lesbians and gays, socialized in the same values, often internalize these negative stereotypes and develop some degree of self-hatred or low self-esteem, a form of internalized homophobia.

When homophobia is combined with cultural and institutional power, the result is heterosexism: a belief in the inherent superiority of heterosexuality and its right to dominance. This is analogous to sexist and racist attitudes, combined with the cultural and institutional power to enforce these attitudes, resulting in sexism and racism. Heterosexism can have a powerful influence on either a woman's or a man's choice to envision, enter, or stay in a dual-career relationship with a person of the same sex. Being "out" on the job can have devastating repercussions to women's or men's career advancement or even to their right to remain employed. Choosing to "be discreet" can have great personal costs in terms of feeling isolated, compartmentalized, and unaffirmed. Few employers extend benefits to an "unmarried" partner or to biological children of that partner, practices that make life more difficult and less fair for same-sex partners in committed relationships.

The anger, discontentment, despair, and stress that all of these discriminatory practices can produce affect how individuals manage their personal and occupational lives. Learning to recognize forms of discrimination and becoming informed about how to work with clients who experience discrimination represent crucial components of effective counseling. [*See* PREJUDICE.]

B. ISSUES OF POWER IN THERAPY

Power is central to situations involving oppression based on sex, race, ethnicity, and sexual orientation. As described earlier, invisibility and assumptions of deviance and pathology have served to perpetuate a society in which it has been assumed that certain groups of individuals had authority and control over other groups and that this situation was as it had to be given the essential natures of the groups involved. Power and authority are also central to the therapeutic process because counseling and therapy involve individuals seeking assistance from persons with unique knowledge and experience. This sets up a power differential between those seeking help and those providing help, with one needing what the other can provide. The situation can put clients in a vulnerable position vis-à-vis counselors, and counselors in a position of unique power and influence.

Historically, psychotherapy adhered to a "medical model" approach in dealing with client problems. Clients, or patients, as they were more typically called, were considered to be "sick" and in need of treatment from a more competent "expert." Clients were expected to defer to the therapists' conceptualizations of their problems and to comply with therapist observations, suggestions, and interventions. Efforts by clients to question or to take control of their own treatment were viewed as a form of "resistance" or "transference," particularly within the psychoanalytic tradition. Although the Rogerian focus on client-centered therapy questioned the expertness of the therapist in determining what was best for the client, it was the feminist and multicultural movements of the 1980s and 1990s that gave the notion of an egalitarian relationship between client and therapist a central theoretical place in psychotherapy. Laura Brown defined the egalitarian relationship as one designed to remove artificial and unnecessary barriers to the sharing of power. This emphasis reflects the importance of a therapist's commitment to analyzing the uses of power in society and how existing power structures deprive women and minority groups of their autonomy, choices, and options.

A primary task for therapists is to examine the power differential not only in the client's social world but also in the therapy room. The hope is that making the power imbalance explicit between therapist and client will create a more egalitarian exchange. According to Laura Brown, "egalitarian" is not synonymous with "equal" in a therapy situation, as some imbalance due to the counselor's expertise is unavoidable and even therapeutic. Therapists can misuse their power and influence in many areas of diagnosis and treatment. Power abuses range from the subtle exercise of control over a client to blatant violations of rights. Abuses might include disregarding the client's needs or concerns, pathologizing a client, breaching confidentiality, or engaging in a dual or sexual relationship with a client. [*See* POWER.]

C. DYNAMICS OF THE THERAPEUTIC RELATIONSHIP

Particularly important to the practice of counseling and therapy is the realization that gender is an actively constructed variable that "gets materialized" in social encounters. This reproducing of gender occurs across cultures. Counseling and psychotherapy is an optimal place for gender to be reproduced because of the power differential that implicitly defines the relationship. Two interrelated active components of gender are particularly crucial to reproducing gender in counseling settings. The first concerns views of gender as difference and of the sexes as opposite, and how language and discourse, both nonverbal and verbal, reflect and reproduce these views. The second concerns gender as enacted and recreated in social encounters.

Language is particularly important to how views of women and men are communicated in counseling. It is not uncommon to use one language when describing women's behavior and a different language to describe the same behavior in men. A woman who is a mother and employed outside the home is called a working mother. A man who is a father and employed outside the home is called employed. An attractive female child is described as pretty, an attractive male child as handsome.

A large body of research concerns gender and verbal communications patterns in four areas pertinent to the counseling setting: interruption, topic control, talking time, and use of silence. The differences observed between women and men in conversation are tied to assumptions about power and status, with those of higher status and power interrupting more, deciding on the topics of conversation, talking more, and using silence more. Thus, similar dynamics would occur in interactions with members of groups having more or less power in a society. To the extent that men as a group are granted greater power and status in our society than are women as a group, these patterns of verbal communication can be viewed as reproducing gender. In addition, if female therapists use the power and influence of their role to engage in these kinds of behavioral patterns with same-sex clients, they, too, would be reproducing gender from

the clients' standpoint of being viewed as the less powerful person in a socially constructed relationship.

Language also becomes important in understanding how women and men interact to reproduce conventional assumptions about gender. Rachel Hare-Mustin introduced the metaphor of the therapy room being lined with mirrors that reflects back only what is voiced within it. If both the client and the counselor hold a certain set of beliefs about what it means to be a woman or a man, these are the only beliefs that can get voiced within the counseling. Describing a woman who offers to help someone as "being mothering," regardless of the kind of relationship between the two people, conveys the larger, powerful discourse that whatever women do, their motivations are ultimately tied to their biological role of mother.

Gender as an active process can also emerge between counselors and clients. Table I summarizes several interconnected factors contributing to the reproduction of gender in counseling. These include using essentialist, gender-as-difference beliefs about women and men to guide work with clients, and isolating or separating the concerns of clients from the context in which they occur, including the context of the counseling relationship. A factor of particular concern is misusing the power and influence of the therapist's role.

One of the most damaging abuses of therapist power is the sexual involvement of a therapist with a client. Sexual misconduct remains the underlying behavior in a sizable percentage of the cases reported to the American Psychological Association's Ethics Committee and state and provincial licensing boards. Complaints in this area have increased each year since 1979, when sexual intimacies with clients were specifically defined as unethical in the Ethical Principles of Psychologists. Moreover, the major area of sexual misconduct violations has continued to be a male psychologist with an adult female client. Many clients are unaware that ethics codes of all major mental health associations explicitly prohibit sexual intimacies with clients. Clients who become sexually involved with their therapists are harmed in many ways. They experience feelings of guilt, an impaired ability to trust others, ambivalence about the abuse, and feelings of emptiness, anger, and alienation. [*See* SEX BETWEEN THERAPISTS AND CLIENTS.]

Factors associated with the reproduction of gender in male–female interactions contribute to understanding this pattern of unethical and harmful behavior. Reasons typically given for why this occurs have to do with traditional gendered assumptions

Table I
Factors Contributing to Reproducing Gender in Counseling/Psychotherapy

Gender-reproducing factors	Examples
Using essentialist, gender-as-difference beliefs to guide work with clients	• Viewing men as competent in instrumental areas and women as competent at relationships • Viewing women as dependent and men as independent • Failing to help female and male clients construct visions of themselves that transcend their traditional sex roles
Isolating or separating the concerns of clients from the context in which they occur, including the context of the counseling relationship	• Conceptualizing a competent women with unabashed ambition as bringing on her own problems at work • Conceptualizing a client's anger as transference when the therapist has acted in ways to silence the client • Fostering a female client's dependence in therapy; failing to acknowledge a male client's dependence
Misusing the power and influence of the therapist's role	• Eroticizing the counseling interaction • Viewing a client who disagrees with the therapist's interpretations and recommendations as "difficult" and "disagreeable" • Using diagnosis as a means of unduly categorizing and controlling the client; failing to discuss clients' diagnosis with them, particularly if diagnosis is required for third-party payment
Conceptualizing client's concerns stereotypically	• Viewing a female client who does not enjoy sex as frigid • Considering a male client's engaging in sex with multiple partners as possibly problematic only if "safe sex" practices are not used • Having the expectation that lesbian and gay relationships mimic heterosexual relationships with regard to masculine/feminine roles (e.g., believing that all lesbian relationships adhere to a "butch/femme" model)
Using gender stereotypic models as the standard for adaptive or healthy behavior and psychological functioning	• Assessing a man's level of functioning on the basis of his success at his occupational work • Viewing a professionally competent man choosing nondemanding employment as compensating for/acting out of unresolved issues from childhood • Adopting the patriarchal stance that a highly individualistic, independent orientation to others is the preferred and ideal style of relating to others

about men's entitlement to women's caretaking and their bodies. These include the needs and wants of the male therapist becoming the focus of the therapy, the therapist creating and exploiting an exaggerated dependence on the part of the female client, and the therapist using rationalizations to discount harm to the client. These reasons concern the nonconscious view that men's emotional and sexual needs take precedence over women's and that women want to meet men's needs in these areas. Because female clients may respond in socialized ways that meet the male counselor's needs—feeling flattered, acting submissively, responding positively to desirable men who find them attractive, or valuing feeling special to a powerful male—the counselor may have little incentive to question his motives.

V. Contemporary Concerns for Clients

Clients come to therapy with a multitude of concerns. Described here are two areas of current concern that reflect societal changes in areas pertinent to gender, race, ethnicity, and sexuality. These topics are sexuality and power and concomitant involvement in work and family roles.

A. SEX, SEXUALITY, AND POWER

Power is often viewed as crucial to men in our culture—power over women, power over other men, and power over themselves. In most cultures, boys and men are more highly valued than girls and women. However, within a particular culture, race and ethnicity can serve as a moderator of male power, with men in some ethnic groups being granted more power than men in other groups. The extent of this differential evaluation may vary, but across cultures, its result is always to grant men more power, freedom, and privilege than women. Generally speaking, men in many societies grow up with feelings of confidence and specialness granted them simply because they are born male. This specialness is an essential aspect of what has become known as male prerogative and entitlement. Male prerogative encourages both women and men to feel that what men do or want to do takes precedence over the needs of women and should not be questioned. The basic sentiment here is that "Men have a right to do what they want to do and women who interfere need to learn their place."

Often overlooked, however, is how little power men may have despite the construction of male power in the culture. Men whose sense of self is closely tied to what they have come to believe are men's prerogatives, especially in relation to women, even small loses of advantage or deference can be experienced as large threats to men's rights and privileges. This can cause difficulties in heterosexual relationships ranging from resentment of women's increased educational and employment opportunities to violence in the form of rape and battering. [See BATTERING IN ADULT RELATIONSHIPS.]

Male entitlement to power over women may take the form of male entitlement to women's bodies, whether in a swimsuit issue of *Sports Illustrated,* the broadcast media, or real life. Other articles in this encyclopedia describe the strong association between sexuality and power and, in particular, the centrality of the male sexual drive discourse to views of male power. Through sexual relations with women, men look for validation of themselves as men. The man must be big where it counts, powerful, and able to take charge. In the past two decades, sexual harassment, acquaintance rape, and sexual abuse have entered into public consciousness. Romantic partners were implicated in 50 to 57% of sexual assaults reported by college-age and adult women, respectively.

Because violence and trauma are often viewed as personal, individual, and separate from the effects of organizational structure and societal norms, battering, sexual violence against women, and incest frequently go unnoticed or unchallenged. Much rape and abuse is hidden, sometimes even from the victims themselves. Most therapists will work with women who have been physically abused at some point in their life. During 1999 it was estimated that a woman reports a rape to the police every 5 to 6 minutes; over 80% of sexual assaults reported by college-age and adult women are perpetrated by an acquaintance. These statistics cross the lines of ethnicity, race, and economic status. An estimated 1 million women each year seek medical assistance for wife battering. Surveys indicate that approximately half of sexual assault and battering victims eventually seek professional help, and many do so years after it occurred. [See RAPE.]

Another aspect of sex, sexuality, and power relates to the prevalent use of women's bodies as constructed objects for display. Women's bodies and women's sexuality are a billion-dollar industry. Historically, being valued and desired by men was an important component of a woman's self-concept because women's worth to men was seen in terms of their virginity, their physical characteristics, and their ability to please, satisfy, and serve men. One result of these gendered processes is narrow definitions of female attractiveness constructed and perpetuated by the popular culture and by advertising.

The narrow cultural definitions of female beauty in our culture, coupled with aggressive ad campaigns, make many women feel unattractive, while at the same time striving to be more attractive. Women more than men spend a great deal of time worrying about their appearance, including their weight. Concerns about weight and thinness are now viewed as chronic stressors in women's lives, crossing lines of race, ethnicity, and class. Many women in the normal weight range diet as a lifestyle and nearly all women who participate in expensive liquid diets regain the weight within one year. Chronic dieting is dangerous to physical health and to self-esteem. The destructive effects of the ideal of female beauty include damage to women's self-concept, depression, chronic dieting, eating disorders such as bulimia and anorexia nervosa, and the misuse of medical procedures such as cosmetic surgery and liposuction. [See BEAUTY POLITICS AND PATRIARCHY.]

B. CONVERGENCE OF WORK AND FAMILY ROLES

Historically, women and men were viewed as primarily suited for the role assigned to their sex—either a caretaker or provider role. This view persisted even though poor women, particularly poor women of color, had a long history of working outside the home.

The situation is quite different today. Employment is now widely recognized as appropriate, normative, healthy, and intrinsically rewarding aspect of both women's and men's lives. Similarly, connections with family—feeling loved and loving and providing interpersonal care and nurturance within families—are also widely recognized as appropriate, normative, healthy, and intrinsically rewarding aspects of women's and men's adult lives. A relatively small percentage of U.S. families today fall into the category of breadwinner father and stay-at-home mother. For example, for married women with children under 6 years old, 63.1% are in the labor force, and for married women with children under the age of 18, approximately 71% are employed. In addition, 12 million people in the workforce are single parents for whom work and family roles converge. Recent data reported by the U.S. Bureau of Labor Statistics indicate that these statistics apply across various ethnic groups.

Overall, engaging in work and family roles is beneficial for women and men. For example, it is well documented that marriage benefits men's health and well-being, and that the health benefits of traditional marriage were greater for husbands than for wives. In addition, employed women report better physical and psychological health than women who are not employed. Extensive work by Rosalind Barnett and her colleagues indicates that the inevitability of a "second shift" for wives is overstated and that although some husbands do far less than their fair share at home, others are in a more equitable arrangement. A good deal has been written about the variations among dual-earner families and how partners manage work and family roles. Overall, men's participation in family work has continued to increase from 1970 to the present time, more so in the area of parenting than in the area of household work.

Contrary to what is often heard in the media, results from the many studies conducted have shown that preschool-aged children are at no added risk if they receive alternate child or day care instead of parental care for some portion of the day. The important factor is availability and affordability of good care. An increasing number of companies are providing flexible policies and parental leave for their male and female employees. [See CHILD CARE.]

In summary, balancing work and family roles, negotiating child and household responsibilities among partners, and finding quality child care are challenges clients are now bringing to counseling settings. [See WORK–FAMILY BALANCE.]

VI. Conclusions

Counselors and psychotherapists do not work in a cultural vacuum; nor do their clients. Our cultural biases have always been with us, but we have only recently begun to develop an awareness of how such factors as gender, race/ethnicity, and sexual orientation shape us, and how the power dynamic between majority and minority cultures operates. History has shown us that those in power—heterosexual White males, predominantly, in the United States—maintain power inequities by excluding, labeling, or pathologizing less powerful groups. Dominant discourses, or the linguistic and cultural practices that affirm and perpetuate the majority culture's values, have largely determined whose needs are served in mental health policy, studies of human behavior, and counseling interventions. As members of the majority culture, counselors and psychotherapists have intentionally and unintentionally participated in these discourses and discriminatory processes over time.

In this increasingly diverse nation, the challenge is for counselors and therapists to develop an understanding of how, historically and currently, women and minority groups have been, and are being, denied opportunities to live full, productive, and authentic lives. Merely acknowledging past and ongoing discrimination is not sufficient, however. Counselors and psychotherapists must attend to the ways in which majority-culture assumptions are coloring their own perceptions and interventions with women, people of color, and lesbian, gay, and bisexual clients as well as with male clients. Without examining their own biases, therapists may unwittingly perpetuate the very power dynamic that is contributing to the client's distress.

What we now know about identity is that it is a complex, unique, fluid, and ever-evolving state of being that arises out of our biological sex and sexual orientation, our gender role, our personal history, ethnicity and race, religious preference, socioeconomic status, age, and a host of other group "memberships." Culturally competent therapists educate themselves about these facets of identity and weave that knowledge into their work with clients. They bring an explicit discussion of gender, race, and sexual orientation into the therapy room, while attending to the universal healing factors that underlie all therapy modalities—empathy, mutual respect and trust, empowerment, a shared worldview, and a strong working alliance.

SUGGESTED READING

Barnett, R. C., and Rivers, C. (1996). *She Works/He Works: How Two-Income Families Are Happier, Healthier, and Better Off.* Harper Collins, New York.

Brown, L. S. (1994). *Subversive Dialogues: Theory in Feminist Therapy.* Basic Books, New York.

Comas-Diaz, L., and Greene, B. (eds.). (1994). *Women of Color: Integrating Ethnic and Gender Identities in Psychotherapy.* Guilford, New York.

Gilbert, L. A., and Scher, M. (1999). *Gender, Sex, and Counseling.* Allyn & Bacon, Needham, MA.

Goldberger, N. R., and Veroff, J. B. (eds). (1995). *The Culture and Psychology Reader.* New York University Press, New York.

Hare-Mustin, R. T. (1994). Discourses in the mirrored room: A postmodern analysis of therapy. *Family Process* **33**, 19–35.

Phinney, J. S. (1996). When we talk about American ethnic groups, what do we mean? *American Psychologist* **51**, 918–927.

Ponterotto, J. G., Casas, J. M., Suzuki, L. A., and Alexander, C. M. (eds). (1995). *Handbook of Multicultural Counseling.* Sage, Thousand Oaks, CA.

Pope, K. S. (1994). *Sexual Involvement with Therapists: Patient Assessment, Subsequent Therapy, Forensics.* American Psychological Association, Washington, DC.

Rogers, C. R. (1942). *Counseling and Psychotherapy.* Houghton Mifflin, Boston.

Westkott, M. (1986). *The Feminist Legacy of Karen Horney.* Yale University Press, New Haven, CT.

Worell, J., and Remer, P. (1992). *Feminist Perspectives in Therapy: An Empowerment Model for Women.* Wiley, New York.

Cross-Cultural Gender Roles

Deborah L. Best
Wake Forest University

Glossary

Cross-cultural research Research that examines similarities and differences in behaviors, concepts, or attitudes across different cultural or ethnic groups.

Culture A dynamic system of rules encompassing attitudes, beliefs, norms, social organizations, and practices presumably related to human behavior and personality development that are shared by groups of people.

Gender Used to distinguish the male and female members of the human species, but emphasizes social rather than biological factors.

Gender roles The social roles (familial, occupational, recreational) that women and men occupy with differential frequency.

Gender stereotypes The psychological traits and behaviors that are believed to occur with differential frequency in the two gender groups (i.e., men are more "aggressive," women are more "emotional"). Stereotypes provide support for traditional sex-role assignments and may serve as socialization models for children.

Individualism-collectivism A dimension along which cultural groups vary in the degree to which they encourage and value the autonomous, unique individual over the connectedness of the individual with the family or social group.

Masculinity/feminity The degree to which men and women have incorporated traits into their self-perceptions that are considered in their culture to be "womanlike" or "manlike."

Pancultural Referring to universal phenomena or behaviors.

Sex The anatomical and physiological differences between males and females and the implication of those differences in procreation.

Sex-role ideology Beliefs that vary from traditional, male-dominated views to egalitarian, feminist views that concern the appropriate relationships between the sexes.

CROSS-CULTURAL GENDER ROLES refer to the different social roles that men and women occupy in various cultures. Travelers visiting different countries are often struck by how some societies emphasize the role differences between women and men, while others show little interest in such diversity. When sex differences are highlighted within a culture, it leads to the expectation that gender is a critical determinant of human behavior. However, it is important to remember that physically and anatomically, human males and females are much more similar than different. Indeed, they are mostly interchangeable in regard to social roles and behaviors, with childbearing being the primary exception. As we explore cross-cultural research on gender, it may be surprising to you to see how little difference gender makes when one considers the substantial variability in psychological characteristics across cultural groups. This article focuses on the general areas of developmental, personality, and social psychology that deal with how males and females view themselves and one another, as well as the way they should and do interact. Cross-cultural studies of gender are concerned with how similar psychological processes and behaviors are across cultures, as well as how they differ.

I. Gender at the Individual Adult Level

A. SEX ROLE IDEOLOGY

In virtually all human groups, women have greater responsibility for "domestic" activities while men have greater responsibility for "external" activities. Such pancultural similarities may originate from the biological differences between the sexes, particularly the fact that women bear and in most societies nurse children. Recently, however, in many societies these socially assigned duties are being shared, with men engaging in more domestic activities and women in more external, particularly economic, activities. The gender division of labor will be reviewed later. Here we discuss the beliefs and attitudes about appropriate role behaviors for the two sexes.

Most researchers classify sex-role ideologies or beliefs along a continuum from traditional to modern. Traditional ideologies maintain that men are more "important" than women and it is proper for men to control and dominate women. In contrast, modern ideologies are more egalitarian, more feminist, and claim that women and men are equally important and that dominance of one sex over the other is inappropriate.

One place where sex roles have been studied extensively is in India where traditional and modern ideologies exits side by side. When Kavita Agarwal,

David Lester, and Nisha Dhawan asked male and female Indian and North American university students what qualities women in their culture should and should not possess, Indian students expressed more traditional views than North American students. Women in both groups were more modern, or liberal, than men. Looking more closely at Indian women, Rehana Ghadially found that the Indian university women who had the most nontraditional sex-role attitudes came from nuclear families, had educated mothers, and were in professional or career-oriented disciplines.

Similar studies by Atsuko Suzuki in Japan have shown that education and professional managerial work are strong predictors of sex-role attitudes for both Japanese and North American women. North American women with jobs, no matter what sort, had more egalitarian attitudes than women without jobs. In contrast, Japanese women with career-oriented professional jobs were more egalitarian than all other women, with or without jobs.

Judy Gibbons, Deborah Stiles, and Gina Shkodriani capitalized on a unique opportunity to study attitudes toward gender and family roles among adolescents from 46 different countries attending schools in the Netherlands. Countries of origin were grouped into two categories: the wealthier, more individualistic countries and the less wealthy, more collectivistic countries. Students from the second group of countries had more traditional attitudes than students from the first group of countries, and girls generally responded less traditionally than boys. [See INDIVIDUALISM AND COLLECTIVISM.]

In many studies of sex role ideology, North Americans have served as a reference group and are usually found to be more liberal, perhaps suggesting that North Americans are unusual in this respect. However, we did not find this to be the case in a 14-country study of university students this author conducted with colleague John Williams. We found the most modern ideologies in Northern European countries (the Netherlands, Germany, Finland, England). The United States was in the middle of the distribution, and the most traditional ideologies were found in African and Asian countries (Nigeria, Pakistan, India, Japan, Malaysia). Generally, women had more modern views than men, but not in all countries (e.g., Malaysia and Pakistan). However, there was high correspondence between men's and women's sex-role ideology scores in a given country. Overall, the effect of culture was greater than the effect of gender.

It is important to remember that, before we conclude that variations seen between countries are due to cultural factors, in cross-cultural research we must show that the variations are related to other cultural variables. For example, in our research we found that sex-role ideology scores were related to economic-social development. That is, sex role ideology was more modern in more developed countries, in more heavily Christian countries, in more urbanized countries, and in countries in the higher latitudes.

B. GENDER STEREOTYPES

Related to sex-role ideology, and often used to justify those beliefs, are gender stereotypes, the psychological traits believed to be more characteristic of one sex than the other. In our research, John Williams and I presented the 300 person-descriptive adjectives from the Adjective Checklist, a standard personality measure, to university students in 27 countries and asked them to indicate whether, in their culture, each adjective was more frequently associated with men, more frequently associated with women, or not differentially associated by gender. Generally, these students agreed about the characteristics differentially associated with men and with women. However, the female and male stereotypes differed most in the Netherlands, Finland, Norway, and Germany and least in Scotland, Bolivia, and Venezuela. Stereotypes of men and women differed more in Protestant than in Catholic countries, in more developed countries, and in countries high in individualism.

Examining the characteristics more closely, in all countries the male-stereotype items were stronger and more active than the female-stereotype items. Interestingly, there was no pancultural effect for favorability, with the male stereotype being more positive in some countries (e.g., Japan, South Africa, Nigeria) and the female stereotype in others (e.g., Italy, Peru, Australia). Using a standard personality scoring system with these stereotype items indicated that across all countries, dominance, autonomy, aggression, exhibition, and achievement were associated with men, while nurturance, succorance, deference, and abasement were associated with women. These stereotype data were recently reanalyzed in terms of the Five Factor Model of personality, which is based on the assumption that the basic dimensions of personality can be encompassed by five dimensions or factors. Examining the stereotypes with the five-factor scoring system revealed that the pancultural male stereotype was higher in the dimensions of extraversion, conscientiousness, emotional stability, and openness, while the female stereotype was higher in the agreeableness dimension.

In addition to these general similarities, there was also variation between countries. For example, strength and activity differences between male and female stereotypes were greater in socioeconomically less developed countries, in countries where literacy was low, and where the percentage of women attending university was low. It appears that economic and educational advancements were accompanied by a reduction in the tendency to view men as stronger and more active than women. However, these effects were merely reduced—not eliminated.

The high degree of cross-cultural similarity in gender stereotypes suggests that the psychological characteristics differentially associated with women and men follow a pancultural model, with cultural factors producing minor variations around general themes. In our model, biological differences set the stage (e.g., females bear children, males have greater physical strength) and lead to a division of labor, with women responsible for child care and other domestic activities, and men for hunting (providing) and protection. Gender stereotypes evolved to support this division of labor. Stereotypes assume that each sex has or can develop characteristics consistent with one's assigned role. Once established, stereotypes serve as socialization models that encourage boys to become independent and adventurous and girls to become nurturant and affiliative. Hence, this model demonstrates how people in widely different cultures come to associate one set of characteristics with men and another set with women, with only minor variations around these central themes. [*See* GENDER STEREOTYPES.]

C. MASCULINITY/FEMININITY OF SELF-CONCEPTS

Manlike or womanlike are the essential meanings of the paired concepts of masculinity/femininity. A person might be masculine or feminine in a variety of ways including dress, mannerisms, or tone of voice. We will restrict our definition to self-concepts and the degree to which they incorporate traits that are differentially associated with women or men. Within this restricted concept of masculinity/femininity, researchers have used different measurement techniques. Some have used self-descriptive questionnaire items, some analyze only socially desirable characteristics, and others examine gender-associated characteristics without reference to social desirability.

Measurement is important in cross-cultural studies, particularly when the researcher is interested in comparing different cultural groups. Problems arise, for example, when a masculinity/femininity scale developed in one country, often the United States, is translated into another language and administered to persons in other cultures. A study of Janet Spence and Robert Helmreich illustrates this problem. They compared the self-descriptive responses of men from the United States and Brazilian men to the Personal Attributes Questionnaire, which contains traits that are male-associated and female-associated in the United States. Men from the United States endorsed more male-associated traits than female-associated ones, but Brazilian men had the opposite pattern. Does this mean that Brazilian men have more feminine self-concepts than do men from the United States? Probably not. This interpretation pays little attention to how a culture defines masculinity and femininity. Cross-culturally, some items in translated scales may be inappropriate due to content, whereas others may be poorly translated.

In our research, John Williams and I used culture-specific measures of masculinity and femininity with university students in 14 countries. Each participant described him or herself and his or her ideal self using the 300 Adjective Checklist adjectives. These descriptions were scored relative to local gender trait stereotypes determined in our earlier study. We found that men in all countries were more masculine than women, hardly a surprising result. Interestingly, for the ideal self, both gender groups wished to be "more masculine" than they thought they were.

While some cultural variation in self-concepts was found, surprisingly these differences were not associated with other cultural comparison variables, such as economic/social development. Across cultural groups, relative to their own culture's definition of femininity and masculinity, there was no evidence that women in some societies were more feminine than women in others or that men in some societies were more masculine than men in others.

In contrast, when using our other scoring schemes for these self-concepts, there were substantial differences across countries in concepts of the self and the ideal self. For example, the differences in the self-concepts of men and women were smaller in more developed countries, when women were employed outside the home, when they constituted a large percentage of the university population, and where a relatively modern sex-role ideology prevailed.

II. *Relations between Women and Men*

A. MATE PREFERENCES

The most extensive investigation of mate preferences was conducted by David Buss and his associates, who gathered data from more than 10,000 respondents from 33 countries. Social scientists usually assume that mate preferences are culture bound and arbitrary, but Buss's findings are contrary. On two similar lists of potential mate characteristics, Buss asked participants to indicate their preferences by rating or ranking the items. Quite surprisingly, there was a remarkable degree of agreement in mate characteristic preferences between men and women. Both sexes ranked "kind and understanding" first, "intelligent" second, "exciting personality" third, "healthy" fourth, and "religious" last. Despite this overall similarity, women generally valued good earning capacity in a potential mate slightly more than did men, whereas men generally valued physical appearance slightly more than did women.

Nonetheless, cultural differences were found for virtually every item, and on some items there was great variation. The greatest cultural effect occurred for "chastity." Northern European groups considered it to be unimportant while groups from China, India, and Iran placed great emphasis on it. Men valued chastity in a prospective mate more than did women.

With the remarkable similarity across samples, Buss suggested there is substantial unity in human mate preferences that may be regarded as "species typical." On the other hand, no sample was exactly like any other, with each group showing some uniqueness in the ordering of mate preference characteristics reflecting at least modest degrees of cultural variation.

B. ROMANTIC LOVE

As with mate preferences, romantic love and intimacy are assumed to be influenced by culture. Genetically, romantic love is valued highly in less traditional cultures, such as the United States, where there are few strong extended family ties. It is less valued in cultures, such as Japan, where strong family ties reinforce the relationship between marriage partners. However, when ethnographies and folklore materials from 166 societies were examined, at least one incident of passionate love was documented in 147 (88%) of the cultures. These findings suggest that romantic love may be a human universal but it may be muted by other cultural variables.

Interestingly, Josephine Naidoo studied Asian Indian immigrants to Canada to see if there were generational changes in attitudes toward love and marriage. Although 63% of first-generation immigrants had arranged marriages, a large proportion of them believed that "love marriages" were an option for their offspring. More than 70% of the second generation wanted more freedom in mate selection and believed that love should precede marriage. [See INTIMACY AND LOVE.]

C. HARASSMENT AND RAPE

Among the few cross-cultural studies of male harassment and hostility toward women is a study by Kaisa Kauppinen-Toropainen and James Gruber. They examined professional and blue-collar women in the United States, Scandinavia, and the former Soviet Union and found that Americans reported the most woman-unfriendly experiences. Scandinavians had fewer job-related or psychological problems, more autonomy, and better work environments than Americans. Former Soviet professionals reported more woman-unfriendly experiences than workers but less than their peers in other regions.

The most comprehensive cross-cultural study of attitudes toward rape victims was conducted with university students in 15 countries by a network of researchers led by Colleen Ward from Singapore. Relatively favorable attitudes toward rape victims were found in the United Kingdom, Germany, and New Zealand, while relatively unfavorable attitudes were found in Turkey, Mexico, Zimbabwe, India, and particularly Malaysia. Attitudes toward rape victims mirror attitudes toward women in general, with more favorable attitudes in countries with more modern sex-role ideologies, and less favorable attitudes in countries with a lower percentage of women in the labor force and lower literacy rates. [See RAPE; SEXUAL HARASSMENT.]

D. MASCULINE WORK-RELATED VALUES

In the area of more general values, Geert Hofstede compared work-related values in 40 countries using attitude survey data collected from thousands of employees of IBM, a large multinational high-technology business organization. One scale he derived in his analysis concerned the extent to which values of assertiveness, money, and things prevail in a society rather than the values of nurturance, quality of life, and people. While the scale could have easily been named "Materialism," Hofstede named the scale "Masculinity" (MAS) because male employees assign greater weight to the first set of values whereas females assign greater weight to the second. Calling the scale "Masculinity" leads to the expectation that variations on these values might be associated with cross-country variations in other gender-related concepts, such as those discussed earlier.

Hofstede computed a MAS index for each of the 40 countries in his study, and the five that rated highest were Japan, Austria, Venezuela, Italy, and Switzerland; the five countries with the lowest MAS indices were Sweden, Norway, the Netherlands, Denmark, and Finland. In high MAS countries there is greater belief in independent decision making, stronger achievement motivation, higher job stress, and work was more central in people's lives.

While it is clear that the MAS dimension is a significant one, the appropriateness of designating this value system as "Masculinity" continues to be questioned. In our research, John Williams and I have found no relationship between our sex-stereotype or masculinity/femininity measures and Hofstede's MAS scores. Other researchers also have not found the expected relationships.

III. Developmental Influences

Having seen the influence of gender on the behavior and relationships of adults, it is natural to wonder about the development of gender-related beliefs and behaviors and the role of biological and cultural influences.

A. BIOLOGICAL INFLUENCES

Researchers who study gender differences in behavior often point to similarities across cultures as support for the role of genes and hormones. This assumes that any biological influence or bias would always lead to an irreversible sex difference. However, the long-standing nature-nurture controversy in developmental psychology has shown that biology does not cause behavior and that such thinking is naive.

Sex chromosomes or sex hormones do not cause behaviors; they simply change the probability of the occurrence of certain behaviors. Genes and the environment influence each other, and somewhat like people inherit genes, they may also "inherit" environments by living close to parents and family. [*See* DEVELOPMENT OF SEX AND GENDER.]

B. SOCIOBIOLOGY, EVOLUTIONARY PSYCHOLOGY, AND ECONOMIC ANTHROPOLOGY

Emphasizing the role of biology in development, sociobiologists, evolutionary psychologists, and economic anthropologists suggest that adaptation to the conditions of life shapes human behavior. While adaptation may be inherited, how adaptation is expressed depends on the events in an individual's life. For example, when variability in gender roles is found, it reflects the fact that different environments trigger different behaviors, even though some of these behaviors may be biologically "prepared" or preprogrammed.

David Gilmore proposed that the male *macho* behavior pattern is an adaptation to extreme risk associated with economic conditions. The dramatic difference in gender roles between two South Pacific islands, Truk and Tahiti, illustrate Gilmore's hypothesis. Trukese males are competitive, violent fighters, and sexually promiscuous, while females are expected to be submissive and protected by the men. In contrast, Tahitian men are not interested in material pursuits or in competition and are expected to be passive and submissive, while the women are generally known to be sexually active. Gilmore accounted for these variations by the dramatic differences in obtaining food. Tahitians fish in a protected lagoon where there is little risk and fish are plentiful. Trukese must fish in the open ocean with the genuine possibility of not returning after a day at sea. Thus, the macho style may be an adaptation to danger that encourages Trukese men to face great risk.

Some aspects of sociobiology and evolutionary theory are consistent with the widely accepted interaction view of nature and nurture. However, there are numerous criticisms of the theory, and research has not supported many of its assumptions.

C. SEXUAL DIMORPHISM

While biology is not destiny, it is certainly an important contributor to the development of gender differences. The term "biological" is usually used to refer to genes, in this case sex chromosomes, but biological also includes the influence of an organism's prenatal and postnatal environments, and often the activities in those environments are culturally determined. For example, the length of an infant's sleep bouts are modified by culturally determined demands on the mothers' time, and when and how an infant learns to sit and to walk are influenced by culturally defined child care practices.

Compared with females, at birth males are somewhat larger and have a higher activity level, higher basal metabolism, more muscle development, and a higher pain threshold. During the preadolescent years (ages 3–10), there are few gender differences in bodily structure or hormonal states, but those that exist are consistent with later development.

By adulthood, males attain greater height and have a more massive skeleton, a higher muscle-to-fat ratio, higher blood oxygen capacity, more body hair, and different primary and secondary sex characteristics. These differences are related to the greater physical strength and stamina of the male and result from the longer growth period of boys and the hormonal changes that appear after age eight. These gender differences, however, only hold within populations, not between and they apply only to group comparisons, not individuals. Many women are stronger and more active than many men.

D. CULTURAL INFLUENCES

Even though biological factors may impose predispositions and restrictions on development, sociocultural factors are also important determinants of development. Culture has profound effects on behavior, prescribing how babies are delivered, how children are socialized, how they are dressed, what tasks children are taught, and what roles adult men and women will adopt. The scope and progression of children's behaviors, even behaviors considered to be biologically determined, are governed by culture. Cultural universals in gender differences are often explained by similarities in socialization practices while cultural differences are attributed to differences in socialization.

One of the best-known, though often questioned, examples of cultural diversity in gender-related behaviors is Margaret Mead's classic study of three tribes in New Guinea. Mead reported that from a Western viewpoint, these societies created men and women who are both masculine, feminine, and who reversed the usual gender roles. Closer examination of these cultures has not supported Mead's claims.

Indeed, the far-reaching nature of sex differences in behaviors are clearly illustrated in the Israeli kibbutz, established in the 1920s, where there was a deliberate attempt to develop egalitarian societies. Initially there was no gender division of labor. Both women and men worked in the fields, drove tractors, worked in the kitchen and in the laundry. However as time went by and the birthrate increased, it was soon discovered that women could not undertake many of the physical tasks of which men were capable. Women found themselves in the same roles from which they were supposed to have been emancipated—cooking, cleaning, laundering, teaching, caring for children.

Indeed, the kibbutz attempts at an equitable division of labor also had little effect on the children. Children reared in a kibbutz held traditional views of sex-role behaviors and made the same sex-typed self-attributions as children who had not had such experience.

E. SOCIALIZATION OF GIRLS AND BOYS

For boys and girls, many behavioral differences are attributed to differences in socialization. In a classic study of socialization practices in more than 100 societies, Herbert Barry, Margaret Bacon, and Irvin Child found that boys are generally raised to achieve and to be self-reliant and independent, while girls are raised to be nurturant, responsible, and obedient. More recent studies have shown that North American parents encourage sex-typed behaviors, and parents in other Western countries use more physical punishment with boys than girls. Differential treatment of boys and girls decreases with age, particularly for disciplinary strictness and encouragement of sex-typed activities. There may be only subtle differences in the ways that girls and boys are treated by parents. However, the same parental treatment may affect girls and boys differently.

1. Task Assignment

Examining children's learning environments in various cultures shows how cultural differences in socialization can affect children's development. The classic Six Culture Study examined aggression, nurturance, responsibility, and help and attention-seeking behaviors of children aged 3 to 11 in Okinawa, Mexico, the Philippines, India, Kenya, and the United States. Fewer gender differences were found in the three samples (the United States, the Philippines, Kenya) where both boys and girls cared for younger siblings and performed household chores. In contrast, more differences were found in the samples (India, Mexico, Okinawa) where boys and girls were treated dissimilarly and girls assumed more responsibility for siblings and household tasks. Indeed, the fewest gender differences were found in the U.S. sample in which neither girls nor boys were assigned many child care or household tasks.

2. Caretaking

Thomas Weisner and Ronald Gallimore analyzed data from 186 societies and found that mothers, female adult relatives, and female children are the primary caretakers of infants. However, when those infants reach early childhood, responsibilities are shared among both sex peer groups. Sibling caretakers are an important part of the socialization process in societies where two- to four-year-olds spend more than 70% of every day with their child nurses. Mothers in these societies spend much of their time in productive activities, not simply mothering activities, though children in all cultures see mothers as responsible for children.

In contrast, in many cultures fathers rarely spend time with their infants, and their relationships are seldom close and involve little caregiving. In most societies, play characterizes fathers' interactions with their children. Nonetheless, fathers have an important impact on children. When fathers are absent for extended periods of time due to war or lengthy sea voyages, their sons display effeminate behaviors (such as feminine game preferences, activities with low physical contact), high levels of dependence, excessive fantasy aggression, and some overly masculine behaviors.

Fathers encourage sex-typed activities more than mothers, but they pay less attention to daughters than to sons. Mothers are equally important as caretakers of sons and daughters, but fathers tended to be more important for sons and spend more time with them. [*See* CHILD CARE.]

3. Peers

Throughout childhood and adolescence, peers play an important role in socialization, and peer influence increases as children grow older. In the Six Culture Study, there was a strong universal tendency for same-sex preference to emerge after age two. By middle childhood, gender segregation was found frequently, perhaps because same-sex peers prefer similar activities, but peers also provide the greatest opportunity for competition and conflict.

4. Education

Educational settings also influence children's behaviors. Observations of fifth graders in Japan and the United States indicate that teachers in both countries paid more attention to boys, particularly negative attention.

Likewise, parents' beliefs about academic performance can have profound impact on children's achievements. Robert Serpell found that in Zambia education was considered more important for boys than girls, and fathers arranged their schooling even though mothers were primarily responsible for childcare. In China, Japan, and the United States, Harold Stevenson and his colleagues found that mothers expect boys to be better at mathematics and girls at reading, even though they perform equally well in some aspects of both disciplines.

IV. Gender Differences in Boys' and Girls' Behaviors

Together, biological and cultural influences lead to differences in the behaviors of males and females, and we look at four areas where cross-cultural gender differences have been found.

A. NURTURANCE

In the Six Culture Study, gender differences in nurturance were most consistent in behavior that children directed toward infants and toddlers than in behavior directed toward mothers and older children. Because infants seem to elicit nurturant behavior, girls who spent more time with infants demonstrated more nurturance than boys who were not engaged in as much infant interaction.

Similarly, Barry, Bacon, and Child found that compared with boys, girls were socialized to be more nurturant (82% of cultures), obedient (35% of cultures), and responsible (61% of cultures). Boys, on the other hand, were socialized to be more achieving (87% of cultures) and self-reliant (85% of cultures) than girls. A later study found more pressure for

boys to conform to their roles (e.g., not be sissies) than girls who also had greater variability in their roles (e.g., tomboys are okay).

B. AGGRESSION

Cross-cultural studies of prepubertal children have consistently shown that boys have higher levels of aggression, competitiveness, dominance-seeking, and rough-and-tumble play than girls. The Six Culture Study found sex differences in aggression and dominance; aggression did not decrease with age and was more physical among the oldest boys. Mothers generally reacted similarly to boys' and girls' aggression, but fathers played a role in socializing aggression in boys.

Acceptance of aggression is similar for males and females in Western European countries, but they show gender differences in the forms of aggressive acts. Initially, males are more restrained but when they act, they are more violent; females are more emotional, using shouting and verbal attacks.

Moving to the other end of the spectrum, Klaus Boehnke and colleagues examined the development of prosocial motivation in schoolchildren from West Germany, Poland, Italy, and the United States. By age 12, but not before, girls demonstrated more mature motives in their responses to hypothetical situations that gave them the opportunity to act in a prosocial way. For example, girls said they would help a friend with a task to "get the job done" or because "that's what friends do." [See AGGRESSION.]

C. PROXIMITY TO ADULTS AND ACTIVITY

Observing the play of five- to seven-year-olds in eight cultures (Australian Aboriginal, Balinese, Ceylonese, Japanese, Kikuyu, Navajo, Punjabi, Taiwanese), Daniel Freedman found that boys ran in larger groups, covered more physical space, and did more physical and unpredictable activities, while girls were involved in more conversations and games with repeated activities. Girls are usually found closer to home and the tasks they are assigned as well as their behavioral preferences may contribute to these gender differences. Furthermore, boys tend to interact more with other boys, while girls tend to interact more with adults. Children's drawings also reflect gender segregation with boys drawing more pictures of boys and girls of girls. Boys drew more vehicles, monsters and violence themes than girls, who draw more flowers.

D. SELF-ESTEEM

Although gender-role attributions are similar, generally girls seem less satisfied with being girls than boys are with being boys, and boys perceive themselves to be more competent than girls do. However, girls' dissatisfaction is not consistently manifested in lower self-esteem. David Watkins found that when compared with boys, adolescent girls in Nepal, the Philippines, and Australia had lower opinions of their physical and mathematical abilities, but girls in Australia and Nigeria felt more competent in reading. Furthermore, Nigerian boys believed they were more intelligent than did girls. [See SELF-ESTEEM.]

In sum, differences between boys and girls in nurturance, aggression, and mobility are robust and consistently found across cultures while self-esteem differences are less consistent. Culture shapes the social behaviors of children by selecting the company they keep and the activities that engage their time. Such experiences can maximize, minimize, or even eliminate gender differences in social behaviors.

V. Development of Gender Roles and Stereotypes

Within the context of cultural stereotypes about male–female differences, children's knowledge of gender roles develops. As early as two years of age, children in the United States stereotype objects as masculine or feminine, and by age three to four they use stereotypic labels accurately with toys, activities, and occupations.

Similar gender stereotyping of toys is found in West Africa where girls play with dolls and boys construct vehicles and weapons. Even though cultural factors determine the content of children's play, the form of only a few behaviors seems to be culturally specific.

A. DEVELOPMENT OF SEX-TRAIT STEREOTYPES

In the United States, children acquire knowledge of sex-trait stereotypes somewhat later than stereotypic knowledge of toys and occupations. John Williams and I developed the Sex Stereotype Measure (SSM) to assess children's knowledge of adult-defined stereotypes. This measure is a picture-story technique in which children are shown silhouette drawings of a male and a female, they are read a story containing a stereotype trait, and they are asked to indicate which person the story is about. European American children showed a consistent pattern of increasing knowledge from kindergarten through high school, similar to a typical learning curve. The most dramatic increases in stereotype knowledge occurred in the early elementary school years, with scores reaching a plateau in the junior high years. African American children's scores increased with age but were lower than those of the European American children, perhaps suggesting slightly different stereotypes for the two groups.

B. CROSS-CULTURAL FINDINGS

In our cross-cultural research, we administered the SSM to 5-, 8-, and 11-year-olds in 25 countries and we found that the percentage of stereotyped responses increased from around 60% at age 5 to around 70% at age 8. Strong, aggressive, cruel, coarse, and adventurous were consistently associated with men at all age levels, and weak, appreciative, softhearted, gentle, and meek were consistently associated with women.

Both male and female scores were unusually high in Pakistan and relatively high in New Zealand and England, suggesting that children in these countries have an appreciable knowledge of sex stereotypes. Scores were atypically low in Brazil, Taiwan, Germany, and France, suggesting that children in these countries did not have consistent knowledge of the stereotype traits. Although there was variation between countries in the rate of learning, there was a general developmental pattern in which stereotype learning begins prior to age five, accelerates during the early school years, and is completed during the adolescent years.

Boys and girls learned the stereotypes at the same rate, though there was a tendency for male-stereotype traits to be learned somewhat earlier than female traits. In 17 of the 24 countries studied, male stereotype items were better known by both sexes than female items. Germany was the only country where there was a clear tendency for the female stereotype to be better known than the male. In contrast, female stereotype items were learned earlier than male items in Latin/Catholic cultures (Brazil, Chile, Portugal, Venezuela) where the adult-defined female stereotype is more positive than the male.

In predominantly Muslim countries, five-year-olds associate traits with the two sexes in a more highly differentiated manner and they learn the stereotypes, particularly the male items, at an earlier age than in non-Muslim countries. Children in predominantly Christian countries initially learn the stereotypes at a slower pace, perhaps reflecting the less-differentiated nature of the adult stereotypes, particularly in Catholic countries.

Looking at older children, 11 to 18 years of age, Margaret Intons-Peterson found that stereotypes of men and women were more similar in Sweden than in the United States. Surprisingly, however, ideal occupational choices did not overlap for Swedish boys and girls; girls were interested in service occupations, such as flight attendant, hospital worker, nanny, and boys were interested in business occupations.

Stereotype findings with children are consistent with the adult model of sex stereotypes discussed earlier. Children's stereotypes seem universal, with culture modifying the rate of learning and minor aspects of content.

VI. Theories of Gender-Related Learning

Most theories of gender-role learning emphasize the gender information readily available in the culture, even though the theories were devised primarily in the United States. Each theory can be adapted to explain cross-cultural patterns of development.

A. SOCIAL LEARNING

Social learning theories consider sex-role development to be the result of cumulative experience. Parents, teachers, peers, and other socialization agents shape children's gender-related behaviors through reinforcement and punishment of behaviors deemed gender-appropriate and inappropriate, modeling, expectations, toy choices, and other differential treatment of boys and girls. Same-sex and opposite-sex parents in the United States react differently to their children, with fathers showing more differential behavior. Boys receive more physical stimulation and are given more freedom and independence than girls. Interestingly, several of the studies conducted in other countries show less differential treatment of boys and girls than found in the United States.

In a study with several colleagues, this author observed parents and their preschool children in public parks and playgrounds in France, Germany, and Italy, and found that parent–child interactions varied across both gender and country. Italian and French parents and children interacted more than German parent–child pairs, and French and Italian children showed and shared more objects with their fathers than mothers, with the pattern reversed for German children. These interactional differences may be related to the cultural differences in sex stereotype learning noted earlier. Perhaps female characteristics are learned earlier by German children as a result of greater interaction with mothers than fathers, a pattern not found in the other countries.

There is substantial cross-cultural evidence that social forces play an important part in gender role learning. However, differential treatment of boys and girls varies greatly across cultures and is not consistently tied to differential behavior. [See GENDER DEVELOPMENT: SOCIAL LEARNING.]

B. COGNITIVE DEVELOPMENTAL

The other prominent theory of gender-role learning, cognitive developmental theory, suggests that the impact of environmental factors is governed by the child's emerging cognitive structures. Children acquire gender knowledge in stages and their level of understanding structures their experiences.

Ronald Slaby and Karin Frey identified four stages in the development of North American children's understanding of gender. Initially, children do not distinguish between the sexes, but by the second stage they begin to use gender categories based on superficial physical characteristics. In the latter two stages, achieved by age 4½ to 5, children understand that gender is stable across time and is consistent.

Ruth and Robert Munroe and Harold Shimmin tested cognitive developmental theory and expected to find cultural differences in progression through the gender stages related to how much the societies emphasized differences between males and females. Contrary to expectation, children in the highly sex-differentiating cultures, Kenya and Nepal, did not attain gender classification at an earlier age than children in two cultures with fewer cultural-level sex distinctions, Belize and Samoa. In all four societies there were differential gender distinctions in tasks and role expectations, and these may have been sufficient for most children to develop gender discrimination skills. The extensive gender differentiation in Kenya and Nepal may have been superfluous. [See SEX DIFFERENCE RESEARCH: COGNITIVE ABILITIES.]

C. GENDER SCHEMA THEORY

Recently, a variation of cognitive developmental theory and social learning theory has evolved: gender schema theory. A schema is a set of ideas used for organizing information, filtering new information, and directing cognitive processing. Gender schema theory assumes the primacy of gender concepts in a culture serves as a basis for organizing information, though there is little evidence regarding the theory from cultures other than the United States. [*See* GENDER DEVELOPMENT: GENDER SCHEMA THEORY.]

VII. *Cultural Practices That Influence Behaviors of Males and Females*

Moving beyond the family and the more immediate factors that influence behavior, there are broader cultural influences.

A. GENDER DIVISION OF LABOR

What is considered masculine and feminine varies across societies, but there are two possible cultural universals: to some degree, every society assigns traits and tasks on the basis of gender, and in no society is the status of women superior to that of men. Roy D'Andrade examined jobs and tasks in 244 societies and found that men were involved with hunting, metal work, weapon making, and travel further from home, while women were responsible for cooking and food preparation, carrying water, caring for clothing, and making things used in the home. Women participated in subsistence activities consistent with child-rearing responsibilities. In another study, men had major responsibilities for child rearing in only 10% of the 80 cultures examined.

Decreases in infant mortality and fertility have reduced the proportion of a woman's life span spent in rearing children. Technology has made it possible to separate childbearing from child rearing, permitting women to participate in the labor force outside the home, but paid employment is only a small part of a woman's economic contributions to the family.

A study of labor trends across 56 countries from 1960 to 1980 found that women's occupational opportunities declined and sex segregation in the workplace increased. Surprisingly, modernization, measured by per capita gross national product and women's education, was positively related to sex segregation but, as expected, women's labor force participation and fertility rate were inversely related. Compared with men, women remain economically disadvantaged and are paid less than their male counterparts. Women prefer traditionally female jobs and those that offer the greatest contacts with other people, while men prefer jobs with the highest income and possibilities for promotion.

Even in societies where women have moved actively into the labor force, they have not had a comparable reduction in household duties. In the United States, Switzerland, Sweden, Canada, Italy, Poland, and Romania, the overwhelming majority of household work is performed by women, regardless of their occupational status. The presence of children and larger homes is associated with less male participation in domestic chores. However, in all countries, blue-collar workers hold more traditional views of the gender division of labor, which suggests that more egalitarian views emerge as education and social class increase.

Gender inequity, however, does not disappear with greater job opportunities for women or with greater education. In four western countries, the United States, Great Britain, West Germany, and Austria, well-educated people and women with employed husbands were less favorable toward efforts to reduce gender inequality than were less educated people or women with no male wage earner.

B. RELIGIOUS BELIEFS AND VALUES

Religious beliefs and perceptions of family honor influence views of women working outside the home. Nadia Yossuf found that Latin America and the Middle East share many family ideals that link the manliness of men (machismo, muruwwa) with the sexual purity of women and influence the division of labor in the family. In both cultures, there is strong resentment against married women participating in the labor force, and if they do work, they must have few public contacts with men. Despite similar economic development, more women are in the labor force in Latin America than in the Middle East. The powerful Middle Eastern male-based family structure tightly controls women's labor force participation, but male kinsmen's control over women is diffused in Latin America by the central role of priests in the social structure. Nonetheless, education leading to prestigious positions overcomes barriers for women in both cultures.

C. ECONOMIC FACTORS

Economic factors also influence gender-related cultural practices. Bride price (compensation for the loss of a daughter's economic contributions to her family) is found most frequently where the bride's contributions are substantial. Dowry accompanies the bride when her economic contributions to her family are small. Theories suggest that when parents have high socioeconomic status, males are favored, but when parents have low status, females are favored. In Kenya, the Mukogodo are at the bottom of the regional hierarchy of wealth, prestige, and ultimately marital opportunities. It is hard for the Mukogodo men to find wives because they cannot pay a bride price. Because men can have as many wives as they can afford, women are in short supply. Mukogodo women easily find husbands, often among their wealthier, higher-status neighbors.

Economic conditions also may influence sex-biased parental investment in children. Among the Mukogodo, the birth ratio of males to females is even, but the 1986 census recorded 98 girls and 66 boys under age four. While there is no evidence of male infanticide, boys' higher death rate may be due to favoritism toward girls. Compared with sons, daughters are breast-fed longer, are well fed, and visit the doctor more often. Parents invest more in offspring who provide the greater economic or reproductive success. When bride price payments are high, the birth of a girl is greeted with fanfare and boys are greeted with little interest.

These cultural practices contrast sharply with those found in other traditional parts of the world (e.g., India, China, Turkey, Korea) where boys are highly valued by their families and their birth leads to great rejoicing. Female infanticide, wife beating, and bride burning are cultural practices that attest to the lack of concern for women in some traditional Indian cultures. Preference for boys continues to be strong in the United States and in many non-Western countries, even though the religious traditions and economic circumstances that created the preference for sons no longer apply to contemporary culture.

D. FEMALE POLITICAL PARTICIPATION

Cross-culturally men are more involved in political activities and wield greater power than women. In a sample of 90 preindustrial societies, Marc Ross found that women were more politically involved when there was high internal conflict and violence within a society and low external warfare.

The long-standing stereotyped dichotomy of public/male versus private/female suggests that men are in the public eye, active in business, politics, and culture, while women stay at home, caring for home and family. However, cross-cultural studies do not always support this dichotomy.

VIII. *Conclusions and Challenges for the Future*

The question of sex differences has fascinated social scientists for decades, and with the growing interest in culture, it is safe to assume that questions regarding their joint effects will continue to intrigue researchers. In spite of the fact that males and females are biologically more similar than different, persons in traditional or modern, industrialized societies can expect to live qualitatively different lives based on gender. Consequently, psychologists will continue to explore reasons for these differences both within and between cultures.

Most striking is the finding that pancultural similarities in sex and gender greatly outweigh cultural differences. Indeed, the manner in which male–female relationships are organized are remarkably similar across social groups. The relatively minor biological differences between the sexes can be amplified or diminished by cultural practices and socialization, making gender differences in roles and behaviors generally modest but in some cases culturally important. Hence, it is reasonable to think in terms of a pancultural model with degrees of variation created by various cultural influences.

SUGGESTED READING

Best, D. L., and Williams, J. E. (1993). Cross-cultural viewpoint. In *The Psychology of Gender* (A. E. Beall and R. J. Sternberg, eds.), (pp. 215–248). Guilford, New York.

Brannon, L. (1996). *Gender: Psychological Perspectives*. Allyn & Bacon, Boston.

Edwards, C. P. (1992). Cross-cultural perspectives on family-peer relations. In *Family-Peer Relationships: Modes of Linkages* (R. D. Parke and G. W. Ladd, eds.). Erlbaum, Hillsdale, NJ.

Hoyenga, K. B., and Hoyenga, K. T. (1993). *Gender-Related Differences: Origins and Outcomes*. Allyn & Bacon, Boston.

Maccoby, E. E. (1990). Gender and Relationships: A Developmental Account. *American Psychologist* **45**, 513–520.

Maccoby, E. E. (1998). *The Two Sexes: Growing up Apart, Coming Together*. Harvard University Press, Cambridge, MA.

Peterson, V. S., and Runyan, A. S. (1993). *Global Gender Issues*. Westview Press, Boulder, CO.

Cross-Cultural Sexual Practices

Patricia Whelehan
SUNY-Potsdam

Glossary

Cross-cultural Outside a given culture. Generally, cross-cultural applies to societies outside mainstream, late-21st-century U.S. culture.

Cultural relativism The ability to accept each culture in terms of its own beliefs and values without passing judgment on them.

Culture The learned, intra- and intergenerationally shared, patterned, beliefs, values, and symbols recognized within a group.

Descent Tracing the members of one's family through either the mother's side (matrilineal), father's side (patrilineal), or both the father's and mother's sides (bilateral) of the family.

Evolution The process of generally gradual, irreversible change from one form to another.

Initiation ceremonies Ritual observances in a social setting, which acknowledge the passage from one stage in the life cycle, usually from childhood to adulthood, to another in a given society.

Menarche The onset of menstruation.

Sex-negative cultures Those cultures that see sexuality as primarily for reproduction, perceive of sexuality as evil, dirty, shameful; provide for little sex education intergenerationally, and have high degrees of shame or guilt about sexuality and sexual functioning.

Sex-positive cultures Those cultures that see sexuality as inherently positive, healthy, and part of being human. Sex-positive cultures may link sexuality with spirituality, provide for intergenerational sex education, and have relatively egalitarian sexual relations between men and women.

Sexuality The biological, learned, behavioral, cognitive, and socioemotional aspects of reproductive and nonreproductive sex and gender across the life span and cultures.

CROSS-CULTURAL SEXUAL PRACTICES include a comparative, cradle-to-grave approach that covers reproductive behaviors, human sexual response, and marital and nonmarital sexual practices. These practices include childhood sexuality, initiation ceremonies, and same-gender sexual behavior, as well as attitudes, beliefs, and behaviors toward gender and sexual aging.

I. Introduction

Human sexuality is a complex interaction of biochemistry and learned behaviors that has evolved with the species. In looking at the expression of modern human sexuality cross-culturally, it is important to distinguish between indigenous practices and beliefs (i.e., those that existed prior to European contact) and current practices and beliefs (i.e., those that are a syncretism of traditional ways and European influence). This article includes both perspectives. Given the emergence of ethnic identities worldwide among a variety of groups and the global effects of diseases such as HIV infection and AIDS, understanding the influence of indigenous sexual patterns, beliefs, and behaviors can help to address ethnic differences relating to sexuality and to foster HIV prevention efforts.

This article looks at sexuality cross-culturally from a life-cycle perspective. The article interprets sexuality broadly. It surveys beliefs and behaviors regarding reproductive and nonreproductive aspects of human sexuality such as birth control; childhood and adolescent sexuality including initiation ceremonies; adult sexual behaviors and models of sexual response; cross-cultural rape; conceptualizations of gender and same-gender sexual behavior; and sexual aging. Much of the existing research and data on human sexuality focuses on modern, industrialized, Euro-American or colonized groups in contrast to foragers and horticulturalists, groups traditionally of interest to anthropologists. In general, contact with Europeans either reinforced negative indigenous beliefs about sexuality or created negative views toward existing practices such as premarital sex or the acceptance of same-gender sexual behavior.

Current sexual practices and beliefs that are considered extreme by Euro-American standards, such as female circumcision in some Islamic African and Malaysian societies, are in many cases probably relatively recent developments. According to Hanny Lightfoot-Klein's research, rather than being deeply rooted indigenous practices, they may be a reaction to Western influences. Traditional sexual philosophies found in Taoism, Tantrism, Confucism, and Islam, attitudes about gender, and same-gender sexual practices have been modified radically by internal political changes within their countries of origin and by Western contact.

There is also a difference within societies between ideal behavior (the societal norms) and real behavior (how people actually behave). The following two examples illustrate this difference. A number of societies do not sanction same-gender sexual behavior. While illegal in both present-day China and some areas of the Middle East, same-gender sexual behavior occurs. The United States presents itself as a model of sexual liberation and choice. However, the double standard of sexual behavior persists between males and females, and discrimination toward gays and lesbians exists nationally in the United States.

II. Conception, Pregnancy, and Childbirth

The reproductive phase of the life cycle from conception through the postpartum period receives cultural attention almost universally. Cultures manipulate reproductive processes because they are crucial to group survival and radically change women's status to mother and adult in most societies. In the latter 20th century, U.S. culture adopted some traditional childbirth practices such as less medication during labor and birth, use of familiar, known people to act as labor "coaches," early infant-mother bonding, and semi-upright positions for birth. Other societies, such as Mayan groups in the Yucatan, trained traditional midwives in biomedical prenatal practices such as regular prenatal care.

A. CONCEPTION

Cultures recognize that penile-vaginal intercourse is necessary for conception. Beyond that, explanations for why conception does or does not occur vary widely. For example, among the Tiwi, a foraging group in Australia, certain totems are responsible for conception. Women seeking to get pregnant invoke these totems; those not wanting to get pregnant try to avoid them or disguise themselves in their presence. The Kgatla of Africa believe that conception occurs when semen mixes with menstrual blood during intercourse.

B. FERTILITY

Fertility concerns are almost universal and are seen as women's responsibility. Research by Becker shows that even in industrialized countries if a man is infertile, his partner assumes responsibility for taking care of both his and her psychosocial needs concerning the situation. Infertility may be diagnosed if a pregnancy and live birth have not occurred within two years of marriage or other forms of a culturally recognized sexual relationship and may result in divorce or the addition of another wife. Steps taken to enhance fertility include consultation with healers known as *dukuns* among the Brunei Malay or *curanderas* among Mayan women in Mexico. These healers may prescribe herbal remedies or specific sexual behaviors to enhance fertility. Fertility problems may also be attributed to witchcraft, sexual transgressions, or taboo violations. In these cases, the witchcraft will need to be counteracted and restitution made for transgressions.

C. PREGNANCY AND CHILDBIRTH

Once pregnancy is socially confirmed, cultures intervene to promote fetal development, the continuation of the pregnancy, and the childbirth process. Women may have food, sex, work, social, or other activities modified during their pregnancy. Food taboos and proscriptions exist to either help determine the gender of the fetus, ensure its healthy development, or provide for an easy childbirth. Among the Sambia in New Guinea, fetal development depends on regular penile-vaginal intercourse between husband and wife. Sambians believe that semen nourishes and develops the baby. Among the Yucatan Maya, massage and binding of the abdomen are common during pregnancy and immediately after birth. Massage and binding help support the enlarging abdomen and are believed to help the uterus return to its prepregnancy size and shape after childbirth.

The cross-cultural management of childbirth spans an intervention continuum. The Manus in New Guinea are one of the few groups studied where women give birth alone and have relatively little cultural attention paid to their pregnancies and postpartum periods. Where childbirth is seen as essentially a normal process, such as in Scandinavia and Mayan cultures, women have attendants with them but receive relatively little biomedical intervention. They tend to give birth in familiar or semifamiliar surroundings with few drugs administered during labor other than herbal concoctions, such as herba buena among the Maya. They rarely have episiotomies. Their perineums are stretched with massage or warm compresses, and they generally give birth in some variation of a sitting or squatting position. Their birth attendants are usually women who are known to them and who stay with them during childbirth and for a period of time after the birth. Among Egyptian women the attendants are known as *dayas*. Among Greek peasant women the attendants are known as *doulas*. They usually stay for several days or weeks after the baby is born to help the women establish breast-feeding. In contrast, in the United States pregnancy and childbirth are seen as biomedical events, requiring much technological intervention, the use of drugs and episiotomies, and hospitalization.

The involvement of men during pregnancy and childbirth varies cross-culturally. In some horticultural groups in South America such as the Jivaro and the Siriono, the *couvade* is common. Men mimic the signs and symptoms of their pregnant and birthing wives. They may experience similar restrictions on food, sex, and activity. Jivaro men experience morning sickness during their wives' first trimester. The husbands in both groups go through simulated labor and childbirth when their wives go into labor. In some patrilineal horticultural societies in the South Pacific, fathers are not present at the birth of their children. Since the late 1960s in the United States, the involvement of men in the births of their children is seen as positive and as a move toward reducing some of the medical aspects of pregnancy and childbirth. [*See* PREGNANCY.]

D. THE POSTPARTUM PERIOD

Postpartum women and their newborns also receive cultural attention. Postpartum sex taboos are common cross-culturally. They can range from several days among some Inuit groups to several years among foragers in Africa such as the San (!Kung). In the United States, postpartum sex taboos last for about six weeks after childbirth. Postpartum sex taboos often accompany extended, regular breast-feeding among foraging groups. Regular, prolonged breast-feeding suppresses ovulation and serves as an effective form of birth control for women in these groups.

In a number of societies, the new mother and infant are secluded from the rest of the group for a period of several days in the United States to six weeks among traditional Greek peasant women. Seclusion serves several purposes. It provides rest for the mother and allows her and her baby to adjust to nursing and to bond. Bonding does not require skin-to-skin contact, but often involves the mother and infant sleeping together. Seclusion also prevents both the mother and infant from being exposed to pathogens carried by others in the group. While babies are born with their mothers' antibodies, seclusion adds another layer of protection against exposure to disease. Last, seclusion serves as its own transitional time for the woman to adapt to her new role as mother.

Women in indigenous groups space their pregnancies and births. Birth intervals average three to five years in foraging societies. This interval helps to ensure the survival of the child by providing the nutrition and attention the child needs. It is also the ideal birth spacing recommended by the American Academy of Pediatrics. A forager woman may have four to six pregnancies during her reproductive life cycle. She spends most of her reproductive life lactating, not ovulating. Women in horticultural and agricultural societies have shorter birth intervals and a greater number of pregnancies and live births. In industrialized societies, particularly the United States during the last half of the 20th century, women have the fewest number of pregnancies and live births and the greatest number of menstrual cycles during their reproductive years. The cross-cultural range of reproductive practices reflects cultural change and continuity.

III. Birth Control

While abstinence is recognized universally as a means of birth control and is the primary method in some societies such as the Inis Baeg in Ireland and the Mae Enga and Dani in New Guinea, there were and are a variety of methods used indigenously and currently. Indigenous foraging, horticultural, and agricultural societies in Europe, China, and South America controlled their population size primarily with abstinence and withdrawal *(coitus interruptus),* but also used abortions, infanticide, herbal remedies, and barrier devices inserted in the vagina to prevent conception. Extended—up to two to three years postpartum—and frequent breast-feeding that suppressed ovulation was common among foragers. Overpopulation in some places such as India is relatively recent and may be a post-European contact phenomenon.

Abortion occurred in all forms of societies prior to European contact. The horticultural Yap in the Philippines performed abortions by inserting herbal-infused, tightly wadded leaves into the cervix to induce abortion. Traditionally, abortions usually occurred to space children or to prevent a first pregnancy. Currently, most societies permit abortion during the first trimester of pregnancy to save the life of the mother. The legality, availability, safety, and affordability of abortions for reasons other than to save the life of the mother currently vary widely from one society to another, including industrialized societies. In India, some women undergo amniocentesis to determine the gender of the fetus. Since boys are preferred in India, female fetuses may be aborted. Even in societies where abortions are legal such as Russia, Italy, and the United States, obtaining an elective abortion can be difficult, expensive, and delayed. [*See* ABORTION AND ITS HEALTH EFFECTS.]

Infanticide is a common form of birth control among indigenous, patrilineal, horticultural societies, particularly in South America. Living in areas with finite resources and ecological pressures that limit expansion, groups such as the Yanamamo in the Amazon River basin kill up to 50% of their female newborns. This practice helps to ensure the needed gender ratios of males to females across the life cycle. Female infanticide also creates a shortage of adult females that is used as a justification to go to war against neighboring groups. Infanticide has been practiced among various European and U.S. groups into the early 20th century. China traditionally practiced female infanticide.

Socially sanctioned infanticide tends to follow certain patterns. Usually, female infants are killed, generally by female relatives, and often by the biological mother. The baby is not named, nursed, or held. She is usually killed within the first 24 hours of life either by suffocation or exposure. Infanticide may also occur in cases of severe physical problems or multiple births.

The most common forms of birth control used cross-culturally currently include the oral contraceptive pill, the IUD, abstinence, and the condom. Condoms are an accepted means of birth control in Japan. In societies that recognize clear distinctions between chaste wives and mothers, and women who have sex with men outside of that context, there is much resistance to condom usage with wives. For example, men use condoms with prostitutes but not with wives and lovers in Mexico and in many polygynous African groups.

Condoms are not only a contraceptive; they can prevent sexually transmitted diseases as well. Correctly, consistently used condoms are the most effective means of preventing HIV transmission among people engaging in penetrative anal, vaginal, or oral sex. Methods of birth control currently used cross-culturally reflect the influence of Western technology and views of sexuality.

IV. Childhood Sexuality

Generally, the attitudes, beliefs, and behaviors a society holds toward childhood sexuality reflect those held toward sexuality in general. Societies begin socializing their young overtly and covertly early in life as to what is considered sexually appropriate. Overall, foraging groups tend to have a positive view of childhood sexuality. They tend to be less restrictive of childhood sexual play (masturbation and peer sexual experimentation) than are patrilineal pastoral, horticultural, or patrilineal and bilateral descent agricultural and industrialized societies. Much of foraging life, including sex, is relatively open. Children who sleep with their parents often overhear or see their parents making love. Childhood experimentation with adult sexual behaviors such as techniques and positions is seen as copying what adults do, as part of being a child and growing up.

Restrictive or sex-negative societies such as the Inis Baeg, the horticultural Trukese, Kwoma of New Guinea, Ashanti, and Manus openly disapprove of childhood masturbation and sex play among peers. They tend to give little direct sex education to the young. They are particularly strict with their females about premarital, penile-vaginal intercourse. Other societies, such as the Alorese, tend to ignore expressions of childhood sexuality as long as incest does not occur and the behavior is not highly visible.

Matrilineal descent societies such as the Hopi, Navajo, and Trobriand Islanders tend to have more positive views of female childhood sexuality than do bilateral or patrilineal descent societies where a female's virginity and chastity are valued to protect the lineage and inheritance. Sex-positive societies such as the San (!Kung), Yap, Hopi, Marquesans, and Manganians accept childhood masturbation, and see peer sex play—which can include both the same and other gender—as part of growth and development. In some of these societies, such as the Hopi, Siriono, Lepcha, and Alorese, adult–child sex that involves stroking a child's genitals or oral sex, particularly with infants

or toddlers, is seen as a way of calming the child. Among the Tiwi and Lepcha, adult–child penile-vaginal intercourse is seen as a way of promoting growth and development in girls. It is not considered to be perverse or child sexual abuse. Generally, adult–child sex is reported more often between men and children than between women and children.

The foraging Tiwi in Australia, for example, "grow a girl" as a way to ensure healthy female sexual and social development. Prepubescent girls are "grown" by an older man selected by the girl's parents. She goes to live with him before reaching puberty. He is her sexual initiator and economic protector. Among the Tiwi, sexuality is vested in females. Totems, animistic protective agents, are passed down matrilineally. Females provide most of the food and are seen as central to the group's survival. Female sexuality is important and respected.

The Sambia, a horticultural group in New Guinea, "grow a boy." Since the Sambia believe that ejaculate is finite, a male may use up his supply in heterosexual intercourse. Therefore, pubescent males engage in fellatio with older adolescent males to build up their *jerungda,* or strength, in preparation for adult heterosexuality. They do not take on a "gay" identity and are expected to behave heterosexually as adults.

Sex education within indigenous groups occurred from observations of adult behavior through sleeping arrangements with adults, through peer education and sex play, and as intergenerational instruction from same gender adults. Additional sex education could occur during initiation ceremonies. Among some African groups, for example, girls engage in mutual labial stretching to increase the eroticism and attractiveness associated with elongated labia. Modern, Western-based sex models of education occur erratically cross-culturally. They may be met with resistance in Islamic cultures in Africa and the Middle East where Western models of sex education are seen as violations of traditional mores.

V. Adolescent Sexuality and Initiation Ceremonies

Adolescence begins with the appearance and development of primary and secondary sex characteristics and ends with the social conferral of adulthood. Some societies formally recognize it as a separate stage of the life cycle. While initiation ceremonies are not universal and do not occur on a societal level in the United States, they are widespread cross-culturally. Initiation ceremonies are more common for females than males. Male initiation ceremonies, however, are usually more elaborate, last longer, and occur separate from females. In general, initiation ceremonies at adolescence are a mark of status change and group identification and affiliation from childhood to (young) adulthood. They realign social relations along gender lines. Often, these ceremonies entail separation and isolation of initiates from the uninitiated. Whereas boys may participate in girls' ceremonies, girls and women generally are not part of the boys' ceremonies. Periods of food, sleep, or other forms of deprivation and disorientation are common in male initiation ceremonies. Initiates are taught the behaviors expected of them as adults.

Cross-culturally, initiation ceremonies occur most often in horticultural societies. Some societies specifically recognize menarche. They include the Mbuti and the Gusii in Africa, some groups in New Guinea, and the Tlingit in the northwest United States. Other groups recognize that adolescent females need a certain amount of body fat to reach puberty. Among the Okrika, a horticultural group in Africa, pubescent girls are removed from the rest of the group, receive elaborate body painting if their families can afford it, and are secluded for several weeks. During this time, their mobility is limited and they are fed a high-fat/high-protein diet. Their seclusion ends with reintegration into the larger society as young women. Initiation ceremonies may involve body transformations. Specific body transformations often include genital surgery that serves as a clear physical sign of a status change, adult sexuality, and reproductive ability. [See ADOLESCENT GENDER DEVELOPMENT.]

A. CIRCUMCISION

Male and female circumcision and other genital modifications occur both in the United States and cross-culturally. In the late 20th century, international and U.S.-based groups have been organized to protest any form of infant and childhood circumcision without the child's ability to give consent.

Male circumcision in the United States began in the mid-19th century to prevent masturbation. The need to retract the foreskin to clean underneath it was seen by various groups to be sexually arousing. Male circumcision in the United States became medicalized by the early 20th century. Males were circumcised in the hospital within 48 hours of birth,

usually without anaesthesia and without family members present. In 1983, the American Academy of Pediatrics stated that male circumcision was no longer medically necessary. The incidence of it has declined from about 95 to 98% prior to the 1980s to about 60 to 65% in the United States as of 2000.

Female circumcision in the United States (specifically the removal of the prepuce or clitoral hood) and clitoridectomy (removal of the glans clitoris) developed in the mid-19th century and was practiced until about 1935–1940. These procedures were done to "cure female insanity" and to stop or prevent female masturbation. These procedures were most often performed on adolescent and young adult middle-class women who either did not fit the middle-class gender role model or who were found to enjoy sex through masturbation, with a number of partners, or to be highly orgasmic with their husbands.

Presently in some sexual subcultures in the United States, tattooing or piercing of the penis, scrotal area, labia majora and minora, and the clitoris are part of body adornment. Some women have their clitorises moved closer to the introitus in the belief it will increase the chances of a vaginal orgasm during penile-vaginal intercourse.

Cross-culturally, male circumcision occurs most often in patrilineal horticultural societies in indigenous South America, Africa, and parts of Melanesia. It also occurs among Jews and Muslims. There is relatively little genital surgery performed in Europe or native North America. Groups practicing male circumcision do so as a rite of passage. Male circumcision practices appear to remain relatively constant cross-culturally. It is a marker of social identity or adulthood and may take on religious and symbolic meanings. In horticultural groups it often occurs as part of an initiation ceremony. Male circumcision cross-culturally currently generates interest relative to the susceptibility to HIV infection. In various parts of West Africa, HIV infection is lower among circumcised males than it is in East and South Africa where male circumcision occurs less often. However, the presence of other sexually transmitted infections or other ulcerative infections on the penis or scrotal area may be more of a cofactor for HIV infection than circumcision or lack of it per se.

"Female circumcision" cross-culturally is a misnomer. Female genital surgery cross-culturally usually involves clitoridectomy or infibulation, not solely the removal of the prepuce. Clitoridectomy and infibulation, usually referred to as female genital mutilation (FGM), generate much controversy with the World Health Organization (WHO) and human rights groups.

Lightfoot-Klein's research in 1989 discusses these practices. There are various procedures performed, with Pharonic circumcision (infibulation) being the most extensive and extreme. Infibulation entails performing a clitoridectomy, removing the labia minora, scraping the insides of the labia majora, and closing the labia majora, leaving an opening for menstrual blood and urine to pass through.

Female circumcision most often occurs in Muslim societies in the Sudan, Ethiopia, Mali, Ghana, and Malaysia. A form of it may have been practiced among Pharonic Egyptians. It is not required by the tenets of Islam. There are data that indicate that the current practice may be about 200 years old. It may have developed in protest against European influence and changes in sexual mores and behaviors that have occurred since European contact. In societies where female circumcision is performed it serves to preserve chastity and virginity; symbolize beauty and cleanliness; allow a woman to be marriageable (only infibulated women can marry); and provide a source of income to the people, generally women, who perform the procedure. According to Lightfoot-Klein, some women report being sexually responsive and orgasmic after infibulation.

Abolishing or modifying infibulation is a complex process involving the socioeconomic spheres of society and values about sexuality, honor, and femaleness in the cultures in which it occurs. Since the WHO banned the practice in the 1980s, performing infibulation has become hidden and more dangerous. There are higher rates of bleeding, infection, scarring, and trauma since it was outlawed. There is internal controversy within cultures that practice infibulation and other forms of female genital surgery whether to continue, end, or modify the practice. Infibulated women who travel or move to Euro-American societies find it difficult to locate health care practitioners who can address their sexual, menstrual cycle, pregnancy, and childbirth needs.

B. OTHER FORMS OF GENITAL MODIFICATION

Other forms of genital surgery performed cross-culturally that continue to serve as part of initiation ceremonies are generally done on males. These practices include superincision, subincision, and penis pins. The Manganians, a horticultural group in the South Pacific, perform superincision. An adolescent male has an incision made from the base of his navel through to the tip of the glans penis. Sometimes semiprecious stones are inserted in the incision. They are seen as increasing the sexual pleasure of his partner during penile-vaginal intercourse. His sexual initiation occurs with an older woman when the scab is healed.

Subincision is most often practiced among some of the foraging groups in Australia, most notably the Arunta. Subincision is initially performed at puberty and may be repeated until the man reaches middle age. The initiates leave their natal compounds and experience a period of disorientation and instruction before being subincised. Older males perform the surgery that entails making an incision from the base of the penis at the juncture of the scrotum to the tip of the glans. The scar resembles a female kangaroo's genitalia, a potent sexual symbol. Subincision is believed to increase a man's virility, serves as a form of male bonding, and distinguishes adult, initiated males from children.

Penis pins usually are inserted under the glans. They serve as a sexual symbol, sign of virility, and status marker. They are most often associated with groups in Borneo. Males believe penis pins increase the sexual pleasure of their partners during penile-vaginal intercourse.

C. PROTEST

Groups that protest any form of female and male genital surgery cross-culturally and in the United States do so for several reasons. Since most of these procedures are done on infants and children, consent is an issue, particularly since these surgeries are largely irreversible. No anesthesia is used with these procedures, including infant male circumcision in the United States. Complications from procedures performed under aseptic conditions include infection, hemorrhage, trauma, and scarring. Last, many women cross-culturally and in the United States experience a reduction in sexual feeling, response, and orgasm after the surgery. Protest groups want infant and child genital procedures abolished as a human rights violation.

VI. Sexual Philosophies and Practices

A. PHILOSOPHIES

There are a variety of sexual philosophies and worldviews that exist cross-culturally. Earliest Taoist,

Confucian, Tantric, and Islamic sexual models were sex positive, only taking on negative connotations more recently either as a function of internal political changes or as a result of contact with Europeans. For example, the loss of a sense of balance, harmony, and the associated positive energy exchange of yin and yang in traditional Taoism and Confucism are reflections of internal and external cultural changes.

All of these early philosophies shared several themes. They believed sexuality was essentially positive and part of the life cycle, something that could be enjoyed and experienced into old age. Taoism specifically addresses sexuality in the elderly. These philosophies consider both men and women to be sexual beings, capable of experiencing sexual pleasure and orgasm. Penile-vaginal intercourse and orgasm unite essential male and female elements that bring harmony, peace, and balance to the individuals and the group, and order to nature. These philosophies originally viewed sexuality as linked to spirituality. Sexual intercourse and orgasm could be a path to spiritual transcendence for both men and women.

Islamic beliefs view sex as inherently human and natural. Islam encourages early marriages to allow men and women a socially sanctioned sexual outlet that will not disrupt the social structure. Men are enjoined to please their wives. Recent restrictive interpretations of fundamentalist Islam are a function of culture contact, change, and reaction against Western influences.

Tantrism encouraged multiple orgasms in women in order to recirculate their energy, while men were encouraged not to ejaculate unless conception was desired since ejaculate was seen to be finite. Men conserved their sexual energy by not ejaculating, and channeled it into higher levels of arousal and spiritual connection.

B. SEXUAL PRACTICES

Sexual practices include norms, beliefs, values, and behaviors about premarital, marital, and extramarital sexuality. In general, societies that have patrilineal or bilateral systems of descent have double standards of sexual behavior for males and females, are more sexually restrictive and sex negative, and, in peasant societies, have the highest degree of body modesty. Overall, these societies restrict female sexuality more so than male sexuality regarding premarital, marital, and extramarital behavior.

In general, foraging and matrilineal descent societies tend to have the most egalitarian rules regarding sexual behavior for males and females. Usually highly stratified groups such as agricultural and industrialized societies have more sex education, more sexual behavioral variety, and more open acceptance of sexuality among the upper classes or castes.

Currently, industrialized societies, regardless of indigenous patterns, tend to accept premarital sex for adults, with greater latitude given to the males. Societies that accept extramarital sex currently include Russia, Bulgaria, and the Czech Republic. Extramarital sex generally is more accepted for the male than the female. Muslims and peoples of Southeast Asia, India, Pakistan, and China presently tend to value premarital chastity, particularly for females. In much of Latin America, premarital chastity is valued for females, but not males.

Most societies, regardless of whether they are polygynous or monogamous, value postmarital monogamy for their women. There are very few societies that practice polyandry, where a woman has more than one male spouse/partner. The Nayar in India are one. Traditionally in some African societies in Zimbabwe, same-gender marriages were permitted.

Specific sexual behaviors cross-culturally run a gamut from very little sex play among the Inis Baeg in Ireland to highly and frequently orgasmic women among the Manganians. Bestiality was accepted within a few societies indigenously. They include the Crow and Ojibwa in North America and some groups in the Middle East where it still occurs.

Kissing in some form occurs in most societies, as does manual genital stimulation and oral sex. Oral sex occurs in North America, Europe, the Pacific Islands, parts of Africa, and traditionally in China and India. Fellatio, oral sex on a man, is reported more often cross-culturally than cunnilingus, oral sex on a woman. Male sexual initiation among the Manganians in the South Pacific includes performing cunnilingus. Sexual positions for intercourse include the man on top, which was not that common among Pacific Islanders before European contact, woman on top, side-by-side, and rear entry. In sex-positive societies such as Mangania, women are expected to enjoy sex, be orgasmic, and initiate sexual activity. In other parts of Oceania such as the Trobriand Islands, "night crawling" was common. Adolescent boys left their huts at night to crawl into the sleeping spaces of girls they liked in order to have sex.

Sadomasochism (S/M) is broadly defined as sexual behavior that stimulates the pleasure-pain boundary.

It can include biting, scratching, slapping, or hitting, and occurs in both traditional and Euro-American cultures. Examples include the horticultural Mundurucuru in South America and Mundugumoor in New Guinea.

Sexual dysfunction occurs cross-culturally as well. The most commonly reported sexual dysfunctions for women are anorgasmia or lack of orgasm, and dyspareunia, pain with intercourse. Erectile problems are the most common problems men report. Depending on the culture, people seek out healers and advisors such as the *dukuns* among the Brunei Malay or *curanderas* in Mexico. A variety of behaviors, potions, and charms are used to restore sexual functioning cross-culturally.

C. RAPE

In U.S. culture, one definition of rape is nonconsensual penile-vaginal intercourse. This definition does not include same-gender rape, nor does it include rape of men by women, a behavior reported among the Trobriand Islanders. Ritual rape is documented in both the United States and cross-culturally. Generally it occurs as either a rite of passage, an ideological threat used to control women's sexual behavior and nonsexual mobility, a real and symbolic expression of power and domination, a punishment, or as spoils of war. According to Peggy Sanday's research in 1992, the occurrence of rape cross-culturally is part of a societal pattern that includes interpersonal violence, male dominance, and gender segregation. Male rape of women is rare in societies that regard nature as sacred, respect the mother–child bond, and see this bond as enduring.

In some patrilineal descent societies such as the Mundurucuru in South America, the threat of gang rape exists in male cultural ideology. The threat of gang rape serves to control the sexual and nonsexual behavior of women. In this gender-segregated society, men see women's sexuality and power to control the food supply as threatening. Women who walk alone along paths are seen as independent and potentially rebellious. They are vulnerable to gang rape by any men who encounter them. It is reported that the threat of gang rape reinforces female conformity. Traditionally, the Cheyenne of North America used gang rape as a punishment for female sexual or other transgressions. It was not used against males.

In the United States, ritual gang rape is part of fraternity initiations on some college campuses according to Sanday. Gang rape is a show of masculine solidarity and bonding more than as a display of virility or sexuality.

Rape of women as part of the spoils of war has been culturally widespread among agrarian and industrial societies over the past several thousand years. These societies generally have either patrilineal or bilateral descent. Raping the women of the defeated groups is a symbolic marker of dominance and submission. It makes a statement of ownership and control over the women and symbolically emasculates the defeated men. It also can potentially disrupt the kinship system and social structure should the women become pregnant. For example, during the late 20th-century "ethnic cleansing" conflicts in Eastern Europe, raped Muslim women are no longer marriageable and are considered to be "shamed, ruined women" within their villages. In summary, cross-culturally, rape is a sexual behavior used more often as a political statement or expression of individual power and anger than as a reflection of desire or sexual attraction and interest. Most sexual behaviors are panhuman; their frequency varies cross-culturally. [*See* RAPE.]

VII. Gender

Gender refers to the label of male or female assigned to an individual based on external phenotypic sex characteristics, while gender identity is the sense of being male or female, and gender role is the expression of one's gender identity. Discussions of gender are culture specific. While all cultures recognize male and female genders, identities, and roles, there is wide cultural variability in their expression. In most cultures, females have more flexibility to express their gender role than do males; the structural boundaries and behaviors are broader for females than for males. Mainstream U.S. culture is relatively rigid in matters of gender. It formally and legally recognizes only two genders, identities, and roles; variations from these are considered pathological and labeled gender dysphoric. Recent attempts to expand the concept of gender in the United States have been met with controversy and challenge.

Cross-cultural views on gender contrast sharply with those in the United States. Will Roscoe's research in 1998 explores the phenomenon of "two-spirit" individuals in more than 500 indigenous societies in North America. These individuals, while chromosomally, anatomically, and hormonally male or female, identify as something other than male or female.

Additional research among the *xanith* in Oman, the *hijira* in India, and the *mahu* in the South Pacific show cultural flexibility in gender identity and role. While there are cross-cultural differences in how third and fourth genders (i.e., men and women who do not fit typical male and female gender roles and identities) live their lives, there are several commonalities. These biological males and females have their gender determined not only by biology, but by a sense of spirituality as well. Third- and fourth-gender individuals are spiritually gifted or blessed by having an alternative gender, and are recognized as different from the other males and females in society. Group elders identify these children early in childhood.

Being a *xanith* in Oman or a *nadle* among the Navajo not only has spiritual connotations and is perceived as special, but is respected and accepted as well. The *hijira* in India, biologic males who are castrated or who bind their genitalia tightly, traditionally held ritual roles. They were seen as capable of spiritual transcendence and attended weddings, births, and funerals as a seer, capable of both positive and negative predictions. Currently, *hijiras* are stigmatized and frequently work as street prostitutes.

In most cultures that recognize third and fourth genders, there are more males than females who fill these roles. A notable female two-spirit role is that of the "manly-hearted woman" among Plains groups such as the Cheyenne in North America. Manly-hearted women wore men's clothes, led war parties into battle, and received full recognition and acceptance in that role. In native North America, most of the female two-spirits were found west of the Rockies and included the Mohave, Navajo, Tlingit, and Apache. However, the Algonkian Illinois in the east recognized a behavioral and sexual female two-spirit.

While there exists a wide variety of different genders, third- and fourth-gender individuals have defined roles in their respective cultures. In traditional China, both men and women could cross-dress for political or social purposes. This behavior did not take on the connotations that transvestism does in the United States. In other cultures, third- and fourth-gender individuals may adopt the behavior, dress, and affect of the other gender. They may engage in heterosexual and homosexual sexual behavior, marry, and be responsible for children while in their alternative role. The specific behaviors of these individuals are highly diverse and may include the roles of shamans or healers within the group.

Culture change and the impact of European concepts of maleness and femaleness, masculinity, femininity, and sexuality affected the status and role of third- and fourth-gender people in their native groups. Europeans mistakenly labeled these people as homosexual or perverse and banned the role from being openly expressed. As indigenous peoples assimilated European behaviors and beliefs, the third- and fourth-gender roles changed, in some cases ended, or became stigmatized. The spiritual connotations associated with the *hijira*, for example, have largely disappeared, and they now are seen much more secularly. Among the Navajo and in Oman, however, the *nadle* and the *xanith*, respectively, continue to be recognized and accepted as they once were. In several native North American societies, the emergence of ethnic identity is serving to question European concepts of gender and replace them with open recognition of third and fourth genders.

While societies recognize biologic males and females and have particular roles for them, the expression of gender varies widely cross-culturally. Several genders, gender identities, and role behaviors are recognized. In contrast, U.S. culture has some of the more rigid gender roles found, particularly for males. "Gender bending," challenging stereotypic male and female roles, is currently one of the areas of sexual questioning and cultural change in the United States. [*See* Cross-Cultural Gender Roles.]

VIII. Same-Gender Sexual Behavior

The causes of sexual orientation—homosexual, bisexual, or heterosexual—are unknown. Orientation is probably a complex interaction of as yet undetermined biological factors that are channeled through a specific culture's beliefs, values, and norms. Same-gender behavior, however, is widespread among both human and nonhuman primates. It has varying interpretations attributed to it based on place and time. As with other aspects of sexual behavior, there are more data for male than female same-gender sexuality.

While same-gender sexual behavior, particularly for males, is recognized cross-culturally and through time, the idea of adopting an identity around the gender of your sex and romantic love partners is relatively recent and culturally restricted. Having an identity as "gay," "lesbian," "straight," or "bisexual" developed about 150 years ago and is largely a Euro-American phenomenon. The cross-cultural limits of creating an identity based on the gender of one's sex partners is evident when conducting HIV intervention and education work or when trying to understand initiation rites that can involve same-gender sexual behavior. Equating behavior with orientation can be problematic in cultures that do not recognize sociosexual identities.

Cross-culturally, same-gender sexual behavior is found even where it is illegal, such as in Egypt and other parts of the Middle East and China. While officially proscribed, same-gender sexual behavior exists in private. In China, it is referred to as "the cut sleeve," after the story of an ancient ruler who had a male lover. Male-male sexual behavior was accepted traditionally among the Mayans, Omaha, Cheyenne, Navajo, Sioux, and Crow in North America. It was and is also found in Indonesia, Java, Thailand, and among Tibetan monks. In Latin America, the inserter maintains his identity as male and heterosexual. He does not experience stigma for his behavior. The receiver in male-male sex in Latin America, however, may be stigmatized and seen as not completely male. In Mexico, the receiver of the penis may be referred to as a *puta* (i.e., whore or prostitute). In Brazil, the receiver takes on a rather limbo status as somewhere between being a male and female.

Ancient Greeks often are used as a model of same-gender male sexual behavior for current gay identity and behavior in the United States. This model may not be the most accurate reflector of gay identity for late 20th-century U.S. culture for several reasons. Adult Greek males were expected to be heterosexually married and produce offspring. Greek same-gender sex focused on male-male sexuality that often involved an adult and younger male. This intergenerational partnering reflected the love of the male body and intellect as much as, if not more than, an erotic interest and orientation. Gay identity in U.S. culture is largely based on peer sex and attraction, not on intergenerational models.

Female-female sexual behavior occurs in China, where they may engage in oral sex and use dildos, and among the San (!Kung), Azande, Dahomey, Nupe, Hausa, and Nyakyusa in Africa. Indigenous groups in India, Indonesia, Peru, and Polynesia recognized female-female sexuality and relationships. Currently, there is a lesbian-identified movement in Mexico. Among the Lesotho in Africa, a "mummy-baby" relationship can occur between adolescent girls. One girl may be older, or the relationship may be more peer-based. The females engage in gift exchange and emotional and sexual intimacy. Female-female sexual behavior is also found in some Australian aboriginal groups and among the Mohave, Klamath, Maricopa, and Cocopa in North America.

Same-gender sexual behaviors among both males and females are part of the continuum of sexual behaviors that occur among heterosexuals. There is mutual oral stimulation, manual and masturbatory stimulation, receptive and insertive anal or vaginal sex with penises and dildos, kissing, use of vibrators, and involvement in S/M behaviors for some people. Where same-gender sexual behavior is proscribed, regardless of the context, it is usually because the behavior is nonreproductive. Same-gender sexual behavior is common among human societies, while an identity as gay or lesbian is recent and culture specific. It is important theoretically and practically to distinguish clearly between orientation, behavior, and identity in order to have an accurate record of cross-cultural sexual practices and in conducting HIV prevention efforts. [*See* Lesbians, Gay Men, and Bisexuals in Relationships.]

IX. Sexual Aging

As with other aspects of sexuality, sexual aging reflects larger cultural norms and beliefs about sexuality as well as the views a society has about its elderly. In societies where the elderly are valued and respected, female status may increase with age. In their postmenopausal years, women may experience greater flexibility in expressing their sexuality. Their sexual behavior is no longer a threat to the social structure, and they have achieved status as older persons and for what they have accomplished. They may be able to choose sexual partners among the younger men, as occurs with the San (!Kung) of the Kalahari Desert in Africa. Among the Abkhasians in the Caucasus, men and women are sexual into old age. For traditional Chinese Taoists, sexuality is considered to be healthy for the elderly.

In contrast, among the Inis Baeg of Ireland, a sex-negative society, postmenopausal women are considered to be nonsexual and susceptible to mental illness. Among the Uttar Pradesh in Northern India, male-female sexual relations are supposed to end upon the marriage of the son. In Western industrialized societies, aging heterosexual men have a greater choice of partners and expression of their sexuality than do women. In the United States, older women are seen as less sexual than older men. It is more acceptable for an older man to be with a younger woman, than for an older woman to be with a younger man. However, recent U.S. research indicates that the happiest people are sexually active married couples in their 60s and 70s.

Sexual behavior among older people is related to the culture's views of sexuality and the aging process, the roles older people have in society, and the status of women. [See AGING.]

X. Conclusions

The expression of sexuality reflects the larger culture's social, economic, and worldviews. Indigenous norms, behaviors, and beliefs about sexuality persist in some form in many parts of the world, although modified by the impact of Euro-American contact. Foraging and matrilineal descent societies tend to have the most open and accepting attitudes about sexuality across the life cycle for both men and women. Societies that associate sexuality with spirituality tend to be more sex positive traditionally and accept women's sexuality as positive. Societies also distinguish between sex for pleasure and sex for reproduction. Patrilineal and bilateral descent horticultural, agricultural, and industrial societies tend to be the most restrictive and have double standards of sexual behavior for men and women. Generally, men have greater expression of their sexuality than do women, including men who have sex with men. Euro-American contact with indigenous cultures has resulted in loss of status for women, repression of their sexuality, and negative views towards third- and fourth-gender and same-gender sexual behavior in a number of societies.

Gender and orientation, while having a biological component, are also socially constructed. A number of traditional societies in North America, the Middle East, and Polynesia recognize more than two genders and have allowed same-gender sexual behavior under a variety of circumstances.

Fundamentalist views of sexuality tend to be a response to Western influence as opposed to being traditional patterns. Western culture is seen as debauched, decadent, and contradictory to Islamic values of women and sexuality. That *Baywatch*, a television series featuring bikini-clad women, is the most popular television show outside of the United States reinforces these views. Some societies, such as Middle Eastern Muslim groups, and those who practice infibulation, have imposed highly restrictive sexual norms on their women as a reaction to Western contact. This is largely due to economic, social, and political changes, and, most recently, the impact of Western media. The range and expression of sexual behaviors, attitudes, and beliefs cross-culturally indicate the diversity, flexibility, and adaptability of the human species.

SUGGESTED READING

Caron, S. L. (1998). *Cross-Cultural Perspectives on Human Sexuality*. Allyn & Bacon, Boston.

DuToit, B. (2000). *Human Sexuality: Cross-Cultural Readings*, 6th ed. McGraw Hill, New York.

Francoeur, R. T. (ed.) (1997). *The International Encyclopedia of Sexuality*, Vols. 1–3. Continuum International, New York.

Gregersen, E. (1983). *Sexual Practices: The Story of Human Sexuality*. Franklin Watts, New York.

Lightfoot-Klein, H. (1989). *Prisoners of Ritual: An Odyssey into Female Genital Mutilation in Africa*. Haworth Press, New York.

Parker, R., and Aggleton, P. (eds.) (1999). *Culture, Society and Sexuality*. UCL Press, London.

Roscoe, W. (1998). *Changing Ones: Third and Fourth Genders in North America*. St. Martin's Press, New York.

Sanday, P. (1992). *Fraternity Gang Rape: Sex, Brotherhood, and Privilege on Campus*. New York University Press, New York.

SIECUS Report. (2000, April/May). *Sexuality: Education: A Global Perspective* 28(4), 5–23.

Depression

Valerie E. Whiffen
University of Ottawa, Canada

Glossary

Artifact A misleading result that occurs because of the way that researchers have conducted their study.

Childhood sexual abuse Sexual contact between a preadolescent child and an adult or another child who is at least five years older.

Depression An emotional disturbance that involves negative perceptions of self, the world, and the future.

Etiology The causes of a disease.

Gender role Personality traits and behaviors that are consistent with societal expectations for girls and boys or men and women.

Longitudinal study A study that follows the same research participants over time, which allows researchers to determine whether or not a variable predicts changes in depression over time.

Marital distress Feelings of unhappiness and dissatisfaction about one's marriage.

Rumination The tendency to think about and try to understand one's emotional responses to life stress.

Sociotropy The belief that one must always get along with other people and that others' approval is needed to feel good about oneself (also known as *dependency*).

DEPRESSION involves feeling down or sad, feeling that nothing is going well, and feeling unenthusiastic about life. These feelings are a common, human response to life events that entail loss, failure or disappointment. The emotion of sadness occurs when we experience losses. This sadness can be profound, as it may be after the death of a parent or spouse. However, this sadness is not *depression* unless it becomes complicated by negative feelings about ourselves and our futures. Depressed people feel badly about themselves, and they blame themselves for things going wrong in their lives. They also have trouble imagining a better future for themselves. Depression that is clinically meaningful involves physical symptoms as well, including appetite changes (either an increase or decrease) and changes in energy level and sleeping patterns. When these symptoms occur together, and are present on a daily basis for at least two weeks, *major depression* is said to be present.

I. Definition of Depression

Depression is the common cold of emotional problems: it is the most frequently diagnosed form of emotional distress. Three clear subtypes of depression have been identified. Major depression is the subtype in which researchers most often have been interested and which is the focus of this article. *Dysthymia* is similar to major depression in that some of the same symptoms may be present. However, fewer symptoms are required and they may be less severe. Individuals also need to be symptomatic for at least two years before they receive this diagnosis. *Bipolar disorder* used to be called "manic depression." The key feature of bipolar disorder is that the individual's mood cycles between periods of depression and periods of elation and intense energy.

The majority of depressive episodes are preceded by one or more stressful life events. These events typically involve loss, such as the breakup of a relationship, the death of a parent, or failure at school or work. Even positive life events or life transitions can entail an element of loss. For instance, when women first become mothers, they may be overjoyed by the baby's birth but at the same time feel that they have lost their freedom and control over their lives. Some investigators believe this is one reason why women are at risk for depression after childbirth. The more losses that an individual experiences in a short period of time, the more likely one is to become depressed. Interestingly, depression often co-occurs with other emotional problems, especially with anxiety, eating disorders, and substance abuse. Thus, depression can be a complex and multiply determined response to a range of life problems.

II. The Gender Difference in Depression Rates

One of the most robust findings in depression research is that women are twice as likely as men to experience depression. Studies of large samples tell us that the lifetime rate of clinical depression is 20 to 25% for women and 7 to 12% for men. The ratio is approximately the same regardless of the method used to measure depression, the definition of depression, or whether the study participants are selected from a community or clinical setting. Studies conducted in a variety of developed countries, including Canada, the United States, the United Kingdom, New Zealand, Italy, Germany, and Sweden, produced similar results. Although the rates for women are always higher, the gender ratio varies from a low of 1.6 to a high of 3.5. However, research from developing countries is less consistent, leading some investigators to conclude that the gender difference is determined more by social than by biological factors. With a few notable exceptions, the gender difference also is present across different cultural and ethnic subgroups within developed societies. The exceptions—which include the old-order Amish, a rural farming society, and college students—have never been adequately explained.

As children, boys are somewhat more likely than girls to experience depression. However, the gender difference reverses by about the age of 14, with girls' rate suddenly increasing. Some studies have shown that the gender difference disappears again at about age 55 when women's rates return to those seen among men throughout adulthood. Because most women are postmenopausal at this age, these studies suggest that females' increased risk for depression occurs only during their reproductive years, which could point to an hormonal explanation. However, the findings of individual studies are inconsistent. One investigator combined the results of 25 studies into a single analysis (called a meta-analysis); over all of the studies, the rates of depression were equal for males and females only before the age of 10 and after the age of 80, which is much longer than females' reproductive years.

Women clearly experience more major depression than men do, and the existing research suggests that they experience more dysthymia too. The rates of bipolar disorder are equal in men and women, which is one of the reasons that it is considered a distinct disorder. Women also are more likely than men to be diagnosed with other disorders at the same time that they are depressed, especially eating disorders, somatization, agoraphobia, panic disorder, and borderline personality disorder. These coexisting diagnoses may partially explain why women are more likely than men to experience relapses after recovering from depression.

Most of the theories that attempt to explain depression do not incorporate what we know about the gender difference in depression rates. Ultimately, a good theory of depression must be able to account for girls' and women's greater vulnerability. However, focusing on the gender difference also may illuminate the most important causes of depression. If we can understand what it is about the lives of girls and women that makes them particularly vulnerable, then we will be better able to understand why both sexes experience depression.

III. Artifactual Explanations for the Gender Difference

Much research has been devoted to determining if the gender difference in depression rates is a real difference or if it is the result of an *artifact*. An artifact is a misleading result that occurs when an apparent gender difference is due to some other variable that is associated with gender. For instance, some critics point out that women may be more willing to seek treatment for emotional problems or more likely than men to admit that they feel depressed. Men may express their depression through aggression or drinking. Research shows that women do not find psychological symptoms to be more socially acceptable than men do. However, they do seek medical help more readily than men do. Nevertheless, men and women with similar depressive symptoms are equally likely to seek treatment. Seeking treatment also cannot explain why rates of depression differ in community surveys where whether or not one is classified as depressed is not dependent on seeking treatment.

Another possible artifact is gender bias. Women may be more likely than men to receive a diagnosis of depression because of gender bias on the part of diagnosticians. Physicians and mental health professionals have read that women are more likely to experience depression than men are. In addition, some characteristics of depression, such as passivity and low self-esteem, are thought to be consistent with the female gender role. Thus, the concern is that diagnosticians are sensitized to seeing depression in their female patients and insensitive to the same symptoms in their male patients. Studies do show evidence of this asymmetry. Clinicians tend to underrate psychological disturbance of all kinds in men and to overrate it in women. Thus, gender bias probably influences the diagnosis of depression in family practice settings. However, most of the studies that established the gender difference used standardized interviews, which require the interviewer to ask the same questions of all respondents. In addition, these interviews leave little room for interpretation in judging symptoms as clinically significant. Thus, it is less likely that gender bias influenced the depression rates found in these studies. To date, no research has assessed the possibility of gender bias in the administration of these interviews.

One factor that is sometimes thought of as an artifact may reflect an important difference between men's and women's depression. Some studies have shown that, among women, depression is more likely to be recurrent—that is, women are more likely than men to have many episodes of depression over their lifetimes. This finding may help us to understand why more women than men are depressed when they are assessed at a specific point in time: for the depressed men this could be a single, lifetime episode, while for the depressed women the episode is likely to be one of many. Individuals who have just had an episode of depression experience more life stress; life stress increases the risk of subsequent depression. Thus, part of the gender difference may arise because more women than men are caught in the revolving door of depression. However, gender differences in recurrence rates are not truly artifactual because women really do suffer more depressive episodes than men do.

IV. Hormonal and Genetic Factors

While the etiology of depression has a strong biological component, there is inconsistent evidence that hormonal or genetic factors can explain the gender difference in depression rates. The fact that the gender difference may coincide with women's reproductive years suggests an hormonal etiology. However, it is difficult to interpret the increase in girls' depression rate at puberty. The hormonal changes associated with puberty, which typically occur over a number of years, coincide with significant social and emotional changes in adolescents' lives. Thus, it is hard to know if the depression rate increases because of hormonal or social factors or even because of the combination of the two. Recent research tried to untangle these effects by measuring pubertal development as well as age. The researchers classified study participants into pubertal stages depending on the extent to which they showed objective signs of puberty (e.g., breast development, menstruation). They found that the gender difference in depression emerged at midpuberty, regardless of the adolescent's age. This is the first direct evidence that links pubertal development to the gender difference in depression.

Women's depression also is linked with such hormonally driven events as menstruation and childbirth. For instance, women diagnosed with premenstrual syndrome (PMS) tend to have a history of depression and their risk for postpartum depression (PPD) is high relative to other women. In addition, women with a history of depression experience a worsening of symptoms when they are premenstrual. However, no research has pinpointed an hormonal mechanism either for PMS or for depressive episodes among PMS sufferers. At first, investigators did not see a connection between PPD and hormones. There is no evidence, in general, that PPD is caused by hormones; in contrast, it is strongly predicted by psychological variables, such as marital satisfaction and social support, which suggests that it occurs in response to life transitions like other forms of depression. However, recent research found a subgroup of PPD women who experience depression only after childbirth. Thus, some women's PPD episodes may be caused by hormones, although, again, the specific hormonal mechanism has not been identified. There may be a subgroup of women who are at risk for depression following reproductive cycle events of all kinds.

It also is possible that reproductive hormones have an impact on the neurotransmitters implicated in depression. Neurotransmitters are chemicals in the brain and nervous system that influence our moods. Female hormones have an impact on how the neurotransmitters are made and used by the nervous system. However, it is important to emphasize that there is no evidence directly linking feelings of depression to hormones. In addition, the hormones that are most clearly linked to depression, such as cortisol, do not differ between the sexes in a way that explains the gender difference.

Researchers also have failed to find gender differences in genetic vulnerability for depression when studies have looked at unselected samples of depressed persons. However, there is a subgroup of depressed individuals whose parents and siblings show either alcoholism or antisocial personality disorder (i.e., criminal or aggressive behavior). In these families, there is a gender difference in the expression of the genetic liability, with the women being more likely to experience depression and the men being more likely to experience alcoholism. In this subgroup of individuals, there is a gender difference in depression rates, which can be explained by genetic factors. These recent hormonal and genetic studies suggest that biological explanations for the gender difference in depression may be uncovered by looking at subtypes of depressed persons.

V. Psychological and Social Factors

An important distinction is made in the psychological literature between variables that are *distal* or vulnerability factors and those that are *proximal* or precipitating. A distal variable increases the risk of depression statistically but is not, in itself, capable of causing a specific episode of depression. A good example of a distal variable is parental rejection. Many depressed adults report that they felt rejected by their parents as children; however, there is no evidence that most adults are depressed about this rejection. Distal variables are thought to influence depression through proximal variables, which are those implicated in the onset of a specific episode. Life stress involving loss or failure is a good example of a proximal variable. If asked, a depressed individual would most likely identify the recent death of a parent or unemployment as the reason that she or he became depressed. The distinction between distal and proximal variables can be arbitrary. In addition, a variable that is proximal at one point in an individual's life may become distal at another time. For instance, parental rejection may be a proximal cause of depression among children—that is, children may feel depressed because they feel constantly criticized and rejected by their parents. In adulthood, parental rejection may be a distal cause of depression through its influence on the way adults interpret negative interactions with their spouses. Despite these complications, the distinction between distal and proximal variables helps clarify the roles played by various statistical predictors of depression.

One approach to identifying the psychological and social factors involved in the gender difference has been to review the research on adolescents. Since the gender difference first emerges in early adolescence, a comparison of adolescent boys' and girls' standing on known risk factors for depression may illuminate the reasons for the difference. After reviewing this literature, Susan Nolen-Hoeksema and Joan Girgus concluded that by the beginning of adolescence, girls are already disadvantaged relative to boys on a variety of risk factors. In addition, these authors believe that girls face more challenges in early adolescence than boys do. Thus, they argue that girls encounter more challenges and that they are less well equipped to cope with these challenges, with the result that they are more likely to become depressed than boys are. Benjamin Hankin and Lyn Abramson narrowed their review of the adolescent literature by selecting only studies that attempted to demonstrate that a given variable could account for the gender difference. Despite differences in the variables reviewed in these two papers, the conclusions are strikingly similar. Both reviews highlight the importance of two variables, childhood sexual abuse and gender role, that also are established distal variables in adult depression.

A. CHILDHOOD SEXUAL ABUSE (CSA)

Statistically, a history of childhood sexual abuse (CSA) is strongly associated with adult women's depression, particularly with chronic, recurrent depression. CSA also is more prevalent among girls than boys. Most important, several studies recently demonstrated that when a history of CSA is controlled for statistically, the gender difference in depression is either reduced or eliminated. In general, childhood adversity is associated with depression during adulthood. When we consider other kinds of adversity, such as physical abuse, girls are not exposed to more adversity than boys are. However, girls are exposed to more CSA, which suggests that this specific form of childhood adversity may be important for understanding the gender difference in depression.

This finding raises an important question: How can CSA explain the emergence of the gender difference during midpuberty? One possibility is that CSA is a proximal variable—that is, girls become depressed because of their abuse. However, this explanation is not consistent with the fact that most CSA occurs before puberty. Therefore, CSA probably functions as a distal variable, even in adolescence. A history of CSA may make it difficult for girls to cope with some of the challenges of adolescence that Nolen-Hoeksema and Girgus described, such as changes in their bodies. Girls who were sexually abused as children may be ambivalent about normal, physical changes that make them sexually attractive because sexual activity was a source of shame in the past. Consistent with this idea, Bernice Andrews has shown that bodily shame may link CSA with depression among adults. In addition, CSA may lead to the development of specific biases in thinking that are associated with depression. For example, children who are sexually abused are typically blamed by the assailant for their abuse. The tendency to blame oneself for negative events may become a stable part of the abused child's personality, such that even life events that are clearly out of one's control are perceived to be one's fault. Very little research

has been done on the cognitive consequences of CSA. This research could help us to link childhood abuse with cognitive theories of depression. Another line of research suggests that CSA may cause permanent changes to the nervous system that increase reactivity to stress. These changes make CSA survivors similar neurologically to patients with adult-onset depression. Thus, CSA survivors may be biologically primed to experience depression in the face of life stress.

CSA also has an indirect impact on adult depression through its influence on relationships. Close relationships, particularly with romantic partners, protect women from becoming depressed when they experience life stress. However, women with a history of CSA have more interpersonal problems than do women without this history. They report difficulties getting close to and trusting other people, and many of those who were abused by family members report that they avoid having close relationships altogether. CSA survivors are more likely to be separated or divorced than are women without this history, which puts them at risk for depression when they experience life stress. In addition, the quality of their romantic relationships may be poor. For instance, CSA survivors are more likely to be physically victimized by their romantic partners or to be sexually assaulted. Revictimization is directly associated with episodes of depression during adulthood.

B. GENDER ROLE

The second factor that is highlighted in both reviews of the adolescent literature is gender role. The term *gender role* can refer either to the socialization of gender-typed personality traits or to the enactment of gender-typed behaviors, such as looking after children. While the adolescent research focuses on the former aspect, the adult literature emphasizes the latter.

The socialization of boys, but not girls, stresses the development of instrumental, self-assertive traits such as independence and decisiveness. As a result, girls and women who identify with the traditional female role possess lower levels of these instrumental traits, which protect both sexes from feeling depressed. By early adolescence, girls possess fewer instrumental traits than boys do. In addition, adolescence is a period of intense identification with gender roles, such that adolescent girls may suppress the expression of instrumental traits (i.e., pretend helplessness) in an attempt to conform to their gender role. Nolen-Hoeksema and Girgus have argued that girls' relative lack of instrumental traits may impede their ability to cope with the challenges presented by early adolescence. Thus, they conceptualized instrumental traits as a distal variable that has an impact on the proximal variable of coping.

One challenge comes from girls' changing bodies. The normal changes associated with puberty mean that girls gain fat, especially in their breasts and buttocks. They lose their prepubescent shape and the thinness that is so idealized in contemporary Western societies. In contrast, boys undergo physical changes that result in their becoming taller and more muscular, that is, moving closer to the ideal for young men. As a result, body dissatisfaction is normative among adolescent girls, but rare among boys. This is problematic for girls because physical attractiveness is a central component of the adolescent girl's gender role. Attractiveness determines girls' popularity with both sexes and often overshadows other characteristics such as intelligence and achievement. Not surprisingly, body dissatisfaction is associated with depressive symptoms in both sexes. Most important, one recent study demonstrated that body dissatisfaction explained increases in depressed mood among 13-year-old girls. This research suggests that gender differences in body satisfaction may account for part of the gender difference in depression.

Paul Bebbington's review of the adult depression literature emphasized the link between gender role enactment and depression. He pointed out that the majority of studies find married men and single women to have the highest levels of emotional well-being. Thus, being married per se may be a risk factor for women. However, being married is almost completely confounded with having children because most married women have children as well. Married women with young children are at the greatest risk for depression, except in countries and cultures, such as Mediterranean countries and the rural Amish, where homemaking is highly valued.

Conversely, being employed outside the home is protective for women, despite the fact that most working women continue to be primarily responsible for childcare and housework in their homes. Most working mothers experience conflict between their roles of worker and mother. They feel guilty that they do not spend enough time with their children,

they feel irritable and tired when they are at home, and they worry that they are not close enough to their children. The vast majority of working mothers report high or very high levels of stress as a result of work-family conflict. However, compared to stay-at-home mothers, working mothers have higher self-esteem and they feel more competent, even about their ability to mother their children. They feel more attractive and less lonely and isolated. These findings indicate that they feel less depressed. However, it is important to emphasize that these studies compare groups of women who have decided either to work outside the home or to become homemakers. It is possible that women who opt out of paid employment do so because they are more vulnerable to feeling stressed and depressed than are women who continue to work. Thus, on the basis of this research, we cannot infer that being a homemaker is necessarily a risk factor for depression.

In previous generations, middle-class women did not typically work outside their homes. Now, in Western societies, the majority do. Men also are more likely now to take on the role of homemaker, and gender roles do not diverge as much now as they did previously. If employment and gender roles are factors in the gender difference, then we should be seeing a decline in the rates of women's depression and in the female-to-male ratio. If anything, studies indicate that rates of depression are higher in younger than in older people, and that depressive episodes are occurring sooner in life. Studies show that individuals born since WWII are more likely to experience depression than their parents. However, there is some evidence that the rate for men is increasing while the rate for women has stabilized. Thus, the gender gap may be shrinking. An increase in the rate for men is consistent with the idea that gender roles play a part in explaining the gender difference. Gender roles also may explain why college students do not show a gender difference in depression rates. The roles and social status of men and women in university are more similar than they are in many other settings.

It may be useful to think of employment specifically and of gender roles generally as distal factors that have a positive impact on the development of instrumental traits and behaviors. For instance, women who work outside their homes may have the opportunity to develop personality traits such as independence and self-confidence that help them to cope positively with difficult life situations.

VI. *Three Theories of Depression: Can They Explain the Gender Difference?*

Most reviewers who delve into the research on gender differences in depression come up empty-handed. They are forced to conclude that we do not have a good explanation for the gender difference at this time. In part, research on this topic is stymied by the same problems that plague depression research in general: difficulties distinguishing the causes of depression from its symptoms and its consequences, and the prohibitive need for large samples and longitudinal studies to adequately test complex models of etiology. However, one of the biggest obstacles to answering this question is the absence of the gender difference in contemporary theories of depression. The most popular and empirically best supported models of depression are virtually silent on the subject of this gender difference. The following sections describe the three major traditions that have attempted to explain why people experience depression. The contributions of each tradition to an explanation of the gender difference are highlighted.

A. COGNITIVE VULNERABILITY

By far, the most empirically tested theory of depression, as well as the most popular, is the cognitive model. Tim Beck first articulated the basis for cognitive theory in his 1967 book describing the treatment of clinically depressed patients. He identified what he called the *cognitive triad*, a set of negative beliefs about the self, the world, and the future, which characterizes the thinking of depressed persons. He also identified the biases in depressed people's thinking that lead to the confirmation of their pessimistic beliefs and expectations. His description of the cognitive underpinnings to depression led to the development of *cognitive-behavioral therapy*, which is an effective and brief psychological treatment for depression. Cognitive theory has been less successful as an explanation for why some people become depressed while others do not. The distorted thinking that Beck identified is a facet of the depression, not a stable way of thinking that is present before and after depressive episodes. Therefore, distorted thinking is unlikely to be implicated in the onset of depression. In addition, traditional cognitive theory does not attempt to explain why women are more vulnerable than men are to depression.

Susan Nolen-Hoeksema is the only investigator whose work falls within the domain of cognitive theory who has formally proposed an explanation for the gender difference. In a review paper published in 1987, Nolen-Hoeksema articulated her argument that the sexes differ in the ways that they cope with negative moods. The sexes do not differ in the amount of life stress that they experience. However, women feel more emotionally distressed than men do at the same levels of life stress. Life stress creates negative feelings in all of us. Nolen-Hoeksema believes that how we cope with these feelings determines whether or not we will go on to experience emotional distress and depression. She has observed that while boys and men tend to distract themselves from their negative feelings, girls and women tend to engage in repetitive thinking about the causes, symptoms, and consequences of their depressed mood, which makes the mood worse. She labeled this tendency *ruminative coping*, and she conceptualizes it as a proximal variable in depression.

In an impressive program of research over the past decade, Nolen-Hoeksema has demonstrated that ruminative coping makes the depressed mood worse and prolongs it. Rumination amplifies depressed feelings by negatively biasing the way individuals think about their problems, and by interfering with instrumental problem solving. Importantly, when rumination was controlled statistically, gender differences in depressive symptoms became nonsignificant. This is a critical finding. Of all the variables considered in this review, only childhood sexual abuse and rumination have been shown to eliminate the gender difference when controlled statistically.

Recently, Nolen-Hoeksema published a study that explored how social factors and rumination work together to contribute to the gender difference in depressive symptoms. She examined the impact of chronic stress, mastery, and ruminative coping on depressive symptoms. The five sources of stress she assessed are some of those that play a distal role in the gender difference: lack of affirmation in close relationships, role burden, housework inequities, childcare inequities, and parenting strains. Nolen-Hoeksema found that, compared with men, women experienced more chronic stress, had a lower sense of mastery, and ruminated more on their depressive symptoms. All three factors contributed independently to higher levels of depressive symptoms, and the effects of chronic strain and mastery were augmented by a ruminative coping style. In turn, rumination was more likely to be used when an individual felt chronically stressed and felt that she could do little to change her situation. In other words, these factors not only contributed to depressive symptoms but also to each other. Nolen-Hoeksema's work stands out as the major contribution of cognitive theory to understanding gender differences in depression.

B. COGNITIVE SCHEMA AND PERSONALITY

In the past 15 years, cognitive theory has been modified in ways that bring its theorizing more in line with traditional psychoanalytic explanations of depression. Although the language used by the cognitivists and psychoanalysts differs, the concepts and etiological mechanisms they propose are strikingly similar. The basic argument is that some individuals are prone to depression because they hold specific beliefs about themselves that exacerbate feelings of depression. While the psychoanalysts maintain that these beliefs form the core of the depression-prone individual's personality, the cognitive theorists conceptualize these beliefs as cognitive structures that are stronger or weaker depending on an individual's life circumstances. Some cognitive theorists maintain that these belief systems are activated primarily when an individual experiences depressed mood.

Both theories proceed from the observation that there are two kinds of depressed people. A sociotropic or dependent individual needs the validation and approval of significant others to feel good about herself, while an autonomous or self-critical individual needs to achieve highly and to strive for perfection in whatever she does to feel worthwhile. These tendencies are thought to be *vulnerabilities* or distal factors that do not contribute to depression directly but that have an impact on how life stress is perceived. Depression occurs when an individual encounters life stress that matches and confirms her or his vulnerability. For instance, a man who needs the approval of significant others to feel good about himself will be at risk for depression after being rejected by someone important to him. Similarly, a woman who strives constantly for achievement and perfection will be at risk if she loses her job. Generally, there is research to support the idea that dependency/sociotropy is a vulnerability factor that increases the risk of depression when individuals encounter interpersonal stressors. The empirical support for self-criticism/autonomy is less clear.

Neither the cognitive nor the psychoanalytic theorists try to explain the gender difference in depression rates nor have gender differences in sociotropy and dependency been systematically studied. However, Dana Jack proposed a concept that is very similar to dependency and sociotropy as an explanation for the gender difference. Jack observed that, due to gender role socialization, women believe that they are responsible for maintaining close and harmonious relationships. When their relationships fail, women's self-esteem suffers. She has argued that beliefs about the importance of relationships put women at risk for depression when they are taken to an extreme, that is, when women feel that their relationships must be maintained *at all costs*. Some women feel that they have to take care of and please other people, especially their husbands and children, even if this caring means putting their family's needs ahead of their own needs. In addition, they believe that they must avoid expressing anger, which might threaten the relationship. Depression occurs when, despite these efforts, relationships are conflicted or they fail. Relationship distress leads women to the conclusion that they have sacrificed themselves for nothing, which is demoralizing. Thus, these relationship beliefs and behaviors are distal factors in depression, which influence the way that marital distress is perceived.

Jack labeled these relationship behaviors *silencing the self*. Some degree of self-silencing is assumed to be normative among women because silencing is consistent with female gender role socialization. In contrast, men are not socialized to self-silence or to self-sacrifice in close relationships, and relationship distress does not have an impact on their sense of self and self-esteem. Thus, Jack's model is consistent with the research showing that girls and women who are socialized to conform to traditional gender roles have less well developed instrumental traits, such as assertiveness, that protect them from depression. She also would agree with Paul Bebbington's conclusion that women's enactment of their gender role, particularly their nurturing of husbands and children, increases their risk for depression because caretaking involves self-sacrifice.

Basic research supports Jack's model. Although women do not self-silence more than men do, their silencing is linked to depressive symptoms while men's silencing is not. Recent research suggests that self-silencing is a relationship strategy that develops when the romantic partner or spouse is critical and intolerant of the silencer. Self-silencing may be a way of avoiding rejection and abuse from this individual. This finding is consistent with the conceptualization of self-silencing as a distal factor in depression that develops in the context of marital problems. However, the key premise of the silencing model has never been tested: Does silencing predict the onset of a depressive episode or the worsening of depressive symptoms over time in the context of a distressed relationship? At this point, silencing is an interesting possible explanation for the gender difference in depression, but the model needs further research.

C. INTERPERSONAL THEORY

The interpersonal conceptualization of depression emphasizes the role of interpersonal relationships in the development and maintenance of depression. In 1976, Jim Coyne observed that depressed women's attempts to gain reassurance from significant others are met with mixed messages. While significant others often are explicitly supportive and reassuring, implicitly they are rejecting and critical. Coyne believed that these mixed messages heighten the depressed person's anxiety and maintain or worsen their depressive symptoms. Subsequent research confirmed Coyne's observation and demonstrated that interpersonal rejection contributes to the exacerbation of depressive symptoms over time. Thus, rejection in close relationships is a proximal variable in depression. As was the case with the two previous theoretical approaches to depression, interpersonal theorists have not tackled the issue of women's greater vulnerability to depression. However, there is an area of interpersonal research that may help us to understand the gender difference; this area focuses on the link between marital relations and depression.

Marital distress seems to have a complex relationship to depression in that, in different individuals, it can precede, maintain, or follow from a depressive episode. However, recent evidence from longitudinal studies suggests that, for women, being in a bad marriage induces depression, while for men the reverse is true, depression has a negative impact on marital satisfaction. This gender difference in the association between depression and marital distress may help explain the difference in depression rates. If a married man is stressed and emotionally distressed, his feelings will have an impact on his marital satisfaction. Women's marital satisfaction is strongly linked to their husbands' satisfaction, so if his distress continues, his wife will become maritally distressed too.

Her marital distress then will increase her risk of becoming depressed. Thus, women's risk for depression comes not only from their own marital distress, but also from their husbands' depressive symptoms and marital distress. Results consistent with this hypothesis were found in a recent study; however, the hypothesis needs to be tested in a longitudinal study, which would track these processes over time.

Marital distress has an impact both on the level of conflict that a couple experiences and on the level of support they provide to one another. Both aspects heighten an individual's vulnerability to depression. Women who are experiencing life stress are protected from becoming depressed by having a confidante. Similarly, once an individual becomes depressed, recovery is facilitated by having a warm and supportive spouse. Interestingly, the relationship between intimacy and depression may be even stronger among women who were sexually abused as children. CSA appears to make women more sensitive to the level of intimacy in their marriages, such that they are more adversely affected by low levels of intimacy than are women without this history.

High levels of conflict in a relationship may promote depression directly. Among women who have just recovered from an episode of depression, one of the best predictors of relapse into another episode is the woman's perception that her spouse is critical of her. Similarly, one study identified a group of pregnant women who were at risk for postpartum depression because they became depressed after a previous pregnancy. The researchers found that critical comments made by the spouse in a brief interview predicted which of the pregnant woman became depressed in the postpartum. Thus, marital distress both creates conflict and reduces the amount of support available to the partners, and both factors may be implicated in the subsequent development of depression. While lack of intimacy and support appears to be a distal factor, conflict and criticism may be proximal.

Gender differences in the response to marital conflict and lack of support may help to explain the gender difference in depression. Women may be more sensitive than men are to both conflict and lack of support. Couples in which one person is depressed tend to have hostile and conflicted interactions, regardless of whether the depressed person is the husband or the wife. However, when the wife is depressed, their interactions are measurably more negative. In addition, depressed women feel even more depressed after a hostile interaction with their husbands than do depressed men after a hostile interaction with their wives. In general, women are more negatively aroused after conflict with their spouses than are men. Women also require more support than men do to maintain their emotional well-being. On average, men and women do not differ in the levels of support that they report receiving. However, if women require more support and if they are more adversely affected by conflict with their spouses, then together these findings may explain why marital distress is more likely to induce depression in women than in men.

VII. *Summary and Integration*

Several distal and proximal variables appear to be implicated in the gender difference in depression rates. Two distal variables are childhood sexual abuse and gender role. Distal variables do not cause depression directly, but they have an impact on other variables that are direct causes. CSA has been shown to eliminate the gender difference when it is controlled statistically, making it an important variable for further study. CSA helps to explain the gender difference in depression rates because girls are more likely than boys to be sexually victimized. However, we do not presently know specifically how CSA is linked to depression. CSA may have an impact on the way that children regard themselves and their close relationships, as well as on how they process information about the world. In addition, trauma may have a negative impact on children's developing nervous systems, such that individuals with a history of CSA are biologically hyper-responsive to stress.

Various aspects of gender role have been considered, and the research suggests that the socialization of girls places them at risk for depression in a number of ways. First, girls are not socialized to develop personality traits, like assertiveness, that help them to cope proactively with life stress. In addition, traditional gender roles exclude women from paid employment, which may prevent them from developing these instrumental traits as adults. Finally, girls and women are socialized to believe that it is part of their role to ensure that relationships function harmoniously. This belief may lead women to silence themselves in relationships. While self-silencing may help women to enact their gender role, especially as it involves caring for children, it also may place them at risk for depression, particularly when their marriages are distressed.

In addition to these distal variables, this review identified two proximal factors that are involved in women's greater vulnerability to depression: a ruminative coping style and marital distress. Proximal factors appear to be direct causes of depression. Women are more likely than men to respond to their own emotional distress with coping behaviors that amplify and prolong their negative mood. Ruminative coping eliminated the gender difference in depression when it was controlled statistically. In addition, women appear to be more susceptible than men are to becoming depressed in the face of relationship difficulties. Marital distress both reduces the amount of emotional support that is available between spouses and increases their conflict. Women's well-being may be more closely tied than men's well-being is to both support and conflict.

Susan Nolen-Hoeksema believes that a ruminative coping style follows directly from socialization practices because girls are not socialized to cope with life stress instrumentally. Gender role also may explain why marital distress has a greater impact on women than on men. If women are socialized to believe that maintaining relationships is part of their gender role, then relationship distress may leave women feeling that they have failed or that they are inadequate; these feelings are the hallmark of depression. Thus, gender role socialization is a theme that pervades the research explaining women's greater vulnerability to depression.

VIII. *Suicide*

One possible outcome of depression is suicide. Approximately half of the individuals who attempt suicide were depressed in the months preceding their attempts. Among individuals who experience many depressive episodes and whose depressions are relatively severe, the lifetime risk of suicide is about 15%. The use of alcohol or drugs also is highly associated with suicide attempts, and many depressed individuals try to make themselves feel better by using drugs and alcohol. Thus, the combination of depression and substance use is associated with an especially high risk of suicide. Paradoxically, suicide can also be a consequence of treating depression. Professionals who work with depressed individuals have long observed that the risk of suicide is greatest in the first months of treatment, when individuals have recovered enough to actively plan for suicide, but not enough to feel that life is worth living.

In addition, there is clinical evidence that the drugs used to treat depression can induce suicidal thoughts in a subgroup of individuals, particularly if the drug is not very effective or if it makes the patient anxious and agitated.

It may seem surprising that only half of the individuals who attempt suicide are depressed. However, it is important to realize that the most common feeling that precedes a suicide attempt is hopelessness. Individuals who attempt suicide feel that there is little hope that their lives will improve in the future. Feelings of hopelessness are common among depressed persons. However, one could feel demoralized and hopeless without feeling depressed. For instance, individuals with a chronic, degenerative physical illness could conclude that the future is hopeless without feeling that they are to blame for their condition or less worthy because they suffer from it. Thus, the connection between depression and suicide is probably accounted for largely by the feeling of hopelessness, which is common to both.

Consistent with the gender difference in depression rates, adolescent girls and women report more thoughts about suicide and they are more likely to attempt suicide than adolescent boys and men. The ratio is on the order of 2:1 for both suicidal thoughts and suicide attempts. However, there is a puzzling reversal in the rates when one considers suicide fatalities: adolescent boys and men are more likely to die as a result of their suicidal acts. In countries around the world, with few exceptions, boys and men of all ages are more likely to die from suicide than are girls and women. In North America, the ratio is about 4:1. Part of the gender difference may be artifactual in that it may be accounted for by the methods used by males and females in their suicide attempts. In developed countries, boys and men are most likely to use guns, while girls and women are most likely to use poisoning, especially with drugs prescribed for emotional distress. Gunshot wounds tend to be fatal immediately, while poisoning with prescription drugs takes time and may be interrupted by others coming across the suicide attempt. In addition, individuals may not know how much of the drug they have to take to complete the suicide attempt. When only suicides involving poisoning are examined, there is no gender difference in mortality rates. However, females who use other methods are less likely than males using the same method to die as a result of their suicidal actions. Thus, part of the gender difference is probably attributable to the methods typically chosen by the sexes, while another part is not.

We cannot know an individual's intent by whether or not the suicide attempt was fatal. Not all deaths by suicide were intended, and not all of the persons who survive a suicidal act actually planned to live. This point is important because women's higher rates of attempting but lower fatality rates traditionally were interpreted to mean that they did not really want to commit suicide but just wanted to get help or attention. Their nonfatal suicide acts were labeled suicidal "gestures," which implies that they should not be taken seriously. The research does not support this conclusion. Only a minority of suicidal persons report that they attempted suicide in order to have an impact on the people close to them. Instead, most explain their behavior in terms of their strong and persistent feelings of hopelessness.

Nonfatal suicide attempts are most likely to be made by young women (under age 30) who are unemployed or housewives, who have low levels of education, and who are working class. These women tend to be separated or divorced and to have financial problems. When married, they tend to have hostile relationships that may include physical abuse by their spouses. They report feeling dependent on others and helpless, and they attribute their suicide attempts to their interpersonal problems. It is not surprising that these women feel hopeless about the future given the many difficulties they face. In addition, they may lack the social and personal resources needed to cope with and solve their problems. An inability to imagine and implement a variety of coping efforts may make suicide seem the only viable option.

Less is known about the characteristics of the men and women who die from their suicide attempts. We do know that they tend to be older. Suicide fatalities in North America and Europe peak in middle age for women and after the age of 65 in men. These individuals also tend to be widowed or divorced and unemployed. It is interesting that the men and women who die from suicide do not differ markedly from each other, except in their ages, and that both groups appear to have much in common with the younger nonfatal suicide attempters. Thus, these studies do not help us to understand why women are more likely to make nonfatal, and men to make fatal, suicide attempts.

Silvia Sara Canetto has theorized that gender role socialization explains this difference. She has cited research suggesting that, in North America and Europe, nonfatal suicidal behavior is associated with femininity, and that fatal suicidal behavior is socially unacceptable for women, possibly because it involves a level of self-determination that is incompatible with the traditional gender role. She has expressed concerns that these cultural messages about gender and suicide may have a particularly strong impact on adolescents and young women who are in process of establishing their identities and who may take cultural messages more literally than adults do. The reverse is true for men: surviving a suicidal act is socially unacceptable, according to the research. Attempted suicide may violate gender role norms about men's emotional strength, their decisiveness, and their ability to succeed, and may risk the disapproval of other males. Canetto has argued that knowing that survival is unacceptable leads men to attempt suicide in ways that are virtually guaranteed not to fail.

While provocative, there is no direct evidence that this theory explains the gender difference in suicidal behavior. Research participants who associate nonfatal attempts with femininity and fatal attempts with masculinity may simply be parroting what they know about the statistics on suicide. In addition, the theory seems to imply that women set out to have nonfatal attempts. Yet there is no evidence that nonfatal attempts were intended to fail.

An alternative gender role explanation was proposed by Stanley Coren and Paul Hewitt who were attempting to explain the preponderance of male fatalities in individuals aged 65 and older. They proposed that gender role socialization leads men to be more concerned about finances and social status, and women to be relatively more concerned with social stability and cohesion. They reasoned that retirement would have a greater impact on the former than on the latter concerns, which may account for the sharp increase in male fatalities from suicide after age 65. To test their hypothesis, they analyzed data collected by individual states in the United States on suicide, indices of financial well-being (such as average annual income and proportion of individuals living in poverty), and indices of stability and stress in the social environment (such as the number of people living in the same house for five years or more and the divorce rate). These analyses supported their hypothesis, in that the suicide rate for elderly males was higher in states with low levels of financial and social status, while the suicide rate for elderly females was higher in states with low levels of stability in the social environment. They suggested that impoverished financial circumstances have a negative impact on men's sense of autonomy and control, which men have been socialized to value, while social instability has a negative impact on women's sense of cohesion and connectedness, which women have been socialized to value.

Again, this is an interesting preliminary hypothesis, which needs to be researched further. The evidence they cite does not directly link financial and social factors to individual men's and women's suicidal acts. The factors they identified may be associated simply with greater stress and emotional distress in the states with the highest suicide rates. In addition, both factors predicted state suicide rates for both sexes, which suggests that both may be implicated in suicidal acts.

At this time, we cannot say why girls and women make more nonfatal suicide attempts and why boys' and men's attempts are more likely to result in their deaths. In both sexes, fatal and nonfatal attempts are associated with depression, marital disruption, and unemployment. Thus, both financial and social instability seem to precede suicide attempts in both sexes, although the former may be particularly vital to men while the latter may be particularly vital to women. Gendered attitudes toward suicide also may play a role in the methods chosen to attempt suicide and in the meaning of the suicidal act. Clearly, much more research is needed to solve the puzzle of gender differences in suicidal behavior.

SUGGESTED READING

Bebbington, P. (1996). The origins of sex differences in depressive disorder: Bridging the gap. *International Review of Psychiatry* 8, 295–332.

Canetto, S. S., and Lester, D. (1995). *Women and Suicidal Behavior*. Springer, New York.

Coren, S., and Hewitt, P. L. (1999). Sex differences in elderly suicide rates: Some predictive factors. *Aging and Mental Health* 3, 112–118.

Culbertson, F. M. (1997). Depression and gender: An international review. *American Psychologist* 52, 25–31.

Hankin, B. L., and Abramson, L. Y. (1999). Development of gender differences in depression: Description and possible explanations. *Annals of Medicine* 31, 372–379.

Nolen-Hoeksema, S., and Girgus, J. S. (1994). The emergence of gender differences in depression during adolescence. *Psychological Bulletin* 115, 424–443.

Sprock, J., and Yoder, C. Y. (1997). Women and depression: An update on the report of the APA Task Force. *Sex Roles* 36, 269–303.

Wolk, S. I., and Weissman, M. M. (1995). Women and depression: An update. *American Psychiatric Press Review of Psychiatry* 14, 227–259.

Development of Sex and Gender
Biochemistry, Physiology, and Experience

Ethel Tobach

American Museum of Natural History and The City University of New York

I. Issues in Sex and Gender Research
II. Developmental Processes Defining Sex
III. Development of Gender Definition: Psychosocial/Societal Processes Integrate Biochemical and Physiological Experience

Glossary

Biochemical processes Those carried out by genes, that is, segments of DNA (deoxyribonucleic acid) that together with RNA (ribonucleic acid) work to produce proteins. Proteins are made of amino acids and are the structural units of all cells, hormones, neurotransmitters, enzymes, and other vital substances.

Development The history of all the changes—biological (biochemical and physiological) and psychological (psychosocial/societal experience)—that an organism goes through, including all life experiences from the time that the gametes (sex cells) from the mother and father fuse to form the zygote. Development starts with the parents, or ancestors, because of what they bring to the gametes and zygote as a result of their experiences. Their contributions and the conditions under which the zygote develops in the uterus of the mother are the foundations for processes of change, including the exit from the uterus into the world in which the individual lives. In the development of sex for both women and men, the experiences produced by the mother's and father's biochemistry and physiology are significant.

Gender Relates only to human beings; women and men will refer to all those who are of an age at which they are presumably physiologically able to copulate (have sexual intercourse), fuse gametes, and produce offspring; this is usually true of people at puberty. Prepuberal individuals (those not yet likely to be able to produce offspring) are designated as girls or boys. Gender is the psychosocial/societal integration of the codes of activity, social relations, and societal status prescribed for individuals on the basis of their presumed sex.

Physiological processes Those functions and structures resulting from the activities of the biochemical entities as they develop and change, producing the foundations for the various developmental stages in the history of the individual's activities.

Sex Reproductive processes, that is, fusing the genetic material of different organisms (biological term: *conjugation*); sex is defined by the gametes carried by the person.

Social behavior Face-to-face, contemporaneous activity of people with each other, in the process of living in a society.

Society That which prescribes the rules for living in groups. The social and societal settings change and are changed by the activity of the individual(s).

THE STUDY OF SEX AND GENDER in this article is based on an integrative levels approach. In this approach, the "biological" factors, that is, the biochemical and physiological processes, and the "cultural" factors, that is, the psychosocial/societal processes, are not apposed. The approach takes into consideration the total experience of the individual as a developmental, historical process, in which all processes are integrated. It views sex as a part of the individual's development, distinct from, but integrated into, gender development. It resolves the apparent contradiction of biology and psychology, of genes and experience. As biochemical levels and psychosocial/societal levels are always functioning in the life of the individual, all these levels must be studied to understand sex and gender. The processes in the histories of sex and gender are interdependent. Sex is differentiated from gender to elucidate how the similarities and differences between women and men develop, without placing all explanations in biology or culture.

I. Issues in Sex and Gender Research

Newspapers, magazines, movies, and television are full of talk about sex and gender. We are led to believe that so much is known about genetics that one's sex and gender can be easily changed. We are told genetic engineering makes it possible to order the sex of the baby one wants, as well as the characteristics of that baby. Genomic research and development to describe all the genes (genome) in different species, including people, using sophisticated computerized instruments, produces genetic information quickly. The genomics industry is on the international stock market, and the announcements of discoveries and stock values encourage us to believe what we are told about the science of genomics in the media. All this makes it necessary for people who are interested in sex and gender to be literate in the science of genetics and behavior, of the relationship among genes, hormones, sex, and gender. This relationship is complex, and learning about genes, hormones, sex, and gender is challenging.

A. SEX AND GENDER RESEARCH

The hereditarian or determinist view about the differences between women and men are featured most often in all forms of media and public entertainment, despite the significant representation of the gender

socializing or learning theorists in psychology and developmental psychology in particular. The three prevailing approaches to the study of gender may be described as (1) determinist, that is, determined by inherited/genetic/biological factors (ethology, sociobiology, and evolutionary psychology); (2) based on learned/environmental/socializing factors (e.g., the sociocognitive perspective concept of K. Bussey and A. Bandura); and (3) "interactionist", that is, seeing both genetic factors and learning or socialization as contributing to gender (behavior geneticists).

The approach to the study of sex and gender in this article is based on an integrative levels approach. In this approach, the biological and cultural factors are not apposed. It takes into consideration the total experience of the individual as a developmental, historical, process. It views sex as a part of the individual's development, distinct from, but integrated into, gender development. It removes the apparent apposition of biology and psychology, of genes and experience. As biochemical levels and psychosocial/societal levels are always functioning in the life of the individual, all these levels must be studied to understand sex and gender.

Each level requires its own methods and instrumentation. When we ask questions about sex, we are asking about biochemical and physiological processes, and the instruments and methods used would not be the same as those used in answering psychosocial/societal questions about gender. Usually, these levels are not studied at the same time, or by the same investigators, but the inferences reached on the basis of the studies of each level must be integrated to understand the processes that produce sex and gender.

This approach differs from the interactionist approach which asks: What and how much is inherited and what and how much is acquired? Several questions are posed by the levels of integration approach: Which biochemical and physiological processes are related to sex? Which psychosocial/societal processes are related to gender? How do biochemical and physiological histories bring about the developmental psychosocial/societal history of the individual? The processes in both histories are interdependent.

1. Why Should Sex and Gender Be Differentiated?

As the dominant approaches to the study of sex and gender emphasize biological processes, the terms "sex" and "gender" are frequently used interchangeably, and the biological processes are seen as fundamental and inherited. However, heredity is not sufficient to explain the apparent differences and similarities between women and men; biochemical and physiological processes are necessary to maintain life and the integrity of the individual. However, these are not sufficient to explain the behavior of the individual. The psychosocial/societal development of the human individual is also necessary. Neither set of processes by itself is sufficient. Seeing the differences between sex and gender helps us understand how the similarities and differences between women and men develop and involve all the processes of behavior, without placing all explanations in one or the other set.

The experiences of the incubating individual, the mother, beginning with the fusion of the two gametes, formation of the zygote, through the placentation period (incubation), are always relevant to the activities of the gametes. Changes in her biochemistry, as a result of foods, climatic processes (radiation, temperature, toxicity), exposure to infecting organisms, and both physiological and psychological stress, are expressed in changes in gene/protein and hormonal function during the development from zygote, to embryo, to fetus. These experiences will reform the activities of the genes, thus producing continuously new foundations for gender development.

2. Why Do People Study the Differences between Sexes and Genders?

a. "Scientific" Method. The strongest stimulus comes from scientific traditions for investigating existing differences or creating differences among individuals or groups to provide clues for understanding a particular phenomenon. By suggesting the sources of differences found, investigators can change the treatment of one group and compare it to the unchanged group (the so-called control group). In looking at sex and gender differences, the proper "control" is difficult to define. As an alternative, qualitative, developmental, long-term studies are being used more frequently. Another technique is to choose two known characteristics that are different in women and men as groups, and then ask whether they are correlated. Correlations do not explain the process responsible for the differences, but they do suggest other possibilities for research.

b. Evolutionary Theory and Behavior. Darwin's concept of sexual selection (competitive choice of partners for mating) was important in his theory of the evolution of species and of behavior. That concept was further elaborated by three theories: ethology, sociobiology, and evolutionary psychology (sometimes called human sociobiology). The three theories consider the differences between women and men, and between female and male animals as evidence of the important evolutionary role of sex differences in species survival.

1. Ethology, the study of inherited behavioral patterns to clarify evolutionary relationships of species, sees reproductive behavior as inherited; gender and sex are not differentiated usually.

2. Sociobiology elaborates the evolutionary inheritance of sexual differences by positing that cultural gender patterns follow the same selective processes as genetic, morphological, and functional characteristics: those gender differences that promote the survival of the species will be maintained and retained in all cultures.

3. Evolutionary psychology integrates sociobiological theory with human genetics and psychology. Cosmides and Tooby posited that the genes that were responsible for human survival early in evolution ($2\frac{1}{2}$ million years ago) are still present in the human genome (all the genes of the human species) and play an important role in cognition, including social cognition (e.g., gender roles). Genes are carried by the nucleus and the mitochondrion (an intracellular organelle that produces most of the sources of energy within all cells and that has its own DNA and RNA). Although the cells of women and men have both structures, the genes in the mitochondrion are usually passed on by the females of the species, whereas the genes in the nucleus are passed on by both females and males. This division of labor suggests to them that the nucleus is the "male" carrier of genes, whereas the mitochondrion is the "female" carrier of genes. Based on a sociobiological tenet that genes are programmed to do anything necessary to assure that they are passed on in the next generation, the "male" genes will do as much as possible to be passed into the next generation, and thus be in conflict with the "female" genes in the mitochondrion. Although the two organelles must work together to maintain the life of the cell, this concept that female/male conflict is inherent has become a popular theory supporting various theories about differences between women and men. [*See* GENDER DEVELOPMENT: EVOLUTIONARY PERSPECTIVES.]

c. Evolutionary Biology, Biomedicine, and Reproduction. Humans were likely always to be curious about the genital and reproductive differences between women and men, although they did not always understand the relationship between sexual intercourse and reproduction. In the course of human history, differences in reproductive function became an essential consideration in regard to labor, when hands were needed to pursue activities for survival. With sedentation, and agricultural societies, women were not only engaged in production of human beings, or reproduction, but also in life-maintaining activities (production). In this era of human history, slavery was prevalent, and women became special commodities. Their gametic sex was the predominant consideration; their gender was secondary in so far as they were seen as good housekeepers, children's care givers, and so on, but also as able to do heavy labor. As Sojourner Truth said, enslaved women were considered able to do the heavy work that was usually considered men's work; gender differences for "hard" labor disappeared.

The biological Darwinian revolution elaborated the interest in reproduction. Evolutionary biologists discovered varied patterns of reproduction: sexual (when two or more individuals mix their genetic materials) and asexual (when cells reproduce without mixing their genetic material with that of another organism). This stimulated interest in the underlying morphology and physiology that makes such diversity possible. The study of the sexual differences between females and males fit in with the early concern with reproduction and production and stimulated research on problems of fertility and sterility in women and men. Concern about sterility and fertility was always intimately related to the formulation of gender roles in society. Being able to produce heirs has been an important societal concern in all classes throughout history because of the economic value of having hands for labor (which contributed to survival) and for the accumulation of wealth. This history suggests how it is that sex and gender are frequently confounded.

As the development of the genomics industry increased our information about genetic processes, evidence was found that the biochemical processes that were different in women and men played roles in life functions other than reproduction. The biochemistry appeared related to many processes in health and disease. Recently, the National Institutes of Health listed 10 studies of the differences between women and men as possibly having a bearing on medical practice: women progress to AIDS with half the viral load that men require; women's blood alcohol levels are higher than men's when imbibing the same amounts of alcohol; brain mapping shows certain language functions are evidenced in both hemispheres in women while men show the activity in only one hemisphere; men synthesize serotonin at a higher rate than women, suggesting why depression is more frequent in women than in men; pain processes are different in women than in men as they respond differently to antipain medications; women's heart attack symptoms are different than men's; liver transplants donated by a woman are less likely to be successful than donations made by men.

It should be noted that these examples may not have taken into account the psychosocial/societal experiences that play a role in the biochemical and physiological processes described, as suggested by the integrative levels approach. Studies of depression in women have shown that gender-related experiences are a major factor in depression. Women and men may respond differently to stresses in part because of the attitudes physicians have toward women as contrasted with their attitudes toward men when both are being examined for the same problems.

These experiences on the psychosocial/societal level are integrated with the biochemical processes in depression. Human and animal research has demonstrated that levels of serotonin, a neurotransmitter, vary with depression. In addition, estrogen and progesterone, produced by the ovary, and testosterone, produced by the testes, have been found to affect serotonin function. Estrogen and progesterone or testosterone can play a role in the function of serotonin in the development of depression. The relationship between psychosocial/societal experiences and the biochemical processes are complex; they work uniquely in each individual.

This does not mean that differences should not be investigated. Rather, it points to the need for biomedical research to ask how genderized medical experiences may affect physiology, requiring different diagnostic and treatment regimens.

B. THE PROCESSES THAT DEFINE SEX AND GENDER

1. How Sex Gets Defined

Humans (mammals) are a sexually reproducing species, that is, humans carry two gametes (egg and sperm), each of which has half the chromosomes that carry the genes, that fuse to form one or more new individuals. The biochemical level of sex definition involves two X chromosomes or an X and a Y chromosome, along with their genes and related proteins; hormonal processes (e.g., the structures and functions of estrogens or androgens); and enzymes. The physiological level involves the systems of cells, tissues, and organs that develop in the individual (e.g., hormonal and neural) and how they function in reproduction. Reproduction is a physiological process. Individuals carrying two Xs are labeled women ("females" in medical practice); those carrying an X and a Y chromosome are labeled men ("males" in medical practice).

Mammals can reproduce by cloning offspring, a process in which introducing appropriate cells from one organism into the nucleus of an appropriate cell in another organism leads to the formation of an embryo. However, this embryo must be incubated in an organism with XX chromosomes, whose hormonal functions will make development, growth, and birth possible. To date, it is not known that humans can be cloned in this fashion. The psychosocial/societal processes whereby this type of reproduction will take place are unknown.

The process whereby the two gametes are usually mixed in humans is complicated and offers many opportunities for unusual combinations of gametes to occur. The psychosocial/societal gender development of individuals carrying such unusual combinations is insufficiently studied and understood.

2. How Gender Gets Defined

Gender is the psychosocial/societal integration of the codes of activity, dress, social relations, and societal status prescribed for individuals on the basis of their presumed sex.

3. How Many Sexes? How Many Genders?

The suggestion that there may be more than two sexes (XX and XY) is based on the fact that individuals usually considered women or men as to their gender may have different combinations of X and Y chromosomes. Based on the chromosomes carried, individuals may be categorized variously as intersexes, or as demonstrating syndromes such as Turner's, Klinefelter's, and so on.

A range of secondary sex characteristics (e.g., stature, hairiness, musculature) are so-called quantitative gender-defined traits, related to hormones and sex organs (ovary and testis), although they may also be related to non-sex organs, such as the adrenal glands, which produce hormones affecting these traits. These are modified by the life experiences of the person as well as by hormonal function. Such variations in so-called gender traits raise questions about the easy definition of girl/boy, woman/man. These are issues of gender, not of sex, which is defined by the gametes carried by the person. Individuals elect to define their genders by clothing and by morphological and physiological manipulations in which secondary sex characteristics are changed in order to assume a particular gender (so-called sex-changing procedures).

Individuals who are homophilic (liking same sex as self: gay men, lesbian women, and bisexuals) may be considered genderized; their sex cells are usually either XX or XY carriers.

4. Psychosocial/Societal Customs of Sex/Gender Definition

In many societies, the genitalia are not displayed. The gender dress is presumed to be concordant with the gametes (e.g., on the visual evidence of a sex characteristic involved in reproduction), such as mammaries. Mammary glands are in evidence in most societies, either conspicuously covered or bare. In men, sex characteristics as represented by the penis and scrotum are not visually evident in most societies. There are some exceptions, such as the wearing of a cod piece (a shell-like covering of the penis and scrotum incorporated into the trousers) in Europe during the Middle Ages or a special cover for the penis (penis gourd; gourds are grown in different shapes for adornment) used today.

The roles that women and men play in the daily life of the group is qualified by the reproductive roles they play: women are producers of the children and their nurturants for early stages of development. However, women and men may engage in food getting and preparation and in building shelters, according to social/societal prescription. [*See* CROSS-CULTURAL GENDER ROLES.]

II. Developmental Processes Defining Sex

The development of sex definition is founded on preceding biochemical and physiological processes reflecting the developmental history of the woman and man who carried the gametes that fused to create the individual.

A. DEVELOPMENT OF GAMETE DEFINITION

The history of the individual begins with what the women and man bring to the egg and sperm (gametes) and the circumstances of the fusion of the egg and sperm. Assuming that the circumstances were usual, voluntary sexual intercourse; that the gametes were fused in the woman's body; that the partners were healthy; that the egg carried a nucleus with 22 autosomal (body) chromosomes and one X chromosome (sex chromosome); that the sperm carried 22 autosomal chromosomes and either one Y chromosome or one X chromosome (sex chromosome); and that the egg and sperm cells fused, a zygote is formed. Each chromosome usually carries one form of a gene; a gene is an arrangement of four nucleotides (adenine, cytosine, guanine, and thymine), each of which may appear a different number of times in different sequences, on a base of sugar (deoxyribose) and a phosphate (gene = DNA = deoxyribonucleic acid). Different arrangements of the nucleotide sequences are called alleles and each chromosome carries one of the alleles of each nucleotide sequence. Parts of the DNA arrangement can move and cause relocation of a part of a chromosome to another chromosome or a different area of a chromosome (transposons). These translocations can affect the function of the nucleotides.

In addition, in the nucleus and in the organelles (small structures in the cell), other sequences of nucleotides (adenine, cytosine, guanine, and uracil) with a sugar (ribose) and a phosphate appear; these constitute RNA = ribonucleic acid. During much of the history of the cells of the body, the chromosomes look like a string that is coiled in a mass in each cell. On each of these chromosomes genes are located in bands.

As the sex cells grow and begin to reproduce, the pairs of chromosomes line up on special filaments (spindles) and begin a process that splits the cell and produces two copies of each of the original pairs of chromosomes, producing four daughter cells, each of which contains one chromosome. In the ovary, the four cells each usually have an X chromosome; in the testis, usually two cells carry X chromosomes and two carry Y chromosomes. This process is called meiosis and the resulting daughter cells are called haploid cells.

Body cells (somatic, autosomal cells) grow in a similar process, called mitosis, except that when the chromosomes line up, they split and reproduce themselves in a pair of daughter cells each of which has a pair of chromosomes, rather than half a pair.

During meiosis, and mitosis, the separation of the chromosomes and their rearrangement usually proceeds as described here; however, their rearrangement is also a matter of circumstances and chance. In these processes of splitting and reassembling in new cells, rearrangements of chromosomes and nucleotides may take place. Chromosomes may lose part of their two arms (one is a short arm, referred to as "p," and one is a long arm, referred to as "q"), which are joined at the center by a structure called a centromere; one part of one arm may get attached to the other arm of the same chromosome or to another chromosome; a part of the chromosome may be lost; some of the nucleotides (genes) on the chromosome may be changed or rearranged (see transposon noted earlier), changing the function of the nucleotide segment; and there may be other changes still to be discovered. These rearrangements and changes may take place in the X and Y chromosomes also. It has been said that the production of a viable, usual individual given all the possible events is astounding.

B. DEVELOPMENTAL STAGES

1. Egg/Sperm Fusion

The two gametes are usually fused, forming the zygote internally in the woman's body. However, in contemporary practice in industrialized societies, the gametes may be fused outside the woman's body; the resulting zygote must be placed in an incubating woman whose hormonal physiology will make development of the resulting zygote possible. This practice is used when sterility of the woman or the man prevents zygote formation in the usual fashion. Sterility or fertility is a function of the biochemical level, involving nucleotide sequences, proteins, and hormones. [See REPRODUCTIVE TECHNOLOGIES.]

The psychosocial/societal processes resulting in the decision to fuse the gametes integrate the biochemical processes with the genders of the woman and man (ancestors). Contemporary societal practices for reproduction in industrialized cultures have been extended to homophilic individuals (gay men or lesbian women) who elect to have children. Foster zygote formation is accomplished by the participation of individuals who carry the appropriate gametes and who can incubate the zygote; sometimes the incubating individual is homophilic, or lesbian.

When the egg and sperm fuse, the zygote may carry one X from the mother and one X or a Y from the father. In the case of the zygote that carries two X chromosomes, the alleles carried on each chromosome could result in a double dose of the same allele. In evolution, through a process that is incompletely understood, one X chromosome remains active, while the other X chromosome is inactivated through the function of a nucleotide sequence on the active chromosome called Xist, the inactivating gene in the inactivating region of the chromosome (XIC), during early embryonic stages. Research with mice (considered a model for humans) has shown that usually the X chromosome from the sperm is inactivated. However, it has recently been discovered that in humans some of the genes on the so-called inactive X chromosome "escape" inactivation. These may be responsible for some of the X-linked characteristics. When the second X chromosome does not become inactivated during embryogeny, the person may show severe mental retardation.

The structures and functions of the egg are significant, first in making the fusion possible and then for the developmental processes that follow.

a. The Egg. The egg is a complex cell containing a nucleus with half the body chromosomes and one X chromosome; yolk proteins deposited from maternal blood in the egg; intracellular structures (e.g., ribosomes carrying the RNA necessary for protein synthesis); the mitochondrion, the energy-producing engine that also carries its own DNA and RNA; proteins that facilitate the activity of DNA and RNA, producing other proteins in the egg and developing organism; and molecules that function in differentiating cell types during embryonic development.

The X chromosome is know as the "sex" chromosome. As of September 2000, 581 nucleotide sequences (genes) have been identified on the X chromosome. Only two genes have been identified as responsible for the development of the ovary that produces estrogen and progesterone, two hormones necessary for reproductive function. Estrogen is active in many other physiological functions. Although most of the research is done with animals, the finding of sites for estrogen activity are important suggestions for further investigation of human estrogen function. There are sites for estrogen activity in the cardiovascular system, liver, immune system, bone, kidney, lung, and thymus. Although it has also been found that estrogen plays an important role in the death of cells, which affects neural function, estradiol (a form of estrogen) plays a role in neuroprotection (e.g., as in stroke).

The association of mental dysfunction with the X chromosome (fragile X, other forms of mental retardation) is well supported in human research. There are estrogen receptors in two areas of the brain associated with learning and memory. These areas are also active in cognitive activity, and areas in which new neurons are formed throughout life (neurogenesis). Again, it should be noted that almost all of these findings are the result of work with animals, but some human research points to its relevance for human behavior. It is also important to point out that estrogen function occurs in women and men, although there are some differences.

b. The Sperm. The sperm consists of a nucleus with chromosomes (some sperm contain an X chromosome and some a Y chromosome), a sperm head with an acrosomal vesicle containing enzymes activating the fusion with the egg, a mitochondrion that is thought not to be functional once the sperm and the egg have fused, and fibers (flagellum) important for the motility of the sperm. Actual movement of the sperm into the egg, however, does not take place immediately after intercourse. The movement of the sperm is facilitated by the muscular activity of the uterus and possible chemical stimulation by different cells in the woman's reproductive tract. Complex chemical processes at the egg's membranes facilitate the fusion of sperm and egg. The sperm mitochondrion and flagellum disintegrate after fusion. Most of the mitochondrial genes in the ensuing individual come from the woman.

The Y chromosome is the other "sex" chromosome, and it is decisive in defining the sex of the new individual as either female or male. As of September 2000, 47 genes have been identified on the Y chromosome; of these a nucleotide sequence known as the sex-determining region (SRY gene) is active in producing the testis, which in turn elaborates testosterone, the hormone necessary for reproduction. No matter how many X chromosomes are in the developing organism, if the SRY area is active on the Y chromosome, the primary reproductive system will be that of a male.

Androgen receptors have been found in the frontal cortex of monkeys, an area involved in cognitive function. It is generally believed that there are no diseases or phenotypic characters (individual traits) linked to the Y chromosome, but this is still a question for further investigation.

2. Embryogeny: Development of Ovary and Testis

Embryogeny occurs during the first two months after fusion. The zygote splits into two cells; each cell, and all later cells that develop, usually has 46 chromosomes: 22 pairs are autosomal chromosomes (body, nonsex cells), and one pair is composed of XX or XY chromosomes. All autosomal cells reproduce mitotically.

After the two-cell stage, in the first few days after fusion, primordial germ cells (sex cells), develop, and by the third week they have moved into an area known as the genital ridge. The cells in the ridge develop into a "bipotential" gonad. Two structures are present in the indifferent gonad: the Mullerian duct is active in forming female reproductive structures, and the Wolffian duct in forming male reproductive structures. The bipotential gonad may become an ovary or a testis, depending on whether the embryo has an X and Y chromosome or two X chromosomes.

If only two X chromosomes are present, the gene, DAX1, carried on the active X chromosome participates in the formation of the ovary, which will produce estrogen. Another gene, WNT4a, that is not on either the X or Y chromosome, but on a "body" chromosome (in a somatic cell), is also active in the development of the ovary. The process whereby these genes act is not yet completely understood. It is interesting to note the activity of a gene on a "sex" chromosome gene and a gene on a "body" chromosome in sex definition.

The participation of nonsex chromosomal material in sex definition is also seen in the activity of the Y chromosome. The sex-determining region (SRY gene) works together with proteins both on the Y chromosome and on autosomal chromosomes, the SOX proteins, to elaborate a testis, which produces two hormones: testosterone and anti-Mullerian duct factor (AMH).

Genes involved in the development of sex definition are also found on other chromosomes: SF1 (in the mouse) on chromosome 9, WT1 on chromosome 11, SOX9 on chromosome 17, and MIS on chromosome 19. The activity of these genes are known for their effects on changing the usual development of sex definition. When the tip of chromosome 9 is deleted, the individual with XY chromosomes develops as a woman, rather than as a man. The process responsible for this reversal is not yet known. Conceptualization of the X and Y chromosomes as *the* "sex determinants" is being modified in the light of new information.

If there is no Y chromosome present, the Mullerian duct, under the influence of estrogen, elaborates the internal feminine reproductive system. If a Y chromosome had been present, and produced a testis, an anti-Mullerian hormone (AMH) would have been produced by the testis. AMH would have influenced regression of the Mullerian duct, and the Wolffian duct would elaborate the internal male reproductive system.

The estrogens produced by the ovary, in addition to those that come from the mother through the placenta, work to differentiate the Mullerian duct into female genitalia. They also produce the secondary sex organs (external: labia, clitoris and mammary gland; internal: vagina, uterus). The development of the clitoris in monkeys responds to testosterone during development. The testosterone produced by the testis is active in developing the secondary male sex characteristics (external: penis, scrotum, which contains primary sex organ, the testis, and the epididymis; internal: prostate, seminal vesicle).

3. Fetal Stage

The fetal stage lasts seven months intrauterine. During the period of incubation (placentation of a biochemical link between embryo/fetus to mother) until birth, the individual develops the sensory, motor, endocrine, and neural systems that are usual in the individual to be born. The various structural (muscle, bone, skin) activating (enzymes), and hormonal proteins are produced from the nutriment from the mother in the placental blood and the activity of the nucleotide sequences and the proteins produced by the embryo/fetus. The input of events outside the body of the mother, such as auditory and tactile stimuli, which have been found to affect the incubating fetus, as well as other stimuli, which may affect the mother's biochemistry and physiology through the activity of neurotransmitters, hormones, and other neural changes brought about by these stimuli external to the mother and the fetus, are transmitted through the placenta. These externally derived changes become integrated with the biochemical (nutritional, hormonal, neurotransmitters, steroids, growth factors, adrenal stress responses, etc.) that develop in the mother in the course of the pregnancy. In the usual situation (usual nucleotide configurations, hormonal function of the mother, etc.), the primary sources of possible effects on the development of sex definition come from the nutritional status of the mother, its effect on the developing individual, and the biochemistry of stress responses.

Evolutionary biologists, biomedical researchers, and now psychologists have been interested in the processes that maintain a developing individual within the mother. The developing organism could act as a foreign chemical stimulus to which the mother's antigenic system would usually react. It has been suggested that the chorion (sac holding the embryo) produces substances that block the antigens, so that the mother does not reject the embryo as a foreign cell. How this process comes about is not yet known. However, it is thought that if the developing organism is the same sex as the mother, certain antigens are not formed.

Ray Blanchard and Anthony Bogaert have hypothesized an explanation for the apparent birth-order effect during the fetal stages on the development of a homophilic man. The more male babies precede the birth of an individual, the more likely the individual will be homophilic. This does not affect homophilia in women, as the process is related to H-Y antigens that are linked with the Y chromosome. The H-Y antigens act like anti-Mullerian Hormone (AMH), the hormone that suppresses the development of the female reproductive system. According to that hypothesis, if the zygote has a Y chromosome, the mother's antibody response is to suppress the "masculinizing" effect of the H-Y antigen, which acts like AMH. As the body has a "memory" for immunogenic experience, her reaction to the Y-antigen is built up in the mother's repeated response to the developing male fetuses, so that there is no suppression of "feminization" processes. Thus, the likelihood of a homophilic male child being born after a number of male siblings in the same family is increased (birth-order effect in homophilia).

The statistical finding that homophilic men are more likely to have more brothers than sisters may be a "sufficient" finding to suggest a relationship between birth order and homophilia in men, but not a "necessary" explanation. To understand how this happens, the pathway from antigen to behavior would have to be clarified. The integrative levels approach would ask: How is it that not all the brothers born after the same number of siblings become homophilic? Could there be psychosocial/societal processes involved that would have to be integrated with the biochemical/physiological levels? Despite the fact that biological factors have been proposed to "explain" homophilia, primarily in men (androgen "insensitivity"; genes; familiality, and hormonal

processes), there is insufficient research attention to the integration of all the psychosocial/societal experiences with biochemical/physiological processes in these individuals.

In 1991, Sandra Wittelson commented,

[A]lthough there appears to be some association among early hormonal events, brain anatomy, functional asymmetry and sexual orientation, there is certainly independence among these factors. This likely contributes to the considerable inconsistency in results among converging lines of evidence. The situation is further complicated by the likelihood that the associations and interactions among these factors are different between the sexes.

Among the factors not sufficiently considered is the psychosocial/societal activity as it refigures the developmental history of gender, leading to the unique complexity of each individual's gender. We also do not discuss why we are asking questions about differences between women and men and about homophilia. Wittelson recognized this in saying: "The challenge to society is to accept, respect, and effectively use the neural diversity among human beings."

4. Birth to Maturity

Although many of the findings resulting from research with humans and animals remain to be verified, they suggest that sex definition may be a process that involves several chromosomes, genes, and proteins, a pattern that has been found for many other expressions of gene function. Broadening the research to include other so-called nonsex chromosomes increases the probability that many experiences that are not usually considered "sexual" play an important role in defining sex and sexual (reproductive) behavior. How experience affects the brain is not yet completely understood, but this is an active area of research.

The usual direction of traditional thought about the relationship between experience and biological factors (such as the organization and activity of the brain) is that the biological factors direct the experience. S. Marc Breedlove considered that perhaps the direction could also go the other way. He found that if one gave male rats copulatory experience, the neurons in the spine that were involved in the activity were changed, whereas if the rat did not have copulatory experience, the neurons did not change. As he says "it is possible that differences in sexual behaviour cause, rather than are caused by, differences in brain structure." One must be cautious about extrapolating from animal behavior to human behavior, but other research supports the concept that experience is reflected in changes in brain structure and function.

5. Continuing Complex Biochemical Processes in Sex and Gender Definition

As indicated earlier, the experience of the mother translates through the placenta into the experience of the developing organism she carries. Psychosocial/societal activity begins with birth and goes on through the life of the person. All the experiences that the individual lives through have different effects on the development of gender. Just as we still do not understand all the processes involved in the development of sex definition, we are far from understanding the processes that are involved in gender development. The profound processes of psychosocial/societal activity have the most valence in the development of gender and many of the biochemical and physiological processes that were begun before birth continue in the person after birth. These continue to be involved in the definition of sex and are integrated in the development of gender.

a. Receptor Function.

When sequences of nucleotides (genes) produce proteins, cells respond to those proteins (e.g., hormones, neurotransmitters, enzymes) when the structure of the proteins fits the molecular configurations in the membranes enclosing the cell, so that the proteins can go through the membrane. The same "fitting" process is necessary once the proteins enter the cell; they must fit some molecule in the cell; there must be molecules in the membrane and in the cell that can receive the proteins, that can perform the receptor function. The receptor process is integral to the expression of nucleotide and protein function in sex definition and other physiological activities.

For example, the evident involvement of androgens in sex definition is complex. Testosterone is changed to estradiol in many cells and tissues (but not in all) and in different systems of the body, including the nervous system, so that it can work.

Receptors for estrogen have been found in the human amygdaloid complex (an area involved in emotional behavior) as well as in the cerebral cortex and hippocampus, both participating in cognitive function. Such receptors have also been found in mouse and rat brains.

b. Aromatization.

The process of change from testosterone to estradiol takes place through the activity of an enzyme (aromatase) and is called aromatization. This takes place during fetal development. It was found that male mouse neurons in the hypothalamus, an important neural area for reproductive activity, show more aromatase activity than female neurons. There may be some proteins that inhibit the aromatization. The increased aromatase activity shows up in late fetal development and is sensitive to amount of androgen circulating in the area. It is suggested by the investigators that this affects the activity of the estrogens in their nourishment of the brain during sexual differentiation of the brain. The processes relate to sex definition, not to gender definition, as this research was done with mice. It is interesting to consider this finding along with the finding that copulatory activity changes the neurons involved in that activity. Copulatory activity, and, in the case of humans, masturbation, may increase the level of testosterone produced and circulating and thus affect the development of the brain's organizational differences between females and males.

c. Androgen Insensitivity.

One set of cells that have testosterone receptors are specialized fatty cells. Testosterone destroys these cells. If these receptors are not functioning, the cells continue to function and grow, producing "breasts" in men who have XY chromosomes. These tissues do not function as mammary glands. These men produce testosterone in the usual fashion. This condition is known as the androgen insensitivity syndrome.

Individuals with the androgen insensitivity syndrome may appear to be women for another reason. The adrenal glands produce androgens that are involved in the development of secondary sex characteristics (hairiness). As these androgens are also not "received," there is no stimulation for secondary sex characteristics. These individuals appear to be women but cannot conceive, because the anti-Mullerian hormone produced by the testis during embryogeny caused the Mullerian duct to regress and internal reproductive organs were not developed. Such individuals may adopt a gender identity defined as a woman. Gametic sex and gender are not necessarily congruous. The psychosocial/societal development of such individuals deserves further study.

d. Location of a Gene Is Important.

Animal research has shown that the DAX1 gene is a complex actor in sex definition. When the DAX1 gene is on both the active and the inactive X chromosome, the individual produces a female sex identity (XX chromosomes) and ovaries. If the X and Y chromosome are present, but the two copies of the DAX1 gene are on the active X chromosome and the SRY gene is on the Y chromosome, testes are produced but they are undescended and nonfunctional; usually such an individual is identified as having a female sex identity. If there is only one copy of the DAX1 gene on the X chromosome, and SRY on the Y chromosome, the normal testes develop and the sexual identity is male. The exact processes whereby this occurs is not yet known. Again, it should be noted that this research was only performed on animals.

e. Origin of a Gene Is Important

1. *Chromosome origin.* Before fusion is achieved, the pronuclei (as the nuclei are termed at this stage) of the egg and sperm may not be equivalent. Based on research with mice, the female pronucleus and the male pronucleus carry genes that are usually equivalently activated. However, it was found that if a nucleotide sequence changed in the female pronucleus and was not able to produce the protein that encourages growth (growth factor), the offspring grew in the usual manner. If the change was in the male, the offspring did not grow properly and were stunted. The activity of the genes depends on whether it came from the egg or the sperm chromosome. Both pronuclei are important for development.

2. *Imprinting.* Unfortunately, the term "imprinting" is also used to describe the behavior of newborn birds that can walk and follow the female bird after hatching. Genomic imprinting results from a different process. If the X chromosome comes from the male, it functions differently than when it comes from the female: this is genomic imprinting. The responsible processes are not yet known.

For example, if the arrangement of a nucleotide sequence (allele) has changed when it is on Chromosome 15 in the mother, it will be expressed as Prader Willi syndrome. If on the father's chromosome, it is expressed as the Angelman syndrome. Although both may feature mental retardation, this is not always true for the Prader Willi syndrome people. In addition, the Angelman syndrome is rarely diagnosed earlier than at two years of age; speech is absent and inappropriate laughter, hyperactivity, and seizures are presented. Life expectancy is of usual length. In the Prader Willi syndrome, dysfunctional characteristics are sometimes seen at birth or during infancy; these are difficulty in sucking, necessitating special feeding techniques; excessive eating seen at about one year of age; and ensuing obesity, which can be life threatening. Although the eating pattern can be controlled, other obsessive-compulsive behavior is seen. Both syndromes occur in girls and boys (women and men).

Genomic imprinting is also being reported in other chromosomal-genomic patterns, such as Down's syndrome; Turner syndrome; and Klinefelter syndrome. The evidence for some clear genomic imprinting in schizophrenia and bipolar syndrome as defined in *DMS-IV* is inconclusive.

The integrative levels approach may be useful in considering the reports of imprinting in individuals with the Turner syndrome (in which the individual has only one X chromosome, XO) as reported by Skuse and his colleagues. They report that an area on the X chromosome from the father facilitates "social cognition." That area is missing on the maternal X. Turner women experience difficulties in social situations, such as peer ridicule, and generally have low self-esteem. To attribute an apparent lack of social cognitive skills would require us to know how the biochemistry of the X chromosome from the mother differs from that of the X chromosome from the father, and how that difference is expressed in protein function throughout the psychosocial/societal developmental history of the individual. Some research is being carried out on the psychosexual development of "imprinted" individuals.

f. Unusual Numbers of X and Y Chromosomes.

Zygotes may have more than one X or Y. The resulting embryo may carry as many as five X chromosomes and one Y, or may not receive the X from the sperm, and therefore have only one X (XO). These and other unusual assemblies of chromosomes are then reflected in the development of the different physiological systems. The fact that these unusual chromosomal patterns usually concern the X chromosome and affect not only the reproductive and nervous systems but other systems (circulatory, skeletal, dermatological) points to the broad involvement of the X chromosome with many aspects of development. The consequent integration of these unusual chromosomal systems with the nervous system leads to many unique gender developmental histories.

Multiple X chromosomes are more frequently reported in industrialized societies than multiple Y chromosomes, but their frequencies throughout the human species are not known. Individuals with XYY chromosomes were at one time thought to be more likely to be aggressive men who were frequently in trouble with the law in industrialized societies. However, research did not support this inference.

The two more frequently found combinations of unusual numbers of chromosomes are the Turner and Klinefelter individuals. The Turner syndrome appears in 1 out of 5000 girls born in industrialized societies; the Klinefelter syndrome appears in 1 out of 1000 boy births. People with these syndromes are clearly genderized, are said to have poor cognitive skills, and are frequently sterile. However, spontaneous menstruation and fertility have been reported in Turner women, although not all pregnancies are carried through.

Although both women with Turner's syndrome and men with Klinefelter's syndrome are considered moderately retarded, research does not always support that contention about Turner women. The gender and cognitive development in individuals with Turner syndrome is considered functional by some researchers. The presence of only one X chromosome in Turner women has been considered to be especially relevant to their visual spatial performance, and Turner women do not do as well as Klinefelter men on spatial ability tasks, but they improve with training.

The implications of underdeveloped internal reproductive systems for understanding "gender" and "sexual" definition and self-identity are demonstrated in a consideration of the research with the two syndromes. The psychological aspects of Turner syndrome function are frequently studied; Klinefelter syndrome individuals are studied less often. Individuals with both syndromes usually have socialization difficulties, but these are not the same. For example, in the Klinefelter syndrome, the man usually has small testes. Depending on the socialization history of the individual, the small testes may not occasion any concern in family and friends. Such an individual may not be thought to have an XXY chromosome configuration and may have identified himself as a "normal" male. Here the sexual identity (because there is one Y chromosome) and the gender identity are compatible but the complete gamete picture is not taken into consideration. Sometimes such individuals have a usual sexual behavioral history, but cannot produce offspring (e.g., aspermatogonia, or low sperm count). Physicians have been counseled to check on the sperm levels when an individual has small testes so that he can be advised "to consider not marrying because of sterility." Modern tech-

niques have made it possible for Klinefelter men to have medical help in obtaining viable sperm (although the count is low) and have the sperm introduced into a woman, producing viable offspring. Sufficient numbers of such children have been born to warrant a call for continued study of them.

In consideration of the social adjustment of Turner women, the attempts to intervene constructively have turned in two directions. In one, the supplemental treatment with estrogen is found to somewhat reverse neurocognitive deficits. In the other, concern about the usual short stature of the women as an important factor of psychosocial/societal adjustment has resulted in programs in which growth hormone was provided to the women. Most of the reports published deal with the anatomical and physiological results of the treatment.

In the Klinefelter syndrome, exogenous testosterone has been given to improve the immune system and to study its effect on brain morphology. It is not clear whether the difference in diagnosis, treatment, and study is related to the fact that the two syndromes are expressed in women and men who usually have different psychosocial/societal experiences in contemporary industrialized societies. In both syndromes, the approach has been to study the development of neuroanatomy and reproductive physiology. Understanding sex and gender definition in the experiences of individuals with Klinefelter and Turner syndromes in sex and gender definition calls for the integrative levels approach to elucidating the intimate interconnection between biochemical/physiological and psychosocial/societal levels.

g. Biochemical and Psychosocial/Societal Integration of Sex and Gender Definition. Activities of genes and proteins at one stage of development usually lead to an expected developmental pattern. When some of the genes and proteins are not functional at the usual developmental stage, as a result of changes in their nucleotide sequences or the amino acid configuration in the proteins produced, individuals do not develop the usual sexual structures and functions at the usual time. During the embryological stage, the testis produces testosterone that is converted to 5-alpha-dihydrotestorene (DHT) by an enzyme. In some males, the nucleotide sequence that codes for that protein (enzyme) is lacking. They develop all the male reproductive internal organs but not the secondary sex characteristics (male urethra, prostate, penis, or scrotum). Accordingly, these infants are considered females and they are genderized as girls, until they begin to develop secondary male sex characteristics at puberty. This developmental sequence illustrates that genes, proteins, and hormones act at different developmental stages to define sex and gender. Julianne Imperato-McGinley and her coworkers have found populations of such individuals in the Dominican Republic, Turkey, Papua New Guinea, Ireland, and Brazil. Their reports indicate that when the gamete identity is revealed, the gender identity usually changes, although it is clear that the "men" cannot produce offspring.

Changes in gender may be related to the class of the individual. In the Dominican Republic, those in the upper classes can marry and arrange for offspring to be born to the wives in those marriages and claimed as their children. Middle-class individuals change gender identity in variable social/societal adjustments. Poor people may become prostitutes or unskilled laborers. Today, individuals diagnosed early with this difference in hormonal function can be treated with appropriate medication to affect further development.

III. Development of Gender Definition: Psychosocial/Societal Processes Integrate Biochemical and Physiological Experience

A. GENDER DEFINITION BASED ON SEX

The neonate is part of a genderizing process that begins at birth with the decision of the caregivers that the visible, identifiable genitalia are sufficient to assign a gender to the child. Usually, this practice is founded on no information about the gametes carried by the child. From that point forward, the ways in which the child is addressed, handled, and dressed are based on that decision. In some cultures, girl babies are fed less than boy babies. The effect of malnutrition on mental growth and development at any stage during the life of the individual is well documented.

1. Genital Awareness

a. Usual Development of Gender Definition. The development of external genitalia become part of the experience of the neonate, infant, and child; the recognition of the relation between the genitalia

and the self may be through self-manipulation or the socialization among caregivers, peers, and the individual. The child integrates self-awareness of bodily changes and the development of secondary sex characteristics with the ensuing societal definitions of acceptable activity, perceptions and cognitive experience of the differences between girls and boys.

Freudians have seen gender development as evidence of psychosexual development; the vagina is seen as an evidence of penis envy. Sandra Bem and Barbara Lloyd and James Stroyan found that children acquire information about genitalia, and that gender differences are seen in children 36 to 65 months of age. The effect of the awareness and information about genitalia on the child's gender development is related to the child's understanding of gender differences in terms of desirability and social/economic inferiority or superiority.

b. Unusual Genitalia and Secondary Sex Characteristics. Differences in genitalia, such as unusual size (e.g., Klinefelter's syndrome), presence of enlarged clitoris, gynecomastia in men ("breasts"), and hairiness in women call attention to the relation between sex and gender. The effects of such awareness have been studied to some extent. Such research requires sensitivity. These individuals should not be considered "subjects" who are "subjected" to being photographed as examples of unusual development of secondary sex and other anatomical characteristics because of biochemical/physiological history, a practice found in many genetic, medical, and reference texts. Such research should be undertaken with the participation of the individuals in developing research questions and methods that address the issues as they affect their lives. Each of these individuals should be considered a national treasure worthy of financial and every other support to make of their lives what they desire.

2. Puberty as a Psychosocial/Societal Process (Maturity of Reproductive System)

Societies decide the point of maturity of both girls and boys and perform rituals to mark it. These rituals may or may not have a basis in reproductive maturity, although they are more likely to be linked to menarche in girls. In societies in which young girls and boys may be married through financial arrangements at ages before puberty, the consummation of the marriage in order to reproduce is usually based on menarche in the girls and the age of the boys.

However, genderization has taken place before the maturity of the reproductive systems. The biology is assumed, the gender is prescribed, and rituals of passage to mature gender roles are customary.

The rituals are frequently tied to age, regardless of concern about reproductive ability, which are assumed. In most societies, such assumed reproductive ability is greeted with approbation and celebration. In contemporary industrialized societies, because of improved nutrition during early stages of development, puberty is reached earlier than in societies with economic problems leading to poor nutrition. In many societies with economic problems, the "sale" of girls and boys for prostitution regardless of reproductive status places the emphasis on sexual activities rather than on self-identified gender. The physiological changes in hormonal function resulting in the evidence of secondary sex characteristics is referred to as "hormonal rush" in some societies, emphasizing the sex of the individual rather than the gender, but acceptable behavioral patterns related to reproductive activity are prescribed by society. In some societies, rituals are performed to recognize a new gender status in society, in terms of assuming responsibilities independent of the reproductive activities expected of them and for the appropriate activity in regard to adults and people of power.

The requirement for women to have children when menarche occurs may change their economic responsibilities in that they must work and bear children at the same time. The type of labor may be genderized in the light of the reproductive responsibilities. However, the girls are expected to be able to labor at muscularly demanding work as well as the boys in societies in which the economic situation is such that each individual must earn the right to be fed. This results in child labor excesses, further affecting biochemical/physiological processes (e.g., exposure to toxins) that may affect reproductive function. The stress of hard labor under poor conditions as well as the psychosocial/societal stress of such conditions changes hormonal activity; hormonal dysfunction leading to difficulties in reproduction becomes a factor in gender status.

In the families where elementary and higher education are possible, the type of profession and jobs to be held are genderized. Women are more likely to be in the service and "helping" professions (teacher, nurse, physician) than in the technical physical sciences and engineering. In industrialized countries, the genderization of academic participation and achievement takes place as early as three years and affects self-evaluation of academic ability and performance so that girls are less likely to acknowledge their abilities. The genderization leads to different access by women and men to appropriate training. It has been found in rats that increased stimulative activity facilitates production of new neurons (neurogenesis), and in birds learning to map an area for food induces neurogenesis. Neurogenesis in areas of the brain that are active in learning has been reported also. Human learning experiences may accelerate neurogenesis and this may facilitate performance. [*See* ADOLESCENT GENDER DEVELOPMENT.]

B. SEX AND GENDER IN NONREPRODUCTIVE (PRODUCTIVE) SOCIETAL ACTIVITES

Two activities reflect changes in the economic and technical character of human activity, and with them, changes in the position of women in society: sports and labor. Both are genderized and rely on biochemical/physiological (biological) differences between women and men to justify the differences in participation by women or men.

1. Sports: Who Does What If It "Takes Brawn"?

In most societies, group and individual games of athletic skill are genderized; boys usually play most of them, but girls do not. In the history of such activities in industrialized societies, most sports remained traditionally genderized until the era of women's activities for equal rights. Women, particularly upper-class European women, began to engage in the sports that had been reserved for men. In recent years in many societies, including those that were originally colonialized and that maintained the European sports traditions brought to them by the colonists (cricket, rugby, football, soccer, tennis, etc.), women have become players in some of those games (tennis, basketball, soccer, swimming). As the globalization of communication and sports developed, many international events increased the financial value of competing in those games. Even though in most sports women have their own organizations, this has sharpened the motivation to "equalize" women with the men in the competition for attracting audiences and honors, which brings financial rewards. This has resulted in sophisticated techniques to determine whether women who compete successfully are using steroids, and whether they are gametic women. Any competence that women achieve is attributed to externally administered steroidal hormones to affect musculature, strength, and performance. The reliability of analysis of urine and blood to discover the use of steroids has been challenged. The identification of gender with gametic sex is clearer, when genomic techniques are used. Reliance on gametic sex without consideration of accessibility to training to develop psychomotor skills disadvantages women in pursuit of sports achievements. The physiological differences between women and men are products not only of the biochemicals (genes, hormones, etc.) but of the ways in which the expression of those biochemicals developed in the physiological history of the individual. Motor differences between women and men are considered to be independent of training by some, but this is disputable. When groups of women and men are compared on various motor measures, there are significant differences in the scores within groups, so that some women are "equal" to or better than some men. The developmental histories of these women and men are specific to their ability, and a study of how those abilities developed would be informative. [*See* SPORT AND ATHLETICS.]

2. Labor: Who Does What If It "Takes Brains"?

a. Some Historical Considerations. Historical studies of postsedentation societies show that the prescription for certain types of labor for women and men was frequently a function of the reproductive activity of women. In many contemporary industrialized societies and those in the process of becoming industrialized, given the advances in technical tools and the drive of women for equity in all aspects of life, it is not necessary to define the division of labor by reproductive role. Both women and men can engage in all types of labor including those requiring mental abilities (computer science, other types of sciences) as well as those requiring psychomotor skills (e.g., construction industries). The jobs that are usually held by men have different, and more desirable, rewards. In industrialized societies, girls and boys learn this lesson early (preschool and primary school children) and understand the genderized nature of the differences in employment of women and men. Much of the research comparing the thinking abilities of women and men may be undertaken to demonstrate a "scientific" basis for the limited accessibility by women to jobs with complex mental tasks.

b. Spatial Abilities as Mental Competence. Spatial abilities in women and men as indicators of mental competence are intensively studied, possibly because they are considered essential in scientific, mathematics, and engineering labor. As Diane Halpern has stated, the term "spatial abilities" refers to a complex interrelationship of many skills (e.g., spatial perceptual, spatiotemporal, visual identification of an object when orientation is changed [mental rotation], and spatial relations between/among objects). She and other investigators, such as Anne Petersen and Kathryn Hood, have noted that gender differences are not found on all tests of spatial ability. Many psychosocial/societal processes are involved (e.g., developmental, emotional, method of observing individual differences, effects of training), and these may be responsible for the variability in the findings. Some studies have found that if the time for response is not limited, there is no difference between women and men; that training will improve the performance of girls more than boys (embedded figures, mental rotation) even after the differences between the girls and boys before training are taken into account; that women do better on map-reading tests than men; and that women do better on spatial memory tests than men. However, despite weaknesses in methods and statistical inference interpretations, most behavioral scientists believe that women are poorer in spatial ability than men. Most researchers in the area of spatial ability seek explanations of gender differences in biochemical factors (biological)—genes, hormones, and neurotransmitters—and at physiological levels (neurophysiological and neuroanatomical processes, reaction time).

C. WHAT ARE THE UNDERLYING RESEARCH ASSUMPTIONS?

Many of the questions are based on explicit or implicit assumptions: (1) the same biochemical factors (genes, proteins, and hormones) that produce different sexes (gametes) produce different neuroantomical and neurophysiological characteristics in groups defined by gender; and (2) as behavioral genetic studies find mental ability differences among differently related people (fraternal twins, siblings, parents) with less shared nucleotide configurations, the differences between women and men are based on their having different genes that correlate with gametic sex differences. Behavior geneticists analyze group differences statistically to state how much of the variation in the scores may be attributed to heredity and how much to the environment. At this time, there is no definitive research about the process whereby spatial ability is inherited, which is not in dispute. Studies with mice and rats in which genes are either removed ("knocked" out) or implanted in other individuals of the same species or of other species (transgenic animals) are cited by behavioral geneticists as evidence for a genetically determined difference between women and men in spatial ability. By studying spatial behavior in people with unusual genes, it is hoped that a gene for spatial behavior will be found. The assumption (which needs to be supported by further research) underlying this approach is that if a mutation of a gene (change in nucleotide sequence or function) as in the Williams syndrome is correlated with a behavioral characteristic, there should be an unchanged gene that will be correlated with that characteristic as it develops usually.

The investigation of genetic processes underlying cognitive behavior is widely carried out with nonhuman animals. In addition to the preceding assumptions of such research, other assumptions are (1) the same biochemical factors (genes, proteins and hormones) that produce different gametic sexes produce different neuroantomical, neurophysiological, and behavioral characteristics in female and male animals; (2) genes will be found in animals to correlate with neural structures and functions involved in spatial abilities; (3) as many nucleotide configurations that correlate with female and male animal reproductive behavior are also found on human chromosomes and the genes must function in humans as they do in nonhuman animals; and (4) the genes that correlate with cognitive ability in animals will be found on human chromosomes and will function similarly in humans.

1. Research Issues

These assumptions are challenged by the following considerations of the ways in which research may be carried out to test them: (1) humans and animals compared; (2) nucleotide functions in gametic sex and neuroanatomy and neurophysiology; and (3) methods and theory: reductionist and integrative approaches.

a. Humans and Animals Compared. Animal research can offer significant suggestions for research on human spatial behavior. It offers necessary information about biochemical, neuroanatomical/neurophysiological processes in animals that suggest similar processes in humans. When an inference can be made from animal and human research, it leads to certain generalizations (e.g., social and spatial experience is a central factor in spatial ability performance). However, the differences between animal and human biochemistry and neuroanatomy/neurophysiology and psychosocial/societal spatial experiences may be significant. Biochemical and physiological information obtained on the basis of animal research may be necessary, but it is not sufficient to understand the processes involved in human spatial ability or how differences in performance develop.

The psychosocial/spatial experiences of animals are based on their gametic sex (reproductive behavior); animals have no societal experiences, that is, there are no group-decided prescriptions as to the behavior of female mice and rats in contrast to the behavior of males as to how they use space or spatial cues. People have psychosocial/spatial spatial experience based on the genderization of their behavior and abilities from early stages of development, from birth through every aspect of their lives through maturity, including the workplace. Spatial experience in rats has been shown to have biochemical/physiological effects and to improve performance; the neurophysiology of people changes as they participate in learning and memory research. However, how the effects of human experience and of rat experience are similar or different has not been studied, as it is not possible to give either species the experience of the other. Yet, based on animal research one can approach the issues of the role of experience in changing human function on biochemical and physiological levels.

How is spatial ability studied in people and animals? In one technique, animals are placed in a pan of water with a platform just below the level of the water. The animal has to solve the problem of finding a platform to avoid having to swim. It should be noted that both mice and rats will avoid swimming in water, and the test is stressful. In another situation, the animals have to solve the problem of finding food or escape from a complex circular maze. Spatial ability in people is observed in situations in which language and reading/writing are involved. An individual is asked to indicate spatial relationships between objects (rod and frame situation), or to distinguish between drawings of the same object from different orientations, or to find subsections in complex drawings, or to visualize changes in shape resulting from manipulations of objects from two dimensions to three dimensions (mental rotation), or read maps, or to use paper-and-pencil mazes. Some animal species (birds and primates) have been trained to record responses to figures or drawings presented in the ways in which they are presented to humans. Experiments have been done with people in mazes similar to those used by animals. However, the converse is not possible with nonhuman animals; they cannot be given problems as presented to humans without special training. People who have been studied in the non-paper-and-pencil mazes similar to those in which animals are studied have not been studied while solving paper-and-pencil problems.

2. What Can We Infer from the Research Results (Statistical Inference)?

First, the data are usually group data. A group is defined by the characteristics chosen by the investigator: strains of mice and rats; girls and boys defined by their location (school, country, etc.) and women and men by their availability for study (e.g., college). The relevance of such findings for other groups needs to be demonstrated before inferences can be made with confidence. Group differences are correlational: the difference is correlated with the groups, but the process responsible for the difference is not demonstrated. Finding differences between groups tells us nothing about the characteristics of any one individual.

Studying a quantifiable characteristic (trait) such as scores on spatial task performance, in groups (populations) raises an issue when those traits are correlated with the supposed existence of particular genes, or neuroanatomy, or neurophysiology. Plant geneticists know that once a genetic or nucleotide configuration is found to be related to a quantifiable trait (height, weight, etc.) and its chromosomal location found, the number of individuals with that trait in a group is affected by the environment in which the individual plant or animal developed. This will result in different frequencies of the occurrence of the particular form of the trait. In other words, if it were possible to rear each group with different experiences, differences between groups might be different. Even though the nucleotide configuration is the same, it expresses itself differently when the organism has different experiences.

3. Genes for Spatial Ability and "Smartness"

The announcement is widely made in the media that a gene has been found for "spatial ability" or "smartness." Genetic manipulations have created mice with changed or missing nucleotide configurations; these "knockout" mice cannot use their spa-

tial memories in water and radial mazes, nor can they solve problems of spatial relationships. The inference is than made that in the intact mouse or rat, those genes are the "spatial ability" genes. One of the lessons that genomics has taught is that a single gene is rarely found to be responsible for a function or a structure.

It has also been found that when a gene is changed or missing, other genes and proteins are affected, and that these may be related to the change in structure or function found when the gene is changed: other genes and proteins may have also been changed, which may have also been involved in the behavior, structure, or function reported. Recognizing this, the investigators of these "knock out" mice also study reproductive behavior; finding that this is the same as that in mice that have not been deprived of the "smartness" gene, they assume that the gene described is independent of other genes or functions. However, it is not possible to state that other genes were not affected. Further, the investigators observe the rodents in more than one spatial task, and when the performances are the same, they take this as further proof of the relevance of that gene for spatial ability. The repetition of observations that yield the same scores does not demonstrate that the "gene" is the same.

4. What Is the Role of Estrogen and Testosterone, or of the Gene or Chromosome for Estrogen and Testosterone?

It is clear that doing genomic research with people would be expensive and time consuming. The creation of a "knock out person" is not possible. However, there are individuals born with certain chromosomal or genetic variations who perform poorly on spatial tasks. One such population consists of people with the Turner syndrome. Individuals with the Turner syndrome typically show other mental patterns that are unusual, as well as poor training and poor social skills. As people with the Turner syndrome lack one X chromosome, the inference is made that this is related to poor spatial ability. The developmental and experiential history of these people is not part of the analysis of the behavioral performance measured, nor has the necessary nucleotide function been reported yet.

Some of the evidence that testosterone or the Y chromosome is responsible for the difference in spatial abilities between women and men is based on men with Klinefelter syndrome. Klinefelter individuals do better on spatial ability tasks than do Turner women.

As testosterone is converted to estradiol in order for it to be active in many cells, tissues, or organs in which it is found, the relationship between genes, hormones, and spatial ability would seem to require some investigation as to the aromatization of the testosterone in Klinefelter men before this complex finding can be understood.

The ubiquity of estrogen receptors in the nervous system and the wealth of protein-producing genes on the X chromosomes are worth investigating in regard to spatial and other cognitive abilities. The recent finding that estrogen is essential for neurogenesis (formation of new neurons and precursors of neurons) also highlights the significance of experience in behavior. The increase in neurogenesis and estradiol activity in significant areas of the brain (frontal cortex, hippocampus) after training or other experiences designed to modify the behavior of the individual also makes consideration of developmental processes important. Investigation of the changes that take place with disease, stroke, or other traumatizing experiences are other traditional means of understanding neuroanatomy and neurophysiological processes behavior.

D. METHODS AND THEORY: REDUCTIONIST AND INTEGRATIVE APPROACHES

Looking for genes, hormones, and transmitters to explain behavior is a reductionist approach and leads to an insufficient analysis. Such information is useful and is used in the integrative levels approach. The integrative levels approach, however, is dependent on developmental information: How do the gametic and other nucleotides produce the proteins? How do the proteins work with the nucleotides? How do these entities work with others? How does the experience of the person affect the ways in which these nucleotides and proteins express themselves in the structures and functions that are involved in the performance defined as spatial ability? Most of the research done with people does not include studies of the neurophysiological/neuroanatomic foundations of the behavior being observed, nor is the developmental history of the individuals taken into account. By defining groups, it is assumed that the experience of the individuals in the group is sufficiently similar to limit the variability of performance. This is the usual behavioral genetic approach: any similarities of the individuals in the group are evidence of their shared inheritance; any variability is evidence of environmental factors.

Information about the biochemical/physiological foundations of behavior in and of itself is necessary, but it is not sufficient to clarify the process of spatial perception or how the differences develop in women and men, however. The information about biochemistry and physiology would have to be integrated with information about the psychosocial/societal developmental history. The significance of using the developmental history is that it resolves the need to choose between the genetic or the experiential process as the preeminent one, the ultimate process. It also obviates the need to quantitatively define the genetic and experiential contribution to the behavior; it seeks at all times to understand how the biochemical/physiological and psychosocial/societal processes become integrated in any behavior pattern, function, or structure.

E. AN INTEGRATED APPROACH TO STUDYING THE DEVELOPMENT OF GENDER

If the societal motivation for the research questions is designed to relate to policies and practices so that equity is possible for women and men, the relative valence of all process are important. To begin to understand the development of gender, questions asked about biochemical/physiological processes need to be answered as well as psychosocial/societal processes: education, training, family, and peer activities. Such research is demanding and challenging; but the demands and the challenges need to be met if the societal goal is to be achieved.

SUGGESTED READING

Alberts, B., Bray, D., Johnson, A., Lewis, J., Raff, M., Roberts, K., and Walter, P. (1998). _Essential Cell Biology._ Garland, New York.

Carson, R. A., and Rothstein, M. A. (eds.) (1999). _Behavioral Genetics: The Clash of Culture and Biology._ The Johns Hopkins University Press, Baltimore.

Fausto-Sterling, A. (2000). _Sexing the Body._ Basic Books, New York.

Ford, D. H., and Lerner, R. M. (1992). _Developmental Systems Theory: An Integrative Approach._ Sage, Newbury Park, CA.

Gilbert, S. F. (1997). _Developmental Biology._ Sinauer Associates, Sunderland, MA.

Griffiths, A. J. F., Miller, J. H., Suzuki, D. T., Lewontin, R. C., and Gelbart, W. M. (eds.) (1993). _An Introduction to Genetic Analysis._ W. H. Freeman, New York.

Halpern, D. F. (1992). _Sex Differences in Cognitive Abilities._ LEA, Hillsdale, NJ.

Rogers, L. (2000). _Sexing the Brain._ Phoenix Press, London.

Smith, E., and Sapp, W. (eds.) (1997). _Plain Talk about the Human Genome Project._ Tuskegee University, Tuskegee, AL.

Diagnosis of Psychological Disorders
DSM and Gender

Dana Becker

Bryn Mawr College Graduate School of Social Work and Social Research

Glossary

Affect A pattern of behaviors that expresses a subjectively experienced emotional state (e.g., sadness, anger, elation).

Antisocial personality disorder An enduring pattern of violation of and disregard for others' rights that originates in childhood or early adolescence and persists into adulthood.

The Diagnostic and Statistical Manual of Mental Disorders (*DSM*) This is the standard assessment guide used by U.S. clinicians to diagnose mental disorders.

Epidemiology The study of the distribution of disease/illness in the general population.

Medicalization The social construction of some types of human behavior as medical disease.

Mood disorders Psychiatric disorders related to pervasive emotional states such as depression, anger, anxiety, and elation.

Multiaxial system of diagnosis A system of psychiatric assessment in which information is gathered in five domains, or axes.

Psychosis Very broadly defined, gross impairments in an individual's ability to be in touch with reality. Frequently, persons who are regularly subject to delusions or hallucinations are said to be suffering from psychosis.

Psychotropic medication Medication given to remediate a psychiatric condition.

THE HISTORY OF PSYCHIATRIC DIAGNOSIS, to a large extent, is a woman's story, although psychiatry has come late to the recognition that gender has an impact on the process of diagnosis. Disorder is located in the eye of the beholder, and psychiatry's *Diagnostic and Statistical Manual of Mental Disorders*, fourth edition (*DSM-IV*) published in 1994, takes a view of disorders as existing within individuals. Problems of living and the distress associated with them are viewed as diseases rather than as behavior that is transactional or socially deviant. This bias may be particularly disadvantageous to women, because personal factors, including gender, have often been used to explain women's behavior, whereas men's behavior is often attributed to external factors. Because women generally have lower status than men in our society, they may be at greater risk for being labeled mentally ill, or "mad," whereas men may more often be viewed as criminal, or "bad."

For the most part, it is our preoccupations as a society that determine our view of what human miseries might be termed "psychopathology." Arthur Kleinman reminded us in 1988 that diagnosis is an *interpretation* of a person's experience that categorizes some types of misery as disease, and it can be argued that gender is the most significant of the cultural constructions that contribute to our ideas about madness. Only a few psychiatric diagnoses actually appear to have cross-cultural applicability.

I. *Gender, Diagnosis, and Disease*

Two recent epidemiological surveys sponsored by the National Institute of Mental Health (NIMH), the Epidemiological Catchment Area (ECA) survey and the National Comorbidity (NCS) survey, have shown that the most common disorders in the general population are depression, alcohol dependence, phobias, generalized anxiety disorder, and drug abuse (note that, in each of the surveys, these disorders were ordered differently). It is much more likely that women will have mood disorders and anxiety disorders than men, whereas men are more likely to have addictive disorders and antisocial personality disorder. Despite the fact that, in the ECA survey, phobias and alcoholism were the disorders most often *reported*, studies of outpatient settings show that depression and anxiety, which both surveys show to be more prevalent among women, are the disorders most commonly *treated*. Women, who often find it easier than men do to seek care, are more frequently seen for psychotherapy in outpatient settings, as Mark Olfson's and Harold Pincus's research demonstrated in 1994.

The actions we take to remedy social problems— and mental health problems are among these—depend, in large part, on whether we find the causes of the problem within individuals or in the environment. We cannot consider the effects of psychiatric diagnosis on women without keeping in mind that the form of classification or categorization that we currently call diagnosis is a powerful form of representation of women's experience. Although the social designation of problems of living as mental dis-

order is a relatively recent phenomenon, the labeling of women as a means of exerting control over them has a history that stretches back for centuries.

As the notion of "evil" gradually gave way to the notion of "illness," control of women through allegations of witchcraft were replaced by another potent means of social control—psychiatric diagnosis. Whereas during the Romantic period of the 18th century, madness had been considered "loss of reason" and the mad were treated as primitive beasts, in the Victorian era of the 19th century the idea began to take root that madness was "moral insanity," or deviance from socially sanctioned behavior. This transformation in thinking about madness made it possible to identify nearly any deviant or disruptive behavior as "morally insane" and brought increasing numbers of behaviors under the scrutiny of physicians.

From the first, women's relationship with the burgeoning psychiatric profession has been an uneasy one. Under the guise of scientific objectivity, male experts became increasingly the evaluators of women's problems. By the mid-19th century, female patients with "nervous" diseases had swelled the practice of many a specialist in "nerve medicine." These women were considered hysterical; they were weak; they were ill. They were defined by the metaphors of illness.

So it was in the beginning, and so has this medicalization of women's problems continued into the present. As Richard Cloward and Frances Fox Piven warned us in 1979, women are being increasingly led to view the stresses they experience in life as substantially related to their health or mental health. The ever-expanding system of classification set forth in the *Diagnostic and Statistical Manual of Mental Disorders (DSM)* and its widespread acceptance by health insurance companies, managed care organizations, the legal system, and governmental programs and agencies has ensured that such will be the case for some time to come.

II. *The Evolution of a Giant: A Brief History of DSM*

The definitions of problems, once arrived at, tend to endure regardless of their validity, and they are not easily replaced by other definitions. When we medicalize psychological problems we individualize them, denying or diminishing the importance of social problems that may contribute to them. For example, a woman whose spouse regularly berates her for her shortcomings may become depressed. It is entirely possible to diagnose this client as having major depressive disorder without acknowledging the depression as symptomatic of a larger problem—the fact of her marital situation and the fact of her subordinate status as a woman in a patriarchal society. Because she has a lesser capacity than her husband to support herself financially, she may be unable to change her circumstances easily.

Those who stand to benefit most from maintaining the social status quo—and, in a patriarchy, most are male—are naturally drawn to an explanatory framework that views the causes of disorder as within individuals. When human problems are viewed as illnesses, the values, beliefs, and politics that influence clinicians when they make diagnoses are concealed behind the mask of a purportedly neutral and objective science.

The history of *DSM* amply illustrates the fact that the "reality" of mental illness is shaped by social forces and psychological theories. *DSM-I*, published in 1952, and *DSM-II*, published in 1968, were slim volumes whose contents were based on little more than the collective opinions of small groups of psychiatrists, and those opinions were virtually ignored by patients and clinicians. All this changed, however, in 1980 with the publication of the much-expanded *DSM-III*. A sign of the times was the replacement of the term "mental illness" with the term "mental disorder," a designation that brought more phenomena under the aegis of psychiatry. The expansion of diagnostic categories from 79 in *DSM-I* to 370 in the current *DSM-IV* has particular significance for women for two reasons. The first of these is that women, as we have just mentioned, constitute the majority of those clients in outpatient psychotherapy; the second is that, until recently, almost all organizationally powerful psychiatrists in the United States have been White men whose thinking, as Hannah Lerman suggested in 1996, has primarily reflected White male values and points of view about the role of women and the causes of mental health problems.

It is widely believed that it was the publication of *DSM-III* (1980) that yanked the psychiatric profession back from the precipice of professional extinction. By distancing itself from psychoanalysis and newly medicalizing the profession, psychiatry gained authority at a time when it had been struggling to attain legitimacy and to differentiate itself from social work and psychology. Prior to this transformation, research funding had all but disappeared. In the wake of the *DSM* revolution, research moneys have been liberally restored. However, much of the psychiatric research performed today has been financed by pharmaceutical companies whose aim has been to develop and test their own psychotropic medications. In fact, the development of *DSM* itself has been underwritten by some of these same pharmaceutical companies.

In 1985, the *New York Times* and other periodicals reported confrontations between feminist psychotherapists and members of the American Psychiatric Association (APA) committee that had authored *DSM-III-R*, the revised edition of *DSM-III*. Although early on its authors had described the projected revision as but a minor recalibration of *DSM-III*, it came to the attention of some feminist psychotherapists that three new problematic categories of mental disorder had been proposed for inclusion in the forthcoming *DSM-III-R*: paraphilic rapism; premenstrual dysphoric disorder, or PMS; and masochistic personality disorder. The psychiatrists were caught short. They had not foreseen the considerable impact the women's movement might have on the practice of psychotherapy.

The chief objection of feminist practitioners to the diagnosis of paraphilic rapism was that it might be used as a psychiatric defense by rapists in criminal proceedings. In the case of PMS, feminists feared the institutionalization of a natural female bodily function as mental disorder. Paula Caplan, in her 1985 book *The Myth of Women's Masochism* and elsewhere, has argued against labeling some women disordered when they display the same selfless, self-abnegating behaviors widely encouraged in the socialization of girls. In the mid-1980s, women who remained in abusive relationships were frequently described as masochistic, even though, as Lynne Rosewater pointed out in 1985, battered women, whose behavior often appears self-defeating, may remain in abusive relationships, not because they suffer from a mental disorder, but for many other practical reasons. These reasons can include fear of death at the hands of their abusers. [SEE FEMINIST APPROACHES TO PSYCHOTHERAPY; FEMINIST MOVEMENT.]

Paula Caplan, Lenore Walker, and others have described in detail elsewhere the arbitrariness of the decision-making processes that eventuated in the determination of the criteria for these new categories of disorder, as well as the difficulties that they encountered in attempting to find a place for their points of view in the proceedings of the psychiatric committees that influenced those decisions. In the end, it was not feminists' compelling theoretical arguments that swayed the committee and won the day; it was the publicity that accompanied their protests and picketing of the 1986 convention of the American Psychiatric Association in Washington, D.C. The attendant mobilization of support from the assistant attorney general and organizations such as the Surgeon General's Conference on Violence, the National Association of Social Workers (NASW), and the American Psychological Association helped remove the category of rapism altogether from the *DSM-III-R*. Feminist protests likewise led to the removal of the category ego-dystonic homosexuality, a diagnosis that had remained in the *DSM-III* even after the "diagnosis" of homosexuality itself had been removed. PMS and masochism—now newly renamed "self-defeating personality disorder"—were placed in the appendix as categories requiring further study. Unfortunately, if one looks very hard in the subsequent edition of *DSM—DSM-IV—* (it is not listed in the index), one can find premenstrual dysphoric disorder, the "disorder that would not die," tucked away as a category subordinate to "depressive disorder not otherwise specified." For the first time in the *DSM*'s history, premenstrual syndrome has been listed officially as a psychiatric disorder.

Over the years, the process of revising *DSM* has become more elaborate, accompanied by invitations to larger and larger pools of participants, the inclusion of whom has rendered the task of revision ever more politically complex. Although the names and titles of contributors are displayed front and center in the *DSM-IV*, lending it an air of spurious legitimacy, no invitations to participate in the process of its drafting were extended to those in social work or nursing, and the psychologists, whose appointments as liaisons had been much ballyhooed, were never consulted throughout the period of its composition.

Despite claims to the contrary, no version of *DSM* has produced compelling evidence of either validity or reliability. As Stuart Kirk and Herb Kutchins summarized in 1997:

Since available scientific data seldom provide definitive answers to questions, most issues must be handled through complicated behind-the-scenes negotiation. Nonetheless, in each new revision the claim is made that the manual has achieved greater validity and more precision. Every change, even ones that are abandoned within a few months, is presented as a science-guided decision in which mistakes have been corrected, ambiguities have been clarified, and new

knowledge has been incorporated. And since the final product . . . is never directly tied through citations to research articles, the claims of science-at-work are difficult to verify or dispute. All of the recent efforts to revise DSM began by discrediting the scientific status of the then current edition. (pp. 37–38)

With each new edition of *DSM*, beginning with *DSM-III*, the biomedical view has become more firmly entrenched, reducing the stated influence of social and psychological theories on the causes of mental illness. Those who have fashioned the various incarnations of *DSM* have maintained that the approach of the manuals, which is to describe behavioral phenomena, is an atheoretical, value-free approach. However, as William Doherty pointed out in 1995, the priorities of the *DSM-IV*'s makers are firmly embedded in its multiaxial system. The first instruction to the clinician in the use of the multiaxial format is to rule out the possibility that the client may have a general medical or physiological condition or any physical condition caused by medication or substance abuse. Only then is the evaluator to move to the individual psychological level (Axis I clinical disorders and Axis II personality disorders), and only then to the level of the social and environmental (Axis IV). In standard practice, clinicians rarely make diagnoses on Axis IV, and even when they do, diagnoses on this axis do not have an impact on the primary Axis I or Axis II diagnoses. For many purposes, both clinical and bureaucratic, only Axis I and Axis II diagnoses are used or required. The priorities of the authors of *DSM-IV* are clear: the attitudes of psychotherapy clients, the meaning these clients give to their symptoms, and the social and historical context of their distress are marginalized in the process of diagnosis. The "medicalized" *DSM-IV* diagnosis, paying only lip service to psychosocial phenomena, remains acontextual and ahistorical in a fashion that denies the very real social problems women face. So, too, does it minimize the substantial contributions that these problems make to the development of the psychological difficulties that eventually bring some women to the attention of clinicians.

The fact that many clinicians use *DSM* more as a necessary tool of commerce with managed care companies than as a valued assessment device should not lull us into believing that it does not heavily influence both our thinking about important social issues and our consideration of social institutions. As Kirk and Kutchins put it, *DSM* sets out a template for new knowledge that shapes which scientific questions will be asked and which will be overlooked.

Lerman warns that unless we adopt an approach that is more contextual, it is unlikely that new knowledge about women's physical and psychological functioning will find its way into the official system of diagnosis.

As an example of how the lack of attention to the context of human problems can work against women, let us again take up the case of the young woman who comes for psychotherapy because she is experiencing subjective distress as a result of her relationship with an abusive partner. In order to ensure that she will garner insurance reimbursement, her therapist gives her a diagnosis—let's say major depressive disorder—that not only describes her distress as more acute than it is but also distorts the extent to which her problems are intrapsychic in origin—that is, the extent to which they exist only in her own individual psyche. Now our young woman, having entered therapy only briefly, will have not only a history of mental disorder, but she may also—if she does not already—come to view her problems as outgrowths of her blighted nature, and her "disease" will be documented in records that may be made available to other insurance companies, the state, and her employer, among others.

III. *Gender Bias and Stereotypes*

Since it is impossible for an individual to process more than a fraction of the information available in any situation, labels can provide a handy means not only for organizing input, but also for determining to what further information the individual will attend. There are inherent dangers in the practice of labeling, however. Clinicians often make diagnoses according to the principle of "seek and ye shall find," paying selective attention to facts that confirm their preexisting biases. Thus, clinicians may be influenced by one salient symptom presented to them to find others that will confirm a given diagnosis. It is so easy to be influenced in this way by a descriptor (e.g., "obsessive") that happens to be a diagnostic category that it is possible to overlook information inconsistent with that diagnosis. Personality disorders frequently provide more handy labels than do some other categories, since most of them carry such descriptors as titles. "Dependent personality disorder" and "histrionic personality disorder" are examples of these. Gender also conveys important information that can act as a convenient organizer for explaining behavior. It can hardly be anticipated that

gender role expectations, which have a significant impact on how all individuals are socialized, would not affect the process of diagnosis.

A. IS *DSM-IV* GENDER BIASED?

As Cynthia Hartung and Thomas Widiger pointed out in 1998, because the information on sex prevalence rates for disorders in the *DSM-IV* was provided by a number of different individuals and no documentation of the rationales for their conclusions was provided, it is difficult to know whether there existed adequate research evidence to support these conclusions. Until the theoretical and methodological problems surrounding the information on prevalence is resolved, Hartung and Widiger maintain, present findings will remain open to allegations of gender bias.

The majority of studies that explore the possible influence of the sex of the client upon diagnosis are studies that instruct the therapist–subjects to read case histories that are identical except for the sex of the client and to select a diagnosis on the basis of the information given. Recently, studies have found gender bias in the diagnoses of antisocial personality disorder, histrionic personality disorder, and borderline personality disorder, among others. Perhaps there will always be differences in the prevalence rates for various disorders because of sex-related differences in biological or environmental factors that contribute to the development and eventual course of a given disorder. However, one can conclude that bias is present when differences between the sexes in their willingness to acknowledge the presence of a problem, the ease with which they seek treatment, or in the responses of others to their problems, among other factors, fail to be taken into account when calculating prevalence rates for various disorders.

Let us consider for a moment how it comes about that, in *DSM-IV*, the sex prevalence rates for childhood disorders are much higher for boys than they are for girls, whereas men are definitely not the majority of those diagnosed with adult disorders. For example, boys are more likely to be diagnosed with major depressive disorder in childhood; women in adolescence and adulthood. This inconsistency may not result from an actual difference in the rates of prevalence of these disorders for males and females. Hartung and Widiger remind us that children's difficulties are often first noticed and viewed as problematic by parents and teachers, not by the children themselves. In adulthood, however, it is generally the distressed individual him- or herself who seeks out treatment, and women have traditionally been more willing than men to seek treatment.

Many of the childhood disorders listed in *DSM-IV* are what are called "externalizing" disorders, or disorders that *others* might find disturbing: enuresis (bedwetting), conduct disorders, reading problems. The sections of *DSM-IV* that are devoted to adult disorders, however, are weighted toward "internalizing" disorders such as generalized anxiety disorder and major depressive disorder, conditions that are problematic for the individual sufferer. In *DSM-IV*, the most common childhood diagnoses—attention-deficit hyperactivity disorder (ADHD), conduct disorder, and oppositional defiant disorder—all of which involve disruptive behaviors, have no equivalents in the adult section. Of course, the decisions about which disorders should be listed in the *DSM* are decisions by committee; committees retain the power to add and subtract disorders.

As Richard Cloward and Frances Fox Piven have noted, even when individuals deviate behaviorally from what is considered the norm, they do so in ways that are influenced by the culture in which they live. Many North American women are socialized to express their distress privately, by internalizing it; males are socialized to express theirs in more overt, "external" ways. The absence of diagnoses for adults whose anger and aggression is out of control (and of these adults, more tend to be men) has been viewed as indicative of bias in the *DSM* by Paula Caplan and others. Thus, it is possible for a man to go to prison on a serious assault charge without necessarily being diagnosed with a mental disorder. Here again, as was mentioned previously, the mad/bad distinction reigns. Women's actions are considered "mad"; men's "bad" (criminal).

Although men and women express certain problematic behaviors differently, the *DSM-IV* does not have much to say about actual sex differences in the ways in which disorders are expressed. For example, research on alcoholism has primarily used male subjects, as Pamela Brett and her colleagues discovered in 1995. When *DSM* criteria are fashioned from research conducted primarily on men, the result may be an underdiagnosis of substance abuse problems in women, if it turns out that women express the symptoms of alcoholism differently from men. Other instances of how symptoms of particular *DSM-IV* disorders are differentially expressed abound. As we shall see, the personality disorder diagnoses offer an ample showcase for gender differences in symptom expression.

IV. Just How Personal Are the Personality Disorders?

Some current psychiatric designations seem to mirror feminine-stereotyped behavior, leading us to question whether gender roles, as Hope Landrine suggested in 1989, are "masquerading as madness," such that these gender role categories and categories of personality disorder are simply "flip sides of the same stereotyped coin." Or is it the case, as Marcie Kaplan argued in 1983, that stereotypical feminine behavior alone can qualify a woman for some personality disorder diagnoses, such as dependent or histrionic personality disorder, whereas masculine stereotyped behavior alone does not lead to a personality disorder diagnosis?

In the *DSM-IV*, a *personality disorder* is defined as "an enduring pattern of inner experience and behavior that deviates markedly from the expectations of the individual's culture, is pervasive and inflexible, has an onset in adolescence or early adulthood, is stable over time, and leads to distress or impairment" (p. 629). It is not surprising, as Jerome Kroll wrote in 1988, that, among the disorders that have been examined for possible sex bias, personality disorders are those most frequently represented, for, of all the disorders, they seem to resemble medical diseases least and to depend most on societal norms and expectations. In 1988, several members of the *DSM-III-R*'s own Advisory Committee on Personality Disorders admitted that some domains of personality problems may have been overrepresented and others underrepresented. They likewise mentioned "overlap" among categories, that is, similarities among criteria that are said to differentiate one personality disorder from another. Kroll pointed out that, as a result of the many difficulties encountered in the attempt to define and categorize the personality disorders, the process has been particularly susceptible to a variety of external influences.

Among the personality disorder diagnoses that are particularly problematic for women is *dependent personality disorder* (DPD). According to *DSM-IV*, some individuals have "a pervasive and excessive need to be taken care of that leads to submissive and clinging behavior and fears of separation" (p. 665) beginning in early adulthood. They fear the loss of approval of others; they are disproportionately fearful of being left on their own to take care of themselves and desperately seek out another relationship when a relationship ends. They find it difficult to make decisions or to assert themselves when they disagree with others. These are but a few of the criteria that characterize dependent personality disorder.

The criteria for DPD exclude the kinds of stereotyped expressions of male dependency that may be expressed in jealous, controlling behavior. As several feminist critics have pointed out, male dependency, in the form of some men's reliance on their wives to take care of their emotional needs and raise their children, is a hidden form of dependency in our culture. The personality disorders section of *DSM-IV* does not include any diagnosis that might describe how male strivings for autonomy may result in disorder if they lead to workaholism or other forms of excessive disconnection from close relationships. Marcie Kaplan, in 1983, only partly tongue-in-cheek, proposed inclusion in the *DSM* of an "independent personality disorder" category in order to underscore the lack of parity between descriptions of male and female difficulties with dependency.

Kaplan underscored the essential assumptions made by *DSM* about dependency, namely, that it is unhealthy and that when it is expressed in an extreme form in women it primarily reflects dysfunction as opposed to reflecting the actual power differences between men and women that may contribute to dependent behaviors in some women. These assumptions have not changed substantially over the two decades in the course of which *DSM* has been revised twice.

In the *DSM-IV*, it is not suggested that the prevalence of dependent personality disorder is higher for women than for men; rather, it is stated that the "sex ratio of this disorder is not significantly different than the sex ratio of females within the respective clinical setting" (p. 667). Robert Bornstein's 1996 research, however, does show that women are being given the dependent personality disorder diagnosis significantly more often than are men, not, he believes, because there are actual sex differences in dependency, but because women are more willing than men to acknowledge dependency.

Although both the dependent and histrionic personality disorder diagnoses, as befits the more "feminine" categories of classification, rely heavily on interpersonal criteria for their diagnosis, the criteria for the histrionic personality disorder emphasize the more active side of dependency. As described in the *DSM-IV*, the "histrionic" individual has a tendency toward "pervasive and excessive emotionality and attention-seeking" (p. 655) beginning in early adulthood. An individual with the disorder may attempt to control a partner through seductiveness or emotional manipulation, while demonstrating a clear dependency on him. She may make suicidal threats and gestures in order to command attention and gain better care from others; she is easily influenced by other people and is inappropriately sexually seductive. Although she is described as "overly concerned" with physical attractiveness, it is difficult to know how the *DSM* committee members were able to separate the socially imposed requirement that women be concerned with their physical attractiveness from clinical levels of "overconcern."

The *DSM-IV*, in describing the "inappropriate" expression of exaggerated emotion said to characterize the histrionic personality disorder, does not describe the social context in which this relationship management style may develop. The histrionic designation not only pathologizes dependency, but it also stigmatizes the way in which some women express anger and aggression, for, although women's direct expressions of anger are often considered socially unacceptable, when women inhibit that anger they may behave in ways that contribute to a stereotyped perception of women as *histrionic*—whining, seductive, manipulative, and covertly controlling.

V. *The Special Case of Borderline Personality Disorder*

According to Widiger and Rogers's 1989 research, almost half of those who meet the criteria for diagnosis of histrionic personality disorder would also qualify for a diagnosis of *borderline personality disorder* (BPD). This is a diagnosis that deserves special scrutiny, since the story of BPD so clearly illustrates how fashions in diagnosis can, over a period of just 20 years, by a sort of diagnostic sleight-of-hand, transform a gender-neutral diagnosis into a "women's" diagnosis, and a particularly pejorative one at that. *DSM-IV* describes the borderline personality disorder as "a pervasive pattern of instability of interpersonal relationships, self-image, and affects, and marked impulsivity beginning by early adulthood and present in a variety of contexts, as indicated by five (or more) of the following" (p. 654):

1. Frantic efforts to avoid real or imagined abandonment.
2. A pattern of unstable and intense interpersonal

relationships characterized by alternating between extremes of idealization and devaluation.

3. Identity disturbance: markedly and persistently unstable self-image or sense of self.

4. Impulsivity in at least two areas that are potentially self-damaging (e.g., spending, sex, substance abuse, reckless driving, binge eating).

5. Recurrent suicidal behavior, gestures, or threats, or self-mutilating behavior.

6. Affective instability due to a marked reactivity of mood (e.g., intense episodic dysphoria, irritability, or anxiety usually lasting a few hours and only rarely more than a few days).

7. Chronic feelings of emptiness.

8. Inappropriate intense anger or difficulty controlling anger (e.g., frequent displays of temper, constant anger, recurrent physical fights).

9. Transient, stress-related paranoid ideation or severe dissociative symptoms.

Because the diagnosis can be arrived at through numerous combinations of its criteria, one individual diagnosed as having the disorder may look quite unlike another with the identical diagnosis (in 1990, Michael Stone tallied up 93 combinations of the *DSM-III-R*'s eight criteria that would yield a borderline diagnosis; with the current nine, one can only shudder to think of how many combinations are now possible).

BPD is the most frequently applied personality disorder diagnosis, both in inpatient and outpatient settings, and it is more commonly diagnosed in women than in men, at a ratio of between 2:1 and 9:1, depending on the research study cited. The second wave of the National Institute of Mental Health Epidemiologic Catchment Area study of the general population showed the prevalence of BPD among a general population sample of 2993 respondents to be quite high—roughly equivalent to the incidence of depression in that same population, and over 73% of those who reported "borderline" symptoms were women. About half the individuals who said they had such symptoms reported having made one or more visits to a mental health facility within the past six months. Women with BPD symptoms, then, are not merely heavily represented in the general population, but in treatment settings as well.

The term "borderline" was not widely used until 1953, when Robert Knight wrote about the "borderline state." There was thought to be a "borderline strip" between neurosis and psychosis, and the "borderline state" referred to a psychotic episode that could break through in an otherwise nonpsychotic individual. As Knight defined it, the "borderline state" did not refer to any sort of stable character structure, as would be required today if it were it to meet the *DSM-IV*'s definition of a personality disorder. With some foresight, it would appear, Knight cautioned his readers that the term "borderline" had more to say about diagnostic uncertainty than about patient psychopathology.

With the publication of *DSM-III* in 1980, descriptions of the borderline syndrome moved away from an emphasis on its schizophrenic-like features toward an emphasis on its affective elements: rage, depression, self-destructiveness (including suicidality), feelings of emptiness, and the like. It does not appear coincidental that such a shift in definition coincided with an increase in clinical interest in and appropriation of financial resources for research on mood disorders, now that the tendency to overdiagnose schizophrenia has been replaced with a more recent tendency to overdiagnose mood disorders. This tendency has had significant implications for women, since a "depressive" group of clients will tend to be female. Michael Liebowitz, M.D., in a paper delivered at the 1990 meeting of the American Psychiatric Association, remarked that, shorn of its affective features, borderline personality disorder would look more aggressive, impulsive, and antisocial. Liebowitz's remark points up how much more "masculine" the diagnosis might look if this were the case.

The borderline personality disorder diagnosis resembles the dependent and histrionic categories in a number of aspects. Many of its criteria, too, represent indices of the difficulties some individuals have in meeting their needs for connection with others and in expressing their anger, such as difficulty tolerating aloneness, engaging in self-destructive behavior, and proneness to outbursts of rage. As Becker suggested in 1997, the problems women have with dependency and anger lie along a continuum, and the symptoms currently called "borderline" are severe manifestations of these problems. Angry or aggressive clients may be said to be "acting out" and an acting-out woman client, particularly one who displays self-destructive or suicidal behavior, is frequently given a diagnosis of borderline personality disorder. Although much current research has demonstrated that many women currently diagnosed with BPD have histories of sexual or physical abuse, the *DSM-IV* makes no mention of this, nor of the numerous studies that have failed to support the validity of the category.

The term "borderline" must surely be one of the most misused and abused in the psychiatric lexicon. In 1992, Judith Herman called it "little more than a sophisticated insult." It has become a catchall diagnosis for the clinician who is confused by what she or he sees and is frequently used as a synonym for the difficult, angry female client who is not making progress in therapy. As Kutchins and Kirk pointed out, the diagnosis has become a vehicle for circular arguments—that a client is demanding or that a therapist behaved inappropriately with her because the client "has" borderline personality disorder, as if BPD were an intractable disease. The waters are further muddied when we read that the "borderline" personality is *unstable* when the *DSM-IV* itself defines the term "personality" as a pattern over time of inner experience that is enduring, *inflexible,* and *stable.* Despite the apparent offhandedness with which the diagnosis is often applied in actual practice, it is no casual matter for a woman to bear a BPD diagnosis. In 1998, Susan Stefan, an attorney studying court law, found that women diagnosed with BPD are often thought to be mentally disabled and, as such, may be subject to involuntary institutionalization, involuntary medication, loss of custody of their children, or termination of their parental rights. In addition, they are frequently discredited as witnesses in court cases that involve rape or sexual abuse. Paradoxically, however, women who carry a BPD diagnosis are not usually considered sufficiently mentally disabled to permit them to receive educational or disability benefits or to recover damages in abuse cases.

VI. *Gender and Posttraumatic Stress Disorder*

Recently, because of the increasing understanding that many women currently being given a borderline diagnosis have histories of childhood physical or sexual abuse, it has been suggested that the *posttraumatic stress disorder* (PTSD) diagnosis may be a less stigmatizing diagnosis, since it points up the connection between external stressors and symptoms. Laura Brown and Lenore Walker have suggested that we view personality disorders as responses to multiple exposures to traumata, sexism, and other forms of oppression that exist in the culture.

The growing recognition of the relationship between traumatic events and psychiatric disorder in the lives of many women has led to an increasing reliance by many clinicians on the posttraumatic stress disorder diagnosis, and no exploration of gender and the *DSM* would be complete without a discussion of its evolution. Given the current popularity of the diagnosis among clinicians, it is difficult to believe that it has been only 20 years since PTSD was first introduced into *DSM-III.* The idea that psychological symptoms could result from traumatic events is far from new, however. Both the Civil War and World War I raised interest in posttraumatic phenomena. It was not until the Korean and Vietnam wars, however, that public attention was focused on PTSD. The efforts of Vietnam veterans were originally responsible for the inclusion of PTSD in *DSM-III.* Although at that time the diagnosis was principally employed to explain symptoms that lingered in the aftermath of soldiers' violent war experiences, it is now often used to describe symptoms that can arise in the aftermath of physical and sexual abuse. This transformation was made possible by a major change in the description of the nature of the traumatic antecedents of PTSD symptoms. In the *DSM-III,* stressful events had to be "outside the range of usual human experience" (p. 236). With the publication of the *DSM-IV* 14 years later, however, there was no mention of such a requirement. In the *DSM-IV,* traumatic events are described as events that involve "actual or threatened death or serious injury, or other threat to one's physical integrity" (p. 424). This redefinition came about because acts of sexual and physical abuse—domestic abuse, rape, child sexual abuse—that are common in the experience of many girls and women were recognized as stressors that might lead to the development of PTSD symptoms.

As they are currently described in the *DSM-IV,* PTSD symptoms include those related to the reexperiencing of the traumatic stressor (e.g., flashbacks, nightmares), those related to the avoidance of the stressor (e.g., a sense of detachment; avoidance of places, people, or activities that evoke memories of the trauma), and symptoms arising from increased arousal (e.g., excessive watchfulness, or hypervigilance; insomnia; impaired concentration). Hannah Lerman suggested that the difficulty in defining the "threat" in "threat to one's physical integrity" (see above) may be problematic for women. For example, a battered women who kills her sleeping husband, fearing he will kill her when he wakes, may find that her claim of self-defense holds little weight in court, because our system of criminal justice requires the presence of a direct and immediate threat in order for such a claim to be upheld. In her book *The Trouble with Blame: Victims, Perpetrators, and Responsibility,* Sharon Lamb questioned why the particular reactions to stressors delineated in the *DSM-IV* should be considered an illness, as opposed to other sets of reactions. She has offered the example of an inner-city youth who shows apathy in school and engages in antisocial activities outside of school. The symptoms are easily discernible, as are the stressors—poverty, possible problems at home, a difficult school environment, lack of employment opportunities—and yet we do not call this aggregate of symptoms or reactions "disorder."

It is certainly preferable to take into account the fact that exposure to external traumatic stressors may have a significant impact on the development of girls and women than to view their symptoms as outgrowths of personality problems. However, broad use of the PTSD diagnosis may not prove the panacea for the problems psychiatric diagnosis poses for women. First, there is something inherently troubling in the attempt to normalize the responses that many women have to abuse traumata while at the same time calling them a disorder. Secondly, the change in the definition of trauma in the *DSM-IV* has brought along with it the possibility that millions of women will become eligible for a PTSD diagnosis, women who then will be said to have a mental disorder. It may also be the case, as Philip Cushman pointed out in 1995, that so many syndromes and situations now fall under the rubric of abuse that the term will eventually be stripped of all meaning. [See POSTTRAUMATIC STRESS DISORDER; TRAUMA ACROSS DIVERSE SETTINGS.]

VII. Whither the Context of Disorder?

As noted earlier, Arthur Kleinman asserted that diagnosis is but an interpretation of human suffering. He further commented that categories—which is indeed what diagnoses are—result from the cumulative effects of cultural influences and historical developments as well as political negotiations. In the attempt to distinguish between distress and disorder, a system of classification may become ensnared in its own rules for deciding when distress is just distress and when distress is disease. Medicalization plucks human suffering out of its context. Consider the case

of the anxiety disorders, which, as shown in the ECA and NCS surveys, appear to afflict women more frequently than men. As Lerman has suggested, specifying behavioral criteria for these disorders can lead, at times, to treatment that is focused on behavior change and symptomatic relief at the expense of understanding context. When we fail to explore the social, relational, and historical backgrounds in which anxieties are rooted, we may be overlooking and even invalidating essential elements of a woman's experience.

Some time ago, a woman in her early 60s came to me for psychotherapy complaining that she had had a panic attack on the highway as she was driving to her son's house. She had been experiencing insomnia and increased anxiety for some time prior to the panic attack. In her very traditional family of origin she had been an extremely responsible daughter who had worked hard and taken care of her younger siblings. She had left her family to marry and she embraced her wifely and maternal responsibilities with an equal sense of duty. Now, with her children grown, as she began to see an opportunity to enjoy a less encumbered life, her younger brother, who had always depended on her excessively, had become ill and was expecting a great deal of care. In addition, one of her daughters-in-law had just given birth to another child. She had been traveling to this daughter-in-law's house to baby-sit when she had had her first panic attack. As is true for many women of her generation, saying no to those who depended on her was not something she had been socialized to do. Although she frequently felt angry at the encroachments others made on her life and how little they gave back, she did not feel entitled to her anger, nor to ask to have her own needs met. Her panic attacks made it unnecessary for her to refuse the requests of others outright; she simply could not fulfill her former role obligations. As this example makes plain, anxiety viewed in a socio-cultural context is not identical with anxiety viewed as an aggregate of symptoms.

The *DSM* story of diagnosis as an objective and scientific enterprise omits the narrative of how social mores determine changing fashions in the definitions of disorder, definitions on which our cultural history is inscribed. We must understand thoroughly the influence of cultural constructions of gender on the process of diagnosis if we are to have the opportunity to remake our present system of classification in a way that takes gender fully into account.

SUGGESTED READING

American Psychiatric Association. (1994). *Diagnostic and Statistical Manual of Mental Disorders*, 4th ed. Author, Washington, DC.

Becker, D. (1997). *Through the Looking Glass: Women and Borderline Personality Disorder*. Westview, Boulder, CO.

Brown, L. S. (1992). A feminist critique of the personality disorders. In *Personality and Psychopathology: Feminist Reappraisals* (L. S. Brown and M. Ballou, eds.), pp. 206–228. Guilford Press, New York.

Caplan, P. J. (1985). *The Myth of Women's Masochism*. University of Toronto Press, Toronto.

Caplan, P. J. (1995). *They Say You're Crazy*. Addison-Wesley, Reading, MA.

Hartung, C. M., and Widiger, T. A. (1998). Gender differences in the diagnosis of mental disorders: Conclusions and controversies of the DSM-IV. *Psychological Bulletin* 123(3), 260–278.

Kutchins, H., and Kirk, S. A. (1997). *Making Us Crazy: DSM: The Psychiatric Bible and the Creation of Mental Disorders*. The Free Press, New York.

Lerman, H. (1996). *Pigeonholing Women's Misery: A History and Critical Analysis of the Psychodiagnosis of Women in the Twentieth Century*. Basic Books, New York.

Showalter, E. (1985). *The Female Malady*. Pantheon, New York.

Ussher, J. (1992). *Women's Madness: Misogyny or Mental Illness?* University of Massachusetts Press, Amherst.

Disabilities and Women
Deconstructing Myths and Reconstructing Realities

Adrienne Asch

Wellesley College

Tiffany S. Perkins

Michelle Fine

City University of New York

Harilyn Rousso

Disabilities Unlimited Consulting Services

Glossary

Disability According to the Americans with Disabilities Act, "a physical or mental impairment that substantially limits one or more of the major life activities."

Discrimination Biased behaviors toward people with disabilities that result from derogatory attitudes or beliefs about people with disabilities.

Handicap Social ramifications of having a disability.

Impairment The biological condition that causes the disability.

Intersections The premise that disability not only impacts other social categories, such as gender, race, ethnicity, social class, age, and sexual preference, but the interpretation of disability is also influenced by historical/situational contexts and internal and external mechanisms.

DISABILITY can happen throughout the life span for girls and women, the cause of which is important to consider, but too complex and multifaceted to contain within this short article. This brief article is designed to educate the reader about the laws surrounding disability rights in the United States; to identify the scholarly literature on the intersections of gender, disability, and race; to highlight many issues that are specific to women with disabilities; and to inform readers of the growing fictional and autobiographical writings by and about women with disabilities.

I. *Introduction*

To begin, three premises organize this article. First, the field of disability studies has long been neglected by feminist scholars, and questions of gender and race have as long been overlooked by disability scholars. This article is an attempt to integrate those literatures, to the extent that they exist, and to invite much more thorough work at the intersections of gender, race and disability. Second, the article documents the dramatic extent to which disability is a civil rights issue that deserves policy and legal attention; that is, persons with disabilities experience discrimination in the fields of work, education, health care, community, and family life, with gender, race, ethnicity, class, age, age at onset, and sexual orientation bias complicating the lives of all women, particularly women of color, poor women, and lesbian women who have disabilities. Third, despite, and of course in part because of, the enormous range of discriminatory practices, there is a vibrant disability rights movement, evident in law, social policy, fictional writing, autobiographies, and disability studies, emerging as a field of scholarly pursuit and disability activism obvious at the federal, state, and local levels. Thus, this article seeks to introduce the scholarship, the evidence of discrimination, and the sense of activism emergent in disability rights movements across the country, across types of disabilities, and across sectors of social life.

II. *Definitions*

Just as feminists have worked hard to distinguish sex (biology), from gender (the social consequences of biological sex), from sexism (the political arrangements based on hierarchical ordering of that which is assumed male and that which is assumed female), and critical race theorists have distinguished race from racism, so too disability scholars and activists have articulated crucial distinctions between impairment, which connotes a biological condition; disability, which indicates a limitation in everyday functioning; and handicap, which refers to the social consequences of a condition. When anthropologist Nora Groce discovered a community on Martha's Vineyard in the late 1800s, in which a substantial proportion of children and adults were deaf but most community members had learned sign language, she found that these disabled children, women, and men were as likely as the general population to be edu-

cated, marry, have children, and work. That is, context matters. When we build environments that exclude, disabilities produce conditions that are handicapping, that is, that limit opportunities. When classroom teachers provide materials in Braille, students with visual impairments or blindness have full access to the texts; when universities and employers understand their legal obligations to accommodate the needs of persons with disabilities, these same persons attend school and work and enjoy far more fulfilling lives than prior to these legal victories; when we construct buildings so that they are wheelchair accessible, persons who use wheelchairs may enter the building and utilize its services; when sign interpreters are hired for plays, the audience may include persons who are deaf.

There are three laws that may be useful guideposts for the reader who is unfamiliar with disability rights legislation or scholarship. On the heels of much grassroots organizing, spawned in the 1970s, Section 504 of the Rehabilitation Act of 1973 was implemented, which provided civil rights protections whenever entities received federal funds. Then, in July of 1990 the Americans with Disabilities Act (ADA) was signed into law, marking the equivalent of a civil rights act for persons with disabilities. With this law, persons with disabilities were now legally recognized as a discriminated against minority group; discrimination was now prohibited in employment, and private businesses, government offices, and nonprofit organizations had to alter their buildings and their practices to be accessible to persons with disabilities. According to the ADA, a disability is "a physical or mental impairment that substantially limits one or more of the major life activities," a record of such impairment, or being regarded as having such an impairment. In a similar spirit, the Individuals with Disabilities Education Act assures, in law, that improving educational results for children with disabilities is an essential element of our national policy of ensuring equality of opportunity, full participation, independent living, and economic self-sufficiency for children with disabilities.

In 1995, it was estimated that nearly 54 million citizens of the United States had disabilities: 10% of the population age 21 and under, 19.9% of all working age people, and 52.5% of all people age 65 and over. Of the 134 million women and girls in the United States, it is estimated that 21.3% have disabilities that affect their daily lives.

While these laws and demographics are rooted in the body, the most exciting and compelling scholarship and activism surrounds the social construction of disability, that is, how does "disability" operate in the world? What are the economic, social, and personal consequences of having a disability, and why has our culture been so committed to locating the disability as in the person, rather than in the social treatment of a large segment of our society?

A word on intersections, before we move into the discrimination literature. As noted earlier, most of the literature on disability assumes disability to have a primary or what Erving Goffman would call a master status, which thereby eclipses all other axes of social and personal life. The evidence presented here challenges this assumption. Again, context matters. First, note that disability impacts gender, race, ethnicity, social class, age, and sexual preference, such that all outcomes reviewed—labor force participation, income, education, health care, and so on—have markedly different consequences for men and women, Whites, African Americans, Latinos, Asians, and Native Americans, elites, middle class, working class, and poor, young workers, elderly workers, heterosexuals, lesbians, and gays. The fact is that most of the existent literature on disabilities—broadly defined—does not attend to "differences" within which makes it difficult to make the argument for intersectionality, but this article will present what little evidence there is on the question of differences within the category "persons with disabilities."

Second, there is an undeniable layering of discriminations such that the more socially disadvantaging characteristics a person has, the more likely her economic, educational, and social outcomes will suffer. That is, the devil is in the intersections—not in any one broad sweeping analysis. We learned this lesson from early feminisms, which did not attend adequately to race; from early civil rights literatures, which did not attend to gender; from the lesbian and gay literatures, which early on (and still) paid lip service to class and race/ethnicity. Now, in disability studies, we "discover" the same—that the intersections matter; to presume that disabilities affect all in the same ways is nonsense, and to argue or study from only one vantage (White, middle-class, heterosexual male with disabilities) distorts the evidence. Type of impairment can also matter, depending on which or how many gender-related functions are affected; whether the impairment is predictable and static, or varies day to day, or is progressive in its manifestations; perhaps whether it is readily apparent or invisible. The following overview of the available literatures on discrimination against persons with disabilities allows us to look at multiple jeopardies and attempts, where possible, to identify the treatment of persons with disabilities.

III. On Discrimination

While research on women with physical and mental disabilities as targets of discrimination is sparse, the evidence is both astounding and consistent in its demonstration of the gross negligence bestowed on women with disability by society. In the past 30 years, both the study and the politics of disability, like gender, race and ethnicity, have undergone dramatic transformation. Using arguments of the 1960s civil rights and women's movements, disability activists and scholars have sought to demonstrate that anatomy need not be destiny. Obstacles to education, community and political participation, independent living, employment, and personal relationships derive not from the incapacities, for example, but from the intersection of impairments and contexts, as well as practices, that refuse to accommodate. We turn, first, to the incidence of disabilities with an understanding that the impact of disability is always contingent on context.

A. THE INCIDENCE OF DISABILITIES

Worldwide, women are at increased risk of becoming disabled throughout their lifespan, and once disabled, they are at increased risk of being sicker, poorer, and more socially isolated than either men with disabilities or than nondisabled women. . . . There is a feedback loop between disability, gender, and poverty which places women, particularly poorer women, at a marked disadvantage at every stage of their existence. . . . This is because poor women are likely to live and work in more physically dangerous environments, to have less to eat, and to receive poorer quality medical care or no medical care at all.[1]

As Nora Groce explicates, having a disability is profoundly related to health care, social treatment, poverty, gender, race and ethnicity, national priorities, immediate social context, family resources, and levels of experienced discrimination. Turning to the United States, the Census Bureau's Survey of Income and Program Participation, an ongoing, nationally representative panel survey of the economic status of

---

[1]Groce, N. (1997). Women with disabilities in the developing world: Arenas for policy revision and programmatic change. *Journal of Disability Policy Studies* 8(1 and 2).

the noninstitutionalized, civilian population of the United States, found the highest rates of disability for Native Americans, followed closely by Blacks and Whites, with Hispanics having a slightly lower rate. Women were found to have a higher rate of disability than men in the general population with this difference being seen within each racial/ethnic group. Likewise, other studies have reported that Black women experience higher rates of some physical disabilities than do their White counterparts. Black women are more likely than White women to sustain serious physical injuries from interpersonal violence. Additionally, one in four Black women will have high blood pressure during her life; rates of cancer for Blacks have gone up by 34%, as compared to 9% over the same period of time for Whites.

B. ON ECONOMICS

Saad Nagi defined disability as "a form of inability or limitation in performing roles and tasks expected of an individual in a social environment." However, statistics on work—one of the most social of environments—and disability characteristics by race and gender are not readily available. Work disabilities have been reported equally by males at 10.2% and 9.9% of females. Analyses by race and ethnicity provide a more glaring set of discrepancies: Blacks report 15.4%; Hispanics report 9.6%; Whites report 9.4%, and all other races report 8.5%. Among people with a work disability, women had a 28.5% participation rate in 1998; for men the participation rate was 32.3%. For persons without work disability, the labor force participation rates were 75.8% for women and 89.1% for men. Across groups, men are more likely than women to be employed or to own a business. Sharon Barnartt and Barbara Altman found, in a study of income among workers with various types of disabilities, that "all groups of women earned less than male peers."

Among those who are employed, women with disabilities tend to be tracked into lower wage positions. Through the 1980s, it was clear that men and women with disabilities were poorer than those without; women with disabilities were at the bottom of the ladder, and Black women with disabilities had less income than any other race/gender/impairment category. Using the 1980 figures, the median income for Black females with work disabilities was 22 cents compared to the White-male-with-no-impairment dollar.

A study undertaken in the early 1990s by the President's Committee on Employment of People with Disabilities, which addressed the issue of "multiple jeopardy" for African American women, found that approximately 1 in every 12 "working-age" Americans has a disability, and that 3 out of every 10 African American women of working-age with a disability have fewer than eight years of schooling. To make matters worse, Marjorie Baldwin reports that "award rates for Social Security Disability Insurance and Supplemental Security Income are lower for African Americans than White Americans and lower for women than men." These findings document the "triple jeopardy," experienced by African American women with disabilities, that is, the additive social and educational consequences of gender, race, and physical or mental disability in a society, which devalues women, people of color, and persons with disabilities.

C. ON EDUCATION

In 1984, the Women and Disability Awareness Project wrote the following:

[A]bout two-thirds of those identified as in need of special education services are males. Researchers have concluded that the male/female disproportion cannot be explained by physiology alone. For example, males labeled mentally retarded have higher IQs than females labeled mentally retarded. The implication is that females are not expected to excel intellectually to the extent that males are and, therefore, are not classified as retarded unless they have very significantly low IQs. In fact, the female stereotype—dependent, emotional, illogical, unambitious, needing protection—has much in common with the stereotype of retarded people. In addition, some observers believe that boys may be too readily labeled mentally retarded simply because of disruptive social behavior.

The 1982 Disability Rights Education and Defense Fund (DREDF) study of 8000 people with disabilities found that physically disabled girls were far more likely than physically disabled boys to be placed in special separate schools. Asserting that such placement seriously limits girls' access to social and educational experiences, the researchers suggest that this difference in treatment comes about because of the assumption that males must support themselves and therefore need a good education.[2] In 1998, the U.S. government wrote the following:

[2] Women and Disability Awareness Project. (1984). *Building Community: A Manual Exploring Issues of Women and Disability.* Education Equity Concepts, New York.

Among school aged secondary students with disabilities, males constitute the largest proportion of each disability category except deaf-blindness, which is almost equally divided between males and females. The disproportionate representation of males in special education seems greatest in learning disability and emotional disturbance categories, which are often considered the disability categories with the most broadly defined eligibility criteria.[3]

The consequences of these placement decisions persist and are severe. In 1997, the Department of Education report on Individuals with Disabilities Education Act (IDEA) documents that girls with disabilities who drop out of school have lower IQ and become young unwed mothers at a much higher rate than their nondisabled peers. Furthermore, there are physiological consequences of child sexual abuse, such as an increased potential for contracting sexually transmitted diseases.

Assessment of level of educational ability typically presumes that all children at any given level of cognitive impairment will receive equal services, that is referrals, one-on-one tutoring, and classroom placement. However, research has shown that factors such as gender and ethnicity interfere with equitable treatment with the result being disproportionate rates of African American children being labeled with mental disabilities or cognitive impairments and girls with any type of disabilities being led down the less challenging educational tracks.

D. ON INTIMACY, SEXUALITY, AND MOTHERHOOD

Research on intimate relationships of women with disabilities reveals another sphere of gender bias, with race and ethnicity rarely addressed. Although marriage, in the traditional sense, may not be the preferred status for many women, of those who are interested, women with disabilities are more likely to get married later in life and more likely to divorce than those without disabilities.

Drawing on the Current Population Survey's data of the early 1980s, research indicates that 60% of men with disabilities compared to 49% of women with disabilities are married. Further, 50% of women with activity limitation are married, as compared to the marriage rates for other groups—64% of women with no activity limitation, 68% of men with activ-

[3]To Assure the Free Appropriate Public Education of All Children with Disabilities, Twentieth Annual Report to Congress on the Implementation of the Individuals with Disabilities Education Act U.S. Department of Education. (1998). U.S. Government Printing Office, Washington, DC.

ity limitations, and 69% of men with no activity limitations.

When women with disabilities are compared to women without disabilities and men with disabilities on rates of divorce and separation, differences again surface. William Hanna and Betsy Rogovsky analyzed 1985 Current Population Survey data on marital status, dividing a subsample of ever-married (but not widowed) men and women into three categories: nondisabled, mildly disabled, and severely disabled. More women than men in all categories were divorced, with significant differences between "severely disabled women" and other groups. Fourteen percent of men termed "severely disabled" were divorced, while 26% of severely disabled women were divorced. Thirty-seven percent of severely disabled women, as contrasted with 22% of severely disabled men who were once married are no longer married, for reasons *other* than death of a spouse.

Research findings indicate that White middle-class women with disabilities have limited opportunities to establish romantic relationships with men (the little research on lesbian relationships among women with disabilities suggests a similar trend) compared to women with no disabilities, are less satisfied with how often they date and perceive more constraints on attracting dating partners, and state that friendships are less likely to evolve into romantic relationships than for women with no physical disability.

For women with disabilities, traditional opportunities to be nurtured and to nurture, with a man or a woman, to be lovers and be loved, to be mothers if they desire, are constrained. Both the constraints posed by physical limitations and the social barriers are formidable. Vicky Daust has confirmed the difficulties: "I want to be attracted to women and I want them to know I am open to having a sexual relationship. This is a harder task than you might realize when you are Deaf and sitting in a wheelchair. There is an assumption of inability and, perhaps, of disinterest."

Women with disabilities historically have been considered unfit as sexual partners and as mothers. Many women have spoken out about the unavailability of adequate counseling on sexuality, birth control, pregnancy, and childbirth from either medical or rehabilitation professionals. Failing to recognize in advance the potential consequence of some birth control devices for women with particular conditions, many gynecologists prescribed unsafe methods. In 1977, Safilios-Rothschild revealed that coronary research has been conducted almost exclusively on men thereby producing data relevant only to men. How-ever, these data were generalized to women so that women interested in resuming sexual activity after a heart attack were advised based on studies of male patients.

At a conference on Women with Disabilities, a woman with spina bifida described a preadolescent encounter with her gynecologist this way:

"Will I be able to have satisfying sexual relations with a man?"

"Don't worry, honey, your vagina will be tight enough to satisfy any man."

Her own satisfaction probably didn't cross the gyne-cologist's mind.

Parenting by women with disabilities is only one of the many roles that may be considered nontradi-tional. Should women with disabilities pursue other "nontraditional" life courses (e.g., the decision to work, to be a single mother, to be involved in a les-bian relationship, or to enter politics), these choices may be regarded as default rather than preference. Ora Prilleltensky's dissertation explored issues con-fronted by mothers with physical disabilities, both women who have children and those who were con-sidering having children. Through the course of 26 interviews and 4 focus groups with 13 participants, she uncovered many of the issues that are central to the lives of mothers with physical disabilities. While all of the mothers expressed joy and satisfaction, most of the mothers had received negative messages about their abilities to attract a sexual partner, be-come a mother, and be a "good" mother.

As noted throughout, issues of sexuality, repro-duction and motherhood confronting women with cognitive, emotional, sensory, or psychiatric disabil-ities have a particularly repugnant history. In the early part of the 20th century, most people with "mental defects" were remanded to mental institu-tions. An even more treacherous fate befell mothers who were labeled "mentally defective" and their chil-dren both believed to be morally and mentally de-generate and inclined to criminal activities. "Treat-ment" for the families included prohibition of marriage, institutionalization, and involuntary steril-ization. In 1927, Carrie Buck, an 18-year-old woman with mental retardation, who lived in the same men-tal institution as her mother, bore a child with men-tal retardation. The court case of *Buck* v. *Bell* argued for sterilization versus euthanasia. The court deci-sion read, in part, "It is better for all the world, if instead of waiting to execute degenerate offspring

for crime, or to let them starve for their imbecility, society can prevent those who are manifestly unfit from continuing their kind . . . [by] . . . cutting off the fallopian tubes . . . three generations of imbeciles is enough!"

The late 1970s and early 1980s saw an increase on research on families in which mothers had mental re-tardation. This research served to soften the public's perspective by challenging stereotypes of promiscu-ity, criminal insanity, and incompetence, and by sup-porting the rights of mothers with cognitive impair-ments to develop intimate relationships.

Many parenting intervention studies reveal not only that mothers with cognitive impairments can provide adequate and appropriate care for their chil-dren, but also that these mothers are capable of learning parenting skills with the proper instruction and followup support. However, the type of support that mothers, themselves, say they need is often not available. Gwyneth Llewellyn constructed case his-tories of six Australian couples—both spouses hav-ing a cognitive impairment—exploring the parents' views of their relationships and their social support for parenting. Extended families were seen by some mothers as playing a crucial role in managing and caring for the children. However, for others, familial support was missing. Friendships, which were viewed as equally important to mothers, were most often a source of discontent. Only 2 of the 12 parents re-ported having friends in whom they could confide or call for assistance. The lack of support for these mothers stems mainly from societal disapproval of parenting by women with cognitive impairments. Llewellyn captures the feelings of isolation and aban-donment that stem from a lack of familial and friend-ship support in the words of Ruth (a mother with mental retardation):

I haven't got family, no family around here, that I can go around and see or they can come around and help me if I am tired with the kids. I have got no one like that to call on to come and get the kids for a couple of hours. I'd like to have family. Other people have said to me, sister, aunty, or mum come and got the kids for a while and do house-work or have a rest or something. I'd like that.

Many states have had laws forbidding people with histories of epilepsy, mental retardation, and psychi-atric disability from marrying. Fears that women with disabilities would produce children with similar conditions (nearly always groundless since the vast majority of disability is not hereditary) have mingled with convictions that they would harm, deprive, or burden children they attempted to rear. Distressingly, recent feminist volumes recounting the richness and diversity of women's experiences of motherhood typically omit discussion of mothers with disabilities. If "disability" is discussed at all, it is in the account of a woman without impairment raising an "exceptional" child with an impairment and the "extraordinary" work involved. The absence of the disabled mother from mainstream feminist and medical literature leads to ignorance and prejudice on the part of midwives, physicians, social service agencies, scholars, and courts. Many obstetricians and midwives refuse to deal with women whose disabilities may complicate their pregnancies. Social service agencies may still decline to let women with disabilities keep children they have borne, and adoption agencies and courts often insist that a parent's/mother's impairment—even if it is not life-threatening—may harm a child and is thus relevant to adoption decisions.

E. ON HEALTH CARE

Since 1994, two major conferences have been federally sponsored, one by the Centers for Disease Control and one by the National Center for Medical Rehabilitation Research, to gain a better understanding of health care issues that affect women with disabilities and to develop resources to that end. The Department of Health and Human Services' Web site provides links to organizations and publications that deal with women with the health issues of women with disabilities. A recent source of information for and about women with disabilities, the Women with Disabilities' Sexual and Reproductive Health Resource Packet, was published in 1997 by the Americans with Disabilities Act and Reproductive Health Project of the California Family Health Council. This packet contains a list of books, manuals, videos, equipment evaluation, listing of the rights of women with disabilities, and a bibliography that covers reproductive health services, pregnancy and parenting, reproductive rights and technology, sex education, the experience of women with disabilities, magazines and newsletters, and national technical assistance resources.

Despite these efforts, women with disabilities in comparison to women without disabilities, still experience serious problems when seeking reproductive health care, such as being refused health care because of their disability; having difficulty finding physicians knowledgeable about specific disabilities and pregnancy; experiencing younger and having

higher incidence of chronic urinary tract infections, heart disease, depression, and osteoporosis; and using public health clinics, specialists, and hospital emergency departments at higher rates than women without disabilities. Issues of gynecological and psychiatric health care become particularly difficult, and buried, for women who are lesbians. Faith Reidenbach, a lesbian woman with manic-depression disability, writes in *Restricted Access: Lesbians on Disability,* that successful treatment was impeded not only by her parents' homophobia (who thought her mental illness was a result of her being a lesbian) but also by what she calls the "anti-psychiatry" interventions of feminist friends and therapists: "I want therapists to stop trying to 'protect' or 'rescue' lesbians from the drug treatment that is now known to be necessary for brain diseases."

F. ON ABUSE

The Women with Disabilities' Network of Canada surveyed 245 women with disabilities and found that 40% had experienced abuse, 12% had been raped, with the perpetrators of the abuse primarily spouses and ex-spouses. Likewise, the University of Alberta's Sexual Abuse and Disability Project conducted a study of 166 abuse cases. Seventy percent of the women, age 16 to 57 years of age, had some type of cognitive impairment. In 96% of the cases, the woman knew the abuser; 44% of the abusers were service providers with 79% of the women being victimized more than once. Furthermore, treatment services were either inadequate, inappropriate, or not offered in 73% of the cases.

A recent review of research on abuse of women suggests that, for women with disabilities, assault, rape, or abuse is twice as likely to occur than for their nondisabled counterparts. Furthermore, depending on how abuse is defined and the frequency of occurrence, not only are the abuse rates for adults with disabilities one and a half to five times greater than nondisabled adults, but also the abuse is often more chronic and severe. Corroborating the finding of longer duration of abuse for women with disabilities, a recent analysis by Marjorie Nosek, Carol Howland, and Mary Young concluded that the incidence of abuse may not be greater for women with disabilities (62% for women with and without disabilities), but the duration of abuse is. These researchers have argued that cultural devaluation, overprotection, increased dependence, economic disadvantages, denial of human rights, less education, social isolation, and the larger culture's refusal to hear or believe these women's complaints may all contribute to the prolonging of abuse. Furthermore, some researchers have asserted that the neuropsychological consequences of abuse may contribute to cognitive declines and perhaps inappropriate mental retardation classification.

G. WRITINGS BY, FOR, OR ABOUT WOMEN WITH DISABILITIES

The past two decades have witnessed a slow, yet progressive increase in writings on and by women with disabilities. Evidence of discrimination has been joined by empirical, fictional, and autobiographic writings on the sensational and the everyday topics of women's lives: joy, arguments, school and work, bodies, self-esteem, community life, wrestling with the law, relations with parents and lovers, community engagement, and political activity. Scholarly journals have, of recent, taken up the academic concerns specific to women with disabilities, such as the 1997 *Journal of Disability Policy Studies,* Vol. 8, (1) and (2), devoted to gender and disability policy and *Canadian Woman Studies* (Summer 1993 edition). In addition, we have witnessed a proliferation of personal narratives, autobiographies, and philosophical and political essays written by and about women with disabilities.

In 1981 Michelle Fine and Adrienne Asch wrote "Women with Disabilities: Sexism Without the Pedestal," which appeared in a special issue of the *Journal of Sociology and Social Welfare.* They reviewed what was then known about the economic, social, and psychological circumstances of women with disabilities. A year later, a group of women with disabilities proclaimed (see Footnote 2 for source):

Until recently, nobody talked much about being disabled. Especially disabled people. Most disabled people . . . were the last ones who wanted to point out that we were different. Well, times have changed. Now disabled people see that this silence has made it harder for us to figure out how to live our lives.

Jo Campling brought to public attention the private lives and stories of British women with disabilities; her book was hailed in the United States too because it spoke for long-silent U.S. women. That same year, Yvonne Duffy authored a significant book on sexuality as a key site for both oppression and ex-

pression by women with disabilities. Since that time, valuable personal accounts and interviews of women with disabilities have been published in Canada, the United States, and throughout the globe. (In addition to articles referenced here, see Deborah Kent's reviews of several books on women with disabilities, 1993, 1994, 1996, 1999.) Several women have written in depth and detail about how disabilities have affected their lives. In addition, there have been works of research and theory on several aspects of the lives of women with various disabilities and a few feminist theorists with disabilities have offered explicitly feminist accounts of the meaning of "disability" for women and men. The last several editions including the 1998 revision of the Boston Women's Health Book Collective classic on women's health attends sensitively and in detail to the concerns of girls and women with disabilities.

The 1990s witnessed the emergence of research that allowed women with a variety of disabilities, including the more recent writings by and about women with cognitive impariments and emotional and psychiatric disorders who wanted to express their wants and needs. These contributions have been particularly significant because they have helped to clarify the confusion created by collapsing all types of mental impairments into one category. In fact, the experiences and needs of women diagnosed with mental retardation may be markedly different from the needs of women diagnosed with Axis 1 psychiatric disorders, such as schizophrenia and bipolar disorder, who may or may not have a cognitive impairment.

The latter part of the 20th century witnessed a worldwide increase in conferences that addressed the topic of women and disability. These conferences included Beijing's 4th World Conference in 1995 on the status of women with disabilities in industrialized and developing countries; Washington DC's International Leadership Forum in 1997 to support the role of women with disabilities as leaders; The Center for Disease Control's Conference on the health and wellness of women with disabilities in San Antonio in 1999; Oakland's conference in 1999 to support funding for all women; Educational Equity Concept's conference, held in New York City in 1999, to update the manual *Building Community: A Manual Exploring Issues of Women and Disability,* which examines the connection between discrimination based on gender and discrimination based on physical disabilities; and the Institute for Basic Research in Developmental Disabilities' conference on parenting issues for women with mental retardation and their children held in Staten Island, New York in 1999.

IV. Internet Resources for Women with Disabilities

The Internet has rapidly become a source for potential research opportunities and a forum where women with physical and mental disabilities can share experiences and receive support. For example, the quarterly journal, *Dykes, Disability, & Stuff,* which can be accessed through its Web site at www.tps.stdorg.wisc.edu/MGLRC/Groups/Dykes-DisabilitiesStuff.html, focuses on health and disability issues for lesbians and also presents news, reviews, verse, art, and controversy with the perspective of the lesbian with an impairment. Additionally, one can post and view comments from female veterans who have physical and mental disabilities at www.geocities.com/CapitolHill/3726. The purpose of this site is to promote the equal treatment of women who are facing disability determination, due to a service-related impairment, within the Department of Veteran Affairs. There is also a Web site devoted to health and aging issues in women with physical and mental disabilities, which can be accessed at www.4women.gov/wwd. From the National Health Information Center, this site includes information on abuse, access to health care, breast health, financial assistance, laws and regulations, older women, minorities, and statistical information on women with various disabilities, including physical, neurological, hearing, speech, and visual impairment.

V. Deconstructing Myths: On Resistance

At the intersection of civil rights, disability rights, feminism, and lesbianism liberation, we witness a generation of women with disabilities who experience oppression still, but many of whom resist gender, race, and disability-based stereotypes and take pride in the identities they forge. Because of or despite their teachers, parents, and peers, they get an education and a job. They live independently, enjoy sex with men or women, become pregnant and carry to term if they choose, or abort if they prefer. They relish their friendships, intimacies, lovers, and activities. Some determine that they will play by the rules of achievement and succeed at meeting standards that are often deemed inaccessible to them. Some accept societal norms of attractiveness and enjoy the challenge of living up to them, impairment notwithstanding. Others choose to disregard anything that seems like "passing" and delight in their difference. Some women demand that the world accept them on their terms, whether those terms be insisting on signing rather than speaking, not covering their burn scars, not wearing clothing to hide parts of their bodies others may see as "ugly" or "deformed," or rejecting prostheses that inhibit and do not help. Girls and women with disabilities are, indeed, everywhere. Demanding that feminist organizations generate a politic that includes disability rights; demanding that their civil rights organizations and churches take on questions of special education and accommodations; and insisting that lesbian and gay centers, battered women's centers, martial arts centers, and abortion clinics design their spaces and practices toward accessibility. There is indeed a legacy of struggle and a growing chorus of voices of resistance.

Turning back two decades, we remember Audre Lorde, who following her mastectomy, refused to wear a prosthetic breast: "On the day after the stitches came out . . . I got so furious with the nurse who told me I was bad for the morale of the office because I did not wear a prosthesis." Likewise, Diane, a quadri-amputee interviewed by Gelya Frank also refused her prostheses in the 1980s because "I knew it would add more sweat, and more asthma, because I would have to work harder with it. So I always saw my body as something that was mine, and something that was free, and I hated anything kind of binding."

More recently, Michele, a 17-year-old Hispanic high school student, explained that she wore her prosthetic arms only to her doctor's appointments. "They are clumsy," she said, "I could manage to do things much more easily without them." Michele was perfectly comfortable having people see her short and "deformed" arms.

Recently a mother with mental retardation who spoke at the Parents with Intellectual Impairment Conference held at the New York State Institute for Basic Research in October 1998 reminded her audience:

"If you want to know what we need, just ask us. We'll tell you. We're adults."

And Eli Claire wrote in *Exiled Pride: Disability, Queerness, and Liberation:*

People who have lived in shame and isolation need all the pride we can muster, not to mire ourselves in a narrowly defined identity politics, but to sustain broad-based rebellion. And likewise, we need a witness to all our histories, both collective and personal. Yet, we also need to remember that witness and pride are not the same. Witness pairs grief and rage with remembrance. Pride pairs joy with a determination to be visible.

VI. Conclusions

The literature on disability and gender has grown substantially since the 1980s, but unfortunately it has remained narrowly self-contained. It is very significant that this encyclopedia entry has been invited on the topic of gender and disability. Indeed, a rich and exciting field of disability studies is emergent. There has, nevertheless, been a reluctance on the part of traditional disciplinary scholars and even women studies scholars to embrace disability as a rich field for intellectual inquiry. Both scholars and practitioners have been slow to introduce disability-based analyses into their research and practice; have been reluctant to shift from disability as biology to disability as a civil rights issues; and have been even more reticent to work at the intersections of gender, race, ethnicity, class, sexual preference, and disability. We ask that readers investigate whether or not issues of disability have been infused throughout this encyclopedia, for example, in areas of achievement, mental health, motherhood, work and family. Only when disability is infused will scholarship be considered adequate to the complexity of women's and men's lives.

SUGGESTED READING

Americans with Disabilities Act of 1990. 42 U.S.C. 12101–12213 (Supp. II 1990).

Asch, A., with Rousso, H., and Jefferies, T. (in press). Beyond Pedestals: The Lives of Girls and Women with Disabilities. In H. Rousso and M. Wehmeyer (eds.) *Double Jeopardy: Addressing Gender Equality in Special Education Supports and Services.* SUNY Press, New York.

Department of Education (1998). To assure the free appropriate public education of all children with disabilities. Twentieth annual report to Congress on the implementation of the Individuals with Disabilities Education Act, Disabilities Rights Education and Defense Fund (DREDF) (1982). U.S. Government Printing Office, Berkeley, CA.

Dreidger, D., and Gray, S. (1992). *Imprinting Our Image: An International Anthology of Writings by Women with Disabilities.* Gynergy Books, Charlottetown, Prince Edward Island, Canada.

Fine, M., and Asch, A. (eds.) (1988). *Women with Disabilities: Essays in Psychology, Culture, and Politics.* Temple University Press, Philadelphia.

Groce, N. (1997). Women with disabilities in the developing world: arenas for policy revision and programmatic change. *Journal of Disability Policy Studies* **8,** (1 and 2), 177–193.

Holburn, S., Perkins, T. S., and Vietze, P. M. (2001). The parent with mental retardation. *The International Journal of Research in Mental Retardation* **24,** 171–204.

Jans, L., and Stoddard, S. (1999). *Chartbook on Women and Disability in the United States.* An InfoUse Report. U.S. Department of Education, National Institute on Disability and Rehabilitation Research, Washington, DC.

Walker, S. (1991). Building bridges to empowerment for minority students with disabilities. *OSERS News in Print* **III**(4), 6–9.

Waxman Fiduccia, B., and Wolfe, L. R. (1999). *Women and Girls with Disabilities: Defining the Issues. An Overview.* Center for Women Policy Studies and Women and Philanthropy, Washington, DC.

Women and disability: Health and aging. Web site: www.4women.gov/wwd

Divorce and Child Custody

Katherine M. Kitzmann

Noni K. Gaylord

University of Memphis

Glossary

Alimony An allowance made to one spouse by the other for financial support pending or after legal separation or divorce.

Child support An allowance made to one spouse by the other to provide for the financial support of children pending or after legal separation or divorce.

Divorce The dissolution of a marriage contract between a man and a woman, by a judge's order or by an act of a state legislature.

Legal custody The right to make or share in making important decisions about a child's upbringing and care. In sole legal custody, only one parent is allowed to make decisions on the child's behalf. In joint legal custody, both parents have a voice in decision making.

Mediation An approach to dispute resolution in which a neutral third party helps disputants to negotiate an agreement that is satisfactory to both parties.

No-fault divorce The ability of a spouse to request that the conditions of marriage be dissolved, without having to prove that the other spouse is at fault and often without having to obtain the other spouse's consent.

Physical custody The responsibility of taking care of a child in one's home. In sole physical custody, the child lives with one parent but may have visitation with the other parent. In joint physical custody, the child splits time between the two parents' households, spending at least 30% of the time with each parent.

DIVORCE is a significant life stressor for many adults and children. This article will consider reasons for the high divorce rates in Western society, the psychological and economic impact of divorce on adults and children, divorce-related changes in parenting and family relationships, the risks and benefits of various child custody arrangements, resources available to divorcing families, and current policies affecting families of divorce.

I. *Current Relevance of Divorce and Child Custody Issues*

Divorce rates in the United States reached historically high levels in the 1980s, making divorce a normative experience in U.S. society. At least half of recent marriages are expected to end in divorce, and about 60% of these involve children. Although the divorce rates in the United States are the highest in the world, many other countries have also experienced a surge in divorce in recent decades, resulting in increased public and scientific concern both about the causes of divorce and about the effects of divorce on adults, children, families, and society.

Divorce can be a significant life stressor for adults, and the problems associated with divorce are magnified in couples with children. Divorce often entails multiple transitions, including changes in living arrangements, family relationships, and economic status. Often the family is still adjusting to divorce when a parent remarries, a transition that presents its own set of stressors. Although most adults and children eventually make a good adjustment to divorce, divorce is nevertheless associated with an increased risk for psychological problems in adults and children, higher rates of involvement in therapy, and a drop in the economic status of women and children. Compared to children from nondivorced families, children whose parents divorce also complete fewer years of education and are at a higher risk for divorce themselves.

One of the primary ways that divorce affects family life is through its impact on the parenting of children, beginning with decisions about custody. More than a quarter of all families in the United States today are led by divorced, single parents. The most common custody arrangement is for the mother to have sole physical custody of the child, with visitation by the father. Researchers and policy makers alike are interested in questions related to the implications of these custody arrangements for children's well-being.

II. *Divorce as a Process Rather Than an Event*

Legally, divorce refers to a specific event—a court ruling that dissolves the conditions agreed on in a legalized marriage. In the study of family life, however, divorce is better conceptualized as a process of transitions in family relationships. For example, in 1991 Andrew Cherlin and colleagues reported results from longitudinal research on more than 17,000 families in the United States and Britain, showing that much of the distress observed *after* divorce actually begins years *prior to* the divorce. In addition, results from the Virginia Longitudinal Study of Divorce, conducted by E. Mavis Hetherington and colleagues, suggest that disruptions in family life continue for several years after the divorce event. Most adults and children make a good adjustment to divorce by the two-year mark, but because most divorced adults remarry, and because divorce rates are even higher in second marriages, many adults and children actually undergo multiple divorce-related transitions.

Divorce usually involves a significant change in family structure—that is, a change in the number and configuration of people in the household. However, numerous studies suggest that it is the quality of family relationships and the family's ability to cope with life transitions, not family structure, that is most predictive of the family members' post-divorce adjustment. For example, research has shown that members of nondivorced high-conflict families are comparable to members of divorced families in terms of psychological problems. This suggests that the psychological problems have more to do with the level of conflict in the family (which is high in both groups) than the family structure per se. In addition, while it is true that single parents face more challenges than do parents with partners, "single-parent status" is not as helpful a concept as is parenting quality in predicting children's outcomes.

The focus on family processes rather than family events or family structure is especially important in light of evidence that "alternative family forms" are becoming normative in the United States. According to the U.S. Census Bureau, in 1999 only about 68% of American children lived with their two biological or adoptive parents. As divorce rates have increased in the United States, there have also been significant increases in the number of couples living together without marrying, births to single mothers, and families headed by gay and lesbian couples. This variability in family forms highlights the fact that stressors often associated with divorce—for example, parents breaking up, single parenting, and custody issues—are not unique to divorcing families.

III. History of Divorce in Western Society

For much of European history, divorce was prohibited by the Catholic Church. After the Protestant Reformation, the regulation of divorce came to be overseen by the government rather than the church, but was still restricted to cases of adultery, cruelty, or heresy. Divorce was also rare in the early years of the American colonies. In the 20th century, however, there was a significant rise in the number of people filing for divorce, and judges began to interpret divorce laws more broadly.

In the United States, divorces are typically granted for one of two reasons. First, the courts in nearly all states have power to give a divorce decree in cases where the marriage was not entered into legally. These include cases in which one partner is already married, the partners have a degree of biological relatedness that is forbidden by law, one or both of the partners is mentally disabled and incapable of making a contract, or the contract was entered into as a consequence of fraud. Second, a marriage may be dissolved by divorce for causes that have arisen since the formation of the contract, such as adultery, cruelty, or desertion. In some states, conviction of a felony or habitual drunkenness can also be sufficient cause for divorce.

In 1970 California passed the first "no-fault" divorce law, allowing a spouse to obtain a divorce without having to prove fault and without having to obtain the partner's consent. By 1985, all 50 states had no-fault divorce laws, although many states continued to provide the option of fault divorce. Typically the only requirement of no-fault divorce is that the couple live separately for a period of between six months to three years, although some states also require mutual consent for the divorce. Canada, Australia, and many European countries also have introduced no-fault divorce laws in the past decades.

IV. Prevalence

A. CURRENT PREVALENCE IN THE UNITED STATES

Demographers have predicted that approximately one-half of first marriages of the baby boom generation (children born between the end of World War II and the early 1960s) and about four in ten "Generation X" marriages (children born in the late 1960s and 1970s) will end in divorce, suggesting that divorce is becoming normative in United States society. In 1997, there were 1,163,000 divorces and annulments in the United States, and the total number of divorced adults in the United States is approximately 19 million, or 10% of the population. Despite the high divorce rate, Americans do not appear to have given up on marriage. Most divorced adults—three out of four divorced men and two out of three divorced women—eventually remarry. In addition, although more and more couples cohabitate before marriage and are delaying marriage, it is common for at least one partner to view cohabitation as a preparation or test trial for marriage.

Approximately 60% of contemporary divorces in the United States involve children. Estimates are that 1 million children are exposed to divorce every year, and nearly half of children will experience their parents' divorce before age 18. In most cases, children are typically very young when their parents divorce. About 40% of divorces involving children occur when children are under 2 years old, and another 25% occur when children are between the ages of 2 and 6.

B. CHANGES IN U.S. PREVALENCE OVER TIME

The increasing incidence of divorce in the United States in the 1960s and 1970s reflects not only recent developments, but also a broad historical trend that has lasted for more than 100 years. This trend, represented in Figure 1, reflects a steady increase in divorce rates since the late 1800s. In 1867, the annual divorce rate was 0.3 divorces per 1000 population. By 1981, the rate had peaked at 5.3 per 1000 before stabilizing and trending downward to 4.3 per 1000 population in 1997. Provisional data from the National Center for Health Statistics indicate that the divorce rate for 1999 has decreased slightly to 4.1 per 1000.

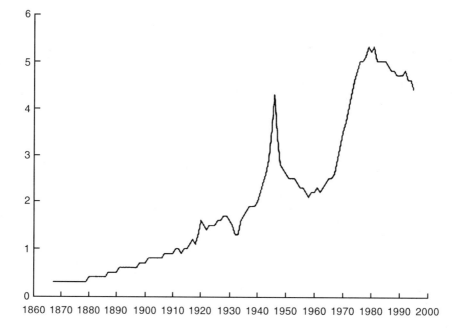

Figure 1   Annual U.S. divorce rates per 1000 population, 1867 to 1990. From *Marriage, Divorce, and Children's Adjustment, 2nd Edition* (p. 13), by Robert E. Emery, copyright 1999. Reprinted with permission of Sage Publications.

Several important exceptions to this overall trend should be noted. The first was a drop in both marriage rates and divorce rates during the Great Depression. The second was a dramatic increase in marriages right before World War II and a subsequent dramatic increase in the number of divorces right after the war. The third exception was the 1950s, a period of unusually strong dedication to marriage following the high divorce rates of the 1940s. The 1960s and 1970s saw a return to the overall pattern of steady increases in divorce rates documented during the past hundred years.

C. VARIATION IN U.S. PREVALENCE DEPENDING ON ETHNICITY

Divorce rates in the United States vary substantially according to ethnicity and race. The highest yearly divorce rates are found among African Americans, followed by Hispanics, then Caucasians. Asian Americans typically have the lowest divorce rates in the United States. In addition, both African Americans and Hispanics are less likely than Caucasians to remarry after divorce. According to the U.S. Census Bureau, these differences remain even after controlling for other factors such as education level and parents' history of divorce. However, it should be noted that there are significant differences within subgroups. For example, within the Hispanic community, divorce rates for Puerto Ricans are about twice as high as those for Mexican Americans.

Ethnic differences in divorce rates are also important to consider when making estimates of the number of children affected by parental divorce. Data from the U.S. Census Bureau show that about 40% of Caucasian children and about 20% of African American children experience parental divorce before turning 16. Thus, despite the higher divorce rate among African Americans, fewer African American children are affected by divorce because the majority (70%) of African American children in recent cohorts have been born to single mothers.

D. PREVALENCE AROUND THE WORLD

Divorce rates in the United States are the highest in the world, but other countries have also experienced a rise in divorce in recent decades. Most notable among these are Canada, Australia, China, Russia, Cuba, and many European nations. In general, countries in Africa and in South America have the lowest rates of divorce. Rates in the Middle East, Europe, and Asia vary significantly from country to country.

V. *Predictors of Divorce*

A. SOCIETAL INFLUENCES

Variation in divorce rates observed among racial and ethnic groups in the United States, and in divorce rates around the world, suggests that a couple's decision to divorce is influenced in part by the sociocultural context in which they live. In the United States, the lower divorce rates during the Great Depression and higher divorce rates after the introduction of no-fault divorce laws provide two examples of such sociocultural influences on divorce. In addition, changes in women's roles and access to resources in U.S. society also appear to have influenced divorce rates. After World War II, many men returned home to find that their wives had attained a new level of independence in the workforce, a societal change that proved to be a contributing factor in the high divorce rates after the war. In the 1970s, the women's movement motivated women to exit inequitable and abusive marriages; more women than men, for example, initiated divorce during this period. Women's incomes have also risen since the 1970s, in part because of the greater educational opportunities made possible by Title IX, including the 1972 Women's Educational Equity Act. Today, couples may be less likely to stay in unhappy marriages if they believe that women are better able than they were in the past to survive economically without a husband. Finally, historians have noted that modern romanticism about marriage, reflected in the ideal of marrying for love, may create unrealistic expectations about long-lasting romance, making modern-day couples more prone to disappointment in marriage.

B. LIFE CYCLE INFLUENCES

Young couples have a higher risk for divorce than couples who marry later, with the divorce rate being two to four times higher among women who marry before age 20 compared to those who marry after age 30. Regardless of the age at which the couple marries, the risk for divorce is greatest early in marriage. Divorce rates are especially high in couples who experience a premarital pregnancy or out-of-wedlock birth. In general, couples who conceive and have children after marriage are slightly less likely to divorce than are childless couples, but this protective factor depends on the children's age. Families with preschoolers have divorce rates about half those seen in childless couples who have been married the same amount of time. For families with school-age children, divorce rates are about equal to those of childless couples, and adolescents in the home may actually increase the risk for divorce. Most divorced adults remarry, and as in first marriages, the birth of children within the remarriage increases its stability. However, the risk for divorce in second marriages is about 10% higher than in first marriages.

C. RELATIONSHIP INFLUENCES

Research by John M. Gottman has shown that certain conflict resolution styles predispose couples to marital dissolution. Interestingly, what appears to distinguish stable from unstable couples is not so much the level of negativity, but the ratio of positive to negative behaviors. Couples in stable marriages show a ratio of about five positive behaviors for every negative behavior, whereas couples in unstable marriages show slightly more negative than positive behaviors. Although constructive forms of marital conflict may actually promote growth in the relationship, certain styles of managing conflict—what Gottman has called "the four horsemen of the Apocalypse"—can be especially destructive. Specifically, wives' criticism and husbands' defensiveness, contempt, and stonewalling are predictive of marital separation and divorce.

D. INDIVIDUAL INFLUENCES

Adults who experienced their parents' divorce in childhood have a 25 to 50% higher divorce rate than those whose parents never divorced. In addition, individuals who cohabitate have a higher risk for divorce, whether they go on to marry the person with whom they cohabitated or marry someone else. This association is thought to be due in part to a selection effect, in that individuals who choose to cohabitate may be more accepting of divorce and less committed to marriage, compared to those who never cohabitate.

In general, psychiatric problems are also associated with an increased risk for divorce, in part because of selection factors in marriage. That is, adults with psychiatric problems have a higher likelihood of marrying someone who also has problems, producing even more marital stress. Both antisocial behaviors and depression have received research attention in this regard. Antisocial behavior is more common in men than women and includes risk-taking behaviors, criminality, substance abuse, and aggression, all of which are associated with an increased risk for divorce. Similarly, depression, which is more common in women than men, is thought to be both a contributor to and a consequence of marital problems.

VI. *Impact of Divorce on Adults*

A. PSYCHOLOGICAL AND PHYSICAL PROBLEMS

Although most divorced adults do not show psychiatric problems, as a group they do show an increased risk for some psychological disorders, most notably depression and alcohol abuse. Even when their problems are not severe enough to require psychological treatment, many divorced adults show milder levels of distress in the form of painful emotions of sadness, anger, guilt, and remorse. Many also report problems of social isolation and loneliness. Because of the multiple losses involved, many clinicians think of the transition to divorce as a period of grief. Like adults who are grieving or experiencing other significant life stressors, divorcing adults, especially men, are also susceptible to compromised immune system functioning and associated physical illness.

Despite the general increased risk for problems during the divorce transition, there is great variability in how adults respond to divorce. For some, divorce brings relief and excitement about the termination of a difficult marriage. Adults' adjustment to divorce may also depend on whether they "left" or "were left." When one partner decides to leave the marriage, he or she may have already started the process of acceptance of the loss of the marriage by the time the other partner learns of the impending divorce. When separation occurs, the partner who leaves the marriage may already have worked through some of the early stages of adjustment, which the other partner is just beginning to experience.

Several factors influence adults' post-divorce psychological adjustment. For noncustodial fathers who want to maintain a close relationship with their children, lack of contact with children is associated with higher levels of distress. For custodial mothers, having responsibility for more than two children, especially young children, is associated with greater feelings of depression. Social isolation also contributes to maladjustment among divorced adults. Although remarriage to a supportive partner is typically associated with a significant decline in loneliness and depression, remarriage also often creates new stressors, especially when children are involved.

B. INVOLVEMENT IN THERAPY

Most adults who go through a divorce do not seek the help of a mental health professional. Nevertheless, men and women going through divorce seek therapy at rates that are about 2 to 3 times higher than those seen in married adults. Adults seek therapy during this transition both to address individual problems of adjustment and to get help dealing with issues related to parenting, parent–child relationships, and children's problems.

C. ECONOMIC IMPACT OF DIVORCE

In most cases, divorce lowers the family's standard of living because running two households is more expensive than running one. However, women typically withstand a greater proportion of this drop in resources. Results from the Michigan Panel Study of Income Dynamics, based on national data collected in the 1980s, showed that by one year after divorce, women's income had dropped to 91% of their predivorce standard of living, but men's income had risen to 113% of their predivorce resources. Five years after a divorce, women who had not remarried still had only 94% of their prior income, whereas divorced women who remarried had 125%, divorced men had 130%, and couples who remained married had 130% of their earlier income.

Several factors contribute to sex differences in postdivorce economic status. First, women on average have less work experience and typically earn less money than men. This is important because fewer than 15% of divorced women receive alimony, and spousal support represents less than 2% of single mothers' income. Alimony is often considered short-term support until the woman can establish her own source of income, either through work or remarriage. Second, mothers typically have additional costs associated with child custody, and child support constitutes less than 20% of divorced mothers' income on average. This is true in part because only about two-thirds of divorced women have a child support agreement in place. In cases where there is an agreement, only about half of mothers receive the full amount owed, and a quarter receive nothing at all. In 1991, for example, $5.8 billion of child support was unpaid. However, although some of the sex differences in postdivorce economic status can be attributed to costs associated with child custody, research comparing custodial fathers to custodial mothers shows that these sex differences remain even when custody arrangements are taken into account. Whereas custodial fathers suffer on average a 10% decline in income following divorce, custodial mothers experience about a 25 to 45% loss in annual family income.

D. INCREASED RISK FOR SECOND DIVORCE

Although remarriage can offer significant benefits in terms of adults' psychological adjustment and the economic security of women and children, second marriages are even more likely to end in divorce, with divorce rates about 10% higher than in first marriages. This risk for divorce is twice as high in families of remarried wives compared to families of remarried husbands. In part, this is because remarried wives often bring children to the new marriage, and the presence of children from a previous marriage increases the rate of divorce in remarriages by about 50%.

VII. *Impact of Divorce on Children*

A. EMOTIONAL AND BEHAVIORAL PROBLEMS

Like adults, most children are resilient in the face of divorce-related stress. Nevertheless, children from divorced families are more likely than children from nondivorced families to show both externalizing behaviors (conduct problems and aggression) and internalizing problems (sadness and anxiety), especially during the first two years after divorce. Conduct problems are the most common, especially in young children. However, the difference between children's problems in divorced and nondivorced families tends on average to be small, with great overlap between the two groups.

B. ACADEMIC PROBLEMS

Compared to children from married families, children from divorced families show slightly lower standardized test scores and grades and have more misconduct in the classroom and suspensions from school. Children from divorced families also complete fewer years of education and are twice as likely to drop out of school as children from married fam-

ilies. These effects can be attributed in part to the disruptive impact of multiple transitions on children's ability to learn and to the fact that single parents have less time to help children with homework and to keep in touch with teachers. However, the economic strains of divorce appear to be even more influential in predicting children's academic outcomes. Adolescents living with divorced single mothers have more economic incentives to work rather than complete high school, and they have also have fewer economic resources available for college.

C. SOCIAL COMPETENCE

Little research has been conducted on the effects of divorce on children's social competence. For some children, divorce many be associated with self-consciousness and a loss of self-esteem. For others, changes in family life may require children to assume responsibilities at an earlier age than peers. These children may appear more mature than other children, but research has shown that children with excessive maturity demands are more prone to depression in adult life.

D. INVOLVEMENT IN THERAPY

Although most children of divorce do not receive psychological services, children from divorced families are nevertheless two to three times more likely to receive mental health services than children from nondivorced families. Although this number may reflect parental overconcern, it also reflects the distress that many children experience during the transition to divorce. Therapy can help treat problems such as conduct disorder and feelings of depression and anxiety, but can also help children deal with milder forms of distress related to divorce adjustment.

E. LONG-TERM EFFECTS OF DIVORCE ON CHILDREN

Research conducted by Paul R. Amato suggests that compared to children whose parents remain married, children whose parents divorce are at higher risk for several types of problems in adulthood. First, these adults show more depression and more life dissatisfaction than adults whose parents remained married. Second, these adults—most of whom are raised in mother-custody families—tend to have poorer quality relationships with their fathers. Third, they enter adulthood with less education, both because of the lower economic resources available to divorced mothers and because of divorce-related disruptions in children's educational experiences. Lower educational attainment in turn is associated with lower incomes and fewer financial assets in adulthood. Finally, adults whose parents divorced have poorer quality marriages and are more likely to divorce themselves, with the risk ranging from a 25 to 50% increase in divorce rates.

F. CHILD CHARACTERISTICS THAT MODERATE CHILDREN'S POST-DIVORCE ADJUSTMENT

Child gender, age, and temperament appear to interact to affect the trajectory of children's post-divorce adjustment. Early research suggested that parental divorce was more difficult for boys than for girls, but recent research finds fewer gender differences than in the past. Although boys are more likely than girls to show problems in social adjustment after divorce, there are few other consistent sex differences. Other research suggests that compared to boys, girls have a more difficult time with the transition to the mother's remarriage, especially when the daughter has become closer to the mother after the divorce.

It is difficult to determine if one age group is more vulnerable than others, because children's age is confounded with other factors such as time since divorce. Preschoolers are often assumed to be at greater risk than are other children, because children of this age group are old enough to have some awareness of what is happening but may have limited coping skills and a limited understanding of what divorce means. However, the largest differences between children from divorced and nondivorced families are found in studies of elementary school and high school children. Older children may also show more difficulties than younger children in coping with a parent's remarriage, in part because the addition of a stepparent may exacerbate the child's struggle with issues of autonomy.

Finally, children who have easy temperaments, who are intelligent, socially mature, and responsible and who exhibit fewer behavior problems are better able to cope with their parents' marital transitions. This is true in part because these children are more likely to evoke positive responses from others and to maximize the use of available resources that help them cope with family stress. Children with difficult temperaments or behavior problems may elicit negative responses from their parents and may have more difficulty obtaining the support of people around them.

G. THEORIES ABOUT WHY CHILDREN ARE NEGATIVELY AFFECTED BY DIVORCE

E. Mavis Hetherington and colleagues have summarized five perspectives on why divorce is associated with an increased risk for children's adjustment problems. First, some children may have characteristics—such as difficult temperament—that make them more vulnerable to the effects of stress, including the effects of divorce. Second, children may be negatively affected by the loss of contact with their father after divorce. A third perspective is that divorce entails a significant change in economic status that is stressful for families, even when prior economic status is taken into account. Fourth, children may be negatively affected by their parents' high levels of psychological distress after the divorce. Finally, children's negative outcomes may be due to the effects of interparental conflict and disrupted parenting that often accompany divorce. No one factor in isolation is likely to explain children's divorce-related adjustment. Rather, these factors probably interact with each other in complex ways to influence child outcomes.

H. RESILIENCE OR IMPAIRMENT?

Clearly divorce is associated with increased risks for children's adjustment problems, but the extent of these risks has been the topic of debate. On one side are those such as Judith Wallerstein who believe that the deleterious effects of divorce on children are substantial and long lasting. This point of view is frequently expressed in the public media and is consistent with clinicians' reports of the negative impact of divorce on the lives of many therapy patients. On the other side of the debate are researchers who have suggested that the effects of divorce on children have been overstated. These researchers note that children are able to adapt to stress, and although divorce is a significant stressor associated with multiple transitions, most children adapt well and emerge as well-adjusted adults.

These seemingly opposite viewpoints are not necessarily incompatible. Researchers who use objective measures of psychopathology typically do not find large differences between children from divorced and nondivorced families, but these measures are not useful for detecting more subtle forms of distress that may be more easily recognized during clinical interviews. Robert E. Emery, a leading researcher on divorce, has proposed that the best approach is one that uses a combination of methods to assess both clinical disorders and milder forms of distress.

VIII. *Impact of Divorce on Family Relationships*

Although divorce terminates a married couple's legal union, it does not necessarily terminate the former spouses' relationship or parent–child relationships. These relationships do undergo significant change, however, during the transition to divorce. For many families, there is even further change in these relationships during subsequent transitions to remarriage and the formation of stepfamilies.

A. RELATIONSHIPS BETWEEN FORMER SPOUSES

Many couples continue to have contact with each other after divorce, especially when children are involved. Although some ex-spouses are able to form a new, cooperative relationship, others experience a great deal of conflict and distress. In some cases, this postdivorce conflict is due to one or both ex-spouses having problems accepting the end of the marriage. Finding emotional closure about the divorce can be especially difficult in cases where the divorce was preceded by multiple separations and reunions. In addition, because couples rarely reach a mutual decision to end their relationship, the two partners may have different levels of acceptance of the end of the marriage, contributing to ongoing negative feelings and post-divorce conflict.

Children make a better adjustment to divorce when their parents are able to cooperate as coparents. However, data from a 1992 study conducted by Eleanor Maccoby and Robert H. Mnookin showed that one and a half years after marital separation, only about a quarter of couples could be described as cooperative. A third of couples still had significant conflict, and another quarter were disengaged. Conflict declined over time, but was replaced with disengagement. Even among couples who were trying to raise their children in joint custody, about a quarter had high levels of conflict throughout the first three years after the separation.

B. CHANGES IN PARENTING AND PARENT–CHILD RELATIONSHIPS

Even several years after the divorce, parents and children have less positive relationships in divorced families than in married families. Residential parents who are depressed, who are cut off from support networks, who have more severe economic concerns, or who have a number of young children are more likely to have difficulties as parents, and these difficulties affect parent–child relationships.

After divorce, residential mothers and children may become closer or more distant as a result of the mother's own emotional needs, the mother's perceptions of what the children need, and loyalty dilemmas in the parent–child–parent triad. As in married families, children in divorced families fare best when their parents are authoritative. However, in part because of the stresses associated with single parenting, divorced mothers on average are less authoritative, less warm, and less effective in discipline compared to married mothers. Divorced mothers also give their children more responsibility at home, and some researchers have noted problems with parent–child role reversals, especially in mother–daughter relationships.

In most cases the father is the nonresidential parent, and in many cases the termination of the marriage brings a significant drop in father–child contact. Although father–child contact tends to be higher right after the marital separation, it declines over time. For example, a recent survey found that about a third of divorced fathers saw their children only once or not at all during the previous year, about 40% saw their children a few times a month or less, and about a quarter saw their children once a week or more. Fathers who want to stay involved with their children sometimes report feeling lonely and isolated because of the loss of contact. Many children of divorce, even as adults, express disappointment that their fathers were not more involved in their lives. [*See* FAMILY ROLES AND PATTERNS, CONTEMPORARY TRENDS.]

C. CUSTODY ARRANGEMENTS

In custody decisions, a distinction is made between physical custody (where the child lives) and legal custody (who makes important decisions on the child's behalf). According to data collected by the National Center for Health Statistics in 1990, nearly three-quarters (72%) of divorced mothers were granted physical custody of children, and fathers were awarded custody in 9% of cases. Joint physical custody, with children dividing their time at least 30/70 between the two parents, was awarded in 16% of cases. Split custody (with siblings being separated from each other) was awarded in 2% of cases, and children were placed with someone other than a parent in 1% of cases. Although most mothers have physical custody, joint legal custody is the norm in most states, meaning that both parents share responsibility for making important decisions regarding the child.

Because of the small number of father-custody households, it is difficult to draw research conclusions about whether mother- or father-custody is preferable for children. The small percentage of cases in which fathers are given custody tend to involve older children, especially boys. However, research indicates that in most cases it is the quality of the parent–child relationship, rather than the sex of the parent, that is important for predicting the success of the custody arrangement. Nevertheless, some older adolescents may fare better when placed with a same-sex parent.

Other research has addressed the question of whether it is better for one parent to have sole custody or for parents to share physical custody. Joint physical custody has several potential benefits, including higher involvement by fathers in children's lives. Although child support tends to be lower in cases of joint physical custody, fathers' compliance with these agreements also tends to be higher. In general, research has shown that children's psychological adjustment is about the same in sole physical custody and joint physical custody. However, an important exception must be emphasized. Because joint physical custody requires a significant amount of coordination between the two parents, couples who continue to have post-divorce conflict may have difficulty managing joint physical custody, and joint physical custody can have negative outcomes for children who are exposed to ongoing acrimony and conflict between parents.

D. THE IMPACT OF REMARRIAGE AND STEPPARENTING

Remarriage, especially to a supportive partner, can be associated with important benefits both for adults' psychological well-being and for children's standard of living. Nevertheless, the transition to living as a stepfamily presents difficulties. Many stepparents report feeling unsure about what role they should play in childrearing, and stepparents on average are less authoritative than biological parents. Decisions about discipline appear to be especially problematic, as rates of physical abuse by stepfathers are estimated to be seven times higher than rates of physical abuse by biological fathers.

Problems in the relationship between the stepparent and stepchild develop in part because children may view their stepparent as an outsider, reject the stepparent's attempt to exercise authority, and feel jealous of the emotional bond between the stepparent and the custodial parent. Because the most common form of stepfamily includes a biological mother and a stepfather, most research has focused on the relationship between stepfathers and children. Younger children may readily establish a positive relationship with a stepfather, but teenagers, especially girls, have more difficulty.

IX. Should Parents Stay Together for the Sake of the Children?

Many parents wonder whether it is better to remain in an unsatisfying, highly conflictual marriage for the sake of the children, or to divorce. Two lines of research have addressed this question. First, longitudinal research suggests that children whose parents eventually divorce actually show adjustment problems well before the divorce, suggesting that children's problems may be due to the marital conflict that *precedes* the divorce. Second, research comparing divorced families to high-conflict married families shows that children show similar levels of adjustment problems in both types of family. When divorce is associated with a move to a more harmonious, less stressful family environment, children in divorced families are similar in adjustment to children in nondistressed, nondivorced families.

However, for some families divorce creates even more conflict than was present during the marriage, and in these cases children show even more problems than children from high-conflict married families. Given the economic strains associated with divorce, it might be preferable in these cases for parents to remain in an unhappy marriage. Whether parents stay together or separate, their challenges are the same: to maintain close parent–child relationships, to provide effective discipline, and to minimize the child's exposure to poorly resolved interparental conflict.

X. Resources for Divorcing Families

Most couples are able to reach a divorce settlement on their own, without litigation, and most adults and children from divorcing families do not seek mental health services. Nevertheless, divorce is associated with conflict and psychological distress that is overwhelming to some families. In these cases, families often rely on lawyers, mediators, therapists, and support groups to assist them in the transition to divorce.

A. MEDIATION

Mediation is an increasingly common alternative to litigation for resolving divorce-related disputes, and in some jurisdictions, couples are mandated to try mediation before being allowed to litigate. In child custody mediation, mediators typically meet with the divorcing couple for between 1 and 20 sessions to promote cooperative negotiation during a time when communication is likely to be difficult. Custody decisions generally do not differ in mediation and litigation, but mediation is associated with higher participant satisfaction as well as faster resolution and fewer court hearings. Compared to fathers who litigate, fathers who mediate have been shown to be more compliant with child support responsibilities and to remain more involved in their children's lives. However, mediation has not been shown to be associated with any mental health benefits for adults or children, is not effective for all couples, and may be inappropriate for couples who have a history of domestic violence.

B. PSYCHOTHERAPY

Therapy can be an important source of social support during the divorce transition and can help family members cope with the emotional distress associated with the family disruption. Individual therapy can provide a safe environment in which family members can openly grieve the multiple losses inherent to divorce, problem-solve about how to cope with the divorce transition, and rectify their misconceptions about divorce. In addition, family therapy can be helpful during the transition to remarriage and stepparenting, a period in which family roles and rules can be in flux. In rare cases, family therapy is also used to help in cases of joint physical custody or frequent visitation with a noncustodial parent, to help parents learn to shelter their children from poorly resolved interparental conflict, and to provide consistent expectations and rewards in the two households. However, there has been no systematic evaluation of the effectiveness of family therapy involving exspouses and their children. [*See* FEMINIST FAMILY THERAPY.]

C. SUPPORT GROUPS AND WORKSHOPS FOR ADULTS

Support groups and group-based intervention programs typically involve 6 to 24 hours of group meetings addressing topics such as finding a new support system, feelings of isolation and lowered self-esteem, and running a household alone. These programs appear to be helpful in decreasing symptoms of depression and overall distress, with average improvement comparable to what is typically found in psychotherapy studies. Many divorcing parents also participate in educational workshops, sometimes by court order. Although there is high consumer satisfaction with the brief workshop format, there has been little research on these workshops' effectiveness. Workshops that have been evaluated with the use of a control group have shown few objective benefits.

D. SCHOOL-BASED PROGRAMS FOR CHILDREN

School-based group therapy programs for children of divorce typically last from 6 to 16 weeks and are designed to lessen children's feelings of isolation and loneliness, foster feelings of support and trust, and clarify children's misconceptions about divorce. In some cases, these groups are formed on an ad hoc basis when school counselors are working with several children from the same school who are showing divorce-related problems. In other cases, school personnel will notify parents of all children in the school that a group therapy program is starting and ask parents to refer their children to the group. Research suggests that these programs typically have modest results, considerably lower than the effectiveness of psychotherapy in general. Two high-quality exceptions are the Children of Divorce Intervention Project and the Divorce Adjustment Project. Children in these programs show significant improvements compared to control groups, in terms of emotional functioning, self-image, and behavior.

XI. *Current Policies Affecting Families of Divorce*

Since the first no-fault divorce laws were passed in the 1970s, divorce in the United States has increasingly been viewed as a private matter, outside the domain of government control. Nevertheless, the past two decades have also seen a proliferation of new policies and laws in recognition of the reality that both the process of reaching a divorce settlement and the terms of the settlement can have an important impact on family members' adjustment.

A. FINANCIAL SETTLEMENTS

In the past, property was divided in divorce settlements by giving each spouse any property for which the individual held title, resulting in inequitable distributions when much of the property was in one partner's name. Since the 1970s, laws have changed so that now all property acquired during the marriage is considered marital property, regardless of which partner has title. Increasingly, nonmonetary contributions to the acquisition of marital property, such as homemaking and child rearing, are taken into account in the distribution of property. In addition, whereas in the past it was common to sell the family home and divide the assets between the former spouses, it is becoming increasingly common for former spouses to share home ownership until the children are of age or until the residential parent remarries.

Because current guidelines for alimony settlements are vague, the American Law Institute has suggested more specific guidelines that take into account length of marriage, contributions in terms of homemaking and child rearing, and support provided by one partner while the other partner pursues an education. Federal legislation also has encouraged the use of formulas to determine child support, and other federal laws, including the Child Support Enforcement Amendments and the Family Support Act, have provided incentives to states to enforce child support agreements. States can garnish wages, intercept tax refunds, deny professional licenses and drivers' licenses, and charge the noncompliant parent with contempt of court. However, these efforts have had limited success, in part because of the low incomes of some nonresidential parents.

B. CUSTODY SETTLEMENTS

For most of modern history, fathers were given custody of children by virtue of their position as the "head of the family." In the 19th century, under the "tender years" presumption, young children began to be placed with their mothers, who were presumed to be more naturally oriented toward parenting. Eventually children of all ages began to be placed with mothers. However, the tender years presump-

tion is no longer built into U.S. laws, in part because of changing attitudes about the roles of men and women in child rearing. Currently, custody decisions are made based on the vague criterion of the child's best interests. This guideline is problematic, both because it is difficult to make reliable predictions about a child's future and because there is no consensus about how to decide what type of future is best for the child. In practice, custody is usually given to the parent who served as the primary caregiver before the divorce, which in most cases is the mother.

Many have expressed concern that the vagueness of child custody guidelines creates uncertainty for parents and encourages even more acrimony, as parents try to produce negative evidence about each other in order to win custody. For this reason, the American Law Institute has suggested the use of the "approximation rule" as a guideline for custody arrangements, stipulating that postdivorce arrangements approximate as close as possible the predivorce patterns of shared parenting. Some states have also begun to require parents to submit detailed plans of how they will coparent after the divorce, in part to minimize conflict in the coparenting relationship. In other cases, parents are court-ordered to attend weekend workshops addressing post-divorce parenting and the importance of sheltering children from conflict.

C. DISPUTE RESOLUTION

Recent decades have seen two important changes in policy about dispute resolution. First, a number of states and many local jurisdictions now require couples to attempt mediation before proceeding to court. Second, there has been an increasing reliance on guardians *ad litem* to represent children's interests and to act as independent fact finders. In some cases, children are asked to state their preferences about custody. The American Law Institute (ALI) has suggested that older children's expressly stated preferences should be taken into account in making custody decisions. At the same time, the ALI has expressed concern about asking children of any age to state a preference if they have not already expressed one, as this requirement would put undue stress on children and on family relationships.

XII. Conclusions

High divorce rates in the United States have prompted concern about the implications of divorce for families and society. However, the current high divorce rate appears to be part of a trend that began more than a hundred years ago, suggesting that there is probably no one explanation for the decreasing numbers of married families in U.S. society. Today, there is less of a focus on legal marriage as the defining characteristic of "family," and what used to be called "alternative family forms" are increasingly normative. As the divorce rate has risen, there also has been an increase in the number of families headed by never-married couples, by single parents, and by gay and lesbian couples. These families experience many of the same stressors and transitions that affect families of divorce, highlighting the need for research identifying family processes that influence family members' adjustment, regardless of family form.

SUGGESTED READING

Emery, R. E. (1994). *Renegotiating Family Relationships: Divorce, Child Custody, and Mediation.* Guilford Press, New York.

Emery, R. E. (1999). *Marriage, Divorce, and Children's Adjustment,* 2nd ed. Sage, Newbury Park, CA.

Hetherington, E. M. (ed.) (1999). *Coping with Divorce, Single Parenting, and Remarriage.* Erlbaum, Mahwah, NJ.

Hetherington, E. M., Bridges, M., and Insabella, G. M. (1998). What matters? What does not? Five perspectives on the association between marital transitions and children's adjustment. *American Psychologist* **53**, 167–184.

Thompson, R.A., and Amato, P.R. (Eds.) (1999). *The Post-Divorce Family: Children, Parenting, and Society.* Sage, Thousand Oaks, CA.

Wallerstein, J., Lewis, J., and Blakeslee, S. (2000). *The Unexpected Legacy of Divorce: A 25-Year Landmark Study.* Hyperion, New York.

Eating Disorders and Disordered Eating

Niva Piran

University of Toronto

I. Phenomenology and Epidemiology
II. Etiological Studies
III. Conclusions

Glossary

Anorexia Nervosa A behavioral and attitudinal cluster that involves the pursuit of thinness, a failure to maintain minimum weight, a fear of weight gain, body image disturbance, and a cessation of menstrual periods (related to weight loss).

Binge eating disorder A behavioral and attitudinal cluster that involves a pattern of recurrent and frequent binge eating behavior as well as distress over bingeing behavior.

Bulimia nervosa A behavioral and attitudinal cluster that involves recurrent episodes of binge eating, purging behaviors, and an emphasis on and dissatisfaction with body weight and shape.

Eating disorders Includes the diagnoses of *anorexia nervosa, bulimia nervosa,* and *eating disorders not otherwise classified.*

Eating disorders not otherwise classified A diagnostic category that includes diverse syndromes of disordered eating patterns (e.g., restriction or bingeing) and of different levels of severity that do not fulfill the clinical criteria of anorexia nervosa or bulimia nervosa. This diagnostic category includes the diagnosis of *binge eating disorder.*

Interoceptive awareness The ability to identify and communicate internal bodily and emotional experiences.

BODY WEIGHT AND SHAPE PREOCCUPATION and varied patterns of disordered eating are common among women who reside in North America. The rapid increase in the prevalence of the clinically diagnosed eating disorders of anorexia nervosa and bulimia nervosa in North America between the 1950s and the 1980s, the current increase in countries going through the process of Westernization, and the significant associated morbidity and mortality have created tremendous interest in their etiology. Further, the much higher prevalence of eating disorders among women than among men has placed gender as a key element in efforts to both understand and curtail this social epidemic. This article examines current knowledge about eating disorders in women by raising and addressing critical issues regarding epidemiology and etiological models.

I. Phenomenology and Epidemiology

Epidemiological studies of eating disorders, disordered eating, and body weight and shape preoccupation reveal a continuum of disruptions in women's

Encyclopedia of Women and Gender, Volume One

eating patterns and body dissatisfaction. This continuum ranges at one end from a low level of body dissatisfaction, through more intense negative body image and varied patterns of dieting and disordered eating, to extreme body dissatisfaction and a severe disruption in eating patterns including a marked intake restriction or regular bingeing and purging behaviors at the other end of the spectrum. The prevalence of body dissatisfaction and disordered eating patterns varies inversely according to severity of difficulties. Body dissatisfaction is common to most women residing in Western countries and has therefore been termed "normative discontent." Approximately 70% of high school girls in North America report dieting to lose weight despite being within the normal weight range. Bingeing is found among about a third of all women, with weekly bingeing in about 15% of them. Purging behaviors, such as vomiting for the sake of weight loss or laxative use, are found in about 8 to 15% of adolescent and young women. Bingeing and purging two times or more a week are found in about 2 to 3% of young women. At all levels of difficulty, adolescent girls experience far more weight concerns and related eating problems than do boys.

Body weight and shape preoccupation, patterns of disordered eating, and eating disorders are associated with morbidity at all levels of difficulty on the spectrum of disordered eating and therefore constitute a significant health issue for women. Even the most benign and socially sanctioned behavior of dieting has been found to be associated with negative impact on mood, work, and relationships. Progressing to the more severe end of the continuum, research has repeatedly documented the social, psychological, and medical complications associated with subclinical eating disorders. At the very end of the spectrum, eating disorders have been associated with severe complications, including death.

The *Diagnostic and Statistical Manual* (version IV), a North American classification system of psychiatric disorders published in 1994 by the American Psychiatric Association, identifies two particular "clinical" syndromes as well as a third, "other," category. The diagnosis of anorexia nervosa (AN) includes the features of pursuit of thinness, a failure to maintain minimum weight, fear of weight gain, body image disturbance, and a cessation of menstrual periods. AN occurs in two subtypes: restricting type and the binge-eating/purging type. The diagnosis occurs in about 0.5 to 1% of girls and women in the age range of 16 to 25. Bulimia nervosa (BN) involves recurrent episodes of binge eating (at least twice weekly), purging behaviors, and an emphasis on and dissatisfaction with body weight and shape. The *DSM-IV* describes two variants of BN: a purging and a nonpurging subtype. Bulimia nervosa occurs in about 2 to 5% of girls and women in the age range of 16 to 25. Prevalence studies indicate that clinical eating disorders are 10 times as common in women when compared with men. While the particular phenomenological expression may vary somewhat, eating disorders and disordered eating patterns seem to be as prevalent across socioeconomic groups and ethnocultural groups. The third, considerably larger, category in the DSM-IV, "eating disorder not otherwise specified (EDNOS), underscores the difficulty of creating dichotomous diagnostic categories within a phenomenological continuum found repeatedly in community-based studies. The EDNOS diagnosis includes most people who display disordered eating patterns. It represents diverse syndromes and ranges of severity. Some of the EDNOS conditions may overlap with, and be as persistent and associated with, a similar degree of morbidity as AN or BN. Further, the severity criteria that make up an aspect of the clinical diagnoses of AN and BN (as opposed to EDNOS) have not been validated.

The clinical diagnoses of AN and BN have been based on observations of clinical samples, rather than community samples. However, clinical samples may be quite divergent from community samples. Access to services, especially in large teaching and research hospitals, is often limited to more privileged, for example White or higher social class members of the broader community. Indeed, studies have shown that only a small minority of women in the community who would be clinically diagnosed with either AN or BN ever seeks professional help. Further, women in the community may tend to display an array of difficulties with body shape and eating not as commonly seen in clinical samples. For example, Black women have been found in some studies to display a lower prevalence of AN or BN, yet they show a higher prevalence of binge eating disorder (part of the EDNOS category of the *DSM-IV*). Moreover, since the North American diagnostic schema is inevitably affected by dominant societal values and mores, this schema may not reflect the cultural diversity held by members of the minority community. For example, Melanie Katzman and Sing Lee suggested in 1997 that particular anorexic patterns of self-starvation among Chinese women did not appear to involve the pursuit of thinness, a key diagnostic element in the North American based *DSM-IV* diagnoses. Alternatively, liposuction surgery, a popular yet not risk-free cosmetic surgery aimed at body shape alteration and the purging of body fat is not labeled as a pathological purging method, while vomiting or laxative use are.

The purpose of discussing discrepancies between the clinical diagnoses of AN and BN and the spectrum of diverse expressions of patterns of disordered eating and body dissatisfaction in the community is not to expand the range of clinical diagnoses and hence pathologize a yet wider spectrum of patterns held by women in the community. Rather, the goal is to suggest that patterns of disordered eating and body dissatisfaction are much more common and more diverse than the clinically diagnosed conditions and that they are associated with multiple risks. Community-based research that examines diverse expressions of problems in the body domain in multiple social contexts, as well as associated risks, has a special role in highlighting the magnitude of these challenges and their presentation as an important social issue. [*See* Diagnosis of Psychological Disorders.]

II. *Etiological Studies*

Similar to the professional exploration of the condition of "hysteria" in the Victorian era in Europe, time and research funding toward the understanding of eating disorders since the 1950s has been channeled to the study of biological, familial, and intraindividual psychological factors, while the social domain remained relatively unexplored until the past decade or so. This emphasis on individual biomedical and pathological factors was dictated by the location of study, typically a clinical setting, and by a dichotomous rather than a continuous view of disorders and risk factors. While leading to important information as discussed here, the exploration of biological, familial, and intraindividual factors has not yet led to the generation of powerful predictive models for the development of body weight and shape preoccupation and eating disorders. Research on social factors has proliferated during the past decade and has started to lead to the emergence of social variables that may hold promise for the development of predictive models in the understanding of body weight and shape preoccupation and eating disorders. Social research has allowed the study of the impact of gender as a social variable that may help explain the predominance of eating disorders among girls and women. Nonetheless, the discussion of etiological factors may reveal that within the context of powerful and multilayered social systems, the interaction of the social context with individual, familial, and biological factors may lead to the blurring of boundaries between the personal, biological, familial, and social. The discussion of etiological factors covers social, familial, intraindividual, and biological factors with a special emphasis on the social domain.

A. SOCIAL FACTORS

The examination of social factors that contribute to the development of a disorder is challenging in that it requires a critical look at existing social institutions and prejudices, a look that is challenging to societal status quo. The examination of the social meaning and practices associated with having a social and gendered body may reveal problematic social domains that likely require social transformation and action. In a recent publication, Richard Gordon described the definition of an "ethnic disorder," coined by Devereux in the 1950s, as "a pattern, that because of its own dynamics, has come to express crucial contradictions and core anxieties of a society" (p. 8). The definition of an ethnic disorder includes the following key criteria: a frequent occurrence and a spectrum of severity of the disorder, the disorder is a final common pathway to varied conditions of psychological distress as well as a vehicle and a "template" to the expression of core conflicts and tensions that are pervasive in the culture, and the symptoms are exaggerations of normal behaviors and attitude and they elicit highly ambivalent responses from others. It indeed appears that eating disorders fulfill these criteria. In a 1993 publication, Susan Bordo similarly described eating disorders as a "crystallization of culture." This article explores four main sources of knowledge that could help to explain the contribution of social factors to the development of eating disorders: knowledge derived in feminist psychotherapy practice, social critical theory, qualitative social research, and quantitative social research.

1. Social Knowledge Derived in Feminist Psychotherapy Practice

While psychotherapy has tended to emphasize intraindividual psychological and, at times, biological factors, a key aspect of feminist therapy comprises the contextualization of presenting difficulties in disruptive social structures of privilege and oppression and adverse social values and mores. Informed by their practice, feminist therapists have constructed social etiological theories that have highlighted the impact of women's social roles and power as well as objectification, relational experiences, and trauma to eating symptomatology. It is important to recognize that this knowledge is constrained by the accessibility of therapy mainly to relatively privileged women who mainly reside in Western countries and by its reliance on prevalent Western values.

The objectification of the female body was highlighted in a 1994 publication by Carol Bloom, Andrea Gitter, Suasn Gutwill, Laura Kogel, and Lela Zaphiropoulos. Expanding object relations theory, these authors examined the impact of women's relational attachment to cultural images and symbols. They suggested that the internalization by girls and women of the cultural objectification of women's bodies, desires, and appetites creates a state of disruption in women's subjective experience of their bodies and desires, which, in turn, impacts on their eating patterns and on their experience of their body.

Susie Orbach, who in 1996 examined women's right to nurturance by self and others, suggested that the restriction mothers experienced regarding their right to self nurturance was inevitably transmitted to their daughters, whose eating problems reflected this restriction. Orbach further examined thinness as an expression of ambivalence toward women's equitable participation in the public work and fatness as an expression of resistance.

In 1986 Catherine Steiner-Adair highlighted the role of disruption in girls' and women's relational needs and suggested that forced suppression of relational knowledge during the process of maturation causes girls to lose their confidence and sense of self, which they then try to restore through fitting into external idealized images of independent women. Feminist therapists such as Ann Kearney-Cook, Ruth Striegel-Moore, and Susan Wooley have examined the impact of sexual abuse on a woman's experience of her body and eating. The devaluation of women's bodies and of fat has been discussed extensively by feminist therapists such as Laura Brown and Catherine Steiner-Adair in 1989 and 1986, respectively.

2. Critical Social Perspectives

Critical social perspectives on women and their bodies can serve to expand the social lens through which eating disorders are examined, as well as guide and anchor social research in this area. A 1963 publication of Karl Marx presents the body as a political entity that reflects individuals' social position. In the same vein, Michel Foucault elaborated in a 1979 publication on individuals', mainly unconscious, learning about their social position, worth, and rights through experiences in the body domain. Individuals' complicity with expected body practices assures, according to Foucault, the maintenance of social institutions of privilege and power. Different feminist theorists have applied this understanding to various challenges that women face, especially in the body domain. For example, Susan Bordo in 1993 as well as Deborah Tolman and Elizabeth Debold in 1994 examined women's constriction of their own appetites and desires in order to fit in patriarchal social systems. In 1986 Adrienne Rich described the body as a politically inscribed domain. Its emancipation, she predicted, would bring massive changes to society. She particularly cautions to be aware of the connections between different phenomena that maintain inequitable "body relations", including the societal sanctioning of a spectrum of violence against women. [*See* FEMINIST THEORIES.]

Within inequitable social conditions women try to adopt various ways of survival. Constraining one's appetites and desires constitutes one way, constraining one's physical size constitutes another, as described by Laura Brown in 1989 and Susan Faludi in 1991. In 1991 Naomi Wolf elaborated on the adaptive function of the hypercritical self-gaze and assessment of fit between one's appearance and the idealized "look" in allowing access to new social opportunities for women. Joan Brumberg has contended in a 1989 publication that consumerism and mass marketing have intensified the construction of the body, especially women's bodies, as a "project" needing shaping and repair, resonating with the cultural deprecation of a full-size woman's body.

These critical social perspectives on women and body image have to be expanded to include the experience of members of diverse social backgrounds, socioeconomic status, and ethnocultural and racial membership. For example, in a 1994 publication, Becky Thompson suggested that privileging sexism over other oppressions and the overreliance on the culture-of-thinness model to explain eating disorders was problematic. Similarly Kim Shayo Buchanan contended in a 1993 publication that the preoccupation with self and body image may seem self-indulgent for Black women considering the prevalence of serious issues such as poverty, single parenthood, and discrimination. Black feminist theory has focused on the ways in which racism, sexism, and economic inequality are integral components of existing political and social institutions; it therefore keeps its focus on radically transforming relations of power, rather than women's bodies. Social transformations experienced by middle-class White women do not parallel the social experiences for Black women, Latinas, lesbians, and single mothers who were part of the labor market prior to the 1970s when new opportunities seemed to have opened for White middle- and upper-class women. Discussing the higher rates of obesity among Black women in 1992, Rosemary Bray highlighted the heavy emotional toll Black women are carrying in raising children alone, mostly in poverty, within the context of racism.

While idealized images of blond, thin, young, and White women do have an adverse impact on Black women's self- and body image, as Kim Shayo Buchanan suggested in 1993, body size may be secondary to skin color and hair texture. White supremacist ideology has made inequality seem natural and inevitable through associating "blackness" with inferior characteristics. Black people have therefore turned to chemical skin lighteners ("fade creams") and damaging hair "relaxers" in order to make them more employable and more likely to survive in the White culture. Within African culture, however, feminine beauty includes a heavier, fuller body, with female curves, which may provide some protection from the White ideal. In 1992, bell hooks suggested that the marginalization of Black women from the dominant cultural ideal, as well as their oppression within patriarchal, racist institutions, can give them more power to resist homogenizing influences and hold a critical, oppositional gaze.

In 1997, Barbara Fredrickson and Tomi-Ann Roberts proposed the objectification theory as a theory that could explain a host of mental health risks for women, including eating disorders. According to this theory, women are acculturated to internalize an observer's perspective as a primary view of their physical selves. This leads to habitual body monitoring, which increases anxiety and shame, affects motivational states, and diminishes awareness to internal bodily states. They further have suggested that the habit of self-conscious body monitoring can profoundly disrupt a woman's flow of consciousness and generates inevitable experiences of shame and, hence, withdrawal. The experience of heightened anxiety and monitoring also affects women's subjective states, intrinsic motivation, and immersion in physical or mental activity. The detection of internal physiological sensations is disrupted as well. These subjective alterations make women susceptible to a host of mental disorders, including eating disorders.

Niva Piran has proposed a related yet somewhat different theory, disrupted embodiment through inequity. This theoretical structure, based on a program of qualitative and quantitative research, suggests that the body is a key domain in the expression of social inequity. Social inequity in the body domain is expressed along three central dimensions: body ownership, prejudicial systems, and social constructions of the body, and leads to different levels of disembodiment. Disembodiment occurs when the body domain becomes associated with acute experiences of personal and social vulnerability, with negative feelings (such as fear, shame, or anger), and with internalized harsh or deprecating attitudes and practices. Disembodiment disrupts one's ability to practice self-care, silences internal dialogues, and disrupts relationships, while enhancing one's tendency to manage or control the body from the "outside." Within this context, it is hard to arrest the development of eating disorders or other self-harm behaviors. Regarding the dimension of disrupted body ownership, within an inequitable social system the body of the less privileged (such as women, visible minorities, and disabled people) is objectified, exploited, and constitutes a socially sanctioned target of a spectrum of violence. Similarly, within an inequitable social system, social prejudices against the less privileged often target the body, the one aspect that cannot be changed and, hence, "embodies" and "justifies" this uncontested "inequity" (for example, terms such as "bitch," "PMS," "dumb blonde," "whore," "brown cow," and "pig" deprecate women's bodies, the bodies of visible minority women, or fat people, respectively). Again, within inequitable social conditions, social constructions of individuals and their bodies tend to fit molds that will maintain the social status quo. For example, women will be equated with their appearance and not their power or instrumentality; they will be encouraged to take less space, to disown desire or appetites, and nurture others rather than the self. Social expressions of inequity in the body domain intensify in all three dimensions of ownership, prejudices, and social construction, during and following puberty. This intensification can relate to the onset of eating disorders and other self-harm behaviors and to the lowering of self-esteem among girls during and following puberty.

This disciplining of the bodies of women and minority group members comprises a political issue related to equity and oppression. A changed experience of women's bodies will have to be associated with larger social transformations.

3. Qualitative Social Research

Research on body weight and shape preoccupation that follows emergent qualitative methodologies anchored in women's voices and diverse life experiences has been limited. However, the few studies that have followed qualitative methodologies and explored the meaning of body weight and shape preoccupation have led to the introduction of social factors not typically considered in etiological models of eating disorders. In 1990 Catherine Steiner-Adair described a qualitative interview conducted with 32 schoolgirls about cultural and individual images of women and administered the Eating Attitude Test (EAT) to them as well. She found that 60% of the girls answered in a way she labeled as the "Wise woman," meaning that they described societal values of independence and success for women and, concurrently, stood apart from these values and emphasized the importance of relationships. The rest of the sample held the "Super woman" pattern, which involved a lack of clarity about, yet the identification with, societal values regarding women, including the devaluing of relationships. Almost all of the girls that held the "Super woman" pattern scored above the cutoff point of the EAT, while none of the "Wise Woman" girls did.

In 1994 Becky Thompson described her life history qualitative inquiry with 18 Black, Latin, and White heterosexual and lesbian women of different social classes and suggested that patterns of disordered eating and eating disorders were reactions to a multitude of social injustices, pressures, and prejudices, including racism, compulsory heterosexism, poverty, and acculturation. Thompson suggested that "trauma" may not only relate to one specific event, but to the accumulation of injuries by the "mundane extreme environment" of racism or other prejudices. In the same year, Mimi Nichter and Nancy Vuckovic reported that among adolescent girls, talk about body dissatisfaction was a way to maintain relationships with other girls.

June Larkin, Carla Rice, and Vanessa Russell reported in 1999 about a qualitative investigation in schools, which examined girls' experiences of sexual harassment. They found that sexual harassment adversely affected girls' body image and was linked to expressions of sexism and racism. Niva Piran described a participatory action research project in a dance school that has led to the emergence of a critical understanding of body weight and shape preoccupation as related to social equity and power. Three main dimensions of expressions of social inequity in the body domain were identified, all contributing to disruption in body-anchored experiences and body image. The first social dimension included experiences that disrupted girls' sense of ownership of their bodies such as external dictations of eating and appearance, objectification, sexualization, sexual harassment, assault, and abuse. The second social dimension related to experiences of prejudicial treatment such as weightism, sexism, and racism. The third dimension included the constricting social construction of women and femininity. Together, these expressions of inequity in the body domain led to a disconnection of girls and young women from their body and to the desire to externally control and manage it. [*See* Sexual Harassment.]

While few and far between, it does appear that qualitative approaches have expanded the social theory of body dissatisfaction and disordered eating and have led to the emergence of more complex and more challenging social factors. Further, this research has illuminated the complex and multilayered nature of the social environment.

4. Quantitative Social Research

Early empirical social research into eating disorders has relied on correlational data to examine trends, between the 1960s and 1990s, toward leaner standards of beauty and to associate these changing media-generated images with the documented higher incidence of eating disorders among women. A similar research strategy was employed to examine the association between diet and weight loss articles and advertisements and elevated incidence rates of eating disorders. The pressures-for-thinness social theory of eating disorders gained wide acceptance even prior to more methodologically stringent inquiries. A review conducted in 1999 by Michael Levine, Niva Piran, and Charlie Stoddard of a large number of studies conducted during the 1990s that employed laboratory-based experimental manipulations yielded mixed results about the relationship between exposure to the media and body dissatisfaction or disordered eating among women. Employing a prospective methodology, Alison Field and her associates conducted a one-year study of more than 6700 girls ages 9 to 14. They reported in 1999 that wishing to look like media models predicted the onset of purging behavior. However, employing a similar prospective methodology with high school seniors, Eric Stice reported in 1998 that he did not find media pressure or media modeling to predict the development of bulimic symptomatology. Further research is needed to explore the hypothesized relationship between media exposure to lean models and body dissatisfaction, with a particular emphasis on the relevance of mediating variables, such as the internalization of societal ideals for thinness or pre-existing body dissatisfaction, to heightened levels of dissatisfaction with weight. In addition, it is valuable to consider criticisms to the "culture of thinness" social theory of eating disorders, in particular the tendency of researchers to problematize models' thinness rather than their objectification or sexualization as disruptive experiences for young women, as well as the tendency to view the "culture of thinness" as a uniform factor without considering the complex, multilayered, and diverse nature of "culture." [*See* Beauty Politics and Patriarchy; Body Image Concerns.]

The impact of different prejudicial systems on body image has been explored mainly in terms of the impact of weightism. While pressures for thinness were explored first as a media-generated effect, social research has progressed to examine the impact of appearance-related pressures in other domains of children's social environment, especially peer groups and families. Michael Levine and his research associates reported in 1994 that teasing by peers has been found to be negatively associated with children's body image and Alison Field and her research associates reported in 1999 that peer teasing predicted eating concerns in prospective designs. Linda Smolak and her research associates reported in 1999 that parental criticality adversely affected children's body image. Piran and her colleagues found that exposure to weightist attitudes by family and friends was significantly related to disordered eating patterns. Similarly, Piran and her colleagues found that disordered eating patterns were related to exposure to sexist experiences, particularly items that deprecated a woman's body and her sexuality. While a growing body of research has explored the prevalence of eating disorders among different ethnocultural and racial groups, quantitative research examining the impact of exposure to racism on body image, especially prejudicial treatment directed at appearance, has been lacking. It has been suggested that Black women may tend to separate how they privately feel about themselves from how they believe others evaluate them. This could relate to an adaptive coping response to chronic and recurring experiences of racial oppression and prejudice. Acculturation, though, as Becky Thompson and others suggested, may comprise a risk factor to the development of eating disorders.

In addition to prejudicial treatment and teasing, additional social processes have been explored quantitatively, especially in interaction with a child's developmental stage. Michael Levine and his research associates reported in 1994 that changes in pubertal status or dating status increased the probability of nonpathological dieting in middle-school girls. Concurrent change in pubertal status, dating status, and academic stress increased the probability of sublinical eating disturbance in girls with a slender body ideal. Social comparison and drive for affiliation were implicated by Susan Paxton in her 1999 findings of a correlation between a girl's preoccupation with body weight and shape and that of her friendship network.

The relationship between the social construction of women and the female body and eating disorders has been examined as well. A meta-analysis of studies that explored the connection between masculine and feminine gender roles among women and eating problems, conducted in 1997 by Linda Smolak and Sarah Murnan, revealed a small positive relationship between femininity and eating problems and a negative relationship between masculinity and eating problems. Newer measures of gender role socialization, such as the Silencing the Self Scale, which was derived through a qualitative inquiry with women, may be more reflective of the relationship between gender roles and eating disorders. For example, in a series of studies Piran and her associates found that patterns of disordered eating were related to adolescent and adult women's tendency to silence their views, feelings, and needs in close relationships as measured by the Silencing the Self Scale. Studies that investigate measures more directly related to the social construction of the female body, such as the Objectified Body Consciousness Scale, may find more systematic results between social construction and eating disorders. Piran and her associates found that the objectified experience of the body was the strongest predictor, among a large number of social predictors, of disordered eating patterns such as vomiting and bingeing in a sample of adult women. Feminist attitudes about appearance have been found to relate significantly to body dissatisfaction while feminist ideology in general did not. Research on sexual orientation and body image has yielded conflicting results among women, while suggesting that men who are gay may experience more appearance-related pressures.

A third main line of research into the social domain in the development of eating disorders has examined the role of sexual and physical harassment and abuse. Most research suggests that sexual abuse comprises a general risk factor to a variety of psychiatric and medical symptomatology, including disordered eating. However, more recent research has expanded to examine the role of sexual harassment, a common experience in the life of girls and women. Piran and her associates have found a significant relationship between harassment and disordered eating patterns. Kevin Thompson and his associates similarly reported in 1999 that experiences of covert sexual abuse, including sexually related comments and similar events, are significantly related to measures of body image anxiety, restrictive eating behaviors, and bulimic symptoms.

Quantitative studies that have compared boys and girls on the patterns of association between social pressures and disordered eating may illuminate protective factors, as well as risk factors to the development of eating disorders. Ruth Striegel-Moore and Ann Kearney-Cooke reported in 1994 that parents of boys and girls were similarly not permissive of obesity in their children. However, the parents of boys were more satisfied than parents of adolescent girls with how much their child exercised. Susan Paxton and her associates also found in 1991 that while BMI was positively related to body dissatisfaction in girls and boys, higher exercise levels were related to higher body satisfaction in boys. Other research suggests that boys place greater value on physical effectiveness rather than appearance. It appears that, even though appearance-related pressures regarding male physique may be intensifying, boys may be somewhat protected by the importance of physical effectiveness. In addition, physical changes associated with puberty bring boys closer to the ideal image of men while placing girls further away from the cultural ideal.

Overall, quantitative studies of social factors have progressed beyond the initial emphasis on media-generated pressures for thinness to social experiences that are closer to the immediate lived social experience of girls and women to include factors such as weightism and other prejudices among peers and parents, sexual harassment, and the social construction of women's bodies and selves. Currently, a host of social variables on all these domains have been found to be associated with eating symptomatology. Prospective research will clarify which of these and other social factors may be able, in community-based studies, to predict the development of body dissatisfaction and eating disorders.

B. FAMILIAL FACTORS

Ample research has been conducted with families of individuals who developed full-blown eating disorders and have received treatment in large treatment centers. Findings may therefore reflect the impact on the family of having a member with an eating disorder requiring hospital treatment, as well as reflecting the concerns of more privileged families (White, middle or upper class). The clinical literature of eating disorders highlights the findings of lower cohesion, affection, and higher rates of enmeshment and conflict among families of women who developed eating disorders. However, these clinically derived familial variables have not been found yet to predict the development of disordered eating and body dissatisfaction in community-based prospective studies. Considering the hypothesized familial genetic transmission of eating disorders, it appears that despite reports of increased prevalence of eating and mood disorders among families of individuals with eating disorders, specific genetic factors in the pathogenesis of eating disorders have not been identified.

Community-based studies that focused on parental behaviors related to body image and eating patterns yielded several findings. Ruth Striegel-Moore and Ann Kearney-Cook reported in 1994 that parental negative evaluations of their children's appearance, eating habits, and exercise behavior increased from the age of 2 to the age of 16. The study further confirmed that parents tend to focus on the body's physical appearance in girls, whereas they emphasize physical functioning such as athletic skills in boys. Linda Smolak and her research associates found in 1999 that parental critical comments on their children's appearance had a negative impact on their children's body image and weight loss attempts. Parents' own dieting patterns and body dissatisfaction were not found to have as large an impact on their children's body image as parental criticality. It therefore appears that the family may serve as a buffer or, alternatively, a conduit of adverse societal influence. If these findings are confirmed in prospective studies, the family will have a special role in the prevention of eating disorders.

C. PERSONALITY FACTORS

Similarly to familial variables, most intraindividual characteristics hypothesized to contribute to the development of eating disorders have been derived based on clinical samples. It has been repeatedly found that psychological symptomatology in eating disorders is affected by emaciation and poor nutritional states. In community-based prospective studies, various personality batteries have not been found to predict the later development of body dissatisfaction or disordered eating among girls, with the exception of poor interoceptive awareness in girls. Poor interoceptive awareness reflects a reduced ability to identify and communicate internal bodily and emotional experiences.

One other important dimension related to individual differences comprises the consideration of temperament. To date, one prospectively study published and conducted by Geoffrey Martin and his associates has found that the childhood temperament factor of negative emotionality predicted the later development of eating and body weight concerns among 12-year-old children, especially girls. This factor was assessed at ages 3 to 4 and onward. This research suggests that a chronic state of negative arousal, combined with environmental factors such as social pressures for thinness, may lead to increased vulnerability for the development of disordered eating.

D. BIOLOGICAL FACTORS

To date, extensive research has been conducted to uncover genetic and physiological etiological factors in the development of anorexia and bulimia. However, most research studies have found physiological abnormalities to be the result, rather than the cause, of dietary restraint and disregulated eating.

A serious examination of biological factors should consider the bidirectional interaction that exists between genetic and neurobiological processes on the one hand and the environment on the other hand. The hypothesized role of serotonin abnormality in bulimia exemplifies this point. As Howard Steiger and his research associates noted, studies have documented serotonin abnormality in women displaying bulimic symptomatology as compared with control subjects who exhibit no eating difficulties. However, these studies could not rule out the effect of binge eating, purging, or prolonged and excessive dieting on this serotonin abnormality. Gender is implicated in these studies as dieting has been found to result in serotonin abnormality in women but not in men. Some women, therefore, may be susceptible to the development of disordered eating following dieting-induced serotonin dysfunction. Further, Bessel van der Kolk and his research associates reported in 1996 that serotin activity was disturbed in people displaying post-traumatic stress disorder. Similarly, animal research has suggested that both genetic background and early experiences affect the functioning of the serotonin system. It therefore appears, as Christopher Fairburn and his colleagues suggested in 1999, that the exploration of a genetic explanation requires the concurrent examination of environmental processes and their interaction with neurophysiological processes.

III. *Conclusions*

Eating disorders, as well as disordered eating and body weight and shape preoccupation, occur overwhelmingly in women. In the past 40 years there has been a dramatic increase in the prevalence of eating disorders in North America and in Westernized countries. Epidemiological studies reveal that body image dissatisfaction, disordered eating patterns, and eating disorders occur on a continuum. To date, the spectrum of phenomena and difficulties evades the classification of eating difficulties into validated "clinical" and "nonclinical" categories. This is especially so when the diverse social locations of women are respected in terms of their ethnocultural and racial heritage, their socioeconomic status, their sexual orientation, and other social factors that, as Foucault and other social critics would suggest, have a major impact on women's experience of their bodies, appetites, and desires. Since disordered eating and eating disorders are associated with social, psychological, vocational, and medical morbidity, it is important to consider the whole spectrum as a challenge to women's health. Research into etiological factors of eating disorders conducted with clinical samples may lead to different derived understandings than are suggested by community-based research. To date, most biological, psychological, and familial studies have been conducted in clinical settings, while most social studies have been conducted in the community. Indeed, clinical findings have often not been validated, especially in community-based prospective studies.

Altogether, theoretical, critical, emergent, and empirical social studies of body dissatisfaction, disordered eating, and eating disorders among women seem to reflect the complex and meaningful nature of the interaction between the multilayered social environment and the domain of the body. The emphasis on appearance, the objectification of women's bodies, the internalization by women of the external gaze, and the ongoing monitoring of the body, all for the sake of fitting in, surviving, and holding on to some social power seems to emerge as an important social dimension in understanding disordered eating and body dissatisfaction and in affecting women's subjectivity and instrumentality. The constriction of appetites and desires, voice, relational needs, and physical space to fit with prescribed social roles that maintain social structures and the status quo appears to constitute another central theme. The prejudiced, intrusive, and violent way in which women's bodies and bodies of women from diverse backgrounds is treated and the internalization of this treatment is another shared theme. Social studies and critical theory further suggest that understanding will be enriched through the exploration of the experience of women from diverse backgrounds along dimensions such as social class, ethnocultural background, sexual orientation, or ability/disability, accepting, as Nielsen suggested in 1990, that these studies may lead to diverse context-specific theories rather than to one universal theory of the development of eating disorders.

Social research further suggests that all social institutions, from macro level social policies, through midlevel institutions such as schools or hospitals, to microlevel institutions such as families and individuals, are affected by dominant social discourses that "shape" women's bodies. Explorations and findings at the microlevel related to familial interactional patterns (such as parents' criticality), individual factors (such as body and self-image or poor interoceptive awareness), and neurobiological processes (such as serotonin dysregulation) are affected by social and environmental processes and therefore cannot be separated from the social context within which they are embedded. Etiological awareness has to involve as a comprehensive and critical understanding of girls' and women's experience of "residing" in their bodies through the course of development and various life transitions. Prospective qualitative and quantitative studies with girls will help clarify the development of body dissatisfaction and eating disorders at the intersection of body and culture. Research to date suggests that a changed experience of the body by women of diverse backgrounds will correspond with larger social transformations.

SUGGESTED READINGS

Bloom, C., Gitter, A., Gutwill, S., Kogel, L., and Zaphiropoulos, L. (1994). *Eating Problems.* Basic Books, New York.

Bordo, S. (1991). *Unbearable Weight: Feminism, Western Culture, and the Body.* University of California Press, Berkeley, CA.

Brown, C., and Jasper, K. (1993). *Consuming Passions: Feminist Approaches to Weight Preoccupation and Eating Disorders.* Second Story Press, Toronto.

Diamond, I., and Quinby, L. (1988). *Feminism and Foucault: Reflections on Resistance.* Northeastern University Press, Boston.

Fallon, P., Katzman, M., and Wooley, S.C. (1994). *Feminist Perspectives on Eating Disorders.* Guilford Press, New York.

Gordon, R. A. (1999). *Eating Disorders: Anatomy of a Social Epidemic,* 2nd ed. Blackwell, Malden, MA.

Piran, N., Levine, M. P., and Steiner-Adair, C. (1999). *Preventing Eating Disorders: A Handbook of Interventions and Special Challenges.* Brunner/Mazel, Philadelphia.

Smolak, L., Levine, M. P., and Striegel-Moore, R. (1996). *The Developmental Psychopathology of Eating Disorders.* Erlbauh, Mahwah, NJ.

Thompson, J. K., Heinberg, L. J., Altabe, M., and Tantleff-Dunn, S. (1999). *Exacting Beauty: Theory, Assessment, and Treatment of Body Image Disturbance.* American Psychological Association, Washington, DC.

Wolf, N. (1991). *The Beauty Myth: How Images of Beauty Are Used against Women.* Morrow Press, New York.

Emotional Abuse of Women

Alisha Ali

Brenda B. Toner

University of Toronto

Glossary

Gender-based analysis An approach to conducting research that takes into account the differential effects of gender role socialization on women's and men's experience.

Partner abuse A form of abuse that occurs within the context of an intimate relationship.

Perpetrator Term used in the literature to refer to the abuser in an abusive situation.

Target Term used in the literature to refer to the abused individual in an abusive situation.

Workplace harassment Various forms of discrimination, insults, and maltreatment occurring within the context of working relationships.

EMOTIONAL ABUSE is defined as any form of violence, aggression, or trauma that is emotional or psychological rather than physical in nature. Emotional abuse can take many forms, including verbal abuse from an intimate partner, workplace harass-

ment, and instances of racial or sexual discrimination. This article explores the phenomenon of adulthood emotional abuse in women's lives, with a particular focus on the conceptualization and assessment of emotional abuse and the long-term and short-term effects of emotional abuse. Directions for future work and the development of intervention programs for emotionally abused women are also discussed.

I. Introduction

Emotional abuse is a relatively new concept in psychological research. It has received far less scientific attention compared to the large number of studies that have investigated physical abuse and sexual abuse. In particular, emotional abuse experienced in adulthood is less frequently studied than is emotional maltreatment in childhood. However, there is now growing evidence that the experience of emotional abuse in adulthood is not only common but can also have severe consequences for a woman's physical and emotional well-being.

The study of emotional abuse has been greatly influenced by feminist researchers who have argued that nonphysical aggression can have detrimental effects on women's lives and on women's self-perceptions. Research in this area has followed a path similar to those followed in the investigation of physical and sexual abuse. This path begins with the identification of the problem, then considers the consequences of the abuse, and finally approaches the issues of how to prevent the abuse and how to develop interventions to help the victims. Accordingly, the consideration of emotional abuse in this article follows this line of discussion. We begin by exploring some key issues in conceptualizing emotional abuse.

II. *Conceptual Issues*

A. TYPES OF EMOTIONAL ABUSE

Theorists generally identify two main types of emotional abuse experienced by women in adulthood. The first type is *partner abuse,* which involves emotional abuse from an intimate partner. This type of abuse is usually at its most serious when it involves a live-in relationship because the perpetrator in this relationship can physically isolate the woman and significantly restrict her freedom and her contact with the outside world. However, emotional abuse can also occur early on in a relationship, even when the woman does not have frequent contact with the perpetrator; in such cases, the perpetrator's goal is to influence the woman to act in accordance with his wishes even when they are physically apart.

Partner abuse typically involves verbal threats and insults, as well as such denigrating acts as putting the woman on an allowance (even when she earns her own money), not allowing her to leave the house alone, restricting her time on the telephone, and criticizing her appearance, her intelligence, her family, and various aspects of her homemaking. When the relationship involves children, the abuse can also include telling the woman that she is an incompetent parent, and threatening to take her children away or to harm them.

The other main type of emotional abuse that has been identified is *workplace harassment.* Workplace harassment generally involves unwanted sexual requests, public humiliation from an employer or coworker(s), and discriminatory abuse. Discrimina-

tion in the workplace is most commonly reported by women who are greatly outnumbered by men within their particular work setting, as well as by women of color. Recent research indicates that more subtle abusive behavior such as deliberate social exclusion, or the "silent treatment," can also have serious detrimental effects on the victim. There is also growing evidence that workplace harassment in male-dominated professions, such as the military, law enforcement, fire fighting, and certain factory jobs, is a common reason for women choosing to leave their jobs in these areas. [*See* SEXUAL HARASSMENT; WORKING ENVIRONMENTS.]

B. POWER DIFFERENTIALS

Emotional abuse, like most other forms of abuse, often occurs against the backdrop of significant differences in power levels between the perpetrator and the target. When a woman is emotionally abused by an intimate partner, it is often the case that a male partner is acting on the assumption that he must maintain power in the relationship and in the household. Similarly, in workplace harassment, the perpetrator is often an employer who has chosen to exploit a position of authority and power. In both types of emotional abuse the woman often has a practical concern around her financial survival. She may be financially dependent on her live-in partner and thus cannot readily leave. In the workplace, a harassing employer often has immense control over the woman's economic future as well as over her career and her chances of future employment. In these ways, we can see how power differentials enable a perpetrator to control the target in the abuse situation by exploiting her dependence and vulnerability.

Theorists are now beginning to recognize power as a key variable in the conceptualization of emotional abuse. As a result, emerging models that explain women's decisions to remain in emotionally abusive relationships now integrate issues of power differentials, as do treatment intervention models for emotionally abused women. Such models follow the assumption that women's disempowerment in abusive situations depends in part on the perpetrator instilling fear in the woman and on the perpetrator's belief that he is entitled to determine the woman's behaviors and actions. The woman's ability to extricate herself from the situation and to recover from the abuse depends largely on her rejecting this belief and recognizing her own sources of personal empowerment. [*See* POWER.]

C. GENDER AS A DEFINING VARIABLE

As with power, gender is a variable that defines the emotionally abusive situation as well as the perception of the situation on the part of the perpetrator and the victim. In most instances of the emotional abuse of women, the perpetrator is a man. This fact is not an arbitrary one; it is directly related to societal doctrines that posit male dominance within the household and within the workplace. In the context of intimate relationships, this assumed dominance can manifest itself through decision making around issues of money as well as issues of social interaction. Money is symbolic of power and is also strongly associated with the stereotypical male role. Research has demonstrated that men who adhere to stereotypical notions of masculinity are more likely to be dominating and controlling in intimate relationships. Similarly, men who follow the societal assumption of male dominance are more likely to try to control a female partner's social freedom inside the home (e.g., restricting time on the telephone or forbidding visits from family and friends) and outside the home (e.g, requiring the woman to wear a pager so she can be tracked or demanding that she spend all evenings at home). [See MEN AND MASCULINITY.]

In workplace settings, harassment is most often directed from a male perpetrator to a female worker. In the majority of professions, men hold higher positions of power than women do, and they are more likely than women to make decisions involving hiring and promotions. In a male-dominated work environment, there is greater opportunity for men to exploit female workers than for women to wield power over men. From a gender analysis perspective, it is also important to note that workplace harassment commonly involves sexual requests from a male employer or supervisor. This type of sexual overture is an overt act of gender-based violation. Women have been found to report fear of rape as a common safety concern, whereas men do not report a counterpart of such concern. Consequently, even a subtle sexual request from a male employer is a fear inducing act to many women. We can thus see how this form of harassment is exacerbated by societal forces that make women's sexuality a source of potential intimidation.

D. DISTINCTION FROM OTHER FORMS OF ABUSE

One final issue to consider in conceptualizing emotional abuse is the question of distinguishing emotional abuse from other forms of abuse. It is important, for instance, to distinguish emotional abuse from physical and sexual abuse, both in research studies and in conceptualizing the effects of different forms of abuse. In the situation where emotional abuse exists without any physical abuse or sexual abuse, there is evidence that damage to the woman's emotional well-being is comparable to that precipitated by physical abuse. In situations involving physical abuse, it is commonly found that emotional abuse existed in the relationship before the physical forms of abuse began. These findings have implications for both research and intervention in the field of emotional abuse. From a research perspective, it is clear that investigators should assess physical and sexual abuse along with emotional abuse to uncover their possible coexistence and to examine whether various long-term and short-term sequelae are differentially associated with different types of abuse. From an intervention perspective, these findings indicate that emotional abuse should be explored as a potential risk factor for women's physical and mental health difficulties. Furthermore, clinicians should be vigilant of emotional abuse as a possible predecessor of physical or sexual abuse in intimate relationships.

It is also important to note that there is considerable conceptual overlap between different forms of abuse. For example, "partner abuse" can be used to refer to physical, sexual , or emotional types of abuse occurring in a relationship. Similarly, workplace harassment can include actual acts of physical abuse in addition to acts of emotional abuse. In later sections we describe emerging domains of emotional abuse that overlap with other types of abuse.

III. Common Components of Emotional Abuse

Although there is a range of behaviors that characterize emotional abuse, there are common components that generally coexist in many emotionally abusive relationships. Researchers and clinicians have identified these components by investigating actual acts of emotional abuse as well as the general atmosphere that exists for a woman living in an emotionally abusive situation. The vast majority of such situations have involved women in live-in intimate relationships experiencing elements of emotional abuse from their male partner.

A. RESTRICTING FREEDOM

In emotionally abusive relationships, the abuser wields much of his power by virtue of his ability to restrict the woman's freedom. This often takes the form of overt restrictions that limit her time outside of the home and make it difficult for her to socialize freely or to have a job. The restriction can also exist in more subtle forms that are aimed at making the woman feel that she must be at home whenever her partner is there. For example, he may indicate that he feels lonely when she is not there or that he cannot prepare a meal without her. Women who experience these more subtle forms of restriction report that initially they feel grateful to be needed so completely. However, the abuse can escalate when the woman chooses to try to go out when her partner wants her at home. At these times, the man may resort to more direct threats.

B. THREATS OF PHYSICAL HARM

Even when emotional abuse is not accompanied by physical abuse, there can be threats of physical harm. For example, women report that their abusive partners terrorize them by threatening to physically attack them in their sleep. Emotionally abused women also report that the threats of physical harm are often very specific; they report that the men describe their threats with details including the time of day, the exact weapon they would use, and the precise nature of the injury the woman would sustain, including the experience of her dying. Theorists speculate that such detailed descriptions are used by the perpetrator to instill a long-lasting and pervasive fear aimed at giving the woman no option but to obey his wishes. These physical threats are also terrifying to the woman because they can be accompanied by the man throwing, or violently breaking, objects in the home. Some women report that these objects are deliberately chosen as possessions that are of emotional or sentimental value to them, including childhood possessions or gifts from family members.

C. THREATS INVOLVING CHILDREN

Physical threats not only involve the woman herself. When the emotionally abused woman is also a mother, threats can involve the children as well. The perpetrator can threaten to discipline the children using extreme physical violence, to take the children away from the woman, and to lie to the children about the woman (e.g., telling them that she is see-ing another man, that she does not love them, or that she is going to leave them). In research studies, women often report that threats involving their children are the most distressing aspect of the emotional abuse. Women who have left emotionally abusive relationships have reported that these types of threats were among their strongest reasons for leaving. It is important to note that there is a connection between threats of physical harm and threats involving children; the man will often remind the woman that her children will be left without a mother if she "forces" him to physically attack her in a manner that could lead to her death.

D. HUMILIATION

Humiliation of the abuse target is a common feature underlying both workplace harassment and emotional abuse in intimate relationships. In workplace harassment, the perpetrator's mode of control over the target often includes public humiliation in front of the target's coworkers. Women have described being yelled at and ridiculed and being publicly labeled as worthless or incompetent. They also describe generalization of the humiliation in which coworkers follow the abuser's behavior and also begin to ridicule the victim. This type of pattern is especially damaging when the woman must work collaboratively with individuals who have publicly insulted her and when her work evaluation is influenced by the opinions of these individuals.

In abuse in intimate relationships, the perpetrator uses humiliation in the home and in front of others. In the home, the man humiliates the woman by forcing her to perform demeaning or menial tasks around the house while he watches and criticizes. Outside of the home, he insults her, forces her always to agree with him in public, and determines when and if she can speak. Emotionally abused women often report that the man uses specific forms of humiliation in front of family and acquaintances, such as stating "don't bother listening to her—she doesn't know what she's saying" or "sometimes I think I'm better off leaving her at home." In these ways the man controls the woman by giving the appearance of colluding with other people against her. Such behavior may be especially common when the couple is socializing with the man's friends.

E. FOSTERING DEPENDENCE

In partner abuse, it is often the man's aim to make the woman believe there is no one else in her life that she can depend on other than him. He achieves this in part by isolating her from family and friends. For example, he will threaten people with harm if they attempt to contact her, and he will lie to her to convince her that other people are against her and that they will harm her or her children if given the chance. After ensuring that the woman is socially isolated, the man then proceeds to establish himself as her sole source of human contact and as the focus of her thoughts and actions. He does this by occupying her time with meeting his demands (e.g., creating meaningless, time-consuming errands for her to do for him) and by forcing her to ask him for permission to leave the home, eat, watch television, or use the telephone. His goal here is to create a childlike dependence on her part wherein she does not question his authority. Part of this dependence is also instilling in her the belief that he basically has her best interests in mind and that no one else can look out for her except him.

F. PSYCHOLOGICAL MANIPULATION

Psychological manipulation in partner abuse is aimed at forcing the woman to question her own judgments and self-worth. In order to make the woman feel that she is inferior and of an unsound mind, the man will try to convince her children that she is dangerous or irresponsible, thereby creating a distance between her and the children. He will also try to make her believe that she is becoming forgetful by telling her that she has forgotten to do something when in fact she has done it. He will also say that he asked her to do something (e.g., dropping off his dry cleaning) when he did not. Psychological manipulation can result in the woman becoming more dependent on the man in decision making and in defining reality. Emotionally abused women report that the man would repeatedly state that others did not trust her and that he was concerned about her mental well-being. Such repeated statements would be used to convince the woman that she should leave a job or stay at home more, thereby increasing her social isolation.

G. FINANCIAL ABUSE

In financial abuse, the man attempts to make the woman financially dependent on him as a means of control. He may force her to give him all of the money she earns or inherits, require her to give him written requests for any money she asks for (along with itemization of each expense and receipts of spending), and not allow her to know the amount of money in the bank account or the details of his own spending. He usually justifies this by stating that he does not trust her to handle money and that his control over the money is in their best interest. Emotionally abused women report that financial abuse is often used to ensure that the woman does not have the financial means to leave the relationship if she wishes to be on her own. This component of abuse also allows the man to have an independent financial existence wherein the woman is kept unaware of how he spends the money and on whom. This further increases the gap between the two partners with respect to their personal freedoms.

IV. *Measuring Emotional Abuse*

In studying emotional abuse and its effects on the women who experience it, researchers must consider a number of influences that determine the overall picture of an abusive situation. As with any relatively new area of research, the findings are largely influenced by the nature of available measures that can be used to assess the construct in question. With emotional abuse research, there are certain questions related to measurement that must be considered in designing and interpreting any investigations. These can be divided into two main categories: issues around how best to define severity of abuse and issues pertaining to the appropriate methodological approach to follow.

A. DEFINING SEVERITY OF ABUSE

Assessing severity of emotional abuse is a crucial issue in both research settings and clinical settings that deal with women's psychological well-being. There are a number of dimensions that constitute abuse severity that must be considered in the measurement of emotional abuse. The following key dimensions should be addressed in evaluating specific measures and research designs.

1. The Abuser's Intent

The intent of the abuser is often not considered a key aspect of measuring the severity of emotional abuse due to practical issues. One practical issue is that researchers who study the effects of emotional abuse on women often do not have any direct contact with the perpetrator; instead, they are interested in the woman's experiences and how the abuse has influenced her behavior and self-perceptions. In such research, the issue of the perpetrator's intent does not directly factor into the methodology because it is not part of the research question. Even in those studies where both the perpetrator and the target of the abuse are interviewed, there is the general sense on the part of researchers that the stated intent of the perpetrator may not correspond to his actual intent. For these reasons, the question of intent is usually inferred by asking the woman how the abusive acts were presented to her and what sorts of statements accompanied those acts. Women report that the man would make such statements as "I can't trust you unless I know where you are all the time," "You're only safe if you have me looking out for you," or "If you were more cooperative, I wouldn't need to set such strict rules." While such statements are not taken to represent the perpetrator's actual intent in the abuse, it can be useful for researchers to ask women about such "justifications," because these statements become part of a woman's lived experience.

2. The Effects of the Abuse

Another dimension that can be considered in defining abuse severity is how emotionally damaging the abuse is to the woman. This dimension is wrought with controversy. Some theorists believe that only the woman's perception of the abuse should be considered. However, there is a risk that a woman who is being emotionally abused may not recognize the behaviors as abusive and may even be unaware of the emotional distress it has caused her. This risk appears to be greatest among women who have experienced long-term childhood abuse as well as ongoing partner abuse and who may therefore have a disrupted understanding of "normal" and "depressed" emotional states. The current consensus among researchers is that an abusive behavior should still be considered abusive even if the target does not label it so; the issue of how it has influenced her (e.g., traumatically, slightly negatively, or not at all) is generally understood to be a separate factor.

3. The Frequency of Abuse

Another dimension to consider is whether one single act of abuse can be used to define a situation as emotionally abusive. Usually, both partner abuse and

workplace harassment are meant to denote an ongoing pattern of abuse. However, it is known from research on the effects of childhood abuse that even one emotionally traumatic event can have serious long-term psychological sequelae. Consequently, most theorists suggest that although ongoing abuse is generally more severe than an individual incident, it is important not to overlook the damage that can be done by one particularly degrading or distressing act. Examples of such acts include forcing the woman to perform humiliating tasks in front of others (e.g., forcing her to eat out of a pet's dish or off the floor) or removing her children from the home for an extended period without informing her of their whereabouts.

B. METHODOLOGICAL ISSUES

Methodological issues concern those aspects of research that relate to a study's design and its implementation. In emotional abuse, the methodological issues generally revolve around the ways of ensuring that the research approach is uncovering the appropriate range of emotionally abusive experiences and adequately assessing the abuse effects on the appropriate sample or group of samples. While these methodological issues can form the backdrop against which a study design can emerge, each of the specific issues must be considered from the perspective of feasibility and theoretical interest within the scope of the particular study.

1. Screening for Physical and Sexual Abuse

As discussed earlier, distinguishing emotional abuse from physical and sexual abuse is a crucial issue in researching the effects of emotional abuse. It can allow for analysis of the differential effects that various types of abuse can have, and it can allow us to further develop the construct of emotional abuse. Researchers should therefore measure physical and sexual abuse in studies of emotional abuse whenever it is feasible. This can be accomplished by using validated abuse screening measures such as Judith B. Brown's Woman Abuse Screening Tool or Frances A. Rodenburg and John W. Fantuzzo's Measure of Wife Abuse.

2. Adulthood versus Childhood Abuse

Similarly important to screening for physical and sexual abuse is assessing research participants for abuse in childhood. This should include assessing sexual molestation, physical trauma, and emotional maltreatment and neglect. This type of screening can allow researchers to examine the specificity of effects of emotional abuse in adulthood, to investigate some of the long-term effects of childhood abuse, and to study the relationship between childhood abuse and adulthood abuse. A related methodological consideration is the question of the cut-off age between childhood and adulthood in studying emotional abuse. Many researchers choose to extrapolate from the domain of sexual abuse research and use similar cutoff ages; in this case, childhood would be considered to end at around age 12 or 13. However, some theorists argue that in investigating partner abuse, adulthood should be considered to begin at the age when the first serious intimate relationship would generally begin; in this case, the cutoff would be around age 18 or 19. Whatever age is chosen to represent adulthood, it is strongly recommended that the same cutoff age be used in the assessment of all types of abuse measured within the same study. [*See* CHILD ABUSE.]

3. Investigating a Range of Samples

One area in which research on emotional abuse needs to develop is that of the inclusion of a broad range of samples across the various studies. For example, there is a need to explore clinical samples of women in attempting to delineate the physical and mental health effects of emotional abuse. In more general studies of different types of emotional abuse experiences, there is a need to move beyond the usual undergraduate student samples and even beyond community-based samples. In particular, more diversity is needed in the composition of study samples with respect to ethnicity, country of origin, age, and socioeconomic status. One final area that must also be considered is the possibility of building a cross-cultural base of knowledge around the construct of emotional abuse. Such a knowledge base could reflect differences in definitions of emotionally abusive behaviors in different cultures, as well as the role of cultural values in influencing women's experiences of emotional abuse. Differences in the types of intervention and prevention strategies that can be implemented in different cultures and in different parts of the world can also be explored. This type of international comparison of samples can be achieved in part through collaboration between researchers in different regions.

4. Checklist versus Interview Measures

Another methodological issue that researchers must deal with in designing a study of emotional abuse is the type of scale or measure to use to assess the abuse. The existing measures are generally quantitative checklist ratings, which list actual acts of emotional abuse and ask the participant to rate the extent to which she has experienced each act ("never," "frequently," etc.). Existing scales such as Hudson and McIntosh's Index of Spouse Abuse, Straus' Conflict Tactics Scale, Shepard and Campbell's Abusive Behavior Inventory, and Marshall's Severity of Violence against Women Scale all include subscales designed to assess adulthood emotional abuse. Because these measures also assess other forms of abuse concurrently, they can be utilized in studies that aim to examine emotional abuse and also screen for physical or sexual abuse. Quantitative scales designed specifically to measure emotional abuse include Sullivan, Parisian, and Davidson's Index of Psychological Abuse and Tolman's Psychological Maltreatment of Women Inventory, both of which cover a range of emotionally abusive behaviors in a psychometrically stringent manner.

Another option for assessing emotional abuse in research is to utilize a more contextualized interview approach. Unlike checklist measures, which do not allow for the gathering of details of abusive acts or the context in which they occurred, interviews can be used to develop a more comprehensive picture of an emotionally abusive relationship. They can also enable the researcher to assess abuse severity along various dimensions concurrently rather than only addressing one dimension (e.g., frequency of abuse). Another advantage of the interview approach is that it can gather information on abusive acts that may not be included on a standard checklist but that may have been experienced by the participant.

There are also difficulties involved in using interview measures to assess emotional abuse. The most obvious is the lack of a valid and reliable interview measure designed to assess this construct. Another difficulty is that the interview process is more time consuming and labor intensive than is the questionnaire approach. One possible solution to these difficulties is for the researcher to use an existing scale and modify it for use as an interview. For example, the questions on the Psychological Maltreatment of Women Inventory can be asked verbally and participants can be asked details about those behaviors that they endorse.

V. Effects of Emotional Abuse

There is growing evidence that emotional abuse can affect women in ways that are as damaging as the effects of physical abuse. While this evidence is based on a much smaller number of studies than those investigating women's experience of physical abuse, there has been sufficient research to allow us to consider effects that have been empirically linked to women's experience of emotional abuse in adulthood. This research has generally considered two main categories of the negative impact of emotional abuse: effects on mental health and effects on physical health.

A. MENTAL HEALTH EFFECTS

Studies exploring the mental health effects of emotional abuse focus either on women in the general population or on women who are seeking help for abuse-related or mental health–related problems. General population studies find that women who have experienced emotional abuse in intimate relationships are at increased risk for problems associated with low self-concept and social isolation; these problems include symptoms of depression and anxiety, as well as body dissatisfaction and symptoms of disordered eating. Even after leaving the abusive relationship, these women are also at increased risk for difficulties with social interaction and can suffer from generalized fear and shyness. Many women also report that they have difficulty trusting others several years after they have left the relationship.

Research on clinical samples of women have found that those who have experienced emotional abuse typically report recurrent depression and accompanying feelings of hopelessness. They also report long-term feelings of low self-efficacy and anxiety and are at risk for substance abuse. Also among the long-term effects are feelings of self-blame and an increased likelihood of social anxiety and withdrawal from social situations. While there is not an extensive literature on the etiological role of emotional abuse in women's mental health problems, these current findings indicate that clinicians working in the area of women's well-being should begin considering emotional abuse to be a risk factor for these types of psychological difficulties.

B. PHYSICAL HEALTH EFFECTS

There has been even less research on physical health effects of emotional abuse than on mental health effects. However, recent studies have found that emotionally abused women may be more likely than their nonabused counterparts to experience chronic headaches and backaches, gastrointestinal problems, dizziness, sleep disruption, teeth grinding, extreme fatigue, and significant weight changes. As there is a need for more research in this area, it would be worthwhile for studies of emotional abuse to include an assessment of physical health difficulties as part of the study protocol.

VI. Emerging Domains of Emotional Abuse

Although partner abuse and workplace harassment are the most comprehensively investigated areas of emotional abuse, recent research has explored other domains that may be important subfields to explore in developing a thorough understanding of emotional abuse and its effects. These emerging domains generally focus on populations that have largely been neglected. Consequently, the information on these domains is not thorough; however, it is important to discuss these emerging domains as they may represent the future of the field of emotional abuse. It is again important to note that these domains can overlap with each other and with other types of abuse. For example, elder abuse can include physically abusive acts as well as emotionally abusive acts. For our present purposes, however, we are interested in the ways in which these domains can contribute to research and conceptualization in the general field of emotional abuse.

A. ELDER ABUSE

Research on rest home communities have uncovered the problem of elder abuse, which refers to abuse of elderly individuals in family homes, hospitals, and other care settings. From the perspective of emotional abuse, the relevant aspects of elder abuse include neglect of the person's basic needs, insults, and threats of abandonment. From a gender perspective, it is important to note that since women tend to live longer than men, they are at particular risk of elder abuse. Community-based research is needed to uncover the prevalence of elder abuse in family homes. There is also a need for the development of interventions aimed at educating health professionals about the risks of elder abuse.

B. MOTHERS ABUSED BY THEIR CHILDREN

The abuse domain of mothers emotionally abused by their children has emerged from clinical work designed to assess and assist youth at risk, particularly substance-abusing youth. This work has uncovered the problems of mothers with live-at-home adolescent sons who become abusive in the home. This abuse is directed at the woman, who in most scenarios is a single mother who has been physically and emotionally abused by her male ex-partner in front of her son. Theorists speculate that it is the witnessing of this behavior that precipitates the son's abusive behavior toward the mother. The abuse usually takes the form of severe criticism, insults, and threats of physical harm. This abuse tends to first appear at around age 14, or when the son is first physically stronger and larger in stature than the mother. It is not known how common this type of abuse is, but it is clearly an important area for future empirical and clinical work.

C. LESBIAN RELATIONSHIPS

The impetus behind research on lesbian relationships has come from feminist theorists who aim to expand traditional restrictive definitions of couplehood and family. The domain of abuse in lesbian relationships is part of this growing field of inquiry. There is reason to believe that women in same-sex relationships are not immune to the problems of partner abuse that heterosexual women can experience. Studies have shown that physical violence does occur between lesbian partners. However, emotional abuse itself has yet to be empirically explored in a comprehensive manner in lesbian relationships. Theorists speculate that lesbians may be at risk for emotional abuse from a partner because they are more likely than heterosexual couples to live without extended family contact, due in part to the possibility of family rejection. This relative isolation can increase the likelihood that the partner who is being threatened and emotionally denigrated will stay in the abusive relationship.

D. RACIAL HARASSMENT

Researchers in the area of traumatic stress have begun in recent years to include racial harassment and racial discrimination among the various forms of life trauma that individuals can experience. This recognition is important since the domain of racism has been largely neglected by psychological research in the past. Emerging theories state that racial harassment in the workplace and in educational settings has negative effects on women of color, including long-term damage to one's self-efficacy and self-confidence, feelings of fear and anger, and symptoms of depression. Racial harassment is also cited by women of color as one of the reasons for leaving a particular job or occupational field.

Racial discrimination can fall under the category of emotional abuse for a couple of reasons. One is that is it helpful for both clinicians and researchers to consider acts of racism to be forms of abuse because of the detrimental effects that racial discrimination can have on the well-being of the target. Another reason is that it is important for work in the area of women's emotional abuse to reflect the experiences of all women, not just White women of certain socioeconomic classes. By considering the abusive effects of racial discrimination, we can more fully develop a picture of the differential manifestations of abuse in women's lives. [*See* Prejudice.]

E. HOMOPHOBIC DISCRIMINATION

The domain of homophobic discrimination has been written about by theorists and clinicians, but there has been a serious lack of psychological research directly examining its effects on women's well-being. Both gay men and lesbians are at risk for homophobic discrimination in their daily lives. The only option to some who may face such discrimination is to keep the nature of their sexual orientation largely hidden. It is important to design research protocols to explore the effects of homophobia on lesbians and on people who are close to them. We suggest that homophobic discrimination be considered a form of emotional abuse when it involves nonphysical violence such as threats, name calling, social exclusion, homophobic "humor," and workplace discrimination. We further suggest that interventions that aim to support lesbians living with homophobia label it as a form of abuse.

VII. *Interventions for Emotionally Abused Women*

Emotional abuse is often addressed in therapy with women who have experienced abusive relationships. However, there is a need to develop protocols to evaluate the efficacy of different types of treatment approaches in helping emotionally abused women. This section explores some of the approaches that have been developed in this area and some of the principles that they follow. In addition to discussing individual and group psychotherapy, we will outline some elements of community-based approaches aimed at reducing the prevalence of emotional abuse and its damaging effects. [*See* COUNSELING AND PSYCHOTHERAPY; FEMINIST APPROACHES TO PSYCHOTHERAPY.]

A. INDIVIDUAL PSYCHOTHERAPY

Models of individual psychotherapy for women in emotionally abusive intimate relationships have been strongly influenced by principles of feminist therapy that focus on reducing self-blame, encouraging personal empowerment, examining the role of gender-related influences, and exploring life options for the woman's future. Most clinicians who work in this area agree that addressing the issue of the woman's self-blame and self-reproach should be a fundamental element of the therapy. This issue is closely tied to the examination of gender-related influences in that women are socialized to take responsibility for their own actions and for the actions of those close to them. In the case of emotional abuse, this overresponsibility can present itself through the woman's belief that her behavior and her weaknesses were pivotal in causing the abuser's behavior. Once the woman has recognized that she is not responsible for the abuse, the clinician can explore different approaches to personal empowerment that may lead the woman to conclude that she does not need the relationship in her life. This realization can in turn lead to the exploration of the different options open to the woman for her future.

Marti T. Loring has developed a clinical model specifically for emotionally abused women. In this model, she espouses a therapeutic stance that values the client as a whole person and demonstrates an interest in the client as an independent individual, thereby establishing a path toward self-acceptance. This model also focuses on validation of the woman's perceptions and involves a particular emphasis on clarifying the components of the abuse and exploring the woman's ability to think about herself with compassion rather than with self-criticism. Like other forms of women-centered therapy, this model opens up options to the client and empowers her to pursue goals that meet her own needs rather than simply focusing on the demands presented to her by others.

B. GROUP PSYCHOTHERAPY

Clinicians who endorse a feminist approach report that the use of group therapy can be beneficial for women who have experienced interpersonal trauma because the group can enable a client to see that she is not alone in her experience and in her perceptions. The group approach also has the advantage of encouraging women to support each other in their decisions and in their exploration of life options. With clients who have been emotionally abused, the decision of whether to pursue individual versus group psychotherapy can be influenced by a number of factors. Most notably, if the woman has been severely socially isolated and suffers from extreme shyness and fear, she may be very uncomfortable entering a group. Furthermore, because emotional abuse can foster a generalized mistrust of others, it is important that a woman only be introduced into a therapy group if she has a basic level of trust of the other group members. Clinicians also warn that there is a potential risk in integrating emotionally abused women into groups designed for women who have been physically or sexually abused because the members of the group may not readily acknowledge that emotional abuse can itself have traumatic effects.

C. COMMUNITY-BASED PREVENTION

Community-based prevention strategies are most often seen in specific communities in which women are at risk for social isolation and partner abuse. In particular, organizations and women-centered agencies within immigrant communities have begun to recognize that women who arrive in a new country with no social connections aside from their husband can easily be socially isolated and often feel that they have no one to turn to if their husband is being abusive. Consequently, prevention strategies aim to develop networks of women who monitor the arrival of new immigrants into their particular ethnic, cultural, or religious community and attempt to establish informal or social contact with women who are newcomers. Integrating the woman into an existing network of support may greatly increase the likelihood that she will receive help when the early signs of maltreatment or abuse begin to appear. Also, some networks establish regular meeting groups for women to attend. In these groups a woman can disclose an emotionally abusive experience and begin to access personal support and practical assistance. [*See* SOCIAL SUPPORT.]

VIII. *Future Directions*

There is a clear need for more research in the area of women's experience of emotional abuse in adulthood. Numerous options are open to scientists who choose to pursue this line of research, both in clinical settings and in general population research. This section outlines some of the identified priority areas for future work on emotional abuse. In particular, we emphasize those areas that could greatly benefit from the integration of feminist methodologies and gender-based analysis.

A. EXPLORING EMERGING DOMAINS

It is important to further delineate the issues at play in the many emerging domains of emotional abuse, and feminist researchers can play a vital role in uncovering these issues. For example, in the domain of emotional abuse in lesbian relationships, there is a need for broad-scale studies that aim to define the types of abuses that can occur in lesbian partnerships and the possible need for intervention and support groups to help women at risk. Similarly, in the area of racial harassment, there is a need to establish research protocols designed to follow the short-term and long-term effects of racial discrimination on women's well-being.

B. DEVELOPING MEASURES

Although there are a number of validated quantitative scales that assess adulthood emotional abuse, the research in this field would be greatly strengthened by the development of more qualitative interview measures. It is important to have such measures because they can increase our ability to tap into the nuances of abusive experiences and can capture detailed information about types of abuse that are not yet well documented or well understood. Furthermore, by establishing the availability of interview measures, we can increase the options open to researchers from a range of disciplines who want to match their measurement tools to the theoretical perspective that informs their work. For example, feminist theorists are increasingly integrating qualitative methods into research designed to explore women's phenomenological experience, and emotional abuse is certainly an area that should be addressed with such a method.

C. INTERVENTION STUDIES

Since clinicians are now developing intervention models designed to help emotionally abused women, this is an appropriate time to initiate research protocols to evaluate the efficacy of different intervention approaches in this field. Randomized clinical trials can be developed for both individual and group therapy protocols, and teams of researchers can contrast the benefits of various clinical approaches. This is also an area where researchers interested in gender-based analysis can play a vital role. We suggest that intervention studies utilize gender-related measurement tools that can readily assess a woman's movement away from self-blame and toward self-acceptance in healing from emotional abuse.

D. CONTEXTUALIZED CONCEPTUALIZATION OF EMOTIONAL ABUSE

One final aspect of emotional abuse that should be addressed is the need for researchers and clinicians to acknowledge the contextualized nature of emotional abuse. As with other forms of violence against women, emotional abuse can be viewed as the manifestation of societal forces that disempower women and reinforce adherence to restrictive gender roles. While many feminist theorists readily endorse this conceptualization, the dominant mainstream literature should reflect the importance of the social context in shaping our behaviors and perceptions. In particular, social messages that assume that the man should have the ultimate decision-making power in the household and that women should be passive and submissive should be directly challenged in research and clinical work. Furthermore, the role of socialization should be considered in framing our understanding of the effects of emotional abuse on women's self-perceptions and behavior. Women are socialized to be strongly invested in maintaining interpersonal relationships and to sacrifice aspects of themselves in order to keep relationships intact. Consequently, women are taught to feel like failures when a romantic partnership does not "succeed." In this respect, we can see why women engage in extreme self-blame when emotional abuse occurs. We can also see the importance of clinical models that encourage women to discover sources of personal strength and resilience outside of the context of the relationship. This type of approach can be beneficial to clinicians and researchers who aim to find solutions to the dilemma emotionally abused women face when they cannot see any options for themselves except to live with the abusive situation.

IX. Conclusion

Feminist researchers will no doubt continue to play an influential role in shaping how we conceptualize and study the emotional abuse of women. Similarly, feminist clinicians will contribute to the emergence of intervention models for emotionally abused women. Individuals working in this area are encouraged to integrate community-based models of research and intervention into their research and clinical perspectives. This integration can include participatory research studies that allow for direct involvement of women who have been emotionally abused. Such involvement can acknowledge the importance of learning from and collaborating with women who have experienced the effects of emotional abuse and who wish to contribute to the development of strategies aimed at preventing the abuse and helping other emotionally abused women.

Community-based approaches to intervention should also be more widely adopted. For example, the formation of grassroots support networks for immigrant and refugee women and other at-risk groups can greatly contribute to the prevention of emotional abuse. Furthermore, prevention strategies should be directed at reaching both women who are at risk for being abused and men who may become abusers. Finally, prevention should also involve broad-based change at societal and political levels. Public awareness about the devastating effects of emotional abuse should be raised. Policy makers and legislators should formulate guidelines and practices similar to those designed to reduce the rates of physical and sexual abuse of women. In these ways, we can begin to counteract the damage and suffering associated with emotional abuse.

SUGGESTED READING

Ali, A., Oatley, K., and Toner, B. B. (1999). Emotional abuse as a precipitating factor for depression in women. *Journal of Emotional Abuse* 1(4), 1–13.

Borkowski, M., Murch, M., and Walker, V. (1983). *Marital violence: The Community Response*. Tavistock, London.

Herman, J. L. (1992). *Trauma and Recovery*. Basic Books, New York.

Loring, M. T. (1994). *Emotional Abuse*. Macmillan, New York.

Marshall, L. L. (1996). Psychological abuse of women: Six distinct clusters. *Journal of Family Violence* 11(4), 379–409.

Tolman, R. M. (1992). Psychological abuse of women. In *Assessment of Family Violence* (R. T. Ammerman and M. Hersen, eds.), pp. 291–310. Wiley, New York.

Van der Kolk, B. A. (1987). *Psychological Trauma*. American Psychological Association Press, Washington, DC.

Empathy and Emotional Expressivity

Pamela W. Garner

Kimberly M. Estep

University of Houston-Clear Lake

Glossary

Display rules Guidelines for dealing with emotions that are used when an individual experiences an emotion internally but does not want to express that emotion externally either in facial expression or verbal response.

Emotion socialization Behaviors enacted by parents, teachers, and peers that directly or indirectly influence children's understanding, experience, expression, and regulation of emotion.

Emotional experience Arousal triggered by a past or present environmental event or an individual action that elicits any aspect of emotion, including characterizing states, processes, and expressions that carry the quality of emotion.

Emotional expressivity Any anatomical, muscular, physiological, or behavioral reaction that is sometimes associated with a felt emotion and functions in the manner in which it is displayed.

Empathy Apprehending the emotional state of another person and experiencing an emotion that is congruent with that state.

Personal distress An emotional response that is focused on alleviating one's own distress.

Sympathy An other-oriented emotional response that can stem from a cognitive awareness of another's emotional state or from the experience of an emotion that is congruent with the feelings of the other.

EMPATHY AND EMOTIONAL EXPRESSIVITY are both critically important to social interaction and to the ability to form healthy social relationships. The popular press has long lauded emotional expressivity and empathy-related responsiveness as feminine strengths. However, differences between females and males seem to be specific to the particular emotion under consideration, the social context, and age. Moreover, there is now evidence that suggests that theorists and researchers must be especially sensitive to the possibility that gender emotion stereotypes may exert a major influence on research findings.

I. Introduction

Much of the work on emotions has dealt with questions regarding the definition of emotion, facial patterns involved in the communication of emotions, the universality of emotional expressions and their meanings, and the connection between internal emotional experience and external expression. Although these issues have not yet been adequately resolved, researchers have recently added another component to the study of emotion, namely the interpersonal and social regulatory functions of emotions. As a result, a considerable body of research has begin to accumulate on the role of emotions in everyday interactions. Because considering all of these issues would be beyond the scope of this discussion, this article focused on the external expression of emotion, the connection between internal emotional experience and external expression, and the role of gender in these processes.

Specifically, this article summarizes the literature on the role of gender in empathy-related responding and emotional expressivity. This is a difficult task given that researchers have generally pursued these topics in separate literatures. Although there has been some debate as to whether empathy itself is an emotion, there is no doubt that empathy-related processes have as their focus the emotions of self and others. Therefore, the bridge that connects these two diverse literatures is the fact that they are both focused on affective processes. We review the portion of this literature that is concerned with gender comparisons. The article is organized as follows. The first section examines the literature on gender comparisons in emotional expressivity. The next section considers research on physiological emotional responses, followed by a discussion of gender comparisons of facial, behavioral, and vocal expressions of emotions. Then, data on gender comparisons of emotional display rules are followed by a review of research on gender and empathy. The rest of the article is devoted to a consideration of how emotion socialization practices may differentially impact the expression and experience of emotions in females and males.

II. Gender Comparisons on Emotional Expressivity

Before beginning a discussion of gender and emotionality, we first provide an account of the current view of emotions as functional. The major premise underlying this view is that social interactions are not devoid of emotion and, as such, emotions are one of the primary means through which individuals communicate with one another. One's own emotional expression may also play an important role in obtaining desired responses from others. This means that to interact effectively, individuals must be aware of their own and others' emotions. That is, emotion expressed by a partner may suggest the need to (1) persist in the current behavior or emotional display, (2) alter social and emotional behavior to correspond with one's understanding of the social partner's feelings, or (3) terminate a particular behavior or emotional display because it is causing the other person distress or because there are negative consequences for displaying a particular emotion. Emotional expressiveness and appropriate responsiveness to one's own and others' emotions may be especially important for negotiating complex interpersonal exchanges because the ability to control the expression of emotion may be useful in reducing miscommunication and misunderstandings between individuals with differing views. There is also evidence that the inability to express emotions has serious negative physical and mental health consequences. For example, the inability to cope with negative emotions can result in stress-related illnesses and can manifest itself in the development of internalizing and externalizing psychological problems.

An abundance of empirical research exists to support such theories. Individuals who are adept at understanding the emotional cues of others are better liked than persons who are deficient in the understanding of emotions. Presumably, this is because they are deprived of important social information, which makes it more difficult for them to respond appropriately to others and less likely that others will respond to them in a positive way. The inability to understand and pose recognizable facial expressions has also emerged as an important correlate of psychopathology. For example, emotionally disturbed children and adults perform less well on emotion recognition tasks than their normally functioning counterparts. There is also evidence that some forms of autism are associated with the inability to share affective experiences with others. Researchers have also frequently reported that maltreating parents are often overly expressive of certain negative emotions and that the facial expressions of their children are generally difficult to interpret. Finally, depressed individuals are less likely to offer constructive strategies for regulating their own negative emotions than nondepressed persons.

There is also evidence that highly expressive children and adults have more positive social experiences than less expressive individuals, and persons who are able to appropriately manage their emotional displays are regarded as more socially competent than others. Several lines of evidence have also implicated the role of emotional discourse in the development of social relationships. In particular, the ability to talk about emotions (especially one's own) seems to be an important determinant of positive social interactions and may also help individuals to manage their displays of negative emotional expressions. People who are able to talk about and describe their emotional experiences may also be more likely to be the recipient of empathic responses when distressed.

Popular as well as scientific opinion has long lauded the belief that major differences exist between females and males in the experience and expression of empathy and other emotions. Indeed, feminist scholars have often asserted that one of the most persistent beliefs about gender differences has to do with emotionality. Women and girls are frequently described as being more emotionally expressive and as feeling more comfortable disclosing their feelings to others than men and boys. The belief that females are more skilled than men at managing their emotions is also a common belief. Specifically, girls and women are believed to express more happiness and joy and dysphoric emotions such as sadness and fear more often and more intensely than men and boys. On the other hand, males are frequently described as inexpressive, except when it comes to the expression of anger, particularly when the target of that anger is a female. These stereotypes persist regardless of whether women and men are asked about their internal experience of emotion or about their style of expressing emotions to others. [*See* ANGER.]

These stereotypic beliefs exist even in childhood. For example, children as young as preschool age believe that anger is more characteristic of males and that sadness is more characteristic of females. Preschoolers' beliefs about the expression of positive emotion are more complex. That is, preschoolers'

beliefs about the expression of happiness vary as a function of the gender of the subject as well as gender of the target. Specifically, boys believe that boys express more happiness than girls whereas girls expect other girls to display more positive emotion than boys. The findings for middle-school children follow a similar pattern with school-age girls attributing more fear and sadness to themselves than to boys, and boys attributing more happiness to themselves.

Multiple channels of emotional expression exist, including physiological responses, facial expressions, behavioral cues, and emotion-based language. According to the literature, gender differences in emotional expressivity are dependent on the specific mode of expression. For instance, when physiological measures are used, males are generally regarded as more emotional than females whereas the opposite pattern is reported when facial cues of emotion are considered. Therefore, we have chosen to organize our discussion of gender comparisons in emotional expressivity around three main areas: physiological responses; facial, vocal, and behavioral displays of emotion; and the discrepancy between internal feelings and external emotional expression.

Before continuing our discussion, it is important to point out that, when found, interpreting gender differences in emotionality is difficult. Much of the research on this topic has employed self-report measures, which are often influenced by social desirability. In studies where observational measures have been used, the observers are typically aware of the gender of the target. Given that gender stereotypes about emotional expression are so widely held, it is also likely that observers' perceptions of emotions are influenced by these beliefs. Finally, there is evidence that the facial expressions of females are more easily interpreted than those of males, except for the emotions of anger and fear. Obviously then, the reported gender differences in facial expressions may actually be the result of methodological issues.

III. *Physiological Responses*

Researchers have been studying gender differences in physiological activity for more than 30 years. Although some researchers have found that physiological responses may be associated with attentional processes, most often, these studies have focused on skin conductance and heart rate as markers for emotionality. In this research, high skin conductance and heart rate acceleration are regarded as indicators of personal distress, overall anxiety, or overall negative emotionality. Conversely, low skin conductance and heart rate deceleration are viewed as indicators of emotional control and, more recently, sympathy. In general, when physiological measures of emotions are used, males and females experience and respond to emotions in similar ways. However, when difference are noted, males tend to have higher scores. For example, when exposed to stressful events or to emotionally evocative stimuli, males typically exhibit higher skin conductance than females, even when they report experiencing less overall distress than females. On the other hand, females tend to have higher scores on physiological measures when they have caused another person pain or distress. This particular finding is interesting in that researchers have begun to use changes in skin conductance as an indicator of empathy-related responding (discussed later). A major problem with this research is that skin conductance may not reflect changes in the experience or expression of discrete-level emotions. For example, sometimes, skin conductance increases during sadness and at other times, changes are seen only for fear and anger.

Although the use of physiological measures to assess emotionality in children is not new, child development researchers have shown renewed interest in these procedures. In this research, differences between girls and boys are rarely reported. Consistent with the adult literature, when gender differences are found in childhood, they seem to favor boys. One exception to this pattern is when conduct-disordered children are considered. In this case, preschool girls show higher skin conductance than preschool boys. Nonetheless, the inconsistent findings across studies make it difficult to come to a firm conclusion about differences in skin conductance for girls and boys. However, a growing body of literature seems to be suggesting that skin conductance may hold different meanings for males and females. For instance, skin conductance is associated with girls' but not boys' reported distress while watching a sympathy-inducing film. In addition, a higher level of skin conductance is associated with low levels of sympathy in boys. By contrast, a high level of skin conductance is related to low levels of prosocial behavior in preschool and school-age girls. Investigators have been increasingly interested in the use of physiological measures in research on children. Most often, these studies have been concerned with physiological indices of empathy-related responsiveness. There-

fore, we will revisit this issue in our discussion of empathy later in the article.

Generally speaking, main effects of gender are rarely reported in studies using heart rate as a measure of emotionality. When differences are reported, they seem to be dependent on the type of emotion under consideration. For instance, women show reduced heart rate in response to anger-arousing situations regardless of whether researchers consider their immediate or delayed physiological response. Conversely, men show an increase in heart rate in response to anger-arousing situations. However, when observed in highly challenging situations, women have been shown to have higher heart rate increases than men. Another important point to make is that, as with skin conductance, researchers are unclear about which emotions are actually associated with heart rate and what these heart rate changes actually mean.

Another physiological measure that has sometimes been used to assess emotionality is facial electromyographic activity (EMG). Because not all emotions are accompanied by specific facial expressions, some researchers have become interested in the specific movements in facial muscles (e.g., brows and corners of the mouth). To their credit, EMG assessments yield information about facial changes associated with overt emotional expression as well as muscular activity associated with emotionality that is too fleeting to evoke a detectable facial movement. Furthermore, this technique has been shown to yield information that cannot be obtained with self-report data or with other physiological measures. Despite the enormous potential that such a technique has for detecting changes in the expression of discrete emotions that may be gender-specific, discrepant findings have been reported with regard to gender. Some studies have shown that females and males show no differences in EMG responsiveness when answering emotionally evocative questions. However, when asked to imagine themselves as a participant in emotionally charged situations or to view affectively laden slides, particularly when the slides are designed to elicit negative affect, females show greater EMG activity than males.

In sum, physiological measures offer great potential for researchers interested in studying emotions. However, there is still much uncertainty about what physiological changes say about emotional expression and therefore the results of these studies are often difficult to interpret. That is, there is very little understanding of which physiological change should occur in response to a specific type of emotion-provoking event. In fact, it has even been suggested that we can only infer what gender differences in physiological responsiveness may mean by interpreting the results of these studies within the context of observational studies on emotion. Another problem with this literature is that there has been very little consideration of the fact that there is tremendous variability in physiological responsiveness within gender and overlap across gender for these measures. Therefore, we urge extreme caution in interpreting gender-specific findings yielded from physiological studies.

IV. Facial, Behavioral, and Vocal Channels of Emotional Expression

Because gender differences in observable emotional expression are often age dependent, we found it helpful to organize the findings in terms of developmental level. For infants, whether gender differences in emotionality are reported seems to be highly dependent on the social context. When observed in solitary play, few gender differences are noted at this developmental period. However, when observed during naturalistic interactions with their mothers, many studies have shown that female infants display more positive affect than male infants and that male infants express more irritability than female infants. Still other research has shown that when the emotion of sadness is considered, male infants display less sadness than female infants, even when the gender of the infant is hidden from the observer. Adults are also more likely to attribute anger to a distressed baby that they perceive to be male and to attribute fear to an infant they perceive to be female, even when the babies display the exact same behaviors.

In a major review of studies of gender comparisons in emotionality conducted in the early 1980s, Haviland and Malatesta found that the literature portrayed male infants as more irritable, more emotional labile, and less emotionally responsive than female infants. More recent research has demonstrated that although gender differences in the expression of positive emotion favoring females are especially apparent when a mother–child play situation is used, this difference is no longer detectable by five months of age. This is an important finding given that some researchers believe that stability in infants' emotional expressivity does not occur until after five months of age. When the still-faced paradigm is used,

whether or not gender differences emerge depends on maternal affective behavior in the play that precedes the still face. In this procedure, the mother is instructed to maintain a particular affective tone (positive, negative, or neutral) in her interactions with her infant. After several minutes, she is then instructed to remain silent and to maintain a neutral or nonexpressive facial display. Female infants of mothers who were affectively positive in the preceding play situation are more likely to maintain a neutral facial expression whereas male infants of affectively positive mothers are more likely to display negative affect in response to the still face. Moreover, male infants tend to have a more difficult time "recovering" from a mothers' still face than do female infants. Although most studies of infants have focused on the expression of primary emotions, a few researchers have examined whether there are gender differences in self-evaluative emotions. In 1992, Michael Lewis and his colleagues reported that female infants displayed more shame than male infants when failing a problem-solving task, especially when the task was regarded as easy rather than difficult.

Research on gender comparisons in emotional expressivity in the toddler and preschool period is also highly incongruent. For toddlers, most studies have shown no gender differences, regardless of whether the children are observed in delay of gratification tasks (e.g., child is offered a highly attractive treat that remains in view and is told that she or he has to wait a few minutes before receiving it) or during separation from the primary caregiver. This is generally true regardless of whether one considers facial expressions of emotions, internal state language (i.e., talk about feelings, wants, or abilities), or behavioral indicators of emotion. For older children, methodology does seem to impact the findings. Specifically, gender-emotion associations are more likely to be found when verbally reported emotions are considered. Preschool girls report more fear and sadness than boys, and preschool boys report more anger than preschool girls in response to hypothetical vignettes as well as affect-inducing films. In addition, preschool girls perceive themselves as experiencing more negative emotional reactions than preschool boys.

Observational data is less consistent, however. Although some studies demonstrate that preschool boys generally display more anger and less sadness than preschool girls, most recent research indicates that gender differences do not exist with regard to the expression of anger in the preschool years. However, studies have consistently shown that the intensity of expressed anger tends to be greater for boys than for girls. The exception to this general pattern is for children who are at risk for externalizing problems. In this case, disruptive preschool girls display more anger than disruptive preschool boys. Disruptive preschool girls also express more anger than boys in hypothetical situations of conflict. Research also indicates that preschool boys and girls become angry for similar reasons. Nonetheless, boys tend to respond to anger in ways that would seem to escalate the anger whereas preschool girls tend to react in ways that would de-escalate the anger situation. It should be acknowledged that most of the above-described studies have focused on observations of preschoolers during interactions with peers. When young children are observed or portrayed (in the case of hypothetical vignettes), gender differences in emotionality are rarely reported. In a 1993 study that considered young children's expressiveness during emotionally charged events in the presence of adults, Amy Halberstadt and her colleagues did not find gender differences in positive or negative emotional expression.

For school-age children, some researchers have found that boys express more anger than girls whereas others have reported no differences in self-reported anger for middle-school girls and boys. Comparable to the data on preschoolers, school-age girls and boys generally seem to become angry for similar reasons. One exception to this pattern is that school-age boys are significantly less likely to make a distinction with regard to intent when the cause of their anger is physical. On the other hand, school-age girls tend to reduce their anger if they later learn that the cause was accidental versus intentional. In response to their own anger, school-age boys report being more likely to act out physically (i.e., retaliate) and girls report that they spend time alone or talking with others to regulate their negative feelings. Overall, girls tend to respond more often with what has been termed relational aggression (e.g., pouting, sulking, social rejection) especially when angry because they themselves have been socially rejected by a peer. Interestingly, however, boys view girls as behaving more physically aggressive in response to anger than girls view themselves. Another finding that is fairly consistent across studies of preschoolers as well as school-age children is that girls seem to have an easier time than boys controlling the display of negative emotion. This finding emerges when observations are used to assess emo-

tion regulation and when teachers or other adults provide ratings of the children's emotionality. Finally, school-age girls' emotional displays are more dependent on the feedback they receive from others than those of boys.

Emotionality has been relatively understudied in adolescence. The lack of consistent research on this topic for this developmental period is surprising given that some theorists have hypothesized that children's gender-role orientations become more stereotypical from late childhood through adolescence and that adolescents frequently encounter situations that elicit extreme levels of emotions. Nonetheless, those studies that have been reported for this age group have suggested that adolescent girls express more sadness, surprise, guilt, and disgust than adolescent boys. Although significant differences have not been found, there is also a tendency for adolescent girls to express more anger than adolescent boys. This finding is opposite of what has typically been reported in research with younger children or adults. In addition to expressing a broader range of emotions, the intensity of expressed emotion is greater for adolescent girls than for their male counterparts. [*See* ADOLESCENT GENDER DEVELOPMENT.]

From adolescence onward, gender differences in self-reported emotions are highly dependent on the type of emotion. Numerous studies have shown that adult women express more positive emotion (e.g., happiness and feelings of love) than adult men in both naturalistic and laboratory situations. These findings are especially apparent when women are observed interacting with other women. Women are also concerned about portraying themselves to others as happy. For example, when asked to select photographs of themselves that will be viewed publicly, females tend to favor pictures of themselves smiling. Such a finding does not emerge for men. For negative emotions, adult females report more shame, surprise, guilt, and sadness than males and males report expressing more contempt than females. In the case of sadness, women report experiencing more intense sadness and they believe that their distress persists longer than that of men. There are also differences in how women and men reportedly respond to their own sadness. Women tend to seek out friends and confidants to talk about their feelings and the incident that caused their sadness whereas men tend to withdraw from social contact with others. Adult female friends also place a greater emphasis on the discussion of emotions during social interactions whereas male friends tend to emphasize shared activities. Women also tend to express their disappointment by crying and men tend to maintain a neutral facial expression, especially in public situations. However, the data for gender differences in self-reported sadness and fear are more inconclusive than for the other negative emotions.

As already noted, females describe their emotional experiences as occurring more frequently and more intensely than males do, but only in situations that emphasize gender roles. For example, women are more likely to express and talk about emotions in interpersonal situations whereas men tend to be more expressive of happiness, sadness, and anger in competitive situations (e.g., achievement settings). Women's perceptions of themselves as more expressive than men is also intensified if they have children. We will return to this issue in the section on emotion socialization practices.

There also seem to be self-reported differences in how males and females respond to anger-provoking situations. When angry, women report they respond by crying whereas men report they feel more comfortable expressing their feelings of anger. Self-report data often do not conform to the stereotype of men being more expressive of anger than women. In fact, many researchers have found no gender differences in the intensity with which anger is expressed or in the self-reported disposition to express anger. Rather, gender-role identity and not biological sex has been identified by some as the determining factor. Specifically, both women and men identified as masculine express more anger than feminine or androgynous individuals. Conversely, feminine individuals tend to surpress the expression of anger.

When observational measures of emotion are used, women are viewed as more emotional than men. These results are most consistent for positive emotions and for the negative emotions of fear and sadness, with differences generally favoring women. Although differences are generally not seen in the expression of overall fear, women express more fear than men in response to specific events (e.g., fear of snakes). When asked to pose emotional expressions, females are better than men at portraying fear and sadness and men are better than women at posing anger. At the same time, however, males are better at posing fear when multiple modes of emotional expression (e.g., vocal and facial cues) are considered. Such differences are not reported for children. Finally, women tend to be better than men at recognizing emotional expressions in the self and others except in the case of anger, where men tend to be regarded as more accurate than women.

Despite the fact that some studies have shown that toddler and preschool girls use more emotion language than their counterparts, researchers have generally demonstrated few gender differences in overall emotion language. However, when emotion language is assessed within the context of discussion of interpersonal events, research with school-age children and adults has shown that females talk more about emotions than males. In addition, preschool girls talk more about emotions than preschool boys when prompted but not during spontaneous speech. Methodological problems exist with research on children's emotion language, however. That is, emotion language is typically assessed during parent–child interactions and measurements are at the dyadic rather than the individual level. This means that children's emotion language is coded as a function of parents' emotion language so that parents who frequently talk about emotion may subsequently elicit more emotion-based language in their children.

V. Gender Comparisons on Emotional Display Rules

As previously noted, emotional expressivity is often determined from facial expressions, vocal and bodily cues of emotions, and activity level. Because people often experience emotions that they do not wish to express externally in facial expression or verbal response, internal feelings may be discrepant from the facial expression of emotion. In concealing their internal feelings, individuals can use a number of strategies including maintaining a neutral facial expression, increasing or decreasing the intensity of an emotional display, or masking their true emotion by displaying a different emotion. There are a several reasons why individuals would wish to offer discrepant internal and external cues of emotion, including wanting to protect themselves from embarrassment or to avoid some other negative consequence (i.e., self-protective reasons) or to avoid hurting some else's feelings (i.e., prosocial reasons). Because women and men believe that their emotions will elicit differential feedback from others, it is possible that the reasons as well as the strategies that people use to "confuse" others about their true feelings may differ for females and males. This is a particularly important issue to address because gender differences in external emotional expressivity are larger than gender differences in internal emotional experience. Theorists have suggested that these findings are largely the result of people's perceptions about how they will be evaluated by others in terms of what is considered to be gender-appropriate emotional behavior. Research supports the view that women expect negative consequences for themselves if they fail to express positive emotions, whereas men expect more positive consequences for the expression of what are considered to be more powerful emotions such as anger and pride. Similar findings have been reported for school-age girls and boys. An additional hypothesis that has been posited as an explanation for these differences is that males and females have different goals about what they think their emotional expressions will achieve. These are important points in that display rule activation requires that there be an awareness that a particular emotional expression is warranted by the situation and that failure to express the appropriate emotion may elicit negative feedback from others.

For the most part, research on display rules has focused on children preschool age and older. Research on preschoolers has shown that when presented a disappointing gift, preschool girls are more likely to display positive emotion than preschool boys. Researchers have taken this finding to mean that girls may be more apt to surpress their disappointment by displaying positive rather than negative affect. When preschoolers are asked about their emotional responses to hypothetical vignettes designed to "pull for" the use of display rules, girls tend to offer more "correct" responses to boys but only when the protagonist in the story wanted to conceal his or her "true" feelings for prosocial reasons. Similar findings have also been reported for school-age children, particularly when the emotions of anger and sadness are considered. Using a similar paradigm with school-age children, three studies have shown no overall gender differences. However, in 1992, Marion Underwood and colleagues reported that when asked to give their responses to videotaped hypothetical scenarios, school-age girls are more likely than boys to report that they would conceal their "true" feelings if what they were feeling was anger. When the facial expressions of school-age children are observed in the disappointment paradigm similar to that described earlier, school-age boys reportedly show more negative affect than school-age girls. This may be because boys expect more disapproval for expressing sadness than girls and expect less disapproval for expressing anger. These findings are further clarified when the emotions of sadness and pain are considered. Using

a similar paradigm in research on adults, David Matsumoto did not report gender differences.

VI. Gender Comparisons on Empathy

In terms of empathy, researchers have mostly been interested in its role in the development of interpersonal relationships. Although the relation between empathy and prosocial behavior is often modest and there are inconsistencies across studies, empirical research over the past 25 years has generally demonstrated that empathy-related responding is an important motivator of prosocial and moral behavior for both children and adults. Other functions of empathy include the facilitation of the parent–child bond and the development of self-concept. Investigators have sometimes speculated on the negative role of empathy, particularly in the development of psychopathology. For example, adults who are regarded as low in other-oriented emotional responsiveness are at higher risk for psychopathology including neuroticism, externalizing problems, and abusive parenting behavior. An inverse relation between empathy and externalizing problems has also been reported for children.

As with emotional expressivity, the literature on gender comparisons in empathy is highly inconsistent. In general, empathy has typically been regarded as a feminine strength. For instance, there is a strong perception that females are more concerned than males about the feelings of others. Instead, males are judged to be more concerned with their own feelings or as unaffected emotionally by distressing experiences. On the other hand, females are viewed by others as more likely than males to provide social support to distressed others and are more likely to be the recipients of such support when distressed themselves. Indeed, the belief that women are more nurturing and more likely to respond with care and concern in response to a needy other is a pervasive one in both the popular and professional literature. Such a belief is also manifested in children's storybooks and television programs.

The literature on gender comparisons in the actual expression of empathy has been reviewed by a number of prominent scholars across the past three decades. The conclusions drawn from these various reviews have sometimes differed primarily because empathy has been defined and measured so differently across studies. In some cases, empathy has been defined solely in terms of cognitive processes such as affective perspective-taking (i.e., understanding that another person's emotional reaction to a situation can differ from one's own). Other researchers have focused on more affective processes in their definition of empathy and have considered social sensitivity to others' emotions (e.g., feeling sorry for a distressed other). More recently, however, both developmental and social psychologists have defined empathy as the apprehension of the affective state or condition of another and experiencing an emotion that is congruent with that state or condition. Indeed, researchers who regularly contribute to the literature on empathy have emphasized the fact that feelings of sympathy or personal distress can result from feelings of empathy. *Sympathy* is characterized as an other-oriented response that can stem from either empathy or cognitive processes whereas personal distress is a self-oriented response that is focused on alleviating one's own distress. Research has supported these distinctions. Sympathy has been positively related to prosocial behavior and social competence in children as well as adults, whereas feelings of personal distress have been strongly associated with self-focused behavior.

Despite this important theoretical advance in the empathy literature, not all of the research we review will make distinctions among the various components of empathy. In including this research, we do not wish to minimize the important advances that have been made in the theoretical and empirical writings on the topic. Instead, we chose to include all available research whether labeled empathy, sympathy, or personal distress and will address issues of definition and measurement as they relate to whether or not gender differences are found.

From a developmental perspective, we know very little about empathic expressiveness in the first year of life. However, in a meta-analysis conducted in 1983, Nancy Eisenberg and Randy Lennon concluded that female infants are slightly more likely than males to respond to another's crying by crying themselves. At the same time, they point out that it is difficult to draw strong conclusions from this early work because in the majority of studies, the crying was that of a female infant. However, in research that focused on more contemporary observational measures that treat empathic concern and personal distress separately, Judy Ungerer and her colleagues did not report gender differences.

The bulk of the work on empathy development of toddlers has been conducted in the laboratory of Carolyn Zahn-Waxler and her colleagues. Some of this work has demonstrated that female toddlers show stronger expressions of empathic concern for others' distress than male toddlers but only for distress that they witness as a bystander. The female toddlers also displayed more referential behaviors (e.g., imitations or enactment of others' distress) than male toddlers. In this research, toddlers' responsiveness to simulated maternal and examiner distress as well as to infant crying are generally included as measures of empathy. In a 1999 investigation that involved similar procedures, no main effects of gender were found. Nonetheless, the empathy responsiveness of girls did seem to be negatively impacted by maternal insensitivity and poor parenting behavior. No such relations were reported for toddler boys. In a third study conducted with an independent sample, no gender differences were found in the empathy behavior of toddler girls and boys. This was true even when discrete measures as well as global ratings of empathy were considered. Research in a different laboratory has also shown that female toddlers expressed more self-distress as well as more attention to the distress of peers than male toddlers. In a paradigm that assessed toddlers' reparative attempts and concerned reparation in response to a doll breaking and juice spilling, no gender differences were reported, perhaps because responsiveness to a mishap does not pull for an empathic response the same way that a distressed other does.

For preschoolers, whether or not gender differences have been found has been dependent on how empathy has been assessed. In a 1995 study with children at varying risk for conduct disorders that included numerous stimuli, Carolyn Zahn-Waxler and her colleagues reported that it was only when viewing mothers' responsiveness to seeing their children in pain that gender differences in facial indices of empathy favoring preschool girls were found. In this same research, there was a tendency for boys to have a lower heart rate than girls in response to sad stories in a mood induction paradigm. On the other hand, the girls displayed more skin conductance and a greater heart rate deceleration than boys in response to the sad stories. Recall that high skin conductance and heart rate acceleration are regarded as indices of personal distress and that low skin conductance and heart rate deceleration are viewed as an index of sympathy. With this in mind, the findings of the above-described study are difficult to interpret in that there was not convergence in the findings for heart rate and skin conductance. In research conducted in a different laboratory, preschoolers were observed watching films that were designed to elicit personal distress or empathic concern. Again, preschool girls were observed to express more facial sadness than boys. However, in research using an affect-matching paradigm, preschool boys and girls do not show differential responsiveness to an affect-inducing slide.

In a series of studies on middle-school children, several researchers have reported no differences in girls' and boys' empathy scores on self-report measures. However, at least one study has shown that differences are found when the self-report measure contain items that assess sympathy as well as personal distress. When affective perspective-taking tasks have been used to assess empathy, gender differences are rarely reported. Nevertheless, first- and second-grade girls report more congruence between their own emotional state and a needy other than boys. For first graders, research has shown that girls display more prosocial behavior after receiving empathic instructions than boys. In a 1997 study of 5-, 9-, and 13-year-olds, Janet Strayer and William Roberts found that girls scored higher than boys on facial and verbal measures of empathy. For both measures, empathy was scored when there was a match (either verbally or facially) between the child's affect and that of a hypothetical story character. At least two studies have shown that gender differences in middle-school children's empathy responses to hypothetical vignettes are intensified when the target child is of the same sex as the respondent. Moreover, the proportion of girls that respond with empathy to hypothetical vignettes is greater than that for males. In a study in which physiological measures were used, kindergartners and second-grade boys displayed more facial distress and higher skin conductance than girls in response to an affect-inducing film. However, gender differences are not found when researchers considered children's responses to only the most emotionally evocative portion of the film.

For adolescents, self-report data has indicated that adolescent girls score higher than boys on empathic concern. This is an important finding given that this measure focuses on cognitive as well as affective components of empathy and distinguishes between empathic concern and personal distress. Adolescent girls also score higher than boys on Davis' Interpersonal Reactivity Index. Using a methodology in which self-report items were differentiated according to sex of target, the majority of adolescents included in a high-empathy group were adolescent girls and the majority of adolescents in the low-empathy group were boys. In addition, both adolescent girls and

boys responded with empathy toward a distressed girl more often than to a distressed boy. In a study that included middle-school children of varying ages as well as undergraduate students, researchers did not find gender differences for facial indices of empathy.

Research on adults has shown that women are more distressed than men at the onset of a distress-eliciting event and remain distressed for a longer period than men. Self-report measures that included items that assess both cognitive and affective components of empathy do seem to differentiate males and females with females demonstrating higher empathy scores than males. In addition, when questioned about their empathy-related responsiveness toward a same-sex peer enduring an uncomfortable electric shock, adult women who expected to face the same treatment reported more empathy than other women whereas men facing a similar fate actually reported less empathy than other men. In addition, after reading a transcript of an adolescent experiencing a distressing event, adult women who reported having had a similar experience as an adolescent reported more empathy than women who had not. No such pattern emerged for men.

Recently, researchers have begun to investigate the influence of gender-role orientation on empathic responsiveness. This research seems to suggest that gender-role identity as measured by Bem's Sex Role Inventory is a better predictor of empathy than biological sex. Specifically, this research has demonstrated that empathy and endorsement of some female-stereotyped traits are positively correlated, whereas endorsement of male-typed traits is a negative predictor of empathy. Other research has shown that males who were characterized as "macho" responded to infant cries with less empathy and more anger than other males. Similar findings have been reported for school-age children and adolescents. Some researchers have theorized that males who reject female-typed attributes have difficulty developing intimate personal relationships with others, which reduces their opportunity for experiencing sympathy in response to other people's distress. An androgynous gender-role orientation is also positively associated with empathic concern. Recall that these findings are similar to those discussed earlier for overall emotional expression. Interestingly, however, females and males do not differ in their overall recognition and responsiveness to infant cry signals, especially if the cries are of their own children.

VII. *Gender and Emotion Socialization*

Parents vary greatly in the strategies and behaviors they use to socialize children's emotions. For example, some parents express high levels of positive emotion during interactions with their children or encourage a broad range of emotional expressions within their families. Other parents express high levels of negative affect during parent–child interactions or discourage their children's expression of negative emotions. In writings in the popular press and the empirical literature, professionals have begun to take note of the fact that parents use different emotion socialization practices with girls and boys. For example, in a study of the popular advice literature, researchers have found that both mothers and fathers are frequently warned about the important role of emotion in everyday parent–child interactions and cautioned about how the expression of certain emotions can be detrimental to the welfare of their children. Interestingly, however, mothers are more likely to be cautioned about their presumed tendency to overreact emotionally and therefore are frequently reminded about the importance of regulating their negative emotions during emotionally charged interactions with their children. On the other hand, fathers are advised to express their emotions more openly, with few comments made about the necessity of managing the display of inappropriate emotions. It should be noted that such advice conforms to gender-related stereotypes about emotional expression.

In the empirical literature, mothers are often described as being more skilled than fathers at managing their own emotions. Mothers also report more positive family emotion than fathers, especially in the presence of daughters. In a 1998 study, Alison Heinhold and her colleagues found that female college students reported expressing more emotions than male students. Mothers of these students also reported more emotion than the fathers. Even more interesting is the fact that both mothers' and fathers' ratings of the daughters' expressivity were correlated with daughters' but not sons' perceptions of their own emotionality.

Research has shown that parents make a major effort to teach girls about emotions and boys often receive negative feedback from parents for expressing emotions that are counter to stereotypical beliefs about male emotional expression. Anger reactions are more tolerated in boys than in girls. Anger responses in girls are more likely to be followed by negative emotional reactions from mothers whereas the anger responses of boys receive more empathic parental reactions.

Regarding affectively laden conversations, both mothers and fathers use more emotion words with daughters than with sons during parent–child discussions and storytelling. In addition, both mothers and fathers also rarely discuss anger with their daughters but do so frequently with their sons. This pattern is reversed for the emotion of sadness. In a 1996 study, Norah Feeny and her colleagues observed mothers as they talked to their preschoolers about the school day, finding that mothers of girls asked more about the emotion of happiness than mothers of boys. There is also evidence that parents of girls expect more emotional control and the use of more sophisticated emotion regulation strategies from their daughters than from their sons. Girls are also more socialized than boys to be more sensitive to the sadness and hurt feelings of others. Researchers have hypothesized that parents may send a message to girls that emotions are important whereas boys may instead learn that expressing and discussing their feelings is inappropriate.

Mothers' and fathers' emotion socialization practices may also influence children's social emotional competence in different ways. For example, the frequency, intensity, and clarity of fathers' positive expressions are related to girls' and boys' peer-related social competence. For mothers, only the intensity of maternal positive expression is associated with preschoolers' popularity among peers. In other research, maternal self-reports of sensitivity to the thoughts and feelings of others have been associated with girls' but not boys' social sensitivity to others. Maternal discouragement of the display of inappropriate affect in reaction to another's distress has also been associated with boys' but not girls' sympathy-related responsiveness. Maternal negative emotion is inversely related to boys' but not girls' understanding of emotions. Maternal perspective-taking in response to emotional events has been associated with girls' and not boys' prosocial behavior. Similarly, girls' and not boys' empathy-related responsiveness has been associated with parents' style of emotional expression. It has been suggested that females may be more aroused when facing a situation that "pulls for" an empathic response and therefore may be more responsive to parental efforts to elicit empathy.

Some researchers have asserted that the transmission of some parental emotions to children may be especially strong for fathers because of their more powerful position in the family. Specifically, it has often been hypothesized that fathers' emotion socialization practices may predict children's social and emotional competence when mothers' emotion socialization practices do not. For instance, fathers' emotion socialization practices have predicted children's ability to control their expression of emotions during peer play and their empathy-related responsiveness even when maternal emotion socialization practices do not. In 1996, Ross Parke and his colleagues reported that fathers who frequently respond with negative affect tend to have preschoolers who are less prosocial than other children. This relation was not found for mothers. In another study, mothers' and fathers' emotion socialization practices both contributed unique variance in explaining young children's emotional competence. In other research, fathers' and not mothers' encouragement of emotional expression was associated with preschoolers' general competence. Fathers who use emotion socialization strategies that encourage the active regulation of emotion tend to have children who are more likely to implement a display rule. It is important to note that the majority of research on this topic has been conducted on White middle-income families. It is not known whether the same findings would emerge in studies that include more diverse samples.

The peer environment also serves as a socialization agent. Some researchers have hypothesized that the small playgroups of girls tend to encourage positive affect and discourage negative affect whereas the larger playgroups of boys maximize the opportunities for conflict and negative emotion. Others have reported that when placed in situations that require emotional control, girls do more social monitoring than boys, suggesting that girls are more concerned about the repercussions of negative emotional displays than boys. For some girls, conforming to socialization pressures for maximizing positive emotional displays may interfere with their ability to attend to other situational demands and could eventually lead to disruptive and inappropriate behavior in the classroom environment. Unfortunately, the peer environment is an aspect of emotion socialization that has rarely been investigated. Given that children spend so much of their time away from home, researchers should begin to more systematically examine the role of peers and teachers in the emotion socialization process.

VIII. Conclusions

In conclusion, this review indicates that, overall, males and females differentially express emotions.

However, these differences are small and are highly dependent on the social context and the specific emotion under consideration. Furthermore, in many cases, the differences reported may be due to methodological artifacts. For example, a good deal of what we know about gender-emotion associations (especially for adults) is based on self-report data. When observational methods have been used, the gender of the participant is typically not hidden from the observer. This has most certainly influenced the outcome of many studies. Given the limitations of current methodologies, researchers must work harder to develop new paradigms to investigate potential gender differences in emotionality. Therefore, before making definitive conclusions about a particular set of findings, the reader should consider the robustness of the finding across the different development periods. Moreover, we suggest that there also be some serious consideration of whether the findings presented here speak more to actual differences between males and females in the expression of emotion or more to gender-emotion stereotypes. Finally, the great majority of this work has been descriptive. Researchers must work harder to develop theoretical models to help explain what differences may mean if found. Clearly, this is an important and interesting topic that warrants further study.

SUGGESTED READING

Brody, L. R. (1999). *Gender, Emotion, and the Family.* Harvard University Press, Cambridge, MA.

Brody, L. R., and Hall, J. A. (1993). Gender and emotion. In *Handbook of Emotions* (M. Lewis and J. M. Haviland, eds.), pp. 447–460. Guilford, New York.

Eisenberg, N., Fabes, R. A., and Shea, C. (1989). Gender differences in empathy and prosocial reasoning: Empirical investigations. In *Who cares? Theory, Research, and Educational Implications of the Ethic of Care* (M. M. Brabeck, ed.), pp. 127–143. Praeger, New York.

Eisenberg, N., and Lennon, R. (1983). Sex differences in empathy and related capacities. *Psychological Bulletin* 94, 100–131.

Feshbach, N. D. (1982). Sex differences in empathy and social behavior in children. In *The Development of Prosocial Behavior* (N. Eisenberg, ed.), pp. 315–338. Academic Press, New York.

Fischer, A. (1993). Sex differences in emotionality: Fact or stereotype? *Feminism and Psychology* 3, 303–318.

Hoffman, M. L. (1977). Sex differences in empathy and related behaviors. *Psychological Bulletin* 84, 712–722.

Lennon, R., and Eisenberg, N. (1987). Gender and age differences in empathy and sympathy. In *Empathy and Its Development* (N. Eisenberg and J. Strayer, eds.), pp. 195–217. Cambridge, New York.

Manstead, A. S. R. (1992). Gender differences in emotion. In *Handbook of Individual Differences: Biological Perspectives* (A. Gale and M. Eysenck, eds.), pp. 355–387. Wiley, New York.

Entitlement

Janice M. Steil
Vannesa L. McGann
Anne S. Kahn
Adelphi University

Glossary

Deserving Refers to the relationship between a person and his or her outcomes; also a set of attitudes about what a person feels he or she is due on the basis of what has been contributed or earned relative to some comparison other. According to most justice theories, failure to receive what one deserves leads to feelings of anger and perceptions of unfair treatment.

Narcissism A pattern of grandiose thinking or behavior marked by an excessive sense of self-importance and the feeling that one is special or unique and should be treated accordingly.

Relative deprivation theory A theory of social justice and social change seeking to explain the frequently observed gap between objective reality and subjective satisfaction. Specifically, relative deprivation theory seeks to explain why the objectively disadvantaged, either as a group (fraternal deprivation) or as individuals (egoistic deprivation), are often satisfied with discriminatory conditions and low outcomes, while the objectively advantaged are often dissatisfied despite favorable conditions and relatively high outcomes. According to the theory, in order for discriminatory outcomes or conditions to be perceived as unfair, individuals or groups must (1) be aware that more favorable outcomes exist, (2) desire these outcomes, (3) believe that they are entitled to these different outcomes, (4) attribute the failure to attain these outcomes to external sources, and, finally, (5) believe that the different outcomes are attainable.

Social comparison theory A theory of self-evaluation proposing that, in the absence of objective standards, individuals will evaluate diverse aspects of themselves, including their opinions, abilities, feelings, actions, and outcomes, through comparisons with others, preferably similar others.

ENTITLEMENT refers to a set of attitudes about what a person feels he or she has a right to, and what he or she can expect from others. Experienced as a moral imperative, the sense of entitlement is strongly linked to perceptions of injustice, and as such has a distinct affective component with strong motivational implications.

Encyclopedia of Women and Gender, Volume One
Copyright © 2001 by Academic Press. All rights of reproduction in any form reserved.

I. Entitlement Defined

Over the past 25 years, there has been increasing interest in the sense of entitlement—as a factor in healthy human functioning, as an important precondition to the perception of unfair treatment, and as a key element in the elimination of current gender inequalities. Yet entitlement as a construct has seldom been defined.

Dictionaries typically identify two branches of meaning for entitle, both stemming from the word "title." The first branch has its roots in the context of nobility or rank, as in giving someone a title or status, and thus implies special rights over others based on special qualities one possesses. The second branch stems from the definition of title that means a right to a possession, as in having a title to a property. This definition pertains not to special rights over others but to the basic and legitimate rights that conform to social rules in the context of a just society.

The first aspect of entitlement that pertains to special rights over others has been used in the clinical literature to discuss neurotic overprivilege and narcissism. This extreme entitlement has been defined by clinicians, beginning with Sigmund Freud, as a non-reality-based and distorted self-perception that consists of grandiose ideas of one's rights without consideration of the rights and feelings of others. In contrast to this pathologic overentitlement, clinicians have also spoken of pathologic restricted entitlement in which one feels a sense of worthlessness, expresses few opinions, acts exceedingly deferential, or fails to require one's just due. It has often been suggested in the clinical literature that these two positions, that of the over- and underentitled, are two ends of a continuum, both characteristic of extreme self-esteem deficits. [*See* SELF-ESTEEM.]

The second definition of entitlement, which pertains to basic and legitimate rights, has been the primary focus of social psychologists, particularly those interested in the psychology of justice. *Black's Law Dictionary* highlights the societal obligation to respect and enforce legitimate entitlements defining the construct as a right that may not be abridged without due process. Sociologists and social psychologists also focus on the legitimate and motivational aspects of entitlement. Eleanor Singer has defined entitlement as an expectation with normative force. Similarly, Melvin Lerner defined entitlement as a cognitive judgment with affective and motivational implications.

A number of scholars have suggested that the sense of entitlement is synonymous with a sense of deserving. Indeed, both constructs are central to sociological and psychological theories of justice asserting that failure to receive valued outcomes that one deserves, or to which one is entitled, leads to feelings of anger and outrage, to perceptions of unfair treatment, and to a desire for change. Others, while agreeing on the importance of both constructs to perceptions of injustice, have proposed that each is based on qualitatively different inputs leading to different outcomes. For example, Janice Steil argued that the sense of deserving is based primarily on earning or achieving, whereas the sense of entitlement is based on more ascribed characteristics. Thus, the sense of entitlement may be more closely associated with socially constructed perceptions of who one is, whereas the sense of deserving may be closely linked to perceptions of what one has done. Given this distinction, entitlement can be seen as a more stable and consistent part of a person, which varies across social roles (wife, mother, student, professional) and across contexts (personal as compared to professional relationships). Deserving, by contrast, may represent a more dynamic attribute changing according to what a person feels he or she has done (performed poorly or well) relative to a particular outcome. Because our sense of who we are can emanate from either an ascribed (e.g., woman) or achieved (e.g., professor) status, the constructs are not mutually exclusive. Yet, as noted later in this article, Steil asserted that the difference in inputs has significant implications for the elimination of gender inequalities.

Taking these varying perspectives into account, then, the sense of entitlement may be defined as a set of attitudes about what a person feels he or she has a right to and can expect from others both as an individual and as a member of a social group. In addition, the sense of entitlement is strongly linked to the perception of injustice and as such has a distinct affective component with strong motivational consequences.

II. The Etiology of Entitlement

In addressing the origins of entitlement, and the sources of individual variability in entitlement levels, clinical theorists tend to emphasize the importance of early family interactions. Social psychologists, focusing more on group differences in the sense of entitlement, emphasize the importance of the socialization process. From this perspective, differences in entitlement levels emanate from differences in status ascribed to various social groups, as well as to the differences in rights and responsibilities associated with different social roles.

Analytic theorists have explained both restricted and excessive levels of entitlement in terms of early childhood disturbances. In 1916, Freud wrote that narcissistic levels of entitlement were related to the feeling of being owed special privileges due to early experiences of suffering in the form of illness or deformity. More recently, excessive levels of entitlement have been associated with lack of attunement, parental rejection, and overgratifying parents. Restrictive entitlement is also said to result from difficult childhood experiences leading to shame or fear. In contrast, a variety of preconditions for healthy entitlement have been posited in the literature, such as adequate parental involvement, including empathic mirroring, strong attachment, attunement, and respect for the infant's most basic needs and desires.

As a child grows, she or he becomes increasingly socialized to cultural norms. Such norms ascribe different statuses to various social groups and assign specific rights and responsibilities to those who perform various social roles. Of particular interest over the past decade has been the extent to which society's differential socialization of men and women, and differential valuing of gendered behaviors, produces a lower sense of entitlement in women as compared to men. Feminist theorists such as Nancy Chodorow and Jean Baker Miller have argued that women are socialized to be nurturing caretakers whose priority is to put others first and to value connections above achievement. Thus, they argued that for women, nurturing, expressiveness, and relationship work come to be valued above independent strivings, competition, and agency. Men, in contrast, are lauded for concentrating on their own needs in order to become independent, successful, and achievement oriented. It has been proposed that these differences result in a lower sense of entitlement in women.

From the social psychological perspective, both gendered expectations, beginning early in family life, and the division of labor along gendered lines affect the expectations and beliefs that women and men hold regarding both their capacities and their opportunities. In addition, gender often covaries with power such that women have access to fewer resources and have less power than men. Gender also covaries with status such that the activities and characteristics associated with women are less valued than the activities and characteristics associated with men. From this perspective, society's system of gendered roles and their attendant statuses leads to gendered levels of entitlement.

Integrating these diverse perspectives, then, the sense of entitlement varies across individuals and groups as a result of early caretaking interactions and the subsequent internalization of societal expectations and social norms.

We now turn to the growing body of studies designed to assess the extent to which differences in entitlement levels can help to explain the persistence of social inequality, particularly the inequalities of women and men at home and at work.

III. *Entitlement in the Workplace*

Seventy-three percent of women are now employed and women now constitute 46% of the paid labor force. Yet, despite recent gains, women continue to be underrepresented in high paying, high prestige jobs and are paid less than similarly qualified men doing comparable work. Indeed, despite decades of educational and legal changes, women still earn only 74 cents for every dollar earned by a man. Neither women nor men are oblivious to these differences, yet findings from both laboratory and field studies suggest that women are not proportionately aggrieved.

Faye Crosby, in a particularly well-designed study, surveyed 345 female and male full-time workers, matched on three levels of occupational prestige. Overall, the findings showed that women in the sample were underpaid relative to men in comparable positions. Further, both women and men reported that women in general were paid less than men; yet the women reported themselves no less satisfied with their pay, their jobs, or their treatment than their more highly paid male colleagues. In other words, women respondents reported that women in general were underpaid relative to men, yet they seemed unaware of their own objective underpayment relative to their male colleagues and expressed no grievance relative to their own salaries or working conditions. Crosby characterized this intriguing pattern of findings the "paradox of the contented female worker."

Evidence from laboratory studies is equally compelling. Callahan-Levy and Messé asked men and women to work on a task for a fixed amount of time and then to pay themselves, as well as others, for their work. Women paid themselves significantly less money and reported less money as fair pay than did men. Subsequently, Brenda Major, and her colleagues, replicated and expanded this self-pay paradigm to construct social psychology's most developed theory of gender differences in the sense of entitlement. Through an intriguing series of laboratory studies, Major showed that, in the absence of external pay standards, women paid themselves less for comparable or better work relative to men and reported less pay as fair. Further, when women and men were given a fixed amount of pay and asked to do as much work as they thought was fair for the amount of money they were paid, women worked significantly longer, did more work, completed more correct work, and worked more efficiently than did men. These gender differences occurred despite participants' expectations that men would pay themselves more than women (study 1) and whether or not they believed their work was being monitored (study 2).

Why do women work longer and harder than men for the same amount of money? Why do women express so little discontent over pay inequities? How do we explain the "paradox of the contented female worker"? Early explanations of this phenomenon focused on gender differences in values. Women, it was argued, value interpersonal relationships and desirable working conditions more than men, whereas men value pay and promotion more than women. This contention, however, is largely unsupported by the research literature. Research focused on social structural variables consistently shows that conditions of employment, rather than gender, are the best predictors of what respondents say they value about their work. Men in low-paying jobs with little opportunity for advancement are just as likely as women to say they value relationships with others more than their actual work; and women in high-paying, high-prestige jobs are just as likely as their male counterparts to say that getting ahead is more important than maintaining relationships.

Rejecting the gendered values explanation, Major argued that gender differences in entitlement emanate from women's pattern of restricted comparisons—including normative comparisons, self-comparisons, social comparisons, and feasibility comparisons.

Consistent with the definitions of entitlement presented earlier in this article, Major argued that internalized social norms not only define what is appropriate for specific situations but also provide normative referents as to what one can expect and feel entitled to. What these referents tell women is that women's work is less valued than men's, and that it is normative for women to be paid less than men. Such normative referents regarding gendered differences in wage standards are internalized to create a lower sense of entitlement in women. Studies conducted in both the United States and Canada by Major and by Serge Desmarais and his colleagues showed that, even when controlling for academic major and career aspirations, college women reported significantly lower income expectations across all points of their careers—including career entry and career peak salaries as well as average annual income. Indeed, when a national sample of Canadian workers was asked, "What was the income you deserved (in the previous year) all things considered?" women reported that they deserved significantly less money than men, even when controlling for age, education, and job factors.

When women internalize a lower sense of entitlement on the basis of normative comparisons, these entitlement expectations are subsequently maintained or challenged through a series of comparisons with self and others. According to Major, the gendered wage gap begins early in life. Boys receive larger allowances than girls, "boys chores" are rewarded with higher wages than "girls chores," and college women earn less in their summer jobs than college men. For women, these gendered wage inequities lead to lower past outcomes and lower future expectations than those of men and, therefore, to self-comparisons that reinforce a lower sense of entitlement.

Comparisons to self, however, are believed to occur less frequently than comparisons to others—preferably similar others. According to Major, three factors are likely to affect the choice of comparison targets: (1) structural factors in the environment, such as proximity, that determine which targets are readily available for comparison, (2) the preference for similar targets, and (3) the goals or motivations of the person making the comparisons. To the extent that women work in female-dominated jobs, see other low-paid women as the most similar and relevant comparison, or are motivated to protect their self-esteem from the failure to achieve higher salaries perceived as unattainable, these factors converge in ways that maintain women's lower sense of entitlement.

This multifaceted position has received substantial, though sometimes qualified support. Laboratory studies have shown that college students have a robust first choice preference for comparing their outcomes to the outcomes of same-sex, same-job others. This preference is ameliorated, however, for participants assigned to cross-sex tasks and for women in high-achieving or "standard setter" conditions. Similarly, Crosby, in her study of employed workers, found that women overall preferred comparisons to other women, but that women in high-prestige positions were more than twice as likely to compare with men as women in low prestige positions. Janice Steil and Jennifer Hay, in a study of high-achieving women and men in primarily male-dominated positions, found that respondents were twice as likely to report that they compared with same-sex others rather than cross-sex others, yet the single most preferred category was combined-sex comparisons. Almost half of Steil and Hay's high-achieving sample participants said they compared with both women and men rather than to either sex exclusively, and almost one-quarter of the high achieving women said they compared primarily to men.

What, then, determines the choice of comparison other? Major suggested that the preference for same-sex comparisons is as much a function of the demographics of the workplace as it is a preference for gender similarity. This hypothesis has been the subject of little systematic investigation. Yet, in a study that directly assessed this issue, Steil and Hay found choice of comparison other to be unrelated to workplace demographics. Although there was considerable variability in the range of gender integration in the jobs respondents held, gender integration of the job was unrelated to sex of comparison other.

What of comparison outcomes? Consistent with the theory, Crosby found that women who compared with men were less satisfied with their outcomes than women who compared with other women. Steil and Hay found that women who compared to men were receiving higher salaries and were in more prestigious positions than women who compared with other women, and Major and her colleagues found that female subjects who had (bogus) information on the self-pay of either same or cross-sex others paid themselves more than subjects who had no information.

To summarize, then, laboratory, field, and contemporary survey studies all show that women continue to be underbenefited relative to men in today's workforce. Yet women do not seem proportionately aggrieved. It has been proposed that women's paradoxical satisfaction emanates from a lower sense of entitlement originating in gendered norms and maintained by a pattern of restricted self/other comparisons. Women compare their outcomes to their own past outcomes or to the outcomes of other women whom they see as similar to themselves. Yet comparing their outcomes to those of other underpaid women limits women's awareness of other possibilities, lowers their expectations, legitimizes inferior outcomes, and maintains a woman's satisfaction with the status quo.

Upward comparisons to those who are more highly paid can increase women's awareness of other possibilities, make them desirous of those other possibilities, enhance their sense of entitlement, and make them desirous of change. Studies have shown that the general preference for same-sex comparisons is ameliorated for women in high-achieving cross-sex contexts and that for women, cross-sex comparisons tend to be associated with higher outcomes and lowered satisfaction with the status quo. One of the biggest barriers to more highly paid comparisons, however, is a failure to believe in the feasibility of change, a topic to which we shall turn in subsequent sections. [*See* ACHIEVEMENT; ANDROCENTRISM; CAREER ACHIEVEMENT; WORKING ENVIRONMENTS.]

IV. Entitlement in the Home

Early interest in issues of gender inequality tended to focus on gender disparities in the paid labor force. A great deal of subsequent attention, however, has focused on the inequalities in men's and women's expectations of relationships and the sharing of the responsibilities of unpaid labor at home. The findings of a vast number of studies have been consistent. Contemporary relationships remain unequal. Wives' increasing commitment to work *outside* the home has not been matched by husbands' commitment to increased work *inside* the home. Indeed, across all domains of domestic life, there are gender-based imbalances; yet, paralleling the findings from the world of work, women do not seem to be proportionately aggrieved.

Husbands are still more likely to work full time, to earn more, and to be in higher status positions than their wives. Yet even when a wife does hold a high-status position, her husband's position is likely to be considered more important than her own. Employed wives continue to do nearly twice as much housework as their husbands do, including two-thirds of the repetitive, routine, and time-consuming tasks such as cooking, cleaning, and laundry. Wives also do from one-quarter to two-thirds more child care and the caretaking gap varies dramatically by the type of task. Mothers and fathers are about equally involved in play time, but mothers spend up to three times as much time alone with the children and continue to shoulder the major responsibility for planning, organizing, supervising, and scheduling activities. Additionally, wives do much more of the emotional work that relationships require, and these gender differences in emotion work result in wives providing better emotional support for husbands than husbands provide for wives.

Yet the majority of both employed and unemployed wives report the division of labor as fair. According to Mary Clare Lennon and Sarah Rosenfeld, it is only when wives' share of the work at home exceeds the two-thirds average that they begin to report the distribution as less than fair.

Why? The explanations for women's lack of grievance at home parallels the explanations of women's lack of grievance at work. A number of investigators including Sampson Blair and Micheal Johnson have suggested that women's lack of grievance is due to differences in what women and men value and want from relationships. According to this perspective, the most highly valued outcomes for women are interpersonal. Women, then, do housework in part as an expression of love and a way of caring for others. Consistent with this perspective, studies have shown that feeling appreciated by their husbands for the domestic work they do is one of the best predictors of wives' perceptions of marital fairness, and husbands' provision of emotional support has a more significant positive effect on wives' perceived well-being than husbands' contributions to housework or child care. From this perspective, then, women perceive their relationships as fair when they receive the interpersonal outcomes they value.

Others argue that women's lack of grievance with the asymmetries of married life is better explained by a sense of entitlement that is lower than their husbands'. Normative comparisons tell us that household work is women's work, that men should be responsible providers, and that women should be nurturing caretakers. Each of these socially constructed roles carries attendant rights and responsibilities; but the distribution of rights and responsibilities associated with the male provider role and the female nurturing role is asymmetrical. For a man, the provider role carries the obligation to earn and provide for the family. These responsibilities, however, generally entitle him to put his career above his wife's career, free him from a number of responsibilities at home, entitle him to a position of greater influence, and allow him to perceive the time he devotes to his paid work as an expression of family caring. For women, however, the provider role is often perceived as interfering with her role as nurturer. Thus, as Linda Thompson and Alexis Walker noted, even when a wife earns more than her husband, she is not entitled to view her career as primary, is not entitled to absent herself from household work, and unlike her husband it would not be acceptable to say that her paid work kept her from her children.

Evidence in support of these contentions comes from the findings of a number of studies documenting the difference in outcomes for high-earning husbands as compared to high-earning wives. When a husband earns more than his wife, he says his career is more important than hers and she agrees. Indeed, the more a husband earns relative to his wife, the greater his say in decision making, the lower his involvement in domestic work, and the better he feels about himself as a spouse and a parent. This is not the case for women. When a wife earns more than her husband, neither she nor her husband is likely to say that her career is more important. Further, women who earn more than their husbands do not feel better about themselves as spouses, and for some women, their husbands actually do less at home.

As in the workplace, the gendered sense of entitlement is maintained through restricted self and other comparisons. As Major and others have pointed out, a number of studies of family work have shown that gender-based patterns of family labor are established at an early age. Boys are allowed to spend more time in leisure activities than girls, and girls are asked to spend more time performing household tasks and child care and to contribute a greater share of family work than boys. According to Susan Oker, both the early and subsequent gendered work patterns in families, particularly women's expectations that they will be the primary parent, raise practical and psychological barriers against women and become crucial determinants of women's opportunities and expectations. Gendered differences in the sense of entitlement, then, are reinforced by women's comparisons to their own past experiences as well as their gendered expectations for the future.

They are also maintained by a preference for comparisons to similar others. When women compare their relationships, their outcomes, and their lives to those of other women, whom they see as more similar to themselves than men, they tend to believe they are faring better than most. When they compare themselves to men, however, they tend to be less satisfied. Arlie Hochschild related the story of Nancy. In the past, Nancy had compared her responsibilities at home, her identity, her life to Evan's (her husband). Yet as time went on and Nancy found herself unable to renegotiate their relationship, she changed her comparison. "Now to avoid resentment she seemed to compare herself more to other working mothers. By this standard she was doing great. Nancy also compared herself to single women who had moved further ahead in their careers, but they fit into another mental category. A single woman could move ahead in her career, but a married woman has to do a wife's work and a mother's work as well. She did not make this distinction for men."

Janice Steil, in her book on marital equality, diagrams the relationship between sociostructural, dyadic, and individual factors relative to partners' sense of entitlement, achievement of relationship equality, and perceptions of relationship fairness. According to Steil, the more that women and men believe that men, but not women, have the responsibility to provide, and that women, but not men, bear the primary responsibility for nurturing the young, the lower the sense of entitlement for women, the more likely they will compare to same-sex rather than cross-sex others, and the more likely it is that they will report unequal relationships as fair. According to Steil, for women to improve their outcomes relative to men, they must adjust their identity from that of nurturer to that of conurturer and coprovider; they must alter the choice of comparison to include cross-sex others, and they must negotiate from a base of entitlement rather than deserving.

Maureen Perry-Jenkins and her colleagues divided employed women into three groups: coproviders, who saw their income as important to their families and saw the provider role as equally shared; ambivalent coproviders, who admitted that their families were dependent on their incomes but were uncomfortable with the reality of shared economic responsibility; and main-secondary providers, who viewed their incomes as helpful but not vital to their families' well-being. Although none of the husbands in her sample shared the work of the home equally, husbands of both coprovider and ambivalent coprovider wives spent twice the time in household tasks as did other husbands, and coprovider wives experienced less depression than did any other group.

Others found that wives who defined themselves as providers were more likely to judge their husbands' contributions to housework as less than fair and to feel entitled to more help. Yet the vast majority of wives, regardless of their earning level, still see their husbands as the primary providers. As a consequence, they fail to claim the rights of the provider role and this leads them to negotiate their relationships on the basis of deserving rather than entitlement. A wife, for example, might believe—on the basis of her financial contributions to the family or her long hours at the office—that she deserves more help at home. But eliciting "help" is not equivalent to shared responsibility. Yet until this high-earning wife redefines herself as a "coprovider," she will not feel entitled to the same "rights" as her husband. She will continue to compare her outcomes to those of other overworked women, rather than to those of her partner; and rather than fighting for equal status and shared responsibility, she will be negotiating for limited goals (help)—and she will be negotiating from a lower-status position. [*See* MARRIAGE; SOCIAL CONSTRUCTIONIST THEORY.]

V. Future Directions

The sense of entitlement is a factor in healthy human functioning, an important precondition to the perception of unfair treatment, and a key element in the elimination of current gender inequalities. In this article we have summarized what researchers have learned about entitlement. In this section we highlight some of the questions that remain to be investigated and some of the limitations that need to be addressed.

We begin with a brief consideration of theoretical and methodological issues. Despite the burgeoning literature on entitlement in both the clinical and social psychological literatures, there have been few attempts to theoretically define and empirically assess entitlement attitudes, and little attempt at integrating the perspectives of the two fields. What, then, is the relationship between social and clinical psychological conceptions of entitlement? Is excessive or pathological entitlement qualitatively different from healthy entitlement? Is more of one always better and more of the other always worse? Or do entitlement levels extend along some continuum, with underentitlement at one end and excessive levels of entitlement at the other? What is the relationship between entitlement and other constructs such as deserving? What are the implications of these constructs for our attitudes toward disadvantaged groups and government "entitlement" programs?

Most of the entitlement literature has focused primarily on issues of gender, seeking to show that differences exist, and with some ancillary attention to the conditions under which these differences are exacerbated or ameliorated. Little empirical attention has been paid either to the specific origins of entitlement or to within-group differences. Some have argued that it is women's socialization to care taking roles oriented toward fulfilling the needs of others that leads to a lower sense of entitlement. Yet studies by Steil and her colleagues have shown that entitlement levels are unrelated to measures of femininity. Rather, preliminary studies showed that the best predictor of the sense of entitlement was self-described levels of agency. Others have argued that it is the internalization of society's devaluing of gendered behaviors that leads to gender differences in entitlement. What, then, can we learn about the origins of entitlement by looking at other socially stigmatized groups? What can we learn by looking at other cultural groups? Likewise, what do within-group differences tell us? What, for example, differentiates highly entitled women from less entitled women, besides a sense of agency? Do the factors differ across contexts?

Both the social psychological and clinical literatures seem to agree that entitlement is important to psychological well-being. In the clinical literature, an appropriate sense of entitlement is viewed as necessary to being an emotionally healthy person who will approach life with a healthy zest ready to claim all of its vicissitudes. In the social psychological literature, the sense of entitlement safeguards one from unfair treatment. According to most theories of justice, failure to receive valued outcomes to which one feels entitled will lead to feelings of outrage and anger, to perceptions of unfair treatment, and to a desire for change. But what if change is unattainable? For how long can one remain angry, and at what cost? Feminist psychologists such as Jean Baker Miller have argued that any group that has been subordinated by another group learns to accept injustices as a way of surviving. According to most justice theories, when desired outcomes to which one feels entitled are perceived as unattainable, a frequent response is to redefine the situation to deny the injustice. According to this perspective, then, a lower sense of entitlement can sometimes be functional. But at what cost to one's self-esteem and sense of self? Dana Crawley Jack, for example, argued that women's depression emanates not from a loss of relationships, but from a loss of self, as a result of women's silencing themselves in hopes of maintaining relationships.

When women ask their husbands to do more work at home, they are often greeted with a repertoire of strategies and justifications designed to resist. When husbands resist, wives often defer. But again we ask, at what cost? According to Hochschild, wives pay a heavy price—including a devaluation of themselves and their daughters as women and the continuation of inequality. So what then is the relationship between the sense of entitlement and women's depression? Clearly, while much has been learned in the past 25 years, fundamental questions remain unanswered as we seek to better understand the relationship between the sense of entitlement, social inequality, and healthy human functioning in the 21st century.

SUGGESTED READING

Crosby, F. (1982). *Relative Deprivation and Working Women.* Oxford University Press, New York.

Hochschild, A. (1989). *The Second Shift: Working Parents and the Revolution at Home.* Viking, New York.

Lerner, M. J., and Mikula, G. (eds.) (1994). *Entitlement and the Affectional Bond.* Plenum Press, New York.

Major, B. (1994). From social inequality to personal entitlement: The role of social comparisons, legitimacy appraisals and group membership. In *Advances in Experimental Social Psychology* (M. Zanna, ed.), pp. 293–355. Academic Press, New York.

Steil, J. M. (1997). *Marital Equality: It's Relationship to the Well-Being of Husbands and Wives.* Sage, Thousand Oaks, CA.

Family Roles and Patterns, Contemporary Trends

Joy K. Rice
University of Wisconsin, Madison

I. Influences on Family Patterns and Roles
II. Changing Family Patterns and Roles
III. Cultural and Religious Differences
IV. The Future of the Family: A Postscript

Glossary

Cohabitation The sharing of a household by unmarried persons who have an ongoing emotional and sexual relationship.

Dual-career family A family in which both partners have a strong commitment to the lifetime development of careers.

Dual-earner family A family in which both parents are employed, but the wife's work is not viewed as a lifetime career.

Egalitarian family A modern family characterized by equal power sharing, decision making, and flexibility in roles.

Family role Expected behaviors associated with a certain family position or status such as parent or provider.

Lesbian or gay family A family in which partners of the same sex live together and share sexual and emotional commitment.

Nuclear family A family group consisting of a husband, a wife, and their child or children.

Patriarchal family A traditional family in which the father exercises most of the authority, power, decision making, and control over resources in the family.

Role ambiguity A stressful situation in which a person is unclear about the expectations of a role or the proper or desired behavior in a social role such as stepmother.

Role conflict/strain Tension that arises when a person fills two or more roles that may clash or compete such as parent and worker.

Single-parent family A family in which one parent cares for one or more children.

Stepfamily A family in which two adults are married or cohabiting and at least one of the adults has a child present from a previous marriage or relationship.

FAMILY PATTERNS AND ROLES have been greatly affected during the past century by contemporary trends that include changes in urbanization, economic modernization, the shift from an agrarian to an industrial economy, and improvement in the status of women in the United States and around the world. Probably the two most fundamental changes in the family over the past half century are the decreased economic dependence of women on men and the weakening of marriage as a basic institution for the formation of family life and form. Changing economic trends and social attitudes have led to more

Encyclopedia of Women and Gender, Volume One

diversity in family patterns and to more alternatives to traditional marriage, including choosing to remain single or childless, entering into cohabitation arrangements, and forming families of choice with people that are not related by blood (created kin). More acceptance of divorce has also resulted in the increasing prevalence of single-parent families and stepfamilies. Women's almost universal participation in paid labor has also dramatically changed family roles. The most common family pattern today is not the breadwinner–homemaker nuclear family, but the dual-earner family in which both spouses are responsible for providing for the family as well as a variant, the dual-career family, in which both woman and man maintain commitments to ongoing careers along with family responsibilities.

I. Influences on Family Patterns and Roles

There is a considerable and growing diversity in North American family patterns. North Americans today face a wide array of choices about cohabitation, marriage and divorce, the number and timing of children, and the division of labor by gender within the family. Family transformation is cutting across cultural, religious, and ethnic groups and is not the simple outcome of values that stress the independence and freedom associated with North American character and values. Instead changing family patterns and roles appear to be part of a broader process of global modernization linked to economic and demographic changes that are increasingly separating family from the economic sphere and changing our ideas about appropriate family roles, especially women's roles. A model of modern family living arrangements assumes that peoples' choices represent the outcome of weighing preferences and constraints, costs and opportunities. Perhaps the most powerful influence on these choices is economic. Since the advent of industrialization, the family has ceased to become the center of opportunities for work. The family is no longer the center of opportunity structure for the individuals in it, and it competes with the workplace and other powerful institutions such as the media for influence over its members.

More income generated outside the family also allows the purchase of privacy and independence and these "goods" are or have become valuable in modern societies. Thus the greater the available income, the more likely it will be used to buy independence from the family. One important result of this trend has been separate living in adulthood apart from families with no family role for longer periods in one's 20s and even later. Another is the growing number of never-married singles who are able to maintain a comfortable life without marriage or the support of parents and their home. As women increasingly have emphasized the place of jobs and careers in their lives, childbearing patterns have also changed. Higher incomes and higher educational levels are associated with lower rates of childbearing. In general, however, marriage and childbearing has been delayed and family size decreased. The contemporary trend of delaying childbirth and spacing births further apart also decreases the average number of children born per mother. While women in general are waiting longer to have a child, they are not always waiting for marriage, and childbearing among single women has increased substantially.

Increasing financial and social opportunities outside the family also make it easier to break family ties and to dissolve marriage. Studies show that divorce is more likely to occur in couples where the wife is able to support herself financially. Historically, stable marriage systems have rested on coercion and inequality in resources and power. Because most women are now employed outside the home, they are not as dependent on their husbands for economic survival, have more power, and can initiate divorce more easily and frequently in an unhappy or abusive marriage. As divorce and remarriage become normative, we are seeing a pattern of "serial monogamy," that is, a series of family relationships maintained and then broken over a lifetime, making definitions of kinship and family roles more ambiguous. [*See* DIVORCE AND CHILD CUSTODY.]

Perhaps the most tenuous position in today's divorced, single parent and remarried families is that of partner-father. It is women who are far more likely to be single heads of households with children and who maintain primary responsibility for children after divorce. Within a year after divorce, half of fathers have virtually lost contact with their children. About two-fifths of divorced men do not pay any child support, and on the average U.S. men pay more for their car payments than they do for their child support payments. If today's modern families are characterized by their diversity, flexibility, and fragility, they are also defined by the remaining centrality of the mother–child bond.

An increasing number of women, however, choose to remain childless for their lifetimes. It is important to remember that many of these so-called new trends have historical precedence. Remaining child-free is not a new phenomenon; in 1940 nearly 20% of married white women between thirty-five and thirty-nine were child-free in contrast to only about 7% of women in this age group in the late 1970s. Again these choices reflect the economic and social trends of their times. Today it is expected that from a fifth to a fourth of American women will remain childless due to a multitude of factors including delayed child-bearing, infertility, and voluntary childlessness.

These trends are not confined to U.S. society. Cohabitation, for example, is not a recent phenomenon nor a uniquely Western one. Societies today and in the past have had large numbers of couples who were not legally married, nor suffered social censure. In Sweden, cohabitation is considered a social institution and is rapidly replacing marriage as a stable couple family form. In the United States, cohabitation is also on the rise, and women may be attracted to cohabitation because of the personal independence and the freedom from traditional marital sex roles it affords. Some refer to all these trends—single living, child-free marriages, cohabitation, divorce, single parent families, stepfamilies, and created kin families—as evidence of the "deinstitutionalization" of marriage, that is, marriage is no longer the primary institution that it once was in providing the structure and means for family formation, economic security, procreation, and child rearing.

The changing relationship of the family to the economy has not only produced pluralism in family forms, but it has also changed *family roles* for men and women. The economic reverses of the 1970s had a profound effect on the social expectations that 1950s families had instilled in their children. Prior to the 1970s, high-profit margins and extra earnings of corporations were passed on to workers at all levels benefiting secretaries and janitors as well as CEOs. Workers were retained even in slow periods as a way of ensuring workplace stability. The government subsidized home ownership as well as higher education, helping young families. The postwar supportive contracts between workers, families, corporations, and governments came to a dramatic end in the 1970s in a revolution of work reengineering. Worker wages were lowered and housing costs increased dramatically. Production, information, and service work became automated. Production was internationalized with manufacturing exported to low-wage areas; cor-porate mergers and reorganization led to workforce "downsizing"; and newly created jobs were part-time and temporary as companies shifted to "no-commitment" hiring.

Families tried to keep up their standard of living by doing four things: they delayed marriage, had fewer children, had both spouses work, and went into debt. For low-income families, the wife's contribution helped to keep the family above the poverty line; for middle-class families, the uninterrupted work of wives became the main route to some social mobility and economic comfort and security.

Other important factors during and since this time, besides economic reverses, have influenced the family. Profound technological advances in the past decades have radically altered work, leisure, and reproductive choices, increased our life span, and affected family and gender roles. As the population ages, women have increasingly become caregivers to the old as well as to the young, juggling the roles of work, career, raising children, and caring for aging parents. Socially, family roles were also greatly influenced by the rise of the women's movement in the 1960s and 1970s that led to far greater participation of women in the labor market and the public sphere and to more egalitarian family roles. By the 1980s and the 1990s the feminist movement began to question the wholesale adoption of a male model of work that emphasized career achievement and economic success at the expense of family life and children. In the model of "New Familism," both spouses were expected to make work concessions for the family, but it was also expected that the wife's contribution and adjustment would be greater, at least while the children were young. These asymmetrical gender role concessions are a central feature of the modified traditional nuclear family, and they often operate in dual-earner families and even in dual career families that are idealized as being more egalitarian. [*See* THE FEMINIST MOVEMENT; MARRIAGE; SOCIAL CONSTRUCTIONIST THEORY; WORK–FAMILY BALANCE.]

II. *Changing Family Patterns and Roles*

How a family is defined has important social, individual, and economic consequences. At the moral level, our notions of family are translated into what we deem appropriate and "right" in terms of roles and expectations about sexuality, having and raising children, and the family division of labor. At the economic and political level, values about the family get translated into family definitions that determine who will benefit from social policies, laws, tax structures, family supports, health benefits, and insurance. How a family is defined also influences whether we think the family is in decline or in transformation. A legalistic, traditional definition of a family has been "a group of people related by blood, marriage, or adoption"; however, public opinion polls have found that two out of three people define the family as "a group of people who love and care for each other" rather than the legal definition. The latter is a nontraditional definition of family and certainly permits diversity in family forms as the norm.

Family definition changes from culture to culture. The United Nations Committee on the Family prefaced its official set of principles about the family with the disclaimer that it would not provide any one definition of family because of the tremendous variety of family patterns and customs throughout the world. This discussion is primarily about families in Western culture and the family in the United States. The traditional definition of family in modern times has meant a nuclear family, a small household of father, mother, and children. It is based on monogamy, a system in which persons cannot have more than one spouse. This is important to note because a majority of the families in the other parts of the world are based on polygamy, primarily polygyny where a husband is able to have more than one wife. The monogamous nuclear family that we have considered the timeless standard in our country in reality represents a minority of families, not only in the United States, but in the rest of the non-Western world.

The idealization of family life in the media gave rise to a popular idea of the typical U.S. family and what it is supposed to look like: middle class and monogamous, with a breadwinner father, homemaker mother, and children living in a one-family household. This model, however, excludes more than 80% of the U.S. population. The nuclear model, while representing only a small fraction of today's families, is nonetheless, deeply embedded in our cultural ideals, government policies, the labor force, and "profamily" political movements. This family standard is a product of falsely assuming the universality of family form and experience. In reality, diversity of family forms has occurred throughout U.S. history. Social scientists once assumed that there was a prevailing type of family at any one time rather than

several types of families in different social classes and regions. Today new research has found that family diversity has been present before and since the beginning of immigration to North America. A historical examination of Native American families, for example, reveals a large range of variation in family patterns. Colonial households commonly included members who were not kin. Rather than the "absent family" assumed to characterize slave life, slaves were connected to one another through extensive kinship networks. And because of immigrant restrictions, until recent decades, many Chinese American households consisted of single men living alone.

Historically, there has also been diversity in family roles regarding division of labor. The strong division of family roles characterized by the 1950s in which the nuclear family came to be the idealized norm does not represent normative family roles for most of our history. For centuries women in families successfully combined child rearing with uninterrupted, lifelong participation in work and the wider economy, although this work was generally seen as secondary to their family roles. Historically, it has been extremely unusual for women to withdraw from subsistence work after childbirth in order to take exclusive responsibility for child rearing and to have their family roles defined by activities assumed to be noneconomic.

Furthermore, it is only more recently and thus more briefly that most working-class men expected to be able to earn a "family wage" that would permit their spouses to stop taking in washing or boarders and to devote full time to the domestic arts developed by the emerging middle class. The concept of the "family wage" emerged in the 19th century; it was the idea that a male industrial worker would be paid sufficiently so that he could unilaterally support a home-based wife and dependent children as a "breadwinner." The breadwinner was a "good provider" for his family: he held a steady job, made a comfortable wage, owned a home, paid the bills, and provided for his family's economic and material needs. Other domestic and child-rearing tasks were assigned to the wife or "homemaker." The breadwinner role is the centerpiece of the patriarchal family, but was not necessarily advantageous to women. In fact, when the ideal of the breadwinner role became dominant, married women were denied the right to work for pay, especially when unemployment was high as during the Depression years.

It is also only in the 20th century that a man's wages were large enough to allow the children of the family to attend school throughout childhood rather than to help the family with work in the factory or field. Children's roles and family relationships also changed with the separation of work and family life initiated by the Industrial Revolution. In earlier times children were considered essentially miniature adults and initiated into many of the same tasks they would have in adulthood. With the separation of work and family life, childhood began to be seen as a special stage of life development characterized by dependency and play.

The nuclear family of the mid-20th century has been romanticized as a special golden age of family stability and comfort, but there is also nostalgia for the prior days of the 19th-century extended family when mutual respect and satisfaction existed between the generations. Yet it is important to note that both the traditional extended family and nuclear family were typically patriarchal families in which family roles were supported by attitudes that legitimized the subordination of women, as well as children, minorities, and the poor. In the traditional patriarchal structure of extended families, respect and obligations to parents were based on parental control of economic resources and reinforced by religious and secular sanctions against those who did not conform.

Most people today value their personal freedom, mobility, and individual decision making and would not want to return to a rigid, inequitable patriarchal family. The diversity in contemporary multiple family patterns reflects a more egalitarian idea about how families should function. As wives have almost universally entered the labor market, they have gained many rights, gradually changing their legal status from being their husbands' dependents to being their equal partners, having the right to contract on their own, to own and dispose of property, to keep their own name upon marriage, and to equally determine their residence.

Another contemporary myth about families is that because so few of today's family patterns and roles conform to older ideas about normative families and our idealization of these forms, then the family is in decline. Instead the family is very much alive as a basic structure and building block of society, but the family has changed, and diversity in family forms is the norm. In addition to the nuclear family, the most common and prevalent family patterns today are the single-parent family, the stepfamily, the dual-earner family (sometimes called the dual-income or co-provider family), and the dual-career family. There

are also increasing numbers of childless families and lesbian or gay families.

A. SINGLE-PARENT FAMILIES

Single-parent families now represent a significant percentage of families, and growing up in a single-parent family is an increasingly common experience for children. The demography of single parenthood has changed a good deal in the past century. In 1900 the typical single parent was a widow. Today most single-parent families are formed as a result of divorce or childbearing without marriage. Single mothers raising children significantly outnumber single fathers raising children. Low-income single-parent families are more frequently headed by never-married mothers than by divorced mothers. Single-parent families have only one parent in the home to provide financial and emotional resources. The daily pressures on single parents to fulfill both work and parental roles can be more intense than in a two-parent family with partners who share these roles. Some single-parent families get significant help from their extended family, friends, kin, and nonkin, creating a network that significantly supports the family and enriches the children's lives. Thus there are both advantages and special burdens in the functioning of the single-parent family.

Generalizations about any family pattern and its functioning can be complicated by cultural, religious, and ethnic factors. The problems of single parenthood tend to be greatest among cultural, ethnic, and religious groups that emphasize nuclear families and traditional roles. Thus family disruption appears to be more likely to produce negative effects among Catholic Hispanics and is less likely to do so among Blacks who have traditionally evidenced more tolerance for family diversity and single-parent family life.

Children who live in families headed by single mothers play a significant role in the household economy. They share more in every kind of household task and take nearly twice as much responsibility for household tasks as those children in nuclear families. The difference between the amount of housework done by children in mother-only and two-parent families is actually larger for teenage boys than for teenage girls. This reflects the fact that girls do so much in all families, while boys in two-parent families do very little housework. Teenage boys in mother-only families share considerably more housework than do teenage girls in two-parent families. Single mothers heading families do not maintain traditional gender roles with the segregation of household tasks by sex, incorporating teenage boys into virtually all traditionally female household tasks. One potential problem in single-parent and divorced families is that the adolescent child may be thrust prematurely into a pseudo-parental role in the absence of a spouse or adult partner and parent to share family responsibilities. Thus an important task of the single parent is to maintain appropriate generational role boundaries.

Growing up in a nontraditional family, be it a single parent-family, a stepfamily, a dual-career family that shares roles, or a lesbian/gay family, appears to have interesting and important consequences for gender roles. Children reared in nontraditional homes have more flexible and less sex-role stereotyped attitudes toward their future roles as parents and workers. Young women who grow up in a nontraditional family (or who experience independent living in young adulthood) not only have more liberal attitudes about female and male roles, but they delay marriage and childbearing and plan to have fewer children than those from families having both biological parents. Some research also suggests that paradoxically, women who have grown up in nontraditional families and have lived as children through family breakup may overcompensate by maintaining traditional family roles and becoming less willing to fight for an egalitarian division of labor when they do marry. [*See* PARENTING.]

B. STEPFAMILIES

Stepfamilies, sometimes called reconstituted families or blended families, are not new. It is only their increasing number that has brought them so much public attention. With nearly half of all marriages ending in divorce and with more than three-fourths of divorced people remarrying, blended families are becoming increasingly common in contemporary North America. These families can consist of parents who have previously been married to different partners, the children born in those previous marriages, and the children born to the current partners. We are rapidly approaching a point where half of all new marriages will involve a remarriage. Note, however, that a substantial number of stepfamilies involve cohabiting couples rather than remarried couples, and a majority of children first enter stepfamily life through cohabitation rather than marriage.

Family roles in stepfamilies can be very complex. There are additional social roles such as stepparents, stepchildren, stepsiblings, stepgrandparents, noncustodial parents, and the spouses of noncustodial parents. Consider the following family ties:

Mike and Kathy are my stepbrother and sister. Gary is my stepfather. Alan and Linda are my real parents, who are divorced. And Alan married Audrey and together they had Carolyn and Chris, my half-sister and -brother. And Linda married Rick and had Lisa, my half-sister. Brad is also my stepbrother from my dad's first marriage.

How are we to understand and make sense of this mixture? We do not have clear norms about the expectations involved in these roles, and even the language describing them is problematic. What name does a child who already has a father call his or her stepfather? In general, people act as they are expected to act in a particular role by society. However, in stepfamilies, there are unclear and often absent societal norms for how to define the remarried family, especially the role of the stepparent in relation to the stepchild.

Women have traditionally taken on greater responsibility for the role of kin-keeper within the family—that is, initiating, solidifying, and maintaining family contact with relatives. That role is more difficult in a stepfamily. Parent–child relationships are fundamentally altered by the existence within a family household of individuals who are not related by blood ties, and the definition of "kin" comes into question within a stepfamily. Thus a significant phenomenon in stepfamilies is that roles are ambiguous and fluid, as are the boundaries about who is in and who is outside of the family. Other parents continue to have influence on the socialization of children, and children often have difficulties accepting any parental authority or discipline from a stepparent. The most complex and ambiguous stepfamilies are those involving children from more than one prior marriage. Stepsiblings may be living in the same house or may be visiting and living in multiple households. The addition of new stepsiblings with a remarriage changes the major sibling relationships and roles in the family. A child may no longer be the oldest child, or the only child, or the only female, or only male child.

Some stepparents choose to forego any parenting or socializing role; they defer these roles to the children's biological parents. However, the reality of living with young children may require that some component of the parenting role be assumed by the stepparent, often with role conflict. The stepparent who lives with the children is far more likely to be a stepfather than a stepmother, and usually the natural father is still alive and present in the children's lives. Research on the stepfather role suggest two contrasting conclusions. The first is that children in these families are as well adjusted and get along with their stepfathers as well as children do with their natural fathers. Another body of research concludes that stepfathers view themselves as less effective than do natural fathers because of the unique problems they experience in the stepfather role. The role is even more peripheral than the natural father's. It may represent "odd man out" in a closed household headed by a mother where the children have a history of defined family work responsibilities and sharing in family decisions. Another problem is that there may be a hidden agenda for the stepfather's participation in the family that is not openly disclosed. The division of household labor in stepfather families is somewhat more "traditional" than in comparable families with a biological father because stepfathers do significantly fewer "female-type" chores, but more of other chores.

The stepmother's new role in stepfamilies can also be stressful. Traditional gender-role expectations for a wife include child care and maintaining the emotional well-being of the family. A stepmother may then try to solve problems between her husband and his children or between the children and their mother, which is usually a no-win situation. Experts agree that the biological parent, whether male or female, should be the primary parent for the children in stepfamilies, which means that women must curb their tendency to try to fix everyone's emotional problems, and men correspondingly must change their tendency to leave the job of emotional intimacy to women. A role that works best for a stepparent, especially initially, is that of an older friend, camp counselor, uncle or aunt or even baby-sitter, a role that has partial and limited authority and responsibility for the child and does not immediately lead to divided loyalties for the child. Realistic anticipation of possible role conflicts and expectations and open communication and cooperation among all the stepparents and parents is important in successful stepfamilies and blended families.

Like children in single-parent families headed by mothers, children who currently live with their mother and a stepfather take a greater role in household chores than do children who live with both their natural parents. The difference, however is much less than that between mother-only and nuclear families. Boys between the ages of 12 and 18 share more in household tasks than younger children in stepfamilies, as they do in mother-only families. It appears that the high proportion of children living for some period in mother-only families, with or without remarriage, is contributing to household competence in men. It is, however, unclear whether this competence will later translate into greater role sharing in their future families and egalitarianism in their attitudes about family roles.

C. DUAL-EARNER FAMILES

As *dual-earner* families have become the majority family pattern in the United States and other industrialized countries, the provider and homemaker role differentiation of husbands and wives has lost some, but not all, of its validity. Child care and housework are still assumed more by the wife than by the husband in most marriages where the woman also works outside the home. The woman who works the same number of hours as does the husband comes home to a domestic "second shift" at night and on weekends. This pattern of women spending more time in unpaid family work than men cuts across age, race, ethnicity, and marital status.

Until recently, family labor was divided into two roles in middle-class White American families: market labor by the husband as provider, and household labor by the wife as homemaker. In this system, goods and services necessary to family life are produced or obtained through the enactment of the "provider" role, while the same goods and services are maintained or converted for family use by someone acting as the "homemaker." Thus these two roles have been seen to complement each other. The provider–homemaker role differentiation, however, is certainly not universal. This division of roles became usual only after the family's place of production and place of consumption became separated. The household became the site of family consumption, and the farm, factory, or office became the location of production. Yet even in traditional agricultural families, the provider–homemaker role division was never rigid, and spouses worked side by side in the fields especially at harvest.

The "good provider" role for men developed in this country during the 1830s. Prior to this time a man was expected to be "a good steady worker," but not the sole family provider. The good provider role for men lasted into the late 1970s, its end officially marked when the 1980 U.S. Census proclaimed that the man no longer was automatically assumed to be the head of the household. The provider/homemaker roles were supported by stereotypes and beliefs that men's personalities tended to be characterized by more *instrumental* character traits that made them succeed in technical and executive roles, in contrast to females who were presumed to demonstrate *expressive* character traits that were best suited to supportive, nurturing roles. Feminists argue that these presumed family roles based on gender are not biological in origin, but are of cultural origin and have been "socially constructed." "Socially constructed" means that they arise not because of innate differences between women and men and their abilities and predispositions, but rather from culturally accepted rules, from relationships of power and authority, and from differences in economic opportunities.

When analyzing family roles, one can use the idea of *conflict,* which focuses on inequality and power in how people act and make decisions. Thus male dominance in the family and the conflicting interests of men and women in the family rests on two sources of coercion: physical force and control of economic resources. From this point of view, the breadwinner–homemaker family role model was not simply an efficient system constructed to provide equal exchange of goods and services, but also a system constructed to maintain the power of men over women, for women's direct access to money and power through paid employment was restricted in this type of family that maintained women's dependence on men. Conflict theorists, then, criticize the traditional breadwinner–homemaker family because they believe it is primarily based on men's domination of women through the control of access to economic independence.

While in today's dual-earner families the role of family wage earner is not just the husband's, many people believe that the man should be the *principal* provider for his family, and the wife's earner role is considered secondary. In dual-earner families, the distinction between the provider and homemaker roles has become less clear as more than half of all married women are employed outside the home and bring in paychecks that are definitely necessary to the economic survival and well-being of their families. Yet there remains a distinction between the breadwinning role and paid employment. Employed wives are not necessarily regarded as family breadwinners. In most dual-earner couples a husband's

status as provider is modified in varied, complex, and dynamic ways by his wife's employment, but it is not eliminated. Today paid employment no longer serves as a visible gender role as it has in the past, but the boundaries of the provider–breadwinner role can be subject to interpretation and modification within each couple dyad. Also, what is voiced about the role may not be in reality practiced. Husbands move to ease conflict by adopting gender ideologies designed to please their wives, but do not necessarily change behaviors. Research on dual-earner couples, for example, finds a great deal of flexibility in expressed ideas about gender roles that often seem to be symbolic substitutes rather than the basis for behavioral changes. Thus the blurring of family and spousal roles is stronger in terms of people's expressed attitudes than in their actual behaviors.

The negotiation of gender roles in families takes place within an existing system of unequal power that affects the ways that women and men construct and contest gender role boundaries. Both use strategies to protect their perceived prerogatives within the family system. Bob can adopt his wife's shared ideas about child care because he knows how improbable it is that he will be called up to give up breadwinning since he outearns his wife four to one. Rebecca goes along with her husband's ideas about males being primary breadwinners because she knows the family needs her income and her husband won't actually ask her to quit her job. Kim who works full time says the division of labor is shared in that she is responsible for the "upstairs" and her spouse the "downstairs," which in reality is the basement and garage devoted to his workbench and hobbies. But the fiction maintains a perception of sharing and an avoidance of conflict. It also maintains some gender distinctions in roles.

According to this line of reasoning, we must continually "do" gender, that is do the work of creating a common sense of what the roles and relations between men and women are like and should be. This way of analyzing how roles and behaviors are socially constructed in a family emphasizes the continuous construction of meaning in our roles and also tells us that these roles are far more fragile, permeable, and flexible than we might think; the appropriate scripts for our roles continually change.

A husband's share of the domestic work does slightly increase when the wife is employed, and his contribution is greater the larger her income, the larger the family, and the younger the children. A husband's contribution to household work, however, is not nearly as large as the wife's, even when they have provided approximately the same income. Wives assume about 70% of household chores. And the more hours a father works, the greater the likelihood that children will take responsibility for household tasks. When it comes to relative availability of two parents in dual-earner families, children substitute for their fathers, not their mothers. Less is known about children's work roles in the family today, as with the advent of child labor laws, children's labor vanished into the home. We do know that children are more likely to share household responsibilities when a parent is disabled or has a health limitation. Overall, however, children's household participation in middle-class families has declined with changes in education and urbanization in the past century. Adolescents have few opportunities to do socially necessary work and the phenomenon of "rolelessness" in contemporary U.S. adolescence has been increasing the past century with the abolition of child labor, extended schooling, and the decline of summer work.

Thus the differentiation of roles in families where the wife assumes a dual-earner role is not simply a function of the work status of both the spouses. Instead the spouses' expectations of the roles and behaviors associated with each gender and how these are constructed and continuously negotiated are very important in understanding the division of labor and family role differentiation in contemporary societies. Another consideration is the influence of societal, ethnic, and cultural traditions and variations, which may influence and prescribe not only individual behaviors, but family roles as well. Black women traditionally have been more likely to expect and approve of working as adults than other women, to have more children, and to involve them more in household tasks, both in single-parent and two-parent families. Black men participate in household tasks less than do White men; thus the experience of involvement in household roles as children does not carry over into more egalitarian marriages. One interpretation of this finding has been that Black men moving into adulthood may experience greater need to succeed in the work world as White men always have, to have intense work roles, and to be taken care of by women at home.

In contemporary U.S. society, sanctions for deviating from family roles have become considerably weakened and family behaviors have become more flexible and innovative, determined by specific family situations, personality, and preference. Today we see two minority groups of individuals who choose not to enter the labor market as dual earners and to be full-time homemakers or househusbands. The full-time homemaker role is possible only in families where a single wage is enough to support the household. Some women choose a temporary stage of full-time homemaking and child care when their children are young in response to society's lack of support for working mothers; the lack of good, inexpensive, child care; and the strong belief they can do better themselves as full-time parents. The other group we know little about because there is a paucity of research about upper-middle-class families. These are women who choose not to work, but nonetheless contribute substantially to their husband's career by cultivating appropriate acquaintances through community and volunteer work and maintaining the social role, lifestyle, and entertaining to support his work role. This family-work pattern has sometimes been called the "two-person" single career, as the wife's role and contributions significantly advance the husband's career and the family's social status. In the past, feminist researchers and some public policy makers have noted that maintaining a household and child care is a job, maybe even a career, one that sets up the infrastructure permitting another spouse to succeed in work outside the home, but a job that has no wages and low status. If all the goods and services provided by homemakers were paid, the amount would be considerable, and the salary for the job would be the equivalent of an average, middle-class wage earner. In this sense all homemakers, as well as males who reverse typical family roles as "househusbands," are "dual earners," albeit unpaid and undervalued in our work-oriented society.

D. DUAL-CAREER FAMILIES

In the *dual-career family*, both the woman and man have a strong ongoing commitment to the lifetime development of careers. Careers differ from jobs primarily because they offer the promise of advancement, intrinsic personal rewards other than money, and require a high degree of motivation, time, and investment. Traditionally women have been concentrated in low-paying service jobs and "pink collar" work, but many more women today have full-time, demanding careers, and they delay childbirth and marriage to advance in these careers. The success of the dual-career family often depends on the willingness of both spouses to actively help and support each other in work and family roles. In dual-career families with children, family life is hectic and often tense as partners juggle division of labor, complicated schedules, travel requirements, the demands of children, and the inflexibility of the work world. These multiple demands may lead to role conflict and some women avoid role strain by compromising their career demands for their home role demands, particularly after the birth of the first child. Even for dual-career couples committed to egalitarian family roles, the transition to parenthood tends to mark a reversion to a more traditional division of roles.

Another way of dealing with career and family overload is to adjust the timing of events over the life course. This adjustment process is referred to as work-family role staging. It may be either simultaneous or sequential. Some individuals choose to continuously perform in the demanding roles of career and home, while other dual-career families postpone some activities in one sphere until a later stage, or trade off periods of more intense work or home involvement. For example, a couple may choose to move to another city to significantly advance the wife's career while the husband takes on more of the parenting, but in the next five years, the situation is reversed.

Some affluent couples alleviate role strain and conflict by "buying out" of part of their family and domestic role by hiring a support system of child-care providers and household help, which depends heavily on their ability to pay. These arrangements are often fragile, complex, and ambiguous, and a dual-career family's heavy dependence on these caregivers and housekeepers can result in catastrophe when the system breaks down or an employee abruptly leaves. The burden of replacing this support system falls almost exclusively to the wife. In essence in these homes, two groups of women trade roles and places, but the career group is highly dependent on the support group.

Again the importance of attitudes and values about appropriate gender roles is also a key to understanding successful dual-career families. Dual-career couples in which each member is equally responsible for earnings are likely to have egalitarian beliefs about household roles and labor. Childless dual-earner and dual-career couples tend to be the most egalitarian, since it is well known that the arrival of children exerts considerable pressure on couples to adopt more traditional family and parental roles along gender lines. Increased education has been found to significantly reduce adherence to traditional family roles. Husbands with more education are not only more likely to espouse egalitarianism in gender

roles, but to participate more in child care and household work. Yet the reality that persists in dual-career as well as dual-earner families, is that the wife is more likely to take on the major responsibility of the so-called second shift of domestic responsibilities.

There is also a generational effect; older women who were among the first large cohort to enter the labor force and to have real careers are more likely to do the "second shift" than their daughters. This group felt more societal pressure to maintain both roles and faced more resistance from spouses. Thus the baby boom generation grew up seeing relatively little change in traditional family roles even though their mothers were working. This "guilt" effect appears to be lessening as baby-boomer couples age into their prime years and couples with modern attitudes and expectations about sharing of family roles create more egalitarian families and role models for children and later generations. Researchers are also encouraged by the fact that men who are more educated hold more modern attitudes and share more in the domestic role. They see this as evidence that the high divorce rates may end, and that "new families" can eventually help stabilize family life and lead to a pattern of more egalitarian marriages and relationships that women desire today. Wives in more egalitarian marriages report greater satisfaction and a lower frequency of having considered divorce. [*See* LIFE SATISFACTION.]

E. LESBIAN AND GAY FAMILIES

While marriage between homosexuals is not yet legally recognized, a number of homosexual couples are raising children and constitute a new family pattern known as a *lesbian or gay family*. Families of lesbians and gays make up at least 5% of U.S. families. Homosexual couples tend to be more egalitarian than heterosexual couples, to share in decision making and in all of the household duties. One likely reason for this result is the fact that both partners, being the same sex, have experienced similar gender role socialization. Another is that most gay and lesbian couples are dual earners, and there tends to be less income disparity that would produce more inequality in the relationship. Most lesbians and gays reject the dominant marriage model that prescribes specific and unequal gender roles. Contrary to the stereotype, partners do not take on the role of either "husband" or "wife" with the corresponding household tasks traditionally assigned to those roles. Lesbian couples who are planning a pregnancy contend with some unique decisions concerning the sharing of the maternal role. Some couples choose to alternate the childbearing role, others attempt simultaneous pregnancies, and some employ state-of-the-art reproductive technology to separate the genetic and gestational components of procreation.

While gay and lesbian families experience many of the stresses and strains of other families including divorced and stepparent families, the overriding and biggest problem remains how the homosexual family manages society's stigmatized attitudes about their sexual preference and lifestyle. Censure and discrimination against gay families leads some gay parents to hide their status. Many homosexual parents fear they will lose their children if they "come out." Children in homosexual homes may be afraid to bring friends home or become involved in activities at school because close contact with others also risks exposure.

A generation of research has found that lesbian and gay parents do not produce particularly different kinds of children than do traditional heterosexual families. There are no significant differences in school achievement, social adjustment, mental health, gender identity, or sexual orientation between the two groups of children. The infrequent small differences between gay and nongay parents tend to show that gay parents are more nurturing and tolerant, in turn, raising more tolerant, empathic, and less aggressive children than nongay parents. Stacey notes that a six-year-old girl from a lesbian family says that she does not "tell other kids at school about my mothers because I think they would be jealous of me. Two mothers are better than one." Her view is echoed by another young woman who, somewhat apologetically, believes she is advantaged to be the daughter of two moms: "I think you get more love with two moms. I know other kids have a mom and a dad, but I think that moms give more love than dads. This may not be true, but it's what I think." A seventeen-year-old male thinks that "the good thing is that you get a more objective view of people in general, being raised by someone who's so persecuted by society. You begin to sympathize with anyone who is persecuted by society. You tend not to be as prejudiced. . . . As fathers go, mine tends to be a little nicer—almost a mother's temperament. I don't know if that's just because of his personality in general or if it's because he's gay. He is a very emotional person; he cries easily. I love him. He's a good dad, and he's more open than other dads." These findings call for more study about how lesbian and gay fam-

ilies differ, rather than deviate, from nongay families, the differences among such families, and the particular benefits as well as burdens lesbian and gay families may give to their members. [*See* LESBIANS, GAY MEN, AND BISEXUALS IN RELATIONSHIPS.]

III. Cultural and Religious Differences

Family roles are also strongly influenced by religious beliefs. Traditional religions hold that a woman's purpose in the moral order is bound by the roles of wife and mother and that women belong in the home. These views have generally characterized Catholicism, Islamic religion, fundamentalist Protestantism, and orthodox Judaism. The Catholic religion has strongly favored the traditional nuclear intact family and reinforces its support of traditional sex roles with its prohibition of birth control and divorce. Divorce constitutes the breaking of a sacrament and those who cannot annul their marriages officially commit adultery by remarrying. However, the divorce rate and rates of the use of birth control by Catholics are similar to non-Catholics. Family life and marriage have been central to Mormonism from its inception, but the specific form of marriage and family structure has undergone significant changes. Polygyny was officially banned in 1890, but the church has become even more firmly committed to traditional views on family life, marriage, and sexual abstinence before marriage. It has opposed legislation that would make gender equality legally binding. Orthodox Jewish groups, too, show a strictly traditional division of family gender roles. Research finds that women in these groups feel tension between the U.S. ideology of equality and their religion's beliefs about female submission, between the ideal of an intact marriage and staying in an inequitable one, and between the economic necessity to work and the religious preference for full-time mothers and homemakers.

Religion, race, ethnicity, and cultural migration may produce tension in expectations of appropriate family roles and forms. Families that have migrated face changing cultural expectations that may cause conflict and threaten the family's structural composition, compromise patriarchal authority, and reverse family roles. Immigrant children take on parental roles in the family if they learn the dominant language more quickly than the parents and must interpret the new culture for the parents. Racial and ethnic prejudice can seriously compound the family's problems and adjustment. Young adults who choose to leave the family or cohabitate may face intense family disapproval and exclusion. Migrant women who work may be seen to betray the traditions of the old culture and country, yet be forced to work in low-paid jobs as their husbands are unemployed, underemployed, or unable to maintain a breadwinner role as they once had before immigration. Other wives experience increased authority, decision making, and power in the family in the absence of their husbands when men migrate alone to take jobs distant from their families.

Some alternative family patterns that appear new to North Americans are actually variant family patterns that have been traditional within Black and other ethnic communities for many generations. The new extended family, single parents who are choosing to live in multigenerational families or with other single-parent friends, has a long-standing precedent in Black families. One of the strongest positive features of Black families have traditionally been strong family ties. African American families historically have frequently lived in three-generational or extended family households with a considerable sharing of resources, assistance, and interpersonal and social support. The assumption of a parenting role is not restricted to blood kin. The use of fictive kin for family support and exchange is well documented; one person may contribute money for a child, another gives nurturing, and still another takes responsibility for medical care and religious teaching. Involved nonkin have the same privileges with regard to children as the children's blood kin. This arrangement allows single persons to raise their children with the help of coparenting relationships with others able to provide financial and other resources. Persons may be members of families or households in some roles and not in others, or for some periods of time, but not others. Permeable family and household boundaries and flexible family roles are functional and even necessary for survival under conditions of poverty. Women have had strong roles in these families, often due to economic necessity, and African American women have labored outside the home since slavery.

In poor Black families, individuals may have children and become grandparents at an early age. Thus family roles are chronologically out of sync with generational position, and the acceleration for one person can create acceleration for others throughout the family. As an example, the teen mother prematurely achieves young adulthood status by becoming a mother, and her young adult mother becomes a grandmother and sometimes a surrogate mother. Family researchers note that the condensing and acceleration of new roles and responsibilities may leave individuals inadequate time to work through the development tasks associated with each phase of the life cycle.

IV. The Future of the Family: A Postscript

Families of the 21st century are facing a socioeconomic transformation as far-reaching and influential as the effects of the Industrial Revolution in the early 19th century. A rearrangement of the links between families and the larger economy has led to a significant reorganization of work, family, and gender roles and to more diverse family forms and patterns. The male breadwinner, female homemaker, nuclear family system that was established in the mid-19th century to resolve that particular societal transition no longer meets the needs of families. Nor does it make sense to use a form of the family as a standard that is attainable only by a minority and may have been dominant for a short period in our history. Individuals increasingly desire egalitarianism, choices in their lives, and flexibility in the formation of their family and kinship ties. These new choices have led to a great diversity and pluralism of family forms in contemporary society today and a profound shift in the role expectations for women and men.

When we simultaneously consider the contemporary family roles of women, men, and children, the results all point in the same direction. At least for young women, living and growing up in a nontraditional family and the experience of nonfamily living in young adulthood result in greater role sharing in the household division of labor with husbands and children. The most important processes that are operating to increase the likelihood that new family forms and patterns will be more egalitarian are economic and attitudinal. The most powerful influence is the growth not only in women's employment, but in women's increased financial contribution to the family and, consequently, their greater power and influence in changing traditional family roles, particularly in modifying the exclusive breadwinner role for men. Secondly, as women and men in families hold more nontraditional views of gender roles, there is likely to be greater spousal sharing of the domestic role. Finally, the emergence of new family forms due to divorce, the declining prevalence of marriage, and the increase in nontraditional family forms is also affecting greater sharing and participation of women and men in both provider and homemaker roles and increasing the participation of young males in household roles in nontraditional families.

Intolerance for family diversity harms not only single-parent families, divorced families, stepfamilies, and lesbian and gay families, but also childless families, interracial couples, many immigrant families, the homeless, the poor, bachelors and "spinsters," househusbands and employed mothers, and today even places full-time homemakers ("I'm just a housewife") on the defensive. Because pluralism of family form has historically been the case not only in our culture but across the world, it is likely that this will be the case in the future as well and that we are entering a new period in which there will be a greater acceptance, maybe even an appreciation of variety, in family patterns and roles.

To effect the kind of egalitarian roles in relationships and families that most contemporary women desire, a social responsibility model of the family would be the basis of family policy. Under this model, there is a strong ideological commitment to minimizing privileges and rights in families based on gender or marital status. Legal marriages are not privileged over other relationships, and a variety of functioning relationships, kin and nonkin, may constitute a family unit. Spousehood is not automatically identified with parenthood, nor the opposite. Social supports and income relief are granted to individuals, rather than to spouses, and the individual is the unit of administration. Thus children in a variety of nontraditional households and families are all equally guaranteed an adequate income. Both parents are held equally responsible for the care of children in cohabitation, marriage, and after divorce; however, the public shares responsibility for the care of dependent children with both parents, and if one parent is absent or is unable to provide child support, the state pays the cost of his or her contribution. Finally, there is no distinction between same-sex and other-sex couples in terms of their treatment by the state. In this model then, there is a collective responsibility that everyone in the society shares for the welfare and well-being of children and for the future of the family.

SUGGESTED READING

Cherlin, A. J., and Calhoun, C. (1999). *Public and Private Families.* McGraw-Hill, New York.

Coontz, S. (1997). *The Way We Really Are: Coming to Terms with America's Changing Families.* Basic Books, New York.

Gelles, R. J. (1995). *Contemporary Families: A Sociological View.* Sage, Thousand Oaks, CA.

Goldscheider, F. K., and Waite, L. J. (1991). *New Families, No Families? The Transformation of the American Home.* The University of California Press, Berkeley, CA.

Gottfried, A. E., and Gottfried, A. W. (1994). *Redefining Families: Implications for Children's Development.* Plenum Press, New York.

Eichler, M. (1997). *Family Shifts: Families, Policies, and Gender Equality.* Oxford University Press, New York.

Mason, M., Skolnick, A., and Sugarman, S. D. (eds.) (1998). *All Our Families, New Policies for a New Century.* Oxford University Press, New York.

Potuchek, J. L. (1997). *Who Supports the Family? Gender and Breadwinning in Dual-Earner Marriages.* Stanford University Press, Stanford, CA.

Stacey, J. (1996). *In the Name of the Family: Rethinking Family Values in the Postmodern Age.* Beacon Press, Boston.

Feminist Approaches to Psychotherapy

Judith Worell
Dawn M. Johnson
University of Kentucky

Glossary

Androcentrism Theories and practices based on the lives and experiences of males as the standard for what is considered normal for women and men in a particular society.

Consciousness raising The process of becoming aware of commonalities across personal experiences that reflect societal practices and structures, such as sexism, racism, and homophobia, that negatively influence the lives of women and men.

Empowerment A broad goal of feminist intervention that enables individuals, families, and communities to exert influence over the personal, interpersonal, and institutional factors that impact their health and well-being. Personal and social empowerment facilitate action toward social justice and equality for all.

Feminist therapy An umbrella term for a range of psychotherapeutic interventions for individual and family distress that employ feminist principles and

consciousness raising in a confidential interpersonal encounter to facilitate personal and social change. Feminist therapy assists women and men to understand and negotiate the gendered personal and environmental factors that impede or promote their well-being and effective functioning.

Gender Culturally constructed beliefs and attitudes about the traits and behaviors of females and males. Gender intersects with other socially defined status categories such as age, race, ethnicity, class, physical ability, and sexual orientation, encouraging questions that are framed in ways other than comparisons between females and males. In any society, gender constructions create images in ourselves and others about who we are and how we should behave as females or males.

Gender analysis A technique of feminist intervention designed to increase awareness of the influence of differential societal expectations for women and men from diverse social groups. Gender analysis includes strategies for negotiation of personal and social change.

Patriarchy A systematic valuing and privileging of male gender and masculinity as culturally constructed in most societies. Patriarchy is characterized by gender-based inequalities and the devaluation, exclusion, and disempowerment of girls and women.

The personal is political A basic principle of feminist intervention that emphasizes commonalities among women and the societal sources of personal malaise. The primary factors underlying women's distress and alienation are considered to be social and political rather than intrapsychic and personal.

Power analysis A technique of feminist intervention designed to increase personal and community awareness and strategies to confront differentials in structural power and privilege between dominant and subordinate socially defined groups.

FEMINIST THERAPIES encompass a range of educational and therapeutic strategies grounded in the knowledge base of the psychology of women and gender. Feminist approaches to intervention are designed to raise personal and community awareness and change related to the gendered expectations and practices that negatively impact the health and well-being of women, men, and families. Contemporary feminist interventions trace their origins to the early consciousness-raising (CR) groups of community women who determined that their individual malaise was a reflection of the inequitable distribution of economic, social, and legal resources between women and men in society (e.g., the personal is political). This entry reviews (1) the background and early beginnings of feminist interventions for the psychological concerns of women in the United States, (2) the major streams of theory and practices that have characterized the development of feminist therapy, and (3) an evaluation of feminist therapy in terms of major critiques and research related to its distinctiveness and effectiveness.

I. Overview

Prior to 1970, recognition of gender issues in mental health intervention was limited. Since then, three decades of enlightenment have achieved public recognition of the separate and inequitable forces that shape the lives of women and men in Western societies as well as globally. With renewed activism in the women's movement, a surge of interest arose that targeted the historic neglect of women's health and psychological well-being. The reawakening of attention to women's issues from the 1960s to the 1980s stimulated both academic and clinical groups in psychology to examine the stereotyping and gender bias that appeared to pervade the fields of mental health practice and research.

Emerging scholarship and research on the psychology of women introduced the "second sex" into the medical and psychological literature and brought the life-span issues of women into sharper focus. In the field of mental health, attention was drawn to considerations of sex and gender in the prevalence, diagnosis, and intervention of a range of human problems. Surveys of both clinical and community samples reveal that a high proportion of individuals with signs of depression, anxiety, panic, eating disorders, and disabling fears and phobias are women. In the United States, overall health and community mental health utilization rates are higher for women than for men, and women are prescribed a disproportionate share of psychoactive medications.

At the same time, new client populations emerged as evidence surfaced about situations that had long been invisible and denied: physical and sexual violence against women, inequitable family arrangements privatized within the home, and widespread exclusion and discrimination of girls and women in education and the workplace. It was also becoming apparent that the mental health needs of women from diverse minority groups were being neglected. To meet these challenges, grassroots community groups mobilized interventions on behalf of women. These included consciousness-raising groups of community women, temporary shelters for battered women, and rape crisis centers that provided information and support for victims of sexual assault.

In the field of academic psychology, a parallel stream of dialogue, theory, and research contributed to the growing conceptual and empirical base of knowledge about women, men, and gender relations. Early research on gender stereotypes by Inge Broverman and her associates in 1968 and 1970 illuminated the gendered stereotypes of women and men by both college and professional groups. On the basis of their findings, these researchers concluded that both female and male professionals held a double standard of mental health, whereby the "healthy male" was seen as more rational, independent, and decisive than the "healthy female," and more similar to the "healthy person." Sandra Bem's 1974 research on sex-role stereotypes led to her position that androgyny, or an equal balance of female- and male-typed traits, was a more desirable model of mental health than adherence to culturally stereotyped sex-role behaviors. The growing field of the psychology of women contributed to an entire new corpus of knowledge about the lives of girls and women and revised views of sex, gender, gender roles, and gender-related behavior.

In the practice arena, new theories and therapeutic strategies were proposed to address issues related to the concerns of girls and women. New models of intervention for women's concerns appeared in the literature, calling for a revision of biased and sexist approaches to women and to their pressing issues. The most revolutionary of these approaches to therapeutic intervention is feminist therapy. Its broad goals are egalitarian, inclusive, empowering, political, and woman-valuing. In feminist therapy, the social construction of gender relocates women's problems from individual and internal to societal and external. The feminist construction of gender defines the nature of women's social and institutional relationships in terms of the expression and maintenance of power. The multicultural construction of gender uncovers and exposes the differentials in power and privilege that appear across diverse social, cultural, and political groups. More recently, the application of feminist interventions to the "new psychology of men" has extended and enriched the possibilities for a feminist psychology that is inclusive rather than adversarial. As a broad and diverse therapeutic approach, feminist interventions have attracted a range of professionals who practice with women, men, families, and institutions. [*See* HISTORY OF THE STUDY OF GENDER PSYCHOLOGY.]

II. *Rationale*

The energy provided by the revitalized women's movement of the 1960s and 1970s supplied the fuel for the emergence of both scholarly and applied approaches to the psychology of women and gender. Two major factors provided the impetus for the establishment of interventions targeted specifically toward the well-being of girls and women: community-based activist grassroots movements and dissatisfaction with many traditional approaches to psychotherapeutic practice with women and their families.

A. GRASSROOTS MOVEMENTS

Three types of grassroots activism served as important precursors to contemporary feminist intervention: community consciousness-raising groups, battered women's shelters, and rape crisis centers. Each of these movements contributed to the gender awareness and activism that characterizes contemporary feminist psychological practice. For the most part, these community groups consisted of laypersons whose concerns about social inequities and violence toward women led them to organize toward the protection and liberation of women and their children.

1. Consciousness-Raising (CR) Groups

In response to the rumblings of a reactivated political women's movement, small gatherings of women began to meet to share their feelings of discontent, self-doubt, and isolation in their traditional roles as wives, mothers, and helpers. Women in these groups exchanged ideas about how their individual problems were rooted in restrictive and stereotyped cultural expectations for how they should live their lives. These discussions led to an escalating awareness that their life situations were connected to their subordinate status in their families and in society. Through these groups, participating women determined that their individual concerns were mirrored by widespread gender discrimination and societal injustices for all women, giving birth to the theme that "the personal is political."

These egalitarian CR groups enabled members to validate their personal resistance to the status quo and provided support and solidarity with other women. Their growing awareness of asymmetrical gender expectations and institutionalized sexism resulted in an activist agenda that demanded change in the sexist and oppressive social structures that they believed characterized a patriarchal society.

In addition to forming the foundation of modern feminist theorizing, CR groups also resulted in positive outcomes for women. Across a number of research studies, women in CR groups were found to develop increased feminist consciousness, autonomy, self-respect, and self-confidence. Contemporary approaches to feminist therapy encompass many of the core beliefs of the consciousness-raising era and focus on issues that still confront today's women. The theme of the "personal is political" concept, in its diverse applications, remains a cornerstone of most contemporary feminist interventions. It confirms the

CR groups' position that a major portion of women's personal distress is embedded in the political, economic, legal, and social inequalities of society that disempower and disadvantage women. Thus, it implies that change must be implemented at the structural levels of society to improve the conditions of all women's lives. [*See* ANDROCENTRISM.]

2. Battered Women's Shelters and Rape Crisis Centers

The analysis of patriarchal and oppressive social structures provided by the CR movement was reflected in two other social movements: the battered women's movement, which provided shelter and counseling for women who were physically abused in intimate heterosexual relationships; and the antirape movement, which supported centers to counsel and assist women who had been sexually assaulted. Both of these movements targeted violence against women as a major social toxin that threatens and endangers all women.

In both movements, male violence against women was viewed as a strategy of control and dominance, intended to "keep women in their place." Thus, accountability and blame for woman battering rested squarely on the abusive perpetrator rather than on women's "masochism" or their desire to be dominated and abused; and all forms of rape and sexual assault were defined as acts of hostility and aggression rather than being motivated by passion and men's uncontrollable sexual needs. This radical approach to woman battering and sexual assault was assimilated into many of the later interventions for women by clinical researchers such as Lenore Walker and Mary Koss. [*See* AGGRESSION AND GENDER; BATTERING IN ADULT RELATIONSHIPS; RAPE.]

B. DISSATISFACTIONS WITH TRADITIONAL THERAPIES

Reverberations from these early women's movements were reflected in the psychological literature as both clinicians and researchers explored their dissatisfactions with traditional forms of treatment. Phyllis Chesler's 1972 book, *Women and Madness*, cast doubt on the ability of the mental health profession to treat women in an unbiased manner and to take their concerns seriously. Early books on feminist therapy, such as *Women in Therapy: New Psychotherapies for a Changing Society*, edited in 1974 by Violet Franks and Vasanti Burtle, and *Psy-*

chotherapy for Women: Treatment for Equality, published in 1977 by Edna Rawlings and Dianne Carter, emphasized how women were disadvantaged by stereotyped and restricted gender roles. Their efforts were aimed at educating practitioners about the critical concerns for which women were seeking relief.

Awareness of professional gender bias led to the 1975 report of the American Psychological Association (APA) Task force on Sex Bias and Sex-Role Stereotyping in Psychotherapeutic Practice, bringing into sharp focus many of the biases against women that existed in therapeutic practice. Women clients reported practices such as the abuse of therapist power with psychotherapy clients, woman-blaming, and biased and demeaning interpretations of women's behavior. These disturbing reports stimulated a conference sponsored by the National Institute of Mental Health on psychotherapy with women, which culminated in the publication of another landmark book, *Women and Psychotherapy: An Assessment of Research and Practice*, edited by Annette Brodsky and Rachel-Hare-Mustin. In addition to proposing alternatives to traditional treatment approaches for women's concerns, these authors called for "new methods of research and evaluation of results to meet the criticisms of feminist and traditional researchers alike" (p. 386).

These early critiques were prophetic. They heralded two decades of cutting commentary on many of the prevailing approaches to psychotherapy with women. It became clear that current theories and practices in psychotherapy were androcentric, being based on the lives and experiences of men and thus reflecting the dominant male culture. The experiences of women from all walks of society were invisible and excluded. Among the more serious of these biases were practices that

1. regarded the "healthy" woman as more dependent, passive, emotional, and submissive than the healthy man. As a result, women were expected to conform to these stereotypes and were viewed as disordered or maladjusted if they rebelled and behaved independently.
2. regarded male stereotyped activities and socialeconomic roles as more important and valuable than those typically reserved for women, interpreting women's legitimate career ambitions in negative and demeaning terms and thereby discouraging women from aiming toward positions of leadership and influence.
3. reflected gender, ethnic, and sexuality bias in di-

agnosis and psychotherapy with women, translating role-resistant behaviors as pathology and culturally normative female behaviors into illness.

4. attributed women's distress and help-seeking to intrapsychic (internal) causes rather than to inequities and toxins in the external environment and dominant social structures.

5. supported asymmetrical gender and power arrangements between therapists and clients as well as between clients and their critical support systems, such as family members and employment settings.

6. ignored the diversity among women, assuming that the experiences of middle-class women from the dominant culture (in the United States) were identical to those of underrepresented minority women or women of color.

7. engaged in "mother-blaming" in family therapy that pathologized women's involvement in family functioning by labeling it as enmeshment or over-involvement. This practice removed responsibility from men for their lack of involvement or their abuse of family power.

8. normalized a patriarchal hierarchy in family therapy that rank-ordered traditional gender roles based on the father as economic provider and head of household and the mother as responsibility for the emotional functioning of family members.

9. medicalized the concerns that women brought to therapy, on the assumption of "woman as biology" with an internal locus of pathology, thereby minimizing women's legitimate situational, economic, and cultural constraints.

Critiques such as these of some of the prevailing therapies reflected many of the dissatisfactions that motivated the call for change.

III. Themes and Variations

The founding "mothers" of feminist therapies are multiple, represented by all those whose work and writings have influenced feminist theories and their applications. Those who identify as feminist in their orientation to psychotherapy reflect both commonalities and differences in their beliefs and practices. The similarities stem from common understandings about the goals of the feminist movement and a general concern for the health and well-being of women as an underserved group in need of attention.

Differences among feminists arise from variations in their beliefs about the origins and solutions to women's disadvantage, as well as differences in their theoretical or applied orientations to psychotherapy. These differences among therapists who identify themselves as feminist or women centered may result in distinctive strategies of intervention, but their common themes provide parallel foundations.

A. COMMON THEMES

A review of the literature on feminist intervention suggests that there is no single definition. Rather, consensual themes appear that form a core of common principles that characterize the writings and research on feminist therapy. Some examples of these principles follow.

Karen Wyche and Joy Rice summarized three broad themes of feminist therapy that were confirmed by consensus in a national U.S. conference on feminist practice in 1993. Conference members included North American and international participants. These three themes included the following:

1. Gender is a salient variable in the process and outcomes of therapy but can be understood only in the context of the other factors in women's lives.

2. Women's experiences must be viewed from a sociocultural understanding that includes an analysis of power asymmetries, as well as an intrapsychic or individual perspective; thus, "symptoms" are seen as a woman's best attempts to cope with a restrictive and oppressive environment.

3. A major goal of feminist therapy is personal empowerment, expanding women's alternatives, options, and choices; the therapeutic relationship is mutual and egalitarian, focusing on a woman's strengths rather than only on her deficits.

Thus, the overall aims of feminist therapy are to liberate and empower women (and sometimes men). In supporting and assisting individuals to assert authority over their lives, feminist therapy educates them as well about the realities of societal contributions to individual problems through gendered socialization, institutional sexism, racism, and other discriminatory practices. It encourages individuals to initiate change, not only for themselves, but in relation to equity for women in all areas of social, economic, and political functioning.

Empirical evidence for the distinctiveness of feminist therapy strategies and goals, in comparison to more traditional approaches, has been demonstrated in a number of studies. Several structured scales have been developed to measure the beliefs and behaviors of therapists who self-identify as feminist or woman centered. Using the Therapy with Women Scale (TWS) developed by Robinson and Worell, Damon Robinson found two broad factors that discriminated therapist beliefs and goals between those who did or did not self-identify as feminist or women centered. Women-centered therapists were more likely than others to affirm and empower their women clients (such a therapist was more likely to "Support my clients in taking charge of their lives") and to endorse woman-centered activism ("Work actively for social change as it impacts on women's improved status").

In a more recent study using a modified form of the TWS, Chandler, Worell, and Johnson reported that clinicians who identified as woman centered or feminist scored higher than those who did not so identify on five distinctive factors: (1) affirming the client ("encourage my clients to explore and assert their own needs"), (2) gender-role awareness ("encourage my clients to explore issues related to societal expectations for girls/women"), (3) woman-centered activism ("provide workshops and seminars on issues pertaining to women and gender"), (4) therapist self-disclosure ("disclose my values, when appropriate, to my clients"), and (5) egalitarianism ("establish an egalitarian relationship with my clients").

Another method of establishing common themes that appear across therapists is to ask their clients. Three recent studies considered the perspective of clients rather than therapists. Worell, Chandler, Robinson, and Blount matched each item on the Therapy with Women Scale with a companion form for clients, documenting that clients do experience in sessions the behaviors that their feminist therapists say they use. In a study by Niva Piran, the Feminist Frame Scale asks clients directly about the feminist behaviors of their therapists in session. The three factors identified by clients on this scale were (1) respectful validation and care; (2) empowerment through collaboration, skills development, and political awareness; and (3) unsilencing trauma: emotional and bodily reactions. On all three factors, clients of feminist therapists scored higher (reported more feminist therapy behaviors) than clients of more traditional practitioners. Thus, there are firm data

that therapists who identify as feminist, regardless of their particular orientations, appear to be practicing a distinctive form of therapy.

In a third study on feminist therapy by Anne Cummings, novice counselors were instructed and coached on the use of four feminist strategies: empowering the client, decreasing power differentials, exploring gender-role conflict, and placing client concerns within a sociocultural context. At the end of training, counselor scores on the TWS and their written diaries following each session confirmed that they were using feminist strategies. Client responses on the client form of the TWS further confirmed that clients experienced these strategies in their sessions. These three studies corroborate that there is a common core of feminist therapy principles that can be reliably measured, can be taught to novice counselors, are experienced as feminist by clients, and are more likely to be implemented by feminist, as compared to nonfeminist practitioners.

B. DISTINCTIVE THEMES

Apart from common themes among therapists who practice from a feminist perspective, specific strategies may differ according to one's theoretical frame concerning the sources and solutions to women's disadvantage and subordinate status. Feminist theories have been identified in the literature in many ways, and they offer a range of explanations regarding women's position in society including what needs to be changed for women to achieve equity. These theories are condensed here according to four primary themes that might be applied in therapy: liberal/reform, radical, relational, and multicultural/women of color. Although the literature points to differences in beliefs among feminist therapists based on theory, there is little empirical evidence linking specific theories to specific practices with clients. There are also number of feminist approaches to feminist practice that emphasize particular populations or specific concerns. A sample of these is discussed in a later section.

1. Liberal/Reform Feminism

Liberal/reform feminism targets the elimination of inequalities between women and men in legal, political, social, and educational settings. In the liberal/reform view, the subordination of women is caused by asymmetrical gender socialization practices and discriminatory laws that exclude women from the mainstream of economic and political life.

Feminist therapies based on a liberal/reform philosophy assist the client in revisioning herself in the context of her gender socialization, or others' expectations for her roles as a daughter, lover, wife, mother, caretaker, and worker. In this process of gender-role analysis, Laura Brown encourages exploration of what each gender role means to the client and how it may influence her satisfaction and distress. A sensitive gender-role analysis enables the woman to explore the potential risks and advantages of alternative gender roles, enabling her to counter self-blame for her current choices and to consider other possibilities. Some therapists encourage androgyny, or developing a relatively equal balance of communal and assertive traits and behaviors. Thus, assertiveness training, or effective confrontation with others when one's needs are not met, may be used to encourage women who have been socialized to be "polite" to overcome their reluctance to ask for equity in interpersonal or work-related settings.

Toward the goal of revisioning herself, the strategy of reframing and renaming of experiences assists the client to transform shame into self-respect and fear into strength, enabling her to acknowledge her ability to cope and survive. In reframing and renaming, socially conditioned behaviors that are frequently seen as pathology, such as being identified and treated as "codependent" for supporting an abusive partner, may be reconstructed as compassionate helping or as the woman's best attempt at coping. Formal diagnosis, which tends to turn coping into pathology, is generally avoided unless required by institutional policies. Women are encouraged to nurture themselves as well as others.

As more women become employed in male-dominated settings, liberal/reform therapy extends its concerns to equality in the workplace. Feminist *employment or career counseling* assists women to explore their work-related concerns and conflicts, such as maintaining a balance between paid job demands and family life, or confronting the abuses of sexual harassment and other evidence of work-related gender discrimination. Self-blame can be reduced by considering the external structural barriers to women in the workplace that maintain them in low-paying dead-end jobs, such as occupational segregation and "glass ceilings" that block career advancement. [*See* CAREER ACHIEVEMENT.]

Liberal/reform feminism also proposed that traditional gender roles are limiting and restrictive for men as well as for women. An early theme of the liberal positions was that "when women are liberated, men will also be free." However, the liberal position focused more on establishing access and opportunity for women than in exploring and challenging the patriarchal power structures underlying women's subordinate status. The radical feminist position moved the conversation and action to another level.

2. Radical Feminism

Radical feminism, in contrast, identifies the locus of women's problems in the politics of institutional power in the creation and maintenance of asymmetrical gender relations. Patriarchy, or the dominance of male privilege and entitlement, maintained through control of political, social, and economic institutions, is responsible for women's systematic oppression and devaluation. Patriarchy is also responsible for heterosexism, viewing as deviant any interpersonal love or sexuality other than between females and males. Cultural stereotypes of women as passive, dependent, and nurturant are social constructions designed to maintain women's compliance and powerlessness. Such stereotypes are internalized by many women and accepted by others as a natural part of their personality, thereby creating a self-fulfilling prophecy (by believing it, they enact it).

Violence against women, sexual objectification, and sexual coercion are also seen as institutionalized control over women to maintain male dominance and women's compliance. Lenore Walker pointed out in *The Battered Woman* that women's apparent "submission" to a battering relationship reflects not masochism or enjoyment of pain but signals her best judgment about how to ensure her safety and that of her children in the face of terrifying violence. In the case of interpersonal violence, reframing and renaming also come into play; coercive and violent strategies by a partner are seen as examples of hostility and control rather than reflections of love.

Feminist therapies from a radical perspective expand the consciousness-raising strategies of liberal/reform therapies. The positive goal of client empowerment becomes the base for a range of procedures. Therapists aim to avoid reproducing with women clients the asymmetrical power relationships they experience in their everyday lives. The first step is to establish an egalitarian relationship with clients. The therapist possesses professional expertise, but the client is respected as an expert on herself. The challenge of creating an egalitarian relationship engages strategic procedures such as collaborative goal setting (rather than diagnosing an illness), sharing one's relevant personal values with clients, demystifying the therapeutic process (informing clients of all relevant aspects of the therapy experience), validating and trusting the experience of the client, and using judicious self-disclosure when appropriate. Client empowerment can also be realized by engaging in social activism, such as becoming involved in activities that benefit other women. Thus, change is directed not only with the client but is aimed at injustices and inequality existing in the larger social structure.

Issues of power imbalance become important in family or heterosexual couples therapy as well, challenging hierarchal structures related to myths about "head-of-household" and who holds decision-making privileges. Thus, societal constructions of masculinity and entitlement are examined for their influence on asymmetrical power relationships between women and men. Considerable research has documented that in both heterosexual and lesbian or gay couples, equality between the partners lead to high relationship satisfaction. In considering the personal concerns that clients bring to therapy, therapists also evaluate the social, political, and economic context of clients' lives. Thus, women can be equally oppressed by gender, race, nationality, and poverty, and these factors are important to explore. [*See* FEMINIST FAMILY THERAPY.]

3. Relational Feminism

Relational feminism (sometimes referred to as cultural feminism) seeks to transform society toward a female-valuing culture based on concern for others, emotional expressiveness, and peace-seeking behaviors. Sexism and oppression are seen as caused by devaluation of traditional female values and overvaluation of male-typed and patriarchical values.

Therapists who practice from a relational or interpersonal perspective consider women's traditional values of caring, cooperation, gentleness, and emotionality as their intrinsic qualities in contrast to the aggressive and competitive values of men. These relational values are translated as strengths rather than weaknesses. In her influential book *The Reproduction of Mothering,* Nancy Chodorow viewed women's development from a psychoanalytic perspective as rooted in the mother–daughter relation-

ship. A leading example of this approach, self-in relation therapy, is identified with the Stone Center at Wellesley College. The self-in relation model of psychotherapy assumes that women develop an enduring capacity for empathy, nurturance, and caring as a result of the early mother–daughter relationship. Some of women's problems also emanate from this early attachment: difficulties in separation and dealing with loss, and developing a sense of a differentiated self and the ability for self-care as well as other-care. Rather than viewing empowerment as a therapeutic goal, relational therapists emphasize the attainment of connection and mutuality in women's interpersonal relationships. [*See* EMPATHY AND EMOTIONAL EXPRESSIVITY.]

4. Multicultural or Women-of-Color Feminism

Multicultural or women-of-color feminism was developed in reaction to White middle-class feminism that arose between 1960 and 1980. The myth of the "universal woman" failed to acknowledge the differing life experiences of women from diverse ethnic, racial, national, and multicultural backgrounds. Women of color in the United States and wherever they represent a minority community are faced with many unique challenges not typically encountered by middle-class women from the dominant culture. They are more likely to be working parents and single mothers, to be economically and politically disadvantaged, and to be subjected to multiple experiences of exclusion and discrimination. For these women, gender is not the only site of oppression.

Multicultural feminist therapies, sometimes referred to as "womanist" rather than feminist, target the needs and interests of specific groups of ethnic women. These include interrelated but distinct therapeutic approaches that address the complex issues that confront women from diverse racial and ethnic backgrounds in terms of the external and reflected internal realities of their lives. Within a sensitive multicultural context, women with diverse racial and ethnic identities can explore their experiences of racism and sexism within and from outside their communities, their personal and cultural selves, their internalization of negative experiences with the dominant culture, and their need to feel connected or distanced from their ethnic/racial community. The therapeutic goal of social activism remains important in multicultural feminist therapy, enabling women to take an active part in shaping their own realities.

Feminist therapists who practice within a multicultural context develop a range of skills that facilitate multicultural sensitivity and competence. For example, understanding the functions of gender as it is interpreted within each community is important. Across the pluralism of cultures, gender roles may be more rigid or more flexible for women with differing group identities. Issues of gender, power, status, and empowerment may assume different contextual frames for members of individualistic cultures as compared to those from more collective or interconnected cultures. Clients may be confronted with conflicting loyalties between commitment to their ethnic community and their awareness of the hierarchies and dominance structures within it. Also, as many North American communities experience an increasing population of immigrants and new citizens from non-Western cultures, issues of bicultural and immigrant identity as well as multicultural loyalties may be of continuing concern. Although the development of informed and competent interventions for specific ethnic groups remains essential, Lillian Comas-Diaz has voiced support for moving toward an integrative and pluralistic feminist psychology and practice that will be of relevance to all women. [*See* COUNSELING AND PSYCHOTHERAPY.]

C. AN INTEGRATIVE MODEL OF FEMINIST PRACTICE

These broad forms of feminist therapies may be practiced in their "pure" form or may be integrated with one or more other approaches. One integrative model has been proposed by Worell and Remer. Their feminist empowerment therapy incorporates several of the unique and critical elements of each of the four major models discussed here. The empowerment model contains four principles, with multiple goals and specific strategies that represent each principle. The overall goals of personal and social empowerment emphasize client strengths and resilience. The four principles are briefly summarized as follows:

1. The *personal is political* principle identifies the major sources of women's problems as political and social rather than internal and intrapsychic. This principle addresses issues of gender-role socialization within the relevant experience and culture of the client, her experiences of sexism and discrimination, her understanding of her symptoms as best-attempt coping strategies, and the possibility of social activism as a therapeutic intervention to gain a sense of personal strength and control over her life.

2. The *personal and social identities are interdependent* principle addresses the importance of exploring a woman's personal identities and the groups with which she identifies and in turn is socially identified. Personally relevant intersects of experience are examined, including those of gender, ethnicity, socioeconomic class, sexual orientation, age, and physical characteristics. Clients are encouraged to distinguish the internal from external in these experiences, including the recognition of conflict and its resolution among them. Critical identity issues may include the realization by some of dominant culture privilege and entitlement, and for others the psychic damage induced by life experiences of discrimination and exclusion from both the dominant culture and their own communities.

3. The *relationships are egalitarian* principle addresses women's lower power and status in most social contexts, both within the dominant culture as well as the power differentials that may exist among women. Egalitarian strategies are established within and outside the therapy session to affirm and empower clients. Particular attention to interpersonal power dynamics is present when therapist and client are from different racial, ethnic, or social groups.

4. The *communal perspectives are valued* principle encourages a process of self-validation and identification of strengths. Qualities of interdependence, concern for others, emotional expression, and cooperation are valued and honored. Language that devalues women is reframed from weakness to strength (e.g., terms such as "enmeshed and fused" may be reframed as "caring, concerned, and nurturing"). Clients are encouraged to nurture themselves, to trust their experience, and to connect and bond with other women who provide community and support.

The goal of personal and social empowerment as an outcome of feminist interventions for women was articulated by Judith Worell in a structured model designed to evaluate women's psychological health and well-being. In contrast to a deficit or illness model that targets mainly symptom reduction, the empowerment model of women's well-being provides a positive and optimistic view of women's strength, ability to overcome barriers, and resilience in the face of stress and trauma. The model offers a theoretical conceptualization that can guide therapy goals, interventions, and the evaluation of therapy outcomes. The utility of this model in assessing therapeutic effectiveness is discussed later in the article.

The 10 hypothesized outcomes of the empowerment model are supported by the literature on women's health and well-being. The healthy woman in a healthy environment is envisioned as having positive self-evaluation and self-esteem; a favorable comfort-distress balance (more positive than negative affect); gender-role and cultural identity awareness; a sense of personal control and self-efficacy; self-nurturance, and self-care; effective problem-solving skills; competent use of assertiveness skills; effective access to facilitative social, economic, and community resources; gender and cultural flexibility in behavior; and socially constructive activism. In brief, she is confident, strong, connected to a supportive community, and resilient.

IV. Special Applications

Feminist principles have been incorporated into interventions for specific high-probability concerns for women such as woman battering, incest, sexual assault and sexual harassment, eating concerns, body awareness, depression, substance abuse, reproductive concerns, and chronic illnesses such as breast cancer, irritable bowel syndrome (IBS), and AIDS. Many of these strategies incorporate individual psychotherapy with women's groups that focus on specific issues such as problematic dieting and purging. In contrast to individual interventions, therapeutic groups can provide normalization of one's behavior through sharing of personal experiences, decreasing isolation through group support, education and practice in skill building, and increased empowerment by diluting the power of the therapist. Feminist interventions have also been developed to address specific concerns of a range of population groups, including adolescent girls, older women, both heterosexual and lesbian or bisexual couples and families, women with disabilities, women from varying racial and ethnic identities, immigrant women, homeless women, and, more recently, men. A sample of issues and feminist interventions for two of these groups, men and lesbians, are considered next.

A. FEMINIST THERAPY WITH MEN

Because the balance of social and political transactions cannot be changed if women are the sole change agents, feminist intervention with men by both female and male therapists has assumed increased visibility and support. Feminist interventions for men have aimed to assist men in dealing with some aspects of stereotyped masculine gender-role expectations that have become problematic in contemporary society. James O'Neill referred to a "masculine gender-role conflict," in which men's socialized needs for power, control, and achievement inhibit the expression of tenderness and positive emotionality. These needs are often accompanied by homophobia (fear and hatred of homosexuality) and excessive focus on the visible trappings of success. Although this pattern is normative for men in North America society, O'Neill suggested that it is dysfunctional for many men in both their work and interpersonal relationships.

Thus, the feminist position that traditional gender socialization has been disabling for women can also be applied to traditional gendered expectations for men. In feminist therapy, the focus might center on uncovering sexist beliefs about women and men, fear of self-disclosure and vulnerability, inhibited emotionality, and overconcern with achievement and maintaining control. Traditional masculinity norms relevant to the client's culture, his own masculinity ideology (what makes him feel masculine and strong), issues of power and entitlement, intimacy and connection in close relationships, and the meanings and expression of sexuality might be some of the topics for consideration. For some men, their perception of White male privilege and entitlement might be of importance. For others, the role of appropriate coping strategies related to anger and violence might be raised. For all men, challenging dysfunctional gender myths and learning to discriminate internal from externally supported ideologies and expectations should be paramount.

For men in minority cultures, many of the themes of exclusion, discrimination, and oppression that are of concern to women will enter into the therapeutic equation as well. However, across groups from three diverse minority subcultures in the United States, Doss and Hopkins found two components of masculine ideology that were similar among men: hypermasculine posturing and achievement. Although the factors of toughness, sensitivity, and sexual responsibility were culture specific, the men in their samples were consistently different from the women on all three measures. Thus, both culture and gender remain important in feminist interventions with men.

B. FEMINIST THERAPY WITH LESBIAN AND BISEXUAL WOMEN

As a theoretical perspective, lesbian feminism takes the position that women's subordinate status and oppression by the patriarchy is maintained by the cultural norm of "compulsory heterosexuality," which regards other sexual orientations as deviant and abnormal. Accordingly, women can free themselves by bonding with one another in more egalitarian and connected relationships.

Therapists who practice within a lesbian feminist framework are sensitive to the issues that confront all lesbian and bisexual individuals in a homophobic society. As is true with other socially devalued groups, feminist therapists may work with the clients' reflected and internalized self-hatred projected by social norms. Anne Peplau and Kristin Beals have pointed out that although many of the relationship issues that lesbian couples confront are similar to those experienced by women in heterosexual relationships, lesbians also represent an oppressed minority group for whom many civil and legal rights have not yet been achieved. One of the more poignant problems raised by these exclusions is the difficulty that lesbian mothers experience in child custody disputes, whereby the assumption is made by most courts that lesbian women are "unfit" for parenting and thus they frequently lose custody of their children. In these cases, lesbian mothers need sensitive support and documentation of their effectiveness as persons and parents that may be provided by the therapist. Feminist therapists who work with lesbian clients also keep current on research that indicates, for example, that no significant differences have been found between children of lesbian and heterosexual parents in social and emotional adjustment or in their sexual orientation.

Feminist therapy specific to this group might also include working with the emotional struggles involved in the "coming out" process (acknowledging to self and others, and coming to terms with one's sexual and affectional orientation), and supporting clients in maintaining a positive, valuing stance sometimes referred to as affirmation therapy. Further exploration of these variations of feminist therapies is worthwhile but is beyond the scope of this article. [*See* Lesbians, Gay Men, and Bisexuals in Relationships.]

V. Evaluation

Is feminist therapy effective? The question of accountability, or demonstrating therapeutic effectiveness, can be raised for any applied practice. Unfor-

tunately, relatively little research has been applied to assess the effectiveness of feminist forms of intervention. There are at last three reasons why research has lagged behind theory and practice in this area. First, like most clinicians, feminist therapists are not likely to be seen as serious researchers and are typically located outside established institutions such as universities or medical settings, where research is supported and rewarded. Second, feminist therapists practice from a variety of perspectives and have merged these with particular theories of psychotherapy as well. This fact makes effective control of the relevant variables in the research endeavor very complex. Finally, only a few graduate institutions train feminist therapists; therefore there are fewer researchers and fewer concentrated groups for researchers to target.

A. DEFINING THERAPY EFFECTIVENESS

If the various forms of feminist therapy are to take their place among the major intervention approaches, it is critical to establish accountability through research that demonstrates outcome effectiveness with clients. But how is effectiveness defined? In most standard therapies, the major focus is on reduction of the distressing symptoms that motivated the person to seek help. Typically, the individual is given a diagnosis according to criteria providing by the *Diagnostic and Statistical Manual* of the American Psychiatric Association (*DSM-IV*). The client is regarded as in remission (returned to her previous level of functioning) when the symptoms of the "disorder" for which she is being treated are reduced or eliminated.

Feminist therapists also aim to reduce personal distress and pain. However, they tend to focus on a client's strengths rather than on her deficits. Symptoms are viewed as adaptive strategies in the context of an unsupportive or oppressive environment. Thus, clients are helped to develop more effective coping strategies, while at the same time working to modify rather than adapt to the toxic elements in their environments. The overall goal for many feminist therapists and counselors is to affirm client empowerment and resilience rather than to return a client to her previous level of functioning. The experience of empowerment prepares individuals to confront and deal with both internal and external threats to their current and future well-being, thus increasing their resilience. Resilience can be conceptualized as a continuum of increasing skills in dealing with adversity and setbacks to health and well-being. Thus, as individuals increase in resilience, they can experience trauma and other aversive life situations without extreme harm to their psychological well-being. Resilient individuals possess sufficient flexibility to resist and overcome future threat and danger, and they use their experiences to further their personal well-being. Standard measures of therapy outcome, such as those for depression, anxiety, and additional trauma-related symptoms of sleep disturbance and dissociation, may be used to assess symptom reduction. It is also important, however, to assess the client's psychological well-being and positive growth.

B. MEASURING THERAPY EFFECTIVENESS

Several new measures of well-being and empowerment have been developed and applied to the task of evaluating feminist therapy outcomes. For example, Worell and Chandler developed the Personal Progress Scale (PPS) to match the 10 goals of the empowerment model presented earlier. The scale measures positive psychological functioning, personal strength, and subjective well-being. In several studies conducted independently by Anne Cummings and by Worell, Chandler, Johnson, and Blount, client scores on the PPS increased significantly following both short-term (four sessions or fewer) and longer-term feminist therapy. In the latter study, a one-year followup of a subset of the clients showed continued improvement on the PPS and scores on two scales of well-being remained stable. These outcomes suggest that even brief interventions from a feminist perspective can impact a sense of personal empowerment. Several other scales that measure psychological well-being, such as those developed by Carol Ryff and by Lambert and Burlingame, also offer promising approaches for assessing the positive outcomes of feminist interventions.

Assessment of therapy outcomes is a complex and arduous undertaking. It is time-consuming and expensive to conduct. Nevertheless, it is clearly important that effectiveness research be continued and expanded. We need to understand how differing theoretical forms of feminist therapy function with differing types of client concerns and with diverse populations. The enterprise has only begun.

VI. The Future of Feminist Therapy

The enthusiasm with which those who practice from a feminist perspective approach their work is tempered by the knowledge that problems have been voiced both within and from without the feminist practice community. Within the practice community, therapists are concerned that more controlled studies using standard empirical methods have not been attempted. Those outside the practice community have voiced some other concerns related to both theory and practice.

For example, some believe that even feminist forms of psychotherapy guarantee continued compliance to an oppressive society. Since most insurance reimbursement requires an official diagnosis, are we not labeling women in distress as ill or crazy when in fact they are being oppressed? By helping women to feel better, are we not lulling them into complacency rather than encouraging them to confront injustice? Are we undermining the goals of the feminist movement, which are to change society rather than those who are oppressed within it? Others have stated that feminist therapy is not therapy but politics, and that therapists have no business imposing their values on clients. From a multicultural lens, some view feminist therapy as a White middle-class invention that has ignored the concerns of those who are less privileged. And those who are critical of the relationship therapies point out that by elevating the "special" valued qualities of women, they fall into the same trap as those who insist that women are less valuable than men. By ennobling the qualities of women, are we not also denigrating those of men?

There are only a sample of some of the concerns that have been voiced about feminist approaches to therapy. The future of feminist therapy lies in efforts and persistence from many quarters to develop useful and testable models of the healthy woman in a healthy environment and to work toward achieving this goal. It is our position that those who are concerned about women in distress and pain can take many roads toward proactive intervention and change. Helping women at the proximal and interpersonal level, we believe, empowers them to work toward change for both themselves and the social institutions that exclude and oppress them.

SUGGESTED READING

Brodsky, A. M., and Hare-Mustin, R. T. (1980). *Women and Therapy: An Assessment of Research and Practice.* Guilford, New York.

Brown, L. S. (1994). *Subversive Dialogues: Theory in Feminist Therapy.* Basic Books, New York.

Comas-Diaz, L., and Greene, B. (1994). *Women of Color: Integrating Ethnic and Gender Identities in Psychotherapy.* Guilford, New York.

Dutton-Douglas, M. A., and Walker, L. E. A. (eds.) (1988). *Feminist Psychotherapies: Integration of Therapeutic and Feminist Systems*. Ablex, Norwood, NJ.

Enns, C. Z. (1997). *Feminist Theories and Feminist Psychotherapies: Origins, Themes, and Variations*. Harrington Press, New York.

Hare-Mustin, R. T. (1991). Sex, lies, and headaches: The problem is power. In *Women and Power: Perspectives for Therapy* (T. J. Goodrich, ed.). Norton, New York.

Hill, M., and Rothblum, E. D. (1996). *Couples Therapy: Feminist Perspectives*. Harrington Press, New York.

Walker, L. E. A. (1994). *Abused Women and Survivor Therapy: A Practical Guide for the Psychotherapist*. American Psychological Association, Washington, DC.

Worell, J., and Remer, P. (1992). *Feminist Perspective in Therapy: An Empowerment Model for Women*. Wiley, Chichester, UK.

Wyche, K. F., and Rice, J. K. (1997). Feminist Therapy: From Dialogue to Tenets. In *Shaping the Future of Feminist Psychology: Education, Research and Practice* (J. Worell and N. Johnson, eds.), pp. 57–71. American Psychological Association, Washington, DC.

Feminist Ethics and Moral Psychology

Mary M. Brabeck

Anmol Satiani

Boston College

Glossary

Alpha bias The exaggeration of differences between women and men.

Beta bias The idea of ignoring or minimizing gender differences.

Ethic of care An idea developed by Carol Gilligan in response to the work of Lawrence Kohlberg. She posited that women prefer this moral orientation, which she defined as one that emphasizes relationships and interdependence and, therefore, more attention to context.

Ethic of justice A distinct orientation with emphasis on justice issues over care; Carol Gilligan argued that men prefer this moral orientation.

Feminist ethics An emerging area that includes several themes. These can be applied in a variety of contexts, including the practice of research, in an attempt to achieve social justice.

FEMINISTS have engaged in critical evaluations of dominant theories in psychology in order to further the goals of feminism. One such challenge has been in the area of morality and ethics. This article describes what feminist theory and feminist ethics bring to the study of moral psychology. We examine the dominant theories of moral development and gender and the responses to claims of gender differences in moral development. We review the empirical work examining claims of gender differences in morality and try to answer the question, "Are there gender differences in moral reasoning and moral orientation?" We conclude by outlining potential cultural influences in moral development and, finally, discuss the implications of studying gender differences without attending to the culture within which individuals develop psychologically and morally.

I. Introduction

Feminist theories have been evolving over the past two decades, and feminist psychologists have contributed to the field as it has expanded over time. Feminist activities of scholarship, professional practice, community activism, and leadership are working toward broad goals of improving the lives of all girls and women, as well as enhancing the lives of families and communities. The scholarship of feminist theory and feminist psychology indicates that a single feminist view does not exist. Instead, a range of feminist perspectives are contained within feminist views, which stem from different philosophical ideas and are supported by empirical research. While, as described in this article, feminists share some common beliefs, they hold a variety of views on how to apply feminist principles to the content and practice of the discipline of psychology.

Psychologists who claim to hold a feminist perspective are of varied geographic regions and encompass a diversity of life experiences and human characteristics, including ethnicity, sexual orientations, race, and socioeconomic status. They occupy various professions, advocate a range of persuasions, vary in beliefs about the ways in which women are affected by patriarchal structures of society, and have differing views in how to solve current problems.

II. Feminist View/Feminist Ethics

Nevertheless, there are shared perceptions that identify a perspective as a feminist view. Models of feminist practice and feminist theories have been available for some time, and the characteristics of a feminist theory of psychological practice were described recently. In 1997, Mary Brabeck and Laura Brown, in *Shaping the Future of Feminist Psychology: Education, Research, and Practice,* wrote about the foundational concepts of a feminist theory of psychological practice, as developed by a group at a working conference. These foundations included the following:

- The goal of feminist practice is social transformation toward a development of feminist consciousness.

- Feminist theory develops out of both personal and professional experiences.
- Gender is not the only site for understandings of oppression; for example, attention to race, class, culture, and sexual orientation provide rich information regarding hierarchy, power, and dominance.
- Feminist theory authorizes voices of the oppressed.
- Feminist theory leads to expanded ideas of identities and multiple subjectivities, and a reformulated understanding of psychological distress from feminist views. (pp. 23–29)

Feminist ethics is an emerging area, which includes five broad themes articulated by Mary Brabeck and Kathleen Ting in *Practicing Feminist Ethics in Psychology,* published in 2000. The themes overlap with the tenets of feminist theory and include the following:

- The assumption that women and their experiences have moral significance
- The assertion that affective responses and subjective knowledge can illuminate moral issues
- The admonition that feminist ethicists engage in analysis of the context and of the power dynamics inherent in that context
- The claim that a feminist critique of male oppression must be accompanied by a critique of racist, classist, homophobic oppressive acts
- The injunction that feminist ethics require action directed at achieving systemic social justice (pp. 5–6)

These ethical frames can be applied in a variety of contexts, such as academic settings, forensic settings, and therapeutic relationships, and they can be useful in guiding research. By examining behavior through these frameworks, we are engaging in feminist ethics while adding to the knowledge base of feminist ethics.

Feminist psychologists and philosophers have raised concerns about theories of moral development and questioned whether focusing entirely on difference or similarity benefits anyone. The discussion that follows describes previous work on moral development and uses a feminist lens to examine this work. The discussion also highlights a shift in the types of questions asked in the area of moral development research as feminists have entered the discussion about the relationship between gender and morality. [*See* FEMINIST APPROACHES TO PSYCHOTHERAPY; FEMINIST THEORIES.]

III. *Theories of Moral Development and Gender*

Morality generally refers to the way in which individuals make ethical decisions and act in moral ways, while ethics is typically discussed as a larger philosophical inquiry into moral obligations and understandings of what constitutes moral good.

Perspectives concerning moral development and gender vary greatly. Evolutionary/Darwinian paradigms posited that "natural," biological differences or differences that naturally evolve over time inevitably result in differences in men's and women's moral capacity. In 1875, Herbert Spencer argued that, although gender differences could change as societies evolve, women were not capable of abstract reasoning. He claimed that women were not able to consider issues of justice, but focused on issues of care in their decision making. Using a similar argument, Sigmund Freud in 1925 posited that because of physical differences that affect psychological development, women have an underdeveloped superego. Superego was thought to be the structure of the mind, which was the internalization of the rules and restrictions of a society. Freud argued that because of this deficiency, women have less of a sense of justice than men and are more likely to be influenced by feelings than by rational, abstract thought. Both of these perspectives support a separation of thoughts and feelings, along gender lines, with girls and women assumed more affectively sensitive and relational, and boys and men more rational and autonomous. [*See* GENDER DEVELOPMENT: EVOLUTIONARY PERSPECTIVES.]

In the early 1970s, Walter Mischel and Albert Bandura, two social learning theorists, introduced an interactionist view of moral development. They suggested that the individual and the environment influence one another. Individuals, according to this theory, can observe and imitate others when making moral decisions. One's environment provides models of behavior that shapes moral action. At the same time, individuals shape their environment by selecting what they attend to. Thus, perceptions of the environment are constructed by the individual. Social learning theorists claimed that whatever gender differences in moral behavior exist result from learning by imitating same-sex models and by consequences to those behaviors. Girls and boys are reinforced for a gender "appropriate" behavior and punished for cross-gender behavior. Thus, being a "good girl" or a "good boy," social learning theorists claim, is acquired behavior.

In the late 1960s, Lawrence Kohlberg's cognitive developmental theory of moral reasoning began to dominate the field of psychology. Kohlberg built on the work of Piaget and developed a six-stage model of cognitive moral development. He posited a sequential, hierarchical, and universal pattern of moral development across the life span. His theory was based on the idea that individuals learn to reason abstractly about moral issues as they mature and encounter life experiences and that the goal of development was to be able to apply universal principles of justice.

In his research, Kohlberg used hypothetical ethical dilemmas. For example, one involves a husband, Heinz, who must decide either to steal a drug to save his ill wife or to let her die. Kohlberg then asked people in an interview what Heinz should do and why. A scoring manual was developed to score people's reasoning about each hypothetical dilemma in the moral judgment interview. Based on interview responses, Kohlberg described three levels of moral reasoning, which contain a total of six stages. The preconventional level involves obeying rules to avoid punishment or to get rewards. For example, someone at the preconventional level might state the husband should not steal, because he might be apprehended and punished by the police. An individual who states that Heinz should not steal because others may not approve, or that the act is illegal, would be classified in the conventional level, according to Kolhberg's theory. Individuals who reach Kohlberg's postconventional level, which involves abstract thinking, might break laws because of internalized standards of justice (e.g., that it might be okay to steal in order to save a life). Participants of civil disobedience movements, who break laws that they believe are socially unjust, might fit into this category.

Kohlberg's original theory was based on an all-male sample. Subsequent research with both men and women found that in a few studies men were reported to reach "higher" stages of development in his research. In one often cited study, by Kohlberg and Richard Kramer (1969), women were found more likely to be at stage 3 (interpersonal) and men at stage 4 (social system and conscience). Since the stages are hierarchical, this is tantamount to saying that men are morally superior to women. However, Kohlberg did not claim gender differences in moral development were innate. Rather, experience and maturation lead to moral development. People of the same age and with similar experiences are likely to be similar in moral reasoning. Kohlberg attributed observed gender differences to differences in role assignments in society. Men's observed "higher" moral development then is due to greater experience with roles that demand abstract, justice-oriented moral reasoning. Subsequent research has supported this claim. [*See* GENDER DEVELOPMENT: SOCIAL LEARNING.]

IV. Response to Claims of Gender Differences in Moral Development

During the 1960s and 1970s, feminist psychologists began to respond to claims suggesting women's psychological inferiority to men. They argued that women had been ignored in research, that psychological theories were developed with males as the norm, and that these theories were being inappropriately generalized to women. Women, they said, were not being viewed centrally and positively in research.

Androgyny theorists, such as Sandra Bem (1974), began to de-emphasize differences between men and women. She argued from a feminist and social learning perspective that there are minimal differences between women and men and if there are differences, these are the result of variations in socialization experiences. Androgyny theorists suggested that women and men were more similar than different, that women could be equally assertive, analytic, dominant, and ambitious as men. However, postandrogyny feminist researchers countered this claim by arguing that androgyny theories were placing higher value on qualities traditionally associated with men and devaluing traditionally feminine characteristics.

In the 1980s, Carol Gilligan and other theorists (e.g., Jean Baker Miller and Nancy Chodorow) began advocating a new norm, which celebrated traditionally feminine qualities that had been pathologized, devalued, or ignored. Carol Gilligan and colleagues articulated a theory of moral and epistemological development that was based on research with women and informed by feminist lenses, viewing women's qualities as strengths rather than deficiencies. As reflected in her title of her 1982 book, *In a Different Voice,* Gilligan emphasized differences in morality between men and women. In response to Kohlberg's work, Carol Gilligan claimed that women

prefer an orientation of care, rather than an orientation of justice, and that a care ethic is as valuable a moral orientation as an ethic of justice. She claimed that justice and care are two distinct organizing frameworks with origins in childhood and that both are equally valid moral orientations. Gilligan argued that, although women and men are capable of using both orientations, women and men prefer one "voice" over another. Gilligan's ideas of gender differences in moral orientation have generated considerable discussion and research.

Carol Gilligan's theory that women and men are guided by different moral orientations or voices was based on results of three studies. In her first study, 29 women, ages 15 to 23, faced with the decision about whether or not to have an abortion, were interviewed before making the decision and two years following their decision. Her second study involved interviewing students in their senior year of college and then five years later. In her third study, commonly referred to as the "Rights and Responsibility" study, Gilligan interviewed 36 males and females between the ages of 6 and 60. Based on these interviews, Gilligan described three levels and two transition periods in the development of a care orientation. The first level, "Orientation to Individual Survival," reflects a concern with survival of the self, while the first transition charts a shift toward the inclusion of others and responsibility toward others. "Goodness as Self-Sacrifice," the second level, involves increased concern for the feelings of others and the possibility of inflicting hurt. Goodness and self-sacrifice merge with the wish to care for others. In the second transition, an individual begins to recognize a responsibility to both care for others and oneself when making moral decisions. In Gilligan's third level of morality of care, "Morality of Nonviolence," the conflict of responsibility to self versus duty to others is resolved in a principle of nonviolence. Care and noninjury become equally applied to issues relating to self and others. No subsequent evidence has supported the existence of these levels, and there is little basis for the claim of the three distinct stages and two transition levels. More evidence has supported the claim that the ethic of care is a moral orientation that can be distinguished from a justice orientation. The main controversy in the work on the ethic of care concerns Gilligan's claims about gender differences.

In 1990, Rachel Hare-Mustin and Jeanne Marecek discussed the complexities of adopting either a position of minimizing gender differences or emphasizing particular perceived differences. They termed the idea of ignoring or minimizing gender differences as "beta bias." In contrast they defined "alpha bias" as the exaggeration of differences between women and men. Hare-Mustin and Marecek argued that both biases have positive and negative consequences, as well as implications that may or may not support the overall goals of feminism and social change. For example, emphasizing differences between men and women (alpha bias) has allowed theorists to express the value of some traditionally feminine characteristics and has prompted a critical examination of cultural values that excuse qualities associated with men, such as aggression. Yet viewing men and women as opposites can perpetuate the status quo and lead to separating the spheres of women and men. For example, if women are more caring, it might provide a justification for assigning them caregiving roles and restricting opportunities for autonomous achievement. If men are more just, ought they be in decision-making roles in government? Hare-Mustin, in 1988, suggested that alpha bias tends to limit understanding of women's multiple roles (caretaker of children, wife, wage earner, etc.) and obscures the differences in overall workload between men and women.

The beta bias has had positive implications for women's increased access to educational and occupational opportunities. If there are no gender differences, it is unjust (and illegal) to deny access to jobs or education based solely on sex. However, this perspective can undermine the importance of particular issues relevant to women and the differences in power and opportunity between men and women. For example, beta bias can divert focus from issues related to maternity leave or the continuation of other social policies relevant to the unique needs of women. How can the ill effects of alpha bias and beta bias be reduced? Many feminists have argued we must begin by critically examining the research that has been conducted on gender differences.

V. Empirical Work Examining Gender Differences in Moral Development

Studies have investigated gender differences in moral orientation over the past two decades. Some studies have examined whether or not there is bias in Kohlberg's theory and asked whether there are gender differences in moral reasoning. Other researchers have examined whether there are two distinct moral orientations (care and justice) and asked if use of these orientations is tied to gender. We look at these issues briefly.

Several studies have found minimal differences in moral reasoning between females and males. In both longitudinal and meta-analytic studies, Lawrence Walker found no significant gender differences in moral reasoning. He used Kohlberg's moral judgment interview and reported that gender only accounted for one-twentieth of 1% of the difference in moral reasoning scores. Likewise, using the Defining Issues Test, a paper-and-pencil measure of principled moral reasoning, Stephen Thoma also found that other variables, such as age and education, were more important and more closely related to moral reasoning than gender. When significant gender differences have been found, it is most often in adolescents. These results point to the complexity of the issue and the relationship between gender and moral reasoning during both adolescence and adulthood. However, most recent empirical research continues to support the idea that men and women do not differ significantly in their moral reasoning.

Researchers have also investigated whether one's moral orientation is dependent on context or a stable trait. For example, researchers have examined whether individuals are consistent in their use of moral orientation across various dilemmas that are used in research. Sometimes researchers used hypothetical dilemmas. That is, like the Heinz story described earlier, they tell a story that depicts a moral problem and then ask research participants to resolve the dilemma as if it were a real one, justifying why they would follow the particular course of action they discussed. At other times, researchers ask participants to identify a moral dilemma they actually faced and then to discuss why they acted in the manner they described. The latter dilemmas are called *real-life* dilemmas. Research suggests that individuals use different orientations depending on the type of dilemma to which they are reacting. Investigators have also wondered about the use of real-life versus hypothetical dilemmas in research. Research has begun to examine whether or not personal experience with the dilemma affects outcomes.

For example, Terri D. Conley, Rosemary A. Jadack, and Janet Shibley Hyde conducted a study in 1997 involving participants who had genital herpes, a sexually transmitted disease (STD), and others who did not. They used two hypothetical dilemmas first introduced by Kohlberg and two hypothetical dilemmas that specifically dealt with the subject of sexually transmitted diseases. While the authors did not find significant gender differences in moral reasoning, they found that participants with herpes had higher levels of moral reasoning than those without this diagnosis. Based on their work, the authors suggested further research examining the role of personal experience in moral decision making. Personal or experiential knowledge of the dilemma and emotional or physical experience may influence moral decision-making processes in complex ways.

In 2000, Sara Jaffee and Janet Shibley Hyde reviewed the research of the past 15 years that focused on this question of gender differences and moral development. Jaffee and Hyde examined 113 empirical studies that posited gender differences in moral orientation. They concluded that distinct moral orientations of care and justice may exist, but these moral orientations are not strongly linked with gender. They found that the literature indicates men and women are using both orientations. Furthermore, age, socioeconomic status, and type of moral dilemma may be moderating the perceived gender differences. In this review of research on gender differences and moral development, Jaffee and Hyde also indicated that their results support previous research that the content and context of the dilemma is strongly related to the type of moral reasoning used by an individual. Overall, Jaffee and Hyde's work supports the idea that there are not large gender differences in moral reasoning and that the study of moral development must be viewed in a more complex manner than attributing care to women and justice to men.

Can research accurately capture the complexity involved in individuals' moral reasoning processes? The dilemmas presented to participants in research studies regarding specific dilemmas involve individual decision making and do not take into account care and justice principles in larger contexts. Individuals within schools, health care systems, justice systems, and the like may know what one ought to do, but might make moral decisions based on particular demands, expectations, and other aspects of these systems. In 1983, psychologist James Rest proposed that morality should be viewed as a multifaceted phenomenon, consisting of four psychological components. The first component, ethical sensitivity, is the identification of the salient ethical aspects of a situation. This includes recognizing possible courses of action and the potential impact of these decisions on others. Component II, moral judgement, entails

formulating the morally ideal course of action. Kohlberg's theory of moral reasoning is an example of component II. The decision of how one intends to act and the moral motivation to carry out one's decision is component III of Rest's model. The fourth component involves moral action and the moral character to persist in a moral task. Rest's model presupposes complexity in moral reasoning processes and moves away from viewing morality as a unitary process. Research conducted over 25 years has supported the efficacy of this model.

Individual differences and contextual factors that impact moral decision making are also important. Research with White, privileged participants may not tell us much about ethnic minorities, individuals of low socioeconomic status, or other groups. Some individuals may confront barriers that prevent them from making particular choices because they lack resources. For example, imagine an immigrant woman with children who is in an abusive marriage. She may feel that she needs to live independently, so that she can guarantee safety for herself and her children, but linguistic, educational, cultural, and economic barriers may prevent her from doing so. This woman may be ethically sensitive, have the ability to form a moral judgment about the ideal course of action, and motivated to act morally. Despite her commitment, however, she may be unable to act due to barriers that prevent her from leaving the abusive situation. Researchers are finding ways to more adequately capture the complexities individuals face in their specific contexts when making and acting on moral decisions. Feminist ethics requires attention to the context that affects and may limit one's options. Feminist ethics also requires one to actively work to achieve social justice by removing barriers to fully realizing one's human and moral potential.

In conclusion, the weight of current research does not support the idea that gender differences in moral reasoning or moral orientation exist. Researchers are now considering more complex questions. For example, in which situations would an individual utilize a more or less "advanced" moral orientation? How does experience with a particular dilemma affect moral reasoning and how might this be related to gender? How might other factors—for example, education level, socioeconomic status, or other contextual factors—influence moral orientations? These questions imply that both men and women are holding multiple perspectives on moral issues. These questions can help us to understand the complex interactions between individuals and contexts, which lead to particular moral responses.

VI. *Culture and Moral Development*

Feminist theorists and researchers assume that many factors affect what we think, feel, and do. Culture is one such factor. However, the relationship between culture and moral reasoning has not been examined adequately in the psychological literature. The difficulty in defining culture makes the study of it complex. Some theorists believe that culture is a set of traditions or practices, such as language, manner of dress, art, music, food, and literature connected with a particular racial or ethnic group. If it is assumed that morality is constructed by members of communities, then it follows that different cultural groups may differ in their ideas about morality and their moral decision-making strategies. In addition, just as differences exist among women, differences may exist within any given cultural group. Since experience changes us, cultural influences are malleable and may change over time, after contact with other cultural groups, and so on. The study of culture and moral reasoning, like the study of gender and morality, should reflect such complexity.

Linda Gump, Harry Triandis, Richard Shweder, Joan Miller, and David Bersoff are all researchers who have examined responses of particular ethnic groups to moral dilemmas. Their research has challenged Kohlberg's notion of moral universality, the idea that all individuals develop the same principles of moral reasoning. Particular ethnic groups (e.g., Asian Indians) may focus on interpersonal obligations over competing justice ones. While North Americans tend to emphasize a more individualistic, autonomous moral view, people in other cultures emphasize more collectivist and communal views, which may emphasize interpersonal concerns. For example, Miller and Bersoff's 1992 study showed differences in the degree of emphasis that North Americans and Asian Indians place on individual rights and justice versus interpersonal violations in communities. The Gump study in 2000, which examined differences in moral judgement between Mexican American and Anglo-American individuals, demonstrated the need to avoid generalizations about gender differences and emphasized the need to look at multiple factors, including cultural values, which may influence moral decision-making processes. These studies highlight the importance of looking at

moral decisions as multidimensional, rather than focusing only on gender. Relevant issues may include, but are not limited to, the socioeconomic status of the individual, educational level, and ethnic background. For example, how do we understand moral development in other cultures? What other factors may affect individuals in another culture to adopt a certain moral stance? How might individuals differ in their moral reasoning within a culture? There is still much to be studied in the area of culture and moral development, and even more to be learned by examining the complex interactions such as gender, culture, age, and socioeconomic status.

VII. *Implications of Studying Gender Differences in Moral Development*

We have briefly reviewed dominant theories of moral development and gender, responses to posited gender differences, and literature that has evaluated claims of gender differences in moral orientation, and we have raised other issues that may influence individuals as they engage in moral decision making. Why do we need to know about gender differences? Who does it benefit to study gender differences in moral orientation? Venturing too far in one direction could result in an alpha or beta bias, so this makes the study of gender differences complicated. Exercising caution in making generalizations is critical in this work. [*See* METHODS FOR STUDYING GENDER.]

We might apply the themes of feminist ethics discussed earlier in the article to Carol Gilligan's theory of moral development. The idea that women and their experiences have moral significance is central to Gilligan's theory. She argued that women's approaches to moral issues are as equally valid as those of men. She raised questions about sexism, which she believed was embedded in psychological research. Gilligan did not engage in a discussion of power dynamics inherent in women's contexts or how these dynamics and other contextual factors might influence moral decision-making processes. Race, class, and other intersections of gender were also not addressed adequately in her original work, though multicultural feminist/womanist theorists are beginning to correct this oversight. Gilligan challenged widely held assumptions about human development, including women's development, with the goal of achieving a greater understanding of women's lives. Her work, however, has not challenged society to remove sexist barriers to women's advancement or to engage in social action to make a more just and caring society.

Many unanswered questions still exist, and research could profit from using a feminist lens to ask these questions. For example, in what contexts might individuals employ various orientations? How do various contexts impact moral development? How does a caring person respond in different ways to particular dilemmas? By using a feminist lens, we might think about how to help foster the development of both care and justice orientations. Research could examine how power, culture, or the absence or presence of other variables might affect moral persons. Studying gender as the only salient variable in this process of moral decision making has removed individuals from their contexts and has ignored other characteristics of individuals and how they might interact within their environments. Feminists advocate a shift from this form of questioning and suggest embracing the complexities in this area of study. This can lead us to investigate moral reasoning in all its complexities. Expanding our frameworks in research can lead to societal change. Feminist ethics should encourage individuals to move from thought to action to improve the human condition and to help to create a just and caring world.

SUGGESTED READING

Brabeck, M. M. (ed.) (2000). *Practicing Feminist Ethics in Psychology.* American Psychological Association, Washington, DC.

Gilligan, C. (1982). *In a Different Voice: Psychological Theory and Women's Development.* Harvard University Press, Cambridge MA.

Hare-Mustin, R. T., and Marecek, J. (eds.) (1990). *Making a Difference: Psychology and the Construction of Gender.* Yale University Press, New Haven, CT.

Jaffee, S., and Hyde, J. S. (2000). Gender differences in moral orientation: A metanalysis. *Psychological Bulletin* **126**(5), 703–726.

Larrabee, M. J. (ed.) (1993). *An ethic of care: Feminist and interdisciplinary perspectives.* New York: Routledge.

Miller, J. G., and Bersoff, D. M. (1992). Culture and moral judgment: How are conflicts between justice and interpersonal responsibilities resolved? *Journal of Personality and Social Psychology* **62**(4), 541–554.

Rest, J., Narvaez, D., Bebeau, M. J., and Thoma, S. J. (1999). *Postconventional Moral Thinking: A Neo-Kohlbergian approach.* Erlbaum, Mahwah, NJ.

Feminist Family Therapy[1]

Louise B. Silverstein
Yeshiva University

Thelma Jean Goodrich
University of Texas-Houston

Glossary

Both/and perspective Holding two apparently contradictory views as simultaneously correct (e.g., holding that battering enacts male power and also that the less powerful women plays a part in constructing the relationship in which she is battered).

Circularity Understanding behavior as interactional patterns that are instigated by people in reaction to one another and reinforced by all parties.

Covert/overt hierarchy In general, a covert hierarchy is an unacknowledged ranking of elements into an order of value and power, whereas an overt hierarchy is an acknowledged ranking. In families, rankings by gender are covert in some cultures (e.g. the United States) and overt in others (e.g. many Muslim countries), whereas ranking by generation are overt.

Gendered power relations Systematic ways of relating between men and women reflecting and recreating the sociocultural ordering of men as dominant over women as subordinate.

Mother-blaming Holding mothers responsible for all aspects of their children's lives.

Nodal point The intersection of several actions. For example, a poor woman of color may be understood as a nodal point reflecting the multiple oppressions of sexism, racism, and classism.

Overfunctioning/underfunctioning dyad Two people create a stable, reciprocal pattern, in which one person carries major responsibility for the relationship or task, while the other carries little. Although the overfunctioning person may appear to be more competent, they are both lending and borrowing self. If the underfunctioning person begins to become more active, the overfunctioning person will begin to underfunction.

Patriarchy The organization of society that elevates men along with their defining attributes and tasks as more important, more valued, and therefore more privileged and powerful than women.

Reciprocity A description of a complex interactional behavioral chain in which each element of the chain shapes and produces the other elements. A change in any one element would therefore cause a change in the others.

Unbalancing/rebalancing interventions Therapeutic moves aimed at shifting focus, power, or direction of interactions away from the usual routine into a new routine.

[1]Parts of this article have been adapted, with permission, from chapters in *Feminist Family Therapy: Empowerment and Social Location* (in preparation) L. B. Silverstein and T. J. Goodrich.

FEMINIST FAMILY THERAPY adds feminist theory to family systems theory. Because the family reproduces patriarchy, racism, and classism, feminist family therapy must address the gendered, racial, and economic power relations that keep women subordinate to men, keep people of color subordinate to White people, and keep poor people subordinate to middle-class and rich people in the broader culture. Feminist family therapy also strives to free men in families from the restricted definitions of self and patterns of relating that exist for men within patriarchy.

I. What Is Feminist Family Therapy?

One important paradox confronting feminists who attempt to define a particular aspect of feminist theory or practice is that there are multiple "feminisms." Thus, even as we attempt to define feminist family therapy, it is changing, evolving, and transforming itself. Leslye Mize articulated this dilemma, outlining the need to reflect diverse voices even as we struggle to speak in a collective voice; challenging us to describe perspectives that are common to all feminist family therapists and, at the same time, to avoid creating a "dominant" discourse.

We have settled on the following: Feminist family therapy, in common with family therapy, holds two main principles about the family. First, it is the primary context for the development and definition of self. Second, it functions as a system (i.e. a stable, changing, and restabilizing set of interactional patterns) that incorporates contributions from each member and at the same time shapes the actions of each member.

Feminist family therapy offers a paradigm for understanding individual behavior in the context of relationship patterns. It is not defined by the number of people in a therapy session. Feminist family therapy can be conducted with one person or with several.

II. Why Feminist Family Therapy?

A. THE FAMILY CONSTRUCTS THE SELF AND RELATIONSHIPS

The word "family" evokes a romance about safety and well-being. However, as with all romance, it fails to ask important questions. For example, we might ask, "Safety for whom? Well-being achieved by whose service, and at whose expense?" Although there are many family structures in contemporary U.S. society with none in the majority, the romance enshrines only one structure: the White, middle-class married couple with the husband as the primary provider and the wife as the primary parent. This ideal obscures the power relations in this "nuclear" family—power relations that are central to reproducing the gendered schemas that hold patriarchy in place. These gendered schemas define what is masculine and feminine, and direct how women and men should relate to one another, (i.e., women should be attuned to men's needs and adapt to them to a degree not reciprocated by men). [*See* GENDER DEVELOPMENT: GENDER SCHEMA THEORY.]

The power relations in this paradigmatic structure affect other family structures as well. For example, gay male partners often strive to avoid the "wife" position; lesbian couples may be vigilant about sharing equal responsibility for money and housework—typical sites of inequality for women in heterosexual marriage. Single mothers are considered handicapped without a man, whereas men who parent as single fathers are seen as heroes. In poor families, men often leave their families when they cannot earn sufficient income to be the primary provider. In very wealthy families, men "leave" the family through overwork or exercise male privilege through overinvolvement in leisure time activities.

Thus the primary site where the basic principles of male dominance are taught is the family—most particularly, the family formed by heterosexual marriage. Paradoxically, women are told that they have power in that arena. In fact, however, women have power only in the areas of family life where men have no interest in exercising power. Although there are differences by race and class, there is no race or class where a wife (or women in general) is not expected to defer to her husband (or to men in general). [*See* FAMILY ROLES AND PATTERNS, CONTEMPORARY TRENDS; POWER.]

Efforts to build egalitarian heterosexual marital partnerships appear to have had some recent success, especially when wives contribute a significant amount of the family income. However, as Betty Carter pointed out in 1995, the new man supports the *idea* of equal partnership but still expects to be able to veto money decisions and to be free to focus on his own career. The new man supports the *idea* of equal involvement in child rearing, but expects the woman to oversee it and to be the primary parent. The new woman supports the *idea* of the involved father who shares housework, as she shares in providing money, but in reality she still thinks she needs to be the primary parent in order to be a good mother. She still expects him to support her financially if she needs to cut back, for she still believes that juggling work and family is basically *her* problem. [*See* MARRIAGE.]

Given the power of the patriarchal family in our cultural ideology, opprobrium attaches to single mothers and lesbian mothers in large part because they are mothering outside of a relationship with a man. Their struggles for legitimacy in a hostile surround can create a view of themselves as inferior mothers. They attribute their troubles not to economic circumstances or to the prejudice against them, but rather to a failure to supply a "male role model." This message reduces what might have been a rich contribution from a second parent to a concrete focus on men.

Women are trapped in this system, but also cooperate with it. They entreat men to take more responsibility for their children, but then excuse them from doing so, often because they are reluctant to entrust men with their care. They find great satisfaction in the very aspect of their life that oppresses them. Paradoxically, mothering provides them with a sense of power and influence not paralleled anywhere else in their life.

In addition to oppressing women, patriarchal culture is also oppressive to men. Just as the gendered division of labor assumes that women should be the primary emotional and nurturing caretakers of men and children, our gendered schemas assume that men should be the primary protectors and providers of material resources for women and children in the context of the family. Why should the provider be a man? Why should only men be expected to sacrifice their lives in war in order to advance nationalist goals of domination or defense? Male privilege can be understood as cultural compensation for the self-sacrifice that men are expected to enact as workers and soldiers. [*See* ANDROCENTRISM.]

Although the designation of primary provider enshrines male dominance in families, it also leads to negative consequences for men. The demand for men to define themselves as workers and soldiers, rather than as loving parents, constructs personality characteristics that are oppressive to both women and men. Good workers and soldiers need to be in touch with their feelings of aggression, competition, and dominance and to keep their feelings of vulnerability, dependency, emotional connection, and nurturance out of their awareness. Much of the male vio-

lence that defines every culture is simply an extreme dimension of cultural definitions of normative masculinity.

B. THE ADVANTAGES OF FEMINIST FAMILY THERAPY

Since family is the mediator and reproducer of patriarchal culture, feminist therapy must address family issues. Seeing a client in the company of his or her family allows us to observe interactional patterns rather than simply individual behaviors. We gain not only in knowledge, but also in the possible points of intervention. We can help family members talk with one another, listen to one another, change routes of communication, specify triumphs, buttress resilience, create room for individuality, find new ways to connect, and link up with support systems. These interventions can create movement in relationship patterns that otherwise hinder a client's progress. Family therapy can offer families opportunities to discuss significant areas that may have found no other arena. For instance, a family may never have put into words how racism has affected its course as a family. Such reflections on injustice and resilience may unify the family.

Even when working with one person alone, the paradigm of feminist family therapy leads us to examine the gendered patterns of dominance and subordination from a multigenerational and extended family perspective. Ways of relating to others and of defining self are transmitted across generations as gendered models and gendered instructions. Examining this multigenerational transmission process places behaviors in a broader context than simply understanding them dyadically or intrapsychically.

Men in the family often follow the patriarchal model to dominate, rather than to nurture. Women may also follow that model and use what power they are allotted to dominate family members who have even less power. Deprived for so long of a significant role in public life, women in families may fight with each other over the scarce territory and resources assigned to them. As therapists, we need to address how the family reproduces this positioning within its own ranks. Otherwise, we may become the handmaid of patriarchy and help squeeze the family into its mold by working toward "adjustment."

A majority of patients in feminist family therapy are women, and a majority of women have subordinate status in their family. Seeing a woman from an individual perspective may mean that she leaves a therapy session with plans for change, only to enter a primary context of influence, the family, that limits her. This positioning occurs even without an adult man in the family. Mothers often hold subordinate status to their own sons. Even in single-mother families in which no man is physically present, the social context of patriarchy renders women subordinate and affects how women view themselves and each other. Feminist family therapy gives the therapist an important way to strengthen and support a woman in her efforts toward her goals.

III. A Historical Overview

A. MAKING GENDER VISIBLE

The earliest phase of the feminist critique of family therapy involved confronting the field's denial of gender as a central organizing principle of family life. In 1978, Rachel Hare-Mustin accused the field of reinforcing stereotyped gender roles by refusing to address gender issues within the family: the importance of the larger societal context in constructing gender roles within the family, the unequal distribution of power between wives and husbands, and the need to work with men in therapy from a feminist perspective.

As the 1980s began, most feminist therapists were working in isolation. In 1984, Monica McGoldrick, Carol Anderson, and Froma Walsh organized a meeting of 50 prominent women in family therapy at Stonehenge in Connecticut. This meeting established a network for women to support each other and to discuss the issues of women in family therapy. The sense of solidarity that emerged from that meeting contributed to an explosion of feminist critiques of family therapy.

In 1987, Hare-Mustin pointed out that mainstream culture was characterized by two forms of gender bias: alpha bias, which overemphasized gender differences in terms of defining women as "relational" and men as "instrumental," and beta bias, which understated gender differences by assuming that women and men have equal opportunities to advance professionally. Hare-Mustin argued that both of these cultural biases permeated all aspects of family therapy practice. She called for a total feminist revision of the field. [*See* FEMINIST APPROACHES TO PSYCHOTHERAPY.]

In 1988, Virginia Goldner observed that family therapy theory defined "generation" as the funda-

mental organizing principle of family life. She labeled the gendered differences in power between husband and wife the *covert* hierarchy, in contrast to the *overt* generational differences in power between parents and children. Her goal was to elevate gender to equivalent status with generation as the two major organizing concepts within family therapy theory.

In 1988, Marianne Walters, Betty Carter, Peggy Papp, and Olga Silverstein created the Women's Project in family therapy, the first public venue where women's issues, both as clients and as therapists, were discussed from a scholarly perspective. These four senior therapists agreed to try both to achieve consensus about women's issues and to preserve their individual clinical approaches to working with families. This model of forming a community, while at the same time maintaining respect for individuality, is a collaboration that is rarely achieved in patriarchal culture.

The project conducted training workshops throughout the United States and England over several years and eventually authored a book. These authors reanalyzed traditional family therapy concepts, such as circularity and reciprocity, from a gendered perspective. The authors devised a series of feminist guidelines for family therapists which identified how gender socialization constructs behavior, recognized the limited access women have to resources, challenged the internalized sexism that inhibits many women, and acknowledged that no intervention is gender-free. Like Hare-Mustin, these theorists called for a feminist revision of the entire field of family therapy.

Several anthologies of feminist family therapy theory were published in the second half of the 1980s. These include books by Marianne Ault-Riche; Lois Braverman, Thelma Jean Goodrich, Cheryl Rampage, Barbara Ellman, Kris Halstead; and Monica McGoldrick, Carol Anderson, and Froma Walsh. Deborah Luepnitz provided a feminist critique of all of the early male family therapists. Taken as a whole, these texts provided depth to the feminist critique and ensured that feminist principles would be taken seriously by the field. In 1988, Lois Braverman became the first editor of the *Journal of Feminist Family Therapy*, establishing a permanent publishing outpost supportive of feminist work.

Another step in the institutionalization of gender in family therapy theory was to ensure that feminist theory was integrated into the family therapy training curriculum. Judith Myers-Avis was one of the first therapists to write about the need to revolutionize the training curriculum. She argued that omitting research about gender was the equivalent of training surgeons with outdated knowledge and skill. She raised many questions about training, such as whether to have a separate course on gender issues or to ensure that gender is integrated into all courses, how to address the political issues raised among other faculty members in response to a proposal for a course on gender, and what to anticipate in terms of the different emotional reactions of male and female students within such a course. [See FEMINIST THEORIES.]

It seems almost incomprehensible now, after more than 20 years of feminist theorizing, that gender was invisible to the early family therapy theorists. However, Luepnitz has made the point that family therapy emerged during the 1950s, a politically conservative phase of U.S. history. Men had just returned from World War II, and women had to be convinced to leave the workplace and return home. Social scientists such as Parsons and Bales provided the rationale for this return by hypothesizing that the gendered division of labor between public and private spheres was "natural." Luepnitz speculated that the early family therapists did not challenge this public-private split in the "normal" family because they were already so embattled fighting traditional psychiatry's exclusive emphasis on individual pathology that they may not have felt they could challenge the normal family as well.

Another factor contributing to the absence of gender issues in family therapy may have been that, except for Virginia Satir, all of the prominent family therapy theorists of the 1960s and early 1970s were White men (e.g., Nathan Ackerman, Gregory Bateson, Murray Bowen, Jay Haley, and Salvador Minuchin). Becoming aware of one's own power and privilege is a difficult task for everyone (see, for example, bell hooks's 1989 critique of White feminists). The early family therapists—White, well-educated, middle-class men—had not faced discrimination based on gender. Thus gender was not a salient variable for them.

Even Virginia Satir did not write explicitly about gender. Videotapes of her work indicated that she supported people to go beyond traditional gender socialization (e.g., by encouraging women to work outside the home and men to express emotion). She also identified *mother-blaming* as endemic to the field. However, she refused to label herself a feminist, preferring instead to call herself a humanist who did not see a need to focus on women's issues as a separate field of study.

In this context of male dominance, family therapy theory conceptualized the family as a "natural" organism within which women and men had complementary, but equal roles. Parsons and Bales' rationalization for the sexual division of labor within families in industrialized society became the cornerstone of family therapy's conceptualization of the "normal" family. In 1966, Nathan Ackerman claimed that attempts to reverse this "normal" division of labor were the root of most child psychopathology.

Early feminists have written about how this acceptance of traditional gender roles structured their own thinking. In 1986, Michele Bograd acknowledged that as she began to rethink her own practice, she realized that many of her interventions were unconsciously gender biased (e.g. asking the mother, rather than the father, about a child's developmental history; asking the father, not the mother, about finances).

B. MAKING POWER VISIBLE

The first task, then, for the feminist pioneers was to elevate gender to an equivalent status with generation as the two organizing principles of family life. The next aspect of the feminist critique was to deconstruct the field's understanding of the "normal" family.

Most of the families referred for psychotherapy were conceptualized as having an "overinvolved" or "enmeshed" mother and a "disengaged" father. The feminist critique pointed out that this pattern of relationships was not a personal characteristic of a specific family, but rather the political construction of patriarchal society. Feminist family therapists noted that men were socialized to overfunction in the public world of work, whereas women were socialized to overfunction within the private world of the family. Thus the enmeshed mother and peripheral father were actually cultural roles created by gender socialization within patriarchy, rather than an expression of the "natural" family. Once the existence of gender and gender roles became salient, the fact that gender roles served to maintain a social system based on male power became clear (to some of us).

The typical intervention of the 1970s, called *unbalancing*, involved moving the father closer to the children and moving the mother out of the discipline arena. In 1981, Salvador Minuchin and Charles Fishman claimed that the need for this restructuring was caused by the mother's unwillingness to "allow" the father to become more involved with the children. The solution to the family problem was to devalue the mother as "inadequate" and to idealize the father as he was brought in to manage the acting out child. The feminist critique that linked these parental behaviors to patriarchal gender roles illuminated this intervention as a blatant example of mother-blaming, rather than a "neutral" *rebalancing* of the family system.

Other concepts of family systems theory were also critiqued, in particular the idea of reciprocity of behavior among family members. From the perspective of natural systems theory, the emotional functioning of individual family members is considered so interdependent that it is the family, rather than the individual, that is conceptualized as the emotional unit. For example, if one family member generally acted very competently, another tended to behave in an incompetent or inadequate fashion. In an *overfunctioning/underfunctioning dyad*, each family member's behavior was tied inexorably to the behavior of the other. This interdependence between family members became translated in family systems theory as the concept of *reciprocity*.

According to family systems theory, if either member of the dyad were to change their behavior, the behavior of the other person would automatically change as well. A common intervention in family therapy was to encourage the overfunctioning partner to stop overfunctioning. Like the example given earlier, this usually involved telling the mother to stop being "overinvolved" with the children. Interestingly, we are not aware of a family in which the husband was encouraged to work less and earn less or where the wife was advised to stop doing the laundry or cooking dinner. Because power was invisible, family systems theory did not acknowledge that women's economic dependence on men made it unlikely that a wife would have the same freedom as her husband to choose to stop over (or under) functioning.

Another factor contributing to the invisibility of power was that family systems theory was derived from natural systems theory. Natural systems are those that occur in nature, like the solar system or an ant colony. Family systems theory assumes that the human family is a natural system, organized by natural laws that are rooted in evolutionary processes. Although there are power differences within the social systems of many animals (especially other primates), we do not ordinarily associate institutionalized power relationships with natural processes. Thus family systems theory originally developed as if power were not a meaningful variable within the organization of families. The theoretical concepts that form the basis of family systems were conceptualized as neutral in terms of power.

In 1988, Harriet Lerner challenged this concept of neutrality by pointing out that families exist within a particular sociocultural context. She argued that simply challenging rules *within* a given family is not sufficient to change dysfunctional relationship patterns. Lerner (and others, e.g., Hare-Mustin, Goldner) pointed out that intrafamily rules are constructed and maintained by the *gendered power relations* in the sociocultural context of patriarchy. Thus the rigid rules of the larger society also had to be confronted. Neither families nor therapists could be conceptualized as neutral. The feminist critique thus moved the locus of therapy from an exclusive focus on the interior of the family to include the need to change external social structures as well.

However, making the issue of power a legitimate subject for therapy has proven to be more difficult than making gender salient. Men, like most dominant groups, are reluctant to give up power voluntarily. Many women, socialized to believe that their only access to power is through men, are similarly reluctant to challenge male authority. This reluctance on the part of women is understandable because being with a man does in reality give most women access to more power and resources than they could have on their own. In the context of intimate relationships, married women typically have less power than their husbands, both because women continue to earn significantly less money than men and also because women have been socialized to avoid power, whereas men have been socialized to embrace it. Thus, empowering women continues to be a challenge for feminist family therapy.

In 1991, Thelma Jean Goodrich organized a collection of papers dedicated to addressing the issue of power discrepancies within the family. This book challenged the field to acknowledge the overwhelming pervasiveness of women's oppression and to recognize that the family is the context within which this oppression is enacted and perpetuated. In the essay that opens the book, Goodrich outlined the connections between power, marriage, and sex. She raised the question as to whether "consensual" sex can be a meaningful concept, even within the confines of marriage, because it occurs between people who are physically and economically unequal. Unless family therapists openly explore the distribution of power within families, she argued that we too are contributing to and legitimizing women's oppression.

In addition to examining how power constructs sexual relations, this book confronted many other controversial issues such as redistributing assets so that wives have as much money as their husbands and raising the question of whether male therapists can empower women. Many of the issues raised in this volume continue to be controversial among family therapists.

These challenges to examine and reconfigure the power relations within families led some feminist family therapists to propose that men be recruited as consumers of feminist family therapy. In 1991, Michele Bograd edited a collection of chapters that articulated the goal of translating feminist practice into caring, effective clinical practice with men. For the first time within the family therapy field, masculinity was examined as something that might be pathogenic to men, as well as to women. The negative effects for men of masculine gender role socialization, with its excessive emphasis on achievement, competition, sexuality, and stoicism, were identified.

Within this collection, Rhea Almeida and Bograd presented an innovative model for working with men's violence against women in the family. These authors pointed out that, just as domestic violence has traditionally been considered a "private" matter because it occurred within the privacy of a man's family, psychotherapy represents a private solution to what is really a widespread social problem. Dealing with domestic violence through psychotherapy further requires that women assume primary responsibility for this problem (i.e., the mostly female mental health profession or the female members of the family). These authors called for men to assume responsibility for other men's violence against their wives through a community mentoring program. This model of intervention described a way that feminist practice can work toward changing the societal context of women's oppression in addition to the internal dynamics of family life.

In 1990, Virginia Goldner, Peggy Penn, Marcia Sheinberg, and Gillian Walker began the Gender and Violence Project at the Ackerman Institute for the Family in New York City. They also focused on innovative methods for working with violent couples. The four women constituting the collaborative team struggled to develop a treatment approach that went beyond the either/or victim/perpetrator approach to domestic violence. They wrote about the challenge of working within the paradoxical world of violent couples. For example, the team had to confront the fact that gender constructed inequalities in each of these couples (i.e., the husband was physically and economically more powerful than his wife). At the same time, they had to acknowledge that some aspects of the couple's interactions were reciprocal (i.e., the wife was sometimes involved in initiating the cycle of violence and she had chosen not to leave the relationship–even when she had a safe harbor and economic independence).

This both/and perspective goes to the very heart of the compatibility of feminism with family systems theory. The authors maintained both that feminism was correct in its deconstruction of battering as an enactment of male power and privilege and that family systems theory was accurate in pointing out that the wife's participation was at times reciprocal, although not equal, in sustaining the cycle of violence.

In 1990, Marsha Mirkin has similarly argued for the integration of a traditional family therapy approach with feminist therapy in the treatment of women with anorexia and bulimia. Mirkin argued that family therapy theory had overlooked the link between the larger cultural context and anorexia. She speculated that adolescent girls were reacting to the unrealistic expectations that our culture has for women: that they be traditional, i.e., fragile and dependent, yet at the same time be more progressive, i.e., tough and independent. The anorexia represented overconformity to the cultural expectations of being beautiful and fragile, and more like a man. Mirkin combined structural interventions, like helping parents keep children out of their power struggles, with a narrative that explicitly valued feminine socialization.

C. GIVING LESBIANS STATUS WITHIN FAMILY THERAPY

For lesbian couples, the impact of their oppression by the larger society is central to a feminist approach to therapy. In 1980, early in the development of the feminist critique of family therapy, Jo-Ann Krestan and Claudia Bepko examined the complex interrelationships between the heterosexual community and lesbian couples. They challenged the idea that lesbians are more likely than heterosexual couples to have a fused relationship. These authors pointed out that within the larger social system, a lesbian relationship is considered either invisible or pathological. This invalidating context creates continual pressure to dissolve the relationship. In reaction to this pressure toward dissolution, some lesbian couples generate rigid boundaries around the relationship and intensify normal tendencies toward closeness into a more fused couple system. Krestan and Bepko defined the central therapeutic task in working with lesbian couples as acknowledging the unique kinds of pressure these couples face while coaching them to deal with these issues without becoming fused.

In 1985, Sallyann Roth described her clinical experience of working with 65 mostly White, middle-class lesbian couples and families in private practice. She delineated six major issues most often presented at the beginning of therapy. These included problems of closeness and distance, sexual expression; unequal access to resources, different stages in the coming out process (i.e., acknowledging their lesbian identities to themselves and to others), choosing to have children, and how to end the relationship. Roth pointed out that, except for the issue of coming out, these problems are all concerns of heterosexual couples as well.

Roth outlined the impact of both the heterosexual and lesbian communities on the particular ways in which lesbian couples deal with these issues. For example, partners who are isolated from a larger lesbian community may have more difficulty negotiating a balance between closeness and distance then couples who have a network of lesbian friends. Similarly, the inability to express physical affection openly because of their stigmatized status within heterosexual society may inhibit the warming up stage and thereby contribute to difficulties with sexual expression. Like Krestan and Bepko, Roth argued for the necessity of addressing the reciprocal relations between the couple and the larger systems in which they are embedded. [*See* Lesbians, Gay Men, and Bisexuals in Relationships.]

D. RAISING THE ISSUES OF ETHNICITY AND RACE

Beginning in the 1980s, the family therapy field began to explore the impact of ethnic, cultural, and racial differences on therapy. However, many authors focused on diversity and did not integrate feminist principles into their recommendations for working with ethnic minority families. The earliest exception to that rule was Elaine Pinderhughes who, in 1986, identified ethnic minority women as the societal crossroads where discrimination based on both gender and ethnorace come together.

Pinderhughes pointed out that ethnic minority women are often blamed for the oppression caused by the larger social system and must also pay the cost for that oppression. Using the stereotype of African American women as matriarchs, she illustrated how these women are blamed for the high unemployment rate of African American men caused by institutionalized racism. When the men abandon their children because their chronic unemployment status does not enable them to provide economic stability to their families, it is the "overbearing" woman, rather than the racist system, that is blamed. Many African American women are then left to suffer the consequences of the system in that they are forced to raise children without the support of the children's father.

Pinderhughes expanded the idea of the African American women as the *nodal point* in a system of multiple oppressions by pointing out that women often agree with the societal view and blame themselves for their husband's/partner's irresponsible and/or abusive behavior. Given the discrimination that African American men suffer in our society, women often feel disloyal if they attempt to hold their male partners accountable for their behavior. Pinderhughes recommended that therapy be conceptualized as liberating minority women from entrapment in their nodal role. Rather than focusing exclusively on intrapsychic or intrafamily issues, effective treatment would include helping them get access to material resources (housing, tutoring), linking them to community support groups, and working from a strength perspective.

An additional important point in this article was Pinderhughes's discussion of Murray Bowen's concept of the societal projection process. In 1978, Bowen hypothesized that the dominant group in society projects its own anxiety onto another group, identifying that group as impaired and needing "help." Rather than helping that group, however, this process actually helps the dominant group manage anxiety by feeling superior and benevolent. Pinderhughes challenged White therapists to give up the "benefactor" role and help minority women gain access to power so that they could help themselves.

After Pinderhughes's complex and challenging chapter was published in 1986, few authors continued to expand on the connection between gender and ethnorace in family therapy. Although the number of books and articles dealing with race, ethnicity, and culture in family therapy continued to proliferate, it was not until the mid-1990s that the interlocking oppressions again became the subject of theorizing within family therapy. This disconnection between gender and ethnorace may have been caused by the fact that the culture of feminist family therapy, like the original culture of traditional family therapy, was made up of primarily White therapists. White feminist therapists were continuing to challenge the field on gender issues, and ethnic minority therapists were ensuring that race and ethnicity became salient variables in family therapy theory. Unfortunately, there was little overlap between these two groups.

We speculate that by 1994, enough of a critical mass of articles and books about ethnorace had been published so that ethnic minority family theorists could now turn their attention to the complex interaction of gender with these issues. Noting that women were often the first members of a family to contact the mental health system, Nancy Boyd-Franklin and Nydia Garcia-Preto in 1994 presented an extensive discussion of issues that were relevant to working with African American and Latina American women in family therapy. In particular, these authors pointed out how racism constructed many aspects of gender socialization. For example, because institutionalized racism has resulted in large numbers of African American men being incarcerated or killed at an early age, African American women have often had to raise children without the benefit of the children's father. Although boys as well as girls are given responsibility for child care within African American families, the likelihood that a girl will become a single mother has led to a tendency to socialize daughters to become overresponsible for caregiving.

Another stress on families is the fact that African American men have been more rigidly kept out of the economic system than have African American women. Thus, African American women often earn more than their husbands. Within the larger context of societal male dominance, this economic and power discrepancy often causes additional problems for couples and families.

These authors also pointed out that Latina American women find themselves in similar cultural paradoxes. On the one hand, the cultural value of *marianismo* suggests that they are morally and spiritually superior to men, while, on the other hand, *machismo* dictates that women should submit to male authority. Like African American women, immigrant Latinas often have less difficulty obtaining employment than their husbands because their domestic skills, such as child care, are in demand. Thus wives entering the workplace create pressure on traditional Latino gender roles.

In 1994, Lillian Comas-Diaz expanded on the complexity of the interplay between gender and ethnorace by looking at the impact of intrafamily racism on LatiNegras, Latinas with dark skin. These multiracial women defy the cultural value of "mejorar la raza" (lightening the family by marrying light-skinned partners). Therefore, although they may be taught how to deal with discrimination based on their ethnicity, they are often not given family support to help them cope with societal racism. Although dark-skinned women and men both suffer from this lack of family support, its absence is particularly difficult for women because of the centrality of family in women's lives. Comas-Diaz introduced the idea of feminist family therapy with one person as a culturally congruent approach for dealing with the multiple oppressions of gender, race, and ethnicity.

All of these authors cautioned White feminist therapists to rethink the primacy of gender in the lives of Latina and African American women, suggesting that racism, ethnicity, immigration status, and socioeconomic class all interacted with gender in the lives of minority women. Just as the early feminist therapists had to rethink theoretical principles such as reciprocity and complementarity, these authors argued that feminist therapists had to rethink their attitudes toward such issues as generational boundaries and reliance on extended family members. Within ethnic minority families, relying on children in the parenting role or on extended family members may reflect economic necessity rather than lack of boundary differentiation.

In 1994, Ruth Hall and Beverly Greene addressed this need to rethink the primacy of gender within White feminist family therapy theory by challenging White therapists to become culturally competent. They proposed that feminist family therapists must recognize that African American (and by extension, all ethnic minority) women and men are bicultural, forced to live within both the dominant White culture and the subordinate African American culture. This biculturalism operates differently for women and men. African American men are part of the dominant gender and the subordinate race, whereas

African American women are members of two subordinate groups. These authors argued further that cultural competence requires, not simply a theoretical understanding of racism, but a personal awareness as well. They proposed that there is an ethical mandate for therapists to confront and understand their own racial identity and racism. [*See* COUNSELING AND PSYCHOTHERAPY.]

IV. Conclusion

This brief summary of the feminist revision of family therapy brings us to the present. From the authors' perspective, gender is now clearly visible within family therapy. However, the thornier issue of how to address power inequalities based on the intersections of gender, race, ethnicity, and class remains a challenge for this field.

SUGGESTED READING

Bograd, M. (ed.) (1991). *Feminist Approaches for Men in Family Therapy.* Harrington Park Press, New York.

Comas-Diaz, L., and Greene, B. (eds.) (1994). *Women of Color.* Guilford, New York.

Goodrich, T. J. (ed) (1991). *Women and Power. Perspectives for Family Therapy.* Norton, New York.

Goodrich, T. J. (in preparation). What does feminist family therapy have to offer feminist psychologists? In *Feminist Family Therapy: Empowerment and Social Location* (L. B. Silverstein and T. J. Goodrich, eds.) American Psychological Association Books, Washington, DC.

Mirkin, M. P. (ed.) (1994). *Women in Context. Toward a Feminist Reconstruction of Psychotherapy.* Guilford, New York.

Silverstein, L. B. (in preparation). Classic texts and early critiques. In *Feminist Family Therapy: Empowerment and Social Location* (L. B. Silverstein and T. J. Goodrich, eds.) American Psychological Association Books, Washington, DC.

Silverstein, L. B., and Goodrich, T. J. (eds.) (in preparation). *Feminist Family Therapy: Empowerment and Social Location.* American Psychological Association Books, Washington, DC.

Walters, M., Carter, C., Papp, P., and Silverstein, O. (1988). *The Invisible Web: Gender Patterns in Family Relationships.* Guilford, New York.

The Feminist Movement

Diane Kravetz

University of Wisconsin-Madison

Jeanne Marecek

Swarthmore College

Glossary

Consciousness raising The process of becoming aware of sexist oppression through ongoing discussion of personal experiences by women in small groups. In consciousness-raising groups, women come to understand the relationship between their personal experience and public, systemic conditions, political structures, and social institutions.

Equal Rights Amendment (ERA) The Equal Rights Amendment was proposed as an amendment to the Bill of Rights of the United States Constitution. Its text is "Equality of rights under the law shall not be denied or abridged by the United States or by any state on account of sex."

Feminism (1) A doctrine advocating political, social, and economic equality of the sexes. (2) Organized activity on behalf of women's rights and interests.

Gender (1) The socially mediated distinctions between men and women. (2) The meaning system by which the relationship between men and women is constituted. (3) A system for the distribution of power and resources that favors men over women.

Second-wave feminism The name given to the mobilization of women in the United States that began in the 1960s. The first wave of feminist organizing began with the Seneca Falls Woman's Rights Convention in 1848.

THE CONTEMPORARY FEMINIST MOVEMENT in the United States is described in this article. This movement, sometimes called the "second wave," rekindled feminism 40 years after women were granted the right to vote. From the 1960s to the present, large numbers of U.S. women (and some men) have allied themselves with feminism. They have joined organizations devoted to securing women's rights and to ensuring that women were fairly represented in policy-making bodies. They have engaged in a variety of projects intended to promote gender equity and to improve the lives of women and girls. They have worked for changes in the law, in societal attitudes and beliefs about women, and for the restructuring of social institutions such as families, workplaces, and schools. They have also worked to ensure women's reproductive rights and

Encyclopedia of Women and Gender, Volume One
Copyright © 2001 by Academic Press. All rights of reproduction in any form reserved.

to combat gender-linked violence by men against women. A new academic discipline, women's studies, grew out of the feminist movement. A variety of business and cultural enterprises have also been developed by and for women. All in all, these efforts have brought sweeping changes in women's status and in their roles in public life and work. However, some of the gains that women have made are precarious. There has been substantial resistance to feminist initiatives, as well as to the principle of equality between the sexes. Moreover, women who are economically disadvantaged often cannot make use of the formal rights they now have and women from ethnic minority groups have benefited less than White women. In sum, the second wave of feminism has yielded more formal equality between the sexes and given many women increased opportunities and more control over their lives; yet the goal of full equity between the sexes remains to be fulfilled.

I. The First Wave of Feminism in the United States

Women's struggles for equal rights and full recognition as citizens have gone on for well over 150 years. The first wave of feminism in the United States set the stage for the contemporary feminist movement, which is sometimes called the second wave. The first wave emerged from women's participation in the moral reform and abolition movements in the 1830s and 1840s. Through their work on behalf of poor women, widows, and the wives of drunkards and their antislavery efforts, these activists became more aware of women's subordinate status. The need for organized efforts to fight for women's rights became increasingly apparent as women abolitionists were criticized for speaking in public and were excluded from antislavery organizations. Barred from participation in the 1840 World Anti-Slavery Convention in London, Lucretia Mott and Elizabeth Cady Stanton began to discuss having a convention on women's rights. Eight years later, in 1848, they organized the Seneca Falls Woman's Rights Convention in upstate New York. This marked the beginning of the women's rights movement.

These activists, including Sarah and Angelina Grimke, Susan B. Anthony, Lucy Stone, and Sojourner Truth, continued to advocate both for abolition and for women's rights. Meetings and conventions on women's rights were held until the beginning

of the Civil War in 1861. After the Civil War, many women's rights activists supported amendments to the Constitution that would provide the rights and privileges of citizens to both Blacks and women. However, the leaders of the abolition movement feared that the inclusion of women in these amendments would jeopardize their passage. Ultimately, the Fourteenth and Fifteenth Amendments granted citizenship and the vote only to Black men and not to women. Women's rights activists recognized then that they would achieve equality under the law only if they secured the right to vote.

In 1869, Susan B. Anthony and Elizabeth Cady Stanton founded the National Woman Suffrage Association (NWSA), an all-women organization that advocated for women's rights. Viewing suffrage as a means of achieving their goals, the NWSA worked for a federal suffrage amendment and on state referendums on women's suffrage. Later that same year, Lucy Stone and her husband, Henry Blackwell, founded the American Woman Suffrage Association (AWSA), a more conservative organization that focused solely on suffrage and worked only on state referendums. Thus began the women's suffrage movement.

The NWSA and the AWSA joined in 1890 to form the National American Woman's Suffrage Association (NAWSA), which continued organizing state referendums. In some states, male voters granted women residents the right to vote in state and federal elections. In 1915, under the leadership of Carrie Chapman Catt, the NAWSA began to campaign at the state and federal levels for a constitutional amendment that would guarantee all women the right to vote. Their efforts were bolstered by the more militant approach of Alice Paul, who founded the Congressional Union in 1913, which became the National Woman's Party (NWP) in 1917. This group engaged in a variety of confrontational activities—marches, mass demonstrations, picketing the White House and the Capitol, hunger strikes—that were widely reported by the press and captured national attention.

Those who supported women's suffrage held two contrasting philosophies. Members of the NWP, for example, held a philosophy of equal rights of the sexes, that is, women should have the vote because women are equal to men and deserve the same rights of citizenship. Other suffragists argued on the basis of women's difference. They held that women would bring a maternal sensibility and feminine values to political life. The caring, selflessness, and superior moral standards possessed by women benefited family life and would benefit society as a whole as well.

These women, often called social feminists, asserted that women (particularly mothers) had special needs and required special protections. In their view, suffrage was a means for women to bring their unique influence into public life.

From the 1890s to the 1930s, social feminists also worked directly to improve the lives of working women and poor women, children, and families. They established the National Consumers' League and the Women's Trade Union League to address the needs of working women. As settlement house activists, they worked to improve public health care, schools, workplaces, and neighborhoods. In the Women's Christian Temperance Union, social feminists fought for legal restrictions on the sale and consumption of alcohol and for other social reforms that would benefit families.

Members of these organizations joined the campaign for suffrage. For example, activists in the temperance movement believed that with the vote, women could curb alcohol use and the poverty, crime, and wife abuse associated with male drunkenness. Women in the settlement house movement, the Consumers' League, and the Women's Trade Union League viewed the vote, for example, as a means to protect women and children from exploitation by their employers.

As a result of the combined efforts of equal rights activists and social feminists, the Nineteenth Amendment was passed by Congress in 1919 and ratified by the states in 1920. After suffrage was achieved, the activities of both groups abated considerably, but they did not cease. In the 1920s and 1930s, social feminists were instrumental in the passage of legislation that funded health care for poor mothers and children; provided widows' benefits; instituted workplace protections specifically for women; and established Aid to Dependent Children, a program that assisted poor families. The National Woman's Party continued to work for equal rights. Every year from 1923 onward, the party proposed congressional legislation to add an Equal Rights Amendment to the Constitution.

II. The Beginning of the Second Wave: Women's Rights and Women's Liberation

The 1960s marked a resurgence of attention to women's issues, generated by changes in women's roles in the family, in education, and in the workplace and by the renewed political activism of women. President John F. Kennedy established the President's Commission on the Status of Women in 1961, with Eleanor Roosevelt as its first chair. The commission was charged with investigating women's subordinate civil status and their legal, social, and economic problems. The commission drew together a diverse group of women, including representatives from the Teamsters, the National Association of Catholic Women, the League of Women Voters, the NAACP, and the B'nai B'rith; women from urban and rural areas; housewives and women in business and the professions. The first report of the commission, *The Presidential Report on American Women*, was published in 1963. Subsequently, all 50 states established similar commissions. The commissions documented female inequality in many aspects of society. They provided activists with important information and they formed a national network of allies.

Two pieces of federal legislation that addressed equal employment opportunities for women were passed. The first was the Equal Pay Act of 1963, which required equal pay for women and men holding the same jobs. The other was Title VII of the 1964 Civil Rights Act. When it was initially proposed, Title VII dealt only with racial discrimination, but through the efforts of Congresswoman Martha Griffiths and the National Woman's Party, sex discrimination was added. This legislation prohibited discrimination in employment on the basis of race and sex and created a federal agency, the Equal Employment Opportunities Commission (EEOC), to oversee compliance.

While these legislative advances were taking place, the publication of *The Feminine Mystique* by Betty Friedan in 1963 catalyzed popular discussion about women's lives. Focusing on middle-class White women, Friedan detailed the debilitating and restrictive aspects of the role of housewife and mother, pointing to the gulf between women's potential and their limited participation in public life. The book crystallized the dissatisfaction felt by many White middle-class women.

The feminist movement emerged in the mid-1960s. Initially, it had two fairly distinct branches: one focused on women's rights and the other on women's liberation. Although their political perspectives overlapped, the two branches emphasized different goals and strategies. In combination, their efforts have led to profound and enduring changes in U.S. society.

A. WOMEN'S RIGHTS ORGANIZATIONS

The women's rights organizations consisted of large, national groups with formal memberships, elected officers, and local chapters. Examples include the National Organization for Women (NOW), the Women's Equity Action League, and the National Women's Political Caucus. These formal, bureaucratic organizations have focused on improving the status of women through reforms in legislation and governmental policies. Their goals have been to eliminate discrimination based on sex in education, employment, and electoral politics and to promote equal rights and opportunities for women.

The leaders of women's rights organizations have mainly been women who had achieved a degree of success in paid employment and were leaders in voluntary and civic organizations. They drew on the skills they had learned in the workplace and as leaders in political, labor, religious, and other community organizations. Because of their experiences in these organizations, these women were comfortable with and functioned well in conventional organizational structures with clearly defined hierarchies of authority and responsibility.

The National Organization for Women (NOW) was the first women's rights organization of the second wave, and it remains the largest. The impetus for NOW emerged during the Third National Conference of Commissions on the Status of Women in 1966. Frustrated by the lackluster performance of the EEOC, conference delegates decided that they needed a civil rights organization for women. This organization was to become the National Organization for Women, founded later that year with Betty Friedan as its first president.

The early accomplishments that NOW and other women's rights organizations achieved in the legislative arena were significant. Under pressure from these organizations, President Lyndon Johnson signed Executive Order 11375 in 1967, which strengthened Title VII of the Civil Rights Act. This order directed employers who received federal contracts to provide equal employment opportunities for women and to develop affirmative action programs to redress the effects of past discrimination. In 1972, under pressure from women's rights organizations, Congress finally gave the EEOC the power to sue employers on behalf of victims of sex discrimination. In addition to investigating individual complaints of sexual discrimination and sexual harassment, the EEOC pursued a number of significant class-action lawsuits during the 1970s and 1980s, including successful litigation against AT&T, General Electric, and General Motors. The EEOC barred airlines from dismissing stewardesses because of their age or marital status and set out regulations that specified the limited instances when an individual's sex could be a determining factor in hiring. Other far-reaching legislation included the 1974 Equal Credit Opportunity Act, which allowed married women to obtain credit in their own names, and Title IX of the 1972 Education Amendments Act, which prohibited sex discrimination in education by institutions that received federal funding. One result of Title IX was a substantial increase in support for women's sports in most universities and colleges, which led to a dramatic upsurge in girls' and women's participation in athletics and the development of women's competitive team sports like basketball and soccer.

From 1975 to 1982, NOW and other women's rights organizations focused their activities on the Equal Rights Amendment (ERA), which read: "Equality of rights under the law shall not be denied or abridged by the United States or by any state on account of sex." The ERA had passed Congress in 1972—49 years after it was first introduced—and required ratification by 38 state legislatures to become part of the U.S. Constitution. At first, ratification by the states proceeded smoothly; in 1972 and 1973, 30 states ratified the ERA. However, resistance to the ERA was gathering momentum. Opponents of the ERA, spearheaded by Phyllis Schlafly and her organization Stop-ERA, promulgated numerous myths about the ERA, claiming that it would force women into combat, legitimate homosexual marriage, require coed public restrooms, deny a woman's right not to be employed outside the home, and place children in state-run child care facilities. The ERA remained three states short of the number required for ratification when the deadline for ratification expired on June 30, 1982. Many of the goals that feminists had in promoting the ERA were eventually accomplished by means of other legislation. Nonetheless, the symbolic value of a constitutional amendment that gives women the same citizenship rights as men was lost. The opposition to this modest yet fundamental goal was a harbinger of the stronger resistance to change that would confront feminism in the decades to come. It also was a reminder of the potent resistance that earlier feminists had faced.

B. THE WOMEN'S LIBERATION MOVEMENT

The women's liberation movement sought to transform cultural beliefs about women, to eliminate the oppression of women, and to transform personal relationships and social structures to reflect feminist values. The women who identified with the women's liberation movement envisioned an egalitarian society based on cooperation, mutual respect, and the equitable distribution of resources, power, and responsibility between the sexes. Many of them were left-wing activists who had been involved in the civil rights, antiwar, and student movements of the 1960s; they identified themselves as radical feminists. Compared with women's rights activists, they tended to be younger women with less professional and workplace experience.

The women's liberation movement consisted of small, local, nonhierarchical groups. Much of their work was conducted in consciousness-raising groups, which discussed and analyzed the everyday experiences of women. They identified patterns of male control over women in work settings, in personal relationships, and in family life and the privileging of male perspectives and needs throughout society. Through the consciousness-raising process, women came to understand how their personal issues and problems were inextricably connected to larger social and political structures. Thus arose the enduring slogan of second-wave feminism, "the personal is political."

Women's liberationists raised the awareness of women across the country by organizing demonstrations and protest marches, giving speeches, and writing newsletters, books, and journals. The latter included *Voice of the Women's Liberation Movement, Notes from the First Year, Off Our Backs,* and *Quest: A Feminist Quarterly.* Collections of essays for mass audiences included *Liberation Now! Writings from the Women's Liberation Movement* (edited by Deborah Babcox and Madeline Belkin, 1971), *Radical Feminism* (edited by Anne Koedt, Ellen Levine, and Anita Rapone, 1973), *Sisterhood Is Powerful* (edited by Robin Morgan, 1970), *Woman in Sexist Society: Studies in Power and Powerlessness* (edited by Vivian Gornick and Barbara Moran, 1971), *Women's Liberation: Blueprint for the Future* (edited by Sookie Stambler, 1970), and *Voices from Women's Liberation* (edited by Leslie Tanner, 1970). The KNOW press, founded by psychologist JoAnn Evans Gardner in Pittsburgh, began circulating essays about women's experiences in sexist society. Books such as Shulamith Firestone's *The Dialectic of Sex,* Germaine Greer's *The Female Eunuch,* and Kate Millett's *Sexual Politics,* all published in 1970, made bold arguments about the extent of male dominance and proposed radical changes in social organizations and male–female relations.

III. Feminist Initiatives

From the mid-1970s, the ideological distinctions between equal rights feminists and women's liberationists blurred. Most women who have identified with feminism have not adopted a revolutionary stance. They have, however, taken part in collective efforts to advance women's interests and to bring about social change. Diverse groups of women have formed organizations in a wide range of arenas: in academia, business, labor unions, the professions, and government. For example, a number of national professional organizations for women were founded, such as the National Association of Black Professional Women and Working Women: A National Association of Office Workers. In addition, many other groups developed national advocacy organizations. In the area of health care, for example, such organizations included the National Women's Health Network, the National Black Women's Health Project, and the National Latina Health Organization. The Older Women's League and the Gray Panthers represented the interests of older women.

Feminists have also created service organizations as alternatives to traditional health, mental health, and social services. These organizations include women's centers, services for women and children who have been raped or sexually abused, shelters for battered women, feminist therapy centers, and women's health clinics. The organizations take a feminist perspective on women's problems, linking them to the social context of female subordination. They are committed to respecting and promoting their clients' autonomy and competence. Often they are staffed by nonprofessional volunteers and former clients, partly in an effort to counteract the mystique of the expert professional and to foster women's self-reliance and self-confidence. Typically, services are offered to women at low cost or free of charge, so that women who cannot afford to pay are not denied services. In addition to providing direct services to individual women, these organizations have worked to transform public understandings of women's problems, to change laws and policies, and to reform the practices of police and district attorneys, physicians and nurses, mental health practitioners, and social workers.

Feminists have pursued change on many fronts. This article describes several major and long-term initiatives. These include a variety of advocacy organizations and service organizations to combat gender-linked violence and to secure and protect reproductive rights, women's studies programs in colleges and universities, and an array of women's cultural enterprises and women's businesses.

A. ACTIVISM AGAINST GENDER-LINKED VIOLENCE

Feminist activism against gender-linked violence began in the early 1970s with the founding of rape crisis centers. At the time, services for rape victims were sadly lacking. Laws, policies, and practices regarding the treatment of offenders and victims were virulently sexist. Rape was considered an act of passion, not a crime of violence; victims were viewed as provocateurs or seductresses. They were presumed guilty until proven innocent and many were disbelieved. Often rape victims likened their experiences with police, hospital personnel, and courts to a second rape.

Rape crisis centers provide 24-hour telephone lines, volunteer counselors who accompany victims to hospitals and police stations, advocates who accompany them through court proceedings, and counseling and group support. Activists have challenged laws, police practices, courtroom tactics, and hospital procedures. They also have challenged public attitudes that blame victims, insisting that the perpetrators be held responsible. They have argued that cultural views that condone male violence and sexual entitlement contribute to its prevalence. Activists also have engaged in rape prevention programs, including community education and women's self-defense courses. They have organized SpeakOuts in which women testify to their experiences of rape and assault, defying the cultural norm of silence. They have also organized "Take Back the Night" rallies and marches to remind communities and campuses that public places are not safe for women at night and to demand community action to ensure women's safety.

As women's sense of shame over sexual assault diminished, more victims began to speak out. Their disclosures of sexual violence in dating relationships and marriages contradicted the image of rape as solely a street crime committed by pathological strangers. Moreover, many women (and some men) reported that they experienced sexual abuse in childhood, often by males living in the household. In response to these revelations, many rape crisis centers expanded their missions to serve women and girls (and occasionally men and boys) who were victims of childhood sexual abuse.

Antirape activism has achieved many positive effects. Most states no longer hold married men exempt from prosecution for raping their wives. Many states have expanded their statutes on sexual assault to cover a continuum of sexually coercive behaviors (including, for example, unwanted fondling and sex acts other than intercourse). Women are now more aware of the prevalence of date rape and acquaintance rape. Still, most rapists are not caught, many who are caught are not prosecuted, and many who are prosecuted are not convicted or punished. Women as a group continue to restrict their activities, especially at night, due to fear of being raped. [*See* RAPE.]

Sexual harassment is another form of gender-linked coercion, one that cuts across age, class, and ethnic lines. In *Sexual Harassment of Working Women* (1979), Catharine MacKinnon argued that sexual harassment in the workplace constituted a form of sex discrimination. MacKinnon's work was the impetus for a number of important legal changes. In 1980, the EEOC included sexual harassment in the workplace as a violation under Title VII. The Civil Rights Act of 1991 permitted compensatory and punitive damages for victims of sexual harassment in the workplace. In 1992, the U.S. Supreme Court ruled that sexual harassment in educational settings was a form of gender inequality and thus was covered by Title IX. These legal changes prompted a number of reforms in workplaces and schools, such as grievance procedures for victims and training for supervisors. They have provided important legal remedies that victims may pursue in the court. Nonetheless, it often remains difficult to pursue formal redress and women and girls who are sexually harassed are likely to put up with the situation or remove themselves from it by dropping classes or changing jobs. [*See* SEXUAL HARASSMENT.]

Much like rape, wife abuse was concealed, condoned, and protected by fear and silence prior to the feminist movement. Social values that sanctified marriage and the family were maintained at the expense of battered women and children. Feeling shame, blaming themselves, and fearing retaliation, few battered women revealed physical abuse by their husbands or partners. When battered women did speak with family, friends, and clergymen, they were likely to be told to return to their homes, to be the loving partners they were supposed to be, and to stop inciting their husbands or boyfriends to violence. Family physicians and emergency room staff exerted little effort to discover the causes of women's bruises and broken bones. Police offered little protection, with many believing that battered women provoked and even perhaps enjoyed violence. To the extent that woman abuse was recognized, it was assumed that it only happened in poor and working-class households or to women of color.

Feminist activists have opened shelters and 24-hour crisis lines to provide battered women with support, counseling, and legal services, as well as temporary housing. Shelters assist their clients in obtaining welfare, child care, housing, and jobs. The response to these services indicates that large numbers of women are physically abused by husbands and partners and that battered women come from all classes and races. Many shelters are constantly filled and must impose narrow limits on the length of time that a woman and her children can remain in residence.

As shelter workers have learned about the needs and experiences of battered women, they have trained police, physicians and nurses, social workers and counselors, and prosecuting attorneys. They have offered public education and antiviolence workshops in schools. Advocates for battered women also have worked for legal changes, such as restraining orders; preferred-arrest policies, wherein making an arrest is the preferred course of action; mandatory arrest policies, which require that offenders be arrested whether or not the abused person has signed a complaint; and statutes that make stalking a criminal offense. The Violence Against Women Act (1994) mandated interstate enforcement of protection orders, created a national hot line, providing training for state and federal judges, and made gender-motivated violence a civil rights violation. In spite of all these advances, battered women still face many difficulties. Many insurance companies deny battered women health coverage. With the severe restrictions placed on welfare in 1996, women who leave a violent relationship have less access to job training, housing, and health care. [*See* BATTERING IN ADULT RELATIONSHIPS.]

B. FEMINIST ACTIVISM FOR REPRODUCTIVE RIGHTS

A key goal of second-wave feminism has been securing for women the right to determine whether and when to have children and how many children to have. State intervention in women's reproductive choices violates their right to privacy and to self-determination. Practically speaking, women's economic self-sufficiency and participation in public life hinges on their ability to control their fertility.

The introduction of the contraceptive pill in the early 1960s provided women with a means of regulating their fertility that was far more effective than what had previously been available. Yet numerous women still faced unintended and unwanted pregnancies. By the late 1960s, the struggle for legal access to safe abortions was underway. Women's access to legal abortion differed from state to state, with many states prohibiting abortion outright and others permitting abortion under certain conditions. Often a woman with an unwanted pregnancy had little recourse other than to bear the child or to seek a "back street" abortion, that is, an illegal procedure carried out in clandestine and often unsanitary surroundings. To remedy this situation, some feminists worked underground to help women obtain safe abortions. Perhaps the most dramatic example of this is Jane, a collective of students from the University of Chicago and other local women, which operated from 1967 to 1973. Jane began as a secret referral service for women in need of abortions, which were then illegal in Illinois. Over time, members of the collective trained themselves to carry out abortions. Operating in secret locations and always risking criminal prosecution, Jane assisted 11,000 women, mostly low-income women and women of color.

The struggle to legalize abortion engaged feminists across the political spectrum. Mass demonstrations and marches were staged throughout the country and in the nation's capitol. NOW and national organizations such as the National Abortion Rights Action League (NARAL), the Planned Parenthood Federation, and the Committee for Abortion Rights and Against Sterilization Abuse (CARASA) worked on the legislative and judicial fronts. In December 1971, the case of *Roe* v. *Wade* came before the United States Supreme Court. This case challenged a Texas law that allowed abortion only when it was necessary to save the woman's life. Jane Roe was the name given the 21-year-old plaintiff to protect her identity. In January 1973, in a seven to two decision, the Supreme Court rendered unconstitutional state laws that denied women abortions. The court based its arguments on the principle that the constitution extends a right to privacy to citizens. However, it retained the principle that the state has a legitimate interest in regulating pregnancy and abortion. Thus, *Roe* held that states could not pass laws that would interfere with a woman's right to terminate a pregnancy in the first trimester of pregnancy (that is, the first three months). In the subsequent two trimesters, however, the state's interests increase and therefore access to abortion can be restricted in a variety of ways. In practice, state laws do not normally permit abortion during the third trimester.

Immediately after the *Roe* decision, women's access to first- and second-trimester abortions was relatively unrestricted. Many feminists who had been active in the battle to secure legal access to abortion now turned to the matter of making sure that abortions were available to women who needed them. Although a number of hospitals and private physicians offered abortions to their patients, *Roe* did not require that physicians or hospitals perform abortions. Moreover, not all women who needed abortions could pay for them. In some locales, activists organized abortion services and women's health clinics that enabled women to receive services regardless of their ability to pay.

Opposition to abortion mounted within a few years. Antiabortion groups issued a stream of legal challenges in state after state, all aimed at limiting access to abortion in whatever ways possible. A number of these cases eventually made their way to the United States Supreme Court and forced the court into a detailed consideration of the precise limits on women's access to abortion. Throughout this time, feminist organizations and other advocacy groups mounted an intensive legal defense of women's right to choose. Although the Supreme Court has not upheld every challenge that antiabortionists have made, the net effect of the court's decisions has been to restrict women's reproductive choice.

Antiabortion groups have succeeded in legislating policies that restrict women's access to abortion. For example, some states now require mandatory waiting periods before a woman can receive an abortion, and some states require that a woman be given "educational" materials prior to receiving services. In some states, publicly funded clinics are prohibited from discussing the option of abortion with their patients. In 1976, Senator Henry Hyde introduced legislation that restricted the use of federal Medicaid funds to pay for abortions. The Hyde amendment, which remains in force at this writing, effectively denies poor women the right to choose an abortion. As access to abortion tightened, feminists have developed new services to help women obtain abortions.

These include referral services to help women locate providers willing to do abortions, services to help women to negotiate complicated regulations, and services that offer loans and grants to women who are unable to pay for abortions.

The activities of antiabortion groups reached fever pitch during the 1980s and 1990s. In some locales, antiabortion groups routinely have undertaken blockades of abortion clinics and hospitals that do abortions. Patients and workers have been assailed by taunting crowds and sometimes subjected to physical threats. Antiabortion activists have resorted to violence toward physicians and other health care providers, including murders, shootings, and bombings. In response, feminist activists have organized escort services and counter-demonstrations. Advocates for women's right to choose have pressed for more police protection of clinics and doctors and for criminal statutes against clinic-directed violence. Despite these efforts, the activities of antiabortion groups have curtailed women's access to abortion. The number of abortion clinics has dwindled, many private physicians have stopped performing abortions, and many hospitals have eliminated abortion services. Providers willing to perform second-trimester abortions are especially few in number. Poor women, adolescents, and women living in rural areas have been especially burdened by new restrictions and decreased availability of abortions. Thus, women's legal right to terminate an unwanted pregnancy has eroded considerably since 1973, and their practical access to abortion services has eroded even more.

Although feminist activism concerning reproductive rights has been dominated by the struggle over access to abortion, abortion is only one dimension of reproductive rights. Feminists have challenged legal policies and practices that denied lesbians custody of their children or visitation rights, as well as adoption policies that discriminate against them. For women of color and poor women, state regulation of fertility has involved not only women's rights to avoid pregnancy and childbirth, but also their right to bear children. Poor women, especially women who are not White, have been pressured into sterilization or sterilized without their knowledge or consent; often these women were receiving public assistance. More recently, state monitoring and control of women during pregnancy has also become a matter of concern. For example, some states have drafted statutes that permit the incarceration of pregnant women for fetal endangerment. These statutes, used to prosecute and incarcerate drug-addicted pregnant women or mothers whose newborn infants test positive for drugs, are more likely to be used against poor women and women of color. Other states have drafted statutes that allow the court to mandate the use of Depo-Provera, a long-acting contraceptive implant, under certain circumstances. Forced contraception, of course, contravenes a woman's right to choose. Feminists are concerned that this too will be used selectively against poor women and women of color. [*See* ABORTION AND ITS HEALTH EFFECTS; REPRODUCTIVE TECHNOLOGIES.]

C. WOMEN'S STUDIES

From its beginnings, the feminist movement has had a strong presence on many college campuses, drawing in women students, staff, faculty members, and administrators, as well as wives of male faculty members and women in the surrounding community. Faculty members at colleges and universities began to teach courses on women and gender in the late 1960s and women's studies programs came into being soon afterward. These programs provided a setting where women faculty and graduate students—who were then few in number and often excluded from the professional and social life of their home departments—could gather. They served as centers of intellectual exchange, collegiality, and personal support for faculty and students in a fledgling discipline. Also, some women's studies programs served as a meeting ground where feminists in the community and those in the academy could join together. This practice, however, was difficult to sustain within the conservative structure of the university and in the face of the workload required to establish legitimacy within the academy. In addition, women's studies programs organized programs and public events on the scholarship on women, and many developed programs that fostered research on women and gender. Throughout the 1980s and 1990s, women's studies programs developed new courses that ranged across the humanities and social sciences. Programs developed new curricular structures as well, including concentrations, minors, and majors for undergraduates and, later, training at the graduate level.

Scholarship in women's studies has left an enduring mark on the humanities and social sciences. A broad variety of journals devoted to women's studies now exist, as well as national and international professional organizations and yearly conferences.

Scholars in women's studies have added knowledge about the lives of women, knowledge that often had been pushed aside and deemed uninteresting. They have also uncovered aspects of social life and experience that had previously been ignored or concealed, such as incest and sexual abuse, female sexual desire, and lesbian experience. Feminist scholars have posed critiques of the methods and practices of traditional disciplines, detailing the hidden assumptions about gender laced through them. In sum, women's studies has succeeded as an academic course of study, as a scholarly project to expand and remake knowledge about women, and as a colloquy of scholars. It has achieved an enduring position in higher education and influenced the curriculum in elementary and high schools as well. Women's studies courses have brought new knowledge about women and gender to many thousands of students. For many of them, women's studies not only provided intellectual knowledge about gender, but also prompted personal changes and political involvement that have contributed to social change.

D. WOMEN'S CULTURE AND WOMEN'S ENTERPRISES

The second wave of feminism has given birth to a vibrant woman-centered culture, one that often intermixes feminist and lesbian themes. Art, music, literature, videos, and theater have been produced and performed by women artists for audiences of women. Women's bookstores, publishing houses, art galleries and museums, spirituality groups, music festivals, and Web sites, as well as restaurants, bars, and coffeehouses, now flourish. Other enterprises developed by women include travel agencies and travel services specializing in all-women's tours, bed-and-breakfast establishments and inns for women, and accounting and law firms specializing in services for women.

Women's culture and women-centered enterprises have provided opportunities for women to work, be entertained, and socialize in supportive environments, where shared values and common understandings can be taken for granted. In a culture that often objectifies female bodies and denigrates female experience, all-women activities provide opportunities for affirmation and celebration; they offer a respite from the restrictions and prejudices of dominant culture. All-women environments have been especially important for many lesbian women, for they often can find little comfort or safety in mainstream culture.

IV. *Dealing with Differences*

Second-wave feminism has embraced women with diverse histories and life experiences, women who are situated in different locations in the social structure, and women who experience different forms of domination and discrimination. Women who have allied with feminism include homemakers, community leaders, clerical workers, factory workers, academics, and professionals; women of different ages and religions; women who were disabled and those who were not; White women and women of color; lesbians and heterosexual women; women who identified themselves as socialist feminists, radical feminists, liberal feminists, cultural feminists, and womanists.

Differences among women have often been sources of tension and conflict within feminist circles. Many groups of women have criticized other groups for paying too little attention to their unique circumstances. Within feminist groups, women have encountered ageism, class bias, racism, anti-Semitism, and homophobia. These experiences are not unique among feminists; they mirror the divisions and hierarchies that exist in society at large. No group of women is exempt from ignorance about and prejudice toward other groups. Yet feminist organizations strive to be inclusive and to advocate for the needs of all women; these high aspirations have necessitated that feminists struggle to comprehend the diversity of women's lives.

The different standpoints of heterosexual women and lesbian women have prompted an ongoing dialogue among feminists. Lesbians' investment in feminism, their high visibility in feminist organizations, and their leadership in many feminist causes ensured that issues of sexual orientation would be addressed. Lesbians have pressed heterosexual women to stand with them to confront heterosexism (that is, the belief that heterosexuality is superior to and more natural than homosexuality) in themselves and in the larger society and to challenge the cultural stigma associated with homosexuality and the social and legal penalties often attached to it. More recently, bisexual and transgendered individuals (that is, persons whose gender identity does not match their biological characteristics; they may choose to change their sex through hormone treatments or surgery) have come forward to insist on recognition of their sexualities and life-style choices. [*See* Lesbians, Gay Men, and Bisexuals in Relationships.]

White feminists and women of color who advocate for women's rights have often had different standpoints and interests. While White feminists have emphasized the subordination of women by men, women of color have been more attuned to the interlocking systems of domination connected to race, ethnicity, class, and gender. Women of color have challenged White feminists to confront their own racism. They have also argued that whiteness confers a privileged position that is difficult for White people to see and pointed out that even though women are oppressed, they can still be the oppressors of others.

From the beginning, many women of color have played a significant part in second-wave feminism. For example, Pauli Murray, a Black civil rights lawyer, was on the President's Commission on the Status of Women and a found of NOW. Aileen Hernandez, a Black union leader, was a founder and early president of NOW. LaDonna Harris, a Native American, worked for both women's and Native American's rights. Shirley Chisholm, a Black congresswoman, was an early leader of the National Women's Political Caucus; in 1972, she became the first Black woman to run for president. Eleanor Holmes Norton, a Black lawyer and civil rights activist, headed the EEOC in the late 1970s. Women of color also established several national feminist organizations in the 1970s, among them the National Black Feminist Organization, the Mexican-American Women's National Association (MANA), and the Organization of Pan Asian American Women.

Black feminists led the way in examining the interconnections between racism and sexism. Early examples include Frances Beale's "Double Jeopardy: To Be Black and Female" (1970); Shirley Chisholm's "Racism and Anti-Feminism" (1970); Pauli Murray's "The Liberation of Black Women" (1975); Gloria Lewis's "A Response to Inequality: Black Women, Racism and Sexism" (1977); and Cellestine Ware's *Woman Power: The Movement for Women's Liberation* (1970). Since then, many women of color—scholars, novelists and poets, lawyers and legal theorists, and activists—have had a powerful influence on feminist thought and feminist practice, although not all of them have chosen to identify themselves as feminists. For example, the African American writer Alice Walker, an ardent activist on behalf of women, prefers to call herself a womanist.

The writings of African American, Latina, Chicana, Asian American, and Native American women have expanded and complicated knowledge of women's experience. Not only have they contributed to the understanding of contemporary racism and prejudice in women's lives, they have also added to historical knowledge by documenting the experiences of women of color during particular epochs. Examples include slave women's life on plantations, Nisei women's internment during World War II, and Black women's leadership during the civil rights movement in the United States. They have added knowledge about women's experiences under colonialism and neocolonialism, as refugees and immigrants, and in the global labor force. This new knowledge about women of color has made it clear that no group of women can rely solely on its own experience to draw generalizations about all women.

Women from different generations also relate differently to feminism. Young women, often called third-wave feminists, have claimed space for their own issues, styles, and ways of working. Just as second-wave feminism took shape within a specific social context, third-wave feminism too is shaped by its social context. The young women who constitute the third wave of feminism derive many benefits from the hard-won battles of the second wave. Yet they are part of an era in which the connection between the rights women now enjoy and earlier feminist activism is not apparent. Many people believe in gender equality but do not see the similarity between themselves and the feminists who brought their beliefs into mainstream culture, hence the common disclaimer "I'm not a feminist, but . . ." Many young feminists have an appreciation of earlier efforts but are also keenly aware of the multiplicity of feminisms developed by women in international contexts and women of color in the United States.

V. Resistance to Feminism

Feminist movements everywhere have always been opposed by those who believed their interests were threatened. Although the 1970s were a time of substantial legislative gains for women and popular support for feminism, the resistance to feminism was considerable. The mass media often ridiculed and trivialized feminists, labeling them "women's libbers" and "bra burners." The media ignored NOW's call for subsidized child care and programs to retrain full-time mothers after their children grew up and instead repeated the myth that feminists disapproved of full-time

mothers and ignored the child care needs of employed mothers. When Congress passed the Equal Rights Amendment, conservatives mounted a campaign to defeat its ratification. When abortion was legalized, militant antiabortion groups agitated against it.

The election of Ronald Reagan as president of the United States in 1980 marked a sharp turn to conservatism and an even stronger backlash against feminism. During the 1980s, and 1990s, legislation and court decisions cut back many of the gains of the 1970s. Access to abortion was curtailed and the size and power of the EEOC was drastically reduced. Congress terminated the Aid to Families with Dependent Children (AFDC) in 1996 and substituted a more stringent program that dramatically reduced the assistance to poor women and children. On many campuses, opponents of women's studies programs mounted public attacks on the rigor of the scholarship and the academic quality of the courses.

At the beginning of the new millennium, the media often support the spurious claims of the New Right that feminists are strident, embittered man haters who oppose motherhood and are determined to destroy the family. Conservative organizations continue to oppose the principle of equal rights for women and men, feminist causes, and feminist organizations. They use their funds to promote rightwing commentators, authors, and spokespersons and to finance antiabortion candidates for legislative and judicial positions. The media seem preoccupied with declaring the purported death of feminism instead of reporting the broad-scale positive changes in women's lives that feminism has made possible.

VI. Conclusion

The efforts of feminists activists have put in place an array of laws and policies that grant women some degree of formal equality in employment, education, and public life. Although abortion remains a bitterly contested issue, women still have access to abortion. Popular views about women's capacities and proper place in the social hierarchy have been irrevocably transformed. It is no longer automatically assumed that men are "naturally" superior to women or that men ought to have more power and privileges than women in the workplace. Women from many social groups have more freedom to make choices about educational pursuits, sexuality, marriage, childbearing, and paid employment. Ideas about the domestic relations of women and men have altered too. Though women still bear the brunt of family work in most households, there have been shifts in the division of labor in many heterosexual couples, with men assuming more responsibility for housework and child care. There is more, but not complete, acceptance of lesbians and lesbian lifestyles. There has been acknowledgment of the problem of gender-linked violence against women, with important institutions such as the American Medical Association, the American Psychological Association, and the American Bar Association speaking out against it. There is less public tolerance of such violence and more public support for protecting women and children. Women's studies continues to enjoy a place in the university curriculum and to draw new scholars to it. Women in minority communities in the United States and women around the world have mobilized to advance their rights, curb violence, and gain access to adequate income, health care, and education. Although much additional work remains to be done, all of these changes speak to the profound and pervasive influence of second-wave feminism.

SUGGESTED READING

Davis, F. (1991). *Moving the Mountain: The Women's Movement in America Since 1960*. Simon & Schuster, New York.

Giddings, P. (1984). *When and Where I Enter: The Impact of Black Women on Race and Sex in America*. Bantam, New York.

Faludi, S. (1991). *Backlash: The Undeclared War Against American Women*. Crown, New York.

Ferree, M. M., and Martin, P. Y. (eds.) (1995). *Feminist Organizations: Harvest of the New Women's Movement*. Temple University Press, Philadelphia.

Garcia, A. (ed.) (1997). *Chicana Feminist Thought: The Basic Historical Writings*. Routledge, New York.

Heywood, L., and Drake, J. (eds.) (1997). *Third Wave Agenda: Being Feminist, Doing Feminism*. University of Minnesota Press, Minneapolis, MN.

Kessler-Harris, A. (2001). *Securing Equity*. Oxford University Press, New York.

Rosen, R. (2000). *The World Split Open: How the Modern Women's Movement Changed America*. Viking Press, New York.

Ryan, B. (1992). *Feminism and the Women's Movement: Dynamics of Change in Social Movement Ideology and Activism*. Routledge, New York.

Staggenborg, S. (1991). *The Pro-Choice Movement: Organization and Activism in the Abortion Conflict*. Oxford University Press, New York.

Feminist Theories

Carolyn Zerbe Enns
Cornell College

Ada Sinacore
McGill University

Glossary

Feminist theories Conceptual frameworks that organize beliefs about the nature and causes of women's oppression and inequality and that propose methods for eradicating oppression and establishing gender equality.

Second-wave feminisms Competing conceptualizations of feminist theory elaborated primarily between the late-1960s and the mid-1980s.

Third-wave feminisms Contributions to feminist theory that both critique and expand on second-wave feminist theories.

FEMINIST THEORIES provide an important foundation for feminist scholarship, research, pedagogy, therapy, and activism. A multitude of feminist theories exist, providing a wide range of perspectives re-

garding (1) why women and men have held unequal power across time and place, (2) why knowledge has historically been accumulated by and for men and excluded women, and (3) how men and women can rectify these problems and achieve equality. Knowledge of feminist theoretical systems is important because these frameworks provide significant information about the various assumptions, goals, and strategies that inform the work of feminists.

I. The Three Waves of Feminism

Recent feminist scholarship proposes that the rich and evolving history of feminism can be characterized by three "waves." The first wave of feminism, spanning the 17th to 19th centuries, encompassed contributions of feminists who worked primarily within the confines of existing systems of rules and laws to achieve equality for women and the right to participate more widely in society. The second wave of feminism, spanning primarily the 1960s to the 1980s, produced a variety of schools of thought about the nature of gender oppression, the appropriate goals of feminism, and the optimal means of reaching these goals. Four major theories associated with second wave feminism are liberal feminism, cultural feminism, radical feminism, and socialist feminism. Third-wave feminisms, which have overlapped with second-wave feminisms, have produced elaborations and critiques of previous theories and include postmodern, women of color, lesbian, global, and generation-X third wave feminisms. Whereas many second-wave theories (e.g., liberal and socialist feminism) were inspired by manmade theories that were modified to incorporate gender perspectives, most recent theories have highlighted women's points of view and have sought to value diversity, flexibility, and multiple perspectives on gender relationships.

This article describes many of the second-wave and third-wave feminisms that are influential at the beginning of the 21st century. It is important to note that the labels associated with these feminist theories allow for efficient communication about specific ideas, but when these labels are applied arbitrarily, they can lead to artificial and inaccurate categorizations. Feminist theory is continually evolving, and the boundaries between feminist theories are fluid and overlapping. Many contemporary feminists are not influenced by a single feminist perspective, but view themselves as eclectic and combine theories in creative and personally meaningful ways.

II. *Liberal Feminism*

Liberal feminism has its roots in liberal enlightenment thought, rationalism, and natural rights philosophies. Early liberal feminist theorists, such as Mary Wollstonecraft, Elizabeth Cady Stanton, and Susan B. Anthony, built their ideas on the foundation provided by liberal male theorists who proposed that men have the ability to exercise rational judgment and are entitled to certain inherent rights, such as liberty, life, property, and dignity. Liberal theorists assumed that these rights are best secured through the passage of laws that allow for equal opportunity and ensure that individuals do not infringe on each other's rights. Liberal feminists noted the ways in which women have been excluded from the liberal framework and argued that women should share the same inherent rights to make productive individual choices as men, participate in the same opportunities and social contracts as men, and receive the same treatment as men. In other words, women deserve equality because they have the same capabilities as men.

As an extension of these values, liberal feminists have historically promoted the use of objective, critical, rational thinking as ways of solving problems. The ideals of individual dignity, autonomy, equality, and the right to seek self-fulfillment are central to liberal feminist analyses. Oppression is thought to be caused by irrational beliefs that women are less capable than men and by rigid or inflexible gender-role conditioning. The solutions to these problems are achieved through logical argument, corrective educational experiences, and reforms and gender neutral policies that ensure that all individuals have access to equal opportunities to exercise their free choice and skills. In general, liberal feminists have focused on reforming existing systems or redistributing persons in existing power structures and have not challenged the basic structures or assumptions that support these institutions. Some important contributors to liberal feminism during the 20th century have included Betty Friedan, Eleanor Smeal, Bella Abzug, and Zillah Eisenstein.

Some of the important values of liberal feminism were reflected in the National Organization for Women's (NOW) Bill of Rights. This document called for legislation related to equal rights, the banning of sex discrimination in employment, the right to control reproduction, access to child care and maternity leave, opportunities to pursue equal and unsegregated education, and access to job training and housing for impoverished women. The NOW Bill of Rights exemplifies a liberal feminist strategy based on the assumption that equality can be achieved through the construction of rational social contracts and legislative means. Many other social reforms of the past 30 years have been consistent with liberal feminist perspectives, including affirmative action policies and policies designed to curb violence such as sexual harassment, rape, and domestic violence.

Liberal feminists assume that the exploration of restrictive gender-role socialization raises women's awareness of how personal issues such as low confidence, low self-esteem, math anxiety, and the fear of success may limit their aspirations. Once aware of internalized restrictions, individuals can develop assertiveness skills that facilitate their success and experience greater freedom to realize their personal potential.

With regard to intimate, work, and friendship relationships, liberal feminists have tended to promote androgyny, or the integration of roles and characteristics traditionally defined as masculine or feminine. This view proposes that when men and women adopt flexible roles, gender differences will be minimal or disappear, and women and men will experience a wider array of life satisfactions. Within the realm of personal relationships, liberal feminists believe that a wide range of nontraditional behaviors is appropriate. Out of respect for individual freedom, however, these choices must be based on personal preferences and should not be externally imposed.

Research and scholarship inspired by liberal feminism have not challenged existing academic methodologies and assumptions but have critiqued the incomplete way in which scientific inquiry has been conducted in the past. They have attempted to eliminate sexism by adhering more strictly to rules of good research design and the empirical, quantitative scientific method. In other words, feminist researchers use objective, scientific inquiry to challenge research-based knowledge that is founded on biased assumptions, questions, or interpretations.

III. *Cultural Feminism*

Similar to liberal feminism, cultural feminism is embedded in a rich 19th-century heritage of ideas proposed by women such as Margaret Fuller, Charlotte Perkins Gilman, and Jane Addams. In contrast to liberal feminists, who argue that women and men are essentially alike and that rational analysis is key to the realization of feminist goals, cultural feminists emphasize the special, unique, different qualities of women and the importance of revaluing intuitive, nonrational aspects of human experience. Liberation involves (1) reclaiming women's caregiving and nurturing roles that have been devalued within an industrial, patriarchal society and (2) using these roles to overcome the problems of society. Cultural feminists have envisioned that social transformation will occur through the infusion of feminine or maternal values into the culture: harmony, an ethic of care and connectedness, and an appreciation for nonviolent and peaceful negotiation. They seek to renegotiate gender relationships by emphasizing altruistic, cooperative aspects of human experience, but they also extend their interests to include ecofeminist concerns, or efforts to build positive, nonviolent, connected relationships with the physical environment.

Important contributors to cultural feminism have included Nancy Chodorow, Dorothy Dinnerstein, Carol Gilligan, Nel Noddings, and Sarah Ruddick, who have theorized about the importance of care, connectedness, and "maternal thinking" in moral and ethical decision making. Other work consistent with cultural feminism has focused on women's relational approach to communication and language, self-development and personality, and ways of seeking knowledge.

The transformation strategies proposed by cultural feminists emphasize finding ways for women to experience communal values, achieve personal and intellectual growth in the context of relationships, and empower women to understand themselves as knowers, creators, and actors, not just as passive receivers. A major assumption of cultural feminism is that women are often silenced and paralyzed by traditional, abstract conceptualizations of knowing, achieving, and considering ethical dilemmas. However, many women are empowered and see themselves as capable beings when they experience connection and resolve issues based on relationship values. In contrast to liberal feminist perspectives that rely primarily on helping women achieve by applying rational, objective strategies, cultural feminist perspectives challenge the androcentric culture's message that in order to succeed, women must learn to "think like a man." Women's lives and women's ways of knowing and experiencing are placed at the center of inquiry. It is important to note that many cultural feminists also believe that the integration of relationship values and abstract, "separate" values represents an ideal way of resolving dilemmas of knowledge, ethics, and personal growth.

Cultural feminist values are most closely related to feminist standpoint epistemologies or ways of seeking knowledge. Standpoint epistemologies propose that as a result of their outsider status in patriarchal society, women are more capable than privileged men of identifying the harmful aspects of theory and culture. Standpoint theorists seek to develop methods that provide a more complete understanding of women's reality than that offered by traditional scientific empirical methods. Consistent with connected thinking, standpoint methods attempt to explore the lives of women through qualitative inquiry that reveals who women are as relational beings. Feminist standpoint researchers place women at the center of inquiry and attempt to erase the boundaries between researchers and the persons who are studied. They reject the notion that inquiry can be value free and objective, attempt to erase the traditional boundaries that exist between researcher and participant, and, through careful qualitative inquiry, make efforts to understand women's experience as it is understood by women.

IV. Radical Feminism

In contrast to the liberal and cultural feminist values of individual autonomy and growth, radical feminism emphasizes the centrality of social transformation that can only be accomplished by the dramatic alteration of cultural values through the vehicle of social activism. Radical feminism, which was born during the "new" feminist movement of the 1960s, identifies women's oppression as the most fundamental and pervasive form of oppression and articulates how patriarchal control over women's bodies has dominated every area of life including paid employment, housework, intimate partnerships, violence, and mothering. Some key theorists associated with this perspective include Kate Millett, Mary Daly, Shulamith Firestone, Andrea Dworkin, and Marilyn Frye.

In order to enact social change, radical feminists have sought to uncover, illuminate, and question the ways in which patriarchy dominates virtually all aspects of human experience. These experiences include thinking patterns, social relationships, dress and physical appearance, and work. The manifestos and writings of radical feminist activist groups of the 1960s and 1970s (e.g., Redstockings, New York Radical Feminists) are important sources of information about radical feminist thought.

Given the centrality of patriarchal values throughout most human institutions, the liberal feminist goal of reforming social institutions and the cultural feminist strategy of revaluing of traditional "feminine" strengths are not seen as powerful enough to initiate true alterations of society at its roots. According to radical feminists, constructs such as masculinity and femininity should be abolished and new, nongendered categories for organizing personal and social life must be formulated and adopted. Similar to the viewpoint of cultural feminists, radical feminists believe that women hold special strengths for understanding and reconstructing a world in which oppression does not exist. However, it is their experience as oppressed beings within patriarchy and

not necessarily their relational characteristics as women that provides the basis for their special knowledge. Patriarchal models of thinking have contributed to a world in which dichotomous thinking and experiencing are pervasive. Thinking is seen as the opposite of feeling. Masculine is contrasted with feminine. Objectivity is considered the opposite of subjectivity. Rationality is contrasted with irrationality. In the transformed, radical feminist environment, participants seek to transcend "masculine" and "feminine" dichotomies by refusing to categorize emotion and subjectivity as women's modes of thinking, but to integrate these processes and to heal the fragmentation that occurs when the worlds of men and women are understood in polarized ways.

The assumption that "the personal is political" is of great importance within radical feminist practice. The consciousness-raising group has been an important context in which women have explored their experiences of oppression, developed theories about women's lives, and proposed methods of enacting social change on behalf of all women. The act of naming oppression and giving it voice, an important aspect of consciousness raising, is seen as empowering in and of itself. In keeping with radical feminist principles, the radical feminist group or organization should be as nonhierarchical as possible, place women and girls at the center of inquiry, and emphasize the importance of participation and dialogue in preparation for resistance and action.

Given the difficulty of achieving a transformed social order within current structures, radical feminists have sometimes advocated for the implementation of separatist communities or organizations in which new values could be clarified in truly egalitarian experimental environments. Within these environments, women can make creative contributions to new forms of religion, art, poetry, science, and literature, rather than being diverted into fighting the inevitable and insidious tentacles of patriarchal values. Collective political and social action are essential vehicles for achieving radical feminism's goal of transforming the culture.

Given the reality that radical feminism has been especially attentive to the reproduction of male dominance through the objectification of women and violence against women, this content has received substantial emphasis in radical feminist writing and research. Radical feminism also devotes substantial attention to the manner in which patriarchy is often reproduced through researcher–participant relationships, the therapist–client relationships, and the application of labels through diagnosis. Radical feminists share with cultural feminists a preference for standpoint theories and epistemologies that seek to transform the content of research studies, the manner in which studies are conducted, and the nature of researcher–participant relationships.

V. Socialist Feminism

Like many other second-wave feminist frameworks, socialist feminist thought originated in the 19th century and was inspired by feminists who envisioned a world in which economic competition and exploitation would be replaced with utopian communities in which men and women would share domestic tasks, household chores, and child care. Socialist feminists share radical feminists' views that gender oppression is a central form of oppression, and they view social activism as essential to meeting their goals. However, they have also sought a more complex analysis of sexism than that endorsed by radical feminists, one that examines the manner in which oppression is shaped by class, economics, nationality, race, and history. In general, socialist feminists attempt to integrate (1) an analysis of the structure of production, class, and capitalism (Marxist perspectives); (2) the control of women's bodies, reproduction, and sexuality and the manner in which this control is shaped by patriarchy (radical feminism); and (3) the impact of gender role socialization (liberal feminism). Some of the important contributors to recent socialist feminist thought include Alison Jaggar, Juliet Mitchell, Iris Young, Donna Haraway, and Ann Ferguson.

Several assumptions of socialism are central to socialist feminist thought. According to this view, human beings are born in a given economic and social structure that substantially shapes individual experience. In contrast to liberal feminism, which starts with assumptions about individual rights, socialist feminists use social realities to explain individual experience. Whereas liberalism proposes that the outcomes of labor result in the expansion of one's private property and satisfaction, socialists argue that work within capitalist systems results in worker alienation from both the product and process of their work. In contrast, communal ownership and cooperation will lead to personal satisfaction. Socialist feminists believe that individual opportunity alone will not lead to an egalitarian world; the realization of human potential will only be achieved through the restructuring of personal (e.g., family) and public (e.g. employment) experiences of men and women. Universal access to economic and work options, education, housing, birth control, and child care is essential.

Traditional socialist theory failed to include any analysis of how men's and women's experiences and roles within economic and family spheres differed and contributed to women's lower social status. Thus, feminist socialist theorists have examined alienation as it relates to women's experiences of sexuality, motherhood, and education. Women have experienced (1) alienation from their own sexuality through sexual objectification and being treated as sexual commodities, (2) alienation from motherhood through the control of obstetric science and other "experts," and (3) alienation from their intellectual strengths by being confined by definitions of intelligence and competence set forth primarily by men.

Socialist feminist theory examines how women are required through structural arrangements to play nurturing and caretaking roles in family contexts, educational settings, and other paid employment roles. The concentration of women in service jobs, low-paying jobs, and caregiving jobs (e.g., as primary and elementary schoolteachers) and men in administrative roles reflects the division of labor within private households in which women are expected to be primary caregivers and men are given executive or decision-making power. Like liberal feminists, socialist feminists pay close attention to the impact of work, education, and family roles on women. However, whereas liberal feminists focus on reforming systems and increasing individual opportunity, socialist feminists see these efforts as useful but inadequate and view the structural transformation of educational life and educational institutions as necessary.

Radical feminists and socialist feminists share assumptions about the necessity of social transformation as a vehicle for achieving feminist liberation. Whereas radical feminists focus primarily on issues associated with patriarchy and male dominance, socialist feminists are especially concerned with the manner in which sexism, classism, and racism are reinforced through economic means. The goal of redistributing power through the transformation of economic structures, including the educational and family systems that prepare individuals for work, is a central goal of socialist feminism. Thus, those influenced by socialist feminist perspectives are especially attentive to the ways in which social policy and capitalism reproduce systems of domination.

More specifically, socialist feminist theory examines how educational, work, and family systems prepare persons to accept their assigned roles as paid and unpaid workers and to fulfill roles that are consistent with their gender, class, and racial backgrounds. Ethnographic and qualitative research programs that reveal "hidden" structural inequities are central to socialist feminist inquiry, as is clarification of how standpoint perspectives can clarify race, class, and gender intersections that cannot be adequately understood through the use of quantitative methods alone.

VI. *Postmodern Feminism*

In recent years, postmodern approaches to feminism have been promoted as ways of transcending the limitations of other feminisms. Postmodern feminisms are influenced by the work of postmodern theorists, who have sought to challenge many assumptions about truth and reality that are often taken for granted, such as the beliefs that (1) people possess a stable and coherent sense of self that transcends circumstances, (2) "objective" knowledge based on reason and experimentation is real and unchanging across contexts, and (3) truth and knowledge can be understood independent of power dynamics and contexts in which they are developed. Postmodern perspectives highlight the limitations of knowledge and the fallibility of knowers, including the tendency for knowers to misunderstand reality, to engage in ethnocentric thinking, and to draw flawed generalizations about human experience.

Feminist postmodernism rejects the existence of any universal female or feminist standpoint. Feminist postmodernist theorists seek to understand how meaning is negotiated, how people in power maintain control over meanings, and how truth is invented, shaped, and modified by history, social context, and the views and life experiences of knowers. These theorists include Linda Alcoff, Nancy Fraser, Linda Nicholson, Jane Flax, and Linda Singer.

A primary tool of feminist postmodern analysis is deconstruction, which involves the breaking down polarities, showing how they are created and often artificial, and explaining how they are related to systems of power. Deconstruction should not be confused with destruction. Rather, it reveals that constructs such as masculine/feminine, heterosexuality/homosexuality, and black/white were created, and that all truth claims and constructs are fallible. No truth is all-encompassing or invariable.

In contrast to feminisms that were centered in social activism, postmodern feminism has arisen within academic disciplines and has become a method for understanding the limitations of knowledge and the changing nature of knowledge. Postmodern theorists examine the contextual nature of knowledge, how power shapes knowledge, and how these realities can be used to develop more complex and relevant views of reality and gender. Postmodern feminism is not a theory in the sense that it does not provide a specific framework for understanding oppression. Instead, it provides a model for questioning the value of other traditional and feminist frameworks.

Of particular importance is the need for theorists, researchers, and practitioners to scrutinize their own practices, assumptions, and beliefs about empowerment and social change. Recognizing one's "positionality" requires theorists and researchers to (1) hone a "third eye," or self-reflective awareness of the many ways in which oppression and empowerment occur; (2) be observant of the complex intersections of power, privilege, race, class, gender, sexual orientation, and other aspects of identity; and (3) use this information to deal with difference effectively and develop flexible ways of seeing themselves and the world. Another closely related value is reflexivity. Reflexivity, or self-reflectiveness, calls on individuals to practice self-awareness and accountability and to recognize a range of human truths. Scholars, activists, and practitioners learn to observe and locate themselves as knowers within certain cultural and sociohistorical contexts and to avoid imposing their personal realities on others.

A social constructionist perspective in psychology is largely consistent with postmodern thought. From a feminist social constructionist perspective, gender is a verb; it is about doing, and thus is shaped and changed by context. Gender is not a unitary set of characteristics that are portrayed consistently or permanently within a person. Gender refers to specific patterns of organizing experience that define or structure relationships, especially power relationships, between individuals. Social constructionist/postmodern perspectives are useful for correcting tendencies to minimize differences or exaggerate gender differences. Instead, important questions focus on the meaning of difference, how gender is created and modified, and how gender is connected to multiple meanings. This perspective is also associated with multiple methods of conducting research. No one method, standpoint or empirical, is seen as completely neutral or objective. A postmodern perspective suggests that all methods have strengths and limitations, and that no one "snapshot," no matter how the rigorous, can provide complete knowledge about women's experience.

VII. Women of Color Feminisms

Women of color feminists share many of the concerns articulated by other feminists, but argue that efforts must be made to make feminist theory more inclusive. The simplistic assertion that "all women are oppressed" implies that all women have common problems and challenges, ignoring the fact that the oppressive forces faced by ethnic, racial, religious, and sexual minorities result in diversity of experience. Thus, the notion of differential oppression becomes a primary theme of women of color feminisms. Important contributors include Angela Davis, bell hooks, Aida Hurtado, Paula Giddings, Elizabeth Spelman, Audre Lorde, Alice Walker, Patricia Hill Collins, Oliva Espin, and Beverly Greene.

Theorist and educator bell hooks views oppression as influenced by an "absence of choices." The liberal feminist notion that women experience a common oppression promotes the class interests of more privileged groups of women by ignoring the additional oppression or lack of choices experienced by women from other ethnic, racial, and class groups. Women of color have criticized White feminists for drawing convenient and presumptuous comparisons between the oppressions of being female and being a person of color. By assuming this similarity of oppression, White feminists overgeneralize and assume that experiences of White women encompass the experiences of all women. Feminists of color note that feminists who propose that gender oppression is central to understanding all other oppression leave women of color with an impossible choice: they may feel forced to choose between their identities as women and identities as people of color, or they may feel forced to prioritize their identities. For many women of color, the personal experience of racism is far more visible, virulent, and commonplace than is the experience of sexism.

Feminists of color propose that exploring differential access to privilege is essential to the creation of feminisms that are relevant to women of color. Due to their relatively privileged status as White people and their connection to powerful White men, White women have access to some forms of power and may come to believe they can share power with men. White feminists have often failed to understand how they have used their privileged position to perpetuate forms of oppression that resemble the types of abuses they have attempted to eradicate. In contrast to privileged White women, poor and working class women of color are subject to additional oppression that they share with men of color. Thus, for women of color, being involved with a man of color cannot lead to sharing power because there is little or no power to be shared. Any analysis of women of color needs to include an understanding of the oppression and double binds faced by men of color of different socioeconomic statuses. White women and men of color can claim to be oppressed but also act as oppressors. Men of color can be victims of racism, but sexism allows them to exploit women; White women can be victims of sexism, but racism allows them to exploit people of color. For women of color, there are no persons of lower status whom they can exploit; therefore, it is their experience that most directly challenges racist, sexist, and classist notions. [*See* POWER.]

Feminists of color can play a central role in creating more inclusive and pluralistic feminisms by proposing theories that reflect their personal experiences and worldviews. For example, Patricia Hill Collins has articulated basic characteristics of Black feminist thought. The components emphasize the centrality of self-definition and self-valuation, the analysis of the interlocking aspects of oppression, and the integration of Black women's culture and Afrocentric values with feminism. Black feminist thought uses the concrete everyday experiences of Black women to inform feminism by (1) emphasizing the centrality of dialogue, which is connected to African and African American oral traditions, to explore and articulate knowledge about women; (2) integrating feminism with an African humanistic ethic of care; and (3) practicing an ethic of accountability, which involves using reason, emotion, and ethics to evaluate the character, values, and ethics of persons who propose knowledge claims.

A major goal of women of color feminisms is to use the standpoints of women of color to rethink feminism and place the life experiences of women of color at the center of inquiry. Many women of color have preferred to use the term "womanist" instead of "feminist" to highlight the centrality of self-definition, the uniqueness of their commitment to women of color, and their rejection of approaches that overgeneralize about all women or propose gender-based dichotomies. The term "womanist," which was coined by Alice Walker, refers to women who love other women and appreciate women's strength and capacity, culture, and emotional flexibility. A womanist is committed to the wholeness of both men and women.

Although both traditional feminists and women of color feminists have identified family life and work as major areas of discussion, their understanding of these issues is very different. For example, the radical feminist notion that the family is an oppressive institution that needs to be eradicated is problematic for many feminists of color. Although the family may be an oppressive institution for many women of color, the kinship patterns, living arrangements, and family structures are extremely different from those of the White middle-class norms of a two-parent family and children living in a single family dwelling with the male as breadwinner. For many people of color, the family is not a system to be eradicated but a primary support system, because it is in the family context that oppressed peoples can find sanctuary from the racism experienced in the public sector. A theory that is relevant to women of color highlights the importance of the family, kin, and community as central support systems for women of color. It identifies ways in which the family may be oppressive, but it does not devalue the family.

A second major issue addressed by women of color feminisms is work. Unlike privileged White women who have had choices with regard to education and work, women of color of lower socioeconomic status may not have access to many job opportunities. Moreover, for many women of color, work is not a choice but a necessity and is often associated with exploitation. Thus, many of the concerns of White middle-class feminists, such as equal pay for equal work and the desire for choice to work outside the home, do not address the needs of women of color. A feminist theory of women of color articulates the necessity of work, its relationships to family survival, and the oppressive and discriminatory practices experienced by women of color. [*See* CAREER ACHIEVEMENT.]

Consistent with radical feminist theory, an important component of feminisms of women of color is activism. Theorizing about the causes of the oppression of women of color is important, but engaging in social change is more important; feminist theory must be dynamic, not static. Women of color feminisms are embedded in real-life issues. Women of color feminists also express concern that theory may be co-opted by academic authors, who tend to elaborate on increasingly complex theories. As a result, theory often becomes obscure, hard to understand, inaccessible to general audiences of women, and of limited use for informing action. For many women of color, activism must be placed at the heart of feminist theory.

Feminists of color state that feminism needs to promote liberation and "decolonization." Many people of color have experienced the suppression or eradication of their own cultures and have been required to accommodate themselves to dominant colonizing cultures in order to survive. Consequences of colonization often include victimization, alienation, self-denial, assimilation within the dominant culture, or ambivalence about one's role in a dominant culture. Through consciousness raising, women of color become aware of how they have internalized the racist and sexist beliefs of the culture and learn skills for countering these beliefs and becoming "decolonized."

As for the content of feminist scholarship and women's studies, feminists of color argue that the content of a discipline needs to be inclusive and pluralistic. Theorists, researchers, and practitioners need to be careful to avoid the "add and stir" approach to women or color, or to rely on content about women of color that is built primarily on the scholarship of White women. Feminisms of women of color explore the lives of women from the perspectives of women of color, are based on culturally sensitive definitions of constructs such as gender roles, and focus on the coping functions of women's behaviors. In light of all these issues, feminist theory must include (1) an analysis of multiple oppression, (2) an assessment of access to privilege and power, (3) an inclusion of the personal experiences and worldviews of women of color, and (4) activism.

VIII. *Lesbian Feminisms*

Lesbian feminist theory has its roots in second-wave radical feminism. Consistent with radical feminism, lesbian feminists have viewed issues related to women's sexuality and sexualized images of women as central to the analysis of women's oppression. However, they have objected to the substantial amount of energy focused on an analysis of male–female relationships and the limited emphasis on concerns that are unique to women. During the second wave of feminism, lesbian feminists noted that heterosexual feminists were vocal and critical about the manner in which women are only valued in relationship to men, but seemed to internalize and act out the very dynamic they critiqued in their own relationships with men. Many heterosexual feminists seemed to have difficulty recognizing the full impact of male oppression in their own lives because of the cognitive dissonance created by their efforts to preserve less than healthy relationships with men. Lesbians who defined themselves as feminists often felt excluded and marginalized by heterosexual feminists who acted as though sexual orientation was irrelevant to an analysis of women's oppression and who appeared to subscribe to the myth that members of an oppressed group (heterosexual women) could not oppress other women (lesbians). During the second wave of feminisms, some heterosexual liberal feminists implied that addressing lesbian issues openly would contribute to negative public images of and efforts to discredit the women's movement. This climate contributed to the invisibility of lesbians in feminism. Lesbians faced a dilemma similar to that of women of color: they felt forced to choose between identifying themselves as lesbian or feminist.

In response to these problems, lesbians began to provide a unique lesbian feminist analysis. Radical lesbians, including Charlotte Bunch, Ti-Grace Atkinson, and Rita Mae Brown, critiqued sexism within gay liberation and homophobia in feminist organizations and directed their energy to understanding women's experience, noting that an overemphasis on problems in relationships with men merely drain women of energy and reinforce patriarchal values. For those who identified themselves as "radicalesbians," choosing to identify oneself as lesbian was seen as a political act that conveyed one's rejection of patriarchy and desire to invest one's energies in women and women's causes.

Lesbian feminisms have made important contributions to the analysis of heterosexuality as a contributor to patriarchy and oppression. Adrienne Rich's classic commentary about "compulsory heterosexuality" pointed out that heterosexuality is presumed to be normative for all people and that this view is a key component of heterosexism. Heterosexism can be defined as the values that promote the notion that heterosexuality is the only natural form of emotional and sexual expression. Lesbian feminists, including Adrienne Rich, Celia Kitzinger, Sue Wilkinson, and Cheshire Calhoun, have highlighted a theme that remains central to lesbian feminist theories: heterosexuality must be analyzed as an institution rather than as merely a sexual preference.

Lesbian feminists examine heterosexuality as a political institution and the manner in which it dictates how some members of society, especially heterosexual men, hold greater power than others. Maintaining an almost universal female heterosexuality is an important mechanism of male domination because it guarantees women's sexual availability to men. Furthermore, women's subordination to men is solidified through various heterosexual norms and traditions, including heterosexual romantic traditions and rites of passage, women's acts of caring for men, prohibitions against cross-dressing, heterosexual pornography and erotica, and heterosexualized humor and dress. In addition to analyzing how heterosexuality organizes social and reproductive relationships, lesbian feminism evaluates heterosexuality as an ideology that conveys prohibitions about lesbianism and homosexuality. Heterosexism promotes the view that male–female relationships are a fundamental building block of society; in contrast, same-sex intimate relationships are seen as holding no social reality. The critical analysis and deconstruction of heterosexist assumptions in society and feminist theory are essential for creating truly liberating feminisms.

Lesbian feminist theories have moved beyond the analysis of "compulsory sexuality," heterosexism, and homophobia and have emphasized themes that affirm lesbian life experiences, such as the cultural components of being lesbian. The components include the impact of growing up lesbian in a heterosexual society, the "coming out" process, lesbian culture and lesbian lifestyles, lesbian intimate partnership and parenting concerns, differences between lesbian and gay identity, and the life experiences of lesbians who represent diversity in terms of race, ethnicity, and social class. Lesbian feminists also critique the work of those who tend to portray lesbians as female counterparts to gay men, which can lead to marginalization or the assumption that lesbian concerns are synonymous with gay issues. Lesbian concerns must be addressed as legitimate in and of themselves.

Lesbians of color have sometimes critiqued White lesbian feminist theorists for not attending to the diversity of lesbians and the multiple discriminations faced by lesbians of color. Lesbians of color may experience triple discrimination for being women, lesbians, and persons of color. Lesbians of color contend that one must understand the specific cultural factors that underpin lesbian oppression within their ethnic group. For example, within the Black community, Black lesbian feminists are often seen as a threat to "Black nationhood," and "lesbianism" is seen as a White woman's problem. For a true lesbian feminist theory to exist, the concerns of lesbians of different races, ethnicity, and social classes need to be addressed.

Queer theory has increasingly informed the work of some lesbian feminists. Queer theory examines the experiences of people who are marginalized or disparaged because of their sexual orientation; these groups include lesbian, gay, bisexual, and transgendered persons. Some lesbian feminists believe that queer theory allows for the deconstruction of traditional definitions of lesbianism and facilitates new and more flexible self-definitions that do not require individuals to choose between identities. Queer theory may allow for a discussion of sexuality that transcends identity categories such as gender and race because it emphasizes the possibility of experiencing a multiplicity of overlapping female sexualities.

In summary, lesbian feminists call for feminist theory to (1) include an analysis of multiple identities and their relationship to oppression, (2) work toward deconstructing the assumption of normative heterosexuality by being inclusive of multiple sexualities, (3) include a social action component, and (4) be attentive to diversity among lesbians. [*See* Lesbians, Gay Men, and Bisexuals in Relationships.]

IX. *Global/International Feminism*

Global feminism has emerged out of efforts to use frameworks from around the world to examine women's experiences across national boundaries, to analyze their interconnections and interdependencies, and to build links and coalitions with feminists around the world. In order to understand interconnections between women, one must explore the interplay between religion, colonialism, nationalism, and gender. Within global/international feminism, there has generally been limited emphasis on developing a central, coherent theory and more emphasis on creating a global perspective that recognizes the diversity of women's experience. Contributors include a wide range of activists and writers such as Nawal el Saadawi, Robin Morgan, Maria Mies, Charlotte Bunch, Angela Gillian, Chandra Mohanty, Annette Fuentes, Vandana Shiva, and Rosi Braidotti.

At one level, global feminists are interested in understanding and comparing the ways in which economics, classism, racism, and sexism affect women

in different countries. More important, however, is the analysis of how women are constrained and oppressed by large multinational systems. Global feminists also operate from the assumption that the circumstances, choices, and experiences of women in one part of the world have an impact on women in other regions. For example, Western women's efforts to ban harmful birth control methods may be successful in removing them as alternatives in the West, but an unanticipated consequence may be the imposition of these devices on women in other, less wealthy parts of the world. Any local feminist efforts must take into account the global implications of feminist activity.

Economic perspectives are especially important to many global feminist efforts. Multinational business practices and international monetary policies have significant impact on the social structure of many so-called third-world countries. For example, multinational companies have often chosen third-world countries as locations for major factories because they are able to pay workers low wages. Health, safety, and pollution standards are often relaxed, and sexual harassment often accompanies these problems. Women are often disproportionately affected by multinational business practices because they make up a large proportion of the factory workforce. A second major economic issue is related to the monetary lending and repayment policies of powerful institutions such as the World Bank and the International Monetary Fund. Debt repayment policies are often associated with structural changes that trigger wage reductions and cutbacks in public services. These consequences often have especially significant consequences for women, who are often responsible for practical matters such as being accountable for the survival of families on whatever resources are available.

Global feminists also concern themselves with the exploitation of women through sex trafficking, prostitution, and sexual violence. Sex tourism is a major economic enterprise and often intersects with modernization, capitalism, and colonialism in the oppression of women. Third-world countries often benefit financially from sex tourism and trafficking, and thus the governments of these countries often overlook or sanction these forms of oppression against women. Women often enter a profession that sells sexual services as a way of ensuring an impoverished family's survival or may be enticed or "sold" into providing sexual services by agencies that claim to be overseas employment agencies or international mail-order marriage agencies. International feminists are working together to provide refuge to women and to challenge governments to create policies that can protect women from these abuses. Another important issue is the use of rape as a weapon of war or a form of destabilization that reinforces the domination of one group over another or that results in ethnic cleansing.

One of the challenges facing Western feminists is their need to recognize their ethnocentrism and their stereotyping of women around the world. Global feminism challenges Western feminists to recognize that each woman lives under unique systems of oppression and to acknowledge that the assumptions of Western women's feminisms have often promoted the intrusive, patronizing, or disrespectful treatment of women around the world. For example, Western women often view the religion of Islam as a monolithic entity that is highly oppressive to women and have difficulty understanding the complexity and diversity of Islamic women's lives. In the minds of many Western feminists, the veil is often associated with Islamic traditions that signify the seclusion, segregation, and subordination of women. However, Islamic women hold a diversity of views about the importance of the veil or the role of the veil. Some see the veil as promoting self-responsibility and modesty, others as providing protection from the stares of men, and still others as providing practical protection from environmental elements. Some women argue that the separation signified by the veil also unifies women and promotes intimacy between women.

Another ethnocentric practice of Western women has been the tendency to view women in other parts of the world as passive victims who need Western women's expertise and insight to overcome oppression. In reality, many successful and culturally sensitive grassroots feminist efforts are being enacted around the world, and Western feminists can learn much by observing these activist efforts, gaining information about the powerful impact of feminist efforts around the world, and forming coalitions and alliances with these women's groups.

A third issue that has sometimes divided international women is the type of concerns they view as most critical to women. Many Western feminist theories highlight the impact of gender oppression, especially as it relates to sexual issues. However, third-world women often see general economic and political issues as more critical to their oppression than issues that are traditionally defined by West-

erners as gender issues. Some global feminists express frustration with Western feminists who express outrage about the practices of female circumcision or genital mutilation, but seem to have blind spots about the role that multinational corporations, which have powerful roots in their own Western countries, play in the exploitation and oppression of women. Finally, many global feminists note that their exploitation as inhabitants of the third world is often more virulent than their oppression as women. As a result, many third-world women prefer the label "womanist" over the label "feminist," because it implies a commitment to the survival of a people and their society.

A major question that continues to demand attention is the degree to which global feminists should adopt the values of cultural relativism. To what degree does one culture or group of women hold the right to judge the acceptability of another culture's standards? A major challenge facing global feminists is to find some balance that allows for the transcendence of ethnocentrism, but the rejection of the form of relativism that seems to condone virtually any behavior as long as it is acceptable within a specific culture. These behaviors including acts such as domestic violence, sexual violence, bride burning, or honor killings of women who have been "dishonored" by rape. Global feminists focus on the importance of respecting difference, but are still struggling to deal effectively with cultural differences that contribute substantially to the oppression of women.

X. Generation-X Third-Wave Feminism

During the 1990s, a group of primarily young adult women (Generation-Xers) began to identify themselves as third-wave feminists. While acknowledging the contributions of second-wave feminism to feminist theory and practice during the past 30 years, they have also been critical of some aspects of second-wave feminism. They have often characterized second-wave feminists as being somewhat inflexible and dogmatic, too concerned with political correctness, and as having promoted unspoken but important "rules" about what one must believe and do to be a "real" feminist. One of their goals has been to reclaim feminism in their own terms and correct some of the inflexibilities and mistakes of the previous generation. Although recognizing the major economic opportunities available to them as daughters of the second wave and the significant social change brought about by new understandings of issues such as sexual harassment, reproductive freedom, and affirmative action, they have expressed disappointment about the previous generation's limited progress combating major social issues such as the AIDS epidemic, violence against women, economic crises, and ecological concerns. Young third-wave feminists have also expressed dismay about stereotypes that portray feminists as hating men or refusing to shave one's legs. Other younger feminists have argued that their efforts to try to live by the "rules" of second-wave feminism resulted in their artificial efforts to "measure up" or gain the approval of the previous generation's feminists. A consequence was a lack of spontaneity and a need to define feminism in their own terms.

Third-wave feminists have sought to fight a feminist backlash in the larger culture by putting forth a feminism that is flexible, that broadens the public's view of what it means to be feminist, and that allows them to express their individuality and uniqueness. In keeping with their desire to endorse a feminism of action, Generation-X women have been involved in a wide variety of activist causes, such as voter registration, affordable health care, parental law related to abortion, better sex education, violence against women, and the combating of subtle forms of racism.

Although the contributions of Generation-X third-wave feminists have been more practical than theoretical, several themes characterize their critique and contributions. First, their writings have often been highly personal. Some young feminists have argued that academic writings on feminist theory have been of limited help to those attempting to live their lives as feminists. Third-wave authors believe that the political implications of feminism are often most clearly revealed in personal writings. Furthermore, personal writings are more accessible to a wide audience, and they truly show a respect and appreciation for the diversity of experience. The Internet and "zines" have become important methods for sharing these ideas and theories as well as for building activist coalitions.

In keeping with other third-wave perspectives, feminists authors such as Rebecca Walker and Barbara Findlen have highlighted the importance of recognizing multiple identities and rejecting polarities or convenient dichotomies such as male versus female or good versus evil. Thus, they tend to express appreciation for feminisms such as global feminism and women of color feminisms. In addition, these third-wave feminists have aspired to be honest about the daily ambiguities, contradictions, and messy dilemmas that confront them. For example, many published personal narratives embrace seemingly contradictory identities such as being feminist and Christian, being male and feminist, desiring to be "treated as a lady" and being feminist, wanting to be married and devote oneself to the care of children while being a feminist, working as a model and participating in the beauty culture while also being feminist, or enjoying hip-hop music (which is often identified as antifeminist) and being feminist.

Second-wave feminists have expressed concern that younger feminists have been inclined to describe the second wave's contributions in monolithic terms and to label these ideas as obsolete or irrelevant. Gloria Steinem has cautioned young feminists against using their energies to "reinvent the wheel." Whatever its limitations, the emergence of this perspective is a reminder of the importance of each generation defining feminism and gender issues in personally relevant ways. It has also encouraged academic feminists, who are the most prolific creators of theory, to rethink and become more flexible about the manner in which they have created and communicated their work.

SUGGESTED READING

Arneil, B. (1999). *Politics and Feminism.* Blackwell, Malden, MA.

Collins, P. H. (1991). *Black Feminist Thought.* Routledge, New York.

Evans, J. (1995). *Feminist Theory Today: An Introduction to Second-Wave Feminism.* Sage, Thousand Oaks, CA.

hooks, b. (1981). *A'int I a Woman: Black Women and Feminism.* South End Press, Boston.

Kitzinger, C., and Perkins, R. (1993). *Changing Our Minds: Lesbian Feminism and Psychology.* New York University Press, New York.

Meyers, D. T. (ed.) (1997). *Feminist Social Thought: A Reader.* Routledge, New York.

Mohanty, C. T., Russo, A., and Torres, L. (eds.) (1991). *Third World Women and the Politics of Feminism.* Indiana University Press, Bloomington, IN.

Tong, R. P. (1998). *Feminist Thought,* 2nd ed. Westview Press, Boulder, CO.

Walker, R. (ed.) (1995). *To Be Real.* Anchor Books/Doubleday, New York.

Whelehan, I. (1995). *Modern Feminist Thought.* New York University Press, New York.

Friendship Styles

Barbara A. Winstead

Old Dominion University

Jessica L. Griffin

Virginia Consortium Program in Clinical Psychology

Glossary

Diary study Research in which participants respond to the same set of questions every day or several times a week.

Gender segregation Separation of people into female and male groups.

Platonic Emotionally close but not sexual.

Script A stereotyped sequence of actions that describes a well-known situation.

Self-construal Definition one has of oneself.

Self-disclosure Telling others personal information about oneself.

FRIENDSHIP is the crown jewel of human relations. Marked by neither the obligations of family ties nor the emotional ups and downs of romantic relations, it is the relationship that can, at times, carry us from youth to old age, an association that is voluntary and based on mutual values and interests. It has received less attention than the other important relationships in our lives (i.e., family and romantic part- ners), but it has received sufficient attention for us to establish a picture of the role it plays in the lives of women and men and the ways in which gender plays a role in the development and maintenance of friend- ships. This article presents definitions of friendship, explores gender differences in friendship, and then traces the interweaving of gender and friendship as they develop over the life span. The effects on friend- ship of sexual orientation and culture and their in- teractions with gender in relation to friendship will also be examined. In addition, we consider both same-sex and other-sex friendships.

I. Definitions of Friendship

In Western culture, friendship is defined by affection, trust, and loyalty. Paul Wright, who has done exten- sive research on friendship, emphasizes the voluntary nature of friendships (unlike the obligatory nature of kinship), the perception of one's friend as a unique irreplaceable individual, and the reflection of oneself in the eyes of a friend as a good and worthwhile person. In young adults, intimacy, help, companionship, and acceptance are most often mentioned as important functions of same-sex friendships.

In 1985 Keith Davis and Michael Todd sought a description of a prototypical friendship. Their research revealed that friends are expected to participate in the relationship as equals; to enjoy one another's company, to trust, respect, and accept one another; to provide each other with assistance and support and to rely on one another in times of need; to be able to "be themselves" with one another; and to confide in one another or do things together. Although friends are expected to be there for you, Pat O'Connor reported in 1992 that practical help is not an inevitable characteristic of friendship. On the other hand, "being there" may indicate emotional support more often than practical or material support and this may be an important characteristic of a close friend.

Friendship is also a socially constructed and culturally constructed relationship. Understandings and expectations of friendships vary among individuals and are affected by gender and culture. Despite personal wishes for friendship, in reality friendships are also constrained by opportunity (e.g., who is available to meet and interact with; how much time there is to establish and maintain a friendship). These opportunities or lack of opportunity are also shaped by age, culture, social class, lifestyle, and gender.

II. *Gender Differences in Friendships*

In 1982 Paul Wright captured the essence of the consistently documented gender differences by describing women's friendships as "face to face" and men's as "side by side." These phrases reflect research outcomes indicating that women are more likely than men to choose to spend time "just talking," whereas men are more likely than women to choose doing an activity with their friend. Women describe their same-sex friendships as more emotionally close, intimate, and satisfying than men do, and women express more affection, verbal and physical, for their friends. Reviews of the research literature on gender differences in friendship have also raised numerous questions to consider when seeking a deeper understanding of gender and friendship: Are gender differences an artifact of self-report methodologies; do women and men define friendship in similar ways; do gender differences in friendship intimacy arise from gender differences in expectations, capacity, or preference?

A. METHODOLOGY

As with most psychological phenomena, especially in adolescents or adults, friendship has been studied primarily by self-reports. Self-report instruments pose several problems, including willingness, honesty, and accuracy. Although human research participants are volunteers, they may vary in their motivation for being in a research project and in their willingness to comply with instructions. They may choose to spend as little time as possible in filling out questionnaires. Despite researcher assurances of anonymity or confidentiality, they may be reluctant to be fully self-disclosing. Even when adequately motivated and honest, they may simply not remember information or not know themselves well enough to give responses that accurately reflect their behavior. These problems with self-report are exacerbated by gender. Gender stereotypes and beliefs about gender differences are ubiquitous. It is difficult for individuals to give information about their own behavior in an arena affected by gendered expectations without having their responses influenced by these expectations. Self-reports of intimacy, emotional closeness, affection, and perhaps even talking may be influenced by participants' beliefs about what is normal or appropriate for someone of their sex to report. Clearly, it is more acceptable in American culture for heterosexual women to self-report close, loving, emotional ties with another, especially another woman, than it is for heterosexual men to report these experiences with another, especially another man.

Although we would prefer more direct measures of friendship behaviors, it is also true that participants are unlikely to behave in completely natural ways in the artificial setting of the laboratory, nor are we likely to see the full range of friendship behaviors. In this review, however, particular attention is paid to those studies that have gone beyond the simplest forms of self-report.

There is also reason to raise questions about who participates in studies of friendship. Psychological researchers typically solicit volunteers for their research, generally for some incentive, such as extra credit for undergraduates or a fee for participation. Robin Lewis, Barbara Winstead, and Valerian Derlega found in 1989 that undergraduate men are less likely than women to volunteer to participate in a study of relationships when given a choice to participate in a more "neutral" (cognition) study. In other situations, researchers attempt to get full participation from an identified sample, but females may still be more likely than males to sign up for or return questionnaires when the subject matter is relationships. [*See* METHODS FOR STUDYING GENDER.]

B. GENDER AND DEFINITIONS OF FRIENDSHIP

If women's friendships and men's friendships are different, then perhaps it is because women and men have different definitions, expectations, or norms governing these relationships. In 1992 Michael Monsour asked undergraduates how they defined intimacy in their same-sex close relationships. Both women and men mentioned self-disclosure most frequently, followed by emotional expressiveness, support, physical contact, and trust. Women, however, were more likely (87%) than men (56%) to list self-disclosure and, although infrequently endorsed over all, shared activities were mentioned by none of the women, but 9% of the men. On the other hand, the second most frequent meaning, emotional expressiveness, was mentioned by 28% of women and 31% of men. Thus, there is substantial overlap but also differences in how women and men define intimacy in same-sex friendships. Monsour also examined definitions of intimacy in cross-sex friendships. As with same-sex friendships, women's and men's definitions were generally similar; but although they do not often mention sexual contact, twice as many men (16%) as women (8%) do mention sexual contact as a meaning of intimacy in cross-sex friendships. On the other hand, in a sample of professional women and men, in 1988 Linda Sapadin asked participants to finish the sentence, "A friend is someone . . ." and found no gender differences in the categories used to code these responses. [*See* EMPATHY AND EMOTIONAL EXPRESSIVITY; INTIMACY AND LOVE.]

In 1999 Diane Felmlee examined social norms in same- and cross-sex friendships. She provided vignettes of same-sex or cross-sex friendship interactions and asked undergraduate participants to rate the appropriateness of the behaviors in the interaction. Participants also provided open-ended responses regarding friendship norms. Felmlee found that, in general, women and men agree that in both same- and cross-sex friendships hugging and crying are appropriate, giving a surprise gift is neither appropriate nor inappropriate, canceling plans is inappropriate, and shoving is very inappropriate. Gender differences were present, but small. Women were more approving of crying and hugging and less accepting of shoving. Felmlee also found that women used more normative words than men did for both female and male friends. Women were more likely to

write that their friends "should," "ought," "must," or "are expected to" behave in certain ways. Also, men were twice as likely to refer to friendship norms when explaining a female friend's behavior compared to a male friend's behavior. Generally, women's and men's definitions of same- and cross-sex friendships are similar and the gender differences that do occur are small. Men's same-sex friendships, however, may be governed by fewer norms than other friendship dyads.

C. GENDER COMPARISONS IN SAME-SEX FRIENDSHIPS

When we observe, through self-reports or other methods, what women and men actually do in their friendships, we find some consistent gender differences. In 1988 Richard Aukett, Jane Ritchie, and Kathryn Mill replicated U.S. findings in a New Zealand sample. They found that when given a choice between doing some activity together or just talking with a same-sex friend, more than three times as many women (57%, U.S.; 58%, N.Z.) as men (16%, U.S.; 18%, N.Z.) chose talking and half as many women (43%, U.S.; 42%, N.Z.) as men (84%, U.S.; 82%, N.Z.) chose sharing an activity. The forced-choice self-report may contribute to these rather dramatic gender differences.

In 1989 Elizabeth Mazur found that when undergraduates described friendship episodes with same-sex friends, women were more likely than men to describe unstructured activities and less likely to describe structured or group activities. Women were also more likely to report episodes with personal self-disclosure and with high levels of personal involvement. Using high school students as participants, Andrea Hussong found in 2000 that young women reported more self-disclosure, affection, and loyalty, but similar levels of companionship, in their same-sex best friendships compared to young men. These gender effects were small to moderate. Young men reported more overt and covert verbal control of best same-sex friends, but this gender effect was small.

In 1999 in a study of a community sample, Kirsten Voss, Dorothy Markiewicz, and Anna Beth Doyle found that although the participants' descriptions of spouses as friends showed few gender differences, women rated their same-sex best friends higher than men rated their same-sex best friends on levels of supportiveness, security, concern, desire to spend free time together, ability to stimulate interest in new and exciting activities, and helpfulness.

Linda Sapadin asked professional women and men what they liked about their friendships. Both women and men most frequently mentioned "sharing/enjoying"; but the actual behaviors described by men tended to have "a group, activity, or fun orientation," while women's responses emphasized sharing and exchanging thoughts and feelings. Also, men were more likely to give responses coded as "sharing/enjoying," while women were twice as likely (28%) as men (14%) to say what they liked most about a same-sex friend was "caring/acceptance."

Many researchers have conceptualized these gender differences in terms of women having more "expressive" relationships and men having more "instrumental" relationships. Paul Wright and Mary Beth Scanlon, however, concluded in 1991 that friendships between women are both expressive and instrumental. They found that women reported their same-sex friendships were especially strong and rewarding compared to their friendships with men and men's friendships with either women or men.

On the other hand, when undergraduates were asked to rate the purpose of actual interactions with friends collected in a diary study, Steve Duck and Paul Wright found in 1993 that both women and men reported that they got together most often just to talk. Shared activities or tasks were the second most frequently endorsed purpose.

Studies of what friends report talking about consistently reveal gender differences. Elizabeth Aries and Fern Johnson have studied what young and older adults report talking about in their same-sex friendships. In studies published in 1983 they found that, among young adults, women talk to same-sex close friends with greater frequency and depth about other relationships, personal problems, and secrets from the past. Men talked with greater frequency and in greater depth about sports; they also talk more frequently about hobbies and shared activities. In a sample of older adults the gender differences were smaller, but women friends still talked more about personal problems and relationships and men talked more about sports and work.

When asked to describe typical conversations with same-sex friends, Lynne Davidson and Lucile Duberman found in 1982 that women compared to men gave almost twice as many personal and three times as many relationship accounts. There were no gender differences in mentions of topical, nonpersonal conversations. Women rated all types of conversation (personal, relational, and topical) as equally important, but men rated topical conversation as more

important than relational or personal. In 1985 Harry Reis, Marilyn Senchak, and Beth Solomon asked same-sex friend dyads to describe their last meaningful conversation and what they talked about on the way to a laboratory study. They found that for both of these reported conversations, women's conversations were rated as more intimate than men's conversations. However, when these same dyads engaged in a meaningful conversation in the laboratory, there were no sex differences in the ratings of the intimacy of the conversations, either by observers or by the participants themselves.

Various measures of the affective qualities of friendship also reveal that women view their same-sex friends more positively than men view theirs. In fact, men are sometimes found to rate their female friends more positively than their male friends. Sapadin found that among professional women and men, ratings of intimacy, enjoyment, and nurturance were highest for women rating same-sex friendships and lowest for men rating same-sex friends. Women are more satisfied with and feel closer to their same-sex friends than men do. Women are also more likely to be affectionate with close friends, including showing more physical attention. Based on research on affectionate communication in dyadic relationships in 1997, Kory Floyd concluded that male-male dyads engage in fewer and less intense enacted affection (verbal and nonverbal) than female-female or opposite-sex dyads and that affection in male-male dyads is considered less appropriate than in other dyads.

Francesca Cancian in 1987 and Julia Wood and Christopher Inman in 1993 have argued that research on intimacy and closeness may be marred by "feminine" definitions of these terms. It is possible that expressions of affection, verbal and physical, are comfortable and acceptable for women but not for men and that men's interpersonal closeness is better captured by sharing activities or doing things for one another. In 1989 Scott Swain reported that when asked to describe meaningful interactions with friends, three-quarters of the men he interviewed named activities other than talking. He also concluded that men's same-sex friendships were characterized by an exchange of favors and assistance. According to Swain, these behaviors and joking relationships may be implicit or covert expressions of affection, which women are able to express directly and overtly. Women tend to seek confidantes with whom to share personal thoughts and feelings; men seek companions with whom to do things. These gender differences contrast, however, with Monsour's finding that women and men both define intimacy in their close friendships similarly, mentioning self-disclosure most frequently followed by emotional expressiveness, support, physical contact, trust, and mutual activities, in declining order.

In an effort to distinguish between gender as a predictor of mean differences in friendship qualities and gender's effect on structural differences in friendship, Hussong examined intimacy and peer control in adolescent friendships. She measured both gender differences in frequency of reported behavior and gender differences in the behaviors that serve as indicators of the constructs, intimacy and peer control. Gender differences in indicators would support the notion that female and male adolescents achieve intimacy or peer control in friendships through different behaviors (i.e., that the structures of female and male same-sex friendships are different). Hussong found only moderate support for this hypothesis. Contrary to her hypothesis, overt behaviors were more indicative of peer control in girls than in boys. As expected, companionship was more strongly connected to intimacy for boys than for girls, but only marginally. Other factors (self-disclosure, loyalty, and affection) were equally strongly indicated by intimacy for both girls and boys. [*See* ADOLESCENT GENDER DEVELOPMENT.]

It has also been suggested that men choose less intimacy, despite similar notions about what it is, because they want less intimacy in same-sex friendships. But when asked by Adelaide Haas and Mark Sherman in 1982 how they would improve their conversations with same-sex others, although many reported no need for improvement (27%), 20% of men mention that they wished for more openness. Research results on gender differences in satisfaction with friendships are mixed. Elizabeth Mazur found that while women and men differed in their manner of engaging in friendship, they were similar in their perceptions of the outcome of friendship. In her study, despite women reporting more personal self-disclosure and involvement in friendship episodes, women and men gave similar ratings to the episodes on meaningfulness, pleasantness, and satisfaction. On the other hand, John Reisman reported in 1990 that men are less satisfied with their same-sex friends, suggesting that some men at least see something lacking in these relationships.

In trying to make sense of the complex research and theoretical literature on gender differences in same-sex friendships, Beverly Fehr in 1996 considered seven possible answers to the question:

Are women's friendships really more intimate than men's? Men are as intimate as women, but only in their closest friendships; men are as intimate as women, they just don't like the word; men appear less intimate only because intimacy is defined in a female way; men simply are less intimate, regardless of the definition; the same definition, but different thresholds for intimacy; men are less intimate, but they like it that way; men can be as intimate as women, but simply choose not to be. (pp. 133–140)

This covers most of the possible interpretations and criticisms of the reported gender differences. Fehr concludes,

[T]he evidence seems to suggest that men's friendships are less intimate than women's are. It is not the case that men are reserving intimacy only for their closest friends. It is also not the case that men simply are reluctant to use the word. Nor is it a matter of being evaluated by the wrong (i.e., feminine) metric or having a different threshold. Instead, it appears that men are less intimate than women in their friendships because they choose to be, even though they may not particularly like it. (pp. 140–141)

D. GENDER COMPARISONS IN CROSS-SEX FRIENDSHIPS

We take for granted that friendship means same-sex friendship; and across the life span same-sex friendships are more common, and generally less problematic, than cross-sex friendships. But among young adults and single adults and in the workplace, cross-sex friendships are increasingly accepted and valued. As women and men delay marriage, as women become an increasing presence in the workplace, and as jobs become less gender segregated, cross-sex friendships become more common in the United States.

Results of research done in the 1980s show that cross-sex friendships are less intimate and less stable, less supportive and less satisfying, and there is less self-disclosure in cross-sex friendships. On the other hand, Keith Davis and Michael Todd found similar levels of trust, respect, acceptance, spontaneity, and enjoyment in cross-sex friendships; and just as Steve Duck and Paul Wright found for same-sex friendships, Kathy Werking reported in 1997 that the most frequently reported activity for cross-sex friends was talking together.

J. Donald O'Meara in 1994 described five challenges to cross-sex friendships: (1) opportunity, (2) sexuality, (3) emotional bonding, (4) gender inequality, and (5) presenting the relationship to the public. Werking suggested yet another challenge: "shedding friendship expectations and behaviors learned in the context of same-sex friendship" (p. 51). That these writers speak in terms of challenges is in and of itself telling of our attitude toward cross-sex friendship. Where same-sex friendship is natural and pleasurable, cross-sex friendship is challenging.

Suzanna Rose found in 1985 that young adults have a specific script to describe how same-sex friendships are formed, but although all participants had a cross-sex friendship, they were likely to describe cross-sex friendships as just happening. One-third of her participants listed sexual attraction as the reason for initiating a cross-sex friendship, although sexual or romantic feelings are usually used as an exclusion criterion for a friendship. One-third simply said they had no strategy for forming cross-sex friendships.

All of the undergraduates in Rose's study reported having cross-sex friendships. High school and college may provide the social contexts that are most conducive to forming and keeping cross-sex friendships. As individuals move into adult work and family roles, numbers of cross-sex friends decrease and a gender gap appears. The workplace is gender segregated and adult gender roles tend to separate men from women. Men may have more cross-sex friendships because their work roles provide more opportunities for developing them. Rose found that among single adults, all the men but just 73% of the women reported having close cross-sex friends, while 67% of married men and only 53% of married women reported cross-sex friends. These age and sex differences reflect the opportunity challenge.

Michael Monsour, Bridgid Harris, and Nancy Kurzweil in 1994 tested whether the other O'Meara challenges were present in cross-sex friendships. They found problems in some friendships, but not in a majority. Issues concerning the emotional bond were reported most frequently. There may be a concern about how close this relationship should be and what kind of priority it should have in reference to other relationships, especially heterosexual romantic relationships.

Following issues of the emotional bond, respondents expressed some concern with public image, sexuality, and equality. Cross-sex friendships can require more explaining and can be a source of jealousy in dating or marital relationships. Men reported more issues with sexuality than women did. Sapadin found equal numbers of women (6%) and men (7%) mention sexual excitement as something they like about their cross-sex friendships, but more men (28%) than women (20%), and a substantial minor-

ity of both, mention sexual tension as something they dislike about cross-sex friendships. As mentioned earlier, more men than women mention sexual contact as a meaning of intimacy in cross-sex friendships. [*See* Sexuality and Sexual Desires.]

The challenges of inequality and gendered expectations in friendship both address the question of how women and men deal with the issue of gender roles in a cross-sex friendship. There is some support for the notion that women and men value in cross-sex friendships the "other" gender's way of doing things. Rose found that women report experiencing more companionship from male than from female friends. But perhaps because an ideal friendship relies on female-gendered skills, men are more advantaged by cross-sex friendships. They report receiving more acceptance, intimacy, and emotional support from their women friends than from their men friends and feeling closer to these cross-sex friends. Both women and men feel more comfortable confiding in and disclosing to women. In a sample of professional women and men, Sapadin found that men, but not women, rated their cross-sex friends higher for overall quality, enjoyment, and nurturance. Although men may benefit from gender differences in friendship behaviors, receiving more from female friends than women receive from male friends, Sapadin also found that what professional women and men like most in their cross-sex friendships was the opportunity to find out what the other sex thought and felt about important relationship and career issues.

Relationship skills have generally been assigned less status than achievement, leadership, or competitive skills. A course on what it takes to be a good friend is far less likely to be found on the market than what it takes to be a good manager. The lack of symmetry in cross-sex friendships—women give more, men get more—can be a sign not just of gendered social skills but of inequality. Sapadin found that some professional women (9%) viewed their cross-sex friends as patronizing.

Kathy Werking, in interviews and surveys asking women and men to compare their same- and cross-sex friendships, confirmed the observation that men find women more receptive, personal, nurturing, and accepting than their men friends. Women in her sample, however, reported primarily similarities between their same- and cross-sex friendships. "The most striking similarity . . . centered on the salience and quality of talk and in the degree of emotional interdependency achieved through that talk" (p. 62).

III. *Gender and Friendship across the Life Span*

Girls like to play with girls and boys, with boys. Preference for same-sex others begins in the toddler years. In 1987 Laura Hayden-Thompson, Kenneth Rubin, and Shelley Hymel found that by two years of age, girls show a preference for same-sex playmates; for boys, a clear same-sex preference occurs by three years of age. Boys are also less cooperative in their play and less responsive to other children. Eleanor Maccoby argued in 1990 that girls may avoid play with boys because their play tends to be more competitive and rough.

A well-established finding in research on children's friendships is that boys play in groups and girls prefer dyads. This sex difference has been observed in kindergartners and is well established by the elementary-school years. Janet Lever in her 1978 observations of children's play found that boys spend more time playing games with complex rules, where players have well-defined roles and outcomes are winning or losing, whereas girls play in dyads or small groups games of pretend or turn-taking games (e.g., jacks, jump rope) with less role differentiation. In 1992 Lora Moller, Shelley Hymel, and Kenneth Rubin observed the free-play of second and fourth graders. They found that boys engaged in more solitary and rough-and-tumble play than girls. By fourth grade, boys engaged in more group games with rules, whereas girls engaged in more parallel, side-by-side, and constructive play. Sex differences were more pronounced in the fourth graders.

A great deal of learning about social behavior occurs among peers. Girls and boys grow up in separate, sex-segregated social worlds where boys learn to vie for attention and dominance and girls learn to cooperate and to be emotionally expressive and sensitive to the feelings of others. Lever concluded that boys learn team membership skills, fair play, and following rules from the types of games they play.

By grades 4 and 5, some of the differences observed in adult same-sex friendships emerge. Girls are more likely than boys to talk with same-sex friends, self-disclose, and share secrets. In 1989 Marcela Raffaelli and Elena Duckett paged girls and boy in grades 5 to 9 and asked them to report on what they were doing at the moment. Girls were more likely than boys to report talking with friends. By grade 9, girls reported spending more than twice as much time (9 hours) "just talking" with friends as

boys did (4 hours). Raffaelli and Duckett also found that in grade 9, girls' conversations were about personal concerns or other people 73% of the time, while these topics made up only 33% of the boys' talk. Boys were more likely than girls to talk about sports and leisure activities.

In a 1996 study of 12- to 15-year-old adolescents, Duane Buhrmester found that girls reported more frequent interactions with friends and they reported much higher levels of self-disclosure and emotional support in their daily interactions with same-sex friends, although they found gender similarities in honesty, straightforwardness, mutual activities, loyalty, and commitment in same-sex friendships. In 1993 M. L. Clark and Marla Ayers found that seventh and eighth grade girls both expected and received more empathic understanding from their best friends than boys did. By adolescence, then, the gender differences in intimacy in same-sex friendships have been established.

Cross-sex friendships are rarely public in childhood. The prohibition that develops in the elementary-school years against interacting with the other sex makes cross-sex friendships difficult. In 1986 John Gottman found that while preschool girls and boys might be best friends, older children who were friends with other-sex children maintained their friendships in secret and often ignored each other at school to avoid being teased. In 1999 William Bukowski, Lorrie Sippola, and Betsy Hoza examined the role of cross-sex friendships in early adolescence. They found that fifth, sixth, and seventh graders prefer same-sex peers, but this preference is more marked for girls than for boys. Both girls and boys who are either very popular or very unpopular are more likely than other children to have cross-sex friends. For unpopular boys, having a cross-sex friend served a positive function by increasing their sense of competence (a "backup system" to same-sex friendship that the authors had predicted). But for girls without same-sex friends, having a cross-sex friend predicted less positive perceptions of personal well-being. As with adults, cross-sex friendships are more beneficial for males than for females. [*See* CLASSROOM AND SCHOOL CLIMATE.]

Much of the research on gender differences in friendship focuses on young adults, most often college students. What happens to friendship as adults enter other stages of their lives: work, marriage, parenting, retirement, old age? Entering marriage or a committed relationship generally means an increase in involvement with kin. Partners are often considered "best friends" and may fill the roles of confidante and activity partner. Forming committed relationships introduces new family relationships (in-laws) and the arrival of children usually intensifies this trend toward focus on family and away from friends. Friendships formed in childhood, adolescence, or young adulthood may also be disrupted by geographic mobility, as adults pursue jobs and romantic relationships that draw them away from established friendships. These "old" friendships do not necessarily fade, indeed they are often valued throughout an adult's life; but they no longer serve the functions of good times or emotional support that require availability. Pat O'Connor found that for lower-middle-class women, geographical stability increased the likelihood of having a confidante. To the extent that men's style of same-sex friendship involvement is less emotionally intense, less intimate, and more based on doing things together, new friendships that meet their expectations may be easier to establish—a golfing relationship can replace a skateboarding relationship. Even "old" friendships, if they did not depend on shared confidences and mutual emotional support, may be easier to maintain. For women the challenge to friendship of these transitions may be greater. Women may form friendships at work, but unlike men they tend not to regard these relationships as close friendships.

O'Connor has explored the paradoxes of same-sex friendships for married women. She discovered that married women acknowledge the primacy of their marital and family relationships, but often find emotional support in friendship that is less readily available from the marriage. These women find in friendships an opportunity to talk about relationship problems and their roles as wife and mother. Women's friendships complement rather than compete with the marital bond. Women also have fewer resources, such as time, money, and personal space to develop and maintain friendships.

Work can provide women with more economic resources, but for women with families, the "double shift" means they have even less time to invest in friendships. O'Connor reported, in a study of college alumnae, that women in full-time paid employment were less likely to have a best friend than women in part-time employment or those not working outside the home. Wright has argued that women in particular are unlikely to find the intimacy they seek in best friends in their coworker friendships. Nevertheless, work does serve as a source of friends for both women and men. [*See* WORKING ENVIRONMENTS.]

Aging often means a further reduction in friendship networks. Retirement, physical restrictions, geographic relocation to be closer to family or to live in a smaller living unit, retirement community, or care facility in addition to losses of friends through illness and death all reduce the availability of friends. Friendship needs may actually increase as their availability decreases. Although women are more likely than men to experience the loss of a marital partner (through a combination of longer life expectancies and the custom of younger women marrying somewhat older men), they may find greater friendship resources at this transition because they have nurtured these relationships, rather than relying solely on a spouse. Men tend to restrict their close and emotionally supportive relationships to their wives. When marital partners are lost, men are particularly negatively affected. Toni Antonnuci found in 1994 that women are more likely than men to report both giving and receiving support from their friends. Widowhood is also more normative for women and there are more same-sex others in similar circumstances to befriend.

The elderly turn to their families for practical support, but the need for help from kin can paradoxically undermine older adults' feelings of self-worth and well-being. In an important 1999 study of the meaning of being a friend, Darcy Clay Siebert, Elizabeth Mutran, and Donald Reitzes found that, in a sample of aging adults, one's role identity as a friend was a stronger predictor of life satisfaction than marriage, income, occupation, and other background variables.

IV. *Sexual Orientation and Friendship*

Nearly all work on friendship has assumed that same-sex friendships are necessarily platonic, whereas cross-sex friends must deal with issues of sexual tension. This is not true for lesbians and gay men. How do they experience same- and cross-gender friendships?

In 1994 Peter Nardi and Drury Sherrod wrote, "It can be argued that cross-gender friendships among heterosexual men and women share some of the same features as same-gender friendships among gay men and lesbians, since both types of friendships contain at least the possibility of sexual attraction" (p. 187). In their 1994 research, Nardi and Sherrod found marked similarities in the same-sex friendships of lesbians and gay men. Specifically, they found no differences in social support, in self-disclosure, or in the number of types of activities performed together. Lesbians did not report more conflicts in their same-sex friendships, but, compared to gay men, they were more bothered by conflict, felt it was more important and were more likely to express their feelings in handling the conflict. Many lesbians (34–59%) and gay men (56–76%) reported having had sex with their same-sex casual, close, or best friends; but gay men were more likely than lesbians to report having had sex with casual or close, but not best, friends.

In a 1987 study of lesbian and heterosexual feminists, Suzanna Rose and Laurie Roades found that lesbian feminists reported lower relationship quality and degree of equality in their friendships compared to heterosexual feminist (and nonfeminist) women. The researchers acknowledged that these differences may be artifactual because they instructed lesbians not to rate their partners as same-sex friends. They conclude that lesbians same-sex friendship needs may be satisfied by their romantic relationship.

To date there is little empirical research on lesbians and gay men in same-sex friendships and none that we know of in cross-sex friendships. Yet the supportive aspects of friendships for these groups are important to understand and variations on friendship patterns in these populations can further our ability to conceptualize the role of gender in same- and cross-sex friendships. For example, the differences between romantic and platonic relationships may be further clarified in a population where these are both with same-sex others. [*See* Lesbians, Gay Men, and Bisexuals in Relationships.]

V. Culture and Friendship

Most of the data presented have come from North American or European samples. Definitions, norms, and expectations of friendship vary by culture. Reisman's research included a sample of Hungarian college students. Lists of topics discussed with friends by U.S. and Hungarian students were similar and the gender differences were the same; women in both countries reported discussing personal problems and feelings more often with their friends than men did.

In 1996 Maykel Verkuyten and Kees Masson examined the effects of collectivism and individualism on perceptions of same-sex friends in a multiethnic high school population, including Dutch, Turkish, Moroccan, Southern European, and Asian students. Collectivism refers to a worldview that stresses interdependence, sharing, identity with the group, and a need for stable and predetermined relationships. Individualism emphasizes autonomy, independence, right to privacy, and personal choice in relationships. As expected, individuals high on collectivism were more attentive and sensitive to their friends; used more social characteristics, such as ethnicity, gender, and religion in describing their best friends; reported having fewer best friends but perceiving these friends as closer; and endorsed more rules for friendships. Conversely, individuals high on individualism were less sensitive to friends and used more personal or achieved characteristics when describing best friends. Men were found to be more individualistic than women; but cultural values did not interact with gender. Verkuyten and Masson found that

women showed a greater attentiveness and sensitivity to their friend than did men . . . women used more personal characteristics in explaining their relationship with their best friend, perceived their relationship with their best friend as more close, shared more intimate information with their best friend, endorsed more the importance of trust and confidence in friendships, and also endorsed rules about relations with third parties more often. (p. 215)

Thus, gender differences typically found in North American and European samples were also found in this multiethnic sample. [*See* Individualism and Collectivism.]

On the other hand, in 1988 John Berman, Virginia Murphy-Berman, and Anju Pachauri investigated the effects of gender and culture on perceptions of friends in India and the United States. They found that in the United States, women gave higher ratings than men to socializing and problem sharing as reasons why someone was their best friend. There were no gender differences in ratings of reasons for choosing someone as a best friend in the Indian sample.

Understanding the norms and expectations for friends and for females and males in a culture must inform our research in this area. In addition to individualism and collectivism, the most frequently studied cultural dimensions, the power differential between the sexes in a culture and the separation versus integration of women in public life are important dimensions to consider when investigating the role of gender and culture in friendships.

VI. *Origins and Outcomes of Gender Effects on Friendship*

A. ORIGINS

If we accept the observation that women and men end up with different sorts of friendships, and, especially, that women have more intimate, emotionally close friendships, we should ask ourselves how did this come about? When we consider origins of gender comparisons, we can hypothesize that there are structural or individual explanations for these differences. Structural explanations emphasize gender roles, social expectations, opportunities or restrictions, and situational demands; individual explanations emphasize personal characteristics, needs, and values that may be the result of biological differences between the sexes or gender socialization. As with most other gender differences in psychological phenomena, the literature on gender differences in friendship has focused primarily on individual differences, but we should be alert in particular to the kinds of structural factors that may influence these gender differences.

In explaining the early occurring differences in friendship and play patterns, the primary structural factors that have received attention are gender segregation and team sports. Adults may separate children into same-sex groups and use gender as markers ("the girls' team and the boys' team") that reinforce the salience of gender to children learning about the social world of peers. Also, the tendency of adults to "romanticize" cross-sex relationships ("girlfriend," "boyfriend," rather than just friend) implicitly supports peers' tendency to tease children engaged in cross-sex friendships. But Eleanor Maccoby has argued that same-sex peer interactions are primarily a choice made by children, as early as preschool. As discussed earlier, aspects of boys' play and interactive style may make boys unrewarding as friends for girls. Boys also tend to avoid interactions with girls; and there is ample evidence that social pressure on boys to avoid the feminine begins very early. Maccoby has argued that girls and boys seek same-sex interactions, and that preference for same-sex interaction (i.e., gender segregation) is more evident, not less, when children are not directly supervised by adults. Even casual observation, however, confirms that adults persist in having children line up by sex and form teams by sex. Thus, whatever the origin, adults generally reinforce the same-sex social worlds of children.

As with gender segregation, one can argue that gender differences in play (i.e., girls play in smaller groups or dyads and engage in turn-taking and less complex games than boys) are the result of child preference, adult directives, or both. Clearly, boys have more often been included and encouraged in the sports arena. A marked change since the 1970s, however, is the rate of participation of girls in team sports. With the passage of Title IX in 1972, prohibiting discrimination, including gender discrimination, in any federally funded educational program, girls' participation in high school and college sports has increased dramatically. According to a 1997 report by the U.S. Department of Education, girls' participation in high school athletics rose from 7.5% in 1971 to 39% in 1996; participation by women in college athletics rose from 15% in 1972 to 37% in 1995. All-girl teams and mixed teams are available in nearly every team sport and the increasing number of women's professional teams (as well as college scholarships) provides not only role models but also incentives for girls to develop athletic and team participation skills. To date there is no empirical evidence that girls' participation on sports teams alters their friendship patterns or preferences, but this is a possibility that should be investigated. [*See* PLAY PATTERNS AND GENDER.]

Many studies exploring gender roles for women and men emphasize the communal or nurturing roles that women are expected to fill and the autonomous and agentic roles that men are expected to play. Researchers have, in fact, placed the gender differences observed in friendships in the context of these well-researched gender roles. To understand these gender roles we can also turn to structural or individual explanations. Alice Eagly's social role interpretation of gender differences in social behavior argues that the major source of these differences is division of labor between the sexes. Women are caretakers and service providers (even in their occupations), roles that require nurturing and socioemotional skills; men are more likely to be skilled laborers, technicians, or managers, roles that require physical, intellectual, or leadership skills. The sorts of interpersonal skills required by a reciprocal, emotionally close relationship between equals (i.e., a friendship) would seem to be those found more often in women's roles, not men's. Fehr has argued, however, that men do not lack skills, but in fact choose to be less intimate with their same-sex friends. It may be that establishing friendships that are similar to other gendered roles is itself reinforcing.

Ever present social norms may, in part, govern gender differences in same-sex friendships. Women have been found to be more physically affectionate with same-sex friends. The norms that might shape this difference were demonstrated in a 1989 study by Valerian Derlega, Robin Lewis, Scott Harrison, Barbara Winstead, and Bob Costanza, which found that pictures of two men putting their arms around one another's waists were judged to be significantly less normal than pictures showing two women or a woman and man putting their arms around one another's waists. In other words, society perceives expressions of physical affection between men as suspect, whereas similar behavior between two women is acceptable.

At the level of individual explanations for gender differences, biological factors may come into play. In 2000, Shelley Taylor and her colleagues argued that female responses to stress have evolved to include a "tend and befriend" in addition to or rather than the "fight or flight" response. If the link between physiological and behavioral differences is confirmed, women's and men's friendship styles may be found to have biological as well as socialization origins. [*See* DEVELOPMENT OF SEX AND GENDER.]

Many have elaborated on the socialization experiences that cause girls and women to be more empathic and attuned to others in close relationships and boys and men to be more autonomous and that cause both girls and boys to acquire and adopt gendered social rules. In 1997 Susan Cross and Laura Madson presented the case for explaining gender differences in social behavior, as well as cognition, motivation, and emotion, in terms of women's and men's different self-construals. Men in the United States, they propose, construct and maintain an independent self-construal, whereas women construct and maintain an interdependent self-construal. "Whereas individuals with an interdependent self-construal [women] may develop skills and behaviors that facilitate the development of close relationships with others, individuals with an independent self-construal [men] may perceive the intimacy created by these behaviors as a threat to their sense of autonomy" (p. 17).

However, Voss, Markiewicz, and Doyle tested the hypothesis that relationship qualities of marriages and same-sex friendships would be more closely related to women's self-esteem than to men's self-esteem. While they found that both marital adjustment and friendship quality are significantly related to self-esteem for both sexes, they did not find that women's self-esteem was more affected than men's.

Seeking the origin of gender differences is a complex task. Both social norms and expectations and biological or learned individual differences should be examined. It is unlikely that any one source will be found to account for a large portion of the variance between women and men.

B. BENEFITS AND COSTS OF FRIENDSHIP

Whatever the origin of the gender differences in friendship, what are the consequences? Friendships are widely regarded as providing important benefits: social support, emotional support, self-clarification through self-disclosure, and identity validation. As described earlier, however, Bukowski, Sippola, and Hoza found that girls without same-sex friends were less well off when they had cross-sex friends than when they had none. This finding surprised these researchers because it has generally been believed that friendship is always associated with affective well-being. It takes only common sense to recognize the benefits of friendships; but are there costs?

O'Connor, while repeatedly citing the many benefits of friendships for women, explored the paradox that friendships may also support the social status quo. Friendships, she wrote, "while strengthening women's individuality, subordinated the claims of that individuality to their marriage and their family responsibilities" (p. 86). By helping us get through the day, a good friend may, perhaps unintentionally, prevent us from asking ourselves how we can change the situation rather than cope with it.

Having a friend means being a friend. Identity as a friend is a strong positive predictor of life satisfaction. But the sort of mutual support and emotional closeness expected of women in same-sex friendships may also be a source of stress. Being a friend means living up to the standards expected of friends. Women endorse more rules for friends about relationships with third parties, and men have fewer norms for same-sex friends than they do for cross-sex friends or than women have for either same- or cross-sex friends. Men make fewer demands of their male friends and are more forgiving of their male friends' mistakes. Men have higher expectations of their female friends and women have higher expectations of both female and male friends. Being held to higher standards in both their same- and cross-sex friendships may also be a stressor for women.

On balance it is likely that women gain more than they lose from the more intimate, emotionally giving and receiving friendships that they develop, especially with other women. But the potential costs of relationships should also be included in our calculations.

VII. The Future of Gender and Friendship

Research on any topic waxes and wanes. After a flowering of friendship research in the 1970s and 1980s, friendship research seems to have withered somewhat. Friendship, however, will always be a cornerstone of human relatedness and should continue to be the focus of empirical study. Cross-sex friendship has received more attention as it has become more of a reality in Western society, but has yet to have benefited from the scrutiny given same-sex friendship. Friendships among gays and lesbians, who may rely even more than heterosexual adults on these relationships for support, are infrequently studied. The impact of culture on the relationship between gender and friendship also deserves further study. Understanding how culture determines appropriate roles for women and men, and for their relationships with others, can help unravel the meaning of gender in relationships.

The events in society today that are most likely to influence patterns of women's and men's friendships are women's entry into the workplace and the gradual breakdown of gender segregation of occupations, changes in women's and men's roles at work and at home, and girls' and women's increasing participation in sports. Gender integration in the workplace provides more opportunities for cross-sex friendships that, to the extent that they are satisfying in different ways from same-sex friendships, may cause individuals, especially men, to reexamine the nature of their same-sex friendships. Or cross-sex friendships may become a more valued source of meaningful and supportive interaction. As responsibilities for economic and family work shift, expectations for women and men in terms of nurturing/cooperative versus achievement/competitive behaviors may also change. Finally, team sports are an arena for learning social relationships that may have shaped men's ability to be team players and assume coordinated roles in a larger social structure. Might team sports likewise affect the more personal, reciprocal, empathic relationships that girls form? Or will girls alter the interpersonal dynamics of team sports? To the extent that gender roles and rules in our society change, so will the connections between gender and friendship.

SUGGESTED READING

Duck, S., and Wright, P. (1993). Reexamining gender differences in same-gender friendships: A close look at two kinds of data. *Sex Roles* **28**, 709–727.

Fehr, B. (1996). *Friendship Processes.* Sage, Thousand Oaks, CA.

Maccoby, E. (1990). Gender and relationships: A developmental account. *American Psychologist* **45**, 512–520.

Werking, K. (1997). *We're Just Good Friends: Women and Men in Nonromantic Relationships.* Guilford, New York.

Winstead, B. A., Derlega, V. J., and Rose, S. (1997). *Gender and Close Relationships.* Sage, Thousand Oaks, CA.

Gender Development
Evolutionary Perspectives

Cheryl Brown Travis
University of Tennessee, Knoxville

Glossary

Adaptive value The extent to which a trait confers relatively increased reproductive success on the individual exhibiting that trait.

Additive effects The cumulative impact of two or more variables, obtained by summing the separate contributions.

Effect size The percentage of variation among individuals on a particular measure that is associated with a predictor or independent variable, such as the variation in math scores associated with academic major.

Emergent A behavior or condition having qualities that cannot be forecast from simply knowing characteristics of the separate components on which it is based (e.g., water cannot be predicted by knowing the separate components of hydrogen and oxygen). In social construction theory, the idea that behaviors and identities are negotiated and renegotiated through ongoing interactions.

Environment of evolutionary adaptedness Environmental conditions thought to have prevailed during the time period when a trait or characteristic and its phenotypic expressions evolved.

Fitness The biological success of an individual in producing offspring that also successfully reproduce, resulting in successive generations with increased frequency of genes carried by the initial individual.

Heritability The percentage of variation in a characteristic or trait that is associated with differences in genetic factors that can be passed on in successive generations.

Kin selection The process where gene frequencies are increased in successive generations by help extended to genetically related individuals (i.e., kin).

Parthenogenesis Asexual reproduction by cloning and where all individuals are genetically female.

Protandrous strategies Species that begin life and early development with a male morphology, but, given certain environmental conditions, have the capability at later stages of life development of becoming reproductively female.

Protogynous strategies Species that begin life and

early development with a female morphology, but, given certain environmental conditions, have the capability at later stages of life development of becoming reproductively male.

Sexual dimorphism The degree to which female and male sexes within a species differ in overall size, distinguishing features (e.g., secondary sex characteristics), and behaviors unique to one sex.

EVOLUTION AND GENDER may be considered in terms of three broad points. First, that environmental factors are quite clearly relevant in the biology, genetics, and evolution of nonhuman species. Second, the influences of biology, genetics, and evolution are associated with a startling range of diversity and variation even among nonhuman species. Finally, compared to these nonhuman species, environmental and social ecology are thus more relevant for human social arrangements, and diversity is especially characteristic of human behavior.

I. Selection and Fitness

General principles of evolution are relatively simple and involve the ideas that individuals vary, some variations are more favorable for survival and reproduction than others, and some of this variation is genetically based and therefore can be inherited. Differential reproductive success may occur as a function of these favorable variations, and differing gene frequencies may appear in future generations (i.e., evolution). Evolutionary models of gender are based on these fundamental mechanisms of differential reproduction and changing gene frequencies.

Evolution is not something that magically occurs in a stand-alone black box. The processes associated with evolution have fairly specific definitions and usually include limiting conditions under which the principle will be operational. Specific social and ecological, as well as biological, conditions may have to be met. These preconditions are often probabilistic rather than lock-stepped and universal. Thus, behavioral expressions of genetic factors are also often probabilistic and conditional. Indeed, the fact that a particular behavior is nearly universal is not proof that it has a genetic component. The interplay of social and ecological conditions shape genetic expressions and additionally will determine the adaptive value, if any, of such expressions.

A. FITNESS

Biological fitness has a specific, genetic, definition in evolutionary theory. Fitness is determined by the breeding survival of successive generations of offspring that carry the genetic features characteristic of the founding individuals. Organisms must themselves survive to reproductive maturity and, in sexually reproducing species, must find and mate with a partner. While producing offspring is important, the sheer number of births is not so important as the number of offspring that survive and who themselves successfully reproduce. The important step is to have children and grandchildren that have children into successive generations.

It is equally important to understand what fitness is not. Fitness refers to gene distributions in successive generations and is not necessarily defined by physical size or prowess. Fitness, for example, does not necessarily require that individuals will live to a ripe old age, or be especially happy, or be especially rich or attractive. Evolutionary fitness does not mean that there is a constant upward gradient of improvements. In fact, some of the oldest and most prolific species on earth have changed very little over the millennia. For example, the horseshoe crab has remained relatively unchanged for millions of years. Beetles, with apparently few improvements to their credit, reasonably can be deemed among the top two or three most successful families of organisms of all time. Furthermore, evolution and natural selection do not result in the ongoing survival of a species. By far the more frequent scenario for any species is extinction, as evidenced by the fact that there are now more species that have become extinct than the total species that currently exist. Thus, noting that something "has evolved" in no way implies that it represents the best or optimal solution, nor does it imply that this evolutionary process has been a success.

B. NATURAL SELECTION

Natural selection operates on phenotypes and involves the various pathways and processes that produce changes in genetic distributions of a population. Natural selection can operate at many levels and life stages, including parenting and caretaking behavior. In some instances these might involve factors that help the young to survive to sexual maturity. Natural selection might also operate on characteristics that improve the chances of finding a mate, or might involve parenting styles, or defense strategies, or interactive social strategies. Natural selection can operate only to the extent that variations in these characteristics have a genetic component. Other mechanisms of evolution include mutations, migration, and general genetic drift.

Natural selection is based on the pattern whereby individuals with certain genetically based adaptations reproduce more successfully than other individuals that do not have the adaptation. The associated genes are then represented with increasing frequency in successive generations. Thus, it is populations of genes that evolve and not individuals.

Natural selection does not necessarily lead to a single perfect solution. There may be several viable solutions to a particular biological or environmental problem. Thus, the same species located in different environments may exhibit very different solutions to the same problem.

C. KIN SELECTION

The fact that biological or genetic factors may be relevant in social behavior does not mean that the behavior will be characterized by greed, brutality, and violence. In some instances selection favors individuals who commit their energy, resources, and sometimes their very lives on behalf of others. This enhances the fitness of an individual if these acts of nurturing and altruism benefit others that have a shared genetic interest, for example, a parent provisioning, warming, teaching, or protecting their own offspring or those of their kin. The factors that favor such genetic selection for helping or collaborative behaviors are called kin selection.

D. ADAPTIVE VALUE

The concept of adaptive value is usually taken to mean those behaviors and characteristics that are favorable for the survival of subsequent generations. These characteristics promote increases in biological fitness and tend to occur more and more frequently, as long as the environment for which they are adaptive remains essentially unchanged. Thus, adaptive value may change over time. Another limiting condition on adaptive value is that some traits may be carried forward in successive generations because they are benign correlates of other traits that are beneficial. Thus, the trait itself may be carried forward, although it has no particular adaptive value, simply because it is correlated with a trait that is

adaptive. For example, the gene associated with sickle cell anemia has remained nevertheless in the gene pool because it also provides resistance to malaria.

It is also important to understand that adaptations in response to some environmental context or problem must be based largely on possible preadaptations that already existed. Thus, adaptations do not necessarily represent the best or ideal arrangement, but rather a cobbling together of what is available. The evolutionary process does not necessarily produce perfection.

E. SEXUAL SELECTION

Sexual selection refers to the higher reproductive success of some members of one sex compared to their same-sex peers. This usually begins with success in obtaining mates and typically is taken to mean contests or competitions among males. The long-term impact of such contests and competitions between males is thought to account for some of the sex differences between males and females in size, coloration, and so on. Such differences are said to reflect sexual dimorphism, and species can range from very little or no difference to extensive sexual dimorphism. These sometimes exotic secondary sex characteristics, such as antlers and colorful plumage, function to the advantage of males in defeating other males, being able to hold a territory, and attracting females. Male-male competition and female choice among potential mates is assumed to be the primary basis for sexual selection. However, this template may reflect a traditional sexism among early theorists who credited only males with dramatic agency. As it turns out, among primates there is considerable female-female competition as well.

F. ENVIRONMENT OF EVOLUTIONARY ADAPTEDNESS (EEA)

The concept of EEA refers to environmental conditions thought to have prevailed during the time period when a trait or characteristic and its phenotypic expressions evolved. Since natural selection is thought to work in a relatively slow process, the genetic components of a behavior reflect more about past, historically distant events (reproductive successes and failures) than they reflect about present circumstances. Successes and failures that affected the gene frequencies may have been played out under conditions quite distant from present circumstances. Further, the fact that a behavior seems to confer prestige or benefits in contemporary human society does not mean that these were effective factors in natural selection in early human evolution. Some of the critical periods for human evolution are found in the last ice age that continued for approximately 100,000 years and ended roughly 12,000 years ago.

II. Assessing Effects: Genes versus Environment?

A. HERITABILITY

Heritability is the percent of variation in a characteristic that genetically can be passed on to successive generations. Heritability is seldom 100%. Genetic factors may account for some, but not all, variation in the attributes and behaviors of interest. Other relevant, nongenetic factors may involve the ongoing social context and historical patterns already in place, as well as ecological factors.

The fact that something is partially shaped by genetic factors does not imply uniformity. Within any given population, there will be a range of patterns and practices. Individuals in the same population may vary in physical attributes, reproductive strategies, feeding preferences, predator defense, and a host of other mannerisms and properties.

Whether traits have high or low heritability depends in part on circumstance. Heritability can take on high or low values in some unexpected ways. For example, if a set of similar seeds were grown under the same conditions, most variations in subsequent generations would be genetic and such variations would by definition have high heritability. If the same seeds were grown in variable environments, then most of the variations in subsequent generations would be due to environmental factors, and heritability by definition would be low.

Assessing heritability among humans can be similarly complicated. This is especially true of twin studies that are often used to assess heritability in humans. Such studies can be very misleading for a number of reasons. For example, one study found that identical twins (with identical genes) had a high concordance of homosexuality (52%). Among fraternal twins, who are no more genetically related than ordinary brothers, the joint occurrence of homosexuality was found to be 22%. This looks like a strong case for a genetic basis for homosexuality, until one is reminded that the joint occurrence of ho-

mosexuality among ordinary brothers [who share 50% of their genes in common] is only 9%. Yet fraternal twins exhibit a much higher concordance of homosexuality than ordinary brothers, even though both share exactly the same 50% genetic commonality. It appears that sharing a common twin environment more than doubles the likelihood of the joint occurrence of homosexuality.

Finding a genetic link to some of the variation in a characteristic is seldom in itself very informative. Saying that something has a genetic basis does very little to explicate the behavior in question. The more provocative science questions involve inquiries about process, context, and function. For example, what is the normal developmental sequence for the behavior, which processes or conditions elicit and sustain the behavior, and which suppress it? One might also want to know how the behavior is situated in the behavioral ecology of conspecifics and how the behavior functions specifically to enhance biological fitness.

B. EFFECT SIZE

Recognizing, characterizing, and accounting for variation is a major goal of science. Effect size is the percentage of variation in an outcome that can be associated with a particular precursor. The standards for considering a factor truly of significant influence depend on its effect size and have been derived from the work of Jacob Cohen on statistical power analysis. These standards are widely accepted and have been around long enough to constitute part of the core of behavioral and social science. In behavioral science research, factors, whether genetic or contextual, that account for 10% of variation in an outcome are considered relatively small, while those that account for 25% are considered moderate, and those accounting for 50% of variation are considered large.

For social behaviors and social roles, such as gender, there is typically a great deal of variation among individuals. The real question is which of the many factors found to correlate with the behavior of interest are worthy of more serious investigation. The fact that variations in a behavior pattern are partially associated with genetic factors is not in itself a notable consideration until the effect size begins to reach a minimal value. Nevertheless, even this level means that over 90% of the variation remains unexplained by genetic factors.

Even when the percentage of variation associated with genetics reaches above 25%, researchers remain interested in other factors that help to explain the phenomenon in question. For example, breast cancer is known to have a genetic component that accounts for approximately 20% of all diagnosed breast cancers. Women born with the critical gene are at greater risk earlier in their lives for breast cancer and often take preventive measures, such as earlier or more frequent mammography. While the genetic component of breast cancer is notable and serious, it is vitally important that causes be identified for the other 80% of breast cancers diagnosed annually in the United States (about 145,000) that do *not* begin with an inherited genetic link.

C. REDUCTIONISM VERSUS HOLISM

A focus on heritability and effect size suggests an implicit model of additive effects. This is based on the idea that genetic and environmental factors each have their separate and unique roles that when added together explain all the variation in behavior. This in turn reflects the reductionist notion that the characteristic of interest is no more than the sum of its parts. This approach to science typically prescribes the breaking down of phenomena into their irreducible, essential elements. These essential elements are then viewed as the permanent building blocks of knowledge.

In this reductionist framework, it is common to think of genetic influence as somehow more important than contextual or contemporary factors. This perspective is reflected in language that refers interchangeably to genetics and the "basics" or the "foundation". However, whether genetic possibilities are actually expressed depends heavily on environmental conditions. Therefore, it is an error to assume that a particular genetic factor always will produce a single definitive outcome.

Another philosophical perspective, holism, views the whole as more than the sum of its parts. In this alternative perspective, behaviors are *emergent*, they cannot be explained by having only information about the separate parts. Behaviors instead should be viewed as the interactive product of a dynamic system. In this perspective, the environment is not simply a static physical element, it is dynamic and interactive.

In this holistic perspective, the dynamic quality of the environment includes the behaviors and social arrangements of peers. For example, whether it is better to be competitive or cooperative in one's social style depends in part on the social environment (i.e., the behavioral patterns of other members of the group). A strategy that might prove functional and stable in one social environment might be profitably changed for another very different strategy in another context. Both strategies could have a genetic basis, but the expression of one or the other would depend on a changing, emergent social ecology. It could be negotiated.

III. *Strategies about Reproduction*

If there is an uncontested finding about reproductive strategies, sex, and gender, it is that there is a broad continuum of variation across all these dimensions. Each is shaped by an interactive ecological and social context, and each variation is associated with certain risks as well as benefits.

Sexual reproduction imposes some relatively risky burdens for individual survival. The process of securing the opportunity to mate can be especially hazardous for males and frequently involves physical assaults and contests with other males or involves a high expenditure of energy in the staking out and defending of a breeding territory. The mating act itself can be fatal for males in species of insects where the female ingests the male. One wonders then why so many species bother at all with this tenuous process. The answer is thought to lie not with the happiness or security of individuals, but with evolutionary benefits derived from genetic mixing and increased genetic variability. This variability is a consequence of sexual reproduction that often (but not always) resulted in the increased survival of successive generations as environmental conditions changed. However, some species get by quite well without sexual reproduction.

Thus, sex, and maleness and femaleness, are not always the basic template for what is natural. As it turns out, sex, maleness, and femaleness are extremely plastic and varied. There is a wide range of variation among nonhuman species, and even among lower organisms environmental factors are found to be very important. Recognition of the diversity and the dynamic quality of sex even among species that we take to be heavily influenced by genetics should lead to an understanding of human gender as being at least as fluid.

A. PARTHENOGENESIS

Sexual reproduction is only one strategy for producing offspring. Asexual reproduction, parthenogenesis, occurs in literally hundreds of species. Some organisms (e.g., coral polyps) follow strategies that opt for the flexibility of both asexual and sexual reproduction. In calm, stable, favorable conditions, asexual reproduction is typical. The same organisms change to sexual reproduction and genetic mixing under harsh or disrupted conditions.

Nevertheless, it is often the case that certain interactive, behavioral events must prevail for reproduction to occur, even in species that reproduce asexually. Many species (e.g., the whiptail lizard) always reproduce asexually. However, in some subspecies, the female will not produce viable eggs unless she has had the opportunity to engage in courtship behavior with another female. In other subspecies, courtship and mating occurs with males of a related subspecies, even though sperm does not function to fertilize her eggs. Thus, interactive behavioral factors are critical to reproductive strategy. If this is true for lizards, it surely is even more relevant for humans.

Simply choosing between asexual and sexual reproduction or between being one sex or another is not the final choice point in the process. The work of zoologist David Crews documents that the production of sexual germ cells (sperm and eggs) may or may not be coordinated with mating behavior, which may or may not be coordinated with fertilization. For example, females of some species may mate and store sperm internally for fertilization of their own eggs at a later date.

The female brown rat may mate several hundred times with most males in her group, but retain only some sperm. She may have no developed eggs at this time. She may then store the sperm and use it at a later time to fertilize eggs she develops when environmental conditions are favorable to the successful rearing of pups. Among brown rats, there are no unwanted pregnancies. The brown rat is just one variation. She is controlled as much by social and environmental factors as by her genetic biology. Thus, a genetic component results not in a single uniform outcome but rather is associated with major variations in format. The fact that humans reproduce sexually and that there is a genetic component for this says nothing about how gender roles will be configured.

B. SEXING THE INDIVIDUAL

There is nothing genetically predestined about what constitutes "real" masculinity or "real" femininity. Males are indeed sometimes large and aggressive, but not always. Females are sometimes smaller and coy, but not always. Individuals in many species possess the genetic potential of exhibiting all variations in between. Thus, noting that there is a genetic male sex or genetic female sex tells us little about what constitutes "maleness" or "femaleness" as these are developed, negotiated, and expressed in individuals. Appreciating just how much variation and flexibility exist among other species leads us to recognize that human arrangements are even more plastic.

One aspect of this variability is reflected in the fact that sex modifications and sex transitions are quite common in species that reproduce sexually. Whether an individual is male or female can be a relative matter and subject to a number of environmental factors. For example, the temperature at which the egg incubates determines the female or male sex in some species. Similarly, all members of some protandrous species begin life as male but as they mature, age, and get bigger, they transform to a female sex and bear eggs.

Other species are protogynous and are characterized by all individuals starting out as female, but in later life stages, some may morph into a male form. For example, Bluehead wrasse (a reef fish) begin life with female coloration, body size, and behavior patterns. A given individual wrasse may later morph into a breeding male with distinct coloration and behavior, but only when there is a convenient space in the social environmental hierarchy.

Other species (e.g., salmon) may have an invariant female or male sex from birth, but there may be significant anatomical and behavioral variations within one sex. For example there may be large, "go-getter" male salmon who go to sea a few years and later return to their freshwater breeding river to compete actively to mate with females. In the same species there are small males who never go to sea and who "sit and wait" in hiding (from big males) only to rush out and release their sperm in synchrony with that of a larger male. All males have the genetic potential to develop in either direction.

Since it takes a lot of energy and exposure to risky situations, one would think that all male salmon would simply adhere to the "small male" strategy. However, only a relatively small percentage follows this developmental path. The problem is that small males without hiding places tend to get eaten before they can breed. Thus, whether it is better for a male to develop as a big hooknose salmon or as a small recluse depends in part on how many natural hiding places occur in the local environment and how many of them are already filled. The demographics and ecological context clearly influence the sexual development of these males. If sexual behavior styles of salmon are influenced by ecology, then without doubt we must recognize that human gender roles and traits are largely a function of context and situation.

IV. Parental Investment and Gender

Evolutionary models of human mate selection and associated gender behaviors have focused on parental investment. Parental investment theory, first proposed by Robert Trivers in 1972, argues that females and males have fundamentally different reproductive strategies, due to differing and conflicting pathways for enhancing their biological fitness. The basic thesis is that everyone tries to produce as many offspring as possible, and that males have the potential to produce many more offspring than females.

Females make a heavy biological investment in offspring by virtue of the fact that individual eggs are bigger and take longer to produce than individual spermatozoa. The energetic burden of females is additionally increased if, as in the case of mammals, they gestate and nurse offspring. The relatively greater biological investment on the part of females makes them less likely than males to abandon their offspring. Likewise, the supposed genetic predilection of females to nurture and protect their offspring makes it easier for males to abandon the same offspring and subsequently to mate again with another female, and another.

This parental investment model seems to be descriptive of some species, but there are many exceptions. These exceptions suggest that there is no across-the-board tendency for males to be sexually cavalier and females to be universally coy. The popularized rendition of parental investment theory as proof of an invariant battle of the sexes is simply false. The range of variation in parenting roles and in gender relationships found in other species suggests that gender relationships among humans are at least as diverse.

In some species, such as the emu of Australia, the female roams from male to male laying eggs in nests provided by the male. She leaves her eggs with him to incubate and nurture upon hatching. A similar pattern is found among some fish (e.g., the stickleback). Male Emperor penguins forego eating for many weeks while they warm a single egg during the darkest months of the Antarctic winter when their female mate is on an extended feeding foray. Thus,

females are not the only ones to make a high investment in offspring.

Nevertheless, parental investment theory is focused on those arrangements where females make a high investment in reproduction. According to the theory, females who make a mistake, of any sort, in mate choice may find it very costly or impossible to replicate the already expended biological resources for reproduction. On the other hand, males who make a mistake in mate choice ostensibly have expended very little investment and it is easier for them to recoup the initial loss through later pairings.

A. GENDER IMPLICATIONS

Parental investment theory forms the basis for several conclusions about gender and human relations and what is popularly referred to as the war between the sexes. According to this model, men evolved to be naturally profligate and promiscuous. They have developed a psychology to facilitate this system so that men are not particularly sensitive to the nuances of close interpersonal relationships. Such a psychology would enable them to pursue their own interests unhindered by doubt, ambivalence, or guilt. Surveys of college students do indicate that relatively more men than women report they would be somewhat comfortable with casual sexual encounters.

In contrast, according to parental investment theory, women evolved to be sexually coy and more attentive to the meaning of events and experiences surrounding romantic relationships. Generalizations of parental investment theory to humans suggest that a culture of domesticity is naturally embraced by females as being in their own best (genetic) interests.

The fact that many girls and women report this apparent preference for home, domesticity, and close relationships does not constitute convincing proof of parental investment theory. Completely disparate models forecast the same pattern. For example, using an entirely different set of principles, one can derive the same prediction from psychoanalytic object relations theory and also from social learning theory. Since all three theories predict a culture of female domesticity, the reported preferences of girls and women cannot be used to confirm or disconfirm any of the theories. Thus, parental investment theory does not offer an explanation of traditionally gendered behavior that is not also addressed by a number of other theories.

The problem is that popular renditions of evolutionary principles are often contorted to justify existing social and political structures. In the past, a kind of social Darwinism was promoted as a way to justify economic class structures, namely that the lower classes were impoverished because they lacked genetic fitness.

Similar overgeneralizations and misrepresentations of evolutionary principles have been used to account for complex social phenomena. Bride price, age differences at marriage, double standards for sexual behavior and rape have been explained as products of sexual selection and principles of parental investment. Supposedly, natural selection has acted on the evolution of genetic frequencies that support such social arrangements. This popularized sociobiology seldom bothers to collect the data necessary to demonstrate increased reproductive fitness associated with these particular arrangements. Simply proposing that something *could* be the result of natural selection does not constitute actual proof. The idea of parental investment indeed may offer a way to account for these social arrangements, but without data, such accounts remain only speculative stories.

B. THE ROLE OF MALES: LIMITING ASSUMPTIONS

A fundamental component of parental investment theory is the proposition that females have a greater initial investment in reproductive efforts than males. However this basic premise about energy expenditure and reproductive effort may not be entirely accurate. The emphasis on absolute difference in the size of individual gametes, eggs or sperm, is arbitrary. In humans, a viable ejaculate should contain 80,000 spermatozoa in order to optimize the likelihood of fertilization. As attested to by a growing fertility industry in the United States, there is considerable evidence that males are not without limits in their ability to produce sperm. Perhaps producing sperm is not as energetically "cheap" as postulated by parental investment theory.

A key feature of the parental investment model is that the most successful males will mate with several females, abandoning each in turn. Remember that for human males to possess a gene for this tendency to mate and abandon offspring, the behaviors would necessarily have evolved tens of thousands of years ago. The actions and events would have occurred in an early environment of evolutionary adaptation. Thus, it is better to think about how sexually promiscuous males of 10,000 to 50,000 years ago would have had more healthy surviving offspring than high investment males, and to think about how, 10,000 to 50,000 years ago, such males would have acquired their multiple mates.

Ethologist John Maynard Smith has stipulated some preconditions of the parental investment model that are often overlooked, but that are necessary if this mate-and-abandon strategy is to result in increased offspring that reproduce. A major precondition is that males who desert their offspring in order to mate with other females must readily be able to find other available fertile females and not be eaten or battered in the process. This would have presented a significant barrier for such males trying to survive in an ice age environment.

Another problem for this mate-and-abandon male involves biological strategies that females may have evolved to upset his strategy. Many primate species (human and nonhuman) have a sex ratio of approximately one to one, thus there is not a great overabundance of females. Further, many females living in proximity follow what is essentially a synchronized breeding season. Human females that live together often report similar synchronizing. A male who spends a significant amount of time courting a female may have invested considerable energy resources and, critically, may have foregone the opportunity to mate with another female. By the time a male courts, mates, and abandons one female, other females may have already mated, be pregnant, or lactating and not ovulating. This would have been fairly typical in the human environment of evolutionary adaptedness. These factors suggest there might well have been selective pressures for the male to be choosy, since the female he courted might well be the only one with whom he mated. Evolutionary principles can be used just as persuasively to create a story that males evolved to have a "natural" desire for domesticity. The fact that such hypotheses are not examined suggests that the application of parental investment models to human males serves more as a rationale and justification for current cultural norms than as a serious scientific exploration.

Another assumption underlying applications of parental investment theory to human gender is that primate males contribute little to the welfare or survival of their offspring. An implicit corollary is that males who abandon their offspring to be nurtured and protected by the female (and perhaps her kin) have at least as many, if not more, offspring living to successfully reproduce as do males who invest more intensively in a monogamous pairbond with a female and their offspring. This corollary seems to run counter to many visions of the evolution of human society where the importance of men as hunters and protectors is highlighted. Are we to believe that human evolution was significantly advanced by male investment in the general group (by virtue of risky hunting and defense behaviors) but that these same contributions were irrelevant to and never specifically directed toward the survival of their own offspring?

Again, all this would have emerged under the early ecology of human evolution. Human males who followed the strategy of mate and abandon would have had to differ genetically from males who did not follow this strategy, and the minimal-investment males would have had to have produced as least as many reproducing offspring as high-investment males. Success would depend not simply on taking advantage of opportunities to mate; the resulting offspring would have to survive, be healthy, and in turn reproduce.

Although males do not gestate or nurse offspring, they can contribute significantly in a variety of ways to the thriving of offspring. Male contributions can include resource acquisition, defense of resources used by the offspring, sheltering, sentinel or antipredator behavior, huddling with and grooming young, transporting or retrieving young, and socialization of young. These are not trivial contributions.

Jeanne Altmann, Thelma Rowell, and Barbara Smuts each have conducted fieldwork finding that primate females with infants tend to affiliate with males, that male–infant bonds are often striking in their affection, and that males often protect very young infants from intrusions by other group members. Primatologist Sarah Blaffer Hrdy noted that among monkeys, Barbary macaque males typically warm and cuddle infants during the winter when their mothers are otherwise taken up with new infants. Even in species such as gorillas where males seem to be generally indifferent or aloof from infants, males may play important roles as primary caretakers and may adopt infants in emergencies.

The social-psychological importance of fathers in families has been endorsed in studies spanning several decades. Evolutionary benefits of the presence of a social father have also been documented by the work of anthropologist Wade Mackey. His work on human fathering behaviors and the adult male–child bond argues persuasively for the benefits of male parental investment. Data from a number of Western societies demonstrate that fatherless children have lowered odds for reaching adulthood and lowered odds of producing grandchildren.

While these roles can be performed by nonbiological fathers, it is likely that for most early humans they were carried out by the biological father. Males could have engaged collectively in group protection that would have benefited all offspring, but evolutionary principles of natural selection operate at the level of the individual. Fathers who were able to make extended investments in their own genetic offspring certainly would have fared better than had they expended their investments in an indifferent way to all.

Among contemporary nonindustrialized societies, fathering and father roles are held to be very important. In these societies, the cultural concept of a father may appear in a relatively elaborate form. A number of tribal groups of the Amazonian basin have constructed complex definitions of a biological father. They believe that the sperm of many men contribute to the layered development of a child. For example, when asked to identify their fathers, members of the Aché almost always list more than one father. Data from similar groups indicate that children with only one acknowledged father are significantly less likely to survive to adolescence than those able to identify a secondary father as well.

C. THE ROLES OF FEMALES: LIMITING ASSUMPTIONS

To work as proposed, parental investment theory depends on some unacknowledged assumptions about females. First, it depends on the stipulation that while there is considerable variability in male reproductive success, there is an assumed limited variability in reproductive success among individual females. The *assumed* lack of variability in female reproductive success means that males have little to lose, or to gain, by being choosy.

Data documenting that there is a significant degree of female initiative in mate selection and data documenting variability in female reproductive success discredit parental investment theory as it is loosely applied to humans. Since humans are primates, data from other primate species are informative here. Primate studies by Barbara Smuts and by Sarah Blaffer Hrdy confirm that there is indeed considerable variability in female reproductive success. Their work documents that females may be active agents in this regard. Female primates often take sexual initiative and may actively attack other females who try to associate with their own preferred male friend.

Hrdy described the female Langurs in her field studies as active, strategic agents, rather than the reluctant and demur female suggested by the parental investment model. She has argued with others that the several primate species that follow monogamous pair-bonds, such as lemurs, langurs, tamarins, and gibbons, do so not only because of environmental pressures but also in response to female-based strategies. For example, females may deploy themselves geographically in such a way as to make other breeding females less available to mating males. The ovulation cycles of these females also may be adapted for keeping a male monogamous. The same females may allow other females in their home territory, but, through a variety of mechanisms, may be able to suppress ovulation in the subordinate female.

Female variability in reproductive success is in part due to dynamic social conditions. It involves position in the social hierarchy and competition among females in general. For the evolution of a genetic basis of behavior, it is necessary to again consider early humans and environmental conditions characteristic of the ice ages and shortly thereafter. The hierarchy and competition among females would have occurred in the environment of evolutionary adaptedness. Thus, individual status could have direct implications for month-to-month survival.

We know that among contemporary nonhuman primates, low-status females (a social condition) may be less healthy, less likely to conceive, less likely to have healthy offspring, and less likely to have offspring that survive to reproductive adulthood. The differential reproductive effect can be quite dramatic, with high-ranking females having reproductive success many times greater than that of low-ranking, inexperienced females. This may be due in part to direct harassment of subordinate females, mishandling of low-status infants by others, and also due to the lowered access of subordinate females to food and water. The offspring of the high-ranking females are themselves likely to rise in the social structure of the troop and thus to carry an advantage in future reproductive efforts. All these conditions suggest that males too have something to gain if they are choosy.

Another key assumption of the parental investment model is that females are generally conservative about any kind of sexual activity and are highly selective in their partners. There are, however, a number of primate species where females do not seem to be all that chaste. Almost every type of mating system has been observed among primates, even within groups of the same species but located in different environmental settings.

Females vary their sexual activity in response to social demographics. For example, nonhuman primate females can and do adjust their physiology and behavior patterns, such as having longer periods of fertility, more breeding days, and more partners when they live in groups having more males. Additionally, when male dominance hierarchies are unstable or when new males enter the group, female breeding days may be increased. One speculation is that females engage in multiple breeding to propitiate males that later might be hostile to offspring.

One effect of multiple copulations is to confuse paternity. A female strategy that may serve this effect is to disguise ovulation and to minimize obvious signs of estrous. In this way, females are free to mate with several males who may be of assistance in various ways and in any case may be less likely to aggress against the female or her offspring. In fact, there is considerable variation among humans in the follicular phase when an egg is matured and developed in the ovary preceding ovulation, and the actual timing of ovulation has a much greater standard deviation than does the luteal phase following ovulation. These biological considerations argue against the evolutionary basis for coy, sexually conservative females.

It is not all exploitation of the duped male, however. There is plenty of evidence to suggest that relationships between primate males and females evolved to be collaborative and mutalistic. Being on good terms with a female and her infant may have immediate benefits for males who engage in caretaking. These benefits would argue in favor of a biological basis for male monogamy and domesticity. For example, socially attached males who are not biological fathers may learn something about the caretaking of their own future offspring. For males who have recently entered the group, caretaking and friendship also may be a way of obtaining effective endorsement by a female and hence socialization into the larger troop. In addition, holding and playing with an infant may be one way for subordinate males to forestall aggression or harassment from dominant males. Males also may use caretaking as a way of building friendships (that are themselves important) with the female and with her offspring who later will become young adults in the group.

In fieldwork among savannah baboons, Barbara Smuts has documented that males and females do develop friendship associations and preferences independent of breeding activity. Friendships are reflected in physical proximity, peaceful approaches, mutual grooming, and sleeping in cuddled arrangements involving the male, female, and her youngest infants. Both males and females contribute actively to the practice of these friendships. An evolutionary advantage for such friendships might be a reduced sense of vulnerability, better immune function, and energy savings when relieved of the burden to be continuously vigilant about potential challenges and attacks.

V. Human Mate Choice

An extension of evolutionary models to human marriage systems has argued that the number and survival of offspring is based largely on the female's ability to make biological investments. Thus, markers of female health, fertility, and general ability to invest biological resources in her offspring come to be valued and sought in marriageable females. The cultural notion of beauty is thought to have evolutionary relevance in this framework because it reflects the cumulative manifestations of such biological markers. According to this account, physical attractiveness and beauty become salient bases by which females are evaluated, because beauty and youth indicate general health and potential reproductive success.

According to this account, the biology, appearance, and age of males do not matter for female choice of mates. Because males cannot contribute directly to the gestation or the nursing of infants, their biology is supposedly less central. In this account, males would be most prized as potential mates if they carried markers for abilities to contribute in other ways to the welfare and well-being of the offspring. The upshot is that women should seek out men for their status and power.

Attitude studies conducted by David Buss and others have found evidence of these preferences. Men do report that physical appearance is important in mate selection and women do report that the financial security of the man is a consideration in their choices. However, these reported preferences are not unique predictions of parental investment theory. The same patterns can be forecast from other explanations for these attitudes. Other cross-cultural studies challenge the evolutionary view of women's preferences for men with money. Studies in Africa and also India indicate that, even more than financial resources, women give highest preference to the quality best summarized as "good sense."

Alice Eagly and Wendy Wood have worked with the same empirical data presented by Buss and arrived at a compelling alternative analysis that accounts for these preferences (i.e., beautiful women and rich men). Their analysis focuses on the political status of women in these cultures and women's access to economic agency. Women look to men to provide financial resources because it is likely, given status differences imposed by the patriarchal politics in these societies, that men will be better able to provide such resources. Thus the supposed "desire" of women to marry for wealth is more likely to be a product of patriarchy than of genetics. Under these conditions, even women with independent means will prefer men with status and wealth because in such hierarchical systems it is always better for a member of the subordinate group (women) to have a powerful ally than simply a pretty one.

VI. Sexual Violence and Rape

Evolutionary perspectives also have been applied to the darker side of traditional gender roles. An evolutionary hypothesis is that men have a genetic basis for rape (of women) because it increases their biological fitness. In this evolutionary account, it additionally is argued that this rape strategy is most beneficial to those males otherwise unable to secure a more committed relationship.

The evolutionary account of rape further implies that males falling into the rapist group are more likely to be from lower socioeconomic classes, criminal subcultures, and those groups with serious psychological or mental deficits. Whether acknowledged or not, this framework for rape corresponds closely to common stereotypes of rape as reprehensible acts perpetrated by criminal or deranged strangers. This is a convenient political belief because it helps disguise the fact that the majority of rapists are known in some capacity by the victim and are often from her same social class and circle of acquaintances. As long as the finger of blame is pointed toward peripheral, "abnormal" males, the normative arrangements of mainstream society that foster rape do not have to be examined. Psychologist Mary Koss, evolutionary biologist Jerry Coyne, and several other scholars have addressed the flaws in this evolutionary account of rape.

A. LIMITING EVIDENCE FOR RAPE AS ADAPTIVE

The rape-reproduction model suggests that victims of rape should be of childbearing age, but national FBI crime statistics and separate national hospital statistics show quite clearly that a high percentage of victims are young children under childbearing age. Another problem with the model is that it draws on stereotypic views of rape as primarily sexual and as primarily intercourse, whereas approximately 20% of rapes do not involve vaginal penetration and approximately 50% do not involve ejaculation. The model additionally offers no evolutionary account for homosexual rape. Furthermore, the rape-reproduction model does not acknowledge or account for gang rape, which clearly reduces the likelihood of paternity. Nor does it acknowledge that wartime rape often results in the mutilation and murder of the victims.

The proposition that rape is an adaptive trait (derived from genetics) is further undermined by the fact that estimates are that only about 2% of rapes result in conception. These are very low odds indeed for the risks incurred. A genetic basis for rape could evolve in some subset of men only if there existed a favorable balance between the likelihood of reproductive success by rape and the risks incurred by rape attempts regardless of the reproductive outcome.

The likelihood of reproductive benefits to the rapist male would be based on the pregnancy rate resulting from rape. However, at the time this rape strategy would have evolved, females were probably less likely than now to conceive from a forced copulation. Most females would have an already existing pregnancy or be engaged in lactation and nursing that would have suppressed ovulation. Thus, the current estimate of 2% conception probably overestimates the likelihood as it existed in the environment in which this behavior would have evolved.

In addition, reproductive gains would have to be balanced against risks. Such risks would be present for all attempts at reproduction via rape, regardless of whether the woman actually conceived and gave birth or not. In evaluating risks of punishment, it is the environment of evolutionary adaptedness (EEA) that must be considered. That is, one must consider the likely conditions and social organization of early human groups thousands of years in the past. In these EEA settings without penal institutions, it is likely that males who tried to violate group social arrangements would be directly killed or driven out. Expulsion in most cases would be tantamount to the

same fatal end. Given the limited benefits and the high risks, it is reasonable to conclude that any genetic basis for rape would have been eliminated by natural selection. [*See* RAPE.]

VII. *Social Constructions and Sexism*

One may argue that gender is best characterized as a social agreement, continually renegotiated and reconstructed in various cultures and times. Gender is not a unitary monolithic phenomenon, but rather varies significantly across cultures.

Unfortunately, stereotypes of human gender regularly find their way into supposedly objective studies of animal behaviors. For example, Wickler in his description of mountain sheep reported that, anatomically and behaviorally, females and males are indistinguishable, even from each other, except for a few senior rams. There is effectively one body shape and size and one repertoire of behavior that is common for all other ages and sexes. However, he continually refers to the females in the group as acting like males. Since their behavior is typical of all females, one wonders why they are not seen to be acting like females. [*See* ANDROCENTRISM.]

Models of human behavior that purport to rely on evolutionary principles, particularly sociobiology, often have been deeply flawed in their logic, in their scientific standards of proof, and in their applications. Stephen Jay Gould and Richard Lewontin, Harvard zoologists, have critiqued sociobiology on a variety of grounds, including the fact that many "predictions" derived from the theory are in fact tautologies that are not amenable to falsification.

Selective use of examples, overgeneralization from animal to human behavior, and frankly pejorative language and sexism (as well as racism) have run rampant throughout much of the theorizing about evolution and the human condition. Ruth Bleier, Ruth Hubbard, Janet Sayers, and Ethel Tobach have further elaborated the political machinations and personal biases associated with Western science and gender studies. For example, popularized sociobiology accounts about hunting apes and territorial apes give almost all credit for human evolution and society to males.

Biological and evolutionary models of gender offer a framework that has the appearance of being especially scientific. By Western sensibilities, such models are understood to be in some fundamental sense True. Nonetheless, personal biases and gender politics do influence science. Great care and effort must be taken in order to remain alert to the possibility that what passes for objective science instead has the potential to disguise political agendas, to camouflage inequity, and to deny the effects of this inequity on the observed behaviors. [*See* DEVELOPMENT OF SEX AND GENDER.]

A. ECOLOGY, CONTEXT, AND POWER

Evolutionary models of complex behaviors often rely on what Stephen Jay Gould referred to as "just so stories." Stories suggesting that evolutionary processes *could* have produced some observed outcome do not constitute compelling proof. Alternative analyses and models propose the same outcomes, but use different explanatory principles. For example, ecological approaches to behavior are also able to account for considerable diversity in social organization (and hence mating patterns) and have led to the highly productive field of behavioral ecology. Studies of the reproductive and social behavior of fish, reptiles, deer, and primates have demonstrated a link between ecological variables, such as the quality and distribution of food, and social organization and reproductive strategies.

Although some scholars have pursued evolutionary theory from a feminist stance (e.g., Patricia Gowaty and Sarah Blaffer Hrdy), other feminists in the sciences (e.g., Ruth Bleier, Ruth Hubbard, and Anne Fausto-Sterling) have argued that most evolutionary models of contemporary gender relationships are social constructions. Ethel Tobach, with other colleagues, has generated a series of books on genes and gender that address many of these issues from a feminist perspective.

Alternative feminist analyses often point to the fact that sex differences in social behaviors are a function of contextual variables, such as status or dominance. The variability of gender-typed behaviors gives further support to the social constructionist view that much social behavior, including gender,

is the result of an interactive process. As such, gender should be viewed as an emergent happening rather than a fixed entity. In this light, some theorists have referred to the phenomena of "doing gender." From a social constructionist perspective, gender is constructed and reconstructed in a dynamic process. Thus, gender emerges as a function of a social context. [*See* SOCIAL CONSTRUCTIONIST THEORY.]

Feminists further suggest that an important aspect of context involves power. Power in this sense involves access to or control of resources, the ease with which different alternatives and choices can be pursued, and the ease by which one can influence others. Research on nonverbal behavior, language, communication styles, negotiating styles, and emotional sensitivity all suggest that those individuals (whether female or male) in higher-status positions tend to behave in ways that are similar to cultural stereotypes of masculinity, while those in lower-status positions tend to behave in ways that are similar to stereotypes of femininity. These studies suggest that much of what is understood as gender is largely a product of social constructions and the differential allocation of power and status rather than a product of evolution.

SUGGESTED READING

Fausto-Sterling, A. (1985). *Myths of Gender*. Basic Books, New York.

Gould, S. J., and Lewontin, R. C. (1979). The spandrels of San Marco and the panglossian paradigm: A critique of the adaptationist programme. *Proceedings of the royal society of London, B* **205**, 581–598.

Gowaty, P. A. (ed.) (1997). *Feminism and Evolutionary Biology: Boundaries, Intersections, and Frontiers*. Chapman & Hall of International Thomson, New York.

Hrdy, S. B. (1999). *Mother Nature: A History of Mothers, Infants and Natural Selection*. Pantheon, New York.

Hubbard, R. (1990). *The Politics of Women's Biology*. Rutgers University, New Brunswick, NJ.

Tobach, E., and Rosoff, B. (1979). *Genes and Gender: Pitfalls in Research on Sex and Gender*. Gordian Press, New York.

Unger, R. (ed.) (1989). *Representations: Social Constructions of Gender*. Baywood, Amityville, NY.

Gender Development
Gender Schema Theory

Carol Lynn Martin
Lisa M. Dinella
Arizona State University

Glossary

Gender schema Organized knowledge structure containing information about the sexes.

Own-sex schema The schema that provides children with information about how to engage in activities and behaviors that they believe are appropriate for themselves.

Schematic consistency The tendency to behave and think in ways consistent with schemas.

Superordinate schema The schema that provides the information needed to label activities and characteristics as being "for females/girls" or "for males/boys."

GENDER SCHEMA THEORY is one of the major theoretical perspectives used to explain gender development. The theory is a cognitive approach in which people are assumed to be actively involved in the process of gender development. The basic idea is that people develop gender schemas, which are knowledge structures about the sexes, that guide their thinking and behavior. Gender schemas encourage schematic consistency such that people often behave and think in ways consistent with their schemas about the sexes.

I. Historical Background

The "cognitive revolution" in psychology encouraged psychologists to consider that individuals play an active role in processing information from the environment. As an outgrowth of the emphasis on cognition, several new theories about gender development were constructed in which the individual came to play a very active role in the processing of gendered information. These gender schema theories, developed in the 1980s, borrowed ideas from cognitive, developmental, and social psychology research.

Three versions of gender schema theory were published within a short span of time: two focused on adult development, and one focused on children. The adult versions, developed by Sandra Bem (1981) and Hazel Markus and colleagues (1982), emphasized how people vary in their use of gender in the processing of information. The child version, proposed by Carol Martin and Charles Halverson (1981), emphasized the development of gender schemas and their functioning for children. Many others were involved in the initial impetus for these theories as well as in their further refinement, including Lynn Liben and Margaret Signorella (1987), Beverly Fagot and Mary Leinbach (1989), and Bruce Carter and Gary Levy (1988).

Although the adult and child versions differ in some ways, there are many common themes running through gender schema theories. In addition to the assumption that people are actively involved in interpreting and constructing information from their social environments, gender schema theories focus attention on how people develop a gendered view of the world. The basic idea underlying gender schema theories is that gender schemas, which are networks of gender-related information, color individuals' perceptions and influence their behavior. Individuals develop gender schemas because of the very heavy societal emphasis on gender. In many societies, gender is one of the most significant social categories, taking on importance because of the way gender becomes associated with how people dress, act, and with the opportunities they have for careers and education. Children are faced with the task of learning about gender categories and with learning about the features that their culture deems to be associated with each sex.

II. Defining and Measuring Gender Schemas

The term "schema" was borrowed from cognitive psychology and has been used widely throughout psychology. Gender schemas, similar to other kinds of schemas, are abstract knowledge structures about the sexes and their characteristics, which are assumed to facilitate how information is perceived and encoded, retrieved from memory, and organized in memory. The content of gender schemas varies depending on one's culture and experience. Gender schemas are viewed as dynamic knowledge structures, meaning that the content associated with gender schemas varies and that the schemas themselves can and do change over time and with experience.

The nature of social influences on the development and the content of gender schemas should not be underestimated. The associations between gender groups and attributes that are developed within one culture, such as about what clothing men wear, becomes the content of gender schemas in that culture. For instance, in the United States, men's clothing usually involves pants. Thus, part of the gender schema content in the United States is that men wear pants but not dresses. In contrast, in a culture where males wear sarongs, sarongs are considered malelike and become part of their gender schemas. Aspects of clothing, appearance, or behavior that are not differently associated with one sex or the other do not become part of gender schemas. For instance, in a culture where both sexes wear earrings, earrings are unlikely to be a marker for discriminating sex, and wearing earrings is unlikely to be part of their gender schemas.

The levels of social and cultural influence on the content of gender schemas range from the cultural context of the broader society, language, and media influences, to other pervasive cultural institutions such as schools, and to the more immediate social influences of the family and peer group. Each level can and does contribute information relevant to the content of gender schemas. More focus and attention has been on the functioning of gender schemas once they have developed than on the particular content of the gender schemas; however, it is important to recognize the far-reaching role of cultural expectations and situations as influences on the content of gender schemas.

The developmental version of gender schema theory describes two forms of gender schemas. The first is a broad gender schema, which contains information about the activities, appearance, personality, behaviors, and roles that are considered to be related to males and females. These broad schemas are called *superordinate schemas,* and they provide the information about how to label things as being "for boys/males" or "for girls/females." Using this information, children can decide whether an object, situation, or behavior is appropriate for themselves or for others. The superordinate schema has a hierarchical structure, with category labels for the gender groups being at the top of the hierarchy (females/girls/ women, males/boys/men) and information about the associated characteristics being lower in the hierarchy (e.g., wears dresses, plays with trucks). Each attribute is linked through association with the category labels at the top of the hierarchy. As schemas develop, the attributes also become associated with one another through their shared relation with "masculinity" or "femininity." For instance, playing with trucks becomes associated with wearing pants as "masculine things," whereas playing with dolls becomes associated with wearing dresses as "feminine things."

The second form of gender schema is a narrower schema that holds information most relevant to one's own personal notions about gender and about one's own interests and behavior. These schemas are called *own-sex schemas.* These self-related schemas may be more complex than the broader culturally shared schemas and contain information about how to carry out the activities and behaviors deemed appropriate for one's own sex. So a girl might hold in her own-sex schema information about how to sew on a button. Thus, own-sex schemas contain detailed plans of action about how to perform an activity as well as the order of events involved in the actions. This view of personal gender schemas is similar to the cognitive psychological idea about "scripts" that can guide individual's actions because they provide information about the ordering of events in time. For instance, a gender-related script might be how to bake cookies. The correct order involved in cookie baking is to prepare and mix ingredients before placing the cookies in the oven. Individuals tend to have more extensive script-related knowledge about activities that are stereotypically associated with their gender group than for activities associated with the other gender group.

When scientists have measured gender schemas in past research studies, they have used a variety of techniques. Many proposals have been made about how to best assess gender schemas. For adults, most often researchers have assessed individuals' self-reported masculine (instrumental characteristics such as dominance) and feminine personality characteristics (expressive characteristics such as warmth and encouragement) or their gender-related attitudes. The assumption is that personality characteristics are most central to gender schemas in adults. In the research on children, many different methods have been proposed and studied including how children behave, the toys they prefer, and the kinds of personality traits they exhibit. The assumption is that gender schemas can be expressed in many different ways and no one way may best capture the nature of gender schemas in children.

Recent writings on gender schemas emphasize that there may be more types of gender schemas, with some being very abstract and others being very narrow in focus. To best predict how someone will behave, it may be ideal to assess many different types of gender schemas, as well as how they are used at different times and in different situations. This more complex view of schemas better captures the flexibility and dynamism of human thinking, especially concerning central organizing categories such as gender.

One example of schemas that are at a very high level of abstraction is children's ideas about gender group similarities and differences. Research studies have illustrated that children assume, even without any specific or explicit information, that girls will tend to like the same things and boys will tend to like the same things. These assumptions about shared similarities within each gender group and the assumption of differences across groups can be viewed as abstract theories about the nature of gender groups.

Gender schemas contain subtle metaphoric associations about gender that children show evidence of understanding, even at a young age. Consider that many children recognize that softness and rounded shapes are associated with females whereas hardness and pointed shapes are associated with maleness. A pointed pine tree is considered to be more malelike to children than a rounded oak tree. These metaphoric associations illustrate the far-reaching range of associations that individuals in many cultures develop concerning gender.

Two general approaches have been used to consider gender schema influences on gender development. One approach is to examine how each individual differs in the specific information within their gender schema and then to assume that these differences relate to other aspects of the individual's behavior and thinking. In this individual differences approach, the issue of how to measure gender schemas is central. Another approach is to focus on the culturally shared aspects of gender, and thus some researchers focus on more general "gender effects" that are common across a broad array of people. In this approach, measurement issues are of less importance than understanding the broad impact of gender on how people think and behave.

III. Development of Gender Schemas

Gender schemas develop through an interaction, over time, of the individual's characteristics with the characteristics of the environment. Infants are predisposed to simplify and organize by categorizing people and objects into groups that have meaning for them. The dimensions that infants begin to focus on and use for developing meaningful groups depends on the dimensions considered significant and meaningful for their culture, such as gender. Research studies have demonstrated that children quickly learn about groups that are given significance, especially when the groups can be distinguished by physical appearance differences. For instance, Bigler and Liben (1992) demonstrated that children learn about arbitrary groups—the "blues" and the "yellows"—when in a school setting that makes these groups salient physically (by wearing T-shirts marking the group color) and conceptually (by teachers asking children to do activities in groups). Thus it is not surprising that children would quickly learn about gender groups.

Many children are exposed to social environments in which gender groups are salient, both perceptually and conceptually. Perceptually, the sexes are marked in many ways by their cultures. Clothing, voices, hairstyles, and adornments are only some of the many cues that can be used to discriminate a person's sex. For example, parents in the United States tend to dress their infants in color-coded clothes to mark their gender group. Even before infants have well-developed gender schemas, they may be developing rudimentary ideas about the sexes based on how their mothers, fathers, and other adults feel, smell, and handle them. The salience of gender in Western culture is apparent, too, in the frequency with which many adults refer to gender groups. Parents and other adults often make vocalizations about

gender groups to children, such as when they remark, "You're a good girl." Adults also socially transmit stereotypes about the sexes, both directly through admonitions to their children (e.g., "boys don't cry") or through stating their own beliefs (e.g., "girls like to play house").

Physical differences between the sexes, both those that are genetically based (e.g., body shape and height) and those that are culturally based (e.g., wearing pink), provide salient markers for children to pay attention to and these markers help them to learn to distinguish between males and females. Even if one marker is not present, others usually are. For instance, children who see a man who is the same size as many women can still identify the person as a male by his clothing and body shape. Once children can distinguish the sexes based on physical appearance differences, they likely have an increased tendency to attend to the sexes to learn more about the characteristics of each group and how these differences relate to their own development. Recent research concerning how adults learn about novel groups suggests that physical appearance differences prime individuals to expect other differences. For instance, when groups are marked by appearance differences, individuals expect the groups to differ in other ways unrelated to appearance, such as in their interests. It is as though "groupness" and all that corresponds to that, such as assuming shared interests, is increased by group members sharing physical similarities.

Recent studies suggest that infants and toddlers notice and attend to the physical differences between the sexes and the attributes associated with the sexes. By the age of one, children may already be developing basic knowledge structures about gender. Two main types of studies have been conducted that shed light on infants' knowledge about gender. The first type of study has shown that infants pay attention to the sex of adults. Infants are shown series of photographs of either male or female adults. The amount of time infants spend attending to each photograph is noted by the experimenter. Infants are found to increase the amount of time they spend attending to a photograph when the series shifts from showing one sex to another, which indicates renewed interest. For example, if photographs of females were shown to infants, they will initially spend a lot of time on the first photograph and progressively less time on each other female photograph. If they are then shown a photograph of a male, the infant will spend longer attending to the photograph of the male because this is new and interesting information. These studies illustrate that infants have the ability to attend to the categories of sex.

The second type of study shows that infants know more than simply the facial characteristics and hairstyles associated with each sex. Infants can make basic stereotypical associations between a person's sex and additional attributes about the person. This finding is clearly portrayed in studies that assess infants' attentiveness when shown women and men coupled with an additional attribute, such as a voice. Infants will look toward women more often when they hear the voice of a woman than when they hear the voice of a man, showing their ability to stereotype sounds of voices into either male or female categories. Older infants tend to show these patterns more than do younger infants. [See METHODS FOR STUDYING GENDER.]

Although the findings from both kinds of studies show that sex is salient to infants, it is premature to conclude that gender schemas exist at this age. It is not clear that infants completely understand the distinction between the two gender categories or that they know what it means to be a male or a female. However, it may be possible that during infancy the groundwork is being laid for the future use of sex and gender as an organizational structure. Very basic associations between sex and attributes appear to be developing at a young age.

Developmental changes in cognitive and motivational processes also influence how the social environment is perceived and interpreted. For schema theories, an important developmental change involves children recognizing their membership in a gender category. Once children attain this understanding, they are more motivated to learn the details and scripts for own-sex-related activities and may attend more to differences between their own group and the other gender group. Research suggests that young children are particularly attuned to gender categories.

Although understanding about one's own gender group may appear to be an all-or-nothing phenomenon, recent evidence suggests that there are phases of understanding one's membership in a gender group. For very young children, the basic understanding is simply, "I am a girl" whereas for older children, their understanding may be more complex, "I am a girl, and I am like most of the girls I know." Cognitive limitations in thinking may influence the simplicity of early personal views of gender. Furthermore, young children are trying to develop a sense

of self, and an important part of that understanding is developing a sense of self as a female or male. As children's understanding becomes more complex and more differentiated as they grow older and gain more experience, subtle variations in personal gender schemas also become more likely.

The basic knowledge about the sexes present in infancy is built on throughout the preschool years and continues developing throughout middle childhood. Research has shown how gender schemas "for self" and "for others" develop in phases, creating a network of direct and indirect associations that children use to organize their world. In the earliest phase of development, children learn to categorize information into the most basic of categories. Many children have rudimentary stereotypes about the sexes that they can describe at the age of two-and-a-half years, and these stereotypes often contain culturally based information about appearance (e.g., girls have long hair), emotions (e.g., girls cry a lot) and activities (e.g., boys play with trucks). At this point the information children hold about gender as well as their ability to use their knowledge is basic. Because of the simplicity of their gender categories and their cognitive limitations in thinking, young children have rigid ideas about gender groups. As children grow older, their knowledge base becomes more extensive and more complex. They add more information that their culture associates with each sex, including differences in occupational preferences, academic choices, and personality characteristics. Children's ability to use gender to make judgments about other's interests and characteristics increases.

Children's gender schemas continue to develop as they grow older. Developmental changes also occur in how they are able to use the attributes associated with the gender groups. In the early school years, children begin to develop the indirect associations within gender schemas, so that they can associate one attribute with another. A surprising characteristic about this phase of development, however, is that these more complex associations can be used only in limited ways. Specifically, children can use same-sex associations, such as a girl being able to recognize that a child who likes dolls might also like kitchen sets. However, they are limited by not being able to use other-sex attributes in the same way. By the age of eight, however, children move into the third phase of development. Children's networks become more complex, and they are able to use the full array of information contained in schemas when making judgments.

As children grow older, the domains of their gender schemas expand and become more elaborate. Although more information becomes associated with each gender group as children grow older and may increase the likelihood of gender schemas being applied, other developmental processes act to offset these influences. As children grow older, the cognitive developmental changes they undergo also influence the development of gender schemas and their application. Older children have more complex ways to represent information and have the ability to use additional classification systems that cross gender categories, thereby decreasing the influence of gender schemas. For example, stereotypes about occupations can be decreased when children are taught decision rules about how occupations relate to interests and skills rather than to gender. Furthermore, as children grow older, individual differences in their values, in the salience of gender, and in gender schema elaboration will modify the use of gender schemas. Furthermore, research on adults suggests that individuals learn to consciously control their stereotype usage. This is a very important point—individuals may have a stereotype come to mind but they can disregard it and override its influence by acknowledging that it is not fair to respond on the basis of a stereotype.

IV. Gender Schemas Influence Attention and Memory

Gender schema theorists propose that schemas influence individuals' attention, thinking, memory, and behavior. The assumption in gender schema theories is that it is not the sheer volume of information about gender that influences behavior and thinking; instead, it is how that information is processed through the knowledge structures that develop to handle the information. Gender schemas guide thinking and behavior through *schematic consistency,* which states that people are motivated to behave and think in ways that are consistent with their schemas. Schemas influence and organize the types of information noticed, encoded, and remembered, leading to the processing of schema-consistent information and the disregarding of inconsistent information. In turn, preferences, behaviors, and even appearances and mannerisms are affected by one's existing schemas. Research has been designed to illustrate the effects of gender schemas on these functions and their outcomes, and the following section reviews the relevant findings.

Gender schemas influence children's attention and memory. Using schemas, incoming information is sorted and categorized as being either schema consistent or inconsistent. Consistent information is deemed relevant, and therefore it is attended to and then further processed. Information that is inconsistent with existing schemas is not considered relevant and tends to be ignored. Thus, gender schemas influence what is noticed and what is disregarded. Furthermore, if information is paid attention to, it can be further processed. The next step of processing includes information being filtered through existing schemas and encoded. Encoding is the process of incorporating new information with existing schemas. Information cannot be encoded without a schema first being present.

Gender schemas are used by children to organize information from the social environment. The information is organized by being filtered through the two main schemas: the superordinate schema and the own-sex schema. Schematic consistency in memory occurs for both types of schemas. These two schemas influence what is encoded in memory and then how the information is retrieved from memory.

Memory is better for information consistent with own-sex schemas. Children remember what is consistent with their own gender group, such as a girl remembering more about objects, attributes, and roles considered appropriate for girls. Also, in many studies, children have demonstrated better memory for information about actors of the same sex as themselves than about those of the other sex. Thus, girls are more likely to remember the actions of a female character in a story or movie, whereas boys are more likely to remember the actions of a male character.

Further evidence of own-sex memory having an advantage comes from studies that have used labeled novel objects to test children's ability to remember gender-typed information. In these studies, children are shown unfamiliar toys, which are labeled for one sex or the other and given names. Children remember the names of novel objects more often when the labels reflect gender typing congruent with their own sex. That is, girls remember the names of objects labeled as being "for girls" or "toys that girls like" more often, and boys remember the names of more objects labeled as being "for boys" or "toys that boys like." In addition, these novel object studies also show how children remember more details about information that is congruent with their own gender group. In one study, children were told the details of how to use novel objects, some of which were labeled as being for their own sex and others of which were labeled as being for the other sex. A week later, children remembered more details about how to use the labeled novel objects associated with their own gender group and less about how to use the other objects. These findings illustrate the influence of the own-sex schema on children's memory.

The implications of these findings are far-reaching. If children remember more about objects and activities that they perceive to be own-sex appropriate but forget information that they believe is for the other sex, then children's competence and skill levels for other-sex activities will be limited. Children may avoid other-sex activities, not simply because they believe that these activities are not "for me" but also because they may have developed limited competence in these activities—they do not know how to engage in them as well as they do activities they perceive as being "for me."

Novel toy studies also have illustrated that children will touch more often and ask more questions about objects labeled as being for their own sex than for objects labeled as being for the other sex, which illustrates their willingness to explore situations that are consistent with the expectations for their own gender group. Developmental trends are found in the exploration of objects associated with children's own gender group, with older children showing more of a tendency to explore gender-consistent objects in comparison to younger children. These findings show how activating the own-sex schema can lead to increased attention and exploration of objects consistent with children's own sex and suggests that this tendency increases as cognitive development increases.

Information consistent with the superordinate gender schema also is remembered at a higher rate than gender-inconsistent information. In several studies, children have shown better memory for gender-stereotypic events than for counterstereotypic events. Children also better remember information that is consistent with their stereotypes about both gender groups as compared to information that is counterstereotypic. For instance, children generally will remember the events of a story that fit their gender expectations, like a girl playing dress up and house, than events that do not, such as a boy playing with a kitchen set. Furthermore, children who hold stronger gender schemas show these effects more than other children.

The impact of gender schemas on memory may be influenced by a number of factors. The first factor is the age or cognitive development of the individual. Many studies have found that as children get older, memory improves overall, and their memory for consistent versus inconsistent information increases. As children's gender schemas develop, their schemas become better organized, they incorporate more information, and they become more complex. It is not clear yet how each of these developmental changes influence schematic processing.

A second factor that appears to influence memory is the type of memory task that is required. More challenging memory tasks seem to increase the likelihood of finding schematic processing effects. When memory tasks are simpler, less bias tends to be seen.

A third factor that influences memory is motivation or having an incentive to remember. Although research shows support for the idea that schema-consistent information is what is noticed, encoded, and then stored in memory, not all schema-inconsistent information is disregarded. In some but not all cases, memory for inconsistent information can be improved when one is motivated to attend, encode, and then remember inconsistent information. For incentives to impact memory, however, they must be salient and attractive. Furthermore, not all studies have found that incentives can increase memory, calling for the issue to be studied at greater length.

Finally, the length of time between exposure and testing affects memory for inconsistent information. Specifically, the ability to remember inconsistent information decreases with longer lengths of time between the original exposure and recall of the information. Additional research is needed to understand why delays influence memory in this way.

V. Liabilities Associated with Gender Schematic Processing, Memory, and Attention

Using gender schemas can lead to faulty information processing in several ways. First, when information is missing from a situation, gender schemas may be used to fill in the gaps and add information where it is missing. When this happens, information that does not exist in reality is created and inserted into a scenario in order to make sense of a situation (or a person). Because these added pieces of new information are remembered as if they are part of the scenario, the actual scenario and the newly contrived scenario are indistinguishable. Furthermore, the contrived information tends to be consistent with gender schemas. These accumulated pieces of additional information have been referred to as *illusory databases*. An example of the use of an illusory database would be a child remembering that the teacher in a newspaper article was a female, even if the teachers' sex was not disclosed. In this case, the child has used his or her gender schema to infer that the teacher is a woman and has inserted this new piece of schema-congruent information into the story to fill the missing information gap, without any awareness of having done so. Although being able to insert information into a scenario to aid the decision-making process can be helpful when the missing information is congruent with the actual situation, sometimes the information is not accurate. These additions can lead to incorrect decisions and memories. In the previous example, the teacher may have been a man, and reliance on the illusory database could have led to faulty reasoning and inaccurate decisions.

Illusory databases are not only used when information is lacking. Sometimes the strength of a schema overrides the existing information, leading to reliance on gender schemas, rather than trying to incorporate or decipher information incongruent with gender schemas. When these types of overrides occur, diverse situations are interpreted to be more similar to one's schema than they are in actuality. An example of this type of faulty decision making would be if a newspaper article reported that a teacher in a story was a male but the child instead inferred that the teacher was a female. In essence, the child has overridden the accurate information with information that is congruent with her or his beliefs.

Another situation in which gender schemas can lead to faulty decision making is through *illusory correlations*. Illusory correlations are when two types of events are categorized together incorrectly or the relationship between two categories is believed to be stronger than it is in reality. Because schemas lead to certain types of information being attended to or disregarded, an incorrect relationship between two categories can be created and maintained. Most of the existing research on illusory correlations is based on the issue of overestimation of associations between distinctive characteristics and minority group members. Few studies have been conducted on how illusory correlations may occur using gender information.

One of the most interesting ways that gender schemas can lead to faulty processing is by causing memory distortions. In memory distortions, instead of information provided by one's schema being applied to a situation as in the use of illusory databases, information within a scenario is *changed* in memory to match gender schemas. One example of memory distortion is when a situation is remembered accurately, but the sex of the actor in the situation is changed. Many studies have tested children's memory distortions by showing pictures of scenes depicting people performing gender-consistent and inconsistent activities. When asked to remember the information, children tend to accurately report on gender schema–consistent scenes. However, when remembering inconsistent scenes, they often change the sex of the person to make the person's sex consistent with the gender-role behavior that was portrayed. For instance, after being shown a female police officer, a child may later say that she saw a police*man*. Another way in which memory distortion occurs is through changing the situation to match the sex of the actor. For example, after watching a scene of a girl playing doctor, a child might later remember the situation as a girl pretending to be a *nurse*.

Just as schemas bias memory more when the memory demands are higher, memory distortions tend to be more pronounced when there are longer delays between exposure and testing. Furthermore, the processes underlying memory biases are yet unclear. Because gender schematic processing involves many steps, it has been questioned as to what point in the process memory distortions occur. For instance, errors may be made during the encoding stage, in which a child might look at a photograph of a girl playing with a truck but encode it as though it were a boy, or in the retrieval stage, in which a child might initially encode the information accurately but later reconstruct it inaccurately by remembering a boy playing with a truck.

Memory distortions have far-reaching implications for understanding gender development. One implication concerns the development and maintenance of gender stereotypes. Although we might expect that viewing counterstereotypic information may help children break down their stereotypes, the research on memory distortions suggests that instead, children may distort this information so that it becomes confirming of gender stereotypes rather than disconfirming them. Another implication concerns the development of programs to counteract stereotypic thinking in children. A number of programs have been developed based on the idea that stereotypes can be challenged by presenting children with counterstereotypic examples. The memory distortion research suggests that this approach may not be effective and may explain why few of these programs have been successful in changing stereotypes. Rather than simply presenting children with counterstereotypic examples with the idea that these will weaken their stereotypes, a more fruitful approach would be to provide children with stronger motivation for changing stereotypes. This may be accomplished by using more detailed explanations about why the actors engage in these behaviors to draw more attention to the behaviors so they are not simply processed as being gender consistent.

VI. Gender Schemas and Impression Formation

Because schemas are used to organize and classify incoming information, they are often used to help interpret ambiguous situations and make decisions when not enough information is present. The process of using schemas as an information base is referred to as *default processing*. Default processing is used by both adults and children in a wide variety of ways. For example, gender schemas are used in making attributions about others when information about the individual is not available, such as when having to guess personality attributes or likes and dislikes of others.

One way children use gender schemas is in making inferences about whether they will enjoy playing with new children. When children are given only basic information about unfamiliar children (e.g., their age and sex), they often decide whether they would like to play with the target child based on their gender schemas. Children of all ages tend to infer that they would enjoy playing with children of the same sex more than children of the other sex. These findings illustrate that children base inferences about others on schemas about what the sexes are like, and they use gender schemas to draw inferences even in the absence of additional information.

Children also infer the specific attributes of unknown children using their gender schemas. Children rely on the knowledge of a person's sex when making judgments about what others like to do. For instance, in one study, preschoolers watched a video-

tape of an infant participating in various activities. For some of the children, the infant was labeled as being a boy; for others, the infant was labeled as a girl. The children reported that the infant had qualities and attributes that were consistent with the label provided. This type of study shows children's use of gender as a way to categorize the qualities and attributes of others, and that generalizations about others are made even when gender is the only information available for making judgments about others.

How children make attributions about new information also has been investigated. In a study of how children make inferences, young children were taught new attributes for a specific girl and boy. Next, they were asked to tell which of these properties a new child would have, and the new child was given a label that did not match their appearance. Results showed that children ignored the conflict between the gender label and the appearance of the new child and relied on the gender labels to decide which attribute should be applied to the child. This shows that children use categorical information as the basis for inferences rather than property information (such as the appearance of the new child).

Children also use gender information to decide if another child would like an unfamiliar toy that he or she likes. For example, a boy who likes an unfamiliar toy will likely reason that other boys also will like the same toy and are less likely to think that girls would like the toy. These findings suggest that children use a gender-matching strategy: if they like a toy, they assume others of the same sex also will like the toy.

Studies have been done to assess how children use gender to help them deal with complex information about others. When young children (five years of age) are told the sex and interests of an unfamiliar person (e.g., Jamie is a five-year-old boy who likes to play with dolls), they tend to base their judgments on information about the other person's sex. So, in this case, they believe that Jamie would like to play with trucks and will not like kitchen sets. Older children (10 years of age) also say that Jamie would like trucks but will be more likely to say that Jamie would also like kitchen sets. Although equivalent studies have not been conducted with adults, the studies that have been done suggest that adults rely more heavily on the masculinity or femininity of the person's interests and that they pay less attention to sex than do younger children. Why this developmental pattern appears is unclear. Developmental trends may relate to adults using subtypes of gender schemas (e.g., having gender schemas about feminine men) or to children's cognitive constraints in processing information.

The advantages and disadvantages of using default processing are clear. Not all information is present in every situation, and many situations are ambiguous. Since frequently inferences need to be made to make everyday decisions, drawing on existing schemas aids in routine decision making, as well as in making predictions about strangers or novel situations. As much as the utility of default processing can be seen, potential disadvantages of relying on schemas to make inferences also exist. Many inaccuracies can occur when situations are not gender-schema congruent. In these cases, inferences may be incorrectly made because the gender schema overpowers the other information that is available.

The extent to which gender schemas influence thinking in other cultures remains to be seen. Although many of the studies have been done only with European American middle-class children, the underlying assumption of this line of research is that whatever one's culture or ethnic group promotes as being sex-linked, those are the characteristics most likely to be influenced by gender schematic information processing.

VII. *The Influence of Gender Schemas on Behavior*

Gender schemas are hypothesized to influence behavior in several different ways. First, gender schemas provide prescriptive information—that is, information about what is considered appropriate for one's own sex and who is considered appropriate to play with. Second, people are motivated to behave consistently with the expectations for their own sex. For children, matching their behavior to the behavior of others of their own sex is one means of self-definition and increases cognitive consistency. Third, schemas provide the detailed plans of action, or scripts, that allow for behaviors to be performed competently.

One powerful phenomenon that has been identified by developmental researchers concerns children's tendencies to play with same-sex peers, which is called sex segregation. From toddlerhood on, both girls and boys tend to prefer to spend time playing with others of their own sex and, for many children,

the majority of their social interactions are with same-sex peers. Sex segregation tends to be more extensive in settings in which children have choices of playmates and where adults provide little structure for play. For instance, sex segregation is very noticeable on playgrounds at school and is less likely in neighborhoods. Sex segregation appears to be more powerful in the early school years and may subside somewhat during adolescence, when dating and mixed-sex group interactions become more common. [*See* SEX SEGREGATION IN EDUCATION.]

Girls play differently than boys in many ways and many of the differences found in U.S. samples have been identified as well in other cultures. When girls play together, they tend to play indoors more than outdoors, they are relatively quiet, and they encourage cooperation among the play partners. In contrast, when boys play together, they tend to play outdoors; their play is characterized by a rough-and-tumble quality of playful, active interactions; and they are more concerned with dominance hierarchies within the group than with promoting cooperative interactions. Furthermore, girls' tend to play with dolls, they enjoy playing house in fantasy play, and they are more likely to use art materials in their play. Boys tend to play with transportation toys, they enjoy playing superheros in fantasy play, and they are more likely to play with construction toys.

The major consequence of sex-segregated play for children is that they are exposed to the play patterns, activities, and interaction styles of only one sex. Through this exposure, children learn and practice the skills and styles of their own sex but do not receive as much experience and practice with other-sex styles and skills. Thus, girls learn how to encourage cooperative interactions, whereas boys learn to be more effective in establishing dominance relationships. Girls learn to be nurturant by playing with dolls and playing house, whereas boys learn to develop spatial skills through construction toy play.

The role of gender schemas in children's play choices has been confirmed in several studies. Very young children may use their ability to discriminate the sexes to help find others who they perceive to be "like me" to play with. As children grow older, their increased gender knowledge may increase their tendencies to choose same-sex playmates as they reason that other children of the same-sex will likely share many of their interests and so these children have additional appeal. Furthermore, children's ideas about what the other sex is like may influence the likelihood of avoiding members of the other sex. Boys may avoid girls because they think their play is boring; girls may avoid boys because they think their play is too boisterous.

Just as children's playmate preferences can be influenced by what they know about gender, so too can their toy preferences and behaviors. Many studies of children's behavior on playgrounds and in classrooms confirms that children tend to spend much of their time playing in gender-stereotypic activities and with gender-stereotyped toys, while spending little time playing with activities and toys, stereotyped for the other sex. Simply observing this pattern does not provide convincing evidence of the power of gender schemas on children's behavior, however. Children may play with gender-stereotypic toys for many different reasons including their prior experiences with the toys (e.g., they are more familiar with them), because their parents have encouraged this type of play, or because they feel that these toys are more interesting.

To directly assess whether children's behavior can be influenced by gender schemas, it is necessary to devise situations that are new to children. This has been done in a number of studies involving unfamiliar toys and activities that are given gender labels ("this is a toy that boys really like" or "this is a game that girls play very well") and then children's play with the toys or games is assessed. The particular toys and games that are used are not stereotyped and the labels are applied arbitrarily to the games and toys so that the particular activity does not influence their responses. The idea is that if children play more with the toys or games that are labeled for their own sex, they are demonstrating the power of gender labels without the confounding issues of prior experiences with the toys and games.

Many studies have been done using the novel toys and games and the results, with only a few exceptions, indicate that children's behavior can be guided by the labels given the toys and activities. Children tend to play longer with, touch more often, and ask more questions about novel toys labeled as being for their own sex than for toys labeled as being for the other sex. Gender labels are more likely to be used by children than information about which sex demonstrates a behavior when the two are put into competition. For instance, if a girl watches a boy play with an unfamiliar toy but the toy is labeled as being for girls, she is more likely to follow the label and play with the toy rather than avoiding the toy because a boy played with it.

Gender labels also influence children's motivation to try hard on a game or task, as shown in studies involving novel games or novel achievement tasks. Children's motivation, accuracy, and their expectancies for success (whether they believe they will do well on a task) are influenced by gender labeling of activities and tasks. When a game is labeled as one that boys do well on, boys perform better on the task than girls; but when the same game is labeled as one that girls do well on, girls outperform boys.

One potential criticism of labeling studies is that the demands of the situation are strong. That is, children are placed in a situation in which they are told which sex usually likes a game or activity. To not follow the guidelines provided by the labels might be difficult. However, several studies have minimized the demand characteristics of these studies by separating the situations of when children learn about the labels from when their behavior is assessed and by having different experimenters involved in the learning versus assessment aspects of the study. Even when the demand characteristics are minimized, children tend to perform according to the gender labels they are given. The one constraint is that they must remember the labels for them to have an impact. When children remember the labels, their behavior tends to fall in line with the labels. Gender labels appear to be more effective with older children than with younger ones and somewhat more effective with boys than with girls. Individual differences in susceptibility to gender labels need to be investigated more fully.

Gender labeling studies have illustrated that gender schemas can influence children's behavior even without any prior experience with games or activities. Children appear to attend to the gender-related cues about who should be better at a game or activity or who might like a toy or activity more and then use that information as a guideline for their own behavior. Parents, teachers, and the media should exercise caution when introducing new toys and activities to children. Even unintended gender messages may be translated by children into messages about who should and should not play with a particular toy or play in a specific activity. Furthermore, the short-term and long-term consequences of gender labels can be serious. In the short-term, children may not engage in activities they believe to be more appropriate for the other sex, thereby limiting their experiences with certain toys or in certain activities. In the long-term, children's behavioral and skills repertoire may be limited because they have not engaged in a wide range of games and activities early in life.

For instance, women may perform less well on spatial abilities tests than men because they spent less time playing with blocks as children, since block play requires practice and skill in spatial relationships. Girls may drop out of math and science classes because they believe that these courses are "not for me" (and not for my sex), thereby limiting later career options. Boys may avoid nurturant play with dolls and thus be less competent and experienced in providing warmth and emotional expressiveness when it is needed to comfort a friend.

In the field of gender development, there is controversy about whether and how gender schemas influence early behavior. Most of the concern has derived from two patterns of findings in the literature. The first finding is that, in several studies, very young children have been found to behave in stereotypic ways about six months before they were able to express stereotypic knowledge. Recent research studies, however, suggest that even toddlers have rudimentary stereotypic knowledge but that this knowledge is more difficult to assess than simply asking them their stereotypes of boys and girls, and so few researchers have attempted these studies. Another finding that questions the role of gender schemas on behavior is that levels of gender schema knowledge do not always correspond with levels of gender stereotypic behavior. A number of potential issues make this question difficult to address, including the difficulty of assessing in depth the levels of stereotype knowledge a person has and the problem that many of the commonly used measures showed little individual variability. Although more research needs to be done to assess when children develop knowledge about the sexes and to understand how and when this knowledge influences behavior, the gender labeling studies provide strong evidence that the potential for influence is strong.

Gender schema theorists tend to assume that gender schemas influence behavior but recognize that this influence is not consistent on either children's behavior or on their motivation. In some situations gender is particularly salient, thereby increasing the likelihood of children showing stereotypic behavior. In other situations, gender may not be salient and children's behavior may not be guided into stereotypic patterns. Furthermore, children vary in their personal gender schemas and the variations among children also influence the likelihood of performing stereotypic behaviors. For instance, some girls may feel like they are not typical of other girls—maybe they see themselves as tomboys—and these girls may

not expect to like what other girls like; in fact, they may expect to dislike those things. Furthermore, gender schemas need not be conscious to be influential—that is, they may become largely automatic as they are practiced again and again, therefore children need not spend excessive cognitive energy thinking about their behavior. [*See* PLAY PATTERNS AND GENDER.]

VIII. *Gender Schemas and Academic Skills and Choices*

Gender schemas influence many aspects of children's behavior and preferences. Although more research is needed on the topic, it has been proposed that gender schemas may affect children's preferences for academic choices and careers. Academic areas and careers are often gender typed, and gender schemas may lead to the narrowing of children's choices in these areas just as they do in toy and peer choices. Children evaluate situations, determine if they are self-relevant, decide if they are for boys or girls, and then decide if the situation is for them or not. What are the implications of gender schemas directing preferences in the areas of academic choices and careers?

Academic choices may be influenced by gender schemas. Children pay more attention to, have better memory for, and are more motivated in gender consistent areas, so when academic areas are categorized as being for one sex or another, differential skill acquisition and performance may occur. For example, if math and science are categorized as "for boys," girls may be less inclined in math and science classes to pay attention and remember, and they may not try very hard if they have trouble in these courses. The same may occur for boys in areas such as reading and writing. In addition, children may not seek out courses in a gender-inconsistent area, therefore limiting their knowledge in this area. A cycle begins in that as children develop fewer skills in a domain, they may struggle to master the course work, which then may contribute to future avoidance of the topic.

Similarly, gender schemas may also influence career choices. Even in early childhood, children have some stereotypes about careers. Just as they can with academic choices, children may use gender schemas to decide whether a career is relevant, whether it is for the same or the other sex, and if the career is for them or not. At an early age children may begin to narrow their choices of possible careers, in that only gender-consistent occupations might be considered viable options.

The influence of gender schemas on academic achievement and career choices may begin very early when schemas influence children's activity choices. As gender schemas influence the activities in which children participate, children's skill attainment is affected. The more children choose to participate in an activity, the more practice they have at the activity's skill requirements. The reverse is also true. When children choose not to participate in an activity because it does not fit their gender schemas, they lose the opportunity to learn the skills associated with that particular activity. Therefore, as schemas lead directly to activity choices, they are indirectly influencing the skills children acquire. Because stereotyped activities for girls and boys often have different skill requirements, children's choice to participate in gender-consistent activities leads to a differential pattern of skill learning for boys and girls. Boys' activities often encourage gross motor skills, spatial abilities, and more mathematically based skills, whereas girls' activities highlight fine motor skills and more language-based skills. Thus the groundwork for children's achievement in academic areas may be directly influenced by their gender schemas. Although conclusive findings for this connection cannot be made without further research, the results of a few longitudinal studies suggests that there is a link between children's activity choices and their academic success in some domains. For instance, it has been found that children who participated in boy-preferred activities in preschool later scored higher on tests of science, math, and spatial abilities. Furthermore, as children decide in which academic areas are important for them to excel, they are also limiting their career options. For example, if at a young age a boy decides reading is not important to him because it is "for girls," his skill in reading is likely to decrease over time, and his chance of becoming an English professor also diminishes. [*See* ACADEMIC ENVIRONMENTS; CAREER ACHIEVEMENT; CLASSROOM AND SCHOOL CLIMATE.]

IX. *Gender Schemas and Appearance*

Even in infancy, children's sex is marked by their appearance. Parents and children use gender schemas in a variety of ways to influence their appearance, in particular, hairstyles and clothing. In infancy, parents often choose to dress their children in ways that make clear the sex of their child, with pink clothing, ruffles, and lace often being chosen for girls, and blue and red clothing more often chosen for boys. This pattern continues as children grow older, with girls often being clothed in skirts and dresses, and boys in pants and sneakers. It has been reported by parents that as children get older they make strong requests to dress in ways that express their sex, even when parents may not prefer this style of dress. From these reports it can be hypothesized that children are aware of the distinction between clothing that is "for boys" and "for girls," and as they begin to choose their own clothing, may use gender schemas to make these choices. Unfortunately, little research has been conducted in the area of gender schemas and dress, leaving many unanswered questions.

Although the influence of gender schemas on clothing for boys and girls may not seem likely to have a profound affect on behaviors, there may be consequences of these types of choices. One consequence is that children's constant exposure to males and females dressing differently may lead to consistent reinforcement of gender as a categorizational tool. Gender schemas are reinforced, and gender stereotypes may become stronger. As gender stereotypes are strengthened, children's views of the opportunities and activities available to them become limited because any option associated with the other sex is disregarded.

A second consequence of gendered clothing styles is that others respond to children and to adults on the basis of appearance. Children (and adults) who appear more gender typed in their appearance may elicit more gender typed responses from others, whereas children who are less gender typed in appearance likely elicit less gender typed responses. The girl in a frilly dress is likely to be treated differently than the girl in jeans.

A third consequence of gendered clothing style is more specifically linked to behavior, in that it is proposed that the clothing children wear may influence the activities in which they participate. For instance, a girl in dress shoes and a skirt may not be inclined to play in sandboxes or participate in activities that require gross motor skills. Few studies have been conducted in this area, and the one or two that have been conducted have not found a direct link between observations of play and dress. However, interviews with children reveal at least an indirect link between style of dress and activity participation. For instance, preschoolers report associations between wearing pants versus skirts with different activities, supporting the idea that gender schemas for clothing may be linked to girls and boys choosing particular activities. Also, preschoolers recognize the advantages of girls wearing pants when they participate in active play. Finally, girls who wear pants more often than dresses are more likely to engage in nontraditional activities, showing a potential link between gender schemas, dress, and, activity choices. More research is needed before it can be concluded that gender schemas and clothing preferences lead to differences in play participation. However, with observational studies showing that boys' activity choices more often than girls' activities are characterized by the use of large gross motor skills, include higher levels of rough-and-tumble play, and have high levels of energy, there is reason to be interested in studying this topic further.

X. *Overview of Liabilities Associated with Gender Schematic Processing*

Gender schemas are useful for helping people to process information efficiently and quickly. They provide information when it is lacking in the environment. Gender schemas provide guidelines that can be used to influence behavioral choices. Some of the most serious consequences of gender schematic processing involve applying gender schemas rigidly to one's own behavior. The major liabilities associated with gender schematic processing of information about behaviors and preferences are the limitations that are imposed when children adopt only one set of activities in which to engage. If children accept and adhere to strictly defined roles for their sex, they will be exposed to stereotypic activities more than to activities associated with the other sex, and they will experience more time playing with same-sex children than with other-sex children. Rather than developing a wide behavioral repertoire, children's skills and behavioral capabilities may be limited to those considered appropriate for their own sex.

To fully understand the potential seriousness of being gender-role limited, it is important to understand the concept of androgyny. The concept of psychological androgyny was originally developed from the idea that individuals can have psychological characteristics that are masculine and feminine. For instance, rather than thinking of masculinity and femininity as representing ends of a single dimension, the idea of androgyny is that two dimensions exist— femininity and masculinity—and people may fall at

any point along each dimension. Research designed to assess the idea of androgyny illustrated that it may be an ideal, that is, psychological androgyny may promote mental health and well-being because individuals with both sets of capabilities are more flexible and can shift their behavior to suit whatever the demands of the situation may be.

Therefore, children who experience only one style of interaction and who have experiences with only one set of skills are not only limited in the ability to perform the other set of skills, they also are limited in their flexibility to adjust their behavior to suit the demands of situations. Children with rigid adherence to gender roles will have more limited experiences, play partners, educational opportunities, interaction styles, appearance, and career options than those children with a less rigid adherence to gender roles. Children with more flexible gender roles are willing to adopt a variety of behaviors and thus should have increased abilities to interact comfortably in a wide variety of situations. To minimize these problems, children should be encouraged to explore many behaviors and activities, and they should be encouraged to think of alternative ways to process information rather than simply using gender categories.

XI. *Summary*

Gender schema theory has been one of the major theories used to understand gender development. Gender schema theorists believe that individuals are actively involved in processing and interpreting information from their social environments, thus they are actively involved in their own development. Gender schema theories, because they emphasize the role of cognitive processes of attention, memory, forming impressions, and making inferences, have added new dimensions to understanding gender development. These theories have been particularly influential in providing insights into how stereotypes about the sexes develop, how they are maintained, and how they are used.

SUGGESTED READING

Bem, S. L. (1981). Gender schema theory: A cognitive account of sex typing. *Psychological Review* 88, 354–364.

Fagot, B. I., and Leinbach, M. D. (1989). The young child's gender schema: Environmental input, internal organization. *Child Development* 60, 663–672.

Liben, L. S., and Signorella, M. L. (1987). Children's gender schemata. In *New Directions for Child Development, No. 38* (W. Damon, ed.). Jossey-Bass, San Francisco.

Markus, H., Crane, M., Bernstein, S., and Siladi, M. (1982). Self-schemas and gender. *Journal of Personality and Social Psychology* **42**, 38–50.

Martin, C. L. (2000). Cognitive theories of gender development. In *The Developmental Social Psychology of Gender* (T. Eckes and H. M. Trautner, eds.), pp. 91–121. Erlbaum, Mahwah, NJ.

Martin, C. L., and Halverson, C. F. (1981). A schematic processing model of sex typing and stereotyping in children. *Child Development* **52**, 1119–1134.

Ruble, D. H., and Martin, C. L. (1998). Gender development. In *Handbook of Child Psychology, Vol. 3: Social, Emotion, and Personality Development.* (W. Damon and N. Eisenberg, eds.). Wiley, New York.

Gender Development
Psychoanalytic Perspectives

Joanne E. Callan

Alliant University and San Diego Psychoanalytic Institute

Glossary

Differentiation The process by which the self (the baby or child) is perceived as different or distinct from the object (the mother or primary caretaker). It is associated by some with the separation-individuation phase and to the larger separation-individuation process, referring specifically to the latter half of the first year of life. To others, it is used to describe the process that is unfolding throughout the first five to six years of life and even longer.

Oedipus complex Named after Oedipus Rex by Sophocles, this phenomenon was identified by Freud as occurring in both girls and boys and is related to the interest that each has toward/in the cross-sex parent, especially during the phallic or oedipal period (from about 30 months of age to five to six years of age).

Psychosexual stages/phases Freud's formulation for conceptualizing the psychological and sexual development of males and females, which related specific body zones to related pleasures and fantasies. Included were the oral, anal, phallic (the latter part of which is sometimes called the phallic-oedipal), latency, and adolescence phases.

THE UNDERSTANDING OF GENDER DEVELOPMENT from a psychoanalytic perspective has advanced considerably since Freud presented his initial views in the middle 1890s. A number of influences, both within and outside of psychoanalytic circles, have shaped the current views, with the greatest interest and attention occurring in the past 40 years. This article reviews the major influences and the theoretical developments and then presents a proposed working model—a developmental sequence—on gender development.

I. Introduction

The various and changing understandings of gender and gender-related development in humans have been influenced by a wide range of disciplines—biology, psychology, anthropology, sociology, religion, philosophy—and by a number of theories within these disciplines, among which have been evolution, psychoanalysis, and sundry sociopolitical and economic views including, more recently, feminist thinking. Although such broadly ranging influences have affected understandings that have evolved over the years, certain developments in and just before the 20th century have been profoundly instrumental in shaping today's formulations of gender development, especially within psychoanalytic thinking. This article focuses first on these various influences and then presents a historical overview of the resulting major theoretical, clinical, and research contributions that have, in turn, led to current psychoanalytic understandings of gender development. Last, the article presents a proposed working model or outline that comprises a developmental sequence of gender development for females and for males, in the specific context of current psychoanalytic perspectives.

II. *Major Influences: 1895 through the 20th Century*

Psychoanalytic formulations and perspectives on gender and gender-related development have been revised significantly since first developed 120 years ago. Since 1895, when Freud announced the affect-trauma theory (his first model of the mind with its essential emphasis on drives), and 1905, when he published the *Three Essays on the Theory of Sexuality*, a number of critical revisions regarding gender development have emerged (specific definitions regarding gender and gender-related development are discussed later in the article). Influences from within and from outside psychoanalysis are discussed next as a backdrop for understanding the resulting theoretical developments and revisions.

A. EXTERNAL INFLUENCES

From the early 1990s through the 1950s, a number of world events had an impact on how analytic thinkers, including Freud, considered human behavior in general. World War I (1914–1918) was one such event, leading Freud and others to examine aggression with renewed interest and to consider issues such as group as well as individual behaviors and motivations. Also influential in the 1930s and 1940s was the world's increasing awareness of "man's inhumanity to man," as a result of Hitler's tyranny and despotism. Psychological casualties in World War II (1941–1945) created urgent need for trained mental health professionals to treat war-related disorders, as did those in the Korean War and, even later, in the Vietnam War. Related to these events were emerging life changes for men and women which led to new roles and responsibilities for both.

In the 1940s, not only were professionals dealing with those directly engaged in fighting, but also with displaced families and children separated from their parents. Anna Freud and Dorothy Burlingame, working in London with such children, were among those whose focus on the special needs of children increased attention on child development, both normal and pathological, opening the door for subsequent attention to early gender development.

Beyond these events influencing psychoanalytic thinking generally, several other developments had a major impact on understanding gender issues, including gender development: the women's rights movement, beginning in the mid-19th century and, more specifically, the later women's movement of the 1970s, the civil rights movement, and the gay liberation movement (see discussion that follows on variance in sexuality). Strong messages from these movements asserted social values and rights that women and minorities—including gays, lesbians, and bisexuals—should enjoy.

Within the women's movement, feminists gained momentum, advocating the essential nature(s) and needs of women. Reflecting both the richness and diversity within and among women, their voices called for a more full awareness of women's development throughout life, their emotions and needs, and their various roles and other life experiences, including their sexuality. Some had strong reactions against a number of major components in Freud's views, most specifically those related to the sexual development and sexuality of women (e.g., his masculinized theories regarding female development and suggested inferiority of women). In reaction, alternative perspectives on female development and life experience came to the fore. As feminist theory expanded, varying views were articulated that constituted a pluralistic rather than a unified body of thinking; accordingly, feminist views and thinking are now described more accurately as feminist theori*e*s. These various theories have been instrumental in a number of the revisions and new formulations within psychoanalytic thinking about gender development. [*See* THE FEMINIST MOVEMENT; FEMINIST THEORIES.]

Other concurrent sociopolitical movements also focused on human needs and values (e.g., the demand for respect of differences, including race and ethnicity, gender, class, and religion). Protest groups who advocated this respect, and others, including those reacting to the Vietnam conflict, contained a common thread: an emphasis on the value and rights of the individual. This emphasis contributed to new understandings of male and female roles and of masculinity and femininity and, thus, to an emerging and expanded understanding of gender development.

Scientific discoveries and advances in related and other disciplines, such as biology and psychology, have informed psychoanalytic theory as well, especially in such areas as human development, adding greatly to the psychoanalytic understanding of gender and gender identity development. John Money and William Masters and Virginia Johnson were among researchers who contributed to an informed understanding of human sexuality. Professionals and their respective professional associations became more sensitive to the complexity and variance that has become more recognized as characteristic of human sexuality. The American Psychological Association and the American Psychiatric Association, followed later by the American Psychoanalytic Association, supported efforts to remove biased language from diagnostic categories and diagnostic manuals, thereby refuting the earlier view of homosexuality as a mental disorder, and academic institutions began supporting informed study on sexuality and gender.

B. INTERNAL INFLUENCES

Psychoanalytic theory has also advanced significantly from within its own circles since the early 1900s, profiting through theoretical and clinical contributions from many analysts and researchers. Its widening scope has dramatically moved both theory and applications from Freud's three models of the mind and other formulations as developed from 1895 through the 1930s. Indeed, particularly critical to discussions on gender development have been those understandings that have moved beyond Freud's views on human sexuality (e.g., male and female sexual development). Among several major theoretical contributions that have had essential influence on current psychoanalytic thinking are the following:

1. *Ego psychology*, with important formulations supporting shifts from Freud's central focus on drives to an emphasis on adaptation; the function of the ego and its defenses; and on normal development, including psychosocial components.
2. *Object relations theory*, with its relational concepts and emphases on the fundamental influence of early mother–child relationships and on the interplay between constitutional factors and critical relationships with others.

3. *Self psychology*, with its formulations on the developing sense of self and the integration of the self.
4. More contemporary revisions, with emphasis on the centrality of the subjective experience and on mutuality in human development and in clinical practice.

Some theoretical developments built on Freud's views, while others departed considerably from his thinking.

Psychoanalytic research related to gender development has burgeoned in the past 20 years, through infant observations as well as studies on child development and families. Findings from these studies have supported the advancement of psychoanalytic theory and its applications, with particular relevance to current understandings of gender development.

Indeed, these various external and internal influences have had a pervasive and broadening impact on psychoanalytic thinking, including the understanding of gender differences and gender development and advancing considerably from Freud's views on how boys and girls develop. Current psychoanalytic perspectives recognize—much more clearly than Freud and his early followers were able to do—both the commonalities and the differences between males and females in gender and gender identity development, and one outcome of this progress is a developing consensus in current theory regarding gender and gender identity development. Even so, unanswered questions remain as do varying explanations that require further attention.

The balance of this article (1) provides further discussion on the development of psychoanalytic thinking regarding gender development and (2) explores the more generally accepted formulations in current psychoanalytic theories as well as remaining questions related to gender identity development. Finally, a developmentally organized sequence describing the complex process of human gender development is presented as a working perspective, drawing on information and understandings presented in the first part of the article.

III. *Psychoanalytic Perspectives: 1895 through the 20th Century*

The following discussion considers major theoretical contributions to psychoanalytic theory on human sexuality, and, in particular, on gender development: first as they developed from Freud's initial publications in 1895 to writings into the 1950s and 1960s and, then, as they developed from the 1960's up to 2000.

A. FROM 1895 THROUGH THE MID-20TH CENTURY

Even though Freud's initial writings on human sexuality were met with a range of reactions from his colleagues and from others, his formulations had, as they continue to have, notable impact. Fundamental to Freud's theory of masculinity and femininity was his belief that maleness and masculinity are the basic and natural states and that, as a result, femaleness and femininity are less valuable. Freud further asserted that as a result of this primary masculinity, boys and girls traverse different developmental paths. Some of Freud's views have prevailed, as noted by various observations and writings (e.g., the presence of infantile sexuality), while others have required revision or correction (e.g., some particularly relevant to this discussion, such as the emergence of early gender identity).

Arguably, Freud's most seminal contribution regarding human sexuality and human sexual development was his notion of infantile sexuality (along with his formulations regarding the unconscious and the Oedipus complex). Although Freud either changed or vacillated about a number of his views throughout his professional life, his commitment to the notion of infantile sexuality persisted. His formulations on masculinity and femininity and those regarding the sexual development of males and females are well known and have been reviewed over the years by a number of theorists. His phallocentrically organized view of sexual development for both boys and girls and the resulting conflicts and anxieties—castration anxiety for boys and penis envy for girls—have received strong criticism, as did his views on girls' inferior sexual and moral development.

Some theorists, among whom are Phyllis and Robert Tyson, believe that Freud's emphasis on sexuality was tied essentially to his formulations regarding infantile sexuality and thus did not really address gender development; yet others, among whom are some feminist theorists, consider Freud's writings—especially those related to his earlier views purporting that women held a status which not only was essentially masculinized, but also considered to be inferior to that of men—directly related to gender differences and how they develop.

Janine Chasseguet-Smirgel, reexamining Freud's writings on female sexuality, developed a summary in the 1930s that remains helpful today in understanding how Freud's theories progressed. In her review, she created two categories of works subsequent to Freud's: those similar to or consistent with and those opposed to Freud's. Chasseguet-Smirgel noted beliefs that Freud continued to hold, in spite of considerable criticism, from 1905 to the time of his death. Her reference to his famous quotation advising those who want to understand more about femininity to turn to the poets or wait for science to provide more information reflects the balance she seemed to seek in her review.

As interesting as her discussions and those of others in the first wave of feminism may have been, there was nonetheless a lull in critical exploration on female sexuality for several decades until renewed interest emerged in the 1960s. Similarly, there seemed to be little real advancement regarding male sexuality in these same years, or regarding gender-related development in general.

B. FROM THE 1960s TO 2000

With the 1960s came renewed and energetic interest about human sexual development among psychoanalytic thinkers, alongside that of others. In Irene Fast's writings in the 1980s on differentiation theory, she identified three specific critical areas around which new data and findings emerged, significantly changing psychoanalytic thinking on gender development (two relating to girls and one to both boys and girls): (1) establishing the clitoris as a female organ, (2) establishing the little girl's early awareness of her vagina, and (3) establishing that social factors override biological ones. Similarly, Ruth Formanek in 1982 pointed to three main contributions up through the 1970s that served to significantly revise Freud's views: (1) Robert Stoller's writings, in part because they took issue with Freud's theory of conflict as it related to gender development; (2) Margaret Mahler's research and resulting theoretical formulations, in part because of the emphasis on gender identity development during the separation-individuation process; and (3) Eleanor Galenson and Herman Roiphe's studies, in part because of the suggestion that developments leading to gender identity formation occur earlier in childhood than Freud had thought.

Stoller's work, in effect, has been so instrumental in advancing the understanding of gender development that many theorists have used his formulations as a critical piece, if not essential foundation, in their work. Indeed, many seem to concur with Formanek that until the 1950s or 1960s there was no real emphasis on gender development, and Stoller is seen as the first to effectively move psychoanalytic discussion on human sexuality and its development toward an explicitly clear focus on gender development. Because of his pervasive influence, a summary of Stoller's formulations that are particularly relevant to gender development is provided next.

1. Stoller's Formulations of Gender Development

Stoller was associated with the University of California at Los Angeles Gender Identity Research Clinic, and initially he developed his work on gender issues based on clinical work with 85 patients plus 63 of their family members. He acknowledged a preference for collecting data through clinical practice, specifically psychoanalysis, expressing his view that it was the best way to find out what really goes on in the mind (as differentiated from the brain). At the same time, he emphasized that a real understanding of the nature and origin of masculinity and femininity could only be fully understood through the integration of biology, learning theory, and psychoanalysis.

Even though Stoller recognized the advances regarding gender identity that were being realized in the 1950s and 1960s, he also acknowledged the importance of Freud's views, noting especially *The Interpretations of Dreams* and *Three Essays on the Theory of Sexuality,* in particular asserting that the greater part of what is called sexuality is determined from infancy on and not just a biological or genetic matter. Nonetheless, Stoller disagreed with much in Freud's formulations regarding gender development, such as Freud's position that female sexuality grew out of conflict. He acknowledged the difficulty of defining sexual behavior, and, although he viewed reproduction as the essential purpose of sexual behavior, he justified this view by saying that it was less true of higher organisms. Explaining further, he said that in humans, sexual behavior may have a psychological purpose apart from reproduction, and he referred to studies discovering that both masculine and feminine behavior are found in higher mammals, with evidence that neither one occurs exclusively in them. He pointed, as well, to the critical finding that for most mammals the basis of sexual-

ity (i.e., sexual tissue) is feminine, and further that masculinization can only occur when some influence is exercised on the female tissue.

Stoller described the focus of his work as pursuing information on the development, maintenance, and manifestations of masculinity and femininity, and he identified three basic conclusions: (1) that the aspects of sexuality called gender are primarily culturally learned, with critical and particular influence, first by the mother and then by the father; and (2) that biological forces contribute to, indeed have a major influence on, the development of gender identity. He explicated and defined the following terms as useful in understanding human sexuality and gender: *sex, sexuality, gender, core gender identity, gender identity,* and *gender role,* careful to note the overlap existing among these terms in their representation of various aspects of human sexuality. He pointed out that sex and gender do not enjoy a one-to-one relationship and moreover that each may take an independent path (in this regard, referring to the similar position already presented by John Money).

- About the term sex, Stoller believed that chromosomes, external genitalia, internal genitalia, gonads, hormonal states, and secondary characteristics must be considered. In short, the emphasis is on the biological, and he used the term in reference to the male or female sex and all the biological parts that determine whether one is a male or a female. He emphasized that the earliest stage in the development of masculinity and femininity involves the sense of one's self.
- To the term sexuality he assigned anatomical and physiological meanings.
- He said that gender is a term referring to "those aspects of sexuality" that "are primarily culturally determined, that is, learning postnatally" using the term to refer to psychological and cultural phenomena rather than biological ones.
- He described core gender identity as the earliest sense of one's sex, of maleness in males and femaleness in females.
- He noted that gender identity deals with several realms—feelings, thoughts, and behaviors—and is to be used when considering psychological phenomena.
- He related gender role to "the overt behavior one displays in society, the role which" a male or a female plays, "especially with other people, to establish a position with them," as that relates to the view of his or her gender.

With regard to *gender*, Stoller asserted that, whereas *male* and *female* are biological terms, *masculine* and *feminine* are terms related to gender. He described gender as an amount of masculinity or femininity existing within a person, adding that usually there is a preponderance of masculinity in males and of femininity in females. He explained that *gender identity* starts with the unconscious or conscious knowledge and awareness that one belongs to one sex and not the other; and he added that as development progresses, gender identity becomes more complicated, giving as an example that one may sense himself as not only a male but as a masculine man or an effeminate man or even a man who fantasizes about being a woman.

Distinguishing *sex* from *gender*, Stoller stressed the biological and anatomical bases of the term *sex*, asserting that one could speak of the male sex and the female sex, yet could speak of masculinity and femininity without referring to biological sex or to anatomy. Explaining his choice of the term *identity*, Stoller said that he used it to mean that of which one is aware, either consciously or unconsciously, about how one exists in the world.

Stoller concluded that, although there can be variance, gender, gender identity, and gender role are usually synonymous in an individual, and he pointed, as did Freud, to future discoveries, saying "It seems likely that in the future another criterion will be added: brain systems. One's sex, then, is determined by an algebraic sum of all these qualities," and he talked explicitly about the "overlapping" of maleness and femaleness (1968, pp. XI, 9, and 10).

Stoller approached the understanding of gender development in ways that both departed from and expanded earlier psychoanalytic views, including Freud's. By grounding his studies and resulting theories in the context of scientific advances (e.g., in biology, genetics, biochemistry, and physiology), he allowed for a more current and comprehensive view of physical, especially sexual, development.

2. Beyond Stoller: Theoretical Developments

As just said, Stoller's identification of new terms and definitions provided a means of clarifying and distinguishing among the major components of human sexuality and thereby allowed for a more explicit and precise understanding of gender development from a psychoanalytic perspective. His key terms have been accepted and espoused by a number of theorists whose work has followed. Increasingly

in the past thirty years, psychoanalytic theorists have built on his works, stressing, in particular, the multiple influences that impact gender development. In doing so, they have moved away from the earlier, more simplistic (and often incomplete, even inaccurate) explanations, such as understanding femininity or female development by relating it to, or comparing it with, male development. The Tysons, for example, have focused on gender identity, gender role identity, and sexual partner orientation, highlighting their interaction or interplay in human development. Beyond demonstrating the usefulness of such distinctions to gain theoretical clarity, the Tysons have illustrated how such knowledge also informs clinical work. Arguably, it is now generally agreed that gender identity develops in individuals through the integration of many factors and that this confluence, which extends beyond childhood, is critical to human development.

Indeed, two concepts—*complexity*, comprising the important distinctions noted previously, and the essential *integration* of various life influences and experiences—are basic to current psychoanalytic understanding of gender development. Although in the past, Freud and others implied that a greater complexity would be required to really understand human sexuality, a full appreciation of just how complex the nature of gender development actually is has only been possible with the increased knowledge and scientific advances that have emerged in the past 50 years. With this greater knowledge came (1) an awareness of how critical and defining is the integration of these many influencing factors and how such integration takes place as well as (2) an appreciation for the variety of experiences and accommodations that can emerge in both males and females.

From studies regarding complexity and those on the essential integration of various components key in the process of gender development, a number of new or reworked concepts and themes have emerged. Concurrently, efforts to develop working models or frameworks for how these myriad influences and aspects can be pulled together have been proposed—for example, those by Irene Fast and Phyllis Tyson. A number of critical areas related to gender development have been and are being explored, among which are (1) *differentiation*, or separation-individuation; (2) *object relations and relationships*, especially early ones with both the mother and father; (3) *variance and fluidity* in normal human sexuality (including issues and new understanding related to heterosexuality and homosexuality), and

(4) *three specific organizers: the oedipal complex, the superego,* and *gender identity.* Brief comment on these areas follow, preparatory to providing a proposed developmental sequence of gender development.

C. CRITICAL AREAS OF EXPLORATION

1. Differentiation

The concept of differentiation has held increasing merit in the psychoanalytic understanding of gender development, indeed, for human development in general. A number of theorists arguing for changes beyond those proposed by the first wave of revisionists have sought to (1) better articulate the process of gender development and (2) support complexity as an essential and defining characteristic of human sexuality. Fast has asserted that both boys and girls move from an undifferentiated view and sense of self to an increasingly differentiated one. She is among those who have pointed to the central organizing function of the recognition of sex differences as signaling the beginning of differentiation. Saying that "children themselves do not categorize their experience in gender terms" (1984, p. 4), she noted that it is within this recognition of sex differences that there emerges a recognition of limits: that boys possess some attributes, girls possess others. Others (e.g., the Tysons) react to Fast's position, pointing to evidence that, early on, boys and girls have an elementary or emerging sense of self accompanied by a sense of being male and female, which includes awareness at some level of having either male or female genitalia; still others have emphasized that achieving differentiation requires an effective sense of one's self and also of the other, so that there is a clear perception and experience of two people.

2. Object Relations: Mental Representations and Relationships

Many psychoanalytic theorists and practitioners use these terms, as comprised in object relations theories, but often with various meanings in mind. These terms are used here to indicate the internal mental representations one has developed, from birth on, of one's self and of one's relationships with others. Regarding gender development, current object relations theories emphasize the critical role of the mother as the primary object, although increasingly they have stressed the nature and importance of the father's presence. Some theorists assert that the nature and

quality of the more close or meaningful relationships that one has with others are essential determinants of one's gender identity.

3. Variation in Human Sexuality

A growing number of psychoanalytic authors and clinicians have presented an expanded understanding of human sexuality, particularly with regard to gender and object choice (i.e., sexual partner choice). Variance in sexuality—that is, the different forms in which human sexual behaviors and fantasies occur, as well as the myriad ways in which one can envision and experience one's self as a sexual being—has been increasingly established in psychoanalytic thinking. For several decades, there has been increasing awareness of the tendency of psychoanalysis to normalize heterosexuality; and there has been a concurrent movement to correct this view (e.g., increasingly, concern has focused on the past tendency to view two normative developmental paths: one for boys and one for girls). In personal communications in June 2000 with several psychoanalysts whose writings, teaching, research, and practices reflect an understanding of variance in human sexuality, the author noted their concurrence regarding advances in just the past decade with respect to increasing openness and attention within psychoanalytic circles on issues of variance. Such progress is also evidenced when one considers that only as far back as the 1970s homosexuality was considered among various professional groups as a diagnosable disorder. Indeed, it is noteworthy that in the late 1990s, the Executive Council of the American Psychoanalytic Association requested its Committee on Scientific Activities to prepare a report on the status of homosexuality and psychoanalysis, coauthored by Bertram Cohler and Robert Galatzer-Levy.

Fluidity in sexual feelings, fantasies, and behaviors is one aspect of this expanded thinking regarding human sexuality that has received considerable attention. The question of etiology of homosexuality has been around for decades, and it takes on new interest with efforts to understand from research as well as clinical data what collection of experiences may lead to sexual partner choice, which is neither only homosexual nor only heterosexual but which changes. Findings reported in the Cohler and Galatzer-Levy book mentioned earlier noted the midlife discovery of a change in sexual preference as constituting just one of the interesting areas of discussion with regard to sexual fluidity. Psychoanalytic thinkers, researchers, and practitioners have much to offer in the pursuit to understand all of sexuality.

4. Organizers

Because of increasing appreciation regarding the complexity of the various processes associated with human gender development, theorists have considered phenomena that may facilitate or otherwise influence these processes, three of which are noted and briefly described here: (1) the Oedipus complex, (2) super-ego, and (3) gender identity.

a. Oedipus Complex. Freud's views on the nature and meaning of the Oedipus complex in human psychological and sexual development, with an emphasis on the different paths taken by boys and girls—in particular, the related shifts in attachments to mothers and fathers and associated conflicts—have been the subject of much writing and debate over the years. Although more recent formulations have continued to emphasize the impact of early relationships on the course of psychosexual development, or gender development, these relationships are considered to be of influence within a multiple set of determinants. Rather than emphasizing biological determinants including drives, theorists have pointed to the increasing awareness of and interest in sex differences that girls and boys have as critical in activating gender differentiation processes. Fast and P. Tyson are among those who have noted more recently such important influences and contributions as (1) the child's awareness and experience of parental relationships, including emerging fantasies and how these contribute to a shift from dyadic relationships to triadic ones; and (2) the father's presence and involvement.

b. Superego. Clinicians as well as researchers have long studied the dtevelopment of the superego and related issues of conflict, anxiety, self-nurturance, and moral development. Even though a retrospective look at Freud's writings on the superego can be confusing due to a lack of clarity and consistency in his views and terms, Freud maintained his beliefs about the differences between boys and girls with respect to superego development, based largely on his model of male development. Indeed, the role of the superego with respect to overall human functioning, including moral development as well as gender development, has been a major topic in psychoanalytic study and thinking—that is, the superego has been associated with the emergence of conflict and anxiety as well as with related feelings of guilt and shame, in both girls and boys, and also to issues of moral development.

Diverging from Freud on superego development, more current views emphasize the instrumental role of object relations, noting in particular the critical role of the mother regarding the myriad messages she instills in both boys and girls; even more recently, early and ongoing influences from the father have also been emphasized. Through verbal as well as nonverbal communications, the mother imparts messages reflecting standards and expectations with regard to beliefs, values, feelings, and behavior, as does the father.

Of interest as well in psychoanalytic thinking have been the role and functions of the superego. A gradual change regarding superego functioning has occurred, moving away from earlier, more singular emphasis on its punitive and judgmental functions to include loving, nurturing, and approving ones, a shift that not only has implications for understanding gender development, but one that can help boys and girls, women and men, gain comfort with their sexuality (e.g., as in accepting and enjoying one's sexuality). Although some acknowledge certain differences between the superego development and functioning of both boys and girls, these differences are now related more to the overall complexity and nature of the life experience of the two sexes—indeed, to that of each child—rather than to biology.

c. Gender Identity. As discussed earlier, Stoller defined gender identity as referring to psychological phenomena and therefore related to a range of experiences and behaviors: feelings, thoughts, fantasies, and actions. Beginning with the awareness that one belongs to one sex and not the other, the process of gender identity becomes more complicated with development, as demonstrated in Stoller's example that a male may sense himself as masculine, or as an effeminate man, or one who has fantasies about being female. Much attention has been given to this construct in recent decades and although there is general acceptance of Stoller's definition, some differences in points of view continue among analytic thinkers.

Another issue of particular interest in understanding the development of gender identity, for both girls and boys, is the quality and nature of the child's relationship with the mother. Through early experiences with the mother (which include being held, fed, cared for physically, and loved) and myriad mutative steps in identifying with the mother, the infant gradually develops a sense of self or self-identity. Both boys and girls must develop a sense of being separate and also of being different from their mothers, and current focus tends to be on how these processes of separation and differentiation are similar but also different for boys and girls. For example, some view as mandatory for forward development that the boy disidentify with—or come to see himself as different from—his mother.

For girls, there is not the same need for disidentifying with the mother; yet it is critical that girls see themselves as distinct from their mothers. Accordingly, whereas boys must disidentify in order to develop a firm sense of masculinity, girls may rely on the oneness or sameness that they experience with their mothers in the ongoing development of femininity. It may be, therefore, that the boy can build on this early challenge to distinguish himself as he moves to meet subsequent developmental stages and tasks. The girl, on the other hand, has to move forward, with respect to becoming separate and different from, in the context of greater ambivalence: ambivalence created out of the pleasure of her closeness and sameness with her mother, but also reflecting the invariable competition, disappointments, frustrations, and restrictions or limitations that she will experience and the resulting anger or hostility that she is likely to feel toward her mother. Accordingly, both boys and girls will experience some sense of vulnerability as they move forward in developing a sense of gender, but this sense, and actual experience thereof, is usually different for the two sexes.

IV. A Current Psychoanalytic Perspective on Gender Development

The discussion up to this point on the past 120 years of psychoanalytic thinking about gender development describes considerable change since Freud's writings, especially in the past three to four decades. Drawing on this material, the author has developed the following perspective on current psychoanalytic thinking regarding gender development: first, through a developmentally sequenced outline, proposed as a working psychoanalytic model on gender development; and second, through a brief consideration of specific issues related to gender development

in girls and then related to that in boys. The content of the developmentally organized sequence relates to gender development in both girls and boys, and this sequence is followed by two related discussions, the first focusing on girls and the second on boys.

A. A DEVELOPMENTAL SEQUENCE OF GENDER DEVELOPMENT

The following sequence on gender development in boys and girls is presented from a developmental perspective—that is, it moves from brief comment on the prenatal influences to developments in the first months of life and on through the oedipal period. These initial descriptive statements related to early developmental stages are followed by some similar comment on gender development as it occurs in later developmental phases. A particular emphasis on the first three to five years of life has been elected (1) because of the attention that has been given historically in psychoanalytic thinking on human sexuality and gender development in the first five years of life, in particular earlier thinking about the oedipal period or phase; but, moreover, (2) because of how important experiences in the first three to five years of life are to a child's developing and overall sense of self, as validated by research findings as well as clinical observations.

• Prenatal influences affect the ways in which both girls and boys develop with respect to gender. Biological factors, including chromosomal and hormonal determinants and functions, have direct influence on sex differentiation among girls and boys. It has also been noted that parental fantasies that develop before and during pregnancy begin to have influence on how both the mother and the father conceive of their child and, thus, how they will relate to a child at birth and thereafter. This parental interaction is ultimately instrumental in how a child comes to see herself or himself.

• Boys come into life as biologically male and girls as biologically female, given an appropriate biological inheritance. In describing the processes of sex differentiation as we now know them to occur in girls, it can be said that embryos develop into the female sex, unless otherwise influenced. Accordingly, neither boys nor girls are only, or all, male and masculine in their early lives, as was thought by Freud and other early theorists.

• Multiple influences impact both girls and boys as they move forward in their overall development, including differentiation. These influences, which are biological, psychological, and sociocultural, have a considerable confluent effect on the gender development of both.

• Both girls and boys are probably usually influenced more by the social environment and their own psychological experiences of their worlds than by biology in their gender identity development. Of particular importance are early object relations; more specifically with regard to gender development, not only the specific ascription or assignment of sex that parents give to a child, but the larger meaning of that assignment to the parents and the related messages they convey based on that meaning are critical.

• From birth on, both boys and girls begin to develop a sense of their bodies, initially mostly from physical sensations and explorations as well as from how they are handled by their caretakers. As they mature, this sense is enhanced by visual cues and observations, by cognitive advances (i.e., being aware of their physical features and gaining labels for them), and through their relationships with others. Over time this process, as described by Ada Burris, leads to a sense of core body image, which, as it is gradually consolidated, uniquely affects gender development in each child.

• For both girls and boys, the capacity for autoerotic behaviors, which can be not only stimulating but also soothing experiences, develops as they move from infancy through the early years of their lives—indeed, throughout the life span. Masturbation is practiced and takes on different qualities, including the development of associated fantasies throughout life. Theorists have noted the organizing function played by masturbatory behaviors in consolidating one's sense of self as a sexual person who can enjoy physical pleasure.

• A major influence on both girls and boys is their early identification with their mothers (or primary caretakers, who in Western cultures are usually female). Both girls and boys identify with and internalize myriad aspects and features of their mothers' emotions, behaviors, roles, and relationships, responding, as noted earlier, to her values and expectations. Interactions with the primary caretaker directly affect how both boys and girls move through the oral and anal phases, specifically with regard to appropriate nurturing, protection, and stimulation, and thus to their overall and developing sense of self, including gender development.

• In the first one to two years of life, the gender experience of girls and boys can be characterized as undifferentiated and also overinclusive. Said differently, they enjoy a narcissistic, or multipotential, sense of self and assume that all people are the same. It appears that they move increasingly from such a posture to one where they know themselves and others—that is, toward a less narcissistic, or more differentiated, perspective.

• At around 18 to 24 months of age, boys and girls seem to be able to identify themselves as either male or female. Current theory places emphasis on the cognitive developments that allow a child to make this identification. More study is needed to fully understand how and to what extent boys and girls experience their maleness and femaleness at this time, particularly in regard to the suggestion that even though they may be aware of being either male or female, boys and girls are not able to be specific about or delimit the various aspects of what makes them male and female.

• An important organizing experience for both girls and boys, thought to happen by the third year, occurs when they become aware of anatomical differences between them. Both girls and boys desire to have or be everything, a desire that can be referred to as the "Baskin-Robbins" phenomenon (a phrase meant to conjure the experience of a child who, when faced with the 31 flavors of ice cream available as choices, would like to have them all). Somewhere between two and three years of age, still in the preoedipal phase, both boys and girls consolidate a sense of self, which involves a gradually differentiated awareness of self and body. At this time, they concentrate on developing identifications that are specific to, or peculiar to, their respective gender. Concurrently, and then increasingly as they move on to the oedipal phase, they concentrate more and more on relationships with their parents. Within these relationships, both girls and boys practice, in the context of their respective gender identifications, how to relate to same-sex objects and to cross-sex objects.

• From birth on, both boys and girls form various identifications with their mothers and their fathers, or primary caretakers, as well as with other family members and, usually, with an increasing number of people outside their families. In this context of multiple, ongoing identifications, they develop a subjective and an objective sense of themselves and thus also of their masculinity and femininity.

• Both girls and boys move through processes in which they alternate between attachment to their parents and others around them and efforts to achieve independence or autonomy. They deal with issues regarding separation and individuation as they also deal with efforts to establish their differentiated, or less narcissistically or inclusively organized, selves.

• From the third year through the sixth year, both boys and girls become increasingly adamant in their preferences and deliberate in their efforts to associate in play with same-sex peers. This preference and behavior are viewed as having socialization value and thus are key to the consolidation of gender identity.

• With a good enough resolution of the oedipal complex (in all of its complexities and components, as ascribed by current theory, including a shift to mastering triadic relationships), both girls and boys move, more or less comfortably, into latency, a period of development that begins at about six years of age. Contrary to some past formulations that latency provides a respite from sexuality and sexual issues, current views hold that gender development persists during these years (indeed, throughout most of life). Boys and girls continue, for the most part, in their preferences for same-sex peer groups, which, as stated earlier, can be seen as an effort to strengthen or consolidate their gender identity. Parents continue to convey expectations regarding roles and activities as well as values they wish their sons and daughters to pursue, increasingly directing them toward the future. Gradually, parental influence is diffused by other forces (e.g., influence from other authority figures, such as teachers and coaches, and also increasing peer influence). Moreover, both boys and girls begin to experience a substantial expansion of their worlds, developing at this time not only new interests but also new means of mastering their environments—as, for example, advancing cognitive skills—all of which impact the sense of self, including gender development.

• Preadolescence is a period of development viewed as an important time of transition from latency to adolescence. Both girls and boys must consolidate gender identity in the context of emerging biological and physical changes, including early development of secondary sex characteristics, such as breast development in girls and voice change in boys. Girls and boys continue to prefer same-sex peer groups and associations for the most part; yet there are emerging cross-sex as well as same-sex interests probably related, to some extent, to future sexual partner choice (e.g., the increasing interest in boys that can be more directly observable in some girls at this time).

• In adolescence proper, generally thought to extend from about age 12 to about 20 (although some now view adolescence in Western cultures as extending into the mid-20s), substantial and rapid changes, which have a significant impact on overall development including gender development, occur in several areas of psychosexual and psychosocial growth and development (e.g., in physical size and body shape, in cognitive functioning, and in social roles and relationships). Major biological changes contribute to increased sexual feelings and urges, and fantasies related to one's gender identity and sexual functioning take on new meaning and intensity. Establishing genital primacy is the goal of adolescence—becoming comfortable with one's own sexuality and gender identity and beginning to think about and seek a relationship with a partner are primary concerns of the adolescent. It is also in adolescence that the capacity for reproduction is usually realized, a capacity that challenges both girls and boys to explore and also consolidate their gender identity. Although they begin to have thoughts about what it might mean to be a parent and even what they might like in a parenting partner, in the early and middle stages of adolescence, these thoughts are often naive and romanticized, whereas in later adolescence, they may become more realistically based (although, of course, teenage pregnancies and motherhood do occur in all three phases of adolescence). [*See* ADOLESCENT GENDER DEVELOPMENT.]

• In adulthood, indeed, throughout life, developmental and maturational processes continue, as described by Calvin Colarusso and Robert Nemiroff, including those related to gender identity and gender development. When possible, both men and women seem to pursue a more comfortable, if not more certain, sense of themselves, a pursuit that embraces their own sexuality as it is integrated with their attachments to, and needs for, others. Influenced by fantasies as well as all past development and experiences, both women and men seek relationships that support and enhance gender identity and a fuller sense of self. Although recent research has focused on stability and fluidity in object choice (i.e., sexual partner choice), further study is needed.

B. GENDER DEVELOPMENT ISSUES IN GIRLS

As noted earlier, Stoller's work set the stage for current understandings regarding gender development in girls. Current theorists generally have supported his assertion that a girl's primary femininity is based on her core gender identity and that, once established, it stands. Increasingly, there is agreement regarding the critical impact of object relations—in particular, the girl's early identifications with her mother (or her primary caretaker) and how the girl, able to rely on these early identifications, is able to discover and affirm herself as different from her mother, as separate from her mother but also like her and dependent on her. Also, increasingly, there is appreciation for the special roles that fathers play in supporting the gender development of their daughters. Not only are fathers critical to development, as, for example, in the oedipal phase, serving in a balancing role as girls begin to move from their initial attachment to their mothers, but they also play a critical role in helping girls deal with their emotions.

A key aspect, and resultant, of the critical early relationships girls have with their mothers as well as with their fathers, is how the girl develops a sense of her body through various somatic and kinesthetic sensations and experiences. Current psychoanalytic theory is more appreciative than in the past about girls' early experience of their genitals and how this awareness helps them in defining gender identity. Indeed, regarding this self-awareness, it has been suggested that girls have less anxiety about their genitals because they are less visible and more protected than are those of boys.

Some agreement has developed as well about the importance of gender development for girls as they move into the second and third years of life—a period in object relations theory known as the separation-individuation phase or differentiation. Key developmental tasks and experiences in this period are directly tied to how a girl pursues her independence and autonomy—her overall sense of self—in the context of remaining dependent on her caretakers.

At this time in their lives, girls seem to develop an enhanced and more defined sense of their bodies and their gender identity through identification with their mothers and through support from their fathers. As girls more through the preoedipal and oedipal phases, fathers may help them in modulating their emotions, including the increasing ambivalence often observed in girls toward their mothers, as previously discussed. It is also at this time that girls, as well as boys, become aware of the differences between female and male anatomy. Although in the past, some theorists have pointed to penis envy and to castration fears as typical reactions girls have to these differences, others have questioned these reactions as being typical

or normal. Rather, they have pointed to the likelihood that girls may be surprised on first noticing anatomical differences between them and boys, but, provided they have had adequate parenting in a balanced environment, girls maintain a sense of pride in their own femininity. Supporting this departure from earlier views, some theorists have firmly asserted the position that castration anxiety and penis envy may be indicative of pathology.

In summary, a girl's gender development, in the context of her overall development, is molded by many influences: biological, psychological, and sociocultural. Particularly critical are her relationships with others, especially that with her mother as primary caretaker. It is critical for girls to establish a sense of femininity through identification with their mothers, because this achievement sets the stage—indeed, is the very foundation—not only for developing a positive, narcissistically invested feminine sense of herself, but also for having stable and fulfilling dyadic and triadic relationships in the future. Having support from one's father is also critical to a girl's developing sense of herself and mastery of her emotions, in particular as the father provides important balance to a girl's relationship and involvement with her mother.

C. GENDER DEVELOPMENT ISSUES IN BOYS

As noted earlier, an embryo must be stimulated hormonally in order to become masculinized. Yet even with this defining influence, a boy's experience and consolidation of his gender identity after birth, and thus throughout the course of his gender development, in many ways parallels that of a girl. As with girls, the major influences with respect to gender development are social and psychological, and among the most important of these are relationships with others. More specifically, the quality and nature of the primary relationship with the mother is viewed as the most influential one for boys, just as for girls.

Within this formative relationship, however, there are major differences between boys and girls. Both before birth, during pregnancy, and after delivery, a mother holds fantasies and expectations about her child, which, being individually, environmentally, and culturally defined, are usually quite different for boys than for girls. Based considerably on this thinking, a mother conveys myriad messages to a boy from the time of his birth about what she expects him to be and how she expects him to become that. Initially, then, a boy develops mental representations and affects that emerge out of his closeness to and identification with his mother or whoever is his primary caretaker. Writings in the past two decades, however, have noted the importance of the father's early relationship to optimal development in both boys and girls. Accordingly, as childrearing practices change, such as with more fathers assuming this caretaking role, theory will no doubt benefit from studies already conducted and those yet to come regarding this parenting shift.

One key difference between the gender development of boys from that of girls involves how boys discover and respond to their bodies and body parts—in particular, to their genitals—which are much more visible and accessible than are those of girls. Discovering their bodies not only increases boys' awareness of themselves, but also increases pleasure, both of which contribute significantly to a developing sense of self. Introduction to his penis—visually, kinesthetically, and physically—is an experience in a boy's self-discovery process that provides various physical sensations and perceptions, thereby contributing to his overall sense of self. Indeed, converging physical, psychological, and cognitive developments contribute to a boy's developing sense of himself and his gender identity. Along with these developments, not only do boys achieve an increasing sense of mastery, often accompanied by pleasure, pride, and confidence, they also experience fears and conflicts around these advances. Crucially important to how a boy reacts to such fears is the nature of the environmental response—in particular, early object relations, especially those with his mother, father, and other caretakers. Nursery school and preschool program teachers, for example, often describe the fears and resulting behaviors of two-, three-, and four-year-old boys as they see and react to little girls whose lack of a penis can be a confusing surprise to them. Teachers recall, as well, little boys' fearful reactions to using the potty at school, including verbalizing their fears about losing a part of themselves (which girls may express as well).

Although the father's role is key in boys' development, just as with girls, it is played out in different and important ways for boys. One example is the critical balancing function that fathers provide in titrating the closeness a boy has with his mother, a function that helps boys disidentify with their mothers. Interactions between fathers and sons are often more physical and sometimes more challenging with respect to the father's expectations for his son's future than are those with daughters. Such interactions

with fathers are necessary for boys so that they may identify with a masculine figure. Fast has developed one description of the differentiation process in boys, wherein they use both their masculine and feminine identifications (gained through associations with both father and mother) as they move toward a masculine adjustment, a movement that can be attributed to their awareness of sex differences and to the resulting sense of limits they must face. Even so, the disidentification process has been viewed as a key and critical factor in boys' gender development, specifically in the process of gender identity formation.

V. Conclusion

Understanding gender development may seem to be a complex, even perplexing, endeavor. As Money said:

The difference between male and female is something that everybody knows and nobody knows. Everybody knows it, proverbially, as an eternal verity. Nobody knows it, scientifically, as an absolute entity for, as day and night merge under the glass of the midnight sun, male and female merge under the scrutiny of empirical inquiry. (1987, p. 13)

Nonetheless, critical advances have been made by psychoanalytic thinkers in the past 120 years in developing a fuller understanding of gender development, and there continues to be much interest and investment in learning more. As Nancy Chodorow said:

No other major theory evinces such continual fascination with and attention to gender and sexuality and such a continual sense of how problematic, contradictory, overpowering, and complex these are—as experiences, as identities, as cultural constructions, as personal enactments. (1994, p. 1)

ACKNOWLEDGMENTS

The substance of this article has drawn on a number of sources: articles and books as well as lectures, classes, and supervision before, during, and beyond the author's formal psychoanalytic training, including those in which she has been the student, analytic candidate, or supervisee and those in which she has been the teacher or supervisor. With such exposure over several decades, the author has found it almost impossible to sort out her own thinking from that of others and theirs from one another. With this awareness in mind, a sincere effort has been made to give credit where credit is due, and deep appreciation is expressed to all who have given of their knowledge and expertise to advance the author's own learning.

SUGGESTED READING

Burris, A. M. (1984). *The Contemporary View of Female Oedipal Development.* Unpublished manuscript.

Chasseguet-Smirgel, J. (1970). *Female Sexuality: New Psychoanalytic Views.* University of Michigan Press, Ann Arbor, MI.

Chodorow, N. J. (1994). *Femininities, Masculinities, and Sexualities: Freud and Beyond.* University of Kentucky Press, Lexington, KY.

Cohler, B. J., and Galatzer-Levy, R. M. (2000). *The Course of Gay and Lesbian Lives: Social and Psychoanalytic Perspectives.* University of Chicago Press, Chicago.

Colarusso, C. A., and Nemiroff, R. A. (1981). *Adult Development: A New Dimension in Psychodynamic Theory and Practice.* Plenum, New York.

Fast, I. (1984). *Identity: A Differentiation Model.* Analytic Press, Hillsdale, NJ.

Formanek, R. (1982). On the origins of gender identity. In *Body and Self: An Exploration of Early Female Development* (D. Mendell, ed.), pp. 1–24. Jason Aronson, Northvale, NJ.

Freud, S. (1959). *The Standard Edition.* Horgarth Press, London.

Galenson, E., and Roiphe, H. (1974). The emergence of genital awareness during the second year of life. In *Sex Differences in Behavior* (R. C. Friedman, R. M. Richart, and R. L. Van de Wiele, eds.), pp. 223–231. Wiley, New York.

Mahler, M. S., Pine, F., and Bergman, A. (1975). *The Psychological Birth of the Human Infant.* Basic Books, New York.

Money, J. (1987). Propaedeutics of diecieous G-IR: Theoretical foundations for understanding dimorphic gender-identity/role. In *Femininity: Basic Perspectives* (J. M. Reinisch, L. A. Rosenblum, and S. A. Sanders, eds.), pp. 13–28. Oxford Press, New York.

Money, J., and Erhardt, A. A. (1996, 1973). *Man and Woman: Boy and Girl.* Johns Hopkins University Press, Baltimore.

Stoller, R. J. (1968). *Sex and Gender: On the Development of Masculinity and Femininity.* Vol. I. Science House, New York, and (1974) Jason Aronson, New York.

Stoller, R. J. (1985). *Presentations of Gender.* Yale University Press, New Haven, CT.

Tyson, P. (1982). A developmental line of gender identity, gender role, and choice of object. *Journal of American Psychoanalytic Association* 30, 59–84.

Tyson, P. (1989). Infantile sexuality, gender identity, and obstacles to oedipal progression. *Journal of the American Psychoanalytic Association* 37(4) 1051–1069.

Tyson, P., and Tyson, R. (1990). *Psychoanalytic Theories of Development: An Integration.* Yale University Press, New Haven, CT.

Gender Development
Social Learning

Bernice Lott

University of Rhode Island

Diane Maluso

Elmira College

Glossary

Culture Ways of behaving, transmitted from one generation to another, that characterize groups of people who share language, history, geography, and social institutions.

Gender Attributes that a culture ascribes separately to human females and males that prescribe appropriate ways of feeling and behaving.

Learning A process that results in a change in behavior following implicit or explicit practice.

Sex Structural and physiological characteristics that distinguish females and males as a result of chromosomes, hormones, and morphological development.

Socialization A process of learning what is normative in one's culture in order to be accepted within it.

THE SOCIAL LEARNING OF GENDER refers to learning how to behave in ways considered gender-appropriate. This article is not about gender differences and will not present a catalog of ways in which girls and boys, women and men behave differently. Instead it is concerned with the construct of gender—as it is embedded in cultures and has variable meanings—and how a social learning approach helps us to understand and explain how gender is acquired and manifested in particular situations and contexts.

I. Definitions and Assumptions

It is important to distinguish between sex and gender. Sex denotes a limited set of innate structural and physiological characteristics related to reproduction and divides animal species (including humans) into female and male. Gender is specific to humans and connotes all the complex attributes that a culture ascribes to each of the sexes. Gender is a social category used by most human societies as a basis for socialization and social status. It is constructed from the particular conditions, experiences, and contingencies that a culture systematically pairs with human femaleness and maleness and reflects the culture's definition of femininity and masculinity.

The distinction between sex and gender has significant implications for politics, social policy, and social action, as illustrated by Bella Abzug's statement at a meeting preparing for an international United Nations conference on women. "The meaning of the word 'gender'", she said, "has evolved as differentiated from the word 'sex' to express the reality that women's and men's roles and status are socially constructed and subject to change."

A. VARIATIONS IN BELIEFS ABOUT GENDER

The specific meanings and extensiveness of the associations implied by gender vary among cultures, in different historical periods, and in different developmental stages. Cultures also vary in the importance they attach to gender differentiation, in how much differentiation there is, and in the strength and importance of gender stereotypes.

The degree of gender differentiation is related to the level of patriarchy and sexism in a society, to differences in the value and power of women and men, and to the allocation of social resources. Kay Bussey and Albert Bandura concluded in their 1999 review that "attributes selectively promoted in males . . . tend to be . . . regarded as more desirable, effectual, and of higher status," but studies of simpler and older cultures indicate that this is not universally true. For example, among the Eastern Chewong of the Malay peninsula, reported on by Signe Howell in 1988, value judgments are not attached to gender: girls and boys are treated the same from birth and follow the same rules, and no gender differences are expected in interests or traits.

Gender in the United States, on the other hand, is a ubiquitous and significant functional category in a broad range of institutions for both children and adults. The extent to which gender expectations influence or correspond to individual behavior, however, is related to individual learning histories, particular current environmental conditions, and personal social contexts (such as position in a family or group). Within-gender differences in how closely behavior conforms to social prescriptions can also be expected because of variations in the intensity of the gender socialization that has been experienced.

B. TWO SEXES OR MORE?

Some have suggested that the assignment of sex to individuals is also a social process. Biologist Anne Fausto-Sterling argued in a 1993 paper that at least five sexes could be produced among humans as a result of variations in chromosomes and morphology. While XX and XY chromosomes typically designate females and males, respectively, variations do exist. There are also variations in hormonal levels and anatomy. Which combination of these characteristics gets labeled female and which gets labeled male is a cultural process. Recognition of this phenomenon is what Celia Kitzinger referred to in 1995 as the "strong" version of social constructionism.

In this article, however, we will adopt the more prevalent view of sexual dimorphism: that there are fundamental and universal anatomical differences, related to reproductive capacities, between the overwhelming majority of females and males (whose chromosomal, hormonal, and morphological characteristics are concordant). Cultures use these anatomical differences to separate people in terms of experience, expectations, social value, and power, but all cultures do not treat these reproductive predispositions in the same way. As noted by Robert A. Levine in 1991, "The new evidence [in anthropology] shows a wider variety of meanings attributed to being male and female than any existing theory could have generated." These different meanings are learned within different cultural groups. [*See* DEVELOPMENT OF SEX AND GENDER.]

C. IMPORTANT ASSUMPTIONS

In our social learning approach, heavily influenced by a feminist perspective, we make use of constructs and formulations that focus on behavior. We attend to the conditions necessary for behavior acquisition and performance, and on the influence of specific situations, general contexts, and expectations. We define gender in terms of what one does, not as what one is. Our view is that gender-relevant behavior is not the result of stable intrapsychic traits that persons carry with them across situations but instead, like all behavior, is responsive to interpersonal social interactions and to the context in which it occurs.

We make the following important assumptions: (1) because of the nature of the human nervous system (i.e., our biology), human development is characterized by plasticity and malleability in response to environmental conditions and experience; (2) gender socialization is a continuing, lifelong process; (3) gender-related behavior in a heterogeneous, complex society is continuously affected by other social categories such as social class and ethnicity as well as by particular family and personal history variables; and (4) gender is a socially constructed concept that varies with culture and historical period.

In the course of gender socialization (i.e., learning to do what is acceptable and normative in one's culture in order to be accepted within it), we learn both what to do and what not to do. We also learn that these prescriptions and prohibitions vary with particular situations. Yet gender seems to be a more powerful regulator of behavior than some other social categories. Thus, the literature supports the conclusion of John C. Gonsiorek in 1995 that, in most situations, lesbians and gay men are more different from each other than similar because they confront situations and problems that are shared in common with other women and men, respectively.

Much of what children learn is in preparation for adult roles. While a major focus of this preparation is the skills associated with being mothers or fathers, there may be other important adult roles associated with gender. For example, a study of poor migrant Puerto Ricans living in Manhattan by Jagna W. Sharff, reported in 1983, found that whereas some girls were reared to be "child reproducers" and were reinforced for traditional "feminine" behavior, other girls were brought up to be "scholar/advocates" and were rewarded for dominance and assertiveness in the interests of the family's upward social mobility. Similarly, Bernard S. d'Anglure reported in 1984 that some Inuit (Eskimo) daughters are trained by their fathers to become hunters rather than to gather and prepare food, especially if the family has no sons. In the United States, children of preschool age have already been taught to believe that men are more competent in certain occupations, like car mechanic and airplane pilot, while women are more competent as clothes designers or secretaries. These findings were reported in 2000 from a study of a sample of children by Gary D. Levy, Adrienne L. Sadovsky, and Georgene L. Troseth.

As Roberta M. Berns pointed out in her 1989 book, the more complex the society, the more we have to learn, and "the more socializing agents and experiences contribute to the process." In this article we first identify the processes that underlie the learning of gender, as proposed by a social learning approach, and then discuss the influence of major socialization agents. Our concern is with the processes and conditions through which sex is transformed into gender, and the article concludes with a focus on variations and changes in gender definitions, or the reconstruction of gender. Much of the empirical literature from the United States that is cited, unless otherwise indicated, is heavily focused on European American, largely middle-class samples, a problem that has been noted by others.

II. Social Learning

The term *social learning* represents a spectrum of assumptions and hypotheses relevant to the antecedents and consequences of human behavior. While there are some differences among social learning theories or perspectives, what is central to all of them is the use of general learning principles to explain complex human social behavior.

A social learning approach to understanding gender was articulated in 1966 by Walter Mischel. He proposed that the same principles that describe the acquisition of all social behaviors are relevant to the development of "sex-typed behaviors," with a central role played by behavioral consequences. These consequences, he noted, differed for girls and boys with respect to different behaviors, could be experienced directly or vicariously (i.e., when observing consequences to others), and could be provided by others or by oneself.

A social learning approach assumes that social behavior is predictable from knowledge of the current situation or context, the individual's previous experience with these (or similar) events, the individual's state of motivation (i.e., what one desires or needs), and the anticipated consequences. This approach includes the following major components or assumptions: (1) every individual of any age has a previous learning history, which provides a repertoire of responses likely to be evoked in particular situations; (2) each situation includes distinctive and general stimuli or cues and has both specific and contextual meaning; (3) motivational factors are either brought to situations or evoked in them; (4) new responses can be acquired if opportunities are provided for their (explicit or implicit) practice; and (5) behavior will be acquired or maintained if it is successful in mediating positive outcomes. We know that individuals learn more behaviors than they display and that performance depends on appropriate conditions.

It is important to distinguish between traits and learned responses (habits). A trait is defined as a behavioral tendency that, once acquired (e.g., through childhood socialization), remains stable, internal, and cross-situational. The concept of habit, on the other hand, ties the performance of a learned response not only to the strength of that response based on prior experience but also to the situational cues and consequences present at the time. There is no assumption of consistency across situations or of intrapsychic stability unrelated to context. There is considerable evidence that human behavior is not well described by traits and that individuals learn responses to, and in, situations continuously throughout their lives. As conditions and opportunities for practice change, so does our behavior. Gender socialization is a lifelong process reflecting changing circumstances and experiences.

We believe that the social learning viewpoint is particularly compatible with feminist psychology. While disagreements continue among feminist theorists about particular issues, there are broad areas of agreement that include (1) recognition of the patriarchal, sexist nature of most aspects of contemporary social life and institutions, (2) recognition of the negative consequences of gender inequities in power, and (3) focus on the entire range of women's experiences. As noted in 1991 by Ruth Perry, among the major questions that feminist scholars across disciplines have asked during the past few decades are "How is human identity constructed in different cultural contexts? How do bodies come to have the meanings they have? How are women and men socialized to think and feel and act?" Such questions can be addressed within a social learning framework; relevant empirically testable hypotheses can be formulated, and data bearing on these issues can be integrated into a theoretical framework concerned with a wide variety of social phenomena. By contributing testable hypotheses about the conditions under which gender learning occurs and is maintained or changed, and about gender's function as a social cue, social learning provides a theoretical and empirical framework for the most basic of feminist assumptions—that gender is an ongoing process of social construction and reconstruction.

A social learning approach to gender includes recognizing the importance of gender as a stimulus for the implicit or explicit behavior of others. Gender evokes perceptual and evaluative responses, expectations, and particular ways of acting. Alice Eagly, in her 1987 book, emphasized that gender functions as a cue for status because it is observed to be correlated with power and prestige across a variety of settings and experiences. Because gender covaries with power and status, persons tend to behave in ways that confirm this. Other social categories, like ethnicity, also function as generalized status cues.

III. Construction of Gender

Each culture defines gender and provides opportunities for individuals to learn and display it by systematically arranging for the experiences of children and adults to differ in association with their sex. We must study these arrangements by first outlining the conditions under which social learning occurs and then focusing on the primary agents or sources of gender socialization. [See SOCIAL CONSTRUCTIONIST THEORY.]

A. CONDITIONS RELATED TO GENDER LEARNING

1. Linguistic Differentiation: Labeling

Children in the United States typically learn to identify gender categories at an early age. Nancy Eisenberg, Carol Lynn Martin, and Richard A. Fabes found in a 1996 study that about 75% of one-year-old children can distinguish between the faces of women and men, primarily on the basis of hair length. By age two, children are showing gender-linked behavior, and by the age of two and a half, they can apply girl or boy labels to themselves and others correctly and show some knowledge of gender stereotypes. Stereotype knowledge increases between ages three and five; by the age of four that knowledge is well developed and closely corresponds with the stereotypes of adults.

Monica Biernat found evidence in a 1991 study for four kinds of gender knowledge or beliefs: physical attributes (e.g., hair lengths), traits (e.g., rough or gentle), behaviors (leader or bakes cookies), and occupations. A variety of evidence, however, supports the conclusion that gender knowledge is not necessarily related to behavior; knowing a stereotype does not mean that one acts in accordance with it or vice versa. As Kay Bussey and Albert Bandura noted in their 1999 review article, one finds variations in gender behavior among children and adults despite their knowledge of gender stereotypes. Evidence also supports the conclusion that gender-relevant behavior by young children is not dependent on a belief about the constancy (or permanence) of gender. As an anecdotal example, an almost five, extremely bright, grandson of one of the authors was overheard asking his grandfather, who was giving his necklace of beads to another grandchild, if the grandfather used to wear the beads when he was a girl.

In order to associate attributes differentially with girls and boys, women and men, it is necessary to distinguish between the genders linguistically. This distinction cannot be taken for granted. Among the eastern Chewong people of Malay peninsula, for example, as reported on by Signe Howell in 1988, no differences are expected on the basis of gender; girls and boys are treated the same, and children are simply called "children." Only at adolescence are they linguistically distinguished as maidens and bachelors. This situation is far different than it is in the United States, where gender labels are highly salient and help to structure our social world. We sort people on the basis of gender and expect that particular characteristics will accompany the gender label.

2. Behavioral Consequences and Opportunities for Practice

A social learning analysis considers the consequences that follow behavior to be the primary mediator of learning and performance. This is the case whether the behavior is based on observation or modeling of others, on direct teaching, or on making responses that are most appropriate to situations. It is, of course, necessary that a behavior be physically within the person's capabilities.

In each society, the major socializing agents and institutions reward children (and adults) for behavior that is gender appropriate and provide aversive consequences or give negative messages for behavior that defines the other gender. These consequences increase the probability that it will be the behavior of same-gender persons that will be modeled. Whether a model's behavior is rewarded or punished will then increase or decrease the probability that it will be imitated in similar circumstances. Kay Bussey and Albert Bandura noted in their 1999 paper that modeling depends on "perceived efficacy to master the modeled activities, opportunities to put them into practice, and the social reactions they produce." Modeling is more likely if the behavior in question produces valued outcomes.

Consequences are often intertwined with opportunities for practice that typically precede, and provide the setting for, behavioral outcomes. Different situations provide differential opportunities to practice particular behaviors and also present demand characteristics that make some responses more probable than others. For example, a doll in a child's hands usually demands hugging, stroking, and tender, loving care in contrast to a ball, which demands bouncing, throwing, and kicking. That dolls are more often put into the hands of girls and balls into the hands of boys is, of course, crucial to the explanation of gender-related behavior in contemporary U.S. culture. A review of research by Marilyn Stern and Katherine H. Karraker in 1989 found that persons reacting to children identified as a girl or boy differed in their responses most consistently in offering dolls to the former and footballs or hammers to the latter.

While there is certainly not a total separation in the play activities of girls and boys, to the extent that they do engage in different play activities we can expect that they will learn and be given the opportunity to practice different skills. This result has been reported by those who have studied games typically played by children in the United States. For example, an investigation of fifth graders by Janet Lever in 1988 found that boys' games and team sports were likely to deal with impersonal rules and to require working for collective goals while girls' games were described as more spontaneous, imaginative, and less competitive. Therefore it is likely that not only will children (and adults) enhance their skills in certain activities through practice, but a greater interest in these activities will be developed and performing them will produce feelings of competence, mastery, or effectance. Such outcomes are predictable even though the gendered activities into which we are channeled may not conform to the potential of our individual abilities. [See PLAY PATTERNS AND GENDER.]

Caregivers influence gender development, as Diane N. Ruble and Carol Lynn Martin pointed out in their 1998 review, "by providing boys and girls with distinct social contexts in terms of toys, room furnishings, and encouragement of same-sex interactions." For example, as reported in 1993, Jacquelynne S. Eccles and a team of researchers investigated whether a sample of parents provided different types of sport activities for their daughters and sons and found that they do. Parents more often watched and played sports with sons, enrolled them more often in sports programs, and encouraged sports participation than they did with daughters; these differences were apparent as early as kindergarten. Within these differing social contexts, children have an opportunity to practice different behaviors and experience positive or negative reinforcement for them. In the United States, most caregivers find it difficult not to provide gender-related toys and activities for children and not to play differently with girls and boys.

Important validation for the role of differential practice in defining gender comes from a cross-cultural study reported in 1988 by Beatrice Whiting and Carolyn P. Edwards. They studied samples from Kenya, Okinawa, India, Philippines, Mexico, and New England by making careful observations of 3- to 11-year-old children in natural situations. The investigators found that the nature of the tasks assigned to girls was "the best predictor of nurturance, compliance, and sensitivity to others." In societies in which boys, like girls, tend babies, cook, and perform other domestic chores, they were also observed to offer help and support to others and to show less egotistical dominance and aggression, and girls were observed to engage in rough-and-tumble play as often as the boys. Across the societies, where there was less difference in the daily routines of girls and boys there was less difference in their behavior.

An analysis of data on 600 U.S. households by Sampson L. Blair in 1992 found that the household chores assigned to children by their parents are typically divided by gender, as they are for adults, and that daughters do more household work than sons. Others have reported similar findings. Claire Etaugh and Marsha B. Liss in a 1992 study also found that the chores assigned to children influenced their career aspirations in gender-related ways. For example, the girls (across a wide age range) were found to participate more than boys in sex-typed household tasks, and more than half of them chose "female occupations such as nurse or teacher." Among the boys, 84% chose so-called male occupations such as lawyer and police officer. This is not surprising since, in expecting different chores to be done by girls and boys, parents provide information about what they consider appropriate for each gender. [See CAREER ACHIEVEMENT.]

Women and men in the United States, as well as children, are typically encouraged to practice behavior in different spheres. Thus, many more women than men find themselves in kitchens and at the bedsides of sick children or adults, where certain responses are clearly more probable, more appropriate, and more likely to be rewarded than others. In 1985 Sandra L. Bem shared the common observation that "women but not men are asked to bake cookies for bake sales and are called home from work when their children get sick at school." Such taken-for-granted "facts of life" have enormous implications for the performance and maintenance of gender-related behavior. Men may know how to diaper babies and take temperatures but they are less likely to do either if a women is present, reducing the probability of their practicing and enhancing these skills. On the other hand, men are more likely to be drafted for war or put into positions of leadership, contexts that demand certain other ways of behaving, providing practice to men but not to women. The greater the division of labor and the greater the limitations in women's social roles, the more gender differences will be observed in behavior and skills. Thus, women and men among the Inuits, as noted by Suzanne Romaine in her 1999 book, are observed to display the same spatial abilities to the same degree; these are necessary survival skills in Inuit (Eskimo) terrain and are practiced by all.

The consequences experienced for behavior may come from others whose reactions are rewarding or punishing, the consequences may be experienced vicariously by observing consequences to others, or the consequences may be self-imposed. As children get older, the regulation of behavior shifts from predominantly external sanctions (both positive and negative) to gradual substitution of internal sanctions applied to themselves. Behavior followed by self-satisfaction and good feelings is more likely to be performed while behavior leading to feelings of guilt or anxiety becomes less likely. Eventually behavior can be regulated by anticipation of self-sanctions.

B. SOURCES OF GENDER LEARNING: MAJOR SOCIALIZING AGENTS

Societies include an array of socializing institutions: parents, peers, language, schools, occupations, heroes, and so on that, for the most part, reinforce each other and are interdependent. Cultural views about gender are omnipresent, are everywhere, in cultural products and in daily life, and gender socialization is accomplished by an entire culture, beginning, in the United States, with color-coded bassinets for newborns in hospital nurseries.

1. Parents and Families

Among the many sources of gender learning, parents are believed to be the most influential. As primary caretakers, sources of nurturance as well as power, gender learning is likely to result from parents' reactions to their children's behavior, their modeling of same and other gender behavior, and their direct instruction. The earliest socialization generally takes place within the family where, as noted by Beverly I. Fagot and Mary D. Leinbach in their 1987 paper, "the child first learns who is male and female, what males and females are and do." Parents inevitably begin gender socialization from the moment of their children's birth and continue the process by what they provide for their children and by their approving or disapproving reactions to what their children do.

The influence of parents is likely to be cumulative since it is they who interact most often with their children on a daily basis, and parents may do a great deal of gender teaching without awareness or intent. For example, research has shown, as summarized by Eleanor E. Maccoby in 1998, that while both parents in the United States tend to use firmer, more punitive tactics and assertive communication styles with their sons, mothers talk more to daughters than to sons, especially about emotions, express more positive emotion in the presence of their daughters, and reciprocate more supportive statements to their daughters.

One study in 1998 by Eva M. Pomerantz and Diane N. Rubin of an ethnically diverse sample of elementary school children and their mothers (who kept daily checklists of their control behaviors) found that the mothers of boys differed from the mothers of girls in being more encouraging of autonomy and being more likely to convey the impression that their child was competent. Robyn Fivush and her colleagues observed a small sample of 21 40- to 45-month-old children and their parents as they discussed past events dealing with emotion. As reported by the investigators in 2000, they found that both mothers and fathers discussed aspects and causes of sad experiences more with daughters than with sons and that, regardless of what emotion was being discussed, there was more of an interpersonal emphasis or context in talks with girls.

In summarizing the research literature in 1984, Carol N. Jacklin, Janet A. DiPetro, and Eleanor E. Maccoby noted that observation of parent and child pairs in play situations has found that "mother–daughter, father–daughter, and father–son dyads all play in ways that are highly sex-typed, [and considered to be] appropriate to the child's sex." Thus, for example, the most rough-and-tumble play was observed in father–son pairs. Research also supports the conclusion that parents, especially fathers, are more accepting of fighting among boys, and that while mothers are willing to accept anger and retal-

iation in their sons, they are more eager to focus on how their daughters can re-establish harmony after conflict with others. The prevailing evidence also supports the conclusion that, in the United States, fathers are more likely than mothers to treat daughters and sons differently, to use different play styles with them, and to try to toughen up their sons so they do not show weakness.

Studies of gay fathers and lesbian mothers, although primarily focused on outcomes for their children's sexuality, seem to support the conclusion that these parents teach much the same gender lessons are heterosexual parents, or do not effectively contradict the gender lessons being learned outside the home. It has been estimated that in the United States there are about 1 to 5 million lesbian mothers, 1 to 3 million gay fathers, and 6 to 14 million children of homosexual parents. A 1992 review of the literature by Charlotte J. Patterson suggests that there are no reliable differences in gender-relevant behavior between the children of homosexual and heterosexual parents. Much of this research, however, has focused on relatively homogeneous White, urban, middle-class professionals. A 1994 study by Patterson of 37 families headed by a lesbian mother found that the preferences reported by most of the children for toys, games, friends, characters from books, movies, and TV indicated that these children had learned the gender associations "considered to be normative." A longitudinal study in 1997 by Fiona L. Tasker and Susan Golombeck that compared the children of divorced heterosexual mothers with divorced homosexual mothers reached much the same conclusion. The investigators, however, suggest that the nontraditional family life of the children of lesbian mothers should encourage them to have less rigid beliefs about what is acceptable behavior for women and men.

There is some evidence that children growing up in families in which there is a nontraditional division of labor learn different gender lessons than other children. For example, in households where mothers are in the paid workforce, children have been found to make less sex-typed choices. Gary D. Levy reported in 1989, from a study of three- to five-year-old children, that girls of mothers who worked outside the home showed greater flexibility in toy choices and other measures of gender-relevant behavior than girls whose mothers were full-time homemakers. In another study, by Campbell Leaper and his colleagues reported in 1995, single mothers were found to encourage nontraditional gender behavior in their daughters, but not in their sons. These results are consonant with those reported in 1997 by Leslie D. Leve and Beverly I. Fagot who found less traditional gender beliefs and values among single parents than among adults in two-parent families. There is cross-cultural support for this finding. A research team headed by J. L. Gibbons reported in 1996 that adolescent children of mothers who work outside the home in Iceland, Mexico, and Spain, as well as in the United States, hold less conservative or traditional attitudes about appropriate gender behavior than adolescents whose mothers are not in the paid labor force.

Evidence that parental gender beliefs and behavior influence those of their children come from a variety of studies. Two-year-old daughters of mothers who do not strongly ascribe to gender stereotypes were observed in one investigation, by Jeanne Brooks-Gunn in 1986, to play more actively and further away from their mothers than daughters of mothers who did ascribe to these stereotypes. A longitudinal survey of 2000 children across the U.S. in 1995, by Constance Hardesty, DeeAnn Wenk, and Carolyn S. Morgan, found that nontraditional gender beliefs in young adult sons were associated with having experienced an ongoing close and nurturing father–son relationship. Thomas S. Weisner and Jane E. Wilson-Mitchell followed a group of nontraditional families in 1990 and compared their children with those from more conventional families. They reported that all the children, in both kinds of families, displayed knowledge of conventional gender associations by age six, and that even the most countercultural parents did not consistently and unambiguously present alternative gender schemas to their children. Nevertheless, children in the least traditional families gave more non-sex-typed responses to objects and occupations than did children in the other families.

The role played by parents' traditional gender beliefs can be illustrated by the findings reported in 1990 by Jacqueline S. Eccles, Janis E. Jacobs, and Rena D. Harold from two longitudinal studies involving 2100 families. They reported that

parents' perceptions of their children's competencies in math, English, and sports are . . . influenced by their children's gender, and by the parents' gender role stereotypic beliefs about which gender is naturally more talented in these domains . . . [and] these influences are independent of any actual differences that might exist in the children's competencies.

Such sex-typed beliefs on the part of parents are apparent even when the children are very young and appear to influence their children's behavior from a very early age. One study in 1984 by Peter O. Peretti and Tiffany M. Sydney, in which 150 nursery school age children were observed daily for a month, found that the children's toy preferences were significantly related to choices made by their parents who believed that girls were more gentle, delicate, and less vigorous than were boys and that boys were more boisterous and strong.

Some investigators have found that parents are less likely than children or adolescents to have sex-stereotyped perceptions of infants, but these findings are based on verbal reports, not observations of parental behavior. A meta-analysis of relevant studies by Hugh Lytton and David M. Romney in 1991 led them to conclude that observational and experimental studies yield more evidence of differential treatment of girls and boys by their parents than self-report studies. On the other hand, there is reason to believe that while parents contribute greatly to the social learning of gender of their children, they are influenced not only by the prevailing norms but also by the individual characteristics of their children and by their own ambitions for them. Because parents tend to respond to the uniqueness of each child, it is not startling to find, as Lytton and Romney noted, that the child's sex is not a significant influence on many of the socialization measures that have been studied (with the important exception of encouraging sex-typed play). Thus, parents may be less rigid than other socializing agents in their view of what is appropriate behavior for their children and may do less direct teaching of gender. On the other hand, gender-differentiated behavior is likely to be influenced by the observations that children in two-parent heterosexual families make of parental interactions. The way mothers and fathers relate to one another presents distinct cultural messages about the expectations for behavior by women and men. [See FAMILY ROLES AND PATTERNS, CONTEMPORARY TRENDS; PARENTING.]

2. Toys, Clothes, and Books

Without directly teaching about gender, parents and others also convey gender messages indirectly through their choice of toys, clothes, and books. In one study by Eleanor E. Maccoby, reported in her 1998 book, in which investigators visited with parents and their 45-month-old children in their homes, the parents were observed to be "more likely to pick out toys that invited high-activity play (such as a toy football) when playing with their sons" and to engage in "rougher, more arousing play with sons than with daughters." Another study, by Claire Etaugh and Martha B. Liss in 1992, found that a sample of children from kindergarten through eighth grade was less likely to receive the gender-atypical toys that they requested from their parents for Christmas and more likely to receive those that were considered gender appropriate. When college students were shown slides of 74 toys in a study by Donna Fisher-Thompson in 1990 and asked the sex of the child they would be most likely to buy the toy for, the results indicated that they were more willing to buy guns, soldiers, jeeps, and carpenter tools for boys and more willing to buy baby dolls, dishes, sewing kits, and jewelry boxes for girls. In contrast, among the eastern Chewong of Malay, previously mentioned, girls and boys are given the same toys and the first possession of all children is usually a small, blunt knife.

In the late 1990s, the U.S. megachain store Toys "R" Us set up sections specifically labeled by gender in many of its branch stores. As reported by Lisa Bannon in 2000, what one could find in the "Girl's World" were "plenty of dolls, kitchen toys and makeup stocked on its magenta shelves. But the trains were over in the red section, designated 'Boy's World' . . . alongside action figures, Tonka trucks and walkie-talkies." As a result of complaints, the specific signs were removed but the sections remained much the same. Similarly, an online toy store (EToys.com) provided suggestions for prospective buyers in their "Birthday Gifts Made Easy" Web site section that vary with the sex of the child one is shopping for. For a six-year-old girl what is considered appropriate is an interactive doll, Barbie Bed and Bath, a phonebook, yoga kit, and ice cream maker. For a six-year-old boy the suggested toys are a baseball pitching machine, walkie-talkies, a pirate ship, an arrow shooter, hot wheels racers, and a superspeedway set. The suggestions for children of other ages are similarly gender typed. Thus, little seems to have changed in the world of children's toys in the United States over the past few decades. There are still a greater variety of toys produced for boys than for girls, and those for boys orient them to the world outside the home while those for girls emphasize homemaking, child care, and attractiveness.

Not to be out stereotyped, Mattel, Inc. began marketing gender-specific computers for children ages 4 to 12, a Barbie and a Hot Wheels model. The former is pink-flowered and comes with half of

the educational software found on the royal blue computer for boys. A visit to the Hot Wheels and BarbiePC Web sites (hotwheels.com and barbiepc. com, respectively) finds the following among the software titles listed for the computer for boys but not for the one for girls: Oregon Trails, a game that teaches history and strategy; Bodyworks, a program that teaches human anatomy and three-dimensional visualization; Kid Pix Studio, for creativity; a thinking game called Logical Journey of the Zoombinis; and ClueFinders for math. Mattel is the company that released a talking Barbie in 1992 that could say "Math class is tough." They eventually eliminated this phrase from Barbie's repertoire in response to heavy criticism.

The world of children's clothes is similar to that of children's toys. A study (cited in a 1987 review by Beverly I. Fagot and Mary D. Leinbach) in suburban shopping malls in the United States found gender clearly proclaimed in what 1- to 13-month-old infants were wearing, a way of perhaps ensuring that strangers will not make mistaken gender identifications and treat the infants inappropriately. When asked, the parents did not say that their child's sex influenced their choice of clothing, but "they dressed baby girls in pink, puffed sleeves, ruffles, and lace . . . while boys wore blue or sometimes red, but nothing ruffled or pink." This is perhaps not unlike the custom among the ancient Aztecs, cited by Suzanne Romaine in her 1999 book, of putting a tiny sword and shield in the cradle of a newborn boy and a toy shuttle and loom in the cradle of a newborn girl.

Jeans and shirts seem to be considered appropriate today for older children of both sexes while at play, but advertisements for higher-priced clothes still feature gender stereotypes. For example, in a six-page spread in the *New York Times Magazine* of February 27, 2000, that featured clothes on computer-imaged child look-alike dolls, an outfit for a boy was displayed on Robo Brain, which had math and soccer chips, while an outfit for a girl was displayed on a robot that had a sunny disposition and a portable boom box built into her stomach. Another girl-robot wearing a pretty yellow dress embroidered with flowers was described as "Good at potsy and girl talk," while still another, called "The Babe" and dressed in sports clothes, was described as "Guaranteed not to throw like a girl."

There are clearly powerful gender messages in parental behavior and the toys and clothes manufactured and purchased for children. There also continue to be traditional messages in many of the books written for and read to and by children. Albert J. Davis reported in 1984 that he found in a sample of preschool picture books that even those judged to be nonsexist, in which the female characters were portrayed as independent and effective, they were also shown to be more emotional and less physically active than the male characters. In 1996 Diane M. Turner-Bowker found, in a sample of prize-winning children's picture books, that adjectives used frequently to describe girls and women differed significantly in connotative meaning from adjectives used frequently to describe boys and men. Adjectives used for girls and women were judged to be less active and potent than adjectives used for boys and men.

A content analysis by Lorraine Evans and Kimberly Davies in 2000 of literature textbooks published in 1997 revealed the same gender stereotypes as those in earlier studies. These investigators examined 132 main characters in 82 stories in 13 books for first, third, and fifth graders. Not only were there more male main characters (54%), but these were "overwhelmingly more often portrayed as aggressive, argumentative, and competitive." Female characters, on the other hand, were "more likely to be characterized as affectionate, emotionally expressive, and passive."

3. Peers

Peers have come to be recognized as significant and major influences on gender learning. Among younger children, peers have been found consistently to influence the activity and toy preferences of others. For example, sex-typed behaviors are more likely to be displayed by children when in the company of same-sex peers while neutral toys are likely to be preferred by children when playing alone. With respect to styles of play, two observational studies in preschools reported by Beverly I. Fagot in 1984 found that boys got more positive feedback for high-activity play from peers than girls did, and that while boys got more reactions from peers and teachers for aggressive behavior, girls got more attention for dependency behavior. Similar findings were reported from a study by Fagot and Richard Hagan in 1985 that analyzed data collected over a four-year period from observations of play during children's first term in preschool. While fewer than half of the aggressive acts by girls received some attention, boys got some response about 70% of the time, most often from another boy. Lora C. Moller, Shelley Hymel, and Kenneth H. Rubin, in a 1992 study, found a rela-

tionship for fourth-grade boys between their popularity or acceptance by peers and the frequency of their stereotypic gender behavior.

In the United States and in other societies, preference for playing and socializing in same-gender groups is observed quite early. Preschoolers with stronger beliefs about gender appropriateness have been found to play in same-gender groups more than other children. Children in New Zealand kindergartens whose behavior was not concordant with sex-role ideology were found by Bernice Lott, in a study reported in 1978, to play more often in areas associated with the other gender.

It makes sense that as children learn about gender and behave in accordance with the prescriptions and proscriptions they are experiencing and observing that they will also influence their peers by their reactions of approval and disapproval. Peers provide gender information through their pattern of play, the toys they use, and their reactions to others' behaviors. The more children are segregated in play, the less is their exposure to other-gender behavior and the greater the influence of gender socialization. Eleanor E. Maccoby has focused attention on same-sex peer groups and concluded in her 1998 book that "[p]eers clearly have a socialization role. Indeed, peers may be more effective carriers of social change than the parent generation."

4. Schools

There is considerable evidence that school functions as a primary setting for gender learning with peers and teachers reinforcing behaviors differentially on the basis of gender, and that gender bias exists in the classroom. While the research findings are not entirely consistent, boys in general tend to receive both more positive and more negative attention from teachers than girls do. Meredith Kimball in a 1995 book cites research showing that both women and men teachers say they believe boys to be better at doing math than girls.

In an experimental study reported in 1995, Rebecca S. Bigler investigated the consequences for gender learning of the use of gender dichotomies in the classroom for separating children for activities and emphasizing gender groups. When the children exposed to gender emphasis classrooms were compared with others on measures of gender associations, the former were found to be more extreme and less flexible in judgments of gender traits. Separate gender worlds are the reality for many children in

U.S. classrooms, affecting the ways of interacting that are practiced and developed by girls and boys. [*See* SEX SEGREGATION IN EDUCATION.]

5. Media

Among the most consistent portrayers of gender stereotypes and sources of gender learning in the United States are the media, with television being particularly influential because of its ubiquitous presence in the lives of families. Kay Bussey and Albert Bandura concluded in their 1999 review of the research literature that a dominant picture of men and women presented in the televised world is that of men as aggressors and women as helpless victims. On television, men are consistently shown as more adventurous and enterprising, more likely to be engaged in occupational and recreational pursuits, more in control, and in higher-status jobs than women. Such gender portrayals are not only present in U.S. media but have been reported also in Great Britain, Australia, Mexico, and Italy.

These same messages appear in programming, commercials, and in special features for children like Saturday morning cartoons. One study of cartoons cited by Frances E. Donelson in her 1998 book found that in the 1990s, just as was true two decades earlier, male characters continued to play more major roles, to talk and achieve more, and to be braver than female characters. As reported by Lisa Bannon in 2000, the Fox cable network has introduced two new digital cable channels, one specifically geared to girls, who are said to be more interested in entertainment that is relationship oriented, and one geared to boys, who are said to be more action oriented. So for preschoolers, a show called *St. Bear's Dolls Hospital* was planned for the girls' channel while *Captain Kangaroo* was slotted for the boys' channel.

The data on television's role in gender learning are generally not unambiguous and reviewers of the literature have pointed out that viewers come to the medium with already learned gender associations. The gender stereotypes presented on television may vary in their influence for children of different ages and in different social contexts. But a natural experiment in Canada provides dramatic evidence about television's influence on gender learning. In this investigation, cited in 1998 by Diane N. Ruble and Carol Lynne Martin, the children in one town were studied before and after the introduction of television and compared with children in a comparable town. The children in the critical town had less traditional gender beliefs than the other children before the introduction of television but two years later showed a sharp increase in adherence to traditional views. [*See* MEDIA INFLUENCES; MEDIA STEREOTYPES.]

IV. The Reconstruction of Gender

Changes in the meaning of girl and boy, woman and man, are already in process as U.S. society experiences significant and enduring changes in institutions like the family, education, and occupations. As changes occur in social, economic, and political life that are accompanied by new experiences, continued reconstruction of the meaning of gender should take place. In the United States today there is more flexibility for girls in single-mother households and, as noted by Beverly Greene in a 1998 review, more flexibility in gender roles in African American than European American families.

Cross-cultural examples illustrate well the plasticity and adaptability of gender-linked standards. As noted in 1988 by anthropologists Beatrice Whiting and Carolyn P. Edwards, all of the behaviors that are gender related in a culture "seem remarkably malleable under the impact of socialization pressure . . . or learning environments." Thus, among the previously mentioned Eastern Chewong of Malay peninsula (reported on in 1988 by Signe Howell), women and men typically work together and most can perform the range of tasks required for daily life; it is only the physiological differences associated with pregnancy, birth, and nursing that produce divisions of labor. Balinese society has been described similarly by Suzanne Romaine in her 1999 book. "Men and women wear almost identical clothing . . . and the male/female distinction is largely irrelevant in everyday life." An example of change in gender meanings under changed conditions of life comes from the Navajo, among whom, it has been argued, traditional gender relationships were greatly altered by contact with the dominant European society and by governmental policies in North America. According to Alfredo Mirande in a 1991 paper, "In traditional Navajo society women exercised a role that was equal to, if not greater than, that of men . . . [but] contact with White culture had the effect of diminishing the power of women." [*See* CROSS-CULTURAL GENDER ROLES.]

A 1992 study in Israel by Menucha Birenbaum and Roberta Kraemer of Jewish and Arab high schools found that among the former, boys were more positive than girls about mathematics and saw its study as more worthwhile, but there were no significant gender differences among the Arab students. The investigators point out that for the Arab girl, school learning is extremely important, and that school is one of the few areas in which she has the same freedom as boys. "[T]he educational arena is perhaps the only context in which girls can legitimately compete for status with boys—and they do it very successfully." The embeddedness of gender within the larger cultural framework can also be seen in findings from a study reported in 1996 by Amy Kyratzis and Jiansheng Guo that compared mixed-sex interactions in public school settings in Worcester, Massachusetts, and Beijing, China. While boys were seen to dominate in such interactions in groups of four- to six-year-old children in Massachusetts, this was not observed in Beijing. The investigators explain that while Chinese men are more powerful in the workplace, women are more dominant in the family and that this domain is as highly valued as that outside the home. What distinguishes Chinese children, then, is that they may learn to shift "readily between two social spheres," illustrating a different construction of gender from that in the United States.

Some researchers have compared samples from the United States with samples from other societies on various measures of adherence to gender stereotypes. For example, unlike what is typically found in the United States, Fijian female and male fifth graders and university students were found by Susan A. Basow in a 1984 study not to self-report significantly different attributes; both groups reported expressive and instrumental traits. Similarly, comparisons among college students in the United States, Germany, and India found new gender differences in self-reported traits within the group from India; these data were reported in 1992 by a research team headed by Virginia A. Murphy-Berman. In another Israeli study, by Liat Kulik in 1998, teenagers from rural *kibbutzim* (collective communities) were found to have more egalitarian views about gender-related behaviors and occupations than their more urban peers from traditional families.

A social learning perspective that focuses on the conditions under which learning occurs recognizes that change is possible and predicts different constructions of gender under different sets of circumstances. A good illustration comes from the study of an ethnically diverse group of 200 widowed men in the United States between the ages of 60 and 96, re-

ported in 1997 by Judith A. Howard and Jocelyn Hollander. Men who reported having provided at least one month of care to their wives before they died were categorized as "caregivers" and were compared with the "noncaregivers." The average score obtained by the former on a self-report measure of "masculinity" (agency) was significantly greater than the score of the latter. Being a "man" was being operationalized by the widowed male caregivers as taking charge, organizing, and devoting time and energy to the care of their wives who needed nurturance and support.

This study of widowed men illustrates that gender is a reliable predictor of social behavior only under certain conditions, a proposition that is central to the social learning approach to gender. Gender-related behavior, as culturally defined, as predictable only where the situation provides strong expectations for such behavior, where prior opportunities for practice have produced gender-associated differential skills, and where there are differential consequences to girls and women and boys and men for what they do or say.

More than 65 years ago Karen Horney, an important voice in psychology and psychoanalysis, gave a paper at the National Federation of Professional and Business Women's Clubs in which she argued that masculinity and femininity were "artificial" concepts and that what women needed to do was "to develop their full potential as human beings" (cited by Meredith Kimball in a 1995 book). Horney would surely have given the same advice to men. Recognizing the "artificiality" of gender constructs leads to identifying the conditions under which gender is constructed and to an appreciation of the varied possibilities for reconstruction.

The diversity among cultures and subcultures in gender meaning provides ample support for arguments like those of Kay Bussey and Albert Bandura, who wrote in 1999 that "[h]uman evolution provides bodily structures and biological potentialities, not behavioral dictates" and "in most domains the biology of humans permits a broad range of cultural possibilities" heavily influenced by "opportunities, privileges, and power." Cultural emphasis on gender dichotomies is universally accompanied by inequities in power and privilege. Where access to social resources is systematically and consistently greater for one group than another, associating the different groups with particular and differently valued skills, attributes, interests, and behaviors would seem to be necessary.

We can anticipate that as differential power begins to no longer distinguish women from men, and as scientific studies and observations of social life challenge stereotypical beliefs about gender differences, gender will become less likely to connote wide differences in expected behavior and its meaning will center on a narrow range of attributes. Sandra L. Bem argued in 1995 that gender distinctions need to rest primarily on the reproductive differences associated with sex. Restricting gender to such a definition would provide the greatest latitude for individual differences since typically gender is the imposition of cultural meaning onto reproductive potentialities.

It has been suggested that movement from one gender to another through surgical or transvestite transformations is a way of bending gender or demonstrating its fluidity. At the same time, however, such transformations seem to depend on unquestioned acceptance of a gender difference ideology and sometimes take cultural gender scripts to caricatured extremes. As Judith Lorber argued in her 1994 book, "Without gender differentiation, transvestism and transsexuality would be meaningless. . . . There would be no need to reconstruct genitalia to match identity if interests and lifestyles were not gendered."

Marge Piercy in a 1976 novel, *Woman on the Edge of Time,* presented a utopian look at the future and projected an egalitarian society in which women and men continued to be identified as such, but in which the work that they did was not gender typed. Adolescents of both sexes went off by themselves for a time to decide on a suitable name and to contemplate their personal choices and interests, and any mixed-gender group of three adults could choose to parent a child together. While we cannot predict a similar state of affairs anywhere in the foreseeable future, we can anticipate significant changes in gender meaning. A future in which gender does not re-strict opportunities or prescribe the directions of one's life is one that holds promise for promoting individual competencies. In such a future, instead of teaching femininity and masculinity we can engage in a continuing socialization process for the maintenance of positive human qualities.

Questioning the meaning and social function of gender does not imply that we should ignore the common gender-specific experiences, problems, values, or directions that define us within the cultural, historical space we inhabit. Only by recognizing these can we ask the important questions about the conditions and process that underlie the construction of gender.

SUGGESTED READING

Bleier, R. (1991). Gender ideology and the brain: Sex differences research. In *Women and Men: New Perspectives on Gender Differences* (M. T. Notman and C. C. Nadelson, eds.), pp. 63–73. American Psychiatric Press, Washington, DC.

Bussey, K., and Bandura, A. (1999). Social cognitive theory of gender development and differentiation. *Psychological Review* **106,** 676–713.

Howard, J. A., and Hollander, J. (1997). *Gendered Situations, Gendered Selves.* Sage, Thousand Oaks, CA.

Lorber, J. (1994). *Paradoxes of Gender.* Yale University Press, New Haven, CT.

Lott, B. (1990). Dual natures or learned behavior: The challenge to feminist psychology. In *Making a Difference: Psychology and the Construction of Gender* (R. T. Hare-Mustin and J. Marecek, eds.), pp. 65–101. Yale University Press, New Haven, CT.

Lott, B. (1997). The personal and social correlates of a gender difference ideology. *Journal of Social Issues* 53(2), 279–298.

Lott, B., and Maluso, D. (1993). The social learning of gender. In *The Psychology of Gender* (A. E. Beall and R. J. Sternberg, eds.), pp. 99–123. Guilford Press, New York.

Maccoby, E. E. (1998). *The Two Sexes: Growing Up Apart, Coming Together.* Harvard University Press, London.

West, C., and Zimmerman, D. H. (1991). Doing gender. In *The Social Construction of Gender* (J. Lorber and S. A. Farrell, eds.), pp. 13–37. Sage, Newbury Park, CA.

Gender Difference Research
Issues and Critique

Janet Shibley Hyde
Amy H. Mezulis
University of Wisconsin

Glossary

Alpha bias Concluding that a difference between groups exists when in fact there is no difference—in this case, concluding that there are differences between males and females when there are none.

Beta bias Concluding that there is no difference between groups when, in fact, a difference exists—in this case, concluding that there is no gender difference when there is.

Effect size The magnitude of the difference between two groups.

File-drawer effect A bias in scientific research in which research that finds no effect or no difference never gets published, but rather is relegated to a file drawer and therefore not known by scientists—in this case, the tendency of research demonstrating gender similarities not to be published.

Gender differences research Research examining differences between males and females.

Meta-analysis A statistical method for synthesizing the results of numerous studies on the same question.

Significance testing An essential component of traditional statistical methods, in which, for example, the difference between the average scores for two groups is tested to see whether it is so large that it was unlikely to occur by chance. "Significant" does not necessarily mean "important."

GENDER DIFFERENCES RESEARCH is research that examines differences between men and women or between boys and girls, in behavior, psychological characteristics, or biological characteristics.

I. Introduction

Few areas of scientific research attract such intense attention from the popular media as research on psychological gender differences. A single study based on data from a small number of people may generate sizzling popular articles. Behind all this, often in the shadows, is an enormous body of scientific research, some of it bad, some simply mediocre, and some quite exceptional. The purpose of this article is not to review the content and outcomes of that research, but rather to focus on methodological and conceptual issues.

Following a brief history of research on psychological gender differences, this article considers the question of whether psychologists should study gender differences and the related issues of alpha bias and beta bias. Next we review various guidelines that have been proposed for research on gender differences and note the importance of connecting such research to theoretical models. Following that is a consideration of two statistical issues: mean or average differences versus within-gender variability, and significance testing versus effect size. We then review the technique of meta-analysis, which is now widely used to synthesize large bodies of research on gender differences. A consideration of the issue of inferences about the origins of gender differences follows. The article concludes with suggestions for future research.

II. The History of Gender Differences Research

The history of research on psychological gender differences stretches back more than a century. The investigation of male–female difference dates from about 1879, the date usually cited as the beginning of formal psychology. Darwinism and functionalism dominated the sciences. Evolutionary theory highlighted the importance of variability, thereby legitimizing the study of variations in behavior, including gender differences. Generally the outcomes of the research appeared to support the notion of the evolutionary supremacy of the White male.

The topic of female intelligence was first investigated by phrenologists and neuroanatomists. The early belief was that female and male brains must be as different in their gross appearance as were female and male bodies in other selected areas. A popular argument was that females had smaller brains than males, that brain size was a direct indicator of intelligence, and that women must therefore be less intelligent than men. Later theorizing was based on the theory of localization of function and, whatever the region of the brain that was identified as being responsible for higher mental function, women were found to be deficient in that region. This work foreshadowed, by more than 100 years, current attempts to explain psychological gender differences in terms of biological factors including evolution and neuroanatomy.

As early as 1910, Helen Thompson Woolley wrote a comprehensive scholarly review of the existing research on psychological gender differences. She was highly critical of the research and concluded that no scientific conclusions could be reached from it, in large part because the constructs that had been studied and the tests used to measure them were so flawed.

Advances came with the mental testing movement, including Terman's publication of an American version of Binet's IQ measure in 1916. In the 1930s and 1940s, Thurstone developed the Primary Mental Abilities Test, which permitted the measurement of specific abilities such as verbal comprehension, numerical computation, and spatial visualizing. Advances in measurement in other areas of psychology, including social behavior and personality, occurred as well. In all areas, researchers were quick to check for and report findings of gender differences.

In 1966, Eleanor Maccoby edited an important volume, *The Development of Sex Differences*. It contained a chapter written by Maccoby in which she reviewed research on gender differences in intellectual functioning; she concluded that girls performed significantly better on measures of verbal ability and boys performed significantly better on measures of number ability and spatial ability. An appendix to the book summarized studies providing data on numerous aspects of gender differences, including aggression, dependence, nurturance, anxiety, and moral development.

In the late 1960s and early 1970s, stimulated in part by the women's movement, an explosion of research on gender differences occurred. Eleanor Maccoby and Carol Jacklin, recognizing the need for a systematic synthesis of this vast body of research, published *The Psychology of Sex Differences* in 1974, reviewing literally thousands of studies of gender differences in a variety of psychological characteristics including abilities, personality, social behavior, and memory. By systematically locating and synthesizing these studies, Maccoby and Jacklin were able to provide definitive answers on questions of widely held beliefs about gender differences. They concluded that gender differences in verbal, mathematical, and spatial abilities and in aggression were well established. At the same time, they dismissed as unfounded beliefs that girls are more social than boys, that girls are more suggestible, and that girls lack achievement motivation. The book, then, was a watershed not only because of the herculean work of synthesizing so many studies, but also because it entertained gender similarities as a reasonable conclusion in some areas.

The next advance in research on gender differences came with the development of meta-analysis in the late 1970s. Meta-analysis and its contribution to gender difference research are discussed in a later section.

III. Should Psychologists Study Gender Differences?

Before considering further the intricacies of research on gender differences, we should step back to consider a predecessor question: Should psychologists even study gender differences? Roy Baumeister, for example, has suggested that studying gender differences may have adverse political and scientific effects and suggested that once "the task of raising consciousness" about masculinist biases was done, psychologists should stop studying gender differences altogether. Rachel Hare-Mustin and Jeanne Marecek suggested that indeed the time has come to put aside the question of gender differences and to turn research attention away from describing differences to exploring the psychological processes underlying the phenomena of gender.

However, whether psychologists *should* study gender differences may be the wrong question to ask. The study of gender differences has shown no signs of diminishing. Review volumes continue to be published. Recent attention has turned to evaluating theoretical models to explain gender difference findings, with a particular interest in bioevolutionary versus social role models. Given the continued interest in studying gender differences, perhaps the appropriate questions are (1) what are the advantages and disadvantages of continuing to study gender differences and (2) what guidelines should researchers adopt to ensure that gender difference research promotes nonsexist political and scientific goals?

Some have suggested that a dilemma exists between pursuing nonsexist research and research agendas that routinely test for gender differences. Particularly given frequent media distortions of research findings, small gender differences may be used to support stereotypes about men and women. In 1985, Janis Jacobs and Jacquelynne Eccles reported how a very small (3%) gender difference in math performance was interpreted nationwide as suggesting a female deficit in math ability. Another researcher reported that women's fine motor and cognitive performance varies across the menstrual cycle, a finding rapidly captured in the media as an example of women's hormonal fluctuations having a negative impact on their abilities. This view suggests that psychologists deemphasize gender difference research and focus instead on gender-neutral or gender-fair examinations of human behavior. Alternatively, researchers should take great care not to report gender differences until their existence and magnitude are validated by replication and theory.

The alternative position argues that it is only by studying gender differences and reporting both nonsignificant and significant findings that researchers can better identify real gender differences, dispel stereotypes about differences where none exist, and test theoretical explanations for the presence or absence of differences. The power of ongoing gender difference research to address these topics is evident in recent research. Meta-analyses in the areas of verbal ability and math ability have dispelled common stereotypes about female verbal superiority and male math superiority by reporting very small differences. Meta-analyses have also demonstrated that some large gender differences do exist, such as in attitudes about sexuality. From this point of view, researchers should continue to ask questions about gender differences and to report significant and nonsignificant findings. This "full information" approach relies on methods for reporting gender differences, such as with effect sizes and percentage of variance accounted for, in the same manner as reporting other psychology findings as a way to discourage sexist reporting and interpretation.

IV. Should Difference Be Maximized or Minimized?

As Rachel Hare-Mustin and Jeanne Marecek articulated in detail in 1988, there are dangers to approaches to gender difference research from either emphasizing or deemphasizing gender differences. The authors cautioned researchers to be aware of the questions they ask in their research, and to evaluate both research questions and interpretations of results for gender biases. One such bias is "alpha bias," or the tendency to exaggerate differences between the sexes. This includes the assumption that male and female are different and opposite, which influences which questions are asked in research, as well as the tendency to report and interpret gender differences in ways that support a view that females and males are fundamentally different. The term "alpha bias" comes from alpha error in hypothesis testing; alpha, or Type I, error, refers to concluding there is a significant difference when one does not exist. Hare-Mustin and Marecek argued that alpha bias is the dominant bias in psychological research on gender, as evidenced in Freudian theory, Parsons's gender-role theory, and the feminist psychodynamic theories of Chodorow and Gilligan. All of these approaches portray men and women as embodying opposing identities and natures; typically, men are portrayed as rational, instrumental, and individualistic whereas women are portrayed as emotional, expressive, and relationship-oriented. Alpha bias leads researchers to emphasize differences between the sexes, at the expense of overlooking similarities.

By contrast, "beta bias" refers to a tendency to minimize gender differences. The term, too, comes from hypothesis testing in which beta, or Type II, error refers to concluding that no difference exists when one does. Beta bias in gender difference research may be associated with a feminist approach that strives for "equality" for men and women, but perhaps at the expense of ignoring key gender differences in social context or experience. Hare-Mustin and Marecek (1988) cited social policies such as no-fault divorces and equal parental leave benefits for men and women as examples of such biases, in that they ignore the differential effects of such policies on men and women. Beta bias can also be seen in Baumeister's suggestion that we abandon gender difference research. Concern with beta bias leads to a belief that, unless we ask the appropriate questions and pursue gender difference research, an unbiased representation of real gender differences and real gender similarities will continue to elude psychologists.

Clearly, there are advantages and disadvantages to studying gender differences. Complete scientific understanding of human behavior, including both gender differences and gender similarities, requires that

we continue to examine gender differences in our research. However, concerns about how findings are interpreted and reported caution us to be wary of both alpha bias and beta bias, so that gender differences are not ignored but neither are they used to promote sexist, antifemale stereotypes and policies. It is important that researchers follow several guidelines to ensure that gender difference research is conducted in the pursuit of better science and on behalf of women. [*See* TEST BIAS.]

V. Guidelines for Research on Gender Differences

In light of concerns regarding gender differences research, we propose the following research guidelines. These expand on guidelines previously suggested by the first author and are generally compatible with other related guidelines for gender difference research. The guidelines are organized according to each stage of the research process.

A. RESEARCH DESIGN

1. Reseachers should clearly state gender difference hypotheses prior to collecting data or conducting analyses, if they intend to report and interpret gender difference findings.

2. Researchers interested in examining origins of gender differences should design experiments and other research designs that enable a *direct* test of relevant theories, including appropriate measures and manipulating key aspects of the experiment.

3. As a general rule, researchers should be aware of their own alpha biases or beta biases, as they may affect what research questions they ask and how they design projects.

B. STATISTICAL ANALYSES

1. Researchers should routinely conduct appropriate significance tests for gender differences on all major measures in their studies.

2. Researchers should calculate effect sizes for all gender differences findings, significant or not, so that readers can easily know the size of the difference.

C. REPORTING FINDINGS

1. Researchers should report the means and variances for men and women on all major measures, as

well as the significance tests and effect sizes for all significant and nonsignificant findings of gender differences, so that the reader can independently examine within-sex variance and between-sex differences and similarities.

2. To minimize publication bias, journal editors should take care to publish reports of nonsignificant gender difference findings, provided the study meets appropriate scientific standards.

D. INTERPRETING FINDINGS

1. Researchers should be cautious in interpreting gender difference findings. Interpretations implying a female deficit should be questioned for other equally valid explanations.

2. Researchers should be cautious in harnessing gender difference findings in support of theoretical models of gender differences when these models were not directly tested. In particular, explanations implying inherent (e.g., biological) differences between the sexes should be made only when appropriate measures were collected and those explanations directly tested.

3. Researchers should be aware that gender difference findings are popular with the media and are often misinterpreted. Researchers should hold themselves to the highest scientific standards in ensuring that their research is appropriately interpretable and accurately interpreted by others, especially nonscientists. The goal is to minimize the extent to which gender difference data are misinterpreted in a manner detrimental to women.

VI. *Linking Empirical Data and Theory*

One reason for the distorted reporting and interpretation of gender differences is that there is a tremendous amount of atheoretical gender difference research, in which researchers test for and report gender differences in the absence of a theoretical model that specifies when and where gender differences should or should not exist. While we support the systematic testing and reporting of gender differences and similarities regardless of whether they were predicted, we contend that theoretical conclusions should not be drawn in the absence of a direct test of the theoretical model. Gender differences results that were not predicted and that were not analyzed

as part of tests of theoretical models specified a priori (before the data were collected) may suggest directions for future research—in which the possible explanations raised by those findings can be directly tested—but they should not be used as evidence in support of a particular theoretical model.

As an example, some studies with findings of psychological gender differences have interpreted those findings as being due to biological factors when in fact no biological measures were obtained in the study. If the biological theory were proposed in advance and followed through the design of the research so that appropriate biological measures were taken, such problematic interpretations could be avoided. Similarly, social-role theorists can design experiments that manipulate the impact of gender roles. An example is Jenifer Lightdale and Deborah Prentice's 1994 research on the impact of gender roles on gender differences in aggressive behavior. They used the manipulation of deindividuation (making the person feel anonymous) to remove people from the influence of gender roles in one condition, and in the other, participants were not deindividuated and therefore were under typical gender-role constraints. The results showed that in the deindividuated condition, in which role constraints were removed or reduced, gender differences in aggressive behavior vanished. [*See* AGGRESSION AND GENDER.]

Researchers testing theoretical explanations for gender differences should be aware of the "level of analysis" problem. Any given gender difference may have explanations at many different levels, from the most proximal (for example, the type of task used in the research) to the most distal (for example, evolution). Explanations at different levels of analysis may not reflect actual theoretical contradictions, but rather a focus at different levels.

Regardless of the theoretical model, researchers should be wary of alpha bias and should endeavor to theorize not only gender differences, but gender similarities and within-sex variation as well. Too often, gender-difference research assumes that gender is a dichotomous, rigid property of the individual. If the extensive examination of gender differences over the past several decades has taught us anything, it may be that gender differences are (1) often small in magnitude and (2) low in frequency compared with the vast similarities between the sexes. Researchers should attempt to explain not only the "why" of gender differences, but also the "when, where, and how" of both gender differences and similarities. With such theoretical approaches, gender can be examined in context, as one aspect of individuals but one with fluid properties depending on context.

VII. *Average Differences versus Within-Sex Variability*

With the emphasis on significance testing, which has dominated psychological research for decades, comes a focus on average or mean differences between two groups, in this case females and males. A finding of mean difference often becomes locked in the memory of scientists and publicized by the media as if there were no within-sex variability and no overlap between distributions of scores for males and females. For example, one study may find that girls score significantly below boys on a measure of self-esteem. The loose translation by the media and some psychologists may be that girls have a lot of self-esteem problems, with an implication that all girls have self-esteem problems and boys have no self-esteem problems. Such a conclusion ignores within-sex variability. Even if girls, on average, scored lower than boys, in all likelihood there were many high-scoring girls whose self-esteem was strong; at the same time, there were boys whose self-esteem was shaky.

Statistically, average differences are reflected in the mean score for each group. Variability is captured by the standard deviation or variance. Researchers must consider within-sex variance as much as mean differences. This principle is captured with the effect size, discussed in detail later in the section on meta-analysis. Generally results of these analyses indicate that within-sex variation is large compared with average differences. A second issue to consider is whether females and males are equally variable, that is, are the variances the same for males and females? Alan Feingold took up this question in a 1992 article. Indeed, the greater male variability hypothesis was first advanced more than 100 years ago to explain why there were both more male geniuses and more males who were intellectually impaired.

Feingold used the variance ratio (ratio of male variance to female variance) to address this question. He found gender differences in variability for quantitative ability and spatial visualization but no gender differences in variability for verbal ability or abstract reasoning. Other researchers found, in several large, nationally representative samples, variance ratios around 1.10 for reading comprehension, 1.05

for vocabulary, 1.18 for mathematics performance, and 1.27 for spatial ability—that is, in each of these measures, males were more variable in their scores than females. Feingold examined the cross-cultural consistency of findings of greater male variability in mathematical performance and spatial ability and found that although in some nations males were more variable than females, in others the pattern was reversed.

Although Feingold's statistical methods have been criticized, the general pattern of his findings appears to hold up when more refined methods are used. This issue of greater male variability is important because it provides an explanation for why considerably more males could score above a high cutoff on, for a example, a measure of mathematical ability even when overall gender differences on the task are small or nonexistent.

VIII. *Significance Testing versus Effect Size*

A war has been raging in psychology—quite apart from issues of gender research—over the past decade concerning the issue of traditional significance testing versus effect sizes and the importance of results. Traditional research on gender differences has suffered from the same problem that has existed in other areas of psychology: statistical analysis has focused exclusively on whether the difference is significant. It is well known, though, that whether a particular difference is significant or not depends in great measure on the size of the sample. A tiny difference can be significant with a large sample size and, conversely, a moderate or large difference can fail to reach significance because of a small sample size and insufficient statistical power. Moreover, an enormous waste of information occurs when complex data are reduced to a single dichotomous result, yes (significant) or no (not significant).

A number of remedies have been suggested including, especially, the use of effect sizes, which convey the size of an effect rather than just whether it was significant. In the case of gender differences research, the effect size is

$$d = \frac{M_M - M_F}{s_w},$$

where d is the effect size, M_M is the mean for males, M_F is the mean for females, and s_w is the average within-sex standard deviation. The *d* statistic conveys how far apart the male and female means are, in standard deviation units. Notice that sample size is not involved in the computation. The *d* statistic is rather like z scores (or standard scores), in that values can be positive (males scored higher) or negative (females scored higher), most values are clustered near zero, and large values, such as 4.6, are extremely rare. Notice that the standard deviation, a measure of variability, features prominently in the formula, thereby representing within-sex variability.

Gender researchers began to report effect sizes around 1980 in conjunction with the development of meta-analytic techniques. The overall recommendation is that researchers report not only the significance test for a particular gender difference, but also the effect size for the gender difference.

IX. Meta-analysis

Meta-analysis can be defined as a quantitative method for combining evidence from different studies. It can be thought of as a quantitative or statistical method for doing a literature review. It is ideal for synthesizing studies on gender differences because typically the number of studies is large; moreover, meta-analysis yields an overall effect size rather than simply a finding of significant or not. A 1986 article by Larry Hedges and Betsy Becker provides a primer on the application of meta-analysis to research on gender differences.

A meta-analysis generally proceeds in four stages. First, the researchers collect as many studies as possible that report data on the question of interest. Computerized searches of databases such as PsycINFO are especially helpful. Care should be taken to locate unpublished studies because of the tendency to publish significant findings and not to publish nonsignificant ones, leading to a file drawer effect in which perfectly good studies that obtained nonsignificant results are relegated to the file drawer and never published and thus are lost from the body of scientific literature. Unpublished studies can be located by searching for dissertations and by using a database such as ERIC, which collects papers presented at meetings.

Second, the researchers extract statistical information from each article and compute an effect size for the gender difference in each article, using the formula given earlier and other related formulas. In the third phase, the researchers compute a weighted average of the effect sizes from all studies to obtain an estimate of the population effect size. In the fourth phase, the researchers test whether the group of effect sizes is relatively homogeneous, representing normal sampling variation, or whether they are significantly nonhomogeneous. In the latter case, the researchers can proceed to moderator analyses that examine whether effect sizes vary systematically according to various features of the studies, such as the age or ethnicity of the participants.

In the early 1980s, some criticisms of meta-analysis in general were raised. It was accused, for example, of allowing the researcher to mindlessly include many poor-quality studies, thus tainting the findings. Meta-analysts, of course, can rate studies for quality on relevant criteria and can exclude poor studies or examine whether they affect the results. Empirical studies comparing meta-analysis with traditional narrative reviews have found meta-analysis to be superior.

Focusing specifically on the merits of applying meta-analysis to research on gender differences, one should first note that meta-analysis has already proved to be an effective tool for synthesizing gender differences in various areas, including mathematics performance, self-esteem, and helping behavior. Some have argued that meta-analysis can make important contributions to the psychology of gender for several reasons. First, meta-analysis can provide powerful evidence challenging long-held beliefs about gender differences, such as female inferiority in mathematics. Second, context is important in the psychology of gender, and moderator analyses conducted in the final phase of a meta-analysis can identify different contexts in which gender differences are large, small, or even reversed. Finally, it is important to study the intersection of gender and race/ethnicity; meta-analyses of gender differences examining race/ethnicity as a moderator can do precisely that.

X. Interpreting Findings of Gender Differences

Researchers should exercise caution when they interpret findings of gender differences. For a variety of historical and social reasons, gender differences are often interpreted as suggesting female deficits despite other equally tenable interpretations. One clear example is the gender difference in self-confidence. Women consistently estimate that they will earn fewer points on an exam than men estimate for themselves, which has often been interpreted as women "lacking" self-confidence. However, an equally strong explanation is that men are overconfident, and, in fact, males appear to overestimate scores as much as women underestimate.

Another concern is speculation about the causes of gender differences when differences are present. Especially given recent interest in bioevolutionary theories of gender differences, there is a tendency for researchers to interpret gender differences as due to biological factors despite an absence of direct evidence supporting such a conclusion. For example, evolutionary psychologists have offered the gender difference in attitudes toward casual sex as evidence for evolutionary theory; however, there is nothing in measures of attitudes that would support biological interpretations over social role theory interpretations. Similarly, other researchers have suggested that their finding that there are more males than females among the mathematically gifted may be due to biological causes, although they had collected no biological measures. Findings being "consistent" with evolutionary or biological theories are not equivalent to directly testing such theories, for example, by using biological measures.

Similarly, researchers often overlook social role or socialization theories when interpreting gender differences, assuming instead that gender differences are due to innate, functional differences between men and women despite abundant evidence that many types of gender differences in behavior may result from gender differences in social roles or socialization. For example, some have cited evolutionary theory as the cause for more male perpetation of homicides and other violent crimes; it is often assumed that males are more aggressive due to sexual selection. However, meta-analyses have demonstrated that men are only moderately more aggressive than women overall, and that the difference depends on the type of aggression. Men are moderately more physically aggressive than women ($d = 0.40$) but only minimally more psychologically aggressive ($d = 0.18$). These gender differences can be interpreted using social role theory, in which social norms dictate male and female expressions of aggression. Women may be less physically aggressive and commit fewer violent crimes than men not because they are biologically less aggressive but because social norms inhibit their expression of aggression in physical or violent ways. Studies of men's and women's attitudes about the expression of aggression support social role theory, not an evolutionary interpreta-

tion. Another example is the assumption that male superiority on standardized math tests or certain types of math problems reflects an inherent female math deficit. However, many standardized tests such as the SAT are taken at the end of high school; girls take fewer math classes in high school than boys do, so they have less math experience when taking such standardized tests. Not only is there a direct nonbiological cause for the gender difference in SAT math performance, but this cause is also predicted by social role theory. If women are socialized to believe they are not competent in math or that math is a male field, they will not elect to take as many advanced math classes in high school. Therefore, the gender difference in SAT performance may be entirely due to social norms and attitudes regarding gender and math, not biologically determined gender differences in math ability.

In sum, care should be taken when interpreting gender difference findings. Biological explanations should not be given for gender differences unless biological theories were directly tested with biological measures. Similarly, findings that are "consistent" with evolutionary theory should also be examined for relevant social role or socialization theories. Researchers should be very cautious about assuming that men and women are fundamentally or functionally different when other explanations are equally valid and less likely to support gender stereotypes or suggest female deficits. [See DEVELOPMENT OF SEX AND GENDER; SOCIAL ROLE THEORY OF SEX DIFFERENCES AND SIMILARITIES.]

X. Future Directions

Two features of research on gender differences will be particularly important for the future: context and process. We need far more systematic research that examines the contexts in which gender differences in behavior appear, disappear, or even reverse themselves. Closely connected to this approach, research must examine the processes involved in producing gender differences and similarities, including the individual's cognitive and affective processes and dyadic and group interactions.

In addition, research must examine questions of multiple identities and multiple differences. Gender is not the only and certainly not always the most salient aspect of an individual's identity; other crucial identities include ethnicity and sexual orientation, which in turn generate a set of social contexts for the individual. Research shows that (small) gender differences found among White Americans can be nonexistent for African Americans; an example is found in a 1990 meta-analysis of data on mathematics performance by Hyde and colleagues. The richest research will examine the contexts and processes involved in multiple identities such as gender and ethnicity.

SUGGESTED READING

Deaux, K., and Major, B. (1987). Putting gender into context: An interactive model of gender-related behavior. *Psychological Review* **94**, 369–389.

Eagly, A. (1997). Sex differences in social behavior: Comparing social role theory and evolutionary psychology. *American Psychologist* **52**, 1380–1383.

Feingold, A. (1992). Sex differences in variability in intellectual abilities: A new look at an old controversy. *Review of Educational Research* **62**, 61–84.

Halpern, D. (2000). *Sex Differences in Cognitive Ability*. 3rd ed. Erlbaum, Mahwah, NJ.

Hare-Mustin, R., and Marecek, J. (1988). The meaning of difference: Gender theory, postmodernism, and psychology. *American Psychologist* **43**, 455–464.

Hedges, L. V., and Becker, B. J. (1986). Statistical methods in the meta-analysis of research on gender differences. In *The Psychology of Gender: Advances through Meta-analysis* (J. S. Hyde and M. C. Linn, eds.), pp. 14–50. Johns Hopkins University Press, Baltimore.

Hyde, J. S., Fennema, E., and Lamon, S. (1990). Gender differences in mathematics performance: A meta-analysis. *Psychological Bulletin* **107**, 139–155.

Jacobs, J., and Eccles, J. S. (1985). Science and the media: Benbow and Stanley revisited. *Educational Researcher* **14**, 20–25.

Lightdale, J. R., and Prentice, D. A. (1994). Rethinking sex differences in aggression: Aggressive behavior in the absence of social roles. *Personality and Social Psychology Bulletin* **20**, 34–44.

Maccoby, E. E., and Jacklin, C. N. (1974). *The Psychology of Sex Differences*. Stanford University Press, Stanford, CA.

Wilkinson, L., and APA Task Force on Statistical Inference. (1999). Statistical methods in psychology journals: Guidelines and explanations. *American Psychologist* **54**, 594–604.

Gender Stereotypes

Mary E. Kite
Ball State University

Glossary

Agency Gender stereotypic characteristics, typically associated with men, that reflect an assertive and controlling tendency and concern for one's own self-interest (also labeled instrumental).

Communion Gender stereotypic characteristics, typically associated with women, that reflect interpersonal sensitivity and a concern with the welfare of other people (also labeled expressive).

Gender polarization The tendency to construe the differences between women and men in unidimensional, bipolar terms.

Gender roles Shared expectations that define how women and men should behave (prescriptive) and how they do behave (descriptive).

Gender role violators Individuals who do not conform to expected gender roles.

Gender schema A classification mechanism developed to process beliefs and cognitions about gender.

Gender subtypes Categories that are more narrowly defined than the basic categories of women and men.

Subtle sexism Beliefs and behaviors that are harmful to women and men but, because people have internalized them as normal or natural, often go unnoticed.

GENDER STEREOTYPES are organized, consensual beliefs and opinions about the characteristics of women and men and about the purported qualities of masculinity and femininity.

I. Overview

The characteristics people associate with men and women are both descriptive and prescriptive. That is, gender stereotypic beliefs describe who women and men *are*, but they also tell who they *should be*. These stereotypes are part of a broader gender belief system that influences perceptions of the sexes. This belief system, conveyed in large part through societal expectations, also includes attitudes toward appropriate roles for the sexes, perceptions of those who violate the modal pattern, and gender-associated perceptions of the self. These multidimensional components have common roots, but are not synonymous. Indeed, research shows elements of this system may be only loosely related. This writing focuses on gender stereotypes, which Kay Deaux and Marianne LaFrance argue are the most fundamental aspect of the gender belief system.

II. *Content of Gender Stereotypes*

Paul Rosenkrantz and Inge Broverman were the first to identify the characteristics typically associated with men and women. These authors determined that two constellations of traits represent gender-associated beliefs: a competence cluster, typically associated with men, that includes characteristics such as "confident," "independent," and "controlling" (labeled agentic or instrumental), and a warmth-expressiveness cluster, typically associated with women, that includes characteristics such as "warm," "kind," and "concerned for others' welfare" (labeled communal or expressive). These beliefs mirror perceptions of one's own characteristics: men self-report greater agency and women self-report greater communion than their other-sex counterparts. [*See* GENDER DIFFERENCE RESEARCH: PERSONALITY.]

These associations have been replicated many times and across many cultures and nationalities. The seminal work of John Williams and Deborah Best, for example, showed that, across 30 nations, there was considerable consensus in perceived attributes, with judgments of men characterized by higher agency and judgments of women characterized by higher communion. These beliefs have also been remarkably stable across time. This resilience occurs despite the fact that self-reports of people's own gender-linked characteristics have changed over time. Jean Twenge, for example, found that women's self-reported agency is higher than in the past, whereas men's has remained stable. Apparently, the gap between the sexes on this measure is narrowing. The sex difference in self-reported communion, however, is not decreasing. Janet Spence and Camille Buckner replicated these findings

and also showed that gender stereotypic beliefs have not incorporated the change. Interestingly, people predict change will follow; Alice Eagly and Amanda Diekman found that people expect the differences between the sexes on these characteristics will diminish over time. They also believe things have changed since the 1950s—before these constructs were consistently measured by gender researchers. This perceived convergence was largely due to the perception that women would be more likely, over time, to take on the qualities typically associated with men. Presumably, these findings reflect a willingness to adjust gender stereotypic beliefs based on perceived changes in gender role behavior. [*See* CROSS-CULTURAL GENDER ROLES.]

Examining the traits associated with women and men remains a central component of gender stereotyping research. Table I contains the traits that constitute the Personal Attributes Questionnaire (PAQ), developed by Janet Spence, Robert Helmreich, and Joy Stapp. This instrument can be used for two purposes: as a self-report measure that assesses beliefs about people's own characteristics and as a measure of gender stereotypic beliefs. The scale assesses the two components of gender stereotypic traits, agency and communion. (The short form of the Bem Sex Role Inventory [BSRI], developed by Sandra Bem, is used in similar ways.) These instruments, and similar ones, have been used in countless studies on gender stereotyping.

A limitation of the pervasive focus on traits is that other central aspects of the gender belief system are often ignored. Yet, as Spence has convincingly argued, gender-associated beliefs are multidimensional and more complex than the constructs measured by the BSRI and the PAQ. Exploring this complexity, Kay Deaux and Laurie Lewis outlined the multidimensional nature of gender stereotypes. These authors showed that perceivers also have gender-associated beliefs about women's and men's physical characteristics and about the roles they occupy. Others have replicated and extended this work; Mary Ann Cejka and Alice Eagly, for example, also showed that these general categories represent gender stereotypic beliefs. In addition, they found that people have gender stereotypic beliefs about cognitive abilities. Men are seen as analytic and good at problem solving, whereas women are seen as creative and verbally skilled. Gender-associated role behaviors, physical characteristics, and cognitive abilities, documented by these researchers and others, are also provided in Table I. [*See* SEX DIFFERENCE RESEARCH: COGNITIVE ABILITIES.]

Table I
Gender Stereotypic Characteristics Associated with Women and Men

	Traits	Roles	Physical characteristics	Cognitive abilities
Associated with men	Active Can make decisions easily Competitive Feels superior Independent Never gives up easily Self-confident Stands up well under pressure	Assumes financial obligations Head of household Financial provider Leader Responsible for household repairs Takes initiative in sexual relations Watches sports on television	Athletic Brawny Broad-shouldered Burly Muscular Physically strong Physically vigorous Rugged Tall	Analytical Exact Good at abstractions Good at numbers Good at problem solving Good with reasoning Mathematical Quantitatively skilled
Associated with women	Able to devote self to others Aware of others feelings Emotional Helpful to others Gentle Kind Understanding Warm	Cooks the meals Does the household shopping Does laundry Is fashion conscious Source of emotional support Takes care of children Tends the house	Beautiful Cute Dainty Gorgeous Graceful Petite Pretty Sexy Soft voice	Artistic Creative Expressive Imaginative Intuitive Perceptive Tasteful Verbally skilled

Another constellation of gender-linked beliefs centers on stereotypic ideas about emotional expression. A recent study by Ashby Plant, Janet Hyde, Dacher Keltner, and Patricia Devine showed that women were believed to both experience and express most emotions more readily than were men. Of the 19 emotions examined, only anger and pride were more closely associated with men than women. Associated with women were emotions such as happiness, embarrassment, guilt, love, fear, and distress. Yet these sex differences were perceived to be larger when the expression, rather than the experience, of emotion was considered. People apparently believe that both women and men suppress emotions when they are inconsistent with their appropriate gender role. As with research on other aspects of the gender belief system, cultural expectations provide a window through which others' emotional reactions are viewed. [See EMPATHY AND EMOTIONAL EXPRESSIVITY.]

III. Development of Gender Stereotypes

How cultural expectations are learned has long interested gender scientists. The sources of people's gender-linked expectations are many: parents, the media, and peers all contribute to ideas about who boys and girls, women and men, are and should be. The relative influence of each of these sources has been debated, but researchers have yet to untangle the exact ways in which these factors interplay. Moreover, it seems unlikely that any one source has undue influence. What is clear is that the weight of the culture supports gender stereotypic beliefs, sometimes to the dismay of those raising children.

To appreciate the staying power of gender stereotypes, one need only consider how early in life these beliefs develop and how accurately children gauge the behaviors deemed appropriate for the sexes. At two months, infants can recognize a shift from a male to a female speaker. By six months, they can discriminate between male and female faces. Children as young as two or three can readily identify which toys are designed for their sex, and they know which activities are stereotypically associated with women and men. Consistent with patterns shown for adults, children's gender role beliefs vary little cross-culturally, although parental influence can speed their development. Beverly Fagot and Mary Leinbach found that children whose parents held traditional views of gender roles learned these associations at a younger age. Early on, then, children understand that they live in a gendered world and this knowledge influences their thoughts and actions. [*See* GENDER DEVELOPMENT: SOCIAL LEARNING.]

Models of children's development assume that gender becomes a lens through which behaviors are viewed and interpreted. According to this perspective, put forth by Sandra Bem, this lens reflects a generalized readiness to process information on the basis of gender-linked associations. Children, then, develop gender schemas that encompass beliefs and expectations about women and men and girls and boys. Carol Martin and her colleagues have detailed how these gender schemas work to organize and bias behavior, thinking, and attention. Their work documents that gender schemas are remarkably stable and that children think and act consistently with their schemas. Yet, consistent with the multidimensional nature of gender stereotypes, these schemas are themselves complex. Margaret Signorella and her colleagues, for example, have differentiated between gender schemas for the self and for others. They further distinguished between knowledge schemas (e.g., information) and attitude schemas (affective judgments). Development of these schemas varied. Children's knowledge about which sex *typically* performs an activity increased with age. Attitudes about which sex *should* perform an activity, in contrast, peaked at around age five and then decreased with age. [*See* GENDER DEVELOPMENT: GENDER SCHEMA THEORY.]

Despite these complexities, the overwhelming evidence suggests that children use knowledge about gender to inform their own behavior and to make predictions about others' behavior. One consequence of this knowledge is the segregation of play partners by sex. The influential work of Eleanor Maccoby and her colleagues showed that children's tendency to play with their own-sex peers begins as early as age two and strengthens with age. Gender schemas also influence what happens during play. Children prefer toys that their own sex likes and avoid toys they believe are for the other sex. The strength of this preference is brought home by the work of Martin and her colleagues. When evaluating a novel, gender-neutral toy, children assume if they like the toy, other members of their sex also will like it and children of the other sex will not. They will also reject even very attractive toys when they believe those toys were developed for the other sex and assume their peers will feel the same. [*See* PLAY PATTERNS AND GENDER.]

At the youngest ages, these beliefs about gender are based mainly on biological sex. Young children predict that a girl described as liking trucks and softball would still generally prefer feminine activities. By around age nine, however, children's networks become more sophisticated and they begin to associate others' activities and interests with global gender-related information, rather than merely biological sex. Now boys who like one feminine activity are assumed to like other feminine activities as well. With development also comes the appreciation that occupational differences and personality cues contain gendered information; children realize, for example, that power is associated with masculinity. Older children are also more willing to acknowledge exceptions to the gender rules (e.g., some girls are good at sports).

IV. *The Structure of Gender Stereotypes*

Certainly by adulthood, societal expectations about how the sexes do and should behave are well learned. Of course, not everyone overtly endorses these beliefs, but most can readily identify them. Evidence also suggests that, at least at first glance, people automatically rely on gender stereotypes when perceiving others. Mahzarin Banaji and her colleagues have examined the effects of this implicit information processing. When research participants are primed for the stereotypically male quality of aggression, they subsequently rate male targets as more aggressive than female targets, compared to those primed by neutral traits. Similarly, those primed by the stereotypically female quality of dependency later rate women targets as more dependent than male targets, compared with those primed by neutral traits. People can also make judgments about gender faster when unconsciously primed with gender-related words. Decisions about the gender of pronouns and names, for example, are made more quickly when the network of associations about men and women has been activated.

Even when these associations have not been directly activated, the assumptions people make about gender are quite predictable and follow a pattern that Sandra Bem has labeled gender polarization. That is, people make the assumption that gender-associated characteristics are bipolar, concluding that what is masculine is not feminine and vice versa. Deaux and Lewis's work supports this assertion. People predict, for example, that a woman described by feminine physical characteristics is also likely to have feminine traits and to occupy feminine roles. Similarly, knowing a person is masculine on one set of characteristics leads to the prediction that the person is masculine on other characteristics. This information, coupled with knowledge of a person's biological sex, also influences judgments of a person's sexual orientation. People believe that men described by female-associated characteristics are likely to be gay and, to a lesser extent, that women described by male-associated characteristics are likely to be lesbian. Predictions about occupations are also linked to gender stereotypes. People expect that traditionally masculine occupations are filled by those with masculine traits and traditionally feminine occupations are filled by those with feminine traits. Finally, judgments of status and power are associated with gender stereotypes. High-status individuals are believed to have stereotypically male traits and low-status individuals are believed to have stereotypically female traits. The higher status of the male role does not always bring higher esteem, however. In a series of studies, Alice Eagly, Antonio Mladinic, and their colleagues showed that women are evaluated more positively than men on global attitude measures, probably because the characteristics associated with women are more likable than the characteristics associated with men. [*See* POWER.]

V. Social Role Theory

As discussed earlier, the tendency to associate gender with a variety of characteristics likely begins in childhood. Yet knowing the origin of these past cultural influences does not, in and of itself, elucidate why these beliefs develop. The current social structure also influences the content of the gender belief system. This influence is a central tenant of social role theory. This perspective, proposed by Eagly, postulates that viewing people in various social roles provides an important basis for beliefs about social groups. This occurs because people consistently observe behaviors that stem from the social roles that group members occupy and, therefore, come to associate the characteristics of that role with the individuals who occupy it. Rather than emerging from biased, inaccurate beliefs, then, ideas about group members are inferred from their recognized behaviors.

The assumption that others' inner dispositions correspond to their observed behavior is a basic principle of social psychology, labeled the *correspondence bias*. All things being equal, people give relatively little weight to how situational constraints influence behavior. Instead, they believe a person's actions tell them about the person's basic personality. To see how this applies to gender stereotypes, consider the well-documented belief that women are communal and men are agentic. Social role theory proposes that these gender stereotypes can be explained by a consideration of occupational roles. Women are traditionally in the homemaker role (or in a lower status employee role) and men are traditionally in the breadwinner (or higher status employee) role. As such, women are disproportionately represented in roles requiring communal traits, such as kindness and concern for others, and men are disproportionately represented in roles requiring agentic traits, such as self-confidence and assertiveness. Because situational factors are given greater weight in judgments of others, viewing women and men in these occupational roles leads perceivers to associate the characteristics of these roles with the individuals who occupy them; hence, people conclude that women are typically communal and that men are typically agentic. A number of studies have supported this hypothesis. When people know a person's occupational role, their judgments appear to be based on that information: employed people are seen as agentic and homemakers are seen as communal, regardless of whether the person in the role is male or female. When occupational information is not specified, women are viewed as higher in communion than men, whereas men are viewed as higher in agency than women.

Tests of social role theory have emerged in a number of domains, including perceptions of leadership ability, beliefs about nationalities, predictions about occupational success, and perceptions of those occupying high- and low-status roles. As noted earlier, an important question addressed by social role theory is whether people's beliefs accurately reflect reality. [*See* SOCIAL ROLE THEORY OF SEX DIFFERENCES AND SIMILARITIES.]

VI. Stereotype Accuracy

At the individual level, guesses about what a woman (or man) might be like are fraught with error. A well-known riddle about why a parent cannot operate on a child works because people often inaccurately assume the surgeon is a male. (People do not guess *she* is the boy's mother.) At the group level, however, gender-based judgments are not far off the mark. To understand this complexity, consider how a gender-linked trait, such as aggressiveness, is distributed for women and men. On average, the distribution for men shows higher aggressiveness than the distribution for women. Yet these distributions overlap, so that some women are higher in aggressiveness than the average man and some men are lower in aggressiveness than the average woman. It is only at the tails of the distribution where men are consistently higher (and women consistently lower) in aggressiveness. Any woman, then, might be more aggressive than would be expected for her group, and any man might be less aggressive than would be expected for his group. Yet at the group level, the assumption that men are more aggressive reflects a documented sex difference. It is at this level that people can most accurately make predictions.

To demonstrate this tendency, Janet Swim asked people to estimate the size and direction of sex differences on a number of categories, including mathematical ability, verbal ability, helping behavior, and decoding nonverbal cues. These estimates were compared to meta-analytic estimates of the actual sex differences on these dimensions. Results showed that people are fairly accurate at predicting the distribution of women and men on these characteristics. Indeed, when Swim found evidence of bias, it tended toward underestimating the sex difference, rather than enhancing it. Similarly, Judith Hall and Jason Carter studied 77 traits and behaviors, demonstrating that people's estimates of sex differences were highly correlated with the results of psychological research comparing women's and men's actual characteristics. Even so, a cautionary note is in order. Methodological questions, such as those raised by the shifting standards model discussed in the following section, limit the confidence researchers can have in comparisons based on self-report measures.

VII. *Shifting Standards Model*

By now, the multidimensional nature of gender should be apparent: when making gender-linked decisions, the perceiver can rely on a wealth of probabilistic information about what another person may be like or will decide to do. Perceivers are aware of the variability among women and men and realize that these judgments are only approximate guesses. The shifting standards model, proposed by Monica

Biernat and her colleagues, proposes that analysis is influenced by relative comparisons—that is, by the yardstick perceivers chose for making judgments.

In the case of gender, suppositions about women and men are made relative to within-group reference points. Hence, people draw conclusions about an individual woman (or man) based on their beliefs about women (or men) in general. Consider a situation wherein a perceiver is deciding whether a woman is tall. According to the shifting standards model, the perceiver generally makes this decision by considering the woman's height relative to other women. In this case, a woman who is 5'11" would likely be perceived as tall. If, instead, the judgment was being made of a man of identical height, he would likely be judged as average height if the analysis was made while comparing him to the average man. Moreover, if the height of the man and the women are directly compared, the woman would be viewed as objectively taller than the man.

According to the shifting standards model, the language of evaluation and judgment is subjective and, therefore, perceivers impose their own meaning depending on the sex of the person being rated. Support for this model has been found for judgments of women's and men's earning potential, athletic ability, job success, verbal ability, and evaluations of leaders in the military, among others. The findings have important implications for understanding gender stereotyping because they suggest perceivers adjust the end anchors of rating scales to reflect the distribution of women (or men) on the attribute in question. Stereotype researchers typically assess gender stereotyping on Likert-type scales (e.g., a numerical rating scale with responses ranging from not at all to very much) or other subjective measures. They also typically take evaluations obtained by this method at face value. In actuality, those judgments may reflect something considerably more slippery. The result may well be that researchers are underestimating people's actual belief about the differences between women and men.

Biernat's work also has shown that, to avoid the problem, researchers can use scales that do not allow research participants to shift or adjust the scale meaning. These "common rule" scales have a constant meaning; for example, height judgments can be obtained in units of feet and inches rather than on a Likert-type scale. Similarly, judges can be asked to rank-order women and men on the dimension of interest. The shifting standards model shows one way assessments are influenced by the research context.

Judgments of the sexes also depend on whether a global or more fine-grained analysis is required.

VIII. *Subtypes of Women and Men*

A two-category system, examining the basic categories of man and woman, is not the only strategy for examining ideas about gender. Although people clearly associate certain characteristics with women and men, these categories are too broad to capture entirely the essence of these social perceptions. Instead, researchers have shown that people can readily identify subgroups of women and men, each of which have unique characteristics. These subtypes do not invalidate the broader concepts, but seem to coexist with them. A number of studies, using a variety of methodologies, have examined these more detailed representations. Although the exact number and type of categories differ across these studies, there is, overall, a remarkable consistency in the subgroups people identify. Subtypes of women that have been consistently noted include the following: athletic woman, businesswoman, housewife, feminist, and sexy woman. Subtypes of men are not as consistently identified, but patterns do emerge. The most commonly noted subtypes include athletic man, blue-collar working man, businessman, macho man, family man, and loser.

The characteristics people associate with these subtypes vary, as do evaluations of the group members. Attributes listed for housewife, for example, focus on the woman's role as caretaker of the home and children, whereas attributes listed for the sexy woman focus on her attractive physical appearance. Macho men and athletic men are similarly described by their body type, whereas blue-collar working men are defined by their social class and work ethic. Evaluations of the subgroup members are, to some extent, based on their perceived gender-associated characteristics. Subtypes defined primarily by communal characteristics (e.g., housewives and family men) are often the most preferred; subtypes defined mainly by sexuality (e.g., sexy women and macho men) are often the least preferred. Feminists are also generally devalued. These differences may reflect the distinction Susan Fiske and Peter Glick have made between *liking* and *respecting* others. These ratings appear to be relatively independent: we may like housewives, but not respect them; conversely, we may respect successful businessmen without necessarily liking them. Beliefs about subtypes may also be linked to

particular contexts and roles. Indeed, the subcategories people generate often center on occupational roles (career woman, blue-collar working man).

IX. *The Influence of Context*

The lives of women and men are complex and the roles they occupy are many. It is not surprising that these complexities interact with stereotypic beliefs to influence interaction. To capture these complexities, Kay Deaux and Brenda Major have proposed a comprehensive model of how, when, and why gender influences behavior. Two assumptions of this model are central: first, gendered behaviors are highly flexible and influenced by context and, second, events are multiply determined. Also central to the model is the idea that neither the perceiver nor the target is a passive participant in any interaction. Instead, both parties work in tandem to influence outcomes. Whether a person is perceived in gender stereotypic terms depends on the perceiver's gender belief system and on how the target reacts to actions and expectancies that stem from those beliefs. Situational influences figure in, too. Some situations are highly gendered, such as a bar scene where heterosexual singles go to find dates; others, such as a business lunch, can be much less so. The ratio of men to women in a given setting matters too. When either sex is outnumbered, gender becomes more central than when the numbers are more balanced.

As this model makes clear, perceivers do not view all situations through the same gender lens, but instead adjust and focus based on information about the situation. Even so, raters are not universally accepting of people in all settings. In particular, individuals who fail to conform to gendered expectations can raise red flags.

X. *Stereotypes and Nontraditional Gender Roles*

When women and men occupy nontraditional roles, evaluations are influenced both by the context and by gender-linked expectations. Women who occupy work roles traditionally reserved for men can thus be placed in a double bind that jeopardizes both their work performance or how they are viewed. This double bind is often rooted in the conflict between the direct and assertive behavior expected of those in traditionally male occupational roles and the warm, nurturant, and supportive behavior more generally expected of women. When these two roles collide, women can find themselves in a no-win situation. Choosing a style consistent with their occupational demands violates one set of expectations, but behaving in a gender-stereotypic manner violates the other. Whether this conflict arises in a boardroom, the classroom, or a steel mill, failure to resolve it can severely hinder a woman's effectiveness and her opportunities for advancement. [*See* WOMEN IN NONTRADITIONAL WORK FIELDS.]

This double bind has been shown to operate in all these settings. An illustration comes from a series of meta-analyses of sex differences in leadership, conducted by Eagly and her colleagues. Their review of the literature on leadership effectiveness showed that leaders are more successful when their leadership style minimizes gender-role violation. Specifically, men are more effective when the leadership task calls for traditionally masculine role behaviors and women are more effective when the leadership task calls for traditionally feminine role behaviors. A companion review of the literature on leadership behavior showed that women leaders are especially devalued when their leadership style is autocratic (traditionally male) compared to when it is democratic (traditionally female) or is not gender stereotypic. Men and women who used a democratic leadership style are evaluated similarly. [*See* LEADERSHIP.]

Relatively few studies have examined how men fare in traditionally female occupations, but the research that does exist suggests that these men are rarely disadvantaged and, indeed, often benefit from their minority status. Outside the work role, however, gender role violation is seen as problematic for both sexes. The pressure to stay within gender-appropriate boundaries begins at a young age: children as young as three punish their peers for gender role nonconformity, and in these younger children, it is male nonconformity that raises the most hackles. Teachers and peers alike are much more likely to notice and correct boys who behave like girls than vice versa. People of all ages believe that feminine boys are probably unpopular, whereas girls' perceived popularity is unaffected by their gender-associated characteristics. College students also report that they would feel worse if their son was a sissy than if their daughter was a tomboy. Finally, people believe it more likely that girls will outgrow tomboy behavior than boys will outgrow sissy behavior.

As adults, passive dependent men and aggressive, assertive women are viewed less favorably than their nonrole violating counterparts. Moreover, people assume that those who primarily display characteristics of the other sex are likely to be lesbian or gay, a category generally held in low esteem. Adult heterosexuals, however, may enjoy greater gender role latitude than either children or gays are afforded. Research by Linda Jackson and Thomas Cash showed that people described as engaging in both male and female role behaviors were preferred over those who endorsed strictly gender-congruent or gender-incongruent roles. Perceptions may also depend on the specific descriptors used. Men described as "feminine" and women described as "masculine" are disliked more than "feminine" women or "masculine" males. Yet people characterized as having communal traits, commonly associated with women, are liked regardless of their gender. Those described only by agentic traits, in contrast, are often disliked—even though for men those descriptors are gender-role congruent. Consistent with this finding, Judith Gibbons, Deborah Stiles, and their colleagues showed that adolescents from eight different countries believed that the most important characteristics a person should possess are kindness and honesty—communal traits. Although it is not particularly satisfying, the answer to the question of whether gender role violators are disliked appears to be "sometimes." People's ambivalence about the sexes is also reflected in theories addressing the subtle ways stereotypes affect judgment.

XI. *Subtle Sexism*

Although gender stereotypes have not changed over time, beliefs about the appropriate roles for women and men have surely become more progressive. Relatively few North Americans will deny a woman's right to work or a man's decision to be involved in child care. National survey data and studies of college students alike show a shift toward considerably greater acceptance of women's rights. Yet the glass ceiling persists; women's options and opportunities have not extended to the highest level: only rarely are women named heads of state or CEOs. Theorists argue that women continue to be limited by sexist beliefs, but that these modern beliefs are ephemeral. Nicole Benokraitis has defined such beliefs as subtle sexism—beliefs and behaviors that are harmful to women and men but, because people have internalized them as normal or natural, often go unnoticed. [*See* CAREER ACHIEVEMENT.]

Psychologists have developed individual difference measures to assess these subtle beliefs. Research shows that even those who profess support for women's rights sometimes report sexist attitudes on these instruments. Those who score high on Swim's Modern Sexism Scale, for example, explain women's failure to become CEOs by pointing to the biological differences between the sexes rather than to discriminatory behavior. Modern sexists also believe that the attention the government and the media pay to women's issues is unwarranted. Relatedly, work by Francine Tougas shows that neosexists—those who believe it is important to maintain the current balance between men's and women's roles—are generally opposed to the women's movement and to programs such as affirmative action. Neosexism theory points to the power of the male role as an explanation for negative attitudes toward women; simply put, men stand to lose if the balance shifts to more egalitarian gender roles. Both women and men can hold attitudes that reject this change. For these individuals, the goal is to maintain the status quo.

Power and status differences between the sexes are an important part of ambivalent sexism theory (AST), proposed by Glick and Fiske. This theory proposes that people actually have ambivalent feelings about the other sex. This ambivalence is fueled by social structural differences between women and men. On the one hand, men have greater status and power than do women. On the other hand, men's relationships with women are a central aspect of their lives. Navigating these waters can produce two categories of sexist attitudes. For men, benevolent beliefs are reserved for the traditional woman, who is seen as needing protection and care. Hostile beliefs are reserved for the feminist woman, who is viewed as making the unreasonable claim that women are discriminated against. Both sets of beliefs patronize and limit women. Yet women, too, can hold ambivalent beliefs about men. Women who envy men's status and power may view men with hostile condescension. But because many women are emotionally or economically dependent on men, they may feel protective and nurturant toward them.

The common thread running through all forms of subtle sexism is that it limits opportunity and serves as a justification for the current patriarchal social structure. These traditional gender roles hinder men and women. Joseph Pleck and his colleagues argue that when men believe they fail to live up to the tra-

ditional masculine ideology, the result is low self-esteem and a variety of harmful behaviors such as problematic drug use, irresponsible sexual behavior, and prejudicial attitudes toward gays.

XII. *Complexities and Limitations*

A limitation of research on the gender belief system is the tendency to focus, implicitly or explicitly, on stereotypes of White targets. How beliefs about ethnicity, culture, sexual orientation, age, and social class intersect with people's gender-associated beliefs has not been extensively considered. At first glance, this may seem justified. As mentioned earlier, the belief that men are agentic and women are communal has been replicated in a variety of populations and settings. Moreover, when categorizing others, perceivers may more readily rely on gender than on other social categories such as race or age. Even so, when these other dimensions are taken into account, the complexity of gender-associated beliefs becomes apparent. Yolanda Niemann and her colleagues showed that when ethnicity of the stimulus person is varied, free response assessments of these more specific targets are quite distinct: White women and men are not described in the same way as Black or Asian women and men. Other work shows that Black women and lower-class women are seen as less feminine than White women and middle-class women. Moreover, the gender-associated beliefs about Black and White men are similar, but Black women are thought to be more like Black men than like White women on male-associated traits.

Views about gender change when other social categories are considered as well. Research shows a double standard of perceived aging, with people believing women reach age markers, such as old and middle age, earlier than men. In the realm of physical appearance, women are thought to decline at a younger age than men do, but this double standard may not extend to other stereotype categories. Both women and men, for example, are viewed as less agentic with age, and evaluations of communion do not vary with age. Beliefs about sexuality and sexual orientation also are tightly linked to beliefs about who the sexes are and should be: recall that subtypes of the global labels "woman" and "man" consistently produce categories reflecting sexuality (e.g., sexy woman and macho man). Moreover, as discussed earlier, people believe that knowing a person's gender-associated characteristics tells their sexual orientation. Mirroring this belief, heterosexuals predict that gay men and lesbians will have the gender-associated characteristics of the other sex. This pattern extends to bisexuals too, but with less consistency and certainty.

A related limitation of the research area is that few studies consider the perspective of ethnic minorities; gays, lesbians, and bisexuals; and members of other social classes. That is, these individuals are rarely sought out as research respondents. The perspectives of residents of different countries also are rarely examined. As one example of the problem with this convention, consider the exception of Williams and Best's work. As noted earlier, these authors found, across 30 countries, considerable consistency in the belief that men are agentic and women are communal. Yet variations emerged as well; in Catholic countries, for example, women were viewed as stronger than they were in Protestant countries. Similarly, differences in women's and men's agency were less pronounced in countries with greater economic development. The recent United Nations report on the status of women provides a look at the issue from another vantage point. This report notes unsettling differences in women's treatment that can only represent chasms of cultural differences. As one example, the illiteracy rate for women in Africa and southern Asia exceeds that for men by at least 20%. Contrast this to the fact that in most developed countries, colleges and universities educated at least as many, if not more, women than men. These statistics almost certainly reflect cultural differences in the way the sexes are perceived.

As in most psychological research, gender researchers have relied mainly on the viewpoints of heterosexual, middle-class, North American Whites; most have been college students. There are notable exceptions, including the comprehensive work described by Survey Research Consultants International. Yet the tendency of researchers to rely on a restricted sample raises a cautionary flag: the influence of a restricted range on variables such as age, education level, sociability, need for approval, and

socioeconomic background has been well documented. And, when international samples are included, reliance on college students becomes even more problematic because the proportion of the population attending colleges or universities varies widely across cultures. The layers of complexity that surround gender stereotypic beliefs will not be completely understood until different perspectives are explored more fully.

Gender scientists have moved from documenting the content of gender stereotypes to an appreciation of the dynamic nature of gender and the centrality of context and process in understanding gender and social interaction. The knowledge gained about gender stereotypes since the 1960s is nothing short of astounding. Research continues on this topic, led by some of the best thinkers and scholars in the social sciences. The future holds great promise for further understanding why and how the gender belief system is so pervasive and how this, directly and indirectly, influences the lives of women and men worldwide.

SUGGESTED READING

Basow, S. (1992). *Gender: Stereotypes and Roles,* 3rd ed. Brooks/Cole, Pacific Grove, CA.

Beall, A. E., and Sternberg, R. J. (eds.) (1993). *The Psychology of Gender.* Guilford Press, New York.

Bem, S. L. (1993). *The Lenses of Gender: Transforming the Debate on Sexual Inequality.* Yale University Press, New Haven, CT.

Burn, S. M. (1996). *The Social Psychology of Gender.* McGraw-Hill, New York.

Deaux, K., and LaFrance, M. (1998). Gender. In *The Handbook of Social Psychology* (D. T. Gilbert, S. T. Fiske, and G. Lindzey, eds.), 4th ed., Vol. 1, pp. 788–827. McGraw-Hill, Boston.

Eckes, T., and Trautner, H. M. (eds.) (2000). *The Developmental Social Psychology of Gender.* Erlbaum, Mahwah, NJ.

Swann, W. B., Langlios, J. H., and Gilbert, L. A. (Eds.) (1999). *Sexism and Stereotypes in Modern Society: The Gender Science of Janet Taylor Spence.* American Psychological Association, Washington, DC.

Unger, R. (ed.) (2001). *The Handbook of the Psychology of Women and Gender.* Wiley, New York.

Hate Crime

Karen Franklin

California School of Professional Psychology, Alameda

Glossary

Identity politics An ideology in which individuals relate to each other as members of specific social categories. Identity politics highlights race, ethnicity, sexuality, and religion while downplaying socioeconomic status and economic power relations as factors in intergroup oppression.

Penalty enhancement The most popular type of hate crime statute in the United States, this form of law adds extra time to the jail or prison sentence of a person convicted of certain classes of crimes if the crime is determined to have been motivated by bias against a protected social category to which the victim belongs.

HATE CRIME, also known as bias crime, is generally defined as a criminal act substantially motivated by prejudice or bias against a specified group, of which the victim is perceived to be a member.

I. Introduction

Intergroup violence has likely been around for as long as humans have divided themselves into social groups. Large-scale examples over the past several centuries include the Holy Inquisition, the African slave trade, the witch hunts in Europe and North America, the Holocaust, recent interethnic conflict in Rwanda and the former Yugoslavia, and the continuing persecution of the Gypsies, to name a few. In contrast, the concept of a hate crime is extremely new, emerging in the late 1970s in the United States.

Hate crime laws are intended to address—at both the symbolic and practical levels—the special harms of crimes motivated by bias or prejudice. Their passage is meant to signal society's moral condemnation of heinous conduct based on prejudice. In contrast to earlier civil rights laws still on the books in the United States, hate crime laws are aimed not at organized hate groups such as the Ku Klux Klan, but at unofficial, individual acts of intergroup violence. As such, their emergence and popularity are part of a larger cultural trend toward the individualization of social problems.

Hate crime is first and foremost a legal term. In the legal context, it refers to a crime in which the victim was selected, at least in part, because of his or her perceived group membership. Extra criminal or civil remedies are applied when a crime that might otherwise be routine (such as assault or vandalism) is deemed to be a hate crime. Some hate crime statutes also require mandatory data collection and special training of law enforcement personnel. The notion underlying all of these laws is that crimes motivated by bigotry are particularly dangerous and socially disruptive.

The exact definition of a hate crime depends on the source. Hate crimes are defined in the federal Hate Crimes Statistics Act of 1990 as "crimes that manifest evidence of prejudice based on race, religion, sexual orientation, or ethnicity, including where appropriate the crimes of murder, non-negligent manslaughter, forcible rape, aggravated assault, simple assault, intimidation, arson, and destruction, damage or vandalism of property." By contrast, the Bureau of Justice Administration defines hate crimes as "offenses motivated by hatred against a victim based on his or her race, religion, sexual orientation, ethnicity, or national origin."

In the United States, where the social movement against hate crimes (hereafter referred to as the "hate crimes movement") originated and where the federal government and a majority of states have enacted hate crime statutes, protected social categories universally include race, ethnicity, and religion. Some statutes also include (in descending order of frequency) sexual orientation, gender, disability status, and other categories.

II. History and Underpinnings

The social movement against hate crimes began in the late 1970s. Criminologist Valerie Jenness has traced its inception to a curious convergence of traditional civil rights groups and the nascent crime victims' rights movement, itself part of a sweeping, tough-on-crime movement that emerged as part of the 1980s Reagan era in the United States. The ideology of identity politics, which arose out of the embers of the vanquished progressive social movements of the late 1960s and early 1970s, has also contributed to the popularity of hate crimes laws.

The genesis of the term hate crime is unclear and indeed is the topic of some debate within the hate crimes movement. The first law that utilized the term was a data-collection statute enacted in Maryland in 1978. Over the ensuing two decades, more than 42 states adopted laws prescribing criminal penalties or sentence enhancements for hate crimes against certain groups. At least 28 states have also enacted laws enabling hate crimes victims to file civil lawsuits, and at least 25 states mandate the collection of law enforcement data on hate crimes.

By the mid-1980s, the Anti-Defamation League of the B'nai B'rith had emerged as a central force in the hate crime movement. Almost all of the hate crime laws in the United States are based on the model statute designed by the league. Indeed, according to Jenness, the public's conception of hate crimes as a serious and growing problem is largely a result of the B'nai B'rith's media campaigns over the past two decades.

National attention to the topic increased with U.S. congressional hearings in 1985 on a proposed Hate Crime Statistics Act. This act, ultimately passed in 1990, requires the U.S. Department of Justice to collect and publish statistics on crimes motivated by racial, ethnic, and religious prejudice. In 1994, as part of the omnibus crime bill, the U.S. Congress also passed a Hate Crimes Sentencing Enhancement Act similar to those enacted by more than three-fourths of U.S. states.

In contrast to the focus on penalty enhancements within the United States, some other countries have enacted hate crime laws that criminalize the sale or promotion of hate-related materials. For example, such laws are on the books in Germany, Austria, France, and Canada. An emerging target of the hate crimes movement is so-called hate sites on the World Wide Web. According to one monitoring agency, the Internet harbors more than 2000 groups that promote racism, anti-Semitism, and other forms of intergroup prejudice.

By the early 1990s, the term "hate crime" (and its synonym, "bias crime") had entered the lexicon of legal scholars. By the end of the 20th century, its use in the media and popular discourse had increased exponentially, and searches for the term "hate crime" on popular Internet search engines produced about 100,000 Web sites.

The term "hate crime" is something of a misnomer, because rather than "hatred" the underlying concept is the social psychological theory of intergroup prejudice, that is, negative attitudes or beliefs toward certain social groups. Intergroup prejudice is hypothesized to encourage individuals to commit crimes against members of scapegoated out-groups. [See PREJUDICE.]

Empirical support for the hypothesized relationship between prejudice and intergroup violence is mixed. Some apprehended hate crimes offenders endorse prejudiced attitudes toward minorities. Others, however, appear primarily motivated by the goals of thrill-seeking or going along with friends. In addition, some high-prejudice individuals commit crimes against members of a different group for reasons unrelated to their prejudice.

III. Prevalence and Patterns

In lobbying for the passage of hate crime laws, proponents have used alarmist language to suggest that intergroup violence is increasing, indeed to "epidemic" proportions. However, due to both the recency of data collection and reporting and to confusion over what constitutes a hate crime, the true severity of the problem remains unknown. Recent increases in intergroup violence, where they have reported, have been in regions with the most comprehensive criminalization efforts, such as in California, suggesting they are a consequence of improved reporting and enforcement practices rather than increases in the crimes themselves.

Indeed, the frequency of hate crimes may never be truly knowable, due to the notorious unreliability of crime data and the complexities of determining prejudice or bias as a primary motivation in individual cases. This is a topic of considerable controversy among legal scholars. For example, legal scholar James Jacobs suggested that the magnitude of the hate crimes problem can be inflated or deflated at will based on how narrowly the underlying prejudice is defined. In other words, if only the activities of organized hate crimes ideologues are counted, there will be very little hate crime; if, however, prejudice is defined quite broadly, most intergroup crimes will fall within the hate crime rubric.

Due to the vagaries of reporting, it is similarly difficult to identify specific patterns that distinguish hate crimes from other types of crimes. From what information is known, hate crimes offenders are primarily distinguishable from law breakers overall by their relatively younger age (a high proportion are juveniles) and their lack of serious criminal records. They are typically not members of extremist groups, although the rhetoric of such groups obviously may influence them.

Overall, hate crimes appear to be disproportionately committed by young men in groups, and to target lone individuals who are strangers to the offenders. Group motivations that have been identified by researchers include peer group bonding, displays of toughness and masculinity, the desire to strengthen one's group or territory against outsiders, and the goal of seeking excitement or thrills.

At the macro level, sociologists remain uncertain about the societal factors that contribute to intergroup violence, or hate crimes. Upsurges in such violence have been documented in White urban enclaves following in-migration by minorities. Additionally, economic and social disenfranchisement and idleness have been implicated by some researchers, especially when political leaders scapegoat specific groups as responsible for economic downturns.

Although the horrendous murders of James Byrd (an African American dragged behind a vehicle by three White supremacists in Texas) and Matthew Shepard (a gay man beaten, tied to a fence, and left to die in Wyoming) garnered widespread media attention in the late 1990s, the vast majority of reported hate crimes are low-level crimes, primarily vandalism, intimidation, and simple assault. Indeed, because hate crime laws typically add extra penalties for acts that are already illegal, their practical impacts are felt primarily by low-level offenders, since perpetrators of major crimes are already heavily punished under existing laws.

In order to prove that a hate crime occurred, prosecutors must establish "beyond a reasonable doubt" that a defendant acted primarily "by reason of" or "because of" the victim's perceived membership in a protected group. Due partly to the inherent difficulties in proving motivation in scenarios that are typically ambiguous, successful prosecutions under hate crime statutes have been rare, although this may be changing as the laws become more well established. Thus, although the social movement against hate crimes has increased awareness of the problem of intergroup violence among the public and within law enforcement, the laws themselves remain primarily symbolic at this time.

IV. Gender-Based Hate Crimes

A. CRIMES AGAINST WOMEN

Around the globe, violence against women is a significant social problem of considerable focus by human rights activists. Although men are statistically at greater risk than women for interpersonal violence, violence against women has a pernicious social effect, often relegating women to a subordinate status by limiting their economic and political rights. Forms of systematic violence against women and girls include rape, sexual abuse, domestic violence, infanticide, and genital mutilation. These acts have been collectively labeled by scholar Carole Sheffield as forms of "sexual terrorism" aimed at maintaining patriarchal control over women.

Despite their pervasiveness and harmful effects, gender-based crimes are often excluded from hate crime laws. Indeed, the model hate crime statute developed by the B'nai B'rith, upon which most existing laws are based, does not include gender as a protected category. This exclusion is typically explained based on practical considerations. Opponents of including gender say it would be too cumbersome. For one thing, crimes against women are more pervasive than other types of intergroup violence. Also, the fact that women frequently know their attacker is raised as an issue distinguishing crimes against women from other types of hate crimes, which are typically conceptualized as targeting strangers as members of a despised social category. Internationally, deference to traditional values that condone the subordination of women has impeded efforts to define crimes against women as hate crimes.

Although women's rights activists have won inclusion of gender in some hate crime statutes, by and large they have focused their efforts on other avenues to protect women from violence. For example, in 1994, the U.S. Congress enacted the Violence against Women Act. This federal law states that women deserve special protection from private violence such as domestic violence and rape, because these are expressions of violent sexism rooted in misogyny (the hatred of women). Recognizing violence against women as a type of hate crime with far-reaching, harmful consequences for families, children, and society, the act grants women the primarily symbolic right to sue their assailants in federal court for monetary damages. [*See* RAPE.]

B. THE GENDER-SEXUALITY LINK

Probably no social groups are as despised and targeted for violence as transvestites and transgendered people, who assume the characteristics and dress traditionally associated with the other sex. Although attempts to systematically catalog violence against these people are just beginning, anecdotal evidence suggests extremely high levels of victimization, including significant state-sanctioned or officially perpetrated violence. For example, in Istanbul, Turkey, ax-wielding police staged a series of raids in 1996 in which they burned down the homes of male cross-dressers, destroyed their property, and beat and tortured those they arrested.

Crimes against transvestites and transgendered people are often conceptualized as a form of "gender terrorism" aimed at punishing gender nonconformity and forcing both men and women to adhere to a rigid gender dichotomy that ultimately serves to maintain the subordinate status of women. Similarly targeted by this gender terrorism are boys and girls around the world who do not conform to cultural norms for gendered behavior. Extreme and continuous abuse forces many of these children to drop out of school, and contributes to their high rates of alcohol and drug abuse, delinquency, and suicide.

There is considerable overlap between this violence against gender nonconformists and the widespread violence that has been documented against lesbians and gay men, especially against masculine women and effeminate men. Indeed, in many cases it is difficult to determine whether individuals were attacked because of their gender orientation or their sexual behavior. For example, research with antigay hate crimes offenders suggests that they may target effeminate men not because of their sexual behavior per se, but because they are perceived as violating mandatory social norms for male behavior or masculinity. Similarly, in one study of violence against lesbians, the victims reported that it was often difficult to determine whether they were assaulted because of their sexual orientation or due to the fact that they were women who were not behaving in submissive or sexually receptive ways toward men.

Despite the natural connections between sexuality and gender, hate crimes activists typically treat gender and sexual orientation as separate, discreet categories. Thus, the aspect of anti-homosexual violence that is based on cultural ideas about masculinity and femininity is rendered largely invisible. And although gay rights organizations have succeeded in getting sexual orientation added as a protected category in many hate crimes laws, few if any laws specifically address violence targeting gender nonconformity.

V. Critiques of the Concept

Both proponents and opponents of hate crime laws agree that intergroup violence remains a serious social problem and that intergroup prejudice is a contributing factor to this violence. They disagree about whether hate crime laws are the best tool for fighting intergroup violence and prejudice. Indeed, the 1990s witnessed both an unprecedented flurry of legislation to outlaw this new category of crime and an answering volley of critiques that by the end of the century had become quite vocal and well defined. Critiques fall into several overlapping categories pertaining to practical enforcement problems, civil liberties concerns, and broader sociopolitical issues.

The narrowest level of criticism focuses on the laws' practical limitations. Primary among these is the inherent subjectivity involved in weighing conflicting accounts regarding prejudiced motivations versus other potential factors in individual crimes. Because crimes are often multiply determined, bias as a primary motivation is typically difficult to prove. For example, disabled people or homosexuals may be robbed not primarily out of prejudice against them, but due to the perception that they are easy targets. Or derogatory epithets may be hurled as "fighting words" in the heat of a confrontation attributable to other factors. Indeed, in one study of reported hate crimes in a major urban area, bias was found to be only a secondary motivation in a sizable proportion of crimes that would have occurred anyway. Thus, critics contend that the laws' subjectivity and openness to multiple, competing interpretations raise almost insurmountable barriers to effective enforcement.

A related topic of considerable concern among legal scholars in the United States is the potential for hate crime laws to infringe on free speech rights. As an example, in a landmark Ohio case that stemmed from an interracial dispute at a campground, prosecutors delved into the defendant's personal life in order to prove that he was a racist. "All these black people that you have described that are your friends," the prosecutor in *State* v. *Wyant* demanded in his cross-examination of the defendant, "I want you to give me one person, just one, who was a really good friend of yours." Whether prosecutors should be allowed to introduce as evidence a defendant's prior prejudiced statements or literary tastes in order to establish bias has been a topic of much controversy.

In a similar vein, hate crime laws are criticized for their potential to be used punitively against the very social groups they were designed to protect. Because the laws are operationalized without concern for societal power dynamics and inequalities, they may naturally tend to replicate the socioeconomic and racial biases within the criminal justice system, thereby possibly creating as much oppression as they ameliorate, critics contend. Indeed, there is mounting evidence that the laws are being invoked disproportionately against African Americans. This trend—which has not been adequately explored or explained—is not surprising, considering that hate crime laws emerged during a repressive, tough-on-crime era that saw the incarceration of an unprecedented number of Americans, especially African Americans.

On a larger, societal level, hate crime laws are criticized for reframing traditional civil rights concepts much more narrowly, framing prejudice as an individual phenomenon removed from its institutional, structural underpinnings. In other words, rather than focusing on larger entities that perpetuate prejudice or discrimination, hate crime laws shine their spotlights on isolated individuals, many of whom are at the bottom of the social ladder themselves and are reflecting rather than creating larger cultural biases. In this way, institutions that perpetuate oppression—such as government, the law, education, psychiatry, medicine, or religion—are distanced from the violence that they may ultimately be responsible for.

This critique implicates the larger ideology of identity politics that underlies the hate crimes movement. With its focus on discreet, fixed, and competing categories based on race, ethnicity, religion, and sexual orientation, the identity politics movement is criticized for negating socioeconomic class and power relations and impeding efforts to create progressive coalitions against multiple forms of oppression and discrimination. Ultimately, critics contend, the hate crimes movement may backfire by simultaneously exaggerating and even exacerbating intergroup tensions.

VI. Conclusion

Hate crime is a new concept that has gained rapid prominence in the United States. During the past two decades of the 20th century, hate crime laws were enacted in the vast majority of U.S. states as well as in many other Western countries. In the same time period, the concept of hate crime and hate crime laws met with growing opposition from civil libertarians and others concerned with their practical impacts. Thus, the validity and usefulness of hate crime as a category of social behavior remain hotly contested topics. Only time will tell whether the hate crimes movement will continue to expand in prominence and acceptability or whether mounting criticisms will lead to its ultimate abandonment as a strategy for combating intergroup violence.

SUGGESTED READING

Davies, M. (ed.) (1994). *Violence and Women*. Zed, Atlantic Highlands, NJ.

Ezekiel, R. (1995). *The Racist Mind: Portraits of American Neo-Nazis and Klansmen*. Penguin, New York.

Herek, G., and Berrill, K. (eds.) (1992). *Hate crimes: Confronting Violence against Lesbians and Gay Men*. Sage, Newbury Park, CA.

Jacobs, J. B., and Potter, K. (1998). *Hate Crimes: Criminal Law and Identity Politics*. Oxford University Press, New York.

Jenness, V., and Grattet, R. (in press). *Making Hate a Crime: From Social Movement Concept to Law Enforcement Practice*. Russell Sage Foundation, New York.

Kelly, R. J., and Maghan, J. (eds.) (1998). *Hate Crime: The Global Politics of Polarization*. Southern Illinois University Press, Carbondale, IL.

Levin, J., and McDevitt, J. (1993). *Hate Crimes: The Rising Tide of Bigotry and Bloodshed*. Plenum Press, New York.

Health and Health Care

How Gender Makes Women Sick

Hope Landrine

Elizabeth A. Klonoff

San Diego State University

Glossary

Carcinogens Cancer-causing agents.

CDC Centers for Disease Control and Prevention.

Clinical trials Studies testing new treatments.

Cesarean section Surgical opening of the uterus and abdomen to deliver an infant.

Developed countries Wealthy countries (i.e., those with a high gross national product) that have modern educational and health facilities.

Developing countries Poor countries (i.e., those with a low gross national product) that lack well-developed educational and health facilities. Also called "third-world" countries.

Episiotomy Surgical enlargement of the vagina to deliver an infant.

First trimester The first three months of the nine months of pregnancy.

Gender Purposeful, structured social inequality based on one's sex.

Mammogram/mammography A test to detect breast cancer.

Maternal mortality Deaths of women during or soon after pregnancy.

Morbidity Frequency of disease or illness.

Mortality Death.

PHS The United States Public Health Service.

Prenatal care Health care received during pregnancy.

Prolapsed uterus A uterus that has descended down the birth canal.

WHO The World Health Organization.

UNICEF The United Nations Children's Education Fund.

HOW GENDER MAKES WOMEN SICK will be explored in this article: we examine how the patterned, purposeful, structured social inequality by sex that constitutes gender contributes to women's morbidity (frequency of disease) and mortality (frequency of death). Around the globe and across numerous cultures, women are viewed and treated as inferior to men (social inequality). This inequality is not random or accidental but instead is patterned. Like a dress pattern, gender is a guide for making lives: it is a guide that determines their shape and content; it is a guide for making the finished articles "woman" and "man" from the raw fabric of biological femaleness and maleness. Not surprisingly, lives socially created (cut and sewn) to be unequal indeed are unequal in health, illness, access to health care, and death.

I. Gender Inequality in Mortality

A. LONGEVITY

According to a 1999 report from the U.S. Bureau of the Census, women in developed (wealthy) countries live for about 81 years. However, race, ethnicity, and social class lead to marked differences in the life expectancy of women in these countries. In the United States, Black women live to 74.7 years compared to 79.9 years for White women. In England, poor women are 60% more likely to die young than well-to-do women. Such differences are even greater when poor (developing, third-world) countries are compared to developed ones. As shown in Table I, women in developing Latin American countries live to age 72, those in poor Asian countries to age 64, and those in poor African countries to age 46. Across developed and developing nations alike, however, women typically outlive men of similar educational and income levels: in developed countries, women live from 6 to 7 years longer than men. In developing Latin American countries, they live 5 years longer than men, and in developing African and Asian countries, they live 2 years longer than men.

Women's greater longevity is the result of both biological and social factors. Female fetuses are less likely to be stillborn or to be spontaneously aborted than male ones, and males are more likely to die than females in the first six months of life, primarily because testosterone (a male hormone) slows the development of male lungs. In adulthood, women's biological advantages continue insofar as estrogen (a female hormone) protects women from several types of cardiovascular (i.e., heart) disease. This biological advantage ceases at menopause when estrogen production is reduced; at that point, sex differences in cardiovascular disease disappear. Where social factors are concerned, women live longer than men because women are less likely to smoke, drink alcohol, be involved in confrontations with guns and knives, and be in motor vehicle and other accidents. Whereas the leading cause of death for women ages 25 to 44 is cancer, the leading cause of death for men of those ages is accidents. For example, Table II displays the leading causes of death among men and women of all ages. As shown, 5.2% of all White male deaths in the United States are due to accidents. This rate

Table I

Life Expectancy at Birth by Sex for Selected Countries, 1999

Country	Men	Women	Difference	Average life expectancy for women
North America				
United States	72.9	79.7	6.8	81.25
Canada	76.1	82.8	6.7	
Europe				
France	74.8	82.7	7.9	81.67
Germany	74.0	80.5	6.5	
Italy	75.4	81.8	6.4	
Hispanic countries				
Equador	69.5	74.9	5.4	72.30
Guatemala	63.8	69.2	5.4	
Peru	68.1	72.8	4.7	
Asian countries				
China	68.6	71.5	2.9	64.15
Bangladesh	60.7	60.5	−0.2	
India	62.5	64.3	1.8	
Pakistan	58.5	60.3	1.8	
African countries				
Kenya	46.6	47.5	0.9	46.6
Uganda[a]	41.8	43.4	1.6	
Congo[a]	45.3	48.9	3.6	

[a]1998 data.

Source: U.S. Bureau of the Census, International Database (www.infoplease.com).

exceeds the rate for women, with the exception of American Indian women, whose rate of accidents exceeds that of White men. The rate of accidents for American Indian men exceeds that of U.S. men and women of all ethnic groups. These accidents among American Indians are primarily due to their hazardous jobs (e.g., in mines and factories).

About 50% of the difference in women's longevity versus men's is due to women's biological advantages, and about 50% is due to men's greater alcohol consumption, smoking, motor vehicle accidents, and death from another man's gun or knife. A few extremely poor countries are exceptions to this longevity rule. In some (e.g., Bangladesh), men outlive women, and in others (e.g., India, Pakistan,

Table II
Percentage of Deaths by Selected Major Causes of Death by Ethnicity, 1997

Cause of death	White men	Women					
		All	White	Black	American Indian	Asian	Latino
Heart disease	31.7	31.9	32.3	30.2	22.6	25.3	27.2
Cancer	24.6	22.3	22.3	21.6	18.3	26.9	21.3
Cerebrovascular disease	5.4	8.4	8.4	7.8	6.2	10.5	6.8
Diabetes	2.3	2.9	2.7	5.0	7.7	3.8	5.9
Accidents	5.2	2.9	2.8	3.1	8.8	4.9	4.75

Source: 1997 data from the National Center for Health Statistics, CDC (www.cdc.gov/nchs/fastats).

Kenya, Uganda) longevity is by and large equal by gender. These exceptions to the gender-longevity rule are (in many cases) the result of the purposeful murder and starvation of girls and women in those countries, as detailed later here. In such countries, women's biological advantage is canceled out by their social worthlessness due to gender (as defined here). In general, however, women have greater longevity than men. But women nonetheless do die needlessly for reasons that men do not.

B. MURDER OF WOMEN AND GIRLS

According to a 1991 report from the United Nations (UN), the murder of women and girls accounts for a significant portion of women's mortality. Specifically, in many developing (poor, third-world) nations in Africa, Asia, and the Middle East, female infants are routinely murdered simply for being female. The murder of adult women also occurs in these countries, with the "dowry-murders" in India and Bangladesh being the most highly publicized. A dowry-murder refers to a husband killing his wife because he was not satisfied with the money and property (dowry) she brought to the marriage. Usually, the woman is doused with kerosene and burned alive. The Indian government reported 4800 dowry deaths in 1990 alone. Women's groups report that the actual figure is significantly higher because many of these murders are officially recorded as cooking accidents; 25% (one out of every four) of the deaths of women between the ages of 15 and 24 in Bombay are due to "accidental" burns with kerosene. In addition, many women in developing countries are murdered because they "dishonor" their families by being rape victims or by violating gender roles and norms.

In the United States, three out of every four intimate murder victims (i.e., people killed by someone close to them such as a husband, ex-husband, or boyfriend) is a woman. According to the U.S. Department of Justice, in 1996 there were 1800 intimate murders, and in 1350 of these cases the victims were women. The percentage of women murder victims killed by intimates has remained the same in the United States since 1976, with the exception of an increase in the number of White women killed by their boyfriends. In many other countries (e.g., Canada, Brazil, Israel), more than 50% of all women murdered were killed by a currently or formerly intimate man.

C. MATERNAL MORTALITY RATES

Maternal mortality rates account for a significant proportion of women's mortality. In the developing countries of Asia, Africa, Latina America, and the Caribbean, 585,000 women die from pregnancy-related causes each year. According to the World Health Organization (WHO), this figure is not only an underestimate, but also reveals that maternal mortality rates (MMR) have been increasing by 16,000 each year. Most of the world's maternal deaths—55% of them—occur in Asia, but Asia also is the site of most of the world's births; 61% of all births worldwide occur in Asia. The highest MMR is not in Asia but in Africa, where 40% of the world's maternal deaths occur, even though only 20% of the world's births occur there. In these poor nations, maternal mortality is due to lack of access to health care. WHO reported that less than 40% of pregnant women in developing nations have access to health care and therefore have seen a health professional during the course of their pregnancies. Up to 66%

of infants delivered in developing nations not only are delivered at home, but also are delivered without the assistance of a physician, nurse, or even a midwife. Hence, many women in these countries die during or soon after delivery.

Those few women in developing countries who have the economic resources to seek medical care during their pregnancies and to deliver their infants in hospitals may die as well. This is because medical facilities and staff in developing nations are poor. Significant maternal deaths due to overcrowding, unqualified staff, and lack of a sufficient supply of blood and of medications have been reported throughout Africa (e.g., in Malawi, Tanzania, Kenya, Senegal, Sudan, South Africa) and other developing countries (e.g., Egypt, Cuba, Vietnam, India, Saudi Arabia, Jamaica, Venezuela). Thus, the health care systems of poor, developing countries contribute to (and indeed often cause) maternal deaths. The MMR in Surinam (a poor, South American country) is 226 (226 maternal deaths for every 100,000 live infant births). The MMR for Africa as a whole is 870; in some parts of Africa, the MMR is 14,285—one in every 7 pregnant women dies.

In contrast, maternal mortality rates are low in developed countries (the United States and in Europe). WHO reported that only 1% of all maternal deaths worldwide occur in developed countries, and these countries have 11% of the world's births. In 1999, the MMR in the United States was 7.5 (7.5 maternal deaths for every 100,000 infant births)—compared to Africa's MMR of 870. While this figure is low in the international arena, it is far higher than the U.S. Public Health Service (PHS) goal of an MMR of 3.3. In addition, while the MMR for the United States and other developed countries is low, it remains high among the poor and minority women of those nations, according to the most recent reports from the Centers for Disease Control and Prevention (CDC): for White women in the United States, the MMR is 5.0, whereas for Black women it is 20.3; Black women are four times more likely than White women to die from pregnancy. The MMR for nonwhite women (taken as a whole) in the United States remains 3.6 times higher than that for White women, and evidence indicates that at least 33% (one in every three) of minority women's maternal deaths are preventable. Likewise, poor women are two times more likely than middle-class ones to die from pregnancy in the United States, England, and other developed nations. This is a result of ethnic and social class differences in access to health care services. The

PHS's goal was for 90% of women to have prenatal care in their first trimester by the year 2000. Cuban American and Japanese American mothers were the only groups to reach this goal. Among Black women, only 68% have first-trimester prenatal care, and the same is true for Puerto Rican (67%) and American Indian (65%) women.

Furthermore, although most women in developed nations have access to hospitals for delivering their infants, the services they receive in these hospitals are often unnecessarily painful or humiliating, and are often conducted without their consent. The routine practices of shaving off women's pubic hair and giving them an enema before delivery are two examples. No scientific evidence indicates that shaving off pubic hair or giving an enema assists in the delivery—but there is sound evidence indicating that these routine enemas cause colitis, gangrene, and other health problems. Similarly, no scientific evidence indicates that routine episiotomy (surgical enlargement of the vagina) improves delivery. This unnecessary procedure is so painful and leaves such an ugly scar (requiring stitches) that some refer to episiotomy as a form of genital mutilation. Episiotomy is one of the single most frequently conducted surgical procedures in developed countries. According to the CDC, 1.2 million episiotomies are performed each year in the United States alone, and these are typically done without women's knowledge or consent. Cesarean sections are all the more problematic. [See PREGNANCY.]

A cesarean section (named for Julius Caesar who was the first to be delivered in this manner) involves making incisions in the abdominal wall and uterus to remove the fetus. The purpose is to deliver an infant when the mother's birth canal is too small for vaginal delivery, and to deliver infants who are in danger due to lack of oxygen, difficult positioning, and so forth. Cesarean sections (C-sections) now account for one in every four live births: 800,000 C-sections were conducted in 1997 in the United States, and 473,000 of those (more than half) were not necessary according to the CDC, the PHS, and the Public Citizen's Health Research Group. These unnecessary C-sections cost $1.3 billion to perform. The procedure is a dangerous one: women who deliver through C-section are three times more likely to die while giving birth than those who deliver vaginally. Hence, the PHS's goal for the year 2000 was to reduce the percentage of C-sections performed from 22 to 25% of deliveries (as of 1997) to 15% of deliveries.

Receiving a C-section is best predicted by a woman's income and the quality of her health insurance: middle-class women (as determined by census tracts) have a C-section rate of 22.9% (of all deliveries) compared to 13.2% for women identified as poor by census tracts. Likewise, the better a woman's health insurance, the higher her chances of delivering via C-section. Women with private insurance have a C-section rate of 29.1%; those in health maintenance organizations have a rate of 26.8%; those who pay out-of-pocket for health care have a rate of 19.3%; and those on public assistance have a rate of 15.6%. Clearly receiving a C-section is predicted by being able to pay for one.

Studies suggest that, in general, a woman's ethnicity does not play a role in her likelihood of having a C-section; however, there are three exceptions to this. The first is that American Indian women have the lowest C-section delivery rate (12%) of all ethnic groups in the United States; their C-section rate is half that of other American women (22 to 25%). The reasons for this low rate of C-sections remain unknown. The second exception to the finding that ethnicity is not related to C-sections comes from a study of women in the navy, all of whom had equal access to precisely the same naval care services and hospitals. This study found that Black women received significantly more C-sections than White women, even when controlling for age; Black women were more than twice as likely to have a C-section than were White women. The third exception to the general finding that ethnicity is not related to C-sections is the numerous women in the United States who have had C-sections against their will, these ordered by the courts when the woman refused but the physician insisted. Almost all of these women were Black; the remainder were Hispanic and a few were Asian. Many of the Hispanic women did not speak English, and 50% of all of the women were poor (e.g., on public assistance and being seen in a university teaching hospital).

C-sections also have other effects on women. For example, a 1996 study published in the *American Journal of Public Health* found that Latinas who deliver via C-section are significantly less likely than those who deliver vaginally to breast-feed their newborns; breast-feeding is known to be better for infant health.

In summary, on the whole, women live longer than men, but how much longer depends on a woman's race, ethnicity, and social class; on whether she lives in a developed or developing nation; and on whether she lives in a "classic patriarchy" nation where women's low social status and low value dictate their untimely deaths. Despite greater longevity, however, women do die unnecessarily, and this is (in the final analysis) the result of gender. Causes of unnecessary mortality for women are murder and maternal deaths. Other causes are discrimination in medical diagnoses, treatment, and health insurance, detailed in later sections.

II. Gender Inequality in Morbidity

Women live longer than men, but, simultaneously, across the world, women are sicker than men: women have both greater longevity and greater (i.e., "excess") morbidity. As shown in Table III, women make more visits to physicians, more visits to hospitals, more visits to emergency rooms, and have more surgical procedures than men, even after controlling for pregnancy.

However, ethnicity and social class play a role in women's visits to physicians and to hospitals. The number of women seeing a physician and the average number of physician visits are both significantly lower for African American women than for White women at all income levels. In addition, women with low incomes are the least likely to visit a physician irrespective of ethnic group. Among the poorest women, fewer African American women are hospitalized than White women. Rates of hospitalization for African American and White women do not differ among the higher income groups. However, Latina women have lower overall hospitalization rates and lower rates of care than White women in every income group.

Table III
Morbidity Data: Women Are Sicker Than Men

Morbidity indicators	All men	All women
Number of annual office visits to physicians	300 million	471.4 million
Number of annual hospital outpatient visits	26 million	41 million
Number of annual emergency department visits	42 million	50.2 million
Number of annual surgical procedures	16 million	40.8 million

Source: 1997 data from the National Center for Health Statistics, CDC (www.cdc.gov/nchs/fastats).

Poor women and minority women make fewer physician visits and have fewer hospitalizations than White and middle-class women because of their lack of health insurance and access to health services. This does not mean, however, that poor and minority women are not sick. For example, self-assessment of health status has been found to correlate reasonably well with objective (i.e., biological) measures of health. Hence, self-ratings of health are collected by the National Institutes of Health as an indicator of the health of the American population. As shown in Table IV, more women than men rate their health as poor, and more minority women (compared to White women and men) rate their health as poor. Specifically, about 1 in 10 women assess their health as fair or poor; however, twice as many African American women and 1.5 times as many Latinas rate their health fair or poor than do White women. Likewise, 1 in every 4 women with incomes under $10,000 rate their health as fair or poor, while only 1 in every 35 (2.8%) women with incomes over $35,000 report similarly. Although across income categories a larger percentage of Latina and African American women rate their health as fair or poor than do White women, these differences between ethnic groups are smaller than the differences by income within each ethnic group.

One frequently used health indicator is the percentage of the population with limitations in major activity due to a chronic condition. About 13% of women ages 18 to 64 report such limitations. The differences in this index among the various ethnic groups is small; about 20% more African Americans (15.6%) and 20% fewer Latinas (10.3%) report limitations than White women (12.9%). However, the differences by income are extremely large; three times as many low-income women (25.7%) report limitations in activity than upper-income women (7.9%).

Another measure of health status is the degree to which health problems limit one's ability to work. Health problems limit the ability to work of more African American women than Latina or White women. This measure also is strongly associated with income; 1 in every 7 (14.3%) women with incomes under $10,000 are unable to work because of their health problems, while only 1 in every 45 (2.2%) women with incomes greater than $35,000 report similar limitations.

In general, then, irrespective of ethnicity and social class, women are sicker than men (i.e., excess morbidity), and poor and minority women are the sickest of all women (highest morbidity).

III. Causes of Gender Inequality in Morbidity

A small portion of women's excess morbidity is due to women's greater longevity: because women tend to live longer than men, more women than men suffer diseases of aging (e.g., Alzheimer's disease, arthritis). The vast majority of gender differences in morbidity, however, cannot be attributed to gender differences in longevity and instead are the result of gender itself: around the globe, it is women's lives (how women are treated) that makes women sick and makes them sicker than men. Nine of the many ways in which gender causes women's excess morbidity are summarized below.

A. GENDER INEQUALITY IN AMOUNT OF FOOD

In developed and developing nations alike, women are responsible for acquiring and cooking food yet often do not eat enough to sustain their health. In several of the developing countries in Asia, Africa,

Table IV
Gender and Ethnic Differences in Two Health Indicators

Health indicators	White men	Women					
		All	White	Black	American Indian	Asian	Latino
Percentage rating their health as fair or poor[a]	8.0	9.7	8.7	16.0	17.8	10.0	14.1
Cases of AIDS per 100,000 in the population[b]	20.0	10.2	2.6	54.1	4.5	1.6	17.6

[a]1997 data from the National Center for Health Statistics, CDC (www.cdc.gov/nchs/fastats).
[b]1998 data from CDC, National Center for HIV, STD, and TB Prevention (www.cdc.gov/nchswww/data).

and the Middle East, girls and women are not allowed to eat as much as boys and men throughout their lives. Consequently, the childhood mortality rate for girls significantly exceeds that of boys in such nations, and hence there are more men than women in the population. For example, in Bangladesh, girls are less likely to be breast-fed than boys, and girls consume fewer calories, less protein, and lower amounts of crucial vitamins than boys. Thus, 14% of girls suffer severe malnutrition compared to only 5% of boys. Likewise, in India, due to the failure to provide women and girls with adequate food, 88% of Indian women have chronic anemia. This is the case throughout the developing nations of Africa, Asia, and the Middle East, where women are fed so little that 50 to 60% are anemic, and all are constantly sick and weak. WHO concluded that this failure to feed women and girls leads to slow death from starvation and from its many associated diseases (e.g., anemia) among women in these "classic patriarchies"—that is, countries where men's lives are believed to be inherently more valuable than those of women. WHO's International Conference on Nutrition concluded that women and girls continue to constitute the majority of the 780 million people in the world who do not have enough food to sustain their health.

In developed countries, menstruation, pregnancy, and lactation increase the number of calories that women must consume to maintain their health, but these additional calories are not forthcoming for poor women. For example, one study found that the welfare funds allotted to poor, pregnant British women pay for only half of the amount of food determined by the Department of Health to be needed. Likewise, many poor women in developed nations feed their children first, and may not feed themselves at all. Similarly, even many middle-class women in developed nations, exhausted from working a job outside the home and then a second job within it, cook for and feed their families and then are too tired to eat anything themselves.

Thus, in developed and developing nations alike, women often do not eat enough to maintain their health; a portion of women's excess morbidity and mortality is due to gender inequality in the allocation of food.

B. GENDER INEQUALITY IN AMOUNT OF WORK

Around the globe and across numerous cultures, women are responsible for domestic work. In developed nations like the United States and England, women are responsible for acquiring food, cooking it, cleaning home and clothing, and caring for children. In developing nations, women are responsible for these tasks as well as for acquiring the water and the fuel needed for cooking. Thus, in developed and developing nations alike, women work longer hours than men.

In developed countries, women have a double-day—they work a paid job outside the home for eight hours and then work a second unpaid job at home. The presence of indoor plumbing, electricity, gas, and various appliances have reduced the heavy, physical domestic labor of women in these countries, but these women still devote 30 to 31 hours per week to domestic chores, compared to 11 to 15 hours per week for men, according to a 1991 report from the UN. Thus, the combined hours devoted to paid work and those devoted to domestic work reveals that the average woman in developed countries works 70 to 71 hours per week compared to 51 to 55 hours per week for men. Consequently, women in developed nations are exhausted, and that exhaustion takes a toll on their health: it is manifested in headaches, backaches, frequent bacterial and viral illness (i.e., higher morbidity than men), and frequent visits to physicians and hospitals. For example, more than 60% of American women report frequent headaches, compared to only 40% of men. Women in developed countries also use numerous toxic substances in their housework. High levels of certain cancers among women are suspected to in part be a consequence of repeated exposure to bleach, pesticides, cleaning fluids, and detergents.

In addition, where paid work is concerned, ethnic discrimination results in Latino, African American, and American Indian women and men being employed in the lowest paid and least desirable jobs. Even when minority groups gain entrance into industry and skilled trades, they are discriminated against in job assignments, and so are assigned to the most dangerous jobs—those that expose them to carcinogenic chemicals and to risk of accidents and dismemberment. Even after controlling for ethnic differences in years of education and work experience, a disproportionately higher number of African American and American Indian women and men are employed in the most hazardous jobs in the nation. In addition, a large percentage of Latinas are employed in the semiconductor and agricultural industries. Workers in the semiconductor industry have work-related illness at three times the rate of other manufacturing industries, and farm workers and their families are routinely exposed to dangerous pesticides and are injured by faulty farm equipment. Furthermore, three out of every five Latinos and African Americans live in areas with uncontrolled toxic waste sites, according to a study conducted by the Commission for Racial Justice. Because race and ethnicity—not income—predict the location of dangerous toxic waste sites, placing these dumps in minority neighborhoods has come to be called "environmental racism." Hazardous jobs and exposure to toxic waste sites play a role in the excess morbidity (cancer morbidity in particular) of Latina and African American women.

The situation for women in developing nations is far worse, because their homes lack electricity, appliances, and plumbing. In these countries, whether women do or do not have paid employment outside the home, the number of hours necessary to accomplish household tasks far exceeds a man's workday. Specifically, women typically must grow and process food (i.e., farm), chop wood (acquire fuel) and carry it long distances, acquire water and carry it long distances from wells to the home, and do all tasks (e.g., laundry, dishes) by hand. They do this during pregnancy and lactation, and later, while carrying young children on their backs. According to the UN's 1991 report, women in the poor nations of Asia, Africa, and Latin America do this debilitating work for 90 hours per week merely to maintain their families' subsistence level, expend far more calories than they consume, and work at least 30 hours per week longer than do men. These women literally are worked to death.

For example, to acquire water in developing nations, women walk about five miles each day to wells or public taps, and then walk back home carrying several gallons of water on their heads; this task alone depletes 25% of the energy they have available from their food intake. In addition to acquiring water for the family, women in developing nations must acquire the fuel that will be used to cook and to heat and light the house. This typically entails walking six miles to acquire 70 pounds of wood, and then walking the six miles back to home carrying that 70 pounds of wood; this round-trip takes four hours. Acquiring water and fuel also places women at risk: they walk miles barefoot over sharp stones, climb trees, and scale cliffs. Falls, cuts, bruises, and bleeding are common, along with permanent back injuries and prolapsed uteruses from carrying heavy loads. They also may be attacked by men when traveling long distances alone.

Once water and fuel have been acquired, women must process the raw food into edible form. For example, raw grains such as wheat or corn must be picked and gathered from fields, then sifted and cleaned by hand, then ground into edible patties, then boiled, then dried, then cooked. Making grains edible requires six hours of arduous work and expends 1800 calories, which often exceeds the amount consumed.

While the health of women in developing nations is not at risk due to exposure to domestic cleaning substances, these women are constantly exposed to wood smoke from the fires burning in their poorly ventilated homes. WHO found that the level of carcinogens (cancer-causing agents) in the wood smoke inside the home in poor countries is equivalent to smoking 400 cigarettes (20 packs) per day. This smoke is responsible for the high frequency of cancers, bronchitis, pneumonia, carbon monoxide poisoning, and respiratory and eye diseases (i.e., excess morbidity) found among women (but not men) in poor nations because it is women and girls who remain in smoke-filled rooms preparing food, cooking, and cleaning.

Thus, a portion of women's excess morbidity and mortality is due to gender inequality in amount of work, in developed and developing nations alike. When this is coupled with gender inequality in the amount of food consumed, it is not surprising that women are often sick.

C. GENDER INEQUALITY IN STERILIZATION

Sterilization is one of the most common methods used worldwide to prevent pregnancy. Sterilizing a man is inexpensive, easy, and does not pose a threat to the man's life, whereas sterilizing a woman is expensive, difficult, and dangerous: women are five times more likely than men to die from sterilization and are five times more likely to exhibit long-term morbidity as a result of the operation. Nonetheless, as Table V shows, around the world, women are far more likely than men to be sterilized—with the exception of Denmark and England, where sterilization rates are equal by gender. Women are often coerced by men and by physicians into being sterilized, and in many cases they are sterilized without their knowledge or consent. Indeed, in the United States, sterilization has been used as a racist weapon against poor and minority women. For example, 45% of Puerto Rican women have been sterilized, along with 42% of American Indian women and 24% of Black women, compared to only 15% of White women.

Table V
Percent of Men versus Women Sterilized in 15 Selected Countries

North America, Europe, and Australia

Country	Percent sterilized	
	Men	Women
Australia	10.4%	27.7%
Canada	12.9%	30.6%
England	12.0%	11.0%
Denmark	5.0%	5.0%
United States	13.6%	23.7%

South and Central America

Brazil	2.6%	40.1%
Columbia	0.7%	25.7%
Costa Rica	1.0%	20.0%
El Salvador	0.0%	31.5%
Mexico	0.8%	18%

Asia

Bangladesh	1.1%	8.1%
China	8.8%	32.1%
India	3.5%	27.4%
South Korea	12.0%	35.0%
Thailand	5.7%	22.8%

Note: Little data on Africa were available.

Source: U.S. Bureau of the Census, International Data (www.infoplease.com).

Medicaid (health care provided by the U.S. federal government for the poor) does not pay for abortions but does pay for female sterilization—and hence women "choose" this procedure. This abuse of sterilization to control poor women occurs in numerous countries, including Brazil, India, Bangladesh, Tibet, Mexico, Bolivia, and others. In these countries, countless poor women are sterilized against their will. In some countries, the government pays poor women to be sterilized. Deaths and excess morbidity from the operation are even more common in developing nations. Hence, a portion of women's excess morbidity and mortality is due to gender inequality in sterilization.

D. VIOLENCE AGAINST WOMEN

Violence against women—including rape, battering, murder, mutilation, and sexual abuse in childhood—contributes significantly to women's morbidity and mortality worldwide. In 1993, the World Bank estimated that this violence is the cause of 20% of the days of life lost by women of reproductive age. As Table VI shows, the frequency of woman-battering is high in both developed and developing nations. The 1993 report of the World Bank also revealed that domestic violence (i.e., battering) accounts for at least 5% of the health problems of women in developed nations and at least 20% of the health problems of women in developing nations. Such violence is more common in some countries than others, because in some countries it is legal and acceptable to beat, torture, and murder women.

Such violence involves stabbing, punching, kicking, biting, and shooting women, as well as dousing them with acid, boiling water, or kerosene. Domestic violence results in millions of concussions, broken bones, burns, cuts, and bruises that require medical attention. It also has been shown to cause numerous long-term health problems for women, including substance abuse, psychiatric disorders, depression,

Table VI
Domestic Violence in 12 Selected Countries

Country	Percent of women reporting domestic violence
U.S. and Europe	
Canada	25%
United States	39%
Norway	25%
Latin America	
Guatemala	49%
Costa Rica	50%
Chile	60%
Africa	
Uganda	46%
Kenya	42%
Tanzania	60%
Asia	
Japan	58.7%
Korea	42%
India	75% (lower caste)

Source: Data are a summary of findings from 25 different empirical studies.

suicides, high-risk sexual behavior, eating disorders, sexual dysfunction, reproductive problems, recurrent vaginal infections, and chronic pain. Depression and suicide are common responses to this violence. In the United States, 30 to 40% of battered women attempt to kill themselves. In Papua New Guinea, two-thirds of all suicide attempts are by women who were battered, and 90% of all successful suicides are women who killed themselves immediately after being beaten. If the battered woman is pregnant (and pregnant women are more likely than nonpregnant women to be battered), there are additional negative health consequences including miscarriages, stillbirths, delivery of low-birth-weight infants, rupture of the uterus, premature labor, and other serious health problems for mother and infant. [See BATTERING IN ADULT RELATIONSHIPS.]

In addition to these implications for women's morbidity and mortality, violence against women also has implications for health care and for the high cost of medical insurance. Studies in the United States indicate that battered women comprise 22 to 35% of all women seeking treatment in emergency rooms, 14 to 28% of all women seeking treatment in clinics, 24% of all women seeking prenatal care, 50% of all women psychiatric outpatients, and 64% of all women in psychiatric hospitals. In addition, according to a 1998 report from the National Institute on Drug Abuse, 60 to 90% of women in drug and alcohol treatment programs have a history of being victims of abuse. One million women per year seek health care for injuries resulting from partner battering alone. Women who are battered seek health care (in emergency rooms, hospitals, and mental health facilities) twice as often as those who are not battered, and the cost of caring for a battered woman patient is double that of caring for a nonbattered woman patient. Thus, much of women's excess morbidity and excess health care utilization is the result of men's violence.

In developing nations, the frequency of violence against women is even higher than the 22 to 35% found in developed nations, and the consequences are all the more severe. For example, the government of Papua New Guinea recently reported that 66% of all married women have been beaten. In South Africa, 60% of married women are battered. In countries experiencing significant social upheaval due to war and other conflicts, the figures are higher, particularly for refugees. In India, wife-beating was not defined as a crime until 1983; since passage of the law rendering it a crime, men have not been charged or punished. In the Papua New Guinea study, most cases involved the husband forcing his wife to have sex (i.e., rape) in addition to the beating. In Latin American countries, 40 to 60% of women report being raped by their husbands.

In February 2000, researchers at the Johns Hopkins School of Public Health published the most comprehensive review of the evidence on violence against women (*Population Reports Volume XXVII*, freely available at www.jhuccp.org). This study found that, worldwide, 10 to 50% of women have been severely and repeatedly beaten by a male partner, and that rape accompanies these beatings in up to two-thirds of those cases. Although violence against women occurs in all populations and cultures, refugees and displaced women are especially likely to be beaten and raped. Women refugees experience constant domestic beatings, rape, and attempted rape. Husbands, relatives, border guards, and male refugees routinely beat and rape refugee women, as do the men whose job it is to protect the women—policemen and soldiers.

E. RAPE

In the United States, estimates of the frequency of rapes (forced, undesired sexual contact) reported to the police range from 4 to 50%. Less than 15% of rapes reported to the police come to trial, and only 1% of those result in conviction. This means that only one rapist in 2500 is ever convicted. Thus, rape is one of the most underreported and the least convicted crimes in the world, despite its damage to women's health. Studies vary in their estimates of the frequency of rape. Ruth Hall's study found that 17% of women had been raped, whereas Mary Koss's studies found that at least 20% of women had been raped. Recent data for the United States indicate that 78 women are raped each hour—1.3 rapes per minute. The situation in developing nations is more extreme.

In developing nations, rape and sexual abuse are not only acts of violence that individual men perpetrate on individual women and girls; instead, they are also a major part of the government's policy for punishing and controlling women. According to a 1991 report from Amnesty International, in numerous countries (including India, Greece, Palestine, Turkey, Uganda, Guatemala, Peru, and Yugoslavia) police officers and other government officials routinely strip women naked, beat them, parade them through the streets, and gang rape them in public for several hours as punishment for minor behaviors such as arguing or traffic violations. The Johns Hopkins School of Public Health February 2000 report found results similar to those of Amnesty International. For example, in Uganda, 50% of women (most refugees) have been raped, and among the Burundi refugees in Tanzania, 25% of women have been raped. Most of these rapes go unreported. The situation among refugees from Burundi in camps in Tanzania can be regarded as prototypical: Burundian refugees tend to remain silent about sexual violence because it is severely stigmatized in Burundian culture. The survivor who steps forward is blamed, ostracized, and punished, and loses her food ration cards.

The physical effects of rape are severe because rape is, first and foremost, an act of physical violence. Studies have found that rape victims have a multitude of physical injuries including scarring, tearing, and bleeding of the genitals and anus; stab wounds, cuts, bruises, and broken bones; venereal diseases such as syphilis, gonorrhea, and HIV/AIDS; and numerous chronic health problems. In addition to these physical injuries, rape victims suffer a plethora of psychological injuries such as depression, suicide, nightmares, phobias, mood swings, eating disorders, and drug and alcohol abuse. Rapes of young girls (sexual abuse of children) have similar physical and psychological consequences. Studies indicate that 25 to 40% of women in developed countries were sexually abused as children (prior to age of 16). The long-term negative consequences of childhood rape are clear in the fact that half of adult women seeking psychiatric help were sexually abused in childhood. [See RAPE.]

Cervical cancer, AIDS, and sexually transmitted diseases among women are related to male sexual domination, sexual coercion, and rape. This is because these diseases are largely a function of the extent to which women can control how, when, and how often they have intercourse with men.

F. CERVICAL CANCER AND SEXUALLY TRANSMITTED DISEASES

Cancer of the cervix is one of the two most common cancers among women, with a half million new cases reported worldwide each year. According to WHO, 75% of these new cases are women from developing countries. In developed countries such as the United States and England, however, the highest morbidity (frequency of cervical cancer) and mortality (death

from cervical cancer) rates are among poor and minority women.

Like HIV/AIDS among women, cervical cancer also is by and large the result of unprotected sexual intercourse with men; the disease almost never appears in women who have had little or no sexual intercourse (e.g., among lesbians). Unprotected sexual intercourse with men can cause AIDS, cervical cancer, and other sexually transmitted diseases in women because, with ejaculation (in the absence of a condom), men deposit several milliliters of semen over the surface of a woman's vagina and cervix. This semen may carry viruses (HIV, genital herpes), bacteria, and fungi (gonorrhea, syphilis, chlamydia) that cause these diseases in women and may carry carcinogens (cancer-causing agents) that men pick up at work (such as dusts, oils, and poisons on their hands). Barrier contraception (condoms) is the most effective way to shield the vagina from these hazards, but whether a man will use a condom is not something women dictate; instead, this must be negotiated with men who often refuse. The high cervical cancer morbidity and mortality rates of women in developing countries, as well as the high rates for poor and minority women within developed countries, are not explained by condom use alone; lack of access to health care also plays a major role.

The best way to prevent death from cervical cancer is to detect the disease early and then to treat it before the abnormal cells spread. Early detection is achieved by a cervical test (Pap smear). Many developed countries have instituted nationwide Pap smear programs to assure that all women have the test regularly. Such countries (e.g., Sweden and Denmark) have reported a 60% decrease in cervical cancer morbidity and mortality. In other developed countries (e.g., the United States) however, many poor and minority women have no health insurance or access to the test. Hence, their rate of cervical cancer morbidity and mortality remains high; only 50% of women in developed countries such as the United States have access to the Pap test and have had the test in the past five years. In developing countries, there are few facilities for or professionals to conduct Pap tests; this is because the nation is impoverished and because the health of women is considered secondary to the health of men. In these countries, only 5% of adult women have access to the test and have had it in the past five years.

Minority and poor women's lack of access to health care in developed and developing nations, coupled with men's sexual domination, explains the high rate of sexually transmitted diseases among these women. In parts of India, 92% of women have a sexually transmitted disease. In Africa, gonorrhea is an epidemic and is the most common disease among women. Gonorrhea leads not only to pain and spontaneous abortion, but also to infertility and to pelvic inflammatory and other diseases. Forcing women to have sex when they do not wish to and without a condom, while simultaneously denying women access to health care, causes numerous diseases and deaths among women, AIDS foremost among those.

G. GENDER INEQUALITY IN HIV/AIDS DIAGNOSIS AND TREATMENT

Data from the CDC indicate that African American and Latina women represent 86% of the AIDS cases among women reported in 1991. AIDS case rates were 14.5 times higher among African American women and 7.4 times higher among Latinas than among White women (see Table IV). Similar rates are found for the incidence of pediatric AIDS cases; children born to minority mothers made up 81% of the cumulative AIDS cases reported through December 1991.

The number of new AIDS cases in the United States has been decreasing thanks to new therapies and decreased by an impressive 6% in 1996. This improvement however is not evenly distributed by gender or ethnicity. In 1996, the incidence of AIDS among American men dropped by 8%, while for women it *increased* by 1%. Likewise, in 1996 AIDS mortality among American men dropped by an impressive 26%, while for women it dropped by only 12%. These differences are the result of the restricted access to health care for HIV-positive women, almost all of whom are poor and 81% of whom are ethnic minorities (Hispanic and Black). Thus, AIDS is quickly becoming a disease of poor minority women: whether they live in New York City, Los Angeles, Bangkok, or Mexico City, the new face of AIDS is a poor woman of color.

For poor women in developing nations, sexual intercourse has financial implications: women must submit sexually to husbands or be left homeless; many of those husbands are HIV-positive. Other poor women in developing nations are forced by their husbands to prostitute themselves to make money because prostitution pays 25 times more than the jobs available to uneducated women. The risk of HIV infection increases with prostitution (i.e., with

the number of male sexual partners). Consequently, 20 to 40% of women prostitutes in India, China, Thailand, and in the developing nations of Africa are HIV-postitive. In other developing countries, the repeated rape of women as part of wars between neighboring countries plays a significant role in the increasing incidence of AIDS among women. In parts of Africa where such wars are common, 4 million women are HIV-positive and they alone constitute 83% of the HIV-positive women in the world. Clearly then, the women in developing nations with high rates of AIDS are not prostitutes (let alone drug addicts). Instead, most are married and were infected by husbands or by other men whose sexual behavior they could not control. Thus, the first case of a woman with AIDS reported in Mexico (in 1985) was a 52-year-old housewife who had never had intercourse with anyone except her husband. Given that the group of women with the highest rate of AIDS are women between the ages of 20 and 29 (in developing and developed nations alike), and given that HIV has a long (up to 10-year) incubation period, this means that most women with AIDS were infected when they were adolescents—and perhaps even during their first sexual encounter with their (future or current) husband. Using condoms would significantly decrease the risk of AIDS for women in developing countries, but only 7% of men in developing nations use condoms.

Of course, developing nations experiencing social upheaval do not make up the entire picture. In the United States, the world's richest country, 130,000 women are HIV-positive and 75% of them are poor minority women. While some of these women are intravenous drug users and others are prostitutes, most are not. Most are married to or cohabiting with a man on whom they are financially dependent, and they often have little choice but to have unprotected intercourse with this potentially infected partner.

Hence, in developed and developing nations alike, gender puts women at high risk for AIDS: women's lack of power and control over men's sexual behavior and over their own bodies—structured social inequality by sex—contributes to AIDS among women. To confront and eradicate AIDS, societies must confront and eradicate gender inequality. Hence, a study published in the *American Journal of Public Health* (1999, Vol. 89, pp. 1479–1482) concluded that

At the heart of women's HIV risk is gender-based discrimination. . . . The actions [e.g., condom use] required to block the spread of HIV cannot be divorced from the

context of sex inequality and its ensuing [financial] dependencies, power imbalances, and threats of violence—in short, the effects of women's status worldwide as second-class citizens.

Gender inequality not only contributes to AIDS in women, but it also plays a role in AIDS diagnosis and treatment. Specifically, women are discriminated against in AIDS diagnosis. Ten years of evidence indicates that the major diagnostic signs of AIDS in women are chronic vaginal infections and cervical dysplasia (noncancerous, abnormal cell growth). Nonetheless, these symptoms have not been added to the nationally referenced lists of symptoms that are distributed by the Centers for Disease Control (CDC). Thus, physicians may not be aware of the possible AIDS-related meaning of these symptoms in women, and no public health-education program to date warns women about the possible meaning of these symptoms. Only in 1992 did the CDC finally propose adding invasive cervical cancer to the list of 23 symptoms of AIDS. Failure to diagnose AIDS in women due to a gender-biased definition of the disease obviously constitutes a serious threat to women's health: because of gender inequality in AIDS diagnosis, many physicians fail to diagnose AIDS in women until late into the disease, when treatments are less effective. Hence, men live for two years and four months after diagnosis, whereas women live *for four months* after diagnosis.

If diagnosed with AIDS, women are then discriminated against in its treatment. Although AIDS cannot yet be cured, treatment can improve quality of life and number of years of survival after diagnosis. Men with AIDS are significantly more likely than women with AIDS to receive the best new treatments. Even in the United States, AIDS clinical trials (studies testing new treatments) routinely exclude women, and hence it is not known if the new drugs would help women. The majority of the participants in AIDS clinical trials have been White men, even though Black and Hispanic women have significantly higher rates of AIDS (see Table IV). Likewise, federal AIDS research money earmarked for women and children routinely is dedicated to children even though the number of women with the disease outnumbers the number of children by six to one. Consequently, in developed and developing countries alike, men with AIDS live at least three times longer than women with AIDS. Among U.S. women with AIDS, survival for Black and Hispanic women is significantly shorter than that of White women because

of ethnic inequality in access to health care services and AIDS drugs. Thus, gender inequality not only contributes significantly to AIDS in women, it also contributes significantly to AIDS deaths among women.

H. GENDER INEQUALITY IN HEALTH CARE AND HEALTH INSURANCE

In the developing, "classic patriarchy" countries of Asia, Africa, and the Middle East, sick boys are significantly more likely than sick girls to be taken to a physician or hospital. This results in higher early-childhood mortality rates for girls than for boys. Likewise, in many of these nations, women's greater morbidity stems from policies that explicitly limit their access to health care. For example, according to a 1990 report from UNICEF, African and Latin American countries purposefully devote more money to health care for men than for women.

More specifically, discrimination against girls and women in the allocation of health care is rampant in developing countries. In India, for example, three out of every four girls (75%) who are sick enough to require hospitalization are denied it simply because of their sex, according to a study published in the *American Journal of Public Health*. Similarly, WHO reported that boys in India are not only 2.5 times more likely to receive medical treatment than are girls, but more money is spent to treat boys than girls, and greater distances are traveled to treat boys than to treat girls despite similar symptoms (e.g., an upper respiratory infection). This is also the case in other developing countries such as Peru, according to a recent report in *Social Science & Medicine*. In Peru, girls and women are considered less valuable than boys and men because of their future or current economic contributions. Hence, girls and women are significantly less likely than boys and men to receive health care (including medications) despite equal symptoms and morbidity.

In developed countries such as the United States, similar gender discrimination and inequality in health care have been found. Many studies have demonstrated that there are significant differences in the medical tests and treatments that patients (with the same symptoms) receive depending on their sex and race. Several recent studies confirm these prior findings. For example, a 1999 study published in the *New England Journal of Medicine* (Vol. 340, pp. 618–626) found that women and Blacks are significantly less likely than men and Whites to be referred for cardiac catheterization (a life-saving heart surgery), despite exhibiting similar symptoms of cardiovascular disease. Another study examined 49,623 Massachusetts (MA) women and men and 33,159 Maryland (MD) women and men who had all been discharged from hospitals after treatment for coronary heart disease. Men were 28% (MA) and 15% (MD) more likely than women to have undergone angiography, and men were 45% (MA) and 27% (MD) more likely than women to have undergone revascularization; men received more comprehensive and thorough diagnostic procedures and life-saving treatments than did women.

Likewise, there is gender discrimination in receiving life-saving organ transplants. Men are significantly more likely than women to obtain heart transplants even when controlling for health care, medical urgency, and prognosis. In addition, women are discriminated against in drug and alcohol treatment: more than 75% of all drug and alcohol treatment programs are designed for men and their beds are reserved for men even though women suffer substance abuse problems of similar severity. Treatment programs designed for male drug abusers also are more comprehensive in the treatment provided than programs designed for women.

Furthermore, women also are discriminated against in health insurance. Numerous studies have found that middle-aged and older women, when compared to men, are twice as likely to have no health insurance, are less likely to have it through their jobs, and, if insured, pay significantly higher premiums than men. Indeed, Medicare coverage specifically discriminates against women in that it provides full coverage for diseases that are common among men (e.g., lung cancer), but inadequate coverage for diseases that are common among women (e.g., breast cancer).

There is also discrimination in federal reimbursement for surgical procedures that are paid for by Medicare. For example, a 1997 study compared reimbursement for biopsy of male versus female genitals, hysterectomy versus prostatectomy, and staging of ovarian versus testicular cancer. Results revealed that male-specific surgical procedures were reimbursed at a higher rate 79% of the time. This discrimination in reimbursement means that women must pay more out of pocket for their surgeries than men. Because the reimbursement standards set by Medicare are used by private-sector insurance carriers, the results of this study mean that this same bias exists irrespective of the type of medical insurance coverage women have.

At least some of this gender discrimination in health care (in developed countries) is a function of the sex of the physician. Data from the National Medical Expenditure Survey were examined to discover if women and men physicians were equally likely to order three gender-sensitive tests (a breast exam, a mammogram, and a Pap test) and one gender-neutral test (blood pressure check). Results revealed that women who have women physicians were significantly more likely than those with male physicians to have the gender-sensitive tests.

The quality of medical care that people in developed countries receive is also a matter of gender and ethnicity. For example, one study in Boston found that 80% of all adverse events (injuries to the patient caused by sloppy, negligent medical procedures) occur in hospitals in minority neighborhoods, and happen to poor, minority women. Sexual preference (sexual orientation) also plays a role in the quality of medical care received. Numerous studies have found that lesbians report receiving poor care from their physicians, and report that physicians respond with hostility, physical roughness, rude comments, and violations of confidentiality when informed of their patient's sexual preference. Consequently, up to 60% of lesbians fail to seek preventive health care (i.e., Pap smears, breast exams, and mammograms). This avoidance of screening is important because lesbians are three times more likely than heterosexual women to develop breast cancer. The reason is that the risk of breast cancer is high in women who have never had a child, and most lesbians have never had a child. While lesbians have high rates of breast cancer, they simultaneously have extremely low rates of cervical cancer, sexually transmitted diseases, and AIDS because these problems in women are by and large due to unprotected intercourse with infected men.

Women in developed countries also are discriminated against in prescribed drugs. Recent studies in several developed countries (e.g., the United States, England, Australia, and New Zealand) reveal that women are significantly more likely than men to be prescribed antibiotics, hormones, ear and nose preparations, drugs for allergies, psychiatric drugs, drugs for cardiovascular disease, and skin preparations even when sex differences in morbidity are controlled. Even though hypertension is more common in men than in women, 62% of people receiving medication for hypertension are women, and the antihypertensive drugs prescribed to women cost more than those prescribed to men. Age and ethnicity also play a role: a recent study examined 574,762 Medicaid prescriptions and found that White patients received significantly more prescription drugs than non-White ones, that older patients received more prescriptions than younger ones, and that women received more prescriptions than men. Older White women received the greatest number of prescription drugs and younger non-White men received the fewest.

Finally, many of women's physical health problems are misdiagnosed as psychiatric disorders by biased male physicians. Our 1997 book, *Preventing Misdiagnosis of Women,* details the high frequency of these misdiagnoses and documents how such medical errors cause needless morbidity and mortality among women. Hence, discrimination against women in medical diagnosis, health care, and health insurance can and does cost women their lives.

I. GENDER INEQUALITY IN HEALTH RESEARCH

Health research also discriminates against women and does so primarily by excluding them from it. For example, women have high rates of coronary heart disease, diabetes, and hypertension, but research on the causes of these diseases rarely includes women. Similarly, clinical trials typically exclude women as participants, and hence it is not known if the new treatments would help women. For example, in the major study testing the extent to which taking aspirin would help prevent heart disease, *all* of the 22,071 subjects were men. Likewise, there were no women in the major study testing the effects of cholesterol-lowering drugs; all 3806 subjects were men. Similarly, there were no women in the major study examining coronary heart disease; all 12,866 subjects were men. This holds for animal studies as well: studies that use animals to test new human drugs use male animals only despite the well-known hormonal differences between males and females of any species: *even the rats are White males.* Women are excluded from clinical trials for heart disease drugs albeit heart disease is the leading cause of death among women and men (see Table II), and even though older women are more likely than older men to develop heart disease because the former live longer. Gender discrimination in health research is so ubiquitous that only 13% of the National Institutes of Health research funds (funds from the tax dollars of women and men) are devoted to the study of women's health.

IV. *Summary*

Gender inequality (social inequality based on sex) causes needless deaths (mortality) and needless, excess disease and suffering (morbidity) in women worldwide. Inequality in the allocation of food and of medical care, coupled with male violence and with inequality in financial power and in the control of sexuality, cause women to be sick much of the time, to be far sicker than men, and to die needlessly. Gender inequality is the cornerstone of the international AIDS epidemic, and also is the crux of rising health care costs: The people who utilize health care services most often are women, and those women do so because they are underfed, overworked, exhausted, battered, raped, depressed, sick from sexually transmitted diseases, or sick from a disease not readily diagnosed or cured because no research has examined the disease in women. To eradicate unnecessary disease and death among women, nations must eradicate gender inequality—gender itself. Indeed, morbidity and mortality have always rushed like rapids through the stable canyons, peaks, and valleys of structured social inequality, engulfing those at the bottom of social ladders while leaving those at the pinnacle dry and unscathed. Hence, to conquer all disease worldwide, nations must conquer all inequality worldwide—by gender, ethnicity, and social class, and by developed and developing world boundaries.

ACKNOWLEDGMENT

This article was supported by funds provided by the Tobacco-Related Disease Research Program Grants No. 8RT-0013 and 9RT-0043 and by the California Department of Health Services Tobacco Control Section Grants # 94-20962 and #96-26617.

SUGGESTED READING

Berer, M., and Ray, S. (1993). *Women and HIV/AIDS: An International Resource Book.* Pandora, London.
Brandwein, R. A. (1999). *Battered Women, Children, and Welfare Reform.* Sage, Thousand Oaks, CA.

Corea, G. (1985). *The Hidden Malpractice: How American Medicine Mistreats Women*. Harper Colophon Books, New York.

Davis, M. (1994). *Women and Violence: Responses and Realities Worldwide*. Zed Press, London.

Doyal, L. (1995). *What Makes Women Sick: Gender and the Political Economy of Health*. Rutgers University Press, New Brunswick, NJ.

Fee, E., and Krieger, N. (1994). *Women's Health, Politics and Power: Essays on Sex/Gender, Medicine, and Public Policy*. Baywood, Amityville, NY.

Klonoff, E. A., and Landrine, H. (1997). *Preventing Misdiagnosis of Women*. Sage, Thousand Oaks, CA.

Koblinsky, M., Timyan, J., and Gay, J. (1993). *The Health of Women: A Global Perspective*. Westview Press, Boulder, CO.

Ravindran, S. (1986). *Health Implications of Sex Discrimination in Childhood*. World Health Organization/UNICEF, Geneva, Switzerland.

Royston, E., and Armstrong, S. (1989). *Preventing Maternal Deaths*. World Health Organization, Geneva, Switzerland.

Ussher, J. M. (2000). *Women's Health: Contemporary International Perspectives*. British Psychological Society, London.

History of the Study of Gender Psychology

Stephanie A. Shields
Kristen M. Eyssell

The Pennsylvania State University

I. Prescientific Views of Women
II. The 18th Century
III. The 19th Century
IV. Psychology of Gender in the 20th Century
V. Gender Research in Psychology Since the 1970s

Glossary

Core gender identity A person's fundamental sense of self as female or male.

Gender role The attitudes, values, behaviors, and beliefs that a culture defines as more appropriate or normal for one sex than the other.

Sex-differences model An approach to gender that focuses on the enumeration of differences and similarities between the sexes.

Sex-typing A term used in 20th-century developmental psychology to describe how and why gender, including core gender identity and gender role, is acquired.

Variability hypothesis The proposition, first put forward in the late 19th century, that differences between the sexes in variability are evolutionary adaptations that can account for differences in social achievement and the status of women and men. The distribution of physical and mental attributes was presumed to reflect a greater range, hence greater variability, among males.

GENDER is the social and psychological representation of biological sex. This article presents a historical perspective on how psychological gender (excluding sexual behavior) was conceptualized and studied scientifically in Western thought prior to second wave feminism in the United States. In providing an overview, it focuses particularly on three periods: 19th-century evolutionary theory's concern with cognitive and emotional features that distinguish females from a male standard; mid-20th-century developmental and social psychology's view of gender as a function of personality manifesting primarily in psychological masculinity/femininity; and, last, second-wave feminist conceptualizations of gender (as distinct from sex) and as multidimensional and culturally embedded.

I. Prescientific Views of Women

Prior to the formation of social science disciplines in the late 19th century, "gender" as a distinct psychological attribute was not differentiated from sex.

Nevertheless, speculations about the psychology of the sexes can be found in the very earliest Western philosophical and religious writings, precursors to scientific study. Academic thinking about the psychology of men and women was largely geared to describing the differences between the sexes and emphasis was on cataloging "natural" differences between the sexes and where these differences originated. Throughout, the emphasis was on describing what makes women different from men. As such, this early tradition typifies what has come to be called the "sex differences approach," that is, a descriptive cataloging of differences and similarities that contains the implicit or explicit assumption of male as standard and female as defective or deficient.

Historically, the study of gender differences has consistently reflected prevailing cultural beliefs regarding the nature of males and females. Early philosophical speculation emphasized the inequality of the sexes on all dimensions of social importance. Sex differences in psyche were accepted as a fact of differences in physiology, thus investigation of sex differences consisted only of cataloging them. This approach is epitomized in Aristotle's *Historia Animalium*:

[W]oman is more compassionate than man, more easily moved to tears, at the same time is more jealous, more querulous, more apt to scold and to strike. She is, furthermore, more prone to despondency and less hopeful than the man, more void of shame or self-respect, more false of speech, more deceptive, and of more retentive memory. She is also more wakeful, more shrinking, more difficult to rouse to action, and requires a smaller amount of nutriment. (McKeon translation, 1941, page 637)

While Aristotle attributed female inferiority to "humors," in later centuries female inferiority was viewed as a function of divine fiat, physiological instability, or defects in the brain. Though the rationale for this belief changed over time, its substance remained the same: females, in every respect, were viewed as lesser beings.

Aristotelian speculation on sex differences was accepted as a complete and accurate description of female nature for centuries. During the early Christian era, scholars and theologians alike asserted that because Adam was made first and Eve was created from Adam, the man must be the standard and woman, the deviant. Eve was also held responsible by Christian thinkers for the sin that caused Adam and Eve's expulsion from paradise. Thus woman was, by nature, inferior and needed to subordinate to men both in the church and in the family.

II. The 18th Century

The Enlightenment, an 18th-century philosophical movement in Western Europe, marked a growing emphasis on male–female differences in intellectual and emotional capacities. This turn in philosophy introduced the notion that the characteristics of women were not necessarily inferior to those of men. Rather that the mental and moral faculties inherent to each sex were complementary. Whereas the earlier tradition emphasized female intellect as an imperfect version of the male, the newer notion was that women have their own distinctive kind of intellectual character, which is the "natural" complement to distinctively male reasoning capacity. Even in the diverse theories of Rousseau, Kant, Hegel, and others, common characterizations of the respective intellectual spheres of the sexes can be found. The rational male world was considered objective and general in scope, compared to the particularistic, commonsense female world. Although reason was ascribed to both sexes, the difference between the sexes lies in the innate intellect that is sex determined. Reason was not construed as an exclusively male domain; rather, highly valued, creative, expansive reason, in short the *better* form of reason, was identified as a male attribute.

III. The 19th Century

With the rise of evolutionary theory in the mid-19th century, sex-related differences became a matter of more serious concern to biological scientists. This is because differences between the sexes were viewed as the basis for describing evolutionary change. Three themes first evident in 19th-century evolutionary theory have persisted to the present day. The first is a tendency to cast the question of gender as one of sex-related difference, with an emphasis on difference. Contemporary social constructivist thinkers remind us that this dichotomizing of gender naturally provides a hierarchical contrast between the sexes. Although each category (male and female) gains meaning in contrast to the other (i.e., it means little to be "White" except in relation to being "not White"), the categories are not value neutral. The dominant (powerful, valued) category becomes as "normal" as the air we never consider when breathing. The subordinate (powerless, devalued) reminds us that "difference" is something to be considered with skepticism.

In the 19th century there was, in addition, a corresponding assumption that difference is exaggerated as a function of race and social class. That is, sex differences were assumed to be greater as one "ascends" the class scale and were greater in more "advanced" races. Social class was assumed to be a reflection of the natural capacities of the individual. By the time distinct social science disciplines formed in the 20th century, race and class came to be considered only rarely by psychologists. Rather, these variables were considered under the purview of sociology and hence not of direct interest to the study of psychological questions.

A second theme stems from the tendency to interpret sex-related differences as a function of biological rather than experiential or environmental factors. A third theme is the conflation of distinctive dimensions of sex and gender. This is the case from 19th-century evolutionary theory, through Freudian psychodynamic consideration of sex, to the earliest attempts to use psychological testing in the 1930s to quantify gender as a trait. In each period biological sex, core gender identity, gender role, and sexual orientation are conflated—that is, measurement or assessment of one feature was presumed to be an indicator of other features. Each of these themes is addressed next.

A. EVOLUTIONARY THEORY

The view that females were inferior in all capacities persisted into the 19th century. For example, Francis Galton, who first systematically studied individual differences, was a proponent of the female inferiority model. Typical of this position, he pointed out that if women's capacities were equal to those of men, then they would be more equitably represented in the achievement of social eminence and positions of responsibility. Charles Darwin believed in general female inferiority in reasoning, creative imagination, and so on. Like other scientists he believed that women had some redeeming emotion and perception-relevant qualities, among them "greater tenderness and less selfishness," greater powers of intuiting, rapid perception, and capacity for imitation. But these characteristics, he argued, were also characteristic of "lower" races and reflected an earlier stage of development.

A refinement of the inferiority theme took shape with the development of evolutionary theory in the mid-19th century. Greater emphasis was placed on the complementarity of the sexes. That is, the strengths of each sex were seen as compensating for the deficiencies of the other. Gender differences were viewed as both a product of evolution and a necessary component of further evolution. Complementarity did not imply coequality. Rather, those qualities most valued by upper-class Victorian society, such as the capacity for abstract reasoning or moral judgment unclouded by sentiment, were those deemed most typically male. Three subjects illustrate the way in which evolutionary theory approached the description of the female as different, deficient, or complementary to the male: the notion of maternal instinct, differences in male and female brains, and cognitive and emotional differences between the sexes.

What was thought to be the basis for sex differences? According to male American and British scientists of the time, the psychological traits of each sex were believed to be a direct consequence of biology. Woman was considered biologically conservative, less variable, neurally underdeveloped, and physiologically vulnerable. She was also genteel, unimaginative, perceptive, modest, coy, dependent, and all of these traits were manifestations of her nature. Although the specifics of any individual account varied somewhat, and despite the fact that each of these accounts was fraught with logical inconsistencies (never mind physiological inaccuracies), the account generally followed this line: Because of innate biological factors the human female's nervous system was limited (or prevented from its full development) either by the simple fact of being female or because of the biological demands of development and maturation of the female reproductive system. The end result was a nervous system that was less capable of sophisticated higher mental processes (creative thought, rational insight) and which comparatively accentuated development of the lower mental processes (emotion and certain aspects of perception). What was not dictated developmentally was ensured by the menstrual cycle and by maternity. It was even seriously proposed that the needs of the uterus took precedence over other organs, and so blood that might ordinarily support brain functioning was, at puberty, diverted to service of the uterus. This belief was often used as an argument against coeducation or strenuous mental challenge for adolescent girls. Pregnancy and maternity were believed to inevitably elicit the instincts for caregiving that would come to dominate her whole personality. The power of this physiological explanation of female psychology persisted into the 1920s, even after behaviorism and a rejection of instinct theory had come to be major themes in North American psychology.

Further proof that the exaggerated differentiation of the sexes was a consequence of evolution came from observations of early anthropologists. "Primitive races" were assumed by these scientists to represent earlier forms of human evolution and they noted that among primitives there were fewer differences between the sexes, physically as well as temperamentally. In so-called primitive races, Western observers asserted that women had flat features and broad bodies like men, in contrast to the marked sexual dimorphism of European women and men of privilege. The wasp-waisted, bosomy Victorian woman was portrayed as a natural product of evolutionary pressures rather than a manufactured product of class privilege and fashion. "Primitive" women were also asserted to show less concern with modesty and more concern with sex than the refined Victorian lady, which was offered as further proof that greater sexual differentiation was an inevitable product of evolution.

Darwin proposed that males were more likely than females to deviate from the physical average of the species. The proposal that, physically, the male was inherently the more variable sex was interpreted by some 20th-century psychologists as meaning that the same was true of the intellectual capacities of each sex. It was originally offered as an explanation for the fact that males of many species had developed greatly modified secondary sexual characteristics while mature females of the same species retained a resemblance of juveniles. Darwin's proposal was based on his belief that there was a greater incidence of physical anomaly in males of all species. Once the connection between individual variation and species development was made, it was assumed by many that variation was valuable per se. Without variation, greatness, whether of an individual or a society, could not be achieved. Male deviations thus became legitimized by evolutionary theory and the hypothesis of male superiority through greater variability became a convenient explanation for the facts of social life. By the 1890s it was popularly believed that the female was the conservative and constant element in the species, while the male, being the more variable, was the source of differentiation and thus further evolution. [See DEVELOPMENT OF SEX AND GENDER; GENDER DEVELOPMENT: EVOLUTIONARY PERSPECTIVES.]

B. THE VARIABILITY HYPOTHESIS

Havelock Ellis, an influential social philosopher and sexologist, extended the concept of male variability from a description of physical traits to all other qualities of character and temperament. He conceded that male variability could explain the fact that there were more men than women in homes for the retarded. But more important, it also explained the fact that genius appeared to be an exclusively male trait. Tests of mental ability had not yet been developed, and so "genius" was defined as achievement of social or professional eminence. The variability hypothesis enjoyed some degree of popularity until World War I. Frequently the discussion revolved around the practical social implications of greater male variation. For example, one debate centered on whether girls, because of the comparative rarity of female genius predicted by the variability hypothesis, should be encouraged to aspire to or be trained for intellectually demanding professions.

The variability hypothesis was met with opposition from its inception. Statistician Karl Pearson, with whom Havelock Ellis had a bitter personal rivalry, challenged Ellis' data, mathematical expression of variability, and his conclusions. The first generation of women psychologists, including Mary Calkins and Helen Bradford Thompson (Woolley), and, most especially and effectively, Leta Stetter Hollingworth criticized the variability hypothesis and conducted research to test it. Opponents disputed three assumptions of the variability hypothesis. (1) Proponents of the hypothesis assumed that all human traits were normally distributed and so smaller variance would indicate a narrower range. Opponents argued that the assumption of normality was not justified. (2) Proponents of the hypothesis based their conclusions on comparisons of simple variance. Opponents argued that there were many other legitimate ways to compare variability, and that some were more appropriate. (3) Proponents believed that sex differences in social achievement were due to biological differences. Opponents argued that social factors were the more important determinants of success. All of the opponents' arguments had merit, but their objections were largely ignored or buried in rhetoric by the proponents of the variability hypothesis.

IV. Psychology of Gender in the 20th Century

The rise of behaviorism in North American psychology temporarily erased empirical research psychology's concerns with questions of sex differences. Behaviorism, as a theoretical paradigm, was concerned primarily with the identification of the principles of learning and motivation that applied to all organisms irrespective of individual differences. Thus, sex-related differences were not a concern. As a result, gender, which was formulated entirely in terms of sex-differences and the psychology of women, came to be identified with the school of psychological theory that took certain individual differences as a central theme, namely Freudian psychoanalytic theory and its successors.

Sigmund Freud's psychoanalytic theory addressed gender as psychosexual development—that is, in terms of the development of personality consistent with biological sex and achievement of a particular form of mature heterosexuality. Like later gender theories, Freud's view of psychosexual development conflates distinct manifestations of gender or gender-relevant attributes into a single notion of gender identity. In this view, core gender identity (one's sense of oneself as essentially female or male), gender role (the attitudes, values, behaviors, and beliefs that a culture defines as more appropriate or normal for one sex than the other), and sexual orientation (one's preference for sexual or intimate partners based on partner sex) are not distinguished from one another. Freud's theories of psychosexual development reveal a perspective of the feminine as pathological. Employing a stage theory of development, Freud postulated that during the third, so-called phallic stage (approximately three to six years of age), children first notice the anatomical difference between the sexes and instinctively recognize that the penis is the more desirable sexual organ. Using ancient Greek myth as metaphors, Freud postulated that boys sexually desire their mothers and view their fathers as dangerous rivals who threaten the boys' bodily, especially sexual, integrity. To resolve the conflictive situation, the boy represses desire for his mother and obtains her vicariously through identifying with his father. The identification process involves the actual incorporation into one's own personality the father's adult masculinity. Girls, on the other hand, never resolve their parallel conflict. Freud argued that, upon recognizing that they have no penis, girls blame their mothers for this perceived mutilation while at the same time longing to maintain the closeness of the pre-Oedipal period. The girl's desire for a penis becomes transformed into a desire to be impregnated by the father, which the girl fears as a physical invasion. Resolution of this conflict for the girl is not as clear-cut as it is for the boy, and her eventual identification with the mother, according to Freud, results in a lifelong feeling of inferiority and a weaker internalization of maternal femininity. [*See* GENDER DEVELOPMENT: PSYCHOANALYTIC PERSPECTIVES.]

Later disciples of Freud reinterpreted the intrapsychic conflicts of early gender development in such a way as to attenuate the phallocentrism and androcentrism characterizing Freud's account. Karen Horney and, more recently, Nancy Chodorow and Ellen Kaschak have offered psychodynamically grounded views that strive to be independent of the masculinist orientation of Freud's theory. Horney rejected the central role accorded to biological determinism in conventional Freudian theory. Moreover, she was quite critical of many Freudian ideas, particularly those about women. For instance, Horney argued that boys suffered as much from womb envy as girls did from penis envy.

Chodorow, a feminist psychoanalytic sociologist, concerned herself with children's psychosexual development. Because most children experience a woman as a primary caretaker, girls can easily find someone with whom to identify. According to Chodorow, this has a profound influence on later functioning, with girls attempting to create that bond with men and experiencing frustration as a result. This also has a negative influence on boys. Her recommendation is for both parents in a household to share caretaking. Kaschak's writings focus on a fresh analysis of the Greek myth upon which the Freudian oedipal conflict was based. Kaschak noted that Oedipus himself was "served" by Antigone, the daughter who was Oedipus's guide. As such, Kaschak argued, males learn that other people exist to serve them. Females, in turn, learn that men are central figures in their lives and are to be served. Only when men and women resolve these myths will they be complete beings, able to relate to one another with respect. [*See* GENDER DEVELOPMENT: SOCIAL LEARNING.]

A. GENDER AS TRAIT: MASCULINITY/FEMININITY AND SEX-ROLE

The systematic search for stable enduring traits that unambiguously distinguish one sex psychologically from the other was an enterprise begun in earnest in the 1930s. Jill Morawski has identified the common features of these early masculinity/femininity tests. They are that masculinity and femininity (M/F) were assumed to represent ends of a unidimensional bipolar continuum, that M/F is a deep-seated and enduring trait, that true M/F is not easily measured by overt behaviors and so requires a sensitive and well-disguised instrument to measure it, and that M/F is an indicator of mental health.

The first M/F scale, developed by Lewis Terman and Catherine Cox Miles, was a questionnaire comprised of more than 450 multiple-choice and yes/no items. Dubbed the Attitude-Interest Analysis Test to disguise its purpose, Terman's M/F scale contained seven subtests that had been normed on elementary and junior high school age students. The M/F scale proved impossible to validate against external criteria as it had low reliability, was uncorrelated with behavioral measures predicted to be related to it, and produced peak scores that were not obtained by adults, but by boys and girls—at different ages. Nevertheless, Terman and Miles concluded that because the "masculine" and "feminine" items were empirically identified—that is, distinguished on the basis of different patterns of response to them by boys and girls—the test was thereby validated.

Today Terman is better known for his contributions to the study of intellectually gifted children. He devised the first self-report masculinity/femininity test because of his concerns regarding the social skills and adjustment of these children. The impetus behind the research was the desire to create an assessment tool that could reliably detect a propensity for what was then called "sexual inversion" (homosexuality in the language of psychology at the time). The homosexual male was presumed to be psychologically feminine, the homosexual female, psychologically masculine. Terman's research was grounded in a presupposition of the preeminence of biological factors in determining the capacities of the individual.

Despite, or perhaps because of, the patently sex-stereotypical content of M/F inventories, psychologists embraced the view that the extent to which an individual is willing to describe himself or herself in terms of stereotypes is a legitimate indicator of healthy psychological gender. M/F scales, however, are not good predictors of either gendered behavior or other traits hypothesized to be related to psychological masculinity and femininity. Other personality tests or psychopathology inventories that included M/F subtests include the California Personality Index and the Minnesota Multiphasic Personality Inventory.

By the early-1970s the assumption that masculinity and femininity represented opposite anchors on a unidimensional, bipolar continuum of "sex-role iden-

tity" was beginning to be challenged. A new generation of feminist psychologists critiqued the notion that masculinity and femininity, as dimensions of personality, should be construed as opposite ends of a unidimensional continuum. The alternative view that rapidly became popular is that masculinity and femininity represented uncorrelated dimensions of personality. Each of these dimensions can be expressed on its own bipolar continuum: high M to low M; high F to low F. Thus, an individual could be located on both M and F continua. The original aim of M/F tests—to identify gender inverts—was eclipsed by concerns with a new kind of psychological health. The search for an ideal way to measure the psychological aspect of sex as a stable, enduring personality trait continued, but with the new assumption that M and F, as independent dimensions of personality unrelated to biological sex and sexuality, would both be expressed to some degree in any individual. This new conceptualization of M and F as combinatory underlay Sandra Bem's proposal that the psychologically healthy individual is one who is androgynous—that is, a person who exhibits a balance of high-scoring M and high-scoring F components. Central to the modern conceptualization of androgyny is the assumption that the traits that identify the well-adjusted individual are not sex specific, but that high quantities of both stereotypically masculine and feminine characteristics are necessary. Jill Morawski pointed out that androgyny became the new standard of mental health for both sexes. Although on the surface the concept of androgyny would seem to be a more gender-fair assessment of psychological health (and indeed, some called the construct revolutionary), the continued reliance on gender-based traits remained in tact. Nevertheless, the new tests continued to measure masculinity as being direct, instrumental, and independent, and femininity as being indirect, expressive, and dependent.

Since the 1970s it has become increasingly clear that M/F is not a rigid trait that reliably predicts an individual's behavior across time and situations. Self-report M/F inventories are now generally agreed to be measures of gender-role self-concept rather than classic personality traits. In other words, it is more accurate to interpret responses on M/F questionnaires as representations of the respondent's self-image than as a quantitative expression of how masculine, feminine, or androgynous a person is likely to appear to be across time and situations.

A second stream of research concerned with gender developed in the post–World War II years in the

United States. It derived from interest in family structures and other social roles occupied by women and men. These sex-role theories shared with the masculinity/femininity tradition a conceptualization of gender as an internalized, stable, and enduring trait, but focused more on the source of sex-role differentiation in the social roles occupied by women and men than a presumptive connection between sexual orientation and healthy psychological gender.

An early notable publication on this sex-roles tradition was Georgene Seward's *Sex and the Social Order*. In that book Seward reviewed the anthropological evidence at the time to illustrate that there was dramatic gender variability across cultures. This variability strongly suggests that the roles played by women and men were not static, predetermined aspects of personality. Rather, Seward suggested, particular aspects of a culture's environment and resources shape what we come to know as "femininity" and "masculinity." She also may have been one of the first to highlight the relationship between gender role and social status or dominance, a point taken up much later by contemporary feminists.

More well known was functionalist sociologist, Talcott Parsons. Parsons argued that, like all animal life, societies seek a homeostatic state, where systems and processes are stable. Parsons saw the nuclear North American family as an exemplar of this homeostatic process. Women's adoption of expressive roles within the domain of the home and men's adoption of instrumental roles within the public domain was believed to serve and maintain this homeostasis. Further, women's subordination to men was required so that they might not come into competition with one another. The stability of the family would be threatened if women sought equal access for "male" jobs. Although not biologically based, women and men were both admonished to maintain their respective roles, for startling the status quo would be disastrous for the family system.

B. SEX-TYPING

Until the early 1970s questions of how and why gender is acquired rested in the province of the study of child development. Under the rubric of "sex-typing," three developmental theories predominated. The first was a stage theory account of psychosexual development from a Freudian perspective. A second perspective grew out of the attempt to splice behaviorism and Freudian psychoanalytic theory into a single perspective. This approach, the social learning the-

ory, developed at Yale in the 1930s, described the role of external forces, via models, reinforcement, and direct training, in creating the conditions for sex typing. To the standard learning theory account, however, it added the notion of "identification" with the same-sex parent, much as the Freudian used the term, to explain the incorporation of culturally approved gender-specific attitudes, beliefs, values, and behaviors into one's own personality. In both theories the challenge was to explain how the boy eschewed identification with the primary caregiver—presumed to be the mother—and how the girl established the identification with the mother despite the fact that she was recognized to be relatively less powerful than male figures. The cognitive revolution of the early 1960s resulted in the addition of a third major model to the account of sex-typing, namely a "cognitive developmental" perspective. This perspective, instead of emphasizing the centrality of identification to the establishment of gender, focused on the capacities of the infant and child to selectively attend to information. This model described sex typing in terms of the processes by which gender as information was assimilated to existing cognitive structures or the ways in which cognitive structures were modified (i.e., accommodated) to the constraints of gender-relevant information. In the case of each of these three major models of the acquisition of gender, however, we encounter the same conflation of distinct and independent gender-related constructs of gender identity, erotic orientation, and gender role that characterized the earlier generation of masculinity/femininity tests and, prior to that, Freudian theory of psychosexual development.

V. Gender Research in Psychology Since the 1970s

The second-wave feminist movement of the 20th century spurred a number of feminist psychologists to attack the biases that had so long been central to psychological practice and research on women. In one of the earliest and most often-cited critiques, Naomi Weisstein dissected the long history of misogynistic bias that underlay North American psychology. She pointed out, like the earlier generation of feminist psychologists had, that socialization and societal expectation, not simply biology, were important in understanding why and how gender differences are produced. Her paper, "Kinder, Kuche,

Kirche as Scientific Law: Psychology Constructs the Female" marks an important statement regarding the psychology of women that spurred a revival of interest in sex differences and the psychology of women, which is the foundation for current work on gender. By the late 1970s, feminist psychologists asserted the research, theory, and practical importance of differentiating between *sex* as categorization on the basis of anatomy and physiology, and *gender* as a culturally defined set of meanings attached to sex and sex difference. In contemporary North American psychology, gender continues to be theorized by the so-called mainstream of the discipline as a biologically based category that is manifested as a fixed, unitary trait.

Despite numerous critiques of the sex-differences approach, gender continues to be construed in much of the published empirical work within the purview of a differences model. Among important critics of the differences model is Janet Spence. She has proposed and demonstrated empirically that gender is a multidimensional phenomenon, which is only partially represented by the expressivity-instrumentality components of conventional masculinity-femininity (M/F) scales.

Four significant trends in gender theory are emerging in current empirical psychology in the United States. One emphasizes gender as a dimension or result of sex-segregation of social role or sociostructural arrangements. This approach has received more thorough treatment among feminist sociologists such as Barbara Risman. The major exponent of this position in psychology is Alice Eagly in her social role theory. A second theme rejects the definition of gender in traitlike terms and instead focuses on gender as a context-sensitive social transaction. One version of gender as process was offered by Kay Deaux and Brenda Major in a much-cited article published in the late 1980s. Their model is compatible with conventional empirical social psychology and has encouraged thinking about gender as a feature of the contextualized social interaction rather than as a fixed, internalized trait. Others whose work takes a view of gender as process and emphasizes its enactment as a social construction include Michelle Fine, Janis Bohan, Jeanne Marecek, and Rachel Hare-Mustin to name but a few. A third perspective is more aligned with feminist standpoint theories and emphasizes the ostensibly unique features of female experience that are posited to have an inevitable influence on the person. This position, most often associated with Carol Gilligan and researchers at the Stone Center, has won a large popular following among educators and community workers concerned with girls' and women's exercise of public voice. A fourth theme is based on a feminist recuperation of Freudian psychoanalytic theories of development. Notable here is the work of Nancy Chodorow and Ellen Kaschak. [*See* SOCIAL CONSTRUCTIONIST THEORY; SOCIAL IDENTITY; SOCIAL ROLE THEORY OF SEX DIFFERENCES AND SIMILARITIES.]

In clinical and counseling psychology, the development of gender-sensitive and feminist therapies has had a pronounced impact on several areas of law and social policy, perhaps most notably in the conceptualization of violence against women. In contrast, theoretical work on gender within experimental psychology has lagged behind gender theory in other social science and humanities disciplines. Experimental work reflects a greater emphasis on devising empirical tests of existing theory than on theory development in its own right. In addition, some evolving perspectives on gender (e.g., queer theory and feminist postcolonial theory) have had limited impact on psychology thus far. An important challenge for the future is the development of a psychology of gender that fully addresses the ways in which gender is a multidimensional construct that is actively created, negotiated, performed, and shaped through social interaction.

SUGGESTED READING

Fausto-Sterling, A. (1985). *Myths of Gender: Biological Theories about Women and Men*, 2nd ed., rev. Basic Books, New York.

Fausto-Sterling, A. (2000). *Sexing the Body: Gender Politics and the Construction of Sexuality*. Basic Books, New York.

Lewin, M. (ed.) (1984). *In the Shadow of the Past: Psychology Examines the Sexes*. Columbia University Press, New York.

Morawski, J. G. (1987). The troubled quest for masculinity, femininity, and androgyny. In *Review of Personality and Social Psychology* (P. Shaver and C. Hendrick, eds.), Vol. 4, pp. 44–69. Sage, Beverly Hills, CA.

Shields, S. A. (1975). Functionalism, Darwinism, and the psychology women: A study in social myth. *American Psychologist* 30, 739–754.

Shields, S. A. (1982). The variability hypothesis: History of a biological model of sex differences in intelligence. *Signs* 7, 769–797.

Humor

Molly Carnes

University of Wisconsin Medical School

Time spent laughing is time spent with the gods
Japanese Proverb

I. Background
II. The Neural Control of Humor
III. Humor and Health
IV. What Is Funny?
V. Gender Differences in Humor

Glossary

Comedy A ludicrous, farcical, or amusing event or series of events.

Conversational joking Informal situational humor that may use verbal devices such as punning, word play, sarcasm and mockery or nonverbal devices such as mimicry or grimaces; created by participants with a backdrop of in-group knowledge; may take the form of teasing, humor directed at absent other(s), or humor directed at oneself (self-deprecating humor).

Funny A property attributed to that which causes mirth in the listener/observer.

Gelastic epilepsy Seizures manifested with uncontrollable laughter, usually without concomitant feelings of mirth.

Humor Refers to either the generation of remarks, actions, or pictures that induce mirth and usually laughter in the listener/observer or to the appreciation of mirth in these occurrences by the listener/observer.

Joke A memorized short story usually with a setup, which creates one perception, and a punch line, which surprises with a brief incongruity (a transient double meaning) that upon resolution is meant to incite laughter in the listener; includes riddles.

Laughter The typical outward expression of mirth although it can occur independent of that emotional trigger and in association with other emotions including fear, embarrassment, contempt, and grief, as well as love and joy.

Mirth The subjective feeling accompanying the perception of something as humorous.

Sense of humor Refers to the appreciation of humor, the ability to find something funny and laugh.

Teasing Behavior directed at a person(s) present meant to incite laughter; may be playful and intended kindly to promote bonding or contain a more aggressive element of disparagement.

Wit Implies a keen intellect and quickness in perception combined with a gift for expressing ideas in a manner that provokes laughter; a disposition to see the ludicrous, comical, or absurd, and to give it expression.

Women's humor Forms of humor identified by contemporary researchers that emphasize social connection, solidarity, resistance, and empowerment, and that acknowledge social and political inequality; relies on stories, anecdotes, and informal repartee more than traditional men's humor; includes domestic humor, self-deprecation, and political subjects.

RESEARCH ON HUMOR has taken several tacks: the physiology of laughter and the impact of humor as a trait characteristic (sense of humor) as well as a state of humor (an episode of laughter in response to a joke or other funny stimulus) on health and biomedical measures, literary histories and anthologies of humor; the function of humor in social and political environments, standup comedy, and comedy in the media (e.g., newspaper cartoons, situational comedies on television). Within each of these domains, to a varying extent, gender differences have been explored. This article reviews aspects of these areas. There is also considerable research on the use of humor in therapy, humor as a tool for education, and the use of effective humor in management. It is worth noting that much of the research on humor has used undergraduate college students, usually of European descent, as subjects.

I. Background

Conventional wisdom and the bulk of empirical evidence indicates that humor is beneficial in our lives. Some theorize that smiling and laughing may have evolved as a means of signaling other members of a social group that an initially perceived threat proved to be a false alarm. The bared teeth and aggressive growl dissolved into smiling and explosive bursts of vocalized laughter to communicate this false alarm to others. This transient incongruity between what is real and what is perceived remains a basic element of humor. For example, a joke "works" because the recipient is led to perceive events a certain way during the setup, but the punch line indicates that events were actually something different. When the incongruity is consciously recognized, indicating the "false alarm," mirth and laughter ensue. Other elements that establish a humorous message include a situational cue that something is meant to be funny (e.g.,

a comedian is on stage), the assurance that the recipient is not in danger, and an element of surprise before the incongruity is resolved in some unexpected way. The ambiguous message (threat or nonthreat) is also part of some humor where the initial act or statement might be perceived or even intended as an aggressive attack, but humor is introduced giving the false alarm (just kidding) message. The ensuing laughter alters the fight posture to one less threatening or even playful.

The ability to generate humor is a valued trait across societies. Although what is considered humorous varies across cultures, the societal function of humor is similar. Humor is a means of reaffirming the social hierarchy, promoting bonding among members of a group, and releasing aggression or tension with relative safety. This is generally accomplished in three ways by humor generators: (1) by directing humor at themselves (self-deprecating humor) to make them appear less threatening and more approachable to other members of the group, (2) by directing humor at another member of the group (teasing) in either a playful or aggressive but nonthreatening manner, or (3) by directing humor at someone or something outside the group to reinforce shared norms among those within the group.

II. The Neural Control of Humor

The neural circuitry involved in laughter and its emotional content is complex and incompletely understood. What is known has been largely inferred from case studies or case series of patients with brain abnormalities. No systematic examination of gender differences could be found. Because humor involves integration of sensory, emotional, motor, and autonomic processes, it is clear that multiple sites are involved. Evidence exists for involvement of areas of the brainstem, limbic system, and cerebral cortex. In one case, electrical stimulation of an area 2 cm × 2 cm in the left superior frontal gyrus consistently produced laughter; low-level current produced a smile and higher current produced hearty laughter. The laughter was invariably accompanied by a sense of mirth indicating that the motor and affective constituents of humor are neurologically closely linked. The location of this area is close to both areas for speech and manual dexterity and has been proposed to be part of advanced evolutionary development of the brain in humans.

Pathological laughter has been described in several

conditions often unaccompanied by mirth. These include certain types of seizures ("gelastic epilepsy"), which have been associated in particular with benign tumors of the hypothalamus but also frontal lobe abnormalities. Laughter as a prodomal warning of an impending stroke has been called "le fou rire prodromique" and reported in acute left hemispheric and left pontine strokes. Pathological laughter has been described with a variety of brain tumors occurring at multiple loci usually without accompanying feelings of mirth. Abnormalities of humor appreciation are seen in right frontal lobe damage.

It is widely observed that the immediate effect of moderate alcohol consumption lowers the threshold for laughter. Greater subjective amusement in response to a humor stimulus has been demonstrated empirically when comparing subjects given alcohol to those given placebo. The underlying neural mechanism for this phenomenon is not known, but it may be that by slightly slowing normal cognitive processes, alcohol enhances the generation of incongruities, which is the setup for the perception of humor. Some researchers in this area go so far as to suggest that the greater laughter of moderate drinkers compared to nondrinkers may be one contributor to their enhanced longevity. Women achieve higher blood alcohol levels with the same amount of alcohol, but otherwise no examination of gender differences in this phenomenon has been performed.

III. *Humor and Health*

Laughter has beneficial effects on the immune system, the reduction of pain, the cardiovascular system, and the respiratory system. Furthermore, it may modulate physiological and psychological response to stress. Norman Cousins is the best-known case study using laughter therapy to combat symptoms and progression of a chronic disabling arthritic disease. Jeanne Calmet, who lived to age 122, attributed her long life to a love of laughter. Anecdotally, humor and laughter have long been viewed as remedies for relieving tension associated with stressful situations. Whereas stress has been linked to suppressed immune system activity and increased vulnerability to disease, humor has been shown to heighten immune system functioning. Some studies have also revealed positive relationships between humor and perceptions of physical health, muscle relaxation, and positive mood states. Watching 12 minutes of Bill Cosby's humor on video resulted in increased feelings of energy in college men and women. Gender differences in these responses to humor have been found in isolated studies. For example, scores on the Situational Humor Response Questionnaire (Martin and Lefcourt, 1984) and the Coping Humor Scale (Martin and Lefcourt, 1983) were positively associated with psychological coping strategies among women but not men. Similarly, in another study, the Coping Humor Scale produced a strong main effect and interaction with stress in the prediction of depression among women but not men. In a study of the physiological response to five experimental physical stressors, female college students with high Coping Humor Scale scores had lower systolic blood pressure measurements than those with low scores, whereas just the opposite was found for men (i.e., higher systolic blood pressures with high coping humor). Based on the existing evidence, some have suggested that humor may play a greater role as a stress moderator among women than men. However, at the present time there is little evidence for gender differences in the health impact of humor as either a state or trait phenomenon.

IV. *What Is Funny?*

Although much of the research on humor has evaluated structured jokes and who finds them funny and why, diary research finds that both men and women laugh about 18 times per day. Spontaneous situational occurrences incite over half of daily laughter, with jokes accounting for only about one-tenth of daily laughter episodes, and mass media and stories of past humorous events accounting for the rest.

Attempts to categorize humor are varied, but there is agreement that to be successful, all humor requires a mutual understanding, a shared experience, between the humor generator and the receiver. Four general techniques are used to generate humor: language (or verbal) humor, which includes exaggerations, irony, insults, misunderstandings; logic humor, which includes absurdity, analogy, coincidence, stereotype, and sarcasm; identity humor, which includes burlesque, caricature, impersonation, parody, and satire; and action humor, which includes the chase and slapstick. In examining what it is that actually causes something to be perceived as humorous, researchers intertwine the purpose and setting of humor with elements that generate humor. For example, several authors describe three broad categories of humor: cognitive-perceptual, social-behavioral, and psychoanalytical and associate these with incongruity or incongruity-resolution humor, disparagement or superiority humor, and suppression/repression or release humor, respectively.

This first theory (cognitive-perceptual, incongruity or incongruity-resolution) has received the most attention. Some argue that it can explain almost all humor, that it is simply the intent of the humor and the social consequence of the humor that differ among other categories. Historical proponents of the incongruity theory of humor include Kant in 1790 and Darwin in 1860. As long as the recipient feels safe and often when some cue is given that something is supposed to be funny, mirth and accompanying laughter are triggered when an incongruity occurs between perception and reality at the moment the humor recipient realizes the incongruity. There is the need for something to transiently have more than one meaning.

Disparagement or superiority humor refers to humor directed by someone in power at those with less power. It is typically directed downward in the social hierarchy with the intent of ridiculing psychological or physical inferiority. It is used to reinforce the status quo in social order. This type of humor has been used more often by men than women because of their historical power relationships. Racist, ethnic, and sexist humor fall into this category. There are clearly elements of hostility and aggression in this type of humor. Teasing that is not playful falls into this category. Thomas Hobbes, the 17th-century English philosopher, building on the teachings of Plato, described the need to disparage as a key element of most humor. More modern humor scholars disagree and even express some discomfort in including disparagement humor as true humor. In the *Handbook of Humor Research* Paul McGhee and Jeffrey Goldstein stress that real "humor is laughter made from pain—not pain inflicted by laughter."

The category of suppression/repression or release humor is based largely on Freud's view that humor and laughter provide a socially acceptable and pleasurable form of release of repressed psychic energy. This theory is the least well explicated and, again, speaks more to the physiological and social purpose of humor rather than the humor itself. While the purpose of the humor may be different, this type of humor can also be subsumed under the incongruity theory of humor because even in tension-releasing humor, it is almost invariably an incongruity that triggers mirth.

In summary, throughout different categorizations

of humor, it is the existence of a transient incongruity, usually accompanied by resolution of the incongruity in an unexpected way, that underlies almost all humor. The social goals of humor can generally be viewed as positive or negative. Positive humor is more collaborative. Its goal is to promote bonding within members of a group, to make others feel accepted, to diminish emotional distress, to correct and reinforce social norms in a positive way. It is very much linked to play. Negative humor, on the other hand, has a bite to it and generally a goal of self-promotion. There are elements of aggression, put-down, hostility, laughter at another's expense. As concepts of humor have evolved, some would exclude such negative humor as true humor.

V. Gender Differences in Humor

A. THE MYTH OF THE HUMORLESS WOMAN AND EVIDENCE TO THE CONTRARY

That women lack a sense of humor is a familiar cliché, and despite voluminous evidence to the contrary it is a firmly entrenched misconception. The woman who does not "get" the joke, the woman who cannot "take" a joke, and the woman who flubs the punch line are all familiar stereotypes. When a woman does not laugh at a joke told by a man, she is told she has no sense of humor; when a man does not laugh at a woman's joke, she is told it is not funny. Feminists, in fact, have been mocked for having no sense of humor with such jokes as, "How many feminists does it take to change a lightbulb? . . . That's not funny!" In a 1981 study, when 200 top executives were asked to select 10 reasons why women should not be placed in corporate leadership positions, "lack of a sense of humor" ranked high on the list emphasizing the abiding stereotype of the humorless woman. A number of reasons have been explored for this phenomenon. One of the most insightful, comprehensive, and also humorous discussions of gender differences in humor including reasons for the persistent stereotype of the humorless woman is provided by Regina Barreca in her book, *They Used to Call Me Snow White . . . But I Drifted.*

Consensus is that the stereotype of the humorless woman reflects more than anything else that those in power (men) have historically defined what is funny. Shared humor depends on shared experiences. Culturally, socially, and biologically, women and men generally share different experiences. Thus, men's humor simply may not be funny to many women and vice versa. In part, this is because women have so often been the butt of jokes that they do not trust men's humor. In many jokes, women have been caricatured as the "bimbo," "gold digger," or "shrew," or the incompetent or physically unattractive wife. As Mary Crawford noted, one simple reason women may appear less humorous is that they are unwilling to participate in their own denigration. Studies of joke appreciation find that women score jokes as less funny when the target of humor is a woman than when it is a man and while both genders find sexual humor funny, women generally do not find humor in sexist jokes. Indeed, it has been argued that all sex differences found in studies of appreciation of sexual humor may have arisen from the confound of sexism in the materials employed. When humor is directed at someone they do not like, both men and women are more likely to think the joke is humorous than when it is directed at someone they like. This may also explain women's apparent lack of a sense of humor when the joke target is another women. [*See* GENDER STEREOTYPES.]

Further complicating the issue of women's sense of humor is the behavioral, expressive, and sociocultural constraints that have been historically imposed on women. Growing up, little girls were frequently admonished that it was not "ladylike" to laugh "too loud" or to be the center of attention, a requirement for the humor generator. Furthermore, much of men's humor involves explicit or implicit sexual content and many women have been warned from an early age that "nice" girls do not laugh at "dirty" jokes because men may get the "wrong impression" that those who laugh are prone to sexual promiscuity. Thus, many women may have been socialized to pretend they do not understand such humor and this could be misinterpreted as lacking a sense of humor.

Promoting the perception of women as humorless has been the omission of women authors of humor from a number of published anthologies and histories of humor, the use of male-defined humor in empirical research to score gender differences in humor response, and even the exclusion of women comedians from a study to determine whether comedians had specific personality characteristics. Nancy Walker noted that the works of women humorists were ignored in literary discussion of U.S. humor until quite recently and that justification for this omission was that the work of women writers of humor was trivial and not "serious" humor. Anthologies of

wit and humor resoundingly confirm that women have always been capable of generating and appreciating humor and, in fact, have made substantial contributions to literary humor. As far back as 1885, Kate Sanborn published an anthology of female humorists, *The Wit of Women*. In 1934, Martha Bensley Bruere and Mary Ritter Beard edited *Laughing Their Way: Women's Humor in America*. Sadly, however, these works were so little known that when Deanne Stillman and Anne Bealls published *Titters* in 1976, they called it *The First Collection of Humor by Women*. More recent anthologies of humor in women's writing include Regina Barreca's *Last Laughs: Perspectives on Women and Comedy* (1988) and *Women's Humor* (1996) and Nancy Walker's *Redressing the Balance: American Women's Literacy Humor from Colonial Times to the 1980's* (1988). (Table I summarizes some of the research on humor and gender.)

Emily Toth in "A Laughter of Their Own: Women's Humor in the United States" (in *American Women Humorists* by Linda Morris, 1994) noted that women humorists, like other women writers, have not been given their due. One notable example is Marietta Holley who was an author from the United States who effectively used her wit to support women's rights and women's suffrage. Her popularity was such that a reviewer of her work during her lifetime wrote that Holley "has entertained as large an audience . . . as has been entertained by the humor of Mark Twain." She published 21 very popular novels infused with humorous satirical comment on the social and political practices of the day that marginalized women. Nancy Walker noted that despite Marietta Holley's importance to the 19th century, she was omitted from a number of humor histories, being dismissed by the male authors of these as being not amusing and irrelevant.

In addition to writing, women have used cartoon humor to make political statements. For example, suffragists in a woman-run press featured weekly or monthly political cartoons (reviewed in *Cartooning for Suffrage* by Alice Sheppard, 1994). Several dozen women published political cartoons from 1910 to 1920 refuting the view that socialization or stereotypes prevented women's political use of humor. Other examples of humorous cartoons with a political function include Betty Swords' Male Chauvinist Pig calendars of the 1970s and the nationally syndicated cartoon, *Sylvia,* by Nicole Hollander, which uses humor to provide commentary on modern social and political inequality.

Table I
Selected Areas of Research on Humor and Gender

Aspect	Finding	Gender difference	Comment
Neurology of mirth and laughter	Multiple brain sites involved; laughter can occur without mirth; pathological laughter can occur in seizures, as prodrome to stroke, in certain genetic syndromes	Has not been studied	Most information from case studies or case series
Conversational joking (conversational humor, situational humor)	Accounts for most daily laughter; three types of humor are involved: teasing, self-directed joking, joking directed toward absent other(s)	Women are more likely to use self-directed joking (self-deprecating humor); men are more likely to use outward directed joking; women find being the target of teasing more aversive than do men	More similarities than differences in what makes men and women laugh but the goals in conversation may be different (self-promotion for men, relational for women)
Social functions of humor	Reinforces status quo when directed at other groups or downward by superiors; challenges existing norms when directed upward at those in power; increases group solidarity; communicates affiliative intentions; changes listener's perception of speaker	Men's humor more likely directed downward and women's upward at those in power; women's humor viewed as more subversive because it is more likely to question societal norms; women more likely to use coping humor	Gender differences primarily due to historical power differential, societal restrictions on female behavior, and different shared experiences
Humor appreciation (sense of humor)	Perceiving the incongruity or incongruity-resolution, which triggers mirth	Women historically portrayed as devoid of humor appreciation; women's humor is said to highlight the absurdities and incongruities of society and human behavior more than men's, which targets individuals	It is noteworthy that articles about using humor to cope in the current health care delivery climate are coming from the nursing (predominantly women's) literature
Use of self-deprecating humor	The target of humor is the speaker; a form of self-mockery	Women are far more likely than men to use this type of humor in conversation and it was the backbone of the routines of the first women comedians; it engenders different responses between men and women: women may perceive the speaker to be more witty and intelligent, whereas men may perceive the speaker to be less intelligent	There may be subgenres of self-mocking humor—some that are meant to induce listeners to laugh at and some to induce the listeners to laugh with the humor generator

Use of other-deprecating humor (disparagement or superiority humor)	Increases group solidarity; helps discharge aggression against outgroup members	More commonly used by men than women in both conversational and public humor; in a classic study senior physicians directed humor at subordinates but rarely did subordinates direct humor upward	Women in leadership positions have not been studied to see if they assume this type of humor
Research tools used for measuring sense of humor	Multidimensional Sense of Humor Scale (Thorson and Powell, 1993), Vitulli's Humor Rating Scale (Vitulli and Tyler, 1988), Situational Humor Response Questionnaire (Martin and Lefcourt, 1984), Coping Humor Scale (Martin and Lefcourt, 1983)	Mean differences in humor scale scores are generally similar between males and females but correlates of humor scores often differ between the sexes	Different tools try to assess both the perception of humorous content in a joke as well as a person's general predisposition to see humor
Moderating effects of humor on stress	Perceived stress and physical symptoms are correlated when sense of humor is low	Inconsistent gender differences in humor as a moderator of self-perceived stress; in response to experimental stressors, high humor appreciation at baseline associated with lower systolic blood pressure in women but higher systolic blood pressure in men	Humor is universally associated with good mental and physical health but mechanisms remain speculative
Humor and leadership	Effective leadership is positively related to the use of humor	Higher frequency of daily laughter was associated with greater Type A characteristics in men, but with fewer in women; lack of a sense of humor cited by men as a reason women should not be chief executives	Leadership training programs for both men and women include the use of humor, but bad humor is worse than no humor

B. WOMEN'S HUMOR

Quite a bit of discussion has centered on whether there actually is a "women's humor" apart from men's humor. There is general consensus that as generators of humor, compared with men, women are more likely to tell an anecdote than a joke, often including themselves and involving common human experiences; are more likely to ridicule a situation rather than a person; and are less likely to use aggressive disparagement humor, but if they do, women are more likely to direct it upward toward those in power (e.g., the sitcom *Roseanne*) than downward toward those with less power (e.g., racist, sexist, and ethnic humor). Women's humor is said to be more subtle than traditional male humor, which has been used to explain why men often do not "get" women's humor and at the same time why much of men's humor seems too obvious or broad to many women. Humor based on the spheres of experience as a wife and mother are easily categorized as women's humor and have been the core of much of the humor generated by women. Other shared experiences like boring dates, inept lovers, and incompetent bosses may also be sources of humor, particularly in all-women groups.

Women and men show differences in the structure and purpose of humor in informal conversation. Conversational joking or situational humor often involves either teasing (which can be aggressive or playful), joking about an absent other, or self-denigrating joking. Men, in general, use more punning, verbal challenges, put downs, and joking directed at an absent other, while women use more playful teasing, "stacked humor" (adding to the humor of another speaker in the conversation), and self-deprecating humor. Mary Crawford has noted and in keeping with the observed gender-linked differences in conversational goals, men tend to use conversational humor in a more competitive mode ("I'm great, I'm the best, aren't we all better than them!"), while women use humor to enhance bonding and support within a group ("That happens to you, too? Good, I'm not crazy.").

Analyses of literary humor, cartoon humor, and television sit-com humor discuss gender differences and, particularly in the case of the latter, how humor reflects the changing roles and acceptable behaviors of women and men in U.S. society. As these have relaxed, women are allowed to be more bold with their humor and to exhibit both wit and intelligence. Comparisons of pre- and post-1980s cartoons also indicates significant change toward a less stereotypical portrayal of female characters. If a joke or cartoon "works" because of the presence of gender-based assumptions, the humor will not persist when the genders are switched. Conversely, if a statement or occurrence becomes funny only when the genders are switched, gender bias or gender-linked cultural stereotypes must have been present.

Women's humor arises from women's experiences. It has functioned throughout history as an effective political tool, serving as a nonalienating, nonviolent, strategic means of expressing anger and frustration over societal injustice. Given that incongruity is the basis of most humor, women, because they have not been part of the dominant male culture, have been in an ideal position to perceive the absurdity of a number of customs and practices. Women's humor rests on using laughter to triumph over institutions and practices that unfairly discriminate against women yet that they may be powerless to change. Because women are usually not in power, their use of humor as a strategic political tool must be cautiously wielded. Women's humor seeks to maintain relationships with those in power even while it calls into question the status quo. Because of the historical power differential, women cannot risk their humor being perceived as too aggressive. Roseanne Barr noted, for example, that she was booed off the stage early in her career as a feminist standup comic because her material was perceived as too hostile. When she "toned down" her material, she hit a chord with her audience with her "Domestic Goddess" routines.

Women must be subtle enough in generating humor to protect themselves even while they are mocking the existing power structure. When a woman uses humor, she takes a chance. If it works, she may gain respect and some power, at least temporarily, as she has controlled the floor and made people laugh. Attempting humor can be risky, however, because if it does not work or is perceived as hostile by those in power, a woman may have much to lose. Wit is linked to intelligence and insight—the jester and the fool are laughed at but are also admired for their insights and introduction of new ideas. Sometimes, however, these humorous characters are beaten or replaced. Barbara Levy noted, for example, that male writers as far back as Chaucer have portrayed women with quick wits as dangerous ones to wed.

C. SELF-DISPARAGING HUMOR

Self-disparaging or self-deprecating humor deserves special mention. This is humor directed at the humor generator him- or herself. Studies of humor in a variety of settings reveal that women use more self-disparaging humor than men. As with many elements of humor, self-deprecating humor is complex. Humor scholars have noted that the first successful standup female comedians (e.g., Phyllis Diller, Joan Rivers) based their routines on one type of self-deprecating humor. They typically targeted aspects of themselves (e.g., physical appearance) to get a laugh and paralleled male sexist humor. Only by debasing themselves, and thus women, a comfortable theme for male comedians, could these women be seen as funny by men and thus even allowed to perform. Women are now cautioned against using self-disparaging humor of this kind, particularly in the workplace, because it may be believed by supervisors and coworkers.

It has been proposed that there are subgenres of self-deprecating humor used particularly by women, which enable the audience to laugh more *with* the humor generator against some custom or assumption rather than *at* them. This type of humor was used, for example, by Erma Bombeck in a piece on how her body will not fit into a bikini. She used self-disparaging descriptions of her body not to put herself down, but to point out the absurdities of the arbitrary and ever-changing fashion ideals of the female form. It is also notable that there are a number of successful female comedians, and these in growing numbers, who do not rely on the self put-downs of the early female comics. Examples include Lily Tomlin, Roseanne Barr, Rita Rudner, Elayne Boosler, and Ellen DeGeneres. While some of their jokes have a self-deprecating element, they themselves are not the target of the joke. In conversational joking as well, it has been observed that women's use of self-mockery often does not result in laughter at the expense of the storyteller, but rather encourages sharing of similar mishaps or negative experiences by others.

Some studies have found that gender is a factor in determining the response of the humor recipient to the generator of self-deprecating humor. In a study of college students, self-disparagement presented in cartoons made the self-disparager, regardless of sex, appear more intelligent to women, but men respond less favorably to this type of humor, perceiving the self-disparager as less intelligent and less witty. In another study of heterosexual attractiveness using photographs and audiotranscripts, self-deprecating humor enhanced the attractiveness to women of high-status men, while even high-status women were viewed by men as less intelligent when they engaged in this type of humor. While no conclusions can be drawn from this work, it is clear that self-disparaging humor must be carefully used and women would do well to avoid the type of self-disparaging humor that targets her own personal traits, especially in a male or mixed-gender group.

SUGGESTED READING

Barreca, R. (1991). *They Used to Call Me Snow White . . . But I Drifted: Women's Strategic Use of Humor.* Penguin Books, New York.

Barreca, R. (ed.) (1996). *The Penguin Book of Women's Humor.* Penguin Books, New York.

Crawford, M. (1995). *Talking Difference: On Gender and Language.* Sage, London.

Finney, G. (ed.) (1994). Look who's laughing: Gender and comedy. *Studies in Humor and Gender,* Vol. 1. Gordon and Breach Science Publishers, Langhorne, PA.

Levy, B. (1997). Ladies laughing: Wit as control in contemporary American women writers. *Studies in Humor and Gender,* Vol. 3. Gordon and Breach Publishers, Amsterdam.

McGhee, P. E., and Goldstein, J. H. (eds.) (1983). *Handbook of Humor Research,* Vols. I and II. Springer-Verlag, New York.

Walker, N., and Dresner, Z. (1988). *Redressing the Balance: American Women's Literary Humor from Colonial Times to the 1980's.* University Press of Mississippi, Jackson and London.

HUMOR ASSESSMENT QUESTIONNAIRES

Martin, R. A., and Lefcourt, H. M. (1984). The Situational Humor Response Questionnaire: A quantitative measure of the sense of humor. *Journal of Personality and Social Psychology* **47,** 145–155.

Martin, R. A., and Lefcourt, H. M. (1983). Sense of humor as a moderator of the relation between stressors and moods. *Journal of Personality and Social Psychology* **45,** 1313–1324.

Thorson, J. A., and Powell, F. C. (1993). Sense of humor and dimensions of personality. *Journal of Clinical Psychology* **49,** 798–809.

Vitulli, W. E., and Tyler, K. E. (1988). Sex-related attitudes toward humor among high-school and college students. *Psychological Reports* **63,** 616–618.

Imprisonment in the United States

Angela Browne
Erika Lichter

Harvard Injury Control Research Center and Harvard School of Public Health

I. Trends in Imprisonment in the United States, 1600s–2000
II. Increasing Use of Imprisonment: Legislation and Social Policy
III. Costs of Incarceration Policies to Taxpayers and the Nation
IV. Who Are the People in Prison Today?
V. Early Trauma Histories: Pathways to Prison for Women?
VI. International Use of Incarceration
VII. U.S. Prisons Today
VIII. Has Increased Incarceration Decreased Rates of Crime?
IX. Summary

Glossary

Burglary The act of breaking into and entering a dwelling with the intent to commit a felony.

Conviction A judgment, based on the verdict of either a jury or a judge, that the defendant is guilty.

Felony Serious crimes punishable by death or more than one year of incarceration. People convicted of felonies are usually sent to prison, as opposed to jail.

Jail A place of confinement under the jurisdiction of local governments usually used to hold people awaiting trial or those convicted of misdemeanors.

Larceny The taking of personal property.

Misdemeanor Minor offenses for which the punishment does not usually exceed one year of incarceration. People who commit misdemeanors usually are sent to jail rather than to prison.

Parole An added period of criminal justice control following release from prison.

Physical abuse/violence The occurrence of at least one act of violence including being kicked, bit, or hit with a fist, hit with an object, beaten up, burned, or threatened or assaulted with a knife or gun.

Plea bargain The negotiated agreement between defendant, prosecutor, and the court as to what a sentence should be in a given case. Plea bargaining avoids the trial process and reduces the time required for the resolution of a criminal case.

Prison An institution of confinement for persons convicted of serious crimes. Prisons may be controlled by either the federal government or the states.

Private prison Correctional institutions operated by private firms.

Probation A judicial requirement that a person fulfill certain conditions of behavior in lieu of a sentence to confinement; it sometimes includes a reduced jail sentence.

Quakers (Society of Friends) A Protestant religious organization characterized by silent meetings for worship and an emphasis on human rights and social activism.

Recidivism A relapse back into criminal activity.

Rehabilitation To restore and bring to a condition of useful activity.

Robbery Stealing from a person using violence or threat.

Sexual abuse/molestation Contact or noncontact unwanted sexual experiences. This includes inappropriate exposure, sexual contact, and any form of penetration.

Violent crimes Defined by the Uniform Crime Reports; includes homicides, robbery, assault, rape, and kidnapping.

THE NUMBER OF PEOPLE INCARCERATED in the United States has risen dramatically since 1985. Although the United States makes up only 5% of the world's population, it now accounts for one-quarter of the world's prisoners. By March of 2000, 2 million people were in U.S. prisons and jails. An additional 3.5 million people were under the supervision of the criminal justice system on probation or parole. At the current rate of incarceration, the U.S. prison population will grow to 7.3 million in 10 years. Given this rapid expansion, it is important to understand the impact this use of imprisonment has on the United States, socially and economically. This article reviews trends in imprisonment in the United States since the 1600s, describes characteristics of people who are in prison today, compares the use of imprisonment in the United States to that of other advanced industrialized nations, and summarizes some effects of this use of imprisonment on crime and social policy. Although most prisoners in the United States are male, women are the most rapidly growing segment of the prison population and the segment about which we know the least. Sections of this article will highlight aspects of women's experiences in the criminal justice system, with attention to how early exposure to violence and other trauma may contribute to a woman's pathway to prison.

I. Trends in Imprisonment in the United States: 1600s–2000

A. PUNISHMENT IN THE COLONIAL AND REVOLUTIONARY PERIOD

The recent increase in the U.S. use of imprisonment reflects a return to an earlier emphasis on punishment. During the colonial period in the 1600s, physical punishment was the predominant response to criminal misconduct. Felons were whipped, branded, publicly shamed, banished, or executed. During the 1600s, there were no state or federal prisons and very few jails. The use of jails and the beginnings of the current prison system began after the end of the Revolutionary War.

When prisons did become established in the United States, they usually confined several inmates in one room. Physical punishment, public shaming, and executions were still used to discipline and control criminal offenders. The first efforts to reform U.S. prison practices were begun in the late 1700s by Quakers in Pennsylvania, concerned about the use of physical aggression against inmates. Quakers advocated less brutal treatment of prisoners and encouraged building prisons with single cells in order to "isolate inmates from the moral contamination of other felons" according to Nicole Rafter. Over time, all U.S. prisons began a shift to single cells. States increasingly took over the imprisonment of people with more serious offense (felonies), leaving those with more minor offenses (misdemeanors) to local governments to control. The first state penitentiary for men, Auburn, was built in 1816 in New York. Sing Sing, on the Hudson River in New York, followed in 1825. By 1870, nearly every state had a penitentiary. By this time, the reformers' emphasis on humane treatment had been replaced with a return to strict discipline and physical punishment.

B. 1870–1970 AND THE PRISON REFORM MOVEMENT

The prison reform movement in the United States began based on pioneering work in England. In 1870, a Declaration of Principles guiding the management of prisons was ratified at a conference of prison administrators in Cincinnati, Ohio. This declaration identified reformation, rather than solely punishment, as the purpose of imprisonment. It ordered prisons to offer educational, vocational, and religious training and led to the invention of indeterminate sentences. Prisoners were held in prison until they were considered reformed by prison officials.

This Declaration of Principles guided prison management for the next 100 years, until the early 1970s. During this 100-year period, most prisons complied—at least in form—with principles of the declaration. Most states had one central prison, which housed people convicted of serious crimes, and several "reformatories," where those with more minor offenses were held. State prisons had single cells and ran on strict rules and discipline. In contrast, reformatories were often structured around a cottage system and offered more programming directed toward rehabilitation.

C. EARLY IMPRISONMENT OF WOMEN

Throughout U.S. history, women have been imprisoned for behavior not conforming to cultural norms of the feminine ideal. Women in colonial America were considered the property of their fathers or, if married, of their husbands. Actions by women that offended husbands were considered quite serious, compared to actions by men that offended—or even injured—wives. Adultery was considered one of the most serious crimes a woman could commit, since it threatened the progression of inheritance. In the early history of the nation, witch-hunts and public executions focused on women who defied Puritan roles for women as the procreators and helpmates of men. Early use of severe punishment as a form of social control of women became a precursor to later use of female imprisonment in the United States.

After the Revolutionary War, women continued to be severely punished for so-called female crimes such as adultery, although there were no similar legal repercussions for men who committed adultery. Women also were imprisoned for other crimes of "sexual deviance" that carried no penalties for men, since the same actions by men were not viewed as threatening to that era's social order. The cultural ideal during this period was that women be pious, pure, and submissive. Women who engaged in acts that deviated from this standard were considered to have "fallen further than their male counterparts in crime, having been born pure," according to Estelle Freedman, a renowned historian of female imprisonment. The use of the imprisonment of women further escalated with increasing urbanization and industrialization. As men moved into formal work settings and gender roles became more differentiated, "deviant" women were viewed as a threat to stability and progress and women were more likely to be imprisoned for minor offenses.

During the early 1800s, people believed that women were incapable and unworthy of reform. Women prisoners were kept in the same facilities as men, but did not receive the care or efforts toward rehabilitation that men did. Their living quarters often were dirty and overcrowded and since prison of-

ficials wanted to prevent contact between male and female prisoners, they were never permitted to leave these quarters. Women were not allowed to go to workshop or exercise areas and their food was brought to them. Medical care was not available, and sexual abuse was common and even accepted. For example, the Indiana State Prison ran a prostitution service for male guards using female prisoners.

The 1920s and 1930s saw a shift in the perception of "criminal women" as beyond help, and the first institutions were opened specifically for women. According to criminologist Joylyn Pollock-Byrne, the goal of this female reform movement was to "establish separate state penal institutions for women prisoners run by women with the purpose of instilling feminine values in the female residents." Hundreds of women who had committed only minor crimes and previously would have been given probation or released now were imprisoned in order to "reform" them. Men convicted of misdemeanors during this period usually were released; male reformatories typically held only juvenile offenders. However, women convicted of minor offenses were sent to reformatories to "restore their feminine status" through removal from the community and "retraining."

Most imprisoned women during this period were young—under the age of 25. Two-thirds were widowed, divorced, or separated. Crimes for which women (but not men) were imprisoned included "moral offenses" such as stubbornness, idleness, disorderly conduct, serial premarital pregnancies, keeping bad company, adultery, and venereal disease. Women and girls also were punished for being sexually molested or raped. The elevated number of categories defined as female crimes rapidly increased the number of women under the control of the justice system.

D. THE GREAT DEPRESSION AND THE END OF THE REFORM MOVEMENT

In the 1930s, due to the stock market crash and the Great Depression, the prison reform movement began to falter. Because of the rapid increase in the use of reformatories for women and juveniles, resources and overcrowding were a serious problem. States could no longer afford to hold people who had committed only minor offenses in prison for long periods of time. Again policies shifted and women were given parole or probation or were sent to local jails instead of reformatories. As the effects of the Depression began to lift, the nation became involved in

World War II. Men left the country to fight overseas and women were suddenly needed in the labor market. Use of imprisonment in general receded as resources and policies focused on the war effort.

The next major change in the use and type of imprisonment in the United States occurred after World War II. A series of studies conducted in the 1960s suggested that treatment programs in the 1950s and early 1960s had no impact on recidivism by men and women prisoners. This finding was especially true of programs based on personality disorder theories. Today there are many questions about the validity of these studies, as well as about methods of rehabilitation used during the reformation period. However, the public was alarmed by study results and sentiment began to shift away from rehabilitation, even for those with first-time or minor offenses. There also were questions about the policy of indeterminate sentencing concerned with inequities in deciding which prisoners were sufficiently "reformed" to deserve release. By the end of this period, the reformation movement had ended. A return to an emphasis primarily on punishment began that continues today.

II. *Increasing Use of Imprisonment: Legislation and Social Policy*

The growth of the U.S. prison population rapidly accelerated during the 1970s. By the 1980s, public sentiment was that the criminal lifestyle was a lifestyle of choice. More behaviors were criminalized for both women and men, and the preferred solution for all levels of crime was to get tough. Mitigating circumstances such as age, coercion, and mental illness were less taken into account. This "get-tough" policy led to curtailing the diversion of mentally ill persons to treatment settings, inclusion of young adolescents in adult prison populations, harsher drug laws, longer sentences, and a greatly expanded use of the death penalty.

Today's prison and jail system is 10 times larger than it was 30 years ago. Instead of being a policy of last resort, imprisonment has become a first-order response for a wide range of nonviolence and petty offenses. The U.S. rate of imprisonment is now 6 to 10 times that of countries in the European Union. Approximately 1 in very 150 individuals in the United States is in prison or jail, a figure no other democracy can match. At this rate, 1 in every 20 children born in the year 2000 will spend a portion of her or his life in prison or jail.

Although more people are going to prison, increased offending cannot explain this acceleration in incarceration. Researchers such as Alfred Blumstein and Allen Beck in 1999 found that only 13% of this growth rate was due to increased offending. Instead, three social policies are primarily responsible for the dramatic increase in the number of U.S. citizens incarcerated: (1) use of imprisonment for drug possession or other drug offenses, (2) three-strikes legislation mandating long prison sentences for third-time offenders, and (3) truth-in-sentencing legislation mandating long prison terms across offense categories.

A. USE OF IMPRISONMENT FOR DRUG OFFENSES

Much of the recent rise in the number of people imprisoned is a result of policies mandating incarceration for crimes that previously received probation or release. The "war on drugs" declared in 1982 by President Ronald Reagan was one of these policies. During the 1980s, new legislation requiring mandatory arrests and long prison sentences for even minor drug offenses was strictly enforced, increasing the number of convictions and prison sentences for drug-related crimes. Since 1989, more people have been sent to prison for drug-related behaviors than for violent offenses. Although most studies show use of illegal drugs is highest among Whites, incarceration as a penalty falls primarily on people of color living in poverty. Also, state laws often require harsh penalties. In New York State, a person convicted of selling 2 ounces of a narcotic, or of possessing 4 ounces, can receive a prison sentence of 15 years to life—the same sentencing range as for rape or second-degree murder. [*See* SUBSTANCE ABUSE.]

B. THREE STRIKES LEGISLATION

Beside the enforcement of drug-related sentencing laws, other legislation adopted in the 1990s produced a sharp rise in the prison population, especially among nonviolent offenders. Many states adopted "three strikes and you're out" legislation. This legislation was first introduced in Washington State in 1993. It stated that anyone convicted of a third serious felony must be sentence to life in prison without the possibility of parole. By 1997, three-strikes legislation had been adopted by 24 states as well as the federal government. In some states, three-strikes laws now mandate sentences ranging from 15 years to life in prison for persons convicted of three crimes, even if some crimes are nonviolent and minor—a policy with no parallel in any other advanced nation. For example, although only 12% of crimes fall under the three-strikes law in Washington State, in California, *all* felonies (e.g., drug possession or witness tampering) are included as the third strike, with a mandatory sentence of 25 to 99 years or triple the recommended sentence, whichever is longer. Statisticians estimate that by the end of the 1990s, 75% of people sentenced under California's law were convicted for crimes classified neither as serious nor violent for the third strike. California leads the nation in use of this law, convicting 3000 people under the mandate by 2000.

C. TRUTH-IN-SENTENCING LAWS

During the 1980s through the 1990s, most states adopted "truth-in-sentencing" laws. These laws require that an individual serve 85% of the maximum number of years specified in the person's sentence; thus, individuals with a 15- to 25-year sentence would be required to serve 21 years and 3 months before being eligible for parole. Historically, judges set a sentencing range longer than was necessary for the crime committed, in case the inmate was a disciplinary problem in prison or gave other evidence that he or she would pose a serious threat if released. Truth-in-sentencing laws require an individual to serve close to the upper limit of her or his sentence, regardless of the person's behavior. Mandatory sentences, such as those for certain drug offenses, removed authority from judges to set sentences based on the facts of a case and led to proportionately longer sentences across cases. Truth-in-sentencing laws increased the length of time individuals spend in prison, increasing both the numbers of persons imprisoned on a given date and the number serving time in maximum security prisons due to the length of the sentence.

As part of the 1994 Crime Act, the federal government established incentive grants, making states that adopted the 85% truth-in-sentencing standard eligible for increased federal money to construct and renovate prisons. As a result of these incentives, prison release rates decreased sharply. By 1999, 14 states had abolished parole board releases for all offenders, regardless of individual case differences or progress while incarcerated; 75% of persons affected by truth-in-sentencing laws in the 1990s were nonviolent offenders.

D. SUMMARY

As a result of mandatory prison sentences for drug offenses, three-strikes legislation, and truth-in-sentencing laws, thousands of persons have been sent to prison since 1990 on sentences lasting 50 or more years. There was a 46% increase in the number of persons serving natural life (no possibility of parole before death, regardless of the number of years served) just between 1990 and 1994. The number of persons serving a mandatory 20 years or more increased form 96,921 in 1990 to 141,026 in 1994—nearly a 50% increase. By 1998, nearly one-quarter of persons incarcerated in all state correctional facilities were serving mandatory sentences of 20 years or more. For the nation, these shifts in policy mean that more prisons must be built to house prisoners with longer sentences.

III. *Costs of Incarceration Policies to Taxpayers and the Nation*

Incarceration as a solution of choice is a costly alternative, both for individual taxpayers and on a state and federal level. Estimates for the cost of building one prison cell range from $52,000 to $94,000 for a maximum security facility. Yet the current growth in the U.S. prison population would require building a 1000-bed prison every 6 days. Annual costs to taxpayers to house and feed every new inmate equal $20,000 or more per inmate. Yet the United States imprisons 1500 new inmates every week. In 1998, taxpayers spent $24 billion to incarcerate nonviolent offenders.

The social choice of imprisonment is costly in human terms as well. Although studies show that the use of illegal drugs is highest among Whites, incarceration as a penalty falls primarily on people of color. By the mid-1990s, one in every three Black men between the ages of 20 and 29 were under some form of criminal justice control. The long prison sentences in the United States combined with discrimination in arrests and application of penalties, also disproportionately affect thousands of children of color, as family members are removed—sometimes for most of their childhoods—and households and communities are fragmented.

Young women and men of all races spend critical adult years in prison, removed from the larger society, their children raised by relatives, foster parents, or the state. These children are at much higher risk for involvement with the criminal justice system and later imprisonment than are the children of parents provided with other alternatives, thus perpetuating the cycle. In addition, it is not only the children of imprisoned parents who are penalized. In an increasing number of states, funds are being reallocated to meet increased demand for prisons, and expenditures for incarceration now surpass expenditures for higher education. In the 1990s, the New York State prison budget grew by $761 million, while the budget for higher education dropped by $615 million. From 1984 and 1994, California built 21 prisons and one state university. Spending on the prison system increased 209%, while spending on higher education increased 15%. During those years, the higher education workforce was reduced by 8100 people, while the number of correction employees increased by 169%. Florida's corrections department budget increased $450 million in just two years (1992–1994) as the impact of new legislation was felt, with corresponding changes in expenditures on education.

Changes in public expenditures are easiest to track on the national level. The total budget to operate the criminal justice system in the United States in 1988 was $61 billion. By 1992, that figure had increased to $94 billion. In a nation struggling over teacher shortages and whether it can afford Social Security and health care for the aged, national expenditures for prison-related costs are now estimated at $41 billion per year.

IV. Who Are the People in Prison Today?

The rapidly growing segments of people imprisoned in the United States today include minorities, teenagers, the elderly, and women.

A. THE "AVERAGE" PRISONER

Most people imprisoned in the United States are young, under the age of 35, with the largest group between the ages of 18 and 24. They are mostly male and approximately 54% are African American. Of the men, over half—62%—lack a formal education; most do not have a high school degree. Many come from single-parent homes or from homes where they experienced physical assaults or neglect. About 20% of incarcerated men are married, and most (55%)

have children under the age of 18. Many of these men were unemployed at the time of their arrest, and more than half had annual incomes of less than $10,000 during the year before their arrest. More than 50% used drugs regularly before their arrest for this incarceration.

Of all persons in both state and federal prison, 67% are there on new charges, 16% are there for technical parole violations (such as failure to report to their parole officer), and 13% are there because their parole was revoked when they were convicted of a new charge. Many of today's prisoners are serving time for nonviolent offenses. A study by John Irwin and James Austin published in 1997 found that over half of their sample committed petty crimes (i.e., their crimes did not result in injury to a person or they obtained only small amounts of money), yet mandated sentencing policies instituted in the 1970s and 1980s often require a prison term. The most frequent crime resulting in a prison sentence is drug possession (22%), followed by burglary (20%), theft and fraud (20%), and drug delivery (15%). Almost half of all federal arrests are for drug or immigration offenses. In 1998 for the first time, 1 million nonviolent offenders were held in U.S. prisons and jails.

B. INCARCERATION OF AFRICAN AMERICANS IN THE UNITED STATES

As noted earlier, although offenses such as the use of illegal drugs are as common among Whites as Blacks, imprisonment as a penalty is used much more frequently with people of color. By the year 2000, African American men were sent to prison on drug charges at 13 times the rate of White men. In 1997, the rate of incarceration among Black males in their late 20s reached 8630 prisoners per 100,000 residents compared to 2703 among Hispanic males and 868 among White males. By the end of 1999, there were 3408 sentenced Black male inmates per 100,000 Black males in the United States, compared to 1335 sentenced Hispanic male inmates per 100,000 Hispanic males and 417 White male inmates per 100,000 White males. Currently there are more African Americans in prison than enrolled in higher education. If this trend persists, by 2020, two out of every three African American men between the ages of 18 and 34 will be imprisoned.

Drug laws since the 1980s are the major contributor to the high rate of minorities in prison. For example, in 1992, 91% of people sentenced under federal drug laws were Black. Currently, possession of

500 grams of powdered cocaine carries the same sentence as 5 grams of crack cocaine. Since crack is a much cheaper version of powdered cocaine, severe sentences for its possession compared to powdered cocaine result in people in poor urban areas being at risk for imprisonment if caught with even small amounts of the drug. Possession of the same amounts of powdered cocaine is almost never prosecuted. In 1995, the U.S. Sentencing Commission recommended altering this sentence disparity between crack and powdered cocaine, but Congress rejected their recommendation.

C. ADOLESCENTS IN ADULT PRISONS

Justice Department data reveal that the number of people under age 18 sentenced to adult prisons more than doubled between 1985 and 1997. All 50 states now have laws allowing juvenile offenders to be tried as adults. In the 10 years between 1988 and 1997, the number of teenagers sent to adult court for drug offenses increased 78%; the number sent to adult court for offenses against a person increased 74%. Most adolescents transferred to adult court are children of color. A study of Los Angeles County in 1996 found that teenagers of Hispanic, African American, and Asian/other ethnic backgrounds accounted for 95% of the cases in which youths were transferred to adult court, although illegal drug use, property crimes, and assaults against persons were committed by White teenagers as well.

Most adolescents sent to adult prisons are male (92%). One-quarter (26%) are very young—between the ages of 13 and 16. Due to the danger of repeated and multiple-perpetrator rapes for male teenagers in adult prisons and other risks faced by children under the age of 18, many teens are seriously damaged and some are killed in adult prisons. Yet many were sent to adult facilities for nonviolent offenses. Among teenagers sentenced to adult prisons in 1997, over one-fifth (22%) were convicted of property crimes, 11% of drug offenses, and 5% of public order offenses, which include weapons offenses, nonviolent sex offenses, liquor law violations, disorderly conduct, and obstruction of justice. Only 7% of adolescents, sent to adult prison committed murder; only 4% committed sexual assault. The majority of adolescents in adult prison for crimes against persons (committed either by themselves or a companion) were convicted of robbery (32% of all teens in prisons); 14% were convicted of aggravated assault.

The sharp increase in sentencing teens to adult prisons in the United States occurred during a period of decreasing severity in crimes by children entering adolescence. For example, in 1998, juveniles made up only 15% of California's felony arrests, down from 30% in 1978. Between 1993 and 1998, the national rate of serious, violent crime by juveniles declined 55%. Although most news coverage of teenage crime focuses on violence, fewer than one-half of 1% of teenagers in the United States were arrested for a violent crime in 1998–1999. Their representation as perpetrators of the most serious violent crimes is also low: contrary to public perceptions, juveniles are responsible only for about 9% of the homicides in the United States each year.

D. THE AGING PRISON POPULATION

Longer sentences and the reluctance of parole boards to release prisoners has resulted in the elderly inmate population now doubling in size every four years. According to Alida Merlo and Peter Benekos, in 1998 there were nearly 84,000 persons age 50 and older in state and federal prisons in the United States. The average annual cost of incarcerating a person over the age of 60 is $69,000—almost four times the average cost to incarcerate a younger person. Elderly people in prison have special needs such as increased health care, specially designed prisons and cells to accommodate physical disabilities, intensive supervision for those with dementia, and hospice care. As thousands more people are given life sentences under new sentencing guidelines, future implications of these needs and their costs will expand rapidly. Ironically, elderly inmates are the least likely to continue to commit crimes if released into the population.

E. WOMEN IN PRISON

The most dramatic increase in the changing rates of incarceration is in the incarceration of women—their numbers have almost quadrupled in the past 15 years. As of June 1997, there were 138,000 women in U.S. prisons and jails. Despite this rapid increase in the imprisonment of women, crimes of violence by women have remained relatively constant. The increase in imprisonment is due primarily to increased use of prison for drug offenses. Only about one-quarter of incarcerated women are imprisoned for violent felonies; for over 50%, their worst offense was drug related.

The average woman prisoner is similar to the average male prisoner in demographics. The majority of women in state correctional facilities are Black (48%), White non-Hispanic (33%), or Hispanic (15%). Fifty percent are between the ages of 25 and 34; 78% have children. More than half were unemployed at the time of arrest; those who were employed had annual incomes of less than $15,000 at the time of their arrest. The majority of women involved in the criminal justice system are at least high school graduates. According to 1999 statistics from the Bureau of Justice, among females in state prisons, 37% have some high school, 39% have a high school diploma or GED, and 17% have some college or more.

Imprisoned women are less likely than imprisoned men to have been sentenced in the past, and those with prior records are more likely than men to have a nonviolent offense. Approximately 55% of women in prison are serving their first prison sentence. Although drug users are less likely to be imprisoned for violent offenses than non-drug users, women incarcerated for drug convictions are still likely to be placed in maximum-security facilities, due to long sentences.

V. Early Trauma Histories: Pathways to Prison for Women?

Rather than being faceless offenders, imprisoned women and men are whole persons, with past histories and choices and past traumas about which they had little choice. Family and intimate violence is often at the core of their life stories and may be a key component leading to present circumstances.

A study by Angela Browne and Brenda Miller in the mid-1990s, at New York State's Maximum Security Prison for women found that the majority of incarcerated women in this setting had suffered severe violence, sexual attack, or sexual molestation prior to their incarceration. Women in the study were an average age of 32; about half were African American, one-quarter were Hispanic, and 13% were White non-Hispanic. Over two-thirds (70%) had been severely assaulted by at least one caretaker during childhood, over half (59%) had been sexually molested before reaching adulthood, and nearly three-quarters (73%) had been physically assaulted by an intimate partner. Three-quarters had been the victim of physical or sexual attacks by nonintimates as well. When all forms of violence were combined, only 6% of these women had *not* experienced physical or sexual assault over their lifetime. Other studies have similar findings.

Lifetime prevalence rates of severe violence found among these imprisoned women far exceed those for *all* acts of physical abuse among women in the general female population of 40% for physical abuse by parental caretakers and 22% for violence by adult partners, as Pat Tjaden and Nancy Thoennes found in a nationally representative study in 1996. Similarly, the 59% lifetime prevalence rate of child sexual molestation stands in stark contrast to the 20 to 27% prevalence rates obtained in community-based samples of women. The majority of imprisoned women had only experienced brief, if any, periods of safety prior to incarceration. Eighty-two percent had been victimized in childhood.

For researchers from the field of family violence, parallels between the long-term effects of violence by intimates and predominant reasons for women's incarceration in the United States are striking. For example, research indicates that female victims of child sexual molestation or of severe physical child abuse by parental figures are at significantly higher risk for alcohol and drug abuse as teenagers and adults than women who have not had these experiences. This is true even when other high-risk factors—such as the presence of alcoholic parents in the home—are taken into account. Girls from physically or sexually abusive homes also are more at risk of separation from their families before adulthood, due to out-of-home placements or running away, and then become at increased risk of involvement in drug- or prostitution-related activities.

Another consistently found aftereffect of child sexual molestation is a marked vulnerability in some survivors to revictimization or involvement with abusive intimates. Drug use also increases the likelihood of relationships with intimates who are violent—both toward the women and others—and who are involved in a variety of other criminal activities. Increased exposure to violent intimates increases the risk of defensive or violent acts by women in protection of themselves or a child, as well as the likelihood that women will be present or will otherwise have "certain knowledge" when a crime is committed by an intimate and will therefore be charged with and convicted of that crime. Thus, some of the long-term effects of victimization by family members may play important roles in the events for which women are locked up. [*See* TRAUMA ACROSS DIVERSE SETTINGS.]

VI. *International Use of Incarceration*

The United States is unique in its use of imprisonment as a solution for social ills. Since 1980, the United States has consistently been a world leader in incarceration. In 1992, Russia surpassed the United States, but the U.S. rate now approaches Russia's and surpasses all other comparable nations. By the year 2000, the state of California held more inmates in its jails and prisons than did France, Great Britain, Germany, Japan, Singapore, and the Netherlands combined.

What causes the United States—with its emphasis on personal freedom—to imprison its citizens at such a high rate? One explanation offered is that the United States has an unusually high rate of crime and thus is forced to incarcerate an unusually large number of its citizens. Another explanation is that criminal justice policies such as those related to drugs and sentencing in the United States are unusually punitive when compared to other nations.

A. INTERNATIONAL CRIMES RATES AND THE USE OF INCARCERATION

Studies of international crime rates do find that there are more assaults and murders committed with firearms in the United States than in any comparable country. Yet the overall U.S. crime rate is not significantly different from other comparable countries. This is especially true for offenses such as larceny, drug possession, and robbery—the offenses for which the majority of prisoners in the United States are incarcerated. What is different in the United States is a propensity to incarcerate nonviolent and drug-involved individuals and to keep them in prison for a much longer time.

B. DRUG USE AND INCARCERATION

The United States is one of the only countries in the world that tries to use incarceration to solve its drug problem. The United States makes more arrests for drug-related crimes and places more drug offenders in prison than any other industrialized nation. An international study conducted by the Ministry of Justice in the Netherlands in 1995–1996 found that the United States made 539 arrests for drug offenses per 100,000 citizens; Germany made 229 per 100,000; England made 162 per 100,000; and the Netherlands made 43. In 1990, British drug offenders were half as likely to go to jail or prison as Americans.

They also stayed in prison for shorter periods. Criminologist James Lynch noted that the proportion of U.S. drug offenders sentenced to more than 10 years in prison is more than triple that of England and Wales. In the early 1980s, Canada declared its own war on drugs, following the lead of President Reagan in the United States. However, drug offenders in Canada are not subjected to the same sentencing guidelines as in the United States. For example, the maximum sentence for possession of cocaine in Canada is seven years. In the United States, the same offender could be sentenced to life.

Has the war on drugs succeeded in reducing drug use in the United States? Despite the high rate of arrests and long sentences for drug offenders in the United States, the number of hard drug users in the United States does not differ from that in nations which much lower rates of incarceration such as Sweden, Germany, and the Netherlands. A recent study by the American Bar Association found that the increased incarceration of drug offenders in the United States also has not decreased domestic drug use over time.

C. SENTENCING POLICIES AND INCARCERATION

With the adoption of mandatory sentencing laws, more U.S. citizens charged with offenses are sent to prison than in other countries. Other nations leave their judges broader discretion in sentencing and, instead of legislation that mandates imprisonment, encourage the use of alternative disciplinary practices such as restitution and community release. For example, in 1996, Canada passed Bill-C41 into law. This law created a community-based alternative to prison called a "conditional sentence." Conditional sentences allow judges to give an individual who otherwise would have been placed in prison a conditional term of imprisonment; the person serves the sentence in the community under supervision. This legislation is partially responsible for a decrease in the number of people behind bars in Canada for the first time in over a decade. Canada's crime rate has steadily decreased, along with the decrease in incarceration. European countries also rely on noncustodial punishment as more humane, cost-effective, and successful. Countries such as Austria, Germany, Portugal, the United Kingdom, and France use monetary fines, conditional sentences, and community service in lieu of prison terms for many offenses.

Mandatory sentencing in the United States not only places more people in prison, it keeps them there longer than in other nations. To date only a few studies have compared the differences in sentencing lengths internationally. One of these studies, conducted by Frase in 1990, examined sentencing practices in the United States and France and concluded that the length of U.S. prison sentences was nearly twice as high as in France. In another inquiry, researchers Young and Brown found that sentence length was a critical variable in determining incarceration rates. They concluded that shorter sentences explained many differences in incarceration rates between the United States and other democratic nations.

VII. U.S. Prisons Today

A. PRISON CONDITIONS

As a result of the growing number of people incarcerated, coupled with the 1980s and 1990s get-tough attitude toward crime, conditions within U.S. prisons are deteriorating. U.S. correctional facilities today are overcrowded and understaffed, often making them dangerous and unhealthy environments. A Justice Department investigation in the first half of the 1990s documented a list of hazardous conditions: in some facilities, toilets and pumping systems were overflowing, kitchen facilities were unsafe and unsanitary, and heating systems were inadequate. Medical care was grossly inadequate and there were few suicide prevention measures. With the rapid growth in the number of persons sent to prison, some incarcerated persons are forced to sleep on the floor without mattresses in unventilated cells, or multiple persons are confined to cells built for one. Overcrowded conditions aggravate violence between inmates and between correctional officers and prisoners as well. For example, in 1997, 69 incarcerated persons were killed by other inmates and thousands were seriously injured.

In addition to dilapidated physical plants and compromised living conditions, many states have made sharp cuts in prison-based education, substance abuse treatment, and other programming. In 1994, Congress passed legislation ending all provision of federal funds for prisoners participating in higher education. Activities, job training, and opportunities for rehabilitation are fewer in today's correctional facilities than in the past. Classrooms, gymnasiums, and program spaces have been converted into dormitories to house incoming inmates.

A unique dimension of the U.S. prison system,

compared to other nations, is its new reliance on "supermax" prisons. By the end of 1997, 36 states and the federal government operated 57 supermax facilities, and many more were under construction. In supermax prisons, prisoners are kept in individual windowless cells for 22 to 23 hours per day. Typically they are allowed out only to shower and to visit the exercise yard for 60 to 90 minutes in a 24-hour period. These activities usually are done alone. Food is passed in to them; they are not allowed contact with other prisoners, and direct contact with prison staff is limited. As much as possible, operations are run by remote control from a central command station on each unit. With the nation's current trend toward extended or life sentences, individuals may spend years living in this sort of solitary confinement. Prisoners in supermax units do not receive work, vocational, educational, substance abuse, or other rehabilitative programming. In 1995, the United Nations declared conditions in some United States maximum security prisons "incompatible" with international standards of human rights, contending they did not meet United Nations Standard Minimum Rules for the Treatment of Prisoners and the Code of Conduct for Law Enforcement Officials.

The punitive and overcrowded environment in U.S. prisons also complicates effective adjustment to communities outside prison once incarcerated persons are released. Empirical studies over the past 20 years document the positive effects of rehabilitative programming—particularly education, job readiness training, and family violence programs—on reducing recidivism. Today's prisoners often are released without skills to find and keep gainful employment. Many leave prison psychologically impaired after years of exposure to isolation. With the abolition of parole in several states, prisoners may be sent back to the general population without preparation or a period of transition. Normal activities of daily life contrast sharply with the prison environments they inhabited for years.

To focus so exclusively on punishment that education and interventions are reduced or eliminated may be harmful, not only for those individuals and their families but also for the nation as a whole. For example, for imprisoned women and potentially for imprisoned men, time spent in prison is an opportunity for direct interventions with individuals with trauma histories that could alleviate some of their suffering while imprisoned and markedly improve their potential for success when they return to the community. Issues of recidivism come into play here as well: if left unaddressed, lack of education, substance abuse, and post-trauma effects—often part of the pathway leading *to* incarceration—would be expected to markedly worsen the prognosis for success outside correctional settings upon release.

A study completed by the New York State Department of Correctional Services (DOCS) Division of Program Planning, Research, and Evaluation found strongly positive effects on recidivism for women in maximum security prison of a program for survivors of family violence. This program was comprehensive, with educational activities, support groups, and individual counseling. The DOCS study followed up all women who had participated in the family violence program from 1988 to 1994 for the first 21 months after their release from prison. Women who had participated in the program for 6 to 12 months had less than half the recidivism rate as women released during the same period who did not participate in the program (10% versus 24%) even when type of crime, prior crime history, age, and ethnicity were taken into account. These findings illustrate the potential benefit for individuals and society of targeted interventions in prisons that deal directly with histories of past trauma.

For both women and men, alternatives to incarceration, when offenses permit, seem to be the most effective deterrent of all. A study by the Rand Corporation comparing persons who were sentenced to jail or prison with persons who received parole and community sanctions for similar crimes found that those under sanction in the community were less likely to offend again than those sentenced to prison or jail.

B. PRISONERS' RIGHTS

Until the 1960s, U.S. citizens who were sent to prison lost their civil rights as defined by the U.S. Constitution. In the 1960s, fueled by the civil rights movement, several cases were brought before the courts that granted selected rights to prisoners. These rights fall under the First, Fourth, Eighth, and Fourteenth Amendments and include freedom of speech, religion, and access to reading material; protection from seizure of legal or religious property; and access to the due process of law. The Constitution also protects incarcerated citizens from cruel and unusual punishment and from discrimination on the basis of sex, race, religion, or other characteristics.

One of the rights lost to many citizens who become incarcerated is the right to vote in state and national elections. In 46 states as well as the District of Columbia, all convicted persons are denied the right to vote while in prison, regardless of the seriousness of the crime. The majority of states (32) forbid persons who are on parole to vote, and 29 states forbid those on probation from voting. In 14 states, people convicted of a crime are barred from voting for life. Voting rights may be rescinded for minor offenses even if the individual is not required to serve a prison term. Passing a bad check, shoplifting, and marijuana possession are a few of the crimes that can permanently cost an individual the right to vote. Many people who plead guilty to minor offenses in exchange for a nonprison sentence, or—even if not guilty—accept a plea for fear they will be convicted at trial, do not realize that they have lost the right to vote.

Although a few other countries remove voting rights for some serious crimes, the United States is the only democratic country in the world with such a high percentage of its citizens absent from the democratic process due to this policy. By the year 2000, nearly 3.9 million citizens in the United States were not eligible to vote because of past convictions; a million of these persons had already completed their sentences. Because of the uneven application of criminal justice penalties to people of color, by 1999, African Americans represented one-third of the persons forbidden to vote. In two states, nearly one in every three Black men had lost voting rights. In eight additional states, one in four Black men could not vote. With prison populations increasing each year, researchers estimate that the number of African Americans forbidden to vote could approach 40% in states where voting rights are permanently lost for ex-offenders.

C. OVERCROWDING AND PRIVATE PRISONS

Since the 1980s, states have been rushing to construct new prisons to house the burgeoning prison population. However, they have been unable to keep pace with the rapid growth. By the year 2000, facilities holding 2500 inmates or more had increased 108% over 1990; those holding 1000 to 2500 inmates increased 65%. Despite increased construction, by 1998, over half of all states (33) were operating 100% or more over their capacity. California was the most extreme example; by 1998, California's prison system was operating at twice its capacity.

This inability to build for and house the people being incarcerated forced some jurisdictions to send their prisoners to other states, far from families and local resources, or to privately owned prisons—often also in other states. Increasingly, state governments turned to the private sector to reduce the exorbitant costs of building new prisons and caring for additional inmates. Beginning in the 1980s, the number of prisoners held in for-profit privately owned prisons gradually increased. By 1997, 6% of the nation's prison population was in private facilities. While this percentage was small, it represented nearly a 300% increase in less than five years.

The use of private prisons was intended to decrease prison costs to states and taxpayers and relieve overcrowded public facilities. However, the business orientation of for-profit corporations may significantly influence corrections and the way prisoners are treated in the future. Leading prison corporations during the 1990s were listed on the New York Stock Exchange, with attendant priorities. Due to private corporations' responsibility to shareholders, decisions in private prisons are made with the generation of profit in mind. In these situations, concerns for the welfare of incarcerated persons are balanced against dividends for shareholders and employee compensation and retention. In the 1990s, private prisons emphasized the use of technology, rather than staff, to maintain security while cutting costs. The goal of cost control was reflected in a preference for the use of isolation (keeping an individual locked up in solitary confinement 23 out of 24 hours), formerly used only for inmates who were serious behavior problems or who needed protection from other inmates. This move toward solitary confinement was paired with decreases in willingness to expend resources for rehabilitation, treatment, or training.

American private prison companies consider the business of incarcerating persons a stable, long-term, high-potential investment. Corrections Corporation of American (CCA) grew by 30% in 1997 alone. As of September 2000, both CCA and Wackenhut's stocks yielded more than 50 times 1999 earnings. In 2000, a Paine Webber research analyst noted that private prison corporations listed on the New York Stock Exchange were "powerful performers and have huge potential, even compared to high-tech stocks." The swelling prison population in the United States and the acceptance of this growth by the public has encouraged their expansion. So far, most private companies operating prisons are confined to the United States. However, by the beginning of the 1990s, private prisons had begun exporting their efforts to other countries, gradually altering the landscape of international incarceration. The first private prison opened in Australia in 1990. By the year 2000, Australia had three private facilities housing 8% of its prison population. All were partially controlled by U.S. prison corporations. U.S. companies were involved in the initial emergence of private prisons in both England (beginning in 1992) and Wales (beginning in 1993). Other countries such as Belgium, the Netherlands, and France have yet to become involved in the privatization of their prison systems, but lobbyists from the private prison sector continue to press for increased involvement in these nations as well.

The incarceration of persons for profit carries with it many policy as well as human rights risks. As with other for-profit corporations, for-profit prisons employ lobbyists and public relations staff to press for legislation and policies favorable to their business and to shape public perceptions of their practices. In the United States, fear of crime is widespread and public misperceptions dominate. Research shows that most citizens believe that juveniles are responsible for a large proportion of all violent crimes, that most persons in prison are there for serious offenses, and that a middle-class persons' risk of being victimized is many times higher than is actually the case. The efforts of private prisons to increase their population base may add to these public misconceptions and the perception of incarceration as the only appropriate response.

VIII. Has Increased Incarceration Decreased Rates of Crime?

Heightened fear of crime in the United States causes many people to see the criminal justice system as the only answer. They conclude that if more criminals are put in prison, there will be less crime. This sounds reasonable, but is it actually the case? Both historical data and current statistics reveal that there is no relationship between crime rates and rates of incarceration. For example, from 1980 to 1985, the U.S. prison population increased 65%, while crime *decreased* 16%. Conversely, from 1986 to 1991, the U.S. prison population increased 51%, while crime *increased* 15%.

Examining crime and imprisonment rates in individual states also fails to yield a clear relationship between increases in incarceration and decreases in crime over time. From 1980 to 1991, 11 of the 17 states with the lowest increase in their prison populations experienced marked decreases in crime, while only 7 of the 13 states that dramatically increased their prison populations experienced decreases in crime. By 1999, Louisiana had the highest rate of incarceration in the United States, placing 776 per 100,000 of its residents behind bars, yet Louisiana's crime rate remains one of the highest in the country.

In California in the 20 years between 1974 and 1995, crime rates actually increased at the same time as the numbers of persons incarcerated increased. In contrast, New York—a state that also has high-density multicultural urban areas, experienced a rapid drop in crime, in concert with slow growth in the prison population. From 1992 to 1997, New York's crime rate dropped 38.6% and its murder rate dropped 54.5%, yet its incarceration rate was one of the slowest in the country, despite an increasing likelihood of conviction if charged. Only two states experienced a slower percentage growth in their prison populations during this time: Maryland and Maine. There are several factors besides increased imprisonment that may explain the decrease of crime in the United States. The booming economy, the aging of the "baby boomer" generation, and a decline in the popularity of crack are more likely explanations.

IX. *Summary*

The United States is unique among democratic and advanced nations in its use of incarceration for social ills. By mid-1999, 1 in every 147 U.S. citizens was incarcerated. The United States now has an imprisonment rate 6 to 10 times the rate of countries in the European Union and is the only democratic industrialized country to continue using the death penalty. The increased use of imprisonment and long sentence lengths in the United States falls most heavily on people of color and has significant effects on family and community well-being. It has also increased the tax burden on citizens and has led to the reallocation of monies formerly dedicated to other social efforts. By 1994, the District of Columbia had more inmates in prisons than students in universities or publicly funded colleges. Yet studies show no consistent relationship between *increases* in incarceration at the state or country level and *decreases* in crime over time. Commenting on trends in imprisonment in the United States since 1980, Alfred Blumstein and Allen Beck ask, if it is policies and not crime rates guiding the imprisonment of U.S. citizens, what will stabilize or reverse this rapid growth in incarceration?

SUGGESTED READING

Browne, A., Miller, B., and Maguin, E. (1999). Prevalence and severity of lifetime physical and sexual victimization among incarcerated women. *International Journal of Law and Psychiatry* **22**, 301–322.

Bureau of Justice Statistics. (2000). *The Sourcebook of Criminal Justice Statistics, 1999.* U.S. Department of Justice, Bureau of Justice Statistics, Washington, DC, www.ojp.usdoj.gov

Chesney-Lind, M. (1997). *The Female Offender: Girls, Women, and Crime.* Sage, Thousand Oaks, CA.

Mauer, M. (1997). *American Behind Bars: U.S. and International Use of Incarceration, 1995.* Sentencing Project, Washington, DC.

Rafter, N. (1990). *Partial Justice: Women, Prison, and Social Control.* Transaction Publishers, New Brunswick.

Tonry, M., and Petersilia, J. (1999). *Prisons.* The University of Chicago Press, Chicago.

Individualism and Collectivism

M. Brinton Lykes

University of the Witwatersrand, South Africa, and Boston College

Dongxiao Qin

Western New England College

Glossary

Being-in-webs of relationships A Confucian notion of the self as embedded in a web of social relations.

Self-in-relation A sense of self as organized around being able to attain and maintain affiliation and relationships, traditionally associated with women.

Social individuality An understanding of the self as an ensemble of social relations developed within a context characterized by unequal power relations.

INDIVIDUALISM refers to a philosophical tradition characteristic of Western liberalism wherein individuals are construed as autonomous, separate, and self-contained entities, clearly distinguishable and independent from their social groups and social contexts. The individual is assumed to be self-sufficient and to utilize rational principles in decision making and social interactions, including, among others, noninterference and equity. Social ties are presumed to be loose and self-determination is a core value. Collectivism refers to an alternative tradition more characteristic of Eastern or Asian societies wherein the common good and social harmony are core values that inform daily reality and decision making. Persons are construed as relational and other oriented, socially indistinguishable from the various in-group relationships to which they belong. From birth onward, a strong, cohesive in-group is the point of reference requiring in-group loyalty and providing social protection. Given the worldwide influence of psychology today and the centrality of self to 21st century psychological theory and practice, this article examines individualism and collectivism as they inform and are informed by psychological self-theories. Further, we discuss selected psychological, cultural, and feminist theories that inform and critique dominant and dichotomous contemporary understandings of the self.

I. Introduction

The concepts of individualism and collectivism are frequently described as opposite poles of a single dimension along which cultures and societies are believed to vary. Cross-cultural researchers have used the terms to describe the relationships between individuals and the social groups to which they belong.

Societies described as individualistic emphasize "I" consciousness, autonomy, emotional independence, individual initiative, right to privacy, pleasure seeking, financial security, the need for specific friendships, and universalism. Societies characterized as collectivist, on the other hand, stress "we" consciousness, collective identity, dependence, group solidarity, the sharing of duties and obligations, the need for stable and predetermined friendships, group decision making, and particularism. An extensive body of literature has developed exploring the implications of these hypothesized differences for social relations and for construals of the self within and across cultures. Harry Triandis, for example, has argued that individualistic cultures have members whose sense of self are self-contained and include more private elements, whereas collectivist cultural representations of the self are more likely to construe the self as sociocentric and relational, including more social or group-based elements. Similarly, Hazel Markus and Shinobu Kitayama have contrasted independent, "Western"/U.S. and interdependent "Eastern" construals of self.

Such global or cross-cultural comparisons have, not surprisingly, provoked debate about within-culture variability. Feminist psychologists, for example, have questioned the adequacy of dichotomous self-theories, suggesting that the Western construal of the self is gendered toward a male perspective, not universal. In this article we summarize the philosophical roots of this hypothesized cultural dichotomy and situate psychological theories of the self therein. Feminist, critical, and cultural perspectives and the challenges they pose for moving beyond dichotomous thinking about individualism and collectivism are critically reviewed. We conclude by exploring more recent efforts to transcend intra-, inter-, and trans-cultural dichotomies.

II. Theorizing the Self and Society

To understand the relationship of culture and self, we trace the philosophical grounding of individualism and collectivism within particular cultures. Uichol Kim, Harry C. Triandis, Cigdem Kagitcibasi, Sang-Chin Choi, and Gene Yoon have argued that liberalism serves as a philosophical foundation for individualism in the West, whereas Confucianism serves as a philosophical foundation for collectivism in East Asian cultures.

Within liberalism, individuals are conceptualized as discrete, autonomous, self-sufficient beings, respectful of the rights of others. Social policies and practices are developed within this framework to regulate behaviors of abstract, universal entities. As a result, in cultures characterized as individualistic, each person is encouraged to be autonomous, self-directing, unique, and assertive and to value privacy and freedom of choice. This philosophical tradition informs self-theories that have been developed by Western (i.e., European and North American) psychologists. The latter have hypothesized a universal, "true" self that transcends specific historical and cultural contexts. The view of the self emergent in the West is consonant with the liberal philosophical tradition and suggests a dialectic between psychological theories and philosophical processes and traditions.

Edward Sampson observed that the boundary of the individual coincides with the boundary of the body, characterizing the Western notion of self as a "self-contained entity." The self-as-individual is thus construed as a private, self-contained, whole and unique entity that exhibits a firm self-other boundary and is self-celebratory. Clifford Geertz argued that the self in Western psychology refers to a bounded, unique, more or less integrated motivational and cognitive universe including awareness, emotion, judgment, and action. Although the self-contained individual is responsive to the social environment and social situations more generally, this responsiveness to social factors derives from the need to verify and affirm the inner core of the self, that is, the unique configuration of internal attributes that constitute the individual. The self is thus construed as a separate entity whose essence can be meaningfully abstracted from his or her various relationships and in-group memberships. The organized whole is set over against other such wholes, a social reality, and a natural background.

In contrast to individualism, collectivism has its roots in an ascribed, communal, and traditional social order. In some East Asian societies, for example, Confucianism is the moral and philosophical basis for a collectivist social order. Collectivist societies that support the basic tenets of Confucianism (e.g., China, Japan, and Korea) prioritize the common good and social harmony over individual interests. Individuals are construed within webs of relationships, socially embedded and situated in particular roles with particular statuses. These connected relationships emphasize the group's common fate. Individuals are encouraged to put others' and the group's interests before their own. At a societal level, duties and obligations are prescribed by roles, and individuals "lose face" if they fail to fulfill these duties and obligations. As a result, interdependence, nurturance, and compliance are important values within these East Asian cultures and societies wherein people experience their fate as interlinked.

The philosophical tradition of collectivism informs self-theories developed by psychologists in such East Asian cultures. For example, the self in these societies or within cultural groups informed by Confucian philosophy is construed as a public-spirited, open system. To involve the other in one's self-construction is not altruistic, it is rather required for one's own self-development. As Wei-Ming Tu argued, self in the classic Confucian sense refers to a center of relationships, a communal quality that is never conceived in isolation. The development of self within Confucian cultures is always within a context of social relations. Thus, the self as "an ultimately autonomous being" is unthinkable. In the Confucian tradition, the more individualistic and narcissistic one is, the less one is a "self." Similarly, self-theories generated to characterize persons in many African, Latin American, and Native American cultures are akin to those within East Asian cultures. Others are intrinsic to one's sense of self.

III. Feminist Commentaries

Developmental theory within Euro-North American psychology describes the self as evolving, through a process of increasing separation, moving toward autonomy and personal independence. Self-theories that are rooted in such understandings emphasize "a separate self," a self-sufficient and self-contained entity. Clifford Geertz's indictment of the universality of such a construal of self and his suggestion that it is "peculiar" constitutes a broader critique of the construct: it is no more more—or less—than the construal of self of a relatively small number of humans, usually White[1] middle- to upper-class men, who are the dominant groups within many Western societies.

[1]Drawing on previous documentation of the political history of the terms "white" and "Black," Lykes and Alice McIntyre have argued elsewhere that although the terms have been defined oppositionally, they are not functional opposites. Black has been subordinated by white and is part of a counterhegemonic practice challenging that subordination. The authors of this article support the differential use of uppercase and lowercase as reflected in this note. The article's use of upper case for both Black and White conforms to an editorial decision.

Feminist theorists echoed Geertz's critique in their challenges of the individualistic bias in traditional psychological theories that they term "masculinist." They have argued that development theorists to date have used male development as the norm and that such theories misunderstand and neglect important dimensions of women's self-development. Jean Baker Miller's path-breaking book, *Toward a New Psychology of Women*, foregrounded for the first time women's senses of self and other. Taking women's subordinate status as a starting point, she developed a "new" psychology of women in which she emphasized gendered power relations and women's relationality. The power to make full development possible was situated relationally, that is, as the power of/for interdependence. Development proceeds through relationship toward a capacity for reciprocal relations. Mutuality is a basic goal of development and aspects of self (e.g., creativity, autonomy, assertion) develop within a primary context of relationality. Women's authentic sense of self-in-relation is therefore incompatible with men's autonomous self, developed within dominant and dominating power in a patriarchal society.

Echoing these concerns, Nancy Chodorow integrated psychoanalytic and object relational theories to analyze the sources of these differences, arguing that "mothering" is a core experience that prepares girls and boys for their respective roles in society. Girls learn to relate to the world as mothers and family members and mothering reproduces itself. Boys—typically mothered by women—become men who devalue women and orient themselves to the external world. Women's greater relationality is due to women's greater responsibility for early child care and their being nurtured by a same-sex caretaker.

Drawing on Chodorow's analysis of mothering as a woman's universal experience in the world, Carol Gilligan suggested that women's sense of self is best characterized by an emphasis on caring. Contrary to traditional theories of moral reasoning and development, Gilligan argued that women reason in a different but no less mature way than men. More specifically, women see morality as a matter of relationship or caring while men view moral issues in terms of a system of law or "impartial" justice. According to Gilligan, attachment, relationships, and intimacy form a connected web through which women come to understand themselves and to define moral behaviors. [*See* FEMINIST ETHICS AND MORAL PSYCHOLOGY.]

Self-in-relation theorists addressed the relative and gendered positions of power within patriarchal societies. Yet their gender analysis implicitly replicated a person-society dualism apparent in the theories they critiqued. The wider society they critiqued hypothesized within-gender homogeneity while other important variables or social markers such as race, class, sexuality, and ethnicity were marginalized in their theories. It is noteworthy that the initial articulation of the theory of self-in-relation was drawn largely from clinical work and research with middle- and upper-middle-class White women. Feminist theories of women's different moral voices, mothering experiences, and senses of self-in-relation have been critiqued as reproducing essentialist assumptions of "gendered," universalized experiences in their neglect of differences among women due to race, class, ethnicity, and sexual orientation.

These theories have been challenged by critical feminists including Mary Brabeck, Kimberly A. Chang, Patricia H. Collins, Rachael Hare-Mustin and Jeanne Marecek, M. Brinton Lykes, Abigail J. Stewart, and Rhoda Unger. Although they agree that women throughout the world develop their identities within patriarchal systems, they argue that they do so in different ways due to social class, power, ethnicity, and sexuality, and within local cultures, at particular historical moments. Insistence on gender as the origin of all relations of domination suggests that all women are dominated by men, a hypothesis challenged by, among others, some Native American women. Equally problematic is the assertion that patriarchal domination of the planet is at the root of all women's experiences of subordination: ideologically, this favors Western women, especially economically privileged women who suggest that racism and class exploitation are offshoots of patriarchy rather than constitutive of and constituted in a complex matrix of power.

Critical feminist theorists argue that culture is not neutral, but rather grounded in material social relations along differing dimensions of power. M. Brinton Lykes investigated selected experiences of White, working, and professional adult women and men and their construals of self. Evidence from this empirical work supported her argument that there are multiple notions of the self and that the culturally dominant notion of the self in Euro-North American societies is rooted in assumptions of autonomy, independence, and separation. A contrasting notion, social individuality, reflects a dialectical understanding of individuality and sociality grounded in an experience of social relations characterized by inequalities of power. The inequalities of power she explored included race, gender, and social class. [*See* POWER.]

Such a model is informative of the experiences of marginalized as well as majority groups because it argues that all humans are embedded in and emergent from a matrix of social relations organized by differing and mobile dimensions of power. Her research was conducted with White and Black U.S. women and poor women in Guatemala, Chile, and Argentina who have formed social movements to protest the state-sponsored violence that targets the poor and those seeking to redress social injustices. Her encounters with these ordinary women engaged in extraordinary actions enabled Lykes to move power to the center of her theory, situating it as central to these women's individuality and sociality.

Subsequent research confirms the centrality of power in psychological theories about individuality and collectivities. Kimberly A. Chang's qualitative study of the moral voices of 30 mainland Chinese men and women studying in the United States challenged Carol Gilligan's gendered interpretation of moral voice by examining the ways in which moral problems and responses were socially constructed in the contexts of power relations based on culture rather than gender. She found that student's responses to moral dilemmas varied with the nature of the power relationship itself, calling attention to the social situatedness of self-construction and moral responses in lived relationships of power.

Because power is dynamic and takes multiple forms, equating power variability and gender differences may be an error found in the writings of the dominant, predominantly White, feminist theorists. Women of color, for example, often recognize more clearly than the former group that some men in their communities are also oppressed, thereby challenging the claim that domination is uniquely masculine and exemplifying once again the complexities of what we call difference. Audre Lorde and bell hooks have proposed that African American feminists take difference, that is, particularity, as their epistemological starting point in building a womanist ethics. Constance W. Turner, for example, described the particularity of Black women's experience in relation to their mothers, the Black community, and the wider White community, thereby countering the notion of a generic or universal woman or mother. She argued that all these differences—race, ethnicity, gender, class, sexuality, and so forth—are interstructured and cannot be separated from each other. Starting with difference or our particularity challenges us to examine multiplicities rather than singling out one dimension, variable, or characteristic as uniquely important. A psychology starting with multiple differences might contribute to less dualistic thinking, invoking categories of difference such as race, ethnicity, class, and sexuality in developing critical theories of the self. The complex interweaving of class, race, and gender calls for a critical approach to self and subjectivity that attends to the multiple dimensions of the social and historic context and the particularities of experience.

IV. Cultural Critiques

Challenges to Euro-North American individualism have also come from anthropologists and cultural psychologists who posit self and culture as co-constituting and co-constituted. As noted earlier, the modern Western view of an isolated or solitary self is peculiar in its cultural emphasis on individualism. Many other cultures value the collective and conceptualize the person within her or his relationships, or, as Edward Sampson has argued, as an "ensembled individual" in which the self versus the nonself boundary is less sharply drawn and others are included within the sense of self. Selected examples from a wide range of studies confirm this position. Hazel Markus and Shinobu Kitayama hypothesized a Japanese, interdependent self, that is, a "self-in-relation-to-other" wherein the experience and expression of emotions and motives are shaped and regulated in consideration of others' behaviors and thoughts. Richard Shweder and Edward Bourne described an Indian self as "sociocentric," since individual interests are subordinated to the good of the collectivity. Drawing on years of clinical experiences and empirical research, Takeo Dio, David F. Ho and Ulchol Kim, and John Berry argued that the self in traditional Asian cultures cannot be defined outside of its relationships. Francis L. K. Hsu and Wei-Ming Tu echoed these considerations suggesting that the Chinese self is embedded in a web of relationships. According to John Smith, the Maorie are not considered to be the primary agents determining their own lives. Mary Brabeck documented a Mayan sense of self in Guatemala arising from and having meaning within "circles of belonging," that is, the community. Drawing on their fieldwork, John Kirkpatrick and Geoffrey White concluded that a non-Western self-conception is one in which some collectivity—family, community, or even the land—constitutes a cultural unit with experiential capacities. Finally, according to Anthony Marsella, a non-

Western self is extended to include a wide variety of significant others and includes a de-emphasis on individual autonomy and independence.

The key characteristics of the non-Western self as described by these cultural theorists are interdependencies or dependencies and fluid boundaries. The various examples briefly summarized here suggest that the degree to which individuals relate to others or society is inclusive, that is, the individual is a self-in-relations-to-others rather than a self-contained, separate entity. The self-construction in these more collectivist societies is in and through the social relations of the community to which the person owes a continuing loyalty.

While cultural psychologists and anthropologists explored the self in a wider context composed of symbolic and behavioral inheritances of a community, they failed to consider selected social factors described earlier, that is, race, class, gender, and power. As such, the hypothesized relationships between independent and interdependent construals of self reaffirm the hypothesized dichotomy between Western individualistic culture and non-Western collectivist cultures where "culture" subsumes race, class, ethnicity, and power. This relativist theorizing of the self is extensive throughout the cultural psychology literature. Cigdem Kagitcibasi critiqued this tendency, arguing that greater differences are found within rather than between cultural and ethnic groups. Moreover, in the absence of a critical reading of social relations of power that vary in terms of class, race, gender, and sexualities within and between cultural groups, cultural psychologists and anthropologists risk reproducing the very psychology and self-theories they are attempting to critique.

V. Beyond Individualism and Collectivism

The use of dichotomies is a heuristic device popular in the West, especially in psychological descriptions of individuals and in characterizations of cultures and societies. When an entire culture or society is pigeonholed along a dichotomous dimension such as masculine/feminine, individualistic/collectivist, or Western/non-Western, subtle and critical differences that may be more characteristic of these social entities are glossed over. Furthermore, such dichotomized descriptions of cultures and societies distort our critical understanding of them, inevitably leading to

good versus bad comparisons. Finally, such glosses minimize the rich variabilities within each of the groups of the dichotomy, assuming commonalities where they may not exist.

In sharp contrast to the interpretations described earlier wherein construals of whole societies and cultures and of the self are characterized as individualistic or collectivist, some social psychologists have defined "culture" from a more critical and local perspective. Lev Vygotsky's studies of cultures and human development focused on human activity, ways of thinking, and tools and artifacts that are both socially constructed and socially transmitted. Culture is a process of human social life and a product of social activity, at the same time that human activity is a product of culture. Person and culture are co-constituted and co-constituting. Because self and culture are co-constituting, one's self is never free from the cultural values and cultural ways of being and doing. One's sense of self is culturally situated and culturally constrained.

The anthropologist Renato Rosaldo argued that culture is dynamically reproduced consciously and unconsciously by each successive generation under different historical and social conditions. Although culture is an ongoing dynamic construct, the reproduction of culture brings dimensions of history into the present and thus creates a sense of cultural continuity. Culture is not necessarily coherent and homogenous and individuals participate in multiple cultures in varying ways. The notion of a uniformly shared culture may be more of a fiction than a reality for most people. Within this view of the heterogeneity of culture, the self is constituted in multiple cultural communities: both culture and self are heterogeneous constructs.

Within critical feminist and critical cultural perspectives, culture is formed and situated at the interstices of complex relations of social class, gender, ethnicity, and sexuality, informed by differing symbolic and behavioral inheritances of the range of communities therein. Cultural practices are grounded in material and social relations resulting in cultural differences between and among different social classes, races, genders, sexualities, and ethnicities. Culture is not determined by any single cultural element (e.g. gender or ethnicity). A given group might share gender or ethnic membership but not cultural membership because of differing access to power in terms of social class.

From a critical perspective, culture results from an ongoing struggle over material and sociohistorical conditions. Rather than a unified culture, a complex combination of critical cultural elements are forged, reproduced, and contested within asymmetrical relations of power that constrain one's self-development and construal of self. Critical cultural theorists hypothesize an embodied self as emergent from *and* engaged by social relations embedded in material and social relations of power and powerlessness.

Oppressive patriarchal, racist, and classist structures are reproduced through cultural practices and ideologies. Critical theorists argue that a neutral conceptualization of culture is due to apolitical scientific rationality and humanistic relativism, which fail to challenge the issue of power and its role in shaping the cultural realities and worldviews that groups hold. Self psychologists are challenged to take a more critical cultural perspective in their theory construction and research, examining the particularities of power that deeply inform self-construals at the intersection of culture, class, race, and gender.

VI. Conclusion

Individualism and collectivism are ideological constructs that underlie theories of self, society, and culture. In defining them, we argued three main points: first, that Western views of an independent self are grounded in a philosophical tradition that emphasizes liberalism and extols the virtues of individualism. In contrast, the interdependent self in some East Asian cultures is rooted in Confucianism, a philosophy that glorifies collectivism. Influenced by its cultural valuing of individualism, Western psychology has produced and reproduced a "universal" model of self-development characterized by separation, autonomy, and personal independence.

Second, we described ways of theorizing the self from feminist, especially critical feminist, perspectives. In contrast to Western developmental theories of the self as a process of separating oneself from the matrices of others, some feminists have argued that women have a distinctively relational self. Although the notion of "self-in-relation" involves a shift in emphasis from separation to relationship as the basis for self-development, the person-society dualism is neither transcended nor transformed. A contrasting, alternative notion, social individuality, was briefly summarized. This construal reflects a dialectical understanding of individuality and sociality grounded in an experience of social relations characterized by inequalities of power.

Finally, we argued for a critical, local interpretation of culture that challenges the dichotomy of individualism and collectivism. Within critical feminist and cultural theory perspectives, culture is not neutral and is grounded in material relations of power and constituted at the interstices of race, ethnicity, class, and gender. This reconceptualization of culture challenges psychologists to rethink self-theories within a critical, cultural perspective.

SUGGESTED READING

Hare-Mustin, R. T., and Marecek, J. (1988). The meaning of gender difference: Gender theory, postmodernism and psychology. *American Psychologist* **43**, 455–464.

Kim, U., Trandis, H. C., Kagitcibasi, C., Choi, S. C., & Yoon, G. (1994). *Individualism and Collectivism: Theory, Method, and Applications.* Vol. 18, Cross-Cultural Research and Methodology Series, Sage, Thousands Oaks, CA.

Lykes, M. B. (1985). Gender and individualistic vs. collective bases of social individuality. *Journal of Personality Psychology* **53**, 357–383.

Lykes, M. B. (1989). The caring self: Social experiences of power and powerlessness. In M. Brabeck, ed., *Who Cares: Theory, Research, and Educational Implications of the Ethic of Care.* Praeger, New York, NY.

Markus, H. R., and Kitayama, S. (1991). Culture and the self: Implications for cognition, emotion, and motivation. *Psychological Review* **96**(2), 224–235.

Ryan, W. (1981). *Equality.* Pantheon, New York, NY.

Triandis, H. C. (1995). *Individualism and Collectivism.* Westview Press, Boulder, CO.

Tu, W. M. (1985). *Confucisn Thought: Selfhood as Creative Transformation.* State University of New York Press, Albany, NY.

Intimacy and Love

Susan S. Hendrick
Texas Tech University

Glossary

Companionate love A type of love characterized by affection, trust, stability, shared values, and a strong emphasis on friendship. This type of love was thought to be characteristic of partners who had been in a relationship for a long period, but it appears that companionate/friendship qualities are important to couples of all ages and lengths of relationship.

Diversity Refers to variety in human groups based on race, ethnicity, cultural heritage, religion, social class, age, and so on. Most research on intimacy and love in the United States has been conducted with college students, typically of European American descent. There is both a desire and a need for more research with persons from a variety of backgrounds, to more accurately represent the diverse population of the United States and the rest of the world. Such research can enrich greatly our knowledge about relationships.

Equality Refers to two persons being equivalent or alike. It can also mean "the same as," but here is used to refer to equivalence of two partners or even balance in the relationship between two partners, rather than two partners being exactly the same.

Intimacy A state of emotional closeness in relationships, wherein relationship partners disclose deeply to one another, experience positive affect and an absence of conflict, and feel understood and able to be empathic toward each other and take each other's perspective. Intimate interactions, intimate behaviors, and intimate relationships are all linked to intimacy.

Love A general term referring to great affection for another that involves a strong emotional connection. Love can be felt for children, parents, romantic partners, siblings, other relatives, and friends and can be expressed in a variety of ways.

Love styles A theoretical and measurement approach to romantic love that proposes six major love styles or attitude constellations: eros (a form of passionate love), ludus (game-playing love), storge (friendship/companionate love), pragma (practical love), mania (possessive love), and agape (altruistic love).

Passionate love A type of love characterized by intense emotional feeling, physiological arousal (often of a sexual nature), and a wish to connect with the partner. Passionate love is thought to involve an intense desire for union with the partner. This type of love was thought to be characteristic of partners who had newly entered into a romantic relationship, but more recently it appears that partners of all ages and lengths of relationship can have a passionate component to their relationship.

Self-disclosure This involves telling or communicating about the self to another person. Such communication is rather intimate and may involve telling about deep feelings, hopes and fears, problems, traumatic events, and so on. Disclosure of this type involves the discloser allowing herself or himself to be open, honest, and vulnerable to another person. Because intimate disclosure is a type of confiding in others, an element of trust is typically necessary.

INTIMACY AND LOVE are two aspects of close, romantic relationships that are linked to relationship satisfaction and other markers of relationship positivity. Here we will consider definitions and theories of intimacy and love, diversity in aspects of intimacy and love, how women and men are both similar and different in intimacy and love, and how the genders might achieve balance in their intimate loving.

I. The Need for Connection

Humans seem to have a fundamental need to connect with one another. We have been described as a group species, wherein our natural tendency is for closeness and bondedness with others. In 1995, Roy Baumeister and Mark Leary proposed a "belongingness hypothesis . . . that human beings have a pervasive drive to form and maintain at least a minimum quantity of lasting, positive, and significant interpersonal relationships" that are constituted of pleasant and frequent interactions in the context of ongoing, stable, and mutually supportive bondedness. Such bondedness is evidenced in varied relating patterns, including the parent–child relationship, romantic partnering, enduring friendships, and the like.

This metatheory of an intrinsic "need to belong" in our species forms the basis of the view of intimacy and love that follows. The focus will be largely on intimacy and love as expressed by adult partners in romantic relationships, but the substrate of such adult intimacy and love is assumed to be the need for belongingness that spans age, gender, race, ethnicity, culture, sexual orientation, social class, and relationship type. The need to belong is a basic aspect of our humanity.

This need for closeness has its roots in our evolutionary heritage, since bonding with others would presumably facilitate survival. Whether we speak of an infant who demands maternal closeness, a pair of

connected adults who foster healthy offspring, or persons who live as part of a group rather than existing in isolation, it is clear that bonding provides the most effective way to ensure provisioning, safety, and ultimate survival. This is, of course, as true today as it was in the mists of our evolutionary past. So where do intimacy and love fit into this fundamental need to be close?

II. Intimacy

"Emotional closeness" is one definition of intimacy, although in fact, intimacy may refer to behaviors and interactions as well as emotions, and even to relationships themselves (as in an "intimate relationship"). Karen Prager has taken a very process-oriented approach to intimacy, choosing to focus on intimate "interactions" and experiences that fulfill partners' needs and enhance the relationship. Intimate experience is typically composed of both positive emotion and feelings of shared understanding. A willingness to be vulnerable (in the sense of being open and honest) to one's partner also characterizes intimate interactions.

Such an approach to intimacy is one-sidedly positive, of course, and ignores the dark side of interaction that occurs within intimate connections—such as emotional and physical abuse. While acknowledging that the potential for the negative always exists, the focus here is on the positive aspects of intimacy.

Attachment theory is an approach that can be considered within the framework of intimacy. Attachment theory was developed based on the ways infants and younger children attach (i.e., seek and maintain proximity/closeness) to a primary caregiver, usually the mother. At least three basic types of attachment have been proposed: secure (a warm relationship between infant and caregiver, allowing infants to explore yet return to a secure base/safe haven), avoidant (a distant and unemotional relationship between infant and caregiver), and anxious-ambivalent (a relationship involving infant protest when separated from the caregiver and infant ambivalence upon reunion with the caregiver).

Attachment theory has been refined and enlarged to include adult attachments between romantic partners, and much research has been devoted to the theory and measurement of attachment. Since over half of respondents in research studies report being securely attached to their romantic partners, and since secure partners are by definition more comfortable with closeness and less anxious about relationships, the secure attachment style can clearly be considered the most intimate of the attachment styles.

A. MEASURING INTIMACY

Although measuring emotions and relational characteristics such as intimacy is elusive, there have been a number of attempts to measure the overarching construct of intimacy as well as measures designed to tap into its various components. One broad measure of intimacy, the Interaction Record Form for Intimacy (IRF-I), requests respondents to rate their intimate interactions and then dimensionalizes these ratings into three broader dimensions: disclosure/communication, positive affect/absence of conflict, and a feeling of being listened to and understood.

Other measures assess the dimensions described here as individual components of intimacy. For example, the Self-Disclosure Index documents the amount of disclosure (the first component of intimacy in the IRF-I) that a person offers to a partner, while a companion measure assesses one's perceived ability to elicit disclosures from others (Opener Scale). Other scales measure the "positive affect" component of intimacy (the second component in the IRF-I) by surveying closeness with the partner or how much one's sense of self includes the partner. Measures addressing the third IRF-I component of intimacy, the sense of being listened to and understood, include measures of perspective-taking, or the ability to "walk in a partner's shoes." Yet whether one measures the components separately or with one scaling instrument, the concept of intimacy is complex and multifaceted.

B. VERBAL AND NONVERBAL COMPONENTS OF INTIMACY

In studying intimate interactions, it is necessary to consider both verbal and nonverbal behaviors. Nonverbal behavior is fundamentally important to intimacy, as when the old song says something about "your words say you love me, but your lips say you lie." When people are truly intimate, they tend to sit close to each other, lean in toward each other, nod their heads in conversation, smile, maintain intense eye contact, and in general "attend." Voice tone and quality are also part of the nonverbal arena. If partners begin drifting apart, their nonverbal behavior shows it. They do not sit as close or touch as much,

they are less attentive and sometimes also less positive. Their gaze may wander, both literally and figuratively.

Verbal interactions in intimate relationships are assessed by the level of disclosure as well as its content. Revealing oneself to another, being unguardedly honest, is a move toward intimacy. Intimate self-disclosures are risky in that they make one vulnerable to the partner, but they seem to be necessary to help move a relationship in the direction of greater intimacy. Expressing affection verbally is also an intimate behavior. Thus a phrase such as "I love you, but it is frightening to tell you that" offers intimacy both in the content of the words and the disclosure of the fear.

C. THE CONTEXT OF INTIMACY

It is essential to remember that intimacy does not occur in a vacuum — it occurs in a "context" — actually a series of contexts. The *individual context* is the personalities, attitudes, values, family background, previous relationship experiences, and so on that each partner brings to the relationship. All of this can be thought of either as personal "resources" or personal "baggage," depending on one's perspective.

The *relational context* has to do with the immediate interactions between partners or the "doing" of the relationship. It is here that the partners' individual qualities mesh or clash, that the partners bring their tendencies to disclose (or not) together and work out their processes of mutual communication. It is in this context that an amorous and sexually experienced partner may slow down the couple's sexual intensity so that the shyer and less experienced partner can be comfortable with sexual sharing.

People also "do" their intimate relationships in a *sociocultural context*, where various social rules can profoundly impact a couple. For example, gender roles may have moved toward greater equality; nevertheless, if heterosexual partners marry, the woman still assumes the man's last name much more frequently than she retains her family name or hyphenates her name. Rarely does a man assume a woman's name. Sexual orientation is impacted severely by social rules, and both lesbian and gay male couples may have to conduct their relationships without benefit of family support and with limited recognition and quite possibly devaluation from the society around them. All too often, the privacy of their intimacy is required rather than chosen freely. [*See* Lesbians, Gay Men, and Bisexuals in Relationships.]

Finally, there is an *immediate context* for a relationship—a context of place and time. Partners may be seated separately at a group dinner, even though they prefer to sit together; this is an occasion when frequent eye contact can keep partners connected. A contrasting example occurs when partners who are getting ready to take a vacation together have a big argument and then have to sit wedged next to each other on a plane. How they handle touching or not touching, talking or not talking, may set the emotional tone (and the level of intimacy) for the vacation.

In summary, if a relationship is like a dance, then the individual context is the dance skills the individual partners bring; the relational context is how the partners learn to move and sway and dance together; the sociocultural context is the dance location (ballroom, disco, college dance); and the immediate context is the quality of the dance floor and the temperature in the room. All contextual aspects are important.

D. GENDER AND INTIMACY

Because the need to belong is a human-based rather than a gender-based need, both women and men require intimacy in their relationships. Although the popular press is filled with dramatic images of the differences between women and men, proclaiming that they are so different they come from separate planets (if not galaxies), actual scholarly research shows that both in and out of relationships, men and women are more the same than they are different. Communications scholar Kathryn Dindia has said that rather than coming from separate planets, men are from North Dakota and women are from South Dakota (although presumably they could also be from North Carolina and South Carolina or even Virginia and West Virginia). In essence, she is saying that for the most part, the differences between women and men are smaller rather than greater.

In the area of self-disclosure (the first component of intimacy in the approach discussed earlier), the conventional wisdom said that women disclosed more than men, and indeed such differences have appeared in a wide variety of studies. But how big these differences are depends on the context and the level of intimacy. When disclosing to a stranger, women disclosed more to women than men disclosed to women, and men disclosed more to men than women disclosed to men. In close relationships, however, women tend to disclose more, but the gender differences are not large.

One should not assume that these differences have the same evolutionary basis as the pervasive "need to belong." Women and men are socialized differently in numerous ways; social structures foster many of the gender differences we see expressed in intimate (and other) relationships. Feminist scholars have offered detailed explanations of how the societal construction of gender roles evolves out of or at least is strongly associated with men's greater power and status. Differing gender roles carry with them a host of differing learned behaviors and skills. One such behavior, sometimes expressed with great skill, may be self-disclosure.

The second of the three components of intimacy discussed earlier, positive affect, is thought to be equally important to men and women. For example, both women and men seek emotional expression, social support, trust, and spending time with a close same-sex or other-sex friend. Also, both women and men seek closeness in sexual contact with a partner, though women may be more focused on the intimacy aspect of sex whereas men may be more focused on sex itself. Of course, much of the extant research has involved college student participants rather than older persons. As men age, there is often a more diffuse affectional tone that surrounds sexual contact and a greater appreciation for physical contact that is not always centered on intercourse.

In an intimate relationship, positive affect needs to be accompanied by a lack of negative affect, and indeed, neither women nor men appear to profit from ordinary relational conflict. Men and women may react to conflict differently, however, with women tending to push their partner to talk about and hopefully resolve the conflict, and men tending to pull back and avoid talking about the conflict. This conflictual dance has been termed the "demand-withdraw" pattern. The goals for the two sexes may be quite similar, however, with women wanting to make the conflict go away through problem solving, and men wanting it to go away through avoidance and "smoothing things over."

Some research on couple conflict has shown that men react physiologically more than women do during conflict (e.g., increased heart rate), and this negative arousal phenomenon has been proposed as one of the reasons that men avoid conflictual interactions with their partner. Yet other research has shown women to experience more arousal during conflict than men experience. A perhaps more plausible reason that has been proffered for men's reluctance to engage an issue is that women are historically disadvantaged both at home and in the greater society. Thus women will raise a conflictual issue in order to improve their situation (e.g., wives asking husbands for greater participation in housework and child care). Men, being more advantaged, have more to gain by avoiding a conflict and maintaining the relational status quo.

The third component of the three intimacy dimensions, feeling heard and understood by a partner, is important to both sexes. Feeling empathy from one's partner—feeling that the partner can take one's perspective, one's point-of-view—is significant for relationship well-being. Both women and men want to support and understand their relationship partners, but their ways of showing understanding may differ. Women, for example, feel understood if they feel listened to. Men, who are typically socialized to solve problems rather than discuss them, frequently offer their partners suggestions or solutions rather than "just listening." Women may then feel frustrated and unheard. Sometimes men just want to be listened to also, but more likely they would appreciate problem-solving behaviors, behaviors that women may be less inclined to enact. So each of the two sexes sometimes gives what they themselves want rather than what the partner desires.

When romantic partners were asked about their empathy (defined as perspective-taking ability) for their partner as well as the partner's empathy toward them, women and men were similar in both their own self-assessed ability to take their partner's perspective and in their evaluation of their partner's ability to perspective-take. And perceived ability of both self and partner to be empathic and perspective-taking was similarly predictive of relationship satisfaction for both men and women. Thus the two sexes are more alike than they are different in this aspect of intimacy. [See EMPATHY AND EMOTIONAL EXPRESSIVITY.]

E. INTIMACY AND DIVERSITY

Most of the research on intimacy has been conducted with heterosexual individuals and couples, and most of these respondents have been of European American descent and middle class. Thus the research very imperfectly reflects contemporary society. What, then, can be said more broadly about gay and lesbian couples, people from different cultures, and partners in multicultural/multiracial relationships?

The need to belong and to bond is a human universal, so the basic concerns of intimacy would not be expected to differ across racial lines or sexual orientation. To the extent that women sometimes disclose more than men, it has been proposed that a lesbian couple might be more communicative than a gay male couple, who might have to work harder at communication. Or to the extent that men may more often initiate sexual interactions, lesbian partners may need to be especially aware of the need to initiate sexual intimacy with each other. Yet overall, gay and lesbian couples are similar to heterosexual couples in their attraction for their partners and their satisfaction with their intimate relationships. Likewise, gay and lesbian partners grieve the loss of a relationship (and its intimacy) in much the same ways that heterosexual partners do.

The universality of intimate connection is present also for couples from different ethnic and racial groups as well as for partners who are in a multicultural/multiracial relationship. Because persons always have unique individual characteristics and particular family background experiences, to some extent every relationship is a cross-cultural relationship. For persons who are from racial or ethnic minority groups, however, the cultural loadings are even more powerful. In addition, social class is a characteristic of "difference" that is often left unexamined.

Recent research examining attachment style and partners' abilities to handle potential conflict in the relationship found that interracial couples have a preponderance of persons who report being securely (as contrasted to insecurely [avoidantly or anxious/ambivalently]) attached to their partner. Such findings are consistent with those for intraracial couples and negate the stereotypes of lower security/more problems in interracial couples.

Although multicultural/multiracial relationships do break up at a rate higher than that of intraracial couples, such relationships are not necessarily problematic. Since similarity is linked to attraction, however, to the extent that partners are dissimilar, they likely will have to work harder to maintain their relationships. And to the extent that their social networks and or the larger society are unsupportive (or even divisive), multicultural/multiracial couples (similar to lesbian and gay couples) also probably need to exert more effort to achieve and maintain a successful relationship.

If intimacy is emotional closeness that is manifested by self-disclosure, positive affect, and empathy, then love is a basic emotion that can drive disclosure, affect, and empathy.

III. Love

Love is a form of intense affection that can involve trust, intimacy, commitment, devotion (typically parent–child love), sexuality (typically romantic love), and a host of other qualities. The focus here is on romantic love, which has powerful emotional feeling as one of its attributes. Some respected scholars even consider love to be one of the select and important "basic emotions."

Ellen Berscheid and Elaine Hatfield made a distinction in the early social scientific study of love between passionate love and companionate love. Passionate love was viewed as a state of intense arousal and emotion, longing for union, and total absorption with the other. The flame of passionate love burns hot. Companionate love, on the other hand, involved the quiet affection of intertwined lives wherein the embers of love glow softly. The explicit assumption was made that passionate love came first in a relationship and, if the relationship continued, evolved into companionate love.

More recently, however, research indicates that passionate love and companionate love tend to co-occur in relationships. Young persons in relatively new relationships rate themselves highly on measures of passionate love but also emphasize features of companionate love, typically describing their romantic partner as their "best friend." On the other hand, long-term married partners, who are presumably quite companionate in their relationships, also rate themselves highly on measures of passionate love, which is in turn a strong predictor of their relationship satisfaction.

Passionate/companionate is not the only descriptive framework for love. Prototype theory considers love in terms of its "best example or set of features;" this example is referred to in turn as the "prototype" of love. Companionate features are particularly important within the prototype approach to love, although when romantic love was the particular focus, passion and sexual attraction were included on a list of central features.

Romantic love can also be considered as a form of growing of the self or self-expansion. The inclusion of self within the partner as well as the inclusion of the partner within the self (essentially the overlap or intertwining of two people) are key aspects of the self-expansion approach.

Still another theory of romantic love describes it in terms of three specific components: intimacy, passion, and commitment. It has been proposed that these three components constitute eight different types of romantic love, and these types of love have much in common with other love approaches. For example, one of these love types is much like passionate love, and another is much like companionate love. Other scholars have focused heavily on the communicative aspects of love or the "ways" in which romantic love is enacted. These ways of both communicating and experiencing love include active love, collaborative love, committed love, intuitive love, secure love, and traditional romantic love, with each love having somewhat different communicational characteristics.

A theoretical approach to love that offers a multidimensional perspective is John Alan Lee's "love styles" approach, which describes several different ways of loving a romantic partner. Most of the research building on this approach has concerned six major love styles: eros (passionate, erotic love), ludus (playful, game-playing love), storge (steady, friendship love), pragma (practical, sensible love), mania (possessive, dependent love), and agape (altruistic, idealistic love). One advantage to the love styles approach, as will be elaborated in the next section, is that the love styles can ostensibly be measured and then related to many other constructs relevant to intimate relationships. Another advantage is that the six "styles" can be thought of as six attitudes or sets of descriptors, perhaps stable in some ways but flexible in others, rather than as six separate types that are immutable. For example, someone could describe herself as a passionate (eros) and friendship-oriented (storge) lover with a heavy dose of practicality (pragma) at one point in time, but could have different love style emphases at another point. Thus the love styles approach offers an array of love options rather than just one or two.

Evolutionary psychology is a framework for looking at love that will be considered only briefly here, since it is not really a love (or intimacy) theory, but rather a metatheory for the psychological sciences to employ in trying to explain much of human behavior. Though its proponents often give love primacy as a mechanism that ensures parental bonding and resulting increased survival rates for offspring, research emerging from this tradition has focused on relatively time-bound events such as mate selection rather than on the processes of intimacy and love in ongoing relationships.

A. MEASURING LOVE

A number of the theoretical approaches to love presented earlier have produced scaling instruments that measure love. For example, there is a measure of passionate love, the Passionate Love Scale. Another measure of love has subscales that presumably assess the relative amounts of intimacy, passion, and commitment. Another measure has evolved from the love ways approach and includes subscales measuring committed, intuitive, secure, companionate, and traditional romantic love.

The love styles approach prompted development of a measure, the Love Attitudes Scale. This 42-item scale has six subscales, each with seven items, that measure eros, ludus, storge, pragma, mania, and agape. The Love Attitudes Scale has been translated into many different languages. The original measure included some items referring to a specific relationship partner as well as other items referring to love more generally, so one form of the Love Attitudes Scale now includes only partner-specific items. There is also a 24-item short form of the Love Attitudes Scale.

The Love Attitudes Scale has been used in relationship research for nearly 20 years, and the various love styles have been related to a number of constructs, thus providing at least a rough sketch of the love styles and their correlates. For example, the erotic love style (eros) is related to greater self-disclosure, whereas the game-playing style (ludus) is related to less disclosure. Eros is also related to higher self-esteem, whereas possessive love (mania) is related to lower self-esteem.

The love styles have also been related to the ability to elicit self-disclosure from others, to sensation seeking, to social support, to conflict tactics, to relational competence, to perspective-taking, to commitment, to various aspects of sexuality, to religiosity, to personal constructs, to attachment styles, to contraceptive behavior, to eating disorder characteristics, as well as to many other variables. In addition, romantic partners tend to be similar in several of their love styles. Overall, love is related to many aspects of close relationships, and gender is related to virtually *all* such aspects.

B. GENDER AND LOVE

The stereotypic view of romantic love in Western culture is in many ways a feminized one. The only facet of love that seems particularly masculine is sex; otherwise, the "moonlight and roses" aspects of romantic passion are readily identified with women. Women are often thought to be more romantic than men are, yet men believe that they also are romantic, and indeed men often rate more strongly than women do on various love measures. For example, using the long form of the Love Attitudes Scale, women have typically been more endorsing of friendship-based, practical, and possessive love, whereas men have been more endorsing of game-playing love. Women and men have not differed consistently on either passionate or altruistic love. These findings are not inconsistent with traditional gender roles wherein women have been more oriented to stable, dependable intimate relationships while men have been permitted or even encouraged to "explore," both romantically and sexually. In fact, some research has shown that gender role (how one views appropriate roles for women and men) makes more difference that actual gender when referring to love attitudes. Differences in love styles seemed to be disappearing, but more recently, research using the short form of the Love Attitudes Scale indicates continuing gender differences, consistent with previous research.

For the most part, however, these differences are relatively small (much like the gender differences in self-disclosure discussed earlier). When women and men are compared on how they relate love to other relationship constructs, they appear to be very similar. For example, in one study, women and men were compared in how love attitudes were related to sexual attitudes. The patterns were very similar for the two genders, with erotic love relating to idealistic sexuality, and game-playing love relating to permissive sexuality, for example. The only really consistent differences appeared in stronger correlations for men between sexual permissiveness and selected relationship questions. Thus, even taking gender role socialization into account, women and men have great similarity in their orientations toward love.

C. LOVE AND DIVERSITY

The need to belong/bond/love is universal, and scholars have proposed that passionate love is universal also. An examination of ancient Chinese literature has revealed references to various types of love (e.g., passionate, obsessive, devoted, casual), dating back thousands of years. Contemporary comparisons of various cultures—Taiwanese, British, German, Russian, Japanese, as well as Hawaiian residents representing European, Japanese American, and Pacific Islander cultures—all appeared to be relatively similar in many of their love attitudes and relational experiences. In other research, Anglo and Mexican American married couples were very similar in their attitudes toward love. Such findings do not negate the need to understand the racial, ethnic, and cultural variations in the expression of love and other romantic sentiments, however. Indeed it is important to contextualize love and appreciate how it might be expressed somewhat differently in a communally oriented society from the way it is expressed in more individually oriented Western society. For example, the phenomenon of "marrying for love" is more typical for Western than for many other (e.g., Asian) cultures. As is true for intimacy, however, we are more the same than we are different.

Similarity also seems to outpace difference for lesbian and gay respondents, when compared to heterosexual respondents. Research specifically focusing on gay men and their love attitudes found that gay and heterosexual men did not differ in their love styles. Other research has also found similarity in closeness and satisfaction for couples, regardless of sexual orientation. Still other work found lesbian couples to report higher levels of intimacy, autonomy, and equality (but not satisfaction) as compared to married couples. Of course, much more work remains to be done in the various areas of diversity.

Age is another aspect of diversity. Though much of the extant relationship research has focused on youthful couples, both love and sexuality are important to couples of all ages. Research on love styles, specifically, found that although married respondents differed from those who were unmarried, people did not differ in their love styles on the basis of age. Other research has also found that college students did not differ greatly from their parents' generation in love styles. Also, as noted earlier, both companionate and passionate love are important to both younger and older relational partners. Sexual activity, as an aspect of intimacy, also continues throughout the life span, given a person's adequate health and an available sexual partner.

D. LINKING LOVE AND SEXUALITY

A facet of love that has been largely unexplored is how love might be linked with sexuality in people's perceptions of their intimate relationships. When people were asked about such links, they offered numerous responses, which ultimately were categorized into several themes. These themes included the idea that love is most important, that love comes before sex, and that sex demonstrates love. Women and men both agreed with ideas such as that love is most important and that sex demonstrates love. [*See* SEXUALITY AND SEXUAL DESIRE.]

What is perhaps most important about such research is that it "scientifically" confirms a finding that might seem to be just good common sense: People really do link love and sex in their intimate, romantic relationships. Surely where sex and love converge, intimacy can be located also.

Some scholars have questioned whether love, intimacy, commitment, satisfaction, or some other similar relational construct is the overarching or most important of the constructs implicated in successful relationships. Research has been variable in articulating which construct is the "most important" one, and it appears that all are different but overlapping constructs and that they are all implicated in describing and assessing successful relationships.

E. INTIMACY, LOVE, AND HEALTH

If we assume that a basis for both intimacy and love is the fundamental need to belong that has been spoken of throughout, then it is clear that love and intimacy are probably part of our intrinsic nature and are linked to human survival on several levels. Thus it is perhaps unsurprising that relationships are also related to both emotional and physical health. The loss of love relationships has been linked to various negative emotional outcomes such as depression, and a relatively recent scholarly emphasis on positive psychology has also underlined how important positive aspects of the human condition (including close relationships) are to human well-being and survival. Both women and men who were in married relationships reported greater happiness than people who were never married, separated, or divorced (although it is important to note that marriage tends to be even more beneficial for men than for women). In a recent large-scale study of sexuality in the United States, those persons who described themselves as the most emotionally and physically satisfied in their relationships were those persons whose relationships were monogamous and long term. Scholars in the medical arena have also recognized that intimate relationships are sources of social support and are also likely to be powerful resources for enhancing the human immune system. Love and intimacy are good for our health.

IV. *Intimacy, Love, and Gender Equality*

Equality as defined here is reflective of equivalence between men and women. This equivalence means both equal rights and equal responsibilities; it does not mean "the same." To subscribe to sameness, one would have to propose that there are no biological differences between women and men, which is patently false, given reproductive and hormonal differences, or to propose that there are no social differences between men and women, which is equally false, given the corporate, political, and financial leadership/reward differences between the sexes. Equivalance, however, implies a fair equalization of resources as well as responsibilities—a balance, if you will. Arguably, it is only through such balance that true intimacy and love can be achieved.

A. HISTORICAL PERSPECTIVES ON INTIMACY AND LOVE

As noted earlier, evolutionary psychologists, and sociobiologists more generally, locate love and intimacy within the bonding mechanisms necessary to unite women and men in the service of procreation, child rearing, and the ultimate survival of the human species. Mate selection is at the center of much of what evolutionary psychology says about love and intimacy. Essentially, men want sexual access to young, attractive (presumably fertile) women, whereas women want men who have economic resources and are good providers. Each wants sexual and relational fidelity from the other (women to guarantee provisioning of offspring, men to guarantee assurance of paternity), which is ostensibly maintained by sexual jealousy, emotional manipulation, and so on, and by bonding mechanisms such as love and intimacy.

The social learning perspective mentioned earlier proposes that many behaviors relevant to mate selection and other relational parameters are learned via social and cultural transmission of gender roles. Thus women, traditionally less advantaged economically and politically, have learned to seek security when choosing a man, whereas men, at least as a group more advantaged, have learned that they can seek youth and beauty as well as good child-bearing potential when choosing a woman—or women.

Some feminist historians take the perspective that patriarchy, or male power and governance, is not an evolutionary mandate but rather a historical artifact arising as societies became agrarian, wealth could be accumulated, and the need for a "state" arose. Before that, women and men were purportedly co-equals. The growth of patriarchy, however, influenced Greek and Judeo-Christian heritages, which informed Western civilization.

Women were not disadvantaged to the same degree in every society and culture; for example, women in Sparta were awarded high status and relatively equal rights. Yet across societies and historical periods, women were typically disadvantaged relative to men (gender dominance predated class dominance). For women (at least class advantaged women) in the middle ages, the best guarantees of longevity were (a) being widowed early in marriage and not remarrying or (b) entering a religious order, presumably because in these situations they were freed from multiple child bearing.

Yet love and intimacy persisted at some level in all societies to the extent that families were formed, children were born and reared, and the human community grew. Some would argue that intimacy and love as we know it did not develop until a conception of the self developed, but ancient writings as well as more modern commentaries from communal societies where the concept of self is relatively less emphasized lend credence to some continuing threads of love and intimacy throughout much of recorded history.

Some of the ebb and flow in intimacy and love (and related romance and courtship myths and rituals) has occurred in tandem with shared spheres of responsibility for family welfare. For example, in some ways there was less romance and more natural sexual sharing in 18th-century United States middle-class society than occurred in the 19th century. It was in the latter period that the Industrial Revolution enticed men off the land and out of the home and underlined the separate spheres of influence governed by the two sexes. Ironically, many romantic customs widened rather than narrowed the gap between men and women because they reified gender differences, and differences between women and men have rarely accrued to women's benefit.

It has been appreciated for some time that differences, particularly substantial differences in power and authority, do not foster intimacy and love. Only equals can be intimate in the fullest sense of the word. As John Stuart Mill noted more than 130 years ago, marriage for two persons "between whom there exists that best kind of equality, similarity of powers and capacities with reciprocal superiority in them" is the best representation of marriage. Mill maintained that only this model

is the ideal of marriage: and that all opinions, customs, and institutions which favour any other notion of it, or turn the conceptions and aspirations connected with it into any other direction, by whatever pretences they may be coloured, are relics of primitive barbarism. (1869)

Though this commentary might have predated the modern feminist movement by a century, nevertheless, the sentiments are congruent with that movement.

B. WOMEN, INDIVIDUALISM, AND COMMUNITY

The feminist movement, discussed in detail elsewhere in these volumes, can be considered the largest flow to date in the ebb and flow of women's empowerment over the centuries. It could even perhaps be whimsically considered a "return" to hypothesized preagrarian coequality. In any case, it has meant a conscious search for economic, legal, political, and social equality, at least in Western society, on a scale never before seen. [*See* THE FEMINIST MOVEMENT.]

Concomitant with this search for equality has come improved and available birth control and the separation of sexuality from reproduction. If part of men's control over women has been (and in many cultures remains) the control of women's sexuality, then an aspect of women seeking equality with men and control over themselves has been women's increasing sexual autonomy, possible only with the freeing of sexuality from reproduction. The journey toward sexual autonomy has sometimes involved attempts to divorce sex from love and intimacy—a stereotypically male strategy—but the divorce has not been successful. The essence of sexuality has remained relational. The need to belong, to bond, to be close has maintained.

The notion that sex can be divorced from intimacy and love is not a new idea, but it is typically a male idea. It is not always an approach disadvantaging women. For example, philosophers and sexual scientists arguing for a naturalistic approach to sex would separate it from love so that it can be appreciated in its own right and would argue for absolutely equal freedoms and prerogatives for both women and men.

The louder voices trying to divorce sex from love, however, are those whose bias is toward unrestrained individualism, with sex as just one more "right of the individual." All too often the individual who deserves these rights has been male, but awarding the rights to women hasn't provided fundamentally satisfying answers either. Unbridled individualism is no better an answer for women than it has been for men, because the cult of the individual lacks the essential humanity of the communal. Societies that emphasize individualism as a central value seem particularly hampered in achieving intimacy and love.

Women have been historically accorded the role of relationship "keeper" within various levels of community—romantic dyad, nuclear family, extended family, social network, voluntary organizations, and the like. This role of relationship maintainer and nurturer has been undeniably burdensome at times yet has been the source of great joy and satisfaction. The emotional communities that women sustain in turn sustain women.

Some gender scholars have proposed that women must continue to embrace community and eschew individualism in order to maintain any sort of morally ordered society, while other scholars have proposed that only male individualism should be eliminated and that a more nurturing female individualism would create a much more "morally ordered society" than we have currently. If women relinquish individualism, they risk relinquishing hopes for gender equality. If women relinquish community, they risk relinquishing their abiding need for emotional connection, including intimacy and love. The answer to the polar ideals of individuality versus community is likely to be an integration of the two, which mirrors the balanced equality that relationship partners must find if they are to achieve and sustain love and intimacy.

C. WHAT WOMEN LOSE BY BEING RELATIONAL EXPERTS

"Women's work" has been, in part, the work of relationships, and in this domain women have ostensibly become the experts. Women are expected to maintain relationships and to do this work well. Women more typically organize marital and family communication, are more disclosed-to by their children, and in general seek to resolve partner conflicts through communication. When things go wrong in a partnered relationship, particularly a marital one, women blame themselves and are blamed by others.

An obvious downside to being the relational expert is this self-blaming and blaming by others that occurs when relationships go awry. A less obvious negative, however, is that it frees men in relationships to be inexpert. This can be a particular problem for gay male partners, if neither partner has been socialized to be the relationship maintainer. But issues of male abdication of emotional responsibility are more apparent in heterosexual couples, where men take for granted their own freedom from relational "upkeep."

There is perhaps a certain similarity between women's and men's typical approach to relationship work and to housework. Women will most often run out of patience first; whether with an unresolved conflict or a dirty kitchen floor; they will intervene to try to remedy the situation. Men will likely address the relationship—or the floor—only when the situation becomes so problematic that it cannot be ignored. Though this is undoubtedly an exaggeration for many couples, for many others it is dead-on accurate. It is a system in which both partners collude, and which is of real service to neither partner. Men will likely not get better at relationship work until women get less good at it; to be true coequals, women and men must convey equality to all venues.

D. THE NEW MASCULINITY

A new psychology of men has emerged, which speaks to men's losses in a gendered world. Though neoconservative men's movements beckon some men, and other men seek (re)connection with fathers or mentoring figures, still other men view the issues in terms of "we" rather than "I," of men's "relational dread" being overcome by the gradual movement toward mutuality in the realm of intimate relationship work. If men are willing to give up their inertia/distance/safety and women are willing to give up their expert status, then women can mentor men in the relational world of love and intimacy, and both sexes can benefit. [See MEN AND MACULINITY.]

V. Conclusions

Research indicates that men and women are overwhelmingly more similar than they are different, whether in intimacy and love or in other relationship characteristics. This is unsurprising if we subscribe to the theory that there really is a fundamental need to belong that is part of the human fabric. Of course we are more alike than we are different, across race, ethnicity, sexual orientation—and gender. Yet women and men are not fully "the same." There are biological and social differences influenced by culture and all too often exaggerated by socialization. Men and women enact relationships both similarly and differently, with differences often emphasized (and reinforced) by the media, social institutions, and others. When understood simply as variant styles of expressing the same underlying need, then the differences can be appreciated and even used to foster new behavioral possibilities for women and men. Both men's and women's relational repertoires can grow.

A metaphor for envisioning the sexes in terms of love and intimacy is an example from medicine. One of the most complex and profound modern medical procedures is a heart transplant. Transplant candidates are rigorously screened and carefully chosen, and both women and men are selected as recipients. Given an appropriate size and type match, a man's donor heart may be given to a woman, just as a woman's donor heart may be given to a man. Our hearts are interchangeable.

SUGGESTED READING

Baumeister, R. F., and Leary, M. R. (1995). The need to belong: Desire for interpersonal attachments as a fundamental human motivation. *Psychological Bulletin 117*, 497–529.

Canary, D. J., and Emmers-Sommer, T. M. (1997). *Sex and Gender Differences in Personal Relationships.* The Guilford Press, New York.

Feeney, J. A., and Noller, P. (1996). *Adult Attachment.* Sage, Thousand Oaks, CA.

Hendrick, C., and Hendrick, S. S. (eds.) (2000). *Close Relationships: A Sourcebook.* Sage, Thousand Oaks, CA.

Latham, A. (1997). *The Ballad of Gussie & Clyde: A True Story of True Love.* Villard, New York.

Prager, K. J. (1995). *The Psychology of Intimacy.* The Guilford Press, New York.

Steil, J. M. (1997). *Marital Equality: Its Relationship to the Well-Being of Husbands and Wives.* Sage, Thousand Oaks, CA.

Sternberg, R. J. (1998). *Love as a Story.* Oxford University Press, New York.

Winstead, B. A., Derlega, V. J., and Rose, S. (1997). *Gender and Close Relationships.* Sage, Thousand Oaks, CA.

Wood, J. T. (ed.) (1996). *Gendered Relationships.* Mayfield, Mountain View, CA

ISBN 0-12-227246-3

90018